THE ARCHAEOLOGY OF

Food, metals and towns

ONE WORLD ARCHAEOLOGY
Series Editor: P. J. Ucko

Animals into Art
H. Morphy (ed.), vol. 7

Archaeological Approaches to Cultural Identity
S. J. Shennan (ed.), vol. 10

Archaeological Heritage Management in the Modern World
H. F. Cleere (ed.), vol. 9

Archaeology and the Information Age: a global perspective
P. Reilly & S. Rahtz (eds), vol. 21

Centre and Periphery: comparative studies in archaeology
T. C. Champion (ed.), vol. 11

Domination and Resistance
D. Miller, M. J. Rowlands & C. Tilley (eds), vol. 3

The Excluded Past: archaeology in education
P. Stone & R. MacKenzie (eds), vol. 17

Foraging and Farming: the evolution of plant exploitation
D. R. Harris & G. C. Hillman (eds), vol. 13

From the Baltic to the Black Sea: studies in medieval archaeology
D. Austin & L. Alcock (eds), vol. 18

Hunters of the Recent Past
L. B. Davis & B. O. K. Reeves (eds) vol. 15

The Meaning of Things: material culture and symbolic expression
I. Hodder (ed.), vol. 6

The Origins of Human Behaviour
R. A. Foley (ed.), vol. 19

The Politics of the Past
P. Gathercole & D. Lowenthal (eds), vol. 12

Sacred Sites, Sacred Places
D. L. Carmichael, J. Hubert, B. Reeves & A. Schanche (eds), vol. 23

The Presented Past: heritage, museums and education
P. G. Stone & B. L. Molyneaux (eds), vol. 25

Signifying Animals: human meaning in the natural world
R. G. Willis (ed.), vol. 16

Social Construction of the Past: representation as power
G. C. Bond & A. Gilliam (eds), vol. 24

State and Society: the emergence and development of social heirarchy and political centralization
J. Gledhill, B. Bender & M. T. Larsen (eds), vol. 4

Tropical Archaeobotany: applications and developments
J. G. Hather (ed.), vol. 22

The Walking Larder: patterns of domestication, pastoralism, and predation
J. Clutton-Brock (ed.), vol. 2

What is an Animal?
T. Ingold (ed.), vol. 1

What's New? A closer look at the process of innovation
S. E. Van der Leeuw & R. Torrence (eds), vol. 14

Who Needs the Past? Indiginous values and archaeology
R. Layton (ed.), vol. 5

Professor Thurstan Shaw, wearing the dress of the Onuna-Ekwulu Ora of Igbo–Ukwu (the mouth that speaks on behalf of Igbo–Ukwu), points out the site of the burial chamber excavated in 1960.
Photo: T.C. Champion.

THE ARCHAEOLOGY OF AFRICA

Food, metals and towns

Edited by

Thurstan Shaw
Formerly, Department of Archaeology, University of Ibadan, Nigeria

Paul Sinclair
Department of Archaeology, University of Uppsala, Sweden

Bassey Andah
Department of Archaeology and Anthropology, University of Ibadan, Nigeria

Alex Okpoko
Institute of African Studies, University of Nigeria, Nsukka, Nigeria

London and New York

First published in 1993 by
Routledge
11 New Fetter Lane, London EC4P 4EE

Simultaneously published in the USA and Canada
by Routledge
29 West 35th Street, New York, NY 10001

Typeset in 10 on 12pt Bembo by Florencetype Ltd, Kewstoke, Avon
Printed in Great Britain by Butler and Tanner Ltd, Frome and London

British Library Cataloguing in Publication Data

The archaeology of Africa: food, metals and towns
  I. Shaw, Thurstan
  960

Library of Congress Cataloging in Publication Data

The archaeology of Africa: food, metals and towns / edited by
  Thurstan Shaw . . . [et al.].
      p.   cm. — (One world archaeology)
  Includes bibliographical references and index.
  1. Man, Prehistoric—Africa.   2. Africa—Antiquities.
3. Agriculture, Prehistoric—Africa.   4. Commerce, Prehistoric—
Africa.   I. Shaw, Thurstan.   II. Series.
GN861.F55   1993
960′.1—dc20   92–13921

ISBN 0–415–11585–X

Contents

List of contributors   *page*   xxiv

Foreword   P. J. Ucko   xxvii

Preface   xxxv

Radiocarbon dates   xxxvii

Introduction   1
P. J. J. Sinclair, T. Shaw & B. Andah
Theme 1: terminology   3
    The 'Neolithic'   3
    The 'Iron Age'   8
Theme 2: innovation and diffusion   9
Theme 3: environmental relations   13
Theme 4: food production   16
Theme 5: urbanism   21
    Northern Africa   25
    West Africa   26
    Central, eastern and southern Africa   28
    Africa as a whole   29
Conclusion   31
Acknowledgements   31

1   *Africa's climate in the Holocene*   32
   A. T. Grove
   Introduction   32
   The end of the Pleistocene in Africa   34
   The Early Holocene   35
     Calculating past rainfall from former lake strandlines   36
     Northeast Africa   38
     West Africa   39
   The Middle Holocene   39
     Onset of current climate   41
   The Late Holocene   41
   Discussion   42

2   *The climatic and vegetational history of the equatorial regions of*
   Africa during the upper Quaternary   43
   J. Maley
   Introduction   43
   The main climatic phases of the late Quaternary in central Africa   44

Soil history   44
Forest refugia and holocene forest expansion   45
Temperature variation and the extension of montane biotopes to low
  altitudes   48
Comparison of the African forest zone with east Africa   50
Conclusions: comparisons between equatorial Africa and dry tropical Africa   52
Acknowledgements   52

3 *The tropical African cereals*   53
  J. R. Harlan
Sorghum   53
Pearl millet   57
Finger millet   57
African rice   58
Teff   58
Digitaria spp.   58
Brachiaria deflexa   59
Abyssinian oat   59
Conclusion   59
Note   60

4 *The spread of domestic animals in Africa*   61
  J. Clutton–Brock
Introduction   61
Guinea fowl: *Numida meleagris* and *Numida ptilorhynca*   62
Domestic fowl: *Gallus gallus*   62
Ducks and geese   62
Rodents   63
The cat: *Felis catus*   63
The dog: *Canis familiaris*   64
Pig: *Sus domesticus*   65
Donkey: *Equus asinus*   65
The horse: *Equus caballus*   65
Camel: *Camelus dromedarius*   65
Domestic cattle: *Bos taurus* and *Bos indicus*   66
Domestic water buffalo: *Bubalus bubalis*   68
Goat: *Capra hircus*   68
Sheep: *Ovis aries*   69
Discussion   70

5 *Ethnographic and linguistic evidence for the prehistory of African
  ruminant livestock, horses and ponies*   71
  R. Blench
Introduction   71
Methods   71
Cattle   73

Introduction   73
Linguistic evidence   73
Dwarf shorthorn cattle   74
Humpless longhorns   75
Kuri cattle   76
Zebu   77
Sheep   78
Introduction   78
Thin-tailed hair sheep   79
Thin-tailed wool sheep   80
Fat-tailed sheep   80
Fat-rumped sheep   80
Goats   81
Introduction   81
Linguistic evidence   82
West African dwarf goats   82
Savanna goats   83
Milking goats   83
Summary and conclusion   84
Cattle   85
Humpless shorthorns   85
Humpless longhorns   85
Zebu   86
Sheep   86
Goats   86
General   87
The history and distribution of horses and ponies in west-central Africa   88
Introduction   88
Horses in sub-Saharan Africa   89
The biological evidence   89
The races of horse and pony in west Africa   89
The dwarfing of the horse in west Africa   89
Disease resistance and fodder   91
Evidence for the antiquity of the horse in west Africa   92
Archaeological and iconographic evidence   92
Linguistic evidence   93
Ethnographic records   93
Classical and Arabic sources   93
Evidence from accounts of travellers   94
Nigeria   94
Ponies on the Niger   97
The pony in central Africa   98
The 'Sara' or 'Laka' pony   98
The Chamba pony   99
The pony west of Borgu   100

The role of horses and ponies in the development of west African
        state systems   100
    Conclusions   103
    Notes   103
    Acknowledgements   103

6   *Nilo-Saharans and the Saharo-Sudanese Neolithic*   104
    C. Ehret
    Nilo-Saharan subclassification   104
    Locating early Nilo-Saharan societies   106
    Reconstructing domestic economy in the early Nilo-Saharan eras   108
    The onset of food production among Nilo-Saharans   109
    Dating early Nilo-Saharan food production   115
    Nilo-Saharans and the archaeology of the Saharo-Sudanese Neolithic   116

7   *Recent developments in African language classification and their*
    implications for prehistory   126
    R. Blench
    Introduction   126
    Changing methodologies in the genetic classification of African languages 126
    The language phyla of Africa   128
        Niger–Congo   128
        Nilo-Saharan   132
        Afroasiatic   134
        Khoisan and isolated languages   134
        Conclusion   135
        Distribution   136
        Methodological implications   137
    Notes   138
    Acknowledgements   138

8   *Linguistic evidence for the use of some tree and tuber food plants in*
    southern Nigeria   139
    K. Williamson
    The names of the plants and their products   139
        Reconstructed languages   140
        Specific languages and groups: classification and source(s)   141
    Tree crops   143
    Tubers   143
    Words indicating cultivation   151
    Conclusion   151

9   *Examination of botanical remains from early neolithic houses at*
    Nabta Playa, Western Desert, Egypt, with special reference to
    sorghum grains   154
    K. Wasylikowa, J. R. Harlan, J. Evans, F. Wendorf,
    R. Schild, A. E. Close, H. Krolik & R. A. Housley

Introduction 154
Archaeological setting 154
Description of *Sorghum* sp. remains from Nabta Playa 157
Infra-red spectroscopy 159
  Procedure 161
  Results 161
  Conclusion 162
Discussion 163
Note 164
Acknowledgements 164

10 *Foraging and farming in Egypt: the transition from hunting and*
   gathering to horticulture in the Nile valley 165
   W. Wetterstrom
Introduction 165
The environmental background 167
Pleistocene, post-pleistocene adaptations and Wadi Kubbaniya 168
  Foraging in the late Palaeolithic at Wadi Kubbaniya 170
    The Wadi Kubbaniya environment 170
    Archaeological remains 170
    Subsistence 171
      Fauna 171
        Mammals 171
        Fish 173
        Water fowl 174
      Flora 174
        'Root' foods 175
        Seed foods 176
        Other plant foods 177
        Missing plant foods 177
    Kubbaniya subsistence through the seasons 178
  Late palaeolithic economy in the Nile valley 179
  The end of the Pleistocene 180
    The changing environment 180
    Terminal palaeolithic subsistence 180
  The holocene climate and the Nile 182
  Epipalaeolithic foragers 183
    Arkinian and Shamarkian industries 184
    Elkabian industry 185
    Qarunian cultures of the Fayum depression 186
      The lake 186
      Qarunian sites 187
        Subsistence – faunal remains 188
        Subsistence – flora 189
        Settlement patterns 190

Tarifian   191
Terminal palaeolithic foraging – an overview   192
The pitfalls of foraging   193
   Annual Nile flood variation   193
   Flood variability and epipalaeolithic foragers   194
   Lean times and cruel floods   195
   Long-term Nile flood trends and epipalaeolithic foragers 196
The earliest farming   197
   The potential of domesticates   197
   Early farming   198
   Incipient domestication   199
Sources for Nile valley agriculture   199
   The Western Desert   200
   Southwest Asia   200
The transition to farming in Egypt   201
   Timing   201
   Process   201
Egypt's first farming communities – a problematic archaeological record 202
   The chronology of Egypt's first farming settlements   203
   Egypt's first farming settlements   204
   The Fayum Neolithic   204
   Settlements   204
   Subsistence – Fayum A faunal remains   207
   Subsistence – Fayum A plant remains   208
   Settlement patterns and the seasonal round   209
   Discussion   210
   The Moerian   211
   Merimde Beni-salama   212
   El-Omari   214
   Badari-Mostagedda-Matmar   214
   Armant-Gurna area   220
   Nagada region   222
Conclusions   224
Notes   226
Acknowledgement   226

11   *The emergence of a food-producing economy in the Sahara*   227
   A. Muzzolini
Introduction   227
North Africa towards the end of the Pleistocene   227
The great Wet Phase of the early Holocene   229
   The first villages   229
   Stone Places (*Steinplatze*) and nomadism on the great plains 230
   The 'Aqualithic'   232
The Neolithic Wet Phase in the central Sahara and the Maghreb   234

Rock art and pastoralism   235
Agriculture   236
Causes and courses of the transition to food production   237
Climate   238
Sedentism   238
Material culture and economy   238
Demographic pressure   238
Conclusion   239
Acknowledgement   239

12 *Identifying early farming traditions of west Africa*   240
    B. W. Andah
Social aspects of food production   240
The environment   241
The socio-linguistic context of agriculture   244
The socio-cultural context of agriculture   244
Valley and upland farming in west Africa   244
Organization of labour   246
Ecology and diet   246
Yam   246
The oil palm   248
Domestication of cereals   248
Archaeological and botanical evidence   250
Tree crops   250
The millets   251
Sorghum   251
Rice   252
The pulses   253
Conclusion   253

13 *The Kintampo complex: a case study of early sedentism and food
    production in sub-Sahelian west Africa*   255
    J. Anquandah
Introduction   255
The Kintampo complex   255
The evidence of sedentism   256
Food production   258
Conclusion   259

14 *Intensification in the west African Late Stone Age: a view from
    central Ghana*   261
    A. B. Stahl
Antecedents   261
The Kintampo complex: the case for intensification   265
The legacy   270
Concluding comments: intensification in the west African Late Stone Age 272
Acknowledgements   273

15 *Agriculture and settlement among the Tiv of Nigeria: some ethno-*
    archaeological observations   274
    C. A. Folorunso & S. O. Ogundele
    The study area   275
    Cultivated plants   275
    Agricultural practice   276
    The farming year   277
        Crop processing   279
    How long have the Tiv been in this area?   279
    Settlement study   280
        Some observed regularities in spatial arrangement   280
        Social organization   282
        Implications for archaeological reconstruction   285
    Appendix: spatial arrangement of settlement features   286
        Ayela, Sar and Tse–Dura   286
        Wombo, Tse–Gbashanam, Lukposo, Adzeger and Alumuku   287

16 *Central Africa and the archaeology of the equatorial rainforest:*
    reflections on some major topics   289
    M. K. H. Eggert
    Bringing central African archaeological into focus   289
    The problem: the rainforest as habitat for humans   290
    The central African rainforest: some basic facts   291
    From savanna to forest: on the emergence of the heart of central Africa 293
    Exploring the rainforest: the River Reconnaissance Project   294
        Stone age forest hunters? On early lithic evidence   296
        Hunters, ceramics and ground stone: focusing on the 'Neolithic' 297
        The Central African Neolithic and early iron metallurgy: cultural
            context and cross-cutting dates   302
        From the periphery to the centre: early pottery in the inner
            Congo–Zaïre basin   304
            The Imbonga Horizon   304
            The Batalimo–Maluba Horizon   306
            The Pikunda–Munda Horizon   311
        Early rainforest pottery: the problem of internal relationship 319
        Early rainforest pottery: the question of external relationship 322
        Surviving in the forest: the problem of subsistence   323
        Early rainforest settlement: stone or iron?   325
    Epilogue: theory, linguistics and archaeological fieldwork   326
    Notes   327
    Acknowledgement   329

17 *Transition from Late Stone Age to Iron Age in the*
    Sudano-Sahelian zone: a case study from the Perichadian plain   330
    A. Holl
    Introduction   330

The emergence of iron technology in west Africa: discussion of hypotheses   330
Systemic analysis of iron technology   332
Earliest iron age sites: chronology and geographic distribution   334
Continuity and change: a Perichadian case study   336
The mound of Mdaga   341
Conclusion   343

18 *The antiquity of cultivation and herding in Ethiopia*   344
    D. W. Phillipson
    Introduction   344
    The archaeological sequence   346
    Botanical evidence for early Ethiopian agriculture   349
        Wheat and barley   349
        Teff   349
        Finger millet   349
        Flax   349
        Noog   349
        Ensete   350
        Chat and coffee   350
        Other food crops   350
    Rock paintings and other evidence for animal domestication   350
        Transport animals   350
        Cattle   351
        Sheep and goats   352
        Pig   352
        Dog and chicken   352
    The linguistic evidence for food production   353
    Archaeological and epigraphic evidence for plant cultivation and
        animal domestication   354
    Conclusion   356
    Note   357
    Acknowledgements   357

19 *The beginnings of food production in southwestern Kenya*   358
    P. Robertshaw
    The environment   359
    Later prehistory in South Nyanza   362
    Later prehistory in the Mara   366
    Conclusions   370
    Notes   370

20 *The rise and fall of nomadic pastoralism in the central Namib desert*   372
    J. Kinahan
    Introduction   372
    The rise of nomadic pastoralism in the Hungorob Ravine   374
    The fall of nomadic pastoralism in the !Khuiseb delta   381
    Conclusions   384

21 *The iron age peoples of east-central Botswana*   386
    D. Kiyaga-Mulindwa

22 *Iron age settlement and subsistence patterns in southern Malawi*   391
    Y. M. Juwayeyi
    Background   391
    The environmental setting   391
    The Early Iron Age   392
        Lakeshore and Shire valley sites   392
        The highlands sites   395
    The Late Iron Age   395
        Longwe pottery   396
        Mawudzu pottery   396
        Nkhudzi ware   397
    Iron-smelting   397
    Conclusion   397

23 *A question of identities: an anthropological enquiry and a historical*
    narrative   399
    J. O. Vogel
    Introduction   399
    The anthropological enquiry   400
        The matter of identity   400
        The cultural identity   400
        The funerary context   401
        The archaeological evidence of African burial practice   403
        The ethnographic record of African burial practice   403
        Another hypothesis   404
            The ethnographic record of the African production of salt   405
            The archaeological evidence of salt extraction and some inferences 406
    The historical narrative   406
    Acknowledgements   408

24 *A perspective on archaeological research in Mozambique*   409
    P. J. J. Sinclair, J. M. F. Morais, L. Adamowicz & R. T. Duarte
    Structuring the interpretive schema: concepts and formulations   410
    A collection strategy for material assemblages   412
    The foraging communities   413
    The farming communities   417
        The southern Mozambique coastal plain   417
        The northern Mozambique coastal plain   421
        The early farming communities: towards a synthesis   426
    Archaeology and national culture   428
    Appendix: ages in radiocarbon years before present   429
        Northern Mozambique coastal plain   429
        Southern Mozambique coastal plain   430
    Acknowledgements   431

25 *New evidence on early iron-smelting from southeastern Nigeria*   432
    E. E. Okafor
    Introduction: earlier studies of iron-smelting in Africa   432
    Experimental and analytical studies   434
    The rise and decline of African iron-smelting   436
    Analysis of iron-smelting residues from Nsukka Division, southeastern
        Nigeria   437
    Acknowledgements   448

26 *Changing perspectives on traditional iron production in west Africa*   449
    F. J. Kense & J. Ako Okoro
    Introduction   449
    Metallurgical background   450
    Ethnographic record   451
    Archaeological evidence   452
    Ethnohistorical/ethnoarchaeological approaches   455
    Origins of iron metallurgy   456
    The end of traditional iron-working   456
    Conclusion   458
    Note   458

27 *Iron technology in the middle Sahel/Savanna: with emphasis on
    central Darfur*   459
    I. Musa Muhammed
    Introduction   459
    The study area   459
    Traditional iron production in the middle Sahel/Savanna   461
    Evidence of early iron production   462
    Discussion   465
    Conclusions   466

28 *Iron-making techniques in the Kivu region of Zaïre: some of the
    differences between the South Maniema region and north Kivu*   468
    N'Sanda Buleli
    Introduction   468
    Prospecting   468
        Nature and method of prospecting   468
            Location   469
            Signs   469
            Prospecting instruments   469
            Grade of the ore   469
            Rites and taboos   469
            Season   470
        Extraction   470
            Methods of extraction   470
            Transportation of the ore   470

Extraction instruments   471
Protection of deposits   471
Preparation   471
  Ores   471
  Charcoal   471
  Construction of the furnace   472
    Maniema type   472
    Interlacustrine areas   473
Reduction process   473
Forging   475
  Tool making   475
  Location   475
  People working in the forge   475
  Tools   475
Conclusion   477

29 Ancient iron-working in Madagascar   478
    C. Radimilahy
    Notes   483
    Acknowledgements   483

30 The iron-using communities in Kenya   484
    H. O. Kiriama
    The early iron-using communities   484
    The 'Later Iron Age'   487
    Archaeological and linguistic correlations   489
    Alternative models: pottery use in a social context   492
    Bantu cultural variation: the Abagusii and Agikuyu of Kenya 494
    Conclusion   497
    Acknowledgement   498

31 Metaphors and representations associated with precolonial iron-
    smelting in eastern and southern Africa   499
    D. P. Collett
    Introduction   499
    Furnaces and products   500
    Smelting and procreation   502
    Reproduction, smelting and cooking   504
    Decoration on furnaces, decoration on pots   506
    A different system of beliefs   508
    Discussion   509
    Notes   510
    Acknowledgements   511

32 The magical production of iron in the Cameroon Grassfields 512
    M. Rowlands & J.-P. Warnier
    Tom Cham – heir to an ancient metallurgic tradition   513

The 'glazed sherds' iron industry 515
  Chronology 517
  The smelting techniques 518
  The smelting process 519
  More on the antiquity and continuity of the industry 522
Fertility and violence 522
Curing a spoilt workshop 528
The smelting process: a synthesis 529
Smithing 530
  Failure, and how to cope with it 533
'Science and magic' 535
  The 'level of ritualization' 538
  The efficacy of magical production 539
Conclusions 542
Notes 543
Appendix 1: Medicinal plants used in the 'glazed sherds' iron industry 543
  A Fertility-inducing smelting cocktail 544
  B Cocktail used in curing a foundry 545
  C The cocktail buried in the smithy 546
  D The herb used in 'curing' a smithy 547
Appendix 2: Glossary (We language) 547
  A Smelting cocktail 548
  B Cocktail used in curing a foundry 548
  C Cocktail buried in the smithy 549
  D Medicine used in curing a smithy 549

33 *Town and village in ancient Egypt: ecology, society and urbanization* 551
  F. A. Hassan
  Introduction 551
  The beginnings of urbanization: a hypothetical construct 551
  The record of ancient Egyptian settlements 558
  Methodology 559
  The urban population of ancient Egypt 560
  Number of villages in ancient Egypt 560
  Town/village ratio 561
  Size of ancient Egyptian villages 562
  The size of ancient Egyptian cities and towns 563
  Settlement hierarchy 564
  Transport 564
  Urban locations in a rural landscape 565
  Settlements and social interaction 566
  Final remarks 568
  Note 569
  Acknowledgements 569

34   *Urbanism in bronze age Egypt and northeast Africa*   570
      D. O'Connor
      Introduction   570
      The regions: environments and cultural histories   571
      Background   576
      Survival and recovery of urban and settlement sites   577
      Urbanism in Egyptian bronze age settlement patterns   578
      Secular aspects of cities and towns   580
      City as cosmos   581
      Urbanism in northeast Africa in the Bronze Age   583
      Conclusions   584
      Notes   585

35   *The land of Punt*   587
      K. A. Kitchen
      Introduction   587
      History of Punt from Egyptian sources   587
         Third millenium BC (Old Kingdom)   587
         Early second millenium BC (Middle Kingdom)   589
         Late second millenium BC (New Kingdom)   591
            Queen Hatshepsut   592
            Mid-XVIIIth Dynasty contacts   597
            Other allusions, Dynasties XVIII–XIX   600
            The Punt expedition of Ramesses III (*c.* 1184–1153 BC)   601
         First millenium BC   602
      Geographical location and extent of Punt   603
      Topography, archaeology, socio-political structure   604
         Topography and archaeology   604
         Socio-political structure   605
      The products of Punt   606
      The eclipse of Punt   606
      Notes   606

36   *State development and urbanism in northern Ethiopia*   609
      S. Munro-Hay
      The earliest evidence for state formation   609
      The Aksumite kingdom   614
      Urbanism in Aksumite Ethiopia   616
         The decline of Aksum   619

37   *Cities without citadels: understanding urban origins along the
      middle Niger*   622
      S. K. McIntosh & R. J. McIntosh
      Identifying urbanism in the archaeological record   625
      Urban origins in the middle Niger: a case study   627
         The excavations   629
         Reconstructing lifeways at Jenne-jeno   631

The regional survey   634
Regional trade and urban effects   638
Conclusion   641
Acknowledgements   641

38   *Urbanization and state formation in Ghana during the Iron Age*   642
     J. Anquandah
     Introduction   642
     Written history   644
     Ethnohistory and ethnography   645
     Archaeology   647
         La and Shai in the Iron Age   647
         Begho   648
         Bono Manso   650
     Conclusion   651

39   *The salt industries of west Africa: a preliminary study*   652
     J. Alexander
     Consumption   652
     Production   652
     Trading   653
     Before AD *c.* 400   655
     AD *c.* 400–1800   655
     AD 1800 onwards   656
     Discussion   657

40   *Trade and politics on the eastern littoral of Africa,* AD *800–1300*   658
     H. T. Wright
     The ninth and tenth centuries   659
     The eleventh to thirteenth centuries   665
     Conclusion   670

41   *Exploitation of marine resources: evidence for the origin of the*
     Swahili communities of east Africa   673
     M. Horton & N. Mudida
     Introduction   673
     Methodology   675
     The ecology of the Lamu archipelago   677
     Fish bones   678
         Identified fish species   678
     Discussion   679
         The significance of fish in Swahili diet   680
         Marine exploitation and the origin of the Swahili   682
     Appendix   683

42   *Coast–interior settlements and social relations in the Kenya coastal*
     hinterland   694
     G. H. O. Abungu & H. W. Mutoro

Introduction   694
Settlement studies in east Africa   694
The Mijikenda *makaya*   697
Coast–interior relations   699
  Ungwana   699
  The Tana basin and ceramic tradition   702
  Coast–interior relations: the Tana delta and basin   703
Conclusion   704

43 *Urban trajectories on the Zimbabwean plateau*   705
   P. J. J. Sinclair, I. Pikirayi, G. Pwiti & R. Soper
Perceiving complexity: the case of the Zimbabwe state   705
Methodological and empirical considerations   708
Great Zimbabwe tradition settlement location: the environmental setting 711
  Site catchment analysis   714
  Soil types and agricultural potential   716
  Vegetation   716
  Discussion   717
Settlement patterns and the context of Great Zimbabwe tradition sites 718
  The survey   720
  The cultural succession   721
    Early Gokomere tradition   721
    Musengezi tradition   722
    Great Zimbabwe tradition   722
  Survey results   722
  Discussion   723
The historical period in northern Zimbabwe: archaeological evidence
for the Mutapa state   725
  Introduction   725
  The site of Baranda: a case study   726
  Baranda in a local and regional context   729
  Archaeological evidence for the Mutapa state   730
Conclusions   731
Acknowledgements   731

44 *Settlement area and communication in African towns and cities*   732
   R. Fletcher
Introduction   732
Method   732
Methodological issues: factors affecting the accuracy of area estimates 733
  The presentation of observational statements   733
  Ambiguity of definition   741
Interaction/communication constraints and the size of settlements   743
  Comment   744
Interaction/communication issues   745
Conclusion   747

Note 748
Acknowledgements 749

References 750

Index 835

List of contributors

George H. O. Abungu, Department of Coastal Archaeology, The National Museums of Kenya, Fort Jesus Museum, Mombasa, Kenya.

L. Adamowicz, Department of Archaeology and Anthropology, Eduardo Mondlane University, Maputo, Mozambique.

J. Alexander, St John's College, University of Cambridge, UK.

Bassey W. Andah, Department of Archaeology and Anthropology, University of Ibadan, Nigeria.

James Anquandah, Department of Archaeology, University of Ghana, Legon, Ghana.

Roger Blench, Independent Researcher, Cambridge, UK.

N'Sanda Buleli, Kivu University Research Centre, Kivu, Zaïre.

A. Close, Department of Anthropology, Southern Methodist University, Dallas, USA.

Juliet Clutton-Brock, Department of Zoology, The Natural History Museum, London, UK.

D. P. Collett, Independent Researcher, Melbourne, Australia.

R. Duarte, Department of Archaeology and Anthropology, Eduardo Mondlane University, Maputo, Mozambique.

Manfred K. H. Eggert, Institut für Altertumskunde, Universität Erlangen–Nürnberg, Germany.

Christopher Ehret, Department of History, University College of Los Angeles, California, USA.

J. Evans, School of Science, Polytechnic of East London, UK.

Roland Fletcher, Department of Anthropology, University of Sydney, Australia.

C. A. Folorunso, Department of Archaeology and Anthroplogy, University of Ibadan, Nigeria.

A. T. Grove, Downing College, Cambridge, UK.

Jack R. Harlan, previously Agronomy Department, University of Illinois, Urbana, USA.

Fekri A. Hassan, Department of Anthropology, Washington State University, Washington, USA.

Augustin Holl, Département d'Ethnologie et Préhistoire, Université de Paris X, Nanterre, France.

Mark Horton, British Institute in Eastern Africa, Nairobi, Kenya.

Rupert A. Housley, Radiocarbon Accelerator Unit, Oxford University, UK.

Yusuf M. Juwayeyi, Department of Antiquities, Lilongwe, Malawi.

Frank J. Kense, Department of Archaeology, University of Calgary, Canada.

John Kinahan, State Museum, Windhoek, Namibia.

Herman Ogati Kiriama, The National Museums of Kenya, Nairobi, Kenya.

K. A. Kitchen, Department of Oriental Studies (Egyptology), University of Liverpool, UK.

D. Kiyaga-Mulindwa, Department of History, University of Botswana, Gaborone, Botswana.

Halina Krolik, Institute for the History of Material Culture, Warsaw, Poland.

J. Maley, Laboratoire de Palynologie du CNRS, Université des Sciences et Techniques de Languedoc, Montpellier, France.

Roderick J. McIntosh, Department of Anthropology, Rice University, Texas, USA.

Susan Keech McIntosh, Department of Anthropology, Rice University, Texas, USA.

Stuart Monro-Hay, Independent Researcher, London, UK.

J. M. F. Morais, Tropical Research Institute, Lisbon, Portugal.

Nina Mudida, Department of Osteology, The National Museums of Kenya, Nairobi, Kenya.

Ibrahim Musa Muhammed, Department of Historical and Archaeological Studies, University of Gayounis, Benghazi, Libya.

Henry W. Mutoro, Department of History, University of Nairobi, Kenya.

A. Muzzolini, Laboratoire d'Archéozoologie, St-André-de-Cruzières, France.

David O'Connor, University Museum, University of Pennsylvania, USA.

S. Oluwole Ogundele, Department of Archaeology and Anthropology, University of Ibadan, Nigeria.

Edwin E. Okafor, Department of Archaeology, University of Nigeria, Nsukka, Nigeria.

John Ako Okoro, Department of Anthropology, University of Toronto, Canada.

Alex Ikechukwu Okpoko,   Institute of African Studies, University of Nigeria, Nsukka, Nigeria.

David W. Phillipson,   University Museum, University of Cambridge, UK.

Innocent Pikirayi,   History Department, University of Zimbabwe, Harare, Zimbabwe.

Gilbert Pwiti,   History Department, University of Zimbabwe, Harare, Zimbabwe.

Chantal Radimilahy,   Musée d'Art et d'Archéologie, Antananarivo, Madagascar.

Peter Robertshaw,   Department of Anthropology, California State University, San Bernardino, USA.

Michael Rowlands,   Department of Anthropology, University College London, UK.

Romuald Schild,   Institute for the History of Material Culture, Warsaw, Poland.

Thurstan Shaw,   previously Department of Archaeology, University of Ibadan, Nigeria.

Paul Sinclair,   Department of Archaeology, Uppsala University, Sweden.

Robert Soper,   History Department, University of Zimbabwe, Harare, Zimbabwe.

Ann B. Stahl,   Department of Anthropology, State University of New York at Binghamton, USA.

Joseph O. Vogel,   Department of Anthropology, University of Alabama, USA.

J.-P. Warnier,   Département d'Ethnologie, Sorbonne, Paris, France.

Krystyna Wasylikowa,   W. Szafer Institute of Botany, Cracow, Poland.

F. Wendorf,   Department of Anthropology, Southern Methodist University, Dallas, USA.

Wilma Wetterstrom,   Botanical Museum, Harvard University, Cambridge, Mass., USA.

Kay Williamson,   Faculty of Humanities, University of Port Harcourt, Nigeria.

H. T. Wright,   Museum of Anthropology, University of Michigan, Ann Arbor, USA.

Foreword

This book is the last to be published of twenty-two volumes resulting from the First World Archaeological Congress, held in Southampton, England, in September 1986, twenty of which have appeared in the *One World Archaeology* series. This series reflects the enormous academic impact of the Congress, which was attended by 850 people from more than 70 countries, and attracted many additional contributions from others who were unable to attend in person.

The *One World Archaeology* series is the result of a determined and highly successful attempt to bring together for the first time not only archaeologists and anthropologists from many different parts of the world, as well as academics from a host of contingent disciplines, but also non-academics from a wide range of cultural backgrounds, who could lend their own expertise to the discussions at the Congress. Many of the latter, accustomed to being treated as the 'subjects' of archaeological and anthropological observation, had never before been admitted as equal participants in the discussion of their own (cultural) past or present, with their own particularly vital contribution to make towards global, cross-cultural understanding.

The Congress therefore addressed world archaeology in its widest sense. Central to a world archaeological approach is the investigation not only of how people lived in the past but also of how, and why, changes took place resulting in the forms of societies and cultures which exist today. Contrary to popular belief, and the archaeology of some twenty years ago, world archaeology is much more than the mere recording of specific historic events, embracing as it does the study of social and cultural change in its entirety. All the books in the *One World Archaeology* series are the result of meetings and discussions which took place within a context that encouraged self-criticism and recognition, among those attending the Congress, of the limitations of their own interpretations of the past. Many participants experienced a new self-awareness and awe about past and present human endeavours, all of which are reflected in this unique series.

The Congress was organized around major themes. Several of these were based on the discussion of full-length, precirculated papers. Other sessions, including some dealing with areas of specialization defined by period or geographical region, were based on oral addresses, or a combination of precirculated papers and lectures. In all cases, the entire sessions were recorded on cassette, and all contributors were presented with the recordings of the discussion of their papers. The Congress organizers felt that if such a meeting of many hundreds of participants did not leave behind a published record of its academic discussions it would be little more than an exercise in tourism.

From the very beginning, in 1982, of the detailed planning for the World Archaeological Congress, the intention was to produce post-Congress books containing only selected contributions; these were to be revised in the light of discussions during the sessions as well as during subsequent consultations with the academic editors appointed for each book. Particularly in the case of sessions based on precirculated papers, all contributors were aware of the subsequent publication schedules: if their papers were selected for publication they would have only a few months to revise them according to editorial specifications, and they would become authors in an important academic volume.

As the Preface to this volume records, *The Archaeology of Africa: food, metals and towns* had its origins in two separate discussion sessions at the 1986 Congress: one, lasting one-and-a-half days, was defined in terms of the 'Neolithic', and the other, of a single day's duration, was defined with reference to 'iron-using peoples'. The former session was under the control of two of the editors (TS & BA) of the present book while the second was co-organized by another editor (AO). Both discussion sessions were specific to Africa; in addition, of course, many important African case studies feature in several of the thematic *One World Archaeology* volumes.

Behind these bald facts of the origin of this book lies much of the central controversy which affected the First World Archaeological Congress, namely the exclusion, late in 1985, of potential participants from apartheid Namibia and South Africa in accordance with UNESCO directives (Ucko 1987; Shaw 1989). This action led to the loss from the organization of the 'iron-using' discussion session of David Phillipson (Ucko 1987, p. 60), and his potential services as an editor of *The Archaeology of Africa: food, metals and towns*. His successor as organizer, John Alexander, was for various reasons unable to assemble for publication a representative collection of papers from the 1986 Congress, and in 1988 Paul Sinclair, who had acted as a session chairman at the 1986 Congress, became the fourth editor of this book.

The above reminder of the history and development of events in 1985 and 1986 emphasizes the symbolic importance of this book as the last of the series to derive from the First World Archaeological Congress.

Why, then, has it taken so much longer to produce this book on Africa than others on different topics in the series, especially since one volume, *Archaeology and the Information Age: a global perspective*, deriving from the Second World Archaeological Congress meeting of 1990, has already been published?

One of the many contributory reasons for this long delay was the result of the crucial decision in 1987 to produce a book exclusively devoted to the archaeology of Africa, as opposed to several books focusing cross-continentally on specific time periods or forms of economic subsistence strategies. This decision inexorably led to the realization in 1989 that major restructuring of the book was necessary, and that several gaps in coverage – for example, some aspects of the archaeology of Egypt, Ethiopia, etc. – still remained to be plugged by the commissioning of many new chapters for the book. It has been one of the several delights of the production of this book to find the willing response to requests for new or revised chapters (see Preface). Among these are contributions by Phillipson, Alexander and several others who were unhappy with the events of 1985/6; the participation of such authors in this book – as in other volumes within the *One World Archaeology* series – is a clear denial of any on-going divisiveness of the 1985/6 academic boycott (despite Chippindale's (1990, p. 9) editorial claims to the contrary). Equally positive has been the willing acceptance by many contributors of the need for severe editing of their manuscripts.

Another major contributory reason for the belated publication of *The Archaeology of Africa: food, metals and towns* is less positive. In order to meet the established, and publicly recognized, high editorial requirements of the *One World Archaeology* series, standardization of terms, the spelling of locations and sites, and the construction of quality maps have proved to be a nightmare. This has been particularly so with regard to publishing the results of C14 dating. The point is not that individual scholars do not exist who are actively engaged in producing high quality scientific work but that, overall, there appears to be an absence of group understanding and appreciation of the implications of such work. One of the results is that African archaeology not only lags behind many other parts of the world in not automatically providing standardized essential information to accompany C14 dates, calibrated and uncalibrated, and other dates obtained by scientific methods, but it is also subject to the cultural preferences and conventions of colonial powers, notably those of Britain, France and Germany, as well as the United States of America. Each of these countries has different traditions, such traditions often also varying according to the particular subdiscipline concerned (e.g. Pleistocene versus Holocene versus Egyptological versus Historic). Treading a success-ful editorial path through the idiosyncrasies of European and American authors in-volved in the archaeology of Africa has proved to be no easy matter. Surely, however, it cannot be long before all those involved in African archaeology must not only agree on, but also implement, agreed conventions (Sinclair 1988, pp. 5, 6, 13) for all publications of its results, within and outside the continent. So far this is far from happening (as also is the case in this book); serious publications such as the *Journal of African History* may not be out of order in continuing the 'established practice [of only giving dates] in uncalibrated form', but clearly it must attempt to do more, since 'in some cases use of the calibration curve results in significant changes in relation to calendar dates' (Sinclair 1991, p. 179).

Nevertheless, pride of place in editorial disenchantment must lie with the problems of referencing. It can presumably be argued that it is historically instructive to trace the development of names and meanings hidden behind journal and institute acronyms: IFAN, for example, metamorphosing in 1966/7 from the *Institut Français-* to the *Institut Fondamental- d'Afrique Noire*, and ORSTOM originally standing for *Office de la Recherche Scientifique et Technique d'Outre-Mer*, but nowadays the *Institut Français de Recherche Scientifique pour le Développement en Cooperation*; or the *Acts* of an organization oscillating between Association and Congress, between Pan and Pan-African, and its coverage altering from Prehistory, to Prehistory and Quaternary Studies, to Prehistory and Related Subjects. Less amusing, however, is the fact that – with a very few notable exceptions – few of the conventions of normal academic referencing standards apply to the vast majority of publications on African archaeology, whether written by Africans, Americans or Europeans, whether published in, for example, the *West African Journal of Archaeology* or *Azania*. In academic journals such as these it is the norm, rather than the exception, to find articles in which quoted references are inaccurate with regard to date, book or article title, journal number or page numbers. In some cases authors cite wrong references even to their *own* published works! Such inaccuracies bedevilled the manu-scripts of many of the authors writing chapters for this book too; it is no exaggeration to report that correcting bibliographical inaccuracies of this kind, together with essential stylistic rewriting and necessary retyping of contributions, demanded editorial work lasting most of two years, and very considerable financial outlay. It was the enormity of this bibliographical work, and its unusually comprehensive academic coverage, that led to the decision to depart from past *One World Archaeology* series practice and to publish a consolidated reference section at the end of this book – an exercise which itself revealed many further bibliographic anomalies and deficiencies, all of which had to be remedied.

De Maret's words (1990, p. 109) regarding the archaeology of Central Africa capture some of the problems well:

> During the colonial era, Central Africa was divided among nearly all the colonial powers, since the ten modern states (Cameroon, southern Chad, the Central African Republic, Equatorial Guinea, Gabon, Congo, Zaïre, Angola, Rwanda and Burundi) which now exist result from the interaction between France, Belgium, Germany, Spain, Portugal and the United Kingdom. . . . Archaeologically the result was a dispersion of effort and a diversity of publications in numerous journals, which often had only limited circulation.

Adequate editing of this book has suffered greatly from this overall situation; with regard to one chapter, for example, despite written enquiries to several Belgian colleagues, phone calls to the Zaïre Embassy and unanswered letters to the Zaïrean author, it has not been possible to obtain any bibliographical details at all! Such problems are not restricted to this part of Africa.

As the Introduction to *The Archaeology of Africa: food, metals and towns* makes plain, much of the history of African archaeology (see, for example, the 'Report of Second Conference of West African Archaeologists' as published in 1967 in the *West African Archaeological Newsletter* 7, 33–5) reveals the problems which have beset the discipline, deriving from the application of terms such as 'neolithic' and 'iron age', which had been developed within a European context, to the material evidence of Africa's past. This main warning message of *The Archaeology of Africa: food, metals and towns* cautions us in the present context to ask whether insistence on a European-derived set of bibliographic standards of accuracy – not to mention the delicate question of exactly *which* particular conventional standards – might also be a retrogressive step. Such a question needs also to be considered in the context of some of the main points made in several of the *One World Archaeology* volumes (for example, chapters by Nzewunwa and by Wandibba in *The Excluded Past: archaeology in education*, edited by P. Stone & R. MacKenzie): namely, that many African archaeologists are unable to consult published literature (let alone any unpublished archives based in the home countries of foreign excavators) without the utmost difficulties, and that differential access to information may easily risk a return to exploitation and domination (see Chapters 11–18 in *State and Society: the emergence and development of social hierarchy and political centralization*, edited by J. Gledhill, B. Bender & M. T. Larsen). It is still much too early to predict (Ucko 1992, p. ix) whether the changing nature of the concept of 'a book' (see the Preface and Chapter 1 of *The Meanings of Things: material culture and symbolic expression*, edited by

I. Hodder, and the Introduction to *Archaeology and the Information Age: a global perspective*, edited by P. Reilly & S. Rahtz) may, in the future, alter current conditions of scholarship so radically that the requirements of academic writing may become unrecognizable, possibly also to the benefit of the African archaeologist.

In present-day Africa, most African archaeologists face almost insuperable difficulties in carrying out their work. These difficulties include not only all kinds of academic isolation mentioned by Ibeanu (1991), but also those resulting from lack of government support, absence of vehicles and petrol, inadequacy of career structures and, in many areas, the impact of antiquities dealing and the plundering of sites. Nevertheless, whatever conditions apply to scholars in Africa which might suffice to excuse inaccurate and insufficient referencing, current bibliographical practices within African archaeology – whatever their derivation – have resulted in distortion of quotations, misrepresentation of published views and, at least, confusion regarding dates and even site localities – in other words, much of African archaeology currently consists of poor scholarship, and poor practice. Whatever may be excused in this respect by the conditions of work for African archaeologists based in Africa, no scholar (African or other) based in Europe, America or Canada working in such academic centres as Cambridge, Calgary, London, Los Angeles, Paris, Uppsala or Washington – all with well-stocked libraries – has any excuse not to insist on, at least, bibliographic *accuracy* (details such as whether or not the names of publishers should be included in references, or whether the citing of page references of chapters within books should be obligatory, are still open to discussion, and demand a consensus view). Not to lead *by example* with regard to the accurate citation of other people's published views is, surely, to encourage the growth of a further unnecessary divide between the nature and practice of scholarship in different parts of the world.

Given the practical difficulties of an archaeological career in most of Africa, given its enormously wide diversity of terrain, culture and language, and given the political and social divisions between anglo-, luso- and franco-phone influence, it is perhaps not surprising that the growth of theory within African archaeology has been stunted and that synthesis has, to date, been exceptional.

It is perhaps surprising that any overall African archaeological picture can be attempted. Yet, this is exactly what the editors have accomplished in their Introduction to this book, not on the basis of a geographical or even temporal coverage, but in terms of thematic cultural developments and cultural diversities. This is one of the features of *The Archaeology of Africa: food, metals and towns* which makes the book almost unique (and see Connah 1987).

In countries such as Sweden, the UK and the USA (and, therefore, no doubt, everywhere else except within the African continent), African archaeology – or the archaeology of Africa – is still considered a peripheral study to mainstream archaeology: except, of course, in the context of the study of early hominids and their possible dispersal from an original African homeland (see *The Origins of Human Behaviour*, edited by R. Foley). *The Archaeology of Africa: food, metals and towns* is an overt challenge to the world archaeological community not to continue simply to reproduce the stultifying descriptive material which constitutes much of the past writings on the later archaeology of Africa. This book offers many novel *analyses* of Africa's past, all pointing to the importance of the African archaeological record.

Another exceptional feature of the present volume is the fact that the majority of authors in this book are those who, having found themselves caught within the limitations of purely descriptive archaeology, have actively tried to remedy it, as well as those from outside Africa who attempt to contribute to the strength of archaeological research in Africa either by excavation or by synthesis. Despite the fact that the traditional influences of European preoccupations, styles and practices continue to form a significant part of the tangled web through which the archaeologists of Africa still have to thread their way, this book suggests that the analysis of the past in Africa may be entering a unique phase of collaborative understanding and cooperation: at this time it appears that *analysis* of *evidence* is the new order of the day and that there is a move away from the deadening parameter of simple 'normative' description which has characterized archaeological writing on the Far East (see, for example, Chapter 18 in *The Excluded Past: archaeology in education*, edited by P. Stone & R. MacKenzie, and Chapter 6 in *Archaeology and the Information Age: a global perspective*, edited by P. Reilly & S. Rahtz) and eastern Europe (see *From the Baltic to the Black Sea*, edited by D. Austin & L. Alcock).

Here we must introduce a note of caution. Current attempts to move beyond the mere description of archaeological material culture and the evidence of past environmental and ecological conditions, towards what is considered to be the fashionable language and format of (American and European) archaeological analysis, are often clouded and defeated by lack of appreciation of the context of the relevant analytical parameters under discussion. Many of those trying to come to grips with the necessary concepts and terminologies are exactly those who have little time for individual study – normally, scholars resident within Africa who are grossly overstretched by teaching and administrative duties with little time or finance to travel to the library resources they need. Only too rarely do they get the chance to spend sufficiently extended periods of time overseas to participate in peer discussions, or to interact with postgraduate research students. Until more of the archaeologists of Africa are also accepted as internationally important theoreticians, the acceptance of African archaeology as a necessary and mainstream part of everyone's archaeological background knowledge (at least at student level) remains unlikely.

One of the hopes for the future is that African governments and world bodies (see Nkwanga 1991) will now recognize the importance of archaeology to the health of nations. Another hope is that, with the return of South African archaeologists to the international forum, the high technical and organizational quality of the archaeology practised in that country will be able to serve as a support to their colleagues in other parts of Africa. One of the fascinations for the future will be to watch the results of interactions between the different archaeological traditions which will now need to develop a social and political framework adequate to assure positive coexistence within the African continent. Meanwhile, the World Archaeological Congress and a few other archaeological organizations recognize as priorities the provision of archaeological literature to African countries as gifts or at prices that they can afford, and the guarantee of an effective African presence at relevant international meetings.

Whatever the difficulties that beset them, the resilience evident among the major contingent of African archaeologists who participated in the First World Archaeological Congress in 1986, and among those who attended the 'Conference in Honour of Professor Thurstan Shaw' in Ibadan in 1989 (Mahachi 1991), cannot and must not be denied. Against all the odds – from lack of adequate financial support to the malfunctioning of postal services and the inadequacies of telephone connections, even (or, in particular) between neighbouring African countries – the latter conference in Ibadan not only took place (and even included the participation of francophone colleagues from Benin who had received no salaries for over six months) but also resulted in the immediate publication of some of its proceedings (e.g. Andah 1990). For those who, following the conference, were privileged to travel east as part of Thurstan Shaw's 'entourage' (Frontispiece) there is no possible doubt concerning the vital role that the archaeological past plays in the African present (and see Chapters 13, 14, 15, 16 and 23 in *The Politics of the Past*, edited by P. Gathercole & D. Lowenthal). For those of us who see the importance of archaeological endeavour in terms of its future and current role within the society of the world, Africa can – despite all its troubles – act as an inspiration.

The archaeology of Africa is, of course, an inspiration in a whole variety of other ways as well. Some of the more positive results of the European colonial past are those examples of genuine cooperation between scholars from outside Africa and those from within; in some cases such cooperation has led to unforgettable images (Ucko 1992, p. viii) and the legacies of such cooperation, be they through the provision of equipment or exposure to specialist training, will undoubtedly live on for a significant period. Equally inspirational are the archaeological insights being provided by indigenous African archaeologists, both to the understanding of the culture history of the African continent (of which there are numerous examples in this book) – through further excavation or by reanalysis of existing evidence – and through contributions to archaeological theory and methodology (of which, again, there are numerous examples in this book). Several chapters are concerned with the evidence from ethnoarchaeology and oral traditions. Through these, a unique African contribution to previous assumptions about cultural continuity and discontinuity, and about the nature of ethnic identity (and see *Archaeological Approaches to Cultural Identity*, edited by S. Shennan), is clearly foreshadowed in the present volume (and see Agorsah 1990). It is exciting to read in this book the way that many current approaches to past environment, ecology and material cultures are transforming the previous orthodoxy of the picture of Africa's past, from pleistocene to very recent times. African archaeology is replacing the past stereotypes of Nilo-Hamites and Bantu peoples with the long overdue recognition of the vitality and importance of local cultural traditions. It is also exciting to find such detailed discussion, in an archaeological volume, of the possible significance of the interplay of modern linguistic evidence, no matter how controversial it is, and archaeological evidence about the past of Africa. A shared feature of all this current work is that it is based on the critical re-evaluation of data which have hitherto been assumed to show a very different picture of Africa's past. Such re-evaluations reveal the difficulties of establishing the exclusiveness of various subsistence strategies of many past African cultures, and the dangers of assuming particular technological practices when there is no firm and direct evidence to demonstrate their existence. Each of these investigations reinforces the conclusion, already mentioned above, that it is dangerous and unwarranted to transfer uncritically any hierarchical systems of classification, and their attendant terminologies, from one body of archaeological material to another.

There remains, of course, the one overwhelming, and single most important, question and message of this book. How has it been possible for knowledge about the past of such a vast continent as Africa, full of diverse, complex and innovative cultures spanning many thousands of years, to have been relegated so ignominiously to universal neglect within the consciousness of world public education? What are the historical, social and political circumstances which have allowed the cultural pride of a whole continent to be ignored, within both formal and informal education curricula all over the world, in favour of the recognition of the worth of only one particular facet of a specific ancient civilization – that of literate ancient Egypt?

Whatever the answer to this question, the future is most unlikely ever to be the same. The achievements in adaptation, in innovation and in social complexity of past African cultures are now beginning to find their rightful places within the materials available within Africa for school, museum and public education. Such an appreciation is not restricted to countries within Africa; thus, for example, the UK National Curriculum for the subject of history now allows study of the ancient Benin Kingdom of Nigeria, while the results of several archaeological investigations within Africa, and of the 'Urban Origins in Eastern Africa Archaeological Project', in particular, have been made accessible in 1991 in attractive popular form in Sweden (*Popular Arkeologi* 9).

Many of the messages of *The Archaeology of Africa: food, metals and towns* continue to concern questions which have long intrigued archaeologists. Thus, in this book, there is much new evidence about the role of plants in pre-agrarian diet, about the beginnings of sedentism and about the domestication of plants and animals in many parts of Africa at different times, and under different conditions, in the past (and see *Foraging and Farming: the evolution of plant exploitation*, edited by D. Harris & G. Hillman; *The Walking Larder: patterns of domestication, pastoralism, and predation*, edited by J. Clutton-Brock). These new analyses all support Thurstan Shaw's original contention at the First World Archaeological Congress in 1986 (Ucko 1987, p. 221) that the term 'neolithic' is not an appropriate one in the African context. There is also much that is intriguingly new about the early exploitation of copper (and see Herbert 1984; Chikwendu, Craddock, Farquhar, Shaw & Gumeji 1989) and the beginnings, development and symbolism of iron-working in different parts of the continent, and especially about how such technological developments may have interacted with social organization and with inter-societal contacts (and see *What's New? A closer look at the process of innovation*, edited by S. van der Leeuw & R. Torrence). There are also detailed analyses of how the lack of recognition of generally accepted archaeological criteria for urbanism could have lasted for so many years; accordingly, the arguments presented here for indigenous urban African developments are revolutionary.

This immensely important book will serve to dispel any doubt about the capacity of archaeology to provide genuine knowledge of the human past, and archaeology's corrective role in assessing the reliability of historical written records, to reveal the actualities of past human endeavours, achievements and activities.

P. J. Ucko
Southampton

Preface

This book has had a long and complex gestation (see Foreword).

Alex Ikechukwu Okpoko derives his position as one of the editors of this book from the early history of the organization of the two sessions of the 1986 World Archaeological Congress (on 'The Neolithic of Africa' and 'Iron-using Peoples in Sub-Saharan Africa') which were exclusively devoted to African archaeology. At that time he worked indefatigably to ensure as major participation as possible from Africans: both in terms of individuals actually being present at the Congress in Southampton and in the soliciting, from authors unable to attend, of papers to be read *in absentia*. He also presented his own academic paper to the Congress. In addition, until 1989, he wrote to Congress contributors asking them for revised versions of their original papers.

We also thank John Alexander for having assisted with the running of Congress sessions and for having begun the process of gathering papers together to be transformed into book chapters. At the Congress we were joined in chairing discussion sessions by B. Andah, F. N. Anozie, J. Anquandah, D. Kiyaga-Mulindwa and S. G. Wandibba.

The real job of making the Congress proceedings into one coherent book has taken place from 1987 onwards – primarily by soliciting and commissioning chapters to complement relevant topics where they were deficient and to try to cover geographic gaps. In this regard, Bassey Andah's editorial role in contacting authors in western Africa to clarify academic content and referencing obscurities proved invaluable. With the assistance of the British Council it proved possible for us to meet with him and the Series Editor in 1989 in England and it was on this occasion that we were able to review the results so far achieved and to determine the final structure of the book and to decide, even at this late date, to seek the inclusion of certain new topics.

We therefore wish to record our particular thanks to two categories of authors in this volume: the early contributors to the book for their patience in staying with us so that we could produce this work in its present form; and the late contributors for responding so enthusiastically to our requests to produce chapters in such a short space of time.

During the years of work on this volume, the *One World Archaeology* series has moved from Allen & Unwin to Unwin Hyman, then on to Harper Collins and, very recently, to Routledge. Throughout these, and other, periods of uncertainty we have been sustained by the encouragement and devotion to African archaeology of the Swedish Agency for Research Cooperation with Developing Countries, in particular the Urban Origins in Eastern Africa Project, which has also provided financial assistance towards the production of this book.

We would like to thank Christina Bendegard for dedicated editorial assistance and Brian Molyneaux for having attempted the impossible in trying to standardize terminology, references and nomenclature throughout the book.

Finally, we should like to express our indebtedness to the monumental efforts of the indefatigable Series Editor of the *One World Archaeology* series, Peter Ucko, without whose persistence and vision this volume would not have seen the light of day. Because of this, and because of the major part he played in creating the form of the final manuscript, we asked him to be named with us as an academic editor of this book, but he declined.

Thurstan Shaw
(Cambridge)

Paul Sinclair
(Uppsala)

February 1992

Radiocarbon dates

Throughout the text, 'bp' (i.e. before 1950) refers to uncalibrated radiocarbon dates, and 'cal BC', 'cal BP' and 'cal AD' to calibrated radiocarbon dates.

Despite considerable efforts, it proved impossible to standardize the book in such a way that calendric and uncalibrated radiocarbon dates ('BC', 'BP' and 'AD') could always be distinguished. This situation accurately reflects the current position in African archaeology.

Even the amount of standardization that has been successfully accomplished offends established practice in some countries.

Introduction

PAUL J. J. SINCLAIR, THURSTAN SHAW &
BASSEY ANDAH

This book is about change in Africa, the changes that have occurred over the last twenty millennia, but principally over the last ten. (We do not deal with the older 'Early Humankind' story revealed in the eastern half of Africa; we are entirely concerned with modern humans, *Homo sapiens sapiens*.) There have been many changes in the environment, there have been changes in the way people have lived, there have been changes in the interactions between these two. In the vast continent of Africa these changes were not uniform: there are today, and always have been, many differing environments in Africa, and the ways different people have exploited these environments have also varied. Change does not necessarily mean a complete break with what went before; change often came to an underlying continuity.

Far and away the greater part of the story of these changes has been written not by contemporary historians, but in the earth; accordingly this story is revealed by the methods of archaeology and of palaeoenvironmental study, assisted where appropriate by oral history and ethnography, including the history of languages, as far as this can be elucidated. From this perspective archaeology is not ancillary to history but, on the contrary, the sources of historical scholarship can be seen as a limited subset of those available to the field of archaeology. Contemporary documents are the texts which historians have to study and interpret; records in the soil form a different kind of text which has to be interpreted by archaeological means. Archaeology has the double task of recovering such texts, and then of finding appropriate approaches or methods of interpreting them (Hodder 1986; Hodder 1989). Other records are embedded in living languages, which only comparative linguistics can reveal. This book attempts to make the double offering of primary textual material and of its interpretation, although the greater part of the book is occupied in presenting and synthesizing the data and less with interpretation.

African archaeology was a relative late-comer in the field of world archaeology (e.g. see Ch. 24) and has not yet accumulated the density of archaeological data that exist from Europe and America. One of the distinguishing features of the development of archaeology in Euroamerica over the last thirty years has been that this density of existing data has fostered a variety of theoretical methods of interpretation. This is not to suggest that masses of data inevitably lead to the development of analytical theory; clearly the case of, for example, Japan or the USSR (Oikawa 1991; Trifonov 1991; Oikawa 1992; Trifonov & Dolukhanov 1992) demonstrates that this is not a necessary consequence. Nevertheless, it must remain true that the stage reached in the archaeology of many areas of Africa is still inadequate with regard to context and content, and without a minimum of such data any attempts at structural analysis become an arbitrary imposition of meaning. It is from their provision of possible analogues for context and content that ethnoarchaeological studies, of which a number are included in this book, e.g. Folorunso & Ogundele, Ch. 15; Vogel, Ch. 23; Rowlands & Warnier, Ch. 32; Okafor Ch. 25, gain their importance.

The main changes which are documented in this book, reflected in the sub-title *Foods, Metals and Towns*, are threefold. They are, first, changes in the ways people gained, processed and distributed their food at different times; second, the change from a technology without metals to a metal–using one; and third, shifts towards urbaniza-tion and the establishment of settlements larger than villages. These changes did not blanket the continent with a technological or socio-organizational uniformity charac-teristic of Africa as a whole. A series of contributions in this book corrects such misconceptions and provides new points of departure for future archaeological contri-butions to the development of theory in African archaeology. In view of the necessity for providing a balanced coverage of the changes in production and social organization which form the central core of the book, and because of the need to free African archaeology from the limitations of foreign terminology, the research topics are dealt with here thematically rather than following the classical European model of Neolithic, Iron Age and Historic, chronologically or sequentially. This is also in order to avoid the implications of unidirectional progress which are inherent in the classical model, and to focus the readers' attention on some of the assumptions which underpin our views of the African past. Such an approach emphasizes the long–term relevance to African archaeology of the themes of terminology, diffusion and invention, environmental relations, food production and urbanism. These themes will cut across the usual categories of traditional archaeological discourse.

The history of the archaeological interpretation of Africa is riddled with assump-tions, as in other continents. In Africa the assumptions differ from those elsewhere only (a) in terms of scale and (b) as a consequence of colonial attitudes. For example, when the 'beaker folk' were conceived of as roaming about in Europe, it was within the continent of Europe itself. At the same time, because of (a) and (b) above, any innovations within the continent of Africa were only considered to be derived from people migrating to Africa from elsewhere. It was only later, in relation to questions concerning the spread of Bantu languages, that an intra–continental frame of reference was established, although still within a migrationist perspective.

Let us look at three sets of assumptions in more detail.

'. . . as far as we know, Africa has never invented anything, but has only received from others' (Ankermann 1905, p. 55). In the early parts of this century, whereas the 'exceptional' events in the African past (e.g. the flowering of Egyptian civilization) were seen as deriving from specific environmental circumstances, the 'norm' was conceived as a hesitant development from the most simple to the more complex, i.e. development was assumed to be a slow crawl towards something more sophisticated. Anything other than this was assumed to come from outside sources.

'Normal' development within such a framework was clearly to be seen and recog-nized archaeologically only in terms of technological development. A convenient framework already existed at this time, that of Thomsen and Montelius from Scandinavia, a framework which became the formative basis for European academic traditions (Daniel 1978; Trigger 1989). In short, from the 1880s onwards, influenced by the widely distributed works of Darwin, the dominant European assumptions in African studies were of an inevitable movement upwards within a sociocultural hierarchy, from hunting and gathering, via pastoralism, to settled agricultural life, eventually leading to 'civilization'. These steps 'upwards' fitted in well with contemporary anthropological and archaeological theories of human progression from savagery to barbarism to civilization, and also with attitudes towards the living representatives of such stages in different parts of the world. Thus, Routledge & Routledge could write, 'the Akikuyu of today are in their civilization and methods at the point where our ancestors stood in earliest times. Present at trial by ordeal, the life of our Saxon ancestors becomes a living reality; watching the pot maker and the smith, the hand of the clock is put back yet farther, and the dead of Britain's tumuli go once more about their daily avocations' (Routledge & Routledge 1910, p. xvii).

THEME 1: TERMINOLOGY

The first theme of the book looks at archaeological terminology in Africa. From the beginning of the twentieth century, writers on African archaeology generally divided the past into 'prehistoric' and 'historic' periods (e.g. Caton-Thompson 1931). In French, and accordingly in French archaeology, the term 'la Préhistoire' indicates the period in world history before any invention of writing, whereas English usage of 'Prehistory' indicates the time before writing was current in a particular place. European archaeological nomenclature, despite difficulties recognized in its application, was imposed on African archaeological material, particularly in the context of the stone tool assemblages (e.g. Deacon 1984; de Maret 1986) which dominated earlier African archaeology. In addition, European terms such as 'protohistoric' and 'iron age' were imposed onto more recent segments of the African past (Schofield 1948; Summers 1950; Mason 1952).

One of the most important European concepts which is still reflected in current literature on African archaeology is that of 'the Neolithic'.

The 'Neolithic'

The concept of the Neolithic current in Europe from the mid-nineteenth to the mid-twentieth centuries was mainly technological, and primarily based on the occurrence in archaeological assemblages of polished stone artefacts. Later, the use of pottery and also, to an increasing extent, the practice of agriculture, were incorporated into the concept, which had an ambiguous usage both as a chronological stage and as a cultural entity. In 1924 McCurdy wrote:

> The Neolithic Period was at first and is still referred to, especially by the French, as the age of polished stone implements. . . . Certain kinds of stone intended for special purposes were polished in Palaeolithic times, but the polishing was not a part of the shaping process. (McCurdy 1924, p. 156)

McCurdy attributed the domestication of plants and animals to the neolithic period, and even foreshadowed Childe's 'Neolithic Revolution' when he wrote: 'The control of the food supply made village life possible, and this, in turn, led to societal organization, without the discipline of which such important works as fortifications, megalithic monuments, lake villages etc., could never have been consummated' (McCurdy 1924, p. 156).

When Childe coined the phrase 'the Neolithic Revolution', he was thinking of it as being in a way analogous to the Industrial Revolution – that is, as a fundamental change in the human way of life that took place in the chronological period, or the cultural phase, which had already been termed 'neolithic' – not something which happened overnight, but over a number of generations (Childe 1936, p. 82). The actual process of domestication of crops and animals was a complex and varied one, not the clearly defined Rubicon that some had previously posited. It was believed that 'the New Stone Age in Europe lasted at the outside 2000 years' (Childe 1936, p. 71). The net result of Childe's drawing attention to the radical changes in the human way of life consequent upon the advent of food production, led to investigations into the dynamics of early food production in southwest Asia (Braidwood 1962; Braidwood & Braidwood 1969). Assisted by the new radiocarbon dating technique, 'cultural evolution' was pitted against 'environmental determinism', the claims of 'the hilly flanks' against 'riverine–oasis propinquity', and these paths of discussion and investigation continue. A second result of Childe's 'Neolithic Revolution' was that, increasingly among anglophone archaeologists, the word 'neolithic', whatever other connotations it might have, came increasingly to mean 'food-producing'.

In Africa, as early as 1929, Goodwin & Van Riet Lowe had recognized that it was inappropriate to try to force the Stone Age industries of South Africa into the mould of European nomenclature (Goodwin & Van Riet Lowe 1929), and had created the South African 'Middle Stone Age'. In spite of this opportunity to escape from the shackles of European terminology, the use of the neolithic terminology still held sway in South Africa, and Goodwin himself applied the term whenever there was an occurrence of three out of the four traditional neolithic traits – 'the polished celt, pottery, agriculture and the domestication of animals' (Goodwin & Van Riet Lowe 1929, p. 278). In the same year that Childe was writing *Man Makes Himself* (1936) (in which he expounded his idea of the Neolithic Revolution), Louis Leakey was writing his *Stone Age Africa* (Leakey 1936). This was conceived essentially in terms of successions of 'cultures', characterized by stone tools which were defined by their morphology. The familiar European names were given to them – Chellean, Acheulean, Aurignacian, Neolithic. Wherever ground stone axes, barbed arrowheads and pottery (or two out of those three elements) were found in Africa, they were dubbed 'neolithic' (Leakey 1936, pp. 70, 98, 136). Some eight years later, before any Childean thinking had reached him, Shaw was not inhibited from christening as 'Guinea Neolithic' a microlithic industry he had discovered in a rock shelter in Ghana, because it also contained pottery and ground stone axes (Shaw 1944, pp. 58–61). There was no direct evidence of food production, and a quarter of a century later Shaw wished to drop the 'neolithic' label (Hugot 1973, p. 598).

There appears to have been a greater reluctance to use the term 'neolithic' in the context of west Africa, and a greater inclination to favour its retention in east and north Africa. This is in part attributable to the fact that evidence for food production tends to be more visible in the archaeological record in east Africa than in west Africa, mainly because of the differences in the preservation of faunal remains. Nevertheless, its usage in west Africa continued into the 1980s; thus, Ellis (1980, p. 123) defined the 'Neolithic' 'as the presence or possession of pottery, ground stone axes and a microlithic industry. The probable domestication of plants and/or animals is implied in the term.'

In the African contexts in which they carried out their enquiries French archaeologists, unlike their colleagues in South Africa, did not have the disturbing sequence of lithic industries that fitted so badly into the European scheme of things. In their archaeological explorations of north Africa and the Sahara, they found no difficulty in designating as 'néolithique', industries which displayed abundant pottery, flint arrowheads and ground stone axes. It is only in more recent years that French archaeologists have become concerned with the necessity to demonstrate the food–producing element, if the term 'néolithique' is to be justified. Part of the reason for this is that Childe's ideas about the Neolithic Revolution did not become as rapidly current on the southern side of the English Channel as on the northern.

Goodwin and Van Riet Lowe's early work had constituted the first real breakaway in Africa from the hallowed European terms, and eventually paved the way for Resolution 6 of the Third Panafrican Congress on Prehistory held in Livingstone in 1955, which recommended that archaeologists should endeavour 'to fit their Stone Age culture sequences into a frame which provides for: Earlier Stone Age, First Intermediate, Middle Stone Age, Second Intermediate, Later Stone Age': there was no mention of Neolithic (Clark 1957, p. xxxiii). Ten years later that scheme was superseded at the Burg Wartenstein symposium of 1965: 'industrial complexes' and 'cultural stratigraphic units' made their appearance, and there was a special recommendation about the use of the term 'Neolithic' (Bishop & Clark 1967, pp. 898–9), which said:

> Owing to the great variety of definitions of the term 'Neolithic', it is recommended: (a) that it be used with the greatest care and that it be clearly defined in all cases: and (b) that the definition of the term 'Neolithic' as applied to cultural–stratigraphic units be further discussed at the forthcoming Panafrican Congress on Prehistory and Quaternary Studies.

Two conferences of west African archaeologists were held which considered the Burg Wartenstein proposals (Shaw 1966a; Shaw 1966b; Shaw 1967); both took the view that the term 'neolithic' was best dropped for Africa, but that, if it were to be retained, it should be used only in the technological sense of indicating the presence of stone tools with a ground cutting edge (Shaw 1966b, pp. 48–9; Shaw 1967, p. 35). This view was communicated to the 1967 Panafrican Congress on Prehistory at Dakar, but the debate there on the use of the term 'neolithic' reached no conclusions (Hugot 1973, p. 598).

Nevertheless, at that same 1967 Dakar congress Sutton reviewed the difficulties of using the 'neolithic' designation in east Africa and recommended its abandonment (Sutton 1973). In his study of the pottery of the East African Neolithic in 1971, Bower was careful to define 'Neolithic', and did so as 'a stage in regional cultural development which is characterized by the introduction and widespread use of ceramic technology (and, also, perhaps, pastoral economies) but precedes the introduction of iron–working in east Africa' (Bower 1976, p. 47). Thus his definition was primarily in technological rather than in economic terms. A ceramic study by Wandibba, a Kenyan archaeologist trained in European archaeological terminology, brought greater clarification to the pottery of what he referred to as 'the Later Stone Age Neolithic' or the 'Later Stone Age/Neolithic period', but without definition of the term 'neolithic' (Wandibba 1980). Meanwhile, a study of 'the Sudanese Neolithic' concluded (Hays 1974; Hays 1976a) that there was no such entity and that the only 'linking features' were the generalized use of ground stone and a common pottery style.

Clearly the situation for east Africa was no more satisfactory than for other parts of Africa, not least for north Africa and the Sahara; Barich's critical re-evaluation of the Neolithic there led her to advise the abandonment of the term 'neolithic'; she suggested instead the sequence of Palaeolithic, Epipalaeolithic with pottery, Pastoral (Barich 1980). This was in stark contrast to previous attitudes which had a long and cherished tradition.

In 1933 Vaufrey had declared that everything in Africa north of the equator was Capsian (Vaufrey 1933), and for many years he continued to expound this view, both for the Epipalaeolithic and for the 'Neolithic of Capsian tradition' (e.g. Vaufrey 1946). He was followed by many authors (see Roubet 1979, pp. 28–51). Balout (1955, pp. 450–1) came to contest this view, declaring that the Neolithic was a culture phase, 'un état de civilisation' and that the term 'néolithique' should only be used if at least one of the following traits was present: 'Polissage de haches et d'herminettes; pointes de flèches de taille bifaciale; céramique modelée, généralement ornée; domestication et élevage; agriculture.' By 1968 Roubet was emphasizing the slow and gradual nature of 'néolithicisation': 'La néolithicisation n'entrâine, dans le cas considéré, ni une révolution, ni des transformations rapides et considérables, mais une adoption progressive de connaissances importées' (Roubet 1968, p. 130), an approach then followed by others (e.g. Camps 1974, p. 216).

The French use of the word 'néolithicisation' has no precise synonym in English and was used to indicate, primarily, the process of adopting food production, and only secondarily, if at all, changes in lithic or ceramic technology. For north Africa, therefore, the French position was that the only acceptable criterion for a neolithic label was food production, implying agriculture and stock-raising. Some archaeologists (e.g. Camps 1974) took another leap into the dark and declared that the mere presence of pottery was sufficient evidence for food production, based on the unwarranted assumption that, although there could be food production without pottery, it was not possible to have pottery without food production. One exception to such an approach which was to change francophone perceptions of this early period in Africa, was the publication of Roubet's volume on the Neolithic of Capsian Tradition, with its demonstration in eastern Algeria of a pastoral Neolithic (i.e. with pottery) without crop-growing (Roubet 1979).

Meantime, in the realm of anglophone archaeology in Africa, there had been two conflicting developments affecting the 'Neolithic'. The first was the advent of a number of British and American archaeologists, particularly in east Africa, for whom the word 'neolithic' meant nothing more than 'food-producing' with, or without, pottery (or, for that matter, stone tools). The second was the emergence of a new generation of indigenous African archaeologists with understandable pride in the achievements of their ancestors, and sensitive to any prejudiced attempts to denigrate those achievements; such denigration had emanated from the white governments and some individuals in South Africa and Rhodesia (Garlake 1973a). (Examples of archaeology being used to bolster a particular polity or ideology are legion; see e.g. Gathercole & Lowenthal 1990.) In reaction to appeals from British and American archaeologists to apply scholarly precision to archaeological terminology, and their questioning of the usefulness of the term 'neolithic' in Africa, Onyango-Abuje – although admitting confusion in the usage of the term 'neolithic' – urged that, in order to prevent the implication that it would have needed Caucasoids to produce 'neolithic cultures', the use of the term 'neolithic' should be applicable to any industry if it contains evidence for *either* animal husbandry *or* crop production (Onyango-Abuje 1980, p. 288).

The term 'pastoral neolithic' then appeared, applied to situations where it was clear that domestic animals were kept but where there was no (or no evidence for) cropgrowing (e.g. Ambrose 1980). The complexities of the east African situation were well described by Bower, Nelson, Waibel & Wandibba (1977), who found it necessary to explain that:

> As a matter of convenient reference LSA is used to refer to Later Stone Age in the technological sense. It is applied to hunter–gatherer societies and pastoral 'Neolithic' societies alike. When LSA and PN are contrasted, LSA should be understood to be referring to hunter–gatherer societies. Pastoral 'Neolithic' (PN) is used to refer to societies with an LSA technology and a pastoral economic base relying heavily on domestic cattle and/or ovicaprids. Pastoral Iron Age (PIA) is used to refer to societies with pastoral economies incorporating iron into their technology. Flaked stone tools of LSA aspect were frequently used as supplements to iron edged tools. (Bower, Nelson, Waibel & Wandibba 1977, p. 119)

With the advent of radiocarbon dating the term 'neolithic' as a time marker is irrelevant; we no longer believe in a succession of culture phases applicable world-wide; and we know that the ways people have organized their economy and their social life, as well as the technology they practised, have varied so widely that we need to describe and define each group separately.

> We are not going to use the conventional terminology based upon broad technological/chronological sub-divisions such as 'Late Stone Age', 'Neolithic' or 'Iron Age'. It has long been recognized that such terms cannot precisely be defined, but their informal use has continued, often at the expense of clarity. (Phillipson 1985a, p. 5)

Substituting such words as 'pastoral', 'agricultural' (*agricole*), 'food-producing' (*producteur*) or 'agro-pastoral' (Holl 1986) gives greater precision, as does the use of 'iron-using' and 'iron-producing' instead of the blanket term 'iron age' (cf. Holl, Ch. 17, this volume and Kiriama, Ch. 30, this volume). It has been well put that 'our objective is a heuristic construct that reasonably approximates to African stone age evidence' (Mehlman 1986, p. 289). Furthermore, in other parts of the world outside Africa, as more radiocarbon dates are obtained and greater precision is given to archaeological entities, there is now a tendency to do without such blanket terms as 'the Neolithic'.

Modern thinking about the beginnings of food production has tended to follow a processual approach. The mesolithic populations of northwestern Europe are now seen, not as all being displaced by immigrant neolithic farmers, but as having been capable of adopting, adapting and developing new economic and social practices (e.g. Madsen 1982; Zvelebil & Rowley-Conwy 1986). Recognition of the complexity of such economic interactions are just as relevant to our understanding of the adoption by many African societies of livestock domesticated elsewhere. The Introduction to another book in the *One World Archaeology* series says:

> We regard human exploitation of plant resources as a global evolutionary process which, in different regions and at varying times in the past, incorporated the beginnings of cultivation and crop domestication. This approach reduces but does not deny the conceptual dichotomy between 'hunter-gatherers' and 'agriculturalists' by treating the development of all techniques of plant exploitation as an integral part of the evolutionary ecology of *Homo sapiens*. (Harris & Hillman 1989, p. 2)

Archaeology in the 1990s has moved beyond a preoccupation with artefacts and distinguishing a succession of 'cultures'; initially the aim was to achieve greater precision concerning the organization of economies and concerning their basis in ecology; more recently, in order to try to uncover the structure of prehistoric societies and to build models of processes of change. It is not to be supposed that, by dropping the term 'neolithic' and substituting phrases such as 'pastoral', 'agricultural', 'farming', 'crop-raising', 'food-producing' or any other expressions, all problems will be solved. Such terms only relate to one aspect of one parameter of living – the subsistence base – and other parameters still have to be taken into account, since societies can only be satisfactorily described in multi-factorial terms. The understanding of the complex issues involved in sedentism, semi-sedentism, nomadism, territorial occupancy and the myriad forms of food production and food usage cannot be assisted by oversimplifying terminology. In addition, the term 'neolithic', imported from Europe, has a series of confusing connotations. Rejection of the term 'neolithic' for African studies would remove at least one reminder of a term with an outmoded eurocentric bias and thus remove a manifest obstacle to good communication between researchers.

The 'Iron Age'

Similar problems of terminology (but with different consequences – and see, in particular, Kense & Okoro, Ch. 26, this volume) have bedevilled later periods of African archaeology. Thus the term 'iron age', discussed as early as 1936 in relation to the Gumban culture of east Africa by Leakey (1936, p. 70), was imported into southern Africa by Summers (1950) and Mason (1952), in part to replace the racial connotations of the often used label, 'Bantu'. It was used to describe and delimit a period during which communities were assumed to have been distinctively different from those that went before. Despite the position taken by Inskeep (1969, p. 31) that 'iron

age' was merely a label of archaeological convenience, its use has led to the identification of supposed particular racial types on the basis of their possession of a particular
technology. Meanwhile, the term has spread to other parts of Africa (e.g. Davies 1967;
Phillipson 1968b), culminating in Shinnie's use of 'The African Iron Age' as the title for
an important compilation of articles (Shinnie 1971). In the same year, the 'Iron Age'
was used as one of the subdivisions of the African archaeological record for the
purposes of organizing the Pan African Congress meeting at Addis Ababa.

Although the term is still strongly embedded in the archaeology of southern Africa
(e.g. Huffman 1989), elsewhere alternatives such as 'early iron age industrial complex'
(Phillipson 1977a) have been adopted, while more recent work in east Africa, as well as
Pan-African syntheses, have avoided it altogether (e.g. Phillipson 1985a).

How iron was adopted for tools and weapons constitutes an old and continuing
debate in African archaeology, which is considered in detail by Okafor (Ch. 25, this
volume). Holl (Ch. 17, this volume) takes another critical look at the issues, distinguishing between iron-using and iron-producing societies. He applies rigorous
criteria in an attempt to interpret the data from around Lake Chad, to determine how
the change came about from 'Late Stone Age' or 'Neolithic' to 'Early Iron Age'. Other
chapters in this book (e.g. Musa Muhammed, Ch. 27; Buleli, Ch. 28) concentrate on
reanalysing previous assumptions about the possible significance of static typologies of
iron-working equipment and furnaces and on authenticating the ethnographic and
historical records.

Recent research in west-central Africa, primarily by scholars associated with the
Centre International des Civilisations Bantou (and see Grébénart 1988), has documented the presence of iron-smelting prior to the first century AD, in Gabon (Clist,
Oslisly & Peyrot 1986). Investigations in east Africa indicate iron-working, possibly as
early as 800 BC, in the area of the Great Lakes (Van Noten 1979; Schmidt & Childs
1985). How such practices may have spread to the rest of south-central Africa is a
matter of ongoing research (Eggert, Ch. 16, this volume; Kiriama, Ch. 30, this volume).

One problem in the use of an imported European terminology and European
concepts is that it is difficult to identify not only the beginnings of the supposed
evolutionary stages but also their ends. Thus, the existence of people who were both
stone tool users and had a knowledge of iron technology challenges the traditional
conceptual framework imported from elsewhere.

THEME 2: INNOVATION AND DIFFUSION

The second theme in the book concerns different attitudes towards innovation and
diffusion which have been of central importance in African archaeology. As has been
seen already, early assumptions were that manifestations of cultural ingenuity of
necessity derived from outside the continent, the only permitted exception being
ancient Egypt. In the case of certain fauna and flora, this may (see Chs 3 and 4) have
been true in one limited sense. However, it is remarkable how far the emphasis of
archaeological enquiry has focused exclusively on the exotic derivations of such plants
and animals, and ignored the equally interesting African role in their exploitation.

Given the explicit or implicit assumptions of colonialism, it is perhaps not surprising that the tradition of assuming an outside derivation for essentially indigenous innovation and development not only covered attitudes to crops and animal husbandry but was also inherent in archaeological interpretations concerning the existence of towns and cities.

Some of these assumptions will now be examined in more detail to show how they have become thematic influences on the archaeological evidence in Africa, whatever the particular culture or chronology.

In Africa, almost every major conglomeration, be it the stone-walled enclosures of Great Zimbabwe (Sinclair, Pikirayi, Pwiti & Soper, Ch. 43, this volume), the cities of Ghana (Anquandah, Ch. 38, this volume) or even the kingdom of Kongo (see Weischoff 1941, pp. 7–13), have been ascribed to the influence of one particular exceptional elite iron age people who were portrayed as having swept across vast areas of land, through innumerable micro and macro environments to impose their authority, usually by replacing (i.e. exterminating) those who stood in their way (reflecting what was indeed happening in some parts of colonial Africa). In cases where no suitable candidates for such migrations could be found, 'explanation' was abandoned in favour of postulation. Royal dynasties, centralized kingdoms (Anquandah, Ch. 38, this volume) and the influence of trading monopolies were usually assumed to be based upon control of long-distance trade with places outside Africa (or, hypothetically, with ancient Egypt).

Two particular 'peoples' have assumed a pre-eminent role in the hypothetical construction of Africa's past, the 'pastoralist' Hamites and the 'iron age' Bantu. These supposedly dominant 'peoples' were given the historical limelight because those who attempted early culture-historical reconstructions underestimated the creative capacities of African peoples; hence they sought external origins for most elements of African culture.

In Germany, cultural historians took a position in favour of succeeding waves of foreign influence bringing a series of different cultural elements to Africa (Zwernemann 1983). The physical migration of people was seen as an important, though not exclusive, mechanism for the diffusion of cultural traits and this was taken to extreme forms by Johnston (1913) and in the Egypto-centric hyperdiffusionism of Elliot Smith (1915). Hamites were seen either as bearers of an intrusive culture, practising divine kingship (originating ultimately from Egypt and the Nile), or they were seen as a shared Nilo-Hamitic substratum of the Nile region in prehistoric times, from which common ancestral basis historic Egypt eventually sprang (Frankfort 1948). State formations from the Great Lakes area of east Africa as well as states in Angola and Zimbabwe were derived either from Egypt (Irstam 1944, pp. 11–13) or through the agency of a south to north spread of the externally derived Erythraean culture (see Weischoff 1941, pp. 7–13). With regard to north Africa, series of maps were produced showing the dominance of the north Erythraean culture originating in Arabia and developing from the Nile to cover large areas of north-central Africa. In northwest Africa, the Surtic culture said to derive from the Mediterranean covered much of the Sahara, while the Atlantic culture penetrated from the coast to influence much of west-central Africa (see Zwernemann 1983, pp. 82–3).

Such diffusionist positions are rejected by modern archaeologists and anthropologists (e.g. Southall 1965, p. 155; Zwernemann 1983, p. 15; Sinclair 1987, p. 22) not only on methodological grounds, but also on the basis of the irrelevant nature of the historical questions which were being posed. Nowadays attention has shifted to answering questions about social dynamics and to specifying internal mechanisms of social stratification (see Kinahan, Ch. 20, this volume; Sinclair, Pikirayi, Pwiti & Soper, Ch. 43, this volume; Hassan, Ch. 33, this volume; MacIntosh & MacIntosh, Ch. 37, this volume). Discredited racial ideas about the physical movement of exceptional peoples were replaced by the famous 'cattle complex' of Herskovits (1926), which described the very widely distributed set of beliefs, rituals and customs centred on cattle, and by the very detailed work by Baumann (1975; 1979) on African culture areas defined on the basis of ecological units and material culture distributions (Zwernemann 1983, pp. 95–100). Such trait distributions have been used to cross-check continental scale distributions of languages and archaeological finds (Heine 1973; Möhlig 1981; Winter 1981). There are many criticisms to be made about such culture areas, including the one that the culture-historical tradition abstracted and compared culture traits without any real regard to their specific societal context (Kuper & van Leynselle 1978); and that they largely ignored ideological/symbolic categories and world-view concepts. The incorporation of insights from symbolic anthropology into archaeological research is increasingly apparent in modern African archaeology. Of particular importance in this regard has been the work of Douglas (1966; 1970; but see Douglas 1990), Kuper (1980; 1982) and Hodder (1982), whose approaches have shed light on such areas as choice of food crops and crafts (see Collett, Ch. 31, this volume; Kiriama, Ch. 30, this volume; and Rowlands & Warnier, Ch. 32, this volume, for ceramics and the complex sets of symbolic categories which may surround the production of iron; Kiriama, Ch. 30, this volume, for household and settlement layout; O'Connor, Ch. 34, this volume; and Fletcher, Ch. 44, this volume, for town organization). In some examples in this book the unit of analysis is the homestead, while in others (e.g. Rowlands & Warnier, Ch. 32, this volume) a holistic approach is adopted in which ideological categories associated with metal working are seen in relation to those of different activities and incorporating a dynamic perspective on how ideology is involved in societal transformations.

Much can also be learned from consideration of hypotheses based on the concept of 'the Bantu' who were, perhaps, the most extreme example of the stereotyped 'bellicose', superior armed 'race' (i.e. Bantu speakers) who feature in many African archaeological books, whether for professional researchers or for secondary- and primary-school students. In many parts of sub-Saharan Africa, Bantu speakers supposedly introduced semi-permanent village life, metallurgy and agriculture (at least in the southern part of the continent), displacing the previous inhabitants. A great deal of archaeological effort – perhaps too much – has been spent on tracing the supposed routes of Bantu expansion from the Niger/Benue region of west Africa, through or around the equatorial forest (Phillipson 1977a; Ehret & Posnansky 1982; Eggert, Ch. 16, this volume), to the region of the Great Lakes of eastern Africa (Soper 1971a; Collett, Ch. 31, this volume; Kiriama, Ch. 30, this volume), and from there south along the Mozambique coast (Sinclair, Morais, Adamowicz & Duarte, Ch. 24, this volume), through the interior via Lake Malawi (Juwayeyi, Ch. 22, this volume) and the Zimbabwe plateau (Huffman 1972) to Botswana (Kiyaga-Mulindwa, Ch. 21, this volume) and South Africa (e.g. Huffman 1988). A fundamental assumption is that we are dealing with the spread of iron-using Bantu-speaking agriculturalists, despite the fact that the contemporaneity of the different traits involved has at various times been challenged (Lwanga-Lunyiigo 1976; Eggert 1981; Andah 1983). A further unwarranted, and potentially dangerous, assumption is the correlation of ceramic clusters with groups of people. The idea that a complex of material culture traits may be equated with a distinctive group of people, speaking a distinctive language has, of course, a long and august pedigree in European archaeological interpretation (Childe 1936, but see Renfrew 1989). In Africa, however, this position has been stated as fact by Huffman (1972; 1980a) but has been challenged by Hodder (1982), and more recently Hall (1987) who questions the focus on ethnic distinctions, especially in relation to the political context of current South African research (see summary by Maggs & Whitelaw 1991). In southern Africa, attempts made to marry the conceptual plan of the 'southern Bantu homestead' of Kuper (1980; 1982) to archaeological data (Huffman 1981; Huffman 1988) have received a mixed reception (Schmidt 1983; Maggs & Whitelaw 1991) and the need to maintain a clearly defined spatio-temporal frame of reference when dealing with symbolic categories is apparent (Sinclair, Pikirayi, Pwiti & Soper, Ch. 43, this volume).

It is from the systematic use of ethnographic source material, as in the contributions of Collett (Ch. 31, this volume) and Kiriama (Ch. 30, this volume) in Kenya and Vogel (Ch. 23, this volume) in Zambia, that further challenges to simplistic ceramic/ linguistic/racial correlations will arise. Uncontrolled pseudo-historical conjecture (as Radcliffe-Brown (1952) and others called it in the 1950s) should have no place in the sophisticated analysis of modern processual and symbolic interpretation. Today it is recognized that these people, whoever they really were (if indeed they were one people – there are, after all, more than 700 recognized subgroupings of the Bantu language family), would have met quite different environmental conditions where they settled, and would have had to adapt in quite differing ways to the different cultures and practices of the people they were to encounter. It is such variation, each a unique expression of cultural activity at any given moment, which should, rightly, be the concern of modern archaeological enquiry. Many would claim that the concept of the 'Bantu expansion' has had the most profoundly negative effects on attempts at sound interpretation of the archaeological evidence.

Are we then to believe that movement of peoples never occurred in Africa? On the contrary: movement at least on the small scale seems to be characteristic of many areas of Africa, and also, in some parts of the continent, occurred on a larger scale, in some cases following the effects of slavery. On the level of general principles, frontier theory applied to African archaeological research by Alexander (1984; Alexander, Ch. 39, this volume) and complemented by recent work by Kopotoff (1987), focuses on the continual 'budding-off' processes in agricultural communities which involve an initial cycle of settlement spread, establishment, split and further spread. The cumulative result of these small-scale movements of individual communities exercising choice and responding in a flexible way to available opportunities is every bit as dramatic as the grand schemes of the diffusionists. Archaeologists need to look at the available evidence to see whether other possible models, such as large-scale movement, also have explanatory power.

THEME 3: ENVIRONMENTAL RELATIONS

The third theme deals with environmental relations. Just as in Europe, so also in Africa, culture history as an exclusive approach to the past has been influenced, and some would say hampered, over the last fifty years by interpretations of the environment. At a gross level such an influence was already present in the early attempts to explain the existence of ancient Egyptian civilization (e.g. Smith 1915). Such an exceptional flowering of culture could only have been due, it was supposed, to an exceptional environmental context that assumed regularity and dependability of the annual flooding of the Nile.

Early attempts at archaeologically oriented environmental reconstruction in Africa in the period before the Second World War (e.g. Wayland 1934; Leakey 1936) derived from the European sequence of glaciations; attempts were made to correlate African pluvials with them, to provide a chronological framework. The period after the Second World War saw great growth in environmental studies. Increasing research showed these preliminary continental correlations to be totally inadequate. With the publication of the landmark collection on *African Ecology and Human Evolution* (Howell & Bourlière 1963), detailed regional sequences became available, e.g. from Morocco (Biberson 1963), east Africa (Bishop 1963) and south-central Africa (Summers 1950; Bond 1963), and these contributions were synthesized on a continental scale in the *Atlas of African Prehistory* (Clark 1967b). In Chapter 1 of this book Grove summarizes important holocene environmental investigations which have been developed in the Nile valley and on lake deposits in Chad, Kenya and South Africa; this chapter is complemented by recent syntheses of lake level studies throughout the continent (Street-Perrott, Marchand, Roberts & Harrison 1989). Together with work on the Antarctic icecap and deep sea drilling programmes, these studies have gone some way towards permitting climatic correlations between western, eastern and southern regions of Africa and even tentatively with Europe and the Americas (e.g. Van Zinderen Bakker 1976; Street & Grove 1976; Street-Perrott, Marchand, Roberts & Harrison 1989).

Further work, notably the geomorphological coverage of east Africa by Hamilton (1982) and the analysis of the climatological implications of the cave sequences of the Cape coast (e.g. Deacon 1984, with extensive bibliography), has done much to provide a chrono-stratigraphic framework for the later pleistocene and holocene eras in eastern and southern Africa, while similar contributions have been made by Andah (1976; 1979c; 1980b) and Andah & Ajayi (1981) for west Africa and, for example, by Wendorf & Schild (1980) for northeast Africa.

As the picture has changed, so fifty years later we have considerable evidence for the quaternary and holocene conditions in Africa at the microlevel, with evidence for the effects of the Nile flooding between 10,000 and 3000 BC almost entirely contradicting the situation assumed by the early investigators: knowledge of recent climatic change has revealed the short-term crises and the environmental uncertainty which past Nile valley populations must have faced.

The present half-century has witnessed how devastating the effects of climate change can be on established ways of life in Africa, and how quite small changes can cross over the threshold between enabling a certain way of life and making it impossible. With rainfall in the greater part of Africa being highly seasonal anyway, the extremes of annual variation may be more disastrous than changes in the annual mean or the variation between decades (Grove, Ch. 1, this volume). So it undoubtedly has been in the past. But availability of water may be more important for sustaining life, or for permitting a certain way of life, than climate as such, which comprises a number of different parameters. This is obvious when the Nile valley is compared with the desert on either side of it. It has been less obvious in the consideration of those prehistoric periods in which the Sahara was 'wetter' than it is now, a fact which is abundantly proven for the early and mid-Holocene; there was certainly greatly increased precipitation over most of Africa around 9500 BP to 8500 BP, following the great aridity at the end of the Pleistocene, when, in addition, temperatures were appreciably lower than at present. How much was contributed by the availability of ground-water sources and how much by increased rainfall in the later fluctuating wet periods in the Sahara 'remains difficult to decide' (Grove, Ch. 1, this volume).

During the period of maximum precipitation, it is reckoned that the zone of sahelian vegetation advanced far to the north of its present northern boundary, and the savanna and forest zones correspondingly (Grove, Ch. 1, this volume). Similarly, extensions and retractions of vegetation zones in the equatorial rainforest seem to correlate with lake levels and the movements of vegetation belts further north (Maley, Ch. 2, this volume; Eggert, Ch. 16, this volume). In periods of increased precipitation from the monsoon there was an additional 'knock-on' effect: the moisture-laden wind released rain over the equatorial forest; evapotranspiration from the forest vegetation re-supplied the southwest winds with water vapour, which was then precipitated as rain yet further on.

Palynological studies, introduced into African archaeology by Van Zinderen Bakker (1951; 1976), have had to face immense complexity and a very wide range of species, as shown by the work of Germeraad, Hopping & Muller (1968) in west Africa and Van Zinderen Bakker & Coetzee (1988) on a continental scale. Despite detailed work carried out in Nigeria (Sowunmi 1981), Uganda (Hamilton 1982), Kenya and Tanzania (e.g. Kendall 1969), Malawi (Meadows 1984), Zambia (Livingstone 1971) and in the eastern highlands of Zimbabwe (Tomlinson 1973) and South Africa (Scott 1982), as well as the detailed work of Burney (1987) and co-workers on Madagascar, there remain very significant gaps in our knowledge (Livingstone 1984).

In recent years there has been growing realization of the importance of the active role of humans in the production of current vegetation and soil regimes. Of particular relevance are the FAO/UNESCO studies on the soils of Africa and land assessment programmes (FAO/UNESCO 1973; FAO 1980) and the vegetation studies of Africa (White 1983). It is now accepted that environment can no longer be conceptualized independently from society, a realization that is reflected in anthropological studies which distinguish environmental categories more precisely (e.g. Ellen 1982).

Theoretical contributions by Higgs (1972), Flannery (1976) and Butzer (1976) also take heed of a differentiated range of environmental factors interacting with past societies in a two-way process (e.g. Hall 1981; Ahmed 1984; Nzewunwa 1985; Sinclair, Pikirayi, Pwiti & Soper, Ch. 43, this volume). A concurrent increase in the precision and sophistication of faunal studies in, for example, Kenya (Coppens & Howell 1976; Horton & Mudida, Ch. 41, this volume), Egypt (e.g. Gautier 1980) and southern Africa (e.g. Brain 1981; Voigt 1981; Crader 1984) now makes it possible to attempt continental-scale syntheses (Clutton-Brock, Ch. 4, this volume; Blench, Ch. 5, this volume).

It is one of the challenges of current archaeological theory, in all parts of the world, to attempt to bridge macroscale environmental frames with the microenvironmental existence of individual humans going about their everyday activities. In Africa the challenge is no less great, as shown above in relation to the Nile, and the many microenvironments occupied by past African societies contrast markedly with the colonial assumptions of scarce resources and cultural uniformity.

Sometimes modern archaeological enquiry produces quite different results from those previously achieved. For example it was an 'easy' assumption in the past that so-called 'iron age' settlement would have been automatically located near water and suitable ores and that nucleated settlement would have grown up as central focal points of an elite based on ownership of cattle. In Chapter 43, Sinclair, Pikirayi, Pwiti & Soper make a rigorous attempt to assess the influence of environment as an explanatory factor in the various stages of settlement in Zimbabwe. They show that previous assumptions were too facile, for it is now clear that although clusters of settlements correlate well with macroscale environmental units, the location of individual settlements has much to do with shifting foci of power, expressed through collateral chiefly succession.

This Zimbabwe example focuses attention on the fact that on the micro level it is no longer adequate to adopt monocausal explanation for individual settlement choice, or even for larger settlement clusters. Environmental analysis alone will not produce satisfactory explanations for past choices and practices. In any society it must be assumed that there has been a range of economic, social and political factors, each with a potentially different spatial domain of operation, interacting to influence the final choice of settlement location, or the adoption of a particular structure of urban complex (e.g. Abungu & Mutoro, Ch. 42, this volume).

Control of the environment – either through organized exploitation of resources, or through access to these resources, or control of hinterland trade, or even through long-distance trade – necessarily includes people's choice regarding which resources are available and how they are to be exploited. There is no reason to think that because humans in Africa have sometimes chosen to live in towns this means an unthinking exploitation of all available resources. For example Horton & Mudida (Ch. 41, this volume) show how the Swahili in c. 800 AD, were able to exploit or reject an enormous range of edible and non-edible marine resources, in contradiction to the assumption that there was little choice of foodstuffs in urban environments.

Contrary to the common stereotype of Africa, the archaeological record shows that choice was available in terms of economic and environmental resources from the earliest times to today. This is exemplified by the variety of food acquisition strategies practised in Africa, of which food production forms the fourth theme of this book.

THEME 4: FOOD PRODUCTION

The different forms of food production practised in many different combinations of methods, on differing soils, in differing environments, using different crops and animals, and at differing levels of intensity present a bewildering array of complexity. So far, in African archaeology, detailed treatments of food production have focused on the period prior to the advent of iron technology. Relatively little work has been carried out on later periods, especially in contexts for which it can be assumed that such information is available in documentary records. In fact, the archaeologist can draw from a far wider range of source materials than can the historian, but African food production in the relatively recent past remains grossly underrepresented in the literature (but see Folorunso & Ogundele, Ch. 15, this volume and Andah, Ch. 12, this volume).

Climate, flora, fauna and water are factors which always affect food getting, but they do not automatically dictate only one kind of response. When there is a change in the availability of natural resources which seriously disrupts an established way of life, one response may involve moving away from traditional territory to lands where conditions are sufficiently similar to enable the people concerned to re-establish their old way of life somewhere else. This is what appears to have happened to the farmer-pastoralists of Egypt's Western Desert who were driven into the Nile valley during the dry period of 6000–5500 BC, because it was no longer possible for them to carry on their traditional methods of food production in their homelands (Hassan 1986b; Hassan 1988). This particular movement may have resulted in the introduction of farming practices to the Nile valley for the first time.

However, there are many other possible reactions to major environmental change. Wetterstrom (Ch. 10, this volume) shows how important it is to study the ecology of hunting-foraging in the Nile valley at a period before the people became farmers. The population had a long, stable, successful adaptation to a rich environment, utilizing a considerable variety of riverine, savanna and desert food resources; but they had to cope with the capriciousness of Nile flood levels, which would have seriously affected the reliability of the crops of tubers, rhizomes and nutlets which they gathered, and which probably formed the staple of their diet. In addition, each group had to compete with other groups for available resources. It was in these circumstances, it is suggested, that crops and domestic animals from the Levant would have complemented the Egyptian hunter-gatherer system by providing predictable resources. In this example the reaction to environmental stress was not to move away but to make qualitative changes to their way of life.

Wasylikowa, Harlan, Evans, Wendorf, Schild, Close, Krolik & Housley (Ch. 9, this volume) show how, away from the river, the grains of wild grasses were an important ingredient in the diet of the farmers' predecessors. Nabta Playa seems to have been on the very verge of changing from the use of wild to domesticated grain. All the houses there contained sorghum remains, but the archaeological problem is to distinguish between wild and domesticated varieties. Whereas the whole plant assemblage points to a food economy based on wild plants, as far as the vegetal component of the diet was concerned, the sorghum itself shows a closer kinship to cultivated specimens than to wild ones. The problems involved in trying to determine, by whatever analytic method, whether archaeologically recovered cereal grains are wild or domesticated, are longstanding (Muzzolini, Ch. 11, this volume). There may even be great difficulty in determining the genus of cereals represented in the impressions on pots. At the early food-producing site of Kadero in the Sudan, impressions at first thought to have been made by grains of finger millet (*Eleusine coracana*) have now been declared to be of sorghum (*Sorghum bicolor*) (Krzyzaniak 1991). These difficulties illustrate how fragile can be the evidence concerning early food production in Africa, and how hazardous it may be to base confident assertions on it. In the majority of areas in Africa, where roots and tubers undoubtedly have an ancient pedigree as important items of diet, their use has hitherto been almost totally invisible to archaeology.

Palaeobotany can thus give a certain amount of information, and it has given most about the African cereals (Harlan, Ch. 3, this volume). Of these the most important are guinea corn (*Sorghum bicolor*) and pearl millet (formerly with the botanical name *Pennisetum typhoideum*, then *Pennisetum americanum*, but now to be known as *Pennisetum glaucum*). It is disappointing, however, that there has been practically no addition to our knowledge of this topic from strictly archaeological evidence during the last fifteen years – thus, for example, the possible uses of the gloss-edged trapezoids from Iwo Eleru, which must have been quite unsuitable for harvesting sorghum (as Harlan rightly points out, Ch. 3, this volume), remain unknown.

Increasing skill and technology in the identification of botanical remains can only go a certain way in aiding interpretation. The Kintampo complex of Ghana (Anquandah, Ch. 13, this volume; Stahl, Ch. 14, this volume) provides examples of a linked series of changes which included an increased investment in food-processing, increased seden-tism, probable exchange networks, increased accumulation of material culture and, in some cases, a measure of food production. These were local responses, and food production is not necessarily the key to understanding these qualitative changes. As Stahl concludes, such changes 'may have had more to do with social parameters than with ecological or demographic variables'.

Conventionally, the role of animals in past societies has been viewed exclusively in terms of either food production or transport. In Africa there is abundant evidence both from rock art and from ethnography (Vinnicombe 1976; Lewis-Williams 1981) that the significance of animals in the lives and the thinking of African hunter-gatherers is far wider than this. Most of Africa's domesticated animals derive from outside the conti-nent (Clutton-Brock, Ch. 4, this volume), partly, it has been suggested, because of Africa's natural wealth in fauna. Several of those introduced domesticates acquired great social and ritual significance in the African context, rather than becoming econ-omic assets for food, transport or hunting. It may even be that some domesticates were not introduced for purely economic reasons; in some parts of sub-Saharan Africa it seems that the horse was acquired as a prestige animal before becoming a military weapon (Blench, Ch. 5, this volume).

Of course this is not to deny the essential role of animals in food production. Cattle, of which there are a number of distinct breeds, are the most important livestock in Africa and, apart from a possible indigenous domestication in north Africa, their ancestors were introduced to the continent in different places and at different times (Clutton-Brock, Ch. 4, this volume). The distribution and dating of many animal species in Africa demonstrates the speed with which changes in distribution can occur. On the basis of the degree of adaptation of modern livestock, it appears that ruminants must have reached west Africa far earlier than is evident from any dated archaeological site with ruminant bones. Such a conclusion is supported by linguistic evidence: 'cattle were part of the cultural repertoire of Niger-Congo speakers at the beginning of their expansion in west Africa which cannot be later than about 7000 BC' (Blench, Ch. 5, this volume).

Linguistic evidence can also be used to support interpretations based on the distributions of African cereals (see maps in Harlan, de Wet & Stemler 1976). It seems to show, on present evidence, that the earliest speakers of Nilo-Saharan were food collectors. The first food producers seem to have been the Proto-Northern Sudanic speakers, who kept some cattle but collected wild grains (tentatively dated to around 8000 BC). Some time later speakers of Proto-Saharo-Sahelian began to cultivate grains as well as keep cattle (around 7000 BC). Later still, goats and sheep were added to the livestock, and gourds and calabashes began to be cultivated in addition to the grains (around 6000 BC). A comparison of the culture history thus constituted from linguistic evidence, when compared with the archaeological evidence from sites of the period in the relevant areas, shows, on present evidence, a remarkably good fit to 'establish beyond reasonable doubt the broad correlation of Nilo-Saharan speakers and Saharo-Sudanese cultures' (Ehret, Ch. 6, this volume). Thus the early Nilo-Saharan peoples are to be associated with stages in the evolution of food production, not with aquatic food-collecting as suggested by Sutton (1974). It is interesting that the postulated areas of domestication of the three most important African cereals, on the basis of their present distributions, lie within the Nilo-Saharan linguistic area.

There are, of course, all sorts of methodological difficulties in placing geographically the original locations of major language phyla. It is even more difficult to equate language speaking with peoples. For example, Ehret (Ch. 6, this volume) uses the 'principle of least moves' and identifies the Nilo-Saharan 'homeland' in the area of the Blue Nile between the Ethiopian highlands and the White Nile, while Blench (Ch. 7, this volume) locates it further west. Nevertheless, it is possible to speculate that the dispersals of the speakers of the ancestral forms of the three major language families of Niger-Congo, Nilo-Saharan and Afroasiatic may have been caused initially by the extreme aridity at the end of the Pleistocene in the zone north of 10°N, which would have forced these foraging groups to move out. When conditions improved, in the earlier Holocene, the more widespread availability of resources would have encouraged the later dispersals (Blench, Ch. 7, this volume). In some instances where humidity has destroyed botanical materials, it is only linguistic evidence that can yield any evidence of depth of time. Thus, in the Niger delta, linguistic roots which can be reconstructed to Proto-Atlantic-Congo, such as those for oil palm (*Elaeis guineensis*), palm oil (from the former) and wine palm (*Raphia hookeri*), indicate a great antiquity, while that for the Guinea yams (*Dioscorea cayenensis, D. rotundata*) may reconstruct even earlier to Proto-Niger-Congo; not of such antiquity are the roots for kola (*Cola acuminata*) and for the aerial yam (*Dioscorea bulbifera*), which reconstruct to Proto-Benue-Congo. Although such linguistic analysis may give some indication of how far back these vegetal sources were important to their speakers, they cannot demonstrate the practice of agriculture. In fact, the search for words and their roots which might indicate the practice of agriculture is only just beginning, but two – 'seed-yam' and 'to plant' (tubers) – suggest that yam cultivation, as opposed to the gathering of wild yams, goes back at least to the period when West-Benue-Congo was spoken (Williamson, Ch. 8, this volume).

Quite apart from questions of the particular nature of food production processes in any particular area, each example of such processes has its own intrinsic importance and serves to demonstrate the multifaceted nature of all food production practices, in particular the subtle relationships which may exist in the various aspects of a particular food production complex. In the Sahara, for example, an area renowned for the claims and counter-claims about food production in the past, Muzzolini shows (Ch. 11, this volume) that the evidence for seed-crop agriculture in the Sahara is slender indeed, but that pastoralism developed early. In other examples it is the interplay between foraging and food producing activities which come under especial scrutiny, and which some-times reveal the inadequacy of the archaeological record, or of archaeological interpret-ative methods to deal with the record. Thus, in the equatorial rainforest of central Africa, although there is no good botanical or faunal evidence to demonstrate food production, such an economic base is usually assumed by archaeologists simply on the basis of the presence, in this area, of a combination of pottery and ground stone edged tools (Eggert, Ch. 16, this volume). Any such assumption seems hazardous, particu-larly in the light of the discovery of a number of ground stone edged tools associated with iron-smelting. The problem is exacerbated by the tendency to draw further conclusions on the basis of such deductions about the economic basis of a particular society. Thus, Eggert does not accept radiocarbon dates which place the beginning of food production towards the end of the second millennium BC, but relies rather on those which date it around the second century BC. It is clear that in this part of central Africa the immediate future of its archaeology must lie in fieldwork. It may also be necessary to use ethnographic information to supplement the indicators of incipient agriculture which tend to be invisible in the archaeological record.

In some areas where there is a paucity of archaeological evidence it is difficult, though no less important, not to accept long-held assumptions that derive from non-archaeological disciplines. Thus, Ethiopia was one of Vavilov's famous potential 'centres of origin' for cultivated plants, and indeed the cultivation of teff and ensete are peculiar to the region. However, although one might expect eventually to find a complex history of cultivating and herding practices, 'currently available archaeological data do not as yet confirm the high antiquity which linguistic and botanical researches attribute to some elements of Ethiopian food production' (Phillipson, Ch. 18, this volume). Archaeological problems of botanical preservation, and the difficulties of accurate identification, do not affect faunal evidence to anything like the same degree, yet there remain numerous enigmas. For example, pastoralists first entered northern

Kenya during the third millennium BC, but did not reach southern Kenya and northern Tanzania until the end of the second millennium (Robertshaw, Ch. 19, this volume). In southwestern Kenya they entered two very different ecological zones, South Nyanza and the Mara. The latter is 'classic' pastoralist country, while the former, carrying tsetse, is less suitable. Efforts have been made to assess the impact of the incoming pastoralists upon the existing populations of hunter-gatherer-fishers, but this has been made difficult by uncertainties in dating and by the non-preservation of faunal remains among such remains as there are of pre-pastoralist activities there. It is therefore only negative evidence that supports the current picture of the pastoralists of South Nyanza having a diversified economy which included hunting, fishing and possibly cultivation (although no carbonized seed evidence has been found in spite of being looked for) and of the Mara supporting 'pure' pastoralists who shunned hunting.

Another area of Africa which saw the development of pastoralism was the drier, western parts of southern Africa. In Zimbabwe and Botswana there is clear archaeological evidence for the build-up of large herds of stock, particularly of cattle but also of sheep and goats (Denbow 1984; Denbow 1986; Kiyaga Mulindwa, Ch. 21, this volume). These herds had considerable potential to act as stores of wealth and means of maintaining and reinforcing social differentiation (Garlake 1978; Denbow 1984; Sinclair 1987). Pastoralism and pottery were introduced to the Namib some two thousand years ago (Kinahan, Ch. 20, this volume), and it has until recently been assumed that the resident hunter-gatherers were displaced by the pastoralists. Kinahan, however, using evidence from the rock art and enclosure remains, advocates the view that in the Namib a hunting society was able to transform itself into a pastoral one. He sees the development of nomadic pastoralism as an indigenous development rather than indicating a new population, despite recognizing the undoubted introduction of livestock from outside, and shows how stock were accumulated in the drier areas of central Namibia in spite of severe environmental impediments.

Archaeological approaches to the beginnings of food production – regarded by some as the most important transformation of any in human societies, by others as the greatest irreversible disaster that has befallen humankind – have tended mainly, as has been shown above, to be economic, ecological, botanical and/or zoological. Andah (Ch. 12, this volume) provides a corrective to the narrowness of such approaches and emphasizes the social aspects of food production (see also Stahl, Ch. 14, this volume), with an examination of west African farming practices. Analysis of the social context within which food production is undertaken has depended predominantly on ethnographic studies, which alone are able to supply information on the intricate details of such socially embedded activities (e.g. Folorunso & Ogundele, Ch. 15, this volume). Whatever the shortcomings of synchronic ethnographic studies carried out under circumstances which are not necessarily reliable indicators of precolonial situations, such studies have focused the attention of archaeologists on the complexities of the means of acquisition, modification and use of different subsistence resources, as well as on the dimensions of symbolic significance.

THEME 5: URBANISM

No meaningful line can be drawn between small rural communities as revealed by archaeological evidence and those which chose to aggregate in larger complexes. According to the European model the latter would have been placed in a higher category of a socio-economic hierarchy, deemed to be well on the way to 'urbanism' and 'civilization'. What, indeed, does 'town' or 'urbanism' mean in the African archaeological context?

The concept of urbanism has been endowed with a great variety of forms and definitions in the social and historical sciences (e.g. summaries by Wheatley 1972; Connah 1987; McIntosh & McIntosh, Ch. 37, this volume; Fletcher, Ch. 44, this volume). For instance, Wirth (1938) defined a city as 'a relatively large dense and permanent settlement of socially heterogeneous individuals'. For archaeologists such as Childe (1950), interested in demarcating the 'urban revolution' as distinct from the 'neolithic revolution' and the 'industrial revolution', urbanism could be identified in the archaeological record on the basis of trait lists, e.g. concentrations of a relatively large number of people in a restricted area; craft specialization; appropriation by a central authority of an economic surplus; monumental public architecture; developed social stratification; writing; science; naturalistic art; foreign trade; and residence-based group membership. This approach was modified in relation to Egypt by Sjoberg, who emphasized the need for a favourable ecological base, an advanced technology relative to the pre-urban one, as well as a complex form of social organization and well-organized power structure (Sjoberg 1960, p. 8). The development of the technological aspects involved in irrigated grain production were taken by Sjoberg as the determinant of the Egyptian urbanization process.

A pioneering archaeological overview of town development for Africa as a whole was provided by Desmond Clark (1962), who analysed the topic in relation to his extensive knowledge of foraging and food producing communities. Strict criteria for the 'achievement of urbanism' were applied, namely the existence of classes of pro-fessionals and a religious hierarchy, a centralized exchequer and public building pro-gramme. Sub-Saharan Africa was found wanting. According to Clark, 'full urbanism was never achieved in southern Africa' (Clark 1962, p. 29); that which did occur (for instance at Great Zimbabwe) was 'stimulated by racial elements deriving from Ethiopia and the Congo basin' (Clark 1962, p. 26). 'Full urbanism was achieved . . . in western Africa, on the east-African coast, and in Abyssinia but this came about in historic times as a result of trade – both overland trade routes and maritime trade – which was usually in the hands of foreigners, Berbers, Moors, Persians and south Arabians' (Clark 1962, p. 29).

Clark's conclusions were essentially negative and his explanations for such a lack of progress focused on the

> climate, which did not require any particular exertion on the part of the population to insure survival. . . . The rapidity of plant growth, malnutri-tion from an unbalanced diet, famine, disease, and warfare have all com-bined to act upon the mentality of the people, so, while they are not usually

slow to adopt improvements that affect the obtaining of food, such
revolutionary inventions and developments as the use of the wheel, irrigation systems, or the growth of classes of professionals or experts seem
never to have been adopted. (Clark 1962, p. 29)

It is significant that urbanism was hardly touched on in Clark's later *The Prehistory of
Africa* (1970).

A similar presumption that Africans could not have been instigators of the processes
of urbanization characterized the work of Kirkman (1954; 1966) and Chittick (1974;
1984) on the east African coast (see Masao & Mutoro 1988). In this area, responsibility
for urban development was placed firmly in the hands of foreigners from the Gulf and
from Arabia. The ramifications of this position, which might be termed the colonial
paradigm, will no doubt be discussed for many years by critical theorists and their
opponents, but an important sentiment expressed by Clark in several places (e.g. Clark
1962, p. 25) was that interpretation was to be based on available evidence – a claim that
might have been better expressed as interpretation based on prevailing opinion. As will
be shown below, in the twenty-five years following Clark's pioneering overview a
wealth of new archaeological data with direct relevance to the topic of urbanism has
become available from throughout the continent. Nowadays, there is not so much a
dearth of evidence as a plethora of data of varying relevance for the understanding of
processes of urbanism in Africa. The current challenge is to absorb and synthesize this
in a comparative framework which encompasses the continent as a whole.

A 'town' is defined here in its widest sense as a collection of houses greater than a
village. Use of this broad definition will allow the inclusion of those urban phenomena
which have been neglected or stand unrecognized simply because the urban definitions
which have been used in the past were based on European or Near Eastern
circumstances.

The mass of historical scholarship and source material ignored by Trevor-Roper
(1963, p. 871) in his famous assertion that 'Africa has no history' is highly relevant to
any consideration of urbanism in Africa. Leaving aside diffusionist attempts to derive
political leadership of African kingdoms from exotic sources (Oliver 1962; see also
comments by Connah 1987, p. 13), a primary focus has been on the occurrence and role
of central authority, as in the survey by Vansina (1962) of African kingdoms and on
forms of recruitment to positions of power (e.g. Southall 1965, p. 155), positions which
emphasize the ephemeral nature of African political formations. Even the settlements
which were their centres of power were rarely accorded urban status. However, there
have been a number of important surveys of urbanism (e.g. Lonsdale 1981), and a more
general coverage by Hull (1976), who has provided a functional typology of towns
using ideology, commerce, government, refuge and 'vision' as categories for distinguishing primary urban functions in Africa. However, it can be argued that such a
functional typology stressing internal dynamics should also include structural analysis,
as well as models derived from the historical record, and that it should also take into
account factors other than the purely material.

A persistent problem for field archaeologists using historical references as points of
departure for archaeological research is the inherent bias of the source material.

Uncritical use by archaeologists of these sources, which cannot be taken as objective statements on the observed situation, has too often led to a skewed emphasis on stone architecture, elite dwellings and objects concerned with foreign trade, culminating in an ascription of exotic origin to the town or trading system (e.g. Kirkman 1957; Chittick 1974). The biases inherent in the written sources become more obvious when the vast corpus of oral accounts is brought into the equation (Vansina 1965), and use of these accounts makes it almost impossible to ignore the African contribution to the establishment and growth of towns. Oral sources have, of course, their own limitations, especially in terms of time depth. Archaeologists may impose contemporary perspectives on their excavated materials and this is a real danger which is at least to some extent unavoidable. Although references to both written and oral historical sources are found widely in African archaeology, attempts to use these sources critically are less common (e.g. Anquandah, Ch. 38, this volume; Sinclair, Pikirayi, Pwiti & Soper, Ch. 43, this volume; Wright, Ch. 40, this volume). There are also large areas of study which are highly relevant, such as the effects of the slave trade and the rise of capitalism on food production, metallurgy and urbanism, and which remain relatively neglected by archaeologists. The pervasive effects of settler ideology and the system of apartheid in warping the historiography of southern Africa is another important source of bias (e.g. Garlake 1973a; Hall 1987) and has been countered by historical materialist approaches in Mozambique (Sinclair, Morais, Adamowicz & Duarte, Ch. 24, this volume) and Namibia (Kinahan, Ch. 20, this volume), which stress the internal capacity of societies to adapt and transform themselves.

Questions concerning African state formation have given rise to a variety of positions among historians, anthropologists and archaeologists, which cut across traditional disciplinary boundaries. The definition of primary and secondary states, as opposed to kingdoms, confederations and chieftaincies, has generated a considerable literature on a world scale (e.g. recent summaries by Gledhill, Bender & Larsen 1988; Miller, Rowlands & Tilley 1989) and in relation to African archaeology (e.g. Connah 1987; Hall 1987; Sinclair 1987). A number of assumptions underpinning these approaches have already been pointed out (e.g. Connah 1987; Sinclair 1987) and cannot be dealt with here in detail. An important point is that there was a tendency in some colonial anthropologists to characterize African economies as primarily subsistence oriented,

> with a rudimentary division of productive labour and with no machinery for the accumulation of wealth in the form of commercial or industrial capital. If wealth is accumulated it takes the form of consumption goods and amenities or is used for the support of additional dependents. Hence it tends to be rapidly dissipated and does not give rise to permanent class divisions. (Fortes & Evans-Pritchard 1940, pp. 8–9)

Such characterizations minimized the capacity for accumulation of wealth in Africa.

An additional assumption was that there was unlimited land for incorporation into different forms of polity:

> in precolonial conditions in Africa land was sometimes of little economic importance, for relatively low population densities (as compared, say, with Europe and Asia) meant that in many regions, land was not a very scarce

resource and hence its tenure could hardly provide the basis for the
differentiation of the 'class' system. (Goody 1971, pp. 12–13)

Current archaeological research has called this assumption into question, not only in
relation to certain specific examples such as Zimbabwe (Sinclair, Pikirayi, Pwiti &
Soper, Ch. 43, this volume) and Meroe (Ahmed 1984), but also more generally in state
formations throughout tropical Africa (Sinclair 1987, p. 22), where control of access to
productive resources (in this case land) is seen as the basis of state power (Connah
1987). To understand the dynamics of the processes leading to urbanization in Africa, it
is necessary to take into account the long-term effects of various systems of small- and
large-scale food production. A consideration of this factor needs to be added to the
already established recognition of the role, in the generation of towns and elites, of the
control of local exchange networks and the injection into them of luxury goods derived
from external trade (e.g. Ekholm 1972; Wright, Ch. 40, this volume).

During the last thirty years more attention has been paid to geographical approaches
in African archaeology ('Archaeology is nothing if not geographical' – Shaw 1963, p.
15), with the massive compilation of the *Atlas of African Prehistory* (Clark 1967b), and
the publication of *Man, Settlement and Urbanization* (Ucko, Tringham & Dimbleby
1972), which enlarged the theoretical concepts of urbanism and provided the comparative base to challenge previous parochial definitions of towns and cities in Egypt and the
rest of Africa. This development has led to the extension of archaeological survey and
the recognition of the need to integrate studies of urban growth with a knowledge of
settlement patterns in the hinterland landscape.

A topic which has been little discussed in African archaeology is the series of
assumptions lying behind the correlation of the most materially visible part of the
largest site with the centre of state power and control. It is this spatial differentiation of
form and function within the settlement system as a whole that archaeologists with a
limited view of a single site are prone to underestimate. Analytical approaches have,
however, become more sophisticated and are often based on data collected with
random sampling procedures stratified according to environmental units (see Sinclair,
Pikirayi, Pwiti & Soper, Ch. 43, this volume). Quantitative analysis of the archaeological record in Africa is also becoming more sophisticated; thus, different forms of
rank/size and clustering approaches to settlement hierarchy have been developed (e.g.
O'Connor, Ch. 34, this volume; Hassan, Ch. 33, this volume; McIntosh & McIntosh,
Ch. 37, this volume; Abungu & Mutoro, Ch. 42, this volume; Sinclair, Pikirayi, Pwiti
& Soper, Ch. 43, this volume). The deceptively simple topic of the size of urban sites
upon which much of the rank/size analyses depend is discussed on a continental scale by
Fletcher (Ch. 44, this volume), who shows the range of spatial variability which must
be taken into account.

From a comparative geographical perspective O'Connor (1983, pp. 28–41) contributed a six-fold typology of African towns: Indigenous, Islamic, Colonial, European,
Dual and Hybrid. Universal indicators of urbanism based on role differentiation were
suggested by Southall (1973) following work on functional specialization in relation to
urbanization by Mabogunje (1968). Measures of social complexity can also be related
to the range of social contacts (Wilson & Wilson 1945); Barth conceptualized

complexity as a function of the interlocking of different domains of social functioning, connecting local communities and regional groupings (Barth 1978, pp. 254–7). Such a view has important potential ramifications for the archaeological interpretation of settlement hierarchy. A corollary of the assumption that the existence of any town must have been due to external influence and control of trade has been a reluctance to accept the idea that urban development in Africa could be an ancient phenomenon.

Much of the early archaeological work in Africa relied on typology to construct stylistic sequences of stone artefacts and ceramics, and sometimes architectural features were also included. The primary aim of these studies was to build up relative chronologies of cultural entities. Whereas this was achieved quite rapidly (albeit sketchily) for the stone-using communities, and somewhat later for iron-using communities in areas such as Kenya (Kiriama, Ch. 30, this volume), Malawi (Juwayeyi, Ch. 22, this volume) and Zimbabwe (Sinclair, Pikirayi, Pwiti & Soper, Ch. 43, this volume), in archaeologically little-known areas such as Mozambique (Sinclair, Morais, Adamowicz & Duarte, Ch. 24, this volume) and the Zaïre forest (Eggert, Ch. 16, this volume) work on primary chrono-stratigraphic frameworks is still being carried out. Urban sites have been under-represented in all aspects of this work. Those few studies which had been made were, at least until the 1960s, flawed by their limited extent (no doubt owing to the expense and difficulty of urban archaeology). The result has been that town organization and growth has been inadequately researched (Robertshaw 1990; Anquandah, Ch. 38, this volume). However, throughout the 1960s and 1970s, with the extension of archaeological fieldwork, both spatially and with an increasing focus on the last two millennia, a greater archaeological involvement with urban research has developed; improvements in chronology, resulting from the application of radiometric methods, have provided significant new analytical tools.

The difference between the complex reality of the past and simplistic assumptions of a uniform lack of development in Africa, is provided by an examination of the data on settlement aggregation, region by region.

Northern Africa

Egypt had been termed by Wilson (1960, p. 124) a 'civilization without cities', and interest in urbanism among egyptologists was comparatively late. Preliminary approaches to urbanism (e.g. Kemp 1972b; O'Connor 1972a) were followed by efforts to construct more applicable urban criteria (e.g. Butzer 1976; Bietak 1979b). A revised list of urban traits of relevance to Egypt was drawn up, namely 'concentrated settlement with a compact form of some size', differentiated internal spatial and functional arrangements, specialized non-agricultural functions, concentration of crafts and goods and stores, division of labour and social hierarchy, religious-cult functions and defensive capability. Alternative analytical models suggested by Kemp (1989) and O'Connor (Ch. 34, this volume), and the analysis of demographic issues by Hassan (Ch. 33, this volume), form an impressive body of analytical approaches to the study of urbanism. The suggestion is, for ancient Egypt, that initial urban development derived from a number of alternative functional perspectives such as centres of food redistribution, defence against pastoralist raiders, religious activity focused on fertility and maintenance of food supply in the face of uncertainty (Hassan, Ch. 33, this volume). Urban development is seen to start *c*. 4000 BC; Hierakonpolis, for example, moves from a grouping of houses to become a large settlement and, with the addition of a fort, is a well-established town by 2700 BC (Hoffman, Hamroush & Allen, 1986). From *c*. 1900 BC the occurrence of planned 'model towns' imposed by central authority, such as Kahun (Kemp 1977a; Kemp 1989), represent an alternative form of urban establishment contrasting with organic growth (Bietak 1979b, p. 104; and see O'Connor, Ch. 34, this volume).

Despite the sophistication of such egyptological approaches to the consideration of the development and functions of urbanism, one old enigma remains: was Punt a real place/area with which important and extensive trading took place and, if so, where was it located? The problems involved in attempting to identify a location for a real Punt are legion (Kitchen, Ch. 35, this volume) – yet this textually attested word meaning southern (but, to date, still lost) area continues to be seen (e.g. O'Connor, Ch. 34, this volume) as a non-mythological place which will one day reveal itself as an early example of local urbanization.

Although some aspects of Nubian archaeology, in particular burial customs, are known in great detail, less has been done on settlement archaeology (and see O'Connor, Ch. 35, this volume). Urban development extended southwards along the Nile, and towns associated with Egyptian forts were established on the second cataract (e.g. at Buhen from *c*. 1900 BC and reoccupied *c*. 1500 BC). Examples of temple towns are known as well. The Lower Nubian sequence continues with important urban sites such as Qasr Ibrim (Adams 1977) occupied from *c*. 1500 BC onwards. The Kerma kingdom, situated around the third cataract and dating from *c*. 1500 BC (Bonnet 1986), was followed by the Napatan (from *c*. 900 BC), and Meroitic kingdoms (*c*. 400 BC to AD 200). This sequence of polities and their associated centres is among the most detailed in Africa (Adams 1977). The development of urbanism at Axum (*c*. AD 200 to AD 600) (Kobishanov 1979), which at one stage controlled the Red Sea outlet to the Indian Ocean and part of the southern Arabian coast as well, resulted in a distinctive political structure which is revealed by historical sources as well as numismatic and archaeological materials (Munro-Hay, Ch. 36, this volume).

Along the western part of the north African coast very little is known about early urbanism, and the main focus of work has been documenting the spread of Phoenician trading stations as far as Cape Mogador, and investigating the classically known centres such as Carthage (Phillipson 1985a, pp. 150–3; Picard 1991). From Roman times, with the notable increase in the availability of both written sources and archaeological research, much more is known of the considerable urban achievement in north Africa which made the region a major provider of food and a range of other commodities to the Roman empire (Decret & Fantar 1981). The rich medieval urban life of the region vividly described by Ibn Khaldun in the fourteenth century has been the focus of detailed intra-site work and comparative spatial analysis by Redman (1986) at Qsar es-Saghir in Morocco.

West Africa

At the beginning of the century early urban developments in west Africa were seen by historians such as Delafosse (1900) as resulting from external stimuli, and as by-products of Islamic influence. Work at Koumbi Saleh (Thomassey & Mauny 1951; Thomassey & Mauny 1956), the presumed capital of the ancient empire of Ghana, examined the extent or absence of this Islamic influence, and the work of Bovill (1968) utilized early Arab writings to paint a detailed picture of 'the golden trade of the Moors' and the trans-Saharan caravan routes. More recently, this presence or absence of Islamic influence in the urban centres on the southern edge of the Sahara, as well as fluctuating environmental conditions, have been explored at the site of Tegdaoust (Robert 1970; Robert & Robert 1972; Devisse *et al.* 1983).

Urban developments at Jenne-jeno (McIntosh & McIntosh, Ch. 37, this volume) in the middle Niger delta from at least the first century AD onwards, have been examined in close correlation with the settlement patterns in Jenne-jeno's hinterland, in relation to food production potentials and the exploitation of other resources. It is an outstanding example of how the dynamics of urban development can only be properly understood by a knowledge of the settlement economy of the whole surrounding area. The work at Jenne-jeno also demonstrated the indigenous nature of urban development; after several centuries of existence the town declined just at the time when Islamic influence was beginning and was formerly assumed to have stimulated Jenne-jeno into existence. The archaeological investigations of the site of Niani, if it has been correctly identified as the capital of ancient Mali, is of great interest as an example of a non-nucleated urban centre of great importance in its heyday (Filipowiak 1966).

Of equal, but of totally different, interest is the site of Begho with its 1500 mounds, at the northern edge of the tropical forest in modern Ghana, whose character was that of an important exchange centre for the gold coming north from the collecting areas of the Ashanti gold fields, before being transshipped north again to meet the southern end of the trans-Saharan caravan routes (Posnansky 1979; Anquandah, Ch. 38, this volume). Much work remains to be done upon the origins of the Hausa/Fulani cities of northern Nigeria, such as Kano, although a modest beginning has been made (Darling 1974).

In the totally different environment of the tropical rainforest, the cities and urban developments of southern Nigeria present a different problem, namely to discover the processes which led to their origin and growth. One of the difficulties is that, because of the vegetation, the settlement patterns of the surrounding areas in former times are archaeologically so much less easily visible. Gathering the necessary data will be much more costly and time-consuming than in areas where the corresponding information can be gathered from a combination of air photographs and rapid ground survey.

Because of the flooding of the world's museums and art markets with objects from Benin, after the British Expedition of 1897, more interest has been shown in its art than in questions concerning the city's origins; the questions have never really been addressed archaeologically, in spite of work having been carried out there with other aims in view (Bradbury 1959; Connah 1975; Andah 1982).

The ideas of Frobenius about Ife are a classic example of the assumption in the earlier part of the present century that African artistic, social and economic development could not have taken place without outside intervention (Frobenius 1913). The theory that Yoruba urbanism was only to be explained by the importation of the idea of a town from the cities of the Sahel to the north, persisted among Nigerian historians and geographers until comparatively recently (Mabogunje 1968). Ife can now be seen as an indigenous development within the nexus of wider Yoruba urbanism. Only after Ife's establishment as the node of a local exchange network and as a religious centre did it rise to wealth and prominence as a result of a process of intensification, deriving from its incorporation into longer distance trade to the north (Willett 1967; Shaw 1988, pp. 481–7).

The remarkable first millennium AD finds of art and craftsmanship at Igbo Ukwu in southeastern Nigeria (Shaw 1970; Shaw 1977) must surely represent some sort of resource concentration and centralization of wealth. What form this took has been a matter of debate but it is likely to have been associated with the office of a supreme social and spiritual dignitary responsible for the well-being of the agricultural commu-nity rather than being associated with the actions of a king and commander-in-chief. However that may be, ethnographers have maintained that before the coming of the Europeans the Igbo had no towns in any real sense and their acephalous and segmentary society was organized in such a way that they did not need them. Such a situation was not owing to a lack of population, since this area provides some of the highest population densities in Africa.

Local markets were important and it seems that towards the end of the first millennium AD, for some reasons not yet adequately explained, this local exchange network became caught up in a wider world – although the nature of this contact remains obscure (Sutton 1991). The solving of the problem of the genesis of centraliz-ation at Igbo Ukwu will not, as suggested by Sutton (1991, p. 141), come from 'the examination of the site of Igbo Ukwu in a radically novel way', nor by speculations about long-distance trading connections, but only from gathering data belonging to the half-millennia before and after the date of the Igbo Ukwu finds from the whole of the Igbo Ukwu hinterland. At present we know practically nothing about the pattern and character of settlement in southeastern Nigeria from the mid-first to the mid-second millennium AD. Until such work is carried out (and see Chikwendu, Craddock, Farquar, Shaw & Umeji 1989), Igbo Ukwu lacks any cultural context.

Central, eastern and southern Africa

Despite the classic historical sources (e.g. Pigafetta 1881), and ethnographic work by Ekholm (1972) on the kingdom of Kongo, in which she analysed the circulation of goods and women, archaeological field research has been hampered by thick rainforest. Only relatively recently, with the extensive surveys of Eggert, have site distributions in the Zaïre basin begun to be recorded (see above and Eggert, Ch. 16, this volume). Further south the finds from a rich burial site at Sanga in Katanga, despite the virtual absence of settlement sites, have led de Maret (1978) to suggest the likelihood of development of social differentiation from c. 800 AD, based on control of local networks of production and exchange, apparently in isolation from east coast trading centres.

In Uganda a number of sites, such as the extensive earthworks of Bigo (Shinnie 1965; Posnansky 1969) and the Ankole capital of Bweyorere (Posnansky 1968), and more recently Bunyoro (Connah 1991), have been investigated. Along the east African coast and the offshore islands there now exist detailed studies of particular town sites, such as

Shanga (see Horton & Mudida, Ch. 41, this volume) and Ungwana, as well as complex settlement hierarchies of the coastal hinterland (Abungu & Mutoro, Ch. 42, this volume). It is now possible to gain an understanding of the growth of early Swahili culture and settlement systems which culminated in the formation of towns with trading contacts extending not only along the western littoral of the Indian Ocean but deep into the interior of eastern and southern Africa, as well as into the Comoran archipelago and the island of Madagascar (Wright, Ch. 40, this volume; Radimilahy, Ch. 29, this volume). Early geographic work on the remarkable central Madagascar highland settlement system in which more than 16,000 hilltop ditched settlements were plotted in the area around Antananarivo (Mille 1970) has been significantly augmented by the archaeological documentation of this region, resulting in some of the most detailed information on field systems and subsistence available anywhere in eastern Africa (Raharijoana 1988; Wright & Rakotoarisoa 1990). Central Madagascar can now be seen to have been in contact with the trading networks of the northwest coast from at least the twelfth century AD onwards (Rakotovololona 1990).

In northern Mozambique, Sinclair, Morais, Adamowicz & Duarte (Ch. 24, this volume) have shown a pattern of autochthonous development over a number of centuries in relative isolation to external trading relations. In northern Mozambique, as in Malawi (Juwayeyi, Ch. 22, this volume), settlements without evidence for imported trade goods seem to be of similar size to those on the Zimbabwe plateau (Sinclair, Pikirayi, Pwiti & Soper, Ch. 43, this volume) and the edge of the Kalahari, both of which were in early and continuous trading contact with the east coast.

In southern Africa, the major focus of archaeological work has been at Great Zimbabwe, which was subject to early and controversial treatment claiming Semitic origin (Bent 1892; Hall & Neal 1902), later to be countered by the classic excavations of Randall-MacIver (1906) and Caton-Thompson (1931) and Robinson, Summers & Whitty (1961). More recent work by Garlake (1973a) and Huffman (1972; 1977) established the urban nature of Great Zimbabwe. Current archaeological interest is to understand the diachronic development and spatial extent of the site in its cultural setting (Sinclair, Pikirayi, Pwiti & Soper, Ch. 43, this volume). Clearly there must have been extensive settlement hierarchies to support Great Zimbabwe and other urban sites, both on the Zimbabwe plateau and in the surrounding regions of Mozambique (Sinclair, Morais, Adamowicz & Duarte, Ch. 24, this volume).

In the northern Transvaal, developments at Mapungubwe (Fouche 1937) are now seen to have preceded those at Great Zimbabwe, and the whole region comprising the Zimbabwe plateau, the Limpopo Basin and areas of the northern Transvaal is now understood to have been involved in significant internal and external trade exchange (Huffman 1972; Sinclair 1987; Huffman 1988; Vogel 1990).

Africa as a whole

This brief overview, region by region, has demonstrated the number of studies focusing on particular urban sites and their environmental surroundings, although few works of synthesis and comparison have been attempted (but see Fletcher, Ch. 44, this volume and Wright, Ch. 40, this volume). Since the work of Clark in 1965, consideration of African towns on a continental scale has only been attempted by

Connah (1987), who recognized that various forms of urbanism were connected with the practice of a variety of subsistence strategies over long periods of time; these allowed for the emergence of elites and the development of urban centres.

In the light of all the above considerations, foreign trade is clearly seen as an intensifier or catalyst of change rather than as a primary mover. No longer can urban developments be seen in isolation from their surrounding settlement hierarchies, or be taken to be simply the outcome of control of long-distance trade, whether on the east African coast or on the southern edge of the Sahara. Factors such as the range of internally based subsistence and exchange practices must now be recognized as being of primary importance not only for the spread of pioneer communities but for the consolidation of regional settlement systems and the differentiation of towns.

Suddenly the body of material available from Africa which is relevant to the understanding and analysis of urbanism has assumed formidable proportions. Thus Connah (1987) has attempted to analyse the nature of the politico-economic relations within which African towns were embedded, whether non-exploitative, redistributary networks or exploitative class systems, locally developed on the basis of the control of internal production, or externally stimulated by invasion or long-distance trade.

The role of long-distance trade in state formation has received a good deal of attention in recent times, with Coquery-Vidrovitch (1975) proposing an 'African Mode of Production' in which such control is seen as the fundamental explanatory factor for the existence of African states. Whether or not such control of trade networks can be accepted as a satisfactory level of explanation to account for the occurrence of state formation, such claims have again brought old debates to the fore. Ranged against such apparently old-fashioned ideas about the primacy of single factor economic control, and dominance of external trade, are those (e.g. Terray 1974) who would emphasize the importance of internal relations of exploitation, such as the maintenance of elites by both indirect exploitation and external trade. It is also possible to argue that surplus production by dependent villages is geared to the needs of a higher order unit which in turn seems to be dependent upon participation in a wider system of exchange. The concept of centre/periphery relations may in fact be extended into the concept of a world system which would treat Africa as an inert and passive supplier of raw materials (Frank 1967; Wallerstein 1974).

Archaeology in Africa as a discipline is faced with a multitude of interdisciplinary questions to which it should be able to contribute its own unique interpretive slant. To what extent can we speak of the 'African town' in a way similar to the generalized models of African kingdoms presented by anthropologists such as Dalton (1981)? How far is it valid to attempt to draw a distinction between state and town in Africa? The weight of the evidence indicates that state formations in Africa from c. 1000 AD were not isolated entities and that they were articulated closely to systems of merchant capital accumulation which operated in the western Indian Ocean and the Mediterranean. However, the earlier periods with their cycles of subsistence and settlement aggregation, as in the Nile and Niger valleys, should not be forgotten, and it will be to archaeology that scholars will increasingly turn for explanations of these and other expressions of early urbanism in Africa.

The future success of studies concerning African urban complexity must depend on the realization that analysis of towns in Africa cannot be restricted to a single society but must also include the fields of contact between different regions. Chronology, the geographical context of urbanism, spatial organization within towns and the provision of ethnohistorical and ethnolinguistic interpretive models for urban growth, must be coordinated (Sinclair 1989). It is clear that successful studies of urban complexity in Africa cannot be separated from an understanding of surrounding settlement hierarchies and inter-regional networks of production and exchange. It may be that archaeological attention will move away from a concern with urban centres (cf. McIntosh & Mcintosh, Ch. 37, this volume) to a consideration of zones of urbanism; in some cases there will be closely knit clusters of settlements, as on the Kenya coast (e.g. Abungu & Mutoro, Ch. 42, this volume), in others they will be more widely dispersed, as in Zimbabwe (Sinclair, Pikirayi, Pwiti & Soper, Ch. 43, this volume). It is highly likely that still more dispersed areas of cooperation will be found in the 'thirst lands' of Botswana and Namibia (Kiyaga-Mulindwa, Ch. 21, this volume; Kinahan, Ch. 20, this volume).

Conclusion

The thematic treatment of the topics we have reviewed here breaks with standard practice in African archaeology. It can be seen that the past of Africa is characterized by a multivariate complexity upon which no easy set of terminological shackles can, or should, be laid. Food production systems in Africa constitute a flexible set of responses to many, and sometimes difficult, circumstances. These systems have succeeded in maintaining populations throughout the continent, often in the face of considerable environmental stress and uncertainty. After more than 100 years of archaeological endeavour it is beginning to be realized that there can be a variety of cultural responses in the face of differing conditions, both societal and environmental.

Communities in Africa have both adapted and adopted, have both given and received. The archaeological record of Africa leaves little doubt about the cumulative importance of the choices made by individual actors in a large variety of circumstances in both rural and urban settings, resulting in forms of socio-cultural organization as complex as any in the world. In the face of the variety and complexity of the archaeological record, there is no justification for excluding Africa from its rightful place on the global stage of cultural achievement.

Acknowledgements

The authors would like to acknowledge the fact that throughout the writing of this Introduction, Peter Ucko not only provided detailed criticisms but was also an important source of ideas. We would also like to thank Jane Hubert, who corrected the text grammatically and worked hard to balance the styles of the contributors.

1   Africa's climate in the Holocene

A. T. GROVE

Introduction

Climate influences every component of the environment – hydrological and biochemical cycles, plant cover, animal life and human activity. Since most of Africa lies within 30° of the equator, temperatures are generally above the global mean and adequate for plant growth throughout the year except at high altitudes and in the extreme north and south of the continent. On the other hand, evaporation losses are everywhere great, exceeding 1000 mm from the rainforest and 3000 mm from lakes in arid regions. So, availability of water at the surface and for replenishing aquifers depends on adequate rainfall; precipitation is the most important of the climatic elements.

Near the tropics the climate is dominated by descending air most of the year and in these latitudes, except on the east side of southern Africa, arid conditions prevail. Polewards of the tropical deserts rain falls in the winter half of the year, being associated with the passage of mid-latitude depressions. Between the tropics rains are monsoonal, derived from moist air masses moving across 'Low Africa' from the south Atlantic between May and September and into 'High Africa' mainly from the Indian Ocean between October and April (Grove 1989). In the wetter regions, long downpours occur at the height of the rainy season, otherwise quite local storms, moving across country often from east to west, are much more prevalent.

Climate is not stable; rainfall records for this century and experience of droughts in recent years have made this quite clear. Years with negative departures from the mean tend to cluster together over periods of a decade or two and affect regions of subcontinental extent (Gregory 1988, Part III). Faure & Gac (1981) have pointed to the remarkable regularity of fluctuations in the discharge of the Senegal, Niger and Logone-Shari rivers in the course of this century with a quasi-periodicity of about thirty-five years. Tyson (1987) has shown regularities in the recurrence of wet and dry periods in southern Africa, the time intervals involved varying from one rainfall region to another and generally being shorter than those apparent in western Africa. Rainfall means over periods of a decade can vary from centennial means by 50 mm (25 per cent) in arid parts of the continent and by over 200 mm (10 per cent) in humid regions (Fig. 1.1).

Rainfall departures from longer term means may also cluster over periods lasting a century or so. The evidence for such medium-term climatic variations is difficult to interpret, consisting mainly of historical records relating especially to the values of Nile levels measured in Egypt, notably at Roda (Grove 1988), and historical records of the occurrence of droughts and famine in the vicinity of the Niger Bend in Mali (Nicholson 1978).

At present there are no good explanations for the fluctuations on a decadal time-scale or the variations on a centennial time-scale. Sea surface temperatures and ocean circulation patterns are probably involved but the ultimate causes may lie in volcanic events affecting solar radiation inputs, temporal variations in the radiation emitted by the sun or events as yet unrecognized. At present prediction is not possible, nor can the climatic record be extended into the past from knowledge of present-day processes and recent climatic history. However, it can be assumed that climate has varied throughout the course of the Holocene on both centennial and decadal time-scales.

An orderliness is apparent in holocene climatic history on the millennial time-scale. This order has become apparent over the last twenty-five years as a result of the application of C14 analyses to lake sediments and studies of their pollen, molluscan and diatom content. The climatic changes in Africa in the course of the Holocene have been

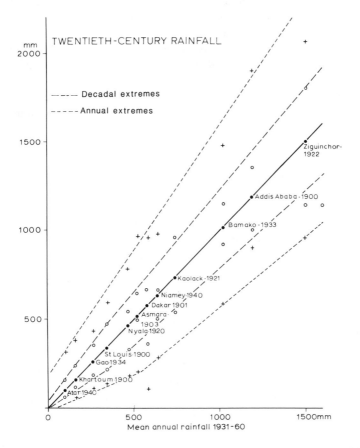

Figure 1.1   The values for the mean annual rainfall at 12 stations on the south side of the Sahara have been plotted on the diagonal. For each station the extreme annual values and the mean values for the wettest and driest decades recorded this century have also been plotted. The results indicate that extreme annual rainfall values differ from mean annual values by between about 300 and 500 mm, whereas mean decadal values differ by between about 150 and 250 mm from the long-term mean.

well marked, much more marked than those in middle and high latitudes over the same time period, impressing themselves on the landscape in the form of old lake strandlines in closed topographical basins. As time goes on and more information throwing light on the holocene climatic succession in Africa becomes available, so does the complexity of the record become more apparent. Nevertheless, one feature remains very striking and that is the much more abundant rainfall between the tropics towards the end of the Pleistocene and in the early Holocene than at any time since.

An explanation for climatic change in the tropics on the millennial time-scale lies at least in part in the regular periodicities long known to occur in the orbital movements of the earth around the sun and especially the variation in the direction of the angle of tilt of the earth's axis giving the precession of the equinoxes (Kutzbach & Street-Perrott 1985). At the present time the axis of the earth is tilted in a direction which results in the north pole being directed towards the sun, giving summer in the northern hemisphere in that part of its orbit where it is furthest from the sun. The situation was quite the reverse 9000 years ago; then the earth's axis was tilted in the opposite direction so that it was closest to the sun at the time of the northern summer. As a result, the solar radiation incident on the northern hemisphere in June, July and August was about 7 per cent greater than at present and in December, January and February about 7 per cent less. In consequence, the monsoonal effect was accentuated, bringing more rain in summer, especially to the interior of northern Africa.

The end of the Pleistocene in Africa

The low level of moraines on the high mountains of east Africa and Ethiopia indicate that snowlines were about 1000 m lower than at present in the last glaciation some-where between about 30,000 and 14,000 years ago. Temperatures were about 5°C lower than they are now, assuming the precipitation was much the same as at the present day, or as much as 9°C lower, taking into account the fact that precipitation between about 18,000 and 14,000 BP seems to have been less than now. The cooling has been confirmed by analysis of pollen from cores taken from mountain lakes which show that the altitudinal vegetation zones were also lowered by something like 1000 m (Maley 1992). The whole of Africa was significantly cooler than now. Periglacial features in South Africa and Lesotho dating from the last glaciation suggest that temperature may have been as much as 14°C lower (Lewis 1988) though a cooling of 5°C is more usually accepted. With the steeper latitudinal temperature gradients, winds were probably stronger than at present, and climatic conditions at both the southern and northern extremities of the continent must have resembled those of Patagonia at the present day. Northern Africa would have been subject to icy blasts in winter from northwesterly winds sweeping across the sea-ice, which extended across the Atlantic as far south as Portugal.

Between the tropics, towards the end of the Pleistocene, the climate was generally much more arid than now. Saharan dunes extended some 500 km south of their present limits, ponding back the Senegal, upper Niger, Logone-Shari and the Nile north of Khartoum. Closed basins where lake sediments remained from earlier wetter conditions were deflated. The entire upper Nile basin was an area of inland drainage with most of the floor of Lake Victoria dry as recently as 13,000 years ago. However, the northern Kalahari some 18,000 to 15,000 years ago was occupied by great lakes flooding 40,000 km^2 of the Makgadikgadi basin and extending from an enlarged Lake Ngami northeast to the Zambezi above the Victoria Falls (Shaw, Cooke & Thomas 1988).

The glaciers on the east African mountains retreated about 15–14,000 BP (Hamilton 1982) and after an interval of a millennium or two lake levels began to rise in Tibesti, the Sahel, the White Nile valley south of Khartoum, southern Ethiopia and east Africa. At about 10,500 BP lake levels fell and a period of desiccation began which lasted about a thousand years (Street-Perrott & Roberts 1983). This was at a time when ice sheets and temperatures were behaving skittishly in middle latitudes for reasons which are not yet understood.

The Early Holocene

The greatest frequency of radiocarbon dates from high strandlines of African lakes is for the millennium between 9500 and 8500 BP. This was the culmination of the last African pluvial period when all the closed basins between the tropics were occupied by lakes, several of which rose more than 100 m above their present-day levels (Grove, Street & Goudie 1975; Street & Grove 1976). Lake Nakuru-Elmenteita in Kenya rose 200 m and overflowed northwards into the Menengai caldera; nearby Lake Naivasha expanded to spill south through Hell's Gate canyon (Fig. 1.2).

Associated with the old shorelines are former beaches or spits containing the shells of various species of molluscs which can be dated by radiocarbon and can also provide information about the microenvironments in which they lived and died. On rocky spurs which once formed headlands protruding into the palaeolakes, stromatolite crusts define former lake levels remarkably clearly. Very often the lakes rose until they reached overflow levels which formed an upper limit to their enlargement so that various kinds of shoreline features are all concentrated at one level. In the Rift Valley of southern Ethiopia, lakes occupying the basins of lakes Shala, Abiyata and Langano merged and combined with Lake Ziway to form one large lake which overflowed northwards and spilled down the Awash river to swell the terminal Lake Abhé in the Afar depression. Further south in the east African Rift, Lake Turkana was fed by a lake 20 m deep in the Stefanie or Chew Bahir basin, which is now usually dry, and also by subsurface flow from a lake in the Suguta valley (Grove, Street & Goudie 1975; Casanova, Hilaire-Marcel, Page, Taieb & Vincens 1988). Turkana rose about 85 m above its present level (which has varied by about 20 m in the course of this century) and overflowed to the Pibor river and the Nile system (Butzer 1980a; Harvey & Grove 1982).

The old strandlines can be traced on air photographs and satellite images. Those of Palaeolake Chad, stretching across Borno in northeast Nigeria, are especially prominent (Grove & Warren 1968). The multiple bars of the old barrier beach, rising 12 m above the general level of the plains and 40 m above the current level of Lake Chad, extend

over 300 km from the Logone opposite Bongor through Bama and Maiduguri to the
Komadugu Yobe near Gashua. The shoreline of the same lake, Megachad it was called
by Moreau (1966), can be traced northwards through the Republics of Niger and Chad
to encompass the Bodélé depression. Occupying about 350,000 km^2 it would have been
exceeded in size at the present day only by the Caspian Sea.

Calculating past rainfall from former lake strandlines

By the time these lakes reached their maximum extents about 9500 BP, mean temperatures and evaporation losses were similar to those of the present day. Insolation in the
northern hemisphere was greater in the summer months but this may have been offset
to some extent by greater cloudiness. Winters would probably have been cooler on

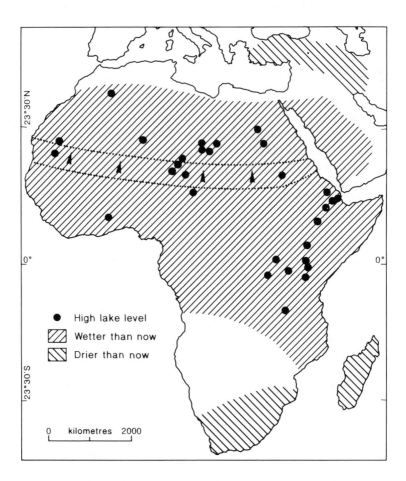

Figure 1.2 Between about 9500 and 8500 BP lakes occupying closed basins in equatorial and
north tropical Africa reached higher levels than they had done for over 10,000 years or have done
since. The dotted lines stretching across the continent show the associated advance northwards
into the Sahara of sahelian-type vegetation.

account of reduced insolation at that season but the increased size of the lakes was mainly caused by greater rainfall than at present.

In attempts to determine the magnitude of the change in rainfall, two approaches have been used: the first involves calculating the water balance of a palaeolake, making simple assumptions about evaporation and runoff coefficients; the second tries to derive better values for evaporation losses by reconstructing energy flows in a palaeolake and its basin.

Calculations of the water balance or hydrological budget involve multiplying the palaeolake area by a figure for the evaporation losses which is derived from the assumed temperature. The result must balance the rainfall and runoff to maintain the lake at the level indicated by its former shoreline (Street-Perrott, Roberts & Metcalfe 1985). In Kenya, Washbourn (1967) calculated that if evaporation from Palaeolake Nakuru in the early Holocene was 1600 mm annually as compared with 1480 mm at the present day and the runoff coefficient of the catchment was 10 per cent as compared with today's 3.26 per cent, the mean annual rainfall required to maintain the lake at the 200 m level would have been 1370 mm as compared with a 1938–65 mean of 965 mm, an increase of 42 per cent. Similarly, Street (1979) calculated for the Ziway-Shala basin in Ethiopia that, with evaporation 2000 mm, the same as today, and the runoff coefficient 16.2 per cent as compared with 12.3 per cent today, the mean precipitation over the basin would have been 1407 mm as compared with 957 mm at the present, an increase of 47 per cent.

Calculations of the hydrological balance utilizing the energy balance to derive figures for evaporation losses and runoff coefficients have been made by Kutzbach (1980) for Megachad. He concludes that mean precipitation over the basin would have been 650 mm as compared with 350 mm today. The total supply of water to the lake in the form of rain falling on its surface and inputs by rivers would have been fourteen times that of the present day, not taking into account the losses by overflow to the Atlantic via the Mayo Kebbi and Benue. Grove and Pullan (1963), using a less sophisticated approach, estimated total inputs at sixteen times those of the present day. About half the supply would have been rain falling on the enlarged lake, while the rest would have come from rivers. Although these would have included rivers from the J. Marra and streams rising in Tibesti, whose deltas can still be distinguished along the northern margins of the Bodele depression, the main inflow would have come, as it does today, from the Shari and Logone; their mean discharges would have been about five times greater than now.

Similar calculations have been made of the precipitation responsible for the greater size of Nakuru-Elmenteita, Naivasha, Turkana and Victoria in the early Holocene (Hastenrath & Kutzbach 1983). Taking into account the accompanying decreases in values for the albedo (reflectivity of the surface) and Bowen ration (i.e. the increase in the proportion of insolation involved in evaporation) resulting from a denser plant cover, increases in annual precipitation were derived of between 140 mm (15 per cent) and 300 mm (35 per cent), rather smaller increases than those calculated from the water balance method used by Washbourn. However, both methods of calculation point to mean annual rainfall totals in the early Holocene having been similar to those of unusually wet years at the present day (Fig. 1.1).

The wetter conditions in the early Holocene extended well to the south of the equator with a very large lake 60 m above the present one in the Rukwa basin of southwest

Tanzania, and an enlarged Lake Chilwa in southern Malawi (Grove 1983). Near the southern tropic, on the other hand, the northern Kalahari in Botswana was semi-arid until after 7000 BP, which is understandable in terms of monsoonal flows in the southern hemisphere being even weaker than at present in the millennia around 9000 BP. The southwestern Kalahari remained dry throughout the Holocene (Lancaster 1979).

Northeast Africa

On the floor of the eastern Mediterranean, layers of saprolitic sediments rich in organic matter result from interruptions of the oxygenation of the bottom waters. This is believed to be attributable to great surface spreads of fresh water brought down by the Nile sealing off the deeper waters from contact with the atmosphere (Rossignol-Strick, Nesteroff, Olive & Vergnaud-Grazzini 1982). The last occasion when this happened was in the early Holocene.

The Nile discharge in the early Holocene required to produce the saprolites would have been much greater than its flow at the present day and the result mainly of greater rainfall over Ethiopia and east Africa.

The rainfall was also greater over the Sudan Republic. Palaeobiological studies indicate that the isohyets in the region of J. Marra were some 400 km north of their present positions (Wickens 1975). From the area between J. Marra and Ennedi, the Wadi Howar flowed to the Nile through an environment which Pachur & Kropelin (1987) describe as characterized by numerous groundwater outlets and freshwater lakes. Further north, Ritchie, Eyles & Haynes (1989) interpret the existence of a deep lake at Oyo between 8000 and 6100 BP as indicating an annual monsoon rainfall of as much as 400 mm where the mean annual rainfall is now a few millimetres a year. About 300 km to the northeast, Selima oasis shows signs of an early lacustrine period and then evidence of a lake 20 m deep occupying the oasis for about a thousand years until 7000 BP (Haynes, Eyles, Pavlish, Ritchie & Rybak 1989).

In Egypt, Neumann (1987) has described charred wood remains from the Gilf Kebir which suggest that between 8000 and 4000 BP water was seasonally available and nomads would have found the area a favourable environment. The wettest period, according to Kropelin (1987), was probably between 6000 and 5000 BP. However, Neumann considers that the annual precipitation need not have exceeded 100 mm and McHugh, Schaber, Breed & McCauley (1989) recognize that storm water may have drained long distances along sand-filled channel systems of the kind that have been revealed by space shuttle radar sensing of this part of the eastern Sahara. Such seepage water might have fed playa lakes and supported vegetation that produced pollen, suggesting a higher rainfall than was in fact experienced. Further north, the floor of the Dakhlah Oasis in the western desert of Egypt was flooded from about 9000 to 8400 BP and groundwater continued to feed lakes there for several centuries afterwards (Brookes 1989). Goodfriend (1988) finds in stable isotope ratios in snail shells evidence of monsoonal rain reaching as far north as southern Israel in the early Holocene.

West Africa

Close to the Gulf of Guinea, Lake Bosumtwi reached high levels about 12,000 BP that were maintained for about 4000 years (Talbot, Livingstone, Palmer, Maley, Melack, Delibrias & Gulliksen 1984) and indicate that rainfall was comparable to or above present values in the high forest zone of Ghana at this time. Relict plant populations point to the equatorial rainforest having extended 350 km north of its present limits and humid associations of plants reaching as far as 21°N (Lezine 1989). The stable isotope content of ocean floor sediments off the Niger delta indicate that its discharge was much increased (Pastouret, Chamley, Delibrias, Duplessy & Thiede 1978). Not only was its flow supplemented by the overflow of Megachad, via the Benue, but the upper river rising in Guinea was much enlarged, flooding the inland delta basin upstream of Timbuktu and spilling over the plains of Azawad after 9000 BP, to flood depressions between old dune lines and occupy an area of 60,000 km² north of the Niger (Petit-Maire & Riser 1987). Rivers from the Ahaggar flowed down wadis to the Tilemsi and the Niger river. Stromatolites dating from 8300 to 6500 BP mark the shore of a lake in the Chemchane depression in Mauritania at latitude 21°N (Casanova, Hilaire-Marcel, Page, Taieb & Vincens 1988). Lakes so large they would have required ten times the rainfall of the present day occupied the Taoudenni depression, and between 9000 and 4500 BP the surrounding areas 300 to 700 km into the Sahara were covered with sahelian vegetation (Petit-Maire & Riser 1983).

The Middle Holocene

Throughout intertropical Africa, there are signs of lake regression in the centuries around 7500 BP, with subsequent recovery but to levels less high than those in the early Holocene (Street-Perrott & Roberts 1983). The curve of Lake Bosumtwi's variations in level (Talbot, Livingstone, Palmer, Maley, Melack, Delibrias & Gulliksen 1984) shows a relatively small recession of 20 m about 7800 BP followed by a prolonged rise between 7000 and 4000 BP when the lake is believed to have overflowed. In the Ziway-Shala basin, Ethiopia, a drying episode from 8000 to 7200 BP was followed by a rise in lake level and then another arid phase about 5900 BP (Gillespie, Street-Perrott & Switsur 1983). In the north of Mali, dunes which had formed in the late Pleistocene and been fixed under a cover of vegetation in the early Holocene were reactivated between 6200 and 5200 BP (Riser, Hilaire-Marcel & Rognon 1983). An arid interval in Tibesti has been placed at 8000–6800 BP, followed by high lake levels from 6000 to 4500 BP and then a marked dry phase lasting a few hundred years (Jakel 1977). At Taoudenni in the central Sahara the sequence of events was even more complicated with two transgression/regression sequences identified between 8800 and 8300 BP, each lasting about 250 years; then there is evidence of four transgression/regression sequences between 8300 and 6900 BP and eight or nine between 6760 and 3840 BP (Fabre & Petit-Maire 1988). Lakes in this basin, lacking subsurface supplies of water and large affluents, were probably more sensitive to variations in precipitation than was the case with some other lakes (Fig. 1.3). It seems possible that after 7000 BP, the Sahara was less arid in the east than it was in the west (Lezine & Casanova 1989).

   Climatic shifts outside the tropics were probably out of phase with those nearer the
equator. In the northern Kalahari, after a semi-arid early Holocene, precipitation
peaked at 6000–5000 BP (Shaw, Cooke & Thomas 1988). This was also a time when the
Shati depression in Libya held marshes and lakes (Petit-Maire, Delibrias & Gaven
1980), and Rognon (1987) refers to a strong increase in the rainfall of the Maghreb on
the northern margins of the Sahara between 6000 and 4500 BP as coming after a long
arid phase. But Fontes & Gasse (1989) are strongly of the opinion that humid conditions
had been established in the northwestern Sahara much earlier, from about 9300 to 7200
BP, and then again from 6200 to 4500 BP. They see groundwater levels building up over
a long period and reaching the surface to give lakes and shellbeds in places like the

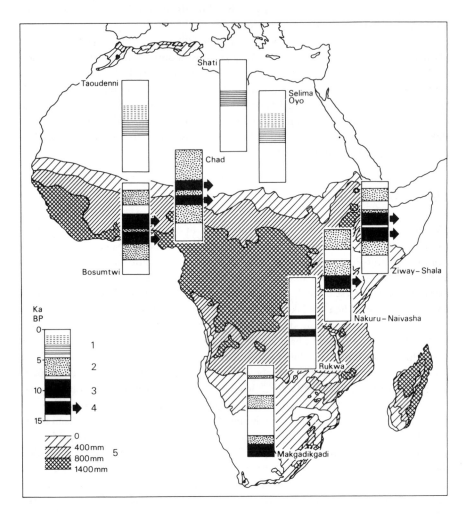

Figure 1.3 Lake-level records from the end of the Pleistocene and the Holocene are plotted
against a background of the distribution of mean annual rainfall at the present day. 1 oscillating
levels; 2 intermediate levels; 3 high levels; 4 lake overflows

Mellala Sebkha and inter-dunal hollows of the Grand Erg Occidental. The quaternary water bodies of the northwestern Sahara may have been connected to large aquifers but the C13 content of the shells shows that their dates are unlikely to have been affected by the presence of old carbon. The organisms present in the thinly bedded sediments point to rapidly varying salt requirements and indicate that the surface levels of the lakes varied markedly according to the abundance of local rainwater supplies.

Onset of current climate

The mid-Holocene humid period in the northwestern Sahara and between the tropics lasted about 2000 years until aridity became more pronounced after 4500 BP. In northwestern Sudan, lake deposits at Oyo indicate a progressive increase in aridity with rainfall diminishing from about 300 mm to less than 100 mm by 4500 BP. The lakes in Taoudenni dried up about 4500 BP though a small saline lake persisted in the basin until 3500 BP. There were arid intervals in Tibesti from 5400–4300 and 3500–2900 BP. Lakes, possibly fed by groundwater rather than overflow from the Niger, persisted in the south of Azawad until about 3500 BP. Near the coast of eastern Ghana aeolian sandsheets and dunes spread over palaeosoils between 4500 and 3800 BP (Talbot 1981). Lake Bosumtwi declined in level about 3800 BP (Talbot, Livingstone, Palmer, Maley, Melack, Delibrias & Gulliksen 1984). Extensive Blue Nile flooding in central Sudan ceased some time after 5500 BP, and the river entrenched its course about 10 m into the floodplain (Adamson, Gasse, Street & Williams 1981). The recession of Ziway-Shala has been placed at 4800 BP (Street 1979). In the Afar depression lake levels fell after 4000 BP (Gasse, Rognon & Strict 1980), as they did in Lake Turkana (Owen, Barthelmé, Renaut & Vincens 1982) and the Western Rift (Hecky & Degens 1973). Lancaster (1987) sees evidence in the dunes and lunettes in the southwestern Kalahari for dry conditions with strong winds during the period from 4500 to 3500 BP, possibly continuing into much later times. However, humid conditions seem to have persisted after 4000 BP along the Mauritanian coast, with sahelian vegetation extending 4°N of its present limits, possibly because the cool Canaries Current extended less far south than at present and the water offshore remained relatively warm until about 3000 BP (Petit-Maire 1980).

The Late Holocene

A final amelioration of aridity took place after 3500 BP in several areas. In the northwestern Sahara, shell-rich sediments occur at 3280 to 3080 BP (Fontes, Gasse, Callot, Plazeat, Carbonnel, Dupeuble & Kaczmarska 1985). In Tibesti aridity was relieved between 2800 and 2300 BP (Jakel 1977). There is some evidence that Lake Turkana briefly rose to +70 m about 3250 BP (Butzer 1980a) but after 3000 BP its oscillations were below a level of about +50 m (Owen, Barthelmé, Renaut & Vincens 1982). Lake Naivasha, which had dried up completely, formed again and persisted through the last three millennia into the present (Richardson & Richardson 1972). Lake Chad rose several metres above its present level and overflowed down the Bahr al Ghazal into the Bodélé depression between 3500 and 3000 BP (Servant 1973). A final rather minor rise of Ethiopian lake levels came a thousand years later (Street 1979). Since 1800 BP lake levels seem to have been low and generally comparable to those of the present day.

Discussion

It is well recognized that the levels of certain Ethiopian lakes such as Abhé in the Afar depression depend on regional groundwater levels; Ziway, Shala and most of the other lakes mentioned here as indicators of past rainfall were much more responsive to local precipitation at the time when the lakes were in existence. This seems to have been the case with the lakes of Taoudenni. The greatest uncertainty arises over the lakes of the northern Sahara. The behaviour of most of them seems to have been influenced by groundwater. There is no doubt that the northern Sahara was a wetter place in the early and mid-Holocene than it is today but it remains difficult to decide how much greater was the rainfall.

In general the changes of lake level in intertropical Africa in the course of the Holocene show a diminishing amplitude and an overall downward trend. The timing varies from one site to another, partly no doubt because of the uncertainties inherent in C14 dating of lacustrine deposits and also according to regional and local geological and groundwater conditions. Atmospheric and oceanic circulation patterns may have varied through time so that exact synchroneity is not to be expected; on the other hand, uncertainties in dating are such that there is a possibility that arid intervals were synchronous over extensive areas.

In general the wetter phases diminish in length and the dry phases increase in frequency as one moves from the more humid regions towards what is now the most arid part of the Sahara. Superimposed on an overall downward trend and long-term variations in lake levels and rainfall are centennial and decadal fluctuations of the kind experienced in more recent times, some of them probably involving quite sharp changes in precipitation over a few years. In general there would seem to be good grounds to suggest that Africa is a drier continent today, at any rate north of Capricorn, than it ever was in the Holocene.

2 The climatic and vegetational history of the equatorial regions of Africa during the upper Quaternary

J. MALEY

(Translated from the French by Thurstan Shaw*)

Introduction

For reconstructing the palaeoenvironments and vegetational history of the equatorial zone of Africa during the late Quaternary, we have direct evidence from palynological and palaeobotanical sources. These two fields of research are often complementary, for macro-remains, especially wood, give precise information, essentially for short periods, while pollen analysis, usually carried out on long sequences dated by radiocarbon, allow one to reconstruct the main vegetation changes over a longer time-scale.

Lakes yielding sequences favourable for pollen analysis have been investigated in Ghana (Maley & Livingstone 1983; Maley 1987; Maley 1989), in Cameroon (Maley 1987; Maley & Brenac 1987; Brenac 1988; Maley 1989; Maley, Livingstone, Giresse, Thouveny, Brenac, Kelts, Kling, Stager, Haag, Fournier, Bandet, Williamson & Zogning 1990b) and in the Congo (Elenga 1987; Elenga, Vincens, Giresse & Schwartz 1987), but since the number of such sites is limited, analyses have also been carried out on marine cores from near the coast when their pollen content was sufficient (Caratini & Giresse 1979; Hooghiemstra & Agwu 1988; Fredoux & Tastet 1988; Fredoux, Tastet, Maley & Guilmette 1989). The frequently smaller quantity of pollen in marine cores is compensated by their long chronological coverage.

Indirect environmental evidence is provided both by various kinds of geological research on lacustrine and fluviatile deposits, and by stratigraphical, sedimentological, geochemical, isotopic and archaeological studies of the soils which support the forest today, or the savannas which fringe or are sometimes contained within the forest. Research on the deep-sea fans of large rivers also give important and often complementary information concerning palaeoenvironments (Pastouret, Chamley, Delibrias, Duplessy & Thiede 1978 for Niger; Giresse, Bongo-Passi, Delibrias & Duplessy 1982 for Congo-Zaïre).

Biogeography, that is, the present distribution of different species of flora and fauna, provides other data which contribute to the delimitation of forest areas surviving

---

* 26 Kingsdale Court, Peacocks, Great Shelford, Cambridgeshire

through previous arid periods, or even to the tracing of migration routes (Maley 1987; Maley 1989; Maley, Caballe & Sita 1990a).

The main climatic phases of the late Quaternary in central Africa

Using data from Africa, De Ploey (1965; 1969) was one of the first to produce a chart of the evolution of the palaeoenvironments of central Africa, in particular naming the main climatic phases. This chart has been completed and further refined by geological, palynological, palaeobotanical and pedological research (Giresse 1978; Roche 1979; Delibrias, Giresse, Lanfranchi & Le Cocq 1983; Schwartz, Delibrias, Guillet & Lanfranchi 1985; Maley 1987; Schwartz 1988a; Schwartz 1988b; Maley 1989).

For central Africa (Congo, Gabon, western and central Zaïre, southern Cameroon and southern Central African Republic) the sequence of the main climatic phases has been established as follows:

The *Maluekian*, placed between 70,000 and 40,000 BP on the basis of prehistoric industries, is regarded as a relatively dry period marked by extensive deforestation.

The *Njilian*, with interpolated ages, and sometimes radiocarbon-dated, lasting from 40,000 to 30,000 BP, was a relatively wet phase corresponding to a definite reforestation.

The *Leopoldian*, dated from 30,000 to 12,000 BP, was on the whole relatively dry. This phase culminated around 18,000 BP in a new and marked extension of open savanna environments.

The *Kibangian*, dated from 12,000 BP to the present, was relatively wet until around 3500 BP (Kibangian A), and was drier since (Kibangian B). Reforestation probably proceeded progressively from the beginning of the Kibangian, but with retreat occurring after 3500 BP.

Soil history

The study of soils yields information on palaeoenvironments, in particular because some of the layers which make up the soils were laid down in succession under different environmental conditions. Various publications have shown that stone-lines, which are fairly frequently found near the bottom of pedological profiles, were laid down in certain periods of the Quaternary as a result of a process of intense erosion during which the forest had disappeared (De Heinzelin 1955; Vincent 1966; Vogt 1966; Marchesseau 1967; Stoops 1967; Schwartz 1990). Above the stone-line there is nearly always a sandy-clay colluvium, in which prehistoric industries are found in some places; and in some, actual workshop floors. These industries are often concentrated at the base of the colluvium, resting on the top of the stone-line. This shows that the tools were left on the surface at a time when the stone-line was uncovered.

Two important questions remain concerning these two layers: how old each of them is and how the colluvium was laid down.

As far as the age of the stone-lines is concerned, it is possible that they were formed at more than one time. The main period of formation would have been during the dry phase of the Maluekian, followed by a rapid deposition of the colluvium during the transition from the Maluekian to the wetter Njilian (Lanfranchi & Schwartz 1990). However, a severe erosional phase, occurring at the transition from the Leopoldian to the Kibangian, between about 13,000 and 10,000 BP, at a time when there was a marked increase in rainfall, could also have produced a coarse deposit (Giresse, Kinga-Mouzeo & Schwartz Forthcoming).

It is not yet known how the colluvium was formed. Was it developed in an open environment, of steppe or savanna character, or was it, on the contrary, formed under forest? Marchesseau (1967), in a detailed morphological and mineralogical study in Gabon, inclined towards an allochthonous interpretation for each interfluve. Allochthony would be connected with alluvial or colluvial transport, and would be associated with soil-creep. However, in the north of the forested area, samples of wood charcoal from the base of the colluvium and just above the stone-line, have given ages of 8560 ± 100 bp and 8470 ± 70 bp in southern Cameroon (Kadomura & Hori 1990), and of 11,200 ± 200 bp, 9150 ± 150 bp and 8685 ± 120 bp in Nigeria, at Iwo Eleru not far from Ife (Shaw & Daniels 1984; Thurstan Shaw, *pers. comm.*). These data seem to show that a stone-line would have been formed towards the end of the Pleistocene and that the colluvium would have been deposited subsequently in a forest environment, since the recolonization of the forest began progressively in these areas from about 13,000 to 12,000 years BP. Nevertheless it is clear that further research, accompanied by precise dating, must be carried out in other areas of the African forest zone before we shall be in a position to reach any definitive conclusion on this subject.

Forest refugia and holocene forest expansion

Various biogeographic data showing the vast wealth of flora and fauna in certain parts of the African forest zone have led to the conclusion that this wealth, particularly localized in certain well-defined areas, is evidence for ancient forest refugia which would have survived the great arid phases of the Quaternary, the last of which took place between 20,000 and 15,000 years BP (Van Zinderen Bakker 1976; Hamilton 1976; Maley 1987; Maley 1989).

Pollen studies recently carried out on lacustrine cores at two forest sites, one in Ghana and the other in western Cameroon, covering a period extending back from the present to about 25,000 to 30,000 years BP, have yielded precise data on this question. The Ghanaian site (Lake Bosumtwi) is situated in a sector where aridification is clearly shown between 20,000 and 15,000 BP by the disappearance of the forest, while western Cameroon benefited from a climate far less dry, attested by the survival of islands of forest forming one of the principal refuges of the African forest block (Maley 1987; Brenac 1988; Maley 1989). Data on the primates of the central Zaïre basin indicate that a 'central refuge' must have existed along certain portions of the great rivers of this basin (Colyn 1987), apparently confirming palaeobotanical surveys conducted in the Congo (Dechamps, Lanfranchi, Le Cocq & Schwartz 1988).

In the Lake Bosumtwi area of Ghana, the forest was completely restored about 9000 BP (Maley 1987; Maley 1989), but pollen results show that in this area the first stages of reforestation became apparent from 13,000 to 12,000 BP.

The holocene forest expansion went far beyond its present boundaries, as can be inferred from the biogeography of the western forest zone. Thus the relatively great taxonomic homogeneity on either side of 'the Dahomey Gap' (which nowadays breaks the east–west continuity of the forest zone in the Republics of Togo and Benin) shows that this sector was probably invaded by forest in the course of the Holocene. This break in the east–west forest zone probably only came into being again from about 4000 to 3000 BP (Maley 1987; Maley 1989).

In central Africa (Fig. 2.1), the beginning of Kibangian A (about 12,000 BP) corresponds to a phase of forest recolonization (Maley 1987; Brenac 1988; Maley 1989), accompanied in Congo by a resumption of podsolization (Schwartz 1988a; Schwartz 1988b). It seems that it was only in the course of the middle Holocene that the forest expanded far beyond its present limits. Thus, near Pointe-Noire, in the coastal zone which is at present covered with savanna vegetation, the bases of tree-trunks of species belonging to rainforest have been observed *in situ* on palaeosols and dated from 6500 to 3000 BP (Dechamps, Lanfranchi, Le Cocq & Schwartz 1988; Schwartz, Delibrias, Guillet & Lanfranchi 1985). This forest extension into what is now savanna, sometimes included in, or adjacent to, the forest zone, indicates that these savannas probably disappeared or were reduced in extent during the second part of Kibangian A (*c.* 7000–3500 BP).

Diverse data for this period have led to the conclusion that there was an increase in rainfall (Giresse and Lanfranchi 1984; Maley 1987; Dechamps, Lanfranchi, Le Cocq & Schwartz 1988), caused above all by a shortening of the southern dry season (Maley 1989). Later, during the Kibangian B (about 3500 BP to the present), the annual dry seasons began to lengthen again, with a corresponding new extension of savannas in, or adjacent to, the forest (Giresse and Lanfranchi 1984; Maley 1987; Maley 1989). The Bantu, who originated from western Cameroon and the neighbouring regions south of the Benue and spread across central and southern Africa in the course of late Holocene times (Vansina 1984), may well have taken advantage of this retreat of the forest, beginning abruptly around 3500–3000 BP, to penetrate certain sectors of the forest. It is

---

Figure 2.1 Schematic map of the forest vegetation of central Africa (adapted from Letouzey (1968; 1985), White (1983) and Maley (1990)).

1   Evergreen forests of southern Cameroon and Gabon with numerous Caesalpiniaceae

2   Atlantic coastal forests with *Sacoglottis gabonensis* and *Lophira alata* in Cameroon, but replaced in Gabon by *Oukoumea klaineana*

3   Congo-type forests characterized by the alternation or mixing of evergreen and semi-deciduous species

4   Open-growing forests with Marantaceae and Zingiberaceae

5a Mixture of forests of types 4 and 5b

5b Evergreen forests with *Gilbertiodendron dewevrei* (*Caesalp.*)

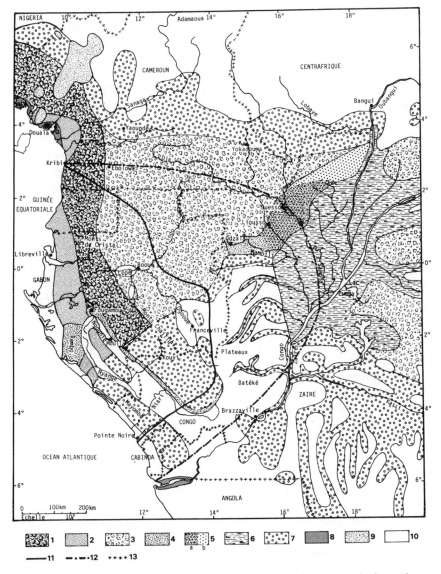

6   Zone almost permanently flooded, with evergreen forests, raphia palms and other moisture-loving species
7   Semi-deciduous forests
8   Mangroves
9   Various montane groups
10   Savannas
11   Limit of *Aukoumea klaineana*
12   Maximum extent of cooler air during the southern dry season (about four months, from June to September)
13   State boundaries

possible, then, that this climatic change – synchronous with comparable changes occurring in the more northerly savannas (Maley 1981; Maley 1982; Maley 1983) – initiated the Bantu migration.

Temperature variation and the extension of montane biotopes to low altitudes

There is now a whole body of data which shows that at the time of the great glacial advances in higher latitudes, culminating around 20,000–15,000 BP, there was also in lower latitudes a marked lowering of temperature. As far as the African forest zone is concerned, various data show montane taxa to have spread to low altitudes, an indication of the lowering of temperature.

First, on the Congo side of the Chaillu massif the existence of a surviving low-altitude (approximately 600–700 m) population of montane taxa (Fig. 2.2), in particular *Podocarpus latifolius* (Maley 1987; Maley, Caballe & Sita 1990a) shows that in the past montane biotopes extended to a low altitude in the forest zone, implying a lowering of temperature of at least 3–4°C. For the Congo sector, this conclusion has been confirmed by pollen analyses carried out by Elenga (1987) and Elenga, Vincens, Giresse & Schwartz (1987) on a short core taken in a depression on the Batéké Plateau at an altitude of 600–700 m. With more than 60 per cent of pollen from montane taxa (mainly *Podocarpus*, *Ilex* and *Olea*), it is clear that a local montane phase continued until about 10,000 BP. Given the altitude at which *Podocarpus* are living today, a minimum temperature drop of 3–4°C may be inferred.

Pollen analyses carried out in western Cameroon and in Ghana, at two low-altitude sites, have also shown the presence of a montane element characterized by *Olea hochstetteri*. From this a minimum lowering of temperature of 3 to 4°C has also been deduced (Maley & Livingstone 1983; Maley 1987; Maley 1989). Furthermore, in the core from Lake Bosumtwi where pollen of *Olea hochstetteri* was identified, Palmer (in Talbot, Livingstone, Palmer, Maley, Melack, Delibrias & Gulliksen 1984) identified many Gramineae fragments as belonging to the Pooideae. Today this taxon is found only in tropical areas on the highest mountains (Clayton 1976; Livingstone & Clayton 1980) such as Mt Cameroon where they grow only above 2000 m (Letouzey 1968; Letouzey 1985). The presence of Pooideae on the hills surrounding Lake Bosumtwi therefore implies a temperature drop which could be of the order of 6°C, a figure comparable to that estimated for east Africa at the time of the last glacial maximum.

Thus, before 9000 BP the rainforest was absent, being replaced by a montane type of grassland with sparse clumps of trees. These trees belonged on the one hand to the montane type of vegetation such as *Olea hochstetteri*, and on the other, not to species of the sudano-guinea savanna but in most cases to the flora of semi-deciduous forests. Today, in fact, it is the montane prairies of the guinea zone at medium altitudes which provide examples of clumps of trees of typically montane species, including numerous ones belonging to the forests of low altitudes, especially semi-deciduous species (Letouzey 1968; Schnell 1977).

Towards the bottom of the Lake Bosumtwi core, dated to around 28,000–27,000 BP,

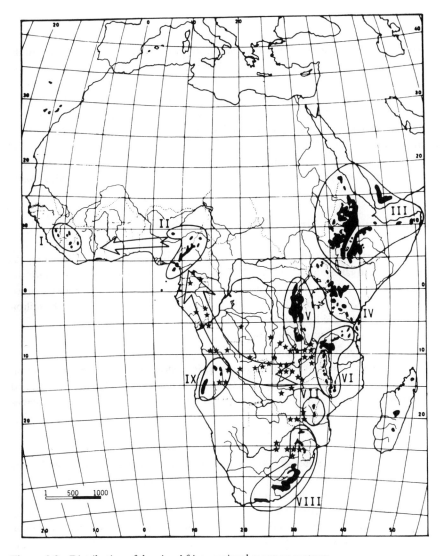

Figure 2.2 Distribution of the nine African regional montane systems.

I West African
II Cameroon-Jos
III Ethiopian
IV Imatongs-Kenya-Usumbara
V Ruwenzori-Kivu
VI Uluguru-Mlanje
VII Chimanimani
VIII Drakensberg
IX Angolan

The stars indicate populations of Afromontane plant species outside the large mountain systems, represented by black areas (adapted and completed from White 1981). The two arrows schematically represent a possible migration path of Afromontane taxa from east Africa to Angola, and subsequently via Cameroon to west Africa (Maley 1989).

the proportion of arboreal pollen reaches about 50 per cent, which is an indication of the presence of a montane forest environment. This tallies with similar data gathered in east Africa.

Pollen data recently obtained from a marine core off the coast of the Ivory Coast (Fredoux & Tastet 1988; Fredoux, Tastet, Maley & Guilmette 1989) show that *Podocarpus latifolius* was present on 'the Guinea Ridge' (in Ivory Coast and Republic of Guinea) during Isotope Stage 5 (in part Eemian) but disappeared towards the very end of the Pleistocene. Today this montane tree no longer exists anywhere further west than the Cameroon mountains, where its spread began in pliocene times (Maley 1980).

Comparison of the African forest zone with east Africa

East Africa, particularly the area between the two branches of the Rift Valley, is relatively rich in lakes and bogs, which have been cored for pollen analysis since the 1960s. Various syntheses have already been published for this region (Van Zinderen Bakker & Coetzee 1972; Hamilton 1973; Livingstone 1975; Flenley 1979; Hamilton 1982; Van Zinderen Bakker & Coetzee 1988).

It should be noted that, since the majority of sites are at altitudes above 1000 m, the results of the pollen analyses apply particularly to montane types of vegetation.

Three principal sites have yielded results from before 30,000 BP: Sacred Lake in Kenya (Coetzee 1967); the peat bog of Kamiranzovu in Rwanda (Hamilton 1982); and Kashiru in Burundi (Bonnefille & Riollet 1988). From these three sites the main stages in the history of the vegetation and the climate are as follows:

Stage 1
This stage began before 40,000 BP and lasted until 33,000–31,000 BP. It was characterized by a climate considerably colder and drier than at present. Sacred Lake, situated at a height of 2400 m and nowadays surrounded by montane forest, was then situated in the Ericaceous zone; as this is nowadays located at a height of 3400 m, this represents a lowering of 1000 m, from which one can infer a lowering of temperature of around 6°C (Van Zinderen Bakker & Coetzee 1988). In Burundi, the Kashiru bog, in which Ericaceae as well as the genus *Cliffortia* (Rosaceae) were dominant, must also have been surrounded by the Ericaceous zone (Bonnefille & Riollet 1988).

Stage 2
From 33,000–31,000 BP to about 28,000 BP there was a wetter fluctuation accompanied by a certain increase in warmth. Montane forest re-established itself around Sacred Lake (Van Zinderen Bakker & Coetzee 1988). At Kashiru in Burundi, Bonnefille and Riollet (1988) deduce a wet, cool climate for this period.

Stage 3
From about 28,000 BP to around 12,000–10,000 BP, the climate was in general considerably colder and drier than today. On the whole, the herbaceous plants, especially the Gramineae and the Cyperaceae, dominated the pollen spectra, corresponding above all to a major extension of the Afro-alpine savannas. The Ericaceous

zone again surrounded Sacred Lake. The coldest and driest period occurred between 21,000 BP and 17,000 BP at Sacred Lake, and between 21,000 and 14,500 BP at Kamiranzovu (Hamilton 1982). The temperature drop must therefore have been between 6 and 9°C. The beginning of the retreat of the Ruwenzori glaciers occurred around 14,750 BP (Livingstone 1967).

Stage 3b
Around 24,000–22,000 BP a brief wet episode has been recognized in various places in east Africa by Perrott & Street-Perrott (1982); it has also been detected at Kashiru (Bonnefille & Riollet 1988) and in other parts of tropical Africa (Maley 1981).

Stage 4
From 12,000–10,000 BP to 4000–3000 BP the climate became considerably wetter and progressively warmer; everywhere the forests began to expand. At Kashiru, Bonnefille & Riollet (1988) observe that before 6700 BP (Stage 4a) the climate was cooler than at present, to become warmer later (Stage 4b).

Stage 5
From 4000–3000 BP modern conditions became established, marked by a decline in rainfall and reduction of the rainforest. Associated with this decline, a marked increase in pollen of *Podocarpus* has been observed at the beginning of this stage, a phenomenon which has continued at certain sites (Mt Kenya) until today (Hamilton 1982; Perrott 1982).

One site north of Lake Victoria, at an altitude of about 1135 m, is worth special mention. In fact, to the north and west of the lake, there are still several extensive areas of evergreen and semi-deciduous forest today. These forests constitute advanced outposts of the wet rainforests of lowland Zaïre (White 1983). An 18 m core taken in Pilkington Bay, not far from the outlet of Jinja, was studied by Kendall (1969). By means of pollen analysis this author was able to reconstruct the forest history of the region:

- After the great dry stage (Stage 3), of which only the final stage is represented, forest recolonization began about 12,000 BP with a certain number of semi-deciduous species.
- Around 9500 BP the forest was completely re-established in the region.
- From 9500 BP to about 6500 BP the forest vegetation had a more evergreen character, indicating high rainfall well distributed throughout the year, with a dry season of no more than two months.
- From about 6500 BP to about 3000 BP the forest vegetation took on a more semi-deciduous character, shown in particular by a marked increase in the pollen of *Celtis* and *Holoptelea*. The dry season was therefore probably extended to three months; the climate was relatively warmer than today.
- From about 3000 BP to today, the forest declined as a result of the climate becoming drier. The widespread character of this decline across tropical Africa shows that, above all, we are dealing with a climatic phenomenon and that the human role in it was much less important than some authors have tried to suggest (for a discussion of this topic, see Hamilton, Taylor & Vogel 1986; Perrott 1987).

In conclusion, the principal climatic phases correlate well between the African forest zone and east Africa, especially after 20,000 BP. Before 30,000 BP the comparison seems more difficult, but the apparent lack of correspondence before this date could be the result of inherent errors in radiocarbon dating operating at the limit of its reliability.

Conclusions: comparisons between equatorial Africa and dry tropical Africa

In the course of the last twelve millennia, the main transgressive and regressive stages of the equatorial rainforest seem to correlate chronologically with lacustrine deposits and vegetation evidence in northern dry tropical Africa (Servant 1973; Maley 1981; Maley 1982; Maley 1983). With regard to the climatic mechanism involved, this correlation could indicate that the moisture-laden air of the monsoon, producing rain north of the forest right up to the central Sahara, derives not only directly from the Gulf of Guinea, but largely also from a recycling of the moisture already precipitated on the equatorial forest and then carried on by evapotranspiration. This repeated recycling of moisture-laden air has been demonstrated for the present period by several isotopic studies (Baudet & Laurenti 1976); from this follows the system elaborated by Monteny (1986; 1987) and well illustrated by the detailed study of an annual cycle by Cadet & Nnoli (1987). Because of this recycling every important change in the African forest block must have had an important effect on adjacent climatic zones.

Acknowledgements

P. Giresse and D. Schwartz are thanked for their advice in the writing of this chapter, and Thurstan Shaw for his kind encouragement. The work is a contribution to the programme GEOCIT and is adapted from Maley 1990.

3   The tropical African cereals

JACK R. HARLAN

In this chapter[1] the domestication, probable areas of origin and agronomic and cultural contexts of the African cereal crops are reviewed. There is as yet relatively little direct archaeological evidence on the antiquity of African cereals, and here only passing reference is made to such archaeological data as are available. Particular attention is paid to sorghum because of its importance in world, as well as in African agriculture, and brief comments are offered on a further seven cereals indigenous to Africa.

Sorghum

Sorghum (*Sorghum bicolor*) is one of the great cereals of the world. From studies at the Crop Evolution Laboratory in Illinois, one can say that its history in Africa is now rather clear, although the same cannot be said of its history in east Asia, which needs to be studied much more thoroughly. Extensive fieldwork over many years, combined with the growing of varieties under controlled conditions in nurseries, and thorough examination of herbarium collections, led to the classification of the varieties of sorghum into five major races and ten two-by-two combinations (Harlan & De Wet 1972; Harlan & Stemler 1976) which turned out to correlate remarkably well with the language map of Africa. (a) The most primitive race, the one that looks most like the wild progenitor, is called the *bicolor* race. It is found just about everywhere sorghum is grown, so it is not much help in identifying the area or areas of origin of domestic sorghum. It has a very loose, open panicle, very like wild sorghum. Its spikelets and grains are larger and do not shatter as well as the wild types, and there are fewer branches, so it is definitely a cultivated, domesticated race, although morphologically rather similar to wild sorghum. (b) The *guinea* race is primarily a west African race. It has special modifications for growing in high-rainfall conditions, i.e. rainfall that is high for sorghum, which is a dry-land crop: the grain at maturity twists 19°, opening up the glumes to permit rapid drying after rains, and the seed is very hard. It is a sorghum primarily of people of the Niger-Congo language family, but, because of its adaptation to high rainfall, a sprinkling of it is found in the highlands of east Africa and southward along the mountain ranges where rainfall is high. It reached India, where it is also found in areas of high rainfall, but basically it is a west African race. (c) The *caudatum* race belongs to the area of the Chari-Nile language group. It is quite distinctive: its grain is flat on one side and convex on the other. It is found primarily from Lake Chad to the Ethiopian border and filtering out from there. (d) The *kafir* race is a Bantu sorghum which belongs to southern Africa. (e) The fifth race is *durra* and it is also quite distinctive. It is a highly derived sorghum, with very dense compact heads and other morphological characteristics which make it easy to identify. In Africa it is grown mainly by Islamic peoples along the edge of the Sahara, and its main centre of cultivation is India.

This curious distribution of the races of sorghum suggests the following history. The first race to be domesticated was *bicolor*, the primitive one, and it was widespread, as it is today. From the *bicolor* race people in west Africa began to develop their own local adaptations of the *guinea* races, peoples in southern Africa developed the *kafirs* and people in the area from Chad to eastern Sudan and Uganda developed the *caudatums*. The *bicolor* race at some time reached India, where the *durras* were developed, and we think it came back to Africa, probably in Islamic times. This history of sorghum makes sense in terms of biology, ecology, history and human linguistic and cultural diversity.

Where did sorghum domestication start? To try to discover this the wild races, of which there are several, have been examined. One of them is the *arundinaceum* race, a west African race adapted to the tropical forest zone. Cultivated sorghum does not do very well in the forest zone; it is grown, but the rainfall is too high and for that reason any great contribution to domesticated sorghum from the *arundinaceum* race can be discounted. The *virgatum* race is a very small sorghum, which is basically a grass of the Nile floodplain which grows along the river and beside irrigation ditches. The race known as *aethiopicum* is of uncertain status. It has never been seen growing in what appear to be natural stands. It just occurs here and there, and I suspect that it is really a secondary derivative of cultivated sorghum by hybridization with wild forms. This leaves the *verticilliflorum* race as the primary candidate for the role of progenitor of the domesticated sorghums. It is extremely abundant in the eastern half of Africa, from Sudan right down to southern Africa, but not in western Africa. In the area of greatest abundance, in Sudan for instance, or parts of Chad, you can drive for a hundred kilometres through tall-grass savanna, a marvellous formation extending as far as you can see, with spiny acacia dotted through it here and there, unploughed, uncultivated, not even grazed very much. This is clearly a primary habitat, and there is a lot of it left. The chief dominant of this grassland is the *verticilliflorum* race of sorghum, present in enormous quantities. It is a very productive plant which can grow 4 m high, with many panicles and lots of seed; if you want to get the seed you have to harvest it over a week or so, but it has enormous productivity in its native state.

Our hybridization studies have shown the *verticilliflorum* race to be fully fertile with cultivated sorghums. They both have ten chromosomes, the chromosomes pair in the hybrids, and the hybrids are fertile. There may be some secondary introgression, particularly in west Africa, and the *arundinaceum* race may have introgressed into cultivated sorghums to help provide adaptation to high rainfall. On grounds of distribution, ecology and morphology, therefore, I think that the primary location of domestication was in the northeastern quadrant of Africa, probably the Sudan-Chad area, where the *bicolor* race was developed and from where it spread through Africa and on to India.

The next question is when this occurred, what time range is involved. But here one comes up against the deficiencies of the archaeological record. The earliest dates for domesticated sorghum are from India (see Kajale 1988), which in effect puts a minimum age on its domestication. It seems to have reached India by around 2000 BC, so it has to be older than that in Africa (Rowley-Conwy 1991). There are, as yet unconfirmed, reports of sorghum from the Khartoum area dated to the sixth millennium BC, and in southern Africa dates in the third millennium BC were initially claimed for sorghum from the cave site of Shongweni in Natal. However, they were obtained from charcoal in the same layer as the sorghum grains, which were later radiocarbon dated independently and proved to be much more recent.

There is no cogency in the argument that the domestication of sorghum in Africa was late because of the absence of stone tools for harvesting it. There is nothing inefficient about using a beating basket (Harlan 1989). The glossed-edge trapezoids from the Nigerian site of Iwo Eleru, probably hafted in a sickle-like implement and making their appearance about 1500 BC, are not suitable for cutting sorghum stalks; they are much more likely to have been used for cutting grasses or reeds for basket-making. Indeed, there is doubt whether one will ever be able to detect the domestication of sorghum from a change in the tool-kit; the tools that one would use for wild sorghum would be essentially the same as those used for sorghum. There are also uncertainties about when and how sorghum reached India. There are reports of pottery impressions of sorghum grains from Arabia dating to about 2500 BC, and there is now evidence in the form of potsherds with Harappan script on them, found on the Arabian coast, for direct connections with Harappan civilization, indicating some sort of intercourse between Arabia and the northwestern coast of the Indian subcontinent by 2000 BC. The whole system of circum-Arabian Sea contact apparently developed quite early and facilitated the movement of material in both directions. However, there is doubt whether sorghum reached India directly across the Arabian Sea; one might think that transmission by coastal shipping was more likely at that time. Finds of sorghum recently reported from highland Yemen and dated to about 2000 BC tend to reinforce that supposition. If there were some dated sorghum from Pakistan it might turn out to be older there than in India. One should not visualize just a single introduction to India; rather that there were contacts over a long period of time through coastal trade. By Roman times, or a little earlier, direct maritime trade was conducted between east Africa and southern India; so a model based on an ebb and flow of material between the two continents could be appropriate. The fact that *bicolor* was the first sorghum to reach India does not help very much with dating the time at which the other sorghums were selected and developed. If the Indian archaeological materials were good enough to identify as to race, it could be very helpful, but, as far as is known, the early sorghums found in India are all *bicolors*.

Despite its primitive characteristics, the *bicolor* race of sorghum has persisted together with all the specialized varieties because it is used for special purposes. The sweet sorghums are of that race and the broomcorns also. People like sweet sorghum, and in a typical village in the sorghum belt of Africa there will be several local varieties grown, and also a few small patches of *bicolor* because the people like to chew it like sugar-cane. Sorghums are high in tannin, some much more so than others. There is selection both for and against tannin content. People tend to prefer high-tannin varieties for beer making, and then there is no need to use hops or some other substitute for hops, so beer sorghums tend to have a high tannin content. Also, some sorghums with a high tannin content are selected because they deter birds from feeding on the grain. I have not studied the distribution of the dye sorghums in detail, but I believe that the dyes which were used in, say, making 'Moroccan' leather came from the central part of the sub-Saharan zone – northern Nigeria and Niger – and that they were selected for an abundance of red pigment; I think these are mostly *bicolors*.

The selection pressures on sorghum in Africa are tremendous. At harvest time the first thing the cultivator does is to go through the field and harvest heads for next year's seed stock. He may have a mixed field of various kinds of sorghum and he will only select what is to be planted next year. So the selection pressure is very strong for what the cultivator wants, and his wants may be very varied and to us unexpected, for example the ease of pounding grain in the morning. In parts of Mali where they grow both the soft-seeded and the very hard-seeded sorghums, women do not like to pound the hard-seeded variety because it is hard work; but they still grow it because it has high insect-resistance in storage. It is therefore saved for the latter part of the season and they eat up the soft sorghums first.

Among the distinctively African techniques of cultivating sorghum two particularly deserve mention: *decrue* and transplanting. *Decrue* is practised primarily along the Niger and Senegal floodplains (Harlan & Pasquereau 1969). When the floodwaters recede in the early dry season, seeds are planted in the mud and the crop is grown on stored moisture, without rain or irrigation. *Decrue* is a complex system of cultivation. Along the great bend of the Niger – the so-called 'inland delta' – the water spreads very slowly and recedes very slowly. Therefore, the closer you are to the river the deeper is the water, the farther from the river the shallower the water; a situation that requires different cultivars for each location. Cultivars are selected for short flooding and long flooding, and there are even very special *decrue* varieties grown down near the river which are harvested by canoe – and sorghum is a dry-land plant!

Transplanting after the rains is another distinctive technique used where the moisture supply is marginal. It is a sort of modified *decrue* in that there are vast areas in the savanna which stand in water during the rains – too much water to grow a crop. After the land dries up the people burn off the grass and sow the crop on residual moisture, but they have to do it quickly. Therefore, they have already started seedlings in a seed bed which are then transplanted, as rice is transplanted in Asia. They uproot the seedlings and plant them in a deep hole dug with a special digging stick, add a little water, and the crop then grows entirely on the moisture remaining in the soil from the wet season.

These two distinctively African techniques of cultivation are applied not only to sorghum but also to pearl millet, and varieties are selected for these special purposes. The same cultivator may have *decrue* varieties and non-*decrue* varieties depending on his land resources. He will adapt his planting from year to year, to adjust to high and low floods, by switching between sorghum varieties and even from sorghum to pearl millet. The cultivators select very intensively for what they want, and they get it. Selection for the non-shattering inflorescence of domesticated sorghum was almost certainly a conscious process, because sorghum is handled plant by plant, and the cultivator knows every plant in his field. In Ethiopia, for example, a crook-neck variety has been selected because it is easier to hang from the roof over the kitchen fire, which keeps the insects out and makes good conditions for the storage of seed stock.

The introduction of maize has in some places caused the cultivation of sorghum to decline or disappear. In most of west Africa, maize has not really become a field crop; it is a garden crop, grown in small patches, although recently it has been more widely cultivated where soils are poor and exhausted, as on the Jos plateau. In parts of east Africa, on the other hand, and in southern Africa, it has become the staple cereal. It fits a niche in which it will grow better with a little more rainfall than sorghum, and it is a niche that was not very well filled before maize became available.

Pearl millet

From the world point of view the next most important African cereal is pearl millet (*Pennisetum glaucum*). The history of pearl millet is different from that of sorghum. The wild forms occur deep in the Sahara and do not extend very far out from the desert into the Sahel. It is the most drought-resistant of all the hot-season millets/cereals. It was probably domesticated in the Sahara, and later moved into the Sahel where it is most common now. It is grown well beyond the Sahel in sub-Saharan Africa because people like it; they generally prefer it to sorghum. It is a very palatable cereal with one of the best nutritional profiles. It has been enormously modified from the wild form. Wild pearl millet has a head no more than 10 cm long, whereas cultivated races have inflorescences up to 2 m long. The changes in the morphology of the inflorescence, and in the size and colours of the grain are astonishing. The colours of the cultivated grain range from brick-red to grey to black, the commonest being grey, which is why it is called pearl millet. These changes are of the same order of magnitude as, or perhaps even greater than, the huge changes that distinguish domesticated maize from the (postulated) form of ancestral wild maize.

The distribution of the cultivated, wild and hybrid forms of pearl millet is somewhat puzzling. In Senegal, large hybrid swarms occur between the wild and the cultivated, and between the cultivated and the weed forms, called *shibra* in that area; very complex populations with all kinds of wild, weedy and cultivated forms all mixed up in the same area. Then there is a geographical gap, eastward as far as J. Marra in Sudan. Perhaps the gap is there because it has not been looked for hard enough. But in the J. Marra area large swarms of wild/weed/cultivated mix-ups again occur. The weed form apparently did not get to India, but domesticated pearl millet did. It is a very important crop in the dry zones of India, where it is the most drought-resistant of the cereals, and it is grown particularly in Rajastan and around the margins of the Thar desert. It probably reached India a little later than sorghum. It is also grown in southern Africa around the margins of the Kalahari desert.

Finger millet

Wild forms of finger millet (*Eleusine coracana*) occur in the highlands of eastern Africa, in Uganda, Ethiopia and Kenya. Again, there are wild, weedy and cultivated forms, including some primitive cultivated races. Finger millet was introduced to India, where it evolved typically Indian races, both in the hill country in the north and in the southern hills. Today, it is used primarily for beer in Africa. At one time it must have been an important food crop, but was subsequently largely replaced by other cereals. The grain is not palatable, but it makes good beer. Finger millet probably reached India around the same time as sorghum and pearl millet. There are no known possible wild ancestors of finger millet, or of pearl millet, in southern Arabia.

African rice

To the rice-eating peoples of west Africa, African rice (*Oryza glaberrima*) is enormously important, although declining in recent times and being replaced by Asian rice (Chang 1989). The progenitor of African rice is quite clear: it is an annual grass of the savanna zone, adapted to water-holes that fill up during the rains and dry out in the dry season. There is a perennial rice related to the wild annual, but it requires more moisture, is a shy seeder, and morphologically would not be a presumed progenitor of African rice. Again, there are the wild, weedy and cultivated forms; in fact the cultivated form can be weedy. One of the more serious problems in growing Asian rice is weedy African rice in the fields.

A distinctive west African culture has developed based on rice: to rice-eating people no meal is a meal without rice. A whole oral literature, and many religious and cultural practices, have grown up based on rice cultivation. There are also specialized indigenous tools for levelling land, digging ditches, conducting water and so on. It is a complete and elaborate rice-cultivation complex, ranging from very simple techniques, such as just throwing the seed into a pond during the rains and then harvesting the crop later, to terrace cultivation with transplanting.

Teff

Teff (*Eragrostis tef*) is seeded on more hectares than any other crop in Ethiopia, although total production is less than that of barley. Teff has an exceedingly small seed, the smallest of all cereals. It is a good yielder, and makes an excellent, nutritious bread, the preferred bread in Ethiopia. In the case of teff, there are no hybrid swarms in the area of native production, probably because of cleistogamy in both wild and cultivated races. The presumptive wild progenitor is *Eragrostis pilosa*, which belongs to the *kreb* complex of harvested wild grasses (Harlan 1989). Presumably it somehow sorted out of the *kreb* complex and was taken to Ethiopia, where the domesticated form was really created.

Digitaria spp.

There are two species of digitaria: *Digitaria exilis* and *D. iburua*. *D. exilis*, or *fonio*, is also sometimes called 'hungry rice', which is a misnomer. There have been two other species of *Digitaria* domesticated, one in India and one in Europe. In fact, *D. sanguinalis* was harvested in Europe until recently. The important characteristic of *fonio* is its quality: it is highly palatable, grown for feast days and the like, even as chief's food. It does not yield very well, but it persists in cultivation. It makes the best couscous, better than wheat. The other digitaria in Africa, *D. iburua*, is grown in very restricted locations. It does not have the quality of *D. exilis* and remains restricted to very small regions in west Africa.

Brachiaria deflexa

As a cultigen, *Brachiaria deflexa* is grown only in Fouta Djallon, in Guinea. It is the most restricted of all cultivated cereals in the world. It has quite large-seeded cultivars and rather well-developed domesticated forms, and although the wild form is quite wide-spread, the domesticated race occurs only in Fouta Djallon.

Abyssinian oat

The Abyssinian oat (*Avena abyssinica*) is a tetraploid, whereas the more widely culti-vated green oat is a hexaploid. The tetraploid developed from a weed, which probably travelled with wheat, barley, lentils and chickpeas when they were introduced to the highlands of Ethiopia. However, it is not known to be deliberately grown in a field. It is a weed in emmer wheat and barley fields, and the cultivators do not try to weed it out of the field, nor do they try to separate it on the threshing floor. They just plant the seed mixture, and so there are non-shattering types, semi-shattering types and shattering types. It makes a good weed and the cultivators do not object to it. Some say that the malt is a little better if you have some oats in it; it makes a better beer. If this is a domesticate, it is a domestication by default rather than by design. Another cereal that has a somewhat similar status to Abyssinian oat is *Paspalum scrobiculatum*, a weed of rice fields in west Africa. This, however, is a real weed, not a positively tolerated one like the Abyssinian oat. It causes digestive problems, and there are some toxins that can come in with fungus infection. But, if the rice crop does badly, the weed may do well and the people may then get a bigger total harvest.

Conclusion

In this brief outline, I have tried to summarize what is currently known from a botanical and agronomic point of view about the origins and early history of Africa's cereal crops. It demonstrates very clearly the dearth of archaeobotanical evidence from the continent. Indeed, it is unfortunately true that little has been added to our knowl-edge of the prehistory of even the most important cereals – sorghum and pearl millet – since the publications of over a decade ago of Harlan, De Wet & Stemler (1976) and Clark & Brandt (1984). Until greater efforts are made at archaeological sites in tropical

Africa to recover direct evidence in the form of charred and other remains of the cereals themselves, we shall not advance our understanding of the 'when' and 'where' of their original cultivation and domestication. The task is formidable, but the archaeobotanical techniques are now available with which to tackle it.

Note

[1] See Harris & Hillman (1989, p. 335n) for the previous history of this newly revised chapter.

4   *The spread of domestic animals in Africa*

JULIET CLUTTON-BROCK

Introduction

In every part of the world where human beings have settled there has been a slow and insidious replacement of the wild flora and fauna by domestic plants and animals, which were either domesticated locally or imported. Africa has been a centre for the local domestication of endemic food plants that have become of world-wide importance, sorghum and the millets being perhaps the most notable of eight species of African cereals (Shaw 1977; Harlan 1989; Harlan, Ch. 3, this volume). In contrast, only one domestic animal, the guinea-fowl, had a wild progenitor that occurred only in Africa; and there is slender evidence for the local domestication in prehistoric times of only three mammals: the ass, the cat and north African cattle. Many other species of African ungulates have been systematically exploited over thousands of years, for example the elephant in ancient north Africa and several species of antelope and gazelle; but these animals have never undergone the process of domestication whereby they have been bred in captivity and become the personal property of humans. Mention should be made, however, of the special relationship that held in southern Africa between the San and the eland (*Tragelaphus oryx*) which Vinnicombe (1976, p. 177) has described as 'at the very heart of Bushman social structure'. Eland were never domesticated although the San did regard the wild herds of this antelope as personal and valued possessions.

Until modern times the diffusion of domestic livestock through Africa was very slow, presumably because of the vast size of the continent and the enormous diversity of its wildlife, which provided an ever-abundant supply of meat. Perhaps for this reason there has been little research on the history of domestic animals in Africa: until recently the only major work on the subject was Epstein (1971). Within the last decade, however, there has been a number of publications on pastoralism and the development in Africa of prehistoric food-producing economies, for example Clark & Brandt (1984), Krzyzaniak & Kobusiewicz (1984) and Hall & Smith (1986). With the increasing number of analyses of animal remains from archaeological sites all over the continent, the history of food production in Africa is now a burgeoning field of research (see e.g. Krzyzaniak 1991; and the following chapters in this volume: Andah, Ch. 12; Anquandah, Ch. 13; Horton & Mudida, Ch. 41; Juwayeyi, Ch. 22; Kiyaga-Mulindwa, Ch. 21; Muzzolini, Ch. 11; Robertshaw, Ch. 19; Sinclair, Morais, Adamowicz & Duarte, Ch. 24; Stahl, Ch. 14; Wetterstrom, Ch. 10; Wright, Ch. 40).

In this chapter, brief descriptions are given of the history of those domestic animals that have been of importance on the African continent. All of them were known to the ancient Egyptians, who apparently also kept in captivity many species of wild animals such as cranes, antelopes, monkeys and hyaena. These are not included in the descriptions given here but they have been described in many publications including Zeuner (1963), Epstein (1971), Houlihan (1986), Boessneck (1988) and Clutton-Brock (1989b).

Guinea-fowl: *Numida meleagris* and *Numida ptilorhynca*

The guinea-fowl is the only domestic animal that certainly originated in Africa. In modern times, two of the four wild species of *Numida* are bred as domestic fowl. These are the helmeted guinea-fowl (*N. meleagris*), which is found wild today in western Africa, and *N. ptilorhynca*, which is endemic to eastern Africa. It was the helmeted guinea-fowl that was first domesticated; it was known as a wild bird to the ancient Egyptians and spread from Egypt to Greece in classical times (Shaw 1977; Houlihan 1986).

There appear to be no references in Europe to the guinea-fowl in the Middle Ages until the Portuguese travellers to the African coast gave the bird its present name in the sixteenth century (Zeuner 1963).

On the few archaeological sites in Africa where guinea-fowl has been recorded, for example J. Shaqadud in Sudan (Peters 1985–6), there is no indication that the birds were reared in captivity.

Domestic fowl: *Gallus gallus*

Chickens were domesticated at some time before the sixth millennium BC in India and Southeast Asia from the red jungle fowl, *Gallus gallus*. Houlihan (1986) states that the chicken arrived late in ancient Egypt, its earliest representation being the sketch of a cockerel on a stone flake from the tomb of Ramesses IX (1156–48 BC). Chickens were not common in Egypt until the Ptolemaic period (332–30 BC).

In western Africa, chicken has been recently identified from the iron age site of Jenne-jeno in Mali, dated to *c.* AD 500–800, by MacDonald (1989; 1992).

In eastern Africa domestic fowl has been recorded from two iron age sites in Mozambique, Manekeni (Barker 1978) and Chibuene (Sinclair 1982).

In southern Africa, the remains of chickens have been recorded from the eighth-century iron age site of Ndondondwane in Natal (Voigt & Driesch 1984; Plug & Voigt 1985).

Ducks and geese

Many species of ducks and geese are represented in the art and hieroglyphs of ancient Egypt. These birds, along with other waterfowl and quails, were an important source of meat and sacrificial offerings, but only two were kept in captivity. These were the grey-lag goose (*Anser anser*), which is the common domestic goose of the present day, and the white-fronted goose (*Anser albifrons*). There are no records of domestic ducks or geese from prehistoric sites in Africa south of the Sahara.

Rodents

The three most common rodent pests world-wide are the black rat (*Rattus rattus*), the Norway rat (*Rattus norvegicus*) and the house mouse (*Mus domesticus*). Strains of the Norway rat and the house mouse are today bred as laboratory animals and pets but historically their association with humans has been only as unwanted commensals which have travelled everywhere with their hosts. Apart from the presumed association of the black rat with early epidemics of plague in ancient Egypt, little is known of the history or distribution of these rodents in Africa. Remains of the black rat (*Rattus rattus*) have been recorded from iron age sites in Zambia and from the twelfth-century AD site of Pont Drift in the northern Transvaal (Voigt & Plug 1981). Black rat has also been identified from the eighth-century AD site of Ndondondwane in Natal by Voigt & Driesch (1984).

The grasscutter or cane rat (*Thryonomys swinderianus*) is found in many forest and savanna areas south of the Sahara. It is a very large rodent that is a valuable source of meat. Within recent years both the grasscutter and the African giant rat (*Cricetomys gambianus*) have been domesticated in western Africa (Tewe, Ajayi & Faturoti 1984). Remains of grasscutter, identified by Bate (1947) from the Early Khartoum site in Sudan as a new species, *Thryonomys arkelli*, are now referred to *T. swinderianus* by Peters (1985–6).

The cat: *Felis catus*

Perhaps the cat was first domesticated by the ancient Egyptians but there is no direct evidence for this. Cats are represented in Egyptian art from the Middle Kingdom (from 1991 BC) but by this time there are records of domestic cat remains from a scattering of archaeological sites in western Asia and Europe. The wild progenitor of the domestic cat was most probably *Felis silvestris libyca*, which is the southern form of the wide-spread species *Felis silvestris*. *F. s. libyca* is the common wild cat of Africa and it is found over most of the continent from the Mediterranean to the Cape, except in the tropical rainforest belt.

There is no information on the history of the domestic cat in Africa, outside Egypt. Unless there was some cultural evidence to suggest domestication it would not be possible to distinguish the remains of domestic from wild cats in an archaeological context. At present in Africa, the wild cat will interbreed with feral and house cats, which makes difficult the separation of even the living cats into wild and domestic forms (Rosevear 1974, p. 385).

The dog: *Canis familiaris*

Finds of canid remains that can be assumed to be at least tamed wolves, if not fully domestic dogs, indicate that domestication probably occurred first in western Asia, around 12,000 years ago and that the progenitor of the dog was the small indigenous wolf, *Canis lupus arabs* or *C. l. pallipes*.

Today, the dog is ubiquitous throughout Africa but, as with all other domestic animals, it was a late-comer south of the Sahara. In Africa, the differentiation of fragmentary bones and teeth found on archaeological sites as dog or wild canid is more difficult than in other parts of the world because of the presence everywhere of species of jackal whose size overlaps that of the dog. In reports on faunal remains it is therefore usual to record merely the presence of *Canis* sp. On the other hand, it is clear that there were dogs in north Africa from at least 4000 BC and innumerable depictions from ancient Egypt show that there were separate 'breeds' from predynastic times. The most common 'breed' appears to have been of greyhound build and probably differed little from the village dogs of Egypt today. How far dogs moved south in the prehistoric period is difficult to ascertain as there are very few records from early prehistoric sites. One find has been reported by Chaix (1980) from the ancient city of Kerma in northern Sudan, dated to the second millennium BC. Domestic dog has also been identified by Peters (1985–6) in his reassessment of the fauna from Esh Shaheinab (*c.* 3300 BC) and from the predynastic site of Toukh in Upper Egypt.

No certain identifications of dog remains, south of the equator, are known until the first millennium AD. From Fagan's iron age excavations at Isamu Pati Mound, Kalomo in Zambia, Degerbol (1967) identified the remains of seven domestic dogs which are dated to AD *c.* 950–1000. More recently, dog has been recorded from a number of iron age sites in South Africa, dated to the late first millennium AD, for example Mapungwe and Schroda (Voigt 1981) and Ndondondwane (Voigt & Driesch 1984). There is as yet no evidence for dog south of the Limpopo before the sixth century AD (Plug & Voigt 1985).

As in other parts of the world, the dog in Africa fills many roles. It is a scavenger that helps to keep villages clean; it can be a companion, bedwarmer, hunter and retriever. Dogs are also eaten for food and in ritual ceremonies; their skins are used, their teeth are made into necklaces and their bones are employed in medicine and witchcraft.

European dogs were probably introduced to the continent from the time of the earliest travels in the Middle Ages, but in southern Africa they were adopted by the San only in relatively recent times. There are nineteenth-century archival reports of dogs being exchanged by the San for stolen cattle (Vinnicombe 1976, p. 57). In her study of 'Bushmen' paintings from southern Natal Vinnicombe (1976, p. 157) reported that dogs made up 5 per cent of the domestic animals represented.

Lee (1979, pp. 142–4) has described the use of dogs for tracking and hunting by the !Kung San in the Dobe area of the Kalahari at the present day. He quotes one man as saying, 'If you don't have dogs you don't even bother to hunt warthog' (p. 144).

Pig: *Sus domesticus*

Wild boar (*Sus scrofa*) were present along the Mediterranean borders of north Africa and in the Nile valley where they were hunted, and domestic pig has been reported from neolithic Morocco by Gilman (1976). Pigs were kept in early dynastic Egypt but they were never abundant and it is possible that the taboos against eating pork first arose in Egypt. South of Ethiopia there have been European introductions of pigs, and the pig is of economic importance in west Africa today.

Donkey: *Equus asinus*

Like the cat, the donkey is traditionally assumed to have been first domesticated by the ancient Egyptians. However, the osteological evidence shows that there were donkeys in use not only in Egypt but also in western Asia by 2500 BC. In Egypt the earliest evidence for donkey comes from a skull that was buried in the tomb of Tarkhan (Petrie 1914, p. 6); recently a radiocarbon accelerator date has been obtained from this skull of 4390 ± 130 bp [OxA-566].

From northern Sudan, Peters (1985–6) has identified a tarsal bone of domestic donkey from the neolithic site of J. Shaqadud.

The progenitor of the domestic donkey is the African wild ass, *Equus africanus*, which is still found wild today as an endangered species in Somalia. In the prehistoric period the wild ass was widespread over the Sahara region and it probably also inhabited Arabia. South of the equator the domestic donkey has been of considerable importance as a beast of burden but its remains are only rarely found in archaeological sites.

The horse: *Equus caballus*

The Hyksos are held responsible for bringing the first horses into ancient Egypt and the earliest recorded remains are from the palace of Buhen, where the skeleton of a horse has been dated to *c.* 1675 BC (Clutton-Brock 1974). From this time onwards the horse was an animal associated with high status and the ceremonial chariot, so frequently shown in ancient Egyptian art.

How far the horse and donkey penetrated other parts of Africa before the arrival of Europeans would be hard to assess because of the difficulty of distinguishing fragments of their osteological remains from those of zebra (but see Blench, Ch. 5, this volume).

Camel: *Camelus dromedarius*

The dromedary, or one-humped camel, is perfectly adapted to life in hot arid deserts, where it will migrate over huge areas, browsing on the sparsest vegetation and surviving without water for longer than any other mammal. There are no wild dromedaries in existence and it is not known when they became extinct. Neither is it known where or when the one-humped camel was first domesticated. The earliest holocene record of the dromedary is from the neolithic site of Sihi on the Red Sea coast of Arabia, where a radiocarbon accelerator date has been obtained of 8200 ± 200 bp [OxA-983] (Grigson, Gowlett & Zarins 1989). If camels were first domesticated in this region they could have entered Africa either through Egypt or through the 'Horn' where there is the highest density of camels today (Bulliet 1975; Gauthier-Pilters & Dagg 1981; Köhler-Rollefson 1988).

In Egypt, a two-strand twist of cord, identified as camel hair, was discovered by Caton-Thompson in her 1927–8 season of excavation in the Fayum. This camel-hair cord, which was more than 3 feet in length (92 cm), was dated to 'the Third or at latest possibly the early Fourth Dynasty' (c. 2613 BC) (Caton-Thompson 1934, p. 21). Much more recently a date of 2690 ± 90 bp [OxA-1061] has been obtained by radiocarbon (Accelerator Mass Spectrometry) on camel dung from Napatan levels at Qasr Ibrim (Rowley-Conwy 1988).

The camel herders of the Sahara exemplify a particular, developed, nomadic way of life which enables people to survive in one of the most inhospitable regions of the world. By following their herds of camels and using water from ancient wells, the desert nomads have exploited a huge region that cannot be used for traditional agriculture. Ecological equilibrium can be maintained as long as there is no reduction in mobility, but any settlement destroys the fragile vegetation and leads to starvation of people and animals (Gauthier-Pilters & Dagg 1981). To the nomad, enforced settlement and losing his herd of camels means losing everything.

Domestic cattle: *Bos taurus* and *Bos indicus*

The history of cattle in Africa is better known than that of any other domestic species; it is also very complicated (and see Blench, Ch. 5, this volume) because for at least three thousand years the continent has been a melting-pot for unhumped cattle (*Bos taurus*) brought in from Eurasia and humped cattle (*Bos indicus*) brought in from Asia, in particular from India. In addition, it is possible that cattle were locally domesticated in north Africa from the endemic wild aurochs (*Bos primigenius*).

At present, the earliest securely dated finds of cattle in a cultural context come from Capéletti in Algeria and date from the seventh to the sixth millennium BC (Roubet 1978). Other early finds have been recorded from sites in the Sahara and in west Africa (see Smith 1980a; Smith 1986; Clutton-Brock 1989b). Whether these cattle originated from western Asia, through Egypt or were domesticated in Africa, cannot be determined, but the earliest records are still at least a thousand years later than the first remains of domestic cattle in western Asia. Gautier (1984) has postulated that the remains of cattle from early neolithic sites, dated to 9000 BP, in the Bir Kiseiba region of the eastern Sahara could be from domesticated animals derived from wild *Bos primigenius* in the Nile valley. However, the bovid remains are very fragmentary and their status is questionable, as recognized by Gautier (see also Smith 1986; Clutton-Brock 1989b; Wetterstrom, Ch. 10, this volume).

By 6000 BP it is probable that cattle pastoralism was well established throughout north Africa and that with the increasing desertification of the Sahara people began to move south with their cattle, only to meet the tsetse-fly belt (Shaw 1977). The archaeological evidence for the presence of cattle in west Africa for a very long time and their continuity to the present day is provided by the small humpless N'Dama breed, which has evolved a natural immunity to trypanosomiasis, the disease carried by tsetse-fly (Epstein & Mason 1984, p. 21).

In east Africa pastoralism became established late in the third millennium BC and over the next 1000 years domestic livestock slowly moved south towards Tanzania (Robertshaw 1989; Robertshaw, Ch. 19, this volume).

These cattle were probably humpless, for the earliest evidence for humped cattle comes from ancient Egyptian paintings dated to around 1500 BC. Epstein (1971) and Epstein & Mason (1984) separate the humped cattle of Africa into two kinds, the earlier cervico-thoracic humped and the later thoracic humped or true zebu. These authors believe that cattle with cervico-thoracic humps (i.e. with humps on their necks) were first introduced by sea into the Horn of Africa. They spread west and by interbreeding with the long-horned cattle of west Africa, developed into the Fulani breed. In eastern and southern Africa humped cattle (at first neck humped but later replaced by thoracic humped) were crossbred with the local humpless cattle to produce the mixed breeds called 'Sanga'. Notable amongst these are the Ankole cattle of Uganda and the Afrikander cattle of South Africa.

Humped cattle can be distinguished in the archaeological record by the shape of the skull or by the posterior thoracic vertebrae which, in the zebu, have bifurcated neural spines.

In the early Iron Age, during the first millennium AD, cattle spread south, together with sheep, and their remains are found on nearly all archaeological sites of this period. Klein (1986, p. 9) supports the view that sheep may have moved south along the west coast of southern Africa, arriving in the western Cape around 2000 years ago, while cattle were introduced along the east coast by iron age farmers who moved into the eastern Cape several hundred years later. The sites in South Africa from where cattle, sheep and goat remains have been retrieved are cited in Klein (1986) and Voigt (1986).

The animal remains from iron age sites in southern Africa show that the meat obtained from livestock was combined with that from hunted animals. This is to be expected in an environment where long periods of drought may decimate herds of cattle that are also subject to lethal diseases, parasite infestations and stock-raiders.

Throughout Africa, cattle have played a crucial role in the social, economic and religious lives of the Bantu-speaking peoples for thousands of years. They have not only provided meat, hides and manure, but have also been used as draught oxen and for providing blood and milk, although, as Voigt (1986) has pointed out, the existence of lactose intolerance amongst west African and some Bantu-speaking peoples argues against a widespread, ancient tradition of milk-drinking.

Domestic water buffalo: *Bubalus bubalis*

At the present day there are domestic water buffaloes throughout the Nile valley. These are all descended from the wild Indian water buffalo, *Bubalus arnee*. The buffalo was not known to the ancient Egyptians and Epstein (1971) suggests that it may have been introduced by Arabs from Syria some time before the tenth century AD. Remains of water buffalo have not been identified from archaeological sites in Africa outside Egypt.

Goat: *Capra hircus*

Domestic goats are all descended from the scimitar-horned goat of western Asia, *Capra aegagrus*. As this wild goat has never inhabited any part of Africa, all domestic goats, throughout the continent, can be claimed with certainty to have been introduced from abroad. The only species of goat or sheep to be endemic in Africa is the Walia ibex, *Capra ibex walie*, which survives today as an endangered species in the mountains of Ethiopia. The ibex has never been domesticated.

The goat was an important livestock animal in ancient Egypt. Zeuner (1963) has described it, from artistic representations, as high-legged and short-haired, and with a long face. He claimed that in the Old Kingdom most goats had straight horns and drooping ears but that later erect ears predominated, and by the Hyksos period the horns were twisted.

Epstein (1971) divided the goats of Africa into four broad categories: dwarf goats of the equatorial belt, savanna goats, Nubian goats and Maltese goats of the Atlas countries. There is little or no evidence from the archaeological record for the early history of these races. Roubet (1978) has recorded an early date of about 6500 BP for goat from the Neolithic Capsian of eastern Algeria. Bate (1953) claimed that the remains of goat from the neolithic site of Esh Shaheinab in Sudan were dwarfed but in his review of the material Peters (1985–6) wrote that there is no evidence for anything but average-sized goat. On the other hand, Carter & Flight (1972) have recorded the presence of dwarf goat at the second-millennium BC sites of Ntereso and Kintampo in Ghana.

South of the equator it seems that the goat was a much less important livestock animal than the sheep and there are very few records of its remains. There appear to be no depictions of goats in 'Bushmen' rock paintings, but Burchell (1822, II, p. 170) wrote the following comment about Khoikhoi living near Klaarwater (now Griquatown in the northeast of the Cape Province): 'The Hottentots who were lying here at this time with their families and cattle, possessed a great number of goats; but I saw among them no sheep.' In general, however, Burchell observed on his travels in South Africa that sheep were much preferred to goats, both by the local people and by the Europeans, because of the fat that could be obtained from the sheep's tails.

Voigt (1986) has identified goat remains with sheep from the fourth-century AD iron age site of The Happy Rest in the Transvaal, while at the eighth-century AD site of Ndondondwane in Natal, 47 elements were identified as goat and 459 as sheep (Voigt &

Driesch 1984). It seems that after their initial introduction into South Africa goats declined in numbers and only sheep and cattle remained as common livestock animals.

Sheep: *Ovis aries*

All the domestic sheep of Africa are descended from introduced stock. Like the goat, the domestic sheep is descended from an Asian progenitor, the Asiatic mouflon, *Ovis orientalis*. There are no species of wild sheep endemic to the African continent; its closest relative in the caprine family is the wild Barbary 'sheep', or aoudad, *Ammotragus lervia*, which inhabits the mountains of north Africa.

The earliest evidence for domestic caprines (sheep/goat) in Africa comes from the fifth-millennium site of Haua Fteah in the north of Cyrenaica, Libya (Higgs 1967; Shaw 1977; Klein & Scott 1986). Although Ryder (1983) has summarized the evidence for the different kinds of sheep in ancient Egypt, their history, as deduced from pictorial representations by writers during this century, including Zeuner (1963), is still rather confusing. It is evident, however, that well-defined breeds of domestic sheep were common in ancient Egypt from 3000 BC. During the Early Dynastic period (3100–2613 BC), screw-horned sheep with lop ears were developed, and fat-tailed sheep began to appear during the Middle Kingdom (1991–1633 BC), according to Zeuner (1963) and Ryder (1983).

From early sites in Sudan, Peters (1985–6) failed to find the specimen identified as '?sheep' by Bate (1953) from Esh Shaheinab, but confirmed the identification of sheep remains from a predynastic site named Toukh, in Upper Egypt, which was excavated by de Morgan at the end of the last century (de Morgan 1897). Within recent years large numbers of sheep remains have been excavated from the tombs at Kerma in northern Sudan, which range in date from 2400 to 1500 BC. The complete skeletons of 55 sheep and 62 separate bones have been analysed by Chaix & Grant (1987), who deduce that they came from a long-legged, thin-tailed breed without the Roman nose of modern desert sheep. Many of the skeletons were 'mummified' so that skin was preserved. The sheep were hairy and most were single-coloured black or white, but there were some black and white piebald sheep.

Caprine remains have not been separated into sheep and goat on many of the early archaeological sites from western and eastern Africa (Shaw 1977, p. 110), but there was enough material for the claim that 'there is now increasing evidence accumulating that pottery and sheep were spreading down the western side of southern Africa from Angola to the Cape by about 200 BC'. This evidence is supported by the work of Klein (1984; 1986) on animal remains from sites in the western Cape.

In eastern Africa, Barthelmé (1985) has recorded the presence of domestic sheep/goat in third-millennium BC sites in the northeastern sector of the Lake Turkana basin. From here domestic caprines with cattle can be traced, from the archaeological record, moving slowly southwards. In Kenya the earliest record of them is from the first-millennium BC site of Prolonged Drift (Gifford-Gonzalez 1984). Then there is a gap until the centuries before AD 900, when caprines have been retrieved from a number of early iron age sites north and south of the Zambesi (Voigt 1986).

Sheep reached the eastern Cape together with cattle by the fourth century AD and are recorded from many iron age sites (Voigt 1984). Klein (1986) has shown that there is well-documented evidence for the presence of sheep in the western and southern Cape from 2000 BP. Goats are quite unknown from these early sites and cattle occur with only very low frequency. Klein suggests that they were introduced later than sheep (?1600–1500 BP).

The best evidence for the kinds of livestock owned by pastoralists throughout Africa comes from the rock art, which is often extremely detailed although difficult to date. Both fat- and thin-tailed sheep are seen on rock paintings from Zimbabwe (Goodall 1946), and Manhire & Parkington (1986) record that fat-tailed sheep are portrayed at eleven sites in the western Cape. Vinnicombe (1976) described two sites in southern Natal where there are paintings of fat-tailed sheep.

The fat tail of the sheep was an extremely valuable source of fat to pastoralists through-out the continent, as it was to the early European immigrants. Youatt (1837), quoting early descriptions of the Cape sheep, wrote that the tail weighed from 6 to 12 pounds. The fat was semi-fluid like thick oil and was frequently used for oil and for butter.

Discussion

Around half of the world's species of wild ungulates, including eighty-seven species of artiodactyls, inhabit the continent of Africa. With this abundance and diversity of wild meat to be exploited, why go to the trouble of keeping domestic stock? The husband-ing of livestock is very troublesome: the animals have to be protected from predators, of which there are a very large number of species in Africa; and they have to be provided with food and water; but above all they have to be owned. And the ownership of much property, whether it is goods and chattels or livestock, entails settlement and an entirely different social and economic basis from that of the nomadic hunter and gatherer of wild foods. There are many cultural, ritual and social reasons why people keep large herds of domestic animals but they only become essential for food when the human population expands beyond the numbers that can be fed from hunted meat, as must have happened with many iron age settlements throughout Africa. Even so, the resources supplied by livestock were always supplemented by hunted animals and the association between pastoralists and their cattle is a very much more complicated matter than the mere provision of food.

Future research on the biochemical analysis of human and animal bone may well go far to unravel the intricacies of diet. It is claimed by Ambrose (1986, p. 707) that the 'Combined use of carbon and nitrogen isotopes permits the differentiation of pastoral-ists from farmers, camel pastoralists from capri-bovine pastoralists and grain farmers from non-grain farmers.'

The relationships between humans and animals in ancient Egypt are still far from understood although the animals have been often described; in the other ancient civilizations of Africa the socio-economic roles of domestic animals are still an open field for research, while the history of camel, sheep and cattle pastoralists has been only glimpsed at.

5 Ethnographic and linguistic evidence for the prehistory of African ruminant livestock, horses and ponies[1]

Roger Blench

Introduction

To the student of African prehistory, the contribution of archaeology to hypotheses about the dates, methods and routes for the introduction of ruminant livestock is generally disappointing. In part this is because finds are relatively few and often late in date. Moreover, in many cases, it is not practical to identify the subspecies or race of livestock at a given site. Rock paintings constitute a more informative source of data but they are notoriously hard to date and give a misleadingly patchy coverage of types. Since it is generally the productivity characteristics of livestock that have implications for economic prehistory, this leaves a large historical lacuna.

Two possibilities suggest themselves to fill this: analysis of the distribution of current and recent breeds in traditional management; and comparative linguistics. Monographs characterizing livestock breeds are more abundant than linguistic studies. The first major description of African domestic stock was Doutressolle's (1947) study of francophone Africa. However, there are two essential texts for this study, Epstein's (1971) massive catalogue of contemporary African livestock breeds and related archaeological and historical data and the recensions of this evidence compiled in Mason (1984a). Animal production compilations such as those of the International Livestock Centre for Africa (ILCA) (1979) and the Food and Agriculture Organization (FAO) (1987) also provide distributional data not available elsewhere.

These sources do not generally consider linguistic evidence and comparative material on livestock terminology. In this field, the broadest discussion is Bender (1982) on domestic ruminants in northeast Africa but there are also smaller-scale studies by Ehret (1967; 1968) and Manessy (1972). Purely linguistic sources such as Westermann (1927) and Greenberg (1966) also incidentally provide valuable evidence for the antiquity of certain species.

Methods

The basic method used in this chapter is to plot the present-day distribution of the various species and breeds of African domestic stock and to explore the historical sources for documented changes. These data are then used to generate a series of scenarios for the possible pattern of diffusion of domestic ruminants.

Comparative linguistics can play a part in unravelling the prehistory of African livestock but it is a problematic part, since there is limited agreement among linguists about fundamental issues of reconstruction. Current ideas about the classification of African languages and the use of linguistic data to reconstruct economic history have been dealt with elsewhere (Williamson 1989a; Williamson, Ch. 8, this volume; Blench, Ch. 7, this volume). Ehret (1989; Ch. 6, this volume) has recently proposed a subclassification of Nilo-Saharan and argued that 'cattle', 'sheep' and 'goat' can be reconstructed to relatively ancient proto-languages. However, as his subclassification has not been accepted by other workers in the field, this claim is difficult to evaluate. It is not the object of this chapter to try and link species or the practice of pastoralism to particular linguistic groups. Evidence from livestock terminology is therefore only remarked in passing.

The core of the present chapter is a series of maps showing the recent or present-day distribution of the major subspecies and races of African ruminant livestock. Some of the unreferenced distributional data were compiled as part of the Nigerian National Livestock Resource Survey (RIM 1991) and working on the survey has provided many useful insights into the processes of change among traditional livestock producers.

Related maps have been published by the contributors to ILCA (1979) and Mason (1984a) but these do not use the distinctions outlined in this chapter. Indeed, for the purpose of prehistory, such maps can sometimes be misleading, as they conflate populations initiated in historical times with 'traditional' populations of unknown antiquity.

Maps of the distribution of mobile entities such as livestock are at best abstractions. Pastoralists are constantly exploring new regions and learning to exploit them on a seasonal or year-round basis. Crossbreeding is constantly taking place, through both conscious policy on the part of producers or simple accidental encounters. In recent times, livestock have been moved around Africa by researchers in pursuit of improved animal productivity. Many types of African stock have been transported out of their traditional habitats and in some cases released to farmers in 'new' areas. Such patterns of distribution are documented in ILCA (1979) but are not reflected on the present maps.

Two other aspects of the maps[2] deserve comment: the enlargement of distribution for very small residual populations and the absence of crossbreeds. Since the humpless longhorns in northern Cameroon may constitute as little as a few hundred animals, to represent them at their true scale on a map of Africa would be an infinitesimal dot. They have therefore been enlarged to draw attention to their presence. Stabilized crossbreeds, such as the Keteku and Baoulé which are both well established and numerically significant, are excluded. There is nothing historically opaque about the development of stabilized crosses at the boundaries of two subspecies, and they are not discussed further in this chapter.

Cattle

Introduction

The most comprehensive overview of the origin of the traditional cattle of Africa is that of Epstein (1971) and Epstein & Mason (1984), who also included historical speculations about the chronology of their introduction into Nigeria. Useful animal production descriptions can be found in Stewart (1937), Gates (1952) and Fricke (1979). Additional archaeological material is reviewed in Smith (1980a), Muzzolini (1983; Ch. 11, this volume) and Clutton-Brock (1989b; Ch. 4, this volume).

All types of cattle interbreed and to that extent they can be regarded as a single species. However, differences between types run so deep that hypotheses as to their origins have often invoked different wild progenitors. Much of the literature on cattle uses the terminology of breeds, types, varieties and races somewhat indiscriminately. In this chapter, 'subspecies' (breeds) are used to refer to the primary divisions of African cattle, i.e. zebu and the humpless breeds. Below this level, the distinctions are treated as races and given upper case initials e.g. Rahaji etc.

TERM	EXAMPLE	COMMON NAME
Species	*Bos*	Cattle
Subspecies	*Bos indicus*	Zebu
	Bos taurus	Muturu
Race	Bunaji	White Fulani

Linguistic evidence

One of the most striking features of terms for cattle – with a quite distinct root from terms for buffalo – in west-central Africa is the apparent time depth for which they can be reconstructed. Greenberg (1966, p. 17) cites cognate forms from all the major branches of Niger-Congo suggesting an original root something like *na. There appear to be no cognates in Kordofanian, arguing that cattle were brought to west Africa after the Kordofanian speakers broke away from the main body of Niger-Congo. The terminology does not clearly distinguish between subspecies, but it is evident that cattle were part of the cultural repertoire of Niger-Congo speakers at the beginning of their expansion in west Africa (which, on conservative archaeological grounds, cannot be later than about 5000 BC).

Contributory evidence is the curious scatter of terms for cattle in Chadic languages (Jungraithmayr & Shimizu 1981), many of them borrowed from neighbouring Niger-Congo languages. This strongly suggests that speakers of Proto-Chadic were *not* cattle producers, at least on their arrival in west Africa.

The linguistic evidence for Nilo-Saharan and other branches of Afroasiatic is summarized in Bender (1982). Essentially, he argues that cattle were brought into east Africa twice: initially from the Ethiopian highlands and then by ancestors of the present-day Nilotic speakers moving in from the northwest. If it is useful to tie in these introductions to cattle subspecies, then it is most likely that the primary introduction

from Ethiopia was the all-but-vanished humpless shorthorns and the secondary introduction the zeboid types.

Dwarf shorthorn cattle

The west African dwarf shorthorn, or *muturu* (a Hausa name), is probably the least-
known breed of cattle in Africa. Little has been published on its distribution, management, anatomical characteristics or productivity. Some useful background material can
be found in Ferguson (1967), Grandin (1980), Beauvilain (1983) and Dineur & Thys
(1986). These cattle are usually referred to in the literature as 'trypanotolerant' cattle
(ILCA 1979; FAO 1987), although humpless shorthorn cattle were historically distributed in almost all ecological zones. However, there are certainly races that can survive
in regions of exceptional humidity, such as the Cross River in Nigeria, where annual
rainfall may exceed 4000 mm.

Far from being confined to west Africa, they were once distributed across the
continent from Liberia to Ethiopia and even reached the islands off the southern tip of
the Arabian peninsula (Epstein 1971) (Fig. 5.1). Isolated populations were recorded in

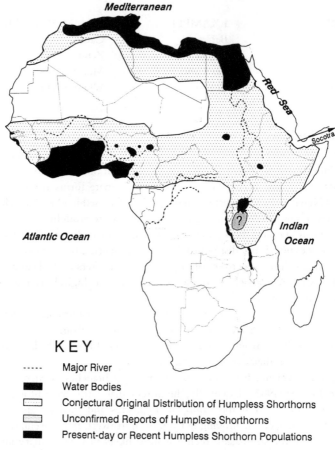

Figure 5.1 Humpless shorthorn cattle.

the Nuba hills in Sudan and in central Tanzania in historical times, and there are still small remnant populations in Ethiopia (Alberro & Haile-Mariam 1982a; Alberro & Haile-Mariam 1982b) and on Socotra island. Humpless shorthorns are the principal breed kept by village producers in northern Africa and down the Nile as far as the cataracts.

Humpless shorthorns are not represented in rock art to the same degree as longhorns despite their extremely broad distribution. Epstein (1971) shows clearly that longhorns were the dominant breed in Egypt, and presumably north Africa, as early as 4000 BC and they were gradually replaced by shorthorns from the third millennium onwards. This makes for a paradox, as the degree of adaptation of longhorns to extreme environments is not matched by that of any other subspecies – which tends to support the speculation that they were the first cattle to cross the desert.

This suggests a controversial speculation – that humpless shorthorns spread into west Africa from the Nile valley and their dispersal through west-central Africa was parallel to but probably earlier than the diffusion along the north African coast. This would explain how they came to be resident when the longhorns were brought across the desert from the Maghreb.

Muturu populations were spread over most of west Africa until the coming of zebu cattle to the semi-arid regions. Their elimination from Chad, Sudan and Ethiopia was probably much earlier and associated with the primary westward expansion of the zebu. It is usually considered that the morphological characteristics of zebu in eastern and southern Africa derive from crossing with resident humpless shorthorns. In west Africa, the *muturu* has come under pressure from the expansion of zebu populations and survives only in pockets in the savannas and in the humid zone forests, where it has had the comparative advantage of trypanotolerance. It seems likely that the rinderpest epizootics that swept Africa in the late nineteenth and early twentieth centuries extinguished many regional *muturu* populations.

Humpless longhorns

The main present-day representative of the humpless longhorn in Africa is the *n'dama*, which flourishes between the Ivory Coast and the western seaboard (Starkey 1984). Humpless longhorn cattle present something of a paradox. They are by far the most common type of cattle in iconographic representations in the Sahara, ancient north Africa and Ethiopia and are also clearly more ancient than the shorthorns. Yet they are today confined to a very small region of western Africa (Fig. 5.2).

The humpless longhorns crossed the desert, perhaps via a western route, as their geographical dispersal was never as broad as the shorthorns. Nonetheless, they seem to have adapted to the derived savanna and the northern forest regions and to have spread between the Senegambia and northern Cameroon. They presumably interbred with the *muturu*, and the brown and white *muturu* types in semi-arid west Africa may be the descendants of these crosses. The humpless longhorns clearly illustrated in Ethiopian rock art have apparently vanished without trace, although they must have made some genetic contribution to present-day zebu races.

Apart from the flourishing *n'dama* populations, there is more fragmentary evidence for a wider distribution of humpless longhorns in west Africa. Rock paintings in Birnin

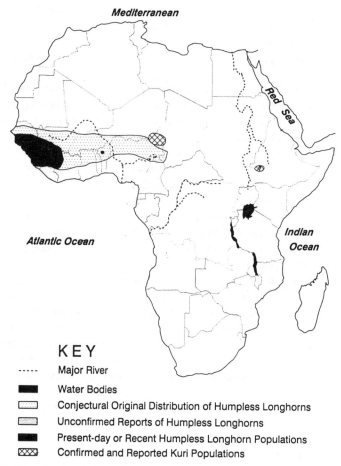

KEY

- - - - -	Major River
▬	Water Bodies
▭	Conjectural Original Distribution of Humpless Longhorns
▦	Unconfirmed Reports of Humpless Longhorns
▬	Present-day or Recent Humpless Longhorn Populations
▨	Confirmed and Reported Kuri Populations

Figure 5.2 Humpless longhorn cattle.

Kudu, northern Nigeria, clearly represent humpless longhorn cattle, and near Zing, in northeastern Nigeria, are traces of a race that appears to be a humpless longhorn. They are kept by the Mumuye people, and are regarded as the 'traditional' type, although they have now almost disappeared on account of repeated crossing. Another residual population of these animals, locally known as *pabli*, has been recorded in northern Benin Republic (Troquereau 1961). Epstein (1971) cites existing populations among the Dowayo (Namji) and Pape in northern Cameroon as well as a record of a population in the Atlantika mountains that became extinct before 1939.

Kuri cattle

A pair of kuri horns had reached the British Museum by the 1820s, but the large-bodied humpless kuri cattle of Lake Chad, with their distinctive bulbous horns, were first recorded by the traveller Heinrich Barth in 1851. He records, 'I saw the first specimen of the "kuri", a peculiar kind of bull of immense size and strength, with proportionately large horns of great thickness and curving inwards' (Barth 1857–8, II, p. 200).

The nucleus of the kuri cattle population is within the region of the former Lake Chad, and along its eastern shores (Fig. 5.2). In Nigeria, kuri are found not only on the lake but along all its shores and along the Yobe valley, as far west as Gashagar. This massive-bodied breed, whose distinctive, inflated, spongy horns are unknown in any other breed, has not been extensively researched. The most comprehensive study of the kuri is that of Queval, Petit, Tacher, Provost & Pagot (1971), which synthesized almost all the available materials up to 1970. Kone (1948), Mason (1976) and Adeniji (1983) contain useful additional materials on the kuri.

The origin of the kuri is unknown. As a humpless longhorn, it resembles the *n'dama* more closely than other subspecies, yet it is remote from the residual humpless longhorns of northern Cameroon, such as the *pape* (Epstein 1971). Alberro & Haile-Mariam (1982a; 1982b) report the discovery of a relict population of kuri in Illulabor Province of southwest Ethiopia. Their report is somewhat invalidated by their accompanying photograph (Fig. 3) which is *not* from Ethiopia but is simply a copy of the photograph of Lake Chad kuri published in Epstein (1971, I, p. 209, photo 220) with the background cut out.

The kuri is not clearly represented in any rock art sites so far discovered, which does argue that it is a local development in the Lake Chad region. It is so significantly different from other humpless longhorns and also highly adapted to an extreme environment, suggesting that it is the relict of a quite separate introduction, possibly earlier than the *n'dama* and related races.

Zebu

The distinctive feature of the zebu is the presence of a fatty hump, a morphological feature that leaves no direct archaeological trace. Zebu can sometimes be detected from skeletal features if the right bones are present. The zebu originates in India and was probably brought to Africa at least 2500 years ago (and see below for the problem of earlier identifications in Egyptian art). Whether it was carried along the 'Sabaean Lane' and spread from the Horn of Africa or via the Nile valley is disputed, but the presence of zebu in southern Arabia tends to argue for the Indian Ocean route. Today zebu are by far the most widely distributed breed of cattle in sub-Saharan Africa (Fig. 5.3).

The discussion is complicated by the many representations of cattle in the ancient Middle East, Egypt and in Saharan rock art that show cattle with some sort of hump. Traditionally, zebu have been identified on this basis in Theban paintings of *c.* 1500 BC. However, Muzzolini (1983; Ch. 11, this volume) has undertaken an extremely detailed investigation of the representations of cattle in Saharan rock art. He concludes that there are some apparently early images of humped cattle that do not fit with the late introduction of zebu and therefore advances the hypothesis of an independent evolution of humpedness in the Sahara.[3] In fact, the identification of humps is by no means self-evident; some humps can simply be high withers. The Damietta bulls of the Nile delta (Epstein 1971, I, Fig. 296) have pronounced withers which could hardly be distinguished from humps in most forms of representation.

Whatever the cause, the zebu must have reached semi-arid west Africa before AD 1000 (Epstein 1971). Zebu would have spread westwards in the early period carried by unknown pastoral groups, until their herders encountered FulBe pastoralists with

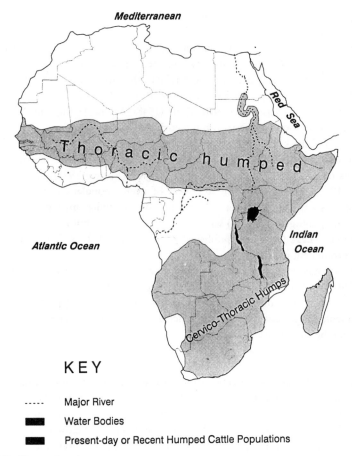

Figure 5.3 Humped cattle.

n'dama cattle in the extreme west. Some FulBe would then have exchanged their *n'dama* for zebu and begun to move eastwards in search of grazing. Zebu appear to have a comparative advantage in the arid zone, and this may have been the element that supported the move eastward. At the same time, zebu would also have spread southwards, colonizing most of central and southern Africa. It is likely that they would have encountered and crossed with humpless cattle, generating the 'Sanga' types.

Sheep

Introduction

There are four basic types of sheep in Africa: thin-tailed hair and wool sheep, fat-tailed and fat-rumped sheep (Epstein 1971; Ryder 1984). All the sheep must originally have come out of central Asia, although they reached Africa by diverse routes.

Linguistic evidence for the antiquity of sheep in Africa is less clear than for cattle and goats and is compounded by the fact that some languages apply the same term to both goats and sheep. In the Niger–Congo languages, there are no convincing reconstructions for 'sheep' further back than Proto-Volta-Congo, i.e. Bantu plus Kwa and Benue–Congo. At this level, a form such as *gwani* can probably be reconstructed. Bender (1982) has reviewed the evidence for goats and sheep in Nilo-Saharan and Afroasiatic and finds a variety of roots that suggest multiple introductions after the nuclei of these language families were established.

Thin-tailed hair sheep

Hair sheep are the most widespread race in Africa (Fig. 5.4) and almost certainly were the first to be introduced as they are the only type well adapted to high-rainfall tropical forest (ILCA 1979; Adu & Ngere 1979). Hair sheep are also present in Saudi Arabia and south India and it is most likely that they were introduced along the same route as zebu cattle, i.e. via the Horn of Africa (Ryder 1984). A Nile valley route is also possible, though there is no immediate ethnographic evidence to support this. The adaptation of hair sheep to humidity argues that they were brought in well before zebu cattle or that they were partly preadapted in India.

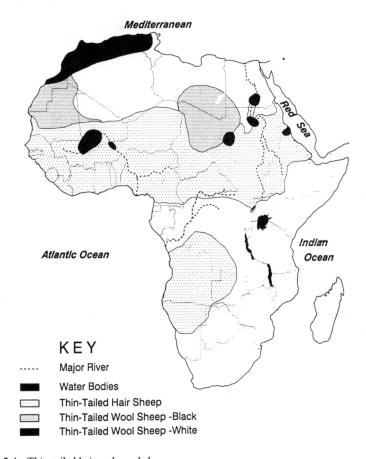

Figure 5.4 Thin-tailed hair and wool sheep.

Thin-tailed wool sheep

Figure 5.4 shows the African distribution of thin-tailed wool sheep. They have a stronger association with urbanization and the development of long-distance trade than hair sheep, which were predominantly developed by pastoralists. Wool is attested in Egypt by 1400 BC and it is probable that coarse-woolled sheep were spread along the north African coast at this period (Ryder 1984). Thin-tailed wool sheep were subsequently replaced by fat-tailed sheep throughout eastern north Africa.

Small numbers of wool sheep were presumably carried across the desert to the inland Niger delta and to Lake Chad. Wool sheep were also taken up the Nile, resulting in isolated populations in Upper Egypt and Sudan. Some pure populations remain but crosses with local varieties also resulted in the black-fleeced sheep currently present in these regions.

Fat-tailed sheep

The third wave of sheep to reach Africa was the coarse-woolled fat-tailed sheep. Epstein (1971, II, p. 111) gives a map of the most important races of fat-tailed sheep in Africa (see Fig. 5.5). The distribution suggests that fat-tailed sheep were introduced independently via the Horn of Africa and into Egypt and north Africa from the Middle East. Fat-tailed sheep are first shown in Egyptian art about 2000 BC. Differences in wool type between these two populations also confirm their separate history.

The most problematic aspect of the distribution of fat-tailed sheep is their penetration into northern Angola. This has given rise to some rather wild and unsupportable speculations about the movement of populations of Khoisan speakers from east Africa. It is simpler to suppose that the fat-tailed sheep were brought by Bantu speakers and then transferred to Khoisan speakers *in situ*. Ehret (1968) has argued that speakers of Central Sudanic languages have to be evoked as intermediaries in the transmission of sheep to southern Africa.

Fat-rumped sheep

The traditional distribution of fat-rumped sheep is limited to a small region of eastern Africa (Fig. 5.5). These are not as clearly defined morphologically as other sheep races and their origins are disputed. Fat-rumped sheep are present in central Asia proper, but there are no populations on the periphery of the African continent and they are not represented. The pocket of fat-rumped sheep shown north of Lake Chad in the map accompanying Ryder (1984, Fig. 9.5) is almost certainly an error [for fleece sheep?]. The fleece sheep in southern Africa on the same map presumably represent European introductions in historical times. Epstein (1971, II, p. 190) proposed that fat-rumped sheep were an independent development within Africa and probably arise from crossing fat-tailed and hair sheep.

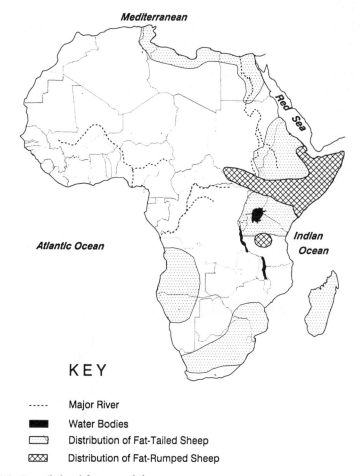

Figure 5.5   Fat-tailed and fat-rumped sheep.

Goats

Introduction

African goats can be divided into three basic types: dwarf goats, savanna goats and milking goats. Whether these can genuinely be distinguished in archaeological contexts remains to be seen. The dwarf goat, often known as the West African Dwarf (WAD), is relatively homogeneous throughout its range. Savanna goats are much more various in both coat colour and body type. There is a clear distinction between prick-eared and lop-eared types, although these may have evolved from the same basic stock. The milking goats are divided into two basic types again, the Nubian or Zaraibi and the Maltese goat. The main sources on African goats are Doutressolle (1947), Epstein (1971), ILCA (1979), Mason (1984) and Ngere, Adu & Okubanjo (1984).

Linguistic evidence

As with sheep, words for goat in Nilo-Saharan and Afroasiatic present a complex picture (Ehret 1968; Bender 1982). There appears to be no evidence for very early domesticated small stock in Ethiopia and eastern Africa, which would be consonant with the multiplicity of terminology.

The situation in west Africa is quite different, as terms for goat in west-central Africa can be reconstructed to a considerable apparent time depth. Greenberg (1966, p. 19) cites cognate forms from all the major branches of Niger-Congo and Williamson (1989a, p. 117) proposes *bhodhi for Proto-Niger-Congo. As with cattle, there appear to be no cognates in Kordofanian, arguing that goats spread to west Africa after the Kordofanian speakers broke away from the main body of Niger-Congo. This puts the introduction of the goat into west Africa well before the introduction of agriculture.

West African dwarf goats

The distribution of WAD goats in Africa is shown on Fig. 5.6. Apart from 'islands' in Morocco and on the Red Sea coast, WAD goats form a continuous group from

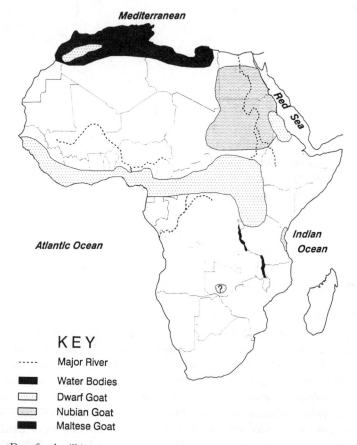

Figure 5.6 Dwarf and milking goats.

Senegambia to the region of Lake Victoria. The WAD goat is usually black, although patched, pied and occasionally all-white animals can be seen. There has been some debate about whether the few archaeological records of early goats in north Africa were dwarfed (Clutton-Brock, Ch. 4, this volume). Whatever the case, there seems little doubt that contact with extreme environments in west-central Africa accelerated the process.

WAD goats are generally associated with the humid zone in animal production literature (e.g. ILCA 1979). However, recent research in Nigeria has recorded 'islands' of WAD goats well into the semi-arid regions (RIM 1991). Like *muturu* cattle, the smaller-bodied goats have been driven into refuge areas with the expansion of larger savanna animals, in this case the Sokoto Red goat.

There are no very early records of goat bones in west Africa, but goats seem to be as ancient as 8000 BP in north Africa and they could well have spread to sub-Saharan Africa by this time, which would be consonant with the linguistic evidence. The late appearance of goats in east Africa is puzzling and can perhaps be explained by the dominance of specialized cattle producers who did not have sufficient labour to allocate them to mixed herds.

Savanna goats

Savanna goats are broadly divisible into the Sahel, Desert or West African long-legged goat, and the Sokoto Red. They are by far the most widespread and significant type of goat in Africa, although their lack of trypanotolerance suggests that they arrived considerably later than the West African Dwarf (Fig. 5.7). The destruction of humid zone vegetation in west-central Africa is permitting them to move further south each year, gradually displacing the West African Dwarf.

Although the Sahel goat is kept mostly in villages today, it is strongly associated with pastoralism. One of the most useful descriptions is by Dumas (1980) whose *chèvre Arabe* of Chad corresponds to the Sahel goat. The most complete overview of the Sokoto Red is Robinet's (1967) comprehensive survey which integrates data from Nigeria and Niger.

The original savanna goat was presumably brought to sub-Saharan Africa by a series of introductions all across its range. Its distribution and diversity of coat colours make it unlikely that it spread outwards from a single nucleus within Africa. Lop-eared goats were probably brought later still, as they are more specialized in arid zone vegetation and have never penetrated very far south. Their distribution suggests an introduction from the northeast, perhaps along the Nile valley to Lake Chad (Fig. 5.7).

Milking goats

Generally speaking, goats are rarely milked in Africa, and the milk is less favoured than that of sheep and cattle. Even in the pastoral regions of the Sahel, the milk is often given to children or drunk by herdsmen in the field rather than taken to market. However, there are two types of goat in Africa that have been brought in especially for their milk-producing qualities, the Nubian or Zaraibi goat and the Maltese goat. According to Mason (1984b, p. 94), the Nubian goat is 'not so much a breed as an idea', as it is phenotypically extremely diverse.

Figure 5.6 shows the distribution of Nubian and Maltese goats. The period of their introduction into Africa is unknown, but their failure to spread into the interior of the

KEY

----- Major River

▬ Water Bodies

▭ Savanna Goats

Figure 5.7 Savanna goats.

continent argues that it is relatively recent and probably associated with Islam. Even so, Islam has spread farther than the milking goats – so they may only have been introduced in the late medieval period.

Summary and conclusion

1. All ruminant livestock must have reached west-central Africa far earlier than any present dated site if degree of adaptation and comparative linguistics are accepted as evidence.
2. There is no need to assume that domestic stock were constrained to move 'around' the Sahara as the arrows on most maps imply. Rock paintings and other evidence suggest that all livestock species could have been carried directly across the desert in earlier periods.
3. The earliest introductions of stock were probably the result of movement by occupationally specialized pastoralists. Livestock were subsequently adopted by village producers and gradually moved into ecological zones outside the orbit of pastoralists.

4. The development of local races similar to the European concept of 'breeds' is particularly associated with pastoralism, where the ancestry of animals is often controlled in various ways. Village producers usually allow free mating, leading to rather indeterminate types spread over vast geographical areas.

5. A later phase was associated with the introduction of races with particular economic interest – for example, wool sheep and dairy goats. This was related to the growth of urban society and long-distance trade.

Cattle

Humpless shorthorns

1. The first wave of cattle to reach sub-Saharan Africa was probably the ancestors of West African Shorthorns, to judge by their degree of adaptation to humid environments. Their closest relatives are north African humpless shorthorns. They would have been introduced from north Africa by occupationally specialized pastoralists in a series of separate introductions. West African Shorthorns were originally spread across the entire continent and also to Socotra and present-day Yemen.

2. The present-day distinction between savanna and coastal races would have developed within Africa, as would trypanotolerance. The red/brown coloration and larger size of savanna races may reflect some genetic input from the now-vanished humpless longhorns.

3. The virtual elimination of the WAD type over the eastern part of its range reflects the incoming zebu populations from the east. WAD cattle only survived in significant numbers in forest regions where they had the comparative advantage of resisting humidity-related diseases.

Humpless longhorns

1. The humpless longhorn or *n'dama* type was probably the second subspecies of cattle to be brought to sub-Saharan Africa, either contemporary with or not long after the humpless shorthorn. It undoubtedly developed from the humpless longhorns of the ancient Middle East.

2. Its date and route of introduction are less easy to determine as its distribution is more limited today than the humpless shorthorns. However, the fact that it only marginally penetrated the high-rainfall regions of the forest zone suggests that it came after the humpless shorthorns. There appear to be no ethnographic examples of humpless longhorns east of northern Cameroon, although they are well attested in rock art in Ethiopia and Kenya.

3. Placing humpless longhorns second in the sequence of introductions makes for a historical paradox: why should there be humpless shorthorns and no longhorns in north Africa if the latter are more recent? The solution proposed here is that the humpless shorthorns spread through west-central Africa from the Nile valley before they diffused along the coast of north Africa. Humpless longhorns then moved across the Sahara and were subsequently displaced in north Africa.

4. The kuri is most unlikely to be a direct development from the *n'dama* type of

humpless longhorn – its conformation and adaptation to environment are too remote from its nearest geographical relatives. It is presumably a descendant of a separate stream of humpless longhorns from the north African region. Whether it developed in isolation in the Lake Chad region depends on the truth of the report of its presence in Ethiopia.

Zebu

1. The zebu was introduced into Africa by sea from India via the Horn of Africa but may also have spread down the Nile valley.
2. Muzzolini's hypothesis of the independent development of humps in the Saharan cattle is possible – but it may also be explained by representations of high withers rather than true humps. Whatever the truth of this hypothesis, African zebu today are largely the result of a movement of stock from further east.
3. Cattle types in eastern and southern Africa reflect crossbreeding with early populations of humpless cattle.
4. Zebu spread into west Africa along the southern fringes of the desert avoiding regions of high tsetse challenge. The present distinctive zebu types in west Africa arose from crosses with the resident humpless cattle.
5. Zebu cattle became a specialized holding of the FulBe people in Guinea who either became pastoralists or switched their herds to zebu. They then began to move eastwards and most of the zebu races in west Africa were developed and introduced from the west. Some of the types bred by the FulBe have spread as far east as Sudan and western Ethiopia.

Sheep

1. Linguistic evidence suggests that sheep were brought to sub-Saharan Africa subsequent to cattle and goats. Nonetheless, the high degree of adaptation to humid tropical forest in west Africa points to the earliest point of introduction via the Sahara in central Africa. Hair sheep are the most widespread race and almost certainly were the first introduced.
2. Hair sheep are also recorded from Saudi Arabia and south India and it is most likely that they were also introduced along the same route as zebu cattle, i.e. via the Horn of Africa.
3. The second sheep race to be introduced was the thin-tailed wool sheep, which probably displaced hair sheep in north Africa and was then carried to a few isolated points south of the Sahara, in some cases producing mixed, black-fleeced races.
4. Coarse-woolled fat-tailed sheep were introduced independently via the Horn of Africa and into Egypt and north Africa from the Middle East. They spread throughout the whole of southern and eastern Africa.
5. The final development of sheep in Africa is the appearance of fat-rumped sheep, which have remained confined to a small region of eastern Africa.

Goats

1. Goats in sub-Saharan Africa probably reflect several waves of introduction: first dwarf goats and then savanna goats. Lop-eared savanna goats may be a subsequent introduction.

2. WAD goats appear to have a circum-Saharan distribution, *if* the Moroccan and Red Sea populations are true relatives of the black goats of west-central Africa. However, the high degree of adaptation and trypanotolerance of the WAD goat presumably marks an antiquity also suggested by linguistics. If so, it is at least possible that the present outlying population in north Africa was carried in the reverse direction, northwards, across the Sahara.

3. Isolated populations of WAD goat still exist in regions dominated by the brown savanna goats, suggesting that their distribution once covered a broader span of ecological zones. Savanna goats were probably introduced many times through a variety of entry points and developed local races such as the Sokoto Red *in situ* in western and southern Africa. These goats probably have more in common with the progenitors of the WAD goats than with lop-eared goats and may have sprung from the same basic Middle Eastern/north African stock developed by different pastoral groups at a slightly later period.

4. The expansion of 'red' races in west Africa is strongly associated with Islam and this is probably a secondary expansion caused by the value of the skins and their consequent importance in trade. As with cattle, savanna goats are gradually pressing further towards the forest as the habitats for tsetse are gradually cleared in west-central Africa.

5. It is unclear whether the lop-eared white goats are distinct from the short-eared brown goats. They have a much more limited distribution and a much stronger association with semi-arid regions. Their epicentre is generally east of the coloured savanna, suggesting that they were brought in by a further wave of pastoral expansion. The centre of the lop-eared goats appears to be in central Africa, implying a movement down the Nile valley to the Lake Chad area.

6. The Maltese and Nubian goats are likely to have been introduced in association with Islam in the last millennium.

General

One of the most striking aspects emerging from the study of current ethnography relevant for the interpretation of prehistoric data is the speed at which change can occur over large regions of livestock production. For example, within this century, West African Dwarf shorthorn cattle have been completely eliminated from many parts of Africa as a result of vegetation clearance and population shifts. The almost complete disappearance of humpless longhorn cattle from most parts of their former range seems less surprising in the light of documented present-day processes.

The combination of evidence from rock art and the current distribution of ruminant breeds provides tantalizing hints of past processes but only the evidence of archaeological sites can confirm or refute the hypotheses they suggest. Unfortunately, many of the morphological features that are so significant to present-day producers, such as coat, horn conformation and milking ability do not leave traces that are preserved in sub-Saharan sites. Only further work on the relationship between these features and what can be excavated, i.e. bones, may make it possible to elucidate the prehistory of African livestock.

The history and distribution of horses and ponies in west-central Africa

The Native Horse of the countries above enumerated [Hausa, Nupe, Borgu, Yoruba, Kontagora, Kebbi] is particularly small and shaggy; it is generally of a mouse colour, with hair as soft and fine as silk: and, like an ass, has a black streak placed transversely on the back and shoulders. (Richard Lander 1830, II, p. 13)

Introduction

In recent years, much has been written on the role played by the horse in the dynamics of west African history. Goody (1971) argued for the importance of cavalry in the formation of a number of the post-medieval savanna states of west Africa, and set up an opposition between the 'horse states' of the savanna and the 'gun states' of the forest. A survey of documentary references to the horse was prepared by Fisher (1972a; 1972b), who argued that the traditional role of the horse in west Africa was more significant as a representation of conspicuous consumption than in terms of military advantage. Law (1976; 1980) has published both an article and a full-length book on the subject of the horse in west African history, constituting an exhaustive compilation of source material on this topic. All of these writers have assumed that all horses are a single species and thus in some sense functionally equivalent. Only a recent publication by Seignobos (1987), focusing on the pony in Chad, has indirectly questioned this consensus.

These discussions concern the medieval and pre-modern period; however, archaeological data may point to an early date for the horse in west-central Africa. In the light of this, it is appropriate to re-evaluate the role of equines in African history and prehistory. Assessments of the distribution and use of the races of horse and the role it may have played in state formation may need to be reconsidered.

This chapter puts forward the hypotheses that:

(a) a domestic horse has been present in west Africa at least as early as 2500 BP.

(b) west Africa has a distinct race of dwarfed horses or ponies, deriving from a variety of north African breeds, and that this dwarfing is a response to local conditions.

(c) horses crossed the desert as domesticates, but may possibly have become feral. They came into the possession of a large number of different ethnic groups, and were consistently inbred. They thereby acquired partial resistance to the trypanosomiases [sleeping-sickness] and the capacity to survive on a broadly-based diet. This in turn allowed them to exploit a substantially larger ecological zone than they occupy at present.

(d) in the hands of acephalous, non-Muslim peoples, ponies were redomesticated (if feral) and subsequently developed diverse local usage patterns. A particularly characteristic formation was the raiding band – the purpose of which was strictly military.

(e) conventional models of the relation of horses to state formation must be re-examined in the light of our knowledge of the capacity of non-Muslims for mounted warfare, particularly in the Plateau area of Nigeria and Adamawa.

Horses in sub-Saharan Africa

The biological evidence

The races of horse and pony in west Africa

The most comprehensive review of the breeds of horses and ponies in Africa is Epstein (1971, II, pp. 401–541). Largely following Doutressolle (1947), he distinguishes the ponies of west-central Africa as a race, quite distinct from the Oriental, Barb and Dongola horses of the north African littoral, the principal horses bred south of the desert today. African ponies have 'a heavy head, thick short neck, [and] . . . may be either bay or chestnut in colour' (Epstein 1971, II, p. 467). A number of different breeds are recognized, with varying characteristics that suggest a derivation from several races of north African horse. Doutressolle's map schematizes various populations according to multiple degrees of *dégénérescence* from supposed original types (Doutressolle 1947, p. 240); few authors would support this type of classification today.

The recognized races of pony in north equatorial Africa, listed from east to west are: Somali, Borana, Kordofani, Kirdi or Laka, Kotokoli, Torodi, Songhai, Kaminiandougou, Minianka, Bobo, Koniakar, M'Bayar, M'par, Cayar and an unnamed breed from the Senegal/Mali border. Figure 5.8 shows the approximate locations of these populations. The pony was evidently widespread and was known in most areas of the savanna with the significant exception of the region corresponding to present-day Ghana.

The dwarfing of the horse in west Africa

Some of these breeds are very small, standing only 90–110 cm high at the withers in the case of the Bariba pony (Meniaud 1912). There would appear to be a general correlation between degrees of latitude south and the height of the pony. Thus the smallest ponies, as with the similarly dwarfed taurines, are found along the edge of the forest.

If the west African pony is of north African origin, then there are two possible explanations for its present reduced size. Either:

(a) at the period when it was introduced from north Africa it was already small in size, and the large north African horses are the result of later introductions of Arab breeds, or

(b) it has undergone dwarfing in west Africa.

Spruytte (1971, pp. 171–6), who experimented with Egyptian chariots to establish the type of horse required to pull them, used ponies in his simulations. This replicated the apparently small size of horse depicted in Egyptian wall paintings, and might be advanced as an argument for a dwarf north African horse. However, Epstein observes (1971, II, p. 428) that 'Egypt is a poor horse-breeding country' and that 'throughout the whole of Lower Egypt . . . native horses are generally small and poor-looking'. Large horses have had to be continually imported throughout the history of the country, because of the humid climate and marshy environment.

Egypt therefore cannot be taken as representative. The original horse of the Berber-speaking peoples of north Africa, the Barb, survives, according to Epstein (1971, II, p. 441) 'with little or no trace of Arabian blood in their appearance'. Barb horses are larger than Oriental horses, standing 135–65 cm at the withers. No archaeological or iconographic material can be unambiguously interpreted to show that the Barb was of the same stature 3000 years ago. Large horses existed in pleistocene Europe, but it is unclear whether or not the horses of the ancient north African littoral were dwarfed.

It cannot be definitely established whether the horse crossed the desert already dwarfed or became dwarfed in west Africa. The most likely solution is a combination of both factors. There is some evidence for the processes that may have been at work. Epstein (1971, II, p. 230) says

> Adverse environmental conditions generally favour domestic animals of diminutive size. Under unfavourable conditions, dwarfed individuals are more highly adapted than the bulk of ordinary stock, the pressure of selection bringing about a gradual alteration of the stock by the slightly higher survival and reproduction rate of small animals.

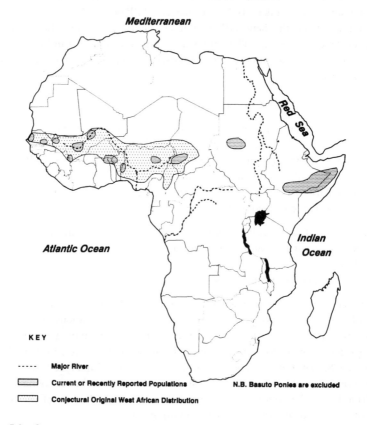

KEY

- - - - -   Major River

☐   Current or Recently Reported Populations   N.B. Basuto Ponies are excluded

☐   Conjectural Original West African Distribution

Figure 5.8   Current or recent pony populations.

Moreover, the inbreeding characteristic of many African domestic mammals kept by isolated communities can further contribute to dwarfing. When the British colonial authorities began to move stock around Nigeria in their quest to improve stock-breeding practices, they rapidly discovered that the resistance of ponies and other domestic stock to disease was highly geographically specific. Although immune in their home range, local stock transported elsewhere rapidly died from fly-borne diseases.

In Africa, both wild animals and domestic livestock have undergone dwarfing. The forest zone has pygmy elephants, hippos, chimpanzees and buffalo, while cows, pigs, sheep, goats and horses all exist in dwarf forms (Epstein 1971, II, p. 231). The evidence suggests strongly that this is a response to inbreeding in an adverse environment. The only animal that has shown no signs of dwarfing is the large Fulani humped cattle – but these cattle are not kept in the humid zone. Intriguingly, these are the only domestic stock in west Africa that are out-bred on a regular basis. Exchanged on a regular basis to minimize losses through epizootics, used to make bridewealth payments, these cows have a broader genetic make-up than the dwarf cattle kept by west African agriculturists.

Dwarfing has been observed in horses in other parts of the world subject to climatic extremes. In the Pacific, horses introduced in the seventeenth century became quickly reduced in size (Hesse 1937). In Mesoamerica, the horse went through a feral stage. Introduced by the Spanish, it spread as an adventive to the southwest, where it was re-domesticated by the Apache and other groups, who rode bareback, as did certain west African peoples.

North African horses may also have become feral in west Africa – selection pressure would then have produced disease resistance and the ability to digest a broad diet. Evidence for feral horses in west Africa is sparse, for by the period when written records begin, most such horses had either been hunted out or recaptured. In the sixteenth century, Leo Africanus (1956, II, p. 558) reported wild horses in the Sahara, and at the end of the eighteenth, Mungo Park (1954, p. 79) saw them at Kaarta on the upper Niger. Although Law (1980, p. 47) concluded that feral horses made no contribution to the supply of horses in west Africa, his remarks only apply to the north African horses introduced across the desert in the medieval period.

Disease resistance and fodder

A feature that seems to have been particularly characteristic of west African pony breeds is resistance to sleeping-sickness. Kumm (1910, p. 252) observed: 'the Bantu [This use of the word "Bantu" appears to refer to speakers of Plateau languages in central Nigeria. At this period, all languages with noun classes were referred to as "Bantu"] mountain tribes ride small ponies which, in spite of their insignificant size are sturdy and very useful. They do not fall as easy a pray to the tsetse fly as the Arab Barb.' Haywood (1912, p. 140), who travelled through modern Mali early in the century, refers to 'large horses showing distinct signs of Arab blood' as especially prone to sleeping-sickness, presumably in contrast to the smaller local horses.

Forde (1934) observed that the dwarf goats of the forest zone have a much greater resistance to fly-borne diseases than their savanna relatives. The dwarfing of some African goats is thought to be an autochthonous development (Epstein 1971, II, p. 231) and such dwarfing is considered to be related to their resistance to disease. The same explanation of dwarfing may well hold for ponies and humpless shorthorned cattle, especially as they appear to become smaller as they approach the equatorial forest.

Some writers (e.g. Fitzpatrick 1910, p. 51), discussing the 'native horse', make the point that it can be grazed anywhere. This contrasts with the Arab horse, that had to be fed on special grasses. Considerable provision had to be made for the collection and supply of such grasses, and tribute in the nineteenth century was often in horse fodder. This suggests an extended period for the adaptation of the pony to west African conditions.

Evidence for the antiquity of the horse in west Africa

Archaeological and iconographic evidence

Law (1980, p. 3) observes that archaeozoological material for equids in west Africa is sparse. Excavations at the rock shelter at Rop in northern Nigeria have yielded a single equid tooth, so far without a radiocarbon result, but dated on stratigraphic grounds to >2000 BP (Law 1980, p. 3). More recently, work by Allsworth-Jones (1982, p. 8) at Kariya Wuro, a rock shelter near Bauchi, has yielded four equid teeth. Again no scientific dating is yet available, but the teeth are associated with the earliest ceramic layer and a date similar to Rop seems appropriate.

In conjunction with other material, these finds may be supplementary evidence for the antiquity of the pony in west Africa. Other confirmation comes from the rock paintings found right across the Sahara. Herodotus first observed that the inhabitants of the Fezzan, the enigmatic Garamantes, used four-horse chariots in 2500 BP (*Histories*, Book IV, p. 183) and this was strikingly confirmed by rock paintings (Lhote 1959, pp. 124–33). Mauny (1978, p. 281) charts some of the most significant rock paintings depicting chariots and demonstrates their increasingly schematic nature further south. By mapping the representations of horses, Mauny (1978, p. 282) can trace the ancient trans-Saharan routes. These seem to have had two distinct starting points, one in the west, leading from present-day southern Morocco to Tegdaoust and Tondia, and the other from the Fezzan, passing by several routes to Gao and the region of Agadez.

Herodotus (*Histories*, Book IV, p. 183) has a reference to the hunting of 'Ethiopian troglodytes' by the Garamantes in their four-horse chariots. Most scholars consider these people may have been the Teda of the Tibesti, who still today use caves as refuges. Their language is Nilo-Saharan, and would be thus unrelated to the Afroasiatic languages used by their pursuers. This may be at the root of Herodotus' unkind comment that they 'squeak and gibber like bats'. Slaving was not the only purpose of these north African ventures into the Sahara: in the south there are also hunting scenes.

In the forest belt of west Africa, there is no archaeological evidence until much later. Equid bones have been uncovered in sites in the area of Nsukka in south-central Nigeria. The site of Igbo Richard, excavated by Shaw (1970, I, pp. 193–5), contains a bronze hilt in the form of a man on horseback. Other material at the site has given a radiocarbon date of 1100 ± 120 bp. Such a date for the representation of a horse seemed so unlikely that Shaw thought it might be occasion to question the dating of the site as a whole. However, more recent archaeological work in this area has confirmed the presence of equid bones in early contexts (Keith Ray, *pers. comm.*, from notes in the possession of Thurstan Shaw). Excavations by Hartle in the Nsukka area of the Ukpo Eze mound, at Umukete near Agaleri, gave horse bones in a context suggesting a date of 750 BP.

Linguistic evidence

If the pony was indeed an early introduction into west Africa, this should be reflected by terminology concerning horses. The first author to approach the problem from this angle was Köhler (1953/4), who examined the distribution of words for 'horse' in Gur languages. Manessy (1972) completed this material with a map of roots in 'Voltaic' languages. Skinner (1979) compiled roots for 'horse' in Chadic and most recently Tourneux (1987) has studied words for 'horse' in central Africa. Most languages do not distinguish horse from pony, especially in the non-Muslim areas.

Law (1980, p. 6) combined Köhler's material with the list of words for 'horse' in Koelle (1854a) to compile a map of the principal roots for 'horse' in west Africa. Two points are clear: an almost complete absence of loan-words from either European languages or Arabic, and the lack of any really widespread roots such as are found for 'goat' and 'cattle'. Some roots cover considerable areas, and they 'jump' the boundaries of language families, suggesting that equine terminology began to spread after the significant divisions in the language families of west Africa were already established.

This scattering of roots matches the polyphyletic racial origin of the west African ponies, suggesting that the horses from which they are descended came across the Sahara along a number of different trade routes. They arrived in prehistoric times, but well after the principal differentiation between the major branches of Niger–Congo and Nilo-Saharan had been established.

Ethnographic records

The archaeological and linguistic data point to an early introduction of horses into sub-Saharan Africa. Classical and Arabic sources are useful to confirm the antiquity of the trade in horses. Ethnographic sources complete the picture by showing the importance and degree of cultural embedding of ponies in various African societies.

Classical and Arabic sources

In discussing the Numidians of north Africa, Strabo (*Geographia*, xvii, 3.7) noted that they rode bareback. Nothing more is heard of horses until references begin to appear in the early Arab geographers. A number of these have been collected together by Fisher (1972, pp. 369–88). The earliest reference appears to be that by Al-Muhallabi in *c.* AD 985 (Levtzion & Hopkins 1981, p. 174). He noted that the people of Gao rode horses bareback. Al-Bakri, writing in 1067 (Levtzion & Hopkins 1981, pp. 80–1), observed that the ruler of Ghana gave audience surrounded by ten horses caparisoned in gold, but remarks that the horses of Ghana were very small, compared, presumably, with those of north Africa.

Al-Idrisi, writing in 1154 (Levtzion & Hopkins 1981, p. 110), has a story that the ruler of Ghana tethered his horse to a gold brick. Al-Maqrizi (Palmer 1928, p. 6) writing *c.* 1400 mentions the small size of horses in Kanem. References multiply as time goes on, and Ibn Fartua's chronicle of Kanem (Ibn Fartua 1926, p. 85) describes the twelfth-century Sultan Dunama as having 100,000 horses. The chronicle of the Bulala Girgam (Palmer 1928, pp. 29ff) records an episode in the political history of sixteenth-century Kanem, when the ruler, Abd el Jalil, defeated the oppressive ruler of neighbouring Kuka, Ali Dinar, fighting with 'small horses'. The text suggests that both large and small varieties of horse coexisted at this period and that different military strategies may have been associated with each type.

A feature of these early accounts that is particularly noteworthy is the casual acceptance of the presence of horses; their introduction is nowhere mentioned – although military innovations are often described in the Kano chronicle and related documents. The reason for not treating horses as an innovation at this period is simple: they had been there since 'neolithic' times. Neither were horses associated with new military strategies, because they were already too widespread. Al-Umari mentions the fourteenth-century ruler of Mali, Mansa Musa, riding out against mounted bowmen who rode gelded horses (Levtzion & Hopkins 1981, p. 268). As gelding horses is a practice normally frowned on by Islam, it may well be that these groups were non-Muslim. Leo Africanus, writing in the early sixteenth century, suggests that only small horses were bred at Kawkaw, for the Songhai empire, and that large animals had still to be brought across the desert.

Evidence from accounts of travellers

Nigeria

Early written sources support the contention that the 'Middle Belt' of present-day Nigeria was occupied by non-Muslim peoples with a 'pony culture'. The pony is usually referred to in the Nigerian literature as the 'Plateau' pony as it first came to the notice of colonial officials on the Jos plateau, although it was actually more widespread in the lowlands. A variety of references from the colonial period and more occasional recent descriptions make it possible to build up a picture of the place of ponies in the traditional societies of this region. Figures 5.9 and 5.10 show the names and locations of peoples and places mentioned in this section.

Some rare photographs survive of traditional pony riders. Isichei (1982a, Plate 13) illustrates an armed Mwahavul [Sura] rider photographed in 1931, while Raphael (n.d., *c.* 1915) gives two pictures of barebacked riders from 'Northern Nigeria' (to judge by the accompanying text, Berom). The pony was formerly favoured by the Berom because of its agility in a rocky environment and ponies were clubbed to death when their owner died and the corpse wrapped in the skin (Davies n.d., p. 179).

The fullest account of the Plateau pony is by Barbara Frank (1981), who was able to photograph a number of riders and animals among the Ron-speaking peoples of the Bauchi area, despite the fact that, by the period of her fieldwork, they had almost disappeared from everyday life. Berthoud (1965, pp. 25–6) describes the elaborate preparations made by the Ten [Ganawuri] before setting off for war on their ponies. Armed with a variety of lances and wicker shields, they used their ponies not only to defend themselves against Hausa slavers, but also to raid their neighbours, the Sholio

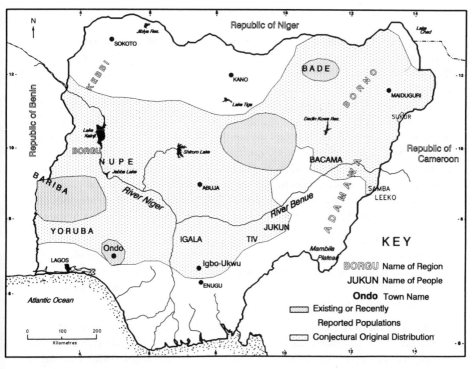

Figure 5.9 Peoples and places mentioned in the text.

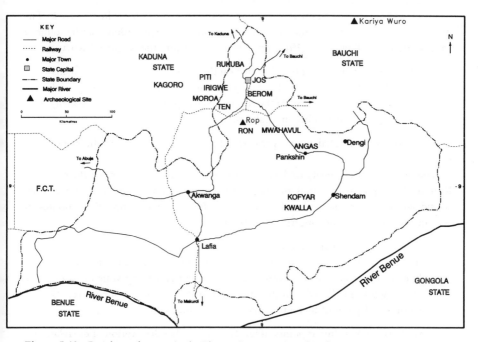

Figure 5.10 Peoples and towns in the Plateau State mentioned in the text.

[Moroa], Irigwe and Berom. The Irigwe themselves, according to Morrison (1982, p. 142), could place as many as a thousand horses in the field, and they apparently used these both for raiding their neighbours and defending themselves against the raids of the FulBe.

Smith (1968, p. 104) describes the 'small hill ponies' of the Piti, who rode bareback with a single piece of cord round the muzzle of the animal to control it. Apart from transport, the principal use of ponies among the Piti was for collective spear hunting of savanna game. Netting (1968, p. 93) mentions the use of ponies by the Kofyar on the plains for war and hunting, while the account in Koelle (1854b, pp. 211–12) of the Bedde shows them using ponies to raid and mount attacks on towns and villages.

One feature of the use of Plateau ponies to excite considerable comment is the cutting of the animal's back before riding it. Kumm (1910, pp. 26–7) describes the Angas thus:

> The natives ride their mountain-ponies bare-backed, and as they them-
> selves wear no clothing, with the exception of a weird loin-cloth of plaited
> grass, riding the frisky ponies is somewhat difficult. So they scratch the
> backs of their animals until the blood exudes, and glue themselves onto the
> beasts with their blood.

If this were the only account of this curious and rather cruel practice, it would be easy to dismiss it as a traveller's tale. But it is also mentioned by Koelle (1854b, p. 211), Barth (1857–8, IV, p. 35), Fitzpatrick (1910, p. 51) and Daniel (1936) with further references in Seignobos (1987, pp. 98ff).

Migeod (1924, p. 88) says, 'In parts of the Bauchi Plateau the pagans who ride bareback and are themselves naked, cut and make great sores on the horse's back. This glues them on, so they run less risk of coming off.' The explanation may be found in some remarks by Tremearne (1912, pp. 298–9) concerning the Kagoro district:

> The saddle, if any, is a goat-skin tied on the back, but some of the pagans
> in the district make a cut in the skin of the backbone about a foot long, and
> open it out so that the flesh of the animal swells up and forms a pad, which,
> after a time, seems to become callous.

The hard pad thus created would provide sufficient friction to keep the rider on his mount.

A number of writers testify to the close relation between the ponies and their owners. Kumm (1910, p. 26) mentions the agility of the mountain ponies and the way they would answer their masters' calls 'like dogs'. Isichei (1982b, pp. 23–4) quotes an account by a Berom man concerning his pony:

> A horse is like a man; you send it out to bring a tired man home, you give
> it water to drink, you walk miles to find it grass to eat, it carries you to
> hunt and to war, when it is tired you dismount and carry your loads on
> your own head. When you die, and they lead it towards your grave, its
> spirit may fly out of its body in its anxiety to find you.

Frank (1981) makes similar points, if less lyrically, in her description of the relation of the Ron to their ponies. Never used as pack animals, ponies were ridden in war, for communal hunting and displays on festive occasions. They were significant elements in the status of married men and were used for bridewealth payments. Wives could show especial affection for their husbands by taking care of their horses. Fitzpatrick (1910, pp. 50–1) points out that ponies rarely seemed to need special feeding and emphasizes how agile the ponies were in the rocky areas southeast of the Plateau.

The pony is now rare in central Nigeria. In the communities that previously kept ponies, only a few remain as prestige possessions, to be brought out on ceremonial occasions. For example, among the Ten [Ganawuri], southwest of the Jos plateau, in 1987 the warriors were able to muster four to take part in a procession for the installation of the ruler. Among the Challa, near Bokkos, ponies are still ridden to market in small numbers. A survey in 1990 uncovered only three ponies still in use. However, in general, competition from other prestige goods, particularly motor vehicles, has tended to eliminate the residual function of ponies as prestige transportation.

Despite their disappearance in reality, the ponies have risen to prominence as symbols of a newly developing ethnic consciousness. Peoples such as the Berom and the Mwahavul, who can no longer muster ponies even for ceremonial occasions, have begun to use old photographs of mounted warriors on locally printed literature. Thus community almanacs and other posters may often reproduce an image of their military past as a rebus to signify present unity.

Ponies on the Niger

The widespread use of the pony survived in the Middle Belt well into the colonial era, and has persisted up till the present in some isolated regions. This is in contrast to the situation along and south of the river, where, despite a wealth of references in early writers, the pony has completely disappeared. In some cases, such as among the Nupe, it has been replaced by the horse. Reconstructing the role it played in these societies is correspondingly more difficult.

A remarkable reference to Ondo in the early colonial period suggests that ponies still remained in use in Yorubaland during this century. Dudgeon (1911, p. 113) says, 'there is also said to be a stunted variety of horse, which is bred for use at Ondo'. Ondo is at approximately 7° latitude and well within the equatorial rainforest. Investigations in 1990 suggested that these ponies have now disappeared, but their recent occurrence makes the data from Igbo-Ukwu more credible.

Apart from its significance among the Igbo-Ukwu bronzes, the early importance of the horse in Igbo areas is argued by its ritual role. The 'horse sacrifice' is one of the most important components of the funeral obsequies of titled men (Isichei 1977, pp. 32ff) in some parts of Igbo territory. Until well into the colonial period, there was an extensive horse market in Nsukka, mostly selling broken-down horses brought from further north, for the sacrifice. Laird and Oldfield (1837, II, p. 180) record the trade in 'horses of a small breed' by 'Eboes' who controlled the river trade down to Bonny.

This sacrifice remains important: the Igbo are still the principal traders in horses within Nigeria. They scour the markets of the far north, especially Borno and Sokoto, for exhausted horses, which are then sent in trailers to the entrepots at Abakaliki and

Onitsha. There is also a certain trade in horses bred on the grassy uplands of the Mambila plateau and adjacent parts of Cameroon. These are trekked by Igbo to the foot of the plateau and then carried in lorries to Igboland.

Oral tradition also gives the horse a significant role among the Yoruba. Law (1977a, p. 43), in his book on the Oyo Empire, recounts traditions that attribute the introduction of cavalry warfare to the Alafin Orompoto in the sixteenth century. According to the traditions, the Alafin could raise a thousand horsemen, and when they went to war branches were tied to the tails of the horses to trail in the dust and conceal their passing. As the Nupe are supposed to have sacked Oyo just previous to this, it is possible that this enterprise on the part of Orompoto was stimulated by the Nupe use of horses.

Apart from oral tradition, there are records dating from the nineteenth and early twentieth centuries. Following Mungo Park's demise at Jebba, a series of travellers visited Nupe and Borgu and later penetrated the Emirates further north. Almost all these authors comment on the livestock kept by the peoples in this area, and most mention, normally with disparagement, the small size of the horses. Lander, for example, in the reference quoted above, distinguishes Fulani horses, large in stature, from small but hardy local animals.

Other writers suggest the character and importance of the pony south of the Niger. Clapperton (1829, p. 56), passing through Yoruba in 1826, mentioned that their horses were 'of a very small breed' and slightly further north, in Borgu, described the 'native breed' as 'small, like the Shetland ponies, hardy, active, and generally of a brown or mouse colour'. Bowen (1957, p. 263), in Yoruba in the 1850s, described the Yoruba pony as 'compact' and 'sturdy' and noted the contrast with the large imported animals, either from the coast or further north, then sold in Ilorin for very high prices. The Igala also reserved an important role for the pony in their royal traditions, for mention of it occurs in a number of 'charter-myths' of their clans and kingdoms (Boston 1968, pp. 66, 94, 105). Lander's observations quoted in the epigraph complete the picture.

Among the Nupe at least, no ponies remain. It seems that the replacement of 'small horses' took place at the beginning of the century since even old men retain no memory of them. There are no reports of ponies in either Borgu or Yorubaland in recent years, and it is likely that they were replaced by motor vehicles relatively early.

The pony in central Africa

There are no clear ethnographic records of ponies in the region immediately east of central Nigeria, in Adamawa, although there were ponies in the semi-arid region immediately due north. Ponies were bred in the Mandara mountains and in adjacent Sukur, but they have now all disappeared from this region. However, in the basin of the Chari-Logone region and further east, references to ponies are again abundant and some ponies are still in use. This section reviews the most significant references and oral historical records compiled by Seignobos (1987).

The 'Sara' or 'Laka' pony

A breed closely related to the Plateau pony is described in a number of early texts referring to Adamawa, the Logone and further east. Barth (1857–8, II, p. 374) pictures a Musgu pony rider from present-day northern Cameroon. The rider is armed with a large spear and two of the iron throwing axes common in this area. The horse appears to have no saddle, and there is only a single bridle without a bit. Brunache (1894, p. 267) pictures a 'Gaberi' pony rider from Lai in the Logone region, riding bareback, but with a wicker shield and a throwing axe. Earlier in his text he describes Tumak[?] horsemen. 'Nos trois cavaliers ont encore le type Sara . . . sur leurs petits chevaux nerveux dont on n'aperçoit que la croupe.' He then refers to the Barth account of slashing the back of the pony and remarks that this practice is unknown in the Logone area.

The most complete account of the use of ponies in this area is by Maistre (1895), whose plates (pp. 193, 203, 207 & 211) depict the role of the pony in Gaberi society. The Gaberi are described as 'une tribu de pillards' and they seem to have made a profession of mounted raiding. The engravings show that they rode with a piece of skin as a saddle, wearing only a leather loin-cloth. Their weapons appear to have been the throwing axe and the spear, and some riders also carried wicker shields. There are leather straps around the mouth of the ponies, and these may have been bits corresponding to those described for the Plateau. Certainly only a single rein is depicted. The plate on Maistre's page 203 has a remarkable image of the Gaberi crossing the Logone in canoes on a raiding expedition, pulling the horses behind the canoes. Maistre (1895, p. 209) saw an army of three to four thousand and he estimated that perhaps one third were mounted, so the Gaberi were clearly able to put considerable forces in the field.

Guillard (1965, p. 312) in his ethnography of the Tupuri, based on research in the 1950s, says, 'Les equins sont de race melangé mais chez un certain nombre on relève des traces nettes d'origine Laka (vulgairement appelée "poneys").' Tupuri ponies were equally ridden bareback and were connected with status and wealth. Tessmann (1929, p. 342) refers to the Laka ponies, and this type of animal clearly played an important part in the economy of this area in pre-Islamic times.

The Chamba pony

One of the most poorly documented military expansions in the history of central Africa in the nineteenth century is the Samba Leeko [Chamba] expansion (Fardon 1988). By comparison with their fragmented neighbours in Adamawa, and the adjacent areas of the Cameroon Grassfields, the Chamba cover a considerable area. Yet they never developed any sort of large-scale polity. Early ethnography of the Chamba is limited to a few pages in Meek (1931a, II, pp. 500–3). Fardon's researches show that the Chamba had an aggressive, militarized society, and that their expansion extended into central Cameroon and back into modern-day Nigeria.

The contributors to Tardits (1981a), writing on the ethnohistory of Cameroon, record the traditions of many grasslands peoples of raids by mounted bowmen, in some cases described as the 'People of the Red Mouth'. In a chronological synthesis, Chilver (1981, pp. 460ff) dates the beginnings of the Chamba expansion to the end of the eighteenth century. The Chamba moved into the Benue valley and began raiding the Tiv and associated peoples under leaders whose names are remembered as Gangkwol and Damashi. This finds striking confirmation in the oral traditions of the Tiv collected by Jones (n.d., p. 487), as yet unpublished. The Tiv record that they were scattered by 'Ugenyi' horsemen while they lived in the Obudu region, and that these were followed by FulBe some years later. It is possible that the Chamba were forced to expand their raiding economy by the attacks of the FulBe. They next appear raiding into the Cameroon Grassfields, a decade later. Muhle (1981, p. 392) records the scattering of the We chiefdom in the 1830s by Chamba raiders. Tardits (1981b, p. 405) records their presence in Bamoum in the early nineteenth century.

The pony west of Borgu

The ponies north and west of present-day Nigeria are probably continuous with the Bariba ponies noted by Clapperton. The most well-known representative of this group is the Kotokoli (Doutressolle 1947, p. 252), described in more detail by Schulken (1922). The Kotokoli pony, exceptionally, was used as a pack animal, negotiating the steep mountains. The town of Sansannémango is today controlled by the Anufo people, originally from the eastern side of the Ivory Coast. They arrived in the eighteenth century, originally mercenaries, and their conquest of this area is traditionally bound up with their possession of horses. When the German colonial authorities reached this area, they found them riding very small ponies, bought from local horse traders to replace the large Arab horses they had previously purchased from the Mossi kingdoms to the northwest.

West of Togo the evidence is sparser, for lack of the detailed ethnographic accounts available for the Nigerian area. However, the stock-breeding literature (Pierre 1906; Schulken 1922; Doutresolle 1947) suggests, by the location of the breeds they describe, that conditions for ponies among the traditional peoples of Togo and eastwards may have resembled those on the Jos plateau and in Adamawa. There is no conclusive evidence for recent bareback riding west of the Jos plateau.

References in Arabic sources suggest similar practices to those on the Jos plateau further west. For example, Al-Muhallabi mentions the people of Gao riding bareback, and Al-Umari refers to the mounted bowmen fought by Mansa Musa of Mali. Rodney (1970, p. 12) quotes an account by Almada written in 1594, showing that when the FulBe moved into the Futa Jallon in the 1470s they already had horses. Chronicles from Timbuktu show that cavalry were used in the invasion of the Songhai Empire in 1512. The eighteenth-century empire of Shehu 'Umar Watara based on Kong in the north of the Ivory Coast seems to have been based on both cavalry and firearms. At these late dates, these may have well been large horses, and the techniques of warfare more closely associated with Islam.

The role of horses and ponies in the development of west African state systems

The introduction referred to scholarly discussion of the part played by horses in the formation of west African state systems. First mooted by Goody (1971), it was further amplified in an article by Law (1976), 'Horses, firearms and political power in pre-colonial west Africa'. Goody (1971, p. 36) asserts: 'unlike military technologies based upon the bow and arrow or upon iron infantry weapons, there is a built-in stratification between the horse-soldier and foot-soldier.' From this he argues that the long investment in time required to produce a trained horseman meant that it was likely to be the product of a system geared to the exploitation of surplus production. Part of the response would be the development of a 'knightly ethic'. Consequently, 'the investment of skill and capital was not a free gift to the nation' but had to be paid for by raiding and the resulting booty. The consequent necessity for centralizing authority over horsemen actually put the cavalry in a position to demand a share of political power.

Evidence for this is drawn from the foundation of states like Gonja, in northern Ghana. Tradition states that Gonja was founded by a group of Mande horsemen perhaps in the sixteenth or seventeenth century, and that their possession of horses enabled them to terrorize the surrounding area. Their Mande origin was a matter of tradition, as, before their arrival, they had been at Bondoukou, where they had exchanged their original speech for a Guan language. The state they established was powered by an almost permanent quest for booty and tribute. Acephalous peoples are pictured as having no effective defences against the speed and mobility of even lightly armoured cavalry. As a result, it was argued, some of the peoples in the area attempted to invoke ritual protection against horses, and thus arose a number of 'anti-horse' shrines described in the chapter subtitled 'The opposition of horse and earth'.

This picture has a pleasing logic to it and may well be true as far as Gonja is concerned. However, elsewhere in west Africa, booty-seeking mounted raiders had the inverse effect on their victims. Most interesting is the case of Mankon in the grasslands of Cameroon (Warnier 1981, p. 427), where the Samba began their raids in c. 1825. Warnier argues that the formation of a centralized polity in Mankon was actually a response to raiding by Samba horsemen. The dispersed lineages that previously characterized Mankon were unable to mobilize military defence against mounted raiders, and thus the following years saw a coalescence of the lineages into a political unit familiar from the ethnography of other groups in the Cameroon Grassfields.

The significant feature is its inversion of the model for the relation between the possession of horses and state formation in west Africa. Here, large groups of mounted acephalous raiders attack settled agricultural peoples without horses. The agriculturalists respond by forming a centralized polity, but without gaining access to the horses that would make their arm longer. Meanwhile, the raiders fail to evolve any political structure more elaborate than the raiding band, except perhaps in the case of Bali-Nyonga, a single chiefdom founded in the grasslands some time in the 1830s (Chilver 1981, p. 463). In the main, as Chilver (1981, p. 458) says, 'It must be stressed that the Bani [Samba] were not a single raiding federation but formed of a number of different semi-nomadic bands . . . which combined for particular raids and then dispersed to different camps.' This recalls the Irigwe in central Nigeria who terrorized other Plateau peoples with mounted acephalous raiding bands.

Another exceptional feature of Gonja was that the raiders did not encounter ponies in the hands of non-Muslim groups. However, elsewhere in west Africa, where these were well established, they could mount effective opposition to the freebooters, often by partly adopting their methods. Morrison (1982), in his discussion of resistance to the FulBe jehad in northern Nigeria of the early–mid nineteenth century, shows that the non-Muslim peoples of the Jos plateau were well able to protect themselves against the incursions of slavers such as the Emir Yakubu (1805–45), who operated out of Bauchi. The Anaguta, the Mwahavul and the Berom seem to have used a variety of military technologies, including the bow and arrow, the spear, and the sword. Their defeat of FulBe cavalry (Hayward 1921, pp. 12–13; Morrison 1982, p. 146) suggests that their response was very different from the acephalous groups of the Volta basin.

This variety of weapons makes it difficult to construct a simple opposition of military technology based upon 'the bow and arrow and iron infantry weapons' to one based on horse-soldiers. Morrison concludes: 'as with all broad definitions, neither of these can really be considered politically or militarily significant in regard to the Plateau.' Similarly, in relation to the stratification argument, the example of the Irigwe cited by Morrison (1982, p. 142) suggests that there is no necessary connection between the evolution of an effective cavalry and a hierarchical polity. The Irigwe were (and are) an acephalous, decentralized people living southwest of modern Jos. In the nineteenth century, they controlled an extensive trade network on the Plateau, operating through Zangon Katab. They exchanged their ponies for larger north African-type horses during the course of the century and used them both for defence and raiding, remaining both undefeated and acephalous.

Such societies, with strong individualist ethics, can retain the social patterns even after they gain access to the 'means of destruction'. The Samba example similarly implies that there is no necessary connection between the possession of armed cavalry and state systems, and even that the incursions of such acephalous groups can lead to the formation of centralized polities in reaction to such attacks.

In this context, it is instructive to look again at a classic debate in African historiography. The Kano chronicle mentions the 'Koroafa', a group of mounted raiders who several times inflicted serious damage on the Hausa Emirates, laying waste the hinterland of Kano in the reign of Muhammad Zaki (1562–1618) and in the reign of Kukuna (1652–60), even burning the town. The implication in the chronicle is that these people were non-Muslims. Historians, taking the lead from Palmer, cast around for a large non-Islamic polity to take responsibility for this uncivil act, and identified the Koroafa with the Jukun, whose empire, based on Wukari, was of unknown extent and antiquity.

The underlying assumption was that a large force of mounted raiders must be the attribute of a centralized polity. This was the view of H. R. Palmer, who requested Meek to undertake an ethnographic survey of the Jukun, and wrote the introduction to the published study (Meek 1931b). Despite Meek's overt acceptance (Meek 1931b, pp. 24–9), his text hints at scepticism. For example, he comments on 'the comparative absence of any suggestion that the Jukun were anything but an unwarlike collection of peoples whose sole interest was the maintenance of innumerable religious cults' (Meek 1931b, p. 29). His elaborate comparative tables showing that the lexical bases of the Jukun language were solidly 'West Sudanic' is a covert demonstration that there is nothing exotic about the origin of the Jukun.

However, once it is accepted that mounted raiders do not have to be sent out from a centralized polity, the identification of the Jukun of the Benue valley with the Koroafa becomes irrelevant. It depends on their being breeders and users of horses on a large scale (Law 1980, p. 19), for which it is noticeable that Meek provides no evidence. The Koroafa raiders are more likely to have been raiding bands mounted on ponies like the

Samba and peoples on the Logone. Possible candidates might be the Bacama or the Bade [Bedde], both of whom were raiders in historical times.

Conclusions

This chapter proposes that the ponies of west Africa were produced by the dwarfing of horses brought across the Sahara in the last three thousand years. This contrasts with the large north African horses which seem to have been introduced (with donkeys) in the medieval period. The ponies became trypanotolerant and were able to digest a wide variety of plant foods. They may have become feral and then been redomesticated. A discontinuous band of such dwarfed horses stretches across the continent to Ethiopia.

The importance of ponies in west Africa has been seriously underestimated because the process of replacement by the larger and more prestigious horses brought across the desert was already advanced during the period when the first observers were writing. Nevertheless, during a long period of west African history, raiders mounted on ponies probably terrorized large regions of the savanna, reaching down well into the forest on occasion.

Notes

[1] What follows are two originally distinct papers which the series editor has insisted on combining.

[2] Lake Chad has deliberately been excluded from the base map as it no longer existed as an open body of water in 1990.

[3] This suggestion appears to gain support from recent research on the DNA of west African cattle (D. Bradley, *pers. comm.*).

Acknowledgements

A first version of the second part of this chapter was delivered to the West African Seminar Series, held in the Centre for African Studies, University of Cambridge on 28/1/83. Since then it has been circulated to a number of interested scholars and benefited from their comments. I would like to mention Philip Allsworth-Jones, who first pointed me towards the equid teeth, and Stephen Hall, for useful discussion of dwarfing. Edoardo Gherzi took the time to look for ponies on the Jos plateau in November, 1990.

6   Nilo-Saharans and the Saharo-Sudanese Neolithic

CHRISTOPHER EHRET

Over fifteen years have passed since Sutton first proposed to a conference at the University of California at Los Angeles that Nilo-Saharan-speaking peoples may have been the makers of what he called the 'Aquatic Civilization of Middle Africa' – the development in the eighth to sixth millennium BC of a set of riverine and lakeside food-collecting economies all across the sudanic belt of Africa (Sutton 1974). The pre-eminence of Nilo-Saharan languages in later times in nearly all the areas where the aquatic adaptations had taken hold lent his hypothesis a strong plausibility. But on the linguistic side of the correlation, essential information was then lacking. A detailed subclassification of the Nilo-Saharan family, which would have allowed inferences about the ancient locations of its speech communities, did not exist; and a systematic reconstruction of phonological history and of ancient vocabulary in the family, which would have provided information on early economy, had not yet been undertaken.

The two gaps in the evidence are now being filled. A reconstructed vocabulary of almost 1500 early Nilo-Saharan root words (Ehret In Progress) offers convincing evidence that the key development in early Nilo-Saharan culture history was the adoption or creation of a food-producing way of life and not a water-based, food-collecting economy. The subclassification of the family which has emerged from this work (proposed in Ehret 1989, and further corroborated in Ehret In progress) shows that the early eras of this history were played out in what is today the southern Sahara and Sahel belt, in other words, on the northern margins and to the north of the focal regions of the aquatic adaptations, but exactly in those zones where the Saharo-Sudanese Neolithic tradition prevailed.

Nilo-Saharan subclassification

The subclassification of the family as it presently stands divides Nilo-Saharan into two primary, coordinate branches, with the second of these branches itself dividing into a complex array of branches and subgroups (language names are in italics):

I Koman
  A Southern Koman (Koman proper)
    1 *Kwama*
    2 Southwestern Koman (*Langa*; *Komo*, *Uduk*)
  B *Gumuz* (with several dialects)

II Sudanic
  A Central Sudanic
    1 East Central Sudanic
      a Balese-Momvu (*Balese, Momvu, Mongbutu*)
      b Balendru
      c Moru-Mangbetu
        i   *Mangbetu* (several dialects)
        ii Moru-Madi (*Moru, Madi, Lugbara*, etc.)
    2 West Central Sudanic
      a Kresh-Aja
        i   *Kresh* (several diverse dialects)
        ii *Aja*
      b Bongo-Bagirmi (after Saxon 1980)
        i   Bongo-Baka (*Bongo, Baka, Beli*)
        ii Yulu-Bagirmi
          (1) *Yulu*
          (2) Kara-Bagirmi
            (a) *Kara*
            (b) Sara-Bagirmi (*Sara, Kaba, Bagirmi, Kenga, Bulala*)
  B Northern Sudanic
    1 *Kunama* (with two divergent dialects)
    2 Saharo-Sahelian
      a Saharan (after Saxon n.d.)
        i   Ennedian (*Zaghawa, Berti*)
        ii Bodelean
          (1) Tubu (*Daza, Teda*)
          (2) *Kanuri* (with several dialects, including Kanembu)
      b Sahelian
        i   *For*
        ii   *Songay*
        iii *Maban* (after Saxon n.d.)
          (1) *Maban, Masalit, Runga*
          (2) *Mimi*
        iv   Eastern Sudanic
          (1) Astaboran
            (a) *Nara*
            (b) Western Astaboran
              (i) Taman (*Tama*, etc.)
              (ii) Nubian (*Nobiin, Dongolawi, Birkid, Midob*, etc.)
          (2) Kuliak
            (a) *Ik*
            (b) Western Kuliak (*Soo, Nyang'i*)
          (3) Kir-Abbaian
            (a) Jebel
              (i) *Gaam; Aka*, etc.
              (ii) *Bertha*

(b) Kir
  (i) Nuba Mountains (*Nyimang; Temein*)
  (ii) Daju (*Sila, Lagawa, Liguri,* etc.)
  (iii) Surma-Nilotic
    [α] Surma (*Majang; Didinga; Me'en,* etc.)
    [β] Nilotic (with three branches, Western, Eastern, Southern)

A detailed subclassification of the last division, Kir-Abbaian, is not included here because its subdivisions reflect stages of history later than those dealt with in this chapter. But a partial subclassification is available elsewhere (see Ehret 1983, where the name 'Eastern Sudanic' has unfortunately been applied to the Kir-Abbaian group, and the Kir branch of Kir-Abbaian has even more unfortunately been termed 'Core Eastern Sudanic').

Some idea of the historical complexity and immense time depth represented by the Nilo-Saharan family can be gained, however, by considering the characteristics of the Kir division of Kir-Abbaian. Kir is by itself as complex internally as the whole Indo-European family of languages, and the Proto-Kir language was spoken in about the fifth millennium BC (see below), at least as early as the Proto-Indo-European language. Yet Kir is just one branch of a branch (Kir-Abbaian) of a branch (Eastern Sudanic) of a branch (Sahelian) of a branch (Saharo-Sahelian) of a branch (Northern Sudanic) of one of the two primary branches (Sudanic) of the Nilo-Saharan family as a whole.

Locating early Nilo-Saharan societies

Inferring the probable locations of earlier speech communities is accomplished by applying the principle of least moves to explain the language distributions of subsequent times: the most probable earlier locations are those which require the fewest population movements or cultural-cum-linguistic expansions to account for later locations. The course of argument in such determinations begins normally with the more closely related tongues and proceeds by stages to the more distant.

The Kir-Abbaian group provides a suitable starting point for the process of establishing probable and possible earlier locations of Nilo-Saharan communities. Previous work (Ehret 1983) has shown that the proto-Kir-Abbaian homeland is best located somewhere in the Blue Nile (Abbai) river region of the modern nation of Sudan. Kir-Abbaian is one of three branches of Eastern Sudanic, the others being Astaboran and Kuliak. The modern locations of the languages of the Astaboran branch – along an axis extending from Tama and its related dialects on the east side of J. Marra, to Nara of the far northwestern Ethiopian highlands – suggest an original spread of the languages of that branch out of an intermediate area, just to the north of the lands in which the earliest Kir-Abbaian speakers are most probably to be placed. In other words, the proto-Astaboran society probably lived north of the latitudes of the Blue Nile, perhaps in the plains of the Atbara region or to the west of the Nile in the same latitudes. (The name Astaboran is taken from the ancient recorded form of the name of the Atbara river.) The third branch of Eastern Sudanic, Kuliak, is composed of languages spoken today only in eastern Uganda, far to the south. But the traceability of both the other branches to adjoining areas of northern Sudan indicates that the proto-Eastern Sudanic society, from which all three derive, is also best located in northern Sudan, probably in northeastern or central northern parts of that country. Only one movement, southward out of that region, is then required to account for the Kuliak presence in Uganda (see Fig. 6.5 below for these locations).

The focus of cultural and linguistic divergence in the several eras immediately preceding proto-Eastern Sudanic times apparently lay in those portions of northern Sudan westward from the Nile. The Maban languages are concentrated in and around the Wadai region of Chad, just beyond the western border of Sudan. In addition to its Eastern Sudanic and Maban branches, the Sahelian group has two other branches which each contain only a single language today. Of these, For is spoken in the J. Marra region (Darfur) in western Sudan, just east of the Maban heartland and adjacent to the span of territory to its northeast in which the early Eastern Sudanic speech areas were most probably located. Songay alone is spoken far away from the other three branches, in areas 2000 km to the west near the great bend of the Niger river. As for Eastern Sudanic, so for Sahelian can all but one of its branches thus be traced to adjoining regions, with the distant location of its remaining branch explainable by a single movement away from the others. The proto-Sahelian country thus probably lay somewhere in or around the northwestern quarter of Sudan. The Songay presence far to the west is evidence that the break-up of the proto-Sahelian speech community was accomplished in part by a major expansion of people westward across what is today the Sahel and southern Sahara (see Figs 6.4 and 6.5).

These inferences about the location of the early Sahelian people are further strengthened by the evidence pertaining to the next earlier era of Nilo-Saharan differentiation, in which the Proto-Saharo-Sahelian language was spoken. The Saharo-Sahelian mother language diverged into two daughter languages, one of which was Proto-Sahelian, the homeland of which lay, as has just been proposed, in or around the northwestern parts of Sudan. The other daughter language was Proto-Saharan, from which the present-day Kanuri, Tibu and Zaghawa languages derive. The work of Saxon (n.d.) has shown that the Proto-Saharan language was most probably spoken in the areas extending from Tibesti on the north to Ennedi or J. Marra on the south – in other words, in the northwestern quarter of Chad, just next to the region where its sister language, Proto-Sahelian, was most likely spoken. The proto-Saharo-Sahelian society can therefore also be placed somewhere in the combined regions of northwestern Sudan and northeastern Chad. (For proposed locations of Saharo-Sahelian peoples just after the end of the proto-Saharo-Sahelian period, see Fig. 6.3.)

The three stages of Nilo-Saharan differentiation preceding the proto-Saharo-Sahelian era shift the focus of historical attention back again eastward. Kunama, which along with the Saharo-Sahelian language group derives from the Proto-Northern Sudanic language, is spoken well to the east, adjacent to Nara in the far northwestern Ethiopian highlands. The Central Sudanic group evolved outside the northern zones of Sudan – the proto-Central Sudanic territory having lain somewhere in or near the Bahr-al-Ghazal areas of far southern Sudan (Ehret, Coffman, Fliegelman, Gold, Hubbard,

Johnson & Saxon 1974). But the Koman languages, which by themselves form one of the two primary branches of the Nilo-Saharan family, occupy a relatively restricted set of areas, along the Blue Nile (Abbai) and its tributaries in far western Ethiopia in the case of the Gumuz, and along the middle parts of the Sudan–Ethiopian border south of the Blue Nile in the case of the Southern Koman. These areas lie roughly at the same longitudes as the Kunama territory and only a few hundred kilometres south of it.

Applying the principle of least moves, the most elegant explanation of these language distributions is that the original proto-Nilo-Saharan lands lay in northern Sudan, perhaps in the general region of the Blue Nile between the Ethiopian highlands and the White Nile. The proto-Nilo-Saharan society then diverged into a pre-Koman grouping nearer the highlands and a proto-Sudanic society nearer the White Nile. A single southward expansion of some of the proto-Sudanic people gave rise to a society out of which the proto-Central Sudanic community would eventually evolve after several thousand years of separate history. Those Sudanic people who continued to reside in northern Sudan became, after an indeterminate period, the proto-Northern Sudanic speech community. A further single era of population movement then spread Northern Sudanic communities across a long east–west belt of territory (see Fig. 6.2). The proto-Saharo-Sahelian society took shape among those who settled towards the western end of this stretch, near the Tibesti region. The Kunama presumably derive their language from those groups who formed the eastern periphery of this dispersal. The actual limits of the Northern Sudanic expansion surely reached northward well into what is today the Sahara desert. For at the eastern extreme ancient Kunama loan-words can be found in the Cushitic Beja language of the Red Sea hinterland (Ehret, research in progress); at the west the inferred location of the proto-Saharan speech community in northern Chad similarly places early Saharo-Sahelian populations in the Sahara.

Reconstructing domestic economy in the early Nilo-Saharan eras

From the proto-Northern Sudanic period onward food production was of increasing importance in the domestic economy of Nilo-Saharans. The evidence for this trend of development comes from reconstructed early Nilo-Saharan vocabularies.

A particular root word can be reconstructed as part of the vocabulary of a proto-language if it meets two criteria, one distributional and the other phonological. First the root must be found in languages belonging to at least two of the coordinate branches of the language group in question. For example, for a root to be traceable back to Proto-Northern Sudanic, it must occur in Kunama, which constitutes one of the two branches of Northern Sudanic, and also in at least one of the languages of the second branch, Saharo-Sahelian. Second, a general characteristic of languages is that phonological change – shifts in the pronunciation of the particular vowels, consonants and tone or stress which make up words – proceeds over the long term according to regular patterns. If a root word of a proto-language continuously has been retained in the vocabulary of an evolving descendant language, then the pronunciation of that root in that language must necessarily conform to the patterns of sound shift by which the language evolved out of the proto-language. Among Indo-European languages, for instance, Proto-Indo-European *p remained *p* in Latin at the beginning of words, but shifted to *f in Germanic; hence, where Latin had *pater*, English has father. The sound shift is thus regular: it conforms to the relevant pattern of sound correspondence between Latin and English.

If the same root occurs in two related languages, but the sound shift patterns are violated in some way, then the word at issue generally must be inferred to have been adopted ('borrowed') by one language from the other at some point in time since they both began to diverge out of their common proto-language. The direction of borrowing can be determined by identifying which language's patterns of sound shift occur in the borrowed word. English *paternal*, for instance, derives from the same Indo-European root as *father*, but conforms to Latin sound shift patterns, *inter alia* by retaining *p*; hence it must be a Latin loan-word in English.

Once in a while the application of these two criteria is not quite enough to allow confident reconstruction of a root. What happens is that occasionally a word may be borrowed early in a history of language divergence, when sound shifts which would otherwise be diagnostic of its 'borrowedness' have not yet taken place in either the borrowing or the 'lending' language. The forms of the root in the two languages will therefore show apparently regular sound correspondences and falsely appear to be independent preservations of a root found in their common proto-language. For preliterate eras this problem in analysis normally arises only in cases of languages which are or were in the past neighbours, because word-borrowing in such eras requires face-to-face contact between speakers of different languages.

The problem case for this phenomenon in Nilo-Saharan is that of Kunama and Nara, which have borrowed a considerable number of words from one another. The two languages belong to different primary branches of the Northern Sudanic group (see subclassification above), but they are spoken in adjoining territories today and probably have been in much the same locations for several thousand years. The attribution to Proto-Northern Sudanic of a root found today *only* in those two can be made only after extremely careful consideration, even if the phonological correspondences appear unexceptionable. A second set of Nilo-Saharan languages among which this problem can sometimes arise is composed of Maban, For, certain nearby Saharan tongues and the Tama and Nubian subgroups of Astaboran, all of which are spoken in or near the Darfur-Wadai regions or, like Nubian, have probable earlier ancestry in those regions. The problem has been avoided here by the simple requirement that, to be reconstructible to an early node on the tree of Nilo-Saharan relationships, a root occurring in languages of either of these two areal groupings must also be found in other, geographically more distant languages of the family.

The onset of food production among Nilo-Saharans

The earliest point in the differentiation of the Nilo-Saharan languages to which some practice of food production can be traced is Proto-Northern Sudanic. For the next successive periods of Proto-Saharo-Sahelian and Proto-Sahelian, the volume of reconstructible vocabulary which is unambiguously indicative of food production continues to increase. It might be thought at first glance that the increase reflects simply greater retention of evidence because the latter two periods are more recent in time. But one key repeated feature of the evidence makes this explanation untenable: at each of the three successive periods, the newly identifiable evidence includes one or more coherent bodies of new vocabulary expressing a suite of practices or knowledge not found at all in the vocabulary reconstructible for the immediately preceding era.

To the Proto-Northern Sudanic language can be attributed the following subsistence vocabulary (with known distributions of each in brackets):

1 *ṇdɔw 'to milk' [Kunama; Eastern Sudanic (Tama; Gaam; Kuliak)]
2 *su:k 'to drive (domestic animals)' [Kunama; Saharan; Eastern Sudanic (Nubian)]
3 *a:yr 'cow' [Kunama; Eastern Sudanic (Nara; Southern Nilotic of Kir group)]
4 *Way 'grain' [Kunama; For; Eastern Sudanic]
5 *ke:n 'ear of grain' [Kunama; Songay]
6 *p'ɛl 'grindstone' [Kunama; Eastern Sudanic (Western Nilotic of Kir group)]

Of these six roots, only the first two are actually diagnostic of food production. Together with the third item, they indicate that proto-Northern Sudanians raised at least some cattle. The root for 'cow' is not diagnostic by itself of food production since cattle would have been known in wild form to early Nilo-Saharans if they lived far enough north in the modern Saharan zones; and the three grain terms would have been as necessary to the vocabulary of wild grain collectors as to that of the cultivators of domestic grains.

Two other Proto-Northern Sudanic roots deserve notice for their archaeological implications:

7 *sa:p or *sa:B 'temporary shelter' [Kunama; Songay; Eastern Sudanic (Southern Nilotic)]
8 *ted 'to make pot' [Kunama; For; Maban; Eastern Sudanic (Western Nilotic)]

No word for any kind of more permanent structure, such as a house, can yet be reconstructed for the Proto-Northern Sudanic language or for the two earlier periods of Nilo-Saharan history. One additional root word applying to an earthenware container may be traceable back to the proto-Sudanic era, however. Its suggested reflexes are Kunama doša 'earthenware bowl' and Proto-Central Sudanic *jɔ or *dzɔ 'water pot'. Its validity remains uncertain because its postulation requires some sound shifts which, though probably regular, are not yet fully substantiated. If it is a validly reconstructible root, it would show the invention of pottery among Nilo-Saharans to predate the Northern Sudanic period and the appearance of cattle-raising. An interesting possibility, in view of the meanings of the Kunama and Central Sudanic terms, is that the earliest ceramic vessels may not have been used for cooking.

In the Proto-Saharo-Sahelian vocabulary two new suites of meanings appear, one with direct and one with indirect implications of the presence of food production. For the first time unambiguous evidence of cultivation turns up, in the form of four verbs referring specifically to agricultural activities, and of a noun for 'cultivated field':

9 *dipʰ 'to cultivate' [Saharan; Songay; Eastern Sudanic (Gaam)]

10 *tɔ:k(ɔ:p) 'to cultivate' [Saharan; *Songay*; Eastern Sudanic (Kuliak)]

11 *p'ad or *pad or *Bad 'to prepare field' [Saharan; Eastern Sudanic (Southern Nilotic)]

12 *kʰay 'to clear (weeds, stubble, etc.)' [Sahara; *Songay*; Eastern Sudanic]

13 *ɗomp 'cultivated field' [Saharan; Eastern Sudanic (Kir)]

Two other verb roots covering aspects of grain preparation, which could as well have been needed by wild grain collectors, can also be reconstructed:

14 *ŋak or *ŋaG 'to grind (grain) coarsely' [Saharan; Eastern Sudanic (Western Nilotic)]

15 *pʰeθ 'to winnow' [Saharan; *Songay*; Eastern Sudanic (Nilotic)]

The second new suite of meanings implies the existence of good-sized and relatively complex settlements among the proto-Saharo-Sahelians:

16 *ɓoreh 'thornbush cattle pen' [Saharan; Eastern Sudanic (Kuliak; Surma of Kir group)]

17 *kʰal 'fence' [Saharan; *Songay*; Eastern Sudanic (Western Nilotic)]

18 *Dɔŋ 'yard, enclosure of homestead' [Saharan: *For*; Eastern Sudanic (Kir-Abbaian)]

19 *ɗor 'open area of settlement' [Saharan; Eastern Sudanic (Nubian; Kir-Abbaian)]

20 *p'er or *per 'granary' [Saharan; *For*]

No root word for 'house' can yet be included in this set, but one piece of indirect evidence, a word for a particular item of house construction, suggests that the Saharo-Sahelians already built the round, conical-roofed house so typical of Sudanic architecture in more recent times:

21 *ɗoŋk'ol 'circular roll of grass which supports roof of round house' [Saharan; Eastern Sudanic (Western Nilotic)]

Additional herding vocabulary can also be identified for Proto-Saharo-Sahelian. As for the proto-Northern Sudanic period, the raising only of cattle is indicated:

22 *yokw 'to herd' [Saharan; *Songay*; Eastern Sudanic (Southern and Eastern Nilotic of Kir group; Kuliak)]

23 *pʰe:r 'cattle' or 'herd' [Saharan; Eastern Sudanic (Southern Nilotic)]

24 *ŋgɛt' 'to milk' [Saharan; Eastern Sudanic (Western Nilotic)]

25 *tʰa 'milk' [Saharan; Eastern Sudanic (Nara; Western Nilotic)]

In Proto-Sahelian vocabulary, however, a quite different suite of meanings relating to livestock raising makes its appearance: for the first time the keeping of goats and sheep can be attributed to Nilo-Saharan peoples:

26 *ay or *hay 'goat' [*For*; Eastern Sudanic (Kir-Abbaian)]

27 *gent 'he-goat' [*Songay*; Eastern Sudanic (Kuliak)]

28 *Wɛr 'sheep' [*For*; Eastern Sudanic (Nubian; Kir-Abbaian; Kuliak)]

29 *meŋkʰ 'ram' or 'sheep' [Maban ('sheep'); Eastern Sudanic ('ram')]

30 *Wel 'ram' [*For*; Eastern Sudanic (Daju of Kir group; Kuliak)]

31 *k'er 'ewe-lamb(?)' [*Songay* 'female kid'; Eastern Sudanic (Kir 'sheep')]

32 *ɗaw 'lamb(?)' [Maban; Eastern Sudanic (*Nara*; Nilotic)]

33 *θagw 'young male goat or sheep (?)' [*Songay*; Eastern Sudanic (Kir)]

Four additional items of herding terminology, referring to cattle, also turn up in Proto-Sahelian:

34 * t̪ ɛ or * t̪ ɛh 'cow' [Maban; Eastern Sudanic (Western Astaboran; Kir-Abbaian)]

35 *oWiŋ 'bull' [*For*; Eastern Sudanic (Eastern Nilotic of Kir group)]

36 *ma:wr 'ox' [Maban; Eastern Sudanic (Kir)]

37 *yagw or *yakw 'young cow (heifer?)' [*Songay*; Eastern Sudanic (Nubian; Southern Nilotic)]

If these are not older Saharo-Sahelian roots which were dropped from use in the Saharan branch, then they may well reflect a growth in the socio-economic importance of cattle in proto-Sahelian times.

A second distinctive set of meanings appearing for the first time in the Proto-Sahelian reconstructions relates to cucurbits:

38 *ɗuT 'a kind of calabash' [*Songay*; Eastern Sudanic (Kuliak)]

39 *kʰul 'a kind of gourd' [*Songay*; Eastern Sudanic (Nilotic)]

40 *Kɛdɛh 'bottle gourd' [*For*; Eastern Sudanic (Nilotic)]

41 *buḓ 'edible gourd' [*For*; Eastern Sudanic (Kir)]

A plausible explanation of this new suite of terms is that the domestication of wild African gourd species had taken place and that by the close of proto-Sahelian times the variety of gourd shapes and sizes so typical of Sudanic agriculture in later eras was already beginning to appear.

Other reconstructible Proto-Sahelian terms reflect the continuing importance of cultivation and relatively sedentary habits:

42 *pʰad 'to cultivate' [*Songay*; *For*; Eastern Sudanic (Southern Nilotic)]

43 *tʰaypʰ 'to clear ground in cultivation' [*Songay*; Eastern Sudanic (Kir-Abbaian; Kuliak)]

44 *t'um 'to sow, plant' [*Songay*; Eastern Sudanic (Gaam)]

45 *pʰa:l 'bush, uncultivated land' [*For*; Eastern Sudanic (Kir-Abbaian)]

46 *tʰɛ:r or *t'ɛ:r 'prepared grain' [*For*; Eastern Sudanic (Nubian; Kir-Abbaian)]

47 *p'ent'uh 'winnowing tray' [*Songay*; Eastern Sudanic (Western Nilotic)]

48 *hwe 'house' [*Songay*; Eastern Sudanic (Kir-Abbaian; Kuliak)]

49 *ka: or *ka:h 'residence, settlement' [*Songay*; Eastern Sudanic (Nubian; Southern Nilotic)]

Any *individual* reconstructed root, it should be noted, might have come into use a stage or two earlier than the extant evidence allows, depending on the vagaries of word retention in particular languages. Specifically, a root word might have been present in a certain proto-language but happen to have been preserved in use only in languages belonging to one of the primary branches into which the descendant tongues of that proto-language diverged. Known to the modern-day scholar in just the one branch, the root could be reconstructed back to the proto-language of the branch, but no further.

Of course, the more branches into which a proto-language has diverged, the less the chance that a root will be retained in only one branch. Similarly, the greater the number of languages in a branch, the less the chance of a root's entire disappearance from that branch, simply because there are more languages in which it could be preserved. The one case where the effects of normal vocabulary attrition might seriously detract from cultural reconstructibility would thus be that of the Kunama branch of Northern Sudanic, which consists of a single surviving language (with two divergent dialects, however). Many root words actually present in the Proto-Northern Sudanic language have surely dropped from use during the millennia since Kunama began to diverge out of that tongue, and some of those undoubtedly had economic connotations. A root like *p^he:r 'cattle' (no. 23), reconstructible on its present distribution to Proto-Saharo-Sahelian, could conceivably be such an item, lost in Kunama but not in all the Saharo-Sahelian tongues.

But while the disappearance of any single root word can be an entertainable conjecture in data such as these, it strains credibility to suppose that a whole mutually connected suite of items could be retained in one branch but dropped without trace in its sister branch, even if that branch did consist of just one language. A case in point is the set of five Saharo-Sahelian roots (nos. 9–13) requiring the proto-Saharo-Sahelian practice of cultivation. Not even one root word necessitating cultivation can be reconstructed back to Proto-Northern Sudanic, yet five can be postulated for Saharo-Sahelian. Kunama does maintain Proto-Northern Sudanic roots indicating subsistence use of grains (nos. 4–6), but not any requiring their cultivation. If just random vocabulary attrition were involved, Kunama should have preserved the one kind of root word as commonly or as uncommonly as the other. The semantic patterning in the retentions thus most probably reflects a material reality: that grains were known and used as food at the proto-Northern Sudanic period but not cultivated until after that time. By the same reasoning, the contrastive implications of the one root word for a structure in Proto-Northern Sudanic (no. 7) and the set of six roots indicative of structures and settlement layout in Proto-Saharo-Sahelian (nos. 16–21) show that a transformation in residence pattern, size and permanence took place between the two periods. Similarly, the existence of six terms referring to sheep and goats in Proto-Sahelian, and of *zero* terms reconstructible to *any* previous Nilo-Saharan era, must be taken as presumptive evidence for the introduction of sheep and goats after the end of the proto-Saharo-Sahelian period and before the end of the proto-Sahelian era.

The data from the more distantly related Koman and Central Sudanic branches of the family reinforce the inference that the Northern Sudanic period was the earliest time of food production among Nilo-Saharans. In both Koman and Central Sudanic the verb vocabularies diagnostic of food production appear, with one exception, to be entirely distinct from those of Kunama and Saharo-Sahelian. The exception, Proto-Central Sudanic *jɔ 'to milk', only strengthens the case, because it is demonstrably a borrowing of the Proto-Northern Sudanic root for that meaning (no. 1), specifically from an early language of the Eastern Sudanic subgroup of Saharo-Sahelian. Its pronunciation in Central Sudanic should have been *nzɔ, and in fact this very root shape can be reconstructed for Proto-Central Sudanic but in what must have been close to its original pre-food-productive meaning, 'to squeeze'. Apparently Central Sudanic preserved the Nilo-Saharan root in its pre-agricultural meaning and at the same time readopted that very root in a new form and meaning from Eastern Sudanic speakers, presumably as a linguistic reflection of the adoption of the trait of milking from the Eastern Sudanians.

Noun roots diagnostic of food production show a very few instances of overlap in distribution between Koman or Central Sudanic and other Nilo-Saharan tongues, but in almost every case phonology or distribution clearly indicates a loan-word origin for the Koman and Central Sudanic forms. One root, Proto-Kir *nay 'goat', turns up in the West branch of Central Sudanic as *-nɛ and possibly in some Koman languages as *nia (*niah?). The vowel lacks proper correspondence in the Koman cases, and so the Koman form must be either a loan, though from which language is unclear, or else a chance resemblance, perhaps of imitative origin (imitative of bleating). The Central Sudanic form, in contrast, has apparent proper correspondence throughout; but since the root is otherwise completely restricted to Kir languages and the Central Sudanic homeland lay in the Bahr-al-Ghazal, just south of the southern fringe of early Kir-Abbaian expansion (Ehret 1983), a diffusion of the term with the southward diffusion of the goat must be suspected. What increases the probability of Kir influence in the spread of the word is the presence of other Kir loan-words in West Central Sudanic (most notably *poɗu 'fire': Ehret In Progress).

Two other root words of food-productive implication known from East Central Sudanic languages – *bilɔ 'sheep' in the Moru-Madi subgroup, and *kala 'thornbush cattle pen' in Moru-Madi and Balendru – are transparently loan-words because of their irreducibly biconsonantal structures. A distinguishing feature of Proto-Central Sudanic was its conversion of all its inherited Nilo-Saharan roots of biconsonantal shape into the shorter shape CV (consonant plus vowel), and these two roots do not conform to that regular pattern. The *bilɔ root is limited elsewhere to the Astaboran branch of Eastern Sudanic (Nara *bile* 'goat'; Tama *bili* 'sheep' etc.), with the Western Astaboran attestations (as in Tama) having the same meaning as the Moru-Madi borrowing and being thus the probable source from which the term diffused to Central Sudanians. The *kala root, on the other hand, is an adoption of the Proto-Saharo-Sahelian *kʰal 'fence' (no. 17), but with the meaning it has in the neighbouring Western Nilotic languages.

In that same meaning, 'thornbush cattle pen', it has also been borrowed into Uduk of Koman. Phonology again certifies its loan-word origin: the regular sound correspondences of Uduk should yield *kʰal instead of the actual Uduk pronunciation *kal*. In both cases the Western Nilotes, who occupy the whole Middle Nile basin between the Moru-Madi lands on the southwest and the Koman territories at the northeast of the basin, are surely the source of the loans.

A further root word, *ti 'cow' in East Central Sudanic, must be reckoned a loan-word in Central Sudanic languages, also for the reason that it lacks regular correspondence with the Sahelian * tɛ or * tɛh (no. 34). Its apparent source was an early Astaboran language (Ehret In Progress). Its historical implications thus are in keeping with those of the borrowed Central Sudanic *jɔ 'to milk' – namely, that livestock-raising diffused to proto-Central Sudanic peoples from other Nilo-Saharans, specifically from Eastern Sudanians living to the north of them in the Sudan belt.

To sum up, the linguistic evidence shows that the earliest Nilo-Saharan societies were food collectors. The first development of food production took place among the proto-Northern Sudanic people, who kept some cattle but probably collected grains rather than cultivated them. Some time later a descendant society of the Northern Sudanians, the proto-Saharo-Sahelians, began to cultivate grains as well as keep cattle. Still later, in the subsequent proto-Sahelian period, goats and sheep were added to the herds, and gourds and calabashes began to be cultivated in some variety alongside the grains. Only at a markedly later time, probably not until after Proto-Eastern Sudanic had broken up into its three branches (see tree of relationship below) did knowledge of this mixed agriculture spread far south of the Sahel and reach the proto-Central Sudanic people of the Bahr-al-Ghazal region. The stage at which the Koman adopted food production is not evident yet; but as their territories lie much closer to the areas of old Northern Sudanic and Saharo-Sahelian food production, the transition may have begun much earlier for them than for Central Sudanians.

Dating early Nilo-Saharan food production

To seek correlation between these findings and archaeology, it becomes necessary to propose some kind of absolute dating, however rough and tentative, for the linguistically attested stages of the Nilo-Saharan development of mixed agriculture. For a distinct stage of language differentiation to be still clearly recognizable at so far a remove from the present as those eras – for sufficient recoverable evidence of the stage to have survived the inevitable attritions of time – a minimum of several centuries' accumulation of linguistic change and innovation would normally be required. A reasonable dating assumption, providing a time span minimally sufficient to meet this requirement while by its vagueness conceding the large degree of guesswork involved, would set a base allowance of half a millennium for each period. Some stages, rather more strongly marked in the evidence, would need to be allowed longer-than-base spans of time. The separation of Proto-Saharo-Sahelian from its immediate ancestor Proto-Northern Sudanic, quite sharply indicated (Ehret 1989) considering its distance in time from the present, is one such case. And the evidence distinguishing the Kir-Abbaian group from the other two Eastern Sudanic branches, even taking account of its being some stages later in time than Proto-Saharo-Sahelian, seems sufficiently greater than that for the two periods on either side of it (Ehret 1983; Ehret 1989) that again a longer-than-base period should be assumed to separate Proto-Kir-Abbaian from the earlier proto-Eastern Sudanic era.

Applying these chronological assumptions begins, as in the inferring of the earlier locations of Nilo-Saharan communities, with the Kir-Abbaian branch of Eastern Sudanic, although in this instance with a particular subgroup of Kir-Abbaian, Nilotic. The proto-Nilotic period, which was three stages of differentiation later in history than the proto-Kir-Abbaian era (Ehret 1983), can with considerable confidence be placed in the chronological vicinity of the middle of the fourth millennium BC (Ehret 1982b, based on cross-ties between relative time-scales for different eastern African language groups and on dated archaeological correlations for some of the cross-ties). Applying

the base allowance of a half millennium per stage, the proto-Kir era at two stages before
Proto-Nilotic would fit roughly in the middle of the fifth millennium, while Proto-Kir-
Abbaian would belong to the centuries around 5000 BC. Proto-Eastern Sudanic, argued
above to have been separated by a longer-than-base period from Proto-Kir-Abbaian,
would date to the early sixth millennium, and the proto-Sahelian period would be
placed close to the middle of the seventh millennium. Proto-Saharo-Sahelian times
would consequently be set at about 7000 BC, but the presumed longer separation
between the Saharo-Sahelian and Northern Sudanic eras would push the proto-
Northern Sudanic period back to the earlier eighth millennium or the ninth millennium
BC.

The tree diagram on p. 117 (Fig. 6.1) arranges the stages of Nilo-Saharan differentiation according to this provisional, estimated chronology. It hardly needs saying that
these dating estimates are the most tentative of propositions. While the relative time-
scale is solid, the spacing of absolute dates and the absolute scale as a whole could be off
by centuries. The direction of error, however, is much more likely to be towards
underestimation than overestimation of the time spans involved.

Nilo-Saharans and the archaeology of the Saharo-Sudanese Neolithic

Combining the inferences as to past Nilo-Saharan territories, the evidence of economy
and habitation offered by vocabulary reconstruction and the estimations of possible
time depths within the family, it becomes possible to outline what the correlative
material manifestations of this linguistically attested history ought to be, and where and
when they most probably might be found.

At the proto-Northern Sudanic period, the first evidence of a food-producing
economy with limited cattle-raising should appear in the archaeology. The habitations
of this era are likely to have been impermanent structures, the accompaniment of what
may have been a transhumant way of life. Grindstones, indicative probably of the
collection of wild grains rather than of cultivation, and pottery should also appear in
sites of this era. This economy and culture should exist by some time around 8000 BC or
before, possibly centred initially on far northern Sudan and spreading out subsequently
across the larger region of the southern Sahara, from the Red Sea hills and the corner of
the Ethiopian highlands on the east, to at least as far west as the areas around Tibesti
(see Fig. 6.2).

The addition of cattle-keeping in the proto-Northern Sudanic period presumes a pre-
Northern Sudanic era in which the Nilo-Saharan communities of the time practised a
purely collecting economy, gathering wild grains among other foods. Thus the sites of
the culture in its pre-proto-Northern phase are likely to resemble fairly closely those of
the proto-Northern Sudanic period itself, with grindstones and – if the possible
Proto-Sudanic root for 'earthenware vessel' is a valid reconstruction – pottery, but
without domestic cattle. The possible geographical extent of this postulated pre-proto-
Northern culture or complex of cultures is not indicated in the surviving language
evidence (see Fig. 6.2).

A number of centuries after the proto-Northern Sudanic era came to an end, roughly

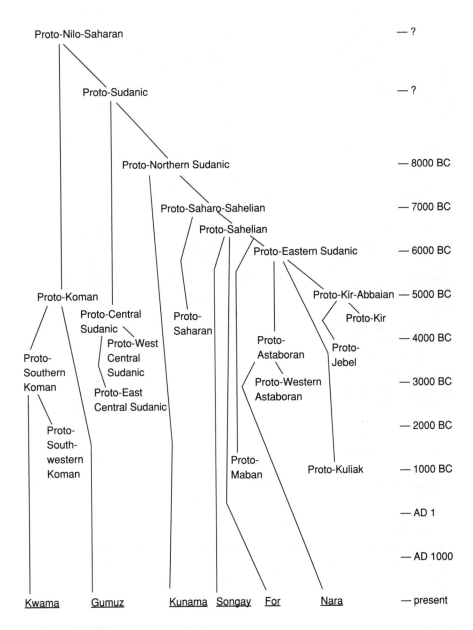

Figure 6.1 The stages of Nilo–Saharan chronological differentiation.

(The chronological placements of Proto–Saharan and Proto–Maban are from Saxon n.d.; of Koman, Jebel and Astaboran, from glottochronological estimates based on data in Bender 1971; of Central Sudanic, from Ehret unpublished work; and of Kuliak, from Ehret 1982b.)

perhaps in the later eighth millennium BC, a more evolved food-producing economy would have been taking shape among the Proto-Saharo-Sahelian-speaking descendants of the earlier Northern Sudanians. The focal area of this second era of food production can be expected to have lain west of the Nile, possibly in northeastern Chad, northwestern Sudan and adjoining parts of Libya and Egypt. The settlements of this era should be larger, more complex and more permanent than those in the preceding Northern Sudanic times, including such structures as round houses, granaries and thornbush cattle pens. In addition to cattle bones, grindstones and pottery, evidence of cultivated grain of some kind should turn up in sites of the period (see Fig. 6.2).

Still later, possibly around the mid-seventh millennium BC, a third stage in the development of food production should begin to appear, attributable to the proto-Sahelian communities, themselves descendants of the Saharo-Sahelians. Again the seminal area of the new developments probably lay to the west of the Nile, possibly in and around northwestern Sudan. But very soon this third stage of food-producing economy and culture must have been spread by various Sahelian speakers far to the west across the southern Sahara, as far possibly as modern western Niger within a few centuries. The salient development in food production in this era would have been the addition of goats and sheep to an already cattle-raising and grain-cultivating economy. The first evidence of cultivation of cucurbits, or at least of their cultivation in any quantity and variety, is likely also to turn up on sites of this period (see Fig. 6.4).

Thereafter, down at least to the proto-Kir period, i.e. until possibly as late as the mid-fifth millennium, Nilo-Saharan food-producing peoples probably expanded relatively little beyond their already extensive territories. On the whole the Sahelian societies of the Sahel and Sahara zones entered into an era very probably characterized for the most part by *in situ*, gradually increasing ethnic and cultural differentiation, with new crops perhaps being added but no major economic transformations intruding (see Fig. 6.5).

This sequence of developments adduced by the linguistic arguments has a strikingly good fit geographically and chronologically with what is known so far of the Saharo-Sudanese Neolithic tradition of the southern Sahara. Currently, the sites indicative of significant changes within the tradition are scattered and few. Once the Saharo-Sudanese world is more fully mapped and dated, the correlations may seem less convincing; but on present knowledge the parallels between the two kinds of evidence are very close indeed.

The earliest Saharo-Sudanese sites currently known date to around the second half of the eighth millennium BC and come from two separate areas, far distant from each other. Those from the far west, in the Aïr of Niger, have grindstones and pottery belonging to the Saharo-Sudanese complex and thus fit the model proposed for the immediate pre-proto-Northern Sudanic era. The contemporary sites to the east, in far southwestern Egypt, also have grindstones and pottery (although its connection to the Saharo-Sudanese complex is in question), as well as bovid bones which are quite reasonably argued by their discoverers to be those of relatively recently domesticated cattle (Wendorf, Schild & Close 1984; radiocarbon dates in this section come from the summary articles of Close 1980 and 1984 and McIntosh & McIntosh 1986a). The materials of the eastern sites match up, in other words, with what the linguistic evidence requires of proto-Northern Sudanic livelihood, and they are located in roughly the time and place predicted for that culture (Fig. 6.2).

The dates would presumably correspond even more closely if the radiocarbon dating could be calibrated. Such dates become progressively younger than the equivalent calendar dates before about two thousand years ago, diverging most rapidly between the late second millennium and the first half of the fourth millennium BC, by which time the radiocarbon dates are eight centuries too young. From then into the sixth millennium the divergence barely increases. Effective calibration cannot be carried back to 8000 BC as yet (Pearson 1987), but even if the dating divergence happens to shrink, the equivalent radiocarbon dates for that era would still have to be a number of centuries too young. Dates between 8950 and 9450 bp would thus very probably reflect actual dates in the early eighth or in the ninth millennium BC for the earliest Saharo-Sudanese finds.

By no later than the first half of the seventh millennium bp, i.e. in probably the eighth millennium BC, cattle bones are also attested at a Saharo-Sudanese site in the far southwest of Libya (Ti-n-Torha Two Caves). Within a few centuries, it would seem, the cattle-keeping version of the Saharo-Sudanese Neolithic had spread across a wide area of the southern Sahara. Except for reaching somewhat further west, beyond the Tibesti region, this expansion is exactly what the linguistic arguments require as the outcome of the differentiation of the proto-Northern Sudanians into daughter societies, and the dating fits as well (Fig. 6.2).

The next two stages of salient correlation between linguistic and archaeological findings depend on recent discoveries from a limited portion of the southern Sahara belt; but the succession of developments in the archaeology of that area, the far south of Egypt, match at key points with the linguistically generated expectations. Until late in the seventh millennium bp (uncalibrated radiocarbon dates) – presumably therefore very early in the millennium in calendar dating, if not before – the cattle-keeping and, apparently, grain-collecting variety of the Saharo-Sudanese Neolithic prevailed in the region. At that point in time a strikingly different version of the Saharo-Sudanese tradition appeared, with precisely the features linguistically reconstructible for the proto-Saharo-Sahelian society and its offshoots – large settlements with granaries and clear evidence of cultivated grain in addition to cattle (Fig. 6.3). The archaeological dating of the change-over is, again, closely in line with what was expected linguistically.

Following this period of early Saharo-Sudanese cultivation in the far south of Egypt came a period of uncertain length, possibly beginning in the first half of the sixth millennium bp, hence probably actually the middle seventh millennium BC, in which goats or sheep finally appear in the material record. Once more this addition to the economy fits the requirements of the linguistic evidence, which shows both goats and sheep becoming part of Nilo-Saharan subsistence by no later than the proto-Sahelian period, which followed the proto-Saharo-Sahelian era and is estimated to have been about the mid-seventh millennium. The linguistic evidence also suggests something not yet followed up in archaeological investigations: thus this period may have seen the domestication of indigenous cucurbits in the Saharo-Sudanese Neolithic (Fig. 6.4).

In tabular form the parallels between the archaeology of the extreme southwest of Egypt (using the terminology of Wendorf, Schild & Close 1984) and the linguistically derived Nilo-Saharan culture history appear as follows:

Archaeological culture	*Linguistically attested culture*
Early Neolithic of el Adam type date: 9450–8950 bp (8000+ BC?);	proto–Northern Sudanic possible date: early eighth or late ninth millennium BC;
features: pottery, cattle, grindstones; ephemeral settlements?	features: pottery, cattle, grindstones; transhumant settlement?
Early Neolithic of el Kortein type date: 8750–8450 bp (mid–eighth millennium BC?); features: cattle; pottery?	
Early Neolithic of el Ghorab type date: 8450–8150 bp (late eighth millennium BC?); features: cattle, pottery, grindstones	
Early Neolithic of el Nabta type date: 8050–7850 bp (late eighth, seventh millennium BC?); features: cattle, pottery, six-row barley, grindstones, granaries, bigger more complex settlement	proto-Saharo-Sahelian possible date: *c.* 7000 BC; features: cattle, pottery, grain cultivation, grindstones, settlements with round houses, thornbush cattle pens, and granaries
Middle Neolithic date: 7650?–7050 bp (6600?–5100 BC) added features: sheep and/or goats	proto-Sahelian possible date: mid–seventh millennium BC; added features: sheep and goats, cultivation of gourds/calabashes

The consistently parallel testimonies of the two kinds of evidence would seem to establish beyond a reasonable doubt the broad correlation of Nilo-Saharan peoples and Saharo-Sudanese cultures. The makers and movers of the Saharo-Sudanese Neolithic, so widespread across the southern Saharan zones, in a variety of phases and facies, from at least the eighth millennium bp (ninth millennium BC?), must in general have been speakers of Nilo-Saharan languages. The different kinds of linguistic evidence place Nilo-Saharan peoples across the same regions of Africa as those in which archaeology locates the Saharo-Sudanese tradition, and places them there during the same long span of time. Moreover, these data require the same sequence of subsistence developments among Nilo-Saharans, down to details of material culture, as the archaeology reveals for the Saharo-Sudanese Neolithic, at least in its manifestations in the far south of Egypt. Throughout, it is with stages in the evolution of food production, and not with aquatic food-collecting, that the early Nilo-Saharan peoples must be associated.

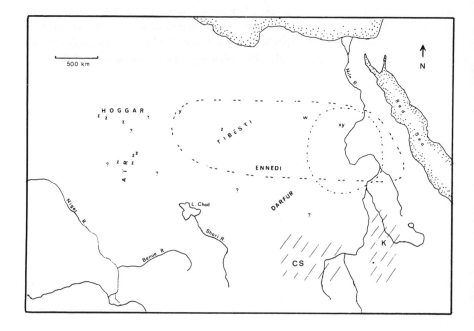

Figure 6.2 Saharo–Sudanese Neolithic sites and proposed Nilo-Saharan speech areas in the eighth and early seventh millennium bc (ninth millennium BC).

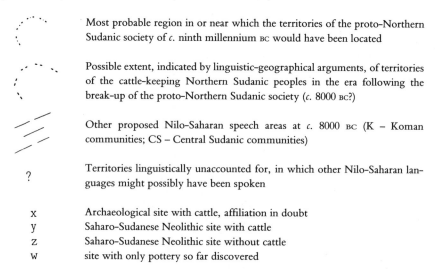

Most probable region in or near which the territories of the proto-Northern Sudanic society of *c.* ninth millennium BC would have been located

Possible extent, indicated by linguistic-geographical arguments, of territories of the cattle-keeping Northern Sudanic peoples in the era following the break-up of the proto-Northern Sudanic society (*c.* 8000 BC?)

Other proposed Nilo-Saharan speech areas at *c.* 8000 BC (K – Koman communities; CS – Central Sudanic communities)

?   Territories linguistically unaccounted for, in which other Nilo-Saharan languages might possibly have been spoken

x   Archaeological site with cattle, affiliation in doubt
y   Saharo–Sudanese Neolithic site with cattle
z   Saharo–Sudanese Neolithic site without cattle
w   site with only pottery so far discovered

Note that Lake Chad is shown at its modern-day maximal size. In the eighth millennium bc it was considerably larger and may have extended several hundred kilometres to the northeast, towards Tibesti. The same manner of representation of the lake is followed on Figs 6.3, 6.5 although it was usually several times its present size in those eras also.

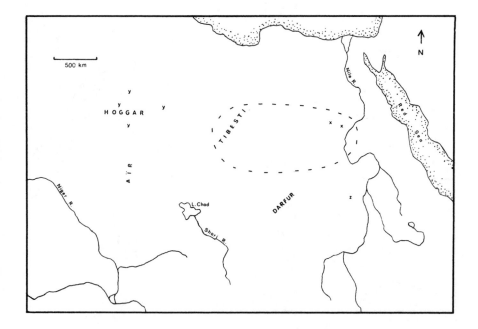

Figure 6.3 Saharo-Sudanese Neolithic sites and the Saharo-Sahelian society in the later seventh millennium bc (later eighth millennium BC).

(dashed oval)	Regions within or near which the territories of the grain-cultivating and cattle-herding proto-Saharo-Sahelian society (of *c.* the later eighth millennium BC) are most probably to be located
X	Saharo-Sudanese Neolithic sites with grain cultivation
y	Saharo-Sudanese Neolithic sites without determinative evidence (as yet?) of cultivation
z	Early Khartoum site

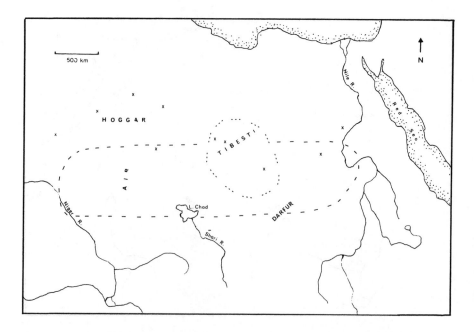

Figure 6.4 The Saharo-Sudanese Neolithic in the sixth millennium bc (seventh millennium BC).

Approximate probable locations of the pre-proto-Saharan and proto-Saharan peoples

Potential extent of the expansion of Sahelian-speaking peoples following the break-up of the proto-Sahelian society (*c.* mid-seventh millennium BC?)

Note that the mapping of the postulated Sahelian expansion does not take into account the presence of Lake Mega-Chad athwart the middle of its span (only the modern, smaller lake shape is marked on the map). The actual westward expansion of Sahelian communities is thus likely to have passed further to the north in the Sahara than the linguistic arguments by themselves would require.

Saharo-Sudanese Neolithic sites of sixth millennium bc date (seventh millennium BC?)

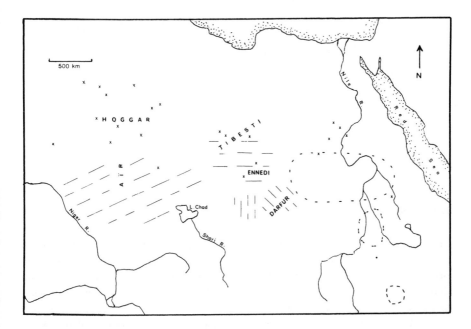

Figure 6.5 Saharo-Sudanese Neolithic and related occurrences and the various Saharo-Sahelian-speaking peoples of the earlier fifth millennium bc (earlier sixth millennium BC).

Region within which the pre-proto-Astaboran society most probably resided (branch of Eastern Sudanic subgroup)

Proto-Kir-Abbaian homeland (branch of Eastern Sudanic)

Possible location of very early pre-proto-Kuliak society (branch of Eastern Sudanic)

Pre-*Songay*-speaking communities (eastward extension of these communities as far as Lake Chad is attested to by the presence of *Songay*-oid loan-words in the Chadic and Kanuri languages which occupied these regions in later periods)

pre-Proto-Maban (branch of Eastern Sahelian)

pre-*For* (branch of Sahelian)

proto-Saharan society

X   Saharo-Sudanese and related sites of fifth millennium bc (sixth millennium BC)

7 Recent developments in African language classification and their implications for prehistory

ROGER BLENCH

Introduction

Prehistorians of Africa who use linguistics for the interpretation of archaeological data are dependent on the work of Greenberg (1966). However, recent research on the principal language phyla of Africa has modified his conclusions, in some cases quite dramatically. The most striking examples of this may be the discovery of isolated languages in east Africa and the internal reclassification of Niger-Congo. Many of these results have yet to be disseminated outside specialized publications and no overall synthesis is available, although a comprehensive summary of Niger-Congo has recently been published (Bendor-Samuel & Hartell 1989).

This chapter sets out the recent conclusions of linguists on the internal structure of the three most widespread African language phyla, Niger-Congo, Afroasiatic and Nilo-Saharan, and refers to summaries of material on Khoisan and the isolated languages. Many uncertainties still remain, and some of these are noted in the text. It is not intended to provide a chronology of the debates that have led to these results; references to many historically important contributions are thus omitted.

This allows the potential for inferences about prehistory to be explored, as well as the types of questions archaeology and linguistics might expect to pose to one another.

Changing methodologies in the genetic classification of African languages

Although Greenberg used the method of 'mass-comparison', the alignment of comparable lexical and grammatical elements to assign individual languages to families, lexicostatistics was a more common technique in the 1960s. Lexicostatistics proposed to establish the relationship between languages through counting cognates on a standard 100-word list, often known as a 'Swadesh list'. With its sister-discipline, glottochronology, which converted these cognacy percentages into estimates of historical time-depth, it seemed to provide a scientific, quantifiable methodology for genetic classification.

Although lexicostatistics has not been entirely discarded, it must now be hedged about with so many restrictions and qualifications as seriously to limit its usefulness.

Glottochronology has almost entirely disappeared. The tighter correspondences that are available between lexicostatistics and archaeological data in the Pacific (Bellwood 1979) have highlighted the problems of uneven decay in particular items on the Swadesh list (Grace 1967).

More promising for the prehistorian is the technique pioneered by Ehret in the 1960s, the cross-comparison of words of cultural significance (Ehret, Ch. 6, this volume). The hypothesis is similar to that adopted by scholars of Indo-European: the reconstruction of specific lexical items to a proto-language is evidence that speakers of that language had the item in their cultural repertoire. Technically speaking, only 'pseudo-reconstructions' are available for African language phyla, since exact sound correspondences for this vast array remain to be worked out. In a sense, though, for the prehistorian, it is enough that a term can be shown to be present in a proto-language: its exact phonological form is irrelevant.

As an example of the use that can be made of these findings, no words associated with cultivation can be securely reconstructed to Proto-Niger-Congo, whereas terms for hunting technology are present. We can therefore infer that the primary divisions of the phylum were in the pre-agricultural phase. This type of inference becomes more secure as data sources expand. An interesting recent use of this technique is Skinner (1984), who has used the reconstruction of names for animals in Afroasiatic to situate its possible centre of origin.

Greenberg, whose language classifications are discussed in this chapter, also made some early contributions to the theory of language and prehistory (Greenberg 1964). An example of the earlier debates of this type is the classic problem of the origin and expansion of the Bantu. The fruitless debates that followed Guthrie's (1967–71) wayward interpretations of his data and consequent disagreement with Greenberg were poor prehistory, but acted to throw the area of methodology into sharp relief. Bouquiaux (1980) presents the most recent classifications of Bantu languages and Vansina (1979a; 1980) has reviewed the history of the debate. In the last decade there have been a number of more detailed attempts to mesh archaeological and linguistic data in the reconstruction of broader aspects of African prehistory, for example Sutton (1974; 1977), Munson (1977), Horton (n.d.) and Williamson (1989a).

A problematic aspect of much of this work has always been the fluidity of linguists' classifications. The availability of improved data has historically been responsible for changes in both the internal classification and external relations of such families. A question that prehistorians can therefore legitimately put to linguists concerns the reliability of their results. If there have been such major revisions in the last two decades, does this not cast doubt on the methods used for classification? May there not be further revisions in the near future that will render present interpretations void?

The only realistic response that can be made is that, although further changes may well occur, they are more likely to be matters of detail than broad continent-spanning revisions. Benue-Congo, for example, has currently been provided with a large number of co-ordinate branches; this is historically improbable. Further analysis is under way to establish more structured subdivisions (Blench 1989a). At present, however, attention should undoubtedly be focused on the implications of groupings at the phylum level. This chapter attempts to stand back slightly further and ask what consequences follow from the recent revisions. It begins by reviewing the latest evidence for particular language families, and then suggests the possible consequences, both in situating their homelands and in reconstructing their expansion.

The language phyla of Africa

Figure 7.1 shows the present-day distribution of the language families of Africa. It is essentially a 'homeland' map; to take into account the large migrant populations, such as Hausa traders or FulBe pastoralists, would substantially increase its complexity. These phyla are now discussed in turn.

Niger-Congo

The concept of Niger-Congo has its roots in Westermann's (1927) 'Sudan-Sprachen' and many of the families recognized today were first established there. Westermann was the first to illustrate the strong links between the Bantu languages and those spoken in west Africa, and his demonstrations have generally been accepted by later scholars. Greenberg's (1966) original analysis of Niger-Congo (or Niger-Kordofanian when he later added the Kordofanian class-languages) set up six co-ordinate branches:

- West Atlantic (Fulfulde, Wolof, Temne, etc.)
- Mande (Mandinka, Mende, Busa)
- Gur (Dogon, Mossi, Dagari, Bariba, etc.)
- Kwa (Kru, Ewe, Akan, Yoruba, Igbo, Ijo, etc.)
- Benue-Congo (Kamberi, Birom, Jukun, Efik and Bantu)
- Adamawa-Eastern (Mumuye, Chamba, Gbaya, Zande, Banda, etc.)

Historically speaking, it is unlikely that a language family would have such a large number of co-ordinate branches – implying a single proto-language that split into six distinct groups at one time. Bennett & Sterk (1977) undertook a complete revision of the internal structure, to suggest the sequence of language-splits. Although not all their suggestions have been accepted, current models reflect their innovatory approach. Tables 7.1 and 7.2 were constructed from Bendor-Samuel & Hartell (1989) on the basis of a consensus among the contributing linguists. In comparison with Greenberg's analyses, the most important developments are as follows:

1. Mande is the second principal division of Niger-Congo, confirming its status as the most separate of the west African branches.
2. Atlantic (formerly West Atlantic) has been promoted to an almost comparable level of distinctiveness.
3. Ijoid (originally part of Greenberg's 'Kwa') has been expanded to include the divergent Defaka and assigned to a separate branch.
4. Bennett & Sterk (1977) first proposed that Gur, Adamawa and Kru be treated as a coherent unit, which they called North Central Niger-Congo. Although the lexical evidence is not conclusive for this grouping, the close relationship between Gur and Adamawa is generally accepted, following Bennett (1983).

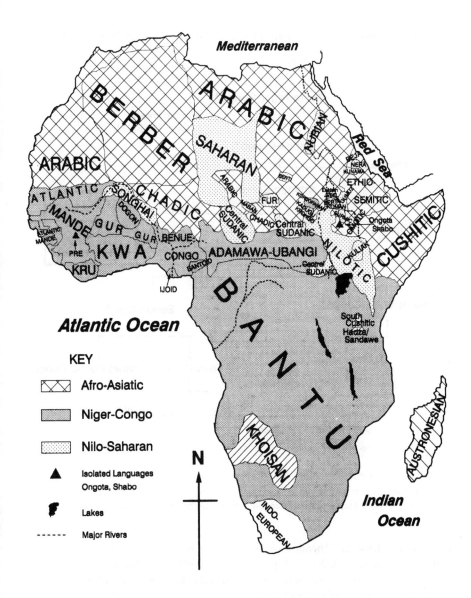

Figure 7.1 African language families.

Table 7.1 Classification of Niger–Congo adapted from Bendor-Samuel & Hartell (1989)

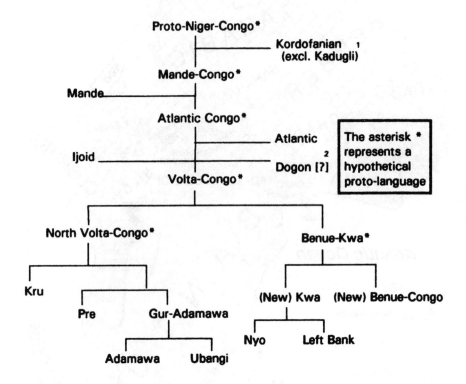

¹ Greenberg included Kadugli in the Kordofanian languages, but Schadeberg (1981) and Bender (1988) have argued that they would be better classified with Nilo–Saharan.
² Dogon has recently been separated from Gur and its classification remains uncertain.

5. The terms 'Kwa' and 'Benue–Congo' have been retained but their application has been radically revised. Kru and Ijo have been expelled from Kwa and many of the language branches of western Nigeria, in particular Yoruba, Nupa, Idoma, Edo and Igbo, have been transferred to Benue–Congo.

Table 7.2 shows the internal classification of Benue–Congo. The principal points to note are:

1. The Yoruboid–Akokoid languages are now called 'Defoid'. This terminology should be regarded as provisional only.
2. The development of Bantoid into Dakoid and Mambiloid is a result of recent work reported in Blench & Williamson (1987). The same paper argues that Tivoid should be regarded as part of Bantu, rather than as a separate branch.

Table 7.2 The principal subdivisions of Benue–Congo: generally based on contributions in Bendor-Samuel & Hartell (1989) and Blench & Williamson (1987)

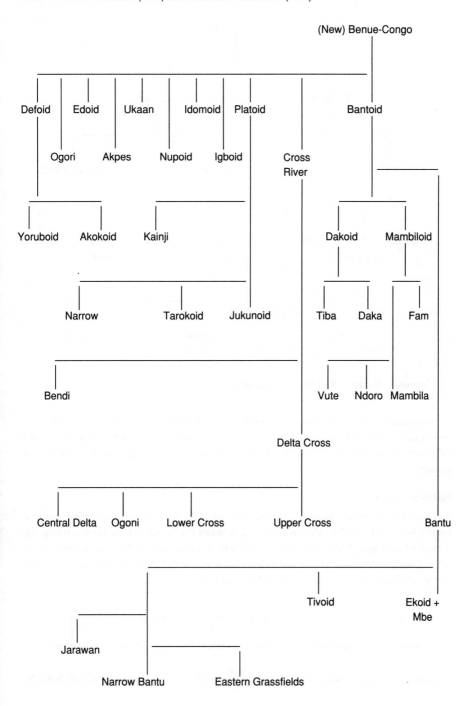

Table 7.3 Internal subclassification of Benue–Congo proposed in Blench 1989a

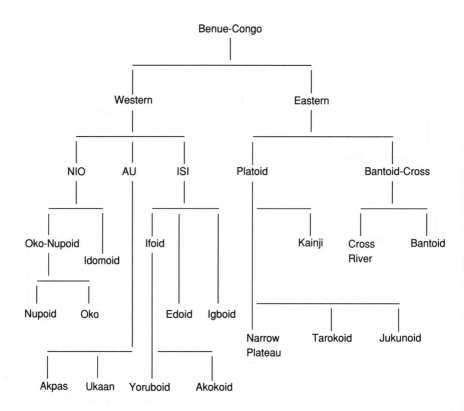

Subsequent to the publication by Bendor-Samuel & Hartell (1989), another analysis of Benue–Congo was undertaken to try and determine the internal structure of the 'Western' group (Table 7.3). It should be emphasized that this proposal is tentative at present.

Nilo-Saharan

Since a new proposed internal classification of Nilo-Saharan has been dealt with at length by Ehret (Ch. 6, this volume), this section is confined to summarizing the published evidence. Nilo-Saharan has always been something of the poor relative of the other principal language phyla, partly because it seems to lack coherence. In Greenberg (1971) it is treated as having six co-ordinate branches:

Senghai   Saharan   Maban   Fur   Chari-Nile   Koman

Doubts were raised about the integrity of some of these, in particular Chari-Nile, by

Goodman (1970). This stimulated a major reanalysis of the phylum by Bender (1976), supplemented in Bender (1988), suggesting nine co-ordinate branches:

- Songhai (A)
- Saharan (Kanuri, Teda, Zaghawa, etc.) (B)
- Maban (inc. Masalit, Runga) (C)
- Fur (D) (now For)
- East Sudanic (Nubian, Nilotic, Ik, Surma) (E)
- Central Sudanic (Bongo, Mangbaru, Lendu) (F)
- Berta (G)
- Kunama-Ilit (I)
- Komuz (Koman, Gumuz) (J)

Since publishing this table, Bender (1988) has reanalysed his material and now proposes a new classification, dividing Nilo-Saharan into 'core' and 'periphery' groups. In the latest version the following groups are 'core' languages or families:

    E East Sudanic including Nilotic and Nubian
    F Central Sudanic including Yulu and Sara
    I Kunama-Ilit
    J Koman-Gumuz

and a new group, the Kadugli languages, formerly classified by Greenberg as Niger-Congo, is added; thus:

    L Kadugli-Krongo-Tulishi

Now on the periphery[1] are:

    A Songhai
    B Saharan
    C Maban
    D For (=Fur)
    G Berta
    K Kuliak (including Ik)

It will be clear that this classification, which has not finally resulted in a 'tree' structure, is incomplete. Nevertheless it conflicts with the classification proposed by Ehret (Ch. 6, this volume), a reflection both of the defects in the data on Nilo-Saharan languages and their differentiation and fragmentation. Although Nilo-Saharan comprises a relatively low number of languages (seventy-eight, according to Bender 1983a), it is the second most diverse African language phylum. This suggests strongly that, after Khoisan, it is probably the oldest.

Gregersen (1972) raised the possibility that there was a deep-level relationship between Nilo-Saharan and Niger-Congo. He proposed a proto-language 'Kongo-Saharan'. The implications of this suggestion have been discussed by a number of authors, for example Boyd (1978). The general conclusion of researchers has been that this question is insoluble until more firm reconstructions are available for the proto-languages of the two phyla.

Afroasiatic

Greenberg (1966) was responsible for the establishment of this phylum. His particular contribution was the dethronement of Semitic from its formerly central position, and the emphasis he placed on its relations with the languages of Black Africa. He proposed 'Afroasiatic' to replace the former term 'Hamito-Semitic' with its slightly bizarre racist undertone. His original classification allowed five co-ordinate branches:

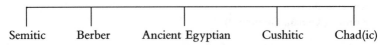

Semitic   Berber   Ancient Egyptian   Cushitic   Chad(ic)

The most significant development since this period has been the establishment of Omotic, a family confined to Ethiopia and consisting of little-known languages such as Nao, Ghimira, Hamar and Dizi (Bender 1975; Hayward 1990). Most scholars have accepted the coherence of Omotic as a group and agree on its assignment to Afroasiatic.[2] In addition, doubts have been raised about the internal consistency of Cushitic, the family to which important languages such as Oromo, Beja and Somali belong. Newman (1980) has proposed a convincing series of isoglosses intended to demonstrate the unity of Afroasiatic, excluding Omotic. In a recent study, Fleming (1983a) has proposed the structure shown in Table 7.4. The most important features of this are the close alignment of Berber and Chadic, the establishment of Omotic as the earliest split and the division of Cushitic into a number of separate branches.

Khoisan and isolated languages

A broad unity of the Khoisan ('click') languages of southern Africa has long been accepted, in the main because of their distinctive phonology. Westphal (1971) listed and classified the Khoisan languages of southern Africa, dividing them into five principal groups. Traill (1978) has pointed out that, despite the distinctive sounds of Khoisan, it is difficult to establish the unity of the group, because of its considerable internal differentiation. Australian languages are similarly characterized by a phonemic unity and comparable lexical diversity.

On the same basis, it has been assumed that Hadza and Sandawe, two languages spoken in central Tanzania, are part of this group, since they also have clicks. Greenberg's (1966) discussion of this group is principally intended to establish that Khoisan is not related to Hamitic. However, he also puts forward a case for the inclusion of the Tanzanian languages in Khoisan. Westphal (1971) expressed doubts, and since that period there has been a considerable expansion of research on Hadza and Sandawe. The latest reviews of this subject (Elderkin 1983; Fleming 1983b) conclude that the relationship remains unproven and the two languages are better treated as isolates.

Classifying languages as 'isolated' seems unsatisfactory, and in earlier work, such as Tucker & Bryan (1956), was little more than an admission of the inadequacy of the data source. Now, however, the reverse is the case, for since the 1960s there has been a

Table 7.4   The principal subdivisions of Afroasiatic (Fleming 1983a, p. 22)

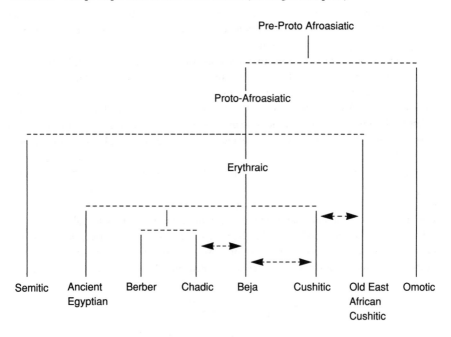

Arrows (◄ -- ►) indicate inter-branch linkages.

massive expansion of both lexical and syntactic data. In addition, the same period has produced evidence for three more languages without any clear affiliations. These are Oropom (Wilson 1970), spoken by an isolated group in northeastern Uganda, Birale (whose correct name is Ongota) (Bender 1983b) and Mekeyir (whose correct name is Shabo) (Fleming 1983b, p. 555) in southwestern Ethiopia. Oropom was recently investigated (Bender, *pers. comm.*) and the wordlist presented by Wilson could not be substantiated. Mekeyir has been treated by Bender as Nilo-Saharan, although its proposed subgrouping remains unclear.

  These languages are spoken by hunter-gatherer groups and their remoteness suggests that they could be survivals from a substratum that has all but disappeared. A parallel situation might be the extreme differentiation exhibited by the languages of hunting groups in northeastern Siberia (Comrie 1981).

Conclusion

The sequence of divisions in Niger-Congo is more clearly established than in Afroasiatic or Nilo-Saharan. The establishment of a large number of co-ordinate branches is effectively an admission of our present inability to reconstruct the intermediate stages. This is partly a reflection of the inadequate data available for certain branches of Afroasiatic and Nilo-Saharan. It would therefore be unwise at present to attempt to correlate archaeological data with particular subgroupings.

Distribution

Figure 7.1 shows the present-day distributions of language phyla and principal families in Africa. They are inevitably simplified, and Ancient Egyptian is omitted, in view of its replacement by Arabic at present.

An aspect of these distributions that deserves comment is the isolation, both geographically and linguistically, of particular families, such as Songhai. The situation of groups such as Songhai or Southern Cushitic, suggests that they were cut off by invasive groups from related branches at an early date. Presumably, Songhai became isolated following a northward movement of Niger-Congo speakers, and the Southern Cushites, the Hadza and Sandawe retained their language while their neighbours became Bantu-speaking.

Figure 7.2 is intended to suggest the possible original location of each of the three phyla, based on knowledge of the present-day and historical distributions. These are derived somewhat crudely, by assuming that the heartland of a phylum is likely to be central to its dispersal, and that it will not be in humid rainforest. Nilo-Saharan is taken to be the most ancient phylum and to have begun its expansion during the Holocene, when the northern margins of the rainforest were considerably south of their present location. The most controversial placement is centring Afroasiatic in the Ethio-Sudan

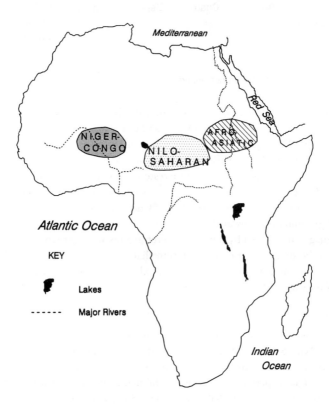

Figure 7.2 Possible original locations of major languages.

borderland. This is based partly on the evidence presented by Skinner (1984) on antelope names in Afroasiatic, and partly on the location of Omotic, which has a special status as the primary branching. In view of the historical evidence for Semitic languages in the ancient Near East, this inevitably suggests a considerable antiquity for the phylum as a whole.

If these assumptions are even broadly correct, then the centre of origin of the three principal phyla of African languages was in the same ecological zone, and roughly adjacent to one another. Niger-Congo began on the southern margins of the Sahara, Nilo-Saharan probably in the former semi-arid zones of present-day Central African Republic, and Afroasiatic in present-day Sudan/Ethiopia borderland.

Methodological implications

Apart from the specific hypotheses advanced here, there are some recent observations derived from lexical reconstruction that should be borne in mind for further research:

(a) The degree of diversity in all phyla is sufficient to suggest that the principal dispersals took place before agriculture. There do not seem to be any terms unambiguously associated with agriculture that will reconstruct. However, words for some domestic animals, in particular goat and cattle, seem to reconstruct at least back to the level of Mande in Niger-Congo. Similar evidence for early exploitation of domesticated animals in the pre-agricultural phase also appears in Nilo-Saharan and Afroasiatic.

(b) If the speakers of proto-languages are assumed to be hunting populations, then the second assumption would appear to be that the principal stimulus to dispersal initially was either pressure on resources or a sudden expansion of their availability. With increasing aridity, movements of game would fragment human groups following particular animal populations. When the climate improved, the expansion of both hunted and gathered resources would allow a corresponding diversification of human subsistence patterns.

According to Street & Gasse (1981), who provide a recent summary of the palaeoecology of the Sahara, 18,000 BP was a peak of aridity. More recent research (A. T. Grove, *pers. comm.*, and see Grove, Ch. 1, this volume) suggests that the height of the drought might have been some 5000 years later, at 13,000 BP. After 12,500 BP there was a significant improvement over a period of some 2500 years, and lake levels rose across the whole of middle Africa. If Nilo-Saharan originated during the extremely arid period, it would explain the deep divisions between its various branches. If both Afroasiatic and Niger-Congo developed during the 12,500–10,000 BP period, respectively east and west of the Nilo-Saharan heartland, this would explain the isolation of some of its branches.

Substantial advances have been made in both the genetic classification and characterization of African language phyla since the 1960s. Although considerable further work is needed, it seems unlikely that the main outlines of present classifications will undergo major revisions. Some progress has been made towards lexical reconstruction of cultural items; however, because wordlists tend to focus on glosses that are specifically acultural, significant terms are often only sketchily collected. A valuable contribution from archaeologists and prehistorians would be the suggestion of terms that are of significance for the elucidation of subsistence patterns.

Although scholars have not been averse to putting forward bold hypotheses relating archaeological and linguistic data, many of these have been rapidly outmoded by new data. Those of a more general nature are harder to test; indeed, it is hard to see what would prove or disprove some of the suggestions offered. Nevertheless, the dialogue between prehistorians and linguists has been fruitful and should intensify as both disciplines continue to refine their data.

Notes

[1] Bender (*pers. comm.*) now regards Mekeyir in southwest Ethiopia as Nilo-Saharan, although its position remains unclear.

[2] Newman (1980) remains a significant exception.

Acknowledgements

The first version of this chapter was written for and presented at the African Neolithic section of the World Archaeological Congress, held in Southampton, 1–7 September 1986. I am grateful to Professor Thurstan Shaw for inviting me to speak, thereby stimulating this contribution. Much of the content has been developed over a number of years through conversation with other scholars of Niger-Congo, in particular Professor Kay Williamson, whose particular contribution is acknowledged here. I am grateful to Bruce Connell and the participants, especially Lionel Bender, at the African Languages Conference held in Boston in April 1988 for additional discussion and comments.

8   *Linguistic evidence for the use of some tree and tuber food plants in southern Nigeria*

KAY WILLIAMSON

It is generally recognized that archaeological evidence of tubers or their cultivation is difficult to find (Coursey 1976, p. 396). The same problem applies to crops from trees which are protected but not cultivated if their seeds do not survive in an archaeological context. It is therefore important to investigate linguistic evidence which could help in the study of the use, domestication or introduction of such crops.

In southern Nigeria, the primary linguistic group is New Benue-Congo, a group which is discussed by Blench (Ch. 7, this volume) in his summary of the new classification of Niger-Congo languages (for more detail, see Bendor-Samuel & Hartell 1989). This classification implies that almost all the languages of southern Nigeria belong to New Benue-Congo. The major exception is the Ijoid group (Ịjọ plus Defaka), which is much more distantly related to *all* other southern Nigerian languages than these are to each other. Tentatively, Ịjọ is placed at the same level of the family tree as the (West) Atlantic family, the node being called Proto-Atlantic-Congo (PAC). According to this structure, if a word can be reconstructed in Ijoid as well as Proto-Benue-Congo, it is assumed to have existed at the PAC level.

The groups of New Benue-Congo radiate out from the Niger-Benue Confluence like the spokes of a wheel. A root which is found in a number of non-adjacent spokes is likely to be reconstructable to Proto-Benue-Congo; those found only in adjacent spokes may be either retained from Proto-Benue-Congo or borrowed from outside. Because many of the proto-languages of these groups have not yet been reconstructed, however, it is not always clear whether these are cognates or loan-words.

The discussion of available evidence which follows concentrates on plant names; at the end a brief mention is made of other words which refer specifically to the cultivation of plants.

The names of the plants and their products

Williamson (1970) discussed food plant names in the Niger delta, a linguistically complex area with seven groups of languages, and showed that the food plant names were of three different types:

(a) Names which were consistent throughout a whole language group and could be reasonably assumed to be reconstructed to the proto-language of that group. The assumption is that the word and probably also the food plant referred to were known to the speakers of the proto-language. In some cases the reconstructed words of one group were also cognate with those of other language groups and could therefore be tentatively reconstructed to the proto-language of a higher group. Such names proved to be those of plants believed on botanical, ethnographic or archaeological evidence to be indigenous to west Africa: yam, oil palm, wine palm, kola.

(b) Names which were often not consistent throughout a language group, but only over part of it, and which were often found in part of a neighbouring group as well. They could therefore not be reconstructed to the proto-language of a group, but rather gave the impression of loan-words which had come into use after the proto-language had begun to split up into the modern languages. Such names proved to be those attributed to the southeast Asian complex: plantain, banana, cocoyam, wateryam.

(c) Names which bore no relation to the boundaries of a group, but spread over a wide area related to well-known trade routes. Such names were those of crops introduced by the Portuguese or in more recent times: maize, cassava, groundnuts.

Some sample roots have been examined in Williamson (1970; 1989b) and are here expanded. Forms outside Proto–Benue–Congo are given first, followed by Benue–Congo forms and a concluding discussion.

Reconstructed languages

CB	Common Bantu	Guthrie 1967–71
CP	Common Potou	Stewart 1973
PAC	Proto-Atlantic-Congo	(tentative only)
PBC	Proto-Benue-Congo	De Wolf 1971

(His reconstructions deal with Old Benue-Congo, equivalent to East Benue-Congo in Blench's (1992a) classification.)

PCJ	Proto-Central Jukunoid	Shimizu 1980
PE	Proto-Edoid	Elugbe 1989
PI	Proto-Ịjọ	Williamson Forthcoming
PJ	Proto-Jukunoid	Shimizu 1980
PK	Proto-Kegboid (Ogoni)	Ikoro 1989
PN	Proto-Nupoid	Blench 1982; Blench 1989b
PP2	Proto-Plateau 2	Gerhardt 1983
PP4	Proto-Plateau 4	Gerhardt 1983
PUC	Proto-Upper Cross	Dimmendaal 1978
PWN	Proto-Western Nigritic	Mukarovsky 1976–7
	(PWN is approximately equivalent to PAC.)	
PWS	Proto-West Sudanic	Westermann 1927
PY	Proto-Yoruboid	Akinkugbe 1978

Specific languages and groups: classification and source(s)

Abini	Upper Cross	
Abuan	Central Delta	Gardner 1980
Akpes	Ukaan-Akpes	Ibrahim-Arirabiyi 1989
Arigidi	Akokoid	Ibrahim-Arirabiyi wordlist
Atẹ	Edoid	
Ayere	Akokoid	
Ban	Kegboid (Ogoni)	Ikoro 1989
Bete	Bendi	
Bokyi	Bendi	Questionnaire: T. Osang
Cen. Delta	Delta-Cross	
Defaka	Ijoid	Jenewari 1983
Degema	Edoid	Thomas & Williamson 1967
Ebira	Nupoid	
Ẹdo	Edoid	Agheyisi 1986
Efik	Lower Cross	
Ẹgẹnẹ	Edoid	Thomas & Williamson 1967
Ekit	Lower Cross	
Ekoid	S. Bantoid	Crabb 1965
Eleme	Kegboid (Ogoni)	Ikoro 1989
Emai	Edoid	Schaefer 1987
Epie	Edoid	Thomas & Williamson 1967
		Questionnaire: N. K. Yakie
Ganagana	Nupoid	Sterk 1977
Gokana	Kegboid (Ogoni)	Ikoro 1989
Gwari	Nupoid	Hyman 1970
Ịbanị	Ijoid	
Ibibio	Lower Cross	Kaufman 1985
Idoma	Idomoid	Questionnaire: E. O. O. Amali
Igala	Yoruboid	
Igbo	Igboid:	Williamson 1972
	Questionnaire:	L. O. Ohanazoeze (Ihiala)
	Questionnaire:	A. Ubani (Umuimenyi)
	Questionnaire:	E. N. Maduakor (Unubi)
Igede	Idomoid	Questionnaire: O. Idoko
Ikwere	Igboid	
Iṣẹkiri	Yoruboid	
Isoko	Edoid	
Iyayu	Edoid	
Ịzọn	Ijoid	
Kakanda	Nupoid	Sterk 1977
Kalabarị	Ijoid	
Kambari	Kainji	Hoffmann 1965

Kana	Kegboid (Ogoni)	Ikoro 1989
	Questionnaire:	G. N. A. Pyagbara
		Notes: N. B. Williamson
Kenyang	S. Bantoid	T. Mbuagbaw (*pers. comm.*, 1991)
Koto	Nupoid	Sterk 1977
Legbo	Upper Cross	
Lẹkọnọ	S. Bantoid	Hedinger 1987
Lokạạ	Upper Cross	
Londo	S. Bantoid	Kuperus 1985
Lungu	Platoid	
Magongo	Ọkọ	
Mambila	N. Bantoid	Zeitlyn n.d.
Mbo	S. Bantoid	Hedinger 1987
Momi	Adamawa	Blench & Edwards 1988
Nembe	Ijoid	Questionnaire: E. I. Gbobate
Nkọrọ	Ijoid	
N. Ibie	Edoid	
Obolo	Lower Cross	
Ọgbịa	Central Delta	Wolff 1969
Ọkọ	Oko	
Okrika	Ijoid	
Pyem	Platoid	
Reshe	Kainji	
Tarok	Platoid	
Tiv	S. Bantoid	Abraham 1940
	Questionnaire:	E. T. Ibuh (Vandeikya)
	Questionnaire:	C. G. Soo (Lessel)
TuNen	S. Bantoid	
Ubeteng	Upper Cross	
Udo	Akokoid	Ibrahim-Arirabiyi wordlist
Ufia	Upper Cross	
Ukaan	Ukaan-Akpes	Ibrahim-Arirabiyi wordlist
Ukue	Edoid	Ibrahim-Arirabiyi wordlist
Ụkwụanị	Igboid	
Urhobo	Edoid	
Vute	N. Bantoid	
Yeskwa	Platoid	
Yoruba	Yoruboid	Abraham 1958
Zarek	Platoid	

If no specific source is indicated, data are from the *Benue-Congo Comparative Wordlist* or from wordlists collected by me or in my possession.

Subdotted letters have been used, following Nigerian orthographic tradition, rather than phonetic symbols: ị, ẹ, ọ and ụ are narrow vowels and ạ is schwa; ḅ and ḍ are implosives, and ṇ is the velar nasal; n immediately following a vowel represents a nasalized vowel. The tone pattern is indicated afterwards by the symbols H(igh), L(ow), M(id), F(alling) and R(ising). The vertical alignment is to show corresponding sounds.

Tree crops

Table 8.1 Oil palm (*Elaeis guineensis* Jacq.)

Proto-Ịjọ			ḍ ẹ	k	ụ	HLH
(New) Kwa						
Common Potou	a	-	d ẹ			H-H
(New) Benue-Congo						
Proto-Edoid	U	-	ḍ i			
Proto-Idomoid	ọ	-	r j			
Proto-Plateau 4	i	-	d i	k		L-H
Lungu	i	-	r e	k		L-H pl. H-
Yeskwa	i	-	l e	k		
Bokyi	u	-	y e			
Central Delta	a	-	ḍ e			
Proto-Kegboid (Ogoni)	a	-	d yi		o	
Proto-Upper Cross		-	d i			H
Tiv	u	-	l e			H-L

Discussion: If the Proto-Ịjọ form is genuinely cognate with the Benue-Congo forms, this root goes back to Proto-Atlantic-Congo.

Table 8.2 Oil palm (*Elaeis guineensis* Jacq.); palm oil

PWN (= PAC)	★	- B I L(A)		'oil palm; frond or nut of oil palm'
Proto-Ịjọ		p u l o	LL	'(palm) oil'
PBC	★	- p i d e		
Akpes	e	- b i r		
Akpes (Akunnu)	im	- b i r i l	M-MM	'oil' (palm oil)
Proto-Edoid	A	- ' b i'di		'oil' (palm oil)
PCJ		b i T	L	'oil'
Vute		b w:r		(w = unrounded u); Cameroon
Ekoid R	u	- b i r	L-F	(i central)
Tiv	i	- v i l e	H-HH	
Common Bantu	★	- b i d a	HL	'oil palm; (nut of oil palm)'

Discussion: This root is clearly PAC; Mukarovsky (1976–7) cites forms from Gur, Togo Remnant and (Western) Kwa as well as Benue-Congo. In view of the preceding root, it is possible that this one originally meant 'fruit or oil of oil palm' and that the first one referred specifically to the tree. Together they strongly indicate that the oil palm was familiar to the speakers of Proto-Atlantic-Congo.
Two other forms that might be cognate here are:

Proto-Ịjọ	★e – b in	L-H	'palm fruit'
Ẹdo	i – v in	H-L	'palm tree; palm kernels'

But if these are cognate, then the forms in the same two languages meaning 'oil' are presumably *not* cognate.

Table 8.3 Wine (Raphia) palm (*Raphia hookeri* Mann and Wendl.)

Proto-Ịjọ	★ k	ọ	r	ọ	HH	
Yoruba	i - k	o			L-H	'raphia fibre'
	ọ - g	ọ	r	ọ	L-LL	'raphia palm wine'
	o - g	u	r	ọ	L-LL	
Ẹdo	ọ - g	ọ	r	ọ	L-LL	'palm wine tapped from the top of
	ọ - g	ọ			L-L	the raffia palm'
Urhobo/Isoko	ọ - g	ọ	r	ọ	L-LL	
Ụkwụanị	ọ - g	ọ	l	ọ	L-LL	
Epie	ụ - k	ọn			L-L	
Ẹgẹnẹ	ọ - kw	ẹ	i		L-LL	
Igbo	n - gw	ọ			H-L	
Abua	ọ - gh	ọ	l		L-L	
Ọgbia	ọ - gh	ọ	l		L-H	
Kana	k	u		ẹ	MM	
Gokana	k	ọ	l		M	
Ban	n - k	ọ		ọ	L-MM	
Eleme	n - k	ọn			L-M	
Obolo	u - g	ọ	r	ọ	H-LL	
Efik	u - k	ọ	d			
Ibibio	u - k	ọ	t		H-F	
Bokyi	n - c	u			L-R	
Kambari (Cent.)	a - kk	u	l	u	H-HH	
	ma - k	u	l	a	L-LL	'palm wine'
Reshe	hi - k	ọ	l	ọ	H-HL	
Zarek (Afizere)	ka - k	ọ	n		M-H	
PP2	i - k	o			L-H	
Pyem	g	o	r	o		
Tarok	in- g	u	r			
Vute	k	w d	w ṇ		(w = unrounded u); Cameroon	
Tiv	i - c	o	r		L-F	

Discussion: This is a very important economic tree in the Niger Delta (Williamson 1970, p. 157). It is used not only for wine: its fruit is edible, it provides raphia fibre, the midribs of the fronds are used for building, it is a fish poison, and edible larvae (*Oryctes* sp.) may be obtained from the rotting trunk. From its occurrence in Ịjọ and many groups of Benue-Congo it appears to be reconstructable to Proto–Atlantic-Congo. The closely similar forms in Yoruba, Isoko/Urhobo and Ụkwụanị appear to be due to recent borrowing in the sense of 'palm wine'.

Table 8.4 Coconut (palm) (*Cocos nucifera* Linn.)

1 Terms mean 'European (oil) palm/European nut'

Nembe	ḅ e k e	im b i	HL LH
Igbo			
(Unubi)	a - k ị	o - y i b o	H-H H-LH
(Umuimenyi)	a - k ụ	b e k ee	H-H LHL
Bokyi	o - k u	o - k a r a	
KoHumono	ẹ - h ụ bh	a - h a r a r a	M-L M-LLL
Abuan	o - z i ph	a - ḅ e k ee ny	L-H H-LL pl. i-

2 From Portuguese *coqueira*

Iṣẹkiri	k o k o d i ẹ	LHML
Ịzọn	o - k o k o ḍ i a	L-LLHL
Epie	o - k o k o ḍ i e	L-LLHL
Ọgbia	o - k o k o ḍ i ạ	L-LLHL

3 Miscellaneous

Yoruba	a - gb ọn	L-M
Igede	ọ - gb ị r ị	H-MH
Idoma	a - kw u m b a	L-HLL
Tiv	i - ky e v e	L-HH

Discussion: The linguistic evidence suggests strongly that the coconut palm was introduced by the Portuguese. The most common terms are either compounds meaning 'European palm' or a direct loan from Portuguese. Other words are quite miscellaneous and no clear pattern emerges.

Table 8.5 Kola (*Cola acuminata* Schott and Endl., *C. nitida* A. Chev.)

Proto-Yoruboid	o – b i		M-L	
Magongo	i – b w	e		
Akpes				
(Ase)	i – b u		M-L	
(Ikaram)	i – b u		L-L	
(Akunnu)	im- b u		L-L	
(Ibaram)	im-gb i		L-L	
(Gedegede)	im-gb ẹ		L-L	
(Daja)	e – m i		L-L	
Ukaan				
(Ikan)	a – b u	e	L-LL	
(Ishe)	i – b u	in	L-LH	
Ẹdo	ẹ –vb ẹ	e	L-HL	
Emai	ẹ –vb e	e	L-LL	
Ibie	ẹ – w u	e		
Isoko	ẹ – w ị		H-H	
Urhobo	ẹ –vb e		L-L	
Epie	ụ – ḅ ị	ị	L-LL	
Ẹgẹnẹ	a – ḅ ị	ị	L-LL	
Degema	ụ – ḅ ụ	ịn	L-HH	
Nupe	e – b i		M-L	
Koto	o – b i		H-L	
Kakanda	ẹẹ- b i		MH-L	
Ganagana	e – b in		M-L	
Abua	e –gb e		L-L	
Ọgbịa	e –gb e		L-LH	
Kana				
(Kono)	gb i	in	HH	
(Kpea)	b u	un	MH	
Ibibio	i – b ọ ṇ		H-H	
Abini	i – b u			
Legbo	le – v u			
Ufia	ri – ḅ u			
Ubeteng	le – b bọ			
Bokyi	di – b e		'kola tree'	
Bete	le – b o		L-M pl. a-	
Londo	– b i o		-LH Cameroon	
TuNen	ni – f u n u		L-LL Cameroon	
Common Bantu	– b i d ụ		LH	

Discussion: This root is clearly widely distributed enough to be regarded as Proto-Benue-Congo.

Gregersen (1967, p. 106, fn. 14) suggests that the Hausa word *gooroo* HL, now found all over northern Nigeria, is borrowed from Songhai *goro*. He notes that the *Kano Chronicle* maintains that kola was introduced from the Nupe, who call it *ebi* M-L, whence Gregersen derives Hausa *ibii* HL, defined by Bargery (1934) as 'a Yoruba variety of kola-nut, with several cotyledons' (i.e. *C. acuminata*), and by Abraham (1962) as a 'type of kola-nut known to Hausa dealers in Yorubaland'. Both Bargery (1934) and Abraham (1962) derive Hausa *ibii* HL from Yoruba *obi* ML. Yoruba *obi* ML might be a loan from Nupe, but this is unlikely, for there are regular sound correspondences in Igala and Iṣẹkiri which show that the word can be reconstructed to Proto-Yoruboid. I suggest, on the basis of the phonology, that Nupe borrowed the word from Yoruba, and Hausa from Nupe.

Tubers

Table 8.6 Aerial yam ('up-yam') (*Dioscorea bulbifera* Linn.)

Ịzǫn (Kolokuma)	ǫ - t ụ m ụ	L-HH
Proto–Nupoid	- d un	
Ikwere	rẹ - dn ụ	H-L
Igbo	a - d ụ	H-L
Efik	e - d o m o	H-HL
Ibibio	i - d o m o	H-HL
Ekit	i - d o m	H-L
Abuan	a - n o m	L-H
Ọgbịa	a - n o m	
Mambila	t u w a r	

Discussion: The occurrence of this word in Nupoid, which is not adjacent to the other groups, suggests that it can be reconstructed to Proto–Benue–Congo. If the Ịzǫn word is also cognate, it goes back to Proto-Atlantic-Congo.

Blench (n.d.) suggests that the tuber is one of the ancient west African crops that formerly had a much greater importance than today. This is confirmed by student reports; it is said to be one of the oldest crops cultivated by the Ikwere and was formerly highly regarded. It was used as a food to wean babies, for birth rituals, and medicinally for boils and to protect the head of an unborn child. An Igbo student reports that it was first used by a hunter who ate it when he was lost in the forest, and that it is used for sacrifices and medicines. An Ekit student also reports a forest origin, the food in this account being fed to the hunter's dog, and notes that when ground it is used as a medicine for dislocated joints. An Ibibio student reports that it was formerly used to treat possession, but is now shunned because it is believed to bring evil spirits to the house. All sources confirm that it used to be far more important than now; in Ọgbịa it was a staple food 40–50 years ago (Dr E. Isukul, *pers. comm.*).

Table 8.7 Yam (general term) (*Dioscorea* spp.)

1	PNC root				
	Proto–West Sudanic	– k i			
		– k u			
	Defaka	i – n i		H–!H	
	Proto–Benue-Congo	– k o d			
	Ọkọ	i – g i l a			
	Ukaan	i – y ọ			pl. a– L
	Ukaan (Ishe)	i – y un		L–H	pl. a–
	Akpes (Gedegede)	e – w u l ẹ		M–LL	
	Proto–Yoruboid	u – c un		M–M	
	Yoruba	i – ṣ u		M–M	
	Ayere	ẹ – s ẹ		L–H	
	Udo	a – j u		L–M	
	Arigidi	e – c i ẹn		M–LH	
	Ẹgẹnẹ	ẹ – ḍ ị a		L–LL	
	Epie	a – ḍ ị a		L–LL	pl. ị–
	Isoko	ọ – l ẹ		L–H	
	Urhobo	ọ – n ẹ		L–H	
	Ukue	u – w ẹ l ẹ		M–LL	
	Proto–Nupoid	– c i			
	Ebira	ẹ – n ụ		M–M	
	Igede	i – j u		M–M	
	Idoma	i – h i		L–M	
	Proto–Igboid	i – j i		L–H	
	Bokyi (Irruan)	ky i – r u			
	Kana (Kpea)	z i an		MH	
	Idoma (Central)	i – h i		L–M	
	Abuan	ẹ – lh ẹ l			
	Ọgbịa (Oloiḅiri)	ẹ – l ẹ l		L–L	
	PP 2 Jaba-Koro	i – ts i t		L–M	
	Proto–Plateau	i – s i r		L–H	
	Proto–Jukunoid	i – k i t		–H	pl. u–
	Ekoid A	e – l o		L–L	pl. be–
	Ekoid F	e – y u		L–L	pl. bi–
	Ekoid R	i – y e l		L–F	
2	Other roots				
	Emai	e – m a		H–L	
	Gwari	– shnam a		MH	
	Bete	ki – p a m			
	Efik	– bya		F	
	Obolo	u – kw a		H–H	
	Tiv	i – y ogh		H–LH	

Discussion: The general name for 'yam' usually refers to the various species of Guinea yam (*Dioscorea cayenensis*, *D. rotundata*). The Guinea yams are indigenous and there are traditions of their being developed from wild forms (e.g. Idoma). They are of very great importance and there are many named varieties in many of the languages.

Guinea yams are normally cultivated by men, unlike wateryams, which are normally cultivated by women. There is usually a ceremonial eating of the first yams, performed either in the family setting (Idoma) or as a public festival (Igbo, Bokyi).

The oldest root is PWS *-ki*, *-ku*, for which Westermann (1927) finds cognates in Mande, Kwa and (New) Benue-Congo (cf. Armstrong 1964, p. 54). It is not quite clear how many of the forms listed here belong to this root; but on the assumption that a velar sound (*k*) could become palatal before a front vowel (*i*), I have assumed that the palatal (*y*), palato-alveolar (*c,j*), and alveolar (*s,z,l,ḍ*) sounds could have developed from it. If all the forms do have a common origin, there must have been nasality in the stem, perhaps in the second syllable, to account for the forms with nasal vowels or with *n*.

Table 8.8 Wateryam (*Dioscorea alata* Linn.)

(1) Most widespread root

Yoruba	e	– w	u	r	a		M-LL	
Emai	o	– vb	i		ẹ		L-LL	
Nupe		w	u	r	a		LL	
Idoma	o	– b	u	n	a		L-LL	
Igbo								
(Umuimenyi)	m	– b	a	l	a		L-LL	
(Ọnịcha)	a	– b	a	n	a		L-LL	
Ibibio	a	– b	i	r	e		L-LL	
Degema	o	– gb		r	o		L-HL	pl. i-
Bokyi (Irruan)	o	– p	u		o			
Tiv								
(Lessel)	ọ	– gb			o		L-L	
(Vandeikya)	a	– gb			o		L-L	

(2) 'Female yam'

Epie	a	– ḍ	ị	a		f ị n a		
Ịzọn (Kolokuma)	ị	– y	ọ	r	ọ	b u r u	LHH LH	

(3) Other

Emai	a k o	– g	u		ẹ	L-L-LL ??	
Kana		g	u	r	a	LM	
Kana		y	a			M	

Discussion: Idoma has four varieties: *ọgbaagwu gwutaje* LHLH HLL, *obuna nẹ bẹ* LLL ? H (white), *obuna nọ wa* LLL M H (red), *obunẹdẹ* LLMH (red but thread-like surface). There are no reports of its use in festivals or rituals. Ibibio: formerly planted only by women. Kana: Of the two types, *ya* is fatter and sweeter; *gura* produces longer tubers. They are grown mainly by women; a man does not boast of wateryams as he does of yams. An annual wateryam festival *ọb ya* 'roasting of wateryams' or *de ya* 'eating of wateryams' is observed in all Ogoni villages, ushering in a period of ten days of preparation for the yam festival. It is generally believed that the wateryam is as old as the Ogoni people. Its importance is shown by its use in proverbs: *O tara loo wiin mẹnẹ, o de zun ya* L HH HH HH HH, L H L H 'By nursing a rich man's child, you eat the tail of the wateryam'. This indicates that the only or most important yam the people had was the wateryam, since the ordinary yam, which is highly regarded today, is not mentioned. Such proverbs as *Bari gaa tẹrẹ kii, a gbaẹn gura* LL HH HM HM, L LL LM 'Before causing famine, God first sent the wateryam' show the wateryam to be the original yam of the people (N. B. Williamson, *pers. comm.*).

The most widespread root (1) stretches from Ibibio to Yoruba. The Degema root cited here is the general word for 'yam'. It is conceivable that PI *ḅuru* LLH 'yam' also belongs to this group, although the vowels seem different. The wateryam is the basic yam planted by the Ịzọn and has a festival among the Kolokuma, confirming its importance among other Delta peoples such as the Ogoni.

There are also a number of names meaning 'female yam' (2), and the plant is strongly associated with women, often explicitly contrasted with the Guinea yam, which is specifically associated with men.

Its cultural importance in the south and east of Nigeria suggests a southeastern coastal entry point. A similar pattern is observed for 'cocoyam'; they are both plants of the southeast Asian complex and could have been introduced in similar ways from the same area.

Table 8.9 Cocoyam (Old) (*Colocasia esculenta* Schott.) (New) (*Xanthosoma mafaffa* Schott.)

Language	Pre	C1	V1	C2	V2	C3	V3	N	Ext	Tone/Notes
(1a) Western forms										
Yoruba		k	o	k	o					HL
Iṣẹkiri		k	o	k	o					HL
Iyayu	-	k	o	k	o					
Atẹ	u -	k	o	k	o					
North Ibie	i -	kh	o	kh	o					
Nupe		k	on	k	o	r	o			MLL
(1b) Eastern forms										
Epie	o -	k	i			l	e			L-HL
Ẹgẹnẹ	i -	k	i			r	e			L-HL
Abuan	o -	k	o			lh	o			L-LL
Ọgbịa	o -	k	i			ḍ	a			L-HL, H-LL
Kana		g	ẹ		ẹ	r	ẹ			MLM
Efik	n -	kp	ọ					ṇ		H-L
Ibibio	i -	kp	ọ					ṇ		H-F
Lokạạ	ọ -	k	a		a	l	a	ṇ		H-HHL
Bokyi	byi -	k	u							
Bete	ki -	ky	e							H-M pl. bi-
Mambila		k	u		e	l				MM
Ekoid A	ṇ -	k	o	g	i					L-LF
also	e-roṇ -	k	o	g	i				L-F-	L-LF
Mbo	ṇ -	k	a	k	ọ	l	ọ	ṇ		L-HLL Cameroon
Lẹkọṇọ	ṇ -	k	aṇ	k	ẹ	l	o	ṇ		L-HLH Cameroon
Kenyang	n -	kw	a			ny	ọ	ṇ		L-LH Cameroon
Adamawa										
Momi		k	ạ			d	ạ	ṇ		MML
(1c) East Ịjọ compounds the root in (1b) with ḅuru 'yam'										
Nembe	i -	k	e			r	e		-ḅuru	L-LL-LH
	i -	k	e			r	e		-ḅu	L-LL-H
Nkọrọ		k	o						-ḅuru	H-LL
Okrika	i -	k	u						u	L-H-L
Kalaḅarị	i -	k	u							H-L
Ịḅanị		k	u						u	HL
(2) A localized root										
Ịzọn	o -	d	u							L-H loan from Isoko
Isoko	o -	d	u							H-L
Urhobo	u -	d	u							H-L pl. i-
Igbo	e -	d	e							H-L 'new', general
Kana	i -	d	ẹ							H-L loan from Igbo
(3) Another localized root										
Gokana		t	o	g	o					HL
Eleme	e -	t	o				o			L-HL
(4) Another localized root										
Tiv		m	o	nd	u					HL
		m	o	nd	o					LL (Abraham 1940)
		m	o	nd	o				udam	(Bohannan & Bohannan 1953)
Vute		m	w	t	u	u				LLH (w = unrounded u)
(5) Miscellaneous										
Igbo (Ọnịcha)	a -	k	a	s	ị					L-LL 'old'
Idoma	a -	gb	a	h	a					L-HH

Discussion: The status of the cocoyam differs greatly from one community to another; in general it is of greater importance to the south and east. In Idoma it is not of great cultural importance, and the idea of having a festival for it is laughed at. In Irruan, in Bokyi, the cocoyam festival Alube is celebrated in May annually. The Tiv name recorded by Bohannan & Bohannan (1953) means 'mondo of the Udam', i.e. the Bendi speakers, suggesting that the Tiv acquired a species of cocoyam from them. In Igboland, it seems that cocoyam was formerly of more importance than now; note the expression *Igbo rie ji rie ede* LR HH !H HH HL 'the Igbo who eat yam and cocoyam'. It is cultivated by women, whereas men cultivate yams. It is used together with yam in the yam festival at Owere (J. N. Uju, *pers. comm.*). It is used for a small festival called *ili ede* H!H HL 'eating of cocoyam' at Umudioka in Idemili LGA, Anambra State (C. Anisiobi, *pers. comm.*). At Ndeaboh in Awgu LGA of Anambra State, rites are performed before eating the new cocoyams; the best cocoyams with palm oil and a white hen with three kegs of palm wine are presented to Ajaḷịnkwọ, the god of fruitfulness; barren women asking for children go with cocoyams; witches, sorcerers and evil spirits hate the smell of cocoyams and can be driven off with them; planting them on the grave of an *ọgbanje* (child who torments the parents by repeatedly being born and dying) prevents it from coming back (M. E. Achi, *pers. comm.*). In the Ogoni group, it was the principal food before the coming of cassava. It is still highly valued, in Eleme more than yams. Its ritual uses include being presented by a woman to her married daughter in the *ndele* LLL ceremony; it is the sole food prepared to entertain the public during the men's yam-tying ceremony *obo* LH; it is served at wrestling matches and marriage ceremonies. The phrase *dee gẹẹrẹ* ML MLM 'eating of cocoyams' refers to the eating of delicious food and enjoyment. In Tai and Bo'ue, it is believed to neutralize the power of spirits and gods (N. B. Williamson, *pers. comm.*). Among the Kolokuma Ịzọn, it has a festival. There are two types of cocoyam, the 'old' (*Colocasia esculenta*), of southeast Asian origin, and the 'new' (*Xanthosoma mafaffa*), of American origin. They are usually called by the same common name, which is qualified as the indigenous or the 'European' type respectively.

Burkill (1985, p. 200) notes that the most common term in west Africa is *koko* or a derivative of it. He suggests that this originates from Arabic *kulkas* or *qorkas* via Fante, the speakers of which are said to have migrated from Sudan to Ghana. This supposed migration seems to be one of the common west African traditions which have no support from linguistic evidence. Burkill also connects Arabic *kulkas* or *qorqas* with *Colocasia*; he then suggests that the *koko* root and Igbo *akasị* both derive from Arabic. It seems unlikely, however, that an Arabic word would be broken up in this way; it does not happen in the case of the more obvious loans from Arabic, such as Hausa *albasa* LHL, Yoruba *alubọsa* LLHL, Igbo *yabaasị* LHLL, Ịzọn *yabasị* LHL 'onion'; furthermore, it is strange that the words should appear in languages near the coast without also appearing in those to the north, especially Hausa and Fulfulde, which are in more direct contact with Arabic, as is the case with 'onion'.

There seems to be a possible alternative suggestion. Nupe *konkoro* MLL seems at once to be connected to the *koko* root and to suggest that the root was originally longer. To the east we find such longer forms, listed under (1b), which find their fullest form in Cameroon Bantu languages, suggesting that the root originally had four consonants, k- k-l-ŋ; it is of course possible that it was originally a compound rather than a simple root. This form was borrowed from east to west; note that the long vowel in Lokạạ and Kana suggests the loss of an intervocalic consonant; subsequent shortening of the long vowel would yield forms such as the Momi one. Further loss of the ŋ would result in k-l- forms, such as the Central Delta ones, while loss of the -l- would give the Efik/Ibibio ones. On the other hand, keeping the second -k- and the -l-, while losing the -ŋ, would result in such forms as Nupe, and a later loss of the -l- would finally yield *koko*. In this form the word then probably spread further along the coast, eventually entering Krio and spreading to the West Indies. The eastern origin is supported by the fact that the shorter forms can fairly easily be derived from the longer ones, the word being longer than Benue–Congo simple words normally are and therefore prone to shortening when borrowed. An eastern origin would correlate with an area where the cocoyam is a very important staple. Blench (*pers. comm.*) has suggested that plantain was introduced into central Africa by Austronesian mariners, and it is plausible that the first introduction of the cocoyam into central and west Africa had a similar origin, with which this name correlates. This would then be an old root which has spread across linguistic boundaries together with the crop.

The English word 'cocoyam' itself appears to be a fairly recent compounding of 'koko' and 'yam'; it seems to be unknown to nineteenth-century writers, but to be in standard use in Nigeria by 1912; it is possible it is a compounding which took place either in Krio or in Nigerian English, which was heavily influenced by Krio in the early twentieth century.

The second root to be considered is found in Isoko *odu* HL, Urhobo *udu* (plural *idu*) HL, apparently the source of Ịzọn *odu* LH, and also likely to be cognate with Igbo *ede* HL, which Burkill (1985), correctly in my opinion, connects with Caribbean *eddo*. I cannot, however, agree with Burkill (1985, p. 201) in the ultimate origins he proposes for *eddo*: 'E is used in Igbo at Umu Ahia and Owerri. *Do* in the Benin area implies an edible tuber. What more easy in a polyglot community [i.e. in the Caribbean] to combine the two as *e-do* or *eddoe*?' I do not find any confirmation of the proposed source words in material available to me, and while it is possible to combine two words of the same meaning in a polyglot community, I would expect one of them to be the lingua franca of the community, in this case presumably a pidginized or creolized form of English. Moreover, it seems unlikely that if a hybrid form of this type were carried back to Africa it would show different forms correlating neatly with linguistic boundaries as these forms do: *odu/udu* HL with South-West Edoid (apart from the borrowing into Ịzọn) and *ede* HL with Igboid; one would expect a single form spread widely over many linguistic groups.

Burkill's (1985) alternative etymology is as follows: 'Or conceivably to the slaves the plant, so well known, might be quite simply the "Edo root", i.e., from Edo, or the old Kingdom of Benin.' This is also unlikely; the tone of Ẹdo is LH and could not be borrowed as HL in either South-West Edoid or Igboid (it is true that Ịzọn shows LH, but this is due to Ịzọn being more of an accent than a true tone language, and the shift is paralleled in other cases, e.g. Ịzọn *aka* LH from Igboid *ọka* HL 'maize'). The distribution for a word reimported from the Caribbean is as unlikely as for the alternative suggestion.

A possible solution is that the root originated in southern Nigeria, perhaps as *ẹdo* HL, and was borrowed from Igbo in that form to the Caribbean while later assimilating the second vowel to the first in Igboid. This still requires an explanation of the vowels in the South-West Edoid forms.

The *Oxford English Dictionary* ascribes a Ghanaian origin to the term, presumably Fante *ọ-do* LH 'yam' (Christaller 1933). The tone is problematic, and it is also difficult to see why a term meaning 'yam' should shift to 'cocoyam' in a community where both were in use.

Words indicating cultivation

Work on this aspect is just beginning as the languages of southern Nigeria are reconstructed to their proto-languages. So far, two words for 'plant' and a word for 'seed-yam' have been reconstructed by Ohiri-Aniche (In Preparation) to a sub-part of New Benue-Congo, Proto-Igboid-Yoruboid-Edoid.

The terminology of yam-growing in particular is elaborate in some languages, and it is quite likely that further explorations in this area would be productive.

Table 8.10   Plant (tubers)

Yoruba	kọ	M	'make a yam heap'
Ẹdo	kọ	H	'plant, grow'
Igbo	kọ̀	L	'plant (tubers)'

Discussion: This root has been recorded only in what Blench (Ch. 7, this volume) calls 'West Benue-Congo', corresponding to the former 'Kwa' of Greenberg (1966). It suggests that yam cultivation, as opposed to the gathering of wild yams, goes back to at least the West Benue-Congo period.

Table 8.11   Plant

Yoruba	gb in	L	'plant (seed)'
Igala	gb ẹ	L	
Ẹdo	gb ọ ọ	LH	'plant (seedlings/cuttings)'
Isoko	kp on	H	
Igbo (Ọnịcha)	gba	H	'cultivate (cuttings)'

Discussion: Like the preceding one, this root can be traced only to west Benue-Congo.

Table 8.12   Seed-yam

Igala	u – gb ẹ	L-L
Ẹdo	ị – gb in	L-H
Emai	i – gb i	H-L

Discussion: This root has been found so far only in Yoruboid and Edoid.

Conclusion

The plant names studied here confirm the observations of Williamson (1970): the old indigenous plants oil palm, wine palm, kola, aerial yam and (Guinea) yam show a consistent distribution not only within particular groups but also across such groups, leading to their reconstruction at a higher level. They are heavily embedded in culture and ritual.

Plants of the southeast Asian complex, old cocoyam and wateryam, are also widely spread but are less consistent within a group; for example, East Ịjọ uses one root for cocoyam while West Ịjọ uses another. They are regarded as indigenous; many languages specify the old cocoyam by their ethnic name and the new one as 'European'. They are regularly associated with women, while men are associated with the indigenous crops, especially the Guinea yam. They are also involved in ritual, more so towards the southeast, which suggests a point of entry from Cameroon. Where both are important, as among the Ogoni, the southeast Asian tubers have a lesser or introductory ritual role *vis-à-vis* the indigenous tubers; one possible interpretation of this is that the southeast Asian tubers were first in use in the area before the arrival of the Guinea yam from further north; this requires proper ethnological investigation.

The plants introduced by the Portuguese, new cocoyam and coconut, are often easily identified as such by their names, which are qualified as 'European' or, particularly near the coast, are known by Portuguese loan-words. They have little or no ritual use.

The southeast Asian tubers, in particular, have been under-investigated (for example, their names do not occur on the standard Ibadan 400-wordlist); possible lines of spread of particular varieties might conceivably be traced through particular forms of the words.

9   Examination of botanical remains from early neolithic houses at Nabta Playa, Western Desert, Egypt, with special reference to sorghum grains

K. Wasylikowa, J. R. Harlan, J. Evans,

F. Wendorf, R. Schild, A. E. Close,

H. Krolik & R. A. Housley

Introduction

During the field seasons of 1990 and 1991 a rich collection of charred fruits and seeds was found at the early neolithic site E-75-6 at Nabta Playa (Fig. 9.1). Samples from 1990 were collected, sorted and tentatively identified by the first author; those from 1991 were collected and briefly examined by Lucyna Kubiak of the A. Mickiewicz University, Poznan. Plant materials from both seasons were generally similar in taxonomic composition.

It must be emphasized that the results presented below are still preliminary.

Archaeological setting

Site E-75-6 was discovered in 1974. It is on a fossil dune and is partially covered by the silts of one of the largest playas in the Western Desert of Egypt. The site was initially studied in 1974, 1975 and 1977 (Banks 1984, pp. 61–129). Almost 1000 m² were excavated, revealing cultural deposits of two different types of early Neolithic but without reaching the southern and southeastern boundaries of the site. The lower layer was assigned to the early Neolithic of El-Kortein type, dating to about 8800–8500 BP. The upper horizon, which was originally thought to represent a single phase of occupation, is early Neolithic of El-Nabta type, dating to about 8100 BP, and showed a patterned arrangement of two rows of features, including the basin-floors of huts, hearths, storage-pits and walk-in wells. This laid-out village was seen as one of the first indications of developing social control within these societies (Wendorf & Schild 1980, p. 269; Wendorf, Close, Gautier & Schild 1990, p. 445).

Excavation of Site E-75-6 was continued in 1990 and 1991 (under the archaeological direction of Wendorf, Schild, Close and Krolik) (Fig. 9.1). An area of 165 m² was opened; it was sealed beneath early holocene playa clays and lay southeast of the earlier

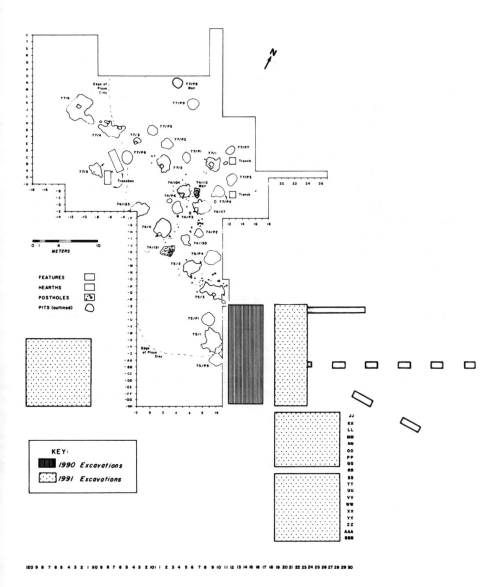

Figure 9.1 Nabta Playa, Site E-75-6: site-map showing the relative positions of the 1977 (unshaded), 1990 and 1991 areas of excavation.

areas (in the direction of the two lines of features) (Fig. 9.2). Removal of the seal of playa clays disclosed a very intricate microstratigraphy, involving several consecutive occupations. Four houses (two oval and two round, all dug to a depth of about 30 cm into the top of the dune), twelve pits and a well were exposed and partially excavated.

The two oval houses are large (8.3 × 4.5 m and 7 × 2.5 m), shallow basins. Hearths in each of them have radiocarbon dates on charcoal of 8550 ± 130 bp (Feature 1/90; Gd-6254) and 8600 ± 140 bp (Feature 3/90; Gd-4587), but these dates are problematically older than AMS radiocarbon dates on *Sorghum* seeds from the same hearths (OxA-3217 and OxA-3219, respectively; see below). In addition, a small hearth cut into the southwestern quadrant of Feature 1/90 gave a date of 7770 ± 110 bp (Gd-6257). The floor of one of them had traces of six hearths (<1 m² in area) and, separate from them, at least 74 small hemispherical depressions, or 'pot-holes', usually 10–20 cm in diameter. The excavated portion of the other oval house had four hearths and 18 hemispherical depressions.

The shallow, circular houses are about 4 m in diameter, and one (Feature 2/90) is dated 7920 ± 100 bp (Gd-6258). One of them had three hearths and seven 'pot-holes' plus an irregular bell-shaped storage pit, while the other had a single hearth and 28 'pot-holes'.

In all the houses, a burned, ashy sediment had been piled up around some of the 'pot-holes' while they held containers, and this sediment was particularly rich in plant remains. This suggests that containers of food were placed in the 'pot-holes' and that hot ash (the brown sediment) was piled up around them to cook the contents, which

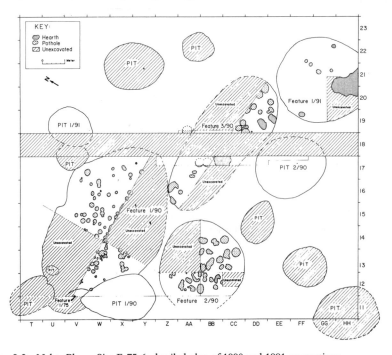

Figure 9.2 Nabta Playa, Site E-75-6: detailed plan of 1990 and 1991 excavations.

sometimes boiled over or fell into the ash, leading to their carbonization and preservation. Many of the 'pot-holes' intersect each other at various levels within the houses, indicating repeated occupations. The house basins as a whole are filled with a grey sand, which is rich in organic remains.

Eleven samples of identified plant remains have direct AMS radiocarbon dates, which cluster tightly around 8000 bp and are in accord with the earlier suite of dates for the site (Haas & Haynes 1980):

8080 ± 110 bp (OxA-3214), Cruciferae? seeds from Feature 1/90
8095 ± 120 bp (OxA-3215), Leguminosae? seeds from Feature 1/90
8020 ± 160 bp (OxA-3217), Sorghum seeds from Feature 1/90
8050 ± 130 bp (OxA-3218), Zizyphus seeds from Feature 1/90
7980 ± 110 bp (OxA-3221), Sorghum seeds from Feature 1/90
8060 ± 120 bp (OxA-3222), Sorghum seeds from Feature 2/90
7950 ± 160 bp (OxA-3219), Sorghum seeds from Feature 3/90
7960 ± 100 bp (OxA-3216), Sorghum seeds from Feature 1/91
8025 ± 120 bp (OxA-3220), Zizyphus seeds from Pit 1/90
7950 ± 90 bp (OxA-3484), Panicum-type from Feature 2/90
7980 ± 95 bp (OxA-3485), Zizyphus seeds from Feature 2/90

Two other radiocarbon age estimates came from the pits: Pit 1/90 gave a date of 8260 ± 100 bp (Gd-6260); Pit 5/75 (in the profile) gave a date of 7450 ± 120 bp (Gd-4586). The microstratigraphy and the radiocarbon dates suggest that the upper occupations, which took place after the dune had stabilized, may cover a period of >1100 years. The presence of wells and the location of occupation near the very centre of a playa suggest dry season occupations.

Pottery was present in some of the features, but was very rare: only nine potsherds were recovered in the 1990 excavation and only three in 1991, including some with herringbone design (from Pit 1/90 and Feature 2/90). Pottery vessels were thus not the usual mode of cooking. In addition, there was almost no burned rock at the site, so pot-boilers were little used, if at all, and food was not commonly roasted on heated rocks. It seems that any containers used in cooking (and the size of most of the plant foods would have necessitated containers) must have been perishable.

All of the houses contained remains of Sorghum, as well as other plant materials. Grains of sorghum type were also present in Pits 1/90 and 2/90.

Description of *Sorghum* sp. remains from Nabta Playa

The genus is represented by numerous charred caryopses and a few charred spikelets. Grains are dorso-ventrally flattened, usually with broad oval or obovate outline; a few are elongated, narrow oval. The large embryo on the dorsal side is as long as 1/3 or more often 1/2 to 2/3 of grain length; the small hilum at the base of the ventral side is oval or obovate. The shape and size of grains show considerable variation (Fig. 9.3). Their dimensions, based on fifteen measurements, are: length 1.65–2.90 mm, average 2.29 mm, breadth 1.25–1.90 mm, average 1.59 mm, thickness 0.85–1.55 mm, average

1.22 mm. Index of the length/breadth ratio is 132–78, average 156; index of thickness/breadth ratio is 61–88, average 76.

All grains are charred, most of them are badly damaged and show deformations characteristic of charred grasses, such as perforations and extrusions of endosperm outside the grain coat in the form of a charred foam. Several grains have glume fragments attached, while some show longitudinal impressions of glume margins along the lateral sides, both features which may suggest that they were charred while still within the glumes.

The ancient charred grains are much smaller and relatively narrower than grains of *Sorghum* varieties cultivated at present and resemble the caryopses of extant wild taxa of this genus. All the ancient charred grains may belong to one taxon but it is also possible that the most elongated specimens represent another form within the same taxon of higher rank.

Spikelet remains (Fig. 9.4) are composed of the second (ventral) glume which at the base is enclosed by the remnants of the first (dorsal) glume. Glumes are thick, with no traces of nervation, which indicates that these are sessile (i.e. fertile) spikelets. In a few

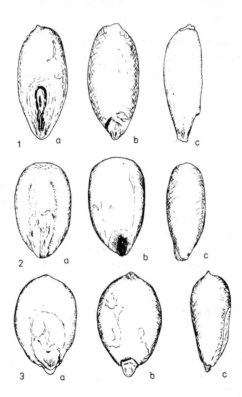

Figure 9.3 Grains of *Sorghum* sp. from Nabta Playa, Site E-75-6: a, b, c – one specimen from each of the dorsal, ventral and lateral sides. 1 – Pit 1/90; 2, 3 – Feature 1/90, southwest quarter. (Average length 2.29 mm.)

specimens, remnants of immature caryopsis are visible inside the glume. Remains of the membranaceous lemmas were not seen, but one specimen has a fragment of geniculate awn inside the glume. The disarticulation scar is rather broad in relation to the spikelet breadth, broader than in mature spikelets of *Sorghum* but comparable to immature ones.

Infra-red spectroscopy[1]

The identification of plant remains from archaeological sites, and the establishment of the phylogenetic relationship of ancient species to modern ones, rely primarily on gross morphological attributes of the plant remains themselves and on appropriate histological criteria. Such identifications are particularly difficult when the samples have

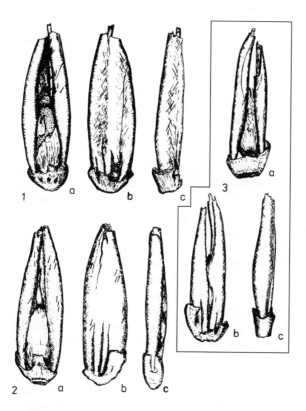

Figure 9.4 Spikelets of *Sorghum* sp. from Nabta Playa, Site E-75-6, Pit 1/90: a, b, c – one specimen from each of the dorsal, ventral and lateral sides. Dorsal glumes broken, immature grains visible inside ventral glume; specimen no. 1 shows a basal portion of twisted awn. (Average length 3.05 mm.)

been charred as, in the majority of cases, their characteristic criteria become distorted, making identification even at species level uncertain. However, it is usually possible to assign seeds to a limited number of alternatives.

A relatively simple, inexpensive and non-destructive method of identifying plant remains involving the use of infra-red spectroscopy (IR) has recently been developed (McLaren, Evans & Hillman 1990). The theoretical background to the concept is that the seed is the product of a series of biochemical processes that take place during its development and which are encoded in the genotype. The morphological changes involved in the process of domestication or other crop development result from a divergence of the gene pools, due both to selection by early cultivators and to natural processes. Thus, each seed variety is unique, as will be its biochemistry, although it will share much of its identity with closely related forms.

Unfortunately, standard methods of chemical taxonomy such as serology or allozyme-electrophoresis are all relatively expensive and require a high degree of skill to carry out successfully. Additionally, the major biochemical components studied are usually proteins or nucleic acids, both of which degrade readily after deposition, or on exposure to heat. Equally, they are easily contaminated by other biological agencies such as bacteria or by exchange with their depositional environment. Consequently, when such studies are undertaken on archaeological materials, the work is difficult, complex and expensive, and thus beyond the reach of most archaeobotanists.

The present method involves the lipid fraction of the seed. Lipids are on the whole stable molecules, well understood chemically, and are easily extracted from seeds without damaging their morphology. They are usually mixtures of fatty acids, glycer-ides, long-chain hydrocarbons and long-chain mono-esters. The actual proportions tend to depend on the species of seed and to some extent the time in the growth cycle. Experience has shown that lipids are archaeologically stable. For instance, beeswax has been detected in sherds from the British neolithic period (Needham & Evans 1987). Also, lipids (unlike proteins, etc.) survive the act of charring. It would appear that the actual charring process causes the lipids to migrate into the body of the seed, thus escaping from the heat source and hence avoiding thermal degradation. Additionally, the actual charring process has two beneficial side effects. First, it tends to sterilize the seed and, second, it coats the seed with an inert wall of carbon. This inert wall protects the sterilized core of the seed from further degradation (biological and chemical) and minimizes contamination from the depositional and post-excavational environments.

Fortunately, the daunting task of unravelling the exact biochemical nature of the lipid residues surviving in the charred seed is not necessary for the archaeobotanist to make an identification. It is equally unimportant for the archaeobotanist to have a detailed knowledge of infra-red spectroscopy. All that is required for identification purposes is to match the overall pattern of the actual infra-red spectrum to a standard spectrum produced under identical conditions. This in itself would be a somewhat lengthy task if the seed was totally unknown but it must be stressed that the technique is employed in conjunction with standard morphological criteria, hence the archaeobotanist will already have assigned the seed to a small number of possibilities.

Procedure

Only one seed was examined at a time. Throughout the extraction process the seed was contained in a lipid-free cellulose thimble. It was thus protected from accidental contamination or physical damage. All solvents used were double distilled in all-glass apparatus in order to have a high purity. All glassware was thoroughly cleaned with detergent followed by 24-hour immersion in chromic acid. One set of glassware was dedicated to each seed to eliminate the possibility of cross-contamination.

The seed was weighed, placed in its thimble and the thimble placed in a soxhlet apparatus. The seed was extracted for three hours sequentially with hexane and chloroform. The extracts were carefully reduced in volume to less than 1 cc. Samples of this solution were spotted onto a previously prepared IR grade potassium bromide disc, the excess solvent being evaporated off by the use of an overhead infra-red heating lamp. A reference disc of identical weight and thickness was similarly prepared using a corresponding amount of pure solvent.

The two discs were inserted into a Perkin-Elmer 781 Infra-red Spectrophotometer and the spectrum was obtained using the multi-scan mode. (Clearly the quantity of lipid present was exceedingly small and consequently the spectrum obtained for a single scan would be very weak – hence the necessity for the multi-scan procedure.) The actual number of scans varied between five and fifteen depending on the amount of extract.

Results

Five archaeological specimens representing different morphological types (2 grains – samples 78/90 (Fig. 9.5) & 16/90 – from Pit 1/90; 2 grains – sample 125/91 – from Pit 2/90 and 1 grain – sample 119/91 – from Feature 1/91) and six cultivated races of

Figure 9.5   *Sorghum* grain no. 78/90 from Pit 1/90. (*c.* 2.9 mm long)

Sorghum bicolor (race *bicolor*; race *guinea*, small-seeded; race *guinea*, large-seeded; race *caudatum*; race *kafir*; race *durra*) and four wild species (*Sorghum arundinaceum*; *Sorghum aethiopicum*; *Sorghum verticilliflorum*; *Sorghum virgatum*) were investigated by the above procedure.

Results obtained for the archaeological specimens were all very similar and the spectra strongly suggest that they all belong to the same species. Unfortunately, three of the cultivated specimens from Kew gave very poor results owing to some form of contamination (probably caused by adhesive, fungicide or something similar). Although other modern, related genera need to be investigated, there is a marked similarity in the general appearance of all the uncontaminated spectra which strongly supports a sorghum designation for the archaeological specimens. A comparison of the various spectra (Figs 9.6, 9.7) showed no exact match but the archaeological specimens showed a nearer kinship to the cultivated specimens than to the wild ones, especially in the hexane extracts.

Conclusion

Clearly, any conclusions drawn must be considered to be highly speculative as a much more detailed study of modern species must be undertaken. With this proviso, the preliminary data support a sorghum designation for the archaeological specimens and suggest the *possibility* that the archaeological materials could reflect some cultivation. Further work is being undertaken, including more detailed analytical studies involving sophisticated chromatographic techniques of the various extracts.

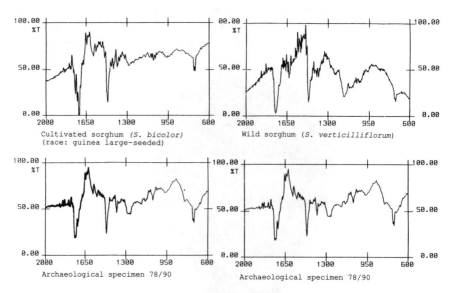

Figure 9.6 Examples of infra-red spectra of hexane extractions from (above) modern grains of wild and cultivated species of sorghum, and (below) a single archaeological specimen of unknown identity from Nabta Playa. (Two spectra of the latter are provided to allow vertical comparison, frequency by frequency.) The horizontal axes represent the wave frequency of the infra-red light (as wave no. per cm); the vertical axis represents the degree of light absorbtion at each frequency (as a percentage of transmission).

Discussion

The identification of *Sorghum* sp. grains from Nabta, based on their morphology, is supported by infra-red spectroscopy. However, the question whether they represent a wild or cultivated form remains unresolved. The lipid analysis does not rule out the possibility that they were cultivated, while grain size and shape, as well as contextual evidence, suggests rather that they were wild.

Sorghum sp. grains were frequent at Nabta, occurring in *c.* 30 per cent of all samples which contained seeds and fruits, but usually in small numbers (1–6 specimens per sample). Thus far, the largest number present in one sample is about 40 specimens. *Sorghum* was found in a botanically rich context which included several other grass genera, other herbaceous plants and at least one tree species. The frequent grasses belong to *Panicum*-type, *Echinochloa*-type and *Setaria*-type, while *Digitaria*-type and *Urochloa/Brachiaria*-type occur only in a few samples. Today, several grass species from these genera are collected for food by nomads living in the Sahara (Harlan 1989). *Sorghum* was the most frequent grass type at Nabta and, since its grains are larger than those of other grasses, we may suppose that it was an important food plant. More detailed estimation of the role it played in the diet of the early neolithic people at Nabta is not possible until quantitative analyses are finished, but Site E-75-6 already gives the first evidence of the use of sorghum grains, whether gathered from the wild or already under cultivation.

Other wild food plants included *Zizyphus* spp. Fruit-stones and seeds of this tree

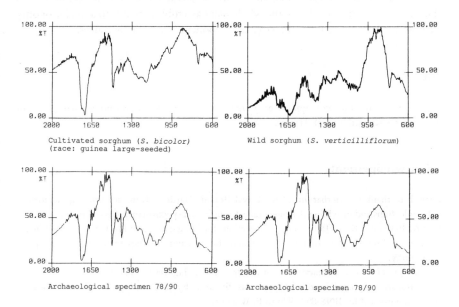

Cultivated sorghum (*S. bicolor*)
(race: guinea large-seeded)

Wild sorghum (*S. verticilliflorum*)

Archaeological specimen 78/90

Archaeological specimen 78/90

Figure 9.7 Examples of infra-red spectra: typical of chloroform extractions from (above) modern grains of wild and cultivated species of sorghum, and (below) a single archaeological specimen of unknown identity. (Axes and units as Figure 9.6.)

were frequent at Nabta. Tubers (undetermined) were also relatively common but were probably of less importance in the diet than they were at the late palaeolithic sites of Wadi Kubbaniya (Hillman, Madeyska & Hather 1989; Hillman 1989; Wetterstrom, Ch. 10, this volume).

Fruits of other plants are so incompletely identified that their usefulness for people is difficult to assess. If we assume that the abundance of remains may be an indication of gathering, then Leguminosae indet., Cruciferae indet. (tribe Brassicae), Cucurbitaceae indet. and Capparidaceae indet. (*Capparis*-type) could represent collected plants. The frequently occurring *Arnebia*-type fruits are inedible and are unlikely to have been gathered for food. Less frequent seeds or fruits at Nabta belong to *Cyperus/Fuirena*-type, *Scirpus/Schoenoplectus*-type, *Rumex*-type, Chenopodiaceae indet. (?) and Malvaceae indet. (?). A considerable portion of the material remains unidentified.

All plant remains were charred with the exception of *Arnebia*-type nutlets. Fruits of most members of the family Boraginaceae do not turn black on burning because of the high content of silica in the pericarp, although they sometimes turn a distinctive pale grey colour (van Zeist & Waterbolk-van Rooijen 1985). Siliceous nutlets of these plants are very resistant to decay and tend to be over-represented relative to remains of species dependent on charring for their preservation. In Nabta, the presence of two charred seeds inside uncharred pericarps indicates that they have been subjected to high temperatures and may be of the same age as the other plant remnants preserved entirely by charring.

The present study did not confirm the occurrence of cultivated barley at Nabta (el Hadidi 1980; Stemler & Falk 1980) and, with the possible exception of sorghum – on which further work is required – the whole plant assemblage points to a food economy based on wild plants, as far as the vegetal component of the diet is concerned.

Note

[1] Infra-red spectroscopy was applied by J. Evans to archaeological and present-day grains of *Sorghum* races selected by J. R. Harlan.

Acknowledgements

We wish to thank the Herbarium of the Royal Botanic Gardens, Kew, for offering facilities to study collections and providing *Sorghum* grains for infra-red spectroscopy. Special thanks go to Dr Steve A. Renvoize, Kew Herbarium, grass section, for his assistance and to Dr Gordon Hillman, Institute of Archaeology, London University, for sharing his experience in ancient plant morphology.

We are grateful to Z. Tomaczynska for the drawings in Figures 9.3 and 9.4.

The research reported in this chapter was financed by a United States National Science Foundation grant (No. BNS-8903585) to F. Wendorf.

10   Foraging and farming in Egypt: the transition from hunting and gathering to horticulture in the Nile valley

WILMA WETTERSTROM

Introduction

In southwest Asia, the beginnings of agriculture go back before 8000 BC, where there were flourishing farming villages and towns by 7000 BC (Moore 1985). But on the other side of Sinai in the Nile valley, lifeways remained unchanged. Old patterns of foraging continued until about 5000 BC when the first farming communities appeared in northern Egypt. About a millennium later farming villages were established in southern Egypt (Hassan 1985, pp. 104–5).

The new farming patterns in Egypt were based on crops and livestock originally domesticated in southwest Asia. The process by which these domesticates were adopted and integrated into an Egyptian foraging economy raises many unresolved questions. Why did Egyptians 'resist' farming so long while their neighbours in the Levant were thriving as farmers (Butzer 1976, p. 9)? Why were domesticates adopted at such a seemingly late date? How did farming techniques and crops and livestock make their way to the Nile valley? How was farming incorporated in a foraging economy? Were foragers displaced by invading farmers or forced to adopt farming because of pressures from neighbouring farmers? How did farming spread through the Nile valley?

We now have a better understanding of hunter–gatherer subsistence in the Nile valley (Fig. 10.1) than even a few years ago, thanks to the work of the Combined Prehistoric Expedition at Wadi Kubbaniya in Upper Egypt (Wendorf, Schild & Close 1989). Wadi Kubbaniya, dated to 18,000 BP, provides a baseline from which one can begin to understand foraging adaptations in holocene Egypt and some of the factors involved in the transition to farming. Although the Kubbaniyan sites are more than 10,000 years older than Egypt's last foraging communities, they nonetheless provide a useful model for understanding later Egyptian foraging. The Kubbaniyan hunting and gathering practices could have been part of a common Nilotic adaptation that may have begun in the late Pleistocene and continued on into the Holocene. With some modification following climate change at the end of the Pleistocene, these patterns of subsistence could have persisted through the Epipalaeolithic.

They may have continued into neolithic times as well. It is proposed here that Egyptian foragers first adopted southwest Asian domesticates as only one more set of resources to exploit, as they continued to hunt and gather. The most attractive feature

of these new foods may have been their predictability rather than their productivity.
Though Egyptians had a seemingly successful and stable subsistence pattern, they were
at the mercy of the annual Nile floods which could fluctuate substantially from year to
year and over time. An unusually high or low flood could devastate the Nile valley,
leaving foragers short. With the domesticates, foragers had a resource that might
effectively compensate for the unpredictability of the floods. Both the location and the
size of the crop and the herds could be controlled to some extent and adjusted in
response to the vagaries of nature. With a grain cache and meat on the hoof, Egyptians
had resources to counterbalance the effects of lean times, thereby allowing them to go
on hunting and gathering. Domesticates were therefore a means to improve the
foraging system by diversifying it rather than replacing it.

Unfortunately, the archaeological data from Egypt's first farming communities are
too sparse to encourage much probing into the causes of the transition to agriculture.

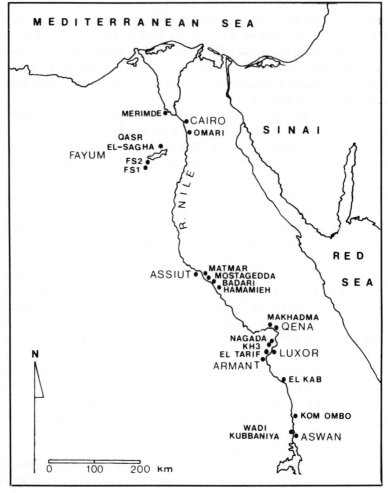

Figure 10.1 Sites mentioned in the text.

But the sites that will be examined here do suggest that initially lifeways were not dramatically changed with the introduction of domesticates, which appear to have been adopted as a whole complex. The first farming settlements are not significantly different from earlier hunter–gatherer camps. They appear to be short-term occupations and left little more than artefact scatters, hearths and pits and, in a few instances, traces of ephemeral structures. Fish remained a major resource while wetland plants were still gathered. Game, the least reliable element of the foraging system, was still hunted, but domestic livestock seemed to play a larger role. In the Fayum this pattern persisted for over 1000 years, but in the Nile valley and on the Delta, change began quickly. Not long after the earliest farming settlements, several trends are evident: storage facilities become more elaborate and more abundant, suggesting a growing role for cultigens in the diet; hunting seems to decline, as suggested by faunal remains and stone tools; and the settlements grow larger and more complex. By the early fourth millennium BC, Egyptians in northern Egypt had shifted to a specialized economy based on crops and livestock. In southern Egypt the transition occurred slightly later.

Finally, it is proposed that the timing of Egypt's foray into food production was not late, but was consistent with events in southwest Asia. Although agriculture and herding were developing throughout southwest Asia between about 8000 BC and 6000 BC, the fully developed Near Eastern complex did not come together until about 6000 BC. Thus it seems quite probable that domesticates came into the Delta sometime between 6000 and 5000 BC, during a period when it has been suggested that there was massive relocation of farming communities in the Levant as a result of climatic deterioration (see below).

The environmental background

It is impossible to understand ancient, or modern, Egypt without considering the Nile and its profound influence on plant and animal life. Flowing north–northwest, the Nile has incised a narrow river valley through pleistocene sands and gravels. Just north of Cairo, it fans out across the wide expanse of delta, channelled today into two branches. Through most of its Egyptian course, some 800 km from the Sudanese border to Cairo, it is virtually the only source of water. The floodplain, now carpeted with acres of irrigated fields, varies widely along the length of the Nile; near Aswan it is little more than the width of the river. Further downstream it is broader, reaching up to 23 km in some places (Issawi 1976). Thus the potential for foraging and farming varied markedly through the river valley.

Skirting the river's floodplain are the low desert terraces, with cliffs rising above them. Beyond lie the deserts: to the east is the Eastern Desert with low rugged mountains, steep scarps and valleys; on the opposite side of the river lies the Western Desert, a flat monotonous plain, barren except for several oases (Issawi 1976).

The Fayum depression, an oasis lying just west of the Nile valley about 60 km southwest of Cairo, was connected to the river via a channel until about the first millennium BC (Hassan 1986a, p. 495). A shallow, saline lake, the Birket Qarun, lies in the northeast corner of the depression, a sad remnant of what was once Lake Moeris, a large body of fresh water. The arid north rim and southwestern corner of the depression have produced some of our best data on epipalaeolithic economies and Egypt's first farming communities.

The climate today is hyperarid, with practically no precipitation south of the Delta except for occasional rain in the Red Sea hills (Issawi 1976). But this was not always the case. Egypt has seen climatic changes and important alterations in the river regime over the last 20,000 years. The period from 20,000 to 12,000 BP was hyperarid, like the present, but cooler. At the end of the Pleistocene as the glaciers retreated, rainfall and temperature increased (Wendorf & Schild 1989, pp. 768–88). Rainfall levels remained higher through much of the early to mid-Holocene, which saw three moist phases. Drier conditions started about 5400 BP and have continued to the present (Wendorf & Schild 1980, pp. 236–41; see also Grove, Ch. 1, and Maley, Ch. 2, this volume).

Partly as a result of these climatic changes, the Nile has had a complex geological history. The river has at various times built its floodplain and at others cut it down, as its water volume and sediment load have varied. This has undoubtedly had far-reaching consequences for the archaeological record in the Nile valley. For example, these geological processes may be responsible for the void in the record for the Nile valley north of the Qena bend. There are no sites in this region between upper palaeolithic and predynastic times, although it is hard to imagine that this potentially rich area would have been ignored by holocene foragers.[1]

The Nile delta also has a complex geological past which has profoundly affected the archaeological record. Nile sediments have been accumulating in the present location of the Delta since the late Miocene with periodic phases of erosion. Between 7000 BC and 4000 BC, as the Mediterranean Sea rose, approaching its present-day levels, the northern third of the Delta was reduced to a vast tract of swamp and lagoon. But at the same time, rapid Nile alluviation was depositing a thick sheet of mud over the Delta, and by 4000 BC it had reached more or less its present dimensions (Butzer 1976, p. 23). With this combination of erosion and alluviation, much of the archaeological record before 4000 BC has probably either been washed away or buried under extensive deposits of Nile sediments, which have amassed 10 m in the last 6000 years (Butzer 1976, p. 25).

Pleistocene, post-pleistocene adaptations and Wadi Kubbaniya

As a result of the work done at Wadi Kubbaniya, more is known about foraging during the late Palaeolithic than at any other time in Egypt's past, and partly for this reason the Kubbaniyan subsistence patterns are used as a model for later ones. But before we consider Wadi Kubbaniya, it is first necessary to ask whether these pleistocene foraging practices are a valid model for epipalaeolithic hunting and gathering more than 10,000 years later. Were holocene hunter–gatherers like late pleistocene foragers?

According to Foley (1988) they were not. He points out that late pleistocene populations show much greater robusticity and sexual dimorphism than modern human populations, which suggests that their foraging and reproductive strategies differed markedly from those of most modern hunter–gatherers. Robusticity probably reflects much greater emphasis on hunting, especially hunting of very large mammals, which were common during the Pleistocene. Marked sexual dimorphism, Foley suggests, indicates very different foraging strategies for males and females. Foley infers that males were responsible for a large proportion of the foraging and provided for the young and females, who contributed relatively little to the food quest. The concomitant social organization probably was quite different, as well, from that of modern hunter-gatherers.

Foley points out that from the end of the Pleistocene, human populations have followed a trend of reduced robusticity and sexual dimorphism, suggesting a reduction in the differences between male and female foraging practices. He argues that this is part of an evolutionary response to depletion of resources. At the end of the Pleistocene, as game animals became scarce, plant foods would have, by necessity, become more important. Males could not have supplied as much food as in the past, while females would have become more critical in the food quest. This could have led to both a decrease in body size and a reduction in the degree of sexual dimorphism. At the same time new social arrangements would have emerged, emphasizing egalitarian relations, a flexible band system and an equally important role for males and females in provisioning the group. Thus hunting and gathering as known today is not an archaic, ancestral way of life, but a post-pleistocene adaptation to the depletion of resources. Foley also argues that agriculture was a parallel adaptation to this situation; that is, modern foraging and agricultural systems emerged together at the end of the Pleistocene in response to a changing environment.

In the light of the potential differences between pleistocene and post-pleistocene adaptations, how does one interpret the data from Wadi Kubbaniya, and what can it tell us about holocene foragers? First, despite its early date, Wadi Kubbaniya follows post-pleistocene trends. The Nile valley, bounded by arid lifeless deserts, was at this time an impoverished environment that supported a limited variety of fauna and a small biomass (Gautier & van Neer 1989, pp. 158–9). Large game supplied only a modest portion of the diet, as suggested by the faunal remains. Like post-pleistocene foragers, Kubbaniyans had to rely on a broad range of resources, including wetland plants and catfish, as indicated by the floral and faunal remains. In this environment, both sexes would have participated in the food quest, with females presumably gathering plants.[2]

The Wadi Kubbaniya sites thus offer insights into foraging systems heavily dependent on Nilotic resources, wetland plants and fish. Archaeological data from later palaeolithic sites suggest that these resources remained predominant up to mid-holocene times, despite some major climatic changes. As the data from Wadi Kubbaniya are far more complete than data from any later sites, they can provide a framework for understanding the foraging systems of Egypt's last hunter-gatherers. The Wadi Kubbaniya work is most valuable in indicating the role of the wetland resources, the ways in which they might have been exploited and the inherent difficulties in such a foraging system. Wadi Kubbaniya sites, however, may not reflect the social organization of epipalaeolithic foragers.

Foraging in the late Palaeolithic at Wadi Kubbaniya

The Wadi Kubbaniya environment

A major drainage system, Wadi Kubbaniya enters the Nile valley from the northwest through a narrow gorge a few kilometres north of Aswan. The Nile valley here from Aswan to the Kom Ombo plain is a narrow floodplain, less than 2 km wide, with steep, sandstone scarps rising on either side (Schild & Wendorf 1989, p. 15).

One of the most important results of the Combined Prehistoric Expedition's work has been a new understanding of the Nile and its floodplain during the late Pleistocene. Through detailed stratigraphic studies and precise geological mapping, combined with information about climate in the Nile headwaters, Schild & Wendorf (1989) determined that the Nile was quite a different river from that of the present. It was a much smaller, seasonal, sluggish river, which probably flowed through several braided channels rather than a single massive stream. Carrying a heavy sediment load, the Nile was depositing sediments throughout this period and gradually raising the level of the floodplain south of the Qena bend. At 21,000 years ago the base level of the river was nearly 16 m higher than today (Wendorf 1989, p. 1).

During the annual flood, the river inundated nearly all of the narrow valley, leaving a thin strip of dry land less than 50 m wide along the cliffs which rise above the floodplain. As a result, there would have been very little access to plant resources during the height of the inundation. Floodwaters also penetrated Wadi Kubbaniya, travelling more than 3 km from the mouth.

Relict vegetation on islands in the Nile (el-Hadidi & Springuel 1978; Springuel 1981; el-Hadidi & Springuel 1989) offer insights into the landscape of both the pleistocene and the later holocene Nile valley. Studies of this vegetation have found (1) a 'strong, water-controlled zonation', and (2) 'a basic association of particular plant communities with water-sediment zones' (Schild & Wendorf 1989, p. 97). The tree zones are always above the line of the flood; the tamarisk and *Leptadenia* shrubs thrive on occasionally submerged sandy deposits; the seasonally flooded areas are occupied by meadows of *Panicum* and *Cyperus*; whereas marshes with *Phragmites*, *Polygonum* and *Cyperus* occur on partially submerged ground (Schild & Wendorf 1989, p. 97). Thus the Nile valley of the late Pleistocene would have been an open landscape of marshes and meadows, with shrubs and trees limited to the edge of the valley along the cliffs. The seasonally inundated Wadi Kubbaniya would have been covered with marshes and meadows. Above these were dune fields, where desert winds continually swept sand into the wadi. Seasonally flooded, these would have supported tamarisk and *Leptadenia* shrubs. Higher dune areas beyond the flood's reach may have had scattered stands of acacias (Wendorf & Schild 1989, pp. 97–100). Beyond the wadi and the Nile valley the desert during this hyperarid period was devoid of vegetation.

Archaeological remains

Between 1978 and 1984 the Combined Prehistoric Expedition carried out survey, excavations and detailed geological studies in the wadi and at its mouth (Wendorf, Schild & Close 1989). As a result it was found that most of the late palaeolithic sites were concentrated on the tops of dunes in a dune-field about 3 km from the mouth of the wadi. The dune sites would have been flooded during late summer, but thereafter offered a commanding view over the swampy floodplain. At three of these sites large-scale excavations were carried out and twenty-four other locations were tested. The principal occupations, which belong to the Kubbaniyan tradition, date from about 19,000 to 17,000 BP (Wendorf & Schild 1989, p. 93). They consist of small camps with concentrations of occupational debris, including bone and charcoal, and stone tools dominated by backed bladelets, heavy grinders and shallow heavy mortars (Wendorf & Schild 1989, pp. 792–3).

Flotation could not be used to recover plant and small bone remains because most of the plant charcoal proved to be very fragile and disintegrated on contact with water. Instead, several hundred cubic metres of dry sediment had to be dry-sieved with specially constructed graded screens. This yielded not only one of the richest assemblages of plant-food remains ever recorded from a palaeolithic site, but also charred remains of human faeces, and the most complete collection of bone ever recorded from the Nile valley, including fragile remains of immature and small fish species.

Subsistence

With this remarkable collection of floral and faunal remains from wadi sites dating to 18,000 BP, Wendorf and his colleagues (Gautier & van Neer 1989; Hillman 1989; Hillman, Madeyska & Hather 1989; Wendorf & Schild 1989) have drawn the most detailed reconstruction of hunter-gatherer subsistence and seasonality ever attempted for the Old World Palaeolithic. They propose a subsistence pattern more akin to post-pleistocene adaptations than pleistocene hunting and gathering. Large game played a minor role, while fish and 'root' foods from wetland plants were staples. At the same time Kubbaniyans had a breadth of dietary diversity comparable to that of African hunter-gatherers in recent times, which probably assured survival through 'lean' periods.

Fauna

The faunal remains, analysed by Gautier & van Neer (1989), were dominated by enormous quantities of fish bones (130,280 from one site alone). Migratory birds were also recovered, as well as small quantities of ungulates. The few canid bones in the samples may have come from animals taken for pelts and claws, whereas the hippo teeth in the collection may have been used for carving. Rodents, toads and snakes were probably intrusives.

Mammals Large mammals would have been important for meat and hides but the faunal remains indicate a very limited role. Little mammal bone was recovered from the Wadi Kubbaniya sites compared with fish and bird. At one site mammals represented only about 1 per cent of the bone (Wendorf & Schild 1989, p. 819). These low quantities can probably be attributed to an impoverished environment. The Nile valley at this time, covered mostly with wetlands and meadows, could have supported neither a large number nor a great variety of game. The monotonous flora would have provided grazing for only a limited number of species; indeed, only three large mammals were common at Wadi Kubbaniya, as well as at later sites in the Nile valley – the hartebeest, aurochs and dorcas gazelle. This stands in marked contrast to the rich faunas at sites in the Sudan (Gautier & van Neer 1989, pp. 156–7). In addition, the river's flood regimen would have severely limited the size of the game populations. During the two to four weeks of maximum flood, people and animals were driven out of the wadi and Nile valley. Between the floodwaters and the arid desert, large mammals would have found a very narrow band of grazing that would have effectively restricted the land's carrying capacity. As a result, the available biomass of the hartebeest and aurochs may have been only a few animals per square kilometre (Gautier & van Neer 1989, pp. 158–9). Finally, the game's behaviour would have rendered them unpredictable and difficult to hunt at times, as described below.

The hartebeest (*Acelaphus buselaphus*) is the most numerous bovid in the Wadi Kubbaniya samples, followed by roughly equal numbers of the now extinct aurochs (*Bos primigenius*) and the dorcas gazelle (*Gazella dorcas*) (Gautier & van Neer 1989, pp. 154–6). The hartebeest and gazelle share several features: they are territorial herd animals easily taken under good environmental conditions, but when the environment deteriorates herds can pick up and migrate great distances in search of new grazing or water.

The hartebeest, no longer found in the Nile valley, used to be extremely abundant in many parts of Africa and in some localities was the dominant species (Kingdon 1982, p. 507). As it was a large gazelle, ranging from 150 to over 200 kg, it would have been a great feast for a successful hunter and his camp. A grazer on bulk roughage, feeding non–selectively on grasses, the hartebeest is generally found in coarse grasslands in an ecotone, usually between woods or scrub and open grassland (Kingdon 1982, p. 509). But wholesale migrations of herds have been seen in some areas during the dry season. Most of the time hartebeest concentrate around sources of food and water during dry periods and disperse when conditions improve. The older males become solitary, spacing themselves out into small territories, while young males join mobile groups of bachelors, and females move with other females and their offspring in herds (Kingdon 1982, p. 516).

During the late Pleistocene, hartebeest would have found grazing in the meadows in drier areas of the Nile floodplain and Wadi Kubbaniya. Here males may have held their territories while female and bachelor groups wandered across the valley. With their sedentary habits and limited ranges they could easily have been hunted (Kingdon 1982, p. 507). In addition, hunters would have had no trouble locating them because they are highly conspicuous (Kingdon 1982, p. 507). Males claiming their territories would have been particularly easy prey. They offset their vulnerability, however, with keen eyesight and great speed (Kingdon 1989, p. 522).

Little is known of the behaviour and ecological requirements of wild cattle, as these creatures have been extinct for several centuries. Gautier & van Neer (1989, pp. 135–6) suggest they were fairly tolerant herd animals, adapted to good grassland with or without wooded vegetation. In Nile valley archaeological sites, wild cattle occur consistently with hartebeest, suggesting that they had similar ecological requirements: an ecotone environment between woods and grasslands.

Dorcas gazelle are a rare sight in the Nile valley today, but they can be seen in the wadis and canyons of the Red Sea hills and the Western Desert and at the margins of oases (Osborn & Helmy 1980, p. 504). Far smaller than the hartebeest, they weigh only 99 to 110 kg (Dorst & Dandelot 1970, p. 239). Like the larger bovid they are territorial herd animals that are easily hunted (Dorst & Dandelot 1970, p. 342). Their staple foods are various species of acacia, including the leaves, flowers, thorns and pods, but they browse on other plants when acacia is not available (Osborn & Helmy 1980, pp. 505–7). Highly sensitive to heat, gazelle require water daily in hot weather, from standing water, dew or vegetation. They confine their activities to the coolest parts of the day and in the summer seek the shade of shrubs and trees in mid-day (Delany & Happold 1979, pp. 160–1), where they are easily stalked and speared (Nicolaisen 1963, p. 157). If need be, they can migrate great distances in search of food and water (Delany & Happold 1979, p. 154). During the late Pleistocene they may have ranged on the outer margins of Wadi Kubbaniya and the Nile valley, where they could have found acacias.

Kubbaniyan hunters may have used spears for taking the larger ungulates and nets and traps for the smaller ones. They may have driven the large herbivores into shallow water where they could have been more easily attacked (Gautier & van Neer 1989, p. 159). Although the hartebeest and gazelle, and possibly aurochs, were easy to hunt, it is unlikely that they were a reliable food source (Gautier & van Neer 1989, p. 159). With the low carrying capacity of the Nile valley, as mentioned above, the herds may have been easily depleted. With their inclination to migrate under poor conditions, they may have abandoned the Wadi Kubbaniya area altogether at certain periods. During the inundation, they may have sought better grazing on the wide Kom Ombo plain and other large expanses of the floodplain.

Fish The fishing patterns seen at Wadi Kubbaniya are repeated throughout the archaeological record into predynastic times. The most important species, accounting for over 90 per cent of the fish bone, was the catfish, *Clarias*. It is a shallow-water fish that could have been harvested in great quantities during its annual spawn, which is believed to occur at the beginning of the flood (Gautier & van Neer 1989, pp. 142–7). During spawning, *Clarias* migrate to the floodplain, congregating in great masses in shallow marginal areas (less than 10 cm to 40 cm deep) where they lay their eggs. Following mating, they lie listlessly for several hours before returning to the main channel. During the one or more consecutive nights of spawning, catfish can be easily caught by hand, or with striking or wounding gear, or cover pots, as is still done today (van Neer 1989, p. 53). The remains of large individuals found in the Wadi Kubbaniya sites have been interpreted as catfish taken during spawning.

A second fishing season occurred in the autumn. As the floodwater receded, adult catfish and later juveniles would have migrated to deeper water, but those trapped in residual pools would have been easy prey. Fishing techniques were probably simple, possibly augmented by stupefying fish with fish poisons or by agitating the mud at the bottom of the pools. Smaller individuals, which were found at Wadi Kubbaniya sites dating slightly earlier than most of the occupation, were interpreted as fish taken during this post-flood season (Gautier & van Neer 1989, pp. 142–7).

During both fishing seasons every able-bodied individual in the community probably joined the fishing parties, including men, women and children. With the spawning run lasting only a short time, each pair of hands that could be added to the workforce was important (Gautier & van Neer 1989, pp. 145, 160). The harvests probably yielded more fish than could be eaten immediately, as suggested by the enormous quantities of fish bone found at some of the sites. Most likely, catfish were sun-dried or smoked over hearths for storage. A cache of dried fish would have helped see the Kubbaniyans through lean periods but would not have lasted more than four or five months before spoiling (Gautier & van Neer 1989, pp. 151–2, 160).

Fishing was not restricted to two seasons, as fish would have been available throughout the rest of the year. But outside these two periods, fish would have been highly dispersed, rendering fishing a more difficult and less lucrative pursuit. Individual fishermen could have fished in the dense vegetation along the margins of flooded areas, using wounding and striking gear or fish gorges attached to lines (Gautier & van Neer 1989, p. 146). Such gorges were found at some of the sites in small numbers (Gautier & van Neer 1989, p. 160).

Water-fowl Another important food resource from the wetlands was migratory water birds. They were important to Egyptians throughout prehistoric and dynastic periods (see also Clutton-Brock, Ch. 4, this volume). At Wadi Kubbaniya the most abundant types are rallids, probably coots (*Fulica atra*), followed by geese and ducks, all of which would have been found in the marshes of the Nile valley through the winter, from October through March, or while they were *en route* between Europe and wintering grounds further south. They may have been taken with nets and traps (Gautier & van Neer 1989, p. 54).

Flora

Ethnographic studies of hunter-gatherers have found that they know and use a broad range of plants, but generally subsist on a small number of productive, reliable staples (Tanaka 1976, p. 105; Yellen & Lee 1976, p. 38; Jones & Meehan 1989, p. 122). The broad base of plants, though not fully exploited, is important as it 'provides an essential margin of safety' during lean periods (Yellen & Lee 1976, p. 38). The antiquity of this pattern is not known, but one might expect to see a broad range of back-up foods in environments where there are stressful periods with marked shortages. Staples might likewise be expected where a small number of foods can efficiently and adequately meet the needs of a community. However, humans clearly do not live on starch staples alone, and the broad spectrum of plant species consumed in small quantities by recent hunter-gatherers have possibly played a critical role in providing essential fatty acids, vitamins, minerals and a range of other components now known to be important to all-round health.

The Wadi Kubbaniya data suggest that there were starchy staples as well as great dietary breadth. Thus far 25 types of seeds, fruits and soft vegetable tissues have been isolated, of which 13 are now identified (Hillman 1989; Hillman, Madeyska & Hather 1989). These are dominated by charred fragments of soft starchy vegetables, most of which are from tubers of wild nut-grass, *Cyperus rotundus*, a type of sedge, which appears to have served as the main source of carbohydrates in the Kubbaniyan diet for at least part of the year. Other starchy vegetables include a large tuber fragment of club-rush, *Scirpus maritimus* or *S. tuberosus*, a rhizome fragment of a dictyostelous fern, as well as five other types of vegetable parenchyma tissue which have not yet been identified. Other foods include fruit fragments of the dom palm *Hyphaene thebaica*, nutlets ('seeds') of club-rush (seemingly the same type that produced the tuber), a receptacle from an immature (edible) flower-bud or an extinct type of waterlily (family Nymphaceae), tiny seeds of what appear to be three different species of the chamomile tribe (Compositae – tribe Anthemidae), a schizocarpous fruit (probably a *Tribulus* species) seemingly charred while still green and edible, and a fragment of the edible fruit of caper (*Capparis* spp.). All of these or their close relatives grow in the Nile valley today and all are edible. In addition, a number of other plant foods, not recovered, were identified through ethno–ecological modelling as almost certainly part of the diet.

'Root' foods Nut-grass is abundant throughout much of the Nile valley today, growing in dense swards at the water's edge and less densely further up the banks and in irrigated fields. It produces a mass of interconnecting rhizomes which bear small, oblong, bitter-tasting tubers. They are rich in carbohydrates, have a very high fibre content, but are very poor in both fat and protein (Bulman 1985; Hillman, Madeyska & Hather 1989, p. 181) and contain a variety of toxins, including alkaloids, ketones and phenols. During the early stages of growth, though, they are still tender and relatively low in toxins and thus probably could have been consumed in large quantities after merely being roasted and rubbed. Once fully mature, however, the tubers would have been hard, woody and toxic, and would have had to be ground and detoxified by leaching to be consumed as a staple.

Grinding stones, which were abundant at the Kubbaniyan sites, were apparently used for this very purpose. Chemical analysis (using pyrolysis mass spectrometry) of a mortar-cum-grinder revealed that the working surfaces (but not any other surfaces) carried 'cellulosics' (starch and/or cellulose) but no trace of protein (Jones 1989), suggesting that it had not been used to grind seeds, but instead had served to grind starchy vegetables such as the tubers.

There are a number of factors which render nut-grass tubers the most probable candidate for a starchy staple at Wadi Kubbaniya. The most important are its abundance, productivity and reliability. At the time the sites were occupied, there would almost certainly have been extensive swards of nut-grass, and these could have yielded enormous quantities of tubers. Hillman (Hillman, Madeyska & Hather 1989, p. 179) found that where nut-grass grew in dense swards at the water's edge, it produced an astonishing 3.3 kg of tubers per m^2 (or 33,000 kg per hectare). In drier areas, where the plants grew less densely, the yield was 37 gm per m^2 (or 3700 kg per hectare). These exceptionally high yields compare favourably with domesticates; barley world-wide averages 16,500 kg per hectare and in the United Kingdom it achieves its maximum yield of 35,000 kg per hectare (Purseglove 1972, pp. 160–1). Nut-grass would not have covered vast acres like modern cereal fields, but ecological data suggest that nut-grass swards were nonetheless rather extensive. A family 'armed with digging sticks could have gathered enough to meet several days' carbohydrate requirements in a matter of hours' (Hillman, Madeyska & Hather 1989, p. 180).

Another great virtue of nut-grass was that it tolerated exploitation – indeed, it probably thrived on it. 'Nut-grass seems to be stimulated into more active tuber production by soil disturbance such as could result from digging wild tubers' (Hillman, Madeyska & Hather 1989, p. 180). 'Heavy annual harvesting of the swards of wild *Cyperus* would thus, of itself, have guaranteed an equally heavy harvest of freshly formed tubers in each ensuing year' (Hillman, Madeyska & Hather 1989, p. 181). In addition, tubers are less seasonal than seeds and fruits and can be harvested over longer periods (Gott 1982, p. 60).

Another factor which suggests that nut-grass, and possibly other root foods, were staples is the ethnographic record. Ethnohistorical records of hunter-gatherer subsistence demonstrate widespread and heavy dependence on root foods as staples (see, for example, the review of Australian evidence by Gott 1982), although it is not clear when these patterns developed. Wherever root foods are abundant they are preferred over seeds (Hillman, Madeyska & Hather 1989, p. 220). Cane (1989, p. 111) observed that native Australians opted for tubers and fruits in preference to seeds, as these require far less time to process. Moreover, the 'feasibility of wild nut-grass having served as a staple at Kubbaniya is reinforced by records of its role as a staple in the diet of Aboriginal Australians who occupied similarly arid terrain and had similar access to seasonally wet areas of riverine vegetation' (Hillman, Madeyska & Hather 1989, p. 227).

Finally, the archaeological record from Wadi Kubbaniya supports this view. Soft root foods have very low archaeological 'visibility' and are rarely found at sites, particularly ones of such great antiquity. The fact that nut-grass tuber remains were recovered at all and that they 'are the only plant food present in all levels of each site suggest[s] that it was, indeed, a dietary staple, and perhaps *the* staple' (Hillman, Madeyska & Hather 1989, p. 227).

Another sedge tuber found at Wadi Kubbaniya, the club-rush (*Scirpus maritimus* or *S. tuberosus*), probably would have grown in extensive stands adjacent to the belt of *Cyperus rotundus*. Like nut-grass, these could have been an ample reserve of carbohydrate-rich tubers. In England, the sea club-rush produces enormous quantities of tubers, which lack the bitterness of nut-grass. If the Wadi Kubbaniya populations were similar, they would have required no more than minimal detoxification before they could be eaten. On the other hand, the mature tubers are even more woody and fibrous than nut-grass tubers and would therefore have required grinding or pounding before they could be eaten. Ethnographic literature records numerous examples of various species of *Scirpus* used as food (summarized in Hillman, Madeyska & Hather 1989, pp. 194–6), and probably it can be said that all species of *Scirpus* tubers were edible.

Seed foods The graded sieves used by Wendorf and his colleagues to recover floral and faunal remains were not fine enough to catch small seeds, but some seeds were recovered within fragments of human faeces found at Wadi Kubbaniya. These small charred bits of faeces probably came from infants, who were presumably 'caught short' while crawling near their family fires. In most fragments the component foods were very finely ground but occasional vegetable inclusions were visible. Most abundant were particles of parenchyma, possibly from tubers, and fragments of folded leaves, but none of these can be identified on the basis of histology. Two seed types, though, were recognizable: seeds of sea club-rush (*Scirpus maritimus* or *S. tuberosus*) and occasional dense concentrations of the tiny seeds of a chamomile (Compositae – tribe Anthemidae).

The seeds of various species of *Scirpus* have been used as a food in both the Old and New Worlds (see Hillman, Madeyska & Hather 1989, p. 196). Where there are sizeable stands of *Scirpus*, large quantities of nutlets can be harvested with relatively little effort. They are almost impossible to chew when raw, but are edible after roasting.

Other plant foods The dom-palm fruit has a fibrous sugary mesocarp which forms a thick layer around the fruit. Fragments of the inedible endocarp were found in the Wadi Kubbaniya sites, presumably discarded from fruits collected as food. A minor food today in Egypt, dom-palm fruit may have been more important among hunter-gatherers. The !Kung San of the Dobe region collect the fruit of another species of *Hyphaene* as a major food from June through October (Lee 1979, p. 169). The consumption of leafy foods is also clear from their abundance in the faecal remains.

Missing plant foods The food plants which have been recovered from Wadi Kubbaniya are inevitably only a portion of the total menu. Plants, unlike bones, require a combination of chance circumstances to be preserved by charring, and many important foods are never represented in the charred assemblage, either because they were eaten off-site, eaten raw, eaten boiled, or because, even if accidentally charred during roasting, they leave nothing that allows their identification. Charred remains therefore provide a very incomplete and potentially misleading record, especially at open sites, such as those at Wadi Kubbaniya, where post-depositional taphonomy is particularly unfavourable.

In order to gain insights into the full spectrum of plants that were likely to have served as staples at Wadi Kubbaniya, ethno-ecological modelling can be used to fill the gaps (Hillman 1989, p. 218; Hillman, Madeyska & Hather 1989, p. 217). The first step involves examining all the available ecological records (e.g. from pollen, wood charcoal, sediments and modern catchment studies) to model the types and abundance of plant food resources that would have been available around the site. The second step is to review ethnobotanical accounts of a range of recent hunter-gatherers with access to vegetal resources closely similar to those modelled, in order to identify cross-cultural common denominators in patterns of preference for specific plant foods from these same habitats.

On the basis of such modelling for the Kubbaniyans, Hillman (1989, pp. 217–26) and colleagues (Hillman, Madeyska & Hather 1989, pp. 217–26) propose that the foods identified above – nut-grass tubers, club-rush tubers and dom-palm fruits – were probably only part of a much broader range of starch staples. These would have included the starchy rhizomes of, above all, catstail or reedmace (*Typha* spp.) and probably also bulrushes (*Schoenoplectus* spp.) and perhaps papyrus (*Cyperus papyrus*) and the common reed (*Phragmites australis*), all of which are wetland plants. All of these reed and rush rhizomes can be eaten while still young after baking, steaming or roasting. After they are fully mature, however, there is little but fibre left – in the *Phragmites* rhizomes, at least. The shoot bases of some of these are also edible and have served as food. The thick rhizomes of the various species of waterlily (e.g. *Nymphaea* and *Nuphar* spp.) are also likely to have been major foods at Wadi Kubbaniya, as they have served as staples among hunter-gatherers and as supplementary foods for farmers and herders in many parts of the world (see Hillman, Madeyska & Hather 1989, pp. 221–2 for ethnographic examples). Rhizomes of various species of *Polygonum* are likewise edible and may also have been eaten at Wadi Kubbaniya. Additional seed-foods would probably have included the seeds of wild millets (*Panicum repens* and *Paspalidium germinatum*, both of which are common in water-edge communities of the Nile valley), a swamp bistort (*Polygonum senegalense*), waterlilies and *Acacia nilotica*. In addition, the nutlets of the sedges could have been a potentially rich source of food, as all sedge seeds appear to be edible. Wild dates could theoretically have grown locally and provided an additional source of carbohydrates.

Kubbaniya subsistence through the seasons

Gautier & van Neer (1989, pp. 160–1), Hillman (1989, pp. 230–2), Hillman, Madeyska & Hather (1989, pp. 213–17) and Wendorf & Schild (1989, pp. 799–802) have proposed the following annual round (see in particular Fig. 13.3 in Hillman 1989, p. 231): the seasons in the Nile valley revolve around the rhythm of the river; the cycle begins with the annual flood, which would have started in early July, reached its peak (c. 7 m or more above low water) in mid-August to early September, and then declined equally rapidly. During the peak flood the waters extended well up the wadi and covered the dune sites.

Sometime after the harvest of spawning catfish the river reached its peak. During this time root foods from wetland plants would have been inaccessible, even though the flood would have stimulated their growth beneath the water. If acacia and date palm were available, however, then the height of the floods probably saw the bulk of the date harvest and the tail-end of the acacia-seed gathering. While the waters covered the dune sites, the occupants probably moved a little up the wadi ahead of the flood to continue fishing and foraging at the water's edge and to hunt large mammals around the floodplain fringe. No occupations, however, have been found higher up the wadi and Wendorf & Schild (1989, p. 801) suggest that such sites may since have been destroyed by deflation.

As the floodwaters began to recede, fishing in the cut-off ponds became rewarding. At the same time, harvesting the root foods of wetland plants began in earnest: first wild nut-grass tubers and, shortly afterwards, club-rush tubers. At this stage in their growth cycle, these tubers would have required only rubbing and roasting to be edible. With the vast swards of these plants available, they could have been gathered in excess of immediate needs and stored for up to several months. Later, as the water receded further, the Kubbaniyans would have had access to the edible rhizomes and flower-buds of waterlilies.

As autumn gave way to winter, the starch content of the tubers and waterlily rhizomes would have increased, while their palatability decreased. Tubers harvested at this stage would therefore have offered rich reserves of starch, but required additional grinding and, for the tubers of wild nut-grass, leaching too. However, it is at this stage that some of the wetland plants started producing edible seeds: nutlets of club-rush, nut-grass, papyrus and other members of the sedge family, grain from the wild millets, nutlets of bistort and seeds of waterlilies. The winter was also the time for hunting water-fowl.

From January and February, the rhizomes of catstail, bulrush, papyrus and common reed would have started to form their starchy storage rhizomes. Some, at least, of these plants would have grown in extensive stands, and providing that digging them from under the floodplain did not expend too much energy, their rhizomes would have offered a worthwhile resource, that could be gathered in quantities sufficient for storage as well as for immediate consumption. The rhizomes of catstail, particularly, were a favoured food of most recent hunter-gatherers with access to mesic wetlands, and it would be surprising if they were not used by the Kubbaniyans. More certain, however, is their use of the fruits of the dom palm, which would probably have been available from February through to April. These, too, are eminently storable, as are the edible seeds of acacia, which were probably available in quantity for several months from spring onwards.

Food needs from spring through to high summer could have been met not only by the acacia seeds, but also by the harvesting of root foods from under the floodplain muds, until they were inundated by the next flood.

Late palaeolithic economy in the Nile valley

The Kubbaniyans' focus on fish and wetland root foods was probably not unique to Wadi Kubbaniya. The post-pleistocene shift away from large mammals to a wider range of resources seems to have begun before 21,000 BP in the Nile valley and is seen in a variety of late palaeolithic sites, all of which are located in Upper Egypt and Nubia. Although the archaeological evidence is very limited, it suggests subsistence practices focusing on wetland resources. Preservation at these sites was often poor and no extensive efforts were made to recover subsistence data. Still, the sites, belonging to a number of different lithic traditions (Halfan, Fakhurian, Ballanan and Silsillian), yielded faunal remains and indirect evidence of plant foods (Wendorf & Schild 1976a, pp. 113–49, 229–310).

Beginning about 21,000 BP, many of the sites began producing masses of fish bones, which Wendorf & Schild (1989, p. 819) interpreted as evidence of a shift to harvesting fish for later consumption. This might mark the beginning of a post-pleistocene type of foraging system with its shift away from large pleistocene mammals. At these sites the mammal remains were nearly identical to those at Wadi Kubbaniya; the hartebeest, aurochs and dorcas gazelle were the only common mammals. But the hippo, which may have been more abundant in the Nile valley than Wadi Kubbaniya, turned up in these sites in small numbers (Wendorf & Schild 1989, p. 818). Some local variations are also seen in the faunal assemblages. The wild ass (*Equus*), which may have roamed the Red Sea hills, appeared in some samples only on the east bank of the Nile (Connor & Marks 1986, p. 182). A mollusc, *Unio*, appeared occasionally in abundance. These sites were probably adjacent to the rare locations where *Unio* beds were accessible (Gautier & van Neer 1989, p. 818).

Wendorf & Schild (1989, p. 820) argue that extensive use of wetland plants, especially tubers, may have begun around 19,000 BP when grinding stones first appeared at Wadi Kubbaniya. Thereafter the implements occur in all other late palaeolithic complexes. As at Wadi Kubbaniya, they are not found at all sites, but when they occur they are extremely abundant, suggesting that these localities were special-purpose camps where grinding stones were used to process plant products or other materials. It seems likely that at least some of the products were wetland plants, as the sites are often near embayments where massive marshes would have flourished (Wendorf & Schild 1989, pp. 820–1).

An alternative interpretation (Hillman 1989, p. 223) is that heavy dependence on wetland and other plant foods may date back much earlier than the appearance of stone grinders around 19,000 BP, with these marking merely a shift from wooden pestles and mortars (or simple stone pounders).

The end of the Pleistocene

The changing environment

As the last glaciers began to retreat, climatic conditions changed dramatically in Ethiopia and equatorial Africa. A warming trend began about 15,000 years ago, followed by increased rainfall around 12,500 to 12,000 years ago. The behaviour of the sluggish, shallow Nile changed profoundly (Wendorf & Schild 1989, pp. 771, 773). Total discharge increased and, as plant cover was restored in the Nile's headwaters, the sediment load declined. Initially there were very high floods, 'wild Niles' as Butzer (1980b, p. 272) called them, which were probably catastrophic. But this period lasted only a short time since the flood levels would have declined as the Nile cut through its valley. The downcutting continued, however, and has persisted until the very recent past. The modern level of the Nile floodplain in Upper Egypt was not reached until Pharaonic times (Wendorf & Schild 1989, p. 773). Thus the regimen of the Nile above the Qena bend shifted from a shallow, sluggish braided stream depositing sediments onto an ever-rising floodplain to a single swifter, deeper river cutting through the valley floor (probably removing archaeological deposits in its path).

Terminal palaeolithic subsistence

Between 14,000 to 12,000 BP, rapid cultural changes were seen in Upper Egypt and Nubia, with old lithic traditions giving way to new ones emphasizing microliths. The bearers of the new cultural entities, the Qadan, Afian and Isnan, faced difficult times with the end of the Pleistocene. The 'wild Niles' 'created ecological havoc in the floodplain' (Connor & Marks 1986, p. 191). Archaeological evidence suggests that Egyptian foragers continued to focus on the river's resources, and Wendorf & Schild (1989, p. 817) believe that they may even have intensified the pattern of specializing in seasonally abundant foods that could be stored.

Most of the sites produced few faunal remains, but the richer ones are informative and seem to repeat the themes seen at Wadi Kubbaniya. Remains at a Qadan site, Site 8905, near Tushka in Egyptian Nubia, suggested repeated occupation of a particularly desirable location for fishing and possibly plant-collecting (Wendorf 1968a, pp. 864–5). The site consisted of over 100 distinct hearth areas clustered near the shores of a fossil embayment. The hearths along the shore yielded numerous remains of catfish (Greenwood 1968, p. 107), which were probably harvested during spawning and possibly smoked for storage. Almost all of the remains were from the skull and anterior part of the skeleton, suggesting that the head was removed before the fish was prepared (Wendorf 1968a, p. 865). Later in the year, marshes, which almost certainly covered the shallow embayment, would have been accessible and ideal for collecting *Cyperus* tubers and other root foods. No plant remains were recovered here but grinding stones were common. These stone implements, however, can no more be considered conclusive evidence for the use of root foods, as they may be employed for many grinding tasks, than their absence can be considered as evidence that root foods were not used (Stahl 1989, p. 174). Krzyzaniak (1991) has had similar reservations about the interpretation of grinding stones in Early Khartoum pre-neolithic sites.

In the hearths located further back from the shore there were few fish remains, but bone fragments of large ungulates, especially the aurochs, were abundant (Wendorf 1968a, p. 865). Hartebeest and red-fronted gazelle, similar to the dorcas gazelle, were also recovered in smaller numbers (Gautier 1968, p. 98). Birds were apparently hunted in the winter, as indicated by remains of duck and teal or garganey, which would have been winter visitors to Nubia (Ballman 1980, pp. 307–9).

The two Isnan sites at Makhadma in the Qena bend of the Nile also suggest seasonal specialization, and offer insights into how epipalaeolithic foragers continued traditional practices, despite the changes in the river's regimen (Vermeersch, Paulissen & van Neer 1989). The two sites, roughly contemporaneous, were occupied between 13,000 and 12,000 BP during the period of 'wild Niles'. Both sites had sizeable middens with large quantities of fish bone, totalling over 3500 elements. At Makhadma 2 nearly all the fish were *Clarias*, which were probably caught during the spawning season. Makhadma 4 was quite different, with an abundance of *Tilapia*, a shallow-water fish of the floodplain, as well as catfish and several other floodplain fish. Vermeersch and his colleagues suggested that these fish were taken later in the flood season as the waters receded.

The topography of the Nile valley here might account for the differences in the two faunal assemblages. Makhadma 2 was located near the first zone of the floodplain; it would have become deep enough to wade in at the beginning of the inundation during the exceptionally high Nile floods. It would, therefore, have been ideal for harvesting spawning fish. But once the flood receded, it would not have been useful for long because the floodplain here is a very narrow strip. In contrast, the floodplain next to Makhadma 4 was much wider and small basins would have remained viable longer than elsewhere during the declining flood. Makhadma 4 may also have seen a different range of fishing techniques than Makhadma 2; fish gorges were found only at Makhadma 4.

The catches at both sites may have been smoked for storage. Charcoal and shallow pits that could have been used for smoking were abundant. In addition, each site produced traces of postholes that may have been the remains of racks used for the fish.

There was almost no mammalian fauna – less than fifty elements, consisting mainly of equal numbers of aurochs, hartebeest and hippo, with no gazelle. The relative abundance of the hippo is surprising, since in earlier sites it represents a small fraction of the fauna compared with the Nile valley trio. There were also small quantities of hare, otter and bird bones. The paucity of the land mammals may reflect a severe decline in bovid populations during the high Nile flood period, a decline that would be expected as a result of the severely restricted grazing for part of the year. It appears that during this stressful time foragers focused even more intensely on riverine resources, utilizing hippo and otter in addition to fish. Unfortunately, no plant remains have been reported from these sites.

During the 'wild Niles', Egyptian foragers may have tried to increase their resources through controlled use of burning. There is stratigraphic evidence of a series of brush fires which occur along the Nile valley over an area 200 km long (Wendorf, Said & Schild 1970, p. 1166), which Clark (1971, p. 250) suggested was due to human activity. Burning is a common method people have used throughout the world to stimulate plant growth, often to attract game (Harris 1989, p. 17). It is most often seen in grasslands and forests, but Eyre (1845, p. 269, cited in Gott 1982, p. 65) observed native Australians burning wetlands. In southern Australia 'firing of the countryside at appropriate times was a regular practice' (Curr 1883, p. 88, cited in Gott 1982, p. 65) and in combination with gathering and digging was a way of managing resources that Gott (1982, p. 65) suggested constituted a form of 'natural cultivation'. In the Nile valley during the terminal Palaeolithic, burning might also have been used regularly to stimulate tuber production and attract game, such as hartebeest, which are 'especially partial to young growth on burns' (Dorst & Dandelot 1970, p. 221). This may have been a new pattern which emerged at the end of the Palaeolithic or it may have been an older practice which was not preserved in earlier sediments because of the geological history of the river. As a new pattern, it would have been another way of increasing food supplies in an impoverished environment.

The holocene climate and the Nile

Egypt's last hunter-gatherers probably faced a more hospitable environment than their late palaeolithic forebears. The hyperarid climate of the late Pleistocene gave way to moister conditions; the lifeless Western Desert saw three major moist episodes which brought both humans and animals to the Sahara (Wendorf & Schild 1980, pp. 236–41). In the Nile valley the river's new regimen may have meant a richer, more diverse floodplain with a greater carrying capacity, at least in some of the broader sections of the river valley.

Monsoonal rains from equatorial Africa appear to have travelled further north, carrying summer rains to much of the Sahel and Sahara (Wendorf & Schild 1980, pp. 240–1), at least as far as 26.6°N (Kutzbach & Street-Perrott 1985), which is a little north of the Qena bend. As a result, several moist phases occurred on a wide geographic scale, but they were not synchronous across the Sahara (Wendorf & Schild 1980, pp. 236–40; Close 1984, p. 314; Haynes 1987, pp. 78–80). In southwestern Egypt in the Nabta Playa and Bir Kiseiba region, there were three major moist periods, from before 10,000 to 8200 BP, 8100 to 7900 BP and 7700 to 5400 BP or later (Wendorf & Schild 1984a, pp. 404–6). In southern Egypt rainfall probably never exceeded 300 mm and in northern Egypt it was most likely much less than that (Hassan 1986a, pp. 493–4; Hassan 1986b, pp. 66–7; Hassan & Gross 1987, p. 91).

During the moist phases, vegetation in the now arid Western Desert was probably limited and concentrated around the seasonal playas and sources of underground water.

Seasonal grasses and forbs probably flourished with the summer rains but there was no surface water year-round. Humans were able to live in the Western Desert during this time by concentrating their settlements around playas and other sources of water (Wendorf & Schild 1984a, p. 408). During dry intervals they may have been forced to migrate, possibly to the Nile valley (Hassan 1986b, p. 70; see also Krzyzaniak 1991).

Before 9000 BP, high Nile floods had penetrated the Fayum depression through the Hawara channel and re-established the lake (Wendorf & Schild 1976a, p. 223), which had disappeared during the hyperarid period of the late Palaeolithic. Through the holocene moist phases and dry intervals the lake levels rose and fell.

Within the Nile valley during the early to mid-holocene period there is some evidence for winter rains in the Red Sea hills in the form of wadi activity on the east bank of the Nile (Vermeersch 1978, p. 146; Butzer 1980b, pp. 273–5). As a result, foragers and animals would not have been so rigidly bound to the Nile valley as their ancestors had been. With limited vegetation in the wadis, game would have had additional grazing lands, and foragers further opportunities for hunting and gathering.

With the beginning of the Holocene, the Nile was well on its way to establishing the modern floodplain. In Upper Egypt the regimen of downcutting begun at 12,000 BP would continue into Pharaonic times (Wendorf & Schild 1989, p. 773). Through much of the Holocene, the Nile valley presumably was a 'convex'-type floodplain, as it is today (Butzer 1959, pp. 70–1; Butzer 1976, pp. 15–18). The natural levees on the banks on either side of the river channel rise a few metres above the floodplain, giving the valley a slightly convex appearance in cross-section. The lowest areas lie further out, often at the outer margins of the valley. In the Nile floodplain, the alluvial flats, before irrigation systems were established, would have been an irregular plain dotted with undulations and hillocks from abandoned river channels and old levees. In the widest areas of the Nile valley, secondary smaller channels probably diverged from the river as they do now (Butzer 1959, pp. 70–1; Butzer 1976, pp. 15–18).

The relict vegetation studies, noted earlier, offer insights into the flora of the Nile floodplain in epipalaeolithic times. Marshes would have been found in the lower areas in the valley margins and in oxbow lakes of abandoned channels (Butzer 1976, p. 18). Acacias, palms and other trees and shrubs may have formed a savanna woodland on active and old levees which were rarely inundated. Tamarisk and *Leptadenia* shrubs may have been common along the sandy, seasonally flooded lands at the juncture of alluvium and low desert or on sandy deposits in the floodplain. Much of the alluvial flats would have been covered by *Cyperus-Panicum* meadows. Some of the sandy soils along the edge of the floodplain may also have supported meadows with a somewhat different grass flora. In this Nile valley there may have been more grazing available than during late pleistocene times, through the year and particularly during the height of the flood. As a result, higher animal and possibly human populations may have been sustained during moister periods. Unfortunately, the archaeological data from the early to mid-Holocene is too scarce to draw any conclusions about population.

Epipalaeolithic foragers

The archaeological record for this period immediately preceding the beginnings of agriculture is unfortunately rather thin and the evidence for subsistence even poorer, with the exception of Nabta Playa in the southwest (Wasylikowa, Harlan, Evans, Wendorf, Schild, Close, Krolik & Housley, Ch. 9, this volume). There are few sites dating from the Epipalaeolithic and there is no continuous sequence in any one area of Egypt. The sites are scattered: from the ninth and eighth millennium BC there are some in Nubia and the Western Desert, from the seventh millennium a number in the Fayum and one in the Qena bend area, and from the sixth millennium a few sites near Armant. Thus vast areas of the Nile valley and chunks of time are not represented. Another difficulty is that sites in the Nile valley are probably an incomplete record of settlement patterns as they are all located on the desert margin at the edge of the floodplain, with none in the floodplain proper. Moreover, this record is too spotty to reveal how foraging patterns may have changed in response to the fluctuating moist phases and dry intervals during the early to mid-Holocene.

Arkinian and Shamarkian industries

The oldest epipalaeolithic industries, the Arkinian (10,580 BP) and Shamarkian (8860 BP) (Wendorf, Schild & Haas 1979, p. 221), are known from a number of sites in Nubia, along the west bank of the Nile just north of the Second Cataract, which were excavated as part of an international salvage effort (Schild, Chmielewska & Wieckowska 1968). Consisting mainly of concentrations of stone tools, the sites suggest seasonal encampments by small groups. In some instances, the same location was used repeatedly, as at Wadi Kubbaniya. At the one known Arkinian site, Dibeira West (D1W1), for example, there were three mounds covered by large quantities of burned stone and chipped artefacts, scattered in twelve very dense concentrations, along with remnants of three fireplaces (Schild, Chmielewska & Wieckowska 1968, p. 651). Each concentration probably represents a separate seasonal encampment by a small group (Wendorf 1968b, p. 1051). This location, like the others used repeatedly, may have been favoured for fishing or collecting roots and tubers. Unfortunately, little more can be said about subsistence except for one important find – evidence of fishing in the main Nile channel – which seems to be an innovation in Nilotic foraging. Although bone preservation was poor, there were remains of three deep-water fish, Nile perch, *Bagrid* and *Synodontis*, in addition to the ubiquitous catfish (Greenwood 1968). Prior to the Epipalaeolithic there are scattered examples of deep-water fish; some appear in a few middle palaeolithic sites in Nubia (Wendorf & Schild 1989, pp. 818–19) and in small numbers at Makhadma 2. But from the Epipalaeolithic onward, fish from the main Nile channel become common along with floodplain types such as catfish (van Neer 1989, p. 52).

The addition of deep-water fish may merely reflect changes in the Nile; with a deeper channel and greater annual discharge the river could perhaps more readily support these species. But other factors were probably involved as well. Exploiting deep-water fish on a regular basis may have been an effort to diversify the resource base, perhaps to solve the problem of seasonal lean periods. Deep-water fish are easiest to catch at the low-water stage, the late spring/early summer, which is a period when other resources would probably have been scarce. At this time Nile waters are less turbulent and access is easier (van Neer 1989, p. 54). Deep-water fish would have been a valuable addition to the diet as they can reach enormous proportions in the main channel; Nile perch, for example, can weigh up to 70 kg and even 120 kg (Brewer 1989a, p. 82). But catching them was probably more akin to hunting, with its attendant uncertainties, than to harvesting spawning catfish.

Van Neer (1989, p. 53) suggests that new technologies may have been involved in the development of deep-water fishing. The simple techniques that were adequate for catching fish during the spawn or in residual pools would not suffice. Hooks, harpoons or nets are required. He proposes that wounding gear was prepared by hafting microlithic tools, the hallmark of the Egyptian Epipalaeolithic, into wooden sticks. Deep-water fishing would be most successfully carried out with the help of rafts or boats, although harpoons and hook and line might be used from shore. Some fish might have been taken on the floodplain during the height of the inundation when the water was relatively deep, but larger individuals and some species, such as the Nile perch, would have been found only in the main channel.

The mammalian fauna at the Arkinian and Shamarkian sites is nearly identical to the Wadi Kubbaniya collections and includes the Nile trio, hartebeest, aurochs and gazelle, as well as hippo and *Canid* (Gautier 1968, p. 98). No plant remains were collected, but grinding stones recovered from several of the sites (Schild, Chmielewska & Wieckowska 1968, pp. 679, 703) suggest possible preparation of plant foods.

Elkabian industry

The Elkabian industry dates from about 8340 to 7885 BP and is known from one site located on the east bank of the Nile about 120 km downstream from Aswan (Vermeersch 1978; Vermeersch 1984). The site consists of eight concentrations of epipalaeolithic cultural debris within the walls of the dynastic site of El-Kab. These concentrations appear to represent one specialized component of the settlement pattern: hunting and fishing camps occupied in the autumn. They were all small; the largest concentration was less than 5 m across. The small stone tool assemblage suggested specialization: backed bladelets were the most common tool type, but there are no scrapers, burins and composite tools. There were three very small grinding stones which had apparently been used to grind red pigment.

The location, in a very narrow segment of the alluvial plain, would offer only a limited range of resources. About 750 m wide, the floodplain would have been even narrower at the time of occupation (Vermeersch 1984, pp. 137–8) and would have supported almost no marsh or meadow community. It might have been a good hunting site, though, where game could have been driven into the water and dispatched.

The faunal assemblage, impoverished because of poor preservation, reflects both hunting and fishing. Deep-water fish predominate, although *Clarias* was also taken (van Neer 1989, p. 50). Open-water fish may have been favoured here because there was almost no floodplain. The mammalian fauna includes aurochs, dorcas gazelle and a medium bovid which may be Barbary sheep, and modest quantities of hartebeest, as well as porcupine. Other riverine fauna include hippo and turtle, represented by a few elements (Gautier 1976a; Gautier 1976b; Gautier 1976c; Vermeersch 1984).

Qarunian cultures of the Fayum depression

Remains of the Qarunian complex, which dates from the seventh millennium BC, are abundantly scattered across the northern and southwestern Fayum depression (and are probably better preserved than Nile valley sites because there has been less disturbance in this barren area). The Qarunian is better known than any of the other epipalaeolithic entities, as a number of sites have been examined by several different teams. Surface concentrations of Qarunian tools were first recorded by Caton-Thompson & Gardner (1934, pp. 2, 55–69) during archaeological and geological studies in the northern Fayum in the 1920s. They designated the industry Fayum B and considered it a lingering mesolithic culture which followed the neolithic Fayum A culture. Wendorf & Schild (1976a, pp. 165–226) examined these same sites and located additional epipalaeolithic concentrations when they carried out a brief survey and test excavations along the north rim of the Fayum depression in 1969. Armed with a better understanding of the chronology, they recognized the industry as a distinct terminal palaeolithic entity and named it Qarunian. More recently Wenke and colleagues (Wenke, Buck, Hanley, Lane, Long & Redding 1983; Wenke, Long & Buck 1988; Wenke & Cassini 1989) excavated a Qarunian site during surveys in the southwestern Fayum. In addition, Mussi, Caneva & Zarattini (1984) located and analysed ten surface concentrations of Qarunian assemblages near Wendorf & Schild's study area. Recent work on the Qarunian has also yielded good data on subsistence. Brewer (1987; 1989a; 1989b) carried out a detailed study of animal exploitation patterns during epipalaeolithic and neolithic times using faunal remains from a number of surface sites. Floral remains, which are currently under study, were recovered from Wenke's Qarunian site by 'floating' enormous quantities of dirt.

The lake

The central feature of the Fayum depression is the lake, and no subsistence pattern here can be understood without reference to its behaviour. During the early to mid-Holocene it was a freshwater lake replenished annually by an influx of Nile flood-waters (Hassan 1986a, p. 493). At the peak of the flood in the early autumn the lake reached its highest point, declining through the following months until the next inundation. The difference between high and low water may have been as great as 2.5 m during periods when the Nile flood levels were extreme (Hassan 1986a, p. 494). The Fayum depression was probably more sensitive to flood levels than the Nile valley (Wendorf & Schild 1976a, p. 311), magnifying the effects of a high flood as well as a low flood. Since the floodwaters had to reach the sill level of the Nile–Fayum divide, the water supply was effectively cut off during particularly low floods (Hassan 1986a, p. 494). At such times the lake would have fallen quickly as the evapotranspiration rate was very high (Hassan 1986a, p. 494). Likewise, the level of the lake could also have risen suddenly with high floods, as drainage was limited to the Hawara channel.

The Combined Prehistoric Expedition found evidence for 'a very complex and not entirely understood series of lake aggradations and recessions during the Holocene' (Wendorf & Schild 1976a, p. 222). There appear to have been four successive lake phases during the early to mid-Holocene (Wendorf & Schild 1976a, pp. 221–6) which are presumably related to rainfall values in the Nile headwaters (Hassan 1986a, p. 495). The lake levels correlate very roughly with evidence for changes in east African lakes (Hassan 1986a, p. 495) and with the data on Nile flood levels in Egypt (Wendorf & Schild 1976a, p. 225).

When the lake was thriving, much of the depression was probably covered by vast marshes, inundated for some time during the height of the flood. Drainage may not have been as good here as in the Nile valley since there was only the single channel through which water could return to the river. As a result, portions of the depression may have remained submerged longer than the Nile floodplain. Evidence of wetlands is seen in the abundant remains of swamp sediments that Wendorf and his colleagues (1976a, pp. 166–7) encountered in their test trenches. The floral and faunal remains from Qarunian sites also offer evidence of marshes in the Fayum depression. Nearly all the bird taxa identified from Qarunian sites nest and feed in areas of shallow-water vegetation. For example, the little bittern and green-backed gallinule prefer areas with thick reed beds (Brewer 1989a, p. 150). The most abundant fish, the catfish, breeds, feeds and lives in shallow water (Brewer 1989a, p. 150). All of the identified plant remains from Qarunian site FS-2 grow in wetlands or on moist soils.

At the margins of the lake there may have been shrubs and scattered acacia, but trees were probably scarce. All of the wood charcoal from FS-2 that could be identified was *Tamarix* (Wetterstrom, unpublished data), which thrives on occasionally submerged sandy deposits (el-Hadidi & Springuel 1978). Grasses would have grown along the margins of the marshes, but they may have formed only a narrow band of meadows if the floodwaters dissipated slowly, as suggested above. Still, there was enough meadow to maintain some ungulate populations, as indicated by faunal remains from Qarunian sites. Beyond the lakeshore the landscape would have been nearly devoid of vegetation, as the summer monsoon rains would not have offered much precipitation this far north (Hassan 1986a, p. 494). But occasional winter rains may have supported ephemeral vegetation in nearby wadis.

Qarunian sites

The site excavated by Wenke and his colleagues (Wenke, Buck, Hanley, Lane, Long & Redding 1983; Wenke, Long & Buck 1988; Wenke & Cassini 1989), FS-2, is located on high ground along an ancient beach and consisted of a series of hearths, pits and surface scatters of artefacts. The most abundant tool type was a small backed bladelet (Wenke, Long & Buck 1988, p. 37). The site appears to be the remains of several overlapping encampments that were used over a long period of time, perhaps seasonally. Three radiocarbon dates for the site range from 8200 to 7600 bp, with a weighted average of 7715 ± 45 bp, or as calibrated dates, approximately 7100 to 6450 cal BC (Hassan 1986a, p. 488; Hassan 1988, p. 143).

The three Qarunian sites that Wendorf & Schild (1976a, pp. 162–211) tested during their survey are similar to FS-2 and are contemporaneous with it as they are dated from approximately 7100 BC to 6030 BC (Hassan 1988, p. 143). Site E29G1 consists of more than six artefact concentrations and is located around two large deflated basins. Site E29H1 duplicates many of these features; a number of artefact scatters overlook a basin.

Subsistence – faunal remains   The one Qarunian site in Brewer's (1987; 1989a; 1989b) study, Site 2, consisted of a surface scatter of lithics and bone which was located along an ancient shoreline on the north rim of the depression. The site, which produced the largest collection of identifiable bone gathered by any Fayum expedition, reflects hunting and fishing practices similar to those in the Nile valley (Brewer 1989a, pp. 68–103). Mammalian fauna included gazelle, hartebeest, *Bos* (presumably wild), *Canis* and hare (Brewer 1989a, p. 111). More common were bones of water-fowl, nearly all of which are found in shallow waters, and remains of ostrich, a desert species. Turtle remains were also abundant, but the bulk of the faunal material came from fish, which were caught by means of two different fishing strategies. Most of the fish were *Clarias*, which were selectively taken in shallow waters along the shore. The second strategy was deep-water fishing, as indicated by remains of *Lates* and *Synodontis* (Brewer 1989a, p. 113).

Working with the annual growth on *Clarias* pectoral spines, Brewer (1987; 1989a, pp. 119–44) determined that catfish were caught during two seasons. The first period, the summer/autumn, corresponds to the annual spawn as in the Nile valley. The second season, however, in the late spring/early summer, is unlike patterns seen elsewhere. Why catfish were taken at this time is a matter of speculation. Brewer (1989a, p. 143) suggested that catfish, which are believed to spawn during the flood, may have bred precociously in the late spring. Another possibility is that they aggregated in masses around a prey species of fish that *was* spawning in shallow waters at this time.

Another explanation proposed by Wendorf & Schild (1976a, p. 162) is that Qarunian folk caught catfish trapped in residual pools when the lake reached its lowest level. All of the sites they examined were located next to basins which would have been ideal for such fishing. At one site they noted that the 'bedrock outcrops would have served as a natural sill behind which fish would be trapped during the low-water stage each year' (Wendorf & Schild 1976a, p. 162). Several lines of evidence confirm that the sites were indeed occupied when water was low. The occupation floors and lithic scatters occur within organic swamp sediments and are almost always associated with a swamp species of snail.

The Qarunian folk who camped at FS-2 seem to have exploited the shallow waters and shore of the lake in much the same way as their contemporaries at Brewer's Site 2. The faunal assemblage has a high proportion of fish, which is dominated by shallow-water types, including *Clarias*. Nile perch is also found in the samples (Wenke, Long & Buck 1988, p. 42). FS-2 was well positioned for fishing during the lake's low-water stage as the site is adjacent to a bedrock basin where water accumulated in seasonal ponds (Hassan 1986a, p. 496). Other lake resources used extensively were birds and turtle. The mammalian fauna at FS-2 includes hartebeest, gazelle, *Bos* and *Canis*, possibly jackal or dog (Wenke, Long & Buck 1988, p. 42; see also Clutton-Brock, Ch. 4, this volume).

At the sites Wendorf & Schild (1976a) tested, mammal bone was recovered from the surface and test trenches and included hartebeest, gazelle, aurochs and hippo (Gautier 1976a; Gautier 1976b; Gautier 1976c). Fish bone was abundant but was not collected systematically.

Subsistence – flora   Site FS-2 was sampled extensively for plant remains but the yield was very low, as is usually the case with forager camps. Many samples produced nothing, while some yielded a few seeds. Several ash deposits, however, were rich with hundreds of small carbonized seeds. This collection provides a complement to the Wadi Kubbaniya material since it includes the spectrum of small seeds that could not be recovered by Wendorf and his colleagues using graded sieves.

Identification of the FS-2 specimens is not yet completed, but it is clear that the assemblage is dominated by vegetation of marshes and moist ground, as might be expected. The most common types are nutlets of the sedge family, including a variety of species of *Scirpus*, *Cyperus* and possibly *Carex*. *Scirpus tuberosus* or *maritimus* is the only one which has yet been identified to species. These sedges would have grown in the marshes along the shore and were probably inundated during the flood season. *Polygonum*, also abundant in the flotation samples, includes species that occur in shallow water and some that grow along canal banks (Boulos & el-Hadidi 1984, pp. 140–4). There were also two aquatic plants, *Myriophyllum spicatum* and *Ruppia maritima*. The latter is a submerged plant in salt and brackish water (Tackholm 1974, p. 622). Several of the other most common types in the samples would have been found along the shore just above the marshes: *Rumex*, Chenopodiacea (probably *Chenopodium*) and *Glinus lotoides*. Various *Rumex* species in Egypt are found along canal banks and on moist ground (Boulos & el-Hadidi 1984, p. 143). *Glinus* occurs on seasonally inundated land (Zohary 1966, p. 602). Members of the Chenopodiacea are often found in disturbed habitats and two Egyptian species, *C. ambrosoids* and *C. murale*, grow along irrigation canals, Nile banks and moist ground (Boulos & el-Hadidi 1984, pp. 17–18). Several as yet unidentified grasses that were found in the flotation samples may have grown in the marshes or meadows.

Some of the plant remains might be traces of fuels or debris from matting but many of them were probably food plants. As noted earlier, *Polygonum* seeds and all sedge nutlets appear to be edible, as there are extensive ethnographic accounts of their use around the world (Hillman, Madeyska & Hather 1989, p. 223). Various species of *Chenopodium* and *Rumex* seeds have been used as a grain by Native Americans (Fernald & Kinsey, rev. by Rollins 1958, pp. 170, 177). Iron age people in Europe harvested *Chenopodium* seeds (Helbaek 1960). The Tuareg in the Ahaggar collect *C. vulvaria* seeds which they grind into flour for bread or porridge (Nicolaisen 1963). The grass seeds may have been eaten as grains. A common way to prepare seeds and achenes is by roasting them, a process by which some might be accidentally charred.

Some of the plants found at FS-2 can be eaten as pot herbs. The tender young leaves and stems of *Glinus lotoides* are consumed as vegetables in some parts of the tropics (Facciola 1990, p. 133). The young shoot tips of *Myriophyllum brasiliense*, a New World species, are used as a vegetable in South America (Facciola 1990, p. 105). Young shoots of both *Polygonum* and *Rumex* have been eaten as vegetables by Native Americans and Europeans (Fernald & Kinsey 1958, pp. 167–77). The Khushmaan Ma'aza Bedouin of the Eastern Desert eat the leaves and stems of *Rumex vesicarius* (Goodman & Hobbs 1988, p. 77).

There were no charred tubers, roots or rhizomes in any of the samples, which is not unexpected since they are so rarely preserved, but they almost certainly were an important food. If the Qarunian people utilized the nutlets of the marsh rushes, sedges and bistort they surely would have been aware of the potential underground. They would also have known of the root crops of *Typha*, *Phragmites* and waterlily. Moreover, it is highly probable that these root foods served as staples for at least part of the year, for the same reasons that they would have been staples at Wadi Kubbaniya – high yield, reliability and extended period of availability. The immature tubers could have been harvested in the autumn once the flood began to recede. Mature, fibrous tubers of some species would have been available starting in the winter and could have been collected until the inundation.

The inhabitants of FS-2 may have harvested only immature tubers here as there is no evidence of grinding stones or other equipment which would have been necessary to render the older tubers palatable. On the other hand, they may have used tools which left no record at FS-2, such as wooden mortars. They may have also carried the stones with them to other, not as yet found, sites or processed tubers at other locations. Another possibility is that the later neolithic folk who camped at nearby Site FS-1 'borrowed' from the earlier sites. If grinding stones had been exposed on the surface of FS-2 and accessible, they would have been tempting. Modern pastoral nomads of the Sahara reuse palaeolithic grinding stones in preference to carrying their own with them (Harlan 1989, p. 84). Most of the Qarunian sites investigated on the north shore of the lake have also yielded no ground stone tools, except site E29G1, where Wendorf & Schild (1976a, p. 182) found both the handstone and quern. A number of seeds and fruits in the FS-2 samples that have not yet been identified might point to another range of resources that were used. Still, it appears that the flora is limited to wetland and lakeshore vegetation. There was no evidence of other taxa which frequently occur in later Egyptian sites where flotation is used, such as the tree fruits, *Acacia* and *Zizyphus*. Their absence may reflect the denuded landscape beyond the lakeshore with its scarce vegetation. As noted above, the charcoal was limited to *Tamarix*. There were also no traces of the desert fruits, *Citrullus colocynthus* and caper, though these are common at later Egyptian sites.

The other Qarunian sites unfortunately were not tested for plant remains, but there were two potential clues to plant use at one of Wendorf & Schild's sites. First, as noted above, a grinding stone and grinder were found at E29G1 resting together in operating position, suggesting that plant foods were ground here. Second, some of the swamp sediments seen in the trench profiles showed evidence of burning, which Wendorf & Schild (1976a, p. 163) tentatively attributed to natural causes. But the burned vegetation might reflect human manipulation, as suggested earlier in the discussion of burned deposits in the Nile valley. Burning could have been used to stimulate plant growth to attract game or increase root harvests.

Settlement patterns   The faunal remains at FS-2 and Brewer's sites, which included one of the sites examined by Wendorf & Schild, indicate occupation during at least three periods, the early summer and autumn when catfish were harvested and during the winter when migratory water-fowl were in the Fayum. The seeds recovered at FS-2 would probably have been harvested mainly in the winter, although with storage they could have been used at other times.

The remaining months of the year, the inundation period and perhaps part of the spring and winter, may have been spent at other types of sites. Mussi and her colleagues (1984) suggested that the ten sites they examined represent another type of camp, as the tool assemblages differed from the classic Qarunian in a number of ways, suggesting 'a different range of activity' (Mussi, Caneva and Zarattini 1984, p. 189). But the sites might represent an earlier phase of the Qarunian industry (Mussi, Caneva & Zarattini 1984, p. 189), which seems more plausible as they are all located at lower elevations along the lake and may therefore be associated with a different lake phase. Unfortunately, there are no radiocarbon dates from the sites, nor any floral or faunal remains which might offer clues to subsistence activities.

Another possibility is that Qarunian folk left the Fayum depression for part of the year. For example, it might have been possible during moist periods to hunt and collect in desert wadis in the winter. Caton-Thompson & Gardner (1934, p. 23), however, found no sites just north of the depression where they were working, whereas the sites along the shore show extensive repeated occupation.

Tarifian

The Tarifian, from the Armant-Gurna area of Upper Egypt, produced the oldest ceramic industry in the Egyptian Nile valley. It is considered epipalaeolithic here for two reasons: Tarifian sites show no evidence of food production and the one radiocarbon date, 6300 ± 180 bp (Ginter, Kozlowski & Pawlikowski 1985, p. 27) (5185 ± 120 cal BC, in Hassan 1988, p. 143), is about a thousand years older than any known farming communities in Upper Egypt.

The Tarifian was discovered in 1978 under neolithic deposits at the site of El-Tarif in Gurna (Ginter, Kozlowski & Silwa 1979; Ginter & Kozlowski 1984; Ginter, Kozlowski & Pawlikowski 1985). Subsequently, five other Tarifian sites were identified during surveys of a 12 km section between Thebes and Armant.

Unfortunately, archaeological remains were scarce at all the sites but indicate that, in addition to a ceramic industry, which was represented by a few very small sherds, the Tarifians had an unusual lithic industry. Intermediate between epipalaeolithic and neolithic levels, it is nearly devoid of microlithic tools but abounding in flake tools.

Yet aside from the lithics and ceramics, the Tarifian communities are no different from earlier epipalaeolithic forager camps, consisting of little more than artefact scatters. A single hearth was found at two sites; one of these also produced traces of a small, shallow pit. Unfortunately, none of these sites offers any evidence of subsistence. No floral or faunal remains were recovered from them, although neolithic sites in the area, which are more than 1000 years younger, produced evidence of domestic livestock and crops, as well as remains of structures.

More dates are needed to establish the chronology of the Tarifian (Hassan 1985, p. 108). But if the one date obtained thus far proves to be reliable, the Tarifian sites offer a window on the sixth millennium BC in Upper Egypt which suggests that changes in epipalaeolithic lifeways were already under way – although there is no evidence that domesticates had reached this far south.

Terminal palaeolithic foraging – an overview

The picture that emerges from this patchwork of sites widely scattered in time and space is of an enduring focus on riverine resources that continued from late palaeolithic times through the Epipalaeolithic. Egyptians followed a generalized procurement strategy (Brewer 1989a, p. 7) that involved two components: (1) reliable, seasonally abundant staples during certain periods of the year – fish and root foods, and (2) a broad base of additional plant and animal resources which filled in at other times and probably provided a safety net for lean periods. This pattern, involving a wealth of plant foods and a role for both sexes, appears to have been part of a broad adaptation which developed in response to post-pleistocene conditions in many parts of the world, although it dates to the late Palaeolithic in Egypt. It probably began to develop in the Nile valley after 21,000 BP and continued to evolve over succeeding millennia. The major changes that can be detected in the scant archaeological record are new lithic assemblages, which may reflect improvements in hunting and fishing techniques, and the addition of deep-water fishing, which would have broadened the resource base and provided food during a lean period. Controlled burning of wetlands and meadows may also have developed in the terminal Palaeolithic. Such a practice would have increased the productivity of one of the major resources, root foods, and perhaps improved hunting success by attracting game.

The settlement patterns of the late Palaeolithic and Epipalaeolithic are largely a matter of speculation for lack of data. Connor & Marks (1986, p. 191), however, have observed that sites dating from the end of the late Palaeolithic include 'a large number of favoured localities which were occupied repeatedly over long periods'. This suggested to them that the territorial range of these groups was probably rather circumscribed. Because of the comparative stability of the environment foragers developed a pattern of successful exploitation which did not require frequent long-range movements to adjust for shortages (Connor & Marks 1986, p. 191). The later Arkinian and Shamarkian people may likewise have ranged over a small area, as many of their sites are highly localized and show numerous repeated occupations. This may have been true of the Qarunians as well, since the sites are localized around the lakeshore, but it is difficult to say how large an area along the lake was used.

In an even more speculative vein, the social dimension of foraging in the terminal Palaeolithic may be considered. As Chase (1989, p. 43) has pointed out, human economy is essentially social in nature. Thus during the Epipalaeolithic and possibly earlier, a set of beliefs, values and rituals probably evolved as procurement strategies developed. These values and beliefs would have supported and regulated subsistence practices, while the social organization and division of labour, likewise, would have helped sustain the foraging practices.

Unfortunately, the archaeological record offers almost no insights into the culture of terminal palaeolithic foragers. It does, however, hint at flexibility in that the innovations noted above, deep-water fishing and burning, may have required changes in the way foragers viewed their relationship with the environment. Burning, if it were indeed practised, required seemingly destructive behaviour.

In any case, although these systems of value and beliefs cannot be reconstructed, it is important to recognize that they would have played a central role in mediating the transition to agriculture, as well as being transformed in the process. The shift from a generalized foraging strategy to a specialized economy based on domesticates represented a radical transformation of lifeways: changes in management of resources, people's relationship to the environment, concepts of territory and ownership, scheduling, division of labour, settlement patterns, sharing and redistribution, to name a few (Chase 1989, p. 47).

The pitfalls of foraging

Epipalaeolithic foragers in the Nile valley were probably more secure than their counterparts in the deserts and savanna but they undoubtedly faced periods of hunger and stress. The greatest threat to their security was most likely the unpredictability of the Nile floods. They could not be certain of the onset of the floods, nor of their duration and magnitude.

Variations in Nile floods occur on two scales, year-to-year fluctuations and long-term trends. During the last 5000 years, flood records show both a great deal of short-term variability as well as significant long-term trends (Butzer 1976, p. 30; Butzer 1984a; Hassan & Stucki 1987). For the Epipalaeolithic, the Fayum depression documents in its ancient shorelines long-term Nile flood trends, which are more or less correlated with the holocene moist phases and dry intervals (Hassan 1986a, p. 495). For the short-term annual variation, however, this geomorphological data is not sufficiently sensitive. But one can turn to records from the late nineteenth and early twentieth centuries for insights into the amount of variation foragers may have faced from year to year.

Annual Nile flood variation

The detailed records of Nile water levels from a gauging station at Aswan are most relevant here as the levels would not have been affected by irrigation works. For the period 1873–1904, Willcocks (1904, pp. 194–201) published a partial record which suggests that variations from year to year can be quite marked. In 1872 the flood crest was 6.3 m, which was 1.5 m below the flood's mean of 7.8 m for the years 1873–1904. Two years later the flood reached 9.0 m, the highest of the century, but three years later, 1877, the flood was again very low with a crest of only 6.3 m. The following year, however, it reached 8.1 m (Willcocks 1904, pp. 194, 201).

Willcocks' (1904, pp. 194–201) daily gauge readings also show great variation in the onset and duration of the flood. During an 'average' year, 1901, the river reached a low (0.08 m below the mean low) at the end of May, and then slowly rose over the next two months to 3.3 m. At this point it began to rise very rapidly, a metre within six days, followed by another 2 m during the next five days, reaching 6.2 m on 10 August. Over the next month it rose another 1.6 m, cresting at 7.8 m on 7 September. During 1874 the flood was early as well as high. It began its period of rapid rise about ten days before the 1901 flood. On 20 July it was 3.4 m and then over the next ten days it rose about 3 m. During the next month it rose almost another 3 m, cresting at 9 m on 5 September. The flood of 1878 was also high but it did not crest until 15 September, about ten days late. In 1902 the flood was both late and low. On 5 August, when flood waters normally are over 4 m, the flood had reached only 2.8 m and it did not crest until 17 September, about twelve days late.

The duration of the flood following its crest also varied markedly during the period of 1873 to 1904 (Willcocks 1904, pp. 194–201). In the average year of 1901 the flood fell more than a metre within a month after its crest and roughly another 2 m over the next month, reaching 4.1 m by the end of October. During 1874, the year of the high and early flood, Nile waters lingered far longer than normal. The river was still at 7.0 m on 30 October, about 3 m above an 'average' flood. It did not reach 4 m for nearly another month, a delay of roughly a month. In 1878 the flood lingered even longer; the river was at 8 m by the end of October and 4.7 m at the end of November, or more than two months behind schedule.

Records from the Pharaonic period are not as detailed but they provide ample evidence of disastrously high and low floods (Butzer 1984a). For example, in records from Nubia, Bell (1975) identified extraordinarily high floods during the period of 1840–1770 BC that were 8 to 11 m higher than present-day floods. Butzer (1984a, p. 107) estimates that the flood volumes were 'three or four times greater than the maximum floods since AD 1869 and probably resulted in crests 2–4 m higher than normal in the northern Nile valley'. The depth of water in basins would have been at least twice that of a normal year (Butzer 1984a, p. 107).

The devastating effects of excessively high and low floods are well documented for historic times.

> Low or short floods reduced the wetted area, the degree of soil saturation, and the amount of fertile silt deposited, but increased the salt concentration of waters reaching fields along the desert margins. . . . This all reduced cultivated acreage as well as unit productivity. (Butzer 1984a, p. 105)

During 1877 flood waters were about 2 m short of a normal flood, leaving 62 per cent of Qena Province unirrigated (Butzer 1976, p. 53). From the Pharaonic period there are accounts of massive famines, extensive desiccation of the Nile delta and scarcity of potable drinking water following poor floods (Bell 1970; Bell 1971; Bell 1975; Butzer 1976, pp. 27–33).

High or lingering floods were equally cataclysmic. The waterlogged soils delayed planting, which pushed the harvest into the late spring when the grain could be lost to desiccating desert winds and heat (Butzer 1984a, p. 105). High floods also encouraged epidemic diseases and soil parasites and destroyed food stores, livestock and seed stock (Butzer 1984a, p. 105). In addition, high floods inundated villages, drowned people, ravaged irrigation works and ruined summer crops (Willcocks 1889, pp. 186–7; Willcocks 1904, pp. 70–1). Butzer (1984a, pp. 105–6) concluded that for farmers in Pharaonic Egypt this variability 'created significant year-to-year fluctuations of food supply, despite the general predictability and reliability of Nile floods'.

Flood variability and epipalaeolithic foragers

For prehistoric foragers the timing and the extent of the flood must have had serious consequences. It is not possible to extrapolate directly from the nineteenth century, with its irrigation works, to the Epipalaeolithic with a 'natural' floodplain, but one can imagine some of the consequences of the flood's vagaries. Hunter–gatherers would have suffered both during and after unusual floods. The onset and timing of the inundation would have affected access to resources. During a late flood, catfish spawning would have been delayed, forcing foragers to endure longer through what was probably a lean time. If the flood persisted in the autumn, fishing in residual pools would likewise have been delayed, as well as access to marshes and meadows. Game herds may have deteriorated, for lack of grazing for an extended stretch.

Unusually high floods probably swamped much of the floodplain, leaving very little dry land. As a result there would have been scant grazing for game. Foragers may also have had less access to resources usually available during the inundation, such as acacia seeds and palm fruits.

A low flood probably caused the greatest havoc. Depending on how much of the valley floor was deprived of floodwaters, large areas may have become desiccated. Meadows and marshes might have dried up, eliminating plant-collecting grounds. With losses to the valley plant cover, game, water-fowl and fish populations ultimately would have dwindled.

An unusually high flood, particularly a long one, would have left a path of destruction too. Floodwaters may have destroyed vegetation that was normally above the high-water mark, such as acacias. Some plant communities might have died after being submerged for longer than they could tolerate. The lowest marshes, for example, might have remained under water for months. The growth cycle of annuals could have been delayed when the natural basins drained late and as a result they may have ultimately produced less seed or fruit. High floods could also have changed the topography of the floodplain, sweeping away levees or forging new channels.

Unusual floods probably had a similar effect on the Delta. Although the Nile flows through several channels here, low floods would still have left large regions of the landscape desiccated, while unusually high floods would have engulfed areas that normally remained dry, such as levees and turtlebacks. Foragers here would have faced some of the same problems as those in the Nile during exceptionally high or low inundations.

Lean times and cruel floods

Extreme floods in both the Nile valley and the Delta would have exacerbated the annual fluctuations in the food supply. The periods that under good circumstances might have been lean would have been times of real hardship. The most difficult periods were probably late spring/early summer and the inundation. During Egypt's 'summer' season, mid-March to mid-August, the soils become very dry, the water level falls to its lowest, temperatures are very high and desiccating winds occasionally blow in from the desert (Butzer 1984a, p. 105). Resources would have dwindled during this time; migratory water-fowl would have flown north and much of the Nile valley would have become parched. The annual winter vegetation would have finished its growth cycle, while some of the perennial vegetation may have died back. Meadows might have turned brown, causing much of the game to disperse. At this point animals were probably at their leanest and offered their least food value, although in some areas they would have concentrated around water sources, rendering them more vulnerable than during the winter months. Root foods would still have been available in the marshes, but by this time they would have been old and woody, requiring, for some types, extensive grinding and detoxification before they could be eaten. Fish resources on the floodplain were probably declining and may have been badly depleted. Deep-water fish from the main Nile channel were most likely taken at this time of low water, filling in the gap. If the previous year's flood had been poor or dangerously high, there may have been very little margin of safety for the Nile valley foragers.

In late August when floodwaters started to wash across the Nile valley, catfish began their spawning runs, providing a major reprieve during this lean period. Nile valley foragers could have harvested catfish and dried them for storage, which would have helped see them through the flood. But with the valley inundated, access to other resources would have been limited. Marshes and alluvial flats would have been inaccessible except during low floods. On high ground some fruits such as dom palm and acacia pods may have been available but plant resources could have been quite scarce. If the floodplain was suffering from a poor flood the previous year, there may not have been enough food to see the foragers through to the flood's end, particularly if the flood drained late.

Long-term Nile flood trends and epipalaeolithic foragers

The long-term trends of higher or lower floods would have meant major readjustments in the Nile valley.

> Lower floods may eventually have favoured channel incisions and a flood-plain of reduced size, with a lower water-table and receiving less nitrogen-rich silts; parts of the floodplain would have been incultivable, and salinization as well as dune invasion could have affected outlying areas. (Butzer 1984a, p. 106)

Large portions of the Delta would have become desiccated. Overall carrying capacity in the Delta and Nile valley would have been reduced with lower floods. A long-term trend of higher floods, on the other hand, would probably have led to a wider floodplain. Ultimately this would have supported more life, but there was probably havoc during the readjustment period. Old vegetation communities would have died while new ones were being slowly established. Former meadows may have turned to wetlands while desert margins became grasslands or backswamps.

Probably the most difficult adjustment would have been to a shrinking Nile valley or Delta. With a decline in resources foragers may have had trouble satisfying their needs during the leanest periods of the year. The dry intervals of the early to mid-Holocene would probably have been particularly trying periods. During the holocene moist phases, Nilotic populations may have expanded as a result of more favourable conditions, although there is too little data to determine whether there were any population changes through the Epipalaeolithic. With the dry intervals, the expanded resource base in the Nile valley and desert wadis probably would have contracted, with devastating consequences for foragers. Additional populations moving into the Nile valley from the desiccated Western Desert (Hassan 1986b, p. 70; Hassan 1988, pp. 144–5) would have compounded the stresses of these times.

The earliest farming

The potential of domesticates

Wills (1988) has argued that the transition to farming in the prehistoric American southwest was an attempt to sustain the productivity of hunting and gathering. The main objective of agriculture was not yield *per se* but control of availability or predictability. With crops, southwestern foragers had a more predictable environment which allowed them to change their land use patterns in such a way as to make wild resource procurement more efficient.

The American southwest is far removed from Egypt in space and time but some of Wills' points are relevant to the Nile valley. Domesticates would have allowed Nile valley foragers to diminish the unpredictability of their food quest and enhance their foraging system. Specifically, domesticates could have (1) compensated for bad floods, and (2) helped Egyptian hunter–gatherers meet the uncertainties of the flood's onset and duration. If an unusually high or low flood had destroyed much of the wild food base, foragers could have planted cereals accordingly to compensate for the losses. Their livestock were always at hand, to provide meat and other products when game was scarce.

Foragers, with their animals and a cache of grains, could have been better prepared for unusual floods than when they relied solely on wild resources. If the floods were late, they could have endured the wait until the catfish spawned. If they were exceptionally high, the domesticates could have replaced the game, wild seeds and fruits that may have been lost or inaccessible. If the floods were unbearably long, and once irrigation had been introduced, the domesticates would have helped see them through the months until the marshes re-emerged and game could graze again.

The domesticates were by no means the only foods that could serve as back-ups and be stored. Indeed, the floral and faunal remains from late palaeolithic sites suggest that Egyptian foragers had a very broad food base and, like recent hunter-gatherers, relied on this diversity to see them through all conditions. But the domesticates could, arguably, have offered the great virtue of being more predictable than wild resources. Foragers had some control over the quantities available as well as their location. In contrast, root foods, which were generally reliable, would have been vulnerable to low floods. After an especially poor inundation much of the area of mesic marshlands in the floodplain would have been desiccated. A flood like the one in 1877, which left 62 per cent of Qena Province dry, would surely have ruined much of the wetlands of a 'natural' Nile valley. The crops of wild seeds and fruits likewise would have deteriorated following a poor flood. Moreover, humans had no control over the location of these resources. The domesticates, on the other hand, could have been planted in suitable locations that assured some success. For example, during a lingering flood, cereals could have been planted in the highest basins, which would have drained first. In poor flood years, cereals could have been sown in low-lying basins, which would have been well watered. Livestock could have been moved to grazing as was necessary, unlike the herds of game that would have migrated under poor conditions. By providing a safety net for Nile valley foragers during the worst periods, domesticates would have helped sustain the basic foraging system and thus complemented rather than replaced it.

Domesticates may have enhanced foraging in yet another way by allowing groups to remain together during lean times. Among recent hunter-gatherers it is common for groups to scatter in order to forage more effectively during the poorest months of the year, if their movements are not limited by water (Yellen & Lee 1976, p. 44). Nile foragers may have done likewise to find adequate game and plant resources. At a time when resources were at a low point they probably turned to the less desirable foods which may have been more widely scattered and less productive than their staples. With domesticates on hand to compensate for the shortages they may have remained together, which could have been advantageous. They would have been better prepared to mount a large workforce to harvest catfish during spawning and may have been in a better position to monitor the most important areas of the floodplain for the spawn. Remaining together in larger aggregations may have also helped Nile valley foragers maintain claims to particular resource areas by staying close to them. Certain locations appear to have been prime fishing or collecting localities, as suggested by the evidence from late palaeolithic sites of numerous repeated occupation over long periods (Connor & Marks 1986, p. 191).

Nile valley foragers may have been particularly receptive to additional food sources when domesticates first appeared in Egypt. The earliest archaeological evidence of crops and livestock is seen in the Fayum around 5200 BC, which is shortly after Fayum lake levels indicate low Nile floods between 5900 BC and 5500 BC (Hassan 1988, p. 143).

Early farming

At first, planting and herding on a small scale would have been compatible with foraging. The crops would have been planted in alluvial deposits where grasses and other herbs may have grown. The major wetland resources would have been untouched and the hunter-gatherer's time and attention would not have been drawn away from the most important wild resources. Farming may have been done in a casual way similar to the methods that Nicolaisen (1963, p. 184) observed among the Tuareg.

> Pastoral Tuareg of Tasile-n-Aijer sow wheat and barley along the river valleys when these have been heavily flooded. Sowing is then done in a very simple way: holes are dug into the sandy soil, usually merely with the hand, and a few seeds are put into these holes. Wheat and barley thus sown grow in tufts with a space of 0.30 to 0.50 metres between each, and there seem to be about fifty straws in a normal tuft – the largest tuft I have seen contained about 130 straws. The plots cultivated in this way are generally very small, the scattered wild plants growing in the plot are not always removed before sowing. The corn plots are left completely to themselves until harvesting, which is done with a sickle.

Livestock could have grazed amicably with the wild ungulates, which are accustomed to sharing waterholes and grasslands with many species (Kingdon 1982, p. 510). Initially they would not have intruded upon the individual territories of hartebeest or gazelle. Only later would competition between game and livestock emerge as population densities increased and people became more dependent on farming and herding.

There were probably no major changes in nilotic diets at first; the epipalaeolithic staples retained their prominent role. The new foods would have been adopted as one of the many elements of the broad base, another back-up food and one more thread in the safety net. Taken into the nilotic economy under these terms, the domesticates would probably have been compatible with the conservative core of hunter-gatherer beliefs, values and norms.

Incipient domestication

Hunter-gatherers in the Nile valley may also have been prepared to adopt southwest Asian domesticates because of their own experiments with incipient domestication (Clark 1971). The evidence for burning wetlands, which first appeared at the end of the Pleistocene and may have been a form of resource management, has been mentioned. Even earlier the Kubbaniyans may have practised a form of 'incidental propagation' (Hillman 1989, pp. 226–7; Hillman, Madeyska & Hather 1989, pp. 180–1). As was noted earlier, the wild nut-grass swards of Wadi Kubbaniya would have responded well to harvesting, a fact that would probably not have been lost upon the foragers. Noticing that the quality of nut-grass tubers was better in those areas that had been harvested the previous year, the Kubbaniyans may have evolved some system of management.

Clark (1971, pp. 55–64) has suggested that a form of incipient animal domestication was practised during the Epipalaeolithic, which involved capturing wild animals and taming, feeding and fattening them for eventual slaughter. Some of these practices seem to have been depicted on predynastic rock engravings in Upper Egypt and more extensively in Middle Kingdom tombs. Tomb paintings indicate that a great variety of animals were subjected to this process, including two types of gazelle, ibex, deer, oryx, addax, cattle, hyaena, small game and birds. Clark (1971, p. 57) suggests that these practices go far back beyond the Predynastic and came about in order to supply a growing population with meat.

Wendorf & Schild (1984a, p. 422) proposed that the Nile valley may have been an independent centre for cattle domestication, although no faunal evidence of early domestic *Bos* has been found. They point out, however, that evidence may be lacking because of the paucity of faunal material in the Nile valley and the possibility that wild cattle were hunted, while the early domestic forms were kept mainly for milk and blood.

Sources for Nile valley agriculture

Scholars have traditionally turned to the Levant and southwest Asia as the source of Egypt's farming practices (e.g. Hays 1964, pp. 91–2; Arkell & Ucko 1965, p. 147; Stemler 1980, p. 505; Trigger 1983, p. 20). But the Western Desert and north Africa have also been considered potential inspirations for Egyptian agriculture (Butzer 1976, p. 11; Hassan 1986b; Hassan 1988, pp. 144–5; Krzyzaniak 1991).

The Western Desert

The Western Desert hypothesis is based partially on discoveries of putative domestic cattle and crops at Bir Kiseiba and Nabta Playa in southwestern Egypt dating before 8000 BP (Wendorf & Schild 1984a, pp. 420–8), which are not convincing (but see Wasylikowa, Harlan, Evans, Wendorf, Schild, Close, Krolik & Housley, Ch. 9, this volume). The remains of the earliest domestic cattle are small quantities of bovid bones, dated to 9500 bp and 8840 ± 90 bp, that were 'tentatively identified' as domestic cattle (Gautier 1984; Gautier 1987, p. 177). But Gautier (1987, p. 179) considers their status inconclusive and states that the possibility of the 'very early appearance of domestic cattle in the Eastern Sahara . . . remains hypothetical'. At younger sites, dating from 7000 BP and later, though, there is good evidence for domestic cattle and small livestock (Gautier 1987, p. 179).

The evidence for crops dated to 8100 BP is suspect as it consists of only three cereal grains (one naked barley grain, two six-row hulled barley grains) and an inflorescence of wheat (Stemler & Falk 1980). If any plant remains were recovered one would expect to see evidence of the wild grasses which were used so extensively by pastoralists in recent times in the Sahara and the Sahel (Harlan 1989).

It is also questionable as to whether wheat and barley could have survived the climate regime of southwestern Egypt. The planting season here would have been in the late summer after the monsoon rains had filled the playas (Wendorf & Schild 1984a, p. 427). Wheat and barley, adapted to the Mediterranean climate, grow in the cooler winter months and would require moisture at a time when the playas were drying out. Normally planted in October or November, they would not thrive if sown at the end of the summer. They would be developing during a period when the days were becoming ever shorter and would probably fail to flower for lack of light. An increase in daylight hours is the stimulus that initiates flowering and fruiting in these cereals (Stemler 1980, p. 50). If any farming was done in southwestern Egypt, summer crops, such as sorghum and millets, would have been more probable crop candidates.

Southwest Asia

Southwestern Asia currently is the most likely origin for Egyptian crops and livestock. The southern Levant is closer to the Nile delta than any of the other regions proposed as potential sources. The complex of domesticates which first appeared in Egypt is the same as that found in the Levant. Moreover, the timing of Egypt's transition can be seen as consistent with the development of farming in southwest Asia (as explained below).

Of the evidence for the emergence of agriculture in southwest Asia, trends in the Levant are those most relevant to Egypt. During the early Neolithic, the Pre-Pottery Neolithic A (PPNA), 8500–7600 BC, a variety of cereals and legumes was cultivated in the Levant, but there is no evidence of domestic livestock (Bar-Yosef & Belfer-Cohen 1989, p. 67; Miller 1991, pp. 141–2). By the end of the Pre-Pottery Neolithic B (PPNB), 7600–6000 BC, domesticated goat and sheep were firmly established in this region (Bar-Yosef & Belfer Cohen 1989, p. 67) and a wider range of crops was cultivated, including emmer, einkorn, two-row and six-row barley, lentil, pea, fava beans and flax (Miller 1991, p. 141). A massive relocation of population also occurred at this time, apparently as a result of climatic deterioration. Farmers abandoned much of the steppe and open forest of Sinai and Transjordan and moved northward and westward to the Mediterranean forest zone of the coast and northern plains (Moore 1983, p. 90).

The transition to farming in Egypt

Both the dates for the transition to farming and the process by which domesticates were adopted are critical issues.

Timing

Hassan (1985, pp. 104–6; 1988, p. 141) dates the earliest farming villages in Egypt at 5200 to 4500 BC in the Fayum and at Merimde Beni-Salama in the Delta. Given these dates, one can assume that farming was established in Egypt sometime before 5000 BC. This can probably be narrowed down to the period between 6000 and 5000 BC on several grounds. First, domesticates appear in Egypt for the first time as a full complex, one which matches the complex that was established in the Levant by 6000 BC. This set of crops and livestock could not have arrived in Egypt much earlier than 6000 BC via a Sinai route since sheep and six-row barley, integral parts of the complex, have not been found in the southern Levant so far.

Second, there is no evidence of domesticates in Egypt before 6000 BC, at least not in the Fayum and Upper Egypt. Given the paucity of archaeological data and complete absence of it in the Delta, however, the possibility of domesticates before 6000 BC in Lower Egypt cannot be ruled out. Some crops and animals might have been introduced earlier but the complement of domesticates at this time would have been limited and, if adopted by local foragers, may not have been sufficiently remarkable to leave a record or stimulate any changes in foraging lifeways. In addition, the wild progenitors of emmer, barley, lentils and peas grow in the oak-park forest belt and in open, steppe-like herbaceous formations, and therefore would not have been available in Egypt (Zohary 1969, p. 52; Zohary & Hopf 1988, pp. 87, 93).

Given the data currently available, it can be proposed that the complex of southwest Asian domesticates was introduced into Egypt between 6000 BC and 5000 BC or possibly earlier but probably not before 7000 BC.

Process

The process by which domesticates were transferred and adopted is far more difficult to explain and cannot be resolved with our present knowledge. The crops and livestock may have moved across Sinai through some of the same mechanisms that transmitted other goods over considerable distances, such as Red Sea molluscs and turquoise. Or they may have been transported from the Levant, but there is no evidence except for ceramics which have been claimed to resemble early Levantine pottery from the oldest level at Merimde (Eiwanger 1984, pp. 61–2).

In any case, whether by immediate or long-distance transfer, domesticates made their way to Egypt and were taken up by Egyptian foragers or some other group of foragers. The earliest known Egyptian farming sites, the oldest level at Merimde and the Fayum

Neolithic settlements, bear no resemblance to PPNB communities and are little more than hunter–gatherer camps.

It is not known how the domesticates would have been integrated into forager lifeways, but it was suggested above that hunter–gatherers added the crops and livestock to their already sizeable repertoire of resources. These new foods, which allowed them to further diversify their generalized foraging strategy, had the special property of being more predictable than the wild foods – that is, if they had already mastered the basis of irrigation technology, at least for those years when the floods failed to reach their normal full extent.

Another issue is the process by which farming spread through the Nile valley after it had made inroads in the Delta. It appears on the basis of Hassan's (1985) tentative radiocarbon chronology that farming gradually moved south, with domesticates appearing first in the Badari district of Upper Egypt, followed by sites south of the Qena bend. Was this a movement of people or concepts and domesticates? Regrettably, the archaeological data do not offer any definitive answers, but lithics from the Badari district of Upper Egypt offer some clues. Holmes (1988) found extensive regional variation in lithic industries that was maintained through all periods of the Predynastic. Such variation would probably not be consistent with a single 'foreign' population moving into an area; some uniformity in lithic assemblages, at least in the earlier phases of the Predynastic, would be more probable. Such regionalism might occur, however, among communities that had already developed regional traditions as forager bands.

Egypt's first farming communities – a problematic archaeological record

Unfortunately, Egypt's archaeological record does not allow us to probe very deeply into the transition from foraging to farming in the Nile valley. The first obstacle is the paucity of sites and the huge discontinuities in the archaeological record. There are few early farming sites and no continuous sequence from forager to forager-farmer in any area. On the contrary, there is a large temporal gap between the last hunter–gatherer sites and the first farming settlements. In the Fayum roughly 1000 years separate Qarunian and neolithic occupations. In Upper Egypt the hiatus between foragers and farmers is about 800 years, if the one date from El–Tarif is counted. In the Delta there are simply *no* sites prior to the Neolithic although Mousterian artefacts have been found in the vicinity of Merimde (Menghin 1932). Another problem with the archaeological record is that the known neolithic sites are almost certainly not *the* first farming settlements and they may not even be very close to the transition stage, temporally or culturally (Wenke & Cassini 1989, p. 144). The Fayum A sites, probably, and Merimde, certainly, followed on the heels of hundreds of years or more of foraging-farming.

Another major stumbling block to understanding the transition to farming in Egypt is the nature of the bio-archaeological record. Although it provides direct evidence of the plants and animals people ate and used in the past, it is by no means a lucid blueprint of subsistence practices. As noted earlier, some classes of plant remains are far more 'visible' than others in the archaeological record on account of taphonomic processes, differential preservation and recovery techniques. Comparing the roles of different classes of plant foods is especially difficult. In the case of neolithic Egypt it is nearly impossible, as one must compare some of the most visible taxa, the cereals, with one of the least visible, the roots and stems of wetland plants. Cereals, especially emmer, are almost certain to be vastly over-represented compared with other classes of plant foods wherever they occur. Both the anatomy of the cereals and the ways in which they are processed enhance their chances of being preserved. Emmer wheat, for example, is often parched before threshing which increases the probability that it will be burned. It has tough woody glumes, glume bases and rachis segments that preserve extraordinarily well, even in an uncharred state. Once charred they are exceptionally hardy, and they are likely to end up burned as this 'waste fraction' is often used as fuel (Hillman 1984, pp. 3–7). As a result one might expect emmer to show up among the plant remains at any site where it was used, even if it was a minor component of the diet. This renders comparisons between relative proportions of wild and domestic plants extremely tenuous.

The faunal record is likewise biased by a host of factors: cultural practices, differential preservation, disposal patterns and deposition processes, as well as the archaeologist's recovery and sampling procedures (Meadow 1980). Fragile bird and fish remains, for example, do not survive as well as dense bovid astragali. Usage patterns can have a particularly profound effect on the faunal record. Where cattle were kept for milk or blood there would be few large bovid remains (Gautier 1984, pp. 51, 67) even though they may have been an important part of the economy.

The chronology of Egypt's first farming settlements

The chronology for the sites discussed here comes from the framework recently developed by Hassan (1985), who evaluated all the radiocarbon age determinations for neolithic and predynastic materials in the Nile valley and the Delta. His work offers a much better chronometric framework than was previously available as he provides a statistical evaluation of dates and makes use of the tree-ring corrections now available. But he cautions, 'Given the present inadequacies, I regard the chronological scheme given here . . . as highly tentative' (Hassan 1985, p. 111).

Hassan (1985, pp. 104–6, 111) dates the earliest agricultural sites in Lower Egypt to the fifth millennium BC and slightly earlier. These include (1) a series of neolithic sites in the Fayum which span the period 5200 BC to about 4000 BC, (2) Merimde Beni-Salama on the Delta which was occupied from about 4800 BC to 4400 BC and probably later, and (3) the site of El-Omari near Helwan which is insecurely placed by a single radiocarbon date at 4100 ± 260 cal BC (Hassan 1985). In Upper Egypt predynastic communities have been dated for many years on the basis of sequence dating developed by Petrie (1920), who also divided the Predynastic into three units, the earliest of which was the Amratian. An earlier ceramic assemblage, the Badarian, was later recognized by Brunton & Caton-Thompson (1928), and this is now regarded as the earliest manifestation of farming communities in Egypt. The Badarian has been dated with material from the site of Hemamieh, which yielded a single date, c. 6050 ± 300 bp (Hassan 1988, p. 141). Appearing roughly 1000 years after the first neolithic settlements in the north, the Badarian is represented by a series of cemeteries and poorly known settlement sites in the Badari-Mostagedda-Matmar district, which were excavated in the 1920s and 1930s, as well as a few sites near Armant.

The succeeding ceramic assemblage in Upper Egypt, the Amratian or Nagada I, has a firmer chronology as it has been dated by numerous radiocarbon age determinations on material from a number of sites in the Nagada region. Hassan (1985, p. 108) places it around 3850 to 3650 BC, although he points out that there are regional variations. This period is much better known than the Badarian because of the abundance of sites. In addition to the Nagada sites, there are numerous Amratian settlements in the Badari-Mostaggeda-Matmar area and sites in the Armant-Gurna region.

To these Egyptian sites must now be added new evidence for early farming at Kadero on the upper Nile (Krzyzaniak 1991).

Egypt's first farming settlements

The Fayum Neolithic

The Fayum offers the oldest and fullest record of the Neolithic of any region in Egypt but it also appears to follow quite a different pattern of evolution from other areas. While forager-farmer camps in the Nile valley seem to have been transformed rather quickly into full-fledged farming communities, the Fayum neolithic people apparently remained mobile hunter–gatherers (Caton-Thompson & Gardner 1934, p. 89; Hassan 1988, p. 149; Wenke & Cassini 1989, p. 153).

Settlements

Most of the sites are located on the northern rim of the Fayum depression and include a number excavated in the 1920s by Caton-Thompson and Gardner (1934) during their geological and archaeological studies in the Fayum depression, several examined by Wendorf & Schild (1976a) during their more recent survey, and a number of sites excavated by Ginter & Kozlowski (1983; 1986; Kozlowski & Ginter 1989) in the Qasr el-Sagha area. Wenke and his colleagues (Wenke, Buck, Hanley, Lane, Long & Redding 1983) working in the southwest Fayum also examined a neolithic settlement.

These Fayum sites span a long period. The oldest, sites IX/81, X/81 and XI/81 (Ginter & Kozlowski 1986), date to about 5230 ± 50 cal BC (Hassan 1985, p. 106). The largest neolithic settlement, Caton-Thompson & Gardner's Kom W, is dated at 4690 ± 45 cal BC (Hassan 1985, p. 99). The youngest Fayum Neolithic sites are VIIA/80 (Ginter & Kozlowski 1986), dated at 5990 ± 95 bp, and Site FS-1 (Wenke, Buck, Hanley, Lane, Long & Redding 1983), estimated at about 4000 cal BC (Hassan 1985, p. 106; Hassan 1988, p. 150).

Although these sites span more than a thousand years, they are remarkably similar and exhibit no discernible change over time except for the youngest sites studied by Ginter and colleagues which date around 4000 BC. All of them, except this last group, produced ceramics and lithics belonging to the Fayum A tradition, Caton-Thompson & Gardner's (1934, pp. 1–2) designation for the Neolithic in the Fayum depression. For the youngest neolithic sites Ginter & Kozlowski (1983, pp. 67–71; 1986, pp. 19–21) defined a new tradition, the Moerian, which will be treated separately later.

All of the Fayum A sites are located along the ancient lakeshore and all, except one, are small camps resembling the earlier Qarunian settlements. The largest site, Kom W, is a low, elongated mound about 200 m long and 175 m wide, which stands some 3 m above the surrounding landscape as a result of deflation around the site (Wendorf & Schild 1976a, p. 215). It is located slightly north and midway between two basins which would have held seasonal ponds. The site may have been inundated occasionally or perhaps seasonally (Wendorf & Schild 1976a, p. 212).

Reoccupied many times over a long period, the mound had accumulated cultural deposits up to about 1.5 m which thinned out to about 30 cm at the edges. Caton-Thompson & Gardner (1934, p. 24) believed that the site was mostly unstratified but Wendorf & Schild (1976a, p. 212) found evidence of three distinct cultural layers in a test trench that they dug just beyond the 1920s excavation.

The deposits consisted of 'chunks and powdered charcoal, numerous potsherds, stone artefacts, and numerous fragments of fish and animal bones' (Wendorf & Schild 1976a, p. 212). The most distinctive features of the site were the abundant 'fire-holes', with diameters from less than 0.30 m to over 1.5 m. In the lowest levels they were sunk into bedrock, whereas in the upper levels they had been scooped out of the midden. All were shallow, none exceeding 0.5 m, with nearly all of them between 15 and 30 cm in depth. At least 248 were found, all of which Caton-Thompson & Gardner (1934, p. 24) regarded as hearths. In some cases this was confirmed by cooking pots set in the holes with fuel packed around them. Nearly all of the pots, which totalled twelve, contained fish or other bones. Caton-Thompson & Gardner found no evidence of structures in the form of postholes, floors or walls. Presumably the Fayum A people used simple shelters of hides or matting set over a frame of branches such as are seen among pastoral people in north Africa today (Caton-Thompson & Gardner 1934, p. 71; Hayes 1965, p. 93; Hassan 1988, p. 148). Nicolaisen (1963, pp. 332–91) illustrates such structures.

The lithic technology, based predominantly on flakes produced by the hard-hammer technique, is distinct from the preceding Qarunian industry, which was dominated by backed bladelets. Bifacial tools and stemmed and concave base projectile points were common (Wendorf & Schild 1976a, pp. 317, 319). Caton-Thompson & Gardner (1934, p. 35) described the pottery as 'hand-made, in coarse clay, full of chaff' and rather asymmetrical.

Kom K, also excavated by Caton-Thompson & Gardner (1934, pp. 37–41), was a miniature Kom W, located next to a basin some distance from the larger site. Roughly 10 by 5 m, its deposits varied between 0.15 and 0.30 m in depth, with the same range of artefacts and features, including 16 'fire-holes' sunk into the bedrock.

Kom K was like Kom W in most respects except for one extraordinary discovery. Up on a ridge approximately 0.8 km northeast of Kom K Gardner discovered 56 granaries, nine of which contained cereal grains and other seeds. These silos, many of which were basketry-lined, were grouped together on a projecting spur of the ridge, along with an additional 11 pits. Another 109 granaries were later located nearby on a flanking spur. The silos ranged in size from about 0.3 m to 1.5 m in diameter with a depth of less than 0.3 m to about 1.0 m. The majority were around 1 m in diameter and between 0.3 to 0.6 m in depth. Fayum A pottery and stone tools, including a wooden sickle with flint blades, were found in the silos, indicating that they were used by Fayum A people. In addition, charred grain in two of the pits produced an average date of 5145 ± 155 cal BC (Hassan 1985, p. 106). Caton-Thompson & Gardner (1934, p. 72) concluded that the granaries were communal storage for Kom K and a nearby surface site since there were no other settlements in the area. The high location would have been preferable to storage anywhere in the immediate vicinity of the shoreline sites as these may have been periodically inundated and the sediments were probably damp (Caton-Thompson & Gardner 1934, p. 91). It is not possible to determine how many granaries were in use at the same time but they probably represent a collection that were dug over a long period, new ones having been prepared as old ones deteriorated.

The grain silos are similar to those used in recent times by the pastoral Kel Tamasheq of Mali, who gather and store wild grasses.

After harvesting the grain is dried and stored in leather sacks, mud-brick granaries rented in town, or in holes in the sand (diameter 0.5 m, depth 1.5 m) lined with matting. Grain which is stored in this latter fashion is usually conserved for times of scarcity. When the first harvests come in, in September, these reserves are immediately replenished, and whatever old grain remains is either eaten or sold. The grain is said to suffer little loss in quality for at least two or three years. The location of the holes is secret but often they are placed near the wells frequented by the group, beside the stands of grain, or on the edge of the village (Smith 1980, pp. 471–2).

The Upper K granaries may also have been secret stores for the Fayum A people, saved for periods of food shortage.

Caton-Thompson & Gardner (1934, pp. 71–87) located a number of additional Fayum A sites on the surface. Nearly all of these were situated at the foot of buttes, presumably for shelter (Caton-Thompson & Gardner 1934, p. 71). The sites are covered with settlement debris – sherds, querns, hammer-stones, grinding stones, lithics – and some have traces of hearths and pot emplacements. All of these sites were probably small encampments, although some of them may have originally been larger settlements which were partially destroyed through erosion, deflation or disturbance during Graeco-Roman times. Caton-Thompson & Gardner (1934, p. 71) also noted places where tools were dispersed in 'sufficient numbers to indicate a well-frequented shore-line, lagoon, or basin'.

Wendorf & Schild (1976a, p. 199) found similar sites during their survey. At Site E29G3, which was probably Caton-Thompson and Gardner's Site R, they located at least 17 hearths in two or three clusters. This site may have been a favourite fishing camp as it was located next to a seasonal pond. Ginter & Kozlowski (1983; 1986; Kozlowski and Ginter 1989) excavated a number of sites with industries comparable to Fayum A which they refer to as Fayumian. These sites were also similar to Caton-Thompson and Gardner's smaller sites. They have very shallow deposits, one or a few hearths, abundant lithic artefacts, sherds from several vessels and occasionally grinding stones (Kozlowski & Ginter 1989, p. 177). Occupied during the lake's low-water stage, they may have been used briefly as hunting and fishing camps, as suggested by the fauna which are described below. Kozlowski & Ginter (1989, p. 177) also found a set of even smaller sites which consisted of hearths with only a few lithic artefacts, fragments of a single vessel and small quantities of bone.

On the southwest shore of the Fayum Neolithic, lifeways were similar. Site FS-1 appears to have been a seasonal camp which was used repeatedly for short-term occupations (Wenke, Buck, Hanley, Lane, Long & Redding 1983; Wenke, Long & Buck 1988; Wenke & Cassini 1989). There were numerous dense concentrations of stone tools and animal bones, many of them scattered around hundreds of small hearths and thinly interspersed with potsherds, grinding stones and other artefacts. There is no evidence of architecture or house floors but there are bones of domestic animals, sickle blades and grinding stones. Unfortunately, the dating of the site is questionable. The one radiocarbon date, 5160 ± 70 bp (Wenke, Buck, Hanley, Lane, Long & Redding 1983, p. 36) (4000 cal BC), places FS-1 much later than the north rim Fayum A sites, although the artefact assemblages suggest that the site is contemporary with Kom W (Hassan 1988, p. 150). Since this is a single date its reliability is questionable (Hassan 1988, p. 150).

Subsistence – Fayum A faunal remains

Brewer (1987; 1989a; 1989b) found in his study of animal exploitation that Fayum A people hunted and fished in essentially the same way as the earlier Fayum B people, except for the fact that they also herded some domestic animals. The wild mammalian fauna included the same taxa found in Brewer's Qarunian site: *Canis*, *Vulpes*, gazelle and hartebeest (Brewer 1989, p. 112). The domestic fauna probably included cattle, but *Bos*, which was found at three of the four Fayum A sites, could not be assigned wild or domestic status because of the sample size and condition of the material (Brewer 1989, p. 102). *Ovis/Capra*, most of which was probably sheep, occurred in all four neolithic sites (Brewer 1989a, pp. 109, 111–12). At Site 1, which had the largest sample, *Ovis/Capra* far outnumbered the other taxa, while at the other three sites the relative proportions of the mammalian taxa were relatively close. Brewer (1989a, p. 109) points out, however,

> that measures of differences in magnitude between taxa have not been substantiated as valid. Nevertheless, one can infer that domesticates were not the sole source of animal protein for Fayum A people and that, in fact, other sources were utilized and perhaps heavily utilized at particular times of the year.

The difference between these sites might reflect seasonal differences or site specialization.

Brewer found that the Fayum A fishing patterns were virtually identical to the Qarunian ones. *Clarias* is the dominant fish in the Fayum A sites, as in the Qarunian, and it was caught during two seasons, the late spring/early summer and the summer/autumn. Deep-water fishing was also practised by the Fayum A people. In addition, the Fayum A folk hunted water-fowl in the marshes, just as their predecessors had done (Brewer 1989, pp. 141–3).

Other faunal studies of Fayum Neolithic sites show results similar to Brewer's, although none were as comprehensive. At the largest Qasr el-Sagha site, IX/81, sheep and sheep/goat predominated, followed by cattle, whereas examples specifically assigned to goat were rare. There were also remains of turtle, crocodile, dorcas gazelle, *Canis* and water-fowl (von den Driesch 1986). At another Qasr el-Sagha site, a hippo was apparently dismembered. This site also produced evidence of a bovid, which was either wild or domestic cattle, an unidentified antelope, as well as some sheep and sheep/goat (von den Driesch 1986).

Fish played an important role at the sites in the Qasr el-Sagha area, as suggested by abundant fish remains as well as the strategic locations next to basins. *Clarias* was the most abundant fish, but the season in which it was caught was not determined as part of this study. The deep-water fish, Nile perch and *Synodontis*, also appeared in the samples (von den Driesch 1986).

Unfortunately, the fauna from the largest Fayum A site, Kom W, was never reported in detail and the collections, stored at the Natural History Museum in London, were subsequently lost (Arkell & Ucko 1969, p. 146). Caton-Thompson (1934, p. 34) briefly reported small quantities of sheep or goat, cattle, pig, which may have been wild, and hippo as well as innumerable fish spines, some turtle and crocodile remains.

Wendorf & Schild (1976a) collected bone at Kom W and another Fayum A site during their survey, which Gautier (1976c, pp. 370–81) analysed. Nearly all the bone from Kom W was sheep/goat, while at the other site sheep/goat far outnumbered domestic cattle bones. A few remains of hippo, *Canis* and dama and dorcas gazelle were also found at these sites. Most of the sheep/goat bones were probably sheep as none was specifically assignable to goat whereas some of it was definitely sheep. Unfortunately, fish bone was not systematically collected with fine screening although it was noted in profiles.

Brewer's study included some of the fauna from FS-1, but additional bones that were not part of his analysis were later briefly reported. These are worth noting as they indicate the diversity of the food base: *Addax*, hare, turtle, hippo, pig and *Oryx* (Wenke, Long & Buck 1988, p. 42).

In sum, there is little to differentiate animal exploitation patterns in Qarunian and neolithic times except for the addition of some sheep/goat and small quantities of cattle.

Subsistence – Fayum A plant remains

The plant remains found in the granaries at Upper K are the only evidence to suggest that the Fayum people were cultivators. Cereals were found in seven of the pits. Seeds of a *Polygonum* species of unresolved identity, and flax, occurred in two others and, supposedly, *Polygonum* 'pods' in yet another silo. In addition, the endocarp (?) of a rather large fruit was found along with *Polygonum* seeds in one of the silos (Caton-Thompson & Gardner 1934, pp. 43–56). Tackholm & Drar (1941, pp. 32, 88) reported that seeds of *Cyperus conglomeratus* were also found in the bottom of one of the granary baskets, although Caton-Thompson and Gardner did not mention it in their report. The cereals include grains and spikelets of emmer wheat, six-row hulled barley and some two-row barley (Caton-Thompson & Gardner 1934, pp. 43–56; Percival 1936). The quantities and relative proportions may not be particularly meaningful, as the grains and seeds appear to have been dregs, left behind when the pits were cleaned, or discards. Moreover, mice nests, which Caton-Thompson & Gardner (1934, p. 53) encountered in some of the pits, suggest that small rodents may have also fed on the cereals.

Some of the grain was probably in storage as it had been left some 6000 years ago, much of it remarkably well preserved. Other specimens were discarded rubbish, as indicated by the fact that they were carbonized. These may have burned while the grain was being parched for threshing or for storage. In one pit a pint of wholly charred grains was found with fragments of tamarisk charcoal (Caton-Thompson & Gardner 1934, p. 50). These were probably the remains of a batch spoiled during parching that had been dumped in the pits. The silos were apparently used for dumps, presumably after they had deteriorated and were no longer suitable for storage. The cereals were probably processed in the vicinity of the pits, as the spoiled batches of grain would not have been carried up the ridge for disposal.

It is impossible to determine what role the cereals might have played in the Fayum A diet. This collection is undoubtedly a very narrow window on the plant foods used by the Fayum A people. The cereals are well represented here as they are eminently storable, but items with a poor 'shelf life' would not be represented, such as stems, shoots, fruits and some 'root' foods. Though some tubers can be stored they probably would not be placed in granaries since they are not suitable for long-term storage, unlike the seeds and grains which are the only types of foods cached at Upper K. From these materials, precisely how much cereals contributed to the Fayum A diet cannot be determined, but it appears that they were used with wild plants; *Polygonum* and *Cyperus* seeds, which also appeared in the flotation samples from FS-2, were stored separately.

At FS-1, unfortunately, no plant remains were recovered, despite extensive efforts to retrieve them (Wetterstrom unpublished data); they simply were not preserved here, possibly because of deflation or repeated wetting and drying. Located adjacent to an area that would have been a marsh, the site may have been a good location for collecting wetland 'roots' and seeds.

From the other Fayum sites no plant remains were reported but at one of the earliest Fayum Neolithic sites, XI/81, there is evidence that the marsh vegetation had been burned (Kozlowski & Ginter 1989, p. 177), as at a Qarunian site noted earlier. If this is the product of intentional burning it would suggest that wild resources, either root foods or game, were still important in the economy.

Settlement patterns and the seasonal round

The larger sites, Kom W and Kom K, and possibly Wendorf & Schild's Site E29G3, are quantitatively and qualitatively different from the small camps Ginter and colleagues studied. Their deposits are deeper and more widely dispersed and include far more hearths. They were clearly occupied for much longer periods and possibly reused more frequently. In addition, the deposits at the larger sites offer a greater range of artefacts, suggesting that a greater diversity of activities took place there; spindle-whorls, shell scoops, beads and pendants were found at Kom W and Kom K and bone awls and bone pins also turned up at Kom W (Caton-Thompson 1934, pp. 33, 40). This diversity also points to a longer period of occupation.

Since some of the dates for the large and small sites overlap, one can assume that they are part of the same settlement system. Groups probably camped at Kom W and similar sites for some length of time, repeating their visits regularly. The small camps were occupied for short stays, but most of them were revisited, presumably because they were desirable locations for fishing and possibly hunting and plant gathering. They may have been used by smaller components of the larger group that split up during periods when resources were scarce, such as the late spring. Alternatively, the Fayum A people may have only camped briefly at the sites that were available during the low-water stage, as these locations were exposed for only short periods. The larger sites may have been above the usual high-water mark and habitable virtually all the time.

Another element of this settlement system is that it might have included yet other sites outside the Fayum, although it was noted earlier that no sites have been found immediately beyond the depression in the areas where Caton-Thompson and Gardner and Wenke and colleagues worked. It is possible, though, that Fayum A people spent part of the year in the Nile valley. There are a number of factors, however, that place them in the Fayum for a good portion of the year. Brewer's fishing data indicate that neolithic Fayumis were on the lakeshore in the late spring/early summer and again during the beginning of the inundation. They would have stayed on after the flood-waters receded in order to plant cereals and flax, unless the crops were grown elsewhere. It is possible that these were carried into the Fayum from the Nile valley but the evidence of charred grains dumped in the granary pits suggests that they were processed there, and presumably harvested nearby. Water-fowl remains indicate occupation at times during the winter. The wild seeds in the Upper K granaries were probably gathered in the winter, as well. The cereals would have been harvested in February or March. Finally, with the dense, rich deposits at Kom K it seems likely that the Fayum A people were on the lakeshore for most if not all of the year. During the winter they may have taken their herds to graze on the plateau above the depression when grasses may have been found during winter rains (Caton-Thompson & Gardner 1934, p. 89).

Discussion

From the archaeological evidence it would be hard to tell that farming and herding had changed Fayum lifeways. As Caton-Thompson & Gardner (1934, p. 89) observed, the Fayum A sites appear to be nothing more than seasonally occupied camps. The largest settlements, Kom W and Kom K, are larger than any of the Qarunian camps but repeat the same themes of hearths and artefact scatters. There is no evidence of structures or any permanent installations. Moreover, Kom K's large mound is the product of repeated occupations over a long period rather than a single, sizeable community. The granaries associated with Kom K appear to be a new feature, not seen in the Epipalaeolithic, but they are not necessarily a sign of sedentary life; such structures are found among pastoral people who harvest and store wild grasses, as noted earlier. Moreover, one cannot be sure that such granaries were not used earlier in epipalaeolithic times and have gone undetected. Gardner only came upon the Upper K pits by chance while doing geological mapping on a ridge. The granaries were not visible on the surface but discovered by workmen sounding the gravel (Caton-Thompson & Gardner 1934, p. 41).

The domesticates appear to be an addition to a forager food base rather than a replacement. Nutlets of sedges and bistort were stored in granaries separately from cereals, suggesting that wild foods were still important, if not more important than the cereals. Domestic livestock was only one component in a large assemblage of fauna. Caton-Thompson & Gardner (1934, p. 89) inferred that they played little 'if any part in this lake-side economy' on the basis of the 'curious absence of sheep or goat dung in the settlements', which contrasted with the abundance of dung in the Nile valley predynastic settlements. Hunting, on the other hand, seemed to play quite a large role, as suggested by the large quantities of concave-base arrowheads found along the ancient lakeshore. Brewer (1989a, p. 171) concluded, on the basis of the changing relative frequencies and the strong presence of wild fauna, that 'domesticates offered merely another resource to be utilized in an overall generalized procurement strategy'. With the addition of domesticates, the Fayum A people had a wider resource base than the Qarunian folk and were 'thus better adapted to the unpredictable environment characteristic of the Fayum Depression' (Brewer 1989a, p. 171).

The Moerian

Ginter & Kozlowski (1986, pp. 19–22; Kozlowski & Ginter 1989, pp. 166–9) identified a second, younger neolithic phase in their sites, which they designated Moerian. Hassan (1985, p. 99) published corrected dates which place the sites between 4275 ± 170 cal BC and 4005 ± 160 cal BC. Since his study an additional younger date has been published, 4820 ± 100 bp (Ginter & Kozlowski 1986, p. 19), which corresponds to c. 3600 cal BC. Ginter & Kozlowski (1983, p. 70) set this industry apart from the earlier Fayumian because of differences in the lithic and ceramic industries. Moreover, they did not believe that this lithic industry, characterized by the blade technique, developed from the preceding Fayumian but was derived from the Western Desert (Ginter & Kozlowski 1983, p. 70).

The delineation of the Moerian is based mainly on materials from the largest and richest site, VII/80, and the only one producing ceramics. Deposits at this site formed a stratigraphic sequence spanning roughly 400 years (Hassan 1985, p. 99). The site covers an area at least 14 by 8 m and has several hearths and a scatter of postholes that suggest windbreaks. The hearths, dug into the ground with rocks piled around, stand in marked contrast to the shallow hearths seen in the Fayumian sites (Ginter & Kozlowski 1986, p. 22). Site VII/80 seems to have been a fishing camp, as nearly all of the faunal remains were fish, predominantly *Tilapia*, a shallow-water type, along with *Clarias*, and some Nile perch and *Synodontis*. Only a few elements of other fauna were found, including sheep/goat, gazelle and a water-fowl (von den Driesch 1986).

Two or three other Moerian sites were located, one of which had a single hearth. One of them yielded a paltry collection of three bones, representing sheep or goat and a small bovid.

The economy of the Moerians, as indicated by Site VII/80, was based on a generalized strategy with even fewer traces of domesticates than earlier Fayum A settlements. For more than a millennium, domesticates played no more than a subsidiary role in Fayum subsistence strategies.

Merimde Beni-salama

Located 45 km northwest of Cairo on the western edge of the Delta, Merimde is far more impressive than most neolithic sites in Egypt. The site rises like a tell above the surrounding floodplain on a spur of terrace that juts out from the low desert. Nearby an ancient channel of the Nile meanders through the floodplain. The site, covering an area 600 by 400 m (24 ha), encompasses a series of successive occupations which Hassan (1988, p. 151) estimates spans almost a millennium (c. 5000 to 4100 BC). The maximum depth of deposits is now 2.50 m but was greater originally as it is clear that erosion has removed overlying levels (Eiwanger 1978, p. 37; Eiwanger 1979, p. 26). Merimde is rare in that it shows a sequence of occupations, which is seen in only two other neolithic sites in Egypt.

Between 1929 and 1937, Junker (1928; 1929; 1930; 1932; 1933; 1934; 1940) carried out seven seasons of fieldwork, systematically excavating 6400 m^2 of the site. In 1977, Eiwanger (1978; 1979; 1980; 1982; 1984; 1988) resumed excavations in the areas Junker left untouched. In five seasons of work he excavated over 1200 m^2 and revised and amplified many of Junker's results.

While Junker (1940, pp. 5–12) had identified only three phases of occupation, Eiwanger established that there had in fact been five. The earliest phase, which Junker had failed to distinguish from later levels, was separated from the succeeding ones by a significant hiatus. It is not clear how long a time span separates Phase I from later ones, but the differences between them are striking (Eiwanger 1980, p. 69; Eiwanger 1984, p. 59). Phase I lithic technology is closer to the Epipalaeolithic with its emphasis on blades than to the bifacial tools typical of the later levels at Merimde. The earliest ceramics are also more primitive than later types and there are marked differences in other classes of artefacts and burial practices as well (Eiwanger 1980, p. 69; Eiwanger 1984, p. 62).

Phase I apparently saw very light occupation as there was only a thin scatter of debris (Eiwanger 1984, p. 12; Eiwanger 1988, p. 13). There were traces of postholes which suggested round or oval structures 2 to 3 m in diameter. These shelters probably consisted of wooden frames covered with matting, hides or other organic material (Eiwanger 1979, p. 26). The only other features were numerous shallow pits and small flat fire-hearths (Eiwanger 1984, p. 12).

Phase II and the succeeding levels saw more intense occupation than Phase I. The deposits were much richer in organic debris, with a dark colour in contrast to Phase I's sandy, greyish yellow fill (Eiwanger 1982, p. 68; Eiwanger 1988, p. 13). The settlements were probably larger as well but their dimensions cannot be ascertained without further excavation. Eiwanger (1984, p. 14) determined, however, that the location and size of the settlement oscillated over time. Thus in one area he encountered the youngest phases immediately overlying the oldest one.

From Phase II on, Eiwanger and Junker documented an increase in the density of occupation and complexity of the settlement. The standard house type, however, remained constant. Throughout the settlement at all levels Eiwanger (1982, p. 68) encountered postholes of the oval houses described above, with numerous hearths standing in front of them. From Phase II on, he also found more substantial evidence of storage structures – large pits lined with Nile mud and bones, located in front of the oval huts. The hearths after Phase I appear to have been used over a long period of time. In these levels small pits were also abundant and appear to have served as trash dumps as well as caches for raw materials (Eiwanger 1982, p. 68).

In the final phase two new types of structures appeared. Oval mud structures, measuring from 1.5 to 4.0 m in diameter, were sunk into the ground about 0.5 m. A foundation was built up to a metre high above ground out of courses of Nile mud or blocks of mud (Eiwanger 1982, p. 68; Junker 1932, pp. 43–51). Junker believed this was the standard house type during Merimde's last phase, but Eiwanger (1982, pp. 68–81) determined that it was concentrated in only one area of the site, suggesting a special function, such as communal storage.

The second innovation of Phase V, the basket silo, was certainly used for storage. Like the silos in the Fayum, the basket silos were large holes lined with basketry and covered with woven lids (Eiwanger 1978, p. 37).

Merimdens' subsistence practices were similar to those of their neighbours in the Fayum, but there is not as much material from Merimde. The following plants have been identified from Eiwanger's excavations in the early neolithic deposits but no details have been published:

> emmer wheat (prevailing); free-threshing wheat? (rare); hulled six-row barley (frequent); lentil (few) pea (few); flax (rare). Wild: *Lolium* and several other weeds, sedges, and legumes (frequent). (Zohary & Hopf 1988, p. 189)

Werth (1939) identified the plant remains Junker collected and found emmer wheat was the most abundant type, followed by hulled six-row barley and very small quantities of free-threshing wheat. He also found meagre amounts of peas and *Vicia* cf. *faba*.

We have only a few clues to the wild plants in the diet. Eiwanger (1984, p. 12) noted that the hearths contained burned reeds or sedges and their rhizomes. He assumed that this was fuel since the hearths only rarely held any charcoal. *Typha* is indeed burned for fuel in Wadi Natrun, west of the Delta (Tackholm & Drar 1941, p. 89), but another possibility is that some of these rhizomes were being roasted to eat. The sedge seeds in the botanical samples may also have been foods.

What role wild foods played compared with crops is impossible to determine. But storage seems to have become more important through time at Merimde, suggesting an increasing role for cultivars. In Phase I levels there was no evidence of special storage containers except the nondescript shallow pits which might have served a variety of other functions as well. The large lined pits that first appear in Phase II indicate a more substantial investment in storage facilities, as do the basket silos of Phase V.

It is possible that Phase I people stored their grains outside the settlement, particularly if they lived elsewhere part of the year. The scant remains in the earliest levels suggest that this might have been a seasonally occupied camp. Unfortunately, little is known about contemporaneous sites in the area that might provide clues to the settlement system. Neolithic material was found during survey scattered in an arc 2 to 3 km from the settlement, most of it badly disturbed, but this material is too sparse to shed light on settlement patterns.

The fauna from the oldest level indicates an important role for fish and domestic fauna. Most of the mammalian fauna were domesticates, the bulk of which were sheep. The remainder consisted of equal quantities of cattle and pig, with small numbers of goat (von den Driesch & Boessneck 1985; von den Driesch 1986, p. 6; Gautier 1987, p. 175). Fishing was an extremely important part of Merimde's economy, as indicated by the abundance of net weights, harpoons and fish-hooks in addition to fish remains (Eiwanger 1982, p. 82). The wild fauna included hippo, crocodile, turtles and some type of antelope.

Although there is no detailed information on the floral and faunal remains from Merimde, two points are clear: the earliest community was small and insubstantial, possibly a seasonal camp. Since there was far less investment in storage facilities than in the later phases, we may infer that the cultivars played a lesser role than later on and may have been a complement to the foraging system. Through succeeding phases, however, Merimdens built increasingly more elaborate storage facilities, suggesting that they were shifting from foraging and farming to a greater focus on farming. Second, fishing retained an important place in the economy, whereas the small quantity and limited number of wild taxa suggest that they contributed less here than in the Fayum.

El-Omari

Located near Helwan about 23 km south of Cairo, the El-Omari group of sites includes one settlement which is roughly the same age as the final occupation at Merimde. The one radiocarbon date from Site A, the oldest of the sites, is 5255 ± 230 bp (4110 ± 260 cal BC) (Hassan 1985, p. 98). Details of the community are only sketchily reported in the very brief accounts which the excavators, Bovier-Lapierre (1926) and Debono (1945; 1948; 1956), published. Still, one can see many of the same features as found in Merimde's final phases. There were over a hundred semi-subterranean circular huts as well as remains of numerous structures of posts and wickerwork. Smaller basketry-lined and clay-lined granaries were also found (Debono 1948; Hayes 1965, p. 117). The plant remains included the crops, six-row barley, emmer wheat, vetch (*Vicia sativa*) and flax, as well as sycamore fig and wild plants (Hayes 1965, p. 119). The faunal remains included the familiar assemblage of goat, cattle, pig and possibly catfish and *Synodontis*, as well as various water-fowl, hippo, ostrich, crocodile and antelope (Hayes 1965, p. 119). El-Omari clearly cannot shed light on the beginnings of farming in Lower Egypt but it does indicate that Merimde was not an isolated case of cultural evolution. The same changes occurring in the Delta were apparently going on elsewhere in the area and at roughly the same time. By this point Lower Egypt's first forager-farmers had given way to more specialized farmers.

Similar shifts in subsistence are also recorded for this date at Kadero, far to the south in the Sudan, in levels dated 4900–3800 BC (Krzyzaniak 1991).

Badari-Mostagedda-Matmar

The region from Matmar, across the Nile from Assiyut, south to the villages of Badari and Hemamieh on the east bank of the Nile has produced the earliest evidence of farming communities in Upper Egypt as well as extensive remains of prehistoric

Egyptian settlements and cemeteries. During the 1920s and 1930s Brunton (1937; 1948) worked extensively in this region, in conjunction with Caton-Thompson (1928), surveying and excavating along a 33 km stretch on the low desert adjacent to the floodplain. He excavated or tested about forty settlements but the emphasis was on cemeteries and grave goods (Brunton 1930; Brunton 1937; Brunton 1948).

It is difficult to ferret out the nature of the earliest farming settlements, the Badarian culture, as the data are scant. The most detailed account of a settlement site comes from Caton-Thompson's (1928) meticulous work at North Spur Hemamieh, which revealed a continuous sequence of occupation 2 m thick dating from the earliest Neolithic in Upper Egypt through the late Predynastic. The site is situated, like Merimde, on a spur of the low desert which projects out onto the floodplain. But it is much smaller than Merimde, measuring only about 37 by 46 m.

The Badarian deposits left few remains at Hemamieh. The lowest level yielded a scant collection of 39 sherds. Above this was a layer of consolidated limestone, or breccia, followed by the actual Badarian occupation. From this upper level Hassan (1984b, p. 3) collected material for two radiocarbon age determinations, which as a weighted average yielded a date of 6030 ± 160 bp. Since there was additional material below the breccia, this date may not encompass the earliest phase of the Badarian at Hemamieh (Hassan 1985, p. 107; Hassan 1988, p. 141). Caton-Thompson (1928, p. 74) described the post-breccia Badarian deposits, which were 75 cm thick, as remains of a 'temporary camping ground'. She found only 106 sherds and a few flint artefacts and no evidence of structures or other facilities.

Brunton (1928; 1937; 1948) recorded numerous sites which he assigned to Badarian on the basis of ceramics, but excavated them hastily and published few details. Like Caton-Thompson, he found the Badarian folk left 'scanty remains' and almost no traces of construction (1928, p. 40). Deposits were thin, consisting of little more than ash and charcoal smears with associated artefacts. Almost the only features at these sites were various pits and granaries (Brunton 1937, p. 15). One of the sites he described as follows:

> A settlement had also existed on the end of this spur; the ground had not been reused in dynastic times, and was therefore comparatively undis-turbed. There was, however, no stratification. Thin layers of ash and charcoal were met with here and there at various depths down to 72 cm, suggesting a series of short occupations. (Brunton 1937, p. 14)

This site produced more evidence of construction than any of the others Brunton examined: three stumps of wooden posts or sticks, 40 to 50 cm tall, standing upright against a vertical scarp about 60 cm high (Brunton 1937, p. 14). A fourth post stood nearby beyond the scarp. This arrangement might have formed part of a wall or windbreak. Another village 'had apparently been of some importance as traces of it were found over a considerable area up and down the spur. But, as always there was no depth of deposits, only occasional thin layers of ash' (Brunton 1948, p. 5).

The only features Brunton (1948, p. 15) observed at this site, like many of the others, were pits and granaries, the largest of which was 95 cm in diameter with a basket lining in the bottom.

The pits and granaries associated with Badarian deposits varied in shape, size and method of construction. At one site there were remains of several large basketry-lined granaries, one of which measured 1.35 m in diameter and 1.0 m deep. At this site there were also some enormous circular pits, measuring up to 2.7 m in diameter and 3 m in depth (Brunton 1948, p. 5). There were also small round pits (Brunton 1937, p. 68) and bell-shaped pits. Two bell-shaped bins were made of sun-dried clay, one of which measured a metre across the base, about 45 cm across the top and 90 cm deep (Brunton 1928, pp. 5, 6). Most of the pits contained Badarian artefacts, which suggested that they dated from this period, but others contained no datable materials and might have been intrusive from later times. Some are associated with village artefacts but others are isolated finds, like the Upper K granaries in the Fayum. Brunton assumed all the pits were granaries but only a few produced any traces of grains and, in one instance, flax capsules (Brunton 1937, pp. 15, 58, 68). Some of the pits may have served a variety of storage functions as well during their lifetimes and may have eventually ended as rubbish dumps. The only other facility Brunton encountered was a small dome-shaped oven, built of 'rough lumps of mud', reddened by fire in a hole 20 cm deep (Brunton 1937, p. 12).

No systematic studies of plant or animal remains were carried out at any of the Badarian sites, but items encountered during excavation were collected and in some cases turned over to experts for identification. This collection is obviously a highly unsatisfactory and incomplete sample of the Badarian economy; it undoubtedly fails to include a wide range of plant foods and wild fauna used by Badarians and is almost certainly biased in favour of large, visible specimens. Still, these meagre remains offer some clues to the plants and animals used by the Badarian folk. Chaff was common at many of the settlement sites and, along with charcoal, was probably some of the most common midden debris, as it is in rural Egyptian villages today. Desiccated and carbonized cereals were occasionally found in village sites in pits, as pockets scattered through the fill, and in pots (Brunton 1928, p. 41; Brunton 1937, pp. 15–16, 18, 31, 58). These were identified as spikelets and grains of emmer wheat and six-row hulled barley (Brunton 1937, p. 33). Flax capsules and the spikelet of a wild grass, probably *Bromus*, were also found in village deposits (Brunton 1937, p. 59). In addition, a pod of a wild vetch, *Vicia tetrasperma* or *V. hirsuta*, was recovered with barley (Brunton 1937, p. 59). John Percival, the botanist who identified the plant remains, considered this a weed (Brunton 1937, p. 59) but since some of the wild vetches are edible this may have served as a food if various toxins were removed.

Cereals and bread occasionally occurred as offerings in burials, usually in pots (Brunton 1937, p. 58). But in the grave of an adult male, grain was found in a leather bag placed at the feet (Brunton 1937, p. 58). In addition, barley which had been ground with its hull was found in the intestines of a mummy (Brunton 1937, p. 58). Castor seeds, probably a wild type, were found in another grave (Brunton 1928, p. 38).

Animal bones were recovered occasionally from settlement deposits, usually in conjunction with cooking pots, but they were more common in burials (Brunton 1928, p. 38; Brunton 1937, pp. 30–1). Unfortunately, they are reported only briefly, often with uncertain identifications. The taxa mentioned are cattle (which might have included wild and domestic types), sheep and goat as well as a variety of wild fauna including gazelle, hippo, fish, turtle and crocodile (Brunton 1928, pp. 7, 12; Brunton 1937, pp. 11, 14, 57). Fish were not specifically identified except for Nile perch (Brunton 1948, p. 7). Meat was apparently included in some graves as offerings; the remains of an immature animal, probably a calf, were found in burials in the form of a leg-bone, blade-bone and rib-bone, usually inside pots (Brunton 1937, pp. 30–1). Animals were also interred in their own burials, wrapped or covered with a mat, including 'pet gazelle', sheep or goat, cattle and dog (Brunton 1928, p. 7; Brunton 1937, p. 57). In addition, gazelle and goat skins were often used as garments in burials (Brunton 1928, p. 40). A skin of an animal with soft black fur, possibly a cat, also occurred in some graves (Brunton 1928, p. 19). Ostrich feathers and night heron (*Nycticorax*), as well as the beak of a spoon-bill, were encountered as well in burials (Brunton 1928, p. 28; Brunton 1937, p. 57; Brunton 1948, p. 8).

Evidence of settlement is much more substantial for the succeeding Amratian period, which Hassan (1988, p. 138) dates to about 3900–3650 BC. At Hemamieh, Caton-Thompson (1928, pp. 82–8) found, in late Amratian levels, the remains of nine hut circles scattered across the site with diameters between 1 and 2 m. Reminiscent of the Merimde oval mud structures, the floors were sunk into the ground up to a metre and a foundation of mud walls was built up to 75 cm above ground. The foundations served as support for a wall of matting or other organic material, as indicated by the imprint of stalks pressed vertically against the wall. There was no opening or step into the structures, prompting Caton-Thompson (1928, p. 83) to remark that 'These sunk hut foundations are, indeed both in dimensions and structure, apparently so impractical, that one would be inclined to regard even the larger of them as store houses only.' She concluded, however, that the larger ones were dwellings because of the remains of a hearth found in one of them. Still, it seems more likely that they served primarily for storage rather than as living quarters, considering their small dimensions and Eiwanger's (1982, p. 68) conclusions that the oval mud huts at Merimde were special-purpose structures. One of the smaller mud circles, measuring about 1 m in diameter at floor level, was apparently used to store fuel; it was filled with a layer of desiccated sheep/goat dung 75 cm deep. Outside the huts Caton-Thompson also found traces of small mud-lined pits that were probably used for storage, as well as the remains of a mud wall a little less than 1 m high, and a row of twelve irregularly spaced posts possibly used to support a windscreen (Caton-Thompson 1928, p. 88). But no traces of frame shelters or other habitations were found.

Although it seems peculiar that Amratians apparently emphasized storage over sleeping quarters, this pattern is not unusual when viewed in the light of recent hunter-gatherers. Yellen (1976, p. 64) observed among the !Kung that

> Huts provide shelter and a place to store belongings; they serve to mark
> out ground which belongs to a single family. Very few activities take place
> inside a hut, and only during a rainstorm do people sleep in them.

In Upper Egypt during the fourth millennium BC people would rarely have required any protection from rain and may, like the !Kung, have used shelters almost entirely for storage.

Hemamieh was not unique during Amratian times. Throughout the Badari-

Mostaggeda-Matmar area Brunton (1928, pp. 44, 47; 1930, p. 3) found similar settlements with mud circle huts which he (Brunton 1928, p. 48) believed were mainly Amratian, although some of them could not be precisely dated. The mud circle huts included types similar to those Caton-Thompson had excavated, as well as other styles (Brunton 1928, p. 44). At one site Brunton exposed a hut in which a section of the wall was built of small rough stones and an area was left open, apparently as a doorway. At another settlement the walls of a hut were built of mud laid upon two courses of mud bricks. At this site Brunton also found the remains of an oblong structure about 1.5 m by 2 m with only north and east walls, which may have been a two-sided shelter (Brunton 1928, p. 47). At another site he (Brunton 1937, p. 78) found what may have been the remains of a windscreen that burned down. It consisted of ten stakes, which had burned off at ground level, stuck in the ground about 7 cm apart in a line about 60 cm long. The stakes had burned off at what seemed to be the old ground level and nearby there was a layer of ash. The depth of deposits in most of the sites was shallow, although some had considerable depth, such as one with deposits up to 105 cm (Brunton 1937, p. 81).

Amratian sites yielded a greater quantity and variety of plant remains than the earlier Badarian ones, probably because the sample of graves and settlements is larger. Emmer wheat and six-row barley are mentioned most often in village contexts (Brunton 1928, p. 63; Caton-Thompson 1928, pp. 77, 85; Percival 1936, p. 272; Brunton 1948, pp. 22–3). Flax capsules were found, as in the earlier Badarian sites. Lentils, *Lathyrus sativus* (the 'grass vetchling') and fruits of *Ficus sycomorus* and wild dom palm, which had not been seen in the earlier sites, appeared (Brunton 1928, pp. 62–3; Brunton 1937, pp. 90–1; Brunton 1948, p. 23), but they were almost certainly not new to the Badari district during the Amratian. Most likely they were missed at earlier sites because of the haphazard recovery methods and sample size. *Asphodelus fistulosus* seeds were also found in a pot (Brunton 1928, pp. 62–3). This member of the lily family, common in the Nile valley (Tackholm 1974, p. 630), may have been gathered for its edible root tubers.

The most abundant wild plants were *Cyperus* tubers, which in some instances were identified as *C. esculentus* (Brunton 1928, p. 63; Brunton 1937, p. 59; Brunton 1948, p. 23). They were found in a pot near Badari (Brunton 1928, p. 63) but were more abundant in burials, many of which may be somewhat later than the Amratian settlements (Brunton 1937, p. 91; Brunton 1948, p. 18). They were also recovered from the intestines of a mummy in a predynastic cemetery at Naga ed-Der, along with grains of *Echinochloa colonum* (Tackholm & Drar 1950, p. 63). *C. esculentus* grows wild in Egypt and is also cultivated for its tubers (Tackholm & Drar 1950, p. 61). During predynastic times tubers were probably collected from wild plants, as suggested by at least one find. Tubers which Brunton (1928, p. 63) found in a pot were 'somewhat smaller than those seen in the market at present', which is consistent with the wild variety. Closely related to the wild nut-grass (*C. rotundus*) found at Wadi Kubbaniya, *C. esculentus* tubers are far more palatable as they are slightly sweet and can be eaten after soaking in water or roasting. They are also used to prepare a beverage and as medicine (Tackholm & Drar 1950, p. 68).

The use of *C. esculentus* tubers in Upper Egypt appears to be a continuation of the palaeolithic practice of utilizing root foods. It is extremely difficult to determine what role the tubers played in the diet, compared to the cereals, but their abundance in burials seems to bespeak some importance. The tubers appear to occur about as frequently in graves as grains, although quantitative data from the burials is not entirely reliable, for a couple of reasons. Plant remains that were not in pots or well preserved may have been missed. In the looted burials, of which there were many, fruits and grains may have been lost or destroyed. Moreover, burial offerings are not necessarily a reflection of the diet of the living; items may have been included for their symbolic value. Indeed the *Cyperus* tubers found in one burial were pierced as if they had been strung, perhaps for medicinal purposes (Tackholm & Drar 1950, p. 62). Still, the Naga ed-Der predynastic mummy established at least that the tubers were eaten at this time. In addition, *C. esculentus* tubers persisted in burial offerings into dynastic times and later (Brunton 1937, p. 111; Tackholm & Drar 1950, pp. 63–4), which suggests that the plants were of some significance.

The faunal data from the Amratian villages are scant but Caton-Thompson (1928, p. 77) reported only domestic livestock at Hemamieh, including sheep or goat, pig and ox. The fauna from cemeteries shows several interesting changes between Badarian and later times which hint at a decline in hunting and an increasing role for domesticates. Brunton (1937, p. 90; 1948, p. 22) noticed in both the Matmar and Mostagedda areas a general increase in the frequency of meat offerings in graves, which he (Brunton 1937, p. 90) speculated was perhaps due to a 'greater wealth of herds'. These offerings were restricted to men, whereas in earlier periods meat occasionally appeared in the graves of women and children as well (Brunton 1937, p. 57). This might reflect increasing restrictions on animal protein in the community. The offerings were 'invariably of small and young ruminants, generally a fore-leg or fore-quarter' (Brunton 1937, p. 90), which would most likely have been domestic animals, in contrast to the earlier offerings which included wild game. 'Pet' gazelles, however, occurred with a number of human burials of both sexes (Brunton 1948, p. 22), which suggests that some form of management was applied to this wild species.

Another burial trend was the decline in the use of skins to cover or clothe the deceased. While roughly one-third of the more than 300 Badarian burials in the Mostagedda district had skins (Brunton 1937, p. 47), only seven of the Amratian graves and one of the Gerzean graves did (Brunton 1937, p. 82). In the Badari area there was a similar decline in the use of skins (Brunton 1928, p. 19). This pattern may reflect a dwindling role for hunting, since many of the skins in the Badarian graves were gazelle. The decline in burial skins may also be related to an increasing role for linen, made from a domesticate, which was also used to cover the body in death and probably in life. Customs were not uniform, though, through this region. In the Matmar area skins were rare in burials of all periods (Brunton 1948, p. 10).

The data from the Badari-Mostagedda-Matmar district do not allow us to draw many conclusions but they offer a hazy sketch of Upper Egypt's first farmers and suggest several trends. First, the scant traces of settlement during Badarian times imply limited, light occupation that was probably seasonal, in contrast to more substantial Amratian settlements. While almost the only features seen in the earlier communities were various pits and granaries associated with artefact scatters and ash dumps, the later settlements left traces of huts, fences, windbreaks and possibly pens, as well as more debris. One of the major changes seen in the Amratian settlements was in storage facilities. Brunton (1937, p. 69) observed that large storage pits and granaries were associated only with Badarian sites. By Amratian times large storage structures seem to have moved above ground in the form of the mud circle huts seen at Hemamieh and many other sites.

These new structures suggest that Amratians were more dependent on cultigens than their predecessors. A greater investment in time and energy would have gone into their construction, which presumably was justified by the value of the products stored in them. The storage capacity of these facilities was probably greater than most of the Badarian pits. Although it is not known how high the mud circles were, most are at least as deep as many of the pits with just the combined height of the mud walls and the depth of the floor. Greater capacity suggests that larger quantities of food were stored, although one cannot be sure that this is not simply a matter of consolidating what might have been stored in many smaller pits.

The above-ground structures also imply more sedentary occupation than seen in the earlier Badarian settlements. Highly visible and accessible, they were probably vulnerable to theft and may not have been left unattended for long periods. Underground structures, on the other hand, were hidden, or easily concealed, and could probably be left. Indeed, the granaries at Upper K went undetected for nearly 7000 years! The Badarian storage pits that Brunton found scattered out in the desert beyond settlements would have been equally compatible with a semi-nomadic pattern, as they would have been safe places to cache grain while the owners were foraging in other areas.

The greater investment in the mud circles is also a reflection of longer occupation, as suggested by ethnographic evidence. Yellen (1976, p. 63) found that the type of huts the !Kung built varied according to the season and the length of time they would be occupied. Far more care and effort went into those used for longer periods.

The mud circles may have been built initially with storage as the primary concern, as suggested above. But over time they may have gradually been improved for the occasions when people moved inside, as suggested by the mud circle huts that diverged from the 'standard' model – the hut with a hearth, the two-walled hut and the mud circle with a doorway.

The indications of a more sedentary lifestyle are complemented by evidence that hunting was dwindling while domestic livestock were assuming a greater role in the economy. Regrettably, there is almost no information on fish exploitation patterns. Although fish bones were occasionally picked up at sites, these samples, limited to the largest, most visible elements, are relatively meaningless.

In sum, several lines of evidence suggest a trend towards longer occupations at individual settlements in the Badari-Matmar district, coupled with an increasing role for cereals and livestock in the economy. Unfortunately, too few data exist to suggest how these settlements were related to one another and communities on the floodplain.

Armant-Gurna area

Ginter and his colleagues (Ginter, Kozlowski & Sliwa 1979; Ginter & Kozlowski 1984; Ginter, Kozlowski & Pawlikowski 1985; Ginter, Kozlowski & Pawlikowski 1987; Ginter, Kozlowski, Litynska & Pawlikowski 1988) located eleven predynastic sites, which they refer to as Naqadian, during their Gurna to Armant survey, mentioned earlier. The sites date from Amratian times; the oldest, Site MA 17, is dated at 3190 ± 60 cal BC (Hassan 1985, p. 109) and the youngest, the final occupation at Site MA 21, at 4890 ± 50 bp (Ginter, Kozlowski & Pawlikowski 1987, p. 60). Hassan (1985, p. 109) notes, however, that the ceramic industry is closer to Nagada II assemblages seen at the site of Nagada South Town than to those from Nagada I times. Regional variation may account for these differences in chronology.

The most detailed information on Nagadian settlements comes from Sites MA 21/83 and MA 21a/83, which lie on the opposite banks of a wadi and were presumably part of a single community. The sites saw three phases of occupation spanning the period of roughly 4000 BC to 3600 BC (Ginter, Kozlowski, Litynska & Pawlikowski 1988, pp. 97, 100). Site MA 21/83 covers about 2500 m^2 and is located, like Hemamieh, on the low desert adjacent to the floodplain. The earliest occupation, which may be contemporaneous with Badarian, left few traces, as in the Badari district; there was a light scatter of artefacts and a few pits. This was followed by another phase of settlement with pits which cut into the lower level. In the last phase there were three successive living floors which span a short period of perhaps 120 radiocarbon years.

MA 21 yielded a wealth of features, nearly all of which occurred in the last two phases, including numerous hearths, pits and traces of various structures. There were four structures with stone foundations, including a rectangular one with a base of cobbles and a row of postholes which may have supported walls (Ginter, Kozlowski, Litynska & Pawlikowski 1988, p. 100). Several round structures with a foundation of limestone cobbles and diameters up to 1.5 m may have been used for above-ground storage (Ginter, Kozlowski & Pawlikowski 1987, p. 61). There was also a rectangular structure delineated by a row of postholes (Ginter, Kozlowski & Pawlikowski 1987, p. 60). Other postholes were scattered across the site in semicircles, rectangles and seemingly random patterns. Some of these may have been the bases of windbreaks or perhaps the remains of light huts or animal pens. The site was riddled with an assortment of pits and hearths, including flat hearths, shallow hearths and oven pits. One of the oven pits, measuring 70 by 20 cm, was particularly well made with stone-lined walls and bottom. It was filled with ashes and partially burned animal dung which had apparently been used as fuel. There were small storage pits, which in some cases were lined with daub and still held the remains of desiccated plants.

Site MA 21a yielded similar sorts of hearths and pits that were both plain and coated with mud. Postholes were more randomly scattered and did not seem to outline structures. The only evidence for a stone structure was a concentration of limestone slabs (Ginter, Kozlowski, Litynska & Pawlikowski 1988, p. 101).

The neolithic site at El-Tarif, for which there is unfortunately no reliable date, overlies the epipalaeolithic deposits described earlier. It consisted of two structures with stone foundations, measuring 3.5 by 2.5 m and 3.0 by 1.5 m (Ginter, Kozlowski & Sliwa 1979, p. 98) and four hearths, about 2 m in diameter, placed in a semicircle around one of the buildings. Unfortunately, neither the age nor precise extent of the site can be determined.

Site MA 6, which has also not been dated, consisted of no more than a concentration of stone artefacts associated with a hearth, although originally it may have been much larger (Ginter, Kozlowski & Pawlikowski 1987). The earliest dated site, MA 17, also produced scant finds; testing revealed a small pit, from which charcoal for radiocarbon age determination was taken (Ginter, Kozlowski & Pawlikowski 1985, p. 31).

Information on Nagadian economy comes from a preliminary report on charred and desiccated plant remains from Sites MA 21/83 and MA 21a/83 (Ginter, Kozlowski, Litynska & Pawlikowski 1988, pp. 93–104). The most abundant item in the assemblage was emmer wheat, represented by spikelets, rachis segments and grains, followed by six-row barley. A couple of lentils were also recovered. The wild taxa include a number of food plants, suggesting a continuing role for collecting. The most common wild type was the seed of *Citrullus colocynthus*, a melon. The seeds of *Echinochloa crus-galli*, an edible grass, appeared in one sample. Carex nutlets found in the samples may also have served as food.

If Sites MA 21 and MA 21a are typical of the Nagadian, communities in the Armant-Gurna area show trends similar to those in the Badari region. The initial settlements were light, ephemeral occupations, while later communities lived in more substantial hamlets with large, above-ground storage facilities. There were no mud circle huts found here but foundations of cobbles were uncovered, suggesting that regional styles of 'architecture' developed in different areas of Upper Egypt during Amratian times. The economy developing at this time was probably shifting towards domesticates but unfortunately there are not enough data available to trace such trends. Although the botanical report suggests that cereals were probably major foods, it does not offer any clues to change over time since it fails to list the levels from which the plant remains were extracted. Nothing can be said about hunting and herding as the faunal data have not yet been published.

Nagada region

Several roughly contemporary communities have been studied by Hassan and colleagues (Hays 1976b; Hassan 1981b; Hassan 1988, pp. 154–5) in the Nagada region between Luxor and Qena on the west bank of the Nile. During several seasons of survey and excavation in the region nine sites were located, spaced at intervals of about 2 km apart on the low desert zone adjacent to the floodplain. Radiocarbon dates were obtained for three early sites and yielded a mean of 3760 ± 40 cal BC; these sites were therefore occupied sometime within the interval from about 3850 to 3650 BC (Hassan 1985, pp. 107–8), placing them in Nagada I or Amratian times. The ceramics, likewise, are similar to those of Late Nagada I or possibly the Nagada I/II transition (Hassan & Matson 1989).

The sites were modest settlements which, like the Badari-Matmar sites, left meagre remains, including traces of hearths, pits, animal pens and possibly huts, as well as middens. At Site KH3 a concentration of debris and various features suggested household and activity areas not unlike those seen in villages today. There were dense scatters of organic refuse and artefacts, a small dump of ash and charcoal, traces of a carbonate-cemented floor, a stone hearth with charcoal, a circular storage pit and an area of compacted dung which had probably been a livestock pen (Hassan 1981b, p. 43). There were no walls or foundations but a posthole with fragments of a wooden post still in place may have been part of a simple hut or windbreak. Dwellings may also have been constructed of blocks of mud and stone, as suggested by the abundance of rubble and Nile mud (Hassan 1988, p. 155). Some of the sites were very shallow but a few had deposits up to 1 m deep. Repeated abandonment and reoccupation seems to have occurred at some of the sites (Hassan 1988, p. 155).

Gautier's (Hassan 1981b, Table 4) preliminary analysis of bone from three of the early sites shows the sample is largely domesticated animals, sheep/goat, pig and cattle. Initially, small livestock was the most abundant type, but it decreased somewhat in favour of pig and cattle, suggesting that subsistence may have become less desert-oriented over time (Gautier 1984, p. 175). Fish remains were common, but have not been identified to species. Fishing may have been done with nets as no fish-hooks or harpoons were recovered (Hassan 1981b, p. 19). Wild fauna was rare and not very diverse. A single element of turtle and bird were recovered and six of dorcas gazelle (2 per cent of the total), in contrast to 347 elements (88 per cent of total) of domestic fauna. Further evidence for a decline in hunting is seen in the tool assemblage; only one projectile point was recovered (Hassan 1981b, p. 19). The sample also included a few *Canid* (probably dog) bones and small rodents, which were assumed to be intrusive.

The plant remains from one of the sites, KH3, currently under analysis (Wetterstrom 1986), were recovered systematically through flotation and show much greater diversity than those picked by hand in the Badari district. In addition to the cultivars – emmer wheat, six-row barley and flax – twenty-three different taxa of wild plants have been identified thus far in deposits from the earlier settlements. The samples, which included charred and desiccated remains, appear to be derived from household rubbish scattered and dumped around the habitation areas. Nearly all of the charred material probably came from household fire-hearths used for cooking and heating and most likely includes fuels, food spills, discards from cooking accidents and refuse. The desiccated material, probably preserved by the relatively dry conditions of the low desert, is not the full spectrum of plants that might have been discarded but is limited to the most resilient materials: chaff, straw, hard fruit stones and tough waxy seed coats.

The plant remains offer no definitive answers but there are several lines of evidence suggesting that cultivars had assumed an important role in the economy by this time. First, evidence of cereals was ubiquitous; virtually every level in every square metre excavated had some traces of cereals. Most of it consisted of tough chaff, which preserves well and is undoubtedly over-represented compared with other classes. But the fact that it occurred in a number of samples where there were no other plant remains suggests that chaff and straw must have been abundant at the settlement. Second, while cereal grains did not occur in all flotation samples, they were the most frequently occurring charred seed type. Since they occurred in small numbers in the samples, it is likely that they were the products of household cooking – grains scattered or spilled in the hearth, or accidentally burned, rather than the product of a single fire or a single batch of ruined cereals. The fact that they occur in many samples suggests that they were perhaps prepared on nearby hearths.

The other common seed types in the flotation samples also offer evidence that cereals were important in the economy. The second most frequent charred seed was *Lolium*-type, which was almost certainly a field weed. *Anthemis*, mayweed, accounted for the greatest number of seeds, nearly all of which were desiccated, and this composite was probably a field weed as well. The flower heads were most likely cut off along with the cereal stalks and later removed from the crop during processing. Once in the rubbish or in piles of straw, the discarded heads would, upon drying out, have shed their many minute achenes, which would account for the large quantity of them in the flotation samples. Empty *Anthemis* flower receptacles were also found in the samples.

Another piece of evidence which suggests a major economic role for cereals at this site is the ratio of charred cereal grains to other seed types at KH3 (roughly one to one). This ratio is the same as for the later site of Nagada South Town. Since the flotation samples from both sites were from midden contexts and were collected and processed in the same way, the similarity is probably not by chance. Nagada South Town, dated to about 3440 BC (Hassan 1985, p. 109), or Nagada II, would almost certainly have been fully dependent on agriculture.

Another sign that the Nagada people were shifting to an agricultural economy might be the abundance of clover, *Trifolium*, seeds. Although this may be a field weed, clover is also a fodder plant, and may have been raised or gathered for livestock at KH3.

There were few potential wild plant foods in the KH3 samples, although they were undoubtedly still used. There was no evidence of tubers and stems of wetland plants, as might be expected, since they usually do not preserve well. Nutlets of *Cyperus*, however, occurred frequently in the flotation samples in small numbers. Most of these were desiccated and could have come from foods or sedges used for utilitarian functions, such as matting. Several ruderal plants in the samples may have been eaten, including *Chenopodium* and *Rumex*, but these may also have been field weeds. The only fruits in the flotation samples, *Zizyphus* and *Citrullus colocynthus*, would also have been consumed.

In sum, the evidence from the floral and faunal remains indicates that the Nagada people relied largely on crops and livestock rather than wild products. The sites, however, seemed to lack evidence of above-ground storage facilities or substantial dwellings, unlike contemporary ones in the Armant-Gurna and Badari regions. Preservation or possibly construction methods may have been poorer in the Nagada area, so that few traces of construction were preserved. It is also possible that storage facilities were missed when sites were sampled. In addition, since there were regional differences in construction techniques and lithic styles, there may also have been differences in social organization as well, which would influence the way in which goods were stored. For example, the desert-edge sites may have been satellites of larger communities on the floodplain that stored the harvest.

Conclusions

By roughly 4100 BC in Lower Egypt and 3800 BC in Upper Egypt foragers had shifted from a generalized subsistence strategy and begun a more specialized one focused on crops and livestock. The bio-archaeological evidence indicates that the broad food base of earlier times had contracted and, although some wild products were still used, they only supplemented the domesticates. The least reliable component of the wild food base, game, seems to have been supplanted by livestock. With this shift in economy, new settlement patterns emerged. The farming hamlets show evidence for extensive, perhaps year-round occupation, and far more investment in storage facilities and habitations. Within the Delta and the Nile valley the shift seems to have occurred rapidly, perhaps within several hundred years after domesticates first appeared at settlements.

We have tried to follow the path taken by Egyptian hunter-gatherers as they crossed the threshold from foragers to farmers. During the Epipalaeolithic they pursued a subsistence strategy that had probably developed during the late Pleistocene in an environment of scarcity. They relied on root foods and fish from the wetlands of the Nile valley to provide the bulk of their diet for at least part of the year. But Egyptian foragers, like recent hunter-gatherers, also utilized a diversity of wild plants and animals, which probably assured their survival during periods of shortage.

It is proposed that they were seeking yet another set of back-up foods when they adopted domesticates. Although the nilotic wetlands abounded with food during certain times of the year, foragers faced seasonal 'hunger' periods, particularly when the Nile floods were unusually high or low or untimely. Indeed, the vagaries of the inundation were probably the single greatest threat to the security of the foragers' food base. Both the volume of the floodwaters and the timing and duration of the floods could have varied widely. In addition, through the Epipalaeolithic, the Nile floodplain and its wealth of resources may have been alternately contracting and expanding as a result of the holocene moist phases and dry intervals. There may have been a period of unusually low floods in the Nile valley, just prior to the first appearance of livestock and crops around 5200 BC, which could have prompted foragers to seek additional resources. The domesticates would have been valued as another thread in the safety net, as additional food during shortages. But they may also have been valued even more highly for their unique property of being predictable. Foragers could to some extent control the location and size of the crops and herds. With this predictable set of resources they could compensate for some of the devastating effects of unusual floods and go on successfully hunting and gathering. Thus domesticates were probably adopted in the Nile valley in order to diversify the food base. They complemented rather than replaced foraging.

In the Fayum there is ample evidence that domesticates were indeed merely added to the food base. Fayum A people continued as hunter-gatherers for nearly 1000 years after adopting cereals and livestock. The earliest farmers in the Delta and Upper Egypt, likewise, appear to have been foragers with a thin veneer of farming tacked onto their economy. But change happened quickly in these areas and within a few hundred years they were squarely set on a course towards full dependence on agriculture.

Perhaps the most intriguing question posed by the Egyptian Neolithic is not why or how domesticates were originally adopted, but what happened to foraging strategies once domesticates were added to the food base. Why were the strategies transformed so rapidly in the Nile valley, but unchanged after 1000 years in the Fayum? Can the differences be attributed to environment? Or to population size? Was the Fayum too marginal to support farming?

Was the Nile valley, on the other hand, a more favourable environment for crops, where they proved so efficient and productive that they offered a better return than wild

foods? Or were other factors gradually nudging Nile valley foragers into more specialized strategies, such as population growth and changes in the environment wrought by
livestock? Was foraging gradually rejected because it was not compatible with the
emerging trend towards sedentism – if, indeed, foragers were not already sedentary in
the late Palaeolithic?

Notes

[1] In the Sohag–Abydos region just north of the Qena bend a few *in situ* middle and upper
palaeolithic sites have been located, but all of these are preserved in wadis outside the Nile valley or
are on protected terraces high above the valley floor (Paulissen & Vermeersch 1987, pp. 32, 34,
37–8, 40).

[2] There is also some evidence from a burial that post-pleistocene reduction in robusticity, which
could be related to changes in foraging practices, was already under way here before 18,000 BP.
The burial, dated to 20,000 BP and found in the mouth of Wadi Kubbaniya, was of a 20–25-year-
old male (Wendorf & Schild 1986). Although his face showed pronounced prognathism, he was
'muscular but slender', and not 'very tall' (Angel & Kelley 1986, pp. 53, 70). He had suffered a
violent death, as indicated by two bladelets in his pelvic cavity, and had been wounded twice
before (Angel & Kelley 1986, pp. 56, 62). Such violence might have been related to competition
over food resources. Unfortunately, this evidence for a reduction in robusticity is not very
conclusive since one individual is not a population, nor is he necessarily typical of his population.

Acknowledgement

I gratefully acknowledge Gordon Hillman's considerable contribution to this chapter.

11 The emergence of a food-producing economy in the Sahara

A. MUZZOLINI

Introduction

The prestige of Pharaonic Egypt has long been such that its aura has been projected backwards onto earlier periods. Indeed, it was until recently considered inconceivable that Africa's so-called 'Neolithic Revolution' could have started anywhere other than in the valley of the Nile. Earlier predynastic villages – especially the Fayum (see Wetterstrom, Ch. 10, this volume) – were long seen as the first stars from which the light of civilization had radiated throughout the whole of Africa. The discovery of the Khartoum Mesolithic (Arkell 1949) extended this theme to the Sudan: henceforth the 'Sudanese crucible' (*creuset*) was lyrically celebrated as the origin of the innovations which were allegedly exported to the vast Sahara area.

The accumulation of archaeological data and of radiocarbon dates has put an end to the development of these fanciful tales (Wetterstrom, Ch. 10, this volume). In their place is a picture of regional contrasts, in which the decisive changes occurred not only in the valley of the Nile, but also elsewhere (e.g. Krzyzaniak 1991) – even in the difficult environments of the Sahara (Fig. 11.1).

This chapter examines the transition from a hunter-gatherer economy (the 'epipalaeolithic stage') in the Sahara to a food-producing one (the 'neolithic stage') there – the term 'neolithic' being used in the sense of 'food-producing', but with reservations because of its ambiguity (see Sinclair, Shaw & Andah, Introduction, this volume; and also Andah, Ch. 12, this volume; Eggert, Ch. 16, this volume).

North Africa towards the end of the Pleistocene

The end of the Pleistocene in north Africa is marked by a period (*c.* 18,000 to 12,000 bp) of extreme aridity (Fig. 11.2; and see Grove, Ch. 1, this volume) which drove out of the Sahara all of its human occupants and practically all of its animals (the 'Post-Aterian Hyperarid Phase'). During this long period, living creatures sought refuge to the east in the Nile valley and to the north in the Maghreb and Cyrenaica. Everywhere there were groups with developed microlithic industries, variously called 'epipalaeolithic', 'late stone age' or 'terminal palaeolithic'.

Some of these hunter-gatherers, such as the 'Ibero-Maurusians' of the Maghreb (*c.* 17,000–10,000 bp) were already semi-sedentary; the greatest departure from nomadism, however, was made by the peoples of the Nile valley: the 'broad-spectrum' facies called the 'Nilotic Adaptation' (Hassan 1980; Connor & Marks 1986;

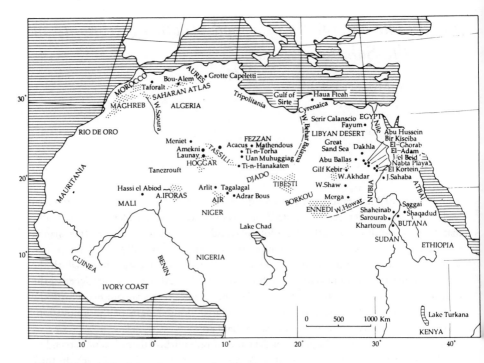

Figure 11.1 Main sites and areas mentioned in the text.

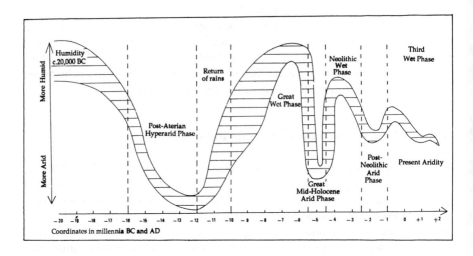

Figure 11.2 Saharan climates: 'more' humid and 'more' arid are in comparison with today's conditions; the width of the curve reflects divergences between regions, contradictory evidence or variations in dating.

Wetterstrom, Ch. 10, this volume), characterized by regular, seasonal occupation of sites for highly specialized food-gathering – including the collection and processing of wild cereals (see Harlan, Ch. 3, this volume; Wasylikowa, Harlan, Evans, Wendorf, Schild, Close, Krolik & Housley, Ch. 9, this volume).

The great Wet Phase of the early Holocene

Towards 12,000 bp the rains returned (Fig. 11.2; and see Grove, Ch. 1, this volume) and, in the period from 12,000 to 7500 bp, watercourses and lakes appeared everywhere. Paradoxically, perhaps, development at this time first took shape in the Sahara, for in the Nile valley, the nilotic adaptation had disappeared. Around 10,000–9500 bp, the desert was reoccupied – the oldest date is 10,100 bp, from Abu Ballas near Dakhla (Gabriel 1986). Groups using pottery appear from 9850 bp at El-Adam and J. el Beid (Wendorf, Schild & Close 1984) in the Egyptian Western Desert, around 9400 bp on the Sudanese Nile at Sarourab (Ali Hakem & Khabir 1989), in Aïr at Tagalagal and Adrar Bous (Roset 1987), and in the Acacus at Ti-n-Torha (Gautier 1982), around 9000 bp in the Hoggar at Site Launay (Maître 1971) and Amekni (Camps 1968) and around 8500 bp at Gilf Kebir in Wadi Akhdar (Kropelin 1987). These groups can only have come from surrounding areas; any claim that humans survived the arid period in the Sahara until the coming of neolithic peoples is no more than speculation – significantly, the latest Aterian date in Africa prior to the arid period is one of 19,000 bp from Taforalt (Morocco) (Close 1984).

These epipalaeolithic pottery-users still lived by hunting, by plant-gathering (attested by the abundance of heavy grinding equipment on many sites and, perhaps, by pottery) and also by fishing, as suggested by evidence that the occupants of Adrar Bous (c. 8000–7000 bp) used harpoons to hunt both large mammals and hippopotami in the nearby lake (Clark, Williams & Smith 1973). Those of Amekni, around 9000–6000 bp, hunted a variety of game, especially large mammals, and fished in the wadi at a lower level (Camps 1968). Those of Ti-n-Torha hunted Barbary sheep (*Ammotragus lervia*) (Gautier 1982) so intensively that it has been proposed that this animal was possibly domesticated (Close 1980; Gautier 1984); however, the criterion used, based solely on the high percentage of this species in the lists of fauna (70 per cent), is not in itself enough to prove domestication (Gautier 1987).

The first villages

In the arid zone, the semi-sedentism resulting from periodic return to the same water sources cannot be considered as a 'revolutionary' innovation – it is a necessity, common to all periods; however, building with durable materials around water sources shows a greater degree of sedentism. This condition is evident in the Egyptian Western Desert, not only in seasonal encampments of the eighth millennium BC (the El-Adam facies around 9500 bp) but also during the seventh, in which the first traces of stone-built houses and of underground granaries are found (starting with the remains of El-Kortein c. 8750 bp and El-Ghorab c. 8450 bp). At Nabta Playa, from c. 8000 bp onwards, encampments appear to be in almost continuous occupation, and fourteen circular houses are arranged in two rows to make a 'street'. At El-Ghorab pits or houses are laid out along the arc of a circle. Associated with these houses are various underground storage chambers and wells, some of which have sunken access ramps (Wendorf, Schild & Close 1984, pp. 1, 414, 425; Wendorf, Close & Schild 1985).

These first developments show that in Africa, as elsewhere, human groups were becoming larger, and that henceforth they concentrated their dwellings, if not their activities, within relatively small 'territories'. This major turning point sowed the seeds from which neolithic and later societies grew. Sedentism and demographic increase, at one and the same time, make possible and necessitate division of labour, storage of food and more complex organization of social relations within the group and between groups.

Stone Places (*Steinplatze*) and nomadism on the great plains

Until recently, studies of the Saharan Neolithic concentrated mainly on the upland massifs and their foothills, for it was known that during the three wet phases following the 'Post-Aterian Hyperarid Phase' of the final Pleistocene both humans and animals had occupied the massifs and that during dry phases these were either abandoned or were reduced to a few refuge zones. By contrast, the great plains, the sandy desert plains and in particular the great Libyan desert which rings Tibesti-Ennedi on the north and east, always remained real deserts, only their boundaries fluctuating slightly according to climatic oscillations. However, the discovery of numerous neolithic sites in the Egyptian Western Desert has made untenable all previous assumptions about the existence of a permanent 'desert kernel' (*Kernwuste*). The dwellings at Nabta Playa and Bir Kiseiba can no longer be treated as merely 'exceptions' – a group of small oases linked to a localized underground source of water – since, in recent years, numerous geographical studies have suggested that the 'desert kernel' hypothesis is faulty. Indeed, numerous sites dating to the early Holocene have come to light on the great plains and the semi-desert steppes to the west.

Gabriel's (1976; 1977, pp. 9–38) studies of 'Stone Places' (*Steinplatze*) showed that they were not only widely distributed, in the centre of desert plains, but that they also sometimes clustered together. He claimed that they were likely to have been encampments and cooking places, as they yielded small concentrations of potsherds, flint blades and the bones of food-animals (including cattle). Gabriel suggested that these Stone Places had been stopping places on the traditional transhumance routes – from highlands to grazing ground in the plains – of neolithic nomadic herding peoples. The question remained, however, how such transhumance would have been possible, sometimes involving hundreds of kilometres from sources of water and stone. Furthermore, radiocarbon dates for these sites ranged from 10,100 bp (at Abu Ballas) to the Middle Ages (Close 1980), dates which Gabriel arranged into chronological 'phases', revealing a noticeable cluster of dates in the Great Wet Phase of the early Holocene as well as a significant grouping in the Neolithic Wet Phase. Clarification comes from various recent interdisciplinary studies – geomorphological, archaeological, hydrological and palynological – showing that these currently desert areas supported hunters or herders during the wet phases of the Holocene, even when the areas themselves were not inhabited. The nomadic peoples concerned simply followed some of the wide valleys (such as Wadi Behar Balama) heading towards the Gulf of Sirte (Edmunds & Wright 1979). Wadis such as these drew fossil water from the Tibesti area, periodically emptying into the Mediterranean and, at other times, presumably reduced to shallow underground flows, emerging in a number of small lakes. Certainly, there was enough water to support at least discontinuous patches of vegetation, allowing fauna to migrate (Pachur & Roper 1984).

Flint and pottery are found on many camping sites well beyond the zones of Gabriel's Stone Places (which have a distribution from Tanezrouft and Saoura in Algeria to Wadis Shaw and Howar in western Sudan) (Gabriel 1986, pp. 14–55). Gabriel's claim that sand plains were crossed by human groups even as early as the ninth or eighth millennium BC therefore appears convincing. At the beginning of the Holocene, however, and in spite of their use of pottery, these groups were undoubtedly still nomadic, epipalaeolithic hunters. There is no reliable or convincing evidence that these people were herders of domesticated cattle – Haynes' claim (Gabriel 1986, p. 19) for a 'probably domesticated' cattle bone at Abu Hussein in a camping place dated to 8150 bp almost certainly being unreliable.

Other claims for domesticated animals are equally unconvincing; thus, Pachur (1982) makes much of the discovery of numerous grooved stones – large stones (c. 50 cm long and c. 20 cm in diameter) with circular grooves carved around their centres clearly designed to have ropes fastened to them – which he interprets as used to hobble (domestic) cattle. However, rock engravings at Mathendous appear to show similar stones as forming parts of traps for capturing wild cattle; they also show archers firing on cattle which have been captured by this means (Jelinek 1985, Fig. 45). Such stones could also have been used to keep tent ropes taut or anchored down. Whatever the correct explanation, unexpected pastures clearly existed in the middle of desert plains.

There is no longer any doubt (Pachur & Roper 1984) that during the early holocene 'Great Wet Phase', during the 'Neolithic Wet Phase' and even, in the west, during the 'Third Wet Phase' – which radiocarbon dates and elephant bones place here as beginning around 3650 bp (Pachur & Braun 1982, p. 43) – areas which are now totally desert at that time supported vegetation (e.g. Serir Tibesti, Serir Calanscio, the Great Sand Sea to the north and east of Gilf Kebir, the Egyptian Western Desert and, further south, the plains around Merga and Wadi Howar). Around 5250 bp, rock art sites such as Mathendous, contemporary with the Neolithic Wet Phase, were associated with lakes 5–10 m above the level of the present wadi bottoms, allowing crocodiles and hippopotami to live there, and explaining their portrayal on rock surfaces (Pachur & Braun 1982). The above climatic evidence (Fig. 11.2) allowed the postulation of a model simulating conditions of water seepage and the calculation of the amount of rainfall necessary to replenish the water table – c. 250 mm per annum (in permeable ground, on the assumption of no interposing layers of clay). Such rainfall would clearly transform a desert into a semi-arid zone, making possible the growth of grazing and the survival of large fauna. The most probable climatic model derived from this hydrological scheme would be that, around 8000 bp, there was a semi-arid regime, possibly accompanied by considerable winter rains.

The 'Aqualithic'

Around the same time, i.e. at the end of the 'Great Wet Phase' or perhaps a little later, increasing sedentism is attested at many (essentially Sahelian) sites scattered from Mali to the Ethiopian plateau, from Lake Turkana to Nubia and Tibesti. These sites, also, are most often confined to river banks or various other water sources, particularly the margins of lakes (whose existence is attested by numerous lacustrine deposits, especially diatomites). Such communities of people are characterized by the remains of aquatic fauna (e.g. fish, mollusca, turtles), which are accompanied by tools, notably harpoons, fish-hooks and pottery. Traces of mud wall construction (otherwise scarcely known outside the 'Mesolithic Khartoum' village, around 7000 bp) are sometimes found, reflecting, as at Nabta Playa but on a more modest scale, the emergence of 'first villages' (see Wetterstrom, Ch. 10, this volume).

Clearly, specialist activities, linked to permanent water, imposed a way of life, at places such as Saggai (Gautier 1983), which was based on almost total sedentism. Here, a virtually static group was fishing (with harpoons) and collecting pila shellfish around 7200 bp (Gautier 1983). Hunting was a merely complementary activity. That the gathering of plant foods also played a part is attested by numerous grinding stones, and by pottery. In the 'Early Khartoum' village excavated by Arkell (1949), sedentism appears to have been complete. Around the large lakes in the north of Mali the way of life combined fishing, hunting and the collection of wild cereals (Petit-Maire, Celles, Commelin, Delibrias & Raimbault 1983).

Such lake and riverside sites – where neither domestic animals nor plants were in evidence – have been ascribed a vivid collective name, the 'Aqualithic' (Sutton 1974), elsewhere (Sutton 1977) also assumed to represent a 'cultural complex'. In fact, however, this classificatory construct is artificial, merely representing an expression of an 'aquatic way of life' – a generalized response, therefore, constructed from numerous and varied cultures dating from the end of the 'Great Wet Phase', to a shared identical economic environment (Hays 1976a; Phillipson 1985a, p.108). Such an aquatic lifestyle continued around many water sources until the end of the 'Neolithic Wet Phase'. For Robertshaw (1982), the Aqualithic represented no more than the current concentration of research on the Nile and the lakes, due to the poor preservation of savanna sites. The Sahara and Sahel were essentially arid and semi-arid, and many of the sites which existed there were linked to essential water sources, but were not really fishing villages: e.g. Amekni in the Hoggar (Camps 1968), Ti-n-Torha in the Acacus (Gautier 1982) and J. Shaqadud in the Butana (Marks, Abbas, Hays & Elamin 1983).

Nevertheless, numerous sites of this period, whether fishing settlements or not, had one feature in common. From Lake Turkana to Nabta Playa, in Tibesti, in the Hoggar, in Niger, whether the first village of Early Khartoum or the seasonally inhabited encampments (which Camps (1974) has grouped together as the 'Saharo-Sudanese Neolithic'), these sites all contained remarkably similar pottery – the earliest to appear were large round-bottomed vessels made of a coarse fabric, the whole surface covered with decoration before firing and with certain common motifs, notably wavy-line and walking-comb. These forms and decorative styles continued throughout the whole of the Neolithic in the south Sahara and Sahel – pots of this kind with wavy-line decoration now having been reported as far afield as Mauritania, around 4000 bp (Petit-Maire 1979).

Should these similarities be attributed to chance convergence? Or should they be interpreted as indicating some genuine cultural or ethnic unit having emerged from the beginnings of the Neolithic? The second suggestion seems hard to credit since such an extended area is involved and, more difficult still, such a long time span. Nevertheless, the ceramic similarities, together with a sedentary mode of existence, constitute the principal justification for the recognition of Aqualithic and Saharo-Sudanese neolithic groupings.

The points of resemblance remain superficial. For the pottery, they concern only the decoration; methods of manufacture vary. Moreover, cultural elements other than pottery and harpoons are very diverse (Hays 1974), and harpoons are not numerous except on exceptional sites such as Hassi el Abiod in Mali – where 200 were found (Petit-Maire, Celles, Commelin, Delibrias & Raimbault 1983, p. 119). Lithic industries are very varied: segments, typical of the Khartoum Mesolithic, are entirely lacking on most sites; the gouges typical of the Shaheinab Neolithic are uncommon outside the Nile valley; and the raw materials used are variable. On the other hand, microliths are common – this 'mode 5' of Clark (1977, p. 23), however, being found in almost all the industries of Africa, Europe and Asia.

It is therefore clear that categorizations such as the 'Aqualithic' or the 'Saharo-Sudanese Neolithic' are far too generalized to be in any way meaningful except, perhaps, as an expression of a common base on which local variations may have been superimposed (see also Andah, Ch. 12, this volume; Eggert, Ch. 16, this volume). In practical terms, such concepts are not useful. Nevertheless, they do serve to underline the contrast in the neolithic period between Saharan and Sahelian Africa on the one hand and, on the other, the lands of the Maghreb and Atlas and nilotic Egypt, where the wavy-line pottery tradition was totally unknown.

Pottery was not transported over great distances; some analyses have shown that manufacture was local (Hays & Hassan 1974; Hays 1976a; Francaviglia & Palmieri 1983). However, even if cultural diffusion of certain elements, such as wavy-line decoration, did take place, the mechanism of its spread – like the extraordinary conservatism over thousands of years – remains unexplained. Shaw (n.d.) has put forward an explanatory model for such diffusion – the practice of exogamy, on the supposition that the potters were women (following common ethnographic models). However, there is no proof, nor any archaeological evidence, to support this suggestion. Indeed, the apparent diffusion of bell beakers in Europe, or of cord-roulette decoration on pottery of the Bantu expansion in the second millennium AD (and see Blench, Ch. 7, this volume; Eggert, Ch. 16, this volume), while involving as extensive an area as that of the wavy-line phenomenon, were both of very short duration, lasting scarcely a millennium. Any explanations based on assumed ultra-conservatism with regard to cultural traits in arid regions seem very weak.

No definitive explanation emerges, the idea of chance convergence seeming as unlikely as a vast cultural unity. More probably, several factors were at work, predisposing the populations of the central and southern Sahara and the Sahel to adopt certain similar features of lifestyle and material culture.

This aqualithic group, albeit of quite vague definition and geographic distribution, appears to occupy roughly the same area as that currently occupied by the large Nilo-Saharan linguistic group. Glottochronology (see Ehret 1984; Ehret, Ch. 6, this volume) dates the origin of this group to the same period, i.e. the early Holocene. Could it be, for once, that linguistic and ethnic events are interdependent, and that the Aqualithic, or the practically identical Saharo-Sudanese Neolithic, peoples broadly correspond to the Nilo-Saharan linguistic block? Ehret (Ch. 6, this volume) recommends this view to archaeologists, and his arguments are impressive.

He dates the divergence of an old branch of the 'Proto-Northern Sudanic' language to around 9000 bp, at a point in time when there appear to have been various terms such as 'cow', 'to milk' and 'to drive', implying the existence of domestic cattle (Ehret, Ch. 6, this volume). Around 8000 bp, the 'Proto-Saharo-Sahelian' adds words implying agricultural activities. Around 7500 bp, words for domestic sheep and goats are included in the Proto-Sahelian vocabulary. The correlations between language and material culture are impressive (e.g. Blench, Ch. 7, this volume; Williamson, Ch. 8, this volume), and archaeologists will have to take a position regarding this linguistic evidence, as they have done in this book (see Sinclair, Shaw & Andah, Introduction, this volume). It is even possible to suggest a very ancient domestication of cattle and the presence of an indigenous 'pre-neolithic' stock of ovicaprines (Muzzolini 1990).

The Neolithic Wet Phase in the central Sahara and the Maghreb

A brief but severe dry phase, the 'Great Mid-Holocene Arid Phase', took hold of north Africa between c. 8000/7500 bp and 7000/6500 bp. In the Levant the fact that sites become rare at this time, after the Pre-Pottery Neolithic B (PPNB), may be linked to this. The Maghreb and Nilotic Egypt were not seriously affected, but the Sahara and the Sahel were. There followed the 'Neolithic Wet Phase' (6500–4500 bp), when territories abandoned during the preceding dry phase were reoccupied and 'true neolithic' societies emerged.

Half a century ago there was much debate as to whether the central Sahara had been a centre of domestication, an idea inspired particularly by rock art, believed to be very ancient, and which clearly depicted pastoral societies. Furthermore, Saharan sites believed to be equally early were classified as neolithic because they already had pottery. These dates were compared to those of predynastic Egyptian sites, equally 'neolithic', but which, in addition to pottery, had domesticated animals and cultivated cereals. At these sites a sedentary lifestyle was practised which is difficult to compare with that of Saharan nomads. Contrary to the beliefs of Vaufrey (1938), among others, who found Egyptian influences in Saharan rock art, a diffusionist idea gained acceptance, namely that a 'Neolithic Revolution' could have spread from the Sahara towards Egypt, and not in the opposite direction.

Other recent theories have emerged from the idea of an essentially Sudanese 'nilotic crucible', clearly centred on Arkell's (1949) 'Khartoum Mesolithic', allegedly sending the influences of its culture towards the west. The prestige of this first black civilization at the dawn of history, at least as old as the Egyptian Predynastic, was welcomed with open arms; it replaced the 'Eastern Hamites', dear to the theorists of the time. However, there is still no evidence to support the idea of either of these heroic sagas for the conquest of the West. Moreover, no diffusionist gradient emerges from the radiocarbon dates which would indicate a transmission from east to west, or the opposite.

Rock art and pastoralism

Discussion about prehistoric life in the Sahara has made much of the 'evidence' provided by the abundant rock art. No examples have been directly dated, but, in spite of this, unbelievably early dates have been put forward on the basis of unverifiable analogies; correspondingly early dates have been attributed to the pastoral activities so profusely represented in the rock art. Echoes still survive from the time when claims were being made for a palaeolithic date for this art (Vaufrey 1938); Mori (1974) once again speaks of an 'Upper Pleistocene' date for the oldest rock engravings. Indeed, the idea of palaeolithic rock art has survived through the Saharan literature in the concept of the so-called 'Bubaline period', a term arising from the frequent representation of *Bubalus antiquus* (*Homoioceras*). This 'period', it is claimed, corresponds to the oldest rock art, showing only wild fauna – thus, a 'pre-pastoral' period. Such a period would have been followed by a pastoral 'Bovidian period', with numerous depictions of bovid herds, allegedly reflecting the beginnings of domestication. The 'Bubaline period' would then be 'pre-neolithic' (using the term 'neolithic' to refer to food production) and therefore at least 'epipalaeolithic'.

However, the supposed 'Bubaline period' does not in fact contain exclusively wild fauna, the animals most commonly represented being domestic cattle – including even a milking scene (Muzzolini 1983; Muzzolini 1986; and see Blench, Ch. 7, this volume). In addition, in the Saharan Atlas, and to a lesser extent in the Fezzan, the same 'Bubaline school' shows sheep with characteristics that leave no doubt about their domestic status (drooping ears and long tails) (Muzzolini 1990). Furthermore, radiocarbon dates on African sheep bones place their domestication after 6000 bp, and domesticated cattle possibly in the fifth millennium BC. Consequently, the distinction between a 'Bubaline period' and a 'Bovidian period' proves to be untenable; the alleged 'Bubaline period' is only a stylistic subgroup contemporaneous with the earlier phase of the 'Bovidian period' (see discussion in Cornevin 1982; Lhote 1984; Le Quellec 1985).

In addition to the rock engravings of the 'Bubaline school' – showing pastoral scenes often attributed to europoid populations and widespread from the Rio de Oro to the Saharan Atlas, the Fezzan, Tassili, the Hoggar and Djado – the 'Early Bovidian' is also found in certain highly distinctive Tassili paintings, the 'Sefar-Ozanéaré group'. These are the only Tassili paintings where the people depicted are exclusively negroid. The favourite subject matter is a herd of cattle, or encampments linked to pastoral activities. The kinds of cattle, the shapes of their horns, and their coat types are already diversified; they cannot, therefore, represent an early stage of domestication but instead an advanced stage in which genes responsible for visible characteristics have undergone a process of selection.

In the early period, sheep are found mainly in the 'Bubaline school' in the Saharan Atlas. These are the famous 'ornamented rams', such as those of Bou-Alem, indisputably domestic sheep, whose genetic traits are of a type which can certainly not be considered archaic (notably the long tail, drooping ears and 'Roman nose' and, in one instance, the horizontal corkscrew horns). A more archaic type, with short tail, is portrayed in the Fezzan, although rarely. Sheep are absent from the engravings and paintings of Tassili and the Acacus in this early period. Although sheep bones were found at Uan Muhaggiag (Acacus), they were absent from horizons of the same age at the neighbouring site of Ti-n-Torha (Gautier 1982).

A much later date must be accepted than that proposed by Mori (1974) and Lhote (1984) for the 'Early Bovidian' of the Tassili paintings, as for the contemporaneous 'Bubaline' stylistic group (at least in its early, more naturalistic, phase). According to faunal and climatic markers, the period should, in round terms, span 6000–4000 bp (Muzzolini 1986) – preceding the severe 'Post-Neolithic Arid Phase' which struck the central Sahara between c. 2500 and 1000 BC. At the time of the 'Neolithic Wet Phase', therefore, a nomadic pastoral economy based on cattle flourished throughout the Sahara – sheep, already acclimatized in the Saharan Atlas, had not yet been introduced into the central Sahara in large numbers.

This picture of Saharan pastoralism, as shown in the rock art, is confirmed by the results of a limited number of excavations: the absence of domesticated animals at Amekni in the Hoggar (Camps 1968), even in the late levels dated to 6850 and 5550 bp. At Adrar Bous domestic cattle do not appear until 5750 bp (Clark, Williams & Smith 1973) – and even then there are some doubts about the date. Even in the Maghreb, in the Aures mountains, among the remains from the lowest levels of the Grotte Capeletti (c. 6600 bp) (Muzzolini 1990), as at Haua Fteah in Cyrenaica around 6800 bp (Higgs 1967; Shaw 1977; Klein & Scott 1986), the domesticated status of cattle and ovicaprines remains uncertain (Muzzolini 1990; Clutton-Brock, Ch. 4, this volume).

The Acacus, on the other hand, has provided some information: a date of 5950 bp from the bottom of the Uan Muhuggiag deposits is associated with a small number of ovicaprine bones, together with cattle, presumed to be domesticated (Gautier 1982). One more date, of 4750–5650 bp, for some twenty bones of probably domesticated cattle, comes from Ti-n-Torha North (Gautier 1982).

The site of Ti-n-Hanakaten in southern Tassili (Aumassip 1984), with dates of 7250 and 4150 bp, attests to the existence of nomadism – reflected by the accumulation of lenses of occupation soils, each one corresponding to a brief sojourn; ovicaprines and cattle are reported, but whether domesticated or not is not clear. At Arlit in western Aïr, domesticated cattle and ovicaprines do not appear until c. 5000 bp (Muzzolini 1983, p. 293).

Agriculture

Saharan agriculture, presumed to have been imported from 'the Nilotic crucible', was the subject of much research during the 1960s – a lush, 'Mediterranean', Sahara was assumed, where cereals must have been cultivated. However, the only supporting finds come from the Hoggar – with cultivation being claimed simply on the basis of the unreliable criterion of the size of a single grain of pollen from 'a cereal' (dated to 5350 bp at Meniet) and two grains of *Pennisetum* pollen (dated to 6850 bp at Amekni) (Camps 1974, pp. 226, 236; McIntosh & McIntosh 1983, pp. 219, 230). Just as unsatisfactory as evidence for cultivation is the imprint of grain, possibly sorghum, on a potsherd from Adrar Bous (Clark, Williams & Smith 1973). All this is inconclusive evidence to confirm any claims for agriculture; nor is the abundance of grinding stones on Saharan neolithic and epipalaeolithic sites any better evidence – since such grinding stones may not have been used in connection with the cultivation of cereals, but only with their large-scale collection (or, according to Krzyzaniak 1991, sometimes only for the grinding of ochre).

In spite of this, arguments from indirect evidence have been advanced. For example, Camps (1974, pp. 217, 230) has suggested that since ceramics are linked to certain culinary practices and dietary modifications which follow from agriculture, the presence of ceramics implies the practice of agriculture. Such a view has been questioned by many, including McIntosh & McIntosh (1983, pp. 219, 230). Additionally, attempts have been made to interpret certain lithic remains as agricultural tools: Milburn (1986) has recently suggested that elongated pounding stones, commonly called stone logs or pestles, were the ard-tips of primitive ploughs. Gouges or adzes for which, without any proof, an agricultural use has been suggested, are similarly abundant on many neolithic sites in the Sahara. Although they are very plentiful on certain Tenerian sites of the fourth–third millennium BC, their use remains uncertain. Thus – although one cannot exclude the possibility that these essentially pastoral communities had very limited seasonal activities connected with the growing of cereals (as happens today in spite of the present aridity) – there is no proof of this.

Even in the Maghreb there is no certain evidence for neolithic agriculture. Flints with silica gloss are known from the Capsian, but it is impossible to determine whether or not the gloss results from cereals – and cultivated cereals at that! The model of transition to food production which the Maghreb furnishes is similar to that of the Zagros mountains – stock-keeping preceding crop-growing – rather than that of the Levant, where crop-growing comes before stock-keeping. Evidence for the ancient practice of agriculture in the central Sahara, the Maghreb or Tibesti is virtually non–existent, as is also the case for the western Sahara. Arguments in favour seem to be based *a posteriori* on a concept of domestication which assumes an aggressive attitude on the part of humans towards animals and plants, derived from the pattern finally adopted by the 'Neolithic Revolution' in the Middle East. It appears, however, that the neolithic nomads of the Sahara relied on animals only.

Causes and courses of the transition to food production

Why did the peoples of the Sahara make the transition to food production at the beginning of the 'Neolithic Wet Phase'? A structuralist 'law' that assumes that the practice of specialized hunting and intensive gathering, and the utilization of a micro-lithic technology are necessarily followed by the adoption of domesticated plants and animals is merely a matter for philosophical debate: such an approach does not answer the questions of why and how it happened in a particular place and at a particular time.

The transition to food production – of which domestication is the most striking aspect – is clearly not merely a matter of cause and effect. It is the response by a social system (social structure, economy, environment and symbolic world) either to an external stimulus (diffusion) or to an internal disequilibrium. What were the events which had not occurred before the Holocene, or what factors might have reached a critical threshold in the Holocene?

Climate

Climate, as Braidwood (1962) has emphasized, is only a permissive condition for a 'Neolithic Revolution'. In fact, comparable climatic conditions had never before produced such a 'revolution'. Climate is a vitally important factor which could accelerate or retard any such change in an arid zone, but it could not, alone, have set in motion the transition to food production.

Sedentism

In an arid zone, a degree of sedentism is necessary to maintain a close link to a water supply. Complete sedentism, with permanent dwellings, appears to be a more or less obligatory condition for the cultivation of cereals, but not for the pastoral system of the Saharan Neolithic. Nevertheless, increased sedentism is clear as compared to epipalaeolithic or earlier times; ethnic groups now became distinct, characterized by, for example, specialized lithic industries and styles of rock art. The people remained nomadic but confined to certain territories, thus producing group identity.

Material culture and economy

In the early Holocene, material equipment was considerably improved. Pottery may have been used for the storage of grain, and was possibly also used for cooking; the lithic industry developed beyond all recognition – edge-ground cutting tools, and above all microliths, allowing for the manufacture of specialized and efficient composite tools. Various skilfully flaked macrolithic tools, such as arrowheads and adzes, were added to the tool-kit. Specialized hunting and fishing, together with intensive collecting of wild grain, which characterized the early Holocene everywhere, may have developed in association with the specialization and the efficiency of these new tools.

Demographic pressure

The density of remains and sites in certain areas of the Sahara gives clear evidence of demographic pressure: for every one Aterian or Acheulean site there are a hundred neolithic. This radical increase in population, immediately obvious from Pachur & Roper's (1984, p. 64) tables, and emphasized by Gabriel (1986, p. 21) for the eastern Sahara, is also illustrated by Tassilian rock art 'villages' with their abundance of engravings and paintings (Muzzolini 1986); a similar trend is observable in Capsian territory (Lubell, Sheppard & Jackes 1984), in the 'late Neolithic' of Nabta Playa/Bir Kiseiba (Wendorf, Close & Schild 1985), in the southern Atbai (Marks, Abbas, Hays & Elamin 1983) and in the valley of the Nile (Hassan, Ch. 33, this volume). The suddenness with which this population explosion burst upon the scene – and the uneven way in which it then progressed in comparison with other factors – suggests that, although not the sole cause of the neolithic upheaval, it must have been a major one.

The principal objections against population pressure models stress that the 'carrying capacity' of a biotope constitutes only a flexible ceiling, and numerous adaptations can modify it (Hassan 1979). However, this objection seems less valid in an arid zone.

In fact, the vital link with a water source, for animals as well as for humans, rigidly determines land occupation as soon as a critical population threshold is reached and all the sources of water are in use (that is, either permanently occupied or regularly visited, according to the 'rights' of each group). Neither animals nor humans then have any further possibility of migrating to another supply of water. This first 'crisis', which had never occurred before the Neolithic, had the end result of creating and fixing 'territories' within finite limits.

As a result of demographic increase all possible 'territories' were occupied; these now included even the most difficult, such as the sand seas. For the first time there was no more virgin land in the Sahara. There followed an increase in sedentism, competition between groups, specialized hunting of the only species existing in the biotope and an intensification of local food-collecting; all this resulted in an accelerated population increase. This continued until a second 'crisis' was set off by the inevitable natural limitations and carrying capacity of the biotope, which is more fragile and, above all, less flexible in an arid zone, if it continues to be exploited in the traditional way by semi-sedentary people. Two solutions were possible. Warfare, in the modern sense of the term, emerged as a new form of relationship between organized groups. Evidence of this exists in J. Sahaba in Nubia, around 12,000 bp, where a burial ground yielded fifty-nine projectile points protruding into twenty-four bodies (Wendorf 1968c). Alternatively, a transition to a still more intensive and planned exploitation of the 'territory' could be made. The possibility had been known; now it became a necessity. It consisted of the regulation of reserves to a far higher degree than simple storage of collected grain in pots or granaries; it involved the accumulation of protein in managed livestock or, where possible, in cultivated cereals.

Admittedly the critical threshold for the breakdown of the equilibrium of the biotope which would set off such a second 'crisis' depended not only on its physical potential, but also on group values, social organization and symbolic worlds (a 'sacred' animal is never hunted) – all features which exclude a hasty environmental determinism.

Conclusion

The lack of correspondence in the emergence of domestication between the Middle East, the Nile valley and the Sahara was not, in this schema, due to time differences caused by an assumed cultural diffusion and for which there is, in any case, no direct evidence. Nor was it due to differences between nuclear areas, which, in any case, cannot be identified in Africa; nor is it attributable to the colonization of 'tension zones'. The differences were solely due to the potentialities that each group recognized in its own territory in terms of its own culture. The territory thus formed a unit that was both ecological and cultural at one and the same time.

Acknowledgement

Work on preparing this chapter for publication in English was carried out by Thurstan Shaw.

12　Identifying early farming traditions of west Africa

BASSEY W. ANDAH

Social aspects of food production

The ecological approach to early agriculture in Africa has clearly been more successful than previous approaches, but in some aspects it still falls short of properly conceptualizing farming in west Africa, either as event or as process. An advantage of the ecological approach is that it correctly perceives farming as much more than the techniques involved in the cultivation of non-African cereals, or the farming of vegetables, root crops, fruit and tree crops, or the technology of the herding or the rearing of a variety of animals. However, ecological analysis still seems to define farming or herding predominantly in technological or techno-economic terms and is largely concerned with the biological phenomenon of domestication. By concentrating on these subjects, ecology excludes from analysis other significant aspects of cultural behaviour, such as diet and the social context of agricultural activity, and wrongly regards the end process of cultivation, which results in some (but not all) instances in morphological change, as marking the beginnings of farming and herding.

　Farming and its inception, anywhere in the world, is more than technological and economic events, innovations and processes – it is a social phenomenon, involving the social meaning of economic resources. We therefore need to know:

(a) who were the earliest farmers in a region, what plants were cropped and what animals kept, and in what kind of ecological setting;

(b) what was entailed in each farming system in terms of crops and animals, what types of activities were involved, the time allocated to these relative to other life-sustaining activities, whether demanding intensive or extensive labour input, carried out by whom (men, women, children, hired hands, slaves or cooperatives), and the kinds of tools used;

(c) where known, the vocabulary of terms for crops, animals, tools, processes, activities and products; which are indigenous and which introduced or borrowed, and for the latter, when and where from, and what they replaced or modified; and

(d) the nature of the households in the different farming communities, and their relationship to the scale or intensity of farming practice; how domestic production was organized; how these farming societies linked up with wider regional systems.

The environment (Fig. 12.1)

Although the west African terrain divides into two clearly defined regions, the dense tropical forest of the coastal belt, extending up to 160 km inland, and the dry upland savannas north of the forest, there is an intermediate zone of forest-savanna mosaic where the forest gradually thins out towards the savanna and, northwards, gradually gives way to the desert. The 'Dahomey Gap' is a break in the rainforest between The Republic of Benin and Cape Three Points in Ghana; the savanna grassland reaches the coast in Togo and the eastern part of Ghana, and the dry Accra plains extend inland for about 16 km and stretch along the coast for about 320 km. The perpetually humid and shady conditions of the rainforest differ fundamentally from the dry conditions of the savannas to the extent that crops of one region are seldom suited to the other. Diffusion of crops and people between the zones have thus always been difficult except via the valleys of rivers such as the Niger, Volta and Bandama. In the savanna regions, on the other hand, east–west and south–north movements have always been easy, using animals of burden overland and by means of canoes along the upper parts of the rivers Senegal, Gambia, Niger and Benue.

Towards the northern and southern extremes of the rainforest, total rainfall quantity was an important factor, as was its reliability everywhere, together with the effect on soil erosion. Towards the drier extremes land management techniques included soil moisture conservation and supplementation (irrigation), as well as control of erosion. In the southern zone the problem was how to make maximum use of the available sunlight and cope with excess soil moisture and erosion.

In the intermediate zone of wetter savannas and drier forests all the above-mentioned

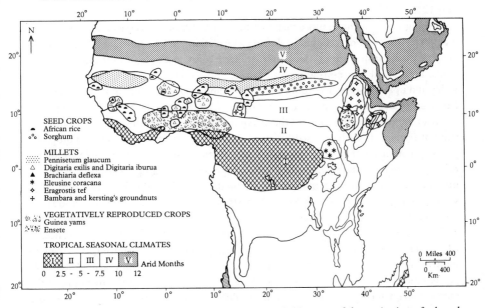

Figure 12.1 Tropical Africa: seasonal climates and probable areas of domestication of selected crops (after Harlan 1971).

management problems still assume some significance, but at different times during the cultivation cycle. In contrast, however, to the northern and southern extremes, the soils of this region are generally better. Moreover, its possession of a long and varied agricultural system has tended to allow much scope for 'riding the system' (Richards 1983b, pp. 24–5). Highly diversified and therefore risk-spreading sets of management strategies, which copy rather than override a number of the natural key characteristics of the ecosystems, are favoured. Indeed, according to Richards (1983a; 1983b), this probably helps to explain the relative lack of gross capital-intensive modifications of the natural environment (e.g. large irrigation schemes and plantation farming) for agricultural purposes in this zone.

In the history of the region, complex land-use combinations have been more typical of the intermediate zones. Examples are agricultural enterprises which combine upland (often shifting) cultivation, valley bottom flood-retreat cultivation, contributions from small domestic livestock and hunting and gathering over fallow and uncultivated land. Adjustments in the balance of attention devoted to these various activities serve to make maximum use through a season, under conditions of climatic variability, of the labour available. In addition, livestock, often subsisting on farm and household by-products, act as savings, and hunting and gathering constitute important buffers against periodic famine (Richards 1983a; Richards 1983b). Other comparative environmental advantages encouraged the cultivation of each crop in its heartland. Thus, for example, the soils of the Sierra Leone/Liberia/western Ivory Coast region tend to be poor in bases; they are concretionary and not very well suited to yam growing. By contrast, the yam has an advantage over rice in the belt of sandy loam soils, developed over unconsolidated sands, which stretches east from Lagos to the edge of the Cross river basin (see Figs 12.2, 12.3).

Farming involves much more than the simple activity once envisaged for this region, e.g. forest or savanna cropping, shifting cultivation or hoe farming. West African peoples distinguish various categories of 'farm': for example, forest and grassland fields, homestead and non-homestead farms, and varieties of these; various types of valley and upland farms, according to the crops and associated soils and vegetation; and labour-intensive and labour-extensive farms. West African farmers have long been aware of the crucial importance of the physical characteristics of the soil in farming their tropical terrain. They have used practices designed to create or conserve appropriate physical conditions for plant growth under intense rainfall, for example: heaping, ridging, mulching, terracing, minimum tillage and managing vegetation cover to minimize erosion; making maximum use of the available labour supply through a season; and generating savings and better stock against famine. Which methods are used depends not only on the environmental situation but the social one: for example, various forms of interdigitation of upland farms are generally of greater significance, in labour terms, than practices such as composting and green manuring designed to improve fertility by organic means. Because of this variety of approaches, archaeologists need to find out what forms of these practices were designed to improve the physical characteristics of local soils in the different ecosystems and when, why and how the different farming societies adopted such practices.

To achieve this we would need to make direct use of data from ethnoecological

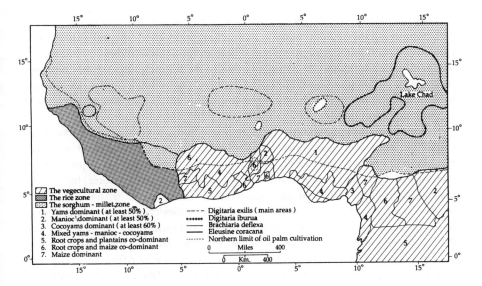

Figure 12.2 West Africa: traditional crop zones (after Harris 1976).

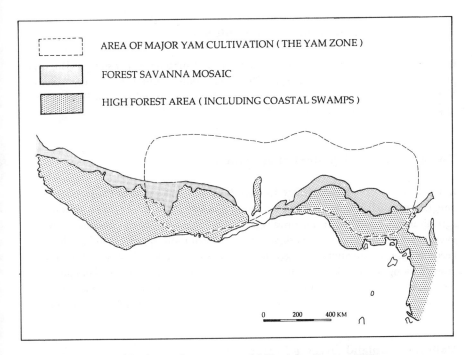

Figure 12.3 Yam cultivation on the west coast of Africa (after Coursey 1976).

investigations being increasingly carried out in the region (e.g. Richards 1983a, p. 22) as well as taking into account some of the newer perspectives on soil management emerging from farming systems research. Our archaeological studies of farming history to date in this region can certainly be faulted for focusing too narrowly on issues such as the use of manure and crop rotation to the neglect of uniquely African-invented techniques concerned with the proper management of the physical and ecological properties of African soils.

The principal crops grown typically exist in association with other crops. Dominant crops have been developed, usually in the context of certain patterns of economic specialization between different peoples and localities within the area, a specialization that was not fixed, but shifted in response to various historical pressures. Indeed, the macro-distributional pattern of the major crops (e.g. rice, yams, the millets and the sorghums) would appear to have derived from a complexity of causes, socio-cultural and economic as well as environmental. In the course of establishing farming traditions for these crops, various types of irrigation, flood retreat and 'shifting' systems of farming were devised by distinguishable cultural groups in west Africa. In special cases techniques unique to a people or area were also developed. Among these were estuarine rice production along the upper Guinea coast and the inland delta of the Niger and the seed yam tradition in some of the valleys of the Guinea forest (e.g. Anambra).

The socio-linguistic context of agriculture

In the light of new work on African languages, and subsequent revisions of language groupings (see, for example, Blench, Ch. 7, this volume; Ehret, Ch. 6, this volume; Williamson, Ch. 8, this volume), classifications based on Greenberg (1963) are in need of reconsideration and revision.

The socio-cultural context of agriculture

In this analysis of agrarian change in west African history some attempt is made to integrate material relating both to agricultural ecology and to the social relations of agricultural production, in historically and geographically specific instances. In our view, if we are to generate hypotheses that are much more specific than have hitherto been the case, productivity and agricultural practices in west Africa would need to be assessed along several distinct dimensions. At the minimum, labour and land productivity measures must be distinguished and some account taken of the way in which changes in productivity are offset or cancelled by changes in variability of output.

Valley and upland farming in west Africa

Early accounts of west African farming systems tended to place undue emphasis on rain-fed shifting cultivation to the neglect of 'traditional' irrigation technology, as well as on the extent and significance of residual moisture and flood-retreat farming practices in valley lowlands. Archaeologists and agricultural botanists have drawn attention to the possibility that flood-retreat conditions constituted a more manageable environment for early experiments in plant domestication than rain-fed uplands. West African rice (*Oryza glaberrima*), for example, appears from this perspective to have been first cultivated in the valleys of the upper Niger drainage system (Fig. 12.2; Richards 1983a; Richards 1983b, p. 23).

As reported by Richards (1983a), recent farming system studies more accurately reflect the strategic importance of valley land suggested by the plant domestication evidence, both for rice cultivation and for cultivation in general in areas of marked rainfall uncertainty. It is clear that there are few areas of west Africa where valley use is insignificant. There are, however, important variations in the extent to which 'upland' and 'valley' land use is integrated by the peasant producer.

Research on northern Nigerian farming systems suggests that dry season cultivation of crops such as wheat and vegetables on 'fadama' land (floodplain), sometimes using simple bucket irrigation, tends to be organizationally independent of cultivation of rain-fed sorghum, millet, groundnuts and cotton. Fadama cultivation is individual work (as opposed to 'gandu', i.e. household work), equivalent to dry season craft employment, trading or seasonal migration. Perhaps as a result, inequalities of land holding appear to be slightly greater for fadama than for upland farms.

In areas where rice and yams are the main staples (Figs 12.1, 12.2), 'upland' and 'valley' cultivation tend to be much more closely integrated. Labour complementarities between valley and upland cultivation are reported from northern Sierra Leone and central Nigeria. Yields on valley soils are higher, and the yams are planted, and therefore harvested, earlier than on uplands.

Diola irrigation systems on the lower Casamance were thought to be unusual for west Africa, but Linares de Sapir (1981) has set these irrigation practices in a broader comparative context: swamp rice cultivation with varying degrees of water control is widespread throughout the west African rice zone and along the Niger. The view that irrigation was not practised beyond the Nile in sub-Saharan Africa is, therefore, wrong.

Temne enterprise created extensive estuarine rice polders on the lower Casamance in the nineteenth century. Leo Africanus observed floating rice being cultivated in the Sokoto-Rima basin (Leo Africanus 1969). Dry season flood retreat (residual moisture) cultivation is of great antiquity throughout west Africa (fadama cultivation in Hausa and Kanuri country) and 'flood advance' techniques are the basis of valley cultivation of rice in northern Sierra Leone.

By the time the first Europeans had made contact with the Diola and their relatives in what is now Guinea-Bissau they had already converted much of the mangrove swamp, fringing the tidal estuaries of important rivers, into a network of paddy fields. Their techniques of dyking, desalinating, ridging and transplanting almost certainly antedate all European contact (Linares de Sapir 1981, p. 559).

Hitherto, economic anthropologists, including archaeologists, have usually claimed that agricultural production in 'pre-market' societies was kinship-based or at best peasant-household-based, and regarded as a primordial relic from the prehistoric past. However, surveys of farming systems indicate that where such economies and productive systems exist they are products of the present historical forms by which such societies were and are enmeshed into a commodity economy dominated by capitalism. Farming systems literature also indicates that in these societies labour cooperatives and other forms of non-kin-based work parties were sometimes of greater significance than kin-based work groups (Richards 1983a; Richards 1983b). A full recognition of the implications of these findings for archaeological investigation would be revolutionary.

Some of the historical aspects are clearly very notable. For example, the yam-based civilization of the Akan peoples developed and was fostered by a centralized political system. To the west of the Bandama river the dry rice cultivators operated more decentralized societies. The coastal Diola established an intensive irrigated rice culture yet remained an egalitarian and 'acephalous' people. The inland Diola, by contrast, had a more extensive cultivation of dry rice – yet were more hierarchical with an Islamized social order. A comparative survey of the rice-growing peoples of the upper Guinea coast and its hinterland from the Casamance to Liberia, both those akin to the Diola and their Mande-speaking neighbours, led Linares de Sapir (1981) to conclude that the 'hierarchization' of social structure in question was as much due to a process of cultural 'Mandigization' as it was to agricultural imperatives.

Organization of labour

It seems that the coastal Diola with their 'weak' lineages and small family holdings, practise close cooperation between husband and wife in rice production and recruit additional labour on an impermanent and intermittent basis through kin networks. The more 'Mandigized' Diola, with larger households and ranked lineages, separate the work spheres of men and women more markedly and make use of formally recruited work groups similar to those widely found in Sierra Leone.

Upland farming is greatly facilitated by membership in an official labour group. Labour groups are less vital for swamp farming, for although swamp cultivation is labour intensive it is less tightly constrained by climatic events. Labour group contracts are specific about the quality of food to be provided for the work party's mid-day meal. The economic advantages of polygamy and numerous children seem to have been developed and stressed only where farming was based firmly, or even solely, on the labour resources of the household.

Ecology and diet

Yam

Ethnographic studies are vital for drawing attention to facts from which we can derive meaningful hypotheses which we can then test archaeologically. As noted by Okigbo (1980, p. 13), the yam – a vine adapted to some months of dry season and needing support on which to climb – appears to be suited to neither the grassland nor the rainforest except to the extent that the yellow yam (*Dioscorea cayenensis*) is adapted to the rainforest area with barely a month of dry season (Fig. 12.3). Similarly, the oil palm requires the moisture of the tropical rainforest zone but also needs adequate sunshine, which is not available inside continuous rainforest. For this reason Okigbo has suggested 'that it is in the forest/savanna ecotone that our ancestors domesticated yams long after periods of experimentation with oil palm and other edible plants' (Okigbo 1980, p. 13). Alexander & Coursey (1969, p. 421) have suggested a date of 3000 to 2000 BC for such yam domestication.

Dietary study of yams indicates some other features important for a proper characterization of early agricultural life in the southern part of west Africa. It indicates, for instance, that 'safe' use of yam tubers by many west African peoples sometimes entailed planting certain poisonous types of *Dioscorea* (e.g. *dumetorum*) around the edges of non-poisonous yam farms in order to scare off monkeys and would-be thieves. Yam utilization commonly entails boiling, peeling, slicing and pounding, and sometimes also steeping them in running or preferably salt water, a detoxification process which generally requires about three days. In the course of tending these tubers over thousands of years there will have been selection for less bitter varieties, for larger size or for specific colours (white and yellow).

The onus is on students of early west African agriculture to identify which west African peoples first commenced the cultivation of this tuber, where in the stress zones, and when and how. What, for instance, was the nature of the relationship with the wild species in the first instance, and how did this relationship progress to cultivation? What manner of interests were first manifested for economic, medicinal or social purposes? What manner of swidden was first established, and with what effect on the plant?

It is generally agreed that at least certain species of yams and the oil palm were first protected and later domesticated in the tropical rainforest zone of west Africa. These crops, in addition to others (see Okigbo 1980, Table 1), occur within the zone of the tropical forest with the length of the dry season ranging from two and a half to five months; it is a region where, according to Harris (1969, pp. 10, 12), the 'origins of tropical lowland vegeculture [should be sought] along semi-deciduous forest margins at riparian, coastal or savanna-edge sites within climatic zones with a dry season of intermediate length'.

Since yams are nitrophiles (Okigbo 1980, p. 15), their unpalatable heads will germinate in rubbish heaps or any other favourable situations into which they are thrown. Preliminary harvesting of these from the wild, leading later to experimentation, did not therefore have to await elaborate clearing of forests, since yams are lofty climbers which can always reach the light even in thick, dense and dark tropical forest, provided the trees are not exceedingly tall. Growing yams in forest clearings using a slash and burn shifting cultivation technique would therefore seem to be the climax of environmental control that may have been attained by the earliest prehistoric farmers of this region.

Okigbo (1980, p. 15) in fact points out that the impenetrable nature of the tropical rainforest today may be a relatively recent phenomenon resulting from intensive forest clearances. In his view, prior to this, farming on periodically flooded river banks did not require much forest clearing. If so, it is likely that the ennoblement of yams occurred on alluvial soils adjacent to river banks, with a relatively open landscape, and one where fishing afforded a means of semi-sedentary culture.

Okigbo (1980, p. 16) also observes that even though yam tubers can be stored so as to ensure that yams are available for about six to nine months of the year, their availability is usually not uniform throughout the year. But there are several edible fruits, seeds and nuts which are abundant at different times of the year and can be used as complementary food items or as substitutes for yams during periods of yam scarcity. Examples of these include the African breadfruit (*Treculia africana*), the native pear (*Dacryodes edulis*), the incense-tree (*Canarium schweinfurthii*), the star apple (*Chrysophylum albidum*) and the African mango (*Irvingia gabonensis*). These are either consumed alone or as a supplement to other items in the diet.

Many other plants thus require to be approached from similar standpoints. Among these would be: the Leguminosae, indigenous to west Africa, which produce edible tubers (e.g. several species of *Vigna*) and edible roots; the all-purpose baobab tree (*Adansonia digitata*); the shea butter tree (*Butyrospermum paradoxum*); edible species in the gourd family (e.g. *Trochomeria dalzielii* – with yam-like roots often produced deep in the ground); and the cultivated species of the sword lily or corn-flat (*Gladiolus*).

The oil palm

The oil palm, second in economic importance only to the Guinea yam, appears to have been protected and extensively multiplied and spread by humans through the west African forest zone (Fig. 12.2). Native to the forest fringe, especially along rivers rather than in the closed canopy humid forest, the present distribution of this tree crop is the result mainly of selective swidden clearance. Although little is known of its origin and early exploitation, a mass interspecific hybridization of wild, semi-cultivated and cultivated varieties appears to have been one ready way in which oil-palm cropping developed in sections of the forest fringes of the Guinea region. Ascenso (1966) has in fact noted the existence of at least three varieties which are concentrated in special areas and which may have developed as a result of human interaction. As with Guinea yams, we need to: (a) identify with what type or types of selective swidden clearance oil-palm distribution is associated – when and where these forms of swidden clearance were first begun and the circumstances leading to their development; (b) define the wild types of oil palm and trace their evolution through semi-cultivated and ancient cultivated types to the present cultivated varieties; and (c) identify what selective pressures led to the development of the species identified. It would help greatly to find out which west African peoples first identified the fruit and kernel of this tree as important sources of food and oils, its sap as an important source of wine, its stem, palm fronds and leaves as important building materials and its fibres for fishing lines, cordage and fish-traps – and to determine when and in what circumstances these discoveries were made.

Domestication of cereals

Harlan, De Wet & Price (1973) were convinced that intensive harvesting of natural stands had no appreciable genetic effects on the plant populations, that in all such settings it was only the seed that escaped the harvester that contributed to the next generation, and that if there were any selective pressure at all, it was always in the direction of shattering, indeterminate growth, seed dormancy and maturation over a long period of time. In fact, it is far from convincing that all cases of nuclear farming resulted only when humans started to plant what they had harvested, and that it was only at this point that two populations were present, exerting selection pressures in opposite directions. Even if this may be so in a cumulative, long-term sense, and viewed from hindsight, it is not so in an immediate short-term setting of varying combinations of chance events and processes of trial and error and experimentation that may well have transpired in those situations where change was locally initiated. Therefore, the questions as to what were the specific experiences different peoples had with specific grasses are real and vital ones, as also are the questions concerning when they actually started selecting deliberately and what they initially actually selected for. These questions can only be answered by unravelling the specific experiences different groups of people had with clearly identified wild species.

Viewed from this perspective, it is far from certain that the earliest farming societies in west Africa actually selected from the outset for those features which are nowadays recognized as separating wild from cultivated cereals, namely: non-shattering, determinate growth; restoration of fertility or reduced or sterile flowers and increase in number or size of inflorescence; greater seed size; lower protein, lighter carbohydrates; loss or reduction of dormancy; reduction of glumes and other appendages; and production of weed races. It is far from clear in our present state of knowledge what features were first selected and if, in fact, the selection of characteristics was as deliberate as some botanists would wish us to believe. If anything, the appearance of weed races should alert us to the fact that some of the selection pressures were accidental by-products rather than deliberate introductions by farming peoples, and that in the earliest phases of farming anywhere in the world deliberate selection must have been of far less importance than it was to become when humans came clearly to appreciate the success of the first sets of changes and how these came to be.

What this means in the case of sorghum and pearl millet, for example, is that these grain cereals, whose wild and weedy species normally have many lateral branches bearing a large number of small heads, have mammoth cultivars with single unbranched stalks bearing enormous single terminal heads as the final stage in the process of their domestication – not the take-off points. The story of the cultivation of these crops begins when reduction of the branching system commences, not when the ultimate is achieved (that is, the large head on a single stalk). The story of early domestication should thus be concerned with identifying when such reduction started and then tracing its progressive evolution to fewer and larger ears at a node until the modern high-yielding cultivars were achieved. For pearl millet we need to find what transpired in between the wild type (*Pennisetum violaceum*), which has numerous small (10 cm or less) heads, and the modern cultivars (with heads over 2 m in some cases).

Recent work on crops like sorghum, pearl millet, rice and cotton have shown that in many cases the evolution of the crop plants took place in genetic contact with the 'wild' progenitors, leading by disruptive selection to several new races of the species, intermediary crops and their weedy relatives – always two races at least at each identifiable stage in the past. In these instances, early domesticates did not become extinct. Rather, gene exchanges continued between wild and cultivated types, and as cultivation dominated the local ecology, so weedy forms arose, subject to selection pressures from attributes that contribute to survival in spite of attempts by humans to weed them out. This disruptive selection has been of great importance in the emergence of weedy sorghums and rices and dooryard cottons.

It seems, then, that in the instance of cereals and legumes, and to a varying extent with other plants, the factors operative in the change from perennials to annuals are some combinations specific to each; these factors include increased desiccation and a wide diurnal and seasonal range between high and low temperatures (Whyte 1977, p. 215).

For example, at the northern limits of their distribution in the Senegal-Mauritanian and Chad regions, the perennial species of *Oryza*, the millets, sorghum and legumes native to these areas must have been exposed to the same factors of aridity and high temperature in the semi-arid zones on several occasions during the Holocene (see Harlan, Ch. 3, this volume). Drought and high temperature, spreading from the north southwards to the zone of vegetation in which the highly drought-susceptible perennial species of *Oryza* occurred, were important factors leading to the initial creation of a number of annuals at different elevations in parts of the Senegal and Upper Niger delta basins.

Archaeological and botanical evidence

Tree crops

Seed husks and kernels of wild or cultivated palms and other tree crops have been recovered from some sites. Outstanding in this regard is evidence from Bosumpra Cave in Ghana of the use and perhaps cultivation of *Canarium schweinfurthii* (a tree whose fruits are eaten) dating to before 3500 BC and for the oil palm, *Elaeis guiniensis*, at a level dating to 3000 BC. Seed husks recovered from Kintampo in central Ghana were obtained from a level dated to 1400 BC (Flight 1970; Smith 1975b; Flight 1976). Oil-palm kernels have also been found from rock shelters in Liberia dating back to 1500 BC (Gabel 1976). In all these sites they were associated with levels containing pottery, ground and polished tools with or without microliths, and it is possible that these associations represent definite techno-economic traditions. Since at sites like Bosumpra, Mejiro Cave (Old Oyo), Iwo Eleru and Afikpo, microlithic tools (which may have been used for specialized hunting) appear, from the evidence on one site, to date back to 9500 BC, it is possible that a tradition of farming oil palms and related crops in the southeast part of west Africa dates back to the terminal Pleistocene. A related techno-complex to the southwest is present in the quartz levels of Yengema and Kamabai (in Sierra Leone) (Atherton 1972) and is characterized by the prominence of choppers, scrapers and heavy cutting tools. Microliths are absent, suggesting little or no hunting. It is possible also that this industrial complex, which is just older than 2500 BC, was used for some form of fallow farming in this part of Guinea.

Around 4000 BP there is some palynological and geomorphological evidence (Sowunmi 1985, p. 128) for the northern forest margin having retreated and for the savanna vegetational belts having moved southwards. This could have caused some environmental stress to the inhabitants and stimulated an intensification of the protection and cultivation of oil palms, and of yams, the inception of which Coursey (1976, p. 402) placed at about this time.

Until 2800 BP the oil palm was only a minor component of the vegetation of southern Nigeria (Sowunmi 1985, p. 127). After that date, not only did it suddenly increase, but weeds of cultivation and of waste places also appeared. This was probably due to human activity, and may indicate swidden cultivation at least by 2800 BP, when forest clearance would have been carried out with stone tools. Because it is difficult to distinguish the pollen of wild and cultivated oil palms, it is not possible now to pinpoint the transition more precisely.

The millets

The millets which are traditionally grown in west Africa appear, except for finger millet, to have been domesticated within the region. Pearl millet (*Pennisetum glaucum*), which is the more widely cultivated millet in west Africa, has two conspicuous races (Harlan 1971, p. 471). The western of these two areas, which occupies part of Senegal and southern Mauritania, is probably the main source area of the pearl millet cultivated in west Africa. Pollen impressions of domesticated pearl millet recovered from Tichitt escarpment in the south-centre of this region (Munson 1968; Munson 1970; Munson 1976) date to between 1000 and 900 BC. Since cultivation did not necessarily commence with domesticated pearl millet, cultivation may in all likelihood have long preceded domestication. Cultivation of pearl millet in this region may be reasonably inferred to extend further back in time than the Tichitt date.

Fonio millet, also cultivated in west Africa, is grown principally in uplands within the sorghum–millet zone (Fig. 12.1). Although its greatest varietal diversity occurs today in the Fouta Djallon plateau and the valleys of the upper Senegal and Niger, Portères (1955, pp. 479–80) suggests it was first domesticated in the inland delta of the Niger and was grown prior to the tenth century AD. It is suggested on the other hand (Harris 1976, p. 345) that black fonio, which has an extremely restricted distribution, originated as a cultivated plant in the Aïr region of the southern Sahara and from there subsequently spread south. Like the fonio millets, a drought-tolerant millet, *Brachiaria deflexa*, grown to a limited extent today in Guinea, may have been more widely cultivated before being subsequently displaced by more productive cereals. Its presence as a minor food item at the Tichitt sites from about 1100 to 400 BC (Munson 1976) suggests that it may have had a long history as a cultivated species in the drier parts of the sorghum–millet zone.

Sorghum

It has been suggested on the basis of botanical evidence that sorghum may have been domesticated first south of the Sahara in the savanna zone stretching eastwards from Lake Chad. Climatically this lies within the long-dry-season zone which experiences seven and a half to ten arid months (Fig. 12.1). Although Harlan & Stemler (1976) claim that sorghum first came under cultivation outside west Africa and later spread to, and was widely adopted in, the semi-arid and sub-humid lands west of Lake Chad, it seems very possible that this plant, which like pearl millet has several modes of variability and a very wide natural distribution, was also domesticated in more than one area and at different times and that the west African region provided more than one nuclear zone. Indeed, there is the strong possibility that the nuclear zones for the African cultivars of this crop are to be found in west Africa – if it is true, as Portères (1950; 1955) asserts, that of the three regions which possessed basic wild stocks of sorghum (west Africa, Ethiopia and east Africa), west Africa's current types, unlike those of the other regions, are unique rather than being crosses between the three primary strains. This suggests that sorghums were spread from west Africa to east Africa and Asia at some time in the past and not vice versa.

Rice

There is little direct evidence concerning the nature of the earliest farming traditions of the rice zone. However, both archaeological evidence on rice cultivation at Jenne-jeno (McIntosh & McIntosh, Ch. 37, this volume) dating back to the first century AD, and existing traditional systems suggest that an early form of rice farming was a décrue (hydraulic) system – utilizing the seasonal flood regime of the Niger (Fig. 12.1). Techniques of floodwater cultivation of rice were developed very early in this area and subsequently extended, on a smaller scale, to other valleys subject to seasonal flooding. Archaeological evidence (e.g. Linares de Sapir 1971) seems also to give some support to the idea that an early development of rice cultivation in tidal swamps and inlets took place in Senegambia and spread later to other appropriate parts of the southwestern coast. It has also been suggested that selection of dry varieties of rice and their incorporation into swidden systems of production probably brought about the most extensive spread of rice cultivation, giving shape to the rice zone as a whole. The transition from small-scale to stable systems of hydraulic cultivation in lowland areas and then to an extensive, mobile pattern of rice cultivation in upland and lowland forests, was to mark a major step in the agricultural transformation of this part of west Africa; but it also raises the question of what, if any, farming systems were already established in the areas penetrated by rice swidden cultivation.

Even if we do not yet know when rice swidden replaced the swidden cropping of other cereal crops, it is certain that cultivation of African rice was well established prior to the entry of Asiatic rice, both within the rice zone and in western parts of the sorghum–millet zone. Portères (1950; 1962; 1976) aptly demonstrated that African rice, which derives from a wild and weedy annual species (*O. barthii* A. Chev – formerly *O. breviligulata* A. Chev; and see Harlan 1989, pp. 88–90) native to the semi-arid interior from Cape Verde to east of Lake Chad, has primary centres of variation in the areas of the upper Gambia and Casamance rivers, extending up to the extensive floodplain of the upper Niger between Segu and Timbuktu in Mali where the Niger divides into several streams and lakes, and floods regularly. He postulated that it was initially taken into cultivation as 'floating' rice in the area of this inland delta well over 3500 years ago and subsequently spread by way of the valleys of the upper Niger and Senegal to the secondary centre of variation where 'non-floating' races were selected and techniques of cultivating rice in brackish water evolved. At the same time the dispersal of cultivated forms to other areas, including the Guinea highlands, led to the selection of 'upland' races adapted to dry cultivation. Whether this was so or not, all available archaeological evidence is in agreement with Portères' (1950; 1976) suggestion that rice cultivation supported the 'megalithic civilization' of Senegambia and some of the early towns of the western Sudan like Jenné which were already flourishing in the early centuries AD.

The pulses

Little is known of the areas of origin and early cultivation history of the pulses thought to be of African origin. If remains of cowpea recovered from a Kintampo site dating to about 1400 BC were indeed cultivated, they attest to a long history of cultivation in these parts, although it is not known where in tropical Africa it originated as a crop. Pigeon pea and sesame (the latter widely cultivated in west Africa for its oil-yielding and edible seeds) were probably native to, and first domesticated in, some parts of west Africa.

Conclusion

Relevant data, archaeological and other, point to the existence of several, rather than one, early seed-cropping complexes in parts of the Sahel and northern savanna regions. Outstanding are: (i) the inland delta of the Niger, the edge of the Fouta Djallon hills in the upper basins of the Niger, Senegal and Gambia (for rice cultivation using hydraulic methods) and some other parts of the western Sudan; (ii) mixed farming and cattle-herding in the central and eastern sahelian regions and parts of the northern savanna regions involving some West Atlantic-speaking peoples, especially the Fulani; and (iii) root, tuber and tree-cropping complexes initiated by Kwa-speaking peoples employing various fallow systems and devices to protect the physical properties of the soil in the forest fringe regions to the far south.

It seems that these early systems of farming had their distinct artefact complexes related to different types of environment and methods of resource exploitation (Shaw 1985a, p. 71), settlement, social patterning and land utilization systems. Generally the hunting and pastoralist complexes in the northern parts of west Africa have industries based on blades and contain geometric microliths, projectile points, with very few or no heavy tools and no ground stone tools. Seed-cropping complexes of the northern grasslands appear to be typified by polished and ground stone tools, a variety of flaked tools (based on blades) with limited occurrences of microliths and projectile points, and a varied range of distinctive pottery. The people cultivating the vegetable (root) crop complexes to the south also used polished and ground tools, but they stand out from all others in having essentially flake-based industries containing heavy, bifacially flaked tools and choppers. Such uniqueness of technological equipment is evident in the ethnographic present in the use of the hoe and digging stick for cultivation, as well as in the ways (deep or shallow tillage) farms are tilled and prepared, taking into full account the type of crops farmed, the nature of soils being tilled and the moisture supplies available in the area.

Lest the import of all this is missed, we note that the management of soil properties, the integration of valley and upland farms and intercropping are only three of many major distinctive features of indigenous agriculture in west Africa. These, as Richards (1983a) correctly notes, are not necessarily survivals from a 'golden age' of traditional agriculture, or evidence of involution (i.e. farmers being forced to pay greater attention to detail as a result of population pressure or capitalist underdevelopment). As principles of ecological management, they differ from those upon which agricultural progress in temperate lands has been based. In consequence, temperate agricultural science and technology have not been, and will not be, readily adaptable to west African conditions. Archaeologists must accept the possibility that west African farmers long ago laid the experimental and practical foundation for an 'improved' agriculture, in much the same way that innovations and experiments by ordinary farmers in England over a period of several centuries provided the basis for what eventually came to be recognized as the 'Agricultural Revolution' (Richards 1983a).

To talk about the 'Neolithic Revolution' along the same old lines, even if in new garb, is to continue to claim that there were no equivalent agricultural revolutions in Africa. To ask why an equivalent revolution either did not take off, or failed, in Africa are inappropriate questions; at best they represent chimeras, and at worst lead to the refusal to recognize several centuries, and in some cases thousands of years, of solid progress towards improved agriculture adjusted to African ecological conditions, in favour of an imported illusion.

Ethnographic investigations are clearly vital for meaningful studies of early farming and farming societies in west Africa. They can provide a basis for generating hypotheses relating to the inception and development of different agricultural traditions known to have existed in various regions of west Africa from prehistoric times. Central to such hypotheses are the identification of the role of local expertise as well as the social ideals and ideas that determined how social knowledge of various kinds was translated locally. The beginnings of farming and its subsequent developments in west Africa can only be satisfactorily understood (modelled) if data derived from specific instances of agricultural ecology and the way people organize their agricultural production are combined.

13 The Kintampo complex: a case study of early sedentism and food production in sub-Sahelian west Africa

JAMES ANQUANDAH

Introduction

For several decades one of the burning issues in African archaeology has been the question of the origin of sub-Saharan food production. It has often been associated, though not necessarily always correctly, with a sedentary form of habitation. In some twenty-seven sites in Ghana's savanna and forest lands and two other sites in the Ivory Coast, recurrent evidence has been found both in excavations and from surface materials which has led to the hypothesis that peoples of the Late Stone Age adopted and practised sedentism and food production shortly after 2000 BC (Davies 1962; Davies 1964; Davies 1967; Flight 1976; Dombrowski 1980; Anquandah 1982; Chenorkian 1983; Posnansky 1984; Stahl 1985b; Stahl, Ch. 14, this volume). Although the hypothesis for sedentism seems to be supported by and large by the available evidence, that for food production appears to be tenuous since it is often uncertain whether faunal remains found in Kintampo deposits represent those of wild, captive, tame or domesticated animals. Similar doubts have been raised about plant food remains found in Kintampo contexts.

However, the balance of the circumstantial associated evidence of polished stone axes, stone beads, buildings of stone, mud and wood, domestic pots and miniature ceramic sculptures depicting humans, cattle, sheep/goats and dogs appears to favour the Kintampo as created by practitioners of pastoralism and horticulture. It thus paved the way towards the establishment of the iron age societies of Ghana and the Ivory Coast.

The Kintampo complex

A typical Kintampo complex site exhibits all or most of the following:

1 Scored soft stone (and occasionally clay) objects variously described as 'cigars', 'rasps', 'potshaping tools' or 'pot-decorating tools' (Anquandah 1965; Davies 1967; Dombrowski and Priddy 1978);
2 Polished axe blades made of 'greenstone' (Calc-chlorite schist);
3 Microliths usually made from quartz;

4 Polished or flaked stone arrowheads;

5 Grooved stones thought to be bead-polishers or arrow-shaft straighteners;

6 Milling equipment;

7 Polished stone arm rings or bracelets and biconically perforated quartz stones;

8 House remains of:

    (a) daub, with or without wooden pole impressions; and

    (b) foundation stones;

9 Domestic pottery characterized by:

    (a) a heavy rolled rim; and

    (b) decoration by combstamp, slip and attachment of modelled figurines depicting humans, cattle, sheep/goat, dogs, tortoise and lizards;

10 Remains of wild and/or domesticated animals and plants.

The Kintampo complex is represented in all the major ecological zones of the area (Fig. 13.1):

Ghana

Coastal grassland	2 sites
Hinterland grassland	6 sites
Forest/grassland ecotone	14 sites
Semi-deciduous forest	5 sites

Ivory Coast

Hinterland grassland (Dabakala)	1 site
Lagoon shell-midden site (Songon Dagbe)	1 site

Under half of the sites have been excavated while the others are known only from surface materials. With the exception of Boyasi and Christian Village, all the Ghanaian and Ivorian sites have radiocarbon age estimations ranging between *c.* 4250 bp (Daboya S-2376) and *c.* 2750 bp. Of the twenty radiocarbon estimations from Ghana and two from Ivory Coast, seventeen range between the nineteenth and twelfth centuries BC (Anquandah 1982, p. 142; Chenorkian 1983, pp. 134–5; Gavua 1985, pp. 138–9; Stahl 1985a, pp. 127, 146).

The evidence of sedentism

Evidence of house remains in the form of daub and/or stone have been found as surface materials in half of the known Kintampo sites in Ghana.

At Christian Village near Achimota it is claimed that 'fragments of baked-clay cylinders must be the remains of clay houses built on very light frames of wattle and sticks' (Davies 1967, p. 217). At the sites of Ntereso, Boyasi, Bonoase and Mumute, clear outlines of house sites were traced and excavated. At Ntereso, thanks to the presence of postholes, Davies was able to find the remains of rectangular houses, each measuring about 4 m², and built probably of wooden poles, mud and grass (Davies 1966b, p. 30).

At Mumute, Bonoase and Boyasi there is clear evidence that granite stones or laterite blocks were used as bases on which wood and mud houses were constructed. The site of Mumute, which is estimated to be about 2100 m², contains not only houses but also granaries and water cisterns. At Bonoase, which is considered to be much larger than

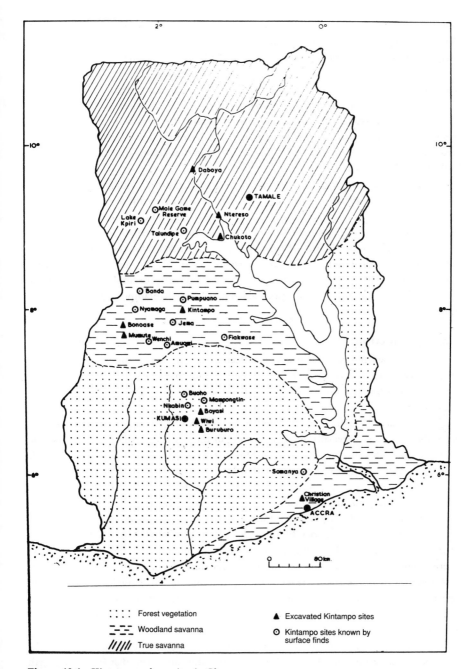

Figure 13.1 Kintampo culture sites in Ghana.

Kintampo (K1, K6 and K8 rock shelters) (Carter & Flight 1972; Flight 1976; Stahl 1985a)

Ntereso (Davies 1966b; Davies 1973)

Mumute and Bonoase (Dombrowski 1976; Dombrowski 1980; Dombrowski n.d.)

Boyasi (Anquandah 1976a; Anquandah 1976b; Anquandah 1982)

Daboya (Kense 1983a; Kense 1983b; Gavua 1985)

Christian Village, Accra (Davies 1967, p. 217)

Mumute, there are clear stone settings representing the bases of huts. Distributions of Kintampo type artefacts found *in situ* in hut squares measuring 4 or 4.5 m^2 have been mapped at Bonoase (Dombrowski 1976). On the basis of a decline in the frequency of artefacts along the transect lines, the rough boundaries of Boyasi were traced and its size calculated to be 11.53 ha. Grooved granite boulders were used at this latter site as 'factory' areas for manufacturing polished stone axes, polished stone arrowheads, stone beads and bracelets. Two excavated rectangular houses measured 6 × 3.5 m and 7.5 × 3 m respectively. Boyasi was a centre for a variety of prehistoric industries and crafts, and the associated evidence of huts and grinding stones argues in favour of a clear tradition of sedentism (Anquandah n.d.b).

The Kintampo complex does not represent a sudden break with the past as far as residence or mobility was concerned. Rock shelters, such as those of the Kintampo area, continued to be used as camp sites alongside the open house sites. At Kintampo K6 rock shelter alone, Flight and Stahl between them excavated an occupation area of some 63 m^2 (Flight 1973b; Stahl 1985b). On the other hand, Nkukoa Buoho, an open inselberg site located near Boyasi and currently used as a Roman Catholic church shrine, is probably the largest Kintampo site and has a dense assemblage of remains of wattle and daub houses, rasps, polished stone axes, Kintampo-type pottery and microliths.

Food production

The issues of sedentism, food production technology and environmental exploitation must be viewed as a corpus of circumstantial evidence that supports the hypothesis for sedentism and food production in the first and second millennia BC in Ghana and the Ivory Coast.

Direct evidence for food production in tropical Africa, though hard to come by, nevertheless exists, especially in rock shelters in the Kintampo and Banda areas, and in a few open sites such as Ntereso and Mumute where remains of *Bos* and ovicaprids have been found (Carter & Flight 1972; Flight 1973b; Davies n.d.; Dombrowski n.d.; Stahl 1985b; Stahl, Ch. 14, this volume). Although there seems to be general agreement that faunal remains of ovicaprids recovered from Kintampo K6 contexts and at Ntereso are those of domesticates (Stahl 1985a), there is no consensus about the character of eight bovid bones found at K6, since the remains appear to belong to creatures smaller than both the grassland buffalo and modern *Bos* spp. Similarly, there is uncertainty as to whether the faunal remains of guinea-fowl (*Numida meleagris*) found in K6 rock shelter level 3 belong to domesticated, tamed, captive or wild species (Stahl 1985a; see also Clutton-Brock, Ch. 4, this volume). Faunal remains of what have been claimed as *Bos* sp. excavated from Mumute have not been scientifically identified.

There is evidence from excavations at the rock shelters of Bosumpra, Akyek-yemabuo, Tetewabuo and Apreku (Smith 1975b; Musonda 1976) that from the fourth millennium BC late stone age hunter-gatherers were exploiting wild plant sources such as the oil palm (*Elaeis guineensis*), incense tree (*Canarium schweinfurthii*) and hackberry (*Celtis* spp.). At Kintampo K6, charred remains of palm and incense-tree oil seeds occur throughout the entire deposit, from Late Stone Age levels to 'neolithic' levels, while remains of hackberry and of an uncertainly identified legume, which may be cowpea, occur mainly in the 'neolithic' levels.

Stahl (1985a) has pointed out that there is an interesting correlation between evidence on subsistence, sedentism and technology (see also Stahl, Ch. 14, this volume). For instance, in Kintampo K6 rock shelter, middle and top levels, there is an increase in daub, ceramics, rasps (Fig. 13.2) and polished stone axes (Fig. 13.3) coupled with the exploitation of rodents (e.g. cane rats and giant rats) normally associated with permanent human habitation (see also Clutton-Brock, Ch. 4, this volume). At about this same time, the artistically minded Kintampo potters were producing pots with modelled decoration depicting cattle, ovicaprids and dogs. If the prehistoric potters were documenting their contemporary experience, then this art evidence supports the argument for sedentism and food production.

Conclusion

The Kintampo complex is a 'neolithic' tradition combining characteristics of sedentism and building technology; a mixed subsistence economy, including hunting, fishing,

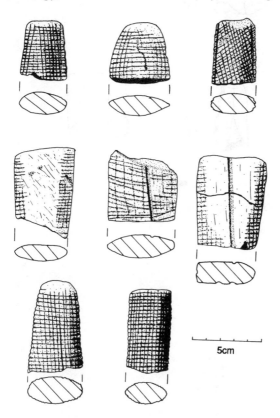

Figure 13.2   Terracotta/stone rasps/'cigars'. K6 rock shelter.

gathering of wild crops and animal domestication; cottage industries and crafts such as potting, various ground and flaked stone implements, milling equipment and stone beads; and the rudiments of terracotta art. It probably owed something to external influences – as is suggested from the evidence of cattle (Shaw 1977), dwarf goats, fishing technology with bone harpoons and fish-hooks, and ceramic decorative motifs such as 'walking comb' (*impression pivotante*) (Davies 1966b). At the same time, there is also some evidence pointing to indigenous developments such as oil palms, cowpeas, guinea-fowl, wattle and daub building technology, late stone age derived pottery and the peculiar rasps. What is now urgently required to prove a fully tropical 'neolithic' is macro – or micro – botanical evidence for yam cultivation.

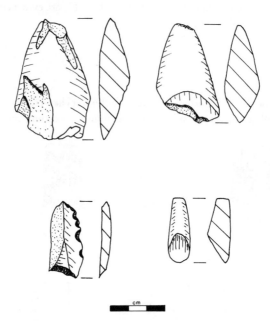

Figure 13.3   Polished stone implements, K6 rock shelter.

14 Intensification in the west African Late Stone Age: a view from central Ghana

ANN BROWER STAHL

Some twenty-five years have passed since Oliver Davies first defined the Kintampo 'Neolithic' (Davies 1962). In the ensuing years numerous sites have been explored, and the parameters of the Kintampo complex are reasonably well-known (see Anquandah, Ch. 13, this volume). In many respects, however, our knowledge of the Kintampo complex represents an oasis in a desert of archaeological time and space; we know little of its antecedents, less of contemporaneous complexes, and virtually nothing of its legacy. Whereas past treatments of the Kintampo complex have been site-specific, the goal of this chapter is to adopt a somewhat broader perspective, considering the Kintampo complex in time and space. By orienting our oasis within what we know of the desert, new perspectives on the Kintampo complex may emerge. The aim is not to provide definitive scenarios; rather, it is to explore the larger implications of certain features of the Kintampo complex with the hope of highlighting areas for future research.

In keeping with recent convention (e.g. McIntosh & McIntosh 1986a), the Kintampo complex is included here in the ceramic Late Stone Age, thereby avoiding use of the term 'neolithic' with all its problematic connotations (e.g. Shaw 1978–9). In the sections that follow, the characteristics of antecedent late stone age occupations will be identified and contrasted with those of the Kintampo complex. Similarities with contemporaneous occupations in west and central Africa will be explored. A concluding section identifies the qualitative differences that distinguish terminal late stone age complexes, and explores the significance of regional variation.

Antecedents

The sparse evidence that exists for the Late Stone Age (LSA) occupation of sub-Saharan west Africa has been reviewed and updated by several authors in recent years (Shaw 1977; Shaw 1978–9; Andah 1979a; McIntosh & McIntosh 1983; McIntosh & McIntosh 1986a; McIntosh & McIntosh, Ch. 37, this volume). A small number of sites scattered from Cameroon to Sierra Leone and spanning the period from the tenth millennium BC to the early Christian era comprise the data base from which to distil an impression of the Late Stone Age (LSA). One problem hindering comparison of these widely scattered assemblages centres on dating. Some sites remain undated, while many more are dated by a single radiocarbon age determination. Only a small number of recently excavated sites are dated by a series of age estimations, thereby providing an adequate basis for comparison with other sites.

Shaw (1977; 1978–9) has tentatively identified two phases within the LSA in sub-Saharan west Africa, each comprising two or more facies that appear to be ecological variants. Phase I comprises aceramic LSA sites spanning the period 10,000 BC to roughly the fourth millennium BC (Shaw 1978–9, p. 65). Within Phase I, Facies A sites are characterized by microlithic assemblages and are located in areas of present-day savanna. Facies B sites lack microliths, and are characterized instead by large flaked implements often referred to as hoes or picks. The two known Facies B sites are located in forested areas of Sierra Leone and Guinea (Fig. 14.1). Phase II, which begins in the fourth millennium BC, is marked by the addition of ceramics to the range of material culture. Shaw associates an increase in regional variation during Phase II with ecological parameters. Facies A sites occur throughout the sahelian zone. Microliths are lacking and a bone industry oriented towards exploitation of aquatic resources (e.g. harpoons, fish-hooks) is characteristic. Facies B sites account for the largest number of known LSA sites and are distributed throughout the present-day savanna. In addition to a microlithic component, Facies B assemblages see the addition of ceramics and ground stone implements (axes/celts/hoes). Facies C sites also yield pottery and ground stone implements, but lack microliths and occur in modern forested environments. The emergence of coastal-based Facies D is associated with the accumulation of shell middens.

A lack of preserved floral and faunal materials at LSA sites has precluded a detailed understanding of the subsistence base of LSA peoples. Most researchers have, however, inferred a generalized hunting and gathering adaptation on the basis of technology. Microliths are presumed to represent components of composite tools, possibly used as

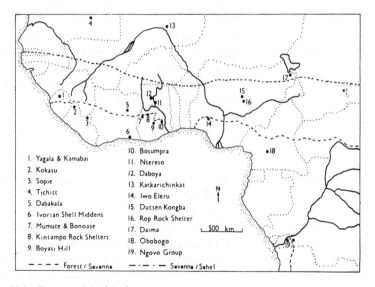

Figure 14.1   Sites mentioned in the text.

projectiles (Shaw 1978–9, p. 58; Andah 1978), processing tools or tools to make tools (McIntosh & McIntosh 1983, p. 236). Shaw (1978–9, p. 58) has suggested that the association of microliths with savanna settings may relate to a reliance on hunting in areas of high animal biomass. This need not imply, however, that hunting was any less important at those LSA sites in more forested areas which lack microliths. Other hunting techniques more appropriate to the pursuit of solitary, territorial and arboreal forest-dwelling species (e.g. use of nets, traps or possibly wooden projectiles, perhaps tipped with poison) are less likely to find expression in an archaeological context. That the requisite weaving and cordage-making skills existed in the LSA is attested by cord- and mat-impressed sherds in the lower levels of K6 rock shelter which are associated with a radiocarbon age determination of 3605 ± 100 bp (Stahl 1985a, pp. 127–34; see also Derefaka 1980). Similarly, economic inferences based upon the presence of chipped or polished stone axes/celts/hoes remain problematic. We do not have a clear under- standing of the function of these implements and cannot to date substantiate sugges- tions that they were used to dig tubers (e.g. Anquandah 1982a, p. 54), clear forests or were employed as woodworking implements (see also Atherton 1980).

Perhaps the best direct evidence for the subsistence base of an LSA population derives from the 'Punpun phase' of central Ghana, the immediate precursor of the Kintampo complex at several rock shelter sites. The four radiocarbon age estimations for the Punpun phase occupation of the Kintampo rock shelters (Fig. 14.1) show a tight clustering in the 400-year period roughly 3700–3300 BP (Stahl 1985a, p. 146). The dates overlap with those from Kintampo complex levels in the area. Punpun assemblages are characterized by an abundance of struck quartz but few recognizable 'tools'. Sparse ceramics with overall impressed decoration are also diagnostic. The Punpun levels at K6 rock shelter comprised deep ashy deposits that yielded an abundance of snail shell, mainly the giant land snail *Achatina achatina* (Flight 1976; Stahl 1985a). The highly fragmented state of the shell suggests their use as food (Stahl 1985a, pp. 140–1). A variety of species were represented in the small sample of vertebrate fauna recovered from the site, including arboreal primates and several large reptiles (tortoise, monitor lizard and freshwater turtle). All these species inhabit both the savanna/forest margin and the fringing forest along rivers in the savanna woodland (Stahl 1985b, pp. 208–14). Seed husks of the edible fruit *Celtis* spp. were abundant in the Punpun levels at K6 rock shelter, suggesting a relatively intensive harvesting of this seasonally available resource. Endocarps of the oleaginous species *Elaeis guineensis* (oil palm) and *Canarium schwein- furthii* occurred in Punpun levels at K6 rock shelter (Stahl 1985a, p. 141). This combination of oleaginous species is also documented at Bosumpra Cave (Fig. 14.1) on the Kwahu plateau, Ghana, and is associated with a single radiocarbon determination of 5303 ± 100 bp (5568 1/2 life). *Canarium* was found in the lowest levels of Bosumpra, and *Elaeis* appeared in combination with *Canarium* in levels from 50 to 80 cm. Above 50 cm *Elaeis* occurred alone (Smith 1975b). Assuming that the single date from the lower levels at Bosumpra is not aberrant, this provides the most ancient evidence for the exploitation of these oily seeds. Other LSA sites that have yielded oil palm include Sopie and Kokasu rock shelters in Liberia (Fig. 14.1), dated from the late to mid-second millennium BC through the mid-first millennium AD (Gabel 1976). Later period sites in Cameroon and Zaïre also attest exploitation of these oleaginous resources (see below).

The temptation must be avoided to overgeneralize from the meagre body of economic data at sites such as K6. Coastal shell middens provide a reminder that LSA populations exploited locally available resources, suggesting disparate patterns of resource utilization in different regions.

Shaw (1978–9) has compared the ceramics from LSA sites across west Africa and has shown that *broad* similarities in decoration occur over a vast area (e.g. in use of comb-stamp, punctate decoration). Sherds are usually too small to make generalizations regarding vessel morphology. Significant, however, are the generally small quantities in which ceramics occur prior to *c.* 1500 BC (3400 BP). Assuming that their paucity in archaeological contexts does not result from depositional biases, it appears likely that the role of ceramics in food preparation and storage was limited. The paucity of ceramics in LSA contexts may reflect greater reliance on dry, as compared to moist, cooking, although moist cooking can be accomplished without use of ceramics (Stahl 1989).

A prevailing notion is that LSA hunter-gatherers were relatively mobile peoples; however, a lack of data hampers assessment of this notion. The majority of excavated sites are rock shelters. This is in part a reflection of the fact that open sites are notoriously difficult to identify (e.g. Gabel 1976, p. 35), combined with the archaeologist's preference for investigating stratified sites. Nevertheless, this may represent a culturally significant pattern, and many of the rock shelter sites exhibit relatively deep deposits that signal intensive use (Table 14.1). Two scenarios might account for this patterning: a continuous occupation by a non-mobile group; or repeated visits of shorter duration, possibly on a seasonal basis (e.g. Shaw 1978, p. 45). Determination of seasonal occupation remains very difficult in tropical settings; nevertheless, at least three resources documented in the LSA levels at K6 (giant snail, *Celtis* & *Canarium*) are seasonal in their availability and suggest a wet season occupation (Flight 1976, p. 216; Stahl 1985b, p. 226). A mobile lifestyle is consistent with the dearth of non-portable material culture in the majority of LSA contexts (e.g. small quantities of ceramics; see also York 1978, p. 160). Repeated use of shelters is thus suggestive of *patterned* mobility, in which groups returned to previously occupied sites.

Use of exotic raw materials is very limited in LSA contexts. Despite the poor quality of the quartz that characterizes the locales of many sites, local raw materials dominate the lithic assemblages of virtually all excavated sites. Thus, apparently no effort was made to obtain more tractable raw material from exotic sources.

Table 14.1　Depth of deposit at LSA rock shelter sites

Site	Approximate dimensions (m)	Approximate depth (cm)	Source
Bosumpra	?	110	Smith 1975b
Dutsen Kongba	7.5 x 3.5	100	York 1978
Iwo Eleru	?	150	Shaw 1973
K6 (Punpun)	18 x 10	90	Stahl 1985a
Kamabai	?	100	Atherton 1972
Kokasu	15 x 8	70	Gabel 1976
Rop	8 x 5	80	Fagg 1972
Sopie	10 x 12	75	Gabel 1976
Yagala	9 x 9	60	Atherton 1972

In summary, the limited data on LSA sites in sub-Saharan west Africa suggests mobile populations repeatedly visiting favoured sites, and possibly practising a seasonal pattern of exploitation. The limited quantity of non-portable artefacts (e.g. ceramics) is consistent with this mobile lifestyle. The dearth of ceramics suggests a cuisine in which boiling and use of sauces was limited, and suggests a limited capacity for the storage of foodstuffs. The presence of mat- and cord-impressed sherds indicates that the requisite technology for the production of woven items was available. Weaving may have been important in the production of hunting equipment (e.g. nets), bags for portage, etc. Unlike the LSA in other parts of Africa, items of personal adornment (e.g. beads) appear to be non-existent or occur in small quantities.

The Kintampo complex: the case for intensification

Our field of vision narrows considerably when we turn our attention to those LSA occupations which provide evidence for increasing sedentism, with the addition of food production. Until very recently, the Kintampo complex of the mid-second millennium BC proved unique in this regard throughout western and central Africa south of the Sahel. In many respects, the Kintampo complex represents a major departure from the 'typical' LSA outlined above; there are aspects of continuity with the preceding Punpun phase which underlie the 'new' elements (Stahl 1985a; Stahl 1986). If there is a single term to describe the numerous changes that occur, it is 'intensification' (e.g. Kaiser & Voytek 1983, pp. 329–30).

Subsistence change has perhaps most interested students of the Kintampo complex. Although there is some disagreement on the precise nature of these changes (see Stahl 1985a; Anquandah, Ch. 13, this volume), there is unequivocal evidence for exploitation of domestic ovicaprids (sheep/goat) at Kintampo sites. The degree of reliance on this exotic domesticate remains unclear. What does seem certain, however, is that addition of sheep/goat to a subsistence repertoire can have far-reaching implications for mobility. Ethnographers working amongst extant hunter-gatherers note that the incorporation of goats into an otherwise hunter-gatherer economy slows travel time, decreases residential mobility, and thereby enhances trends towards sedentism (Vierich 1982; Cashdan 1984). Apart from the evidence of ovicaprids, inferences regarding the reliance of Kintampo peoples on food production are based upon indirect evidence. Management of tree crops is inferred from the dramatic increase in *Elaeis* pollen that occurs in the Bosumtwi core at around 3500–3000 years BP (Talbot, Livingstone, Palmer, Maley, Melack, Delibrias & Gulliksen 1984, p. 185). The close connection between oil-palm and yam cultivation in contemporary west African contexts has led some researchers to suggest that this combination of managed/cultivated resources very likely characterized Kintampo complex subsistence as well. Clearly, we are in no position yet to confirm or disconfirm this linkage. Given comparable environmental settings in the past, it is ecologically feasible. Many Kintampo sites are clustered in areas of the modern forest/wooded savanna margin or in upland savanna outliers in forested regions where oil palm, *Canarium* and yams may have flourished. We are in a better position to assess the contribution of hunting and gathering to the Kintampo economy.

Both continue to be of considerable importance despite the addition of domesticates (Stahl 1985a, pp. 138–45; see also Posnansky 1984). Hunting is indicated by a range of vertebrate fauna at K6 shelter, although the species differ from those of the Punpun levels. Some forest-dwelling species (e.g. duiker, royal antelope) are attested; however, exploitation of large rodents and other species normally associated with more open settings suggest either environmental modification during the Kintampo as compared to Punpun occupation, and/or a change in hunting strategy that favoured exploitation of species attracted to clearings and settlements. These changes are not inconsistent with a shift to garden hunting (e.g. Linares de Sapir 1976) or opportunistic exploitation of species attracted to settlements (Stahl 1985a, pp. 143–4). Gathering of wild plant foods is documented for the Kintampo complex, although declining exploitation of seasonally available resources in the uppermost Kintampo levels at K6 may reflect changing scheduling priorities (Stahl 1985a, p. 144).

By focusing on the study of stylistic variables, students of the Kintampo complex have largely overlooked the implications of ceramic evidence for changes in culinary style, and perhaps by extension changes in subsistence patterns (e.g. Davies n.d.; Rahtz & Flight 1974; Stahl 1985a; Stahl 1985b). Nevertheless, several observations may prove worthy of future investigation. First, there is a *dramatic* increase in the quantity of ceramics in Kintampo contexts by comparison to the preceding Punpun phase occupation (Stahl 1985a) (Figs 14.2, 14.3, 14.4). Presumably this reflects greater reliance on ceramics for cooking or storage purposes. Two basic vessel forms dominate Kintampo ceramic assemblages: jars and bowls (Davies n.d.; Anquandah 1976a; Dombrowski 1976; Stahl 1985a). The rims of bowls with an estimatable diameter recovered from the 1982 excavations at K6 rock shelter (n = 28) ranged from 10 to 30 cm. Jars exhibited greater variation, ranging from 12 to 44 cm (n = 21). Manufacture of a range of jar sizes opens new possibilities for cooking (e.g. boiling, preparation of sauces) and storage (e.g. foodstuffs or water). Increased reliance on oil palm may be linked to the increasing importance of ceramics because processing of the nut requires prolonged cooking. Thus we must pay closer attention to the problem of vessel function amongst Kintampo ceramics. For example, researchers should be alert to the presence of residues, especially on interior surfaces, for these can provide important clues to the range of foods consumed and to methods of preparation (Hastorf & DeNiro 1985). Presence of external charring may provide clues to those vessels used in cooking as compared to those used for storage.

Small grindstones are a ubiquitous feature of Kintampo complex sites. Although we are unable to identify the type of foodstuffs that may have been processed, their abundance in Kintampo complex sites probably signals increased involvement in plant food-processing. Elsewhere, I have suggested that more elaborate processing can lead to an increase in the nutritive value of foods and may provide an avenue for intensification of plant food exploitation (Stahl 1989).

Anquandah (Ch. 13, this volume) has outlined the evidence for more intensive settlement patterns associated with the Kintampo complex. A pattern of decreasing residential mobility is witnessed in the erection of relatively substantial structures clustered into small hamlets, and in increased accumulation of material goods such as ceramics. Decreasing residential mobility has important implications for exploitation of wild food resources. Foraging from a fixed base results in declining availability of resources which, under constant foraging pressure, are unable to regenerate (e.g. Bahuchet & Guillaume 1982; Hitchcock 1982; Vierich 1982; Hitchcock & Ebert 1984). It should be noted, however, that Kintampo peoples were not necessarily fully sedentary. Some sites appear to be the product of more ephemeral occupations (e.g. those in the Banda hills; Stahl 1986) and a degree of seasonal mobility cannot be ruled out (see also Holl 1985).

In contrast with earlier west African LSA sites, evidence of ornamentation and 'decorative' art is associated with the Kintampo complex. Large numbers of small shell beads are documented at Ntereso (Fig. 14.1; Davies 1980, p. 219) and K6 shelter (Stahl 1985a, p. 138). Small quantities of stone beads were recovered from Boyasi Hill (Anquandah 1976a). Polished stone 'bracelets' are considered a diagnostic feature of the Kintampo complex and occur at numerous sites. Clay figurines also appear for the first time in Kintampo contexts (e.g. Anquandah 1982a, pp. 60–2), although I am less optimistic than Anquandah (1982a, p. 62; Ch. 13, this volume) about our ability to identify the species represented. This increased investment in the production of ornamentation and figurines, involving in some instances use of exotic raw materials, may signal a qualitative change in social parameters (e.g. Bender 1981).

Another aspect of intensification that characterizes the shift from the Punpun to the Kintampo occupations is increased procurement of exotic materials. This is especially apparent in the materials used in production of polished stone implements. Suitable raw materials are lacking in many areas of Kintampo occupation. For example, at K6 shelter, the nearest source of the preferred greenstone was 70–80 km distant (Stahl 1985a), and it is not until the advent of the Kintampo complex that polished stone implements are in evidence. This is in contrast to sites where suitable raw materials are locally available and polished stone implements occur in early ceramic LSA contexts (e.g. Bosumpra: Shaw 1944). Similarly, increased use of non-local materials is expressed in increased use of mica inclusions in ceramics from the upper Kintampo complex levels of K6 shelter. Again, the closest source of mica is 70–80 km distant (Stahl 1985a). Whether this increased reliance on non-local raw material is a product of exchange or procurement expeditions is unclear. One line of evidence does, however, underscore the possibility that Kintampo peoples were linked in exchange networks. The recovery of two small marine shells at K6 (Flight 1976, p. 217; Stahl 1985a, p. 138) strengthens the likelihood that the numerous shell beads in Kintampo levels at K6 were manufactured from marine rather than terrestrial or freshwater shell, an interpretation that is consistent with the thickness of the beads (see Stahl 1985a, p. 138). Given the distance to the coast, it seems plausible that the occupants of the K6 site obtained shell through exchange.

Also suggestive of widespread communication networks amongst Kintampo peoples is the remarkable homogeneity of Kintampo ceramics from widespread areas. Not only is there homogeneity in decorative technique, but perhaps more importantly there exist close similarities in the zonation and placement of designs on vessels. Though detailed comparative study remains to be undertaken, examination of both published and unpublished collections indicates that the application of diagonal comb-impression in horizontal bands is a common feature of bowl forms at a number of sites, e.g. K6 (Stahl 1985a) (Fig. 14.4), Ntereso (Davies 1980), Bonoase (unpublished material). Pendant zones of comb-stamping are commonly placed between the neck and shoulders of jars (e.g. Davies 1980) (Figs 14.2, 14.3). Alternating triangular zones of comb-stamped and plain surfaces forming an interlocking pattern are a common feature on the body of both jars and bowls (e.g. Daboya: Shinnie & Kense 1989). Grooving or scoring often appears in a reticulate pattern on the necks of jars (e.g. Ntereso: Davies n.d.; K6: Stahl 1985a; Daboya: Shinnie & Kense 1989; Bonoase, unpublished material). Such similarities signal linkages of populations from as far north as Daboya, south to the Kumasi area, and possibly extending to the coast (see Anquandah, Ch. 13, this volume) (Fig. 14.1). It seems unlikely that this homogeneity is the result of trade in ceramics (e.g. Anquandah 1982a, pp. 61–2). The variations in paste exhibited between sites seems more consistent with local manufacture, homogeneity being the product of widespread communication of a common style.

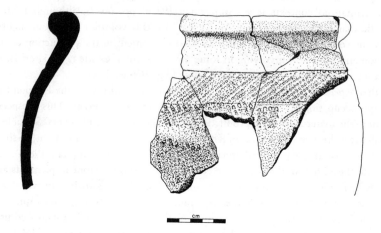

Figure 14.2   Unpublished reconstructed Kintampo jar, K6 rock shelter.

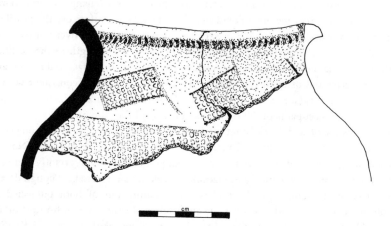

Figure 14.3   Unpublished K6 jar form.

Increasing reliance on exchange might be viewed as a natural outgrowth of decreasing residential mobility. What is striking in the case of the Kintampo complex, however, is that those goods which were probably obtained through exchange (e.g. mica, marine shell, metamorphic rock) are materials not utilized by peoples of the local preceding LSA. Thus, exchange was not simply a mechanism that a sedentary group substituted for mobility as a strategy for procuring required raw materials; rather, *new* demands for exotic raw materials characterized the Kintampo complex. These new demands signal qualitative changes in patterns of consumption, and very likely relate to changing patterns of group relations in comparison to the preceding LSA. At a somewhat earlier date, the upper levels of the Iwo Eleru sequence in Nigeria (Fig. 14.1) also attest to the import of raw materials used in the manufacture of ground stone implements (Shaw 1978, p. 47). This suggests that similar changes characterized other areas as well.

Thus, the Kintampo complex is characterized by intensification along a number of dimensions: subsistence, food-processing, settlement, communication networks, exchange and personal ornamentation and art. Until very recently, it appeared as a unique configuration in the prehistoric landscape of west and central Africa south of the Sahel. Recent research, however, suggests that comparable developments characterize other areas as well. Specifically, the work of de Maret at the site of Obobogo, near Yaounde, Cameroon (Fig. 14.1) has revealed evidence of extensive (2500 m²) village deposits associated with pits that overlie a generalized microlithic level. The later occupation is dated to the end of the second/beginning of the first millennium BC. Associated material culture included polished stone implements, grinding stones and grooved stones. Use of both *Elaeis* and *Canarium* is attested. Iron slag occurred in association in several pits (de Maret 1982a; de Maret 1982b, pp. 2–3; de Maret 1985, pp. 134–5). Subsequent investigations revealed similar sites in neighbouring areas (de Maret, Clist & Mbida 1983; in Gabon, see Clist 1989a). Though analysis of Obobogo and related material is ongoing, preliminary reports are highly suggestive of similar

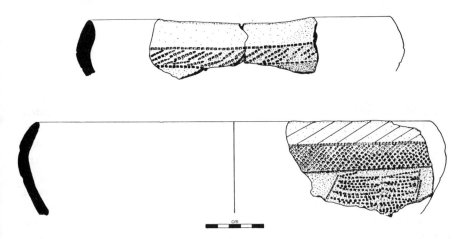

Figure 14.4   K6 bowl forms.

processes of intensification as expressed by the Kintampo complex, albeit at a slightly later period.

Further south along the forest/savanna margin in lower Zaïre, excavations have revealed a series of sites with polished stone implements and abundant ceramics including large vessels (de Maret 1986). Ngovo group sites include both rock shelters and open sites that are preferentially located on prominant points near water and wooded areas. The sites are dated in the range 395 BC–AD 230 and are associated with exploitation of *Canarium* and *Elaeis*. Although domestic fauna was not attested, the range of wild fauna at Ngovo group sites includes duikers, a large rodent, forest pig and the giant African snail. Thus, hunting and gathering remained important activities and, as de Maret (1986, p. 129) has stressed, although food production is a possibility, its economic importance and social consequences may have differed from other areas of west and central Africa.

Tantalizing hints of comparable developments come from the site of Dutsen Kongba near Jos in northern Nigeria (York 1974; York 1978). The main excavations (Site A) revealed evidence of a microlithic LSA which saw the addition of ceramics at a very early date (fourth millennium BC). Ceramics in the lower levels of the shelter occurred in small quantities and included sherds impressed with a triangular stylus (York 1978, pp. 150–1). Upper levels in the main shelter witnessed an increase in the quantities of ceramics, some of which are comb-stamped (York 1978, pp. 150–1). Of special interest were test excavations in a corridor leading off the main shelter (Site B). Here a hollow-based flaked arrow point found on the surface was analogous to those found at Ntereso, and excavations revealed ground stone implements and ceramics similar to those from upper levels at Site A. Although the excavated area was small, ceramics were recovered in abundance (York 1978, p. 162). Deposits at Site B were associated with a date in the mid-second millennium BC.

According to the limited data available LSA occupation in the far western extreme of west Africa (e.g. Atherton 1972) did not undergo the same processes of intensification as we have seen elsewhere. Nevertheless, here too, there is evidence for the addition of oil palm to the subsistence base (e.g. Gabel 1976).

The legacy

Rock shelters in the Kintampo area appear to have been abandoned some time before about 3000 BP. This has led some to suggest that the Kintampo occupation of central Ghana ended somewhat abruptly (e.g. Flight 1976, p. 220), and indeed, until recently, the ensuing period up to the earliest evidence of iron metallurgy in Ghana (early first millennium AD) appeared a virtual blank (e.g. Anquandah 1982a, pp. 67–8). Recent excavations at the site of Daboya on the White Volta appear to bridge this chronological gap (Shinnie & Kense 1989). Areas of the site along the river yielded roulette-decorated ceramics characterized by new vessel forms (Ware B) which are stratified above the characteristic comb-stamped Kintampo ceramics. The nature of the transition between these disparate ceramic traditions remains unclear, and dating in the relevant units is somewhat problematic (Kense 1983a; McIntosh & McIntosh 1986a, p. 423).

Nevertheless, Ware B ceramics are securely dated to the late first millennium BC with the possibility that they extend into the early first millennium BC. Kense (1983a, p. 10) interprets Ware B as representative of the 'Early Iron Age' although published reports give no indication of the economic basis of the 'Ware B' occupation. Kense points to similarities of Daboya Ware B to ceramics from intrusive, later levels at Ntereso (Davies 1980, pp. 222–3) which may be associated with a radiocarbon date of 1890 ± 110 bp (SR-90; Davies 1980, p. 221).

The limited evidence thus suggests that the gap between the end of the Kintampo complex and the advent of the Iron Age reflects the inadequacy of our database rather than a hiatus in occupation. Nevertheless, several patterns of possible significance emerge from a consideration of continuities and discontinuities in site use. For example, the long-standing pattern of occupation associated with rock shelters apparently ceased with the passing of the Kintampo complex. Of the Kintampo shelters, only K1 yielded evidence of significant use after the Kintampo complex, and only then as a special-purpose site – a 'quern factory' (Rahtz & Flight 1974). A middle level of the post-Kintampo occupation yielded a single date of 57 ± 68 bc (Birm 28: Rahtz & Flight 1974, p. 8). This pattern of rock shelter abandonment need not imply an abandonment of the area; rather, it may signal changing priorities of site placement. The inselbergs of the Kumasi area also appear to have been abandoned, suggesting that the factors that made them attractive to Kintampo peoples ceased to be of importance. By virtue of their geological characteristics, these inselbergs are characterized by thin soil cover that probably accounts for the associated savanna cover in an otherwise forested area (see Newton & Woodell 1976; Newton 1980). Erosional rather than depositional processes have dominated these upland sites, processes which contribute to the visibility of the Kintampo complex sites. The apparent lack of 'post-Kintampo' settlements could then be a product of people moving, for whatever reason, into lower lying areas where deposition rather than erosion was the predominant geomorphic process. Simply stated, post-Kintampo sites may be deeply buried.

Sites for which we have hints of a continued post-Kintampo occupation (e.g. Daboya, Ntereso) point to the continuing draw of major rivers as a magnet for settlement. This may reflect the attraction of fishing, water, ease of transport or, at Daboya, salt (Kense 1983b, p. 10). Again, depositional factors may lead to poor visibility of sites on the alluvium; it is significant that both the Kintampo and post-Kintampo occupations at Daboya were deeply buried (Shinnie & Kense 1989).

Finally, we must consider the extent to which settlements not focused on specific, localized resources will be visible. The shifting villages of extensive farmers living in small groups are likely to be difficult to detect, especially if they are located in topographic contexts where they were likely to become buried. This is in contrast with the focal, continuous occupation that might characterize sites associated with special-ized or spatially restricted resources such as salt (Daboya), or special soils capable of supporting more intensive cultivation (e.g. *firki* near Lake Chad: Connah 1985). Thus, we may obtain a skewed image of the overall settlement patterning if we generalize on the basis of the few known first millennium BC sites.

Concluding comments: intensification in the west African Late Stone Age

Available evidence suggests that a series of related changes characterized the ceramic LSA occupations of west and west-central Africa from the beginning of the second millennium bc. These linked changes included: decreasing residential mobility; probable involvement in exchange networks; increased accumulation of material culture; increased investment in food-processing; and a series of subsistence changes that, in some cases, included a degree of food production. This chapter has focused on the evidence from central Ghana, but similar changes appear to have taken place in west-central Africa (e.g. Obobogo, Ngovo) and along the margins of the Sahel (e.g. Daima: Connah 1981) and the Sahara (Tichitt: Munson 1976; Holl 1985). A number of authors have attempted to place these changes within a larger west African context, and have singled out food production as the primary factor to be explained from among the many interrelated changes that occurred (e.g. Clark 1976; Shaw 1977; Smith 1980b). Almost inevitably, this has led to formulations with a northern bias that see the adoption of food production in sub-sahelian west Africa linked to events in the Sahara and Sahel (Stahl 1984). North–south connections, and consequently similarities between Saharan/Sahelian and savanna/forest expressions of the ceramic LSA, are stressed (Clark 1976; Shaw 1977; Smith 1980b).

While I do not deny that such connections existed, they have been overstressed and have blinded us to other possibilities (Stahl 1985a; Stahl 1986). A theme that suggests itself from the material reviewed here is an east–west patterning of the terminal ceramic LSA in several broad zones which correspond roughly with Shaw's classsification of earlier ceramic LSA sites reviewed above. Especially significant is the emerging pattern of intensification at ceramic LSA sites in a broad arc that follows the contemporary forest/savanna margin, extending roughly from the eastern Ivory Coast (e.g. the Kintampo complex site of Dabakala: Chenorkian 1983), through Nigeria (e.g. Dutsen Kongba) and Cameroon (Obobogo), as well as on the southern margin of the forest and savanna in lower Zaïre (Ngovo group; see Fig. 14.1). Although the database is frustratingly limited, common themes along this arc appear to be: patterns of decreasing residential mobility; increasing reliance on ceramics; and, in contrast to sites further north, a subsistence economy characterized by continued reliance on hunting and gathering, perhaps supplemented by arboriculture (e.g. exploitation of oleaginous species), horticulture and probably limited reliance on domestic animals (sheep/goat). This pattern contrasts with what is known of the subsistence base of sites in the Sahara/Sahel margins, where investment in food production during the last two millennia BC appears to have been greater (e.g. Karkarichinkat: Smith 1974; Smith 1975a; Daima I: Connah 1981, pp. 137–9; Tichitt: Munson 1976; Holl 1985). Thus, as during Shaw's Phase II, the few known sites in the broad arc following the Sahara margin and Sahel may share more features with each other than they do with sites further south. Conversely, the coastal facies of Shaw's Phase II (e.g. Ivorian shell middens, Fig. 14.1) exhibits greater continuity during the final two millennia BC. Here, successive technological changes (e.g. addition of ceramics, iron) appear to have had little impact on the subsistence base of the populations exploiting coastal lagoons (Chenorkian 1983).

Thus, I suggest that qualitative economic differences distinguish the terminal ceramic LSA occupations in these three broad arcs or geographical regions. It would appear that, whatever the underlying processes that promoted intensification in disparate areas of west and central Africa during the last millennia bc, the 'response' was a local one and the timing of resultant changes varied from area to area. Whereas the advent of food production has been stressed as the most important change at northern sites (e.g. Smith 1980b), evidence from more southerly latitudes suggests that food production is not necessarily the key to understanding the qualitative shifts that took place during the terminal LSA. We must not overlook the multivariate nature of change (Stahl 1986), nor forget that the range of changes witnessed during the terminal LSA may have had more to do with social parameters (e.g. Bender 1981) than with the ecological or demographic variables that have loomed so large in past discussions.

Acknowledgements

Thanks are extended to Thurstan Shaw, who encouraged me to participate in one of the sessions from which this book originates. His helpful suggestions regarding the direction of this chapter were particularly appreciated. The ideas expressed benefited from conversations with Paul Richards and Peter Stahl, and from participation in several seminars at University College London and Cambridge University during the period 1985–7.

15 Agriculture and settlement among the Tiv of Nigeria: some ethnoarchaeological observations

C. A. FOLORUNSO
& S. O. OGUNDELE

In the late 1970s and early 1980s a number of ethnoarchaeological studies were conducted in the area south of the river Benue in Nigeria inhabited by the Tiv (Fig. 15.1). The prime objectives of this Bantu 'Homeland' Project, as it was called, were to

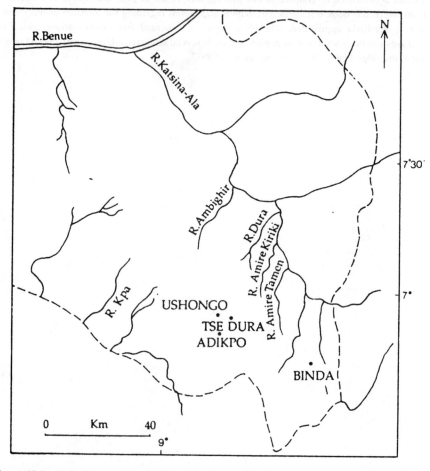

Figure 15.1 Main sites mentioned in the text (after Andah 1983, Fig. 1).

trace the character of settlement, land use patterns, technological and social developments 'and to use such data to test closely various hypotheses derived mainly from linguistic evidence regarding the earliest decipherable phases of "Bantu" cultural history' (Andah 1983, p. 23). A report on excavations in two rock shelters at Tse Dura carried out as part of this project has already been published (Andah 1983, pp. 33–60).

An understanding of the subsistence practices pursued in the area over the last three thousand years was a desired goal of the research project, but in the absence of any noticeable patterns of field boundaries or terracing and in the face of the difficulty of obtaining data on early subsistence from excavation, ethnographic data were collected about cultivated plants, agricultural practices and food-processing methods. Similarly, ethnographic data were collected about settlement patterns, with a view to having a basis from which to assess the potential and the limitations of such data in interpreting archaeological findings (Allan 1972; Cranstone 1972).

The study area

The study area is located in the Katsina-Ala valley, in the southeastern part of Tiv-land in central Nigeria (Fig. 15.1). The Tiv are the largest ethnic group in Benue State, covering an area stretching from approximately 6°30' to 8°00'N and from 8°00' to 10°00'E. The study area is situated approximately between latitudes 6°45' and 7°00'N and between longitudes 8°40' and 9°50'E. The climate is tropical, having a wet season from May to October and a dry season from November to April. From December to February a dry northeast wind, known as the 'harmattan', blows off the Sahara, causing a marked drop in humidity. The vegetation is principally Guinea savanna grassland consisting of tall grasses interspersed with trees of moderate height. The vegetation is thick during the wet season and becomes parched and sparse during the dry. The soils are generally characteristic of tropical ferruginous types derived from crystalline rocks with an appreciable quantity of ferromagnesium minerals. The area is well watered by rivers and streams such as the Amire Tamen, Amire Kiriki, Ambighir, Dura and Kpa, all tributaries of the Katsina-Ala, itself a major tributary of the Benue. These rivers and streams are usually flooded during the rainy season and inundate wide stretches along their banks. Gallery forests and thick vegetation line these rivers (Fig. 15.1). The area possesses several archaeological sites, consisting of rock shelters and open settlement sites on hilltops, but no signs of field systems or terracing.

Cultivated plants

The Tiv (Abraham 1933; Bohannan & Bohannan 1953; Bohannan 1954a) are principally subsistence farmers whose staple crops are yams (*Dioscorea* spp.), bulrush millet (*Pennisetum* sp.) and guinea corn (*Sorghum* sp.). The Benue valley area allows participation in both the grain-based economies to the north and the yam-based economies of the regions to the south. This fortunate ecological position permits year-round farming activity. Yams are harvested in July or August; guinea corn ripens in May or June.

Yams are the basic and the most highly prized crop in Tiv-land. They start the rotation cycle of the farming year and are the crop planted when fallow is broken. They form a major part of Tiv diet, and an outside observer might think that the Tiv eat only pounded yam. Indeed, it is not unusual to see yam being pounded in the early morning for breakfast.

Sweet potatoes, cocoyams, maize, cassava and groundnuts – all crops introduced from outside Africa in the sixteenth century or later, with the possible exception of one sort of cocoyam and one sort of groundnut – are considered as mere substitutes for the main staples, and are planted on lands lying fallow from other crops. Locust-bean trees (*Parkia* sp.) are valued for their produce and are owned by the person on whose fallow land they occur. Peppers and beniseed (*Sesamum indicum*, probably introduced) are grown, and vegetables and condiments include leaf greens of many kinds and beans of several varieties. Other introduced crops are the citrus fruits, guava, tomatoes and onions.

Agricultural practice

The choice of land for farming is normally determined by its closeness to the compound, allowing easy accessibility, yet far enough away not to be menaced by goats. The compounds are part and parcel of farms, surrounded by kitchen gardens where a large proportion of the vegetables are grown, including garden eggs, as well as tobacco and cotton, mostly for local use. A minimal amount of livestock is kept in the compounds. Most kitchen gardens adjoin orchards where oranges, grapefruit and guava are grown. Immediately beyond the orchards are the farmlands.

Although it can be said in general that the Tiv live on their farms, people in need of additional farming land may move away from their compounds. In such cases, they have camps on the farm where they stay for the period that they want to work, and return to their compounds after a few days. Usually people go to their collateral kinsmen to seek such additional farming land, and they are provided with one or two rooms in the compounds of their hosts, which they use while visiting their farms.

Both men and women clear the land, but men do the hoeing of mounds and ridges, as well as preparing the land for planting, while women do the planting and weeding. Women harvest yams and other root and vegetable crops, but both sexes perform complementary tasks in the harvesting of grain crops. Both see themselves first and foremost as farmers, and any other craft they practise is carried out after they leave the farm. It has been estimated that only about 40 per cent of farming labour is contributed by men (Briggs 1941).

Every married woman in Tiv-land has a right to own a farm sufficient to cater for the needs of herself and her dependants. It is obligatory for her husband to provide such a farm and to perform, or oversee, the heavy work on it. Farm produce is kept in granaries or store-huts which are the exclusive reserve of the women. Women therefore play an important role in subsistence activities in Tiv-land.

The farming year

The bush is cleared for a new planting season around mid-August. The clearing of the land and the making of mounds go hand in hand. On the day clearing starts, the compounds are left virtually empty as all hands are put to work. Women take food to cook on site, while children of working age join in the clearing. Children under working age and babies are all taken to the clearing site where they play or are nursed. When the land is being cleared, the scene is one of much noise and singing.

Tiv men and women do most of the rest of the farm work separately and alone, but sometimes they work in groups, particularly for the really hard work of mounding yam fields. The men who habitually work together are usually from the same compound, often full brothers or half-brothers. Men may also call in outside help. Younger men call on their age-sets and in return give them food and locally brewed beer. The older men ask a younger age-set, to whom they are the patron or adviser, to work for them. They may also ask a friend to bring his kinsmen to work for them and the work normally ends with feasting.

When land is first cleared, it is planted with yams, so the hoeing of yam mounds therefore follows the clearing of the land. These mounds are laid out in rows, starting from the centre row, which is also the biggest. When the mounds have been finished, dried grass and leaves, left on the field after clearing, are gathered into small bundles and set on top of the mounds, weighted down with clods of soil. This is said to be both to prevent erosion and the crumbling of the mound, and to afford protection from the sun for the sprouting yam during its first few days above the surface. Soon after the mounds are finished, a piece of freshly cut cassava stalk is inserted low in the side of the mound. Planted several weeks or months before the yams, the cassava is given a chance to grow high enough to provide a trellis for the yam vine to climb.

The clearing of the grass usually lasts until the end of November, while the digging of the mounds, which takes longer, is preferably done before the dry season sets in and the ground becomes too hard to dig easily. However, many people do not finish digging their mounds until well into the new rainy season, sometimes the middle of May, though early planting produces better crops.

The planting of seed yams begins in February, as the best and biggest yams are those which are planted then, and continues well into the rainy season. The seed yams are sometimes stored in huts in the compound or in trenches or in the old mounds of the previous year's field. They are taken to the new field by women, who sort them by types and lay them out, one seed yam on top of each mound. They are planted by both men and women, the men using a heavy hoe and the women a digging stick. The grass cap is first removed, and the hoe is used to slice a sizeable portion off the top of the mound, leaving a place where the yam is to be inserted. The sliced-off soil is then allowed to fall back gently. The digging stick is held in both hands, and with a sharp downward stroke, the stick is forced into the top of the mound. By twisting and working it about, a hole is created into which the yam is inserted. The top is then closed over by hand. In all cases, the grass cap is replaced on the mounds and again weighted with soil. During the month of May when the rainy season is well under way, yams that have not sprouted are removed from the mounds and replaced by others. The planting completes the men's work; the subsequent weeding, done with a small hoe by women, sometimes lasts into the dry season. Yam fields are also used to grow cassava, groundnuts, beans, pepper, corn and cotton. Most of these are planted by women during and after the first weeding, usually low in the sides of the mounds. Only women plant and harvest these crops.

The first yams are harvested in early July while the general harvest takes place in late December and in January at the height of the dry season, after the guinea-corn harvest is finished. Most of the harvesting is done by young women with digging sticks. The stick is driven into the top of the dry mound, then with a forward movement one whole side of the mound is peeled off, leaving the yam exposed on one side. The dry soil can be loosened round the yam and the yam is lifted out undamaged. The yams are gathered and then sorted into their different types, particularly into eating yams and seed yams. After this careful sorting, the yams are cached about the field in trenches, covered with a matting of dried grass. Seed yams are either carried to the compound or to the new field.

As soon as the harvesting of yams and cassava is over, the land on which they grew becomes a second-year field. In March/April, usually after the harmattan has stopped, but before the rains, what remains of the old mounds is levelled by the men. Then, after the first big rain, bulrush millet is planted by scattering the seed on the ground, which is then turned and worked quickly to bury the seed. This is mainly men's work but women may assist. Millet is considered a delicacy; it must be planted following a soaking rain, ideally followed by four to five days of cloudy weather but no rain. A successful planting is usually considered a matter of luck.

The most common crop interplanted with millet is guinea corn, planted about four weeks after the millet. Cassava is also found growing in the field before millet is planted. Millet is harvested about eight to ten weeks after planting, usually in June. The men break down the stalks and cut the base with machetes and lay the stalks in rows for the women to cut off the heads and tie them into bundles for carrying back to the compound. Millet is valued for the quality of local beer produced from it. It is used for meal, particularly during the period when guinea corn is exhausted and before new yam is dug. Guinea corn is harvested in the same way as millet and harvesting occurs after the first harmattan.

In a three-year rotation, after two years of cropping, a piece of farmland is usually allowed to lie fallow, although certain crops may be grown on it. Beniseed may be planted in April and harvested in June, and sweet potatoes, groundnuts and cassava may also be grown.

Women usually do the clearing of fallow for these fallow crops. When fallow land is cleared for planting, fallow crops, grass and small stems are allowed to dry and are burned. The ashes are mixed with the soil when mounds or ridges are made. The time for recultivation of a piece of fallow is determined by the type of grass which it produces. The fallow land is expected to grow sword grass. Year after year the sword grass reduces in volume and is replaced by more luxuriant grasses until it disappears from the land. Thus the land is ready to be farmed again when the sword grass has disappeared.

Crop processing

The harvested crops are brought to the compound for processing, since the farm is always in the vicinity of the compound. Each family in a compound has its own granaries or, more commonly today, store-huts located at the periphery of the circle of living houses. Food-processing is carried out in the communal shelter, which is usually located at the centre of the circle of living houses in the central open space, as well as under the trees found immediately outside the compounds. Women peel the skin off cassava and soak it in water for some days to detoxify it in preparation for making it into the granular form known as 'gari', which is a staple food. Women process locust-bean seeds, thoroughly washing them in perforated pots called *buufu* (also used for roasting meat). Women also do the processing of millet and guinea corn.

How long have the Tiv been in this area?

Four decades of observation of Tiv agricultural technology and techniques have shown little variation or change (Bohannan 1954b). The crops cultivated and the methods of cultivation reflect an intimate understanding of the environment. Tiv farming traditions no doubt have a long history, although changes must have taken place with the adoption of crops introduced from Asia (e.g. the citrus fruits) and the New World (e.g. cassava and maize). The question is, how long have the Tiv been in this region? Oral traditions claim that the Tiv moved from the southeast. This would imply that the present study area would have been the area first settled by Tiv. There is no sure way of dating this tradition but the fourteenth or fifteenth centuries AD can be inferred from the Bohannans' assertion (Bohannan & Bohannan 1958, p. 4) that the Tiv had been in the area long before they became engaged in wars with their neighbours at least three hundred years ago; and from the genealogical charts of Abraham (1933).

Radiocarbon dates from one of the settlement sites associated with Tiv fall within this period (Folorunso 1989a). Excavations were carried out in two rock shelters at Tse Dura, which yielded three occupation phases (Andah 1983; Folorunso 1983a). The earliest contained stone chopping tools and a small number of sherds of pottery; these were decorated with incised grooving and punctation, together with the use of string roulettes. Then there was a break in occupation. The second occupation phase yielded iron slag, 'neolithic'-type artefacts and pottery predominantly decorated with mat impressions. The latest phase in the rock shelters was restricted to the topsoil and belongs to the historic period, as it contained clay smoking pipes; pottery with mat-impression decoration still predominated, however (Folorunso 1989c). Radiocarbon dates suggest that the second, iron-using, occupation began about the third century BC and that it ended towards the end of the first millennium AD (Calvocoressi & David 1979, p. 26).

In the study area, ancient hilltop settlements – with circular-based houses and granaries resembling present-day Tiv compounds – can be identified in many places. Excavation at one such site on Ushongo hill yielded pottery predominantly decorated with the impressed mat patterns, and two radiocarbon dates placing it somewhere in the fifteenth century AD (Folorunso 1983b; Folorunso 1989a).

The archaeological and ethnographic data suggest that these open hilltop settlements were occupied by Tiv (Bohannan 1954a). The question still remains, however, as to when the Tiv first settled in the Benue valley. Who were the people who inhabited the rock shelters? The only links between the rock shelters and the present day are the pottery types and their decoration. Such parallels are between the present-day Tiv and the iron-using people of the second phase of occupation in the rock shelters spanning the period from the later part of the first millennium BC to the end of the first millennium AD. The fact that mat-impression decoration on pottery is the most popular among Tiv potters today is not sufficient evidence by itself to say that it was the Tiv who were responsible for the second phase of occupation in the rock shelters.

Settlement study

Studies of human settlement in different parts of the world have become increasingly sophisticated both in practice and in terms of their theoretical framework (Udo 1966; Udo 1982, pp. 10–50). Udo (1966, pp. 130–6; Udo 1982, pp. 12–48) has observed that settlement is a concrete expression of the workings of a society and economy over time in a single place. The forms of settlement express the ideas, attitudes and feelings of the occupants both past and present. Human geographers treat spatial arrangements of societies in terms of local situations, in conjunction with the variables of climate, vegetation and resources. Historical geographers, as well as demographers and archae-ologists, study settlements of different time periods within a given space and for different spaces or locations. As a result of the added dimension of time, most scholars have become increasingly aware of the complex nature of human settlements and the corresponding need to depend to some extent on larger-scale models (e.g. locational and central place models developed from such disciplines as mathematics and anthro-pology) (Hodder & Orton 1976, pp. 15–49).

Ethnographic observation can map present-day settlement units and record the economic, social and political organization of the living community. From such studies we can learn a great deal about the internal organization of a settlement: how the people arrange themselves on the ground, as well as how they make, use and dispose of some of their materials – from pottery to houses. We have therefore mapped and studied the present-day compounds of Sar, Ayela and Tse-Dura, all located in the Tse-Dura area (as well as the Tse-Dura archaeological settlement site), and Wombo, Tse-Gbashanam, Lukposo, Adzeger and Alumuku, all located in the plain around the Binda hills (Figs 15.2–15.6). An additional reason for conducting a modern settlement study here is that oral traditions suggest that the present-day settlements are directly related to the former settlements on hilltops and slopes, now archaeological sites (Bohannan 1954a). Consequently, this ethnographic approach has been used to assist in the interpretation of the archaeological sites (Folorunso 1989b).

Some observed regularities in spatial arrangement

Following detailed examination (Appendix) of settlement units in the study area, some regularities in spatial arrangement were observed. The houses are circular in shape, with the exception of one or two rectangular houses in a very few of the compounds. Each compound has a central shelter, with a roof set on strong wooden posts, usually open-sided but in two cases with low walls. In two compounds, mango trees replace the central shelter. These communal shelters are usually larger than the living houses and are at least 3 m away from them. The doors of the houses face the central shelter, whereas the newly constructed living houses are often located further away from them. Most of the cooking structures are located outside the living houses, in front of the doors. Women may decide to turn a living house into a kitchen. A few houses serve both for sleeping and for cooking. Similarly a former drying rack might be turned into a kitchen. Bathrooms are usually situated at the edge of each settlement unit, with an average diameter of 2 m.

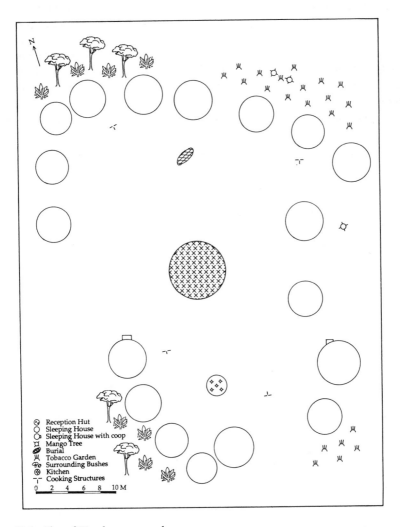

Figure 15.2   Plan of Wombo compound.

The Tiv use a raised platform when constructing their houses, and the clay floors are normally beaten hard before occupation. During the period of occupation, living floors may be refilled with clay, especially when depressions have been created in them as a result of intensive use. A bed constructed from raffia-palm trunks is always located at the left-hand side of the entrance to each house. This is to ensure privacy even when the door of the house is open. Abandoned houses gradually disintegrate through time. The mud bricks of which the walls are constructed start falling down once the houses have been abandoned. In this way the walls are in time reduced to the foundations, while the mud bricks litter the surroundings.

Social organization

A compound or settlement unit can be established either by a single male and his immediate family or by a group of people forming an extended patrilineal polygynous family. This arrangement usually consists of one or two elders, their wives, the children – unmarried adult daughters and the adult sons together with their wives and children. Thus a settlement unit can be made up of as few as two or three houses at the initial stage; and the number of houses may gradually increase to between ten and twenty.

A compound is called by the name of the founder who is, apparently, the head. The

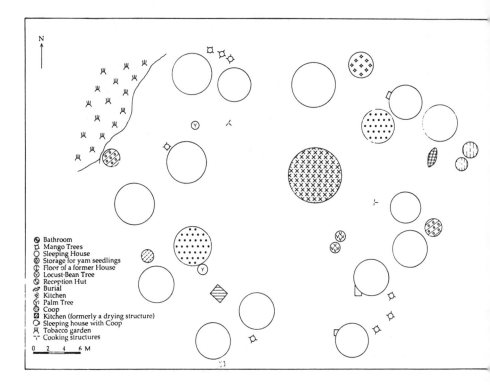

Figure 15.3 Plan of Tse-Gbashanam compound.

Tiv social and political structure is hierarchical; the compound head is usually granted some degree of authority within a given settlement, presides over meetings and also controls most, if not all, the magical forces (Bohannan 1954b, pp. 1–14; Downes 1971, pp. 15–32; M. Nagu, *pers. comm.* 1987). Above him is the clan head and finally the *Tor* Tiv. The *Tor* Tiv is the supreme chief of the Tiv people and the symbol of their aspirations and world-views. In the compound, however, the head plays the role of a father to all members of his compound. All the wives in the compound usually give some food to him, and the children as well as other members of the settlement unit are free to partake of it. When a compound head dies, the next oldest male member of the compound takes over the leadership of the settlement.

Each central shelter of a compound serves, among other things, as a meeting place for recreation, to settle disputes and to eat and drink. Representatives from neighbouring settlements hold meetings in a chosen compound to discuss such issues as the construction of community roads, bridges, churches and market squares. In fact, the central shelter is one of the major activity areas in any given settlement unit. It also

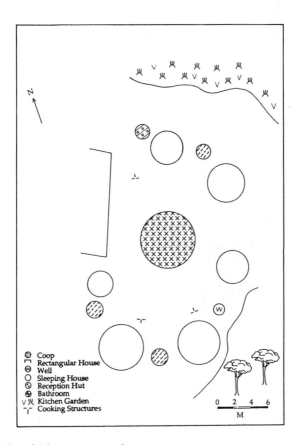

Figure 15.4   Plan of Adzeger compound.

serves as an effective information centre at both the intra- and inter-compound levels. In some compounds, the shade of mango trees may serve as the central meeting place. Bigger meetings involving the entire clan (made up of many neighbouring compounds) are presided over by the clan head (*Tor*).

Members of a settlement unit usually carry out such activities as cloth-weaving, mat-weaving, wood-carving, basket-making and pottery-making in the large open space within the settlement. At times, a bachelor may have his own separate house while the unmarried female children can be living together. However, this arrangement may change if and when need arises. Thus, for example, a bachelor may later be living with some younger male children in the same house, while in a similar way, a wife's house may be changed to a children's house. In sum, the functions of living houses cannot be neatly compartmentalized. One of the reasons for having the central shelter is to enable the compound head to keep watch over the other members of the settlement during the

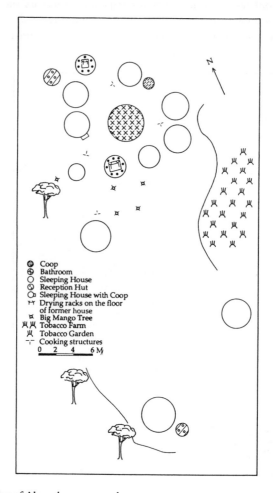

Figure 15.5   Plan of Alumuku compound.

daytime, and, occasionally, at night. The older houses in a settlement are nearer the central shelter than the newer ones.

Implications for archaeological reconstruction

The concept of circular construction observed among the present-day Tiv in making their houses and laying out compounds may still be recognized in the archaeological settlement sites investigated (Tse-Dura Fig. 15.6 and Binda). The houses in these archaeological sites were circular in shape, and some clusters were identified. These clusters appear to be the equivalent of the present-day settlements.

Each one of the present-day clusters contains two to twelve houses. These modern settlement units or compounds are smaller in size than the settlements in the archaeological sites (usually located on hilltops and slopes). Thus, Alumuku, Adzeger and Lukposo, near the foot of the Binda hills and on relatively higher ground, have smaller houses and the settlements are more compact than on the archaeological sites. The Wombo and Tse-Gbashanam present-day compounds, located on lower ground, are larger.

It is probable that several groups of Tiv, belonging to different extended patrilineal polygynous families, were living together on habitable hilltops and slopes in ancient times. These groups appear to have tried to maintain their different identities, as shown by the various clusters in each archaeological settlement. As a result of this development, later houses tended to be smaller in size, so that the hilltops and slope could accommodate several different families belonging to some particular major lineages. This is a nucleated mode of settlement as opposed to the present-day dispersed

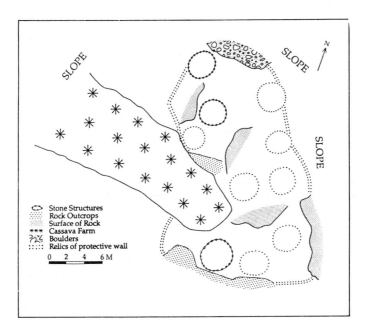

Figure 15.6   Plan of Tse-Dura open settlement site.

settlement system. The different settlement patterns through time in this study area are forms of adaptation to changing social, political and ecological challenges (Ogundele 1989).

The nature of settlements at the time the ancient Tiv descended from the various hilltops and slopes is yet to be properly understood. We still have gaps in the evolutionary history of Tiv settlement. Sites that could throw light on this aspect of settlement history have either been destroyed by farming activities or by the resettlement of subsequent generations.

It is difficult to know the exact range of functions of houses in an archaeological context because of the problem of reuse, as revealed by our ethnographic findings. For example, a living house might later be changed into a kitchen. Similarly, a bachelor's house may be turned into a storage room as need arises. At times, a house may serve as a kitchen and sleeping apartment simultaneously. Archaeologists using ethnographic information to throw light on archaeological settlement in an area have the advantage of avoiding the mistake of automatically assuming that structures and other material artefacts always had the same unchanging function.

Appendix: spatial arrangement of settlement features

Ayela, Sar and Tse-Dura

Ayela, Sar and Tse-Dura, present-day compounds located about 1 km east of the Adikpo–Ushongo road, were mapped. They were all oval in shape, with lengths ranging from 45 to 50 m, while the average width was 38 m.

There were two rectangular houses (non-traditional) in each of these settlements, while the remaining round houses were constructed of sun-dried mud bricks.

During the investigations, three house sizes were identified, as follows: (i) small houses ranging between 4 and 5 m in diameter; (ii) medium-sized, ranging between 6 and 7 m in diameter; (iii) large (central meeting places) ranging between 7.5 and 9.5 m in diameter. Medium-sized houses were most frequent.

At Ayela the foundations of a new house were observed to the south-southwest of the compound, while at Sar three new houses were identified. One was located to the north, while the remaining two were at the western and southeastern corners of the settlement respectively.

At Ayela there was one abandoned house located to the south-southwest, while at Sar two were identified and mapped; the latter were situated in the northeastern quarter of the compound. One abandoned house was also identified at Tse-Dura, located to the northwest of the settlement.

Only Sar had a central shelter, with a diameter of 8.6 m. At Ayela and Tse-Dura the central meeting places were represented by a mango tree.

Both Ayela and Sar had three cooking structures (an arrangement of three stones) while Tse-Dura had two. The average distance of each of them to the nearest living house was 2 m. These cooking structures were usually located in front of the doors of the houses.

Sar compound had two drying racks, roughly 2 m square, and Tse-Dura one.

Both settlements had orange orchards and kitchen gardens. The ones at Ayela were located at the southern end of the settlement, while at Sar they were to the northwest and south of the settlement respectively. Similarly, at Tse-Dura the orange and mango orchards and kitchen gardens were located to the east and south-southeast of the settlement.

Hen-coops were attached to three of the houses in Ayela and Sar compounds, while two separate coops were identified at Tse-Dura. One was located to the east and the other to the west of the settlement. Houses were located at least 1 m away from each other.

Two circular bathrooms were found in each of these compounds, their sizes ranging between 2 and 2.5 m in diameter. They were situated on the circumference of the three compounds. There was one water well each at Ayela and Tse-Dura, about 1.5 m in diameter. The nearest house to each of these wells was about 2 m away.

Two burials were identified at Sar compound; one was located to the north, while the other was to the northeast of the settlement. Each of them was at least 2 m away from the nearest living house.

Wombo, Tse-Gbashanam, Lukposo, Adzeger and Alumuku

Wombo (Fig. 15.2), Tse-Gbashanam (Fig. 15.3), Lukposo, Adzeger (Fig. 15.4) and Alumuku (Fig. 15.5) compounds, all located in the plains and within the Njorov sub-clan area, grade from circular to oval shapes. The length of these present-day settlements ranges from 36 to 72 m.

They all consist of circular houses, with the exception of Lukposo and Adzeger, each of which has one rectangular house. The houses were constructed of sun-dried mud bricks, except for one at Tse-Gbashanam which had been constructed of mud by the coiling method.

The houses were located at least 1 m away from one another. At Alumuku, Adzeger and Lukposo (on the higher ground near the foot of the Binda hill complex) houses were generally smaller and the settlements more compact than at Wombo and Tse-Gbashanam, located on lower ground and further away from the Binda hills. These settlements were larger, with lengths ranging between 56 and 70 m, while the average width was 53 m. The houses were also bigger: at Tse-Gbashanam, the majority of houses were medium-sized, with the central shelters the largest.

In all these settlements the single door of each house directly faced the central shelter. The distance of the nearest house to the central shelter ranged between 3 and 11 m.

Both Alumuku and Tse-Gbashanam had two abandoned houses. At Lukposo, the foundation of a new house was identified and mapped.

Cooking structures were identified in all the five present-day compounds investigated in the Binda area, Alumuku and Wombo with four each, Adzeger three and Lukposo and Tse-Gbashanam two each. The average distance of the cooking structures from the nearest living house was 2 m. In addition, Tse-Gbashanam and Wombo each had one house that was being used as a kitchen.

At Alumuku, two drying racks located inside the floor area of two former houses were mapped. One was to the north-northwest, while the other was to the west of the settlement. On the other hand, the only drying rack at Tse-Gbashanam had been turned into a kitchen.

Two storage structures for yam seedlings were situated about 3.5 m from the burial and 3 m away from the nearest living house. All the settlements have kitchen gardens located on their peripheries.

There were nine mango trees at Tse-Gbashanam; Alumuku and Wombo had five and three respectively. Adzeger and Lukposo did not have mango trees at all. Tse-Gbashanam also had two big locust-bean trees and two palm trees located within the settlement.

All the settlements (with the exception of Adzeger) had hen-coops attached to some of the circular houses in addition to separate coops. Adzeger compound had only separate coops, three in number. The separate coops are circular in shape with an average diameter of 2 m, while the ones attached to houses are rectangular in shape.

Lukposo and Adzeger had one bathroom per compound, while Alumuku and Tse-Gbashanam had two each. These bathrooms averaged 2 m in diameter, and they were situated on the circumference of the settlement. They are usually circular in shape, constructed of sticks or pieces of wood, with matting wound round to make the 'walls'. Each bathroom has a boulder at the centre, on which people squat or stand when taking their baths.

At Wombo a burial was located in the north-northeast quarter of the compound. This was approximately 22 m away from the central shelter and about 3 m from the nearest living house. A burial was also located to the northeast of Tse-Gbashanam compound. This burial was about 1 m from the nearest living house and 15 m from the central shelter.

16 Central Africa and the archaeology of the equatorial rainforest: reflections on some major topics

Manfred K. H. Eggert

Bringing central African archaeology into focus

In the last four decades the archaeology of Africa has seen a development which would have been unimaginable to even the most optimistic mind fifty years ago. From a concentration on some quite limited areas, fieldwork has gradually been expanded to cover the whole of the continent. From a strong topical and/or temporal bias resulting in a predominantly selective approach to the remains of the past, e.g. early man and rock art, interest and, consequently, field activities have been expanded to include all aspects and facets of the many-sided phenomena of the human past in Africa. An ever-increasing number of newsletters, journals and conferences as well as an unprecedented output of scholarly and popular articles and books devoted uniquely to African archaeology are ample proof of this – as is the publication of this *One World Archaeology* book.

We are supposed to be ready, then, to tackle the intricate questions of cultural development in Africa instead of concentrating on the more immediate and mundane aspects of archaeological endeavour. This may well be so but some necessary qualifications need to be made. In spite of the immense progress of African archaeology there are still many regions, and quite a few of them exceedingly large, in which archaeological research has only very recently begun, or which are still virtually unexplored. It is with these regions in mind that we may question our readiness to address the complex issues of major transitions in the realm of cultural evolution.

One of those less fortunate regions is central Africa, in some parts of which archaeological research is not much older than about two decades – in most others it is, in fact, much more recent. A case in point is the territory of Gabon, where systematic archaeology started with the establishment of an archaeology department at the Centre International des Civilisations Bantu under the direction of Bernard Clist in 1981/2. Although the results achieved in the short span since the department's inception are very impressive indeed (Clist 1989a), our knowledge of the country's prehistory is of course still very fragmented. It simply seems premature to offer anything but some broadly informed guesses on the basic culture-historical problems associated with the archaeological remains of this west-central African state. What we need here, as in central Africa generally, are not models integrating diverse data into a supposedly coherent pattern of potential evolution but the data themselves – more first-class field data to be used effectively in more or less intricate schemes of regional and inter-regional integration.

Having hinted that the whole of central Africa is among the late-comers to the continent's archaeological progress, we now turn to our immediate concern. What is proposed here does not pretend to cover central Africa in the modern sense of the territories of what is now the Cameroon, Gabon, Central African Republic, southern Sudan, Zaïre, northern Angola and Congo. Rather, we limit this chapter mainly to a particular region situated in the very heart of central Africa, i.e. the equatorial rainfor-est. We cannot claim to have anything to offer to the more theoretical archaeologist in the sense of adding to the growing body of all-embracing 'culture models', let alone 'general theories'. Rather, we are concerned to make some reflections on several major issues of the current state of equatorial rainforest archaeology. As the attentive reader will soon realize, we are nevertheless dealing, although implicitly, with some rather important themes of both a factual historical and a theoretical nature.

The problem: the rainforest as habitat for humans

If we are to deal with the ancient human settlement of the equatorial rainforest we are immediately faced with a number of problems, some of which are only indirectly related to the human past in this specific natural environment. Thus, we have to address the question of the age and the development of the forest during the Quaternary. Another major area of concern would be when and how this habitat was occupied by human groups, once its particular character had been formed.

In dealing with the nature of human penetration and occupation of the rainforest, one is prone to stumble into an abyss of anthropological theorizing involving a number of disciplines, the most prominent of which are historical linguistics, cultural anthro-pology and, of course, prehistoric archaeology. What is alluded to here is generally known as the Bantu Problem. This still hotly debated topic can be conceptualized as being mainly the outcome of a highly selective approach, i.e. some rather incoherent and premature linking of partial data with hypotheses from various disciplines that are not easily compatible with them. In this presentation, we try to steer clear as far as possible from this thorny problem.

An important topic to be discussed is related to the broader issues mentioned in the introductory remarks. On the one hand we have to address the basic questions of how to survive in an environment usually judged hostile to human settlement. What were the pre-existing natural conditions? Are we justified in projecting the traditional economic pattern, i.e. the subsistence base which prevailed at the point of European penetration of the forest, into the past? These are some of the basic questions to be faced concerning the settlement of the forest.

There is another complex topic. How are we to conceptualize the transition from stone-using to iron-producing and iron-using? Did this transition really occur in the equatorial forest or were those groups of people who first settled this habitat already versed in the art of iron-working? The emergence of pottery manufacture is a structur-ally related problem.

In the sections which follow I try to address some of these topics in a more or less systematic manner. It is to be hoped that the resulting picture will not only provide a succinct review of the present state of equatorial rainforest archaeology, but that it will also highlight the more general problems involved in the prehistory of this particular region.

The central African rainforest: some basic facts

As any physical map of Africa shows, the continent's land surface is made up of plateaux of different altitudes. Even the so-called 'basins', while being depressions in relation to the surrounding mountainous regions and plateaux, still represent plains with an altitude of several hundred metres above sea-level. Central Africa is a case in point: its major geomorphological feature, the Congo-Zaïre basin, rather low-lying as it is in general physical terms, still has an average height of about 400 m above sea-level.

With an extension of about 382,000 km^2 the Congo-Zaïre basin represents the largest basin of the African continent. Geomorphologically speaking, its principal internal features are vast plains built up by accumulation processes during the Pliocene, Pleistocene and Holocene. These inner plains are structured by a gentle relief of about 20 to 40 m of relative height. This rather flat relief is dissected by large erosion zones marked by creeks, rivers and lakes. Swamps and inundation forests are an omnipresent phenomenon. Because of this internal structuring, the basin's main ecological features are relatively low-lying, with large inundation zones on the one hand and smaller, more elevated areas of permanently dry land on the other.

The Congo-Zaïre basin's climate is linked to the basin's geographical position with respect to the equator. It forms part of a zone stretching from latitude 10°N to 10°S which is characterized by an average monthly temperature of 24° to 29°C. The annual temperature at Mbandaka on the equator shows an average of 25.4°C. Rainfall in the forest is high, with an annual average of about 1750 mm on the equator. The monthly average varies considerably but lies – July excepted – above 100 mm. The variation of rainfall exerts a very direct influence on the level of the numerous rivers, swamps and other water features.

In the equator region proper there are two main phases of more intense rainfall in the course of the year, i.e. from April through May and from October through December. With increasing distance from the equator there is some seasonal variation and a gradual decrease in this two-peak pattern to be found.

Analogous to the more or less accentuated phasing of the rainfall, the course of the year is marked by a regionally linked pattern of high and low water levels culminating in two fairly clear-cut phases in the area adjacent to the equator. There, the difference between the highest and the lowest mark can amount to about 3 m. Generally it can be said that seasonal rainfall, and thus the level of the waters, is marked by considerable, sometimes even extreme, fluctuation. It is not altogether unusual, therefore, that last year's average represents this year's lowest or highest level.

The very existence of the evergreen tropical forest is dependent on an average annual rainfall of about 1700 to 2000 mm, a maximum of two more or less arid months and an average annual temperature of at least 20°C. Given these climatic restrictions, we find the evergreen forest to both the north and south of the equator. In the west the forest borders the Atlantic coast of Gabon, extending north to southern Nigeria. Interrupted by the so-called 'Dahomey Gap' in southern Benin and Togo – a gap due to relatively low annual precipitation of about 800 to 1000 mm – the forest continues over a distance of about 200 km along the Upper Guinea coast from Ghana to Sierra Leone.

The central African rainforest forms one of the main types of the continent's natural environments. Situated between the Atlantic Ocean to the west and the east African Rift Valley to the east, it borders on a savanna belt to the north and south. According to current estimates it represents about 8 per cent of the continent's surface. Extending over about 2500 km in an east–west, and over about 1600 km in a north–south, direction, the forest forms what may be called a 'transcontinental barrier' (Fig. 16.1 and see Maley, Ch. 2, Fig 2.1, this volume). If this points to its physical character it should be added that the forest is generally perceived as a barrier to human settlement and human expansion as well.

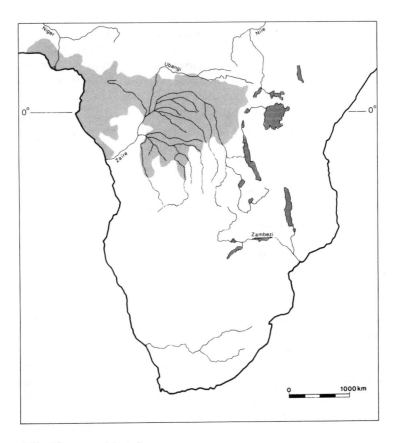

Figure 16.1   The equatorial rainforest.

From savanna to forest: on the emergence of the heart of central Africa

Any consideration of the human occupation of the rainforest has to address the problem of the development of this specific biotope, i.e. its palaeoecology. As the palaeobotanist John Flenley (1979, p. v) has pointed out, thirty years ago the rainforest was regarded 'as essentially static, a museum piece, a survival from far into the geological past'. In this view, the pleistocene climatic fluctuations of the temperate regions were believed to have left the tropics largely unaffected, or to have been reflected there as 'pluvials'.

Subsequent research has very substantially altered this view. Today, the equatorial rainforest is perceived as having changed considerably in the late Pleistocene and Holocene. The pluvial theory has been largely modified to accommodate new findings, resulting especially from research in lakes, bogs and swamps in east Africa, from submarine drillings off the central African coast as well as from geomorphological, sedimentological, pedological and palynological work in the Congo-Zaïre basin and in northwest central Africa. According to current thinking the glacials of the northern latitudes have been more or less reflected on the African continent as 'interpluvials' or 'interglacials'. These interpluvials are believed to have been caused by shifts in wind circulation and ocean current systems which themselves are considered as being a consequence of the glaciations in the northern hemisphere.

In the central part of the Congo-Zaïre basin pertinent palaeoecological research started only in the late 1970s with the fieldwork of the geomorphologist Johannes Preuss. Preuss, who collaborated closely with our archaeological rainforest project, recently published an important paper synthesizing the relevant work done in east Africa and on the Atlantic coast.[1] In the overall picture his own preliminary results from the central forest fitted in rather well (Preuss 1986a; Preuss 1986b; Preuss 1990; see also Grove, Ch. 1, this volume; Maley, Ch. 2, this volume).

From Preuss's findings there emerges a rather complex picture of climatic and vegetational variation in central Africa. In the central part of the Congo-Zaïre basin we have to allow for at least two phases of accumulation between about 42,000 and 35,000/25,000 years bp.[2] The accumulation processes were interrupted by periods of considerable precipitation and dense vegetation. This presumably rather complex and very poorly understood pattern of climatic variation appears to have been part of what is called the 'Ndjilian' wet phase (Preuss 1986a, pp. 139–40, 146).

Between about 25,000 bp and 18,000/16,000 bp the Congo-Zaïre basin was dominated by a rather dry climate resulting in an open type of vegetation. This phase has to be attributed to the 'Leopoldvillian' dry phase (Preuss 1986a, pp. 140, 146).

From about 16,000 bp onward the central Congo-Zaïre basin saw another phase of increased rainfall, apparently characterized by a trend towards a more dense vegetation. This phase, which perhaps constitutes a transitional period between the 'Leopoldvillian' and the 'Kibangian', appears to have ended around 11,500 bp (Preuss 1986a, pp. 142–3, 145).

We unfortunately lack radiocarbon dates and associated sedimentological and palynological information for the time between 11,500 and 2000 bp from the central part of the Congo-Zaïre basin (Preuss 1986a, pp. 143–4). This particular period, mostly belonging to the 'Kibangian' wet phase, seems to have been crucial for the development of the equatorial rainforest. However, according to evidence from southeastern Zaïre, the 'Kibangian' appears to have been followed by a rather dry climate lasting from about 4000 to 2500 bp (Clist 1989a, p. 63).

From 2000 bp onwards Preuss's (1986a, pp. 144, 145) results, as well as other data (Clist 1989a, p. 63), suggest a trend towards a humid climate, bringing into existence the rainforest, which has survived, though much modified by human agency, into modern times.

In assessing the current knowledge of the palaeoecology of the equatorial rainforest in general and of the central part of the Congo–Zaïre basin in particular, we have to admit that it is founded on an extremely small database. Nevertheless, there seems to be sufficient evidence to attribute the development of the evergreen forest, as it is known today, to the early Holocene. We have to keep in mind, however, that at this point we can sketch central Africa's ecological history in only its barest outlines. We must not forget that we are generalizing from rather widely spaced, i.e. more or less isolated, empirical evidence. In doing so we are forced to interpolate where it would be of utmost importance to rely on hard evidence. Thus, at this moment we are not able to assess the specific role and the overall influence of the predominantly dry climate indicated by palynological evidence in southeastern Zaïre between 4000 and 2500 bp. The important point is the effect this dry episode might have had on the nature and extension of the rainforest, which is believed to have been formed by that time.

Preuss has demonstrated that the inner Congo–Zaïre basin harbours an enormous potential for providing important empirical evidence needed for understanding the development and environmental fluctuations of what is now the equatorial rainforest. At the present time, however, we are far from being able to assess adequately human relationships to, and interaction with, the emerging forest.

Exploring the rainforest: the River Reconnaissance Project

Having set the stage in broad outline with some basic facts regarding central Africa in general and the rainforest in particular, I shall now concentrate on a much more limited area. The following will deal with a particular region within the equatorial forest. This region is situated in about the central part of the forest or, more specifically, to the south and the northwest of the great Zaïre river bend. Its most important physical elements are several major rivers which form an extensive network of natural communication routes. First and foremost, there is the Congo or Zaïre river, as it is officially called in the Republic of Zaïre, forming the main watercourse in the whole of central Africa. To the south of it, the region in question is characterized by the Lulonga-Lopori-Maringa river system, the Ikelemba river, the Ruki-Busira-Tshuapa and Momboyo river systems and finally by an inland lake, Lake Tumba. To the north, our focus region is dominated by the Ubangi river, the upper part of which is beyond the northern limits of the forest. Somewhat more to the south, we have the Sangha-Ngoko and its tributary, the Likwala-aux-Herbes.[3]

Initial experience in the forest in 1977–8 (Eggert 1980) led us to devise a specific project aimed at surveying as much of the hitherto archaeologically unexplored forest territory in as short a time as possible. From the very beginning it was quite evident that to accomplish this goal one had to use the waterways in much the same way as the early European explorers did. The resulting River Reconnaissance Project still aims at surveying archaeologically all major river courses (Eggert 1983). So far it has been implemented during four field seasons, namely in 1981–2, 1983, 1985 and 1987. As a result, we are now fairly familiar with the archaeology of all the rivers mentioned above. The overall distance covered amounts to some 5000 km (Fig. 16.2).

In sum, we might say that our expectations of this project were met. One has to keep in mind, however, that the archaeological knowledge thus gained is necessarily river-centred. The very few surveys into the hinterland cannot compensate for this fact.

At the very heart of our reconnaissance project lies the conviction that in an area totally unknown in archaeological terms we ought to set out by establishing age-area schemes based on whatever archaeological material we happen to have. Thus, the major objectives are regional cultural sequences which will eventually serve as a backbone for more comprehensive as well as more detailed studies of a local as well as regional focus.

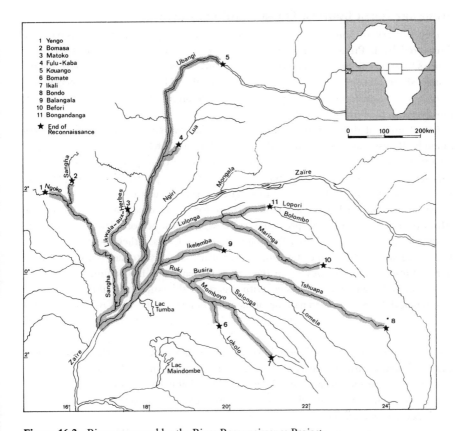

Figure 16.2 Rivers surveyed by the River Reconnaissance Project.

From a methodological and theoretical perspective there is indeed very 'little of compelling interest' in our reconnaissance strategy (Bower 1986, p. 35). For all its simplicity, however, the water-borne approach to archaeological surveying of a rather difficult territory, severely biased as it is, has allowed us to explore a very important part of the major rivers in the inner Congo-Zaïre basin. The archaeological material thus obtained consists almost exclusively of ceramics showing a very impressive range of formal and decorative variation in both time and space. It served as a basis for devising the cultural sequences that had been envisaged for the region.

The main lines of the age-area sequences resulting from our River Reconnaissance Project have been presented in a number of papers (Eggert 1983; Eggert 1984; Eggert 1987a; Eggert & Kanimba 1987).[4] Rather than repeating what has been detailed there it is proposed to concentrate here on three topics of prime importance: (1) lithic evidence of an early human presence in the region, (2) ceramic evidence of early settlement of the inner part of the forest by pottery-producing populations and (3) the question of the subsistence base and technology of these early settlers. To be discussed adequately, these topics will have to be visualized not only in a regional setting but in the wider context of central African prehistory as well.

Stone age forest hunters? On early lithic evidence

Evidence of penetration of the inner Congo-Zaïre basin by preceramic hunters has been discovered by J. Preuss. In 1982 and 1983 he found a number of stone artefacts at various locations on the Ruki and the Busira-Tshuapa rivers as well as, above all, on the eastern shore of Lake Tumba (Preuss & Fiedler 1984; Fiedler & Preuss 1985; Preuss 1990). Apart from some flakes, segments, cores and unmodified waste the artefacts are mostly projectile points made of quartzite.

As yet none of these stone artefacts has been discovered in context. The material found by Preuss was collected from the surface. Unfortunately, most of the stone tools discovered in what is now forest territory do not come from primary or undisturbed deposits (see, e.g., de Bayle 1975, pp. 157–93; Clist 1989a, pp. 63–75). Thus inferences based solely on form, technique and raw material have to suffice.

Judged in terms of J. Colette's nomenclature for the Kinshasa area of west-central Africa (Cahen 1976), Preuss's projectile points would best be considered as belonging to the so-called 'Djokocien' and 'Ndolien'. This would place them within the upper Lupemban (or, perhaps, the 'Lupembo-Tshitolian') and Tshitolian. This attribution does not lead very far, however, for there is, as Cahen (1978) has demonstrated, much confusion and many inconsistencies with regard to the empirical nature, definition, geographical distribution and naming of the lithic industries of central Africa. The main problem at the base of this is the notorious lack of sufficiently secure and stratified contexts.

Given the present state of central African stone age studies and the non-stratified nature of Preuss's artefacts it seems reasonable to assign them tentatively to a late stone age context. The interesting point is what kind of habitat the people who made and used these artefacts lived in. Would it be a reasonable assumption to envisage them as forest hunters and fishers?

In this context attention has to be drawn to Van Noten's (1977; 1982, pp. 31–4) excavation at Matupi cave in northeastern Zaïre in 1973 and 1974. He recovered a microlithic industry distributed over about 2 m of deposit and dated between 3000 and at least 40,000 bp. Today Matupi cave is situated in the rainforest but palynological and faunal evidence indicates that for most of the time when the cave was occupied by stone age hunters it was lying within a savanna environment. However, riverine or gallery forest was to be found in the vicinity of the cave. It was only during the latter part of the occupation, somewhere between 12,000 and 3000 bp, that the cave came to be situated in a rainforest environment (Van Noten 1977, p. 36; Van Neer 1984).

Likewise of interest are two rock shelters near Bamenda where de Maret carried out some test excavations in 1978 and 1980 (de Maret, Clist & Van Neer 1987). Of special importance is Shum Laka rock shelter where a microlithic industry, mainly of quartz, is associated with larger and bifacially retouched tools made of basalt in the upper layers of the deposit. Some of these basalt artefacts resemble hoes or axes, although no real polished tools of that type have been found. One of the basalt specimens, a flake, has a polished surface. Radiocarbon dates place the beginnings of the microlithic industry somewhere in the ninth millennium bp while the basalt artefacts are thought to appear within the fifth millennium bp.

In the same layers as the basalt assemblage thirteen ceramic sherds were found. Some of them seem to have been decorated by means of twisted cord roulettes. Because of the contamination of two relevant charcoal samples these potsherds could not be dated properly; although associated with the basalt industry, de Maret believes that they nevertheless appeared 'a little bit later' (de Maret, Clist & Van Neer 1987, p. 580).

Today, Shum Laka rock shelter is surrounded by open savanna vegetation. Van Neer's analysis of the fauna recovered from the deposit has shown, however, that the rock shelter was once situated near the border between montane and semi-deciduous humid forest (de Maret, Clist & Van Neer 1987, pp. 572–3). According to the faunal evidence the hunters exploited both environments so that there is no way to decide in precisely which of these two types of forest the shelter was situated – assuming the vegetation remained unchanged throughout the occupation.

Matupi cave and Shum Laka rock shelter are cited here as examples of two types of utilization of forest resources by late stone age hunters. While the hunters at Matupi probably operated from a savanna-based shelter located in the immediate vicinity of some riverine forest, those who occupied Shum Laka were decidedly much more adapted to forest conditions.

With respect to the stone artefacts collected by Preuss in the inner Zaïre basin, these two rock shelters are important in another sense as well. They exemplify the fact that lithic industries in themselves, even if they are stratified, do not help us in determining the kind of environment they were used in. We can by no means be sure, therefore, that those people who perhaps knapped, or at any rate used, the projectile points at the shore of Lake Tumba, did so in a rainforest habitat.

Hunters, ceramics and ground stone: focusing on the 'Neolithic'

Among the stone artefacts of J. Preuss's surface collection from the eastern shore of Lake Tumba there is one specimen which does not fit in with the others. It is a polished adze made of quartzite with an overall length of 5.2 cm. It was found at Ibonzi-

Moambo and Preuss & Fiedler (1984, p. 242; Fiedler & Preuss 1985, p. 186) tentatively assigned it to a ' "neolithic" settlement' still to be found.

The adze of Ibonzi has to be considered an isolated item not only with regard to the Lake Tumba area but to the rainforest as a whole. The nearest parallels in shape and size I know of are two ground tools from the upper Ouham river in the Central African Republic (Vidal & de Bayle 1983, p. 124, fig. 11,3.5). The site, Toala island, lies far to the north of the forest. Since these tools are axes, their similarity to the adze of Ibonzi is limited. Of course, even a closer resemblance would be of no necessary significance.

Unlike other regions of central Africa (e.g. de Maret 1986 for Lower Zaïre) in the rainforest there is as yet only the site of Batalimo on the Lobaye (Central African Republic) where stone axes are associated with pottery (de Bayle 1975, pp. 206–20).[5] About half of the 227 stone axes found there were broken and several others were but partly finished. Just one of the axes was polished and only partly at that. Thus, the excavator interpreted the site as a workshop for stone axes.

The material found at Batalimo is usually considered to belong to a 'neolithic' culture. However, this interpretation is based on a rather restricted view of what it is reasonable to call 'neolithic'. In this case, the criteria used are of a somewhat extraneous nature in that they only take into account material found in association, i.e., partly polished stone tools and pottery. This concept of the 'Neolithic', most often further reduced to just polished stone axes, has a long tradition in African studies. This view has long been criticized (Shaw 1966a, p. 10; Shaw 1966b, pp. 46–9; Shaw 1967, p. 35; and Sinclair, Shaw & Andah, Introduction, this volume), and more recently for the central African area (Clist 1986).

In reviewing ground stone tools from secure contexts in central Africa, Clist was able to show that such tools are not restricted to a food-producing way of life. Rather, they appear already in late stone age contexts, as is demonstrated by a number of sites. De Maret's test excavation at Shum Laka rock shelter mentioned above might serve as an example. Another case in point cited by Clist (1986, p. 228) is from the Batéké plateau in the Kinshasa area, i.e. on the southwestern rim of the Congo-Zaïre basin. There, Mortelmans recovered a number of artefacts from what seems to have been a camp site of late stone age hunters (Cahen & Mortelmans 1973). Apart from about 80 per cent of unmodified waste the assemblage consists mainly of bifacially worked foliate points and arrowheads, segments, cores and flakes. Some bifacially retouched tools with more or less parallel edges resemble axes. One similar, although unifacially retouched, artefact made of a flake has an asymmetrical cutting edge which is partly ground (Cahen & Mortelmans 1973, Pl. IV, 1).

Although the archaeological context of this assemblage which Cahen and Mortelmans (1973, pp. 37–8) assign to the late Tshitolien has not been documented properly, Cahen, the principal author, and Mortelmans (1973, p. 37) consider it as belonging to a one-component site. As to the partly polished tool, they refer to the Zambian site of Gwisho, where late stone age material was associated with polished axes and adzes (Fagan & Van Noten 1971).

Given a number of unquestionable as well as some probable associations of late stone age industries with polished stone artefacts as presented by Clist, the traditional view of correlating ground stone axes and adzes with a neolithic way of life must be abandoned.

It is an altogether different question, however, whether those tools are associated with pottery. This point has been only implicitly touched upon by Clist.

It has to be stressed generally that the production and/or reuse of polished stone artefacts is not limited to a stone age context but might also occur in an iron-producing and iron-working cultural setting. Thus, relevant discussion of the association of such tools with pottery has to be limited to a pre-metallurgical context. With respect to Shum Laka rock shelter, de Maret is, as we have seen, somewhat ambiguous about the association of several pottery fragments, some apparently decorated by rouletting, with a late stone age industry in the upper layers of the deposit. Clist (1989a, pp. 69–73, 77), on the other hand, seems to be less hesitant in accepting and interpreting an association of a microlithic industry with some small potsherds at the Libreville-'Sablières' (Nzo-gobeyok) site in the Estuaire province of Gabon. For him the fact that several sites with what he calls 'neolithic assemblages', situated some 20 km away on the opposite side of the Gabon estuary, might indicate that pottery was being exchanged between early neolithic farmers and late stone age hunters is proof enough.[6]

Apart from the possibility considered by Clist, there seems to be no evidence for assuming a 'genuine' association of ceramics and a hunter/fisher and gatherer way of life. It still appears to be valid that wherever pottery is produced and used in a primary prehistoric context we are dealing with settled people. Excluding the site of Batalimo, which will be dealt with later, there are six sites in central Africa where polished stone tools and early ceramics have been found closely associated. One of them is Obobogo, a suburb of Yaounde (de Maret 1982a; de Maret 1982b, pp. 2–3; de Maret, Clist & Mbida 1983; de Maret 1985, pp. 134–5; Clist 1986), the others are Okala, Lopé and Tchengué in Gabon (Clist 1987a; Oslisly & Peyrot 1988; Peyrot & Oslisly 1990) as well as Ngovo and Sakuzi in lower Zaïre. The latter two belong to what de Maret (1986) came to call the 'Ngovo Group'.

At Ngovo, a cave about 10 km to the southeast of Mbanza-Ngungu, de Maret excavated a very thin archaeological layer immediately below the surface in 1972. He recovered a ground stone axe and 161 potsherds of a very characteristic style which Mortelmans (1962) had labelled 'Group VI' pottery. An associated charcoal sample yielded a date of 2145 ± 45 bp (Hv-5258) which was confirmed in the following year by a date from a charcoal sample taken from a sondage immediately adjacent to the first one (2035 ± 65 bp, Hv-6258) (de Maret 1975; de Maret 1986, pp. 106–13).

At Sakuzu, about 100 km to the northwest of Ngovo cave near the Zaïre River, de Maret & Clist (1985) excavated a variety of features in 1984. One of them, Feature 37, an almost circular pit with a diameter of 85–90 cm and a depth of 1 m, yielded a fragment of the cutting edge of a ground axe with a number of Group VI potsherds. A radiocarbon date run on associated endocarps of oil-palm nuts yielded a date of 2110 ± 55 bp (Lv-1471) (de Maret 1986, p. 121).[7]

At the Okala 1 site twelve shafts or pits with diameters between 0.5 and 2 m and depths between 1.2 and 1.8 m, excavated in 1986–7, have yielded a rather distinct early pottery. It is flat-based with channelled rims and decoration characterized by incision and impression, sometimes by means of a rocking comb. In Shafts XIV and XV this pottery was associated with cutting-edge fragments of ground stone axes while Shaft I contained a grindstone (Clist 1987a, p. 26). Endocarps of the nuts of oil palms have also been recovered from various pits (Clist 1989a, p. 70, Table 1 nos. 21, 25, 29, 33–5). This complex of pits has been dated between 2460 ± 60 bp (Beta-25549) and 2120 ± 60 bp (Beta-25548) (Clist 1988, p. 46, Fig. 2; Clist 1989a, p. 70, Table 1).[8]

The Okala 1 site is the type-site of what Clist (1988; 1989a, pp. 77–9) introduced as 'a new neolithic complex' under the label of 'Okala Group'.[9] Another site of this new group is Lopé 12 where one of two pits contained Okala-type pottery as well as a fragment of a ground stone axe. A radiocarbon measurement run on associated endocarps of nuts of the oil palm gave a date of 2280 ± 80 bp (Gif-7525) (Oslisly & Peyrot 1988, pp. 64–5) (Table 16.1).

At Tchengué near Port-Gentil on the Atlantic coast in Gabon a polished adze with a constricted neck is reported to have been found associated with ceramic sherds, microlithic flint artefacts and shells of various species (Peyrot & Oslisly 1990, p. 14). The pottery is said to resemble Okala ware. Unfortunately, no radiocarbon sample has been obtained from this site (Peyrot & Oslisly 1990, p. 17).

The sixth site containing an association of early pottery and polished stone tools, Obobogo, represents a somewhat more intricate case. As no detailed analysis has been published yet, we have to rely mainly on Clist's (1986, pp. 219–20; 1989a, p. 79) summary of the site. According to that summary, as well as preliminary notes published by de Maret (1982a; 1982b; 1985, pp. 134–5) and collaborators (de Maret & Clist 1985), four shafts up to 3.1 m deep yielded a very considerable amount of a fragmented flat-based pottery decorated by incision, impression and rocked zigzag. Associated with this rather distinctive pottery were upper and lower grinding stones, grooved stones, a small polished adze and a cutting-edge fragment as well as several flakes of ground stone tools.[11] The shafts are being interpreted by Clist (1986, p. 219) as representing storage pits. As to botanical evidence, endocarps of nuts of the oil palm as well as kernels of the edible fruits of the tree *Canarium schweinfurthii* have been recovered. The site is interpreted as representing a village settled by neolithic food producers (de Maret 1982a, p. 12; de Maret 1982b, p. 3; de Maret, Clist & Van Neer 1983, p. 5; de Maret 1985, pp. 134–5; Clist 1986, pp. 220, 227). The radiocarbon dates associated with the various features are of particular importance in the context of the socio–economic organization of the people of Obobogo (Table 16.2). Its very interest-

Table 16.1 Selected radiocarbon dates for the association of polished stone tools and pottery (for Obobogo see Table 16.2)

No. Site	Radiocarbon age (bp)	Calibrated age (cal)	Lab. no.
1 Okala 1[10]	2460 ± 60	770–408 BC	Beta-25549
	2120 ± 60	341–322 / 204–96 BC	Beta-25548
2 Lopé 12	2280 ± 80	402–353 / 308–234 BC	Gif-7525
3 Ngovo	2145 ± 45	349–315 / 207–116 BC	Hv-5258
	2035 ± 65	151–148 BC / 117 BC–AD 22	Hv-6258
4 Sakuzu	2110 ± 55	198–94 BC	Lv-1471
5 Batalimo	1590 ± 90	AD 380–562	Gif-5894

Sources: de Maret 1985, pp. 135, 146; de Maret 1986, pp. 109, 121; Oslisly & Peyrot 1988, p. 65; Clist 1989a, p. 70, Table 1

ing patterning leads to the question of whether there are any differences in the pottery associated with Shafts II through IV on the one hand and Shaft VII on the other. Unfortunately, the preliminary publications on Obobogo do not address this rather important issue. It is interesting to note in this respect that the only date retained of Shaft II in an unpublished MA thesis (Claes 1985) is the one from the intermediate level (Hv-10832). Clist (1986, p. 220), who reports this fact, does not present the arguments but rather summarily offers an alternative explanation in suggesting that the conflicting dates might result from a possible superposition of two pits of different age.

With respect to Obobogo there is thus much more detailed information needed before its association of polished stone tools and early ceramics can be properly appraised. So far, this site appears to have yielded the oldest association of this kind in the whole of central Africa. For those who have to rely solely on the published evidence, de Maret's and Clist's acceptance of this early dating is somewhat surprising.[13] In this context, attention must be drawn to the fact that all these early dates derive from one laboratory, the same laboratory which has furnished rather old dates on other occasions (Eggert 1987a, pp. 132–3). A control test on Obobogo material run by a different laboratory would be very welcome indeed.

Obobogo poses problems in still another sense which is directly relevant to the present context. According to Clist (1986, p. 220), Shafts IV and VII contained not only archaeological material of the kind summarized above but also iron slag. Although he concedes that the early dating of Shaft IV does not conform to our present knowledge of the beginnings of iron production and iron-working in Africa, he apparently questions neither the archaeological context nor the date as such. Rather, he proceeds by suggesting that Shaft IV belonged to a group of pits 'the radiocarbon dates of which have to be calculated jointly in order to obtain a mean date' – which seems to me a somewhat peculiar proposition.[14]

At the present time I should like to take exception to Clist's (1986, p. 227) statement that from now on one should envisage a 'true Neolithic' in the northwestern zone of central Africa by the end of the second millennium BC. As long as the Hanover dates of Obobogo have not been confirmed by independent evidence I propose to adhere to the dates yielded by the Louvain laboratory. These dates, centering around 200 BC, are in general agreement with the above quoted radiocarbon determinations which both the

Table 16.2 Radiocarbon dates for some features at Obobogo

No. Feature	Level (cm)	Radiocarbon age (bp)	Calibrated age (cal)	Lab. no.
1 Shaft IV	130–150	3625 ± 165	2273–2245 / 2210–1850 BC	Hv-11046
2 Shaft IV	?	2310 ± 100	410–357 / 289–251 BC	Lv-1432
3 Shaft II	040–050	3070 ± 95	1436–1256 / 1238–1223 BC	Hv-10583
4 Shaft II	140–170	1990 ± 65	94 BC–AD 75	Hv-10832
5 Shaft II	200–280	2955 ± 110	1385–1338 / 1320–1010 BC	Hv-10833
6 Shaft III	140–160	2635 ± 100	900–780 BC	Hv-11045
7 Shaft VII	050–070	2120 ± 70	349–315 / 207–91 BC	Lv-1394
8	260–290	2120 ± 150	380 BC–AD 20	Lv-1395

Sources: de Maret 1985, pp. 135, 147; Clist 1986, pp. 219–20[12]

same laboratory and Hanover have furnished for the association of polished stone tools and early pottery in lower Zaïre. They also agree with four of the six dates from the Beta laboratory for Okala 1 in the Gabon estuary as well as with the Groningen date for Lopé 12 in the same country (Table 16.1).

Considering the socio-economic implications of the concept 'neolithic' or, for that matter, Central African Neolithic, there is almost no hard evidence to rely on. Apart from a number of sites where early utilization of the oil palm (*Elaeis guineensis* Jacq.) has been established, we do not possess any botanical and/or faunal evidence suggesting a domestication of plants and animals. Consequently, any use of this concept has to be based on secondary criteria, the most important of which at this stage seems to be an archaeological context of primary association of polished stone tools and early ceramics in the sense discussed above.

The Central African Neolithic and early iron metallurgy: cultural context and cross-cutting dates

If we apply the very indirect and restricted definition of an early, i.e. pre-metallurgical, food-producing way of life proposed above to the central African empirical evidence, we are faced with a problem. In some areas the archaeological material used as criteria to define this 'Neolithic', e.g. ground stone implements associated with early ceramics, appears to be at least partly connected with evidence of iron production and iron-working.

As has already been said above, Shafts IV and VII at Obobogo yielded polished stone artefacts and – probably – early pottery as well as iron slag. Clist (1986, p. 220), who apparently accepts this association as being original, was quick to point out that this leads to the question of the contemporaneity of polished stone artefacts and iron tools. He did not discuss this question, however. In doing so we have to be precise as to which polished stone artefacts we are talking about. The point is that we have to be concerned only about those artefacts which are associated with what appears to be the earliest pottery in whatever region we are discussing. This would be true for Obobogo.

With respect to lower Zaïre the oldest pottery known as yet is Mortelmans's 'Group VI', i.e. the kind of pottery which is the diagnostic element of de Maret's 'Ngovo Group'. So far no genuine association with either iron slag or iron implements is known. According to Clist (1986, p. 225) iron metallurgy appears there first in the context of the so-called 'Kay Ladio' pottery which succeeds Group VI pottery in the first three centuries AD. Interestingly, there seems to be some evidence that Kay Ladio ceramics were associated with ground stone axes as well (Clist 1986).

As to Okala pottery in Gabon, no association with the products or by-products of iron metallurgy has been reported as far as I am aware. However, ongoing research in Gabon has presented us with a rather surprising picture with respect to the temporal and areal distribution of neolithic and early iron age cultural contexts.

At the Otoumbi 4 site, in the savanna zone around the middle Ogooué river, a fragment of the cutting-edge of a polished axe has been found embedded in the shaft of an iron-smelting furnace which yielded a date of 1980 ± 80 bp (Beta-15066) (Clist 1986, p. 222 note 4; Oslisly & Peyrot 1988, p. 65; Clist 1989a, p. 71, Table 1, nos. 56, 79). This association is presumably due to chance but Clist's (1989a, p. 79) statement that the date can be considered to be a *terminus ante quem* for the use of polished tools in the central savannas of Gabon seems nevertheless premature. This is not to deny, however, that there is a strong case for assuming that iron metallurgy had been practised in several inland areas of Gabon for quite some time by that date.

In the Otoumbi area Clist (1987c, p. 381; 1989a, p. 71, Table 1) had two charcoal samples from a shaft-bowl furnace at the Otoumbi 2 site dated to 2640 ± 70 bp (Beta-14834) and 2400 ± 50 bp (Gif-7130). From the north of Gabon he has reported two pits at the Oyem 2 site containing pottery as well as iron slag and dated to 2280 ± 55 bp (Lv-1521) and 2220 ± 75 bp (Lv-1520) respectively (Clist 1989a, p. 81). In southwestern Gabon at the Lac Bleu site to the north of Mouila a shaft-bowl furnace, yielding two dates of 1920 ± 80 bp (Beta-12208) and 1670 ± 90 bp (Beta-10301), was excavated in 1984 (Schmidt, Digombe, Locko & Mouleingui 1985, p. 17). A circular slag heap at the same site gave a date of 2100 ± 90 bp (Beta-12207) (Schmidt, Digombe, Locko & Mouleingui 1985, p. 17).

The most important sites related to early iron production in Gabon yet discovered occur in the southeastern rainforest part of the country. The most promising of these are located at Moanda. Initial survey and excavation work in 1984 and 1985 led to the testing and partial excavation of shaft-bowl furnaces and refuse dumps at the Moanda I and II sites (Schmidt, Digombe, Locko & Mouleingui 1985, p. 17; Digombe, Schmidt, Mouleingui-Boukosso, Mombo & Locko 1987a, p. 10; Digombe, Schmidt, Mouleingui-Boukosso, Mombo & Locko 1987b).

The radiocarbon datings obtained for Moanda I are 2050 ± 100 bp (Beta-15738) for a shaft-bowl furnace and 2050 ± 60 bp (Beta-15741) for the centre of a refuse dump about 4 m away containing slag and tuyère fragments.[15] A small sondage on the western side of an undisturbed second furnace gave a date of 2350 ± 140 bp (Beta-14427) (Digombe, Schmidt, Mouleingui-Boukosso, Mombo & Locko 1987a, p. 10; 1987b, p. 713).

The site of Moanda II has yielded a radiocarbon date of 2330 ± 90 bp (Beta-14428) for a furnace; another date of 2220 ± 90 bp (Beta-15742) was obtained for an industrial dump lying about 12 m north of this furnace (Digombe, Schmidt, Mouleingui-Boukosso, Mombo & Locko 1987a, p. 10; Digombe, Schmidt, Mouleingui-Boukosso, Mombo & Locko 1987b, p. 715).

To these and other Gabonese early iron age industrial sites (Table 16.3)[16] we have to add an early date for iron metallurgy from the Mayombe mountain chain in Congo. The site, located some kilometres to the west of Les Saras, yielded a considerable quantity of charcoal and charred endocarps of palm nuts which were associated with iron slag and fragments of tuyères. A radiocarbon determination run on the charred material gave a date of 2110 ± 60 bp (Arc-373) (de Foresta, Schwartz, Dechamps & Lanfranchi 1990, p. 10).

Thus we are presented with a somewhat incongruous picture with respect to the temporal relationship of so-called 'neolithic' and iron technology sites. Clist (1989a, p. 81) tries to minimize this in maintaining that after 2500 bp a 'neolithic tradition' thrived on the coast while in the interior there were areas 'where iron metallurgy was practised on a wide basis'. However, the neolithic site of Lopé 12 and the early iron age sites of Otoumbi are situated on the same stretch, although on opposite sides, of the middle Ogooué. In this context we are reminded of the fragment of a polished stone axe in the clay shaft of the furnace at Otoumbi 4 mentioned above. At the Libreville-'Sablières' (Nzogobeyok) site on the coast a charcoal sample of a feature containing some lithic waste and iron slag was dated to 2490 ± 50 bp (Gif-6678). Clist (1989a, p. 83) reminds us, however, that the slag could have descended into its present position through the sand mantle from above. Finally, at Kango, located in the inner part of the Gabon estuary, we do have both 'neolithic' as well as iron technology occurrences (Clist 1989a, pp. 77, 83–5). Nevertheless, the distribution maps provided by Clist (1989a, p. 76, Fig. 9, p. 81, Fig. 11) demonstrate that the 'neolithic' sites tend to cluster within a distance of about 60 km from the coast while the major iron technology sites are clearly situated in the interior. However, how far this tendency of areal distribution is due to survey bias remains to be seen.

Currently, the contemporaneity and partial areal coexistence of 'neolithic' and iron technology communities suggested by radiocarbon dates denies any straightforward explanation. Due to very intensive field research in the last decade this double phenomenon has been almost exclusively restricted to Gabon. Considering the speculation-ridden character of early iron age studies in sub-Saharan Africa (Eggert 1981) it comes as no surprise to see the current Gabonese findings immediately woven into a speculative model of invention and transcontinental diffusion by Digombe, Schmidt, Mouleingui-Boukosso, Mombo & Locko (1987a; 1987b).

From the periphery to the centre: early pottery in the inner Congo-Zaïre basin

The Imbonga Horizon

The discovery of some very early pottery in the central part of the equatorial forest can be considered one of the major results of the River Reconnaissance Project. As

Table 16.3   Selected radiocarbon dates for early iron metallurgy in Gabon and Congo

No. Site	Radiocarbon age (bp)	Calibrated age (cal)	Lab. no.
1 Otoumbi 2	2640 ± 70	843–795 BC	Beta-14834
2 Otoumbi 2	2400 ± 50	752–707 / 531–400 BC	Gif-7130
3 Moanda I	2350 ± 140	762–678 / 662–626 / 600–360 / 289–252 BC	Beta-14427
4 Moanda II	2330 ± 90	487–436 / 425–370 BC	Beta-14428
5 Oyem 2	2280 ± 55	398–363 / 280–261 BC	Lv-1521
6 Oyem 2	2220 ± 75	392–190 BC	Lv-1520
7 Moanda II	2220 ± 90	394–177 BC	Beta-15742
8 Mouila	2100 ± 90	349–315 / 207–9 BC	Beta-12207
9 Moanda I	2150 ± 90	370–96 BC	Beta-17043
10 Moanda II	2150 ± 110	380–50 BC	Beta-17044
11 Makokou	2150 ± 70	362–282 / 259–105 BC	Lv-1514
12 Lopé 4	2130 ± 110	370–40 BC	Beta-15063
13 Koualessis	2110 ± 70	340–322 / 204–49 BC	Beta-15059
14 Les Saras	2110 ± 60	332–329 / 200–91 BC	Arc-373

Sources: Clist 1989a, p. 71, Table 1; Schmidt, Digombe, Locko & Mouleingui 1985, p. 17; de Foresta, Schwartz, Dechamps & Lanfranchi 1990, p. 10

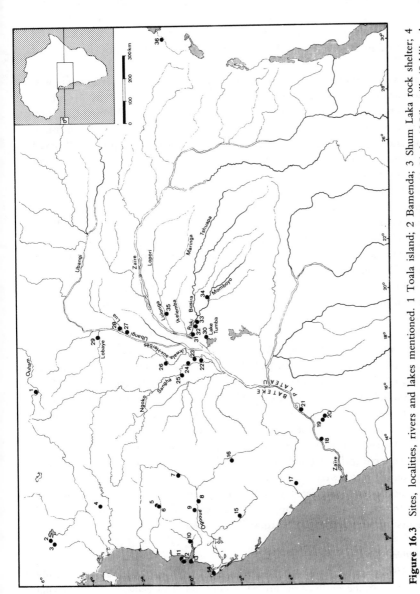

Figure 16.3 Sites, localities, rivers and lakes mentioned. 1 Toala island; 2 Bamenda; 3 Shum Laka rock shelter; 4 Yaounde–Obobogo; 5 Oyem; 6 Oualessis; 7 Makokou; 8 Lopé; 9 Otoumbi; 10 Kango; 11 Okala; 12 Libreville-'Sablières' (Nzogobeyok); 13 river Denis site; 14 Tchengué; 15 Lac Bleu site; 16 Moanda; 17 Les Saras; 18 Sakuzi; 19 Mbanza-Ngungu; 20 Ngovo; 21 Kinshasa; 22 Mobaka; 23 Likwala-aux-Herbes, Kilometre 186; 24 Mitula; 25 Pikunda; 26 Munda; 27 Dongo; 28 Maluba; 29 Batalimo; 30 Ibonzi-Moambo; 31 Mbandaka; 32 Bokélé; 33 Bokuma; 34 Imbonga; 35 Boso-Njafo; 36 Matupi cave

discussed elsewhere (Eggert 1984, pp. 256–7, with note 20), we used the term 'horizon' for any distinctive pottery group showing a certain degree of areal distribution. Thus, the earliest ceramics yet discovered were labelled 'Imbonga Horizon' after their type-site, Imbonga on the Momboyo (Fig. 16.3).[17] Their characteristics have been described in three papers (Eggert 1983; Eggert 1984; Eggert 1987a); we can therefore be very brief here.[18]

The main types of Imbonga pottery are globular pots and open and in-turning bowls. While they are of different size, the pots are usually characterized by a rounded shoulder, a concave neck and a fluted, more or less out-turned rim. Without exception Imbonga ware is flat-based. Its decoration is executed by means of grooving, incision, impression and appliqué. Comb-stamped as well as incised zigzag patterns ('rocked zigzag'), often covering the outer surface of the bases as well, are its most salient diagnostic trait (Figs 16.4, 16.5).

Our River Reconnaissance Project revealed a very interesting distribution pattern for this pottery. Quite obviously, it is centred on the Zaïre river where Imbonga ware has been found on its left bank in the Mbandaka area. It is also present on the Ruki, Ikelemba and Lulonga rivers, which discharge their waters directly into the Zaïre. As to the big rivers in the hinterland, i.e. the Tshuapa and Maringa, no Imbonga pottery has been found. The only exception is the Momboyo, on the middle course of which the type-site is located. The situation is quite different to the north and northwest of the Zaïre river, for Imbonga ware was entirely absent not only on the Ubangi but also on the Sangha-Ngoko and Likwala-aux-Herbes rivers.

In addition to eleven radiocarbon dates for the Imbonga Horizon published and discussed recently (Eggert 1987a, pp. 132–3, with Table 1), two other dates for a closed ceramic assemblage at Bokuma on the Ruki have been processed in the meantime. The dates are 2090 ± 70 bp (GrN-14003) and 2025 ± 70 bp (KI-2433) respectively.[19] Two pits filled with Imbonga pottery at Boso-Njafo on the Lulonga yielded dates of 2440 ± 150 bp (GrN-14005) and 2260 ± 80 bp (GrN-14006) respectively. Finally, an additional sample from a ceramic complex at the site of Imbonga itself gave a date of 2160 ± 90 bp (KI-2428).[20] As has been pointed out in the article quoted above, some of the dates published then have to be rejected as a result of specific inconsistencies in an inter-laboratory comparison. Two others, much younger, seem to have been run on charcoal which was not genuinely associated with the pottery in question. Thus, we end up with the fact that Imbonga pottery first appeared and saw its florescence during the second half of the first millennium BC (Table 16.4).[21]

The Batalimo-Maluba Horizon

During our 1985 reconnaissance of the Ubangi river we found a flat-based and richly decorated pottery to the south of the great Ubangi bend. This ware showed a striking resemblance to some of the ceramics published by de Bayle des Hermens (1975) from the site of Batalimo, already referred to above (Fig. 16.6–1). At Maluba on the Lua, a small eastern tributary of the Ubangi, we were able to excavate two pits containing this pottery. This led to the creation of a 'Batalimo-Maluba Horizon' (Eggert 1987a). A fair sample of this pottery has been obtained from an erosion gully at Dongo on the Ubangi.

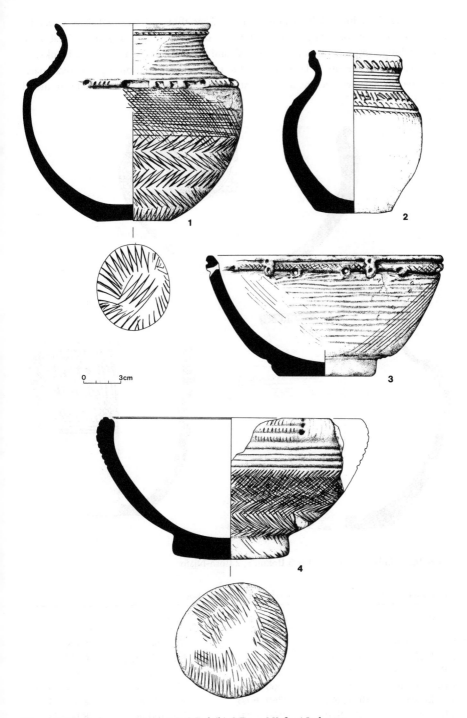

Figure 16.4 Imbonga pottery. 1 & 3 Bokélé; 2 Boso–Njafo; 4 Imbonga

In general, Batalimo-Maluba pottery is a rather thin and well-polished ware. Its decoration, mainly consisting of alternating horizontal and vertical zones of elaborate cross-hatching, impression motifs, incised and grooved lines as well as blanks, is usually very well executed. To judge by the material collected during our reconnaissance, the main types present are well-structured globular pots and wide-mouthed bowls (Figs 16.6, 16.7).

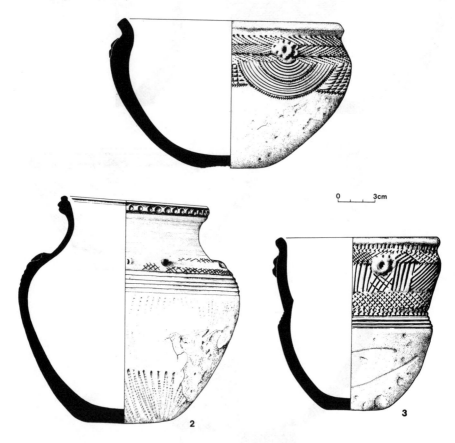

0   3cm

Figure 16.5   Imbonga pottery. 1 & 3 Bokuma; 2 Boso–Njafo

Table 16.4   Currently accepted radiocarbon dates for Imbonga pottery

No. Site	Feature	Radiocarbon age (bp)	Calibrated age (cal)	Lab. no.
1 Boso–Njafo	BSN 85/1	2440 ± 150	800–390 BC	GrN-14005
2 Bokélé	BKE 81/1	2290 ± 70	402–257 BC	GrN-13583
3 Boso–Njafo	BSN 85/3	2270 ± 70	399–234 BC	KI-2439
4 Boso–Njafo	BSN 85/3	2260 ± 80	399–203 BC	GrN-14006
5 Bokuma	BOK 83/1	2260 ± 60	396–234 BC	KI-2363
6 Imbonga	IMB 81/9/I	2160 ± 90	375–100 BC	KI-2428

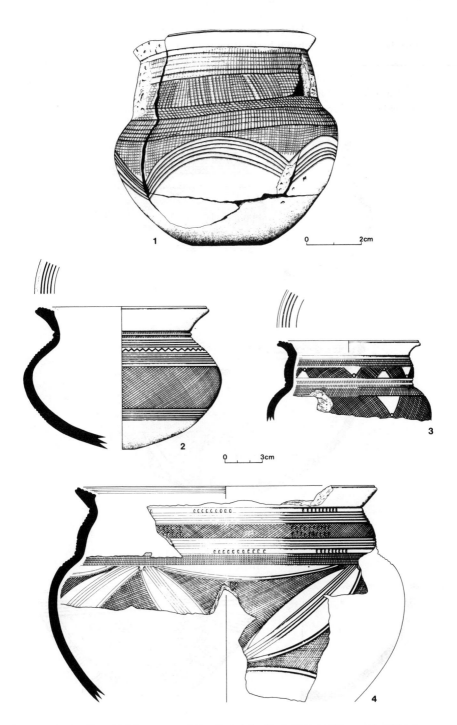

Figure 16.6 Batalimo–Maluba pottery. 1 Batalimo (after R. de Bayle); 2 Dongo; 3–4 Maluba

At present, Batalimo–Maluba pottery shows a rather restricted distribution in the area to the south of the Ubangi bend. It remains to be explored how far it extends on the Lobaye, where the site of Batalimo is situated, into the hinterland. From our 1987 reconnaissance of the Sangha–Ngoko and Likwala it is evident, however, that this ware was not distributed along the banks of these rivers (and see below).

As has been said recently, the stylistic boundaries of Batalimo–Maluba ware and its

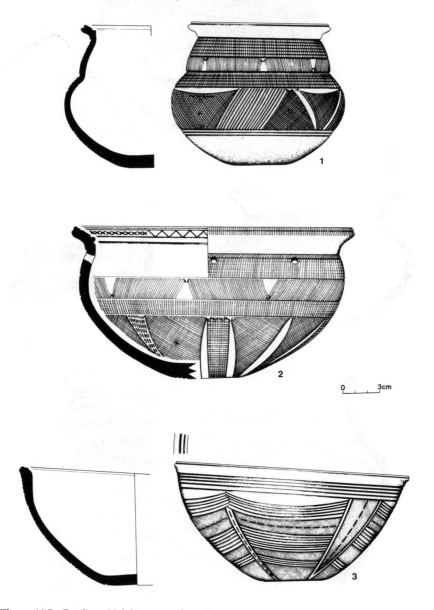

Figure 16.7 Batalimo–Maluba pottery from Dongo.

precise relationship to some other presumably early pottery on the Ubangi are still ill-defined (Eggert 1987a, pp. 140–1). Much more reconnaissance and excavation work is needed before we can be sure of the extension and internal differentiation of this ceramic horizon.

So far only four radiocarbon dates have been processed for Batalimo-Maluba pottery from Maluba (Table 16.5). They have been commented upon recently (Eggert 1987a, pp. 139–40). In this context reference has to be made to a thermoluminescence determination on pottery from the site of Batalimo itself which yielded a date of 1570 ± 220 yr (OxTL-154a-4) (Aumassip 1975, p. 233). In 1982 Vidal obtained a charcoal sample at the site which provided a date of 1590 ± 90 bp (Gif-5894). Unfortunately, its precise association has not been reported (de Maret 1985, pp. 135, 146; Vidal 1987, p. 23).

Taking all the dates for Batalimo-Maluba pottery known so far together we realize that they represent a considerable time span. Its clustering in the first half of the first millennium AD is nevertheless obvious. Therefore, this ware has to be considered as being somewhat younger than Imbonga pottery. However, a partial overlapping cannot be excluded at this stage of investigation.

Table 16.5 Radiocarbon dates for Batalimo-Maluba pottery

No. Site	Feature	Radiocarbon age (bp)	Calibrated age (cal)	Lab. no.
1 Maluba	MLB 85/1/2	2140 ± 200	400 BC–AD 70	KI-2445
2 Maluba	MLB 85/1/2	1990 ± 60	92 BC–AD 72	GrN-13585
3 Maluba	MLB 85/1/1	1930 ± 120	90 BC–AD 220	KI-2444
4 Maluba	MLB 85/1/1	1670 ± 110	AD 240–460 /476–530	GrN-13584
5 Batalimo		1590 ± 90	AD 380–562	Gif-5894

The Pikunda-Munda Horizon

During our 1987 reconnaissance of the Sangha-Ngoko and Likwala-aux-Herbes in Congo we excavated a rather distinctive pottery at Pikunda on the Sangha and at Munda on the Likwala.[22] The features from which the pottery was obtained were pit structures of various dimensions. At Pikunda a shaft with a depth of about 3 m was partly excavated while the same was done at Munda with two shafts about 1.5 m deep. In the latter village a shallow bowl-like pit was also dug.

The pottery recovered from the pit structures at Munda displayed a general stylistic homogeneity. Its main type is a wide-mouthed bowl with approximately parallel sides and a flared rim. Very rare are open bowls without rim and with a profile the upper part of which approaches the vertical. The same is true for globular pots and bottle-like vessels both with everted rims. There is no doubt that this pottery was uniformly round-based with the centre of the bottom sometimes slightly incurved. Not one single fragment of a more or less flat base was recovered. The decoration consists of horizontally arranged bands of various designs produced by means of incision and grooving. The designs, exclusively based on linear elements, are usually characterized by interspersing and by alternating patterns of positioning which sometimes include festoon-like arrangements of lines and grooves (Figs 16.8, 16.9).

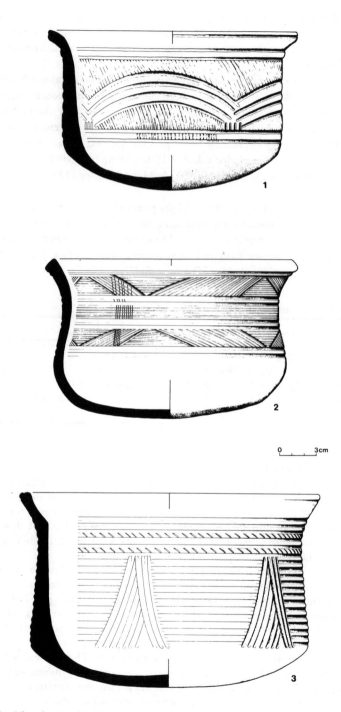

0   3cm

Figure 16.8 Pikunda–Munda pottery. 1–3 Munda, Shaft 1.

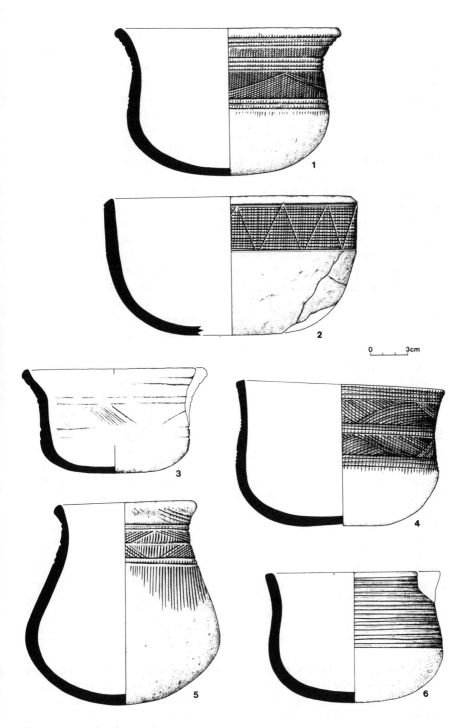

Figure 16.9 Pikunda-Munda pottery. 1–6 Munda, Shaft 3.

At Pikunda the ceramic fill of the deep shaft was not homogeneous. While the upper part of it contained a rather young pottery partly characterized by roulette decoration (Fig. 16.10), its lower layers yielded a ware shaped and decorated differently. This older pottery, which is rather limited in quantity, does not appear homogeneous in the sense of having very clearly defined boundaries of shape, decoration and fabric (Figs 16.11, 16.12). Some of the fragments recovered from the shaft as well as from the surface (Fig. 16.13) show a considerable similarity to the ceramics of Munda which led me to create a 'Pikunda-Munda Horizon'. In addition to the pattern of decoration already described for Munda ware some fragments from Pikunda display horizontal bands of wavy lines (Figs 16.11–6, 16.12–8). Moreover, the bottom of one largely preserved pot from the shaft is decorated with superimposed patterns of rocked zigzag produced by means of a toothed instrument (Fig. 16.11–1). This specific comb-stamped decoration and a slightly different rocked zigzag executed with an edged tool occur on other fragments of Pikunda-Munda pottery as well (Figs 16.8–1, 16.12–1, 16.13–4).

At the present time the chronological position of what is called here Pikunda-Munda pottery depends on nine radiocarbon determinations (Table 16.6). The two shafts at Munda yielded six dates which overlap at the 68 per cent confidence level. The shallow pit at the same locality provided two dates. While they are internally consistent, they are considerably younger than those of the first two features. It has to be stressed in this respect that the pottery associated with all three features was absolutely homogeneous.

For the lower part of the Pikunda shaft we have only one radiocarbon date at our disposal. It fits in very well with those of the shaft structures at Munda.

Table 16.6   Radiocarbon dates for Pikunda-Munda and other early pottery

No. Site	Feature	Radiocarbon age (bp)	Calibrated age (cal)	Lab. no.
1 Munda	MUN 87/2–1–1	2020 ± 180	353–306 BC / 240 BC–AD 140	KI-2887
2 Munda	MUN 87/2–1–1	1990 ± 45	47 BC–AD 63	KI-2881
3 Munda	MUN 87/2–1–1	1910 ± 80	AD 7–146 / 162–194	KI-2886
4 Munda	MUN 87/2–1–1	1800 ± 90	AD 113–269 / 272–338	KI-2885
5 Munda	MUN 87/2–1–3	1990 ± 65	94 BC–AD 75	KI-2888
6 Munda	MUN 87/2–1–3	1980 ± 41	37 BC–AD 67	KI-2876
7 Munda	MUN 87/3	1680 ± 90	AD 244–435	KI-2890
8 Munda	MUN 87/3	1650 ± 80	AD 261–289 / 327–448	KI-2889
9 Pikunda	PIK 87/1	1980 ± 100	110 BC–AD 120	KI-2877
10 Mobaka	MKA 87/102	2270 ± 160	520–160/139–124 BC	KI-2894
11 Mitula	MIT 87/103	2230 ± 100	400–180 BC	KI-2895
12 Likwala	LKW 87/186–1	1960 ± 90	92 BC–AD 124	KI-2893

As has been mentioned above, the pottery fragments from the lower part of the shaft at Pikunda, while certainly different from the material characterized by roulette decoration, are not uniform since they did not represent only Pikunda-Munda formal and ornamental characteristics. Considering the Sangha-Likwala area as a whole the situation with respect to early pottery is even more complicated by the fact that we

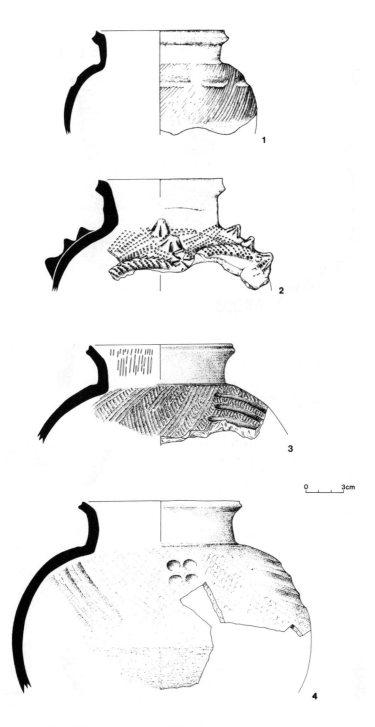

Figure 16.10 Pottery from Pikunda (upper part of shaft).

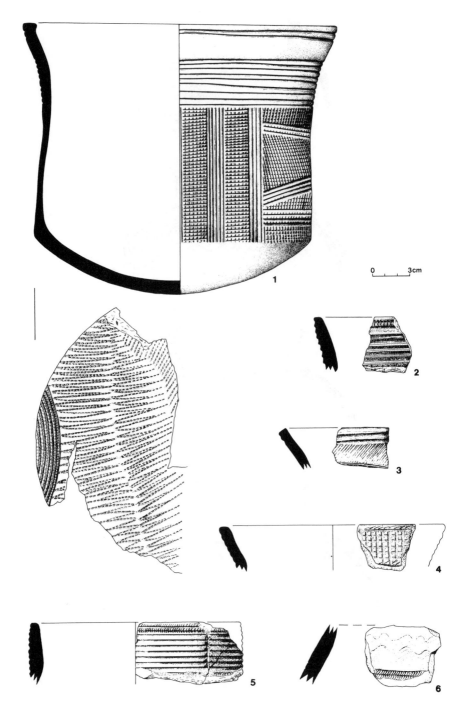

Figure 16.11 Pottery from Pikunda (lower part of shaft).

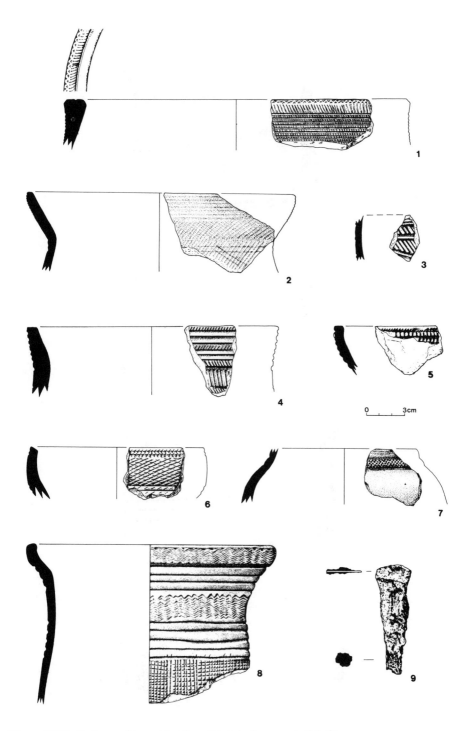

Figure 16.12 Pottery and iron object from Pikunda (lower part of shaft).

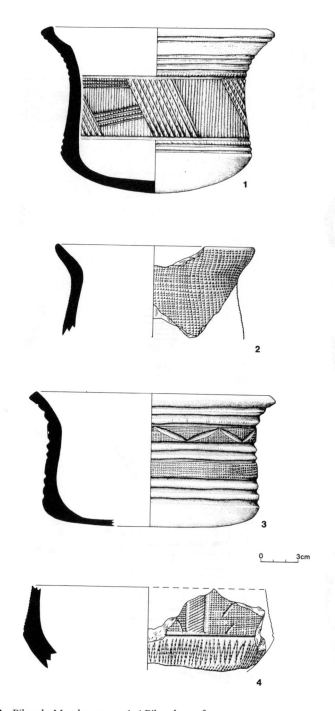

Figure 16.13 Pikunda-Munda pottery. 1–4 Pikunda, surface.

obtained three rather early radiocarbon determinations for ceramics at Mobaka and Mitula ('Mitoula') on the lower Sangha and for an unnamed location on the river bank on the middle course of the Likwala (Table 16.6). In the first two instances a few fragments of pottery with some charcoal in what appeared to be a primary association were found partly eroded out of the village surfaces (Fig. 16.14). At Likwala, Kilometre 186, however, a pit of about 1.75 m depth had been exposed by continuous erosion of the steep river bank consisting of clay and other alluvial soil. It contained a partly broken pot and some sherds (Fig. 16.15). The radiocarbon determination was run on charcoal from the fill of the pit.

The problem is that none of the pottery found associated with the dated charcoal samples appears clearly to belong to the Pikunda-Munda type. For the moment we can only acknowledge this rather peculiar situation. It has to be kept in mind, however, that in contrast to the Pikunda-Munda ware the other three dates and the associated pottery are currently isolated phenomena which only future work will allow to be properly understood. This specific case might nevertheless serve as a reminder that one ought not to try to infer too much from too little – for it is quite true that, for all its obvious benefits, one single river reconnaissance in a virtually unexplored region is but a drop in the bucket when it comes to assessing adequately its archaeological potential.

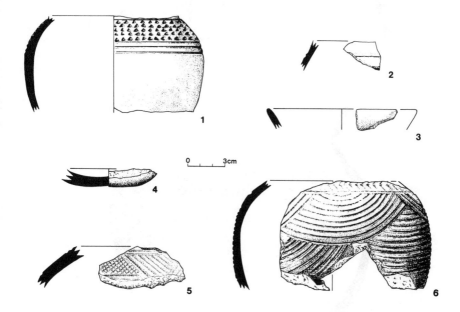

Figure 16.14 Pottery from Mobaka and Mitula. 1 Mobaka; 2–6 Mitula.

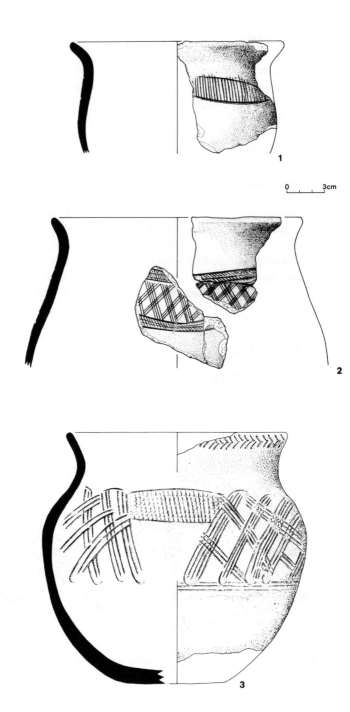

Figure 16.15 Pottery from Likwala-aux-Herbes, Kilometre 186.

Early rainforest pottery: the problem of internal relationship

To summarize our quick survey of the earliest pottery in the inner Congo-Zaïre basin we may conclude that we are confronted with three more or less well-established regional ceramic styles introduced here under the labels of 'Imbonga Horizon', 'Batalimo-Maluba Horizon' and 'Pikunda-Munda Horizon'. In the Sangha-Likwala region other early pottery, the precise nature and temporal position of which cannot be appropriately determined at this time, seems to have been in use. Disregarding the respective isolated cases, the other ceramic entities, taken together, are clustered around the end of the first millennium BC.

Considering the nature of radiocarbon dating and the limited number of dates at our disposal, a partial temporal overlap of the three pottery styles discussed here cannot be excluded. Even more important, however, is the question of whether or not these particular ceramic entities evolved independently of each other. Stated somewhat differently, the historically important point is whether there is anything in the ceramic evidence at hand which would argue for some sort of 'genetic' relationship between either of these entities. Or are they even, to mention just one slightly different possibility, part of one and the same ceramic tradition?

When I originally set out to address this question with regard to Imbonga pottery on the one hand and Batalimo-Maluba ware on the other, I found that they shared a number of elements such as flat bases and main vessel forms, as well as some decorative techniques and motifs. On closer inspection it became clear, however, that even in what appeared to be common to both there was much variation between the two ceramic groups (Eggert 1987a, p. 141). This led me to conclude, then, that a direct relationship between Imbonga and Batalimo-Maluba pottery was highly improbable and that each represented a quite distinct ceramic configuration. For all that, I indicated the possibility of a common ceramic tradition out of which both groups might have evolved (Eggert 1987a, p. 143).

When speculating on the possible origins of Imbonga and Batalimo-Maluba pottery in 1986, I drew attention to the fact that these two groups centred on the Zaïre and Ubangi respectively. Therefore, a hypothesis of a possible common ceramic antecedent to the northwest of the Ubangi-Zaïre confluence did not seem too far-fetched at that time (Eggert 1987a, p. 143). In fact, our 1987 reconnaissance of the Sangha-Ngoko and the Likwala-aux-Herbes rivers was devised as a deliberate test of this hypothesis. Consequently, we now ought to be in position to judge the adequacy of that proposition.

As has been detailed above, the 1987 reconnaissance produced evidence of early pottery in the projected region. Contrary to what had been hoped, however, this pottery does not provide the key to the problem. Rather than having traced back Imbonga and Batalimo-Maluba pottery to a common ceramic 'ancestor', we are now faced with reconciling three different pottery styles instead of two. I do not see how Pikunda-Munda ware can be considered directly related to Batalimo-Maluba pottery and much the same holds for its relationship to Imbonga ware. This is not to deny, however, that the overall pattern of layout and techniques of decoration, as well as the fabric of the Munda pots, recall Imbonga ware. This rather vague impression notwith-standing, there are more differences than similarities between these two ceramic groups. It suffices to draw attention to vessel shape in general and base form in particular.

When it comes to comparing the absolute dating of Imbonga, Batalimo-Maluba and Pikunda-Munda pottery our initial hope that early pottery in the Sangha-Likwala region might represent a ceramic tradition ancestral to the first two groups was in vain. The dates obtained for Pikunda-Munda ware very clearly demonstrate the priority of Imbonga pottery. We thus have to accept the fact that Imbonga ware is still the oldest securely dated pottery as yet discovered in the equatorial rainforest.

Our 1987 extension of the River Reconnaissance Project into the Sangha-Ngoko-Likwala region of Congo and the adjacent southeastern part of Cameroon did not provide the key to the settlement of the inner Congo-Zaïre basin by pottery-producing populations. As to its temporal position, the early ceramics found at Pikunda on the Sangha and Munda on the Likwala are roughly equivalent to Batalimo-Maluba pottery. In this respect, the discovery of apparently older pottery at Mobaka and Mitula on the lower Sangha should be kept in mind. Somewhat surprisingly, the dates are the same for this quite different pottery.

Early rainforest pottery: the question of external relationship

In a paper written in early 1985 and devoted to a detailed analysis of the Imbonga Horizon and related problems, an attempt was made to relate the specific pottery in question to ceramic entities known from outside the rainforest (Eggert 1984, pp. 277–86). On the whole, the result was completely negative despite the fact that as far as only single elements of shape or decoration were considered some parallels could be drawn.

In the meantime de Maret (1986) published the ceramic material at the heart of his Ngovo Group and Clist (1988; 1989a, pp. 75–80) discussed the pottery of his Okala Group. This does not affect, however, the outcome of my 1984 paper for there do not appear to be any convincing resemblances between either Ngovo or Okala pottery and Imbonga ware. Thus, there is still no material known from outside or within the forest with which to connect Imbonga pottery in any comprehensive, i.e. broadly based, manner. The same is true for Batalimo-Maluba and Pikunda-Munda ware.

In his recent review Clist (1989a) approached the problem of possible relationships between the different groups of early central African pottery in much the same way as I had done for Imbonga and Batalimo-Maluba ware in 1987. Having reviewed the evidence, he concluded that the various ceramic groups were isolated from each other and that no direct link existed between them. Focusing his attention on single elements, such as 'rocking comb impressions, zigzag incisions and impressed designs on the flat bottoms' which are common to all his groups considered, he felt confident to suggest a 'common ancestry' to all of them (Clist 1989a, p. 80). In fact, he believed that this ancestral ware might be represented in the pottery from Obobogo and the river Denis sites 1 and 3 in the Gabon estuary which he had briefly discussed before (Clist 1989a, pp. 76–7).

As I have pointed out elsewhere (Eggert 1988, p. 34) the only elements common to both Obobogo and Imbonga pottery are flat bottoms and rocked zigzag decoration. Therefore, and with respect to what has been said above on the absolute dating of the Obobogo shafts, I must differ from Clist.[23] To understand fully his line of reasoning one has to be aware of the fact that he tends to think of his early 'neolithic' villages in Cameroon and Gabon in terms of Bantu-speaking groups. For him, it is quite possible that the first 'neolithic' settlers represented those Bantu speakers who certain historical linguists tell us spread from the Nigeria–Cameroon borderland both to the east and to the southeast. Thus, Obobogo and other early sites with ceramics are considered by Clist (1989a, p. 90) to be the material remnants of early Bantu speakers slowly advancing southwards following the coastal savannas. However, there is nothing in the archaeological record with which to support this latest attempt at linking archaeology and historical linguistics.

Surviving in the forest: the problem of subsistence

As has been shown above, Imbonga pottery is chronologically linked to the last half of the first millennium BC and thus represents the oldest ceramic group of the inner Congo–Zaïre basin. It is tempting to equate the people who made this pottery with those populations who were the first systematically to settle the central part of the equatorial forest. Considering the early dating of this settlement we are at once faced with the problem of how these populations managed to survive in the forest environment.[24]

Today, manioc (*Manihot utilissima* Pohl) constitutes the staple food *par excellence* of the rainforest. Being a food plant of south American origin, its distribution in Africa beginning in the early seventeenth century was due to European, especially Portuguese, seafarers (Bontinck 1972, p. 82; Vansina 1979b, pp. 11–12). As has been discussed elsewhere, there are some indications that plantains (*Musa paradisiaca* L.) served as staple food in the forest before the introduction of manioc (Eggert 1984, pp. 264–5). This was still true in parts of the central forest when the first Europeans arrived there in the late nineteenth century (Eggert 1987, pp. 7–14).

It is still very much a matter of debate when and where the plantain and the banana (*Musa sapientium* L.) arrived from southeast Asia and how they were propagated on the African continent. Since, according to current thinking, they were introduced to the east African coast in the first half of the first millennium AD (Simmonds 1966, pp. 311–12), it appears quite unlikely that the people who produced and used Imbonga pottery subsisted on plantain. Yam (*Dioscorea* spp.) seems to be the best candidate to have provided these people with a staple food.

Unlike the plantain, yam is not especially adapted to rainforest conditions. While it does thrive there as well, it is more at home in the forest-savanna mosaic characterized by less precipitation. There are quite a few species of yam, some of which originated from South America and Asia. However, two species (*Dioscorea rotundata* Poir. and *Dioscorea cayenensis* Lam.) are considered autochthonous to Africa (Coursey 1967; Alexander & Coursey 1969; Coursey 1976). As to the possible antiquity of its general use as a food plant, some west African evidence appears to be of interest. There the prohibition that it must not come in direct contact with iron tools in a specific ceremonial context, i.e. during the 'New Yam Festival', is fairly widespread. This has been interpreted as indicating that the plant's introduction into general use predates the introduction of iron metallurgy (Coursey & Coursey 1971, p. 478).

In view of the fact that the botanical structure of yam is not very resistant, and thus preservable, chances for direct archaeological evidence of its cultivation are very slim.

The same is true for pollen evidence since domesticated species flower only rarely or under circumstances that impede free, i.e. wind-borne, propagation of the pollen (Coursey 1967, pp. 32, 35–6). However, current work on chemical analysis of remains of tubers and roots preserved in pottery seems rather promising (Hill & Evans 1989). Also, some indirect indicators of yam cultivation may result from botanical and ethnoarchaeological experiments (Chikwendu & Okezie 1989). The importance of an ethnographic and ethnoarchaeological approach to identifying indirect evidence of yam cultivation had already been outlined twenty years ago (Alexander 1970).

For the time being, however, we have to look for more tangible botanical evidence than that left behind by yam cultivation in our search for cultigens used by the early pottery-producing populations in the forest. As has already been mentioned, there is fairly widespread evidence of the use of the oil palm (*Elaeis guineensis* Jacq.) in connection with early sites in central Africa. This is true for the inner Congo-Zaïre basin as well. Endocarps of the fruits of this tree were recovered at Imbonga, Maluba and Munda in connection with early ceramics.

At Imbonga these endocarps were associated with the kernels of the fruits of the wild *Canarium schweinfurthii* Engl. After they have been put in warm water for a moment the fruits of this tree are still being eaten today in the equatorial forest as well as in other parts of Africa. Moreover, in the equator region the resin of this tree is being used to seal cracks in pottery (Irvine 1961, pp. 508–10; Hulstaert 1966, p. 33, no. 93). As has been seen above, de Maret found oil palm and *Canarium schweinfurthii* associated at Obobogo as well. The same has been reported for west African sites (Eggert 1984, p. 269).

With respect to the oil palm commonly thought to have originated in west Africa, it may be stressed that the rainforest proper is not its natural habitat (Hartley 1970, pp. 2–4). To thrive it needs sufficient light provided only by open village spaces and agricultural clearances. Its occurrence in forest stretches devoid of human settlement is thus a sure sign that the area was once settled (Opsomer n.d., pp. 503–4; Van Moesieke 1929, pp. 402–3; Allison 1962, p. 246).

Still today, the oil palm is of prime importance in the rainforest. While the nuts are eaten raw, boiled or roasted, the various other parts of the tree serve multiple functions, e.g. as material for construction, as the source of palm wine, etc. Moreover, the oil extracted from the nuts still covers the greater part of the fat requirements of the forest population (Hulstaert 1962; Hulstaert 1966, pp. 128–32, no. 429). While the oil palm thus plays an important role it is not – and never was – a staple food.

In the archaeological literature there seem to be some misconceptions with respect to the early use of the oil palm. Thus, Shaw (1976, p. 131) speaks of 'the early protection' of this tree and de Maret (1982b, p. 3) takes the occurrence of palm nuts and the fragment of a grinding stone in a shaft at Obobogo as an indication of 'some sort of sedentary food producers'. In the same context, the latter (de Maret 1982b, p. 12) even talks about the 'process of domestication' of the oil palm.[25] Considering the morphology and physiology of this palm, concepts like these appear to be somewhat inadequate. In fact, once utilized the oil palm is propagated quite easily and without any premeditation simply by the throwing away of the palm nuts. It is interesting to note in this context that, while the oil palm is utilized everywhere in the equatorial rainforest of Zaïre, it is never cultivated in a traditional setting.

It is clear, then, that at the moment the evidence concerning early food plants remains somewhat inconclusive. Nothing has been said about animal sources of food because at present we lack evidence about this in the equatorial area; that is mostly because faunal remains are so scantily preserved.

Early rainforest settlement: stone or iron?

When the Belgian administrator H.-J. Lothaire (1907) travelled in the Lulonga region of the central forest in 1890 he claimed to have seen ten to twelve shaft furnaces in full operation. While he may not have used the correct terminology for the installations that he saw,[26] there is no doubt about the widespread practice of iron production in pre-European times in the inner Congo-Zaïre basin (R. K. Eggert 1987, pp. 53–61). Still today abundant remains of this activity consisting of both single slag dumps and whole fields with up to sixty and more slag heaps are scattered throughout the equatorial region. Unfortunately, there is very little evidence concerning either the antiquity or the development of iron metallurgy in this region.

Lately much has been written on early iron metallurgy in tropical Africa. We have been told by Schmidt and co-workers that the methods of iron production developed during the early Iron Age in what is now Tanzania were especially advanced. The early smelters are said to have discovered and systematically used the principle of preheating the incoming air of the furnace – a procedure that is claimed to have yielded a technically superior carbon steel (Schmidt & Avery 1978; Schmidt 1980; Schmidt & Avery 1983; Schmidt & Childs 1985). It has been demonstrated, however, that these far-reaching claims are not supported by the available data (Eggert 1985; Eggert 1987b; Rehder 1986). It may be noted in passing that there seems to be a similar tendency on the part of some authors, among them Schmidt, to find some supposedly uniquely advanced early iron metallurgy in Gabon as well (Schmidt, Digombe, Locko & Mouleingui 1985, p. 17; Locko 1987, p. 25). As yet, however, nothing substantial has been published in this regard.

As has been discussed above, early iron metallurgy in northwest-central Africa is currently dated to the last half of the first millennium BC. This early appearance of iron production and iron-working in the interior of what is now Gabon stands in apparent contrast to the dating of central African 'neolithic' cultures. We have had to admit that at present there is no immediate answer to account for this puzzling phenomenon. We now have to consider the corresponding situation in the region lying to the east of Gabon, e.g. in the central part of the equatorial forest.

This is not the place to document meticulously and discuss whatever sources on traditional and ancient iron production in the inner Congo-Zaïre basin we have at our disposal.[27] Rather, we have to concentrate on the question of whether the technical equipment of the first pottery-producing populations in the central forest was based on stone or whether these people already had the knowledge and experience to extract iron from lateritic ore.

I have stressed on several occasions the curious fact that no other material than pottery is found in Imbonga Horizon contexts (Eggert 1984, p. 277; Eggert 1987a, p. 131; Eggert 1987c, pp. 3233–4). It is therefore impossible to decide to which techno-complex the earliest ceramic group in the central forest should be ascribed. It goes without saying that a solution to this problem will have to await further fieldwork.

According to the site of Batalimo one would have to interpret the Batalimo-Maluba Horizon as being the material representation of a stone tool-producing and stone tool-using culture. One would like to see additional empirical evidence in support of this view, however. Unfortunately, our own sondages at Maluba did not provide any material evidence to substantiate or refute the current interpretation.

Considering the Pikunda-Munda Horizon we have clear evidence that it possessed an iron technology. In the lower part of the Pikunda shaft we found a small iron tool of unidentified function. While one end was worked into a spatula-like blade, the other seems to represent a badly corroded handle (Fig. 16.12–9). As has been said above, however, the pottery from the lower part of the shaft does not appear to be entirely homogeneous. At Munda, on the other hand, one of the pottery-packed shafts showed unmistakable signs of intense heat. Furthermore, its fill contained a very considerable proportion of iron slag. While we have not yet completely analysed this structure and a related one, there appears to be sufficient evidence to assume that it was somehow related to iron techniques. It could have been a bowl furnace.

With respect to the basic technology of the early pottery-producing populations in the inner Congo-Zaïre basin we are thus presented with a situation that is in some way similar to that of Gabon. While it is still uncertain whether Imbonga pottery is associated with stone or iron techniques, the somewhat younger Pikunda-Munda Horizon appears to be firmly connected to iron metallurgy. Strangely enough, however, the youngest horizon of early pottery in the central forest, Batalimo-Maluba, purports to have been based on a 'neolithic' technology. This somewhat incongruous picture demonstrates how fragmentary is our current insight into one of the most formative periods of central African culture history.

Epilogue: theory, linguistics and archaeological fieldwork

Generally, sub-Saharan archaeology or, more specifically, the later part of it, has had its fair share of theory or, rather, speculation, with its studies on 'Bantu origins' and the like. These studies had their heyday in the 1960s and 1970s, in the time before systematic archaeological work in most parts of central Africa really started. Consequently, this part of the continent was either left out altogether or the blanks filled in with broad strokes of imagination. The pertinent studies themselves were a peculiar blend of a variety of elements predominantly borrowed from cultural anthropology, archaeology and historical linguistics. The underlying theoretical assumptions were of both a very general anthropological and a linguistic nature. One lengthy critique came to the conclusion that the model on which these writings on the problem of Bantu expansion were based was surprisingly simplistic, with basic cultural mechanisms such as migration, adaptation and acculturation hardly conceptualized in other than a most superficial manner (Eggert 1981, p. 323). As to general linguistics, the studies had to be judged very lopsided in their almost unique reliance on lexicostatistics and glottochronology. This was counteracted only recently by Möhlig's (1981; 1989) phonological approach to Bantu linguistics leading to what he called the 'strata- or stratification model'. Interestingly, his results differ considerably from those of Heine (1973; 1984) and Heine, Hoff & Vossen (1977).[28]

The lesson to be learned from the writings of the 1960s and 1970s is that the historical interpretation of the younger prehistory of sub-Saharan Africa has been almost exclusively dependent on the changing hypotheses proffered by Bantuists. As has been demonstrated elsewhere (Eggert 1981), archaeologists have been largely discredited in the course of attempting to transpose these views into their own field. Nor has it been reassuring, in these processes of circular reasoning, to find the Bantuists then taking such dependent archaeological findings as independent confirmation of their own results.

The archaeological situation in central Africa has changed considerably since the 1960s and 1970s. For all the lacunae still very much part and parcel of central Africa's archaeology, a solid empirical footing is beginning to appear for some selected topics, as has been shown in this chapter. However, some of the newer attempts at synthesis are only slightly different from what has been criticized before (Vansina 1979b; Vansina 1984; Vansina 1989). For all the acclaim that these speculative schemes gain for their supposed 'plausibility' (see, e.g. Phillipson 1985b, pp. 71–2; Clist 1989a, p. 90) they remain anachronistic (Eggert 1984, pp. 270–1; Eggert & Kanimba 1987, p. 482). While the basic theoretical problems persist and need to be tackled without further delay, empirical data can no longer be displaced by speculation, no matter how 'nicely' such speculation may fit in with a supposed intricate web of inter-regional connections. This chapter must therefore conclude with the realization that for central African archaeology at least, armchair pseudo-history must make way for a historical discourse that is theory-based *and* factual. The future of central African archaeology, at this time, lies in fieldwork.

Notes

[1] For a very brief summary of the pertinent palaeoecological data from east Africa and the Atlantic coast see also Clist (1989a, pp. 61–3). There, information which was not available to Preuss from northwest as well as south-central Africa is considered.

[2] The calibration of conventional radiocarbon dates to 'BC' and 'AD' given in the following tables have been calculated according to Stuiver & Pearson (1986) and Pearson & Stuiver (1986).

[3] According to the official French spelling of geographical names in the People's Republic of Congo this river is spelt as 'Likouala-aux-Herbes'. Attention must be drawn to the fact that there is another river by the name of 'Likouala' (sometimes called 'Likouala-Mossaka') in that country. Lying to the west of the Sangha, this second river flows largely parallel to the Likwala-aux-Herbes. In the following text 'Likwala' refers to 'Likwala-aux-Herbes'.

[4] For the region to the south of the Zaïre river the cultural sequence presented in these papers has been very much elaborated and documented in impressive detail in an unpublished doctoral dissertation by Hans-Peter Wotzka (1990).

[5] See Eggert (1987a, pp. 134–7) for some reservations as to the homogeneous nature of the pottery at the site of Batalimo.

[6] The three radiocarbon dates given by Clist (1986, p. 227; 1989a, pp. 69–70, Table 1) for this association refer to the first half of the fourth and the beginning and middle of the third millennium BC respectively. The cautious wording by Clist (1986, p. 227) leads me to express some

reservation as long as no details with respect to the precise nature of the relationship of the lithic industry, the sherds and the charcoal samples used for dating are published.

[7] According to Clist (1986, p. 225) this pit contained another fragment of a polished stone artefact, possibly an axe.

[8] The six radiocarbon dates listed by Clist (1988, p. 46, Fig. 2; 1989a, p. 70 Table 1) are not specified as to the archaeological features from which the corresponding charcoal and palm-nut samples were derived.

[9] I do not put much trust in the dating of the river Denis 1 and 3 sites in the Gabon estuary where early ceramics are reported to be associated with what seems to be late stone age lithic material. The pottery is said to show a number of common traits with Okala pottery. The dates for the sites in question are 4810 ± 80 bp (Beta-20789) and 3400 ± 70 bp (Beta-17061) respectively (Clist 1989a, pp. 70 (Table 1), 76–7; see also Clist 1987a, pp. 27–8).

[10] Of the six radiocarbon dates published only the oldest and the youngest have been retained here (see note 8).

[11] Unfortunately, the precise association of the ground stone items and the pottery within the different shafts has not been specified in the publications quoted.

[12] Together with the date Hv-10583 quoted above, de Maret (1982a, p. 11; 1982b, pp. 2–3, 15) published two other dates from Obobogo, run on charcoal and affiliated with a 'trench A': level 40–50 cm, 2055 ± 70 bp (Hv-10580); level 130–140 cm, 2900 ± 110 bp (Hv-10582). No details about the archaeological contents of Trench A are given. The Hv-10580 date was rejected by de Maret (1982a, p. 11) as 'probably contaminated by modern disturbances', whereas the other two were retained.

[13] However, de Maret (1985, p. 135) seems to reject the Hv-11046 date as too early (see note 14).

[14] The Hv-11046 date is apparently rejected by de Maret (1985, p. 135) as too early because of its association with iron slag. It is puzzling that the Lv-1432 date, which de Maret accepts, is not cited and discussed by Clist (1986, p. 219). In another publication, however, Clist (1987c, p. 381) refers to this date while omitting Hv-11046.

[15] A younger date of 1560 ± 100 bp (Beta-15739) for this refuse dump has been rejected on statistical and stratigraphic grounds while another one of 1850 ± 70 bp (Beta-9082), although derived from a sample from beneath the dump, has not been considered further (Digombe, Schmidt, Mouleingui-Boukosso, Mombo & Locko 1987a, p. 10; Digombe, Schmidt, Mouleingui-Boukosso, Mombo & Locko 1987b, p. 713). While Digombe, Schmidt, Mouleingui-Boukosso, Mombo & Locko (1988) commented on the Beta-17043 date from Moanda I and the Beta-17044 from Moanda II, no detailed information is available for the dates from Makokou, Lopé 4 and Koualessis listed in our Table 16.3.

[16] Some information on the sites not discussed here is to be found in the literature quoted for Table 16.3 as well as in Clist (1987b, pp. 7–8; 1989b, pp. 82–7).

[17] For all sites and other geographical indications, see Figure 16.3.

[18] What I called 'Imbonga Horizon' has been divided up into four partly contemporaneous groups – Imbonga, Ingende, Bonkake and Inganda – by H.-P. Wotzka (1990).

[19] More specifically, Wotzka (1990) assigns the associated pottery to what he calls the 'Inganda Group'. We have no radiocarbon dates for his two other ceramic groups which I included in the Imbonga Horizon, his 'Bonkake' and 'Ingende Group'. The situation is somewhat more complicated in that he now assigns the pottery associated with three of the dates published by me as belonging to Imbonga ware (Eggert 1987a, p. 133, Table 1, nos. 4–6) to his 'Monkoto Group', which is apparently younger than Imbonga pottery. I accept his classification.

[20] The ceramic complex in question is IMB 81/9/I which had been dated to 3775 ± 105 bp by the Hanover laboratory (Hv-11574). This date belonged to those furnished by Hanover that have recently given rise to some critical comments (Eggert 1987a, pp. 132–3). The new date provided in 1989 by the Kiel laboratory only corroborates the criticism expressed then.

[21] This dating of the Imbonga Horizon has unfortunately been wrongly assigned to 'the second half of the first millennium AD' in Eggert (1987a, p. 133).

[22] Officially, the two villages are spelled in the French manner as 'Pikounda' and 'Mounda' respectively. In what follows the official version of any geographical designations mentioned will be given in brackets.

[23] Eggert 1988 was written in 1986, i.e. before our reconnaissance of the Sangha-Likwala region. While I left no doubt about the extremely limited number of elements common to Imbonga and Obobogo pottery, I then felt that the latter might have been some kind of connecting link between the ceramics of the Saharo-Sudanese territory on the one hand and that of the rainforest on the other (Eggert 1988, pp. 34–5). Thus, at that time my concept of a possible 'ancestral' role of Obobogo pottery was similar to that of Clist.

[24] For a somewhat more detailed discussion of the following see Eggert (1984, pp. 264–9). A very thorough general review of early crops in Africa has been provided by Shaw (1976); specifically for west Africa see Shaw (1977).

[25] See also the remarks of de Maret (1986, p. 129) on evidence of oil palm and *Canarium schweinfurthii* utilization in the context of his 'Ngovo Group' and similar presumably neolithic phenomena ('a sort of aboriculture', 'a process of domestication', 'a form of agriculture').

[26] Lothaire (1907) used the term 'hauts-fourneaux', i.e. 'shaft furnaces'. Judging from the evidence known to me I believe that in the central part of the forest iron production was practised with bowl furnaces.

[27] For a brief discussion of pertinent evidence see R. K. Eggert (1987, pp. 53–61) and Eggert (1987c, pp. 3235–7).

[28] For a detailed analysis of the current situation involving central African archaeology, Bantu linguistics and cultural anthropology see Wotzka (1990).

Acknowledgement

I should like to thank Peter Ucko who insisted that this chapter be written. I also thank Rita Volbracht, Christl Meyenburg and Peter Mlodoch (all from Hamburg) as well as Bianca Sommer and Wolfgang Taubeld (both from Erlangen) for the preparation of almost all the maps and line drawings used in this chapter, and also Ines Balzer (then also of Erlangen) for help in preparing the map in Figure 16.3.

17   Transition from Late Stone Age to Iron Age in the Sudano-Sahelian zone: a case study from the Perichadian plain

AUGUSTIN HOLL

Introduction

In traditional archaeological classification, the past is divided into successive sequences based on technological transformations (see Musa Muhammed, Ch. 27, this volume). These broad divisions are certainly valid, but they are very general and tend to overshadow many other changes which occurred in past societies. The purpose of this chapter is to analyse a very short temporal sequence of west African late prehistory pertaining to the appearance of a new technology and new kinds of artefacts – metallurgy and its products – and to discuss through a case study various kinds of processes attested by archaeological data. This chapter is a study of change: transition means a process of change from an earlier stage A to a later stage B. These different steps are from the 'Neolithic' or Late Stone Age, broadly defined as food-producing economies without knowledge of metallurgy, to the Early Iron Age, which witnessed the appearance of the first iron artefacts in the prehistoric assemblages. But the division is not so simple, because the mere presence of iron artefacts or debris does not inevitably indicate a 'conventional' iron age site; many other factors must be sought. According to Kense (1983c, p. 12), an iron age society can best be considered as one which has a working knowledge of iron technology and has integrated that technology within the various aspects of its social structure. An important differentiation can thus be made between iron-using communities which received their iron artefacts through exchange or trade, and iron-producing communities which have mastered iron technology. The blurring of this distinction often leads to confusion in the discussions of hypotheses concerning the emergence of iron technology in Africa.

The emergence of iron technology in west Africa: discussion of hypotheses

There is a considerable literature dealing with the problems related to the origin of iron technology in west Africa (Lhote 1952; Mauny 1952; Mauny 1953; Huard 1960; Huard 1964; Arkell, Fagan & Summers 1966; Diop 1968; Shinnie 1971; Mauny 1973; Tylecote 1975a; Andah 1980; van der Merwe 1980; Rustad 1980; Treinen-Claustre 1982; Echard

1983c; Schmidt & Avery 1983; Phillipson 1985a). Two main traditions of explanation coexist: one of them, initiated by Leo Frobenius and the German 'Culture Historical School', consists of various kinds of diffusionist theories, and the other is put forward by proponents of local evolution.

According to diffusionist hypotheses (Mauny 1952; Mauny 1953; Huard 1960; Mauny 1964; Arkell, Fagan & Summers 1966; Mauny 1973; Tylecote 1975a), the problem of the development of iron technology in west Africa has already been solved; some propose a north African or Carthaginian origin with hypothetical Lybico-Berbers or Berbers as middlemen, while others prefer an oriental origin, the Meroitic hypothesis. Thus iron technology expanded from Mediterranean and/or Meroitic centres to west Africa because 'it seems impossible . . . that a discovery of iron technology independent of the Mediterranean area occurred there. This complex technology could not emerge in a context totally ignorant of metallurgy' (Mauny 1973, p. 533).

Recent archaeological research does not support this opinion (Grébénart 1979a; Grébénart 1979b; Van Grunderbeek, Roche & Doutrelepont 1982; Grébénart 1983; Holl 1983; Lambert 1983; Schmidt & Avery 1983). The proponents of local evolution hypotheses disagree with diffusionist theories (Lhote 1952; Diop 1968; Andah 1980) and believe that, considering the wide distribution of iron ore in west Africa, iron technology was an indigenous development. Diop (1968, p. 37), for instance, after a short review of different explanations for the origin of iron technology in west Africa, concluded that 'it now seems certain that traditional African iron technology is very ancient, widely distributed and autochthonous, but we still have to determine zones of origin of that metallurgy, their exact dating and the hypothetical iron routes throughout the African continent'. In other words, nothing is known, all is to be done.

The simplicity of arguments mobilized by this old debate is misleading. The analytical level of the discussions is too general, and sometimes mainly a matter of faith. It is clear that iron technology is a complex system of interactions between societies, environment, technical skills and social demands. According to Rustad (1980, p. 232), it is clear that iron technology must be broken down into its component parts to permit valid comparisons. Since the component parts of iron technology have alternative manifestations, the question 'Did iron technology diffuse?' is too broad and vague (see also Musa Muhammed, Ch. 27, this volume). Many of the components could have diffused independently of the others. The appropriate line of thought is to begin with specific traits which are capable of comparison. Using archaeological assemblages, one must first select useful criteria for comparison; they may be divided into two kinds: intrinsic, pertaining to the various properties of archaeological finds, more specifically iron artefacts, and extrinsic, dealing with archaeological context; both kinds of criteria are included in a more general systemic framework.

Intrinsic criteria deal with three main properties (Gardin 1979, p. 123). Physical properties (P) are all those characteristics of iron artefacts related to their mineralogical constituents (Tylecote 1983). Archaeometallurgical techniques developed in recent years make possible the investigation of provenance, the nature of the iron ore exploited and the level of technological skills. Geometrical properties (G) are those characteristics related to the form of iron artefacts. The analysis of specific forms present in each assemblage may allow the delimitation of specific craft traditions, and radiographic investigations assist the study of the specific modes of transformation used. Finally, semiological properties (S) pertain to the analysis of decorative design systems. They are more culture-dependent and must therefore reinforce the presence and/or absence of specific craft traditions, and their geographic distribution.

Extrinsic criteria also consist of three properties: that of place (Pl) (the site, the stratigraphic unit, the archaeological structure), or the specific activity area in which the artefact has been found; the property of time (T) (the exact or relative dating of the finding's context), and the property of function (F), which may allow a functional classification of iron artefacts (e.g. jewels, weapons, agricultural tools) and the appreciation of their relative part in the global assemblage of a specific site or stratigraphic unit.

Through a combination of these different properties, P, G, S, Pl, T and F, it may be possible to build our inferences on more solid empirical bases, and to make inter-site comparisons easier.

Systemic analysis of iron technology

Archaeologists are concerned with generalizations and explanations of cultural transformations and process; our specific concern here is an empirical understanding of the relationships of environment, social dynamics and iron technology. According to Arnold (1985, p. 2), as attractive as assumptions are about the interpretive significance of (ceramic) types for the interpretation of the past, it remains to be demonstrated that (ceramic) classifications and chronologies do more than group (ceramic) assemblages in space and time. This argument is equally applicable to the study of iron artefacts. Classifications based on fragmentary iron artefacts are very limited in scope. An iron blade is not a behavioural unit. Like all cultural behaviour, the behaviour used in the production, decoration and use of iron products is structured: 'behaviourally meaningful units are structured into higher level patterns and sequences . . . it is not the units themselves that carry information, but rather the way these units are structured relative to one another' (Arnold 1985, p. 5).

Contrary to the analytical/mechanical paradigm, the systems approach is more concerned with relationships between entities than with the entities themselves. It concerns the principles of organization rather than the intrinsic properties of these units of organization. Its focus is on the 'how' of organization more than the 'what'. Systems are therefore concerned with wholes and causation is not mono-causal but multi-causal.

The acceptance of a new technology is a matter of opportunity, costs vis-à-vis earlier situations, e.g. previous use of stone or other materials; such acceptance is determined by a combination of social, economic, technological and ecological circumstances. Iron technology may thus be conceptualized as a system consisting of varying degrees of interaction between environment (resources, weather and climate), technical knowledge, and, in social organization, between conflict scheduling, social differentiation and demands. Each pair of these interaction sequences can be seen as a feedback mechanism either limiting (negative feedback) or stimulating (positive feedback) iron technology development.

The production of iron artefacts may be divided into four main sequences: the procurement of raw materials, the reduction process, the smithing and the distribution of final products. These different steps are differentially coordinated according to societies. In some, there are peoples specialized in iron ore procurement. Their products are sold to iron smelters who sell their own products, the blooms or ingots, to blacksmiths. In some others, the four sequences, from iron ore procurement to iron artefact production and distribution, are accomplished by the same individuals or group of peoples. The social position of people engaged in an iron-producing system is also very variable. In some societies they have no specific status (Monino 1983). In some others, the Mossi (Izard 1983) and the Tuareg (Bernus 1983), for instance, they are granted special treatment: 'a small minority, blacksmiths are a fundamental element of Tuareg society. Complex clients' relationships had allowed the establishment of rules between necessary partners with complementary roles' (Bernus 1983, p. 248).

Obviously there is a long labour sequence in the production of iron objects. The first step is the acquisition of raw materials – iron ore, clay and fuel – which constitute environmental requirements. This phase may lead to specific social division of labour. The building of smelting installations, furnaces, tuyères and crucibles and their spatial locations are also socially conditioned by societies' value systems and rules (Echard 1983b; Monino 1983). Depending on the amount of iron needed, the reduction process may last some hours or some days in relation to schedules conflicting with subsistence activities in each specific society and in relation to weather conditions. This activity may therefore be seasonal. The smithing sequence which takes place after the

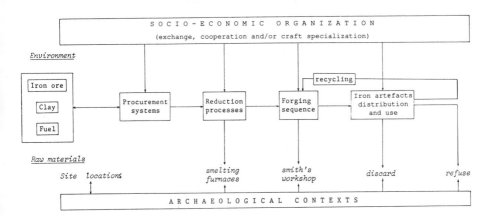

Figure 17.1 Model of iron-working system with archaeological correlates.

production of iron blooms is partly conditioned by the quantity and the quality of social demand; the same argument is valid for the nature of the distribution system and the degree of discard and curation of iron objects. The paucity of iron artefacts in some sites may be related to the low rate of discard and high degree of curation (Fig. 17.1).

The partial conclusion is that a systems approach tries to fill the gap between archaeological data and the past societies which produced them. However, in the present state of archaeological research on this specific topic in Sudano-Sahelian Africa, we are obliged to formulate some questions in order to devise their archaeological test implications:

1. When and where did the earliest iron artefacts occur?
2. What are their archaeological contexts?
3. What is their nature and their relative importance in the archaeological assemblages?
4. Is there concomitant change or continuity in other parts of the archaeological assemblage?

Earliest iron age sites: chronology and geographic distribution

Pre-iron age metallurgy is known to have been present in two areas of west Africa, the Akjoujt region in Mauritania (Lambert 1983) and the Agadez region in Niger (Grébénart 1979a; Grébénart 1979b; Grébénart 1983). In Mauritania, in the Guelb Moghrein area, copper metallurgy was established between the eighth and third century BC and production consisted of small weapons and ornaments (Lambert 1983, p. 73). Nothing is known about the relations between this copper-producing society and late stone age societies in that region. In the Agadez region, in contrast, more substantial information is available.

Grébénart (1983) found two phases in the Niger copper metallurgy: an earlier phase – Copper I – present at Afunfun Site 175, Sekkiret valley sites and Aghtauzu Site 178. This early copper metallurgy consists of the production of artefacts in native copper, and its dating, from fourteen radiocarbon dates, ranges from 4140 ± 90 bp (furnace) to 2700 ± 70 bp (Grébénart 1983, pp. 111–12). A later copper metallurgy – Copper II – has been found in the same area, at Afunfun Site 162, Ikawaten Site 193, Sekkiret valley sites, Azelik Site 210, Tyeral Site 207 and Tuluk Site 211, and dated, from seventeen radiocarbon determinations, from the ninth century to the first century BC. Furnaces, slag and copper objects are present. The products consist of spindles, spatulas, thin arrowheads, burins, hammered bracelets and small ingots weighing from 30 to 160 grams. The amount of slag varies from 10 m^3 at Afunfun Site 162 to 32 m^3 at Ikawaten Site 193. According to Grébénart, the copper metallurgists were nomadic, engaged in probably seasonal small-scale production and supplying Saharan neolithic communities.

These data on pre-iron age metallurgy are a real challenge to earlier diffusion theory (Mauny 1953), but the problem is still not resolved: what are the relations between copper and iron technology? The debate is still very intense among archaeometallurgists; according to van der Merwe (1980), there is no direct link between copper and iron technology and there is no logical sequence of technological progress from the first to the second. Whatever the truth, copper technology attests the mastery of a considerable degree of pyrotechnology. Iron technology did not develop in contact with Mauritanian copper-producing societies, but this did occur in the Niger area. The earliest occurrences of iron technology have been found at Do Dimi, 2628 ± 120 bp (Dak 145); Azelik, 2490 ± 90 bp (Gif 4175), 2480 ± 90 bp (Gif 4330) (Calvocoressi and David 1979, p. 25); and Ekne Wan Ataran, 2400 ± 90 bp (MC 2397) (Sutton 1982, p. 213). In the latter area there is an important difference from Copper II settlement patterns. The early iron age settlements are represented by forty permanent habitation sites. Their surface areas vary from some 10 m² to more than a hectare. They are located on the southern side of the Tigidit cliff, stretching for more than 200 km from east to west. This early iron age complex is dated from the fifth century to the first century BC. Furnaces, slag and iron objects attest local iron production, on a small scale. Products consisted of small objects such as ornaments (arm-rings, spindles, pendants) and weapons (arrowheads, harpoons). Considering the distribution of the sites, the dating and similarities in ceramics, Grébénart (1983, p. 115) thinks that there were relations between early iron-producing and Saharan neolithic communities through exchanges. It is worth noting that stone artefacts were always present in early iron age habitation sites in the form of small scrapers, bifacially flaked and polished axes and arrow points. From this development we can see that early iron objects were above all status objects. The basic toolkit was not radically affected by the early development of this new technology. It seems that the production of prestige items, such as ornaments and weapons, was the main social demand which led to the development or adoption of metallurgical technology by late stone age societies.

This transition did not take place at the same speed in the whole Sudano-Sahelian zone; the shift is gradual (Figs 17.2, 17.3, Table 17.1). Nineteen securely dated Sudano-Sahelian sites are selected for discussion here. Seven of them are in Niger, four in Nigeria, four in Chad, two in Mali, one in Ghana and one in Senegal. If we divide these sites into three chronological periods, the first composed of sites possessing iron artefacts dating before 500 BC, the second of sites dated between 500 BC and 200 BC and the third sites dating between 200 BC and 1 BC, we see that the earliest occurrences of iron artefacts are in Niger and Nigeria. Sites dated between 500 BC and 200 BC are distributed in Niger, Nigeria and Mali, and finally sites dated between 200 BC and 1 BC are distributed in Niger, Nigeria, Mali, Chad, Ghana and Senegal. All these sites do not have the same potential for the investigations of the transition from the Late Stone Age to the Early Iron Age. Some good opportunities are offered by stratified mound sites. This is the case for Daboya (Kense 1979; Kense 1985b) in modern Ghana:

> Research at Daboya . . . had clearly demonstrated an unexpected antiquity
> of occupation. The site had been inhabited, possibly continuously, since
> about the early 2nd millennium bc and thereby represented one of the
> oldest and most consistent sites in Ghana to date. (Kense 1985b, p. 19)

At that site, the earliest iron artefacts occurred in a layer dated from the first century BC: 2010 ± 140 bp (Gx 6133) (Sutton 1982, p. 297). Sites of the 'Nok culture', Taruga and Samun Dukiya, do not have pre–iron age archaeological deposits (Rustad 1980). In contrast, sites of the Perichadian plain (Lebeuf 1969; Connah 1981; Lebeuf 1981) are well-stratified mounds in which an investigation of change in material culture is possible. These kinds of settlement mounds are widely distributed in northeastern Nigeria, northern Cameroon and western Chad. They result from the gradual build–up of structural remains and domestic refuse from successive human activities formerly located for long periods of time on the same site. According to Connah (1985, p. 779), they are also an archaeological indicator of the existence of intensive agriculture. The rather limited distribution of such high settlement mounds in west Africa, and their tendency to be confined to river valleys and floodplains, would indicate that this may indeed be the case.

Continuity and change: a Perichadian case study

The Lake Chad basin is a generally flat terrain, situated in the middle of the transcontinental Sahel zone stretching across Africa from the Atlantic in the west, to the Gulf of Aden. It is composed of seasonally flooded plains, swamps and higher patches of sandy soils sloping gradually from 320 m above sea-level northwards to Lake Chad at 282 m.

The environmental sequence for the Pleistocene at Lake Chad is complex (Servant-Vildary 1978; Servant & Servant-Vildary 1980; Maley 1981). During the Holocene, the palaeo-Chad reached the 320 m contour and formed the Bama-Limani-Bongor ridge, an old shoreline, between 8000 and 2000 BC. The lake level has gradually dropped since 2000 BC, allowing progressive human settlement. For much of the Holocene, the

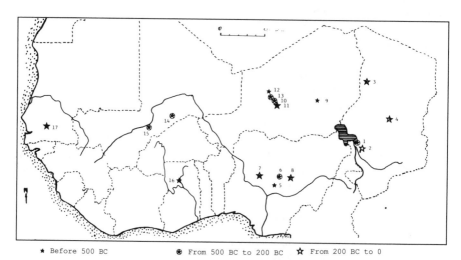

★ Before 500 BC   ⊛ From 500 BC to 200 BC   ☆ From 200 BC to 0

Figure 17.2   Earliest iron age sites in west Africa. 1 Mdaga; 2 Amkoundjo; 3 Toungour; 4 Zoui; 5 Taruga; 6 Nok and Samun Dukiya; 7 Rafin Ndoko; 8 Rop Shelter; 9 Do Dimi; 10 In Talaylen; 11 Teguef n'Agar; 12 Azelik; 13 Ekne Wan Ataran; 14 Nokara A; 15 Jenne-jeno; 16 Daboya; 17 Tiekene Bassoura

Perichadian plain was devoid of human habitation. Mound sites appear to be an adaptation to the occupation of seasonally flooded flat land. According to Lebeuf's *Carte archéologique* (1981, p. 14), 822 mounds have been recorded: 432 in Cameroon, 140 in Chad and 250 in Nigeria. Only a very small sample of this large number of sites has been excavated or tested. Archaeological research confirms the beginning of mound occupation by late stone age populations around 2000 BC. The earliest sites occupied are: Bornu 38 (11°32′N, 13°40′E), dated to 3830 ± 250 bp (N 793), 2960 ± 160 bp (N 794), 2880 ± 140 bp (N 795) and 2590 ± 170 bp (N 796); Bornu 70 (11°55′N, 14°21′E), 2680 ± 180 bp (N 791) and 2720 ± 120 bp (N 792); Kursakata (12°19′N, 14°14′E), 2880 ± 140 bp (N 480); and Daima (12°12′N, 14°27′E), 2520 ± 110 bp (I 2945) and 2400 ± 95 bp (I 2372) (Willett 1971, pp. 354–5; Connah 1981). At Sou Blamé Radjil, there are seven radiocarbon dates ranging from 3280 ± 360 bp (Ly 2284) to 2280 ± 170 bp (Ly 2004) (Lebeuf 1981, p. 11), with additional dates from Mdaga (12°12′N, 15°03′E), 2375 ± 150 bp (Gif 742) and 2150 ± 135 bp (Dak 10) and finally Amkoundjo (12°26′N, 15°02′E), 2070 ± 180 bp (Gif 435) and 1910 ± 180 bp (Gif 432) (Lebeuf 1969, p. 8) (Figs 17.4, 17.5, Table 17.2).

Not all of these sites have the same potential for the study of the late stone age to early iron age transition; some of them, Bornu 38 and Bornu 70, were occupied by hunter-fisher-gatherers possessing a bone and stone technology. Some other sites, like Amkoundjo, were settled by early iron age populations. Among the remaining sites,

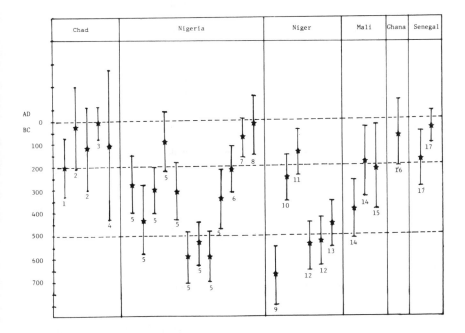

Figure 17.3 Radiocarbon dates of earliest iron age sites in west Africa.

Table 17.1 Early iron age sites : radiocarbon chronology

Sites	Radiocarbon dates (bp)	Lab.no.	References
Chad			
1 Mdaga	2150 ± 135	Dak 10	Lebeuf, Lebeuf, Treinen-Claustre & Courtin 1980, p. 12
2 Amkoundjo	1980 ± 180	Gif 432	Lebeuf 1969, p. 8
	2070 ± 180	Gif 435	ibid.
3 Toungour	1960 ± 60	Hv 3804	Close 1980, p. 165
4 Zoui	2065 ± 320	Hv 4498	ibid.
Nigeria			
5 Taruga	2230 ± 120	I 1459	Calvocoressi & David 1979, p. 26
	2390 ± 140	I 2960	ibid.
	2250 ± 100	I 3400	ibid.
	2042 ± 126	BM 532	ibid.
	2269 ± 116	BM 533	ibid.
	2541 ± 104	BM 938	ibid.
	2488 ± 84	BM 940	ibid.
	2541 ± 104	BM 941	ibid.
	2291 ± 123	BM 942	ibid.
6 Nok	2160 ± 95	I 4913	ibid.
7 Rafin Ndoko	2020 ± 75	N 2585	ibid.
8 Rop rock shelter	1975 ± 125	I 406	ibid.
Niger			
9 Do Dimi	2628 ± 120	Dak 145	Grébénart 1983, p. 120
10 In Talaylen	2210 ± 90	Gif 4170	ibid.
	2010 ± 90	Gif 4171	ibid.
11 Teguef n'Agar	2090 ± 90	Gif 4172	ibid.
12 Azelik	2490 ± 90	Gif 4175	ibid.
	2480 ± 90	Gif 4330	ibid.
13 Ekne Wan Ataran	2400 ± 90	MC 2397	Sutton 1982, p. 313
Mali			
14 Nokara A	2340 ± 115	Gx 0231	Calvocoressi & David 1979, p. 23
	2130 ± 150	Gx 2888	ibid.
15 Jenne-jeno	2160 ± 180	RL 807	McIntosh & McIntosh 1980b, p. 195
Ghana			
16 Daboya	2010 ± 140	Gx 6133	Sutton 1982, p. 312
Senegal			
17 Tiekene Bassoura	2126 ± 110	Dak 167	Calvocoressi & David 1979, p. 27
	1980 ± 60	NY 357	ibid.

there were occupations of the Late Stone Age at the base of the mounds and, later, iron age occupations. This transition has been the subject of a masterly study by Connah (1981; 1985) for the Nigerian part of the Perichadian plain (e.g. Daima). We await an understanding of this process in the Cameroonian as well as Chadian part of this ecological setting (an archaeological report on Mdaga has already been published (Lebeuf, Lebeuf, Treinen-Claustre & Courtin 1980) and research on Sou Blamé Radjil (Rapp 1980) is being published). Here we focus on the Mdaga mound and then compare it to the Daima sequence.

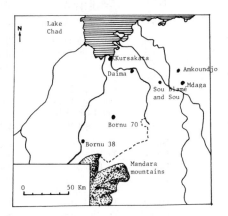

Figure 17.4 Main sites in the southern Perichadian plain mentioned in the text.

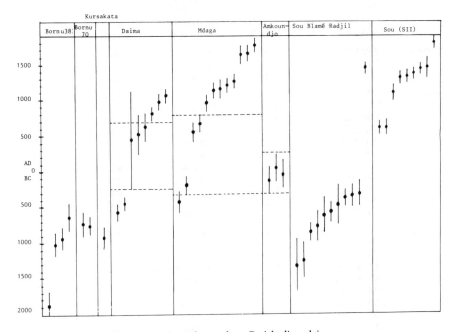

Figure 17.5 Radiocarbon dates from the southern Perichadian plain.

Table 17.2 Mounds sites and radiocarbon chronology

Sites	Radiocarbon dates (bp)	Lab. no.	Stratigraphy	References
Bornu 38	3830 ± 250	N 793	Cutting I spit 14	Connah 1981, pp. 85–6
	2960 ± 160	N 794	Cut. I spit 11/12	ibid.
	2880 ± 140	N 795	Cut. II spit 12	ibid.
	2590 ± 170	N 796	Cut. II spit 1—10	ibid.
Bornu 70	2680 ± 180	N 791	Cut. I spit 3	Willet 1971, p. 355
	2720 ± 120	N 792	Cut. II spit 2	ibid.
Kursakata	2880 ± 140	N 480	spit 16 5.40/5.80 m	Connah 1981, p. 91
Daima	2520 ± 110	I 2945	Cut. I spit 49/50	Willet 1971, p. 355
	2400 ± 95	I 2372	Cut. I spit 47/48	ibid.
	1500 ± 670	I 2371	Cut. I spit 33/34	ibid.
	1470 ± 270	I 2370	Cut. I spit 31/32	ibid.
	1320 ± 190	I 2943	Cut. I spit 39/40	Lebeuf 1981, p. 11
	1140 ± 90	I 2368	Cut. I spit 13/14	Lebeuf 1969, p. 8
	970 ± 90	I 2369	Cut. I spit 15/16	ibid.
	890 ± 90	I 3181	Cut. I spit 3/4	Lebeuf 1981, p. 11
Mdaga	2375 ± 150	Gif 742	Tr. IV 4.90 m	Lebeuf 1969, p. 8
	1260 ± 100	Gif 741	Tr. IV 4.20 m	ibid.
	910 ± 100	Gif 740	Tr. IV 3.20 m	ibid.
	2150 ± 135	Dak 10	Tr. VII 3.15 m	ibid.
	1383 ± 125	Dak 26	Tr. VII 1.80/2.00 m	ibid.
	981 ± 117	Dak 28	Tr. VII 1.60 m	ibid.
	330 ± 120	Gif 429	Tr. VII 1.50 m	ibid.
	794 ± 120	Dak 11	Tr. VIII 3.50 m	ibid.
	170 ± 90	Gif 1367	Tr. VIII 0.90 m	ibid.
	680 ± 95	Gif 1172	Tr. XII 4.20 m	ibid.
	750 ± 95	Gif 1171	Tr. XII 3.80 m	ibid.
	284 ± 109	Dak 27	Tr. XII 1.00 m	ibid.
Amkoundjo	2070 ± 180	Gif 435	Tr. I 2.60 m	ibid.
	1910 ± 180	Gif 433	Tr. I 1.00 m	ibid.
	1980 ± 180	Gif 432	Tr. I 0.30/0.60 m	ibid.
Sou Blamé (SI)	3280 ± 360	Ly 2284	C 4.30/4.40 m	Lebeuf 1981, p. 11
	2430 ± 250	Ly 2283	C 4.05/4.15 m	ibid.
	3200 ± 250	Ly 2282	C 3.40 m	ibid.
	2470 ± 210	Ly 2281	C 3.04 m	ibid.
	2570 ± 240	Ly 2280	C 1.50/2.00 m	ibid.
	2800 ± 110	Gif 4934	S. 79 4.00 m	ibid.
	2530 ± 120	Ly 2005	S. 79 3.00 m	ibid.
	2280 ± 170	Ly 2004	S. 79 2.60/2.67 m	ibid.
	2310 ± 150	Ly 2003	S. 79 2.40/2.47 m	ibid.
	2340 ± 100	Gif 4821	S. 78 2.78 m	ibid
	500 ± 60	Gif 4820	S. 78 0.49 m	ibid.
Sou (SII)	1340 ± 90	Gif 4933	Tr. XIX 7.30/7.40 m	ibid.
	500 ± 130	Ly 2002	Tr. XIX 1.00/1.10 m	ibid.
	850 ± 90	Gif 4932	Tr. XI 4.20 m	ibid.
	620 ± 80	Gif 4504	Tr. XI 2.00/2.50 m	ibid.
	650 ± 80	Gif 4151	Tr. XI 0.90/1.40 m	ibid.
	1340 ± 100	Gif 4822	Tr. II 3.80/3.85 m	ibid.
	520 ± 80	Gif 4152	Tr. II 0.50 m	ibid.
	580 ± 80	Gif 4149	Tr. I 1.90 m	ibid.
	150 ± 80	Gif 4150	Tr. I 1.70 m	ibid.

The mound of Mdaga

Mdaga is an elliptical-shaped mound 300 m long, with a mean width of 185 m, and 8 m high, located 14 km to the north of N'Djamena. It is situated on the shore of the Linia, a seasonal tributary of the Chari, and it is surrounded by an impressive earthen wall, with an average width of 6 m at the base, with four entrances. The site was excavated from 1960 to 1968 (Lebeuf, Lebeuf, Treinen-Claustre & Courtin 1980) and fourteen trenches were dug. The maximum thickness of the archaeological deposit was 5.50 m in Trench IV. The earliest deposit is dated to 2375 ± 150 bp (Gif 742). The total area excavated covers 1290 m² out of a mound surface of 5.5 ha, 2.12 per cent of the site. Cultural remains consist of ceramics (Fig. 17.6), terracotta statuettes, animal bones, a small number of bone tools (points and harpoons) (Fig. 17.7), stone artefacts (stone hammers, polished axes and grinding tools) (Fig. 17.7) and metal objects of iron and, later, in copper alloys (Fig. 17.8). At Mdaga, two of the fourteen trenches, Trenches IV and VII, had late stone age occupations; they did not prove to be rich in artefacts. Two of the first units with eleven occupation levels belong to the Late Stone Age (Levels 10 and 11 (4.40 to 5.00 m deep)); Level 9 was dated to 1260 ± 100 bp (Gif 741). Iron artefacts appear in Level 5 in the form of two hoe blades. In Trench VII there were twelve occupation levels, among which levels 10 to 12 (3.50–4.80 m deep) belong to the Late Stone Age. The earliest iron artefacts occurred in Level 8, dated to 2150 ± 135 bp (Dak 10), in the form of slag, and in Level 7 there was an iron axe (Fig. 17.8–8).

Dwelling structures have not been clearly identified, but they are often attested by cooking features like hearths, fire-hardened floors, cooking-places and *in situ* pots. Some burials were also discovered.

In levels of the Late Stone Age (Tr. IV, Levels 9–11; Tr. VII, Levels 10–12), seven burials were excavated. Inhumations were in extended positions, lying on the back, with arms at the side. Six were in a south–north orientation, whereas one without any grave goods had a north–south orientation. Stone artefacts consisted of a small number

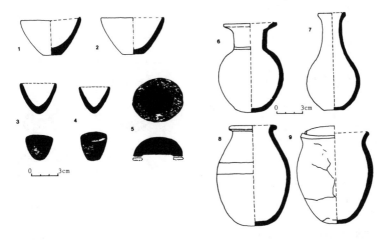

Figure 17.6 Mdaga cultural material. 1–2 late stone age bowls; 3–5 crucible types; 6–9 early iron age vessels

of upper grinding stones, two stone polishers and one polished stone axe (Fig. 17.7–7); bone tools consisted of a nicely polished bone axe (Fig. 17.7–9) and a broken piece of spearhead or harpoon. Ceramic materials included thick undecorated sherds, pot-lids and the entire base of a four-legged pot; a majority of sherds were decorated with twisted cord and roulette impressions. The only faunal remains were fish bones, *Lates niloticus* and *Gymnarchus niloticus*.

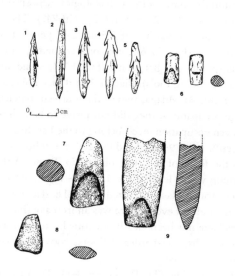

Figure 17.7   Mdaga cultural material. 1, 3–5 harpoons; 2 spearhead; 6 bone whistle; 7–8 stone axes; 9 bone axe

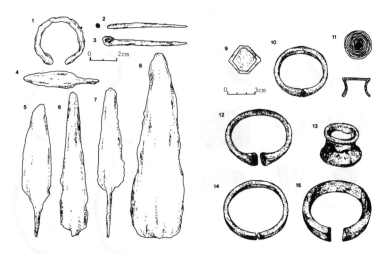

Figure 17.8   Mdaga cultural material. 1 iron arm-ring; 2–3 iron spindles; 4–7 iron spearheads; 8 iron axe; 9 undetermined alloyed copper artefact; 10, 12, 14–15 alloyed copper bracelets and arm-rings; 11, 13 lip plugs in alloyed copper

In levels of the Early Iron Age (Tr. IV, Levels 6–8; Tr. VII, Levels 7–9), three burials were excavated, one of which was a double burial containing a man and a woman (Lebeuf, Lebeuf, Treinen-Claustre & Courtin 1980, p. 51) possessing the earliest occurrence of grave goods, in the form of ostrich eggshell beads and a terracotta headrest. Inhumations were in extended positions, lying on the back, arms on chests and hands on faces. Two bodies were buried in a southwest–northeast orientation, and the remaining in a northwest–southeast one. Stone artefacts consisted only of a broken greenstone polished axe. Iron equipment was attested by an iron axe and slag. Ceramics consisted of large sherds of 'Sao pot' and well-fired thin sherds, mainly decorated with twisted cord and roulette impressions. A terracotta statuette representing a tortoise was also found. Faunal remains consisted of hippopotamus and elephant bones as well as tortoise–shell fragments. Surprisingly enough, no remains of domestic stock were found in these earliest occupation levels of Mdaga. The earliest occurrence of *Bos taurus* came from Tr. I, Level 4, in association with glass beads (Lebeuf, Lebeuf, Treinen-Claustre & Courtin 1980, p. 30), thus indicating a later date. Evidence for ovicaprines is totally absent from the whole Mdaga bone sample. The explanation may be twofold: either as a bias in the excavation's sampling procedure or as a peculiarity of Mdaga settlers. This problem needs further archaeological investigation.

From the archaeological data presented above, some changes appear between levels interpreted as representing the Late Stone Age and Early Iron Age. The most obvious is shown by burials: the orientation of the burials changed from a dominant north–south axis to a southwest–northeast one. The inclusion of grave goods appears in iron age levels. The earliest iron equipment consisted of agricultural tools. The paucity of bone tools does not allow definitive conclusions, but it appears that with the advent of iron, the manufacture of bone tools decreased and later disappeared. The subsistence economy appears to have been based on hunting, gathering and fishing. Cattle husbandry and millet (*Pennisetum* sp.) agriculture are well attested in later early iron age contexts but we do not possess enough archaeological data to certify their earlier existence. The presence of slag may indicate the existence of at least a part of iron technology on the site, probably forging. In comparison with the Daima sequence (Connah 1981; Connah 1985), the Mdaga sequence is very poorly understood. An understanding will only be achieved through explicit and systematic model-building.

Conclusion

We have seen that many of the questions formulated in the earlier part of this chapter remain unanswered. The main purpose of the chapter was to formulate a set of archaeological test schemes for future research. Current archaeological investigations in the Houlouf region in Cameroon (Lebeuf & Holl 1985; Holl 1987; Holl 1988) will be used in this way. The most important conclusion is that a site-specific approach alone is ineffective in the search for explanation of the transition from the Late Stone Age to the early Iron Age: a regional approach is undoubtedly a more suitable analytical unit.

18   *The antiquity of cultivation and herding in Ethiopia*

DAVID W. PHILLIPSON

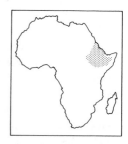

Introduction

The later prehistory of Ethiopia offers several important contrasts with that of other African regions, both in the emphasis of the research that has so far been conducted and in the results obtained. The first point to note is the physical isolation and environmental variety of Ethiopia. Its territory includes not only one of the continent's largest mountain massifs, reaching a maximum altitude of over 4600 m and with extensive high plateaux between 2000 and 3000 m above sea-level, but also the arid lowlands of the Danakil which dip more than 100 m below the water level of the adjacent Red Sea. The highlands are bisected by the Rift Valley and also by the huge and precipitous gorges of the Blue Nile and Takezze, up to 600 m deep, through which much of the highlands drain and by which great quantities of silt from soil erosion are transported annually to the Sudanese plains.

To the northeast, Ethiopia borders on the Red Sea with – from north to south – the steep and rugged escarpment, 2000 m high, behind Massawa, then the arid Danakil lowlands extending southwards to Djibouti and northern Somalia. To the southeast and south the highlands fall gently and with increasing aridity to the plains of Somalia and northern Kenya; while to the southwest the land is increasingly forested as it drops to the Sudanese lowlands. Further north again, especially beyond the Blue Nile, the edge of the northern Ethiopian highlands becomes more precipitous until, in their northernmost part, they merge imperceptibly with the Red Sea hills. For the greater part of their length, the land borders of Ethiopia follow quite closely the line of the 1000 m contour.

Within these borders it is useful to consider Ethiopia as comprising the following geophysical and ecological zones (Fig. 18.1):

1. *The northern highlands*, comprising the Simyen mountains and the high ground of Eritrea and Tigre lying to their north. Most of this region drains westwards to the Nile, via the deeply incised Takezze and its tributaries.
2. *The central plateau.* To the south of Simyen, this region includes the high grasslands of Shoa and Gojjam separated by the Blue Nile gorge, together with the more rugged country to the east of Lake Tana.
3. *The Danakil depression and Rift Valley* is for the most part a hot and arid region extending along the Red Sea coast at the foot of the escarpment which marks the eastern boundary of the northern highlands and central plateau. The Rift Valley extends southwestwards to Lake Turkana (Rudolf) at a relatively high altitude,

bisecting the southern highlands.

4. *The eastern highlands,* to the south of the Danakil depression, extend from west to east through Harar to the borders of Somalia. To the southeast they merge imperceptibly with the Ogaden.

5. *The Ogaden,* the extensive region drained by the Juba and Webi Shebele rivers, sloping gently down to the southeast, with increasing aridity, to the Somali plains.

6. *The southern highlands,* on either side of the Rift Valley, comprise extensive areas of hilly, temperate country only slightly lower than those of the northern and central regions.

7. *The western and southwestern lowlands,* peripheral to the central plateau and the western part of the southern highlands, are forested, well-watered regions bordering the Sudan.

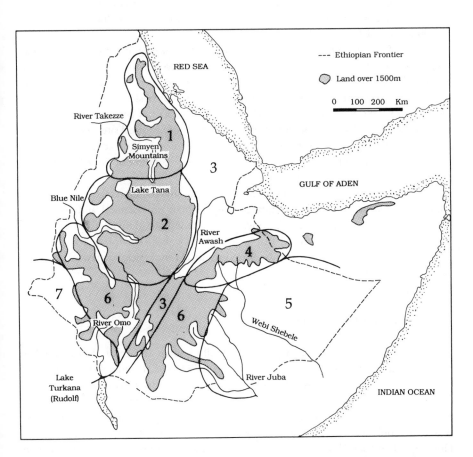

Figure 18.1 Geographical regions of Ethiopia, as defined in the text. 1 The northern highlands; 2 The central plateau; 3 The Danakil depression and Rift Valley; 4 The eastern highlands; 5 The Ogaden; 6 The southern highlands; 7 The western and southwestern lowlands

This environmental diversity is reflected in the variety of recent traditional farming practices (Huffnagel 1961). The plateaux and highlands comprise the principal area where the cultivated cereals include not only wheat and barley, which are generally believed to have their ultimate origin in southwestern Asia, but also African millets and other cereals, notably teff and (perhaps) finger millet, which are of local Ethiopian derivation. A wide variety of non-cereal crops is also grown in Ethiopia, of which the most important is *ensete* – a banana-like plant, the pulp from the base of whose leaves forms the staple food of the Gurage and other peoples in the southern highlands. The *ensete* is an exclusively Ethiopian crop; others are *noog* and *chat*, while coffee appears to have been originally cultivated in southwestern Ethiopia. This brief and incomplete survey suffices to indicate that the history of Ethiopian agriculture must be long, complex and of exceptional interest. Indeed, Ethiopia has been recognized as a centre of indigenous plant domestication since the pioneering botanical research of Vavilov in the 1920s (Harlan 1969). The agricultural technology is also of considerable significance, not least because this is the southernmost African area where the ox-drawn plough was used in precolonial times.

In view of the circumstances outlined above, it is surprising and disappointing that very little archaeological endeavour has so far been devoted to elucidating the early history of Ethiopian food production. Indeed, only one localized field project has so far been devised specifically to illuminate this matter (Dombrowski 1970) and, as will be shown below, the post-pleistocene prehistory of Ethiopia has been investigated only cursorily. More archaeological work has been devoted to historical sites, notably in the northern highlands of Tigre and Eritrea, but even here very little attention has been paid to the problem of illustrating the food-producing economy of the Aksumite and pre-Aksumite societies (cf. Phillipson 1990).

As a result of this dearth of relevant archaeological investigation, the survey which follows must depend to a disappointingly large extent on botanical and zoological evidence and also on the relevant conclusions that can be derived from historical linguistic studies. It is recognized that many of the conclusions offered remain extremely tentative and that, in particular, the absolute chronological framework remains very poorly known.

The archaeological sequence

The period of Ethiopian prehistory conventionally known as the Late Stone Age has recently been surveyed by Brandt (1986). By the early Holocene, microlithic industries, whose history in several areas extends far back into the upper Pleistocene, are known from several parts of the Rift Valley and from rock shelters at Laga Oda near Harar and at Gobedra near Aksum. Although the investigated occurrences are few, there is no reason to doubt that such industries were ubiquitous in Ethiopia during the early Holocene. High lake-levels at this time encouraged concentration of settlement in places where aquatic resources could be exploited, as at Lake Besaka some 100 km east of Addis Ababa, although hunting of land animals also continued on a substantial scale. The date at which pottery first appears on these sites is not accurately known, being perhaps around the fourth or third millennium BC at Gobedra and somewhat later both at Laga Oda and at Gurgussom in the Danakil (Roubet 1970).

It is this later period, the last 5000 or 4000 years BC, that is particularly relevant to the present discussion, but archaeological detail is exceedingly scant. Several ancient village sites near Agordat in Eritrea have been described by Arkell (1954). They are known only from surface examination and have not been excavated: their age and duration of occupation are thus unknown. The ground stone 'axes' and 'maceheads', together with the pottery and items of personal adornment, are stated to show affinity with material from further west: in particular a connection has been proposed with 'C-Group' artefacts of the late third millennium BC in Nubia (Clark 1967a; see also Phillipson 1977a). Elsewhere, archaeological knowledge of this period comes only from the upper levels of the small-scale excavations at open sites and rock shelters noted above (Fig. 18.2).

Ethiopian evidence for the beginnings of metal working is particularly incomplete. It is possible, but cannot yet be proved, that copper/bronze metallurgy locally preceded that of iron, as was the case in the Nile valley. Iron objects, together with bronze, are

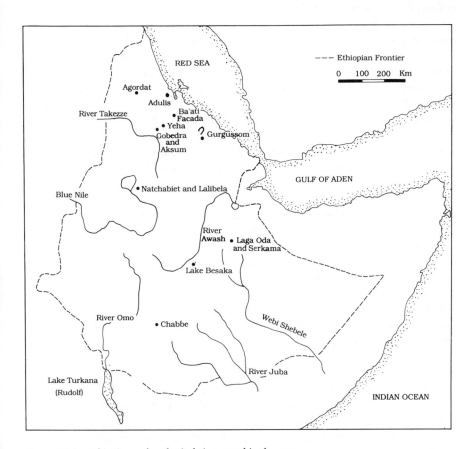

Figure 18.2 Ethiopian archaeological sites noted in the text.

first attested on sites of the so-called pre-Aksumite period in the mid-first millennium BC (de Contenson 1981), which is generally assumed to mark the beginning of the historical period in northern Ethiopia. It has been usual to link this development with the arrival of settlers or colonists from south Arabia. Some writers have gone so far as to suggest that pre-Aksumite culture was essentially a transplant from the latter area. It may be suggested that this view is a result of the current emphasis of archaeological research in this area on monumental architecture and sculpture, inscriptions and imported luxury items, all of which have undoubted south Arabian affinities. Scholars such as Fattovich (1990) and Anfray (1968), who have paid particular attention to the local ceramic traditions, have recognized the strong indigenous element/s at these sites. It can hardly be doubted that the seemingly sudden appearance in northern Ethiopia of dressed-stone architecture such as that exemplified by the Yeha temple, of figurative stone sculpture and of Himyaritic inscriptions, does indicate a close degree of contact with south Arabia, involving the physical presence of some persons from the latter area. There is, however, no reason to believe that such immigrants represented more than a small proportion of the total pre-Aksumite population. (The linguistic implications of this conclusion will be considered below.)

Between the last one or two centuries BC and the mid-third century AD arose the more truly urban Aksumite civilization of northern Ethiopia. The periodization and terminology of this process are confused in the literature, and this is not the place to attempt a clarification. The main historical source, now dated with some confidence to the mid-first century AD, is the *Periplus of the Erythraean Sea* (Casson 1989) which indicates that manufactured luxuries from the Mediterranean world were already being imported to Aksum via the Red Sea port of Adulis, in exchange for ivory and other interior commodities. Significantly, grain (σιτος, generally translated as wheat),[1] which was noted as an import to what is now Somalia, is not included in the list of things brought to Aksum, implying that northern Ethiopia was already self-sufficient in that commodity.

Archaeological research has demonstrated the existence, in the northern Ethiopian highlands, of a string of towns extending inland from Adulis to the capital at Aksum, near the inland, western, edge of the highlands. The most recent report on excavations at Aksum (Munro-Hay 1989a) provides a useful overview, but little that is directly relevant to a consideration of the food-producing economy. The inscriptions and other historical sources (Kobishchanov 1979), however, are somewhat more informative; their evidence is summarized below.

Archaeological fieldwork on the Aksumite period has been largely restricted to urban sites and those with evidence for elaborate burials and/or monumental architecture. The only exception is a survey undertaken by Michels in 1973–4, the results of which have not yet been fully published (Michels 1976; Michels 1979; Michels 1990). The survey, of an area of some 500 km[2] between Yeha and Aksum, revealed numerous rural settlements: surface collections of pottery and other artefacts have been seriated and linked with obsidian hydration dates to provide a chronological framework extending from a 'late Neolithic' of *c.* 800 BC into late Aksumite times *c.* AD 1100. The chronology of the first seven centuries AD has been refined through the work of Munro-Hay (1989a; Ch. 36, this volume).

Botanical evidence for early Ethiopian agriculture

The principal crops that have been traditionally cultivated in Ethiopia in recent times have been noted above. The relevant botanical information may now be summarized.

Wheat and barley

These two cereals are almost certainly derived in cultivated form from southwestern Asia, where their wild prototypes occur and where their domestication is attested from at least the ninth millennium BC. The distribution of wild barley, however, extends into Egypt – where it was exploited for food, as at Esna (Wendorf & Schild 1976b), as early as 10,000 BC – and it is possible that future research will indicate initial cultivation in that part of Africa also. At present, the earliest confirmed African attestation of cultivated barley is also in Egypt *c.* 7000 BC (Wendorf & Hassan 1980; see also Hassan 1984a and Wendorf & Schild 1984b). The great number of varieties of wheat (*Triticum* spp.) and barley (*Hordeum*) known in Ethiopia, some of which are exclusive to that region, strongly suggests that their local cultivation is of high antiquity (Simoons 1965 and references cited).

Teff

This small, hardy and nutritious cereal, a member of the widespread genus *Eragrostis*, is today cultivated for human consumption only in Ethiopia, where it grows at higher altitudes than those which sustain wheat and barley (Simoons 1960). It is the preferred ingredient of the traditional flat sour bread *injera*. The suggestion has been made (Shaw 1977) that the initial cultivation of teff must have preceded the introduction of wheat and barley to Ethiopia, on the basis that the domestication of such a tiny grain would have had no rationale at a time when larger ones were already available. This hypothesis does not, however, take account of teff's unique qualities and advantages noted above, and it cannot be sustained.

Finger millet

Eleusine coracana is widely cultivated in sub-Saharan Africa. Harlan (1971) considers its original homeland to have been in the general area extending between northern Uganda and central Ethiopia. In many areas it is the preferred base for the making of beer. It flourishes at lower altitudes than wheat, barley or teff, and also in parts of the highlands.

Flax

Although generally regarded as a source of fibre, flax (*Linum*) is traditionally grown in many areas of Ethiopia for the oil which may be obtained from its seeds. It is widely distributed elsewhere, having been grown in Egypt from at least the fifth millennium BC.

Noog

Another source of vegetable oil, *Guizotia abyssinica*, is an exclusively Ethiopian cultigen.

Ensete

Also a uniquely Ethiopian crop, *Ensete edule* is cultivated as a staple food in the southern highlands. It is also grown in parts of Shoa for fibre and for its leaves, which serve a variety of functions including protection of foodstuffs during cooking. *Ensete* seeds are rarely fertile and it is generally propagated vegetatively, a practice which has permitted its cultivation at altitudes significantly higher than those which are favoured by wild forms. When fertilized with cattle dung, *ensete* is capable of supporting an extremely high density of population – up to 150 persons per km^2 being recorded among the Gurage. Beyond the implications of its distribution and dominance, there is no information concerning its antiquity.

Chat and coffee

Both these stimulants which, in their very different ways, have achieved considerable economic significance, appear to be indigenous to Ethiopia: the former to the eastern highlands and the latter to the forests of the southwest. Coffee (*Coffea arabica*) was originally chewed, as *chat* (*Catha edulis*) still is; its use as a beverage is believed (Purseglove 1976) to be a relatively recent development.

Other food crops

A significant number of crops, in addition to those noted above, are traditionally cultivated in Ethiopia. Some, such as sorghum, are of African origin, some (lentils and chickpeas) were probably introduced from Asia at an early date; while others, including tomatoes and the now ubiquitous chilli pepper, have an origin in the Americas and were unknown in Ethiopia prior to the last few centuries.

Rock paintings and other evidence for animal domestication

The history of Ethiopian domestic animals is essentially simpler than that of the cultivated plants. Cattle, sheep, goats, horses, donkeys, dogs, chickens and (at lower altitudes) camels are currently held. All are known from adjacent areas, both in the Nile valley and in Arabia as well as, with the exception of the horse, in east Africa to the south. There is no reason to suppose that any of these animals was initially domesticated in Ethiopia, although in several cases specifically Ethiopian varieties have developed. The evidence of rock paintings (Joussaume 1981; Brandt and Carder 1987) offers valuable insights into the history of animal domestication in Ethiopia.

Transport animals

The donkey was known in Egypt as early as the mid-fourth millennium BC and is commonly depicted in a fully domesticated guise (Clutton-Brock 1987; Clutton-Brock, Ch. 4, this volume). It may have been originally domesticated in Egypt. It is not attested in Nubia before the eighth–seventh century BC, at which time the horse also made its appearance in the Nile valley. Neither animal seems to be represented in the earlier Ethiopian rock art, which would be in accord with the view that they may have been brought to the area from Nubia late in the last millennium BC. The camel, likewise, is generally believed to have been a late arrival to Ethiopia, perhaps around the beginning of the Christian era. It is mentioned in Aksumite inscriptions and is recognizable only in the relatively recent rock art. However, evidence has recently come to light for its presence at Qasr Ibrim in Nubia by about the seventh century BC (Alexander 1988). Indications both archaeological and linguistic from northern Kenya (Phillipson 1984) suggest that the camel may have been present in northeastern Africa for rather longer than is generally believed (see also Bulliet 1975).

Cattle

By contrast, cattle seem to have a significantly longer history in Ethiopia, not only as providers of meat, milk, leather and horn, but also as sources of motive power and embodiments of wealth. Several varieties are involved: humped and humpless, long-horned and short-horned. Both in northern Ethiopia and in the east, around Harar, the earliest and most numerous representations in the rock art are of humpless long-horned cattle attended by herders carrying spears (Fig. 18.3). The emphasis given to depicting udders suggests that the cows were milked. Similar features occur in the somewhat more stylized rock engravings at Chabbe in the southern highlands (Anfray 1967a). Since the majority of cattle depicted in south Arabian artworks are short-horned, it has been suggested that the long-horned beasts shown in Ethiopian rock art may be earlier than the main extension of south Arabian influence in the mid-first millennium BC. This argument is far from conclusive, and should in any event presumably be applied only in the northern zone, and not to the Harar area where direct south Arabian influence is not indicated. Particular interest attaches to a painting at Ba'ati Facada near

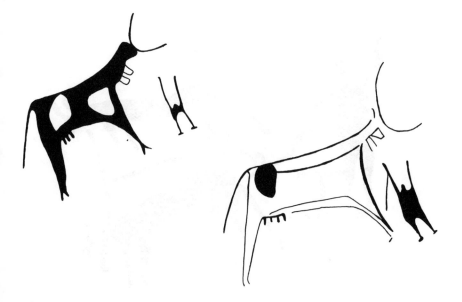

Figure 18.3 Rock paintings of cattle and herdsmen at Serkama in the escarpment of the eastern highlands near Dire Dawa (after Clark & Williams 1978).

Adigrat (Drew 1954; Clark 1980) which depicts an ox-drawn plough (Fig. 18.4): unfortunately there is no evidence for the age of this representation, but its degree of stylization suggests a relatively late stage in the rock-art sequence.

Sheep and goats

Both these animals are of ancient southwest Asian origin and were known in the Nile valley from at least the fifth millennium BC. Rock paintings in the Harar area, as at Serkama (Clark & Williams 1978), include clear representations of fat-tailed sheep (Fig. 18.5). There is general agreement that this variety developed in Arabia but the dating evidence offered by Anati (1968) is inconclusive (see also Khan 1988) and there seems no reason to follow Brandt (1984) in assuming that the presence of fat-tailed sheep in Ethiopia must postdate the mid-second millennium BC.

Pig

The pig may have been kept by the earliest farmers in Lower Egypt (Hassan 1984a). It is not now kept in Ethiopia, where the general Semitic prohibition of pork is maintained by the Christian church as well as by the Muslim population. Whether the pig was kept in Ethiopia in earlier times is not currently known.

Dog and chicken

Although both these creatures are now widespread and important, they are not represented in Ethiopian rock art and their local antiquity is unknown. It may be assumed that, as in many other parts of the world, the domestication of the dog is very ancient, and that the chicken was at some time introduced from an Asian source.

Figure 18.4 Rock painting of an ox-drawn plough at Ba'ati Facada near Adigrat, Eritrea (after Drew 1954).

The linguistic evidence for food production

The majority of Ethiopian languages are classified in the Cushitic, Omotic and Semitic branches of the Afroasiatic language family. The last-named branch now accounts for the largest number of speakers, for it includes Amharic and Tigrinya as well as the old liturgical language of Ethiopian Christianity, Geez, descended from the Ethiopic represented on Aksumite inscriptions. There are, however, a number of Cushitic languages surviving in the northern half of the country, particularly in remote or peripheral areas, and these are conventionally classed together as Agau. Cushitic languages, with those of the Omotic group, are general in the south and east. It is clear that the Cushitic languages have been established for longer and, indeed, that the history of Semitic speech in Ethiopia is relatively short; the linguistic evidence is in keeping with the view that the region's first speakers of Semitic languages were immigrants from south Arabia during the pre-Aksumite period of the first millennium BC. That the latter were indeed Semitic-speakers is demonstrated by their Himyaritic inscriptions: it seems probable, but cannot be proved, that they were the first speakers of such languages to settle in what is now Ethiopia.

It appears that some of the vocabulary in recent Ethiopian Semitic languages relating to cereal cultivation and, remarkably, the plough, was borrowed from Cushitic sources (Simoons 1965; Ehret 1979). This strongly suggests that plough-cultivation of cereals was practised in Ethiopia before the advent of Semitic speech, but there is as yet no indication whether this priority is to be measured in centuries or in millennia. Leclant (1956) has noted that some words relating to iron-working in recent Ethiopian Cushitic languages appear to be loans from Semitic sources; but, again, many others are not from Semitic, including the name for iron itself – *bir(t) (C. Ehret, *pers. comm.*).

The argument has been presented by Ehret (1979) that the Afroasiatic language family as a whole may have developed in northeast Africa bordering the Red Sea some 15,000 years ago. His proposal that intensive use of wild cereals was in some way a

Figure 18.5   Rock paintings of fat-tailed sheep at Serkama (after Clark & Williams 1978).

prerogative of these initial Afroasiatic speakers has little to support it. More relevant to the present discussion is his view, based on the incidence of common vocabulary roots in different branches of Afroasiatic, that the herding of domestic animals and the cultivation of cereals (and perhaps of *ensete* also) may have an antiquity in Ethiopia in the order of seven millennia.

Archaeological and epigraphic evidence for plant cultivation and animal domestication

With the exception of the rock art noted above, so few Ethiopian sites have yielded evidence relating to animal domestication and/or plant cultivation that it is appropriate to discuss them separately. A geographical arrangement, from north to south, will be followed here.

In the north, excavation at the small rock shelter of Gobedra near Aksum revealed seeds of cultivated finger millet which appeared to be contemporary with the earliest pottery, around the third or fourth millennium BC (Phillipson 1977b). Radiocarbon accelerator dating of the actual seeds, however, has shown them to be only about 1000 years old, so they must be regarded as intrusive to the layer in which they were found. A camel tooth from the same layer is perhaps less likely to be intrusive, and an accelerator date on it is awaited. Domestic cattle are tentatively identified from a higher level, dated to the last millennium BC (Phillipson 1977b).

At Aksum itself it is only during the most recent excavations, directed by the late Neville Chittick, that stratified animal bones were preserved for identification. Flotation techniques for the recovery of plant remains were, however, not employed; and circumstances since the 1974 excavations have prevented examination and identification of the fauna. Primary archaeological data relating to food production at Aksum are thus not yet available. Some secondary indications may, however, be noted (Munro-Hay 1989a). Clay figurines of both humped and humpless cattle were recovered, together with one representation of a pair of yoked oxen. A detailed examination of the pottery by Wilding (1989) has shown that only in late Aksumite times do ceramic vessels occur that resemble modern *injera* trays and coffee pots. It is possible, therefore, either that these items of diet were introduced to Aksum around the sixth century AD, or – perhaps less likely – that they were enjoyed in earlier times but with metal utensils, which were replaced with pottery ones as the state's prosperity declined.

The nature of the bread that was consumed in earlier Aksumite times may be illustrated through several lines of enquiry. The coins of the kings of Aksum, from the late third to the early seventh century AD according to the chronology most recently proposed (Munro-Hay 1984a; Munro-Hay 1984b), frequently portray cereal ears, usually on either side of the potentate's bust (Fig. 18.6). Detailed enquiries seem rarely to have been made as to the identity of the cereal thus shown, which has been described variously as barley (Head 1887; Munro-Hay 1984a), wheat or barley (Munro-Hay 1989b), or by a non-committal term (Anzani 1926; Kammerer 1926). Close examination of a number of specimens leads to the conclusion that emmer wheat is represented (see caption to Fig. 18.6).

Aksumite inscriptions (Kobishchanov 1979) refer to loaves of bread, which were evidently quite small as consumption at the rate of five per man-day appears to have been normal. Although there is (S. Munro-Hay, *pers. comm.*) controversy over the precise Ethiopic qualificative used with the noun h̲bst = loaf (Drewes 1962), the Greek version of Ezana's inscription provides the translation ἄρτους σιτινους (Salt, in Valentia 1809), which leaves little doubt that wheaten bread is meant. The optimum altitudes for wheat cultivation in Ethiopia, including emmer, are between 1800 and 2200 m (Huffnagel 1961), which coincides with the height of the plains around Aksum. It may be that the wheaten loaves then consumed were analogous to the modern Ethiopian *dabbo*, which may itself be paralleled in ancient Egypt (Kemp 1989).

The inscriptions make several references to cattle and small stock in large numbers, generally as tribute, booty or army provisions (Kobishchanov 1979). They also refer to camels and 'pack animals' – presumably donkeys – which must have been of major importance in Aksum's long-distance trade. The mention of camels is of particular interest in view of the recovery of a tooth of this animal from nearby Gobedra. Camels are not currently kept around Aksum, where the rainfall pattern, significantly different from that of the adjacent lowlands, inhibits breeding in camels acclimatized to the latter area. In other parts of Ethiopia, however, camels are regularly used to transport goods, notably salt, from the lowlands to the plateaux (O'Mahoney 1970; Belai 1987). Aksumite inscriptions also indicate that wine was sometimes available. Small-scale wine imports are noted by the author of the *Periplus* in the first century AD: they are also indicated archaeologically by the presence of Mediterranean amphorae at Aksum (Wilding 1989). Representations of grape vines in Aksumite architectural decoration (e.g. Littmann 1913) raise the possibility that wine was also produced locally.

Two caves near the eastern shore of Lake Tana, Natchabiet and Lalibela, were excavated in 1966–7 by J. Dombrowski with the specific aim of obtaining archaeological evidence for early food production. Unfortunately neither site yielded material older than the last millennium BC. At the latter site the earlier of two occupation phases, dated *c.* 500 BC and lacking any trace of iron-working, yielded evidence for barley,

Figure 18.6   Aksumite coins showing cereal ears. All are British Museum specimens. From left: gold, Endybis, 1989.5.18.1 (late third century); bronze, Ouazebas, 1989.5.18.244 (late fourth century); gold, Ebana, 1989.5.18.257 (early fifth century); bronze, Armah, 1989.5.18.435 (early seventh century). The cereal ears show increasing stylization – indeed, the representation on the reverse of Armah's coin could be mistaken for a wreath were its antecedents not known. The repeated representation of paired grains, of long terminal whiskers and short lateral ones, leaves little doubt that emmer wheat is depicted.

chickpeas and legumes, with bones which have been provisionally identified as those of cattle and sheep/goat. The pottery belonged to a tradition distinct from that of the later occupation, dated to the early second millennium AD and best represented at Natchabiet. At the latter site the upper, iron age, levels contained evidence for the processing of cotton and for the preparation of *injera* (Dombrowski 1970; Dombrowski 1971).

South and east of the Rift Valley, two areas have been investigated by expeditions under the leadership of J. D. Clark. At Laga Oda rock shelter in the Chercher mountains west of Harar, a long sequence of occupation has been noted by Clark & Williams (1978). In the later levels, dating from the mid-second millennium BC, wear on the microlithic tools suggests their use was to harvest grasses (Clark & Prince 1978), although there was no indication whether or not these were cultivated. The same level yielded pottery and bones of domestic cattle. Camel remains were first attested early in the second millennium AD. Two hundred km further west, in the Rift Valley, open sites near Lake Besaka also provide evidence for domestic cattle at this time. Unlike their predecessors of several thousand years earlier, the inhabitants of sites used pottery and a stone industry in which scrapers were the dominant type (Clark & Williams 1978; Brandt 1980).

To complete this account of archaeological evidence for early Ethiopian agriculture it is necessary to note that the oldest (indeed the only) physical trace of ancient teff comes not from Ethiopia but from Hajar bin Humeid in south Yemen (van Beek 1969), where a potsherd from stratum B – dating probably to the first century BC/AD – bore a clear impression of this cereal.

If the archaeological evidence for early food production in northern and eastern Ethiopia, outlined above, is lamentably incomplete, that from the south and southwest is almost non-existent. In Wollega and on the Tuli Kapi plateau, a number of ground stone tools were recovered some fifty years ago, which M. D. Leakey (1943) has compared with certain Kenyan examples. R. P. Azais found analogous artefacts in the region north of Lake Rudolf, associated with decorated pottery and, in some instances, with metal tools (Bailloud 1959; see also Phillipson 1977b). Since Azais' discoveries are not fully documented, and have apparently not been preserved, there is now no way – pending further fieldwork – of confirming their associations or ascertaining their age. If, as seems possible, these ground stone artefacts are to be associated with pre-iron age cultivation, they may eventually provide evidence for the antiquity of the southern Ethiopian *ensete* complex.

Conclusion

In conclusion, it may be noted that the sparse archaeological data currently available do not as yet confirm the high antiquity which linguistic and botanical researches attribute to some elements of Ethiopian food production. Several such elements may be recognized and each is in need of detailed investigation. Cereal cultivation, which in some areas (initially or subsequently) involved the use of the plough, affected both indigenous and derived species. The *ensete* planting culture of the south is but one of several locally developed facets of food production which has made a major impact on the region's economy. Domestic animals have been of significance not only as food and wealth, but also as providers of labour and transport. The environmental diversity of the region adds to the expectation that the prehistory of Ethiopia's cultivating and herding practices will prove to be complex and varied.

Note

[1] Σιτος cannot be assumed to have signified 'wheat' at the time of the *Periplus*. Its general meaning, according to Liddell and Scott, is 'grain' or even 'bread'. This is confirmed by Jasny (1944), who notes that the word probably did not take the specific meaning of 'naked wheat' until about AD 300.

Acknowledgements

I thank Dr Martin Price for permission to examine coins in the British Museum and Dr Richard Duncan-Jones for the reference to Jasny 1944.

19   The beginnings of food production in southwestern Kenya

PETER ROBERTSHAW

The explanation of the origins of agriculture, and by extension the origins of animal domestication, is rightfully regarded as one of the 'Big Questions of Archaeology' (Binford 1983a, p. 26 and see Clutton-Brock 1989a; Harris & Hillman 1989; Clutton-Brock, Ch. 4, this volume; Harlan, Ch. 3, this volume). Since east Africa[1] boasts no wild progenitors of either domestic animals or agricultural crops, with the possible exception of finger millet (*Eleusine coracana*) in northern Uganda, the relevant questions in this context are, first, by what process were domesticates introduced into the region; second, how did the earliest food producers adapt to east African environments and, third, how did these adaptations evolve into those encountered by early European travellers and ethnographers in the last hundred years? East Africa is renowned for its pastoral peoples, who spurn both agriculture and hunting-and-gathering; therefore, the explanation of the evolution of this pastoral adaptation and its socio-cultural framework is an important goal of both archaeological and historical research, which I have attempted to address in other publications (Robertshaw 1982; Robertshaw & Collett 1983). In this chapter I focus upon the adaptations of early food-producing peoples in east Africa, confining myself to an outline of the evidence from southwestern Kenya, where I have been engaged in field research for several years. However, to locate this work within the broader canvas, I shall first outline current thought on the first question – the process by which domesticates were introduced to east Africa.

Domestic animals make their appearance in east Africa as part of what seems to be a 'package deal', which includes new styles of ceramics, lithic artefacts, burial practices and settlement patterns. While the evidence is by no means entirely unequivocal, it thus favours a model of population movement, but on what scale is very difficult to judge, given the sparseness of archaeological research. Pastoralists first entered northern Kenya during the third millennium BC, but their arrival in southern Kenya and northern Tanzania is on present evidence dated only to the end of the second millennium.[2] However, similarities between ceramics from northern Kenya and undated sites in the south suggest that future research will bridge the chronological gap. This early pottery is subsumed within the Olmalenge tradition.[3] There are relatively few sites containing this pottery, an indication perhaps that early pastoral settlement in the region was sparse. From about 1000 BC onwards there are many more sites, the pottery from which is mostly assigned to either the Oldishi or Elmenteitan traditions. Whether the appearance of these traditions is to be tied to further population movements into east Africa is not certain, since so little is known of the earlier

parts of the ceramic sequences. Those who have faith in linguistic-archaeological correlations reason that the population movements by which Southern Cushitic and Southern
Nilotic languages spread into northern Tanzania are manifested by these ceramic traditions
(e.g. Ambrose 1982).

However, the early pastoralists did not enter a depopulated wilderness; rather they
encountered hunter-gatherers, who, in the central Rift Valley at least, adapted their lifestyle
to take advantage of the new possibilities offered by the presence of domestic animals but
without abandoning their hunting-and-gathering existence (Ambrose 1984a). While 'post-
pastoral' foragers are generally a neglected aspect of archaeological enquiry (Cable n.d.),
study of the pastoralists themselves in east Africa has not progressed very far either, being
mostly confined to the establishment of culture-stratigraphic sequences, a task not without
pitfalls. Efforts to go beyond classification are restricted to a handful of studies (Bower 1978;
Ambrose 1980; Gifford, Isaac & Nelson 1980; Robertshaw & Collett 1983; Robertshaw,
Collett, Gifford & Mbae 1983; Ambrose 1984a; Bower 1984a; Bower 1984b; Gifford-
Gonzalez 1984; Gifford-Gonzalez & Kimengich 1984; Marshall 1986; Robertshaw 1989).

The environment

Southwestern Kenya (Fig. 19.1) is one region where recent research has focused on
early food-producing communities and their hunting-and-gathering antecedents.

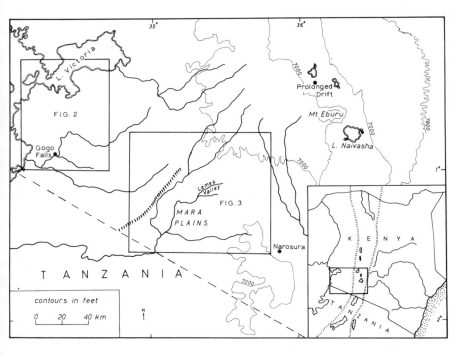

Figure 19.1 The area of research.

Archaeological fieldwork has been undertaken here in two rather different environmental mosaics. The first of these, in what is now South Nyanza district, begins with the shores of Lake Victoria and climbs eastwards, through a series of impressive ancient volcanoes, into the pre-Cambrian rocks of the Kanyamkago hills (Fig. 19.2). Rainfall increases with altitude, from 790 mm per annum on the lakeshores to over 1000 mm in the Kanyamkago hills, the rain falling mostly in two rather indistinct seasons from March to May and October to November. Vegetation varies with altitude and precipitation, shifting from *Euphorbia* and *Acacia* bush and grassland near the lakeshore to *Combretum* and allied broad-leafed savanna species in the hills. Tsetse fly abound in parts of the region carrying both animal, and in some areas human, trypanosomiasis.

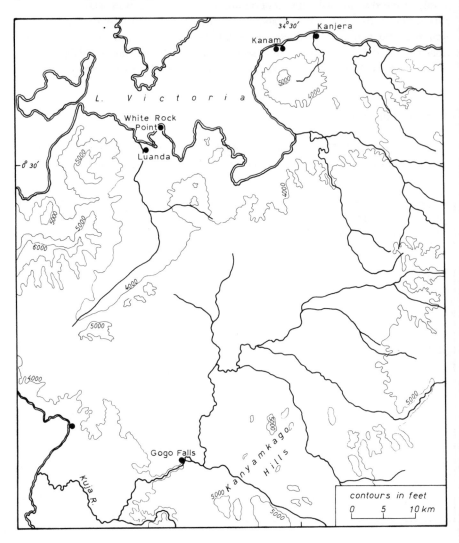

Figure 19.2   Archaeological sites in South Nyanza.

The present inhabitants of the region are in the main Nilotic-speaking Luo farmers, who keep a few domestic animals. They displaced or assimilated earlier Bantu-speaking groups during the eighteenth and nineteenth centuries (Ogot 1967), though Suba fishermen still live along much of the lakeshore.

By contrast the Mara region (Fig. 19.3) is in many respects classic pastoralist country inhabited by the pastoralists *par excellence* of east Africa – the Maasai. The Mara is the northern extension of the vast Serengeti ecosystem, in which open, high-elevation grassy plains are interrupted by ranges of quartzitic hills and occasional inselbergs. The archaeological research discussed here was undertaken in the northern part of this region, bounded to the west by the Siria escarpment, to the north by the Amala river and the forests of the Mau and the east by the Loita plains. Here we can contrast two areas – the Lemek valley and the Mara plains. The Lemek valley, with reddish-brown sandy soils derived from the quartzitic hills, receives some 700 mm of rain per annum, mostly in the first half of the year. The presence of springs on the hill slopes and permanent water-holes in the stream-beds makes the valley attractive for year-round settlement. The pastoralists tend to locate their settlements at the bottom of the steep hill slopes, where they have easy access to a range of resources – the bush of the steep slopes for firewood and building materials and browse for goats, the springs for water, and the gentler, lower grassy slopes for grazing their cattle. Rainfall is somewhat higher

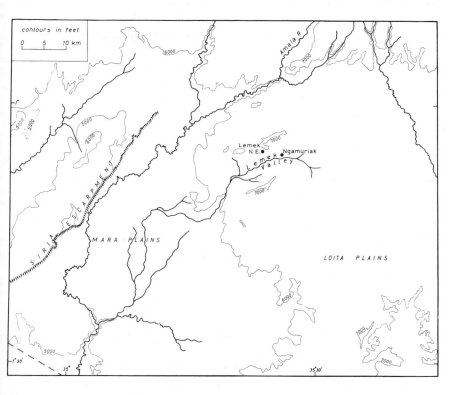

Figure 19.3 The Mara region.

on the Mara plains, where nutrient-rich black cotton-soils are derived from the underlying volcanic peneplain. The grass plains are interspersed with bush-lined stream courses, where pastoralists locate their settlements on the sandy soils which flank the streams and are more conducive to the well-being of their livestock than the heavy, poorly drained soils of the plains. The pastoralists compete for grazing, particularly in the dry season (June–October), with vast herds of wildebeests and other ungulates, whose numbers have increased enormously since the eradication of rinderpest. At times in the past bush cover was greater and the presence of tsetse fly restricted settlement to the Lemek valley and immediately adjacent areas (Lamprey 1984).

These two regions, South Nyanza and the Mara, with their varied environments, promoted rather different adaptations among the early food-producing communities who settled there, despite the fact that they appear to have belonged to a single cultural tradition. We also know something of the lifestyle of their hunter–gatherer antecedents in South Nyanza, but the archaeological record of this period in the Mara is elusive.

Later prehistory in South Nyanza

The later prehistoric sequence in South Nyanza begins with the shell middens on the shores of Lake Victoria first investigated by Louis Leakey (1936, p. 69) and subsequently examined in more detail (Robertshaw, Collett, Gifford & Mbae 1983). The contents of the middens document broad-spectrum hunting-and-gathering subsistence. Shellfish were gathered from the shallows of the lake, where a variety of fish, notably lungfish (*Protopterus aethiopicus*), were also caught, perhaps with the aid of various basket traps. There is a substantial component of mammalian fauna, which is composed exclusively of wild species, mainly medium to very large ungulates. A broad range of species, both gregarious and non-gregarious, was obtained from a wide variety of habitats. Buffalo and hippo are the most commonly represented species, but there are also numerous antelopes, pigs and birds, as well as crocodiles and Nile monitors (*Varanus niloticus*). Gifford has suggested that 'this wide range of animal species taken might reflect a foraging system in which "first choice" animal species were not locally available in sufficient proportions, necessitating expansion of the animal food base to include less energetically rewarding species' (Robertshaw, Collett, Gifford & Mbae 1983, p. 32). When considered in the light of the evidence from the site of Gogo Falls discussed below, it seems reasonable to infer that the shell middens represent only a part of a regionally diverse system of subsistence and settlement, much of which may have operated well inland of the lake.

The stone artefact assemblages from the shell middens, like many of their east African later stone age counterparts, are typically nondescript. Backed microliths and scrapers dominate the assemblages, which are manufactured in a variety of raw materials. Obsidian and crypto-crystalline silicas were favoured for the manufacture of shaped tools; the former, present in only small quantities, derives from the central Rift Valley about 230 km to the east (Merrick & Brown 1984), while the latter was probably obtained from hills some 50 km to the east. This again indicates that the middens should be seen as part of a regional system of exploitation of resources. The middens have also yielded highly decorated pottery, now placed within the Kansyore phase of the Oltome tradition (Collett & Robertshaw 1983b), and several barbless bone points (Robertshaw, Collett, Gifford & Mbae 1983).

Similar pottery and stone artefacts have been discovered at Gogo Falls, a large and complex open site located beside the rapids of the same name on the Kuja river 22 km inland from Lake Victoria in the Kanyamkago hills (Collett & Robertshaw 1980). A very small excavation at the site in 1981 yielded cattle remains apparently in association with Oltome pottery; this prompted speculation that the shell middens may have been a lacrustrine-oriented facies of what was for the most part a farming or pastoralist subsistence system (Robertshaw, Collett, Gifford & Mbae 1983, p. 37). However, more extensive excavations, carried out in 1983, have served to show that domestic animals are not in fact associated with Oltome ceramics at Gogo Falls or, for that matter, anywhere else. The evidence for subsistence during the Oltome occupation of Gogo Falls is in many respects very similar to that from the shell middens. There are shellfish, but in lower densities than in the lakeshore sites; they were collected both from the lakeshore and from the river (P. Kat, *pers. comm.*). Analyses of the fish and mammalian bones are not yet complete, but preliminary results show the presence of a wide variety of large mammals, among which buffalo and hippo again seem to be common. Thus, considered as a whole, Oltome subsistence appears to have varied little spatially or perhaps seasonally. The archaeological evidence suggests a very broad-spectrum, but not internally differentiated, opportunistic foraging adaptation, in which parts of the lakeshore and Gogo Falls may have acted as 'magnet' locations (cf. Binford 1984, p. 263). In this respect Gogo Falls was renowned historically as a natural weir where fish could be easily collected (Butterman 1979, p. 103).

The dating of Oltome settlement in South Nyanza is a problem. Apart from some dubious readings on bone apatite, there is a date on shell from one of the middens of 6740 ± 80 bp (Pta-3139), from which at most 100 years should be subtracted, based on a correction factor obtained by dating modern shell from the lake (Robertshaw, Collett, Gifford & Mbae 1983, p. 7). Recently the Oxford Accelerator Mass Spectrometry laboratory has attempted, generally without success, to extract collagen from several bone samples. However, one date of 5700 ± 100 bp (OxA-828) was obtained from a sample of bone collagen from the shell midden at Kanjera West, but the laboratory comments that this probably represents a minimum age (Gowlett, Hedges, Law & Perry 1987, p. 147). Inland at Gogo Falls the dating of the Oltome occupation is perhaps even less satisfactory, where on the basis of radiocarbon and obsidian hydration dates (Table 19.1) one may choose a 'short' or 'long' chronology. Thus, on the one hand, if one accepts the charcoal date from the Harwell laboratory and the hydration dates, then the ash midden in which the Oltome materials were deposited dates within the last two millennia BC.[4] If, on the other hand, one considers the Oxford AMS date obtained from a charred buffalo tooth as more reliable, then one must argue that the hydration dates are simply wrong and that the charcoal date may be the result of mixing of older and younger charcoal, a real possibility since the sample was composed of scattered fragments of charcoal rather than a single 'lump'.

The dating issue at Gogo Falls is of fundamental importance. If a 'long' chronology is correct, then the Oltome occupation of the site was pene-contemporaneous with that of

Table 19.1   Radiocarbon and obsidian hydration dates for the Oltome occupation of Gogo Falls

Excavation spit[1]	Radiocarbon date (bp)	Calibrated date (cal)[2]	Hydration date[3]
M3	3020 ± 100	1420–1110 BC	667 BC ± 194
M4	7300 ± 500	6670–c. 5500 BC	
M6			146 BC ± 93
			1663 BC ± 115
M7			524 BC ± 65
M9			16,058 BC ± 383

[1] The deposit was excavated by arbitrary levels (spits) each 10 cm thick and numbered from the bottom of the topsoil (M1) to the base of the deposits (M10).

[2] Calibration based on: Pearson & Stuiver (1986); Kromer, Rhein, Bruns, Schoch-Fischer, Münnich, Stuiver & Becker (1986).

[3] Dates by MOHLAB.

the lakeshore middens, indicating that they were indeed part of a single subsistence system. The other implication of a 'long' chronology is that there may then have been a substantial hiatus between the period of Oltome settlement and the first appearance of pastoralists in the region, dated to about the beginning of the first millennium AD. However, if a 'short' chronology is correct, then not only would the Oltome settlement of Gogo Falls not be contemporary with that of the shell middens, but also there can have been little or no hiatus between this hunter-gatherer settlement and the coming of pastoralism. Therefore, whichever chronology is chosen, there are important consequences for understanding the process of the advent of food production.

The earliest evidence of food production in South Nyanza is also found at Gogo Falls in a rather spectacular manner. An enormous ash midden, 2 m or more thick – almost certainly the burnt dung of livestock – and chock-full of well-preserved bones, potsherds and stone artefacts, partially overlies the Oltome horizons. The majority of the pottery consists of undecorated hemispherical bowls and globular pots with occasional spouts and lugs typical of the Elmenteitan tradition. However, the presence of pots with panels of crudely incised cross-hatching below the rim suggests that this may be a hitherto unrecorded facies of the Elmenteitan in a region well to the west of the previously known distribution of this tradition.[5] What is certain is that this pottery is so vastly different from the Oltome material that there is little alternative but to view the advent of food production in the context of the immigration of new groups of peoples with a different cultural system.

With the advent of the Elmenteitan there are also major changes in the pattern of stone raw material usage at Gogo Falls. In the Oltome horizons quartz predominated and most of the small quantities of obsidian were of a translucent grey colour. In the Elmenteitan midden 80 per cent or more of the artefacts are now made in obsidian, most of which is of a bottle-green colour, shown by chemical analysis to derive from sources on Mt Eburru in the central Rift Valley (Merrick & Brown 1984). A predominance of Mt Eburru obsidian is typical of Elmenteitan assemblages everywhere and demonstrates that the inhabitants of Gogo Falls were part of the wider Elmenteitan world, which succeeded in moving large quantities of obsidian over considerable distances. The location of Gogo Falls at the most distant point from the source of the distribution network, if such a network did indeed exist, meant that obsidian was more highly valued here than elsewhere. This is manifested by the very small size of most of the artefacts, the abundance of *outils écaillés* and the rarity of the modified blades which are so characteristic of the Elmenteitan industry as a whole (Nelson 1980).

Remains of domestic animals – cattle and caprines – were recovered from all levels of the Elmenteitan midden at Gogo Falls. Caprines dominate the faunal assemblage numerically, followed by cattle and then an array of wild animals, represented in considerable numbers. Topi/hartebeest, oribi, zebra and reedbuck are the most commonly represented species. This faunal assemblage would appear to reflect hunting of local populations of small antelopes and pigs in a variety of habitats, combined with seasonal hunting of larger migratory ungulates (Marshall 1986), as well as some fishing and fowling. The combination of frequent hunting with pastoralism is rare in east Africa both in the ethnographic literature and the archaeological record (see e.g. Horton & Mudida, Ch. 41, this volume). Only one other site, Prolonged Drift in the central Rift Valley, has produced a similar mixture of abundant wild and domestic animals (Gifford, Isaac & Nelson 1980). Therefore, the interpretation of these assemblages is a matter of some interest. Gifford-Gonzalez has proposed several alternative models of subsistence and settlement systems to account for the Prolonged Drift assemblage (Gifford, Isaac & Nelson 1980; Gifford-Gonzalez 1984), while the suggestion has also been made that the site was occupied by poor pastoralists compelled by necessity to hunt while attempting to establish viable domestic herds (Robertshaw & Collett 1983). The latter hypothesis would also fit the Gogo Falls situation (Marshall 1986; Robertshaw 1989), particularly as the abundance of tsetse fly in South Nyanza is likely to have depressed livestock numbers. The alternative suggestion that the Gogo Falls assemblage is the result of hunter-gatherers supplementing the products of the chase by rustling or exchange with pastoralists does not bear detailed scrutiny: first and most cogently, the faunal assemblage was found in an enormous pile of livestock dung; second, the absence of animals with claws, nails and fur is in accord with common taboos among food-producing peoples on the eating of such animals; and, finally, the age profile reconstructed from the cattle teeth is indicative of long-term culling of a pastoral herd rather than opportunistic rustling (Marshall 1986, p. 169).

Four radiocarbon dates on charcoal samples place the Elmenteitan occupation at Gogo Falls between the first century BC and the end of the fourth century AD. In the topsoil overlying the midden were found considerable quantities of early iron age Urewe pottery, some of which had worked its way down into the upper levels of the midden. Iron bracelets, blades and other objects were found in association with this pottery, but there is no evidence that iron-smelting took place at the site. A single ornament made from marine shell can be attributed to either the Early Iron Age or the latter part of the Elmenteitan occupation. The differences between the Elmenteitan and the Urewe pottery are so radical (cf. Collett 1985, Ch. 5) that, as with the appearance of the Elmenteitan, immigration of new groups of people is the obvious explanation. Indeed, the appearance of Urewe pottery in South Nyanza is undoubtedly part and parcel of the well-documented expansion of Bantu-speaking farmers through eastern and southern Africa (e.g. Phillipson 1977a). Thus, major changes in subsistence, settlement and technology in South Nyanza are linked with immigrant populations.

Gogo Falls has provided a fascinating glimpse of the adaptations of stone age food producers in the region, but our understanding is limited by the absence of other, contemporary sites in South Nyanza which might permit the recognition of regional patterns of subsistence and settlement. A recent, but brief, survey designed to rectify this situation produced disappointing results (Robertshaw, Pilgram, Siiriäinen & Marshall 1990). There is clear evidence that the Elmenteitan pastoralists of Gogo Falls combined hunting with herd management, but did they also grow crops? Much effort was expended in the flotation of samples of deposit during the excavations and a good number of carbonized seeds were recovered, but it appears that no cultigens are represented (W. Wetterstrom, *pers. comm.*). However, it is well to remember that absence of evidence is not the same as evidence of absence.

Later prehistory in the Mara

The Mara region has been subjected to a great deal more archaeological fieldwork than South Nyanza. Thus, some 150 sites have been recorded, though only seven of these have been excavated (Robertshaw, Pilgram, Siiriäinen & Marshall 1990). Surface collections have been made at several more sites. A considerable suite of obsidian hydration dates has also been processed in order to establish the culture-historical sequence for a region in which virtually every site has only a single occupation horizon.

The later prehistoric sequence in the Mara apparently begins with later stone age (LSA) sites that lack pottery. They occur generally as small, light-density, surface scatters of artefacts found on a broad range of hillslopes. Faunal remains are not preserved at any of these sites. Thus, the Mara region presents a marked contrast with South Nyanza with its rich evidence for LSA foraging adaptations. Indeed, the absence of LSA sites with faunal remains from the Mara was a shock, for we had expected to document prehistorical exploitation of the vast herds of game that roam the Mara plains. Moreover, such evidence has been forthcoming from further south in the Serengeti (Bower & Chadderdon 1986). The obsidian hydration dates for one of the Mara LSA sites fall in the first few centuries AD. Thus, we are confronted with the possibility that all these so-called LSA sites may date to the period of pastoralist occupation of the region. Perhaps they are the result of pastoralist activities, for example a casual flaking episode of a group of men out herding cattle, and bear no relation to hunting whatsoever. Therefore, we have as yet no unequivocal evidence of LSA occupation of the Mara prior to the advent of pastoralism.

On present evidence the earliest sites in the region, at which bones of domestic animals – cattle and caprines – are found, contain pottery of the Oldishi tradition similar, but by no means identical, to that from Narosura (Odner 1972). The associated stone artefact assemblages are predominantly made from grey obsidian, from the Naivasha region of the central Rift Valley, some 100 km to the east (Merrick & Brown 1984), and chert, the latter being preferred for the manufacture of backed microliths. Oldishi sites have been found only in the Lemek valley, where obsidian hydration dates from several sites indicate occupation between very approximately 800 and 400 BC. The identified faunal remains from the major excavated site, Lemek Northeast, are all domestic, caprines being far more numerous than cattle (Marshall 1986). As at Gogo Falls, there is no evidence of cultivation.

After about 400 BC, possibly somewhat later, sites of the Oldishi tradition disappear from the archaeological record of the Mara to be replaced by other pastoralist sites, the pottery and stone artefacts from which belong without doubt to the Elmenteitan tradition. Again, the implication is that population movements are involved. More than thirty-five Elmenteitan sites have been recorded throughout the region in a distribution pattern closely similar to that of the modern pastoral Maasai settlements (Lamprey & Waller 1990; Robertshaw, Pilgram, Siiriäinen & Marshall 1990). A histogram of the maximum dimensions, as measured by the extent of the artefact scatters, of these Elmenteitan sites shows something of a bimodal or perhaps trimodal distribution (Fig. 19.4). While possible sampling errors, such as differential preservation and exposure of sites, cannot be dismissed, it is clear that the larger sites are not simply the product of greater post-depositional movement of artefacts caused by sheetwash. Two of the six largest sites contain extensive deposits of animal dung indicative of central livestock enclosures. These data raise the possibility of economic differentiation, both between possible pastoral camps and more agriculturally oriented settlements and concomitantly between larger (semi-permanent?) and smaller (seasonal?) settlements. However, with our present knowledge, these are little more than speculations, which may serve to focus future fieldwork priorities.

Large-scale excavations at the Elmenteitan site of Ngamuriak in the Lemek valley have uncovered several middens, dung accumulations, one or two house-floors and vast quantities of artefacts and faunal remains. The last have been the subject of detailed analysis by Marshall (1986; 1990). More than 99 per cent of the identified bones belong to either cattle or ovicaprids. Reconstructions of slaughtering patterns, herd management practices and herd sizes demonstrate that the occupants of Ngamuriak had large herds of cattle compared with small stock by the standards of modern subsistence pastoralists in east Africa. The fact that they allowed their animals to reach maximum meat-weight before slaughtering suggests, too, that ecological and economic constraints on pastoral herd growth were few (Marshall 1990).

Elmenteitan sites

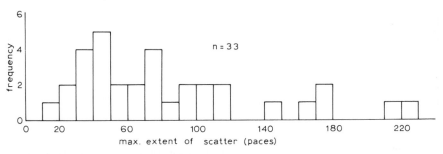

Figure 19.4   The maximum dimensions of Elmenteitan sites in the Mara region.

In contrast with the abundant evidence for pastoralism, no carbonized seeds of any cultigens have been found at Ngamuriak despite considerable efforts aimed at their recovery. Nor are there many grindstones, though of course grinding equipment need not be made of stone. The large quantities of pottery at the site and the spatial organization of debris is suggestive of long-term occupation, which is arguably incompatible with a subsistence economy based entirely upon pastoral produce.[6] Site catchment analysis has also shown the potential of the Ngamuriak area for farming (Robertshaw & Collett 1983, pp. 70–1). In a wider context, analysis of nitrogen isotope ratios in putative Elmenteitan skeletons, unfortunately not from the Mara region,[7] has revealed a considerable plant-food component in their diet (Ambrose & DeNiro 1986).

Obsidian hydration dates from several sites suggest that Elmenteitan occupation spanned the period from approximately 400 BC to AD 600, possibly even as late as AD 1200 if dates on artefacts collected from the surface of sites and, therefore, in dubious context, are to be credited. There also seems to be some geographical patterning to the dates (Fig. 19.5), the Mara plains being first settled by Elmenteitan pastoralists around AD 250, several centuries after their appearance in the Lemek valley. While an explanation invoking sampling errors cannot be discounted, a more exciting alternative

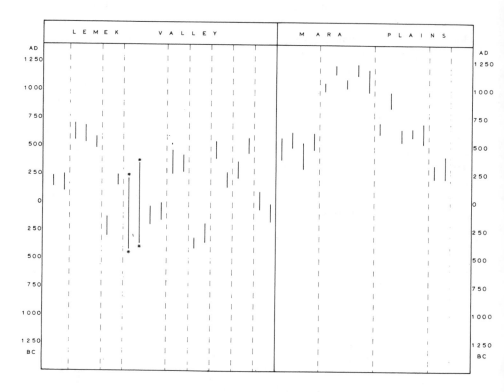

Figure 19.5 Geographical patterning in the dates for Elmenteitan sites in the Mara region. Starred dates are calibrated radiocarbon dates; others are obsidian hydration dates.

would propose that the expansion of settlement onto the Mara plains represents a shift in economic emphasis, following a reduction in cultivation, towards more mobile pastoral strategies aimed at exploiting the rich grasslands of the plains. This would have been facilitated by the spread of iron age farming communities, from whom grain could be traded, into the highlands to the north and west (cf. Robertshaw & Collett 1983).[8] Another alternative hypothesis would suggest that expansion onto the Mara plains may have been facilitated by a reduction in bush cover and hence in the distribution of tsetse fly. This hypothesis is not mutually exclusive with the previous one, since the proposed reduction in bush cover may have come about as a result of pastoralist intervention rather than any climatic or environmental changes.

Our knowledge of the later part of the prehistoric sequence in the Mara, that of the present millennium, is in many ways as intractable as that of the pre-pastoralist LSA. A considerable number of sites have been discovered on the Mara plains that defy easy attribution to any of the known cultural traditions. These are mostly surface occurrences with stone artefacts made from a variety of obsidians and other raw materials, together with undecorated pottery, which lacks the mica temper characteristic of Elmenteitan ceramics in this region. However, a few sherds with rouletted decoration are a common feature of many of these sites. Since this form of pottery decoration is generally found on sites dating to the middle of the present millennium, there is an indication that the Mara sites may postdate the Elmenteitan. However, we can also not dismiss the possibility that these sites are palimpsests of several occupations, particularly since artefacts from one of them have been dated to around AD 400. What these sites may be documenting is not population replacement but a continuation of Elmenteitan settlement into the period when traditional lithic procurement strategies were breaking down under the impact of the spread of iron tools and weapons, and when new techniques of ceramic decoration were being rapidly diffused.

Several authors have suggested on the basis of either historical linguistics (Ambrose 1982) or ceramic design structure (Collett 1984, p. 87; Robertshaw n.d.) a link between the Elmenteitan and speakers of Southern Nilotic languages. Therefore, it is of considerable interest to note that Maasai traditions identify the original inhabitants of the Mara region as 'Il Tatua', who are often equated with the Tatoga of northern Tanzania but are perhaps best viewed as an archetype of all earlier Southern Nilotic-speaking inhabitants of what became Maasailand (Lamprey & Waller 1990). Thus, one may posit an equation between the Elmenteitan of the archaeologists, 'Il Tatua' of oral tradition and the Southern Nilotes of the linguists. To take a rather more conservative stance: if further archaeological research confirms the hypothesis that Elmenteitan settlement continued well into the present millennium, then Elmenteitan pastoralists and their descendants occupied the Mara region for the best part of two thousand years. This is a marked difference from the relatively brief episode of Elmenteitan occupation of South Nyanza, where it was perhaps harder to eke out a pastoral existence in the face of tsetse flies. The abundant rainfall and rich agricultural soils of the alluvial floodplain in the vicinity of Gogo Falls also attracted incursions by farmers with hoes and spears with iron blades.

Conclusions

The later prehistoric sequences of the South Nyanza and Mara regions of southwestern Kenya are remarkably different. In South Nyanza a broad-spectrum, gathering-hunting-fishing adaptation is replaced by, or perhaps assimilated into, the Elmenteitan cultural tradition of immigrant pastoralists some two thousand years ago. However, Elmenteitan settlement in South Nyanza is apparently rather short-lived, since radiocarbon dates for other sites in the Lake Victoria basin with Urewe pottery suggest that early iron age farmers probably occupied this region by the middle of the first millennium AD at the latest. In contrast, in the Mara there is little evidence for occupation by foraging peoples prior to the advent of the pastoralists, whose material culture is assigned to the Oldishi tradition. These pioneer herders settled in the Lemek valley, from which they would appear to have been displaced around 400 BC or somewhat later by the makers of Elmenteitan pottery and stone artefacts, who were to occupy the region for the best part of two thousand years.

Not only was the duration of Elmenteitan settlement very different in South Nyanza and the Mara, so also was their subsistence economy. South Nyanza appears to have been ecologically marginal for viable pastoral production, compelling diversification of subsistence into hunting, fishing and possibly cultivation. However, the Mara region was capable of supporting large numbers of livestock. Thus, hunting was shunned,[9] despite the fact that the herds of the pastoralists had to compete for grazing with large populations of wild herbivores. Whether cultivation was also shunned is a more difficult question, which can only be answered by more fieldwork. However, there is some evidence to suggest that the earlier phases of Elmenteitan settlement were basically restricted to the Lemek valley and that an expansion of settlement onto the Mara plains occurred in the first centuries AD. It has been mooted that this expansion took place within the context of a shift from agro-pastoralism to more mobile pastoralism, with agricultural produce obtained when required through exchange networks. In this shift may lie the origins of the so-called 'pure' pastoral economies which have so enchanted anthropologists.

One might argue that east Africa has little or nothing to offer towards finding the answer to the 'Big Question' of the origins of agriculture, but to do so would be to deny the fact that consideration of the 'where', 'when' and 'how' of food production is really of secondary importance compared to the explanation of the process of the spread of food production across much of the globe and what that involved in terms of human interactions and adaptations – those of farmers, pastoralists and foraging peoples.

Notes

[1] By 'east Africa' I refer to Kenya, Uganda and Tanzania.

[2] See Collett & Robertshaw (1983a) for a detailed discussion of the dating evidence and a refutation of much earlier 'dates' for domestic animals in southern Kenya.

[3] Formerly Nderit ware.

[4] The much older hydration date from the base of the deposits presumably represents the chance

incorporation into the midden of a much older artefact that does not date the main occupation.

[5] Sherds which belong within the rather enigmatic 'Akira ware' were also found. However, discussion of these interesting pots is beyond the scope of this chapter (see Bower 1973b; Langdon & Robertshaw 1985).

[6] The point has been made elsewhere that no pastoral society can survive indefinitely without access to agricultural produce (Monod 1975, p. 134). The implications of this statement for our understanding of the subsistence systems of early pastoral communities in east Africa have been discussed by Robertshaw & Collett (1983).

[7] No human skeletal remains have been found in the Mara region.

[8] The appearance of iron age (Urewe) farmers at Gogo Falls may be relevant in this context.

[9] Less than 1 per cent of the identifiable faunal remains from Ngamuriak belong to wild animals (Marshall 1986).

20   The rise and fall of nomadic pastoralism in the central Namib desert

JOHN KINAHAN

Introduction

The Namib desert is the most arid region of sub-Saharan Africa, extending along the Atlantic littoral from south of the Orange river for more than 2000 km to the north, across the Cunene river and into Angola. In Namibia the inland limits of the desert are between 100 km and 200 km from the coast, coinciding with the 200 mm isohyet and the foothills of a broken longitudinal escarpment. Several episodic river systems drain from the savanna highlands, cutting across the desert to enter the sea at widely separated intervals.

This chapter reports an archaeological investigation carried out in the central parts of the Namib desert, north of the great dune sea. The area between the !Khuiseb and Ugab rivers (Fig. 20.1) is dominated by extensive gravel plains with scattered mountain ranges. Of these by far the largest is the massif once known as Dâures, the 'burning mountain', renamed Brandberg during the colonial era. Archaeological interest in this massif was aroused early this century by the discovery of important rock art sites (Jochmann 1910). Although the earlier research was antiquarian rather than scientific (e.g. Breuil 1948), more systematic enquiries soon followed (Mason 1955; Rudner 1957; Viereck 1967) and in the last two decades detailed studies have established the framework of a radiocarbon sequence for the last eight millennia in the Namib as a whole (Wendt 1972; Sandelowsky 1977; Wadley 1979).

Evidence for the introduction of pottery and livestock to the Namib during the last two millennia (Sandelowsky, Van Rooyen & Vogel 1979) is in general agreement with data from elsewhere in southern Africa (Deacon 1984; Klein 1986) which point to the spread of nomadic pastoralism throughout the more arid western parts of the subcontinent. The establishment of European settler communities during the last three hundred years led to a rapid collapse of nomadic pastoralism everywhere in southern Africa (Elphick 1977), and in the Namib desert pastoralists were reduced to abject poverty within only two hundred years. When colonial rule was established at the turn of the century large areas were already depopulated, the desert nomads having settled near the small towns, mines and trading posts. Archaeological research in the Namib has, however, subsumed these economic processes within a paradigm of ethnic succession which has served until now as a general framework for the precolonial sequence. This view, which relies heavily on the somewhat romantic ethnography of Vedder (1938), is of uncertain relevance to the more distant past.

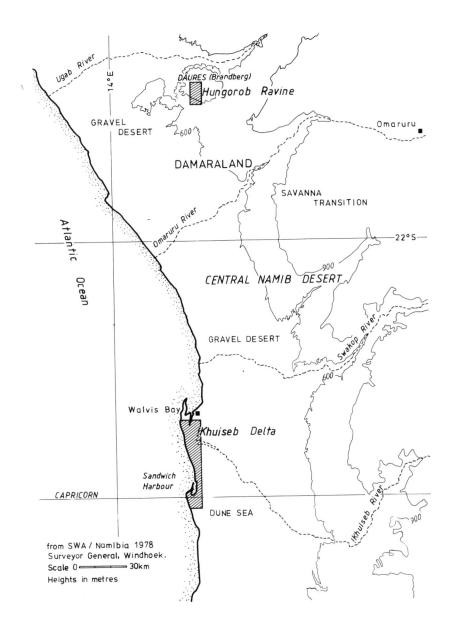

Figure 20.1 Map of the central Namib desert, showing the location of the Hungorob Ravine and !Khuiseb delta research areas.

Rudner (1957) and Jacobson (1980) considered the rock art to be the work of hunting communities displaced several centuries ago by the arrival of pastoral people with pottery and metal. Others such as Wadley (1979) used the ethnological observations of nineteenth-century settlers as a detailed explanatory framework for the archaeological sequence and, indeed, Shackley (1985) argued that the establishment of ethnic affinities should be the first goal of research in this region. The two most recent syntheses of archaeological research in the Namib (Sandelowsky 1983; Shackley 1985) further emphasize this approach despite its failure to establish useful correlations between the material evidence and the ethnological record. Empirical weakness is not the only failing of the ethnic succession paradigm; its denial of any social evolutionary potential in precolonial society is equally questionable in the light of modern anthropological theory.

For example, Ingold (1980) and Meillassoux (1981) have emphasized the capacity of hunting society to transform itself, which suggests an alternative to the conventional view on the rise of nomadic pastoralism in the Namib. Other workers such as Bonte (1981) and Lefébure (1979) have pointed to specific social relations which are associated with nomadic livestock production, in a social and ecological setting where each family is, as Marx once observed, 'an economy unto itself' (Marx 1973, p. 433). If these basic considerations also determine the physical layout of pastoral encampments, they should provide more useful archaeological insights than ethnographic observations compiled long after the collapse of the nomadic economy. As to this final process, work by Vercruisse (1984) and others on the penetration of precapitalist economies suggests that it may be possible to determine from archaeological evidence the cause of the pastoral demise.

Given the importance of the Dâures massif in previous research, I chose to test my hypotheses there, in the Hungorob Ravine on the southwestern side of the mountain (Fig. 20.2). The ravine descends almost 2000 m in little more than 10 km between its source near the summit of the massif and the point at which it reaches the desert plains. A number of reliable water-holes have ensured the importance of the Hungorob over the last few millennia, although no one lives there today. In an attempt to corroborate my observations I also investigated the archaeology of the !Khuiseb delta, near the present port of Walvis Bay. Places such as the Hungorob were initially unaffected by mercantile penetration, but coastal communities fared differently since the bay was the main European trading entrepôt during the eighteenth and nineteenth centuries. Using complementary data from these two research areas I will first consider the rise of pastoralism in the Hungorob Ravine and then its collapse in the !Khuiseb delta.

The rise of nomadic pastoralism in the Hungorob Ravine

There are more than sixty rock art sites in the Hungorob, ranging from single figures and cryptic marks to large friezes crowded with animals and groups of people. Of the 815 paintings recorded, roughly 75 per cent could be identified to species or some higher taxon. Human figures dominated the paintings, leaving rather less than 20 per cent of the sample to be filled by a variety of antelope, with giraffe, zebra, lion, elephant, ostrich and snake in order of decreasing frequency. The rare subjects such as elephant and snake occurred only at those sites with the greatest overall number of paintings. These sites, six in total, were situated at the most reliable water-holes in the upper ravine and thus appear to have served as central places in a variegated pattern of settlement.

Two of the central sites contained deposits suitable for excavation; of these, Falls rock shelter provided the basic stratigraphy for a local sequence, correlated with a test excavation at the other site, Snake Rock. At both sites the deposits were composed of sandy silt layers with varying admixtures of decomposed granite, ash, charred plant material and dung. Three phases of occupation could be discerned from the stratigraphy, and these were corroborated by the sediment characteristics, dating of organic material and the presence of key associations. In this sequence, the pre-pottery phase dated to between 4500 BP and 2500 BP; pottery was introduced during the second phase which dated from 2100 BP to 1600 BP, while the final phase of occupation is linked to only one date of 730 BP for a substantial accumulation of domestic animal dung at Falls rock shelter. According to this evidence, neither site was occupied during the last five hundred years.

Stone tool assemblages from these two excavations include a small range of formal artefacts dominated by *en écaille* thumbnail scrapers, mainly in crystalline quartz, and a variety of points and other projectile components with *abrupt normal* retouch. The relative numbers of tool types did not vary to any marked degree through the sequence, suggesting that stone tool technology remained practically the same throughout the

Figure 20.2 Hungorob Ravine from the southwest.

sequence. A detailed attribute analysis was performed to test this observation using the Frequency Modulated Homogeneity Function of Beavon and Hall (1972). The results of this procedure, more fully discussed in Kinahan (1984), are summarized in the dendrograms in Figure 20.3. With the *en écaille* and *abrupt normal* tools treated as two groups, the Falls rock shelter assemblages show the same similarities between phases. These similarities are retained both in the combined scores for this site and in the combined scores for Falls rock shelter and Snake Rock. Assemblages from the pre-pottery and pottery phases are so much alike that if the innovation of pottery is related to the changes in the stone tools of the pastoral phase, the delay alone suggests more complex processes than a shift in the composition of the toolkit.

However, faunal remains from the two excavations showed a similar continuity throughout the sequence, with one small species of antelope, as well as hare and hyrax,

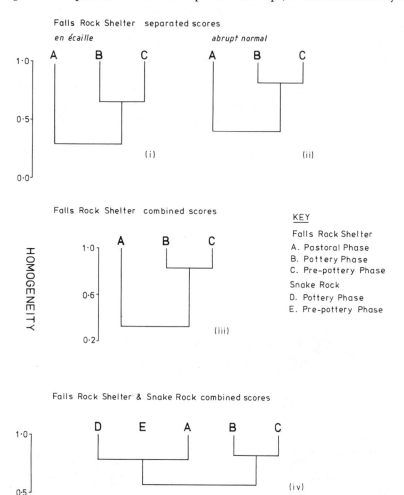

Figure 20.3 Homogeneity dendrograms for Hungorob Ravine stone tool assemblages.

represented in almost unvarying proportions. The selection of these species appears to have been governed by local abundance rather than any particular cultural preference and when the remains of leopard meals were occasionally found in the course of fieldwork, their species and skeletal parts composition resembled those of the archaeological samples. No sheep or goat remains were positively identified from the pastoral phase deposits and it is therefore likely that, while the dung accumulated from the use of Falls rock shelter as a stock enclosure, the animals were slaughtered and consumed elsewhere.

These observations are grounds on which to reject the ethnic succession hypothesis and consider the alternative, that the hunting economy in the Hungorob Ravine was able to adopt the appropriate social relations for the control of property in livestock. There is reason to doubt the appropriateness of subsistence technological evidence as a reflection of changes in social organization, particularly when a far more pertinent source is to be found in the rock art. Although the paintings in the Hungorob sites are undated, studies elsewhere in southern Africa have established that the rock art of this region directly refers to ritual healing practices in which the egalitarian ideological precepts of hunting society were reproduced (Lewis-Williams 1982; Lewis-Williams 1984).

A large painted frieze at Snake Rock (Fig. 20.4) well illustrates this phenomenon, with several clear representations of ritual healing. Painted in the same style and in the same shade of red-brown pigment, groups of human figures can be linked together as perhaps the earliest of many superimposed subjects at this site. In these groups, rows of women are shown clapping their hands while men appear in various dancing postures and stages of physical collapse; some men are depicted as if moving in file, using short walking-sticks, while others are supported by their companions and one lies prone, with blood streaming from his nose.

All these are common features of the so-called trance dance described from among Kalahari hunting communities by Marshall (1969) and other anthropologists. More recently, however, Guenther (1975) described Nahron hunters in the same area as having assumed the function of ritual specialists, or shamans. These individuals appear to have altered the egalitarian ethos of trance performance by using their ritual skills to acquire personal herds of domestic stock in exchange for their services among neighbouring pastoral communities. In effect, the shaman is a powerful agent of social change generated from within hunting society.

The frieze at Snake Rock in the Hungorob Ravine superimposes upon the monochrome dancers figures with elaborate clothing and decoration. These figures seem to represent the final episode of painting at this and several other sites. They incorporate various animal attributes that are common in the rock art and are therefore clearly a development of the same tradition. However, they are all men, appearing either singly or in small groups, but without showing any of the conventional postures and attitudes of the trance dance. The paintings clearly suggest a shift in religious practice towards the end of the rock shelter sequence. Taken together with the introduction of pottery and the abandonment of the rock shelter sites once livestock was established in the area, the evidence on the whole favours a local transition to pastoralism rather than the displacement of hunters by immigrant pastoral groups.

Figure 20.4 Detail of the main frieze at Snake Rock (scale 1:10).

After AD 1000 a new pattern of settlement arose in the Hungorob. Large encampments of stone-walled habitations appeared at the ravine entrance where previously there was little settlement at all. In the upper reaches of the ravine, close to the rock art sites and the main water-holes, small homesteads with stock enclosures were constructed. The upper and lower ravine sites were opposite poles of a transhumant pastoral cycle which exploited a striking altitudinal difference in pastures. The higher parts of the massif support lush perennial pastures, but these are beyond reasonable daily range of the encampments at the entrance of the ravine where the pastures, best described as ephemeral, have a far lower carrying capacity.

Elsewhere (Kinahan 1986), I have described the archaeological characteristics of this settlement pattern in considerable detail. The sites in the ravine entrance include several hundred features which are differentiated in separate encampments greatly varying in size. Each encampment consisted of several household clusters, centring on one relatively complex hut feature with elaborate storage cells. The surrounding features would include freestanding storage cells, mainly coops for the young of small livestock, as well as cooking shelters and simple hut features. Apart from their outward appearance, the complex and simple huts were distinguished by other characteristics, including the placement of hearths and stone pestles. The ash from hearths in the complex huts was removed to middens elsewhere on the site, suggesting that these huts were serviced by the rest of the household. That the simple huts were probably occupied by women is indicated by their repeated association with stone pestles which in no instance were found with the complex huts.

These characteristics lead me to propose that households in the pastoral encampments formed discrete entities, internally structured according to a distinction of status probably based on property ownership and gender. It is of particular interest that the herds were kept mainly at stockposts near water-holes several kilometres away. Spatial expression of pastoral relations of production and ownership was clearly as important an element of the encampment site as the livestock itself. The sites are clearly temporary aggregations of autonomous households on annual pastures with highly localized water sources. It is difficult to estimate the combined size of the herds. The pasture conditions are such that even with herds of a moderate size there would have been little left within grazing range of the encampments after about two months.

With the onset of the dry season the herds would have been moved up the ravine where they could be maintained until the first rains of summer. If the summer herding alliances changed from one year to the next, it is likely that the layout of the aggregation encampment would have to change as well. This explains the great number of encampments at the foot of the ravine which probably represent a series of separate occupations during the last millennium. In contrast, the homestead sites in the upper ravine were repeatedly occupied and some have considerable midden accumulations. Figure 20.5 summarizes the hypothetical pattern of Hungorob transhumance in the form of two successive annual cycles which also illustrate the major archaeological characteristics of this movement.

Pottery occurs in far greater quantities in the upper ravine than on the encampments at the foot of the ravine, in almost inverse proportion to the actual size of the sites. This is in keeping with the occupation history of the sites and closer examination of the

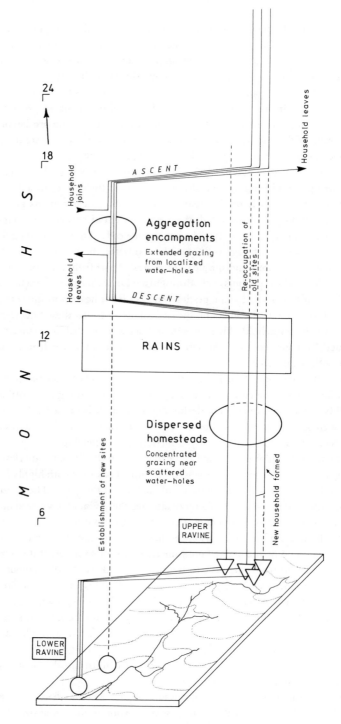

Figure 20.5 The Hungorob Ravine biannual transhumance cycle.

pottery and its context provides some useful additional insights into the pastoral economy. The Hungorob pots are generally bag–shaped with paired lugs and basically fall into two overlapping groups: pots with necks usually have lugs and are invariably decorated, while pots without necks are sometimes decorated if they have lugs, but always lack decoration if they have no lugs. Chronologically, the necked pots precede pots without necks, but both have pierced lugs. This style eventually gave way to a preference for vestigial lugs and then no lugs at all. In contrast to the most recent pottery which is entirely plain and often covered by a thick accumulation of soot, the earlier examples are highly burnished. Although the pots clearly represent a local development in style, the change from necked storage vessels to wide–mouthed cooking vessels points to a change in the function of the pottery.

Considering the associations of the pottery, the most likely reason for this change is an intensified exploitation of an unusual cereal resource contained in the underground caches of grass seeds gathered by harvester ants on the plains of the Namib. The stone seed pestles mentioned already occur mainly on the summer encampments and the fact that most of the pottery is found on the homestead sites indicates that the seed caches were robbed at the start of the dry season, winnowed and taken to the upper ravine as food for the dry season. The same would have applied to the many bees' nests at the foot of the Hungorob which were opened as the herds left for the upper ravine, cleared and closed up again for the following year.

Close as the adaptation of herding to the ravine may appear, the environmental setting obviously can neither indicate nor explain the specific characteristics of social organization in the nomadic pastoral community. Still less are these insights available from the colonial ethnography, which invariably stresses ethnic affinity rather than social and economic structures. Once developed as practical tools of archaeological interpretation, the essential structures of the pastoral economy lead to even more detailed reconstruction of a land–use pattern that is now completely extinct in this region (Kinahan 1990).

The fall of nomadic pastoralism in the !Khuiseb delta

Environmental conditions on the Namib coast are in dramatic contrast to those further inland. Whereas the desert plains below the Dâures massif receive very little rain, the coast receives virtually none, its vegetation being mainly confined to river courses such as the !Khuiseb where sufficient underground water supplies exist. The archaeological site distribution in the !Khuiseb delta reflects a small range of feasible subsistence strategies, all inevitably tethered to the somewhat fickle and brackish water supplies.

Shell middens are the most numerous archaeological sites in the delta. They occur all the way from Sandwich Harbour to the outskirts of Walvis Bay, in small groups, each centring on one large midden up to 10,000 m^2 in extent. None of these midden sites has potable water today, but protruding from the surrounding dunes are always to be found the desiccated stumps of substantial reed–beds. It is indeed likely that constant shifts in the water supply have resulted in a greater density of sites, although it is still possible to discern a variegated pattern of distribution closely resembling that of the Hungorob Ravine.

All the large central shell middens included remains of whale, fur seal and a variety of marine birds. Furthermore, all were found to include small amounts of finely decorated and burnished pottery dating to between 1800 BP and 1400 BP, approximately the same time range as the early Hungorob pottery. During the present millennium these fine wares were also replaced in the !Khuiseb by robust bag-shaped pots, usually found with heavy encrustations of soot. This pottery was widely associated with cattle and small stock remains, as well as elegantly finished and decorated bone knives. It is known from several early historical sources that the knives and the pottery were used together in the cooking of !nara melons from which a nutritious and long-lasting extract was made (Budack 1977).

Although the !nara is quite prolific among the coastal dunes, neither robust pottery nor bone knives were found at Sandwich Harbour. It would appear that the acquisition of pottery had initially no effect on subsistence in the !Khuiseb and that the technology of potting was only adopted after a considerable time, when it formed part of a subsistence pattern based primarily on livestock production. Sandwich Harbour has abundant fresh water but very little grazing, and this need must have necessitated a shift in pastoral settlement on the coast to the area around Walvis Bay, 50 km to the north.

Pastoral encampments near Walvis Bay were evidently positioned to ensure access to water, !naras from the dunes, fish from the coastal lagoon and grazing for livestock along the course of the !Khuiseb. However, by the mid-eighteenth century the number of encampments at the bay appears to have dropped to only one. This change is not linked to any evidence of declining resources, for the bay encampments were probably occupied all year round, to judge from the faunal remains (e.g. Avery 1984). A more likely explanation is that pastoral settlement at the bay gained so much in importance after initial trading contacts with European merchants that it quickly fell under the control of one powerful encampment at the water-hole of ≠Khîsa-//gubus, 5 km inland from Walvis Bay.

The most significant early documentary record of contact is the narrative of Thomas Bolden Thompson who commanded HMS Nautilus on her voyage to survey the Namib coast in 1786 (J. H. A. Kinahan 1990). Finding the people at Walvis Bay friendly and unafraid, Thompson accepted an invitation to visit their encampment which lay about 10 km inland over the dunes. Being an acute observer and talented watercolour artist, Thompson noticed and recorded many details of dress and decoration, including the use of glass trade beads. He noted particularly the absence of livestock and although their spoor were everywhere to be seen, he could not obtain sufficient animals to reprovision his ship at short notice. When he attempted to espy the land beyond their encampment the people became considerably agitated. Later visitors such as Alexander (1838) confirmed that cattle could not be purchased from the pastoralists at the bay without giving several days' notice. This indicates that the animals had to be brought from stockposts much further inland.

Archaeological remains at ≠Khîsa-//gubus comprised large quantities of cattle and small stock remains, as well as a variety of European artefacts including 2500 glass trade beads. The assemblage of pottery from this site includes a number of vessels with highly unusual axially pierced lugs, the only other examples of which are from five widely scattered sites up to 100 km inland at the foot of the escarpment. The implication is that these finds represent an extensive pastoral network of inland sites linked with the trading outlet at the coast. This is given further weight by the fact that one of the inland pots contained more than two thousand glass trade beads, many of which matched the range of types found at ≠Khîsa-//gubus. The distribution of these sites and the evident lack of large seasonal aggregation encampments suggest that, in contrast to the Hungorob, there existed in the !Khuiseb area a system of stock rotation between relatively fixed points.

However, the circulation of livestock and commodities in this area was already established well before the arrival of European merchants. Copper beads in particular were produced in the highlands of central Namibia (Kinahan & Vogel 1982), and found their way in large numbers to the site of ≠Khîsa-//gubus. It is further significant that both glass and copper beads were restricted to the pastoral sites and therefore integrated with the livestock economy. Copper beads served as a means to acquire livestock, and this equivalence of value would have meant that the hoarding of beads was a viable technique of herd management in a grazing environment as uncertain as the Namib. Although glass beads were evidently treated in the same way, their trade value was arbitrary and their equivalence in livestock would therefore have dropped as the beads became more abundant. Indigenous copper production in central Namibia ceased early in the nineteenth century, and this in all likelihood reflects a decline in livestock production along the !Khuiseb.

The glass trade bead sequence in Figure 20.6 shows a series of informative changes during the two and a half centuries of contact in this area. Blue cylinders and red-on-green beads were initially restricted to the bay site and two of its stockposts, one of

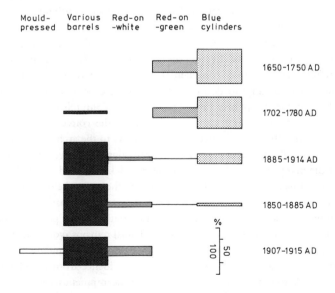

Figure 20.6 Sequence of glass trade bead distribution in the central Namib desert.

which accumulated a large hoard, dominated by the great variety of beads that were introduced towards the end of the last century. These often large and colourful beads were also found at Sandwich Harbour and on some recent sites near Walvis Bay, where people lived as squatters without any livestock. Whereas glass beads were at first an important trade commodity for the Namib pastoralists, it is clear they eventually became worthless trinkets. Certainly, effective occupation of inland pastures was only a memory by 1885, when a colonial commission of inquiry recorded that fishing establishments at Sandwich Harbour took on destitute people as additional labour (*Proceedings* 1885). According to the glass bead sequence and the other archaeological evidence, pastoral production seems to have absorbed all labour until the economy collapsed entirely about one hundred years ago.

Conclusions

Although previous research in the Namib established the general archaeological characteristics of the area, no wide-ranging and systematic surveys were available until the present study. Moreover, the investigation reported here also approached the archaeology of the Namib from an entirely different perspective, with the purpose of investigating basic economic processes rather than of supplementing the colonial ethnographic record.

While previous studies did not hesitate to attribute the abundant rock art of this region to extinct hunting communities, they were unable to place the rock art in the archaeological sequence. Noticing the presence of a second pattern of settlement marked by large concentrations of stone features, earlier studies inferred a simple process of ethnic succession. In the absence of positive verification for such immigration events, the archaeological evidence of sustained continuity in settlement, technology and subsistence points to a different interpretation. Favouring this is the evidence from the rock art which indicates that a radical ideological shift allowed for the rise of shamanism as a means of effecting the establishment of a fully pastoral economy.

Critics of this approach may complain that it does not resolve the origins of the domestic stock which came to dominate the regional economy. This is so, but the evidence I have adduced supports a more plausible and comprehensive explanation for the establishment of a pastoral economy than does the conventional view. Future research may clarify the actual source of the stock. As to the archaeological characteristics of fully pastoral settlement in the Namib, previous studies were frequently unable to interpret the many stone-walled sites in this area which lacked physical evidence of domestic stock. I have now shown that not only do these sites belong to a specifically pastoral pattern of land use, but that they exhibit certain diagnostic layout characteristics which provide detailed insights into the organization of the pastoral community. This is important, first because it is unlikely that faunal remains would survive on large summer aggregation encampments where the majority of slaughter animals were probably first-year males; and second, because the evidence from the Namib is very clear that livestock were not necessarily kept at the encampment itself.

The pattern of land use which emerges from this study is very different from that encountered by the first colonial settlers. Indeed, since the pastoral economy in the Namib desert had already collapsed by the turn of the nineteenth century, the notion of a degenerate and unproductive indigenous economy was easily established. The state of this economy in recent decades also served to justify a system of land distribution which did not take into account the dry season pasture needs of peasant farmers. As a result, the rural livestock economy in the arid western parts of Namibia has steadily declined over the last few decades, its reserves of pasture depleted to critical levels. Precolonial land use was not only more extensive, but appears to have incorporated a number of vital principles of sustained-yield pastoralism. For example, summer aggregations entailed very intense grazing over the short period that ephemeral pastures could last, leaving the maximum possible period of rest. In the dry season the herds were more widely dispersed, allowing more sustained grazing if the rains were delayed. The evidence that encampments were simply temporary alliances indicates that household autonomy was a necessary feature of the grazing strategy. The pattern of archaeological sites further indicates that herd owners moved about in a very extensive network of alternative water-holes and pastures, which they exploited according to distribution of rainfall. Far from being a random search for grazing and water, nomadic pastoralism in the Namib operated according to a set of rational techniques and precautions which ensured a high level of productivity.

The articulation of nomadic pastoralism and merchant trade in itself reflects the high productivity of the Namib economy, for prior to contact there were already in place measures which reduced the size of the herds through the circulation of indigenous commodities. It is, however, apparent that the accumulation of pastoral wealth was susceptible to sudden reverses and that the entire livestock economy could collapse if too large a proportion of the herds was lost through commodity exchange. Finally, both the evidence of contact and exchange and that of land use and settlement emphasize the important contribution archaeology can make towards understanding the internal dynamism of the precolonial economy.

21   The iron age peoples of east-central Botswana

D. KIYAGA-MULINDWA

The notion that southern Africa was once an empty land (Marks 1980), a claim most strongly encouraged by agents and sympathizers of South Africa's regimes in order to justify white domination in southern Africa, has created a general problem in the presentation and interpretation of the past. Since there are only minimal cultural distinctions between the peoples of this region, such myths eventually spilled over into neighbouring countries, such as Botswana, ultimately affecting the theoretical interests and research strategies of archaeologists.

Botswana lies to the north of the Republic of South Africa. It is currently inhabited by Setswana-speaking people in the south, east and northwest of the country. The northeast is mainly inhabited by Kalanga-speaking groups, many of which share various ethnic affinities with some Sotho-Tswana-speaking groups to the south, while a few Kalanga groups, sometimes referred to as the proper Kalanga, have affinities with the Shona of Zimbabwe. To the west, southwest and most of the northwest, the country is inhabited by small groups of San, variously referred to as Basarwa, the Yei, Humbukshu, the Banooka and Herero.

Much of the existing literature has created an impression that there were no iron-using farmers or pastoralists in the area until the arrival of the Setswana-speaking groups across the Madikwe (Marico) river in the Transvaal. This event took place as recently as the middle of the seventeenth century AD at the earliest (Ngcongco 1979). Until then, according to some sources, Botswana is supposed to have been occupied 'largely if not exclusively, by the hunter-gatherer people of the Late Stone Age Stock' (Phillipson 1969, p. 35).

In the long-standing debate on the spread and settlement of iron-using Bantu-speaking peoples in southern Africa, many archaeologists have been convinced that the movement was accomplished by eastern and western 'streams' (Phillipson 1977a). These streams seem to have bypassed Botswana. Although Phillipson has since revised his stand in favour of the Chifumbaze complex (Huffman 1982; Phillipson 1985a), his earlier theory largely contributed to the false assumption that Botswana was only settled at a much later date by iron age people, coming into the country from neighbouring South Africa to the east and the southeast. These later migrations, which are supported by oral traditions as well, were those accomplished by the ancestors of the present-day agro-pastoral and mainly Setswana-speaking peoples. If these interpretations of Botswana's past were tenable, there would have been no iron age communities in Botswana prior to c. AD 1650, when the present Tswana groups are known to have started moving into the country.

Evidence from recent excavations carried out mainly in eastern Botswana is beginning to question such assumptions (Fig. 21.1). It is also beginning to show that, far
from being marginal to the historical developments in the region, this area, today
covered in part by the Republic of Botswana, was one of the main centres of settlement
and population movements in the region from the early centuries of the first millennium AD. We now have an early iron age chronology from as early as the fourth

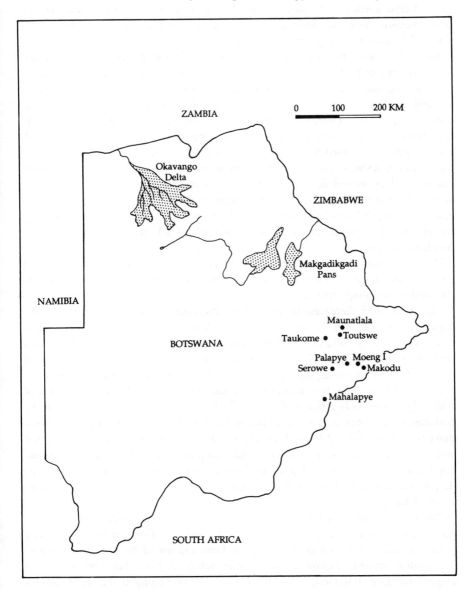

Figure 21.1 Sites mentioned in the text.

century AD. This is particularly interesting because the area of east-central Botswana forms part of the Shashi-Limpopo confluence, which seems to have played host to the growth and development of the most famous iron age cultural system in this subcontinent, popularly known as the Zimbabwe tradition. It is now believed that the Zhizo group of southwestern Zimbabwe and east-central Botswana (where they are known as the Toutswe people) were the earliest iron age groups so far known to have lived in this area. These were later, in the tenth century, replaced by the Leopold's Kopje people who, in their northerly expansion, established themselves at the site of Schroda, the largest known Zhizo site, located in the northern Transvaal. This expansion forced many of the earlier Zhizo groups to migrate westwards into Botswana.

The bulk of our information on iron age communities in the area comes from the work carried out by Denbow (1983; 1986) on a group of sites that have produced material now included in the Toutswe tradition. Denbow carried out a systematic archaeological survey in an area covering almost a 100 km radius around Serowe, the capital of the Central District of Botswana. His thorough investigations revealed the spread of some three hundred or so similar sites dating between AD 680 and AD 1300. A study of pottery collected from a sample of these sites revealed great similarities with Zhizo pottery in southwestern Zimbabwe and northern Transvaal. This pottery mainly has stamped or incised decoration. The vessels are mostly of simple forms with undifferentiated rims. Other common features of these Toutswe sites are the huge deposits of vitrified cowdung, now easily observed on aerial photographs as they are clearly marked by patches of the grass, *Cenchrus ciliaris*, which usually grows on such cowdung mounds.

Denbow suggested that these sites were structured in a hierarchy which correlated with size and location. He noted in particular three distinct categories, which he classified in ascending order of physical size.

Class 1, of which there were 159 examples in his research area, was the smallest in the hierarchy. Excavation at Kgaswe B55 revealed nineteen hut foundations. Kgaswe was dated to between AD 990 and AD 1010 (Denbow 1986, pp. 18–21). Carbonized sorghum seeds and millet were found in storage bin structures, as well as several thousand glass beads and ostrich egg shells, suggesting long-distance trade from the east African coast. Such Class 1 sites tended to cluster around medium-sized sites of Denbow's Class 2, of which there were only a few in the area. Taukome, near Serowe, and Sung, in the Mahalapye area, both in east-central Botswana, have large mounds of vitrified cowdung as wide as 20 m and 1.5 m deep. The single largest settlement in this hierarchical system was the Class 3 site of Toutswe, which lends its name to the complex. Toutswe has a central midden measuring up to 5000 m^2 and excavations have revealed the deepest and most extensive vitrified cowdung mound in the entire system. The well-known Class 3 sites have an area upwards of 50,000 m^2 each.

This hierarchy of Class 1–3 settlements seems to reflect some stratification between the people who lived in or controlled the settlements. This settlement hierarchy correlates well with the observations on the depth and size of the cowdung mounds. The small settlements of Class 1 had little or no such dung at all, while Toutswe had the largest and deepest mound, hence the reason for considering it the centre of this settlement system. The medium-sized settlements such as Taukome had cowdung mounds with an average depth of about 1.5 m. The evidence seems to signify that there were large cattle herds at Classes 2 and 3 sites over a very long period of time. This is an obvious sign of wealth in cattle and, along with this, economic and political power in the hands of those who were in control of these communities. Denbow concluded that the Toutswe people were agro-pastoral communities living under a nascent state system in this area during the Iron Age, a system which was mainly based on the control of wealth in cattle.

Denbow's work was the first to bring to the fore concrete evidence for the presence of very early iron age communities in an area which had hitherto been thought to have been occupied only by the San until the arrival of the Setswana-speaking people. However, this interpretation does not tally with the prevalent explanation of the spread of Bantu-speaking people in the region. This new evidence replaces the two-streams theory in favour of multiple streams over a broad front. It is on the basis of this evidence that the proposed Bantu (Leopold's Kopje) movement to the north of Limpopo from the south around the tenth century (Hall 1987; Huffman 1982) is now beginning to find favour.

The Toutswe tradition came to an end in Botswana at the close of the thirteenth century, a period which coincided with very severe droughts in the area (Cooke 1975; Grey & Cooke 1977). It is presumed that the Toutswe communities, having had a close affinity with the Zhizo peoples of Zimbabwe, would have moved eastwards in search of better grazing for their large herds of cattle. This is also the time when the Zimbabwe state was rising in the east, to which the Toutswe emigrants must have been a welcome addition, especially with their massive wealth on the hoof.

There is only scanty and sometimes indirect evidence of iron-making on typical Toutswe sites. Denbow noted only one smelting site and one iron mine in his research area (Denbow 1983) and made no collection from either of these sites. However, there were other groups of people in the area adjacent to Toutswe who seem to have specialized in the art of iron-making. This area to the east of Toutswe, specifically in the Tswapong hills to the east of the modern town of Palapye, abounds in direct evidence of iron ore mining, smelting and smithing. Extensive archaeological surveys have been carried out in these hills which have revealed several iron ore mines and iron-smelting sites on the hill slopes, and excavations have been carried out at two sites (Moeng I and Makodu).

Excavations at Moeng I (Kiyaga–Mulindwa 1983) revealed a total of 2789 pieces of tuyères, over half of which were encrusted with slag on one side. Some were recovered joined together in twos or threes, suggesting multiple tuyère insertion for increased draught into the furnace. The excavations also revealed the remnants of a furnace base. The furnace was round, measuring 78 cm inside diameter, with a wall thickness of up to 16 cm. From an examination of the furnace debris, which was abundant, it was possible to reconstruct the original shapes of the furnaces, which appear to have been bell-shaped and probably about 1.5 m in height. The inside of the furnace had a small, round, bowl-like depression which corresponds well with what in other iron-smelting traditions has been referred to as the medicine hole (Küsel n.d.), apparently intended as a receptacle for molten slag during the smelting process. No remnants of bellows were recovered, suggesting, perhaps, that the bellows were reused several times, unlike the tuyères, which appear to have been disposed of as waste after every use. No material relating to human settlement was recovered at the site. We therefore interpreted Moeng I as an industrial site, confirming observations elsewhere that in many areas of Africa iron-smelting processes were normally carried out secretly, some distance away from residential settlements (McCosh 1979). Several iron ore mining pits were also discovered about 1.5 km away from the site. Charcoal samples from this excavation produced radiocarbon dates ranging between AD 654 and AD 1355.

The other excavated site at Makodu is uniquely different from Moeng I. This site, covering over 8000 m² and with an additional extension some 800 m to the east, is located on the hill slopes above the villages of Majwaneng in the Central District of Botswana, some 10 km east of Moeng I.

Makodu was both a residential and craftsmen's village, yielding pottery (5895 potsherds), faunal remains (3266 bones), glass and shell beads and copper chains. It also had stone cairns and pole and *daga* daub, as well as innumerable broken pieces of tuyères mixed with furnace wall debris, dumped in heaps of up to 1.7 m. Most of the pottery had simple forms with rounded or square rims, decorated mainly with either incised bands and triangles, or stamped/impressed decorations occurring mainly on, or below, the neck. This pottery compares in several ways with the pottery of the Limpopo-Shashi valley reported by Hanish (1980).

On the basis of this new evidence, we can now begin to see a high degree of economic specialization in what appears to have been a very restricted area of east-central Botswana. There is now irrefutable evidence of the spread of cattle sites, clearly corresponding to Denbow's hierarchical settlement system and associated political stratification. There are also hundreds of sites such as Kgaswe and Maunatlala with clear evidence of agricultural specialization, also corresponding well with their location on good sand/clay soils and favourable water resources. In addition, we now also have the evidence of mining and working of iron at sites like Moeng and Makodu in areas which are rich in iron ore deposits.

The presence of a heavy scatter of faunal remains at Makodu, but without any associated vitrified cowdung deposits in the area, is obvious evidence of exchange networks between the cattle sites and the iron-smelting sites. These sites also share in the foreign exchange networks, either directly or through the well-established site of the Toutswe political elite. There must have been many other sites in the area which specialized in other items of trade or subsistence which are still awaiting exploration but, from the evidence available so far, this area of east-central Botswana had both political and economic networks, which sustained these iron age communities at hitherto unimagined levels. These networks obviously stretched beyond the confines of the area to the east, and possibly also elsewhere. We now know of several iron age sites in both the north and southeast of the country which appear to have existed contemporaneously with the Toutswe communities but belonging to different cultural traditions.

22 Iron age settlement and subsistence patterns in southern Malawi

Yusuf M. Juwayeyi

Background

Intensive archaeological research of Malawi's Iron Age was begun in the mid-1960s by the late Keith Robinson. From 1968 to 1975, Robinson conducted extensive archaeological site surveys in southern Malawi and made many small-scale excavations in the area around the southern tip of Lake Malawi, along the entire length of the Malawi section of the Shire river valley and in the area east and north of the Mulanje plateau. Later, other researchers worked in the Bwanje river valley and on the Shire highlands complementing his work (Cole-King 1973a; Kurashina 1973; Juwayeyi 1981). One of Robinson's major achievements was to establish an iron age archaeological sequence for Malawi and as a result, the Iron Age of Malawi became one of the better known sequences in this part of Africa.

The environmental setting

The Great Rift Valley which extends from the Red Sea to the Zambezi valley traverses Malawi from north to south and it is her most outstanding topographic feature. The Shire river, Lake Malawi's only outlet, follows the rift to the Zambezi river.

The relief of southern Malawi is characterized by changes of elevation within short distances. Within a distance of 160 km, for instance, the land rises from 46 m above sea-level in the lower Shire to 2133 m above sea-level on the Zomba plateau and 3048 m above sea-level on the Mulanje plateau. The Shire highlands too range from 610 m to 1097 m above sea-level and are surmounted by several residual mountains. Bounded by the Shire valley on the west and on the east, it gradually merges with the well-drained agriculturally rich Lake Chilwa/Phalombe plain.

The presence of several lakes, and the varied topography have given rise to a diversity of climates and varied ecosystems. As many as fifty-five natural regions have been identified within Malawi's small land area (Stobbs & Young 1972). There are many gradations between dry and wet and hot and cold (Lineham 1972, p. 26). The windward side of mountains and hills on the Shire highlands, for instance, tend to get more rain, sometimes as much as three times more than the adjoining areas. The mean maximum temperature for July is 12.5°C in the Mulanje area but 20°C in the Shire valley 70 km to the southwest. The result of these climatic variations is that Malawi has an extremely favourable agricultural environment, as all but 5 per cent of the land area receives at least 76 cm of rainfall a year, the minimum required for dry land farming in central Africa (Agnew 1972, p. 33). The basic vegetation type is Miombo forest characterized by *Brachystegia globiflora*.

The environment was very suitable for both hunter-gatherers and iron age agriculturists. Malawi has one of the highest population densities in Africa south of the Sahara.

The Early Iron Age

The Early Iron Age in southern Malawi is represented by Nkope ware (Cole-King 1973b). This pottery is closely related to other early iron age wares such as Kwale, found originally at Kwale near Mombasa in Kenya, and Lelesu from Tanzania dating to about AD 200, and other wares recovered at Gokomere and Ziwa in Zimbabwe and at Dambwa in Zambia (Robinson 1964; Soper 1971b; Phillipson 1977a). In Malawi, Nkope pottery has a very wide distribution. Besides being found in the whole of southern Malawi, it has also been located in the Dedza and Nkhotakota districts of central Malawi and in the Kasitu valley and Kandoli mountains in northern Malawi (Robinson 1970; Robinson 1973a; Robinson 1973b; Mgomezulu 1978; Robinson 1979; Robinson 1982; R. C. Greenstein, *pers. comm.*). Nkope pottery has also been found in adjacent areas of eastern Zambia and Mozambique (Phillipson 1976).

Unlike the later iron age wares, Nkope vessels are easily identifiable by their fabric, which is usually thick for their sizes, and by their pronounced and usually decorated rims. The basic vessel forms of Nkope ware are globular pots with everted rims and bowls with flattened and thickened or inturned rims.

In southern Malawi, most Nkope pottery sites have been located along the shores of the southern tip of Lake Malawi and along the Shire river and its tributaries at altitudes of between 100 and 200 m above sea-level and on the Shire highlands and the Namwera and Mulanje plateau areas at altitudes of over 500 m above sea-level (Figs 22.1, 22.2).

Lakeshore and Shire valley sites

The distribution of Nkope sites is heavier along the shores of the southern tip of Lake Malawi and the Shire valley than it is on the Shire highlands and other plateau areas. One reason for this is that, unlike the lakeshore and Shire valley areas, the highlands have been subjected to fairly intensive agricultural exploitation by large estate owners as well as by small farmers since the turn of the century. Many open sites have disappeared as a result. The location of the lakeshore and Shire valley sites argue for considerable reliance on the lake and rivers as a source of food. Most of the sites are conveniently located, often only a short distance from the lakeshore or river bank so as to make prolonged or overnight fishing trips unnecessary. Although the excavated sites have produced negligible amounts of molluscs and fish bone, this may be a preservation problem, for bones of large animals are not plentiful either. However, the available evidence also suggests that hunting of terrestrial animals was an equally important occupation, particularly in the Shire river valley. The early iron age inhabitants of the valley apparently hunted on the highlands as well (Robinson 1973a).

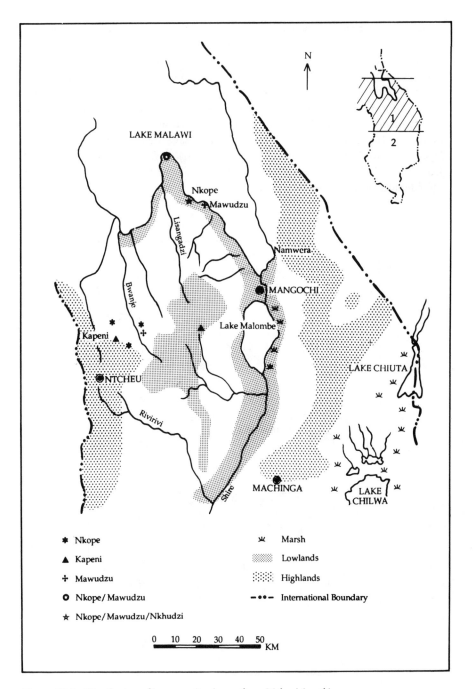

Figure 22.1 Distribution of iron age sites in southern Malawi (north).

At Matope Court site, the presence of house remains, bones of domestic cattle and grinding stones suggests that the hunting expeditions originated from permanent bases. Glass beads and a cowrie shell suggest some kind of contact with the coast.

Dates for Nkope ware along the shore of the lake and the Shire valley range between 220 ± 90 and 995 ± 60 AD (Robinson 1973a, p. 122). Except for an AD 550 date from Nasiyaya site north of the Mulanje plateau, most of the lakeshore and Shire valley dates are apparently older than the dates presently available from the highlands. At some sites on the highlands, both Nkope and Kapeni pottery have been recovered from the same layer dating to the tenth century AD (Juwayeyi 1981). A full transition from the early Iron Age to the later Iron Age does not appear to have been fully accomplished on the Shire highlands until about the twelfth century AD.

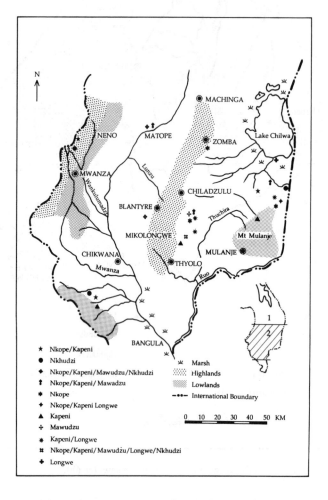

Figure 22.2 Distribution of iron age sites in southern Malawi (south).

The highlands sites

On the highlands, the location of settlements of the Early Iron Age was influenced by the topography, availability of resources such as iron ore, good, deep and easily workable soils and proximity to water. Most sites tend to be at permanent stream junctions or along permanent streams where farming activities could be undertaken both during the rainy season and, by means of irrigation, in the dry season.

Preservation of sites on the highlands that have survived recent intensification of agricultural practices is better than at the lakeshore and Shire valley sites. This could be a result of their relatively younger age. The sites here are quite large. Some of them extend to at least 2 ha in size and others such as the Chirombo Iron Age Village site in Thyolo district and Site TO 17 in Chiradzulu district are much larger (Juwayeyi 1981).

Hut floors and hut *daga* that were observed at some of the sites suggest that huts were constructed to last a long time. However, the huts were quite small. None of the hut floors observed at Chirombo Iron Age Village site, for instance, exceeded 2.4 m in diameter.

Although subsistence strategies generally suggest that early iron age inhabitants were not as dependent on cultivation and rearing of cattle and other animals as those of the later phases of the later iron age period, there was still a relatively high degree of self-sufficiency at most sites. Cultivation and rearing of cattle were often supplemented by hunting, which has always been a major part-time activity of most people in Malawi even until relatively recent times. Although other areas with a village tradition on the Shire highlands were not any different from those of the lakeshore and Shire valley areas, remains of iron-working such as iron slag, tuyères, raw iron ore, iron implements, as well as of iron furnaces themselves, show that more villages here had their own iron-working facilities than those of the lakeshore and Shire valley areas.

The Late Iron Age

In Malawi, the transition from the Early Iron Age to the Late Iron Age has been arbitrarily set at about AD 1000 (Robinson 1973b, p. 8). Kapeni pottery, which until recently was not known to be older than that date, was thus classified as Late Iron Age in spite of the fact that it has features which clearly suggest a closer relationship with the earlier Nkope pottery than with the rest of the later iron age wares. Recent research, however, has shown that Kapeni pottery should perhaps be reclassified as terminal Early Iron Age; for in addition to early iron age features, the pottery is now known to be at least two centuries older than the AD 1000 date. On the Shire highlands, both Nkope and Kapeni have been found *in situ* in the same levels. Kapeni pottery, however, was still in use for at least a century after the use of Nkope pottery had ceased.

The distribution of Kapeni sites suggest that factors determining site location had not changed from those of the Nkope period and that Nkope lifestyles continued with no discernible changes. Just like Nkope sites, there is a heavier concentration of Kapeni sites along the Shire valley than on the Shire highlands. Sites were located at roughly the same distance from the river as they were in the earlier period. Stratigraphic evidence shows that reoccupation of Nkope sites by Kapeni inhabitants occurred frequently.

Longwe pottery

Because of its resemblance to Mawudzu pottery, Longwe pottery was originally classified as Mawudzu ware (Denbow 1973). More discoveries of the same pottery in the north and east of the Mulanje plateau has resulted in its present name (Robinson 1977).

On the Shire highlands and in the north and east of the Mulanje plateau area, Longwe pottery has been dated to AD 1020 ± 40 and AD 970 ± 50 respectively (Robinson 1977, p. 14; Juwayeyi 1981, p. 102). These dates are older than the oldest Mawudzu dates and they overlap with some of the Kapeni dates. At some sites on the Shire highlands, Longwe has been found in the same levels as Kapeni. The two wares, however, do not closely resemble each other.

Unlike Nkope and Kapeni, Longwe pottery has a restricted distribution. At present it has been observed in the area north and east of Mulanje plateau, in the lower Shire area, on the Ntaja-Namwera hills and on the Shire highlands. Most of the sites are located at altitudes of over 500 m above sea-level. Although none of the sites excavated in the north of Mulanje plateau are rock shelters, six of the seven excavated sites on the Shire highlands are. Longwe pottery from these sites was often recovered from levels that also contained later stone age lithic artefacts. This type of mixing, particularly on the Shire highlands, argues for less reliance on normal iron age subsistence strategies such as cultivation and rearing of cattle and other animals, and greater dependence on hunting and gathering. However, although some late stone age communities elsewhere are known to have made or used pottery (Cook 1963; Robinson 1964; Robinson 1966), more research on the Shire highlands is required in order to interpret and fully understand this type of pottery. More about the Longwe sites themselves needs to be known. If preservation permits, their economy and other related activities must be ascertained. Further, non-Longwe sites in the area also need to be studied in greater detail.

Mawudzu pottery

Mawudzu pottery was first described by Robinson from the Mawudzu hill site in the lakeshore area. This pottery is quite distinct from the earlier Nkope and Kapeni wares and it is unlikely to have evolved from either of them. Recent radiocarbon dates place the inception of this pottery to the twelfth century AD (Mgomezulu 1978). This is a time when Kapeni pottery was no longer in use and Longwe pottery was being phased out. The period beginning from the twelfth century AD apparently coincides with the period of Chewa migrations into central and southern Malawi. This has resulted in the speculation that Mawudzu pottery may have been introduced by Chewa-speaking people.

Despite the lack of discernible early iron age features on Mawudzu pottery, the distribution pattern of Mawudzu sites appears to have followed that of the early iron age period. Later on, however, the Mawudzu inhabitants spread out rapidly to cover most parts of southern Malawi. On the Shire highlands and in other areas, the location of Mawudzu sites and artefacts associated with Mawudzu pottery show greater dependence on cultivation and the rearing of cattle, and the intensification of long-distance trade, than during the Early Iron Age. Most of the sites are in areas that are very fertile and close to permanent water sources. Artefacts such as Indian glass beads and copper have been recovered.

Nkhudzi ware

Nkhudzi pottery, first recorded at Nkhudzi Bay (Inskeep 1965), is quite distinct from any of the earlier types of pottery mentioned above. Its introduction into Malawi from about the eighteenth century AD was probably a result of the long-distance trade which was practised by a number of tribes including the Yao, the Makua and the Bisa. Robinson (1973a, p. 108) has indicated that the Bisa were, at one time, using typical Nkhudzi-type pottery.

The distribution of Nkhudzi sites is quite similar to that of Mawudzu. Most sites were located in areas which were clearly fertile and close to water sources. There is no clear evidence that rock shelters were ever inhabited during this time. Archaeological and particularly ethnographic and historical evidence indicates that Nkhudzi settlements were very large. Cultivation, rearing of cattle and smelting of iron were the main economic activities.

Iron-smelting

Very little research into the smelting of iron during the Iron Age has been undertaken in Malawi. Our present knowledge is limited to a few oral traditions and casual field observations. The distribution of iron-smelting sites, though not yet mapped, appears to cover the entire country and suggests that Malawi had enough natural resources for the manufacture of iron implements.

Oral traditions emphasize that, besides good iron ore, and the observance of certain taboos, the type of soil used in the construction of iron furnaces, and trees used to provide the charcoal that was burnt in the furnaces, were very crucial for the production of iron. In southern Malawi, soils from termite mounds and trees that produced the smallest quantity of ash, such as Mbanga (*Pericopsis angolonsis*), were often preferred to other types of soils and trees. There is need, however, to know more about this economic aspect of the lifestyle of the iron age inhabitants. Further work, including dating of the iron-smelting sites, studies of the types of charcoal used and other related studies, needs to be carried out.

Conclusion

The earliest iron age pottery in southern Malawi is called Nkope ware and it has been dated to the third century AD. It continued to be in use until about the eleventh century AD. At the type-site, Nkope ware is overlain by a distinct pottery type called Kapeni ware. The earliest known date for this pottery is the eighth century AD (Mgomezulu 1978). Kapeni ware is considered the earliest of the late iron age pottery. In the areas north and east of the Mulanje plateau, another late iron age pottery tradition was described by Robinson. He called this pottery Longwe ware (Robinson 1977). More research needs to be done in order to define fully and more precisely its distribution and chronology. Present indications are that this pottery overlapped with Kapeni ware from the tenth to the eleventh century AD. At some sites, both Kapeni and Longwe pottery are overlain by Mawudzu and Nkhudzi pottery, which have been dated to the mid-twelfth century and eighteenth century AD respectively. The dates for Mawudzu pottery coincide with the arrival in Malawi of the Chewa-speaking people, so that it is generally assumed that they may have been responsible for its introduction. Variants of Nkhudzi ware, on the other hand, are still in use in some parts of southern Malawi.

Most of the sites were conveniently located to enable their occupants fully to maximize the exploitation of aquatic and terrestrial food sources. Cultivation of crops, rearing of cattle and other animals and the smelting of iron were also major economic activities. In later centuries, these activities were intensified to include long-distance trade.

23 A question of identities: an anthropological enquiry and a historical narrative

JOSEPH O. VOGEL

Introduction

Archaeology is not only a process which unearths different things used in the past, but one which requires its practitioners to recognize the articles discovered and then to establish likely cultural contexts for them. To that end we often try to uncover their function, their utility, in some past cultural circumstance. This chapter posits that the articles archaeologists encounter in their investigations sometimes had complex careers and that some pottery discovered in ancient settlements in southern Africa recast their cultural personae from time to time. By analysing the kaleidoscope of the several uses of these African artefacts and their allied cultural contexts, we can also illuminate other aspects of the lifeways of the early inhabitants of the Victoria Falls region.

There is a more general principle to be observed as well: that many different artefacts transform persona and function over time with respect to differing cultural circumstances. As a consequence, archaeologists sometimes need to cast their analytical nets broadly, in order to determine not only the function relative to the locus of the find, but to search out clues to other uses and the changing fortunes of the cultural identity of material culture through time.

Objects which have been discarded as rubbish by their owners can, nonetheless, be identified with reference to some original use. The act of discard implies a culturally moderated decision, within a more complete lexicon of culturally predetermined decisions. Not all transformations of cultural persona, or function, are as evident, or as universal, as discard, though all are the consequence of choices mediated by other cultural programmes.

While working at the headquarters of Senior Chief Mukuni, outside Livingstone, Zambia, I requested permission to collect some of the discarded grinding stones littering the fields around the town. However, when my assistants and I went to gather them we were soon pursued by a covey of old women who drove us away from the grindstones in one field, which appeared to be under their safekeeping. Elsewhere we were allowed to gather several of the heavy grindstones unimpeded. Some months later I returned to observe Mukuni's burial. This took place in the field of *protected* grindstones. There were other royal graves there and each was marked by a carved wooden peg and a used grindstone. None of the stones differed from the ones we had collected: each was a spent grindstone discarded from domestic use. They may even have once been the domestic property of a now dead chief. Perhaps the grindstones marking graves once functioned in mundane domestic contexts, were worn out and discarded to become the object of ritual beer libations on royal anniversaries. As a result, we may posit two cultural formulae: one establishing the domestic tool and another determining use as a grave marker, as well as culturally moderated acts transforming some into trash and others into objects used in important ritual performances.

Our experience showed that grindstones could be discarded as trash without further thought: those we were allowed to collect. Others were retained in the cultural inventory, but given a new function. But why grindstones as grave markers? Pragmatically, we can posit that they were the most durable household article available. But why a domestic article? . . . and so forth into other questions of cultural perceptions and symbolism. This chapter asks such questions about some pots found in prehistoric African villages, places them in suitable settings within the broader context of early savanna farmer lifeways, and then draws some speculative conclusions.

The anthropological enquiry

The matter of identity

During the excavation of the cemetery at Chundu, in the Zambezi valley, near the Victoria Falls (Fig. 23.1), two pottery vessels were found whose bottoms had been broken out (Fig. 23.2). Nothing like them had been found previously. A search of ethnographic sources was no help in identifying them, nor in ascribing a function to them. Nowhere did the literature describe the breaking of pottery as a part of funeral ritual. However, the style of the pottery was definitive, easily identified with other pottery of the late first millennium AD and assigned to the Dambwa phase of the local Early Iron Age (Vogel 1972; Vogel 1980; Vogel 1982).

The pots were found in sets. From this, we reached the naive conclusion that they functioned in tandem. These sets consisted of one globular jar, whose base was intentionally broken out, and a bowl-like vessel formed from a jar base. The pierced opening in the globular vessel and the upper edge of the 'bowl' each showed signs of wear. Although metal vessels with intentionally pierced bases are sometimes placed on recent Kaonde and Bemba graves near Kanshansi mine in northwest Zambia (M. Bisson, *pers. comm.*), the Chundu specimens were intriguing because of the traces of use on them. These pots had had some usage prior to becoming grave inclusions. They not only performed some function in tandem, but they retained that relationship following the transformation to grave objects. These modified pots had probably begun their existence as common domestic vessels with no relationship to one another. How they came to be identified as a pair becomes a relevant matter of enquiry.

The cultural identity

Early iron age pottery of the Victoria Falls region is segregated into stylistic types, distributed into temporal phases, identified by stylistic elements with specific spatial and time relationships (Vogel 1980; Vogel 1984). A portion of that sequence, Dambwa phase, is associated with a population living on the Sinde-Maramba Divide throughout the late eighth and early ninth centuries. The villages at Chundu and Zambezi Farm

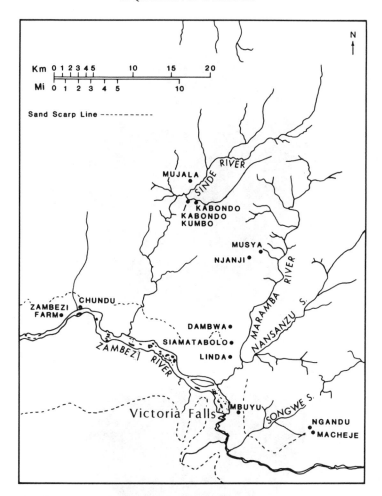

Figure 23.1 The Victoria Falls region during the eighth century.

both belonged to this period and can be associated with a settlement system, which is contained within a small portion of the region (Vogel 1984).

The funerary context

Since the first set of vessels was found with eighth-century graves at Chundu Farm (Vogel 1973, pp. 26–30; Vogel 1982), maybe they had been ritually 'killed' before their burial. Broken vessels located in purported burial shafts at the Kalambo Falls site had been identified as 'killed' vessels, but no trace of the burial remains was associated with them (Clark 1969, p. 141; Clark 1974, p. 64). These pits and their contents may have been graves as the excavators suspected, but their contents and pattern of loose in-filling bore a closer resemblance to a pit found at Kabondo Kumbo (Vogel 1975b) than any of the graves excavated elsewhere in the subcontinent. Such an explanation was not confirmed by either the archaeological or the ethnographic record. Though there was

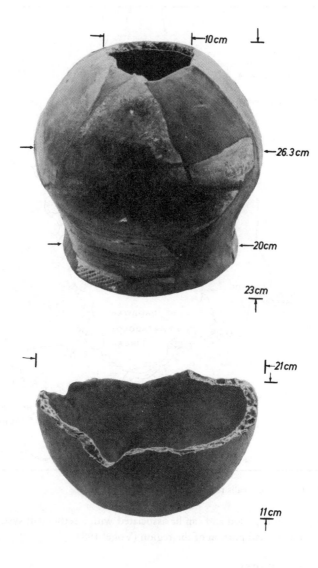

Figure 23.2 *upper* Kumadzulo Class 9 vessel, with hole broken out of base.
lower Evaporating dish made from base of large pottery vessel.

no indication of the practice of burying pierced pots, the vessels, their makers and their
ritual life belonged to a world some 1200 years in the past. A heretofore unknown
window into that world seemed prepared to open, illuminating the ritual and social
behaviours of those times. The ethnographic accounts from southern Africa do chronicle some funerary practices and the graves examined by archaeologists permit another
perspective as well.

The archaeological evidence of African burial practice

Iron age sites with substantial evidence of graves and grave goods include: elaborately furnished burials at Sanga and Katoto, from the upper Lualaba river valley of southern Zaïre (Nenquin 1963; Hiernaux, Maquet & De Buyst 1968; de Maret 1978); graves containing gold beads at Ingombe Ilede in the Gwembe valley (Chaplin 1962a; Fagan 1969a); Soli graves with worked iron and iron bells from central Zambia (Fagan 1961; Chaplin 1962b); and some graves from near Simango in southern Zambia containing iron hoes (Vogel 1974). A nineteenth-century cemetery at Nkudzi Bay, in Malawi, contained many iron implements (Inskeep 1965).

The cemetery site at Chundu (Vogel 1973, pp. 26–30; Vogel 1982), near Livingstone, had whole and broken pottery, cattle bone, iron tools, copper strips and shell beads in association with the grave contexts. Copper jewellery, iron tools and imported shells were buried in pottery vessels found there. Sixteenth-century graves found at Simbusenga, in the Victoria Falls region, were of small children buried in the centre of the village (Vogel 1975a) and nineteenth-century graves at Simbusenga and Nansanzu all contained many large pottery fragments (Vogel 1971; Vogel 1975a).

This sparse sampling of grave contexts, spanning some hundreds of years and associated with different cultures in the subcontinent, shows a long-established pattern of grave furnishings. The Soli graves were of chiefs, and the kind and quantity of the grave goods may be somehow related to rank. Iron bells do denote a chiefly rank. A nineteenth-century grave at Simbusenga was probably not that of a high status individual (on the evidence of Chief Sekute), although it contained much pottery. The Simonga hoes were unused and the extravagant furnishings of the Zaïrean graves suggest specialized mortuary pottery. Otherwise there is a multi-ethnic pattern of grave contexts furnished with domestic pottery and commonplace iron tools.

The ethnographic record of African burial practice

Throughout southern Africa, land represents the most valued asset of descent chartered combines (as descent groups). Even conquered people retain the special rights of ownership (Bucher 1980). Individuals may clear land for their own use, but at death title passes to their lineage, to be administered as part of corporate holdings. These lineage-administered combines legitimate continuity of their title and claims to authority by invoking a hierarchy of ancestral spirits: those who once owned the land who willed responsibility to it to their heirs.

The Shona call their chiefs *mwene we nyika*, owner of the land. But *nyika* signifies not only the land, but the people dwelling on it and their rights (Bucher 1980). This rationalization seems to be held throughout the subcontinent, and African societies there seem to value the mediation of benefits and obligations. The 'owner of the land' holds title as a sacred trust. The 'owner of the land', representing a bridge with the ancestral past and future aspirations of production, is at once manager and mediator, authority and benefactor. He is required to act in the best interests of the commonweal and respect the claims upon his service held by the ancestral dead, as well as the living. Keenly aware of their role as mediators of the supernatural, as well as the natural worlds, leaders maintain a continuing three-sided arbitration between the stewards and the people, and the living and the dead. It is this world-view of mediation and perceptions of benefit which we detect in the mortuary proceedings.

The published reports (e.g. Colson & Gluckman 1951; Holleman 1953) describe funerary practices and suggest some of the underlying intent. As a result, we may characterize funerals as part of a process which extends over a period of years, and as having importance to the stability of descent groups. We may identify four steps: (1) death; (2) burial; (3) funeral; and (4) recurrent memorial observances. Burial occurs soon after death. The preparation and burial of the corpse seems of less importance to the process than do some later activities. The funeral requires preparing food and brewing beer before the mourners are brought together. All this requires time, with the result that funeral observances occur sometime after the death and burial. The memorial observances recur over a subsequent period of time, until they merge with the more general rites commemorating the ancestral spirits in general.

Although there are several different stages, each with its own symbolism, the archaeologist finds evidence only of the preparation and burial of the corpse. This usually occurs within hours of death (Richards 1951, p. 185; Holleman 1953). The burial is a modest affair following the washing and draping of the corpse. This duty usually falls to the in-laws of the deceased. The idea of the burial preparations is that the deceased spirit must be given its proper due; in this way it is appeased and any hostile intentions it may harbour are assuaged. At the same time, it is introduced into the company of ancestral spirits (Holleman 1953). In preparing the corpse, the intention is to suggest an appearance of prosperity, in order to make the spirit of the newly dead presentable to the ancestral hierarchy, and successfully induct it into their ranks, while substantiating the propriety of the deceased stewardship of, and the heirs' interest in, the corporate holdings held in trust by the lineage.

This process is one of transformation, a passage from the world of the living to that of the dead, acknowledging the world order in which the ancestral spirits retain an active interest in guiding the welfare of the descent group. Following the prescribed ritual practices and performances gives the heirs confidence and they begin to distribute the estate. Burials and subsequent memorial observations are an important part of these intergenerational compacts, dedicated to transfer of wealth and preservation of claims on property within descent groups. The individuals memorialized merge with the company ancestors. Grave goods can be construed as validating this shift in status and thereby parallel other material transactions (including marriage payments) meant to mediate other kinds of status change (as in Berry 1989, p. 42).

Another hypothesis

Even if these vessels were important to this kind of process of mediation, the question remains: how did they come by this importance? Our examination of them suggested that they were a common variety of domestic ware, modified by perforation of the base or removal of the body above the base. If the pots were not altered as part of the burial ritual, and the signs of wear on the edges of the openings suggest prior use, we need to understand their previous use and posit how this gave them a special status.

Vessels similar to those of this study were found in a hut at Zambezi Farm without burial associations. Oral tradition suggested that vessels such as these were used in the making of salt.

Although we commonly refer to salt and salt-making as if they are a single compre- hensive entity, in fact they encompass many different processes and products. Some extraction – mining or the reduction of soils – is intended to produce sodium, whereas the reduction of plant salts results in potassium. Both have nutritional value, but each performs a different function as regards body chemistry (Denton 1982); and potassium is often used as a taste substitute as seasoning during food preparation.

What we identify as salt – food or flavouring – may matter little to our reconstruction of extraction processes, but it can bear on broader generalizations involving exchange, dietary and taste preferences, social interaction or whatever.

Whereas hunters may satisfy their physiological need for salt by the consumption of blood and flesh, the mainly vegetarian diet of farmers makes it necessary to obtain salt from other sources (Denton 1982, p. 569). The sodium requirements of settled farmers and an acquired taste for salt in tropical Africa (as noted for the Bemba by Roberts 1973, or a hunger for salt referred to by Denton 1982) have had important implications regarding the extraction processes and exchange networks used to obtain it.

The ethnographic record of the African production of salt

Salt, for human nutrition, and the taste for salt, have long been a significant economic and social force (Multhauf 1978; Alexander, Ch. 39, this volume). At times, its production incurred social obligation, as among the baLozi (Mainga 1973, p. 37); at other times it was an economic commodity and marketed, as in the Spanish Sahara (Mercer 1976). As a staple of African trade, from the salt mines of the Sahara to the Uvinza marshes (Howe 1966, p. 54; Fagan 1969b; Roberts 1973, p. 186; Schmidt 1978, p. 40; Denton 1982, pp. 80–2; Saad 1983, pp. 28–9), it motivated fabled caravan routes and the meeting of peoples in its collection. Salt was produced close to home, as well.

Although there are anecdotal accounts of traditional salt manufacture (*pers. comms.* from Mubitana and Corbeil), more formal accounts are not common or very different in their descriptions of the process. Aldridge (n.d.) recorded traditional salt-making in the Lukanga swamp, and Bisson (*pers. comm.*) observed Chewa women making salt at a mineral spring in eastern Zambia. In each case the process began with the collecting and burning of grasses. The ash was dissolved in water. In the Lukanga, the brine was filtered through grass laid in a pierced pot. In eastern Zambia, after the sediment had settled, the brine was decanted into another pot and then boiled away to produce a salty residue. Each day's work produced only a small quantity of grey coarse salt. Bisson estimates that four adult women cutting the grasses and collecting the firewood altogether produced only around 250 g.

The various methods for making salt may be summarized. Shona women used boiling water to reduce salt-bearing soils (Bhila 1982, p. 39) and the Gwembe Tonga also dissolved crusts skimmed from salt pans in boiling water before straining the residue, which was left to evaporate (Reynolds 1968, p. 187). At Ivuna, brackish waters were first boiled and then allowed to evaporate (Fagan & Yellen 1968). Salty brines were sometimes used to prepare vegetable relishes (Scudder 1962, p. 248; Reynolds 1968, p. 187), but the salty distillate was more commonly allowed to evaporate, forming lumps or cakes. Such cakes may be found for sale at village markets. Other sources of salt include the processing of the dung of small stock (Reynolds 1968, p. 187n), leaching minerals from the ashes of saline grasses (Reynolds 1968, p. 187; Roberts 1973, pp. 186–7) or simply consuming ashes mixed into broths (Scudder 1962, p. 248; Denton 1982, pp. 85–6). Salt extraction entailed, generally, solution in boiling water, filtration, cooling and crystallization. Among the Bemba, a brine was produced from the diluted ash of saline grasses and then filtered into pots, where it was allowed to crystallize (Roberts 1973, p. 187 & Ill. 10). Something like this can be inferred from the Zambezi Valley pots.

The archaeological evidence of salt extraction and some inferences

Among the Gwembe Tonga (Reynolds 1968, p. 187) filtration took place in a clay pot, through the bottom of which holes were bored, or a single large hole was made with a hammer. Pottery sherds with small holes bored into them were found at the seventh-century village at Kapwirimbwe, in Lusaka, and identified as salt strainers, because of their similarity to modern ones seen in Tonga villages (Phillipson 1968a, p. 12).

Similarly, the Victoria Falls region specimens (Fig. 23.2) resemble the percolators used in the Gwembe, where a filter of dry grass was placed in the closed vessel, covering the hole or holes, into which a boiling brine of water and ash was decanted, to percolate into an open vessel placed below it (as reconstructed in Fig. 23.3). The evaporator from the Zambezi Valley archaeological site was a base broken off a large pot.

The historical narrative

We began with the assumption that we could determine the uses of some archaeological objects and then utilize that information to tell us something about the lifeways of

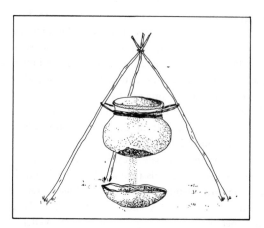

Figure 23.3 Sketch of salt-making apparatus. The percolator is suspended from the tripod, while the percolant drips into the evaporator.

prehistoric people in Africa and the cultural environment producing such objects. Consideration of the circumstances of these pots led us along three separate lines of enquiry and towards a varied set of explanations; each was couched in a different aspect of African cultural life.

Underlying one of the enquiries were two inferences: that burial displays were an integral part of a category of social transaction meant to mediate transfers of property and validate successive claims on lineage holdings. A fitting metaphor may be social transactions involving the payment of bride price or blood wealth (Schneider 1981). Grave wealth may be perceived as a necessary part of a warrant balancing the ongoing account between the descent group's spiritual guardians and the heirs to property: metaphorically melding the past, present and future interests of the claimants.

This explanation is suggested by the fact that not only were grave goods everywhere an integral part of traditional mortuary ritual, as verified by a consistent record of grave furniture in archaeological contexts, but by their selection from the same class of things customarily used to mediate other social contracts: iron hoes and axes.

Even with this understanding of the socio-economic value of grave goods, we still have no sure impression of the intrinsic value of the grave wealth or its relation to social ordering or status. In other covenants sealed by transfers of wealth, value is intended as compensation for a perceived loss. We can posit in funerals and their ritual a similar principle at work, but one moderated by the need to impress the afterworld: to convince the ancestral guardians of the present generation's abilities as stewards, creating a context in which a calculated facade of exaggerated worth may be expressed. As a result, the mortuary programme becomes a definitive act of political theatre casting a serendipitous image, rather than an explicit portrayal of reality. The archaeologist's usual reading of the social persona of the dead, based upon assumptions about the quantity and value of grave goods, becomes muted. The social and economic success expressed is not necessarily that of the deceased individual, but of the corporate entity.

We must therefore posit that the burial environments found at the old villages in the Victoria Falls region and elsewhere originated in a world-view requiring validation of legitimacy by giving the deceased their proper due and by material transactions meant to balance accounts by an equitable transfer of wealth. The suggestion is that traditional burial customs were stereotyped, protracted acts dedicated to mediating ongoing relations between heirs and ancestral guarantors; that African graves are a culturally mediated format formalizing social contracts. The pottery found with the Chundu burials somehow fits into this programme; the archaeologist, in order to move beyond mere description, must attempt to formulate a paradigm explaining the suitability of these pots to this culturally critical process.

By its presence in graves, the pottery demonstrates that it is important in this transaction. Even if the pots had been used in salt-making, how did they become part of the burial programme at Chundu?

Eighth-century farmers in the Victoria Falls region were producing and filtering salty brines: whether sodium or potassium-laden ones cannot be decided from analogy alone. But there are neither salt pans nor salt deposits in the Victoria Falls region. Therefore it is likely that potassium was produced locally, by reducing vegetation, and that sodium was obtained by exchange from elsewhere. Chundu and Zambezi Farm are the only early villages in the Victoria Falls region sited near the river margins, where suitable grasses are available (Vogel 1984, Fig. 5).

During the nineteenth century, the Livingstones reported salt-producing centres in the lower valley (Livingstone & Livingstone 1865, p. 225). The suggestion is that the settlements in the Victoria Falls region were similarly engaged in the manufacture of salt and that they represented salt-producing centres for local circulation. If the salt produced there was potassium and their sodium was obtained elsewhere, the salt makers could have extended their social commissions as producers to an entrepreneurial one. If their salt moved along the same ethnically enfranchised inter-regional routes which brought copper, ostrich eggshell, cowries and glass to the region (Vogel 1990), then we may be permitted to posit a speculative scenario relating the social importance of salt production, organization of exchange and the iconic significance of their marking in the graves.

The burials transformed, by social or ritual associations, many different objects – whether manufactured as status items, ritual paraphernalia or domestic tools – metamorphosing the domestic cultural roles of the Chundu vessels over time, transcending apparent function to encrypt particular kinds of information, and defining richer contexts of cultural relevance. In the end, identification leads on to matters of social role and beyond to other, more comprehensive, fields of transaction residing beyond a limited sketch of village salt producers. Though the full implications of the role of salt producers as the mediators of transformation and the accumulation of graves at a salt-producing settlement still fall beyond the scope of the information presented here, they nevertheless inhere in understanding these 'domestic' objects, and become intriguing as examples of the analytic possibilities offered by even limited ecological evidence. The manifold identification of function, even of superficially simple objects, ultimately rests in sundry contexts, variously embedded in elaborate cultural matrices, beyond the range of casual analogies.

Acknowledgements

The research at Chundu and Zambezi Farm was supported by the Director and staff of the National Museums of Zambia, Livingstone Museum. The plate was photographed by Mr Geo Lupiya, Technical Officer, at the Livingstone Museum. Mike Bisson gave us the benefit of his observations, which I gratefully acknowledge here. The figures were sketched in the field by my wife, Jean. Reproduction of the illustrations was aided by a grant from the Dean of Arts and Sciences at the University of Alabama.

24   A perspective on archaeological research in Mozambique

P. J. J. SINCLAIR, J. M. F. MORAIS,

L. ADAMOWICZ & R. T. DUARTE

Mozambique has not been as well developed archaeologically as some other African countries, but this deficiency is now being offset by a consolidated effort by the country's major academic and governmental institutions. This task began prior to independence in 1975 (SARQ 1980) and was intensified with the establishment in 1980 of the Department of Archaeology and Anthropology at Eduardo Mondlane University in Maputo; at the same time, the National Museums and Antiquities service has extended its involvement in teaching, recording and cultural development work on a national scale.

At the university, the problem of the production of archaeological knowledge has been debated in relation to the compilation and explanation of archaeological data (cf. Gardin 1980) and the role of archaeology as a discipline in Mozambican society. In order to provide a basis for the study of archaeology in the particular intellectual and practical circumstances of postcolonial Mozambique, a multidisciplinary effort was made to evaluate the historical roots of material culture studies in the country (SARQ 1980). This chapter outlines this history and provides a set of research strategies appropriate to the further development of archaeology in Mozambique.

Archaeology began in Mozambique in the early eighteenth century with isolated references to rock paintings, but along with other parts of Africa, the first archaeological emphasis was on the Palaeolithic, exemplified by the important work of Barradas from 1942 to 1960 on quaternary stratigraphy (Barradas 1961). Until the 1960s, the periods covering the last two millennia received little attention except from visiting scholars who concentrated, like Wieschoff (1941), on the zimbabwe culture or, like Van Riet Louwe (1943) and Breuil (1944), on coastal shell middens. This was in contrast to the contributions of resident missionary anthropologists such as Junod (1912–13) and Earthy (1933). Since then, the study of later periods in colonial and immediately postcolonial times has expanded, as, for example, in the later work of Barradas (1967), Rita-Ferreira (1975; 1982) and the more than forty articles by Oliveira, Senna Martinez, Leisegang, Dickinson, Derricourt and Smolla (quoted in detail in Duarte, Cruz e Silva, Senna Martinez, Morais & Duarte 1976; Sinclair 1987, pp. 26–7; Morais 1988, pp. 40–3).

Archaeological work in Mozambique has tended to emphasize intersite comparisons using typological studies. For example, a number of attempts were made to relate Mozambican assemblages to more established sequences in South Africa, Zimbabwe and Zambia. This tendency is understandable in view of the arbitrariness of colonial boundaries and the relatively small number of archaeological sites known in the mid-1970s in Mozambique (approximately 160). The need to compare has resulted, however, in a conception of material culture which is abstracted from economic, ideological and political aspects of a society and from the environmental context.

Within this limited perspective the theoretical framework was poorly developed. Considerable effort was made in typological analysis, but few if any attempts were made to conceptualize the interrelationships between different facets of social structure and social change.

However, attempts to offset some of these inadequacies have appeared in a number of areas. Important contributions to the archaeology of later periods occur in the series of papers by Duarte, Cruz e Silva, Senna Martinez, Morais & Duarte (1976), and these have opened up new directions in the study of ceramic distributions and technology. A substantial contribution to the study of the interrelation of economic and environmental variables was provided in 1975–6 by the Eduardo Mondlane University project at the zimbabwe stone wall enclosure of Manyikeni, 50 km inland from Vilanculos, conducted with the assistance of the British Institute in East Africa (Garlake 1976a; Garlake 1976b; Barker 1978). In addition, new theoretical departures were developed by Morais (1978), building on previous work by the FRELIMO's *Historia da Africa* (1972). For the first time in Mozambique, precolonial social groups were conceptualized and their material culture examined from a historical materialist perspective; most importantly, the archaeology was determined by the concrete needs of Mozambican society (see below).

Structuring the interpretive schema: concepts and formulations

Extensions of this initiative have entailed both theoretical and empirical work. In the development of a theoretical archaeology the need to draw from a wide range of approaches in the social sciences was recognized. In this regard the work in Mozambique should be seen as an attempt to open a scientific discourse on the aims of African archaeology and the extent to which these are addressable from a materialist perspective.

Interpretation in postcolonial Mozambican archaeology has been dominated by a historical paradigm. This has partly been a response to the pressing need for illustrative material for the newly universalized school and adult education system and also a reflection of the interests and training of Mozambican archaeologists (Morais 1988, pp. 50–1). At the university in Maputo, however, multidisciplinary discussions focused on the object(s) of historical, anthropological and archaeological analysis, drawing on current debates in African and west European historiography concerning the nature of the past. The conflicting positions of structuralism (e.g. Bernstein & Depelchin 1978; Bernstein & Depelchin 1979) and eclecticism (e.g. Samuel 1981) were considered in relation to the more subtle empiricism of Thompson (1978), the 'scientific history' of Althusser & Balibar (1970) and the outright rejection of the past as an object of knowledge by Hindess & Hirst (1975; 1977). The concern of Africanist anthropology with modes of production was also assimilated, as seen in concepts ranging from the generalized domestic community of Meillassoux (1975) and the African mode of production of Coquery-Vidrovitch (1975) to more specific notions of social formation. Further contributions from Scandinavia, notably those of Friedman (1974) and Ekholm (1981), have also been influential.

A particular concern was to link the theory of specific modes of production to social and material contexts. Here the approach of Godelier (1972) was favoured over the positivism of Binford & Binford (1968), and Watson, Leblanc & Redman (1971). An additional concern was the archaeology of historically specific social entities, especially in terms of the relationship between social formation and empirical data (see Klejn 1973). It is in this context that problems concerning the base/superstructure metaphor (Danilova 1971; Friedman 1974; O'Laughlin 1975; Tilley 1982) and the dangers associated with a confusion of analytical and structural categories in an empirical situation are most acute and remain somewhat unresolved. A flexible theoretical framework incorporating economic aspects (with an analytical equivalence between the material means and social relations of production, cf. O'Laughlin 1975), ideological aspects (incorporating symbolic categories) and political aspects (emphasizing the spatial expression of power relations) was best suited to integrate the available archaeological evidence (Sinclair 1987, p. 28).

First attempts at assessing the range of empirical data from Zimbabwe and Mozambique in terms of this approach have been carried out (Sinclair, Morais & Bingham 1979; Sinclair 1981). Archaeological evidence relating to previous typologically defined entities was assessed and efforts were made to focus upon systems of production, division of labour, extraction of surplus product and the cycles of reproduction of the material and social aspects of society. Attention was also focused on data relating to the processes of social differentiation in the Zimbabwe state (SARQ 1980; Sinclair 1981; Sinclair 1984b; Sinclair 1987, pp. 150–6). The broad temporal scale encompassed (from the lower Pleistocene to the recent past) included a range of social forms from foraging bands to centralized states. This necessitated consideration of various typologies of social organization and their relative archaeological visibility. Difficulties encountered with the articulation of economic, ideological and political aspects of the interpretive methodology have led to a discussion of the range of meanings embedded in material remains and a more refined use of ethnographic source material to pose new analytical points of departure (Adamowicz 1985; Sinclair 1987; Morais 1988, pp. 120–35).

Changes in the above position developed from the theoretical concerns of the 1970s and mid-1980s and were already apparent in the emphasis on incorporating environmental as well as societal complexity into analytical frameworks (Morais 1988). Problems in operationalizing the various available concepts of social formation in terms of the spatial complexity of archaeological data, in particular from Zimbabwe (Sinclair 1987, pp. 29–33), introduced new theoretical challenges. Current concerns with network and hierarchy theory which integrate local, regional and global systems hold out new possibilities of integrating the disparate archaeological data sources into an historically coherent and socially relevant discipline.

A collection strategy for material assemblages

Any attempt to apply a concept of societal organization to a specific empirical situation is subject to significant limitations. Are these limits determined by the methodology or do they in fact exist in the archaeological material? How far should one use a concept of society to interpret archaeological taxonomic units in the archaeological record of eastern and southern Africa? How can one discern in past societal forms the equivalent complexity of modern ethnographic situations? So often the units of analysis impose a spurious simplicity or logical coherence more related to the present than the past.

Traditionally, analysis in African archaeology has been defined in terms of ceramics with underlying assumptions of correlations with groups of people, as with Fagan's (1965) 'cultures' or Phillipson's (1977a) 'tradition' and 'stream', and Huffman's (1980a) 'style system and facies'. Discussion of the socio-cultural and political implications of these categories has been an important component of recent archaeological work in South Africa (see Maggs & Whitelaw 1991, pp. 19–20). Given improvements in our knowledge of production and usage of pottery there seems little doubt of the inadequacy of ceramic typology used in isolation for defining the limits and forms of past societies, and this is reflected in the marked reluctance to use ceramic categories as a basis of analysis by some scholars (e.g. Hall 1987). A multivariate approach to the archaeology of the farming communities of southern and eastern Africa is certainly needed.

In Mozambique, faced with very substantial gaps in our knowledge of the farming communities, a consensus was reached that ceramics constituted an important and addressable source of archaeological information. Work aimed at constructing a primary but polythetically defined chronostratigraphic framework through identifying or discounting the existence of 'consistently reoccurring sets of ceramic attributes' (cf. Clarke 1968) or 'non-random association groupings' (cf. Hodder 1982), rather than aiming at a narrow definition of ethnic units (cf. Huffman 1980a). The analytical methods used relied upon concepts of ceramic typology developed by Nordström (1972) and Hulthen (1977) (see details in Sinclair 1986; Sinclair 1987, pp. 164–7). The emphasis has been upon analysis of form and decoration of ceramic assemblages with the important addition of thin sectioning and technological analysis pioneered in southern Africa by Hulthen (1988).

In Mozambique, many constraints have affected this archaeological work: severe logistical and financial problems, a small trained workforce and the uncertain situation in areas affected by conflict. These difficulties have in part been overcome through support from Eduardo Mondlane University and the British Institute in East Africa (1975–6) and, more recently, substantial financial support from SAREC (the Swedish Agency for Research Cooperation with Developing Countries) and the participation in various projects of the Swedish Centre of National Antiquities (Lindqvist 1984). Support from the latter in particular has been orientated towards developing the potential of archaeology in Mozambique in education and providing the necessary infrastructure to enable a broader range of archaeological research to take place.

Archaeological research has also been severely limited by the lack of infrastructural development. In the absence of osteological, botanical, cartographical and environmental collections and compilations, securely dated representative samples of ceramics were used to provide entry-points for exploring the different levels of variability in the archaeological record of Mozambique as a whole. The first priority was to establish an initial chronological framework in three widely separated areas of the country: Maputo in the south, Inhambane in the south-central region and Nampula in the north (Morais 1984; Sinclair 1987; Duarte 1988) (Fig. 24.1).

Having developed this framework and established the usefulness of a location sampling analysis and comparison of ceramic assemblages we were well aware of the limitations imposed by this strategy in generating data suitable for interpreting socio-economic aspects of past societies and, consequently, saw the need for developing new excavation strategies. At Manyikeni excavations involving an extensive random sampling programme (Morais & Sinclair 1980; Sinclair 1987) provided a test case for future work. The adoption of a statistical sampling procedure was aimed both at reducing the amount of excavation and spreading the scope of data collection over an area of sufficient size to provide a basis for the assessment of a range of questions on the socio-economic, political and ideological aspects of the site (Sinclair 1987, pp. 91–8). This approach also highlighted the limits of interpreting archaeological data dependent upon a series of contextual assumptions and subject to the operation of post-depositional factors (e.g. Schiffer 1976; Hodder 1978b; Binford 1981; Carr 1985).

An integral part of this approach has been the development of information technology (IT) applications to process the data in order to develop a diachronic model of site growth (Fig. 24.2) (Sinclair 1987; Sinclair 1991). In northern Mozambique, Adamowicz (1985; 1987) has standardized the recording of large amounts of data from more than 100 sites, while Duarte (1991) has concentrated on a very detailed contextual register of individual excavations. In all these IT applications, once the data is formatted (often a time-consuming task), the result has been a marked reduction in the time needed to obtain analytical results, thus accelerating the need to reformulate questions. At the University Campus (Sinclair, Nydolf & Nydolf 1987) it was possible to integrate the statistical analysis of the contents of the excavation into the excavation procedure as part of the search process. Further developments of this minimalist approach have been undertaken as part of the current Urban Origins in Eastern Africa Project with the microstratigraphic investigation of Great Zimbabwe and sites on the east African coast (Sinclair, Kokonya, Meneses & Rakatoarisoa 1992).

The foraging communities

In spite of valuable research in rock art, particularly from central and northern Mozambique (e.g. Castro 1956), remarkably little is known of the foraging communities of the Holocene (Sinclair, Morais & Bingham 1979; Sinclair 1987, p. 59; Morais 1988, pp. 40–3). This lack of information is owing to the fact that during colonial times earlier periods were emphasized, whereas since independence, attention has been consciously directed to farming communities. This emphasis was deemed necessary in view of the lack of scientific infrastructure, the expense of excavation and analysis of stone tools and associated finds and the absence of sophisticated geomorphological and

Figure 24.1 Site locations.

osteological technologies for interpretation. Recent efforts in both southern and northern Mozambique are, however, changing this situation.

From southern Mozambique a sequence from the Middle Stone Age through the Late
Stone Age and the Matola tradition has been excavated from the cave sites of Caimane I
and II by Morais and Jonsson (Morais 1988, pp. 113–16). A series of late holocene dates
(St 8880, 8889, 8890, 8893, 8894) all of which are associated with late stone age deposits
is now available (see Appendix) (Sinclair 1991) and this is complemented by the recent
reassessment of the available collections by Meneses (1988) and a comprehensive
overview of previous stone age studies in Mozambique.

In northern Mozambique, test trenches were dug in six rock shelters in order to
develop a chronostratigraphic framework for settlement systems analysis in the
Nampula region (Adamowicz 1985; Adamowicz 1987). Fifteen radiocarbon dates
ranging from the sixth millennium BC to the sixth century AD are available on charcoal
associated with assemblages containing microliths, excavated from the rock shelters of

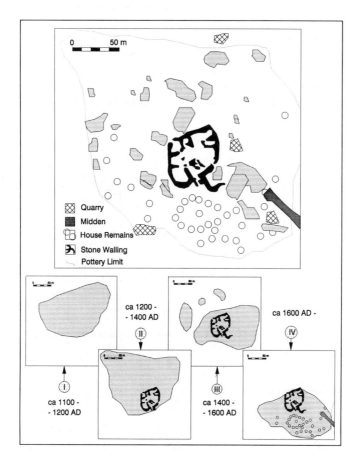

Figure 24.2 Diachronic model of occupation at Manyikeni based on results of multivariate
analysis of ceramic finds.

Riane (St 9022, 9023, 9024, 9025), Nakwaho (St 8194, 8195, 8196, 8197, 8198, 8200) and Xakota (St 8694, 8695, 9201) (see Appendix) (Adamowicz 1987; Sinclair 1991). The new work carried out by Adamowicz provides the firmest chronology so far for the later foraging communities in Mozambique, expanding the chronologies already published (Morais 1984; Sinclair 1987; Morais 1988).

Available evidence for the economy of the foraging communities is discussed in detail by Sinclair, Morais & Bingham (1979) and Adamowicz (1985; 1987), including current perspectives on the transition from foraging to farming and the likely extensive overlapping of these subsistence strategies. The first faunal reports from northern Mozambique reveal a range of wild species and some sheep/goats (Adamowicz 1990). There is little doubt, notwithstanding the dearth of research, that foraging communities were well established in most parts of Mozambique throughout the Holocene. Evidence from Nampula points to a stable settlement pattern over time with some possibilities of sedentism in favoured areas (Fig. 24.3). There is less evidence than might be expected from surveys of coastal areas, particularly in the southern part of the country.

When the onset of farming is being considered, simplistic models of migration and ethnic succession - with a sharp distinction between 'late stone age' and 'early iron age' populations – do not seem appropriate. It is clear that models must allow for the high degree of receptivity shown by foraging communities elsewhere in southern Africa. In northern Mozambique, the repeated use of sacred sites from mid-

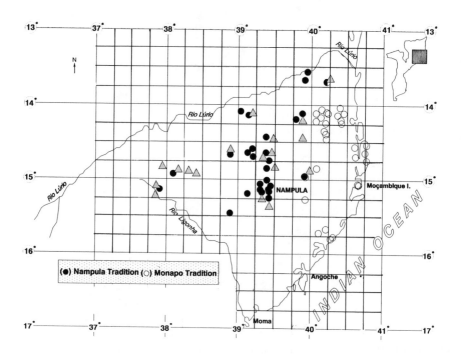

Figure 24.3 Late stone age and early farming community sites in Nampula province.

holocene times to the present (Adamowicz 1987) points to continuity rather than disjunction.

The farming communities

The southern Mozambique coastal plain

In southern Mozambique considerable progress has been made in creating the chronological framework through the identification of early farming community sites. Preliminary findings on chronology have been previously reported in Sinclair, Morais & Bingham (1979), Hall & Vogel (1980) and Morais (1984) and more detailed work is now available (Sinclair 1987; Morais 1988).

Beginning in 1975, Cruz e Silva (1979) excavated the important site of Matola, which has ceramic material (Fig. 24.4) similar to that previously reported from Silver Leaves near Tzaneen in the Transvaal (Klapwijk 1974) and also from middens along the Gaza coast north of Maputo identified by Senna Martinez (1976) and Smolla (1976). The site, re-excavated by Morais and Jonsson (Morais 1988, pp. 90–8), is securely dated to the early and mid-first millennium AD (St 8546, 8547) (see Appendix) and has given its name to the Matola tradition, which is stylistically similar in terms of ceramics to Kwale tradition material from the Tanzania coast. We do not know whether the Matola ceramics reflect the adoption of pottery by resident foraging communities or, as presently seems perhaps more likely, they were introduced together with iron-working technology by immigrants from the north. The Matola tradition does, however, represent the earliest farming community in Mozambique and is amongst the earliest in southern Africa as well.

Excavations at the University Campus (Sinclair, Nydolf & Nydolf 1987; Sinclair 1987, pp. 73–9; Morais 1988, pp. 85–8) indicate a Matola tradition occupation associated with iron-smelting debris from around the second to the sixth centuries AD (St 9836, 9837, 9838). At Zitundo the same material, with extensive evidence for iron-working, is dated from the second to fourth centuries AD (St 8909, 8910, 8911, 8912) (see Appendix) (Morais 1988, pp. 98–109). Very little osteological material has been recovered, representing only wild species, but these sites are major occupations and are considerably more substantial than those reported by Hall (1981) from Lake St Lucia in Natal. At Zitundo, the sequence described by Maggs (1980) in Natal is repeated and Morais (1988) has argued for a cultural continuum from the early Matola assemblages to the mid-first millennium Lydenburg assemblages, characterized by ceramics with cross-hatched incision. Huffman (1982), however, emphasizes stylistic disjunctions, using examples from the interior, dividing the ceramic assemblages into two separate traditions. At Caimane I and II, three readings (St 8873, 8874, 8892) probably postdate Matola deposits (see Appendix) (Morais 1988, pp. 114–15; Sinclair 1991).

Later first-millennium AD assemblages from southern Mozambique such as that from Massingir dated to c. AD 900 in association with cattle bones (Duarte 1976) are less well known than the Matola tradition (Morais 1988, pp. 116–20). Farming communities of the second millennium AD are very little studied, with the best known sites being the middens of the Gaza coast (Senna Martinez 1976). The coastal middens probably represent accumulations of debris from short-term discontinuous seasonal exploitation of shellfish resouces by agriculturalists resident up to 40 km from the coast – a pattern described ethnographically by Earthy (1933). The available evidence is detailed by Morais (1988, pp. 176–85), who also includes the environmental contexts and a comprehensive discussion of economic evidence (Morais 1988, pp. 130–5).

Further north, evidence of the Matola tradition in Vilanculos Bay is limited to a single fluted fragment of pottery from the beach. However, other early farming community traditions are represented on the Bazaruto archipelago (Sinclair 1982; Sinclair 1987, pp. 86–90) and the nearby coastal and hinterland areas. The Gokomere tradition settlement of Hola Hola on the river Save is a particularly clear example of the

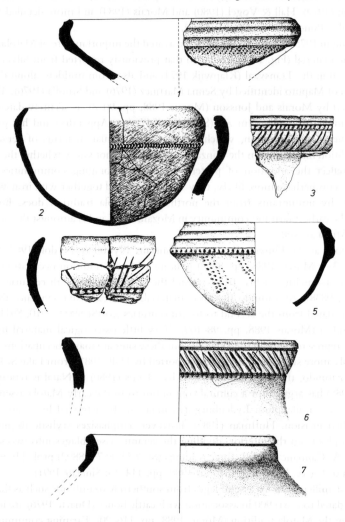

Figure 24.4 Ceramics. 1–14 Kwale tradition from coast and interior of Nampula province, *c.* 40 BC – AD 100; 5–7 Matola tradition (scale 1:2)

spatial layout of a farming community settlement from the first millennium AD (Sinclair 1985; Sinclair 1987, pp. 81–3; Morais 1988, pp. 109–12).

The series of dates from the early trading site of Chibuene in Vilanculos Bay is also of particular interest. Two occupation levels are clearly visible in the stratigraphy and a third level may exist. The lower occupation at Chibuene has been dated to the later first millennium AD, contemporary with Kilwa Ib on the basis of ceramics (Fig. 24.5) (Chittick 1974), and a series of radiocarbon dates (St 8494, 8495, 8496) are all within the first millennium AD (see Appendix). The possibility that the basal levels reflect a mid or perhaps even early first-millennium, pre-Islamic occupation of the site has been strongly enhanced by the identification by H. Wright (*pers. comm.*) of a fragment of imported green glazed ware known from Sohar on the Omani coast. In east Africa, wares associated with the green glazed ceramics at Sohar are known only from Ras Hafun in northern Somalia and are dated there from the first century BC to the fifth century AD. Some very friable contemporary earthenware has been identified at Chibuene and similarly decorated material, dated to around the seventh century AD (St 8497), has been recovered from the hinterland at Nhachengue (see Appendix). Some attributes of later earthenwares (Fig. 24.5) at Chibuene, found in association with Sassanian Islamic and tin glazed wares, are similar to the Gokomere/Ziwa tradition, which is very clearly represented at Dundo on Bazaruto island in association with blue-green glazed Sassanian Islamic sherds. The local economy of Chibuene is discussed in detail by Sinclair (1987, pp. 86–90) and Morais (1988, pp. 71–2) and both sheep and cattle remains have been recovered from the lower levels of the site. Further south near Inhambane a site found by Adamowicz (*pers. comm.*) with earthenwares similar to those at Chibuene (Fig. 24.5) but without any imports, has been dated to the eighth century AD (St 11590) (see Appendix) (Sinclair 1991).

The uppermost occupation at Chibuene is dated by four readings from the thirteenth century AD to the present (St 8491, 8492, 8493, 9703) and is therefore at least partially contemporary with Manyikeni and the zimbabwe tradition (see Appendix). The ceramics from Chibuene show definite similarities with those of Manyikeni and other sites on the islands of the Bazaruto archipelago (Sinclair 1987, pp. 86–91) and also with coastal wares known from the Save river mouth (Barradas 1961; Dickinson 1975), Sofala (Liesegang 1975) and the northern Mozambique coast at Sancul and Ibo Island Upper (Sinclair 1985; Sinclair 1986).

The trading site of Chibuene, occupied from at least the mid-first millennium AD, is of crucial importance for our understanding of the articulation of the offshore islands of the Comores, the southern extension of the east African coast and the southern African interior. Developments of the very substantial urban settlements at Mapungubwe and Great Zimbabwe from the late first millennium AD were preceded by the development, around the edges of the Limpopo basin, of extensive settlement hierarchies based on agro-pastoralism, with evidence for intensive metallurgical production (Sinclair 1987). Accompanying these developments was the penetration as far as the edges of the Kalahari desert (Kiyaga-Mulindwa, Ch. 21, this volume) of exotic trade goods in the form of glass beads identical to those found at Chibuene.

Excavations at the zimbabwe stone wall enclosure of Manyikeni (Fig. 24.1) extend our range of consideration of the spatial interaction of variables on the semi-micro (intra-site) level of Clarke (1977, pp. 11–16) and provide the possibility of testing the categories implicit in our conception of social formation against empirical evidence. The 1975 and 1976 seasons resulted in a developmental sequence of the stone wall enclosures and the analysis of faunal remains from the site (Garlake 1976a; Garlake 1976b; Barker 1978).

In 1977 and 1978, a stratified sampling procedure at the 1 per cent level using 1 × 1 m trenches provided a more systematic coverage of a *c.* 10,000 m^2 area than would have done a haphazard location pattern of larger trenches (Morais & Sinclair 1980).

The 7 per cent success rate in encountering house floors in the sample led on to upper and lower estimates for the number of house structures in the settlement around the outside of the stone enclosure; and detailed study of the ceramic distributions from the different stratigraphic units of the site using correspondence analysis (Sinclair 1987)

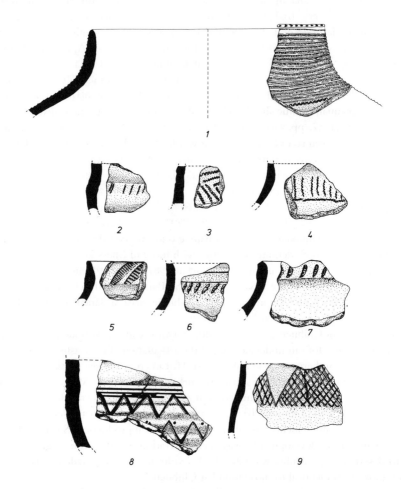

Figure 24.5 Chibuene ceramics. 1–7 shell-stamped earthenware; 8 water jar from the Gulf; 9 earthenware similar to Kilwa Period 1 (scale 1:2)

permitted a reconstruction of horizontally overlapping areas of occupation at different time periods (see Fig. 24.2).

These statistical techniques have also been applied to other variables selected from finds of gold, imported glass beads, work implements and dietary remains. Questions derived from our different levels of theory and from ethnographic sources were framed in terms of null hypotheses and then tested statistically against the database. In terms of dietary remains functional information relating to the economy in terms of herding practice and the species hunted and environments exploited were obtained from species identifications. Further information based on more sophisticated analyses of the faunal remains relate to relative status- and gender-based spatial preferences (Sinclair 1987). The random sampling approach has facilitated an estimate of the number of houses in the sample area and, by extension, a figure of 150–200 for the population of the site. Current work is focused upon the food production potential of the area surrounding the site based on the catchment analysis provided by Sinclair and the detailed FAO land assessment (Sinclair 1987).

The northern Mozambique coastal plain

Archaeological work in northern Mozambique was initiated by Duarte, Cruz e Silva and Sinclair in the late 1970s (Sinclair 1985; Sinclair 1986) with the investigation of twenty sites in the Nampula and Cabo Delgado provinces. These early efforts have been surpassed by Adamowicz (1985; 1987), who has reported more than one hundred sites from Nampula province. In Nampula, recent surveys have covered the coast, hinterland and interior of the province, providing information on late stone age occupation as well as preliminary evidence of two major ceramic traditions. Forty-seven radiocarbon dates have been reported from northern Mozambique.

Sites of the early farming communities are increasingly well known from Nampula. The first phase sites have ceramics which are similar to Kwale wares from Kenya and Tanzania (Fig. 24.4). From the coast, a single site, Mwakoni, has been reported, while three occurrences of the same material have been found at Riane, Namolepiwa and Namialo II in the hinterland less than 100 km from the coast. In the interior near Nampula town, five sites (Muhekani, Nampula I, Murrapania IV, Namikopo and Mutawania) are known. No dates are available for this phase but, as will be seen below, stratigraphic relationships may be inferred from a number of sites. Two later traditions, the Monapo from the coast and the Nampula from the interior, have been identified by Adamowicz (1987). The Nampula tradition has been divided by Adamowicz into three phases which have recently been summarized by Sinclair (1991).

The major sites of the Nampula A phase are Xakota, Muhekani, Nampula I, Makohere, Namikopo I, Mutawania and Murrapania IV. Characteristic pottery (Fig. 24.6), decorated with incised bands and some bevelling, might be derived from the earlier Kwale phase. A second-century AD reading is available from Murrapania IV (St 11006) from a seated burial associated with pottery and an elephant tusk (Fig. 24.7) (see Appendix). At Xakota a third-century AD reading (St 9200) is associated with Nampula A pottery, which appears to extend at the same site to the fifth century (St 9198) (see Appendix). An important find of sorghum (mapira) is dated to around the seventh century AD (Adamowicz 1987, p. 68). Contact with the coast is indicated with some shell-stamping motifs on Nampula A pottery from Murrapania and also Muhekani.

Nampula B pottery decoration is characterized by dentate stamping on both jars and bowls (Fig. 24.6), similar to Nteope material from southern Malawi. This phase is dated between the sixth and seventh centuries at Riane (St 9021), Namikopo I (St 9704, 9705, 9770) and at Nakwaho I (St 8194) (see Appendix). Nampula C is characterized by jars with single bands of dentate stamping just below the lip, and other motifs comprising punctates and plant impression and thin lines of vertical impression also occur (Fig. 24.8). The Nampula C phase is dated from about the seventh century AD to possibly the thirteenth century by a radiocarbon series from Mutawania (St 11005), Muhekani (St 9194, 9196), Murrapania IV (St 11004), Xakota (St 9199) and Tototo II (St 9020), where it is mixed with later material (see Appendix). Later pottery in the

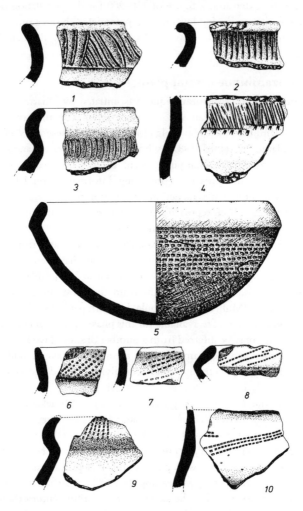

Figure 24.6 Ceramics from the interior. 1–4 Nampula A tradition, *c.* AD 100–350; 5–10 Nampula B tradition, *c.* AD 350–700 (scale 1:2)

Nampula town area is characterized by carinated jars decorated with bands of cross-hatching and multiple bands of incised triangles, punctates and dentate stamping. Dates from *c.* sixteenth/seventeenth century AD are available on charcoal associated with this material at Xakota (St 8692) and Muhekani (St 9706) (see Appendix). Adamowicz (1987) has compared the pottery to assemblages of the Luangwa tradition.

On the coast and adjacent hinterland, pottery of the Monapo tradition (Fig. 24.9) occurs stratified above Kwale tradition wares at Mwakoni, Namialo II and Namolepiwa. Monapo Phase I pottery (Fig. 24.9) is dated at Namolepiwa to the fourth century AD (St 9449) (see Appendix). The fact that some of these sherds at Namolepiwa were coloured white, apparently from use as palettes for the production of the white paintings executed on the cave walls, may be chronologically significant. Phase II of the Monapo tradition is dated at the same site to the sixth century AD (St 9775) (see Appendix). Pottery jars decorated with zigzag shell-stamping motifs, bands of

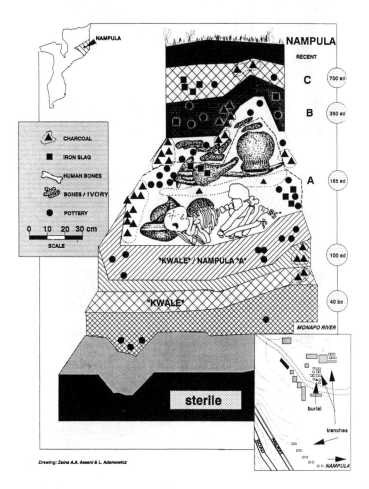

Figure 24.7   Murrapania: burial plan and section.

horizontal shell impression and space motifs are characteristic of Monapo Phase II, but bowls are rare (Fig. 24.9). Other sites include Namialo II and III, Tikinyia and Serra Mesa as well as a number of surface scatters near the coast (Adamowicz 1987; Sinclair 1991).

The sequence at Namolepiwa continues with the interesting occurrence of Nampula C pottery dated to *c.* seventh/eighth century AD (St 9451) (see Appendix). Above this Adamowicz reports the close association of a number of different pottery bowl forms dated (St 9450) to *c.* seventh/eighth century AD (see Appendix) – indicating perhaps the use of the site as a ceremonial offering place, as is strongly suggested by modern ethnographic data. Contact with the interior is evidenced *c.* eighth century AD by finds of pottery with dentate stamping similar to Nampula C material at Namolepiwa and

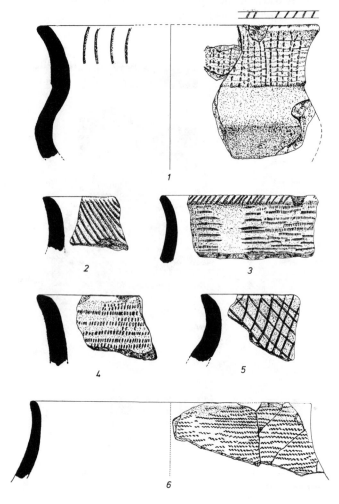

Figure 24.8 Ceramics from the interior. 1–5 Nampula C tradition, *c.* AD 700–950; 6 shell-impressed ware indicating coastal contact (scale 1:2)

Tikinyia, another ceremonial centre. The final later farming community assemblage of the Namolepiwa sequence is dated (St 9448) to the seventeenth century AD (see Appendix) (Adamowicz 1987; Sinclair 1991).

Later pottery traditions were first systematically recorded at Lumbo and Ibo Island Lower by Sinclair (1985; 1986). Pottery from these sites has been compared to Kilwa Period III and is dated at Lumbo to the fourteenth century AD (St 8498) (see Appendix). Material from the upper occupation at Ibo is very similar to that recovered from the Sancul middens in front of Mozambique island and has even been recovered from the wreck of the *St Antonio de Tanna* in Mombasa harbour which dates to *c.* 1697. The same motifs, notably the raised appliqué wheel-made ware and the open bowls decorated with red colour and graphite, are found as far south as the mouth of the river Save in south-central Mozambique (Sinclair 1985; Sinclair 1986). This material, together with

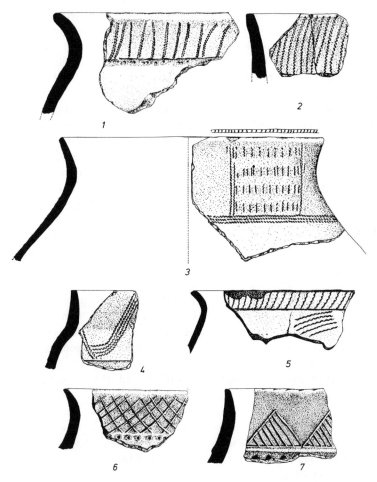

Figure 24.9   Coastal ceramics. 1–2 early Monapo tradition, *c.* AD 300–600; 3–5 late Monapo tradition, *c.* AD 600–1200; 6–7 typical examples (cf. Chibuene), *c.* AD 600–900 (scale 1:2)

that from more than twenty newly reported sites dated at the mouth of the river Lurio to the twelfth century AD (St 11007), at the Armazia site to the seventeenth century (St 9772) and at Muhekani to less than 250 years ago, has been subsumed by Adamowicz (1987) into the 'Swahili Tradition'. This controversial label has not found broad acceptance and is probably better termed the Sancul tradition (Duarte 1988; Duarte 1991) (see Appendix). Further south at Xokas, Maravi pottery has been dated to recent times (St 9018) (see Appendix) (Adamowicz 1987; Sinclair 1991).

The first detailed survey work on Swahili settlements on the northern Mozambique coast has been carried out by Duarte (1988; 1991). He also outlines previous efforts in colonial times. Mapping and architectural analysis and test excavations have been carried out at a number of stone-built sites, especially Somana, Pangane and Gomene. Somana has been dated on the basis of architectural parallels and Lumbo-type ceramics to c. twelfth/thirteenth century AD. The site was inhabited prior to the building of the coral structures, as shown by the occurrence of Monapo tradition pottery. Pangane is a later Swahili site dated to c. eighteenth/nineteenth century AD on the basis of architec-tural parallels and Sancul tradition ceramics. Particularly interesting information on shellfish-gathering is available from both Somana and Gomene and eight glass beads have been recovered from Gomene but not from Somana, indicating that not all sites are recipients of exotic goods.

Duarte (1991) has developed a model of the articulation of the coastal settlements to the agricultural communities of the hinterland through extended kinship networks. He argues that the environmental variation and uneven risk of drought were countered by extended exchange networks. This ability to spread uncertainty, he argues, enabled the settlements of the coast to survive a variety of threats from land and even from sea raiders. The possible undermining of these networks by the increase in number of individual traders still remains to be tested against archaeological data.

The early farming communities: towards a synthesis

The research of the last fifteen years in Mozambique has demonstrated a remarkable ceramic continuity, from Kwale tradition assemblages in southern Mozambique, Natal and the eastern Transvaal (and even southern Zimbabwe) through northern Mozambique to the Usambara mountains in northeastern Tanzania and the coastal lowlands in Kenya. Dates from the southern extension of this distribution are as early as those from the north, suggesting a very rapid north–south spread. Claims by Chittick (1983) that this material is represented in collections from Barawa in southern Somalia are so far unsubstantiated.

The extent to which stone-using communities overlapped with iron-using agricul-turalists remains uncertain. Rather surprisingly, few stone artefacts have been re-covered from farming community sites in southern Mozambique, with the notable exception of Hola Hola. The best hope for answering questions about such settlement relations comes from the work of Adamowicz (1987) in northern Mozambique.

The exploitation of marine resources among the coastal farming communities of the early first millennium AD is especially evident in southern Mozambique and Natal. Agriculture is less well known, but sorghum and millet were grown and sites of the early farming communities do seem to occur in areas of high productivity. In

Mozambique no evidence for animal husbandry occurs in Matola tradition contexts, the only exception being possible cattle remains from the later occupation at Zitundo. A similar situation holds in other Kwale contexts, with the notable exception of the mid-first millennium Kwale sites from Kenya, where both cattle and sheep/goat remains have been reported. Sheep and cattle remains are known from south-central Mozambique at Chibuene from the mid–late first millennium AD (Sinclair 1987) and cattle are reported from the south at *c*. AD 900 at Massingir (Duarte 1976).

Iron-working is an important technology, with the demand for charcoal potentially affecting the ecological balance in the sandy soils of southern Mozambique. However, recent modelling of the farming economy of southern Mozambique by Morais (1988) and the contributions of Adamowicz (1987) in northern Mozambique have transformed our knowledge of settlement patterns over a considerable area. In the first millennium AD, the early farming communities appear to have been small in scale and orientated towards subsistence, with communal access to land. Each community appears to have been relatively self-sufficient, but alliances and contacts such as marriages and local exchanges may still have been significant (Sinclair 1987, p. 152). Decentralized control is a notable feature of early farming communities and is accompanied by a tendency towards fragmentation and the relieving of contradictions by the setting up of new communities. This tendency is suggested by the rapid spread of farming communities throughout the subcontinent. Enough sites have been investigated along the coast and in the hinterlands of the eastern Transvaal, northern Mozambique and Tanzania to permit at least a preliminary statement that the penetration of exotic trade goods – if it did occur – was not on a significant scale in this early period. With the possible exception of Chibuene, no evidence for glass beads occurs in the first half of the first millennium AD, and marine shell finds can be adequately accounted for by the exploitation of marine resources and the result of local exchanges.

Early reports of first-millennium Kwale/Matola sites in Natal and Mozambique suggest a restricted coastal distribution. However, finds of similar ceramics from the eastern Transvaal, the Mt Buhwa region in southern Zimbabwe and the substantial sites from the interior of Nampula province in northern Mozambique show that it is necessary to conceive of a geographical context which encompasses the coastal plain in its broadest sense. The balance of evidence does, however, favour a primary correlation with the Zanzibar/Inhambane floral mosaic extending southwards into the Tongaland complex, with perhaps a secondary extension into the interior. Available interpretative models emphasize a rapid dispersal from the area of the Great Lakes but the links between the early Lake Nyanza occurrences and those of the coast need further investigation, particularly in view of the close similarity in dating between the two regions.

Recent work by Horton (1984) on the offshore islands from the Lamu archipelago to Zanzibar has failed to recover evidence for Kwale ceramics. However, a single fluted sherd recovered from Unguja Ukuu on Zanzibar (Juma, *pers. comm.*), and the Kwale site on Kilwa island reported by Sinclair, indicates that island environments were in fact occupied in the early first millennium AD by farming communities. Mid-first-millennium Gokomere/Ziwa wares have also been reported from Bazaruto island in southern Mozambique (Sinclair 1987). No pottery similar to the early Kwale/Matola wares, nor to the Gokomere/Ziwa wares, has been observed in any of the collections housed in institutions from the Comoran archipelago or Madagascar. Current surveys in the Comores and planned work in northwestern Madagascar are aimed at confirming this picture. Nevertheless, it is important to recognize the remarkable correlations between the early imported wares from Ras Hafun and Chibuene and, later, the equally impressive distribution of red-slipped wares which occur at least as early as the late first millennium AD onwards from Somalia in the north, down the Kenya/Tanzania coast across to the Comores and northern Madagascar and as far as Chibuene in southern Mozambique. The associated earthen wares are quite possibly derived from Kwale antecedents. This is important because evidence for social differentiation begins to occur in the form of stone architectural features towards the end of the first millennium AD and very often in association with exotic trade goods (Sinclair 1987, pp. 143–56; Duarte 1991). The provision by archaeology of a dated series of indigenous farming community sites from the early first millennium AD onwards is crucial for a balanced understanding of the development of urbanism in the region (Sinclair 1991).

Archaeology and national culture

Throughout the practice of archaeology in Mozambique, but particularly at the excavations at Manyikeni, a number of issues concerning the connections between society at large and the production of archaeological knowledge have been raised. Archaeology is one means of collection, interpretation and transmission of historical information in specific social contexts and not merely a way of accumulating knowledge of past human behaviour. The focus and frame of reference should be susceptible to discussion. What is the object of study? For whom? What emphasis should be placed on which set of meanings embedded in material culture? How should the work be implemented – mass involvement or small, highly trained technical teams? Should research be oriented academically towards theoretical advances or should resources be redirected to convey an awareness of the existence and characteristics of the precolonial past to Mozambican peasants and workers?

Some of these questions may well be superseded, for it is to be hoped that a situation develops in Africa in which there is no contradiction between academic interest, both foreign and local, and development needs. To achieve this it is necessary to distinguish between foreign and national research workers exploiting the archaeological heritage for their own ends and the much more difficult task of genuinely contributing to knowledge and awareness of the country's past. However, the inadequacy of framing the discussion of appropriation of knowledge in only national terms is underscored by an assessment of the contradictory interests between urban and rural frames of reference. In southern Africa forms of this opposition date back at least to the first state formation and class differentiation at Great Zimbabwe in the thirteenth century. Later historical developments in the region south of the river Save, from gradual foreign encroachment to the setting up of colonial administration and the involvement of men in migrant labour contracts in South Africa, to the anticolonial struggles, and to the present civil strife, provide a complex matrix of class interests as foci for applied archaeological work.

In this context the work carried out at Manyikeni, about 700 km to the north of the capital in a rural zone, resulted in a form of praxis which integrated scientific and cultural work and established the first links between the practice of archaeology and popular involvement and education. From 1977 more than 400 people from the surrounding region participated voluntarily, and the first open-air archaeological display in the country grew from the daily educational tours around the site (Sinclair 1990, pp. 154–8). The implementation of the project at Manyikeni in an area which was adversely influenced by the war situation symbolized for a wider audience in Mozambican society the people's determination both to comprehend and to affirm their historical role in the struggle for nationhood. More recent experience in northern Mozambique, with the development by Adamowicz (*pers. comm.*) of teacher training programmes and archaeology by correspondence courses, shows clearly the depth of interest for archaeology amongst ordinary people in Mozambique. In view of the urgent need to establish archaeological heritage management programmes – especially with the rapid move to a free market economy – it is this reservoir of public concern which must be tapped for the further development of the archaeological discipline in Mozambique.

Appendix: ages in radiocarbon years before present

Northern Mozambique coastal plain

St 8194	Nakwaho I	1260 ± 105
St 8195	Nakwaho I	2470 ± 115
St 8196	Nakwaho I	3335 ± 115
St 8197	Nakwaho I	4285 ± 125
St 8198	Nakwaho I	5145 ± 170
St 8200	Nakwaho I	3670 ± 160
St 8498	Lumbo	600 ± 75
St 8692	Xakota	325 ± 145
St 8694	Xakota	1935 ± 100
St 8695	Xakota	5115 ± 170
St 9018	Xokas	<250
St 9020	Tototo II	660 ± 100
St 9021	Riane	1485 ± 170
St 9022	Riane	4600 ± 200
St 9023	Riane	5590 ± 130
St 9024	Riane	6555 ± 130
St 9025	Riane	5020 ± 120
St 9194	Muhekani	940 ± 215
St 9195	Muhekani	<250
St 9196	Muhekani	1230 ± 100
St 9198	Xakota	1460 ± 100
St 9199	Xakota	890 ± 205
St 9200	Xakota	1665 ± 110
St 9201	Xakota	2730 ± 230

St 9448	Namolepiwa	280±70
St 9449	Namolepiwa	1635±80
St 9450	Namolepiwa	1195±140
St 9451	Namolepiwa	1245±90
St 9704	Namikopo I	1280±100
St 9705	Namikopo I	1320±170
St 9770	Namikopo I	1375±100
St 9772	Armazia	290±95
St 9775	Namolepiwa	1435±100
St 11004	Murrapania IV	1150±140
St 11005	Mutawania	1370±140
St 11006	Murrapania IV	1785±85
St 11007	River Lurio	835±140

Southern Mozambique coastal plain

R 1327	Matola 2532 Cd 1	1880±50
R 1328	Matola 2532 Cd 1	1120±50
R 1329	Xai Xai 2533 Ba 3	<250
R 1337	Chongoene 2533 Bb 1	<250
St 8491	Chibuene (Upper)	<250
St 8492	Chibuene (Upper)	<250
St 8493	Chibuene (Upper)	665±80
St 8494	Chibuene (Lower)	1270±80
St 8495	Chibuene (Lower)	1400±85
St 8496	Chibuene (Lower)	1155±85
St 8497	Nhachengue	1254±80
St 8546	Matola 2532 Cd 1	1720±110
St 8547	Matola 2532 Cd 1	1470±80
St 8548	Matola 2532 Cd 1	2025±80
St 8585	Chongoene 2533 Bb 1	<250
St 8586	Xai Xai 2533 Ba 3	<250
St 8587	Chongoene 2533 Bb 1	<250
St 8588	Bilene 2533 Ac 3	<250
St 8589	Xai Xai 2533 Ba 3	510±165
St 8590	Chongoene 2533 Bb 1	880±100
St 8591	Chongoene 2533 Bb 1	<250
St 8592	Xai Xai 2533 Ba 3	<250
St 8873	Caimane II	880±210
St 8874	Caimane II	715±90
St 8880	Caimane I	8010±115
St 8889	Caimane I	3745±355
St 8890	Caimane I	5035±260
St 8892	Caimane I	795±270
St 8893	Caimane I	5950±315
St 8894	Caimane I	3100±250
St 8909	Zitundo	1775±105
St 8910	Zitundo	1435±105
St 8911	Zitundo	1760±105
St 8912	Zitundo	1685±105

St 8913	Zitundo	1575±105
St 9703	Chibuene	445±160
St 9836	University Campus	1775±85
St 9837	University Campus	1355±100
St 9838	University Campus	1590±75
St 11590	Inhambane	715±150

Acknowledgements

Different aspects of this work were carried out collectively. It owes a great deal to a wide range of people in Mozambique, and in particular to T. Cruz e Silva, A. Lo Forte and B. Bingham. M. Stephen and C. Lindqvist also participated in surveys, excavations and discussions, as did the various members of the team from the Swedish Central Board of National Antiquities from which the contributions of Dr G. Trotzig, L. Jonsson, P. Lindqvist, N. and G. Nydolf and D. Damell are particularly appreciated. Sincere thanks are due to SAREC for financial help and to the Departments of Archaeology and Anthropology at Eduardo Mondlane University and the Departments of Cultural Anthropology and Archaeology at Uppsala University for providing facilities. Keith Ray provided much kind help and criticism of an early draft of this chapter.

We wish, also, to record our thanks to O. Cabral, Z. A. A. Assani and A. Branco for assistance with the preparation of illustrations.

25   New evidence on early iron-smelting from southeastern Nigeria

EDWIN E. OKAFOR

Introduction: earlier studies of iron-smelting in Africa

Initial attempts to study African iron-working were geared towards finding the origin of this technology in the continent rather than towards studying iron-working *per se*. Nearly all earlier major works on African iron-working were devoted to this question (Lhote 1952; Mauny 1952; Huard 1966; Shinnie 1966; Arkell 1968; Diop 1968; Shaw 1969; Trigger 1969; Tylecote 1970; Tylecote 1975a; Todd 1976, pp. 5–25; Andah 1979, pp. 135–42; Van Noten 1979; Rustad 1980; van der Merwe & Avery 1982, pp. 150–2; Schmidt & Avery 1983, pp. 432–4; Phillipson 1985, pp. 148–86; Kense 1985; Keteku n.d.; Okafor n.d.a). The study of African iron-working should investigate first all the ramifications of the processes of the technology as practised in the various communities of Africa, in order to acquire the data for comparative studies. Without such a database no study of origins will lead to objective conclusions. It is only when the technological processes of bloomery iron-smelting in Africa have been established that we can have the raw data for making comparisons with others. It is only by means of such studies that it can be determined whether early African iron-working was due to diffusion from the posited donor areas or was an independent development or an amalgam of both processes (see Holl, Ch. 17, this volume).

There have thus been three schools of thought on this topic, which may be called the diffusionist, the indigenous and the cautious (Okafor n.d.b, p. 2). Arkell (1968) and Shinnie (1966) belonged to the diffusionist school, and held that African iron-working was derived from Egypt through Meroe and the Sudan; this view was modified by Huard, who proposed that African iron-working diffused from Meroe and the Gulf of Syrte in Libya. However, the position of Meroe as the centre of diffusion was undermined by work on the iron-smelting site of Taruga in Nigeria (Tylecote 1975a; Tylecote 1975b) and at Meroe itself (Tylecote 1970), which initially suggested that Meroitic iron-working was later in date than that practised at Taruga from the fifth or sixth centuries BC; later, however, sixth- to third-century BC dates from materials associated with slag were obtained from Meroe (Green 1975). Trigger (1969) postulated that African iron-working originated from east Asia through Madagascar or the east African coast. Williams (1969; 1974) believed that African iron-working came from Meroe and Carthage. The view that Carthage was the source of African iron-working is presently the most favoured by the diffusionists. This idea was originated by Mauny (1952) and has since been developed by others (Shaw 1969; Shaw 1975; Tylecote 1970; Tylecote 1975a; van der Merwe & Avery 1982). Mauny speculated that Berbers from the Phoenician settlements of north Africa were the agents through whom iron-working diffused into Africa. Not much is yet known about iron-working in Punic north Africa, although excavations at Carthage revealed a bloomery iron-smelting site using tuyères (Lancel 1978; Shaw 1985b), and an iron-smelting furnace at Do Dimi in the southern Sahara yielded a ninth-century radiocarbon date (Calvocoressi & David 1979). Mauny (1952) had also speculated that iron-working might have been diffused by trading voyages along the coast of west Africa, but later accepted that the account of Hanno's voyage is a forgery (Mauny 1970, pp. 78–80).

Opposed to these diffusionist models are the protagonists of independent invention, from Lhote (1952), who based his supposition on the lack of iron-working among the Saharan Berbers, to Diop (1968) and Keteku (n.d.). Because carbonized wood in the alluvial deposits at Nok producing Nok-style figurines gave a mid-fourth-millennium BC radiocarbon date and Nok-style figurines are associated with the iron-smelting site of Taruga, Diop saw no reason why iron-smelting should not have been indigenously developed at this date. Rustad (1980, p. 237) supported an indigenous origin because iron-smelting could not have come from Meroe and he thought an ultimate Carthaginian source unlikely. Schmidt & Avery (1983, p. 433) date their suggestion for an indigenous development of iron-smelting out of copper-working to the turn of the first and second millennia BC, taking place at Taruga in Nigeria and in the Kagera district of northwestern Tanzania. The latter area also saw the innovation of preheating the inflowing air in the tuyère to obtain higher furnace temperatures (but see Egert, Ch. 16, this volume).

The view that iron-smelting could not have been independently developed in Africa because there was no pre-existing pyrometallurgical tradition there (Wertime 1973; Tylecote 1975a, pp. 4–5; Wheeler & Maddin 1980; van der Merwe & Avery 1982, pp. 150–1) is challenged by discoveries in Mauritania and the Republic of Niger. In the former, there is evidence of copper-mining and working at Akjoujt dating from the ninth to the sixth centuries BC, while in the latter, in the Agadez region, the exploitation of native copper goes back to the second millennium BC and smelting to the early to mid-first millennium BC (Calvocoressi & David 1979; McIntosh & McIntosh 1983, p. 241). These discoveries have led Avery & Schmidt (1979; Schmidt & Avery 1983) to propose a hypothesis that iron-smelting might have developed independently from a copper-smelting technique using iron oxide as a flux.

The third school of thought on the origins of African iron-smelting comprises 'the cautious group' (Okafor 1984; Okafor n.d.b), represented by Andah (1979) and Phillipson (1985a), who take the position that more data are required before making a choice between the other two possibilities.

Much of the debate on origins hinges on the reliability or otherwise of radiocarbon and thermoluminescence dates and their interpretation. Those from Nok and Taruga in Nigeria are well known (Fagg 1969; Shaw 1969; Calvocoressi & David 1979, p. 10; Shaw 1981), clustering fairly strongly with a beginning in the mid-first millennium BC; also in Nigeria, the Tse Dura rock shelter produced a date for iron-working in the fourth century BC (Calvocoressi & David 1979, p. 11), and the Baha mound in the second century BC (Shaw 1978, p. 97). More recently the Nsukka Division of south-eastern Nigeria has produced three Accelerator Mass Spectrometry (AMS) dates from iron-smelting furnaces at Opi spanning the fifth to the second century BC (Appendix). In Ghana mid-first-millennium BC to mid-first-millennium AD dates have been accepted for iron-working at Daboya (Kense 1985a, p. 16). From the Congo basin, de Maret, Van Noten & Cohen (1977, p. 495) have accepted fourth- to third-century BC dates for the earliest iron-working there, while from Buhaya in northwestern Tanzania dates of the ninth and fifth centuries BC have been accepted for early iron-working (Schmidt & Avery 1978; Avery & Schmidt 1979).

At one time it seemed as if the spread of an iron technology over a large part of sub-Saharan Africa was to be associated with the spread of Bantu-speaking peoples from their ancestral homelands in the Nigerian–Cameroonian border area (Greenberg 1963; Fagan 1965; Davies 1966a; Hiernaux 1968; Mason 1974, pp. 211–16). However, a number of archaeologists now believe that the Bantu diaspora, whatever it was, began before a knowledge of iron technology. The linguist Ehret (1982a, pp. 57–65) has adduced evidence indicating that the beginning of the Bantu dispersal occurred in the third millennium BC. Those who still wish to associate the spread of iron-working with the spread of Bantu speakers find in this earlier dating for the Bantu spread some justification for accepting older dates for iron-working which others have hitherto rejected as 'unacceptably earlier', 'impossibly old' or 'earlier than what is assumed'. Such dates include a 3265 ± 65 BC date from the Nok gravels (Barendsen, Deevey & Gralenski 1957, pp. 916–18); dates of 3190 ± 129 and 3580 ± 130 BC (Davies 1966a, p. 471) and 1630 ± 130 to 1240 ± 120 BC from the confused site of Ntereso in Ghana; and a second-millennium BC date from Buhaya in Tanzania (Schmidt & Avery 1978).

It seems in fact that the radiocarbon and thermoluminescence dates associated with iron-working activities are not at present sufficiently precise or reliable to settle the question of origins.

Experimental and analytical studies

A number of studies have been carried out with a view to understanding better the processes involved in African iron technology. Investigations by Sassoon (1964), Sutton (1976a), Anozie (1979), Effah-Gyamfi (1981) and Okafor (1983; 1984; 1988; n.d.b) demonstrated that extensive and complex iron-working was practised in various parts of Nigeria. Goucher (1983) and de Barros (1988) have studied iron-working sites in Bassar, Togo, and the former applied analytical techniques to the products of the technology to determine their chemical and mineralogical composition. In northern Ghana, Pole (1974a; 1975a; 1975b; 1985) has described the various furnace types and smelting techniques employed in that area.

A number of 'imitative experiments' (Childs & Schmidt 1985, p. 122) in reconstruct-ing techniques of African iron-smelting have been carried out, based on ethnographic models, aimed at providing a better understanding of archaeological iron-smelting remains: Friede & Steel (1977; 1988) in South Africa, Todd (1976; 1979) in Ethiopia at

Dimi, Haaland (1985) in Darfur, Pole (1974b; 1975a; 1975b; 1985) in Ghana, Sassoon (1964) in Sukur in Nigeria and Van Noten (1985) in the Madi and Gisagara areas. Schmidt's replications of Haya smelting in northwestern Tanzania were specifically designed to test the hypothesis of air preheating in the tuyères (Schmidt 1980; Childs & Schmidt 1985). Except for the smelts at Sukur and Dimi, observed by Sassoon and Todd respectively and carried out by practitioners of the trade, these experimental proceedings produced little or no iron; this is not surprising inasmuch as they were conducted or directed by people acting from hearsay or distant memory.

In pre-industrial technologies, steel (with *c.* 2–4 per cent carbon) was produced in various ways, e.g. in the eastern Mediterranean by carburizing low-carbon blooms during forging, or in China by decarburizing blooms with high carbon content during forging. Wrought iron (with less than 1 per cent carbon) is the usual product of the bloomery process, but African smelting methods developed ways of producing medium carbon steel direct from the furnace (van der Merwe 1980, p. 497). Schmidt (Schmidt & Avery 1978; Schmidt 1980; Schmidt & Avery 1983; Schmidt & Childs 1985) has associated this with the practice of placing the tuyère deep within the combustion chamber so that the air blown in has been preheated by its passage through the tuyère, thus achieving a higher temperature in the furnace. Tylecote (1987) has denied the significance of this.

A large volume of literature has been produced on furnace description and typology (Bellamy & Harbord 1904; Forbes 1933; Cline 1937; Francis-Boeuf 1937; Sassoon 1964; Tylecote 1970; Tylecote 1975a; Tylecote 1975b; Sutton 1976a; Pole 1985; Sutton 1985; Friede & Steel 1988; David, Heimann, Killick & Wayman 1989). Typologically they are grouped into four: the simple bowl furnace (regarded as the earliest), the low shaft furnace with no provision for slag-tapping, the low shaft furnace with a hole for removing bloom and tapping slag and the tall shaft furnace 2 to 7 m high operated without any bellows (Van der Merwe 1980, pp. 490–1). Outside Africa this type of shaft furnace with self-induced draught is only known in India and Upper Burma (Tylecote 1965). In Africa it is known from Nigeria, Ghana, Togo, Cameroon, the Congo basin, Zambia, southern Tanzania, Malawi and the Horn of Africa. A unique type of furnace from northern Nigeria and Cameroon is so constructed that the bellowsman is protected from the heat of the furnace by a wall and the tuyère descends into the base of the combustion chamber, thus also probably providing some preheating of the draught (Sassoon 1964; Tylecote 1965, p. 345; David, Heimann, Killick & Wayman 1989, pp. 189–91). At one time it was hoped that a plotting of the geographical distribution of the different types of furnace would indicate routes of diffusion, but this hope has proved illusory.

In all the research that has been conducted into African iron-smelting, the least amount of attention has been paid to the analysis of residues. This has been due partly to a lack of realization of the information that can be obtained in this way, partly to the lack of facilities in many parts of Africa to carry out such analyses.

In west Africa, the earliest published attempt at residue analysis was that carried out by Tylecote (1975a), which gave bulk analysis of slags from Taruga and Meroe, together with four other analyses of ores from both sites. However, only the oxide constituents of the samples was given and nothing is known of the the mineralogical phases of these samples. The number of specimens used in this study was very small, so the results are inadequate for comparative purposes. From sites in Igboland, Okafor (1984; n.d.b) analysed four specimens of slag, but only the major elements were sought and minor and trace elements were lumped together as 'others'. Nothing is known about their mineralogical phases, their free-flowing temperatures, density and viscosity. These deficiencies make this work less useful for comparative studies.

From Togo, Goucher (1983) published a summary of analyses of fifteenth-century Bassar slags. Although details of the oxide constituents were not published, major phases were identified as wustite, fayalite and glass. From the Ivory Coast, Zacharia & Bachmann (1983) made an analysis of slags from the Senufo: major phases were identified as fayalite, wustite, spinel, hercynite and magnetite. Their viscosity was found to be very low and their free-flowing temperature to range from 1160°C to 1190°C.

Work among the Dimi ironworkers of Ethiopia (Todd 1976; Todd & Charles 1978) remains to date the most detailed study of African iron-working residues. Ores, slag and metal specimens were analysed and the results compared with the analysis of residues from Hani in Ghana, and from central and western Sudan; most of these slags had a high flowing temperature of around 1400°C. From these analyses it was realized that it is difficult to do provenance studies from slag analysis using trace elements.

In South Africa, van der Merwe & Killick (1979) analysed smelting residues from Square near Phalabora; they identified the sources of ores used in early smelting from comparative studies of titanium/calcium and titanium/iron ratios. Friede, Hejja & Koursaris (1982) made analyses of iron-smelting slags from South Africa, Swaziland and Botswana, determining not only the oxide constituents but also their free-flowing temperatures and mineralogical phases. Analyses of slags from iron-smelting sites in the Magaliesberg area (Friede 1977) and the Melville Koppjes Nature Reserve are of limited value since they only give the oxide constituents.

The rise and decline of African iron-smelting

It thus seems that African bloomery iron-smelting was distinguished by three characteristics: the direct production of medium carbon steel direct from the furnace; pre-heated draught arrangements; and the development of shaft furnaces with self-induced draught. In spite of these distinctive achievements and this level of technical sophistication, it is not surprising that the industry gradually declined, at different rates in different areas, in the face of cheap steel imported from the blast furnaces of Europe and actively promoted by colonial governments (Flint 1974, p. 387; Williams 1974, pp. 69, 72, 86). However, there may have been two additional factors which contributed to the decline: an environmental one, occasioned by deforestation as a result of the tremendous demands for charcoal made by an iron-smelting industry (Goucher 1981; Haaland 1985); and a politico-economic one caused by a shortage of labour for a labour-intensive industry (Pole 1982; Oguagha 1982, p. 58; Oguagha & Okpoko 1984; de Barros 1988; Okafor n.d.b, pp. 66–7).

Analysis of iron-smelting residues from Nsukka Division, southeastern Nigeria

In the course of research by Okafor (Forthcoming), excavations were carried out on sites with iron-smelting furnaces at Opi, Owerre-Elu, Orba and Umundu (see Figs 25.1, 25.2). From these smelting furnaces eleven AMS radiocarbon dates were obtained. Three charcoal samples were collected from the three iron-smelting furnaces excavated at the foot of Opi hill. The samples were sealed by slag and tuyère fragments on the floor of the furnace. Samples OW/17/90 and OW/18/90 were collected from the base of the smelting furnace in the ploughed farm within the Owerre-Elu site; sample OW/18/90 consisted of twigs and grasses used to temper the clay used in the making of the tuyère. The three charcoal samples from Orba were collected at various points within a badly damaged smelting furnace in the dry valley at the Agu-Amaorba smelting site, all encased in slag and cinder. The three samples from Umundu had a similar provenance.

The dates derived from these samples are as follows:

Lab no.	Sample no.	Date bp
OxA-3201	OP/3/91	2305 ± 90
OxA-2691	OP/1/90	2170 ± 80
OxA-3200	OP/2/91	2080 ± 90
OxA-2738	OW/17/90	1060 ± 60
OxA-2739	OW/18/90	570 ± 60
OxA-2693	OR/2/90	300 ± 90
OxA-2694	OR/3/90	215 ± 100
OxA-2695	OR/4/90	295 ± 85
OxA-2688	UM/1/90	200 ± 80
OxA-2689	UM/2/90	205 ± 80
OxA-2690	UM/3/90	130 ± 80

When these dates are calibrated (Stuiver & Pearson 1986; Van der Plicht & Mook 1989) the results are as given in Table 25.1 and 25.2.

The three dates from Opi span the fifth to the second centuries BC, the two from Owerre-Elu fall in the tenth and the fourteenth centuries AD, and the six from Umundu and Orba cluster around the eighteenth century AD. These three groupings have therefore been referred to as the early, middle and late phases of iron-working in Nsukka Division. Morphological and microscopic analytical investigation led to the following conclusions concerning bloomery iron-smelting in this area:

1. Bloomery iron-smelting probably began around the fifth century BC, much the same time as at Taruga; the two sets of radiocarbon dates are not sufficiently discriminatory to say whether one or the other was earlier.
2. The technology was efficient in terms of iron extraction; very little free iron oxide was left in the slag, especially in the late period when extraction was more efficient in this regard than in the early period.
3. Smelting was conducted in various forms of slag-tapping, forced draught shaft

Table 25.1 Radiocarbon dates from Nsukka iron-smelting sites

Lab. no.	Sample no.	C14 date bp	SD	Calibrated dates*	
				One sigma	Two sigma
OXA-3201 Opi	OP/3/91	2305	90	520–200 cal BC	765–120 cal BC
OXA-2691 Opi	OP/1/90	2170	80	380–110 cal BC	400–20 cal BC
OXA-3200 Opi	OP/2/91	2080	90	345 cal BC–cal AD 15	370 cal BC–cal AD 75
OXA-2738 Owerre–Elu	OW/17/90	1060	60	895–1020 cal AD	810–1155 cal AD
OXA-2739 Owerre–Elu	OW/18/90	570	60	1300–1420 cal AD	1285–1435 cal AD
OXA-2688 Umundu	UM/1/90	200	80	1640–1950 cal AD	1490–1950 cal AD
OXA-2689 Umundu	UM/2/90	205	80	1640–1950 cal AD	1490–1950 cal AD
OXA-2690 Umundu	UM/3/90	130	80	1660–1950 cal AD	1640–1950 cal AD
OXA-2693 Amaoba	OR/2/90	300	90	1460–1950 cal AD	1430–1950 cal AD
OXA-2694 Amaoba	OR/3/90	215	100	1520–1950 cal AD	1450–1950 cal AD
OXA-2695 Amaoba	OR/4/90	295	85	1460–1950 cal AD	1430–1950 cal AD

*The dates were calibrated using the calibration curve of Stuiver & Pearson (1986) and the calibration program of Van der Plicht & Mook (1989).

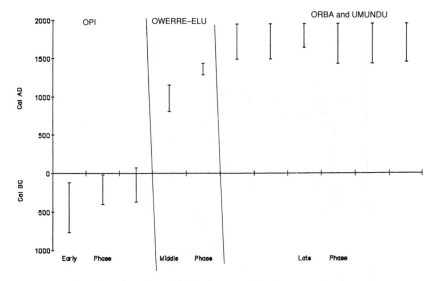

Table 25.2   Radiocarbon dates from Nsukka iron-smelting sites.

furnace in the early and middle periods, but in the late period these were replaced with self-draught furnaces in which the slag was not tapped as smelting progressed.

4. No pit or bowl furnaces were found. What were thought to be bowl furnaces (Anozie 1979) were discovered to be pits into which slag was tapped.

5. Local geothite and haematite were the ores smelted. Nsukka ores are rich in Al_2O_3 with significant levels of TiO_2. Initially the high presence of Al_2O_3 in the iron ores led to the use of high temperatures in smelting them; later, the temperature was lowered by the use of a sand flux.

6. Major mineral phases in Nsukka slags are fayalite, hercynite and wustite; minor phases present in some are glass, leucite and magnetite.

7. Nsukka slags have very low basicity; the smelters did not use any lime or lime-rich flux.

Ethnographic enquiry revealed the following:

1. The location of iron ores determined the siting of the industry; when ores were exhausted, smelting sites were relocated.

2. Bloomery iron-smelting was conducted by a specialized group of craftsmen, who moved from one site to another as ores became exhausted.

3. The smelters limited themselves to the production of blooms; they never refined or forged them, but sold them to smiths who carried out these operations.

4. The prevalent economic and political situation influenced the development of the various phases of the industry. For example, a shortage of labour in the late period may have favoured the adoption of the self-induced draught furnace.

Leja (Figs 25.1, 25.2) is a small town 14 km south of Nsukka which has the largest quantity of iron-smelting residues in southeastern Nigeria. They consist of cylindrical blocks with an average height of 28 cm, a diameter of 43 cm and weigh between 34 kg

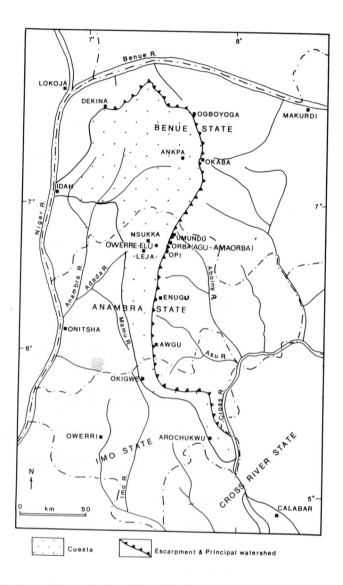

Figure 25.1 Some of the main sites mentioned in the text.

and 57 kg. There are more than 500 of these blocks in the Otobo Dunoka quarter of Leja (Fig. 25.3) (Anozie 1979, p. 125). During the ninth Panafrican Congress on Prehistory and Related Studies held in Jos in 1983, F. N. Anozie and K. Ray presented a paper on the bloomery iron-working at Leja and Umundu. They described innumerable furnaces containing a bowl-shaped matte of iron and slag left behind at the base (Anozie 1979, p. 125; Anozie & Ray 1983), suggesting that these represented stores or

Figure 25.2 Some of the main sites mentioned in the text.

reserves for an extensive iron industry or 'bloom bank' (Clark 1983, p. 1). Some disagreement with this interpretation was expressed at the congress, but until recently no attempt had been made to test this speculation by trying to forge tools from these iron-working remains. Early in 1991, however, the present author was able to collect samples for this purpose, after protracted negotiations with the chief priest of Leja, Eze-Leja (Fig. 25.4). In order to obtain the iron residues, it was necessary to provide certain items for sacrifices and the propitiation of the gods and, after the rituals, to accept samples collected by somebody appointed by Eze-Leja himself. The first two blacksmiths approached with the request to forge something from the specimens thus obtained from four different places (weighing between 1.5 kg and 2.8 kg) refused to attempt it on the grounds that the lumps were waste and not ore, and second that it would require too much charcoal. A third blacksmith, from Umundu, a town with a long tradition of iron-working (Anozie 1979, p. 129; van der Merwe 1980, p. 492), was eventually persuaded to make the attempt on condition that he was provided with however much charcoal might be needed (which in the event, cost the equivalent of £45 for all of the experiments undertaken) and that payment should be made for his services whatever the outcome.

Figure 25.3 Blocks of slag.

Figure 25.4 Eze–Leja and his advisers at the 'bloom bank'.

Table 25.3 Leja slag analysis

Wt % of oxides	Lej/1/90	Lej/2/90	Lej/3/90	Lej/4/90	Lej/5/90	Mean	SD
FeO	59.42	65.17	61.29	65.35	63.05	62.85	2.27
Al_2O_3	9.48	7.04	10.51	7.30	7.27	8.32	1.41
MgO	0.31	0.50	0.08	0.39	0.31	0.32	0.14
SiO_2	25.93	25.08	23.59	25.01	27.66	25.45	1.33
TiO_2	1.00	0.81	0.91	0.72	0.73	0.83	0.11
MnO	0.11	0.18	0.06	0.31	0.24	0.18	0.09
P_2O_5	1.32	0.95	0.95	0.63	0.65	0.90	0.25
CaO	1.41	0.11	1.54	0.07	0.07	0.64	0.68
S	0.18	0.08	0.18	0.10	NA	0.13	0.05
V_2O_5	0.05	0.04	0.21	0.10	NA	0.10	0.07
K_2O	0.78	0.04	0.68	NA	0.02	0.38	0.35
Total	99.99	100	100	99.98	100	100.10	
$\dfrac{CaO}{S_1O_2}$	0.05	<0.01	0.07	<0.01	<0.01	0.02	0.03
K	1.78	2.07	1.89	2.05	1.83	1.92	0.12
Melting Temperature	1180°C	1155°C	1280°C	1150°C	1160°C		

NA = Not Analysed
K = Viscosity Coefficient

Table 25.4 Leja slags: phase analysis

Sample number	Wt % of oxides	Fayalite	Hercynite	Wustite	Glass
Lej/1/90	FeO	65.42	48.20	95.40	41.10
	Al_2O_3	0.39	45.97	1.58	13.16
	MgO	0.22	0.32	0.55	ND
	SiO_2	32.94	0.82	0.85	30.32
	TiO_2	ND	3.62	1.60	1.42
	MnO	0.30	0.32	0.02	ND
	P_2O_5	0.34	0.27	ND	3.11
	CaO	0.35	0.03	ND	5.69
	S	ND	0.08	ND	0.87
	V_2O_5	0.04	0.14	ND	ND
	K_2O	ND	0.15	ND	4.31
	Total	100	99.92	100	99.98

ND = Not Detected

Table 25.5 Leja slags: phase analysis

Sample number	Wt % of oxides	Fayalite	Hercynite	Wustite	Glass
Lej/2/90	FeO	68.61	49.58	98.03	64.30
	Al_2O_3	0.60	46.82	ND	3.48
	MgO	ND	ND	0.20	ND
	SiO_2	29.99	0.57	0.66	17.79
	TiO_2	ND	1.73	0.53	0.65
	MnO	0.40	0.30	0.12	0.35
	P_2O_5	0.25	0.05	0.46	11.86
	CaO	0.06	ND	ND	0.69
	S	0.90	0.05	ND	0.82
	V_2O_5	ND	0.90	ND	ND
	K_2O	ND	ND	ND	0.06
	Total	100	100	100	100

ND = Not Detected

Attempts were made to forge iron from the four samples on four separate occasions, but in each case the result was the same: after sufficient heating, as soon as the sample was tapped by the blacksmith's hammer on the anvil, it shattered and the fragments were scattered around. It became evident that no tool can be forged from the Leja residues. They behave just like iron silicate slag, which softens and melts when subjected to high temperature. Confirmation that these residues are not blooms but lumps of slag was obtained by analysing samples under the scanning electron microscope at Sheffield University. The results of the bulk analyses of these samples are given

Table 25.6 Leja slags: phase analysis

Sample number	Wt % of oxides	Fayalite	Hercynite	Wustite	Glass
Lej/3/90	FeO	66.25	48.98	97.28	27.26
	Al_2O_3	0.50	46.98	0.26	12.07
	MgO	1.07	0.60	ND	0.20
	SiO_2	31.05	0.75	1.04	27.24
	TiO_2	0.20	1.95	1.12	0.89
	MnO	ND	0.08	0.04	0.10
	P_2O_5	0.26	0.12	0.02	11.86
	CaO	0.49	0.10	0.12	12.01
	S	0.04	ND	ND	0.94
	V_2O_5	0.12	0.44	ND	0.24
	K_2O	0.02	ND	0.11	7.19
	Total	100	100	99.99	100

ND = Not Detected

Table 25.7 Leja slags: phase analysis

Sample number	Wt % of oxides	Fayalite	Hercynite	Wustite	Glass
Lej/5/90	FeO	62.76	48.13	77.62	29.28
	Al_2O_3	0.89	48.02	15.23	16.56
	MgO	ND	ND	ND	0.36
	SiO_2	34.66	0.61	3.41	48.10
	TiO_2	0.24	2.83	3.60	0.23
	MnO	0.38	0.29	0.14	0.37
	P_2O_5	1.06	0.12	ND	3.17
	CaO	ND	ND	ND	1.68
	S	0.01	ND	ND	0.25
	V_2O_5	NA	NA	NA	NA
	K_2O	NA	NA	NA	NA
	Total	100	100	100	100

ND = Not Detected
NA = Not Analysed

in Table 25.3. Spot analyses of their individual mineral phases show that they are essentially fayalitic slags with some wustite, hercynite and glassy phases (Tables 25.4–7 show the analyses of the individual phases). The fayalitic phase makes up more than 60 per cent of the mineral constituents of each of the samples analysed (see Table 25.8). Normalized values of the major oxides in the bulk analyses plotted on the Al_2O_3–FeO–SiO_2 phase diagram show that the Leja slags have melting temperatures of between

Table 25.8 Mineral phases in Nsukka slag samples

Leja samples	Fayalite	Wustite	Hercynite	Leucite	Glass	Others
Lej/1/90	68% massive grey crystals	5% white dendrites	16% dark grey euthedral crystals	AB	11% dark siliceous pools	
Lej/2/90	85% massive grey crystals	AB	13% dark grey euthedral crystals	AB	2% dark pools in air holes	Thin bands of magnetite
Lej/3/90	66% massive grey crystals	6% white dendrites	18% dark grey euthedral crystals	AB	18% dark pools in air holes	Thin bands of magnetite
Lej/5/90	86% massive grey crystals	3% white dendrites	10% dark grey euthedral crystals	AB	1% dark pools in air holes	Thin bands of magnetite

1150°C and 1280°C (Table 25.3). This temperature range is within the melting temperature of bloomery slags (Morton & Wingrove 1969; Morton & Wingrove 1972; Tylecote 1987, p. 313).

An interesting result of the Leja slag analysis is the discovery of bands of magnetite that separate individual slag tappings (Figs 25.5, 25.6). Until now Leja iron-smelting has been described as having been conducted in a bowl or pit furnace and the residues as resembling furnace bottoms (Anozie 1979, p. 126). However, visual inspection of the external surfaces of these blocks reveals that they are made up of various layers (Fig. 25.7). These layers seem not to extend into the core of these blocks when they are fractured. This can be explained by the fact that the slag nearest to the walls of the pit cooled faster than that at the centre with a lower rate of heat loss. This meant that the outer parts of the individual tapping would almost solidify before the next tapping, while the centre was still molten. This results in the slag at the centre fusing with the next superimposed batch. The two layers fused together are impossible to distinguish with the naked eye; but under the SEM samples taken from the core of these blocks reveal individual layers separated by bands of magnetite, products of oxidation after the slag was tapped from the furnace before another batch was superimposed on it. The different mineral structures and texture observed on the opposite sides of the magnetite bands show that the slags had different cooling rates and temperatures, which further shows that they were formed under different conditions.

Leja iron-smelting, therefore, appears more likely to have been conducted with the same techniques as those used by the Opi smelters, where similar remains exist. At Opi a forced draught shaft furnace was used, with slag pits connected by channels at the base. Slag from the furnace was tapped intermittently from openings at the base of the furnace and run through the channels into the pits. The slag later solidified in the pits, giving rise to the cylindrical blocks that are observed at both Opi and Leja.

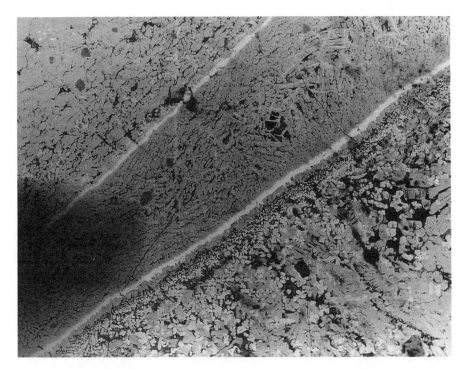

Figure 25.5 Thin white bands of magnetite (sample Lej/5/90) (scale 0.1mm).

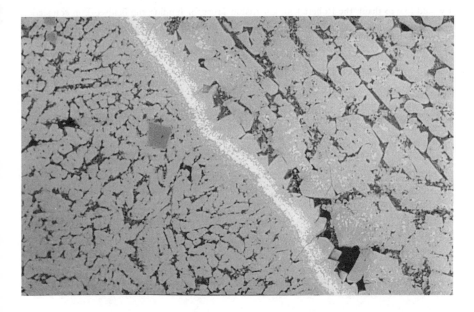

Figure 25.6 Thin band of white magnetite (sample Lej/3/90) (scale 0.1mm).

Figure 25.7   Layers of individual tapped slags (cm scale).

Acknowledgements

I would like to thank the Robert Kiln Charitable Trust for funding the fieldwork in connection with the tests carried out on the 'bloom bank', and the Oxford Laboratory for having provided accelerator dates.

26 Changing perspectives on traditional iron production in west Africa

FRANÇOIS J. KENSE & JOHN AKO OKORO

Introduction

For over a century, indigenous iron production in Africa has been the focus of considerable scholarship (see Cline 1937; Pearce 1969; Kense 1983c). The study of the iron industry has undergone several distinct phases – each reflecting specific interests on the part of the ethnographers and specialists concerned.

For most of the early years, the African evidence was generally interpreted as demonstrating 'living' examples of early forms of furnaces and techniques. This belief reflected the need to validate the evolutionary paradigm which saw a universal sequence of the major technological achievements. Detailed descriptions were made of both the technology used by smelters and smiths and of the cultural practice necessary to ensure a successful smelt. As the data tended to be sporadic and unbalanced in both their geographic distribution and their detail, this perspective invited erroneous conclusions as to the antiquity and importance of African metallurgy (e.g. Beck 1884, as referenced by, and supported in, Gowland 1912; Francis-Boeuf 1937; Arkell 1948; Mauny 1952).

The next phase saw an increased emphasis upon the ethnographic study of iron production, with more careful examination of both the construction of the furnaces and the components of the smelting materials. These studies often included measurements and diagrams of all aspects of the smelt. The phase is characterized by the first scholarly attempt to review and organize the available African data into a coherent study (Cline 1937). This and other more specific studies formed part of a larger pool of research that attempted a global synthesis of Old World iron-working (Forbes 1950; Coghlan 1956). It is clear, however, that there remained a number of implicit assumptions about African iron production that biased even these more careful studies.

One of the principal limitations imposed on these early studies of traditional iron production was the inability to establish a temporal framework for African traditions. The third phase, therefore, was characterized by the use of archaeology to determine both the antiquity of smelting and the location of the earliest production centres on the continent (e.g. Huard 1966; Fagg 1969; Willett 1971; Flight 1973a; Posnansky & McIntosh 1976; Calvocoressi & David 1979; McIntosh & McIntosh 1986a).

Concurrent with, and largely because of, this attention to the temporal record of iron-producing sites was a renewed interest in the metallurgical aspects of the process. Through a comparative analysis of the chemical properties of ore, slag and bloom, the physical and chemical changes in the material of the furnace linings and tuyères, the structure of the furnaces themselves and the effects of different types of draught arrangements, metallurgists determined a broad range of possibilities in the smelting techniques of pre-industrial societies (e.g. Tylecote, Austin & Wraith 1971; Tylecote 1976).

Over the past two decades, studies of traditional iron-working have become more complex and diversified. We identify four major lines of investigation. First, some researchers are concerned specifically with the overall historical impact of iron production within a particular region. This group examines the environmental repercussions of intensive metallurgical technology and seeks a better understanding of the complex interplay between this and economic and political factors that control of iron production entailed for particular societies, or their elites, in the past (Goucher 1981; Haaland 1985; de Barros 1988). Second, a methodical exploration of the extent of indigenous practices has sought to demonstrate that the knowledge and skill of the traditional smelters and smiths were far more sophisticated than had previously been recognized (Todd 1979; Avery & Schmidt 1979; van der Merwe & Avery 1982). This research has included extensive efforts to reconstruct the smelting process through re-enactments by individuals once familiar with the technology (Pole 1974a; Pole 1974b; David, Heimann, Killick & Wayman 1989). Third, the socio-economic and environmental repercussions of intensive metallurgical technology are closely examined. And fourth, the role and socio-economic importance of smelters and smiths themselves are studied within their own respective societies.

This chapter reviews these aspects, with particular emphasis on the most recent issues as they concern traditional west African iron production. The discussion is prefaced by a brief review of basic metallurgical principles regarding iron-smelting, a synthesis of the older ethnographic record and a summary of current interpretations of the relevant archaeological data. The vexing, and perhaps increasingly irrelevant, question of the origins of African iron-working is addressed at the conclusion of this discussion.

Metallurgical background

Traditional iron-smelting requires four elements: an iron ore; a combustible material (usually charcoal) to raise the temperature to a point where the iron ore is reduced; air; and a combustion chamber within which the whole process takes place. Smelting can produce one of several products in the furnace, each dependent on the quality of ore and combustible material used, the temperature achieved and sustained and the degree to which reduction takes place.

Conventional understanding of pre-industrial iron metallurgy determined that only two products were possible and that only one was usable for further work at the forge. Wrought iron, a spongy ferrous mass low in carbon ($< 0.1\%$ C) and relatively high in impurities, was considered the desired 'bloom' for traditional smelters. Wrought iron results from a furnace temperature of around 1150°C and is associated with a slag material that is generally not liquefied. Wrought iron is the product of direct reduction and is usually termed a bloomery process.

One of the more exciting results of recent metallurgical and archaeological investigation into indigenous African smelting has been the recognition that the production of a second type of iron was possible using 'traditional' technology. Although the production of steel had been suggested and even recorded by earlier researchers, it was not until the experimental work of Schmidt (Schmidt 1980; Schmidt 1981; Schmidt & Childs 1983; Childs & Schmidt 1985) and others (van der Merwe 1977; van der Merwe 1980) that it became clear that a medium content carbon (2–4% C) steel could be produced by non-industrial technologies (van der Merwe 1980). The requirement that the furnace achieve a higher smelting temperature of some 1200–1300°C was met through the practice of preheating the draught air through the tuyère by inserting the tuyère into the combustion zone of the furnace (Schmidt 1975). This discovery showed that steel was produced intentionally and not as a byproduct of a misdirected smelting process. It also demonstrated that a sophisticated technology had evolved around how to procure steel in the furnace as well as how to treat and fashion it in the smithing forge (see Okafor, Ch. 25, this volume).

The third type of product is cast iron, a hard and brittle mass that is high in carbon (> 4% C) and low in siliceous impurities and virtually unworkable by the smith with a traditional technology. The temperature required to produce cast iron ranges from 1400 to 1500°C and as a result usually yielded a vitreous slag run-off. As the product of a failed smelt, cast iron was usually discarded by the smelter. Recent work by David (David, Heimann, Killick & Wayman 1989), however, has demonstrated that traditional smelting may have intentionally produced cast iron, along with both wrought iron and steel, in a given smelting operation. More importantly, he shows that the smelter knew how to decarburize the iron appropriately to prepare the samples for smithing (David, Heimann, Killick & Wayman 1989, p. 198).

The recognition that pre-industrial African smelting could produce three types of usable iron products using indigenous technologies has only deepened our appreciation of the complexity of these technologies and heightened our awareness of the complicated interplay between such variables as furnace structure, selection and preparation of the ores and fuels, source of draught, types and construction of tuyères and smelting times.

Ethnographic record

A principal objective of the studies by Cline (1937), Pearce (1960), Mauny (1961) and Kense (1983c) was to summarize the known ethnographic data for smelting practices. As these works were based almost wholly on the available documentary evidence (and not on actual field observation), they relied heavily on the interests and expertise of the ethnographers reviewed. There was, consequently, a considerable emphasis upon the preparation of the ores, the construction and structure of the furnace, the type of bellows employed and the time involved in the actual smelting. Unfortunately, this information is often at the expense of details concerning the type of ores and charcoal utilized, the manufacture of the tuyère and its exact placement within the furnace and a careful description of the resulting position in the furnace of the bloom and slag after the smelting was terminated.

The focus of early ethnographers, and one that remains important today, reflected a desire to devise a classificatory system for African iron-smelting technology. Since any such system would inadvertently focus on the physical aspects of the process, such as furnace and bellow variations, it is not surprising that most conventional comparisons of iron practices have been based on typologies established from furnace construction or form (e.g. Klusemann 1924; Cline 1937; Forbes 1950; Coghlan 1956; Tylecote 1962; Sassoon 1963; Tylecote 1965; Williams 1969; Williams 1974). Most of these classifications distinguish furnaces as 'pit' or 'bowl', 'domed' or 'shaft' furnaces and often employ exotic names to establish 'types' (e.g. Catalan, La Tène, etc.). The basis for these terms, however, and their relative significance, are derived from European data and, as Sutton has recently pointed out, these designations have little value in Africa where a combination of elements can be found in a single furnace (Sutton 1985, p. 167). In the same publication, Pole selected a three-fold classification as exemplifying most recent systems and showed clearly how such a system is meaningless in the African context (Pole 1985, pp. 155–8). He went on to suggest that he could identify at least sixteen varieties of furnace construction in west Africa alone!

The primary weakness of these classifications lies with the heavy emphasis upon the structure of furnaces and the near absence of any consideration of the other variables involved in the smelting process. Although this is most understandable in an archaeological context, where little else of the process may be recoverable, it should not deter us from appreciating and acknowledging the complexity of the technology.

Archaeological evidence

Archaeologists have assigned the term 'iron age' to the chronological period associated with the use and/or knowledge of iron technology. As a result of such a broad distinction, iron age studies have encompassed a wide range of research interests. Only one of these has focused on the range and scope of smelting technologies.

Unlike the creation of the ethnographic record, in which observers deliberately concentrated on the primary physical characteristics of the smelt, the nature of the archaeological evidence has largely pre-empted consideration of much else beside furnace, tuyère and bellow types and a basic reconstruction of the primary metallurgical reactions.

Traditional archaeological investigations were concerned with two issues: assigning a particular technology to the established ethnographic classification and determining its place within a chronological scheme. Neither of these issues was addressed independently of the parameters set by current ethnographic and historical reconstructions.

Since archaeological classifications largely paralleled the ethnographic work, its evidence was interpreted as confirming what others had proposed. Inconsistencies in the archaeological data were not stressed or were viewed as reflecting an incomplete record. Furnace remains were described as 'pit', 'bowl', 'domed' or 'shaft', even if the remains were often too disturbed to indicate the overall structure or if the reconstruction did not quite seem to resemble any of the set types.

Archaeological data proved to be more substantive in providing a temporal framework for the development of iron production. Sites were eagerly sought which would extend the origins of African iron technology back to an ever greater antiquity. But even here the archaeological data were used to support the accepted chronological sequence, that envisioned iron metallurgical knowledge diffusing from the Near East and spreading throughout Africa from the north and northeast. It was the questions of the route and rate of this transmission into Africa that have remained the controversial issues.

The areas of Africa considered crucial for an understanding of the origins and diffusion of iron knowledge include north Africa (Mauny 1952), the northeast (Egypt and Sudan), the interlacustrine region of east Africa, various Saharan oases and the tropical forest zone of central Africa. Most of west Africa, therefore, does not figure prominently in *current* hypotheses on metallurgical development.

Two regions in west Africa (Fig. 26.1), however, have provided some clues to the antiquity of iron. One is the area of the Nok culture, which flourished in central Nigeria during the mid to late first millennium BC (Fagg 1969). This iron-producing culture used low shaft furnaces, of which several have been uncovered and described (Tylecote 1975b). Although the use of bellows is suggested on the basis of the furnace construction, none have been found (Tylecote 1975b; Tylecote 1976). The furnaces had a depression at their base for collecting the slag and it appears that the iron produced was of the direct bloomery type.

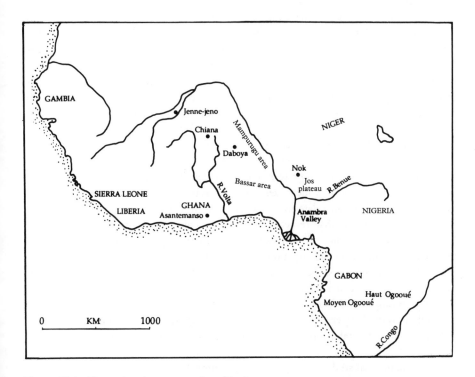

Figure 26.1 Sites and main areas mentioned in the text.

The second area lies in the Haut Ogooué region of Gabon, where smelting remains from at least two sites have been dated to the mid-first millennium BC (Digombe, Schmidt, Mouleingui-Boukosso, Mombo & Locko 1987). These dates are only slightly earlier than those reported from Moyen Ogooué which spanned the mid to late first millennium BC (Clist 1987b). Few metallurgical data concerning the smelting technology associated with these sites are available at the present time.

Evidence for smelting, or at least the presence of iron production, from a number of other sites across west Africa has often raised more questions than it has resolved. This occurs most frequently when the archaeological research is either directed to other issues or the record is largely incomplete, with the result that metallurgical details are often tantalizingly brief. This category includes work such as that at Asantemanso (Vivian 1990), Jenne–jeno (McIntosh & McIntosh 1980b), several sites in Niger (Grébénart 1987), Daboya (Shinnie & Kense 1989), Sierra Leone (Atherton 1979), Liberia (White 1974) and Gambia (Hill 1981).

But there has also been considerable research directed explicitly to finding and analysing information about iron production practices. This approach usually consists of a survey and subsequent excavation of furnace sites. Much information has accumulated concerning furnace construction and variety. Knowledge of details regarding the chemical and physical properties of the process itself (from the slag, furnace linings and the rare occurrence of residual iron bloom) has also greatly improved.

Some recent research will indicate the range of current scholarship. We identified three types of furnace structures from sites in the Mampurugu Kingdom of northern Ghana (Okoro 1989; Kense In Press). Only furnace types 1 and 2 made use of tuyères; furnace type 3 employed naturally induced draught. Only one group of furnaces resembled the straight standing type identified by Pole (1975b) from Chiana in northwestern Ghana. Interestingly, this furnace too had the tuyère and slag-tapping holes placed at the opposite sides of the furnace's lower section. Type 1 and 2 furnaces were low structures with upright shafts while type 3 had a larger rounded chamber over 1.5 m wide at the base. We await the dates for these furnaces, although one associated carbon sample dated to the mid-second millennium AD.

These latter furnaces have a general resemblance to the furnaces described by de Barros (1986; 1988) for northwestern Togo. He recovered numerous furnaces in the area of Bassar, many of which were of substantial size. These furnaces and the associated cultural remains date from the late first millennium AD through to the late nineteenth century. In that respect, they are probably contemporaneous with the Mampurugu material. Since de Barros was working in Togo prior to the Mampurugu research, his comments concerning the widespread distribution of Bassar iron products into eastern Ghana can now be challenged, as the Mampurugu area was undoubtedly an important iron-producing region in its own right and possibly just as extensive in its distribution range. The work in Bassar and Mampurugu has demonstrated the significant relationship between the iron technology employed, the control of the iron industry and the establishment of political structures in second-millennium west Africa.

Iron metallurgical studies of large smelting centres have increased in several areas of francophone west Africa (Echard 1983c). In Nigeria, the search for iron sites has intensified in several areas, particularly in the northern states. Investigators seem anxious to locate all three principal types of furnaces and are accomplishing that goal. Anozie has identified many iron-smelting sites across much of Igboland (Anozie 1979), while Okpoko has concentrated his research in the Anambra valley (Oguagha & Okpoko 1984). Jemkur has surveyed and investigated sites among the Berom people and their neighbours on the Jos plateau (1989) and suggests that the basic technologies employed by these groups have affinities with the Nok traditions. One of the observations that Jemkur makes is that many of the furnaces are constructed along stream beds (Jemkur 1989). We also found this to be a favoured spot for placing many Mampurugu furnaces (Okoro 1989). The extensive survey and excavations by David and the Mandara Archaeological Project in Cameroon demonstrated that the iron production technology described above could be documented in the archaeological record for several centuries (David & MacEachern 1988; David & Sterner 1989).

The reliability of the archaeological evidence for dating of early smelting sites has been challenged recently by Killick (1987). He suggests that in many instances of preparing charcoal for the smelt, the smelters used old, dry wood gathered from the ground. This has special significance for sites in the southern Sahara and Sahel where such wood may be of considerable age. The value, therefore, of this charcoal as a carbon sample to date the antiquity of a particular smelting site may be greatly misleading.

Ethnohistorical/ethnoarchaeological approaches

Recognizing the limitations inherent in the archaeological record, archaeologists renewed their interest in the rich source of information available in the ethnographic and historic records. This time, however, these records were viewed in the light of recent archaeological data.

A number of interesting studies have examined the archaeological evidence in comparison to the ethnographic record for a particular region and have been able to suggest that particular traits and forms of behaviour from the recent past can be attested in the more distant past (Sassoon 1963; Anozie 1979). Many of these studies have included a re-enactment of traditional smelts under 'real' conditions, thereby enriching understanding of the process and perhaps identifying traits that may linger in the archaeological remains (e.g. Pole 1974a; Schmidt 1974; Todd 1979; Childs & Schmidt 1985; David & MacEachern 1989).

Considerable attention is also directed towards appreciating the extent of smelting that the archaeological record manifests. Haaland (1980), de Barros (1988) and Okoro (1989) have all made estimates of the slag volume present at sites and on this basis have attempted to extrapolate the amount of charcoal, ore and iron bloom that may be represented by that slag. Okafor (1989) has also done estimates of the number of trees required weekly to provide fuel (1460 kg of hardwood) for the smiths now living in a Nigerian community and deduces an enormous figure (and see Okafor, Ch. 25, this volume).

Origins of iron metallurgy

It has long been a goal of researchers into the Iron Age to determine when and where
iron production began in Africa. From an initial belief that iron-working originated in
Egypt, to one that saw African smelting as an imported industry that remained
unchanged for a thousand years or more, current views place the growth of African
iron metallurgy within a development distinctive to a number of regions on the
continent. Although a number of archaeologists and others argue strongly in favour of
an independent origin of iron technology in Africa (e.g. Diop 1968; Andah 1979b),
most researchers feel the current data do not clearly support these claims (Huard 1966;
Kense 1985a; Close 1988; Shaw 1989). The chief obstacles to accepting an indigenous
origin for African iron-working include the lack of evidence for any pyrotechnologies
in sub-Saharan Africa predating the beginning of iron production (McIntosh &
McIntosh 1981), the absence of cultures demonstrating a transitional state between
dependence on stone and then iron for its technological basis (Sutton 1985) and the fact
that there has yet to be found a site that predates the beginning of iron production in the
Near East (Kense 1983c). In our view, the necessary data to confirm the position that
Africa was an independent centre for the discovery of iron production are not yet
available. We are increasingly uncomfortable, however, with the view that the accumulating evidence for technological diversity can be attributed only to adaptation of
introduced ideas (and see Okafor, Ch. 25, this volume).

Perhaps the reality lies somewhere in between. It is clear that iron-working technology, once introduced to various regions of Africa in a multitude of forms during the
first millennium BC, underwent a remarkable period of development and change over
the next two and a half millennia. This development, responding to differing environmental circumstances, the type of ores available, socio-cultural factors and economic
needs, resulted in the wide range of technologies that have manifested themselves in the
archaeological and ethnographic records. It is meaningless to speak of 'the development
of iron-working' in Africa, as if there was a single and uniform linear process of
development across the continent. Iron production has been a flexible and adaptive
technology, continually responsive to a changing natural economic environment.

The end of traditional iron-working

Although the iron-smelting industry has been defunct across west Africa for several
decades, it is clear that its demise did not occur at a uniform rate nor that common
causes existed for its demise. In fact, determination of the circumstances involved in the
cessation of iron production in different areas of Africa has become a significant field of
enquiry in itself, attracting the attention of a growing number of specialists.

Interest in the demise of iron production grew with the recognition that, although
imported iron was available to Africa from the mid-seventeenth century onwards, it
was not until the early part of this century that smelting finally stopped. If the
conventional view were true, that the imported iron was both 'cheaper' to buy and
'superior' in quality than the indigenously produced iron, how do we account for the

tardy disappearance of an intensive, time-consuming and risky enterprise such as iron-smelting?

One of the more controversial suggestions for this demise revolves around the effect that iron technology had on any particular environment. Even though ethnographers and metallurgists had long recognized the heavy demand for charcoal that iron-working made, few appreciated the environmental cost exacted by the cutting down of trees to prepare the charcoal. Haaland (1985), Goucher (1981), Shaw (1981a, p. 158) and de Barros (1986) have argued effectively for the destructive results tree cutting has produced in the areas of their research and have suggested that the extinction of certain tree species and even deforestation were not unlikely consequences.

Goucher (1981) indicated one possible evolutionary factor in the seemingly random variation of smelting techniques. She suggests that with the competition from European iron, indigenous smelters may have come under pressure to produce greater quantities of iron and to do so more efficiently in terms of the amount of ore and charcoal used. These considerations may account for the modifications noted in furnace dimensions, number and placement of tuyères and the development of preheating the forced air from the tuyères. These factors may also have affected the types of ores utilized, its preparation and the clays used in the construction of both the tuyères and the furnace itself. While this model is certainly attractive in relating general smelting developments to economic pressures, the interpretative significance is somewhat reduced by the evidence that preheating has a far greater antiquity than merely responding to European competition. This again shows how intricate are the variables controlling iron production.

A different approach has been proposed by Pole (1982). He places more emphasis upon socio-economic factors of labour input, price, the ritual value of local iron and the social organization of the iron-working groups themselves, in explaining the gradual disappearance of smelting. Indigenous production required a high level of skill and a heavy investment of time. If the market value was not sufficient to compensate such commitment by the smelters then there would be little encouragement of the industry.

The colonial regimes actively supported the importation of foreign iron into their areas of influence and helped to ensure that it was widely available. And precisely because of the quantity and the inferior quality of the imported iron (often mixed with sulphur to keep costs low (Goucher 1981)), the indigenous blooms were difficult to sell for an equitable price.

It is important to point out that the preceding discussion refers principally to smelted iron and not to the finished products of the smiths. It was the smith who finally determined whether he would continue to use locally smelted iron or turn to imported bars or ingots. Obviously, the two controlling factors for the smith would be the availability and price of the imported iron and a recognition of what the market would bear for his products.

It is obvious from the ethnographic record that smelting and smithing were two separate technical operations and that each was carried out by a distinct group of specialists. It is not at all clear whether the two activities were ever undertaken by the same individuals, at least not as a regular practice in the past.[1] Okoro (1989) observes that the smiths he interviewed in northern Ghana were clearly uncomfortable about smelting techniques, even though they thought that traditional smelters may have known the principles of smithing.

Conclusion

This chapter has shown that the emphasis in the study of iron production has broadened substantially over the past twenty years. No longer are researchers primarily interested in locating and dating a particular furnace or smelting site or in determining the furnace classification of a specific structure. As Pole (1985) has convincingly demonstrated, there is little need to view a static furnace classification as a meaningful or even desirable objective in interpreting technological variation. Other than serving as a general descriptive device for distinguishing one furnace structure from another, the use of terms such as 'domed', 'pit' and 'shaft' furnace has little significance in the understanding of traditional iron technology. There is no clear geographic or temporal importance associated with any of these types in the west African context. On the contrary, with additional archaeological work, it is increasingly clear that numerous types of furnaces coexisted in the same areas and/or in the same time periods. The significance of the 'discovery' of a new furnace type, therefore, is minimized (e.g. Ekechukwu 1989). This realization may surprise, and perhaps even distress, some archaeologists who are trying desperately to interpret the variability within some model of cultural determinism.

The confusing, and seemingly random, picture presented by the data is clearly not the fault of the archaeological record. Instead, it demonstrates that the research operated within a faulty paradigm which, consequently, posed questions inappropriate to the African data. The furnace structure and the type of bellows used are important attributes of the technology and comprise a key portion of the data for the archaeologist. They are not, however, an end in themselves, significant factors in understanding the development of iron-smelting within a particular society. The interplay between the natural environment (e.g. types of ore and hardwoods available, presence of water), local needs (range and quantity of iron goods required), regional and interregional trade potential (the markets), socio-cultural factors (how societies are organized) and political factors (who controls what) are all important in influencing the way in which a particular technology develops and changes. Seen in this way, each technology can be viewed as the unique response to a distinct set of variables.

The challenge, therefore, is to reconstruct, as well as possible, the societies within which iron production occurs. Through an analysis of the differences in the factors noted above, general correlations can eventually be identified between technological manifestations (e.g. furnace type, smelt process, use and placement of tuyères) and different types of west African societies.

Note

[1] In David's re-enactment (David, Heimann, Killick & Wayman 1989, p. 198) the smelter carries out some smithing as well.

27 Iron technology in the middle Sahel/Savanna: with emphasis on central Darfur

IBRAHIM MUSA MUHAMMED

Introduction

This chapter describes the development of iron technology and its achievements in central Darfur. Ethnographic observations, historical reports and archaeological evidence are used to present a historical perspective of iron-using and technology and its impact on middle Sahel/Savanna communities.

There has been a general lack of archaeological research in the region, with the exception of Lebeuf & Griaule (1947), Arkell (1951; 1952), Coppens (1965; 1969), Huard (1966), Lebeuf (1980), Connah (1981), Treinen-Claustre (1982), Musa Muhammed (1986) and Holl (Ch. 17, this volume). Such absence of research has made it vulnerable to scholars' speculations, especially in connection with food production, the rise of civilization and diffusion of iron technology. Because these were based on very little evidence, they produced a confused picture of cultural development in the region. This prompted the writer to undertake planned archaeological investigations in central Darfur in 1980–1 where, in selective surveys, forty-six archaeological sites were recorded (Musa Muhammed 1986). In many of them, evidence of iron-using and production was found associated with cemeteries, settlements and other structural remains.

The study area

The present study is confined to the area between the Nilotic and the Chadic basins, and to the Sahara (latitude 17°N) and the southern forested area (latitude 5°N) (Fig. 27.1). This region is rather flat, sometimes extending for hundreds of kilometres without major natural barriers. Exceptions to this are ranges of hills such as J. Miedob, J. Tagabo, J. Furrung and J. Marra/Si. The latter is the highest, being more than 3000 m above sea-level, and is a watershed mid-way between the Nilotic and the Chadic basins.

The surface is mostly composed of sand-dunes (known as the Qoz) which extend between northern Darfur and northern Kordufan, and westwards to join the 'ergs' of the eastern Sahara. To the south, where there is more rainfall and denser vegetation, the dunes are more stabilized and the soil is of clay-sand until it changes gradually to swampy, alluvial seasonally flooded clay plains around Lake Chad.

Annual rainfall is less than 100 mm in the north, increasing southwards to more than

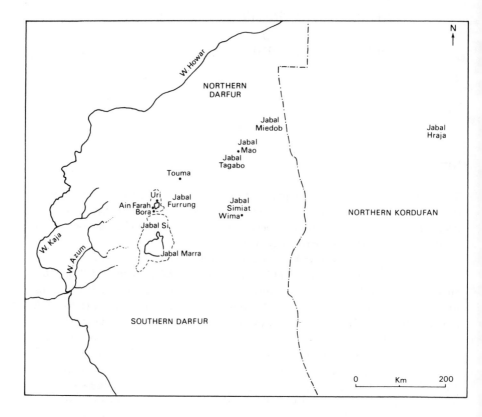

Figure 27.1 Darfur and its surroundings.

400 mm, mainly falling in the summer between July and October. The region has no permanent rivers, but is crossed by many wadi systems such as the Wadis Azum, Howar and Kaja. In the north the vegetational cover is rather sparse, consisting mainly of semi-desert shrubs and a few trees such as *Balamites aegyptiaca*, *Acacia nilotica* and *Tamarindus indica*. In the south, and with increasing rainfall and/or altitude, the vegetational cover becomes denser and gradually merges into savannah vegetation of richer grass and taller trees such as *Acacia albida*, *Acacia tortiles* and *Acacia sayel*.

Living in the north are nomadic and semi-nomadic groups who breed camels and have, to a large extent, similar modes of life. The centre, especially the highland areas, is inhabited by sedentary agriculturalists who cultivate grain (millet and sorghum), breed cattle, and have donkeys and dogs as their main household animals. In the south there are cattle nomads.

Traditional iron production in the middle Sahel/Savanna

The few travellers who visited the region before the early twentieth century (Browne 1799; al-Tunisi 1845; al-Tunisi 1851; Nachtigal 1971) gave some information about iron-using in the region, including iron tools and their production.

Browne (1799, p. 267) reported that iron ore was plentiful in Darfur and was smelted (and probably forged) by pagan negro people (probably indigenous) who were looked upon with contempt by the Muslims.

> The method by which I observed a workman supply the defect of a furnace for fusing metals appeared worth noticing. He had a leathern bag, which, on compression, forced the air through a wooden pipe for bellows, and placed over the fire, made in a small hole in the earth, the remains of a water jar, with which simple apparatus, the effect was rapid and not inconsiderable.

He also described the type of iron they produced as: 'soft and perishable, with increased trouble in renewing the edge, the tools formed of it answer all the purposes of their rude workmanship'.

Al-Tunisi (1845; 1851) referred to blacksmiths in Darfur, Wadai and Bornu as a hereditary caste. He said they were dishonest and, living mostly confined to their own community, did not mix with non-smith members of society. No ordinary non-smith would make marital links with them, and they were disliked by people in the region. Those of Darfur were traditional hunters who organized long-distance hunting groups for big game, such as giraffe, and sold the hides.

Nachtigal (1971) described smiths as despised groups confined to their caste in Bornu, Wadai and Darfur. He reported that smiths in Darfur and in Wadai were organized in 1873–4 under the Malik al-Hadaddin, minor officials who were responsible for all the smiths of these sultanates. They administered justice among them and collected taxes, in the form of iron tools. Such offices have ceased to exist, the last evidence for them in Darfur being in 1916.

MacMichael (1912; 1922) and Arkell (1937a; 1937b), who worked as Sudan Government officials in the region, confirmed travellers' remarks about iron-working and the position of those engaged in its production. More recently, Haaland (1985, pp. 55–6) asked local people familiar with the traditional iron-smelting process in Touma village in the Tunjur area of northern Darfur to carry out an experiment in iron-smelting, from quarrying of ore to collection of the smelted bloom, including production of charcoal, building of furnaces and smelting of ore. They dug a depression in the ground, the size of which depended upon the size of furnace required. For a large furnace the diameter of the depression is about 1.70 m and for a small one about 80 cm. A shaft about 1 m high is constructed above the depression with a wall thickness of between 4 cm and 5 cm. The number of tuyères (made of heavy red clay) also depends upon the size of the furnace; large ones usually have ten tuyères inserted around the middle of the shaft, and small ones about six. The furnace is broken after smelting and never reused.

The use of bellows seems to be similar to that described by Browne (1799) and to examples observed by the writer, currently used in Darfur and Kordufan for forging. The main type currently used in the region is a bag bellows made of tanned goatskin with two openings: one is attached to an iron pipe of 20 cm long and 5 cm diameter inserted in the charcoal or fire, the second with a wider opening is held by the person working the bellows. Two straight wooden slats are fixed to the second opening with leather straps for the fingers of the person who pumps air in, by squeezing the bag down and pulling it up continuously. When two bellows (also called double bellows) are used, they are placed very close to each other so the pipes lie touching one another. The two pipes are then inserted in a clay or wooden nozzle to hold them together. Sometimes a heavy stone is placed over them to make them more stable during the process of pumping the air (see Connah 1981, p. 161; Haaland 1985, p. 56, for photographs of double-bag bellows).

Haaland's observations seem to be very similar to a description of the smelting process as given to the writer by an informant (Hassan Hare) in 1980 in the J. Mao, suggesting that such technology was widespread in Darfur.

Another type of furnace very similar to the one described by Haaland is reported to have been in use in Kordufan in the nineteenth century (Wilson & Felkin 1882, II, p. 302); the only difference is that in Darfur bag bellows were used, while in Kordufan they were pot bellows. Pot bellows are sometimes called drum bellows, consisting of a round container made of clay or wood with a diameter roughly twice its depth. Its top is usually covered with a leather lid and it usually has one or two clay nozzles. When the skin is moved up and down the air blast is forced through the nozzles into the fire.

It is known that a high cylindrical furnace with bag bellows was in use in northern Chad until the beginning of this century. It was possible to reproduce this type using local expertise as late as the 1950s. Such furnaces are very similar to the Darfur one described by Haaland.

The historical and ethnographic observations described above suggest that iron technology in this area has remained similar for the last two hundred years. This apparent continuity between the historical and ethnographic data is regarded as a useful background which may illuminate the archaeological evidence of early iron production in the same ecological zone.

Evidence of early iron production

During 1979–81 the writer discovered three areas of iron-working in the hills of central Darfur, J. Tagabo, J. Si and J. Simiat (Fig. 27.1). In the first area twenty-five iron furnaces and a possible iron-forging area (no smelting furnace remains were found) were located at Mao; in the second an iron-working area was surveyed at Wima. Two others were found in Bora. These constitute the first archaeological evidence of early iron technology to be reported from Darfur.

More than twenty smelting furnaces were located by the writer at the southern end outside the walled settlement at Mao in the Tagabo range. All were of circular shape and built 3–4 m apart in an area of 150 m^2. The surviving remains revealed that each furnace had had a circular superstructure (50–80 cm diameter) with clay walls 5–7 cm thick projecting above the ground surface. Excavation of two of these furnaces revealed circular pits, 80 cm in diameter and 50–60 cm deep. The pits had been lined with clay and slightly smoothed by rubbing. The clay was about 5 cm thick. Although nothing is known about the upper parts of these furnaces (if they ever had any), the remains suggest a similar structure to that described by Haaland (1985). No tuyères were found complete or *in situ*, although fragments lay nearby. Some were well burnt and vitrified, and had slag fused on them, showing that they had penetrated the furnace wall.

Inside the furnace, iron slag was loaded with charcoal, layers of each lying alternately. These materials had probably been packed in this manner and then the whole fired with grass, as suggested by Haaland's experiment (Haaland 1985, p. 55). A charcoal sample from one of the furnaces has been dated to the first millennium AD (Musa Muhammed 1986). In the area surrounding the furnaces many small (7 × 3 m) heaps of slag, similar to those from the furnaces, were found distributed in an irregular manner. It seems that iron waste was thrown away within a specific area. The furnaces were probably not repeatedly reused, as Haaland's experiment suggests.

Evidence from central Darfur shows an iron-producing society with a fully developed iron technology and objects well integrated into different aspects of the life of the community. However, more evidence from stratified iron contexts is needed to show the relationship between non-iron-using and iron-using communities in the area.

Recently, research carried out by Treinen-Claustre (1982) confirmed that Toungour (north Chad) (Fig. 27.2) had been a very important iron-producing area, with extensive evidence for early iron production. The remains of the furnaces there are rather different from that of Darfur, having a separate chamber for slag collection. The only similarity is the presence of bag bellows. Differences in burial orientation and the appearance of brick building associated with the beginning of iron-using in the area are innovations which are difficult to interpret at present.

Koro Toro (Fig. 27.2) is an important iron-producing area. Iron slag in Bochianga (Koro Toro) has been dated to AD 450 ± 100, AD 935 ± 80 and AD 1220 ± 90 (Posnansky & McIntosh 1976, p. 193). These dates are important because the sites in this area have many mounds of iron slag which Arkell had guessed belonged to the ninth century AD (Arkell 1951; Arkell 1952). The amount of slag and remains of iron furnaces suggest that iron was in considerable use in the region; it is associated with pottery and stone structures, but more research is needed to understand the full impact of such a probable extensive use and production of iron here.

Daima (Fig. 27.2) is the best stratified site of the eastern Lake Chad area where the earliest iron object (a spearhead?) has been dated to the first century AD (Connah 1981, p. 156). It was found in a layer directly succeeding a layer of stone artefacts. Other levels associated with iron are dated to the fifth, sixth and eleventh centuries AD. Remains of iron slag in level 7 suggest that iron was probably produced there. Such evidence suggests that iron was the first metal ever to have been used in the area. Communities in this zone therefore appear to have moved directly from a stone-using to an iron-using economy without passing through any transitional period of using bronze or copper.

Mdaga Mound, 14 km north of Daima, is another important eastern Lake Chad site which reveals evidence of iron-using and working. Hoes and blades were the first iron

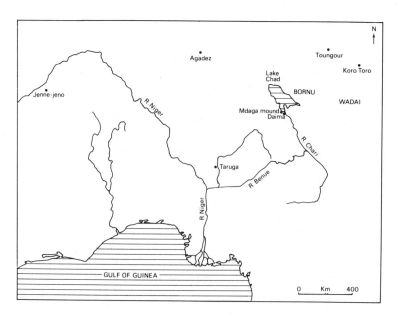

Figure 27.2   Main sites mentioned in the text.

tools to be found, in a layer dated to 200 ± 130 BC, above a layer containing only stone tools. Iron slag was also found in an upper layer associated with iron objects. The sequence of this mound suggests that there were some changes in the burial orientation when iron was introduced. For instance, the iron age dead are buried on a southeast–northwest axis instead of the pre-iron age practice of burying along a north–south axis. More data are needed to understand the factors behind such changes.

MacMichael (1922) reported remains of iron furnaces and great quantities of slag in the J. Hraja, Kordufan. The surface remains suggest that iron was probably produced in considerable amounts. Other important sites in northern Kordufan show evidence of iron-using associated with pottery and structural remains of large settlements, but they remain to be excavated. Several other localities in the border region between the Republics of Chad and Sudan, within this zone, show remains of an iron industry, but these also have yet to be excavated and dated.

A long-necked socketed hoe was excavated from a pit at Mao. It has an overall length of 17 cm, of which 14 cm constitute the neck. This is the oldest dated example of such a hoe, belonging to the first millennium AD. Several similar hoes were reported by Arkell from the surface of ruined settlements in Darfur which he dated to the thirteenth century AD. This later type was also found in north Kordufan (Penn 1931, p. 184) and further west in Senegal (Mauny 1961, p. 153). Such hoes are no longer in use in Darfur, having been replaced by small short-necked ones.

Three double-edged knives, around 12 cm long and 4 cm wide, were excavated from a Bora midden. These date to the first millennium AD. Knives similar to this one are still in use in Darfur and Kordufan.

A reaping knife (locally known as Tigidi) with a total length of 30 cm, with a right angle at each end forming points which could be fixed to a handle, was excavated from Bora. Another excavated example came from Mao. It is 9 cm long and 2 cm wide. They can be dated to the first millennium AD. Reaping knives of similar type were found by Arkell (1937b, p. 306) at Uri and elsewhere. He suggested that they might date to the sixteenth century and considered them very efficient tools for cutting crops. Similar tools were also reported from Kordufan (Seligman & Seligman 1932).

Several hundred iron beads were found in excavated graves at Bora. All of them are round and each has a central hole of less than 3 mm. They had rusted together. Some 210 examples of a similar but rather smaller type were found at Ain Farah. They are very reminiscent of a type of bead excavated from a grave at Daima (Connah 1981, pp. 150–1). At all three sites the beads were associated with bodies buried in contracted positions and belonging to the first millennium AD.

Four bracelets have been found in excavated graves, one from Bora being dated to the second half of the first millennium AD. Broken pieces of possible anklets were found beside the legs of a body in a grave at Bora and in another at Ain Farah.

Discussion

The material reviewed above has shown that there are close affinities between the traditional iron technology and artefacts of Darfur and Kordufan and those of the Chadic area and that they should be seen as part of the middle Sahel/Savanna tradition and may have a common origin. The beginning of iron-using in this zone was rather late in comparison with its neighbours. Nevertheless, the numerous mounds of slag and other remains of iron production suggest that this was an important zone for the adoption and development of iron technology. This was probably associated with environmental conditions which provided the vital elements for iron production, ore, fuel and clay.

In contrast, the origin and development of iron-using in this zone has been seen by archaeologists as merely transitional (Kense 1985a; Musa Muhammed 1986), with knowledge of iron technology deriving from one or other of its advanced neighbours, the Nile valley or west Africa (Arkell 1951; Arkell 1952; Mauny 1961; Huard 1966). Darfur has been considered the bridge between the Nilotic and Chadic basins through which iron technology was transmitted from Meroe to west Africa during the Christian era (Arkell 1951; Arkell 1952), but this is refuted by recent C14 dates (mentioned above), which suggest that the west African iron technology is as old as that of Meroe and made use of a different type of iron furnace. So, Darfur's iron technology does not seem to be of Meroitic origin.

Mauny (1978), in opposing Arkell's ideas on the grounds that there is no archaeological evidence of Meroitic iron technology in west Africa and that iron production in the latter area was earlier than the supposed dates for the diffusion, instead proposed that knowledge of iron-working had been disseminated from the north African littoral to west Africa, from where it spread to some parts of Lake Chad (Connah 1976).

Against the Meroitic hypothesis are the early dates for the west African sites. Most of them were contemporary with, if not earlier than, Meroe and no object of Meroitic origin has as yet come from excavated contexts in the area. Also, the suggestion that the Taruga furnaces have affinities with north Africa make the Meroitic hypothesis unlikely.

As long ago as the 1950s Lhote (1952), and more recently Andah (1979b), suggested that iron technology was achieved locally by indigenous groups in the area. Those who support local development accept the early dates of iron technology associated with Nok culture sites, but because these dates were obtained from alluvial deposits, some scholars now doubt their contexts and association with iron objects. Andah argues that iron technology in sub-Saharan Africa developed in a different way from that of Egypt because the metal in west Africa did not require a complicated method for its smelting and, consequently, the technology did not need to have evolved from a pre-iron copper or bronze metallurgy.

Other authors have suggested the idea that iron technology may have developed from the copper metallurgy of Akjoujt (e.g. Tylecote 1982). There is new evidence of early iron production in the same vicinity (Agadez) as copper production, dated to the beginning of the first millennium BC. As yet, however, there is no evidence to suggest that the Agadez copper technology was ancestral to iron-working in the area, indicating that west Africa had an 'advanced' pre-iron metallurgical tradition (see Okafor, Ch. 25 and Kense & Okoro, Ch. 26, this volume).

The region covered in this chapter shows many archaeological and ethnographic affinities with areas to the west and the desert to the north. Research in central Darfur has not revealed any affinities with the Nile valley (Meroitic or Christian), but has confirmed that the Darfur furnaces were similar to those of Taruga. Consequently, the earlier dates of iron production in the triangle of Agadez–Taruga–Jenne-jeno make this area an important region of iron production in its own right which badly needs further investigation in connection with iron production in the middle Sahel zone.

Finally, it must be realized that the possibility that iron technology came from outside the continent may not be in direct conflict with the position that it was invented locally by African communities. Iron-working could have developed locally and also diffused to neighbouring areas within a zone where perhaps the most serious barriers restricting movement of ideas and people would have been socio-political ones (McIntosh & McIntosh 1983, p. 216; McIntosh & McIntosh, Ch. 37, this volume).

Conclusions

The adoption of iron seems to have affected the environmental conditions and changed the vegetational cover of many parts of the zone (Haaland 1985). According to some authors, the resulting massive deforestation of some areas caused depopulation (e.g. Agadez area, Grébénart 1983), and possibly caused the decline of some political powers such as the Kingdom of Mema (Haaland 1980).

The distribution of iron remains suggests that iron-working was carried out in specific areas, perhaps already by organized groups within the communities. Such restriction of first-millennium AD iron-working remains to special areas in the surveyed sites suggests a rather low status for smiths and may be signs of the beginning of an endogamous group in central Darfur society at that time.

Iron technology may have brought about changes in other areas of material culture (see also Rowlands & Warnier, Ch. 32, this volume). It could have been used for quarrying and/or digging stones for building such huge structures as the platforms at Mao, Wima and Uri. In the well-stratified site of Daima a round mud building was found for the first time associated with a layer which showed evidence of iron-using, while layers beneath this revealed only grass and wood buildings. Potsherd pavements were found for the first time associated with a layer which showed evidence of iron-using (Connah 1981, p. 148). This may reflect that iron-using was associated with new trends in building techniques in the zone; however, more data are needed to substantiate such a suggestion.

Iron-making techniques in the Kivu region of Zaïre: some of the differences between the South Maniema region and north Kivu

N'SANDA BULELI

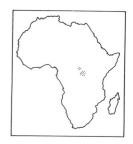

Introduction

In Kivu, according to most traditions, the people of the region had mastered iron-making before their arrival in this part of Zaïre. Given the use of a rich variety of techniques, including prospecting, reduction and manufacture of tools, two principal iron-making methodologies can be identified, corresponding to two areas: (a) the Maniema area, where the main characteristic is a smelting apparatus cut into the ground; and (b) the interlacustrine area, where the main characteristic is a raised round smelting apparatus made of bricks.

In May 1984 a research team from the Kivu University Research Centre reconstructed the methods of smelting iron practised by the Banyabwisha or Hutu from the Rutshuru area, and this information was correlated with oral information recorded among the Mamba–Kassenga and Benye–Mikebwe in South Maniema in July 1983.

Prospecting

Nature and method of prospecting

Prospecting in the two areas shares one important feature: it was never carried out systematically. Much was left to chance and tradition and was not practised on a regular basis. Intuition and empiricism played substantial roles. There were no systematic methods of detecting sites.

The first important differences concern those involved in prospecting activities. The Mamba-Kasenga from the Kasongo area had no specialist ore prospectors. Everyone helped. This was probably due to the proximity of deposits which could be found on the slopes of Mt Mwanakusu in the northeast of Kasongo. The ore was easily recognizable as heavy, black stones often found on the surface. The Benye-Mikebwe, from the Kabambare area, on the other hand, had a group of specialist 'ore hunters', the Bayazi. A similar group was known as the Abacuzi by the Banyabwisha. This, however, was a group without common goals or common interests – for example, each individual Bayazi kept what he found. In Bwisha, the right to prospect was limited, deposits being considered the property of the landowner on whose land they were found. This is the chief differentiating factor between the South Maniema deposits and those of the interlacustrine area. The former were collective in character, belonging to the entire community, whereas the latter were, in essence, privately owned.

Location

Deposits were usually found on mountain sides and never in valleys or on the floodplains of rivers, as in North Maniema. In the Rutshuru area, lacking rivers, there were no alluvial deposits.

Signs

The Mamba-Kasenga and others recognized deposits by the size, shape, weight and colour of the stones (*matadi*), which were, in fact, black and heavier than ordinary stones. The Banyabwisha made a distinction between two kinds of ore: *buro*, dark blue in colour and shiny; and *kanyenga*, reddish in colour. The Benye-Mikebwe, however, looked for chalky rock, or traces of it in the soil, as a guide to the presence of deposits; dead or dying grass was similarly seen as a good indicator. The Banyabwisha also considered the presence of dwarf reeds to be a sure sign of a deposit. The presence of these dwarf reeds on a mountain, coupled with dry soil, led them to believe that a deposit existed.

Prospecting instruments

There was a considerable assortment of tools, most being for both prospecting and extraction and often for certain domestic tasks such as sowing, hunting and fishing. The Mamba-Kasenga used picks and iron bars; the Benye-Mikebwe used a very hard wooden stake, which they called *musolo*; and the Banyabwisha used a hoe.

Grade of the ore

The grades of ores varied from site to site. In some places large rocks were found, in others only small stones. The Banyabwisha prized the large, blue-coloured rocks (*buro*) above the reddish ones (*kanyenga*) which, according to them, produced iron of an inferior quality.

Rites and taboos

Sexual abstinence was widespread among most of the Kivu peoples for all metallurgical activities including prospecting, extraction of ores, their reduction and forging. For the Benye-Mikebwe, this sexual ban was rigorous and lasted throughout the prospecting period. In addition, the prospectors would sacrifice a chicken before departing on a search, to increase the chance of success. For the Mamba-Kasenga and Banyabwisha, on the other hand, where supplies of ore were abundant, prospectors had no such prohibitions. The discovery of a deposit gave rise to great celebrations, in the course of which goats were strangled and prospectors drank banana beer.

Season

The dry season was the most favourable for prospecting, allowing other production activities, such as hunting, to be carried out in other seasons. When the need arose, however, as in time of war, prospecting and extraction could be carried out at any time of year.

Extraction

Methods of extraction

The method of extraction depended on the morphology of the terrain. In some cases, a simple pit of the necessary depth was dug. However, for mountain deposits, galleries were cut. At Bwisha, for example, a tunnel was dug into the mountainside where a seam was located, reaching a maximum depth of 30 m. However, because of the dangers inherent in this sort of operation, miners preferred to dig vertical shafts. Elsewhere, however, extraction took place in the open, either by collecting blocks of ore protruding from the surface of the soil, as was done by the Benye-Mikebwe, or by wearing away the ground, as in certain Bwisha deposits. In the latter case, the miners started at the bottom of the hill or mountain and worked upwards.

As far as the organization of labour was concerned, all societies relied on teamwork, but with different motives. In Maniema, extraction involved the entire family. Moreover, the legal status of the deposits recognized exploitation by the whole community. Teamwork here reflected more the solidarity of the clan or family than gain. In the deposits of the interlacustrine areas, on the other hand, exploitation was a personal affair. At Bwisha, for example, all deposits belonged to the landowner, who owned all rights of exploitation. Thus relationships between the miners reflected only the interests of the individual. The next logical step was then payment for the rights to exploit deposits. Each miner looked for his own ore. Not necessarily being a smelter, he could sell the fruits of his labour to dealers or to smith-smelters. Such a way of working made the miner appear as an independent worker.

Transportation of the ore

As soon as the ore had been extracted and cleaned, it was transported to an appropriate place, either to huts equipped for just this purpose or to the foundry itself. The Mamba-Kasenga put the ore into *itumbi*, the smelter's shed, and the Benye-Mikebwe into *yazu*, the smith's shed. The Banyabwisha stored their ore in huts called *imiririmbo*. Each smelter had his own huts. The ore had to be protected against rain, which, according to tradition, could adversely affect its quality at the time of smelting, and also against spells. In certain parts of Bwisha, ore was also stacked in the open air, in holes called *agitabiro:* this practice, according to custom, permitted the regeneration of the ore.

The task of transportation was usually left to women, although men did help out if the need arose. The ore was put in reed baskets (called *mwembo* by the Mamba-Kasenga) or baskets made from creepers (*mu'umbila* to the Benye-Mikebwe), which were then carried on the head or back, or alternatively, as was done by the Bwisha, placed in carrying hammocks made from strips of bamboo. Among the Banyabwisha, for whom extraction was a matter of individual enterprise, the transporters, who were also often the excavators, had a list of prices for transportation: one load for between one and three goats, or for *ubutega*, bracelets made from vegetable fibres, or even for certain iron instruments.

Extraction instruments

Among the Mamba-Kasenga and the Benye-Mikebwe, prospecting tools doubled up as tools of extraction. The Banyabwisha, however, employed a range of specific instruments: *ifumi*, a sort of worn-out hoe, *imihunda*, a spear tip used as a mine bar, *iserieri*, a metal tool used for leverage, and a series of heavy hammers of which the *impuro* was one.

Protection of deposits

In general terms, the way in which deposits were protected depended on the juridical nature of the estate. In Maniema, for example, where ownership was collective, the deposits were under the protection of the chief of the clan or group of clans. Other tribes were denied access under pain of war. Thus, each community put in place an infrastructure to protect its deposits. The Mamba-Kasenga and the Benye-Mikebwe combined this activity with hunting, agriculture and gathering, thus allowing the land to remain under constant surveillance.

In the interlacustrine areas, on the other hand, in particular among the Bwisha where deposits were privately owned by estate owners or the *mwami*, security was ensured by guarding the sites day and night. The exploitation of deposits and the transport of ore were normally carried out in the dry season, avoiding accidents, landslips and shaft flooding.

Preparation

Ores

Having been pulverized with a hammer, the ore was then washed and dried. Drying often consisted of heating by building a fire on top of it. Among the Banyabwisha, such grilling was carried out in the same apparatus as the smelting itself. Ore was usually prepared the day before reduction.

Charcoal

Charcoal was prepared several days before smelting, the process being the same for all Kivu peoples: tree branches were removed and then placed in a specially dug ditch, then incinerated. Care was taken to cover the ditch completely so that the wood burned without air. The Mamba-Kasenga used the *kaluma* tree, and the Banyabwisha the *umugimbu*. The Benye-Mikebwe, in contrast, did not use charcoal, their system being to heat the ore to melting point together with the dried wood of the *muzim'yezu* tree.

Construction of the furnace

Maniema type

We shall concentrate on two types: the Mikebwe from the Kabambare area and the (Mamba-)Kasenga version from the Kasongo region. With reference to the Mamba-Kasenga group, the Mamba specialized in forging, whilst the Kasenga concentrated on smelting. The Kasenga could have developed smelting skills (which they had, more-over, learnt from the Mamba) because they were based near the Mwanakusu deposits, whilst the territory of the Mamba lacked such deposits. For this reason the former refused the latter the right to exploit their deposits, fearing that the Mamba, should they become too rich, might constitute a potential threat. The one group comple-mented the other, since one produced the iron and the other forged.

The Kasenga furnace was called *nyungu*. It was usually cut into a level area. It included a circular pit, approximately 50 cm deep and 40 cm across, dug on a fairly wide terrace, to provide shelter for the bellows (Fig. 28.1). This central pit served as a hearth inside which the reduction process took place. This furnace had only two pairs of bellows, positioned opposite one another.

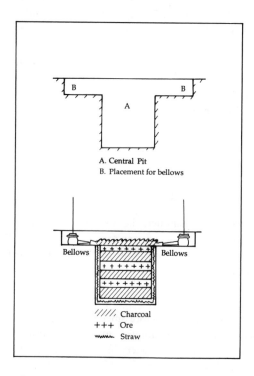

A. Central Pit
B. Placement for bellows

Bellows   Bellows

///// Charcoal
+++ Ore
www Straw

Figure 28.1 Kasenga furnace.

The Benye-Mikebwe furnace was called *nyundu*. It was a raised furnace cut inside a termite hill. This comprised a central shaft approximately 1.5 m high, open at the top and from the bottom of which three small channels ran off towards the exterior (Fig. 28.2).

Interlacustrine areas

The Banyabwisha call high furnaces built in brick, of loam, marl or clinker, *uraganda*, having the following characteristics (Fig. 28.3):

> Form: conical.
> Material used: loam reinforced with marl.
> Number of pipes and bellows: 20 units.
> Description of base: central hole dug in the ground, above which the
> furnace was erected.
> Dimensions: 30 cm deep, 1 m diameter at base and 60 cm at top.

A furnace was built by a team from the Kivu University Research Centre in a single morning, although certain preparations could be made the day before. The round pit was dug, then ferns burnt in it and the ore, which was to be smelted the following day, dried. After the ferns had been lit, the nozzles were put in position and the masonry construction then built. In theory, the fire was supposed to smoulder all night underneath straw before construction began the following day, in order to allow the loam to dry before smelting commenced.

All building work was directed by a specialist, with the aid of assistants. It was he who made the plans and he who modified them to increase efficiency. For the most part, builders relied heavily on models they had seen in the past.

Reduction process

Reduction processes usually began very early and lasted between five and eight hours. The operation began with a religious ritual: this included the sacrifice of an animal, anointing of the furnace with the animal's blood, and an invocation to the spirits. Directly afterwards charcoal was loaded and lit. Among the Banyabwisha, a first layer was tipped in which, coming into contact with the fire which had been smouldering in the hearth since the day before and encouraged by the bellows, caught alight immediately. The furnace was then filled to the top with alternate layers of charcoal and ore. At the same time, the bellows were being worked flat out and would not be stopped until reduction had taken place – the reduction being judged by the molten ore coming out of the nozzles. Once the smelt had subsided, work stopped and the smelt was broken into to gain access to the metal. However, the iron obtained in this way was not pure. It was, in fact, of such mediocre quality that it had to be reworked in the forge.

The Kasenga began by covering the walls of the pit with a coating of dry straw. Then the alternate layers of charcoal and ore were loaded. After the fire was lit, a creeper (species unknown) known as *muzi wa nyungi* or *kakulamuna* was hung over the hearth. According to local belief, the sap of this creeper was supposed to help in the reduction

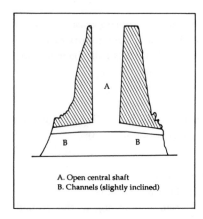

Figure 28.2   Benye–Mikebwe furnace.

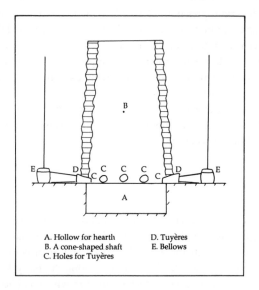

Figure 28.3   Banyabwisha furnace.

of the ore. The sign of fusion was the drop in volume of the material contained in the furnace bowl. Furthermore, the smelter pushed in a rod to check and confirm that reduction had taken place. The bellows were then stopped and the fire allowed to go out, so that access could be gained to the reduced metal.

The Benye-Mikebwe began by covering the bottom of the pit with a bed of pieces of wood, which was in turn covered with a thin layer of earth. Then the ore, which had been crushed and heated beforehand, was loaded. Finally, wood was placed on top and lighted. As there was no charcoal or bellows, the principal task was to ensure that the furnace was always full of wood, thus maintaining or increasing the intensity of the fire. This operation could last the whole day and required considerable perseverance. Reduction was known to have taken place when a thin thread of glowing metal flowed through the run-off channels.

The Mikebwe furnace has a twofold advantage: first, the metal is easily collected as it runs off to the exterior; second, it could be reused, in contrast to the Banyabwisha and Kasenga versions. On the other hand, it was fairly labour-intensive, especially the feeding of the fire.

Forging

Tool-making

As soon as the metal was taken out of the furnace, it was given to the smith who worked it and who had to produce the necessary tools. Often, however, the same specialist was responsible for both smelting and forging, except among the Mamba-Kasenga group, where the former were the smiths and the latter the smelters.

Location

In contrast to the foundry, which was located outside the village, the forge was always a part of it, most often being housed in a shed-like construction with a thatched roof and a hearth in the middle. Among the Mamba and the Benye-Mikebwe it was situated next to the smith's hut. In Bwisha, the building took the form of a hut with a conical roof made from the bark of a banana tree. Two wide doors on either side of the building facilitated ventilation and allowed rapid evacuation in case of fire.

People working in the forge

The forge was most often manned by a master smith, a bellows operator and a hammerer, all members of the same family. However, other families were often able to send them apprentices, providing some sort of payment was made. There were, among the Mamba, two sorts of smith: the *sendwe*, the master smith, a specialist in the use of all tools, and the *mutumbi*, who only made certain tools. Both used a bellows operator (*mukuluti*) and a *mushitahi*, a hammerer. They also employed an apprentice, *mutushi*, to run errands. The same three roles existed among the Banyabwisha:

umerakera:	master smith;
umubenzi:	hammerer and errand boy;
umuvuguzi:	bellows operator.

Tools

The same basic tools were used in all traditional forges in the Kivu although local variations are apparent:

Bellows: usually a light piece of wood, roughly triangular in shape with two cavities in the base, into which led two converging tubes. A gazelle or sheep's skin covered the two cavities, thus forming two air pockets. A rod was attached to each of these, in order to work the apparatus. The Banyabwisha used a variety of clay bellows.

Nozzle: a cylindrical piece of baked earth placed in front of the bellows to compress air.

Hammers: several different kinds, made either of iron or very hard earth. Among the Banyabwisha they were named according to size and purpose:

> *impuro:* hammer-block used to beat or shape the iron;
>
> *umwangate:* smaller hammer used to finish instruments;
>
> *wgarushora:* medium-sized hammer used as an anvil in the production of arrows, spears and swords;
>
> *indangato:* hammer with four facets used for more delicate work;
>
> *mupunduriro:* hammer intended to shape iron spear points.

The peoples of South Maniema used two main categories: a very hard stone mass (*nyundo, nondo, musanya*) to beat the iron (in contrast to the interlacustrine area, where an iron hammer was used) and a series of small iron hammers (*ihama, nkondo*) for detailed work and finishing.

Anvil: usually a large, very hard stone, more or less flat and smooth taken from a river bed. Among the Banyabwisha the anvil consisted of a block weighing several kilograms which had to be transported over long distances (from the streams flowing down from the Mikeno volcano in Busanza or at Jomba in the streams of Nybugendo).

File: a very hard stone with a flat and ridged surface. Stone files are still found among the smiths of Maniema, where they coexist with iron ones brought by colonization.

Tongs: made from two strips of iron or wood fixed to a handle. A piece of wet cloth, skin or bark was wrapped around it when in use at the forge. The Benye-Mikebwe used palm branches split down the middle. The Banyabwisha had a tool which they called *inbirindi by' ibiti* made from the roots of forest plants called *imisa* and *imufumzo* (species unknown).

Chisel: usually in the form of a piece of iron with a very sharp tip and without a handle and used to divide up the iron and to make reliefs, drawings, etc. The Banyabwisha used a sort of billhook called an *agachero* or *impango*.

In addition to this equipment, which was widespread throughout the region, there was also an assortment of tools peculiar to each group. The Banyabwisha, for example, used an *urugarama*, an iron rod with a handle and a rounded end, to unblock the nozzles during smelting. They also used an *ikizimo*, a sort of spray made from banana-tree fibres and fitted with a handle, used to put out the fire or to lessen its intensity, or to wet the iron before heating or beating. During forging the smith also used the dust of a soft rock, called *imongi*, which was thrown into the hearth of the forge at regular intervals to soften the iron and thus to reduce the number of tools which were broken or cracked.

Most tools for forging were made by the smith himself but certain equipment was only produced by specialists. The specialist smiths of the Banyabwisha worked the *impuro* for at least five days, on a special anvil. Moreover, the manufacture of hammers was so time-consuming that they were very expensive; in Bwisha, for example, their prices varied between ten and fifteen cows.

All the instruments used in the manufacture of iron were tempered. The technique involved consisted of heating the tool until it was white hot and then, already shaped, it was plunged into cold water. The Mamba used salt water and added a little oil. Hammers were worked even after smelting. Among the Banyabwisha, for example, a ball of iron was heated until it turned red and then hammered on the anvil. This hammering gave it its final shape and it was then retempered, in the same way as among the Mamba, to harden it.

Conclusion

The above review has revealed two distinct communities. The reduction techniques practised in Maniema differed from those of the interlacustrine areas. The former are characterized by raised furnaces, the latter by circular masonry constructions. The Maniema hunters and farmers possessed, as far as metallurgy was concerned, a culture of their own which differentiated them from the interlacustrine regions, the majority of whose population were herders and farmers.

Despite this diversity, however, both groups shared certain common techniques: for example, prospecting techniques; those used for ore extraction; and tool manufacture. Indeed, certain tools are found in both cultural entities: bellows, nozzles and forge equipment. There was, therefore, a certain amount of technological borrowing between these peoples, but it would be premature to suggest that they may have had a common origin.

29   Ancient iron-working in Madagascar

CHANTAL RADIMILAHY

Even though traditional iron-working is still an honoured profession in Madagascar, there has been no detailed ethnographic study made of this tradition and its practitioners. Yet such studies could help resolve many enigmas concerning metallurgy that are facing archaeologists more and more frequently in their investigations of Malagasy prehistory, as shown in a recent compilation of the evidence (Radimilahy 1988). This chapter assembles and presents a résumé of what information is currently available from various sources on this subject. These sources include historical, ethnographic and technological information and a series of unpublished results from recent archaeological work in the southern region and the central highlands area of Madagascar.

The observations made by early voyagers to Madagascar on the use of metals, and less frequently on the technology of metal-working, while superficial and haphazardly scattered through their writings, do nevertheless afford some insights into this aspect of Malagasy cultural history (see Radimilahy 1988 for detailed references). European explorers were particularly interested in the armaments of the early Malagasy. Many of these early explorers, driven by dreams of commercial profit, certainly came to Madagascar in search of iron and other metals. The later the account the more precise becomes the information contained in it and the more detailed become the observations on technology. Among other things, the information contained in these accounts allows us to compare ancient metallurgical practices with those presently practised by traditional specialists on the island.

If one accepts the postulate that there has been a continuity of Malagasy cultural practices over time, then we can use information obtained about the contemporary practice of metallurgy to help in the interpretation of archaeological remains. Consequently, it has been possible to reconstruct aspects of a number of archaeological sites that show evidence of metal-working (Radimilahy 1988). Some of the archaeological features found at such sites bear a striking resemblance to contemporary furnaces found among the Merina and Betsileo of the highlands. Such material culture correlates between past and present societies suggest that iron-working was part of the cultural repertoire from the time of the first peopling of the island (Radimilahy 1988).

The social organization of metal-working societies is a reflection of a philosophy that also finds expression in oral literature. This philosophy involves an attitude of both distrust and respect on the part of society towards iron-working specialists. Traditional ideology proposes that originally metalworkers were the aristocracy of society, but they fell from this social position after having committed an offence against the prescriptive rules of the social order. One finds such conceptions among most groups in Madagascar, whether this be the Amoronkay, the Betsileo or populations in the extreme south of the island. Such ideology is not without parallels on the African mainland.

There are certain similarities between Malagasy and African iron-working technologies, although linguistic evidence points to a critical contribution to Madagascar from southeast Asia. To this initial contribution Islamic populations added their part in the development of workshops and trade. Trading outposts on the island ensured the integration of Madagascar into the international commercial network of the Indian Ocean and probably stimulated the development of iron technology (Vérin 1986).

At a time when the depth of Malagasy prehistory was as yet unsuspected, Decary posed the problem of the origins of metallurgy in Madagascar in surprising terms:

> Ironworking found across the island is remarkable because of the double pistoned bellows for the furnace. Metallurgy would have been introduced by Malaysians during their earliest migrations . . . it would have been king Andriamanelo who taught his subjects, during the sixteenth century, how to work metal, and how to make spears 'that fly and that kill'. At the same time the locals began to manufacture axes: they could thus build canoes to replace rudimentary rafts of bamboo. At least, this is as legend has it.[1]
>
> (Decary 1951, p. 157; translated from the French)

During the last twenty-five years, archaeological research carried out by the University of Madagascar has shown that the origins of Malagasy culture go at least as far back as the end of the first millennium AD, and that the arrival of Indonesians was not a late phenomenon (Vérin 1986; Dewar 1987; Wright & Rakotoarisoa 1990). Furthermore, the Indonesian ancestors of the Malagasy had contact with Bantu-speaking peoples who, like themselves, already at that time had a knowledge of iron-working.[2] In addition to the archaeological evidence from numerous sites showing that iron-working was already known very early on the island,[3] it is worthwhile examining the various cultural influences that could have contributed to Malagasy traditions of metallurgy.

Madagascar, an area of contact between different peoples and civilizations, was a natural meeting place for various techniques and traditions of iron-working. Though Indonesians contributed to the peopling of Madagascar, the precise location from which Indonesian migrations took place is as yet undetermined. It thus makes sense to look for the roots of Malagasy metallurgical traditions in peninsular southeast Asia as well as in the adjacent archipelago.

Continuing work on contact with Indonesia (e.g. Van Heekeren 1958) was relatively unconcerned with metal usage except for the problem of the provenance of imported bronze drums. Recently, Glover (1990) has suggested that bronze could have appeared in Thailand as early as the late third millennium BC, and quite definitely by the mid first millennium BC. Trade relations in the region began during this period, with Indonesia and India supporting an extensive exchange network by the late first millennium BC (Glover 1990). This trading system with its associated circulation of goods eventually led to the florescence of Indian commercial relations during the early centuries AD and the beginning of Indian influence in southeast Asia dates to this period.

A little before the beginning of the Christian era, iron-working was known in peninsular southeast Asia and it subsequently spread to Indonesia. The technique, later called 'Catalan', made its appearance first in India and Persia. Iron was smelted directly in a depression in a furnace, this depression consisting of a 'lower hearth' with alternating layers of minerals and wood charcoal. Smelting took an average of four to six hours, and the product obtained underwent a second heating, with hammering, to eliminate residual slag.

From a linguistic point of view, Dez (1965) has drawn attention to the close correspondence in the terminology of metal-working between Indonesia and the 'Great Island', claiming that such technical terms find their origins in a common linguistic fund called 'Common Indonesian'.

> Malagasy [MLG] and Common Indonesian [INC] provide some related words which occur in both iron-working and potting techniques:

anvil	*landaizana* [MLG]	anvil	*landhat'an* [INC]
bellow	*tafoforana* [MLG]	to breathe	*puput* [INC]
charcoal	*arina* [MLG]	charcoal	*ag'egn* [INC]
iron	*vy* [MLG]	iron	*bet'i* [INC]
lead	*firaka* [MLG]	silver	*pilhak* [INC]
pot	*vilany* [MLG]	vessel	*balagna* [INC]
a dish	*finga* [MLG]	dish	*pingagn* [INC]
forge	*tefy* [MLG]	forge	*tempa* [INC]

> (Dez 1965, pp. 205, 211; translated from the French)

These observations complement those of Dahl (1951), according to whom the term *tefy* in Maanjan signifies 'the work of the potter, the ironsmith, the goldsmith as well as the tinsmiths'. Since this radical signifies 'to give form' or 'to strike and to pound' (*te (ni) pa* = formed, pounded), the action of the ironsmith is included in this image because iron is 'formed by blows of a hammer'. Similarly, the bellows of the furnace make reference to another image. In Maanjan *ka/puput* means 'the count of breaths/blasts'; in Malagasy *fofotra* refers to the action of working the bellows.

Further material aspects of the Malagasy forge are comparable to its Asiatic counterpart:

> The bellows of Malagasy ironsmiths and those of all Malaysia consist of two alternating pistons which are vertically coupled. The blowpipe used by Temoro housekeepers in order to kindle their fire, and the blowpipe of both the Sakalava and the Betsimisaraka belong, with the piston bellows, to the same Malaysian cultural assemblage.
>
> (Molet 1948, p. 725; freely translated from the French)

But such comparisons are not only limited to the domain of technology. They also concern myths originating in Indonesia about metal. According to Ottino (1983, p. 256), the notion of 'civilizing heroes' (*héros civilisateurs*), which is widespread in Madagascar, finds its origins in Malaysia. Thus, the legend of Iboniamasiboniamanoro concerns an individual who personifies the instruments used in iron-working as well as the 'inventions' of the sovereign Andriamanelo. In Indonesia, as in Madagascar, ironworkers hold a privileged but ambiguous position. 'In ancient Java the relationship between prince and smith was comparable to that existing between brothers' (Eliade 1971, p. 87). In Madagascar, ironworkers are considered to be close to the sovereign by virtue of the service they offer him. Even though their position is not economically advantageous, their influence is no less important. They were granted certain privileges. For instance, among the Tanala they had the right to quasi-royal sanctuary and among the Imerina they belonged to the aristocratic class of the Andriandranando. Eliade (1971, pp. 87–8) has remarked that in Indonesia the 'workers of metal' have a royal and aristocratic lineage. Malagasy metalworkers fell from such ranks but were later able to reclaim an aristocratic status.

Iron-working techniques, social organization and royal status therefore seem to be closely aligned in Madagascar. Indeed, according to Domenichini-Ramiaramanana & Domenichini (1983), the special role of iron is possibly indicated in oral sources which refer to an early society whose technology was based on wood and in which, while knowledge of iron existed, its use was reserved for ritual purposes. Such a special significance for iron is suggested in the relation between the meaning of a word for anvil and the role of the ironworker in the marine economy. The Tsimihety ironworker is 'the master of fish-hooks', but remains dependent on others for his nourishment because he does not take to the sea; and one of the names for the anvil, *landaizana*, literally means 'the refusal of the sail' (*la* 'refusal' + *na* 'of/through the' + *laizana* 'sail'). The royal aspect of the position of iron is suggested by the relationship between alternative forms of the words for blacksmith (*andriandriana*), anvil (*riandriana*) and prince (*andriana*) (Domenichini-Ramiaramanana & Domenichini 1983).

The ironworker was conceptualized as 'a mysterious being who must be isolated from the rest of the community' (Eliade 1971, p. 89) and this is even more prevalent in parts of Africa than in Indonesia. The fear of their craft and of their person confers on them an ambiguous status in both societies. Among Africans, as among the Malagasy, myths concerning the working of iron are often associated with divine intervention. A Betsileo myth recounts that it was the Zanahary (deified ancestors) who brought to earth the minerals necessary for their craft (Renel 1910). The intermingling of Indonesian and African cultures in Madagascar is such that it is not possible to separate the respective contributions. Yet there are notable differences in the traditional iron-working technologies employed (Kense 1983c). Among the Fouta-Djallon there are very large furnaces which necessitate a smelting period of 24 to 36 hours, and in some cases 72 hours (Appia 1965). There are also smaller furnaces, where the smelting process lasts all night. In Niger, among the ironworkers of Ader, the erection of a furnace follows a well-ordered ritual in which the attention devoted to details guarantees a high-quality production (Echard 1965). Sexual abstinence is practised on the eve of the smelting operation and, as in Madagascar, certain types of wood are chosen for the fuel. None of the bellows in Africa are double-pistoned as they are in Madagascar and Indonesia, but are of the 'bag' ('*poche*') type. On this subject, Vérin (1977–8) notes that, if the use of leather bellows were demonstrated for an earlier period, this would be an indication of a late arrival of Indonesians. We know that leather bellows exist also in Madagascar but are used uniquely for the working of precious metals. If one could establish the relative chronology of the different bellow types some precision would be added to the controversy concerning the populating of Madagascar.

Generally speaking, African ironworkers do not seem to claim to belong to the highest ranking social category. They do not, however, play a less important societal role because of this. Among the Mafa of Cameroon, Podelewski (1966) tells us that three-quarters of all diviners are also ironworkers. Further, the operations involved in childbirth devolve upon them: the ironworkers deliver two-thirds of all Mafa newborn. Funerary arrangements are among the obligatory tasks that are assigned to them. Endogamy seems to be the rule among groups of ironworkers. In the case of the Mafa, once certain members of such groups no longer practise assigned social services they no longer practise strict endogamy.

The earliest known Malagasy archaeological sites contain objects of iron as well as furnace debris and these are associated with ceramic remains from the Persian Gulf. Already in the ninth and tenth centuries AD, the 'Great Island' found itself part of the exchange network of the Indian Ocean, a network which continued to develop in succeeding centuries (Vérin 1986). One Arab source of the twelfth century, Al-Idrisi, reported that African iron from the east coast was one of the trade products much in demand in India:

> One goes from Medouna, following the coast to Melinde, a town of the Zendj, in three days and nights by sea. Melinde is situated on the coast at the mouth of a river of soft water. It is a big town whose inhabitants live by hunting and fishing. On the land they hunt tigers and other dangerous animals. From the sea they catch different species of fish which they salt and from which they base their commerce.
> They own and exploit iron mines, and this is for them a commercial undertaking and the source of their major revenue.
>
> (Al-Idrisi; translated from Guillain 1856, p. 205)

Further, concerning Sofala, Al-Idrisi continues:

> The people who live there are poor, miserable, having no other resources to live from except iron; in effect there are a lot of mines of this metal in the mountains of Sofala. The inhabitants of the islands of Zanedj (the islands of Raneh) [Comoro islands – Madagascar?] and of the other surrounding islands come here to find iron, to take it to the mainland and to the islands of India, where they sell it at a good price; because it is a very valued object of trade and is greatly consumed in India, and, although it exists in the islands and the mines of this country it does not however equal the iron of Sofala, either in terms of its abundance or in terms of its quality [goodness] and malleability. The Indians excel in the art of working it and in preparing mixtures of substances with which, through fusion, one obtains soft iron which is commonly called 'the iron of India'.
>
> (Al-Idrisi; translated from Guillain 1856, pp. 224–5)

Chanudet (1988) stresses the role of India as the centre of demand for metal in order to develop its industries in the eighth century. Lombard (1971, pp. 178–9) notes that indeed 'the Islamic world is poor in iron' and thus it 'turns toward India and the barbarian West', and continues:

> This steel, manufactured in southern India, is made from a mineral coming from the east coast of Africa, from the country of the Zenj, a mineral which is judged superior to that from India for the steel of the crucible. This mineral, crudely extracted by the blacks, is distributed through India by Moslem merchants, and then transformed into Indian steel and distributed through the Moslem world either as unworked steel or already made into swords.
>
> (translated from Lombard 1971, pp. 178–9)

Madagascar could have been one of the areas of production that fed such commerce. Islamic sites such as Mahilaka in Ambisindava Bay in the northwest (Vérin 1986; Radimilahy 1990) are particularly rich in material remains. From such commercial activities, lasting over centuries, there developed a metal-working tradition wherein Indonesian knowledge was confronted by the combined intellectual experience of African migrants from the Swahili-speaking region.

Notes

[1] This tradition which is found in the chronicle of the Tantara ny Andriana has hardly any more substance in fact than does the tradition that attributes to King Ralambo a half-century later, the introduction of the practice of eating zebu cattle meat. Archaeological excavations at Talaky have shown that the consumption of cattle goes back as far as the eleventh century AD (Battistini, Vérin & Rason 1963).

[2] For contact between Indonesians and Africans, see Vérin (1989). Domenichini-Ramiaramanana & Domenichini (1983) maintain that the populating of the island occurred well before the ninth century AD.

[3] Bloch & Vérin (1966) and Ottino-Kellum (1969) have noted the occurrence of isolated lithic fragments at certain sites, and Vérin (1977–8) has suggested that such fragments may be evidence for the manufacturing of gunflints. Gunflints are known from numerous areas since at least the sixteenth century AD (for example at Maliovola in the region of Anosy (Rakotoarisoa, *pers. comm.*), at Ambanoro in the north of the island, and in the Androy region).

Acknowledgements

The editors wish to record their gratitude to Susan Kus for her work in preparing this chapter for publication in English and to Henry Wright for helpful comment.

30 The iron-using communities in Kenya

HERMAN OGOTI KIRIAMA

The early iron-using communities

The early Iron Age in Kenya is part of a large tradition, extending into southern Africa, which sometimes (at least in east Africa) combined both iron and stone technology in the exploitation of domesticated and wild animals and plants (Bower, Nelson, Waibel & Wandibba 1977; Bower & Nelson 1978; Ambrose 1984a; Phillipson 1985a). There is still considerable controversy, however, as to the precise definition of this supposed complex.

Soper (1971b) was the first to attempt a comprehensive analysis of the early iron age pottery styles in eastern and southern Africa. He suggested that two major groupings existed in the region in east Africa: Urewe and Kwale; and he linked these groups to pottery in Zimbabwe (Ziwa and Gokomere wares) by what he called the transitional Nkope assemblage from southern Malawi. He also suggested that material from Kalambo and Mwabulambo may also belong within this group, but that the other material from Zambia formed a separate subgroup.

Soper's analysis was followed by Phillipson's (1975; 1977a), which tried to demonstrate that, after the period represented by Urewe ware, there was a north to south ordering in the chronology of the early Iron Age, thereby implying that there was a north to south movement of either ideas or populations. Phillipson divided the pottery styles from both east and southern Africa into an eastern stream, comprising material from Kwale, Lelesu, Mwabulambo, Nkope, Gokomere, Ziwa, Dambwa and Transvaal, and a western stream including Kalambo, Chondwe and Kapwirimbwe. He then used a floruit analysis of C14 dates to show a north to south temporal ordering for the eastern stream and suggested that the same might be true for the western stream. This evidence enabled him to hypothesize the existence of a population migration from eastern Africa into southern Africa and, furthermore, a correlation between the two streams and Bantu speakers.

This hypothetical grouping, first known as the 'Early Iron Age Industrial Complex of Eastern and Southern Africa' (Soper 1971a; Phillipson 1977a) and later as the 'Chifumbaze complex' after a rock shelter in Mozambique where the characteristic pottery was first excavated (Phillipson 1985a, p. 171), is here called the Mwitu tradition, indicating the forested ecozones in eastern, south-central and southern Africa in which most of the sites are found (Collett 1985; Kiriama 1986; Kiriama 1987).

The Mwitu tradition is represented by sites with typologically related pottery styles generally dated to the first millennium AD. This pottery is either the earliest known pottery where it occurs, or contrasts markedly with existing pottery traditions (Huffman 1970; Soper 1971a; Soper 1971b; Phillipson 1977a; Huffman 1982; Soper 1982; Collett 1985). In Kenya, the Urewe group is the first pottery linked to iron-using communities, occurring on the northern side of Lake Victoria, notably at Yala and Alego; it is reported in the interlacustrine area and on the eastern side of Zaïre; and it extends northwards to the Chobi area in Uganda. Soper (1982) suggests that the pottery from Uvinza in western Tanzania may also belong to the Urewe group or may show some transition to Kalambo.

This stylistic generalization has come under recent criticism, however. Van Noten (1979) has shown that there is a great heterogeneity in the decoration of Urewe pottery in those areas where it occurs, suggesting that it may be misleading to assign it to a single type. Indeed, not only are the C14 dates for the pottery fairly well distributed in the first few centuries AD throughout the area of occurrence, but a group of earlier dates has also been obtained. When dates from Buhaya in northwestern Tanzania and also from Rwanda (Schmidt 1975; Schmidt 1978) are calibrated, these dates appear to extend the Urewe ware back to the eighth century BC. There has been some hesitation in accepting these dates, however, as they make this area contemporaneous with, if not older than, early dates for iron-smelting in Meroe (Van Noten 1979; de Maret 1982b; Soper 1982). Soper (1982, p. 225) also argues that the samples used for dating might have come from charcoal from a very old tree, therefore inflating the antiquity of the dated event. On the other hand, Collett (1985) maintains that the Mwitu tradition in the interlacustrine area goes back to about 2800 BP.

One of the two later groupings of the Mwitu tradition in east Africa is named the Kwale, extending from slightly north of Mombasa on the Kenya coast, through the highlands of northeastern Tanzania from Kilimanjaro to the Usambara mountains and, maybe, as far south as the Ngulu hills. In inland Kenya, examples of this group occur at Kilungu and at Ithanga hills and in the Tana valley east of Mount Kenya (Fig. 30.1). Affinities of this group have been found in the pottery from Taita and Kwamboo (Collett 1985; Diblasi 1980). It has also been shown that some traces of this group persist in the later iron age Gatung'ang'a ware of central Kenya (Siiriainen 1971). Soper (1982) suggests that some of the early pottery from Manda, dated to the eighth century AD may have some affinities with Kwale but he thinks that these Manda finds should not be subsumed within it. Radiocarbon dates from the type-site of Kwale indicate that the site may have been occupied between the first and second centuries AD (Soper 1967). Other dates from Usangi hospital in north Pare in Tanzania are from the ninth or tenth century AD (Odner 1971), while in central Kenya, a related pottery has been dated to the seventh century AD at Gatare forest in Nyandarua, and to the twelfth or fourteenth century AD at Gatung'ang'a. The geographical and temporal spread of Kwale ware leads one to suggest that this, like Urewe, is not a homogeneous group, and that the diversity needs further investigation.

According to Collett (1985), the Mwitu tradition is succeeded by a second culture which he calls the Kapwirimbwe/Lydenburg/NC3/Roan Antelope group in parts of south-central and southern Africa.

Despite controversy about the linkage of pottery types with specific groups of people and hesitation in accepting the various dates, it is now generally accepted that the inter-

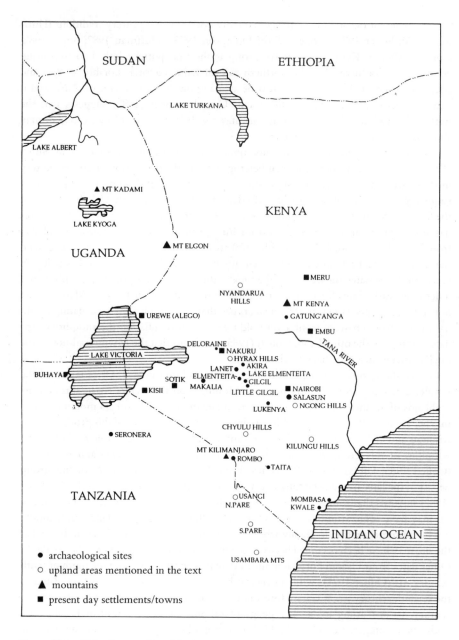

Figure 30.1 Main sites mentioned in the text.

lacustrine region had an underlying stylistic similarity among these wares and provides the earliest dates for the iron-using communities in eastern and southern Africa.

The 'Later Iron Age'

From the scant evidence available from the later iron-using communities of Kenya, there is some indication that this period witnessed a diversification of the ecological zones which were occupied and exploited. Whereas the known early Mwitu tradition sites were concentrated on the wooded highlands, had compact settlements and may have been involved in agriculture, most of the later sites, both in the woodlands and in the savanna, had dispersed settlements and an economy based on stock-raising and milking as well as on cereal agriculture. It seems that there were two complementary modes of life. The apparent association between the later sites and a new type of pottery – a rouletted ware, found in those areas previously occupied by later stone age pastoralists – has encouraged some scholars to associate the iron-using communities of this region – the central Rift Valley of Kenya – with Nilotic speakers. It may be incorrect, however, to describe these communities as later iron-using, since they are the earliest iron-using communities in some regions and are only later in comparison to those who inhabited the areas previously occupied by groups represented by the early Mwitu tradition ceramics. It has also not been established whether these communities are ancestral to the present communities of these areas.

In the central highlands of Kenya, the introduction of iron-using led to a decline in the workmanship of the obsidian tools which hitherto had been used in the area. This is attested at Deloraine Farm, where a degenerate industry reminiscent of the Elmentaitan was found (Chittick 1979; Ambrose 1982). This is the earliest iron age site in the Rift Valley, dating to between 1300 and 1100 BP. Similar pottery has been found at Makalia burial site and Gilgil River burial site (Fig. 30.1). Related wares may be represented in the Gusii area (Bower 1973a; Kiriama In Press).

A more widespread iron-using culture appears prior to about 1185 BP. This is represented by Lanet ware (Posnansky 1967), a pottery assemblage with elongated gourd-like or bag-shaped vessels, which have handles and spouts and a twisted cord roulette decoration. This pottery is often associated with shallow depressions, fre-quently lined with dry stone walling and commonly referred to as Sirikwa holes (Sutton 1973b). Sutton (1987) identifies them as stock pens of the ancestors of the Kalenjin who may have occupied the whole of the western highlands and the adjacent parts of the Kenyan Rift Valley until the Maasai dislodged them in the eighteenth century. However, some scholars are now arguing that the so-called 'Sirikwa holes' are not a Nilotic, but, in fact, a Bantu phenomenon. The argument is that in those areas where these features occur, there is oral testimony from the various Bantu groups in Kenya that they lived there at one time or another during the late seventeenth/early eighteenth centuries, the same time period from which these Sirikwa holes date. It is also informative that the Sirikwa holes are abundant in the Sotik area and at a time (eighteenth century) when the Abagusii claim to have occupied the area. It is worth noting that the present occupants of the area, the Sot Kalenjin, are a Kalenjinized Abagusii (Kiriama In Press).

In the early phases, the late Iron Age has a degenerate lithic industry – for instance, at the northeast village at Hyrax Hill, Salasun, Rombo and at Akira – which drops out almost entirely by 350 BP, as it does at Lanet. Trade goods, including glass beads and cowrie shells, are represented in the later phases, indicating contacts with the coast and, possibly, with more distant lands.

Regional variants of Lanet ware have been found at Mount Kadami in northeast Uganda (Robbins, McFarlin, Brower & Hoffman 1977; Wandibba 1984), Mount Elgon (Chapman 1966) and, as stated above, at Hyrax Hill (Leakey 1945), Lanet, Salasun and Akira in the western highlands of Kenya, east of the Rift Valley at Lukenya (Gramly 1975) and in Tanzania at Seronera (Bower 1973a). It has been argued that similar pottery is presently used by the Okiek (Blackburn 1973) and is widely used by the Maasai and other eastern Nilotic groups (Sutton 1973a) as well as by some northern Kalenjin groups (Sutton 1973b) who were previously in close contact with the Maasai.

According to Soper (1982, p. 235), later developments in areas occupied by the early Mwitu tradition should parallel the historical developments that led to the emergence of the people who are occupying these areas in modern times. Soper hopes that the language and material culture of these areas may reflect the broader cultural trends and continuities of the basic population. In central Kenya, Siiriäinen (1971) found a degenerate variant of Kwale ware bowls associated with necked pots with rocker-stamped decoration. This is represented at Gatung'ang'a where C14 dates range from the twelfth to the fourteenth centuries AD. This association also extends as far as the eastern slopes of Mount Kenya, the Nyandarua ranges, Ngong hills and south to the Kilungu hills. Sites with these later assemblages have also been found in Embu, Meru, in the Chyulu hills (Soper 1976) and at Rombo (Kiriama n.d.). However, the Chyulu hills and Rombo assemblages do not have any Kwale elements in them. The Chyulu hills material has been dated to the sixteenth century AD, but the Rombo one is as yet undated, although circumstantial evidence points to its contemporaneity with the Chyulu ones.

Soper (1982, p. 236) suggests that the origins of the necked pots in Gatung'ang'a ware should be sought in Kwale ware. He also argues that the bowls which occur in both wares are an indication of ceramic continuity from Kwale to Gatung'ang'a ware, and that this may suggest population and language continuity. However, he does not take into account the possibility of borrowing and interaction between different communities. On the basis of the distribution of these later assemblages, and because both of them follow a trend towards resemblance with present-day pottery assemblages in these regions, Soper attributes these assemblages to Bantu speakers. But this attribution does not extend into the central Rift Valley.

Most workers at one time correlated the southern Nilotes with the later iron age assemblages of the central Rift Valley (Sutton 1973a; Sutton 1973b; Phillipson 1977a). But the 1180 BP dates for Lanet wares are far earlier than the linguistic evidence allows. It is now argued, therefore, that this date is approximate to that given for the presence of the Ongamo-Maa cluster of the eastern Nilotes in the highland area (Ehret 1974; Ambrose 1982). It is also argued that the rouletted ware is presently associated with eastern rather than southern Nilotic speakers, and those southern Nilotes who use this type of pottery, the Kalenjin, are those groups which were in close contact with the Maasai and other eastern Nilotic groups (Sutton 1973a). The reconstruction now advanced is that the Ongamo agriculturalists, who were the earliest Maa speakers to live near Mount Kilimanjaro, may have absorbed the southern Cushites who hitherto lived in the area, and may also be responsible for the extensive settlements in the Rift Valley. They would also have absorbed southern Nilotic groups on the west side of the Rift Valley, pushing them back to their present distribution in the western highlands (Ambrose 1982; Ambrose 1984a).

Archaeological and linguistic correlations

The association between the start of iron-using in Kenya and the spread of Bantu languages, as proposed by historical linguists and adopted by some archaeologists, is based primarily on the fact that in these areas the distribution of iron age culture and of the Bantu languages is broadly coterminous and thus a manifestation of the initial southward spread of Bantu speakers (Oliver 1966; Soper 1967; Soper 1971a; Soper 1971b; Phillipson 1977a; Soper 1982; Phillipson 1985a, p. 179). It is also argued that the close degree of linguistic similarity which may be demonstrated among the Bantu languages of the subcontinent indicates that they may have been derived from a common ancestor in the recent past (Soper 1982; Phillipson 1985a).

Oliver (1966) was the first to use both linguistic and archaeological data in order to reconcile the views of the linguists. Oliver's stage 2 was an expansion from a Katanga nuclear area at the beginning of the Christian era, west from Zaïre to the Atlantic and eastward to the Indian Ocean. During the second half of the first millennium AD, another expansion, which Oliver called stage 3, took place. This was an expansion into the interlacustrine area of western Tanzania and Uganda with a further settlement along the Indian Ocean. The final stage (stage 4) took place in the second millennium AD and filled the rest of Kenya, Tanzania and southern Africa.

Oliver's model was based on Guthrie's (1962) assumption that there was a Bantu nuclear area in Zaïre. However, this model has often been criticized because Oliver used random C14 dates to support postulated population migrations and their routes. He did not have sufficient archaeological data to allow him to posit a realistic correlation with the linguistic evidence. He thus treated archaeological phenomena as prehistoric phenomena (Schmidt 1978).

Using the evidence of a decline in the similarity of ceramics through the region, Soper (1971; 1982) argued that the Bantu expansion happened in a wave. He held that the differences were not an indication of different communities, but a function of distance: the further one wave moves from the homeland, the more different it becomes. This model does not, however, offer a mechanism for differentiation. Is such variation because of contact with other groups or is it an inherent desire to become different? This model has also been criticized for proposing a slow Bantu movement, whereas C14 dates reveal a fast movement (Collett 1985).

Huffman (1970), on the other hand, suggests that the migrants had dispersed from the nuclear area like pellets from a shotgun. In other words, he saw the movement as having been extremely rapid, with groups of people walking long distances before settling. Thus it was an instantaneous dispersal and, according to Huffman, this accounts for the existence of co-traditions of pottery in the region.

Phillipson (1977a) accepted Heine's (1973) linguistic classification and saw an initial movement into the lakes area, with two subsequent principal spreads, one to the east and the other to the south and southwest. Phillipson's classification as regards the Kenyan situation can be summarized as follows:

> Stage 3, 400–300 BC: Bantu speakers move along the northern edge of the forest from Cameroon to the interlacustrine area. These are the people responsible for Uwere ware.
>
> Stage 6, 100–200 AD: movement from the interlacustrine area to southeast Kenya and northeast Tanzania. This gives rise to Kwale ware.
>
> Stage 7b, 300–400 AD: spread along the east coast as far as South Africa.

According to this postulate, the first wave of migration, originating in the lakes region in the early centuries AD, was responsible for the introduction of iron to the Kenyan coast.

David (1982) rejects both Phillipson's and Oliver's postulation of a Bantu movement round the equatorial forest. He argues that the Bantu speakers may have first occupied the forest and then, following the river valleys, moved into the interlacustrine area where Urewe ware developed. The use of iron, according to David, also spread from west Africa along the same route (river valleys) but later this innovation reached the interlacustrine area via the forest. David, however, accepts Phillipson's views about the spread of the eastern Bantu from the interlacustrine area to parts of the east coast and South Africa.

Collett (1985) compared neolithic ceramics with those of the early Iron Age. His results showed that the decorative themes used in neolithic ceramics were quite different from those of the early Iron Age. He also discovered that, whereas coil breaks were prevalent in neolithic ceramics, they were not common in early iron age ceramics. This difference suggested that, in typology and technology, the early Iron Age was different from the preceding time of the neolithic pastoralists, leading Collett to conclude that the early iron age inhabitants may have migrated into this region from elsewhere.

Collett (1985; 1987) has offered an explanatory model based on a simulation study. Underlying this model is a presumption that the Bantu expansion was motivated by social stress derived from the increased friction in human communities as populations grew and approached a social carrying capacity. Thus, according to this model, as population increased, the frontier gradually moved forward. However, behind the frontier, population continued until it reached a socially defined carrying capacity. This increase in population led to conflicts which in turn led to part of the population moving past the advancing frontier and then settling. The same process then started all over again.

According to Vogel (1986), however, while the increased population and expansion proposed by the model may be ideal for explaining expansions within settlement systems, it cannot explain why there are large areas associated with the early Iron Age. Vogel applies this model to the study of the early iron age settlements in Zambia and concludes that, whereas there was some fission in the settlements, it was not a social/ecological split into mother and daughter communities. Rather, he argues, the fission suggests the actions of a population adapted to a particular microenvironment of limited settlement opportunities; after the existing patches of suitable land had been exhausted, a settlement was moved to a similar but as yet unused microenvironment. As a result, the movement of settlement system loci did not leave a significant remnant occupation at the last locus – unlike the moving frontier hypothesis. After the earlier place of occupation had replenished its resources to an acceptable level, it was at least logically possible for the people to move back there again.

Collett may have been misled in differentiating neolithic and early iron age populations through his use of correlation cluster link analysis for the ceramic data. Technology also changes depending on the circumstances that people find themselves in, and the mere fact that coil breaks are prevalent in the Neolithic and not in the early Iron Age does not in itself show these people to have been different.

A number of criticisms of the correlation between linguistic and archaeological evidence, and others of the Bantu migration hypothesis as a whole, have been voiced by archaeologists, linguists and anthropologists.

Soper (1982) has rejected some of the linguistic evidence, arguing that it does not tally with the available archaeological data. He argues (p. 234) that

> a straight one to one correlation of Early Iron Age variants with modern Bantu subgroupings does not seem to be tenable, and perhaps it should never have been expected, implying as it does a sort of columnar development through all the vicissitudes of history for nearly 2000 years.

Lwanga-Lunyiigo (1976) argues that the Bantu speakers appeared on the east African scene very early, and that the expansion from west Africa never took place. He also argues that it is difficult to spot the exact origin of Bantu languages. He maintains that iron-smelting was an independent innovation of the east Africans and that the interlacustrine area was the centre from which metallurgy, Urewe ware and agriculture spread to central and southern Africa. He supports his arguments by asserting that the sickle cell gene originated in east Africa and spread to other regions.

Gramly (1978) also denies the idea of a Bantu migration. He argues that pottery, food production and iron-working did not spread simultaneously into eastern and southern Africa and, in any event, that none of these features can be associated with the spread of Bantu languages. According to Gramly, Bantu was spoken for millennia in most of the same regions where the languages are prevalent today, and the peoples of these regions have remained in the lands they occupied since before the advent of food production, ceramics and metals. Inherent in this argument is that the ceramics of the Bantu may be similar, either technologically or typologically, to those of the preceding neolithic pastoralists.

Other archaeologists such as de Maret & Nsuka (1977) have wondered whether Proto-Bantu as reconstructed is not a false creation, a synchronic projection by linguists of a diachronic process. Some linguists are adding their voices to the criticisms. Möhlig (1979), for instance, rejects the idea of family-like relationships among languages. He argues that convergence among Bantu languages has been so strong that no family can ever be reconstructed and that linguists who have tried to do so have completely ignored socio-linguistic findings as well as the findings of general dialectology. In such cases dialectological approaches are the only valid ones; both neo-classical comparative linguistics and lexicostatistics lead only to false results (Vansina 1980).

Möhlig claims that the Eastern Bantu languages (those spoken in Kenya and other parts of east Africa) did not originate from a single ancestral tongue but are a representative of blends of different genetic strata. However, despite this, he still sees all the ancestors of the Eastern Bantu speakers as having come from an area located between the northeastern fringes of the forest and the western shores of the great lakes.

For Kuper (1980), the main question is not to look for the origins of the various Bantu languages but rather to discover whether a common Bantu culture ever existed. If so, he argues, cultural anthropology can help reconstruct Bantu expansion. He argues that the study of cultural processes can help indicate how an eventual Bantu migration could, or could not, have proceeded. This approach has been adopted by many archaeologists, especially those working in southern Africa (e.g. Huffman 1980a; Huffman 1982; Huffman 1986b). But this approach is not really different from the historical-linguistic/archaeology link, as both emphasize that there was a common core Bantu culture in eastern and southern Africa. These arguments also assume that the Bantu culture was somewhat 'superior' to that of the people they encountered on their way, forcing the 'natives' to abandon their culture in favour of that of the Bantu 'colonizers'. Such arguments do not allow leeway for the Bantu speakers to have integrated with contact peoples, either by being completely or partially absorbed or by absorbing them.

It is because of the apparent similarity of Bantu languages, therefore, that linguists, other anthropologists and archaeologists have been attracted by the notion that these peoples migrated into the region. However, none of the hypotheses, models and archaeological constructs used to support this notion have real evidence to back them up. As yet there are no data to show that an advancing frontier was associated with a gradual change in ceramic similarity or that long-distance migration was associated with a rapid change in material culture and other items. Indeed, it has been shown that people can, in certain circumstances, move long distances and, in spite of being dominant, abandon their material culture and even languages for those of the people they encounter on the way (Collett 1987).

Alternative models: pottery use in a social context

From the above discussion, we can see that archaeologists have tried to link archaeological phenomena – primarily ceramics – with linguistic phenomena. This is unfortunate as it presupposes that there is or has been a cultural unity among the Bantu speakers of eastern and southern Africa. This is really the same as arguing that the Bantu speakers of this general area have had a columnar development over the last two thousand or so years. As useful as linguistic evidence may prove to be in indicating the general direction of the supposed Bantu movements, such linguistic evidence can tell us nothing about how and why iron production took place and prospered in some areas earlier than in others. That is, linguistic evidence cannot tell us about the internal diversity within iron-using groups or reveal the historical development from a pre- or proto-Bantu ancestor, and linguistic evidence itself cannot resolve the problem as to whether the languages which we now recognize as Bantu do indeed constitute a defined linguistic group.

The study of the distribution of pottery styles is similarly flawed. In Kenya, the ceramics of iron-using communities have been studied as a system of stylistic attributes, using a methodology similar to the linguistic approach. The lexicostatistic of the archaeologist has been decorative style, the argument being that at any one time an ethnic group can be identified by the stylistic features of its pottery (Huffman 1982, p. 134), and thus stylistic unity exhibited in any area is said to be indicative of a common historical origin (Phillipson 1977a). The problem with this line of argument is that it denies the makers or the users of such pots the ability to interact with their neighbours and also the ability to have individual variability within the group itself.

A modern example that reveals the problem is that of the Agikuyu potters of central Kenya. Pot-making among the Agikuyu is the preserve of women; however, because of the economic viability of the trade, one man decided to join it. In order for him to be seen to be different from women potters, he invented his own distinctive styles. An archaeologist excavating the area in the future and using diagnostic keys as a basis of his analysis (as used in Bantu studies) will inevitably conclude, wrongly, that two communities lived in this area (Wandibba 1984, p. 79). Furthermore, because of the popularity of Luo pottery (Luo are a Nilotic-speaking group in western Kenya), Agikuyu customers often bring Luo pots and ask their own potters to copy them. Luo pot forms are therefore widespread in the area (Wandibba 1984, pp. 79–80).

Perhaps a similar situation prevailed among the iron age communities. There may have been itinerant potters who roamed over the area selling their skills to the various communities. In this case the variability represented in the pots would not be due to within-group differentiation but would reflect a real variability between various groups. A study of stylistic variability alone cannot enable us, therefore, to establish the identity of the makers of such pots. A more contextual approach is necessary, considering, for example, whether there is any relationship between form, function and size, and what the relationship is between these variables and decoration. Such a study may lead to questions concerning the specific circumstances within which these variables acted.

Indeed, the basic question remains, after all these archaeological and linguistic analyses, whether there exists what can be termed an exclusive Bantu culture.

In pursuing this problem further it is necessary to understand the social realm within which ceramics and iron objects were created and used. This is because the social context within which an item of material culture functions can enable one to understand the similarities and differences that do exist between various societies. For example, if one were to look at the contexts in which iron occurred among the various Bantu groups in Kenya, one would notice remarkable differences that make it a folly to talk of a common core Bantu culture (see Huffman 1980a; Huffman 1982; Kuper 1982).

Bantu cultural variation: the Abagusii and Agikuyu of Kenya

The Abagusii and Agikuyu are Bantu speakers inhabiting the western and eastern highlands of Kenya respectively. Both groups are mixed farmers and traditionally practise(d) male circumcision and female clitoridectomy. In their oral traditions, both groups claim to have been brothers in the distant past, though they emphasize that they came to their present areas from different directions (Ochieng' 1971; Muriuki 1974). These groups were, and to a certain extent are, iron smelters. However, they exhibit differences in the forms of furnaces they use, the Agikuyu using the induced and possibly natural draught furnace (i.e. Mweiga), while the Abagusii use the induced bowl furnace. Archaeological evidence for iron-working in both areas is indicated by remains of furnaces, slag heaps or tuyères. Pottery, thought to belong to the Iron Age and dating to between the fourth and eighteenth centuries, has been recovered from both areas (Siiriäinen 1971; Bower 1973a; Kiriama In Press). The Agikuyu still make pots today but the Abagusii buy their pots from the neighbouring Luo.

Both groups are patrilineal, patrilocal and exogamous. Bridewealth in both cases was paid in the form of cattle, sheep/goats and millet (among Abagusii) or honey (among the Agikuyu). However, it is in the production and use of iron that these supposedly related groups exhibit differences. According to Kenyatta (1938), among the Agikuyu the whole family of a smelter took part in the work of procuring ore for smelting. There was division of labour among the members of the family: 'When a man is busy washing the sand, his wife or wives and children are busy spreading the ore in the sun to dry' (Kenyatta 1938, p. 72). While Leakey (1977) states that the smelter and his apprentices were prohibited from having sexual intercourse with their wives the day prior to, and during, the smelting period, he makes no mention of women being prohibited from approaching the smelting site. Taking into consideration the fact that women participated in the procurement of the ore, it can be inferred that they were also allowed near the smelting site. This behaviour can be interpreted in two ways. First, while the actual act of sexual intercourse was considered to be dangerous to the smelting, perhaps because both resulted in the creation of a new substance (child and iron), the woman was not herself seen as being dangerous. Or, second, the wife was seen as an integral part of the family and so there was no reason for excluding her from participating in the smelting process. The link between procreation and smelting among the Agikuyu has been adequately described by Collett (1985). The Agikuyu view the furnace as female and the bellows as male. Thus, the whole process is seen as an act of intercourse leading to the procreation of iron.

The Abagusii, on the other hand, present a marked contrast. Women are not allowed to participate in any iron-smelting activities. It is believed that if a woman touches any of the iron-smelting apparatus before the smelt is done, the smelting will not succeed.

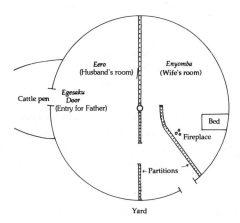

Figure 30.2 Spatial arrangement of an Abagusii dwelling.

One may argue that this is because of the fear of not only the fertility of the woman, as in the Agikuyu case, but also fear of the person of the woman herself.

If there was any link between procreation and smelting, what Collett calls fire transformations (Collett n.d.; see also Kuper 1982), we could expect this to be depicted in the homesteads of these groups. The argument here is that because fire is significant in procreation, iron and cooking, the three processes will always be opposed to one another whenever they happen to occur together. For instance, in the dwelling we could expect the hearth to be in an opposing position *vis-à-vis* a woman's bedroom.

The significance of this ideological and technological relation to the problem of the cultural history and identity of the Bantu is that if a core Bantu culture exists, then some fundamental similarity may be expected between basic aspects of Agikuyu and Abagusii society.

Among the Abagusii, the world of the homestead is experienced by its inhabitants as a unit of economic expansion and social control. The behaviour of an individual *vis-à-vis* other members of the society is expressed in the homestead patterning. Thus, for instance, the senior wife of a man has her dwelling built at the centre of the homestead while those of her co-wives are built to the right and left of hers. So, whenever a visitor comes to the homestead he knows how to behave towards the women he finds in these dwellings. This kind of structuring is extended to individual dwellings, and the ordering of space within the dwelling also reflects the relationship between the various members of that group.

The Abagusii dwelling was divided into two rooms: a woman's room (*emyomba*) in which cooking takes place, and a man's room (*eero*) in which the male entertainment, beer drinking and most domestic rituals occur (Fig. 30.2). A man's room was always on the right hand side, and the woman's room always on the left, and the placement of the doors reflected their different concerns. The door of the man's room faces the cattle pen and can be used by the man and his male relatives. This was called the door of the 'tribe' (*egesiari giagesaku*) (also known as the *egesaku* door). The other door enters directly into the woman's room and is used by the wife and her friends. If he wishes, however, the husband can also use this door.

The arrangement of the doors shows the strong attachment that the Abagusii had to the patrilinear lineage and the role cattle played in the enhancement of the lineage. The cattle were used to bring more women into the village and thus more children, thus prolonging the lineage. The Abagusii then can be said to be a cattle culture complex people (Kuper 1982).

This patterning of the house also reveals the Abagusii's attitude towards women. They are seen not only as outsiders – who should not use the lineage door and so be in direct contact with cattle, which are important in the continuity of the lineage – but were/are also inferior to men and should always be in the background. This inferiority of women is nowhere better depicted than in the way items are spatially ordered in the house. All articles which were made by women, such as pots, were usually stored in the woman's room or in the store built beneath the roof and which was supposed to be exclusively used by women. On the other hand, all male articles, such as hoes, pangas and baskets, were stored in the man's room. This is despite the fact that in their daily life, these things were either used mostly by women (hoes and baskets), or used by men (beer pots). In addition, women are not allowed to wear any iron ear-rings or hand bangles. These are only worn by men. A woman only wears iron anklets after she has been married and she is only allowed to remove them after the death of her husband or after her divorce. The idea of women wearing anklets may be seen as an assertion of the man's right over not only the fertility of his wife, but also over her offspring.

With the Agikuyu, the reverse is the case. The whole family is allowed to participate in the iron-smelting activities, possibly indicating that women are seen as equals, or that they are fully accepted as members of the patriclan. That women are seen as equals was stated by Cagnolo (1933), who reports that while publicly a man may appear to dominate his wife, at home or in the house it is the wife who is superior. This egalitarianism is also seen in the patterning of the Agikuyu dwelling. Unlike the Abagusii dwelling, among the Agikuyu the woman's room was in the centre-back of it (Fig. 30.3), a position from which the occupant of the room can command all that is in the dwelling and also see whoever is entering it. While the man has his own dwelling (*thingira*), where he entertains his visitors, all the articles, whether male or female, are stored in the woman's dwelling. This shows the prominent role that Agikuyu women may play in the society, that despite publicly being the wife, in the house the woman was mother of all (both her offspring and husband), and thus had controlling power over her house. This can also be seen from the fact that the Agikuyu woman is allowed to wear iron rings, unlike her Abagusii counterpart. Hobley (1922) also states that before an Agikuyu smith embarked on his smelt, he had to make iron bracelets for his wives. This independence of an Agikuyu woman can be partly explained by the fact that her lineage still played an important role in so far as her marriage was concerned. For instance, if there was a divorce or a separation, the woman always went away with her children. In addition, all the property in her house is hers and she can dispose of it in any way she likes without seeking her husband's permission.

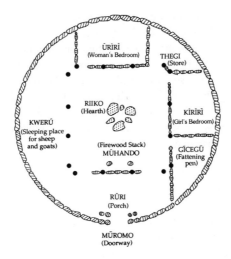

Figure 30.3 Spatial arrangement of an Agikuyu dwelling.

The above examples show a marked contrast between two contemporary groups who could both be classified as belonging to a generalized Bantu cattle culture. But if we were to extend this to the archaeological record, could such differences be discerned? The Agikuyu *thingira* is built near the cattle pen, while the Abagusii *egesaku* door faces the cattle pen. If these sites were to be excavated, and the structure of both dwellings and pens was visible, the occupants of the sites could be shown to have owned cattle and to have made use of iron, but their social manipulation of these resources would be very difficult to determine. It is reasonable to suggest that these distinctive groups would have been lumped together in a single classification.

Conclusion

From the above discussion it can be seen how archaeologists have tried to use linguistic evidence to explain archaeological phenomena. This failed because it has created homogeneities where there was heterogeneity. Such use of linguistic evidence has also caused archaeologists to overlook other equally important issues – social contexts – which can be very important in explaining the similarities or dissimilarities that do exist among the Bantu speakers. The ethnographic evidence has also shown that, despite the apparent linguistic similarity amongst Bantu speakers, there are various cultural differences – especially as far as the use of iron is concerned – and that this may militate against not only the concept of a common core Bantu culture, but the whole idea of Bantu expansion from a common origin and also the idea of an area from which iron-working originated.

The basic question to look at, then, as far as Bantu are concerned, is the relationship between Bantu language, culture, society and physical population. How does one extrapolate from language to culture to society – as Murdock (1959), Oliver (1966), Phillipson (1977a) and Johnson (1989) have done?

Thus, instead of archaeologists concentrating on demonstrating mechanisms and routes through which the Bantu – and thus knowledge of iron-using – spread, they should strive to look at the social context in which this technology was adapted and used. Understanding the context of adoption and use of this technology, as the ethnographic examples have shown, may enhance understanding of their societal meanings and thus the social strategies that the society employed, and eventually help to explain how social change occurred (Hodder 1986).

Acknowledgement

I am indebted to Dr Simiyu Wandibba of the National Museums for his encouragement when I was writing this chapter, and also for reading numerous drafts of it.

31 Metaphors and representations associated with precolonial iron-smelting in eastern and southern Africa

D. P. COLLETT

Introduction

In recent centuries European culture, in its scientific manifestation, has treated technology as a series of physical or chemical processes that can be predicted and controlled through the application of materialist, causal theories. While this approach is useful in the understanding of technology in scientific terms, it is less useful when it is employed as a method for understanding productive processes in societies that do not employ European scientific concepts. The problem with the scientific approach in the latter context is that it leads the analyst to divide the activities that occur during the production of an item into 'technological' acts and 'magical' or 'symbolic' acts. However, activities are rarely, if ever, divided into these two categories by the participants. Rather, they perceive all the acts that occur during the productive process as essential for a successful outcome (see Rowlands & Warnier, Ch. 32, this volume).

From the perspective of the participants, all the activities associated with a productive process are efficacious. The analyst may therefore see the division by European science of acts into those that are technologically efficacious and those that are magical or symbolic as masking a unity that underlies both 'productive' and 'magical' actions. In this case both 'technological' and 'magical' activities are techniques for controlling the world (Gell 1988; Rowlands & Warnier, Ch. 32, this volume). The failure of a scientific analysis to recognize this underlying unity means that it has to dissolve and eliminate the culture of the participants during its application. Eliade (1971) has made this point in the context of 'primitive' smelting and alchemy by pointing out that attempts to assimilate these techniques to chemistry suppresses the fundamental break that occurs during the change from a sacralized to a profane approach to technology.

Many recent attempts to understand precolonial iron-smelting in eastern and southern Africa have employed scientific approaches to the understanding of the technology (Schmidt & Avery 1978; Friede, Hejja & Koursaris 1982; van der Merwe & Avery 1982; Childs & Schmidt 1985; Todd 1985). In virtually all of these cases the analyses of the processes are divorced from the cultural context in which they occur. This chapter attempts to redress this imbalance by exploring the beliefs that are associated with precolonial iron-smelting in this region and by examining the ways in which these beliefs are also linked to a wider set of productive practices.

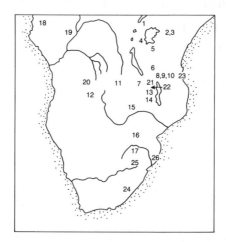

Figure 31.1 Location of groups discussed in text. 1 Nyoro; 2 Kikuyu; 3 Mberre; 4 Haya; 5 Rongo; 6 Fipa; 7 Ushi; 8 Nyakusa; 9 Bena; 10 Kinga; 11 Kaonde; 12 Chokwe; 13 Ngoni; 14 Chewa; 15 Ila and Lungu; 16 Shona; 17 Venda; 18 Ithumba; 19 Kamba; 20 Chokwe; 21 Chisinga; 22 Bemba; 23 Nyiha; 24 Zulu; 25 Kgatia; 26 Thonga.

Furnaces and products

Ethnographic accounts of iron-smelting in eastern and southern Africa indicate that the traditional furnaces in the region can be divided into three major types: (a) forced-draught bowl furnaces; (b) low-shaft, forced-draught furnaces; and (c) tall-shaft, natural-draught furnaces. Air is pumped into the first two furnace types by hand-operated bellows while in the third type air is drawn into the furnace by the 'chimney effect'.

The first furnace type simply consists of a pit in the ground and there is no above-ground superstructure. The superstructure of the second furnace type rarely if ever rises more than a metre above the ground, while the third furnace type has a much taller superstructure that may rise anywhere between 2 and 7 m above ground level (van der Merwe 1980).

An examination of the distribution of these three furnace types indicates that the region (Fig. 31.1) can be divided into three distinct zones. The northeastern area is characterized by a patchwork distribution of bowl furnaces and low-shaft furnaces. The former class of furnaces has been reported for the Kikuyu (Routledge & Routledge 1910, pp. 82–90; Kenyatta 1938, pp. 70–3; Leakey 1977, pp. 304–7), Kamba (Hobley 1910; Lindblom 1920, p. 258), Mberre (Brown 1977), Ithumba (Last 1883) and the groups in Rwanda/Burundi (Celis & Nzikobanyanka 1976), whereas the latter class has been reported for the Nyoro (Roscoe 1923, p. 220), the Haya (Schmidt & Avery 1978), the Rongo (Rosemund 1943) as well as the Bena and Kinga of southern Tanzania (Sutton 1985) and the Kaonde of northern Zambia (Chaplin 1961).

The second zone coincides broadly, but not exactly, with the central African matrilineal belt. Both tall-shaft and low-shaft furnaces occur in this area and both types are used by the same groups but for different stages of iron production. This pattern has been reported among the Fipa (Lechaptois 1913; Wykaert 1914; Grieg 1937; Wise 1958a; Willis 1981), the Nyiha (Brock & Brock 1965), the Ushi (Barnes 1926) and the Lungu (Chaplin 1961). Only the tall-shaft furnaces are mentioned in some of the accounts of precolonial smelting in this area – for example for the Chewa (Hodgson 1933), Chishinga (Brelsford 1949), Ila (Gouldsbury & Sheanne 1911, p. 279; Smith & Dale 1920, pp. 203–10), Ngoni (Stannus 1914) and Chokwe (Lima 1967) – but it is probable that both furnace types were used by all these groups. The southernmost boundary of the second zone, at least in the recent past, appears to have been the Zambezi river. All of the ethnographically reported furnaces to the south of this boundary fall into the low-shaft class. These furnaces have been reported for the Shona-speaking peoples in Zimbabwe (Taylor 1926; Franklin 1945; Cooke 1966; Hatton 1967) and the Venda (Stayt 1931, pp. 59–61).

It is clear from the ethnographic accounts of smelting among the Fipa, Ushi, Nyiha and Lungu that more than one furnace type can be used during the process of iron production. It might be expected that the use of two furnace types reflects some difference in the chemistry of smelting among these groups when compared with the chemistry of smelting among those groups who use only one furnace. However, there is no indication that the products of any one furnace type are necessarily different from the products of any other furnace type. This can be illustrated by a simple example: three products of the smelting process are recognized by the Fipa, who smelt ore in a tall natural-draught furnace, and the Rongo, who use a low-shaft furnace. The products are slag, crude iron and a mix which needs further smelting, which is called *mtale* by the Fipa (Wise 1958a) and *msilo* by the Rongo (Rosemund 1943).

The recognition that the products of smelting in different furnace types may be the same raises some problems for a simple chemical interpretation of the technology. The Fipa resmelt *mtale* in a small induced-draught furnace (Lechaptois 1913; Wykaert 1914; Grieg 1937; Wise 1958a) while the Rongo break up the *msilo* and add it to the ore used in the next smelt (Rosemund 1943). The former group treat *mtale* as a material that is in some way different from iron ore while the latter group treat *msilo* as iron ore. It could be argued that the difference in the treatment of the product that needs further refining is a reflection of the different furnace types used for ore smelting and that a low-shaft furnace is essential for the refining of *mtale/msilo*. However, the Kaonde smelt ore in a low-shaft furnace and refine one of the products in a second low-shaft furnace (Chaplin 1961). This indicates that they treat the product that needs further refining in the same was as the Fipa although they use the same furnace type as the Rongo. The comparison of the way in which *mtale* and *msilo* are refined therefore suggests that the treatment of the products of iron-smelting reflects the way in which the products are classified rather than any technological necessity.

A second example serves to reinforce the importance of cultural classifications in the overall understanding of iron-smelting in eastern and southern Africa. The initial smelting of ore amongst both the Nyoro (Roscoe 1923, pp. 217–23) and the Mberre (Brown 1977) produces iron blooms that are subsequently welded into ingots. A separate class of metalworkers are responsible for the welding of the blooms amongst the Nyoro and they use separate furnaces that are smaller versions of the ore-smelting furnaces. However, amongst the Mberre the conversion of blooms to ingots is the responsibility of the smelter and he uses the same furnace as the one used to smelt the ore. Thus, in the Mberre case the blooms can be treated in the same way as ore, while the Nyoro treat the blooms as a separate category.

The link between the number of furnaces used to produce iron and the cultural classifications of the products of smelting highlights the importance of cultural classification in the understanding of the technological processes. This further indicates that the beliefs associated with different stages of the production process need not be the same and the next section focuses on the beliefs associated with the smelting of iron ore.

Smelting and procreation

It has been recognized for many years that the smelting of ore in eastern and southern Africa is often metaphorically linked to human reproduction and childbirth. Perhaps the clearest account of the sexual nature of ore-smelting is provided by the Chishinga, who explain the prohibition of intercourse during smelting in the following way (Brelsford 1949, p. 48):

> The furnace . . . was regarded as the smelter's wife for the period of the work and to sleep with his human wife meant . . . adultery . . . to commit adultery whilst the wife is pregnant means . . . that the child will die, and so by analogy the furnace would not produce good iron.

Although there are other ways of explaining the prohibition against intercourse, the statement made by the Chishinga smelters shows that smelting is seen as a form of procreation. A similar link is shown by the 'lewd' rhymes sung by the Ila during smelting (Smith & Dale 1920, p. 209):

> Oh it is boiling / It is boiling, the medicine / When this physic is ready / I shall free a woman and child / It is boiling, the medicine.

The statement by the Chishinga smelters and the song sung by the Ila smelters indicate that the ore-smelting furnace is like a pregnant woman.

Both the Chishinga and the Ila use tall, natural-draught furnaces to smelt the ore and the metaphorical link between smelting and pregnant women is confined to this furnace type. The use of procreation as a metaphor for the transformation of ore into iron is not confined to those groups who use a natural-draught furnace; it is also found amongst groups who use low-shaft furnaces. For example, the furnace is described as the reproductive organs of a woman in one of the lessons in the Venda *domba* ritual while the tewel pipes are described as being symbolically male (Blacking 1969, p. 167).

The same metaphorical link between smelting and human reproduction is also found among some of the groups who use bowl furnaces. In Burundi the songs chanted during ore smelting draw an explicit analogy between smelting and procreation, for example (Celis & Nzikobanyanka 1976, p. 125):

Tu as brisé mes membres et tu les as sondés
Mais qui ne brassez pas de la bière plate
Comme c'est beau!
Choisis, choisis, choisis au-dessus
Choisis au-dessus ainsi, le fer au-dessus, le machefer en dessous
Agnouille-toi, agnouille-toi et enfante.

Similarly, Leakey (1977, p. 306) states that for the Kikuyu 'there is no doubt that the furnace was seen as female'. Therefore, the metaphorical link between ore-smelting and procreation appears to be widespread in this part of Africa and it is associated with furnaces of all three types.

The evidence for a metaphorical link between smelting and human reproduction has so far been confined to verbal statements. However, this link may also be iconically represented by the decoration of the furnace. One of the more interesting, and less durable, examples of this form of representation is produced by Fipa smelters. When the furnace is built it is decorated with red *nkulu* powder (Lechaptois 1913; Wise 1958b). This powder is worn by girls at the onset of menarche and when they are getting married. Thus the furnace is initially decorated as a young, fertile bride[1] and the elaborate rituals at the end of furnace construction are analogous to a wedding ceremony (Wembah-Rashid 1969). Once the furnace is charged, it is painted black and this mimics the veiling of the young wife's, hopefully pregnant, body with a black cloth (R. G. Willis, *pers. comm.*).

Amongst other groups, the representation may be more direct and the furnace may be decorated with moulded female attributes, normally breasts: for example, moulded breasts are added to the tall-shaft furnaces used by the Chokwe (Lima 1967). This form of iconic representation is also found amongst some of the groups that use low-shaft furnaces. The Karanga ore-smelting furnace, a low-shaft induced-draught furnace, is decorated with breasts and 'cicatrization' marks (Taylor 1926; Franklin 1945; Cooke 1966). Similarly, Bernhard (1962) has described recent prehistoric furnaces from Ziwa Farm, Zimbabwe, which are decorated with pictures of women giving birth.

Although both the tall-shaft and low-shaft furnaces may be decorated to represent women, the absence of a superstructure on bowl furnaces makes the moulding of recognizable iconic decoration impossible.

Attention so far has been focused on the furnaces that are used to smelt iron ore and it is clear that these furnaces are associated with ritual and symbolism. If one looks at those groups that use two furnaces in the production process, one finds that there is virtually no ritual or symbolism associated with the second furnace. For example, there is no explicit symbolism associated with the low-shaft furnace used by the Fipa to purify *mtale* (Wise 1958b) and the small refining furnace used by the Lungu is conceptualized as part of the forging process (Chaplin 1961).

The ritual and symbolism associated with the ore-smelting furnace and the lack of any ritual or symbolism associated with the purifying furnace needs some explanation.

The boundary between ore and iron cannot be drawn at any particular point in the smelting process. Leach (1976, pp. 35, 82) has pointed out that transitions across a boundary involve an ambiguous period when an object or person is in neither one state nor another. These periods represent a problem in classification and they are treated as being 'sacred', subject to 'taboo' and are associated with ritual activity. Therefore, it is not surprising that the furnaces in which the transformations take place and the people who are involved in the activity are surrounded by ritual and taboo.

While the idea that the ore-smelting furnace is associated with a period of ambiguity can be used to explain why these furnaces are ritually and symbolically important, it does not explain why they are thought of as women and why smelting is seen as a form of procreation. However, smelting is only one part of the conceptual system associated with sexual metaphors.

Reproduction, smelting and cooking

The idea that sexual intercourse makes a couple 'hot' is common in eastern and southern Africa: it is reported among the Bemba (Richards 1956, p. 30) and the Kgatla (Schapera 1971, pp. 170–1). The information from the Zulu is more explicit and shows the importance of heat in human reproduction. They explicitly state that the male's semen and the woman's blood are transformed into a child by the heat of intercourse and that the 'heat' of intercourse is used by ancestors to mould the child (Berglund 1976, pp. 117, 232). Among the Thonga of southern Mozambique sexual intercourse is said to release heat (Junod 1912–13, p. 188) and the child 'is the product of a successful firing' (Junod 1912–13). Similarly, among the Kikuyu a woman who is barren because she has been cursed by her mother's clan goes through a ritual in which members of the mother's clan say (Leakey 1977, p. 546): 'We bless this for you and put heat into you if it is evil words that we use to you that prevented your bearing a child.'

While there is no explicit statement to show that the Ila believe that sex makes people 'hot', the lower pieces of wood in a friction drill used to make fire is called 'the female' while the drill is 'the male' (Smith & Dale 1920, p. 143). In all of the groups described above 'heat' is essential for procreation because the child will not be formed without it, and the same is probably true for most of the groups in eastern and southern Africa.

Unfortunately, clear descriptions of indigenous concepts of procreation are rare and it is difficult to provide clear evidence on this point. This lack of clarity is especially true for the Nyakusa (Wilson 1957; Wilson 1959) but this group seems to show most clearly that the common conceptual link between smelting and procreation is the process of heating and a detailed examination of these data is therefore appropriate.

Wilson (1977, p. 10) suggests that the Nyakusa obtained their iron from neighbouring communities and therefore she does not describe smelting. However, some of the features of her description of smithing are more reminiscent of smelting. For example, she states (1959, p. 153): 'Smithing and coition are felt to be alike, and the molten iron that trickles out of a forge is linked with menstrual blood.' But smithing cannot produce liquid iron (iron melts at 1536°C, which is well above the temperatures which can be achieved in an open forge) while it is common for liquid slag to run from the furnace through the tewel pipes during smelting. It seems more likely, therefore, that some of her descriptions of the symbolism of forging are probably descriptions of the symbolism of smelting.

Wilson (1957, p. 140) states that among the Nyakusa, 'a pregnant woman has a great fire in her body. . . . That fire is strong.' When a man has intercourse with a woman he puts his blood in her (Wilson 1957, p. 142) and this blood is presumably transformed into a child by the fire of intercourse (fire is a symbol of sexual intercourse – Wilson 1957, p. 143). The developing foetus is likened to iron. For example, the Nyakusa avoid the smithy if their wives are pregnant: 'Only when it is seen that the "iron" is there [when the wife is pregnant] do I fear' (Wilson 1957, p. 142).

The stress placed on the process of heating in both human reproduction and smelting suggests that other heat-mediated processes may also be metaphorically linked to these two processes and the most obvious link is found with cooking. For example, the Kikuyu conceptualize smelting as a form of procreation but they refer to the furnace as *nyungu*, the word for a cooking pot (Leakey 1977, p. 305). But this link between furnaces and pots is not confined to the Kikuyu: the Venda also talk about 'smelting in a pot' (Stayt 1931, p. 61) although it is clear that they smelted in furnaces. Although other groups do not draw an explicit analogy between pots and furnaces, they may refer to women as 'pots'. For example, when an Ila woman looks for a wife for her son she will go to neighbouring villages and ask for a pot (Smith & Dale 1920, p. 46). More importantly, the 'lewd' song of the Ila smelters that refers to medicines boiling makes it clear that smelting can be seen as a form of cooking. These examples indicate that women, furnaces and pots are all metaphorically linked and it is the nature of this linkage which will now be explored.

The central element of heat-mediated transformations is basic to the metaphorical triad of cooking, procreation and smelting and the importance of this mode of thought needs some explanation. If meat or vegetables are heated, they are changed and this change is irreversible; they cannot be converted back into raw meat or vegetables. The same is true of the transformation of ore into iron, given the available technology, and also for procreation where the foetus cannot be converted back into semen and blood.[2] In all three cases the heat changes a substance from one state to another and once it has been changed it does not revert to its original state.

The concept of an irreversible transformation mediated by heat provides a cultural solution to the crossing of boundaries. In their simplest form heat-mediated transform- ations can be used to convert the raw, natural world into cultural 'cooked' products (see Lévi-Strauss 1970 for a fuller discussion of this point). Thus the mode of thought enables humans to 'control' the boundary between culture and nature and so impose order on their world and this is clearly represented in oral traditions from south-central Africa where fire and cooking are used to differentiate 'cultured' from 'wild' people (Wilson 1959, Ch. 2; De Heusch 1982). However, the mode of thought is not only a charter for differentiating culture from nature. The metaphor of irreversible heat-mediated transformations can also be used as a plan for acting upon and producing change in both the physical and social world. Therefore it seems likely that the metaphorical links between furnaces, pots and women, and smelting, cooking and procreation are part of a pervasive mode of thought or system of beliefs in eastern and

southern Africa. This mode of thought provides a plan for cultural action in the world
and consequently it allows humans to 'control' nature.

Decoration on furnaces, decoration on pots

It has already been pointed out that in some groups furnaces may be iconically
decorated so that they look like women. Given the metaphorical links between women,
furnaces and pots, one might expect that pottery would be treated in a similar way, and
this possibility will now be explored within the context of a particular group of people,
the Karanga of southeastern Zimbabwe.

Ethnographic and archaeological descriptions of Karanga furnaces show that they are
iconic representations of women (Bent 1892; Robinson 1961; Sinclair 1984a; W. Ndoro,
pers. comm.). At a minimum they have moulded breasts but a relatively complete iconic
representation appears to be more common, with the furnaces having moulded breasts,
cicatrization marks on the stomach and moulded genitalia immediately above the rake-
hole (Fig. 31.2). More importantly, the decorations of the furnaces make them look like
Karanga women (Bent 1892). Pots are not decorated in the same way as furnaces and
one might think that the metaphorical link between pots and women and furnaces is not
represented by the surface treatment on pottery. However, there is a clear conceptual
link between pots and women amongst the Karanga and this link has been explored in
some detail by Aschwanden (1982). The informants that he quotes draw specific links
between fertile women and some classes of pots but his failure to examine how the
decoration on pots fits into this scheme makes his analysis incomplete. Research on the
significance of pottery decoration has recently been undertaken in an attempt to
improve our understanding of the link between pots and women.[3]

The two most frequently used cooking pots are *hadyana*, used for cooking meat and
vegetable relish, and *shambakodzi*, used for cooking *sadza* (stiff maize or millet porridge). The decoration on *hadyana* can take one of three forms: (a) a single or double
incised line around the 'neck'/shoulder junction, (b) a band of hatching or cross-
hatching on the 'neck'/shoulder junction and (c) either of the previous two decorations
with four pairs of pendent triangles below the band which can be either plain or filled
punctates (Fig. 31.2). The decoration on *shambakodzi* is confined to single or double
incised lines at the 'neck'/shoulder junction.

Attempts to elicit information about the meaning of the motifs during fieldwork are
often met with the simple explanation that it is traditional. However, many more
informants than one would expect can give some information on the meaning of
decorative motifs, although the degree of knowledge is very variable. In a number of
cases, informants state that the punctates used to fill the pendent triangles represent
beads and most informants also say that the triangles represent *zvikwati*. This term
refers to the chevron pattern, normally worked in beads, that was common on the front
apron worn by a woman.

Information on the bands of hatching or cross-hatching is difficult to obtain and in
the absence of further research cannot be commented upon. However, informants are
clear about the meaning of the incised lines that run around the 'neck'/shoulder junction

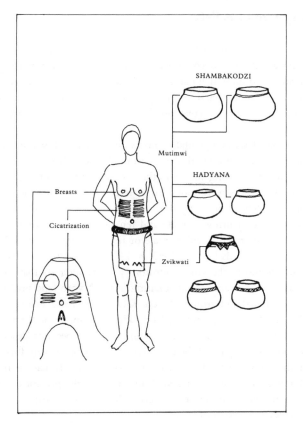

Figure 31.2   Adornment on furnaces, women and pots.

of *hadyana* and *shambakodzi*. These lines are called *mutimwi* and they represent the string worn around the waist of females and young boys. This information indicates that items of female clothing are represented by the decoration on cooking pots and so Karanga pots are decorated like women.

Although it is possible to state that both Karanga furnaces and pots are decorated to be like women, it is interesting that the exact form of representation is different. In the case of furnaces, the superstructure is made to look like a naked woman with sexual attributes explicitly represented and the representations are therefore iconic. However, the decoration on pots represents items of female attire and the decoration is therefore a metonymical form of representation for a woman. So, although the two different forms of decoration have the same referent, one has to be aware that in material culture the same referent may have multiple meanings.

A different system of beliefs

In the examples which have so far been examined the furnace is the vessel within which the transforming agent, fire, is contained. Therefore, it is the furnace which is surrounded with ritual and on which cultural re-presentations of the system of beliefs are placed. But there are some societies in eastern Africa that conceptualize smelting in a different way and this alternative conceptualization of the smelting process will now be reviewed.

Lanning (1954) has described genital symbols on smiths' bellows[4] from a number of 'capital' sites in Uganda. These symbols consist of clay protuberances that can be either large or small. Enquiries among smiths in the Nyoro and the Njulunga areas indicated that the large protuberances were found on male bellows and that the small protuberances were found on female bellows. Both a male and a female bellows were used to feed a single tewel. The pairing of male and female bellows is somewhat surprising because bellows are described as either male or female in the societies that have been discussed in previous sections (Wilson 1957, p. 142; Leakey 1977, p. 306), and the two categories are not found in the same community. This suggests that there may be a difference between the concepts about smelting in the Nyoro (and probably the other interlacustrine kingdoms) and groups like the Kikuyu, Fipa and Venda.

Roscoe (1923, pp. 217–25) has provided a detailed description of Nyoro smelting and some of the associated symbolism. Unfortunately, he does not describe how the furnace is conceptualized or any of the ritual which is associated with furnace construction. Whether this means that there is no ritual or that the furnace is not 'seen' as a woman is unknown and is not particularly important in the present context. What is important is the ritual and concepts associated with bellows because they are obviously important in the Nyoro system of beliefs.

Roscoe (1923, p. 220) points out that sexual intercourse is prohibited during the construction of bellows and that the breaking of this 'taboo' leads to the bellows filling with water. This suggests that there is an opposition between wind, which bellows produce when they are working properly, and water. Further evidence for this opposition can be seen in the practice of some Nyoro rain-makers. For example, one Nyoro rain-maker covered holes on a sacred mountain from which the wind was supposed to come in order to stop the wind blowing the rain away (Roscoe 1923, p. 31). However, a simple opposition between wind and rain does not fully describe the importance of wind. Kahola Hill is the home of a special earth-spirit and people come to this place to make requests for prosperity, children and rain (Roscoe 1923, p. 44). There are four holes on this hill, from which violent gales are said to emerge and, when the gales are destroying the crops, sacrifices are made on the hill and the holes are covered to stop the wind. Thus, wind can be seen as destructive and is opposed to rain, which brings fertility, a constructive process. But wind can also bring rain and Roscoe (1923, p. 219) recounts how when ore is being mined, a hole on the hillside is covered 'lest the wind blow from it and bring rain before they had finished work'. This suggests that wind is best seen as an agent of change rather than as a term in a binary opposition.[5]

There is also some evidence to suggest that wind may be a manifestation of the ancestral spirits. Thus, if a man is ill and is possessed by a hostile spirit, meat is cooked and placed in a pot to attract the spirit. The top of the pot is covered with pieces of grass and when these are disturbed by a passing wind, the pot is covered and the spirit is caught. It is then burnt or thrown in a river (Roscoe 1923, pp. 286–7). What is interesting in the above account and in the description of transferring a spirit (Roscoe 1923, pp. 285–6) is that 'cooling', the metaphor that would be used by those groups that use the women–furnace–pot metaphors, is not used to control the transformation of an individual from a sick to a healthy state. Instead, the healer 'controls' the spirits, and in the case of the hostile spirits this is done by controlling the 'wind'. It is also apparent that the spirits affect the state of the world and controlling the spirits, in this case controlling the 'wind', provides a system through which people can act on their world.

If controlling the 'wind' is a way of transforming and changing the world then the symbolism associated with the Nyoro bellows is not surprising. It is through the bellows that the smelter and the smith control the wind and produce the transformation of ore into metal.

Discussion

The data on precolonial iron-smelting are extremely patchy and can rarely if ever be fully integrated into the detailed ethnographies for particular groups. Despite these limitations it is possible to gain some understanding of the way in which beliefs about the process of smelting fit into a wider cosmology. It is also possible to see that cosmology and practice in precolonial iron-smelting are inextricably interlinked.

This chapter identifies two distinct systems of belief that are linked with precolonial production of iron in eastern and southern Africa. The first system emphasizes a link between smelting and human reproduction while the second system draws a link between smelting and controlling wind. These two symbolic systems are not correlated with any obvious difference in the tools used for smelting but those tools which are symbolically significant in the two systems are different. The difference can be most easily summarized in the following way:

heat : furnace :: wind : bellows

The difference between the two systems in the location of symbolic emphasis is reflected in the treatment afforded to furnaces and bellows. Where the significant element in the transformation is heat it is the furnace, the container of fire, that is decorated, while it is the bellows that are decorated when the significant element in the transformation is wind. Despite this difference, it seems likely that both symbolic systems ultimately link smelting to some form of sexual symbolism.

The difference between the two systems is not confined to the location of decoration but reflects a more fundamental division in the source of the agent of change. Fire, the source of heat in smelting, is a natural element that has been 'domesticated'. It can be produced by the use of friction drills and is found in the kitchen hearth at the very centre of domestic space. The same is not true of the wind, which appears to be capricious and is largely controlled by mechanical means – the placing of covers over holes. Thus the symbols used in smelting may be derived from either the domestic domain, fire and heat, or from the natural world, wind, and the choice of the source of the symbols as well as the symbols themselves may ultimately help one to understand how people perceive their world.

In the Introduction it was suggested, following Eliade (1971), that when science divides up the practices of non-scientific societies into 'efficacious' and 'magical' acts it destroys the view of the participants, who see all their practices as essential if a technological process is to have a successful outcome. Once it is recognized that both 'magical' and 'technological' acts refer to the same system of beliefs it becomes obvious that 'magic' is itself a technology because it is a technique for controlling the world (Gell 1988). It should therefore not be surprising to find that beliefs about technological processes inform ritual acts. This point can be illustrated by an example.

Both the Kikuyu and the Maasai have a 'smiths' curse' which is believed to be very powerful. When the Kikuyu smith is cursing someone he heats up a piece of iron and then cuts it on his anvil saying, 'May so-and-so be cut like this iron. Let his lungs be smashed to smithereens. Let his heart be cut off like this iron' (Kenyatta 1938, p. 76). In this case, heat is central to the operation of the curse. The Maasai smith uses a different technique. He utters the curse while manipulating the bellows and fire is not necessary for the curse to be effective (R. Waller, *pers. comm.*). Here it is the bellows, and presumably the control of the wind, that is central to the operation of the curse.[6] Thus 'technology' may be as much a part of 'magic' as 'magic' is a part of 'technology'.

One of the central elements in the present discussion of precolonial iron-smelting is the way in which the participants conceptualize the productive process. This conceptualization may be present in the songs that smelters sing, it may be present in the actions of the smelters (for example when the Fipa smelter is 'married' to the furnace), or it may be present in the decoration of the furnace or bellows. Thus, the links that exist between beliefs and actions need not be physically represented in material culture and, even when they are, they may be difficult to decipher in the absence of any social context. This is illustrated by the material representation of the metaphorical links between furnaces, pots and women amongst the Karanga. While furnaces look like women and pots are decorated to be like women, the decoration on pots and furnaces is so different that one would not recognize the link from the decoration alone. This discrepancy between the decoration on pots and furnaces arises because, although a set of signs may have a single referent, the material manifestation of each sign may be based on different tropic forms. It is also possible that when the tropic form is either metonymic or synecdochal then different parts may be used in different contexts to represent the same whole. It is this ability to use different signs for the same referent that can make it so difficult to 'read' the conceptual links between different processes from material culture alone.

Notes

[1] In a recent reconstruction of Fipa smelting the furnace was painted white to be like a bride and this presumably reflects the spread of the western symbolism of a white wedding (see Wembah-Rashid 1969).

[2] I would like to thank Dr R. G. Abrahams for pointing out to me the importance of irreversible changes produced by heating.

[3] Data on the meaning of decoration on Karanga pots have been collected over the last four years as part of a larger project on the semiotics of Karanga pottery. This work has been undertaken by the present author, J. N. Knowles, W. Ndoro and O. Nehowa.

[4] The bellows are also used in smelting.

[5] Beattie (1971) points out that Roscoe (1923) is not always reliable. However, holes in mountains and 'wind' bringing the black scent of 'death' are common elements in Nyoro mythology (see Beattie 1971, Ch. 3). I would argue that there is a consistent representation of the link between ancestors, holes in the ground and wind in the ethnographies of both Beattie and Roscoe.

[6] It is probable that the cosmology of the Maasai is different from the cosmology of the Nyoro. Fire is important in the Maasai system of beliefs and lighting fires is a common component of many rituals, for example the lighting of fire at the beginning of a new age set by the *olpiron* (fire-stick elders). It should also be noted that the friction drill used by the Maasai has the same symbolism as that used by the Thonga. However, as Jacobs (1965, p. 282) notes, 'in the act of intercourse, it is the male who breathes life into the smouldering kindling'. He also notes that the word *akut*, to blow, is used as a metaphor for ejaculation. It is the link between male blowing of the kindling and ejaculation that probably underlies the use of the bellows in the curse of the smith.

Acknowledgements

This chapter is in large part a revision of one section of a PhD thesis submitted to Cambridge University. I would like to thank J. N. Knowles and my supervisor, J. Alexander, for their comments. The data on the meaning of decoration on Karanga pots were collected in Zimbabwe and I would like to thank the National Museums and Monuments of Zimbabwe for funding part of this research. The views expressed in this chapter are those of the author and are not necessarily those of National Museums and Monuments of Zimbabwe.

32   The magical production of iron in the Cameroon Grassfields

MICHAEL ROWLANDS

& JEAN-PIERRE WARNIER

The latest publication to address the question of the relationship between African 'magic' and 'ritual action' on the one hand and iron-working technology on the other, is that by van der Merwe & Avery (1987). We find the paradigm within which their work is set is unsatisfactory in their use of the opposition between productive techniques and magic as defined by Evans-Pritchard (1937). The problem is by no means new and there have been several recent and successful attempts to address the question in terms of symbolism (e.g. de Maret 1980; de Heusch 1982, pp. 180–93; Echard 1983b; Monino 1983; Herbert Forthcoming) in order to deduce some deeper social purpose behind apparent explanations for the production of iron.

Our intention is not to lose sight of the role of technical efficacy in magic, since one of its advantages is as a concept over a symbolic perspective, which tends to reduce practical action to an *idéologique*. In his distinction between practical and magical action, Lévi-Strauss reversed the usual formula by claiming that, from the point of view of the agent, practical actions are subjective since they result from his/her interference in the physical world, whilst magical operations are objective since they 'appear to him as additions to the objective order of the universe: they present the same necessity to those performing them as the sequence of natural causes' (Lévi-Strauss 1966, p. 221). In the 'savage mind', culture does not determine nature but rather the reproduction of nature determines social reproduction in much the same way as the classification of nature must precede the building of culture (e.g. most famously in his argument that totemism had to precede exogamy in human evolution or that 'religion consists in the humanisation of natural laws and magic in the naturalisation of human actions', Lévi-Strauss 1966, p. 22).

This disposed of the idea that 'primitive technology' was just a simpler version of the rational action of an agent on an inert object. Clearly Frazer had had a point when he argued that, to the 'primitive mind', what we understand to be 'nature' is instead the product of 'animistic' forces lodged in things and substances whose reproduction does not depend on human intentionality. Human ritual action was directed to the naturalizing of culture and the recognition that cultural reproduction ultimately depended on, and was inseparable from, the propitiation of nature. Whilst no one subscribes any longer to an inferior 'primitive mentality' sunk in irrational superstition, nevertheless it seems that magical action has to be credited with a more profound role than 'a symbolic commentary on technical strategies in production, reproduction and psychological manipulation' (Gell 1988, p. 8). Lévi-Strauss' (1966, p. 220) definition of magic as 'the belief that man can intervene in natural determinism to complete or modify its course' allows us to proceed instead with understanding how, in our case, people believed they were participating in a natural process of the transformation of matter from one state into another. The idea that a technical process recapitulates more general ideas about natural reproduction in a mythological and cosmological context re-establishes the link between magic, fertility and technology made by Malinowski (1934) and by Evans-Pritchard (1937).

We shall be concerned with showing that the logic of such transformations was perceived to be more associative and relational than mechanically causal, although it is part of the practical efficacy of such reciprocity of perspectives that the two should not be seen as contradictory (see also Collett, Ch. 31, this volume). The case study is the metallurgical industries of the Grassfields, with a particular emphasis on what we have called the 'glazed sherds industry'. Our purpose is to describe this material, to place it in its regional, historical and economic context and to address the question of the technical efficacy of magical rites in iron production.[1]

Tom Cham – heir to an ancient metallurgical tradition

In 1984, the village of We, previously described by Geary (1976), had only one active blacksmith, by name Tom Cham. Another smith was building a workshop around a big granite anvil standing about 100 cm above ground, and was slowly assembling equipment: bellows, stone and iron hammers, water trough, medicines. The peasant farmers of We, and of eight other village chiefdoms considered in this chapter, still need a number of iron implements that cannot be found ready-made from the stock of industrial products sold in local markets. They need knives to tap the oil and raphia palm trees for wine, bells for their hunting dogs, spears to hunt the occasional cane rat in the dry season, double-edged farm and kitchen knives for the women, long knives for the local butchers and a few, less common, items. The demand is important enough to keep Tom Cham busy two or three days a week, and presumably much more if he were willing to devote less attention to his yam and coffee farms and to pig-breeding. The demand is met only thanks to imports of 'traditionally' manufactured iron goods from the Ndop plain, about 150 km away, by itinerant traders.

In this remote part of the Grassfields, the pace of change has accelerated over the last twenty years. The rapid improvement of road transport, various development projects, primary education for all the children, and secondary school for the few, the hospital in Wum, coffee-farming, etc., have expanded economic opportunities. School teachers and petty traders ride motor-bikes. People travel fairly easily by bush taxis. More or less sophisticated goods, from the transistor radio to soap and the bush lamp, are readily available in local stores or through the daily or weekly markets.

In such a fast-changing context, the ethnographer finds it difficult to date and periodize the implementation of iron-working techniques and the associated symbolism he describes. Tom Cham does perform the appropriate 'rituals' in his workshop. But does he still perform pregnancy and delivery rituals when one of his four wives is having a child? Probably not. Perhaps he did perform them ten years ago and would revert to them in case of misfortune. But for the time being, the procedures followed at the government or mission maternity clinic will do as 'rituals'. Despite the change, Tom keeps his mind trained on a number of material and symbolic bearings provided by what we call tradition, that is, on the landmarks left by a long history of iron-working that we shall now sketch. In so doing, we wish to assess the economic and cultural importance of iron production in the area, and to establish the chronological framework of what will follow.

According to David (1981) and de Maret (1985, p. 135), iron production in the Grassfields is about 2000 to 2500 years old. The extreme diversity and density of genetically related languages within the Grassfields language group, and available archaeological evidence indicate that the Grassfields have been fairly densely and continuously settled for at least a couple of millennia.[2] The advent of food production in the area dates back to c. 4000 BC.

In the nineteenth century, towards the end of the chronological sequence, the Grassfields were fairly densely, though unevenly, settled, with an average density of perhaps 15 to the square km. The lowlands surrounding them specialized in the mass-production of palm oil for exchange against commodities produced in the highlands. This pattern of economic specialization and trade has been analysed by Rowlands (1979) and Warnier (1985). The basic types of political organization ranged from chiefdoms in the highlands, to acephalous societies in the palm-oil-producing areas. They have been described by numerous scholars: Pradelles (1975; 1986), Warnier (1975; 1985), Geary (1976), Nkwi (1976), Tardits (1980) for the more centralized polities; Dillon (1973) and Masquelier (1978) for the more 'acephalous' ones.

In the nineteenth century, iron production had become the preserve of a number of Grassfields chiefdoms (see Fig. 32.1). A first survey was undertaken by Jeffreys (n.d.a; n.d.b) during World War II, and subsequently partly published (Jeffreys 1948; Jeffreys 1952; Jeffreys 1961; Jeffreys 1962). The highest concentration of sites is found in four chiefdoms of the Ndop plain surveyed by Warnier & Fowler (1979). The quantitative approach to African iron production in their publication coincided with similar concerns by other scholars such as Goucher (1981; 1984), Robert-Chaleix & Sognane (1983), Grébénart (1983), Pole (1983) and de Barros (1986), who provided comparative material. It appears that with 220,000 m^3 of slag and smelting debris, the Ndop plain metallurgy is among the very few large 'traditional' industries of west and central Africa. The village chiefdom of Babungo, for example, was geared entirely to the production of iron and mostly for export.

After the Warnier & Fowler (1979) publication, the next step in the study of the Ndop plain industry would have been to periodize it and to perform laboratory analyses coupled with experiments in the field. However, these projects fell through for various reasons. Instead, in 1982, one of us (J.-P. W.) chanced upon a number of metallurgical sites, in Fundong, north of the Ndop plain, that belonged to a different technological tradition. They were part of what we shall call the 'glazed sherds' smelting industry,[3] which is better documented than the Ndop plain industry.

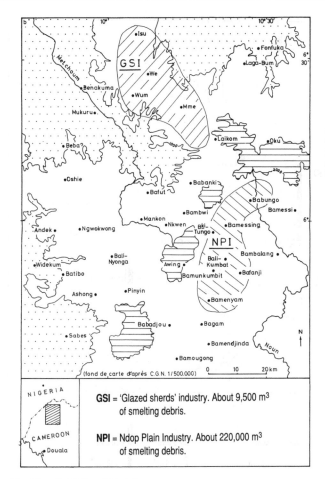

Figure 32.1   The Grassfields iron industries.

The 'glazed sherds' iron industry

From north to south, this industry extends from Isu to Fundong (Fig. 32.2). We did not have the opportunity to survey east of Nyos and Fungom, and a few sites could perhaps be found in the direction of Bum. The industry itself is quite homogeneous and can be treated as representing a distinct technological and cultural tradition of its own.

We carried out a survey aimed at making a census of all smelting and smithing sites of the area, including all periods, to collect quantitative and qualitative data allowing us to periodize the industry and to assess possible changes in techniques and economy. Altogether, 98 smelting sites and 48 smithing sites were found (see Table 32.1).

As a prerequisite to the study of techniques and symbolism, we shall now describe the glazed sherds smelting industry and its chronology, the smithy and the concepts of violence and fertility associated with it. The 98 smelting sites fall into two broad categories: small, scattered sites around Fundong (21 sites, each averaging 6.44 m³ of

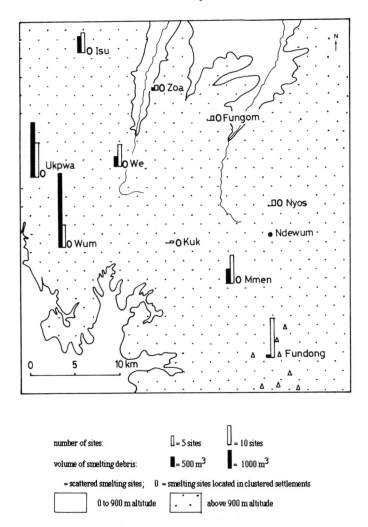

Figure 32.2   The 'glazed sherds' iron industry.

smelting debris), and rather bigger sites concentrated within clustered settlements (77 sites with 12 to 330 m³ of smelting debris each). Figure 32.2 shows the distribution of smelting sites and of the volume of smelting debris. One can see that the sites are fairly evenly distributed over the whole area. Yet the volume of smelting debris is heavily concentrated in the northwest, where two settlements (Wum and Ukpwa) possess 75 per cent of the smelting debris of the whole industry. Only in Fundong, to the southeast, are small sites found, scattered in the countryside. Everywhere else, they are concentrated in clustered settlements.

Table 32.1 Smithing and smelting sites, 'glazed sherds' industry

Locality	A	B	C
Fundong	0	21	135
Mmen	11	15	783
Nyos	1	3	?
Kuk	2	1	20
Fungom	5	2	25
Wum	6	12	3960
We	13	12	538
Zoa	1	2	150
Ukpwa	0	19	3152
Isu	9	11	902
Total	48	98	9665

A = number of smithing sites in a given locality. 'Smithing sites' = sites identified by oral tradition, and by at least one of the many items indicative of the presence of a workshop: raised platform, small or big anvil, water trough, granite hammers.

B = number of smelting sites in a given locality. 'Smelting sites' = sites identified by oral tradition and at least the presence of smelting debris (slag, tuyères, glazed sherds).

C = estimated volume of smelting debris in a given locality, in cubic metres.

Chronology

A hoard of eighteen polished stone axes was found in Fundong in 1979 (a discovery which eventually led to the investigation of the iron industry). At the time, it seemed reasonable to think that the iron age site that appeared to be associated with the hoard (the matrix of the hoard was destroyed in the digging that led to its discovery, and the association cannot be firmly established), and other sites in the Fundong area were somewhat older than the others, located in the north of the area (Isu, Zoa, We), where smelting was still undertaken until after World War II. We had seven sites dated by radiocarbon. The results are given in Table 32.2.

The cluster of the three older dates – collected around Fundong – even if FUN 2t and FUN 3t may be contaminated to some extent, give an indication that iron production in the area is about ten to fifteen centuries old. As expected, the northern sites, about which much can be learnt from eyewitness accounts (e.g. Jeffreys n.d.a; Jeffreys n.d.b) and from oral tradition, are recent. We thought that the Mmen sites would date somewhere in between, but this (on the basis of only one date, however) does not seem to be the case.

None of the Fundong furnaces is preserved. As a result, one cannot fully demonstrate that the recent sites are linked to the early ones by an unbroken technological tradition. But the smelting debris are nearly identical on all 98 sites, and quite distinct from the debris left by neighbouring industries (especially the Ndop plain industry). The distinctive nature of the smelting debris is sufficient proof of the continuity of the tradition.

As regards the economy, there are four indications that this industry was producing iron for export to lowland populations west and north of the area: (1) Palm-oil producers in the lowlands did not produce iron at the end of the nineteenth century, and

Table 32.2 Recalibrated dates, 'glazed sherds' industry

Site	Date no.	Date (cal)
FUN main site	Ly-3065	AD 245–915
FUN 2t	Ly-3066	AD 1305–1669
FUN 3t	Ly-3067	AD 610–1260
FUN 1t	Ly-3722	modern (contaminated?)
FUN 9t	Ly-3723	modern (contaminated?)
PWA 2t	Ly-3720	modern
MEN 1t	Ly-3721	modern

FUN = Fundong; PWA – Ukpwa; MEN = Mmen. The samples FUN 1t, 2t, 3t and 9t were collected in the shallow heaps of smelting debris, and are likely to be contaminated. The three other samples were collected in deep, apparently undisturbed contexts, and the measurements are consistent with expected results.

do not seem to have ever produced any. No ethnographer, traveller or natural scientist has ever found smelting debris in the lowlands; (2) Oral traditions indicate that this pattern of specialization and exchange is as old as oral history can tell; (3) Similar patterns are very well documented for the rest of the Grassfields, and it seems reasonable to think that they obtain in this area as they do elsewhere; (4) The volume of smelting debris in the smelting area is of such a magnitude as to indicate production for export. However, this last contention can admittedly be challenged, as we know little of the number of people thus provided with iron, their level of consumption and of the time periods concerned.

The smelting techniques

Smelting techniques can be reconstructed from Jeffreys' survey and publications, from informants' accounts and from the material found on smelting sites. Smelting furnaces are preserved, or were destroyed within living memory on 14 out of the 98 sites surveyed. Out of those, 13 had twin furnaces, and only one (in We) had a single furnace, that had been built alone 'for lack of manpower', said the informant. This was considered unusual, but not unfortunate. We shall now describe a site in Isu and complement the information with whatever can be gleaned from elsewhere.

Site ISU 4t is located in the Kege quarter on the land of Buta Dum. Nze Kage, the last smelter to use the workshop, died in 1942. The workshop has been abandoned for several decades. The area where it stands was planted with coffee, now overgrown with bushes. Two furnaces, about 90 cm in external diameter and 70 cm in height, stand 120 cm apart. In between is a water trough lined with stones, a small 'moon' granite anvil and two grinding stones.

Another site, ISU 5t, shows the same pattern. But, in addition, the square raised platform on which the workshop was standing is preserved. It measures 6.60 x 6.50 m, and the only doorway, with a stone threshold, is located to one side of the furnaces. On Site ISU 8t, where the platform is also preserved, the door is located at the other side. The orientation of the door, the furnaces and the walls was so diverse on the different

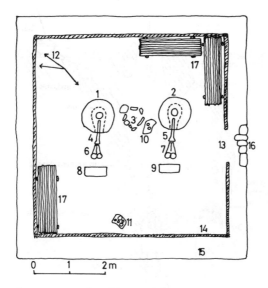

Figure 32.3 Layout of a reconstructed smelting workshop.

1 & 2 furnaces; 3 water trough; 4 & 5 tuyères; 6 & 7 bellows; 8 & 9 benches; 10 & 11 'moon anvil'; 12 geographic north as observed on the three sites Isu 4t, 5t and 9t; 13 doorway; 14 lattice wall; 15 raised earth platform; 16 paved threshold; 17 beds

sites as to appear haphazard. The informants said it was purely a matter of practical convenience. In We and Isu, informants said that the smelting and smithing workshops were built at a sufficient distance from any compound so as to minimize the risks of destruction by fire, should the thatch roof of the workshop be accidentally ignited. From available evidence, the standard layout of a smelting workshop can be reconstructed as in Figure 32.3. The furnace can be reconstructed as in Figure 32.4 (and compared to a Ndop plain furnace in the same figure).

The smelting process

The smelting process was observed by Jeffreys in 1941 in the chiefdom of Isu (Jeffreys n.d.a, Appendix A, pp. 84–102):

84. *ISU.* The iron-workers' quarter lies about half a mile to the north of the village. There are only two foundries, each with two small furnaces, shared among five families of workers. Two families operate the furnaces in one foundry and three in the other.

85. The furnace . . . is a small, mud cylinder about 30″ high with a mouth whereby the blast is delivered and through which the bloom is extracted. This is at ground level. Then there is the vent or chimney through which the ore and charcoal are fed. Originally there were nine foundries but cheap European iron has caused seven of them to go out of commission. The foundry-men have taken up smithying instead, buying scrap iron. I noticed in places that old tins were used as a source of scrap iron.

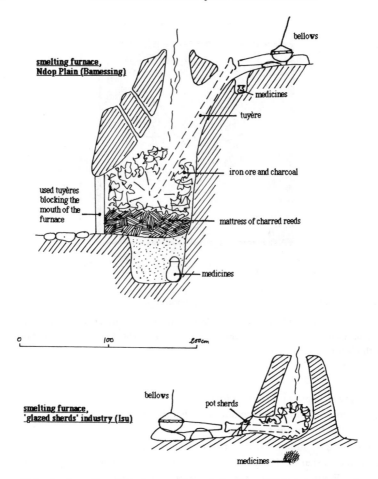

Figure 32.4 Sections of smelting furnaces, 'glazed sherds' and Ndop plain industries.

(86. . .) 87. Of these five families of foundry-men one of their number, the oldest, BENDOP, was both foundry-man and smith. His smithy, like all the other smithies, was a building distinct from the foundry. The buildings for both smithy and foundry are rectangular, lattice-walled, bamboo structures with thatch roofs. All the other foundry-men were smelters pure and simple. Their blooms however did not have a wide sale. It was bought only by the ISU smiths.

88. On my arrival one furnace was in full blast. The next day both furnaces were at work and I was informed that preparations were afoot to set the other furnaces in commission.

(89. . .) 90. When I arrived five blooms had already been made and their weights were 4.5 lbs., 4.5 lbs., 6.75 lbs., 6.75 lbs., 9 lbs., average weight 6.25 lbs. A basket was used as a measure of the ore for each blow. The weight of ore carried by this basket was 31.5 lbs. Hence the ore produced only about 20% of its weight of metal and that is a liberal

allowance because though the bloom had been shingled there was still a good deal of slag mixed with the iron and the weight of this slag is included in the 6.25 lbs.

(91. . .) 92. I arrived just when a blow was finishing. These smelterers use a calcining or roasting furnace and not as the OKU smelterers, a catalonial hearth. The heat generated by these furnaces appeared to be greater than that secured by the OKU workers. On arrival the calcined ore, heated red-hot round the mouth of the furnace was being removed for breaking up into pieces not larger than 2″ diameter.

93. The tools used are primitive. Young saplings are cut into pointed stakes and with these the glowing embers of the furnace are scraped out till the bloom was located. A wooden shafted iron prong or rabble was used to prise out the bloom which was then picked up by a pair of raphia bamboo tweezers some four feet long which immediately burst into flame.

94. The bloom was then promptly dropped into a pool of water which foamed and bubbled from the heat. The bloom was not shingled with a wooden batter on being taken out of the furnace as is correctly done at OKU and BIKOM. When it was cool the amorphous mass was taken outside and then beaten with a heavy stone on a slab of granite. The bloom was now ready for the smithy, but was very impure.

95. The furnace mouth is also the air inlet for the forced draught. No sooner was the bloom removed than the furnace was prepared for another charge. The tuyère was examined because it had an air-leak due to a recent crack. The tuyère, made by the workers themselves, was snapped off at the crack and the useful end thrust well into the depths of the glowing furnace. The furnace mouth is not closed with mud so as to compel the forced draught to go up the feed vent or chimney. On the contrary large potsherds are so packed round the tuyère that more than half of the blast blows back and out between these potsherds, which are covered over with charcoal. Thus an exterior hearth is formed. In this hearth the raw ore for the next charge is heated red-hot and thus becomes calcined.

96. The furnace was now filled up with charcoal and the blast started. As the charcoal sank down more was added until between three and four baskets had gone in. The weight of charcoal in each basketful was 11.25 lbs. so that some 35 lbs. of charcoal were put in and fired. While the furnace was being stoked up another worker had pounded up the calcined ore. A small quantity – about a handful of this pounded ore – was taken in a crude wooden scoop and loaded into the furnace followed by a full shovel of charcoal. As the ore and charcoal sank down the process was repeated till all the ore had been loaded in.

97. Small quantities of a special dust called NDAN, collected from the floors of smithies were added at regular intervals. Its function was to prevent the slag from adhering to the iron – presumably a flux of sorts.

98. I was informed that after the last load of ore had been put in, the blow was continued for only a short time. I asked if there were any indications which showed when the iron was ready and was told that the flame at the vent of the furnace, instead of remaining blue and red, turned white. I watched several times for this change but never saw it occur. What happens is that the bluish-red reducing flame gives place to

the yellowish–orange oxidising flame as the charcoal becomes burnt off and the blast now supplies sufficient air to turn the reducing flame into an oxidising one.

99. At intervals the potsherds in the furnace mouth were partly removed with the wooden tweezers and the charcoal scraped away with green stakes so that the rabble could be inserted to stir up the ore and to drag out any slag that had formed. On looking into the furnace the slag appears as a bright cherry red and the bloom white hot and glowing.

100. It took about eight hours to produce 7 lbs. of iron. In twenty four hours I saw three such blooms produced from one furnace. Once the foundry is started it is worked continuously for twenty four hours each day for two weeks: after which time all workers are exhausted. They take spells at the work and sleep in the foundry whither also is brought their food.

101. At every blow some six inches of the tuyère is lost. When the blow is over and the furnace mouth opened it is found that the ore and the slag are resting on the furnace end of the tuyère. The bellows end is then held in the hands and slowly twisted round. The furnace end which is plastic with heat then sheers off. In other furnaces this loss does not occur as the tuyère is not thrust in so deeply.

102. . . . The WE people use the same ore and the same processes.

More on the antiquity and continuity of the industry

At the end of the smelt, the tuyère and the potsherds at the mouth of the furnace were removed, and some of the semi-liquid slag was allowed to flow into the small gulley in front of the furnace. It solidified very quickly. Thus, each smelt left a cake of slag, 8 to 20 cm in length, in the shape of a half-truncated cone (Fig. 32.5).

The potsherds, as appears in Jeffreys' account, were submitted to high temperature. As a result, they were heavily glazed, and often fused together (Fig. 32.5). A remarkable feature of all 98 smelting sites – whatever their location and presumed date – is that they all contain vast quantities of half-truncated cones of slag, and glazed potsherds, often fused together. We take this as an indication that the furnace type and size, and the smelting techniques, were reproduced with little change over the time period considered, that is, ten or fifteen centuries, and that there is a continuity in both technique and human settlement. This view is consonant with other types of evidence analysed in another publication (Warnier 1984).[4] Since the glazed ceramic is found on all sites, we named this industry the 'glazed sherds' smelting industry. From now on, we shall assume it is homogeneous enough both in technique and associated concepts to allow us to lump together information collected in any of the eight chiefdoms considered. There are, of course, local variations. But in our opinion, they are of an 'etic' nature that does not affect the basic technical and symbolic patterns.

Fertility and violence

We now turn to the concepts of fertility and violence that underlie the production techniques associated with this industry. The data comes from interviews with elderly

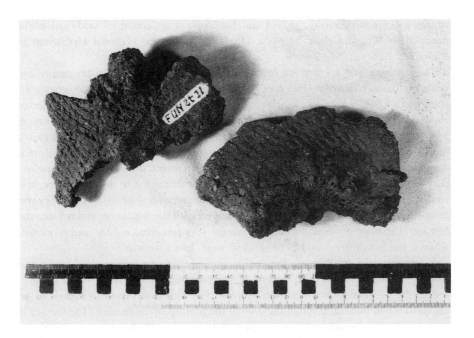

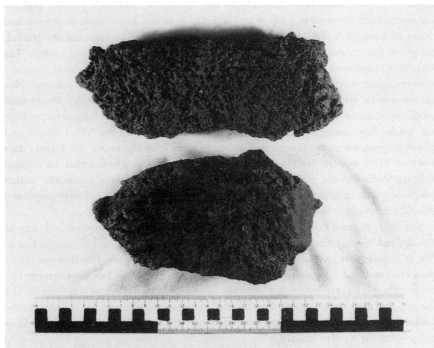

Figure 32.5 Glazed sherds and slag cakes, 'glazed sherds' industry.

Above: potsherds, fused, glazed, and with adhering slag, from Fundong. Scale in cm
Below: two cakes of slag seen from above (Fundong). Scale in cm (the ruler is 30 cm long)

smiths and smelters mostly in We and Isu, from a collection of medicinal plants obtained in We, and their botanical identification by the National Herbarium in Yaounde.

The smelting process is quite explicitly likened to the process of pregnancy and delivery. Besides charcoal, two types of inputs are fed into the furnace through the chimney: a 'male' ore and a 'female' one. The male ore is a ferralitic gravel collected about 6 km north of We, by the road to Isu, on the hillside, about midway to the top, in a grassy and fairly dry area. The female ore (not an iron ore at all, perhaps not even a flux) is a clay, collected in the banks of a local stream.[5] Once collected, the female ore is dumped in the stream, soaked and pounded. It is then mixed with crushed slag and iron dust from the smithy. This is then shaped in a cake that is left to dry. Once dry, it is pounded again and broken into pieces. The male ore is never washed. It is kept dry and pounded into small bits. Then it is roasted, mixed with the female ore and fed into the furnace. The male ore is said to be like semen. It is perceived as 'dry' and powerful, whereas the female ore is said to be wet and weak 'like a woman'.

As regards iron production, the conjunction of these two principles – male and female – is seen as the cause, as it were, of the conception of the bloom in the furnace, and of the pregnancy-like reduction process. The bloom is seen as a foetus, to be delivered when mature, through the door at the bottom of the furnace. The furnace is considered to be female, and to participate in the fertility which is associated with the female sex, with dampness, humidity, water, 'coolness', and with a lower position consistent with the woman's lower position during sexual intercourse, as streams and water are found downhill. Male ore, on the contrary, is found on high and dry ground, far above the streams. It is kept dry, and made more powerful by being roasted. The furnace is not shaped as a female body with breasts or other female attributes, contrary to some other west African smelting industries (see Collett, Ch. 31, this volume). Nor are the double bowl wooden bellows and the clay tuyères seen as male, despite their phallic appearance, and the fact that the stiff tuyère is thrust into the furnace throughout the smelt. The analogy with the reproduction process does not affect shapes and physical appearances, but processes. The ore does not look like semen, the furnace does not look like a woman, the bloom does not look like a baby. The fact that the wooden bellows looks like the male sex organ is irrelevant. The truth of the matter is that pregnancy and smelting participate in the same fertility process and that pregnancy provides a paradigm for iron production only at a fairly abstract level.

Similarly, the two furnaces are not seen as husband and wife. They are both seen as female, and, from Jeffreys' account and the opinion of Dongari and Washman Chi in We, it appears that local smelters found it more practical to work two furnaces rather than one, and that a single furnace would have done in case of labour shortage. The tuyères, manufactured by the We smelters, are made of two types of clay, which, like the ore, are 'male' and 'female'. The 'female' one, said to be 'brown', is collected in the Ndzong quarter, as is the 'female' iron ore, and the 'male' one, said to be 'red', is collected in the Kiwem quarter.

Washman Chi, an old We man, said that every now and then the bloom would come out in two separate lumps. It would then be considered that the furnace had delivered twins, and the smelters would perform the same birth celebration as for twins, with twin dances and songs. They would slaughter a goat and the whole ward would rejoice. Indeed, in the Grassfields, twins are considered as 'gods' and are believed to work wonders (cf. Jeffreys 1947).

In the Cameroon Grassfields, therefore, as among the Bassar of Togo, procreation, as pointed out by Herbert (Forthcoming), provides a paradigm for iron production. Whereas Herbert's paper focuses on the convergence of technology and gender, we wish to focus first on the avoidance of violence and its relationship with iron and procreation, and, second, on the technical efficacy of the 'paradigm of procreation'.

As regards the paradigm of procreation and the avoidance of violence in the production process, three points deserve mention: first, apotropaic medicines are buried under the furnace; second, there is a taboo on violence in the workshop; third, there is a curing 'ritual' in case of failure in the smelting process, or a breach of taboo.

When the furnace is built, a cocktail of herbs[6] is buried underneath, either in a pot, or under a stone, or even directly in the ground with no stone on top, as was the case in the We and Isu furnaces which we excavated. These herbs were called the 'spear of the workshop'. Some smelters buried medicines at the threshold, to 'trap' people who entered the workshop with ill feelings. Appendix 1 lists the herbs put under the smelting furnace and occasionally at the doorway.

All medicinal plants have to be collected when young, that is, 'fresh' and full of sap that can be extracted by squeezing the plant. The men who collect the medicines take along dried tadpoles, fried in palm oil, for the occasion. Before any plant is cut, they detach a piece of tadpole and deposit it at the foot of the herb they are about to cut. The only comments that could be elicited were of the kind: 'The elders have always done it.' Very tentatively, we can only remark that tadpoles belong in the water. Further, among the neighbouring Bamileke, another Grassfields people studied by Pradelles (1986), the doubles of the souls of children to be conceived are supposed to live in the swampy areas at the bottom of the hills, and to look like frogs and tadpoles. However, neither of us could come across similar beliefs in the We area, where enquiries on the folk theory of conception and pregnancy in women remained without any clear resolution – perhaps a result of several decades of intensive Christian proselytizing and primary school and adult education. Nevertheless, we seem again to come across water and procreation. Besides, one can see from Appendix 1 that most plants are collected in shady and damp areas, on hydromorphic soil. As such, they are associated with the female sex, with fertility and with female attributes: low ground, water and coolness.

Similarly, in nearby Bafut, the 'breath-life' of important men would be released at death to wander and finally settle in a wet place, with the implication that they were 'souls' to be reborn (Rowlands 1985). In Nso, Chilver reports that conception is believed to take place at six months when 'divinity' breathes life into the foetus and makes it move (Chilver n.d.). This is part of a more complex image in which a person may acquire form and breath through the patriline but acquires *sem* (a substance commonly associated with the liver or the stomach in general) through the patriline from the MF. The association of descent with corporeal form and life, i.e. the person as a moral being, contrasts with the transmission of *sem* through affines. Only important and powerful men and women are recognized as possessing *sem*, which conveys two qualities, the ability to transform into natural things and beings (strong winds, hailstorms and leopards, buffaloes and elephants), and clairvoyance, to see with two or four eyes and identify the source of hostile actions. In their transformed state such men and women may travel to foreign lands and rob people and things of their breath-life and bring it back to 'fatten' their own people, and they can visit mysterious under-worlds where the cunning can evade evil spirits and return to the living world with fabulous riches. We begin to see that iron production is therefore only one element of a more sustained discourse concerning the practical efficacy and achievements of those who possess the power to transform and acquire wealth.

On being asked if these plants have been selected for their therapeutic properties in curing human diseases, Washman Chi replies:

> No! The furnace is not sick, and cannot be treated like a sick person. It is a matter of experience. At the beginning, the dead elders found that those leaves were successful in ensuring good smelting, and restoring things into order if there had been something wrong in the workshop.

However, Jonathan Kum and Dongari are of the opinion that the herb used in 'curing' a spoilt smithy (see Appendix 1, sample 22) is the same that is used in treating women who have suffered a miscarriage, because, they say, 'a mishap in the smithy is likened to a miscarriage' or may cause the iron to 'cook' in the fire and disappear, which is a miscarriage of sorts.

A number of medicines are said to cure oedema and swelling (see Appendix 1). These symptoms are said to be characteristic of witches. Witches often die with swollen feet or a swollen belly, and this is why dying with such symptoms is considered a bad and shameful death. What is most characteristic of witches is that they cause barrenness and death by eating away the strength of their victims. Besides, they are known to be quarrelsome. There is a hint, in the list of medicines used in the foundry, of the fact that iron production may be the object, and also a potential instrument, of witchcraft through the association of iron and violence. The medicines thought to cure oedema are also said to trap witches or violent people crossing the threshold of the workshop, and to affect them with oedema and swelling of the limbs.

Iron production is explicitly expected to be a non-violent process. Blood should not be spilt in the workshop, once the blood of a fowl has been sprinkled on the medicines and on the furnaces at the time of their construction and at the four corners of the building. Should a smith wound himself, he must run out of the workshop, pressing the wound with his hand so as to contain the blood. In the past, blacksmiths and smelters used to protect themselves with leather aprons made of the skin of a particular species of antelope (unfortunately unidentified). No menstruating woman is admitted in the workshop. And, in the past, only men who had begotten at least one child were admitted to the smelting workshop. Here again, we find an association between smelting and fertility. No one should quarrel in the smithy, because quarrelling is the beginning of violence. No one with a red feather on his cap is admitted in the workshop – wearing a red feather of the turaco being the privilege of someone who has killed an enemy at war, or a large, noble game animal (elephant, python and, above all, leopard). No one carrying a bag of medicine is admitted.

Men should abstain from sexual intercourse the night before they participate in a smelt. However, says Dongari, if a smelter has a very quiet wife, who is never involved in any quarrel, he can meet her secretly the night before a smelt and have intercourse. Jonathan Kum is of the opinion that the emphasis here is not put on the avoidance of sex as such, but on the avoidance of jealousy and quarrels often associated with sex. A smelter, says Washman Chi, should never have a dispute with his wife or a relative who comes to work with him. He should never compel a wife or a son of his to do anything. Since no one should quarrel in the workshops, these can be taken as refuges by people – even criminals – who are pursued by regulatory societies. The latter (the 'jujus' as they are called in Grassfields pidgin) are prohibited from entering these sanctuaries.

What is true of the smelters and the foundries also obtains to a certain extent with blacksmiths and smithies. We were struck by the personality of Tom Cham, the only active smith or smelter we had the opportunity to meet: he is a very quiet, unassuming person, gentle and speaking softly, yet physically very strong, obviously knowing exactly what he wants, and quite determined. It was easy to work with him. He would take us to a quiet back room in his compound, listen to the request, state precisely what he could do for us and what he could not, and always kept his appointments.

Washman Chi explains, 'Iron is a very dangerous thing because it can be used to kill.' Women are not allowed to use a knife to spill blood, because women are associated with fertility. When they want a fowl for the pot, even one they personally own, they must ask a man to kill it. The manufacture of iron should be accomplished in a non-violent context, otherwise it will get out of hand and achieve the destruction of the community. In Zoa, smiths and smelters were not allowed to go to war. In We, however, they did. In all the chiefdoms under consideration, as in the Grassfields as a whole, there is a taboo on the use of iron weapons between allies or within a descent group or a local community, and Grassfielders distinguish and oppose wooden weapons and iron ones. Brawls and quarrels within a descent group or a polity, or between allies, can be resolved by fighting with wooden clubs. The equipment is made up of a fibre helmet to protect the head, a wooden club held in the right hand as an offensive weapon, and a wooden bar furnished with a handle as a defensive weapon held in the left hand.

War proper was undertaken outside the polity (and still is to some extent), and was carried out with iron weapons: spears, machetes and, in the second half of the nineteenth century, flintlock guns. The distinction/opposition wood/iron duplicates the opposition between inside and outside, brawl and war, for which there are distinct words in most if not all Grassfields languages – words listed elsewhere (Warnier 1983, p. 464). Drawing blood with an iron implement within the descent group or between allies or members of the same community causes misfortune (*ndon* in the Ngemba and Menemo-speaking groups) – another concept first analysed by Dillon (1973) in the case of the Meta, but which is found, with little variation, all over the Grassfields.

Thus, iron production stands at the intersection of two independent lines of thought: (a) it is a fertility process, and (b) iron is potentially very dangerous. These two lines of thought intersect at the very point where violence comes into consideration: (a) violence – especially the peculiar form of violence constituted by witchcraft – adversely affects the process of fertility, and (b) violence plus wood can be contained within limits, whereas violence combined with iron is highly dangerous, and is destructive of alliance and descent connections. In both cases, the substance that focuses fertility and violence is blood: the blood of fertility and birth opposed to that of wound and death. Blood has to be avoided at any cost, especially blood drawn by iron.

Curing a spoilt workshop

The third symbolic element is what happens in the case of a breach of prohibition and failure. When the smelt does not produce any bloom, or when the blooms are light and spongy, or when a dispute occurs in the workshop, or when blood is spilled in it, then the workshop is spoilt and has to be cured. Failure to cure the workshop would end up in permanent barrenness, that is, in the end of the production process. It might even affect the workers with barrenness, ill-health, leprosy and death. The sacrificial blood of animals can cure the bad blood of humans, and the blood of fowls is often spilled in contexts where this has to be done. Washman Chi said that this was normally done to cure a workshop. In similar circumstances that we witnessed, the fowl was not, however, slaughtered with a knife. The man officiating seized the lower part of the bird's beak in his right hand, and tore it away in a sharp gesture. The blood oozed from the throat and the fowl soon died. On the other hand, when a fowl is slaughtered for the pot, its throat is split open with a knife. However, we did not check whether this difference was perceived as being significant by the informants.

All informants agree that, using a fowl or not, the spoilt workshop has to be cured with a concoction of herbs (Appendix 1) – a different cocktail from the one that is buried under the furnace. The herbs, collected young, were put in a water pot, and squeezed to extract their sap, which was mixed with the water. The water was then sprinkled on the furnaces, at the doorway and at the four corners of the workshop. 'While sprinkling,' says Washman Chi, 'the men called the name of God to obtain his blessings. They could never see God, but they called on him.' It can be seen from the medicinal use of the herbs (cf. Appendix 1B) that they are supposed to facilitate childbirth, alleviate pain, promote fertility and peace.

One feature of this pharmacopoeia deserves mention: the *ikenge* (*Dracaena deisteliana*), which is, everywhere in the Grassfields, a peace symbol, does not appear in the context of iron production. We have no explanation for this state of affairs. Jonathan Kum, Elias Kum and Simon Chu of We, of whom we asked the question, could not find any answer. 'The elders never did it,' they said.

One can speculate on the connection between iron, agriculture, fertility and the reproduction of people and society. Austen (1987, pp. 14–15) remarks that iron production, in Africa, is first and foremost geared to destruction, the use of violence and authority, and that the history of food production and people does not seem to be closely related to the advent of the Iron Age and the development of metallurgy. We could not elicit any clear statement from any of the informants regarding the relative importance – economic or symbolic – of agricultural implement vs. weapon. Yet they all said that the first thing that was expected from a blacksmith was to turn out machetes to clear the bush (the agricultural implement of the men), and hoes to dig the ground (the implement of the women). Newly smelted iron was used to produce those implements and only those, and more hoes than machetes. Most other implements, including spearheads, were turned out from scraps collected from worn-down hoes and machetes. In addition, the smelters' avoidance of war and violence in general is well documented in the Grassfields, as is their connection with agriculture and fertility. According to Austen, this association between iron and reproduction might be recent, but we would challenge this position in view of the 'paradigm of reproduction' so characteristic of African smelting techniques, and so widespread as presumably to be very ancient.

Expressed in the local categories, the type of power named *sem* in Nso, *ifinti* in Bum, *ndim* in Bafut, is generally associated with achievement, imposition of will and hence with a potential for quarrels, bloodshed and evil. The 'male iron ore' of the We may be seen as the domesticated equivalent of that sort of power, and as a requisite for conception and reproduction.

The smelting process: a synthesis

A platform, *c.* 6.5 × 6.5 m, is built and a shed erected on top, with a thatch roof, and raphia 'bamboo' lattice walls. The selection of a suitable site, and the heavy work of building used to be a collective responsibility of the residential ward. In the past men did it free of charge, because each ward needed a number of smelters and smiths at hand. (Tom Cham, when he built his smithy twenty years ago, had to invite people and provide them with food and drink at his own expense.) The smelters and/or medicine men collect 'fertility-inducing' medicines, in sufficient quantity to make a heap about 1 m across. They chop them into bits, dig two holes about 1 m in diameter at the place of the pair of furnaces, and two smaller pits at the centre of the big ones. They stuff the medicines into the smaller pits, and sometimes in a hole dug at the threshold, inside the workshop. Alternatively, they can stuff the medicines into small pots, buried at the same places. They slaughter two chickens and sprinkle the blood on the medicines. They bury the head of one chicken with the medicines. They put a stone slab on top of the herbs, and fill the hole with clay. Then they build the two furnaces, above the filled holes, with ferralitic clay mixed with better quality clay collected in hydromorphic soil. The workshop is equipped with a water trough lined with stones blocked with clay, located between the two furnaces, benches facing the furnaces, bellows, tuyères, occasionally one or two 'moon' anvils (see below) and beds for the men who sleep in the workshop.

Before a smelt, four kinds of inputs are collected: a 'male' ore, and a 'female' one (a clay), ferruginous dust from the smithy and charcoal. In the past, the customers who wanted a hoe or a machete were responsible for collecting the inputs, charcoal included, and, presumably, brought potsherds to put at the mouth of the furnace. The charcoal was made from five trees listed in Table 32.3.

Some customers were also expected to help in the workshop, by bringing food, fetching water and raphia wine, etc. Tom Cham says that wine is an absolute requisite in smelting as in smithing: 'If there is no wine, I cannot enter the workshop. I cannot

Table 32.3 Trees used for making smelting charcoal

Sample no.	Vernacular name	Family	Species
15	*ketsale*	Euphorbiacea	*Macaranga* cf. *heterophylla*
19	*ugay*	Irvingiacea	?
20	*ugam*	Anacardiacea	*Pseudospondias micrantha* (A. Rich.) Engl.
21	*Kelum*	Euphorbiacea	*Bridelia micrantha* Baill.
31	*ndang*	?	?

work without wine, because there is too much heat, and I shall feel pain from my shoulders to my abdomen.' Teams of smelters were taking turns at each of the two furnaces. The smelters themselves manufactured the tuyères and replaced them when cracked. People were working in a festive mood, and 'there were always quantities of food and wine in the workshop', say the informants. The bloom was extracted after about eight hours of work, quenched in water and a new smelt started immediately. Between one and six blooms were needed to make a hoe, depending on the quantity of iron contained in each bloom.

The smelting debris – tuyères, slag and potsherds – was dumped on a heap by the workshop and abandoned. The blooms were carried to the compound of a smelter who owned a 'moon' anvil, standing usually in the open, most of the time in the courtyard of the compound. There was only one anvil for several workshops, with the exception of a few small ones kept in the workshops, as illustrated in Figure 32.3 (items 10 and 11). The moon anvil was a block of granite, of various shapes (rectangular, square, round), flat on the top, and about 50 to 80 cm across, and standing *c.* 40 to 50 cm above ground. The bloom was crushed cold, on the anvil, by being pounded with heavy granite hammers. In the crushing process, a number of craters were excavated on the flat top. As a result, it resembled the surface of the moon with its many craters of different sizes. The pounding process reduced the slag to powder, and left the iron crystals free of adhering slag. After sifting, the bits of iron were brought to the blacksmith, put on the hearth, heated, welded together by pounding, and worked into the shape of a hoe or machete.

Smithing

According to Tom Cham his workshop was erected some twenty years ago. By that time, smiths were not turning out hoes any longer, and the residential ward did not feel concerned about Tom's project. He invited men to roll the large stone anvil from an old site to his compound, and to help him with the building. Then he invited Blandi, from whom he learned the craft, and went with him to the bush in order to collect the herbs under the guidance of the elder. Tom provided a fowl. The fowl was slaughtered, and its blood poured on the medicines before these were put in a pot that was buried in the ground where the hearth was to be located (Appendix 1). The fowl was eaten by all the

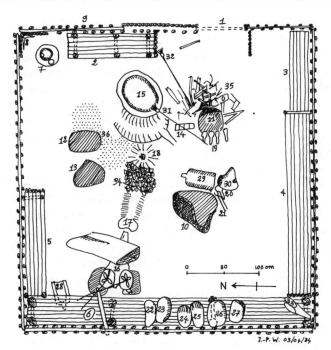

J.-P. W. 03/04/84

Figure 32.6   Layout of Tom Cham's smithy (1984).

The building: 1 sliding door; 2, 3, 4, 5 bamboo benches; 6 raised bench; 7 shrine; 8 raphia bag and spear; 9 lattice walls

Standing equipment: 10 main granite anvil; 11, 12, 13 small anvils, about 30 cm high; 14 small anvil with grooves; 15 water trough; 16 bellows; 17 tuyère; 18 smithing hearth

Mobile equipment: 19 & 20 iron hammers; 21 iron tongs; 22 to 27 granite hammers; 28 log of wood used by Tom Cham as a stool; 30 log of wood; 31, 32 brooms with long handles, to quench the burning charcoal; 33 spare frame of wooden bellows

Materials: 34 charcoal; 35 scrap iron; 36 ashes

men present at the inauguration ceremony, except those who had had sexual intercourse the night before.

Then Tom gave a goat to Blandi as payment for teaching him the list of medicines, and as a fee to start his workshop. All the blacksmiths of the We chiefdom were present, and he gave to each of them at least a fowl. The present layout of the workshop is illustrated in Figure 32.6. In the corner to the right of the entrance to the workshop is a shrine, with a round earth structure at ground level and, above it, in the corner, a raphia bag pinned to the wall, a few dried raphia palms stuck into the 'bamboo' lattice and a spear. Tom, on practical grounds, did not want anything touched – the whole place, he said, was rotten and could collapse. The raphia bag, he said, does not contain any medicine, but only the calabash in which the herb *ulu* is soaked before being sprinkled in the workshop when things go wrong (sample no. 22 in Appendix 1).

We shall now describe the production process of a knife used to tap raphia wine, as performed by Tom Cham, with Jonathan Kum, our research assistant, in his workshop on 10 April 1984. One of Tom's wives brings a piece of wood glowing at one end. Tom takes it, puts it in the hearth and heaps charcoal on top of it. The woman walks to the high bench at the back of the workshop, without a word being uttered by Tom or herself, sits on it, and starts blowing the bellows. Meanwhile Tom selects a piece of car spring, and puts it into the fire. Within seconds, the iron is white-hot. Tom takes it with iron tongs, puts it on top of the big granite anvil, and asks Jonathan to hold the tongs. Tom takes a cold chisel and cuts the car spring into two along its length, then reheats it, carries on the process, and severs about 15 cm of the halved spring. He has two pieces about 15 cm long and 2 cm in width.

He now abandons one of the two pieces and works on the other one. He flattens one end of the piece, hafts that end on a piece of wood, and puts the other end in the fire. Every time Tom puts the iron into the fire, the woman starts blowing the bellows gently without being asked. Tom heaps charcoal on top of the iron, and, every now and then, takes a sort of broom hafted on a 120 cm stick, dips it into a large water trough and quenches the charcoal with a generous quantity of water. Thus, the top layer of the charcoal is not wastefully burnt away, and the consumption is kept very low. In fact, at the end of the whole process, it does not look as though the quantity of charcoal, however small it was to start with, has significantly diminished. Tom takes a granite hammer, weighing about 10 kg, and pounds the piece of iron rhythmically (Fig. 32.7). He shouts 'weh' at each blow, and starts singing short phrases towards the end of the pounding process. On another occasion, Tom says that pounding with a granite hammer on a stone anvil, and shouting at each blow to increase one's strength and to control one's breath, is the first thing that an apprentice must learn when he studies the craft.

Tom now has a piece of iron which is thin, long and nearly flat. The implement is almost completed. Tom sits on a log, facing a low stone anvil that stands between his legs, and starts shaping the tip of the tapping knife with an iron hammer, going a couple of times through the routine of heating the iron and quenching the fire. The iron is never quenched. The only use made of the water basin is to help to control the combustion of the charcoal through the opposing actions of pumping the bellows and spreading water. The hammer is a solid lump of iron, as illustrated in Figures 32.7 and 32.8. It is not hafted, and its long part is firmly held with the right hand.

Tom has finished within five minutes. He straightens his back, holding the tapping knife right in front of him, for the last photograph (Fig. 32.8).

In the past, a much larger team of smiths and apprentices was needed because they were working locally produced iron instead of car springs. This required a special type of charcoal from the unidentified tree called *ndang* in the We language, and the presence of a couple of specialists used to assessing the correct heat at which the iron crystals would weld together, and to hammering the raw iron in such a way as to pound it into a workable piece. In the past, before the end of hoe manufacture, smithies were noisy and busy places. A lot of drinking and cooking would go on inside the workshop. Only people who had paid a fee could share in the food. If someone who had not paid ate some food, the smiths would not make any remark nor would they quarrel. But they would experience failure, and they would have to cure the workshop.

Figure 32.7 Hammering on the big anvil. Tom Cham flattens a piece of car spring with a granite hammer. On the ground, to the left and behind the log of wood, are the iron hammers (We, April 1984).

Failure, and how to cope with it

Failure in the smithy is dealt with in nearly the same way as in the foundry, since the aetiology of failure is cast in a single paradigm, expressed as follows by Washman Chi: 'The medicines [said to promote fertility] do not like quarrels.' The symptoms are that the iron 'burns' in the fire, or breaks up when beaten. The fire burns irregularly or without producing sufficient heat. Such failures will trigger a curing process, as will

Figure 32.8 Tom Cham and his raphia-tapping knife. In front of him, and under his right foot, are the iron hammers. Behind him is the big granite anvil. In the background is the high bench on which the granite hammers are stored (We, April 1984).

any breach of taboo, e.g. entering the workshop with a bag of medicine or a red feather, or blood being accidentally spilled in the workshop, etc.

The curing process consists in collecting the herb *ulu* (Appendix 1, sample 22), squeezing it in water and sprinkling the water all over the workshop, especially on the furnaces, the hearth and the door. No fowl is sacrificed, this being done once and for all when the workshop is built. (Yet Washman Chi says that the curing process of a *foundry* may involve the sacrifice of a fowl *in* the workshop.)

Anyone can apprentice himself to the craft by paying the fees and studying with a master. Thus, smiths and smelters do not belong to any special caste, contrary to what obtains in many societies of the Sahel. They enjoy a prestigious status that puts them somewhat apart from others. Anyone can look at the workshop and what it contains. But before being allowed to touch anything, one has to pay a fee of one fowl. When a son is born to a smith or smelter, the latter invites all his colleagues and entertains them with fowl meat, which is taken as a fee allowing the boy to touch anything in the workshops. Tom was offered a cup of raphia wine by a Quarter-Head, who poured a generous libation, drank from the cup, gave it to Tom, who held it in his right hand, then took it in his left hand, had it refilled, poured a libation and drank while holding the cup with the left hand. Smiths and smelters have the privilege of taking and drinking with the left hand – something which is prohibited by standard etiquette.

'Science and magic'

According to van der Merwe & Avery (1987, p. 143) three aspects of iron-smelting are universal in 'traditional' sub-Saharan African industries:

1 For iron-smelting to be successful, the smelters must be technically expert and a variety of supernatural forces must be propitiated. This propitiation takes the form of ceremonies and ritual and involves the application of special materials or medicines. The combination of ritual and medicines is referred to here as magic.

2 The iron smelters, especially the leaders, command the knowledge to carry out both the technical and magical components of smelting. This makes them more than ordinary craftsmen and gives them special status, usually high; alternatively they may be outcasts.

3 Sexual symbolism and taboos accompany smelting, often expressed through the exclusion of women from smelting in progress, compulsory celibacy for the smelters or female anthropomorphic details added to smelting furnaces.

There are two different issues to be considered. First, what is the relationship between 'magic' and 'production' techniques? Can the functions of 'ritual' or 'magical' practices be made explicit? Second, how can one explain the great amount of variation that occurs in the ritualization of production techniques in different societies? We wish to show that, expressed in these terms, the questions are nearly impossible to answer, and that, instead, the facts should be assessed in their symbolic contexts.

We would classify the explanations of magic vs. technology provided by those who have studied the craft (as reported by van der Merwe & Avery) under three headings:

1   Dismissal of 'magic' as superstitious practices without any impact on the practical outcome. This is the position of Kjekshus (1977, p. 91); an explanation of it being found in the economic domain: esoteric knowledge is 'a type of trade-union secrecy aimed at maintaining monopoly over an important economic enterprise'. If this were the case, smelting 'magic' could be perceived as hocus-pocus, even by the master-smelters themselves.

2   Acceptance of magic as a technology in its own right. This is the position of van der Merwe & Avery (1987, p. 144): 'we did not find that magic has a scientific contribution to make to iron smelting technology, but nevertheless concluded that iron smelting could not be conducted without it, because it is too important to the smelters.'

3   Adoption of a functionalist explanation, whereby magic is seen as a technological charter. This is the position of Bronowski (1973, p. 171) in his report on Shinto ritual which accompanies the making of samurai swords.

In the first paradigm, 'magic' is denied the status of a technology, a status which is reserved exclusively for the smelting technology as such. In the second paradigm, 'magic' is taken as a technology in its own right, distinct from the smelting technology, and with equal status. In the third paradigm, the smelting technology is absorbed into the 'magic' technology and the latter provides the mnemonic devices, the concepts and the work organization needed to perform the whole process successfully.

In some respects the Grassfields case does not fit the third paradigm, in so far as 'ritual' actions were performed *before* or *after* a complete chain of operations (building a workshop, smelting, smithing) and not *during* the production process, which is conspicuously un-ritualized, as can be seen from Jeffreys' account of the smelting process and our account of Tom Cham's work. Thus, the ritual techniques could not operate as a charter of the production techniques. In other respects, the Grassfields case fits the functional explanation (Malinowski 1948, pp. 1–71) since the ritualization of iron production can be seen as providing a cloak of sanctity that increases the seriousness of the performers, an organizing force in the labour process, and as producing confidence in those who have to cope with the unknown. However, there is no way that the above interpretation can be either verified or proved false, and any such explanation would apply equally to *any* production process, even those of industrial societies. In this respect, the ideological constructs produced by the working class, or the society at large, in any workshop or factory can be seen as fulfilling the same functions as the smelting 'magic'.

As regards the first paradigm ('ritual' = secrecy), in the Grassfields, *within* a community, anyone could learn the trade, at a cost which was not out of proportion considering the complexity of iron technology and the prestige attached to it. Smelters and smiths do not seem to have ever enjoyed any kind of monopolistic position arising from their esoteric ritual knowledge. However, learning the craft *across* cultural and political boundaries seems to have been a different matter altogether. According to Tardits (1980, pp. 348–9), the Bamoum kingdom used to obtain its iron from the Ndop plain chiefdoms. However, when the king of Foumban (the capital town of the kingdom) wanted to import the smelting technology, the latter was not introduced from the Ndop plain, as one would expect, but from the Mbam valley, east of Foumban. There are two other indications that ritual and production techniques were shrouded in secrecy from the outside. The first is the fact that, next to the iron-production centres, there were peoples who were entirely dependent on such chiefdoms as Wum and We for their iron supply. This was the case of the Metchum valley peoples described by Masquelier (1978), who considered themselves as *beu ongu* ('peoples of tribute') to the highland chiefdoms. The latter raided the former for palm oil, and purposely restricted the quantities of iron goods traded to the palm-oil producers. There is no positive indication that there was a ban on the transfer of technology. But such a transfer would have reduced the dominant position of the highland chiefdoms, and our guess is that there must have been such a ban until the import of cheap European iron made it futile.

Second, it is striking to see that, within the Grassfields, there are at least three quite different smelting technologies embodied in the Ndop plain, the 'Kom' and the 'glazed sherds' industries. Warnier (1985) has described the intensive exchange and communication networks within the Grassfields (and see Chilver 1961). In such a context, one would expect that the most efficient technological innovations would diffuse fairly rapidly, despite the economic constraints of comparative advantage costs, the dimension of the markets and the organization of labour. But this was not the case (and see Buleli, Ch. 28, this volume). Iron technology did not diffuse, and the know-how did not cross political boundaries, although the productivity of the various industries differed greatly. Undoubtedly the Ndop plain industry ranked at the top, and the 'Kom' open hearth technique described by Jeffreys (1952) most probably at the bottom, with the 'glazed sherds' industry somewhere in between. One would not expect such a diversity of techniques if the information was circulating freely. However, in such a situation, we admit that it is difficult to weigh the role of environmental constraints, of economic constraints (comparative advantage costs, access to market, size of market and availability of labour) against the role played by a ban on the transfer of technology effected by the enforcement of secrecy.

The second paradigm is certainly the most appropriate, but it raises a problem that was not discussed by van der Merwe & Avery, namely the fact that neither in the Grassfields nor in Malawi do the smelters and smiths make any 'emic' distinction between 'ritual' or 'magic', and 'production' techniques (see also Collett, Ch. 31, this volume). Western-educated scholars have a certain concept of causation as regards the reduction process – a concept provided by the natural and physical sciences. It gives us criteria to discriminate between 'production' and 'ritual' techniques in a traditional industry. The expression 'production technique' tends to be a gloss for whatever *we* perceive as the components in the chain of operations that seem to be technically needed for the success of the smelting and smithing processes, whereas 'ritual technique' tends to be a gloss for whatever component *we* perceive as technically useless from *our* point of view. In the opinion of Washman Chi, Tom Cham or Dongari, the medicinal herbs, and the taboo on blood and violence, are pure and simple *production* requirements of the smelting/pregnancy process.

In terms of the Western idea of technical usefulness, the 'male' ore (a ferralitic gravel) would not belong to the 'magic' or 'ritual' domain, whereas the 'female' ore (a clay), which does not seem to be technically required (although this contention could be revised after further analysis) would belong to the 'magical' or 'ritual' domain. This would obviously be an absurd conclusion. As Barley (1983, p. 10) says, this simplest and most pervasive viewpoint in anthropology can be summed up as: 'This looks crazy. It must be symbolism' (or, we would add, it must be 'magic', 'ritual', etc.).

In other words, the whole production process is cast in a more or less coherent symbolic code that allows the producers to have a fairly clear representation of what is going on, and how to cope with technical breakdowns (see also Collett, Ch. 31, this volume). In line with the central thesis developed by Lévi-Strauss (1966), one can see these representations as an intellectual *bricolage*, that is, as functionally equivalent to the scientific and empirical knowledge of the metallurgical engineer. In the words of Barley (1983), it is not symbolism which is the 'crazy' part of the intellectual construct. It is the totality of the mental repertoire, and it is found throughout the production process, even in the components that are technically required from a scientific point of view. Its basic concepts are provided, first, by sexual reproduction and the categories of male and female, hot and cold, dry and wet; and, second, by the experimentally deduced conclusion that iron + violence is dangerous and mutually exclusive to the reproduction process. Therefore they should be disconnected by the enforcement of strong prohibitions.

Van der Merwe & Avery raised the question of whether the production process could be successfully performed if its 'ritual' aspect (defined as technically useless) were to be dispensed with. This question, from our point of view, is meaningless, because every step in the production process, whether technically required or not, is perceived in terms of the symbolic code. The true question is: how does such a symbolic code or such 'magic' allow the workers to achieve technical success in iron production?

The 'level of ritualization'

In Malawi, van der Merwe & Avery (1987, pp. 159, 163, 165) observe that 'Phoka ritual . . . is more elaborate and more firmly grounded in tradition than that observed at Chulu.' They offer two kinds of explanations: first, the Phoka are located further away from town, they are less acculturated and more traditional, therefore they are more expert at rituals and esoteric knowledge; second, that 'magic' can be seen as producing 'confidence in those who have to cope with the unknown'. They then add (van der Merwe & Avery 1987, p. 165): 'a technology which is based on sufficient knowledge to make it work but not enough to predict the outcome falls in the same category as agriculture, hunting, fishing or love.' If this were the case, one would expect *more* 'magic' among the *less* expert and more acculturated Chulu. Yet the reverse is observed, because the Phoka are said to be more 'conservative'.

If 'ritual' is seen as the expression of a symbolic code, which is again seen as the technological language of the 'savage mind', then there must be a symbolic and a 'ritual' component in *any* technical process, *even if its outcome is entirely predictable*. In fact, if one listens carefully to what Dongari, Washman Chi and Tom Cham say, their symbolic discourse is entirely cast in the categories of the most rigorous determinism. Everything is perceived by them as predictable, or at least subject to explanation, after the facts: a drop of blood in the workshop will cause the iron to 'cook' and disappear. The 'male' ore causes the conception of the bloom in the furnace. If there is blood, quarrelling and breach of taboo, then one can predict without any risk of error that the production process will fail, even if the timing of the failure is somewhat unpredictable. The alleged unpredictability of the outcome is such only in the eyes of the Western engineer. There are, of course, unexpected and unpredicted mishaps . . . but *ex post facto* they are always explained, or can always be explained, by the craftsmen in the most deterministic terms provided by the symbolic code.

Nevertheless, we must attempt to account for the fact that some societies have developed their magical constructs out of proportion, and beyond what seems to be functionally adequate for grasping the technical processes. Such is the case of the Phoka rituals. In that respect, in the 'glazed sherds' industry, the symbolic discourse is kept at a low ebb. A number of strategic operations (building a furnace, feeding the inputs into it, etc.) are cast into the categories of gender, reproduction and taboo on violence, but many are not, at least in the present state of our documentation (pounding the iron on the anvil, pumping the bellows, shaping an implement). Eighty years ago, a visiting anthropologist, even over a period of several months, would have witnessed very few episodes about which he could have said, 'This looks crazy. It must be a ritual.' Elsewhere Warnier (1983, p. 37) observed that, in Babungo, there are taboos on pre-nineteenth-century furnaces, and not on the more recent ones. With the vast production increase that took place in the nineteenth century, a secularization or, in Weberian terms, a disenchantment of the symbolism of iron production seems to have taken place.

The efficacy of magical production

Lévi-Strauss (1958, pp. 205–26) addressed the problem of the practical efficacy of magical techniques in the context of shamanistic curing: a case of a difficult delivery. By comparing the psychoanalytic and the shamanistic cures, he describes how in both the patient alters her own representation of her body and of the delivery process. Consequently, mental and physical blocks were overcome and, thanks to the cure, the delivery assumed a normal course.

As we have seen, African smelters and smiths commonly conceived of the iron production process as a form of pregnancy-delivery. It might be thought that a significant difference here would be that the shamanistic cure acts on psychosomatic processes (which change personal volition, intentions and representation), whereas the symbolic action of the iron producer deals with technical, extra-somatic processes. But this is precisely the ethnocentric separation of person from thing or culture/nature dichotomy that our ethnographic case has striven to deny. Preoccupation with denying any primitivist aspersions to do with 'fetishism' has served to obscure the significant fact that the transformation of person into thing in either reversible or irreversible time is a theme of the utmost importance in African religions. In the Grassfields this is most clearly seen in the context of births and funerals.

Birth involving an irreversible transformation from inanimate to animate foetus to moral being is accompanied by a reversible process, the giving of breath or spirit to the child which at death returns to be reborn as a future spirit whilst the corporeal form, buried on compound land, continues as an ancestor to be summoned by striking a bell and giving libations when required by living descendants. In many Grassfields societies there also exists a concept that, in addition to people with common sense (lit. 'to have a head'), there are people with extraordinary powers of clairvoyance who are said to see with two or four eyes and who may see the hostile intentions of enemies in far-off lands, or recognize the source of some danger. Some of them are able to transform into natural phenomena (e.g. strong winds or storms) or into animals, in particular the leopard, to combat these enemies or predate on them instead (i.e. to rob them of breath-life). We have already mentioned that such people acquire these powers through the matriline. The MF transmits to the children of his daughter a substance, commonly associated with the liver or generally the stomach, that may be activated through appropriate use of medicines or by dropping special water in the eyes. The possession or activation of such substances are reversible, in the sense that they can be removed or made quiescent by ritual means. For instance, in the past, if a leopard were killed, it would be assumed to be a foreign transform which had to be brought to the palace so that a chief (or *fon*) could remove its liver or heart so that its power to transform could be redistributed to important men. In the Grassfields kingdom of Nso, the name for councillor (*kibay* sing.) and 'those who have eaten the leopard' (*vibay* pl.) are the same. More significantly, it is a form of power that facilitates the transformation of person to thing and vice versa as part of a single natural continuum.

We can now argue that in Grassfields' cosmology there is a common theme in the concept of the person, in birth and funeral rites and in metaphors associated with production, of which iron-making was a particularly potent form. We can, for example, associate several aspects of the symbolism of iron production with the ideal that the person should be composed of wet, cool substances of ancestral origin, activated by breath-life from 'divinity' and made powerful by a substance from the wilderness transmitted through affines. We can see the analogy to female and male ores and types of clay for the tuyères. Moreover, the power to transform is not only associated with violence in the continuous nightly battles that men of title engage in to despoil each other's populations of life essence, but it is also the power, used with selfish intention, that leads to sorcery. Hence there are prohibitions on the entry of those connected with shedding blood, whether members of the regulatory societies or menstruating women, and limits on sexual intercourse due to its association with quarrels and, perhaps in particular, with affines. These prohibitions imply that the real danger stems from the fact that the substance that can bring about all these bad effects is in the workshop and forms a necessary part of the production of iron. The real issue is that it does so only under certain controls that the smith exercises in the production process.

We have emphasized that interpreting iron-working solely in terms of symbolic meaning would be inadequate because magical techniques intervene in a *process* of production. Here the observation by Lévi-Strauss concerning the role of shamanistic cure in overcoming blocks in the process of delivery is relevant to Evans-Pritchard's question (1937, p. 464), 'How do Azande think their medicines work?' Azande offer what he termed a 'spiritual explanation', i.e. Azande believe in the existence of a 'soul' acting to produce certain empirical results in technological activities when a gap exists between action and result. Such a gap was defined as a stage in the natural process of production where nothing could be seen to account for what was happening, e.g. it was the 'soul' of eleusine which accounted for the gaps between the planting of the seed, its germination and its appearance above ground. The problem is, of course, that such gaps are precisely the moment when technical skill is meaningless and the 'spirit' of the natural process may be interrupted or defeated by the intervention of those with malevolent intention. Such a view obviously rests on a preconceived notion that a production process should be continuous and uninterrupted for it to be successful. Hence gaps both in terms of knowing what is going on, and in time (particularly in irreversible time), share the common feature of being the occasions when things can go wrong through the intervention of malicious spirits or foreign transforms who would extract the breath-life from the iron and use it for their own purposes. No doubt this lies behind the ideal that iron-making should be a continuous and uninterrupted process and why the participants will eat, sleep and work in the workshop until they are exhausted, involved in a continuous round of production without 'gaps'.

The majority of magical actions in the iron-working process that we have reconstructed were concerned with protecting the furnace and the workshop from hostile forces. The furnace was protected by 'medicines' called the 'spear of the workshop'; the entrances had medicines that would cause oedemas or swellings to trap witches or violent people crossing the threshold of the workshop. Quarrels within the workshop were likely to break the protective barriers and expose it and the production process to dangers.

Our evidence also suggests that the tendency to use human fertility as a metaphor or a paradigm in studies of African iron-working (e.g. Herbert Forthcoming) is inappropriate (but see Collett, Ch. 31, this volume). Iron-making, like most other forms of production, was not seen in different terms from human procreation, and the latter was not seen as providing the model of all other types of procreations. On the contrary, smelters and smiths appear to have regarded themselves as facilitators in what we would call a *natural process* by which certain materials in nature transformed themselves into a substance which could be adapted to culturally useful ends. Humans were there to facilitate this process and help remove impediments, and protect against sources of danger to the natural process. By achieving these ends, humans could direct a natural process into a socially useful direction, i.e. could come to believe that they were participating in a natural process of transformation, which was equally their image of the relation of persons to things in general.

The curing of a spoilt workshop most effectively demonstrates this point. The workshop is barren; the workers might even be affected with barrenness, ill-health, leprosy and death. Curing the workshop depends on attracting the blessings of divinity to act through the medicines that would also be used to cure infertility or ensure successful pregnancy. Clearly there is no reason to assume that one of these situations is more real than the other; both were equally serious, were part of the same conception of procreation and could be affected by the same causes and potentially cured by the same techniques. Magical production of iron implies therefore a conception of 'production' that is ideologically constrained by the belief that it is part of a larger natural process of transformation of persons and things in either reversible or irreversible time.

Conclusions

What, then, do we know about the 'glazed sherds' industry and associated material culture? It appears in the archaeological record some ten to fifteen centuries ago. Since then it has always been part of the pattern of economic specialization and regional exchange in the northwestern Grassfields. It reached unprecedented developments in Wum and Ukpwa in the nineteenth century. As such, it has occupied a key position in the economy, daily life and identity of the inhabitants of the nine chiefdoms concerned. The production technique is fairly well known. The knowledge of the technique was expressed by the craftsmen in terms of gender and reproduction. By providing the basic material component of agricultural implements, especially the hoe, it contributed to the production of food and the reproduction of society. Iron-working was seen as a step in the process of transformation of people, crops and things. Yet it was perceived as highly dangerous, because iron weapons could kill. It was shrouded in ambiguity, and the symbolism of the production process took this ambiguity into consideration. The techniques of production aimed at eliminating violence and witchcraft from the very inception of the reproduction process of iron, food and people.

What we do not know exceeds by far what we know. This enquiry has focused on iron production, the associated material culture and its symbolism. But these are part of a much larger setting about which we know little. The symbolic discourse on human reproduction and food production remains nearly unknown, partly because it has been superseded by other discourses (religious, scientific), partly because our research was not designed to elicit such a discourse. For example, if iron is perceived – as we think it is – as part of a much larger process of transformation of things, crops and people, then the men who produced iron could perceive themselves as participating in the reproduction of society, hence their high status, perhaps also the taboo on sexual intercourse before a smelt, and the fact that only fertile men (who had had at least one child) could work in the foundry.

The highland chiefdoms, engaged in iron production, provided the lowland peoples with their agricultural implements. If iron-working was perceived as participating in the reproductive cycle of crops and people, then it means that the highland peoples contributed to the reproduction of the lowland palm-oil-producing peoples. The latter had no control over one of the requisites of their own reproduction. This is consistent with their low status in the regional hierarchy, on which Warnier (1985) has commented extensively, their tributary relationship to the chiefdom of Wum in the nineteenth century described by Masquelier (1978) and the fact that highland peoples considered them as 'slaves'.

What this shows is that any narrow conception of production is essentially faulty and that any study of Grassfields' (African?) iron-working should exceed the limits of wanting to know only the material conditions of making things. Iron-working practices contained and objectified instead much wider ideas about those Grassfields' cosmologies which provided unitary organizing frameworks within which production could be organized.

What needs to be questioned ultimately is the adequacy of modern Western-derived social models which have a propensity to distinguish and separate levels of social analysis (e.g. cultural – political – economic). The problem we have had in grasping what has been presented to us archaeologically and ethnographically lies as much in the inadequacy of our conceptualization as in our empirical success in acquiring new 'facts': a condition made no easier by the spread of scientific rationality and Christianity from early European contact which has now largely destroyed indigenous discourse. However, criticism of Western models is not an argument for absolute relativism but, on the contrary, for the recognition that understanding cultural difference can only be achieved through the systematic comparison of social worlds and their historical development.

Notes

[1] Research on the 'glazed sherds' industry was conducted by M. J. Rowlands and J.-P. Warnier with the help of R. Asombang, M. Poulibé, Th. Ngouné, Jonathan Kum and the elders mentioned in this chapter, between 1982 and 1985, thanks to the financial help of the Cameroon Institute of Human Sciences for J.-P. W., and Central Research Fund, London University, for M. J. Rowlands. May all of them find here the expression of our gratitude. We also thank the Cameroonian authorities for having granted research approval, the Cameroon National Herbarium in Yaoundé for botanical identifications, the chiefs of all the chiefdoms visited during the research, Ch. Geary for having helped us in the field, J.-C. Villié for the photographs reproduced in Figure 32.5.

[2] Warnier (1984; 1985) gave a detailed discussion of the evidence.

[3] Occasionally, in other communications, Warnier has referred to this industry as the 'Chap group industry', from the name of a group of chiefdoms where the industry is found. However, the industry extends beyond the group and is better characterized by a technological feature.

[4] Samples were collected on selected sites in order to assess the nature of the technical process and possible indications of continuity and change in techniques. However, they have not yet been analysed.

[5] Samples have been collected but have not yet been analysed.

[6] The botanical samples were collected and named, and their local use ascertained, with the help of Dongari, Washman Chi, Jonathan Kum and Tom Cham in We. At the beginning of the enquiry, there were some discrepancies in the information. It was reduced by cross-checking with the various informants. None of our informants was a professional traditional healer. In an attempt at knowing more about the use of these herbs in the local pharmacopoeia, Warnier tried to interview a well-known and successful local healer. The latter was understandably reluctant to communicate his knowledge out of the framework of standard apprenticeship, and we had to abandon this part of the research. The uses stated in this chapter are the common ones known to everyone.

Appendix 1: Medicinal plants used in the 'glazed sherds' iron industry

Each botanical sample is listed below with its number in J-P.W's herbarium, a vernacular name in the We language, the botanical identification by the National Herbarium of Cameroon when available and local medicinal uses. For comparative purposes, we added comments by Dalziel (1937). The vernacular names are given in phonetic transcription in the glossary (Appendix 2).

A Fertility-inducing smelting cocktail

8 *Nang kaze* 'cocoyam of God'. *Urginea altissima* Bak. (Liliaceae). A big onion, with leaves and flowers, growing on dry and sunlit ground, on the hills. Its leaves remain green nearly all year round. Only the onion and leaves are included in the smelting medicines, not the flower. No known other medicinal use in We. Dalziel (1937, p. 479) mentions cosmetic and diuretic uses.

9 *Tey utimenyam* 'medicine (like) the liver of an animal'. *Marattia traxinea* Smith (Marattiaceae). Grows beside rivers, in the shade, all year round. Used in treating sores, wounds and abdominal pains. Diuretic.

10 *Teywi sange* 'medicine broom-stick'. *Pilea microphylla* Liebm. (Urticaceae). A small plant that grows all year round on hydromorphic soil. Used to treat bad stomach.

11 *Ketsa.* No translation. *Pteridium aquilinum* (Dennstaedtiaceae). An evergreen fern that grows nearly everywhere. Used as a 'juju' against theft. Herbalists use it extensively, but the informants do not know for what purpose.

12 *Kelenge* 'caterpillar', because of its hairy stem that resembles a caterpillar. *Emilia coccinea* (Sims.) G. Don. (Asteraceae). Grows all year round on hydromorphic soil. Used to be given in decoction to warriors who had cut the head of an enemy to prevent oedema of legs and feet.

13 *Ambwat 'Bwat'* is onomatopoeic. It is the noise made by the dry fruit when it is split open. No translation. *Fuirena umbellata* (Cyperaceae). Grows all year round in swampy areas. Used to cure asthenia, by rubbing it into scarifications made at the joints, or drunk as a decoction. Given to toddlers, to make them walk. Dalziel (1937, p. 518): plant relished by stock at all times in 'Gold Coast', and burnt in Liberia for ashes to make salt.

14 *Teywu zabi tawu* 'medicines illness leprosy'. *Erythrina* sp. A tree that grows on the hills. The bark is ground into powder and applied on sores caused by leprosy. The powder itches. Dalziel (1937, p. 242): bark in high repute, and the tree is often injured by stripping and cutting. In Nigeria for jaundice. Worn as charm. Diuretic, and used as such in horses. Probably for the same reason, used for gonorrhoea, as infusion mixed with spices, honey, etc. In 'French Guinea', women after childbirth are given decoction of pounded bark. In 'Gold Coast', the bark and leaves are pounded and mixed with palm soup to cure barrenness in women (Irvine). For dysentery the root may be used along with the bark. Seeds used as ornaments, beads and in games of chance. Various 'superstitions' attached to the tree.

15 *Enumi.* No translation. *Palisota bartari* Hook (Commelinaceae). Grows all year round on swampy ground. There are two varieties, one 'male' and one 'female'. Used against swelling and oedema. Large leaves are softened on the fire. Young shoots are cut small, squeezed in water, wrapped in the large leaves in a bundle, and the bundle is rubbed on the swelling. Dalziel (1937, p. 466): used by Pygmies in the preparation of arrow poison, though not poisonous.

16 *Gue.* No translation. *Commelina* sp. Grows all year round on hydromorphic ground and in the shade. Eaten ground in powder and mixed with palm oil, drunk in decoction, washed on the face or carried around the neck to cure swollen eye, vision disorders and dizziness. Also put as a 'juju' against theft on farms and piles of firewood.

It will effect in the thief the sort of ailment it is supposed to cure (eye disorder and dizziness). It may also cause epilepsy. It is also used, macerated in raphia wine with other plants, to treat barrenness of women. Promotes fertility.

17 *Ufe*. No translation. *Vitex grandifolia* or *doniana*. An evergreen tree that grows in forest galleries. Bark (or leaves?) ground and mixed with castor oil is rubbed into scarifications on swollen parts of the body, to cure oedema. Dalziel (1937, pp. 457–8): *V. grandifolia* bears a plum-like fruit that has a thin edible pulp. Used (where?) to make a spirit said to taste like rum.

B Cocktail used in curing a foundry

1 *Fesangang*. No translation. *Spilanthes filicaulis* (Schum & Thonn.), C. D. Adams (Asteraceae). A small plant (10–15 cm high) that grows everywhere except on hilltops during the rains, and on hydromorphic soil in the dry season. The orange flower is used in case of difficult childbirth: six buds or flowers are thrown in a water pot. If they float with the flowers on top, the omens are good and the flowers are squeezed in raphia wine that is given to the woman to drink. The delivery is said to proceed easily thereupon. If the omens are bad, the woman is sent to the Wum Hospital. Also drunk in decoction by the notables of *ukum* before their annual festival at the beginning of the dry season.

2 *Fezaame*. No translation. *Achiranthes aspera* Linn. (Amaranhaceae). A very small plant (5–10 cm) which grows all year round on hydromorphic ground. Used together with other plants in decoction against scabies. Also against stomach disorders. Never used alone. Dalziel (1937, p. 34): plant used in Shari-Chad to make ash-salt. In India, root macerated in water is applied to relieve the pain of scorpion stings, a use not recorded in west Africa.

3 *Tey ukebang adzeng* 'medicine red back' (the back of the leaf is classified as 'red'). *Dichrocephala chrysantemifolia* (Blume) D. C. (Asteraceae). Grows in the shade, but not in swampy ground. Squeezed in water and given to drink to people who have been hit by lightning.

4 *Gue* (see sample no. 16 in the 'fertility-inducing' smelting cocktail).

5 *Fekau*. No translation. *Sida veronicifolia* Lam. (Malvaceae). Grows in shady, wooded areas, but not on hydromorphic ground. A creeper. Squeezed in water with plant no. 1, and given to pregnant women during labour, to facilitate delivery. Also taken during pregnancy to the same effect. Said to relieve abdominal pains. Dalziel (1937, p. 132): *S. linifolia* Cav. (J.-P. W.: not *S. veronicifolia* Lam.): 'herbalists give it to women in pregnancy in Lagos, without any known efficacy.'

6 *Teywi ndzange* 'medicine of *ndzange*' – *ndzange* being a plant vaguely reminiscent of the castor oil plant (*Ricinus communis* L.). *Hibiscus manihot* Linn. (Malvaceae). Grows in the wild, in shady places, but can be cultivated like okra (*Hibiscus esculentus*) for its fruit. But the sauce made with it does not draw like the okra soup. Medicinal use: leaves squeezed in water are given to pregnant women to drink. Relieves pain and promotes the health of the foetus.

7 *Tey useng*. No translation. *Ipomoea* sp. (Convolvulacea). Prospective husbands take their immature brides to their compounds during the annual festival, and give them this plant squeezed with other plants in raphia wine, to drink, while fattening them. It is

supposed to promote physical growth and sexual maturity. Also macerated in a
successor's raphia wine for three weeks after succession, to promote patience and
forbearance. Ceremonial use: put around a successor's neck during the succession ceremony. Also worn around the neck by twins and their parents. When a
father of twins dies, men put the plant around their neck before they can handle the
corpse.

C The cocktail buried in the smithy

23 *Nya fengang* 'garden egg of divination'. *Solanum torvum* Sw. (Solanaceae). A shrub
that grows everywhere, and bears yellow fruits that shrink and become brown when
drying. The fruit, roasted and mixed with raphia wine, is eaten to treat heart conditions. Also used to treat oedema by rubbing the fruit into scarifications performed on
the skin with a razor. The oedema and the heart condition are thought to be caused by
the 'heat' that is accumulating in the affected organs. The fruit takes the heat out of the
organ. The leaf, mixed with other herbs and eaten, is used to treat coughs. Dalziel
(1937, p. 435) writes: 'the small orange-red berries are eaten cooked or sometimes raw.
A decoction of the fruit is used in Sierra Leone by some peoples as a cough medicine for
children.'

24 *Ineng*. No translation. *Paspalum orbiculare* Forst. (Poaceae). Grows in the village, but
not cultivated. When a smith is burnt by a spark, he takes a young shoot of the plant,
peels off the leaves and squeezes the juice directly on the wound. This is a treatment
specific to the smith. When high, used in basketry to make the core of the coils, sewn
around with a needle.

25 *Tey keteu* 'medicine head'. *Dichrocephala chrysantemifolia* (Blume) D. C. (Asteraceae).
Grows along house walls in the shade during the rainy season. Neither planted nor
cultivated. Leaves baked on the fire to soften them and rubbed on the head and inhaled
to treat headache (that is, in vernacular, 'burning of the head').

26 *Sa*. No translation. Dubious identification: ? *Lannea* sp. (Anacardiaceae). A tree that
grows everywhere. Mentally disturbed people are washed in a decoction of the leaves,
and given some to drink. Also used in treating recurrent fever.

27 *Tey febom* 'medicine small calabash'. *Bidens bipinnata* Linn. (Asteraceae). Grows all
year round in half-shaded places, e.g. banana and coffee plantations. Squeezed always
in a small calabash, in water, and given to new-born babies to drink. Said to soften the
intestines and ease their movements. Has some obscure relation to the navel. Dalziel
(1937, p. 416): 'the juice of the fresh plant warmed is used to drop in the ear or eye for
earache or conjunctivitis, and also as a styptic to stop bleeding from a wound. The
young leaves can be used as a pot-herb. An Ashanti proverb says that the black seeds of
Bidens pray that the yellow *Aspilia* may become equally black.'

28 and 29 Same sample: *Tebang kaze* 'tobacco of God'. *Cynoglossum amplifolium* var.
macrocarpum, Brand. (Boraginaceae). Grows and blooms all year round in semi-shaded
places, e.g. banana and coffee plantations. Medicinal uses: smokers who suffer from
bad sight smoke the leaf in their pipe.

30 *Fanga*. No translation. *Polygonum limbatum* (Polygonaceae). A small tree that grows
on hillsides. An evergreen, it seems. The informants said they had never noticed any
flower or fruit on it. The bark is boiled in water, and the decoction is applied on chronic

wounds, but not drunk. The bark is used as medicine, and the leaf – not the bark – is collected with the other leaves and herbs to be buried in the smithy.

D The herb used in curing a smithy

22 *Ulu.* No translation. The sample provided in 1984 by Tom Cham was incomplete and could not be identified. In 1985, Warnier collected a complete sample identified as *Sida veronicifolia* Lan. (Malvaceae), identical to sample no. 5, known as *fekau* in the We language. It could be either two varieties of the same species, or two different parts of the plant, or again two different names depending on the context and use of the plant. Warnier did not have any opportunity to check. It is a plant about 50 cm high, that grows everywhere all year round. Has a reddish flower. In the smithy: squeezed in water that is sprinkled all over the place in case something has gone wrong. Medicinal use: in case of miscarriage the herb is squeezed in raphia wine, and drunk morning and evening by the woman. Comments by Jonathan Kum and Dongari: a mishap in the smithy is likened to a miscarriage.

Appendix 2: Glossary (We language)

The languages of the nine chiefdoms under consideration are genetically related within the 'Ring' subgroup of the Grassfields language group. Yet most of them are not mutually intelligible, as is the case between Wum and We, only 10 km distant from each other. These languages are tonal languages and have noun classes. They are closely related to the Bantu family. They have been described and analysed by members of the Grassfields Bantu Working Group. The vocabulary of the iron industry (a 'cultural' vocabulary) is fairly homogeneous over the whole area. For comparative purposes with other African iron industries, we present here a glossary in the We language. Each word is given in singular and plural forms (if any), and with the possessive concord, so as to allow linguists to identify the noun classes.

— anvil	sg.	zìɤəm	kənám	kŭŋ
	pl.	zìɤəm	únám	wŭŋ
		stone	furnace	my
— bellows	sg. & pl.	súət	wúŋ	
		bellow(s)	my	
— bloom	sg. & pl.	bʷəɤə	wûŋ	
		bloom	my	
— charcoal	sg. & pl.	kǎy	tùŋ	
(cf. 'trees')		charcoal	my	
— foundry see 'workshop'				
— furnace see 'workshop'				
— hammer (stone)	sg.	ŋgɔ'ɔ	nàm	zúŋ
(cf. 'anvil')	pl.	ŋgɔ'ɔ	tɔ́nàm	túŋ
		stone	furnace	my

- hammer (iron)   sg. *m̀bì: zúŋ ìtsə̌zə̀*
                   pl. *mbɪ: túŋ tə̀tsə́tə́*
                       hammer my smithing
- hoe   sg. *fʷə̀ zúŋ*
                   pl. *fʷə̀ túŋ*
                       hoe my
- iron   sg. *bvú' kùŋ*
                   pl. *bvú'ù wûŋ*
                       iron my
- machete   sg. *kûŋ kúŋ*
                   pl. *kûŋ wúŋ*
                       machete my
- medicines.   The list of medicines is given here in the same order as in Appendix 1. Each species is preceded by its sample number.

A Smelting cocktail

- 8   sg. *nâŋ kázə̀ kúŋ*
        pl. *nâŋ wúzə̀ wúŋ*
            cocoyam (of) God my
- 9   sg. *téy úíí mə́nyàm wúŋ*
        pl. *téy ŋ́íí mə́nyàm múŋ*
            medicine liver (of) animal my
- 10   sg. *téyɪ́wɪ šāŋə̀ wúŋ*
        pl. *téyŋ́ɪ šāŋə̀ mùŋ*
            medicine broom-stick my
- 11   sg. *tsá kúŋ*
        pl. *tsá wûŋ*
- 12   sg. *kə́lèŋé kúŋ*
        pl. *lə̀ŋé wúŋ*
            ('caterpillar my')
- 13   sg. *kàmbwát kúŋ*
        pl. *wambwát wúŋ*
- 14   sg. *téywú zàbì táwú wúŋ*
        pl. *tɛy ŋ́zàbì táy mûŋ*
            medicine illness leprosy my
- 15   sg. (male): *vǝ́nzúŋ ènùmì*   sg. (female): *èzáni*
        pl. (male): *vǝ́ntúŋ tǝ̀númtə̀*
- 16   sg. *gúə̀ zúŋ*
        pl. *gúə̀ tə́ŋ*
- 17   sg. *fə́ wûŋ*
        pl. *fə́ mûŋ*

B Cocktail used in curing a foundry

- 1   sg. *sàŋàsàŋ fûŋ*
        pl. *sàŋàsàŋ mûŋ*

  — 2   sg. *zàámɔ́ fûŋ*
                pl. *zàámɔ́ mûŋ*
  — 3   sg. *téyú kɔ̀bâŋ àdzɔ́ŋ wúŋ*
                pl. *téyú rkɔ̀bâŋ àdzɔ́ŋ múŋ*
                medicine red back my
  — 4   sg. *gúɔ̀ zúŋ*
                pl. *gúɔ̀ tôŋ*
  — 5   sg. *káú fûŋ*
                pl. *káú mûŋ*
  — 6   sg. *téywí ǹdzàŋɔ́ wúŋ*
                pl. *téymì ǹdzàŋɔ́ múŋ*
                medicine *ndzange* my
  — 7   sg. *téyúsɔ̀ŋ wûŋ*
                pl. *téyǹsɔ̀ŋ mûŋ*

C Cocktail buried in the smithy

  — 23   sg. *nyà fɔ́ŋgàŋ fúŋ*
                pl. *nyá ŋgàŋ múŋ*
                garden egg (of) divination my
  — 24   sg. *nɔ́ŋ zùŋ*
                pl. *nɔ́ŋ tùŋ*
  — 25   sg. *téy kɔ́tɔ̀ù wùŋ*
                'medicine head my'
  — 26   sg. *sà zúŋ*
                pl. *sà túŋ*
  — 27   sg. *teý fɔ́bɔ̂m wúŋ*
                pl. *ntéy nɔ̀fɔ̀bɔ́m múŋ*
                medicine small calabash my
  — 28 and 29   sg. *tébâŋ kázɔ̀ kúŋ*
                'tobacco (of) God my'
  — 30   sg. *fàŋgà fúŋ*
                pl. *màŋgà múŋ*

D Medicine used in curing a smithy

  — 22   sg. *lû wúŋ*
  — ore   sg. *táý zúŋ ìnàm támkɔ́*
                pl. *táý wûŋ ànàm támkɔ́*
                stone my furnace smelting
  — slag   sg. *tsàỳ nàm zúŋ*
                pl. *tsàỳ tɔ́nàm tûŋ*
                slag furnace my
  — smith or smelter   sg. *tsɔ̀ánàm wúŋ*
                pl. *ɣɔ́tsɔ̀ánàŋ wúŋ*
  — smithy (see 'workshop')
  — trees for charcoal:

- 18   *kə́tsàlè*
- 19   *úɣâì*
- 20   *úɣàm*
- 21   *kə́lùm*
- 31   *ǹdàŋ*
- tuyère   sg. *sə̀ŋə́ nàm kúŋ*

              pl. *sə̀ŋə́ nàm wúŋ*

              tuyère furnace my
- workshop or furnace (the word is the same. Only the context makes the difference.)
- foundry   sg. *nâm kúŋ kə̀támkə́*

              pl. *nâm wúŋ wùtám^{w}ə́*

              workshop my smelting
- smithy   sg. *nâm kúŋ kə̀tsə́ə́kə́*

              pl. *nâm wúŋ wùtsə́wə́*

              workshop my smithing
- smelting furnace   sg. *tsínàm támkə́ zúŋ*

                    pl. *tsə́nàm támkə́ wúŋ*

                    furnace smelting my
- smithing hearth   sg. *tsínàm tsə́kə́ zúŋ*

                   pl. *tsə́nàm tsə́kə́ wúŋ*

                   furnace smithing my

33 Town and village in ancient Egypt: ecology, society and urbanization

Fekri A. Hassan

Introduction

[The Teaching of King . . . for his son Merikare, Dynasty IX–X]
See, [the land] which they destroyed is made into districts and every great city [is restored]. The governance of (each) one is in the hands of ten men, a magistrate is appointed who will levy [. . .] the amount of all the taxes. The priest is provided with a farm, and men work for you like a single gang. How is it that disaffection does not occur? (Because) you will not suffer from a Nile which fails to come.

(Simpson 1973, p. 187)

The achievements of the Egyptian civilization dating back to *c*. 3000 BC and lasting for three millennia thereafter loom high as one of the earliest manifestations of the great artistic, literary and intellectual potential of humankind. These achievements were inseparable from agricultural production and a system of accumulating wealth, mobilizing a massive labour force for monumental works, patronizing crafts, marshalling armies and pursuing lofty intellectual concerns. The achievements of this great civilization were associated with the emergence of towns. The towns were characteristically relatively larger than farming villages, but more importantly they were distinguished by the concentration of managerial, religious, military, commercial or 'industrial' activities. This concentration was a manifestation of a new political landscape. In this chapter I develop a model of urbanization in early state societies, explore various aspects of towns in ancient Egypt, their development, size and hierarchy, and examine their relationships to agricultural productivity, transportation and social interaction on the basis of hypothetical constructs.

The beginnings of urbanization: a hypothetical construct

The beginnings of town life may be traced back to the upper layers at Merimde Beni-Salama (Fig. 33.1), *c*. 4000 BC. The settlement was large, with perhaps as many as 1300–2000 persons, and with rows of huts with dug floors and walls made of plastered mud, as well as workshop areas (Hassan 1988; see also Wetterstrom, Ch. 10, this volume). By 3500 BC, two towns were prominent in the cultural landscape of Upper

Egypt – South Town in the Nagada region (Qena) and Hierakonpolis (Edfu) further south. They were associated with the cult/religious centres of Seth and Horus, respectively. The inhabitants of these towns were perhaps no more than 900 persons for Nagada South Town and 1500–2000 persons in Hierakonpolis (Hassan 1988, p. 161). These two towns were connected with agricultural communities in southern Egypt (see Wetterstrom, Ch. 10, this volume). By *c.* 3000 years BC, most of Egypt was unified in a single nation-state extending over a north–south distance of about 1300 km. A capital of the emerging nation was established in Memphis. The kings were buried in Abydos further south in a cemetery in the low desert west of the floodplain. Closer to the floodplain, ceremonial buildings for royal mortuary cults were situated. The royal cemetery was moved to Saqqara near the new capital during Dynasty II. In later periods, other capitals of the nation were established (e.g. Thebes, Tanis, Tell el Amarna). The kings ruled over a country consisting of administrative divisions, which were later called 'nomes' by the Greeks. A total of twenty-two nomes in Upper Egypt were fixed by Dynasty V. For Lower Egypt the number of nomes was fixed at twenty later in Roman times (Baines & Malek 1984, p. 15). Occasionally, the boundaries of some nomes shifted. At other times, the divisions were altered. Accordingly, in some cases there is more than one capital for the same nome.

In a pioneering contribution, Butzer (1976) presented a comprehensive inventory of cities, towns, villages and fortresses from textual sources. The inventory included 217 settlements from Upper Egypt (twenty-two nomes), the Fayum and the first Lower Egyptian nome. Butzer subdivided these settlements into a hierarchy of city, large centre, small centre and large village. He used the term 'city' to refer to the two main capitals: Memphis and Luxor-Karnak (Thebes). Large and small centres most probably represented, not unlike today, towns serving as the nodes in a regional hierarchy of administrative, economic and religious activities. Each nome, like a modern governorate, was characterized by a nome capital connected to a number of smaller provincial towns, like today's *markaz*, which serve as administrative nodes and local market-places. Egyptian nome capitals were most probably primarily rural in character, as they are still today, with fields, shops and mansions. The nome capitals were primarily seats of political and religious power and as such served as centres for economic activity including manufacture, services and distribution of goods. The nome capitals were the major centres for the collection of annual taxes on cereals, cattle and other products (Helck 1974). The nome capitals also commanded and controlled the rural labour force (O'Connor 1972b) and mobilized such force for local agricultural projects (e.g. building dikes) as well as for military operations. The nomes were connected to the nation's capital via the Nile. Boats sailed up and down the river to transport taxes (collected in kind) and bring back goods and gifts.

Towns may have emerged initially as (1) centres of redistribution of food or exchange of resources, (2) fortified settlements to ward off nomadic marauders and (3) religious centres within an agrarian context characterized by great anxiety and stressful seasonality. Some of the capital nomes may have developed from earlier villages located at the terminus of desert routes. Such towns would have included Memphis, Atfih, Cynopolis, Assyut, Abydos, Dendara, Coptos, Armant/Gebelein and Edfu. Some of the first towns may also have been religious/cult centres that later served as capitals for

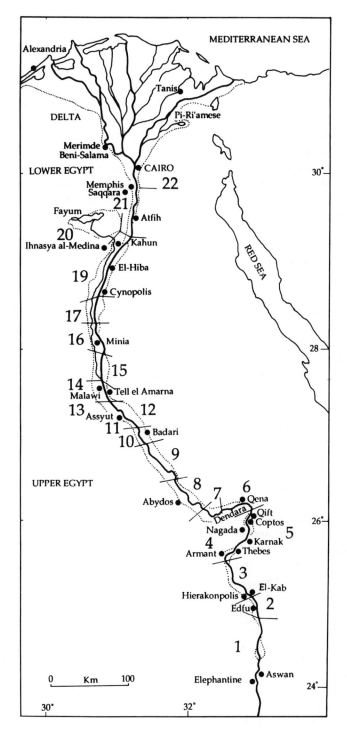

Figure 33.1 The twenty-two nomes of Upper Egypt and the major localities referred to in the text. Dotted line represents the edge of cultivation.

the earliest petty states that preceded the unification of Egypt into a single nation. Such centres may have included Edfu and Abydos. A predynastic state commanded by Hierakonpolis may have consisted of the union of the three southernmost nomes (Elephantine, Edfu, El-Kab). In the meantime, a polity centred in Nagada may have dominated the nomes associated with Karnak, Qift and Dendara.

The fluctuations in agricultural yield were particularly important in the development of vegetation cults and ritual and regional integration of resources. Towns were the centres of these key developments. Agricultural productivity is remarkably variable. Sedentary communities which depleted the wild resources around their settlements and became dependent on plentiful harvests were particularly vulnerable. They must have watched with fear and apprehension the sinking level of grain in their silos during the last months before the ripening of grain. Disastrous floods, inclement weather, pest infestations and other unforeseen calamities must have been a basic ingredient in the psychology of early farmers. Jubilation and gratitude within a context of ritual and a cosmogony of death and resurrection must have marked the season of plenty. This was also a time for feasting and frivolity, of marriage and partying and of a temporary relief from the climate of apprehension and fear. Chiefs, who rose to integrate and co-ordinate the resources of neighbouring villages, were closely identified with the spirit of divine mercy and benevolence. In addition, chiefs were also likely to arbitrate disputes about land and debts. They were also the likely candidates for mobilizing the male youths into a cadre of warriors whenever any of the villages within their domain came under attack.

Ritual and economic co-ordination among neighbouring villages were advantageous in overcoming periodic food shortages and in alleviating anxiety and fear. Ritual and economic integration would not have been possible without chiefs, who would have come from a recognized lineage, with a personal reputation for justice, wisdom and courage. Inevitably, conflicts might have emerged as kin-based organizations clashed with hierarchical institutions based on occupational and managerial relations (Gailey 1985). Occasionally the power of the chief to collect food for his household, function-aries and for redistribution may have been challenged by other village headmen wishing to renege on their commitments. A chief could not have survived, safeguarding the federation of villages, without the ability to extract a share from agricultural yield by supernatural, juridical and coercive powers. A militia to enforce collection of food contributions would have thus emerged. As the number of administrative transactions increased, the need for book-keeping became essential. Clerks and scribes were added to the retinue of the chief.

The rise to chiefly status is likely to have been marked by the display of insignia of supernatural or military power. In Egypt, such items included lionskins, maces, beads, feathers and headgear. A chief maintained alliances by rewarding village headmen with gifts of such status goods. Local community leaders were also drawn into an inter-regional network of ritual, economic and coercive privileges. Gradually, their alle-giance shifted away from kin-based obligations towards the higher source of power and prestige. Status goods were secured through trade for rare objects and patronage of craft specialists.

The aggrandizement of chiefly power guaranteed long-term survival of an agrarian economy. However, tribute to the chief rose in proportion to the increase in the number of managerial personnel, craft specialists and priests. Demands to integrate the allied client chiefs and the population through feasts, gift-giving and ostentatious display also mounted as more territories came under control. In some cases, agrarian failures, ecological disasters, subjugation by neighbouring groups or a breakdown of an alliance might have aborted the process of development. Economic growth might also have been arrested in certain ecological settings. Thus, after 500 years of agricultural developments in the Nile valley, provinces of various degrees of political integration (Frankfort 1948) still marked the stage before inter-regional integration.

Realization of the benefits of regional integration is likely to have led to progressive enlargement of the co-operative units. Neighbouring towns established networks for reciprocal relief from occasional food shortages, defence or trade. Certain towns, in favoured locations or under the command of capable leaders, served as centres for collection and redistribution. The chief in charge of co-ordinating the complex re-lationships between families, heads of villages and district chiefs accumulated more revenues, supported more artisans, commanded more people and had access to more foodstuffs and goods than any village headman or chieftain. For example, if five districts were integrated and if every district chief kept 50 per cent of the revenues for his town and transmitted 50 per cent to the paramount chief, the latter would have had access to revenues five times that of any district chief. The paramount chief could divert a good part of his income to public works and activities such as ship-building and mounting military campaigns and still have sufficient funds to have a town three times as big as any provincial town. It is possible that in a vast region with great agricultural potential (e.g. the Nile valley or Mesopotamia) several such principal towns may have emerged simultaneously in different parts of the country. This may have led to a situation in which petty states with capital towns commanding political provinces in different parts of the country coexisted. Rising demands by an expanding elite for labour, trade goods and agrarian products set the stage for conflicts and coalitions. Large political units are likely to have fared better than smaller units and would have been able eventually to dominate the countryside. At that point, military conquests and federations set the course for the emergence of a nation-state. The head of the state commanding great administrative, religious and military powers emerged as the symbol of a new political order. Within this order, kin-based institutions were overridden, but not obliterated, by central authority and hierarchical organization. The residence of the head of the state or king became the material expression of royal authority – an authority sanctioned by divine power. The royal town outshining all other towns by its high walls, monuments and temples became the first town, a capital city – magnificent, powerful and eternal.

The size of the capital city, as well as towns, was and still is ultimately bound up with the resource base and the amount of food and tribute that can be transported, as well as the facility by which the king or chief can extend his control (ideological and military) to the districts in his domain. Steponaitis (1978), in his examination of Mississippian chiefdoms, has properly identified the reciprocal relationship between the power of the chief and his ability to maintain continued access to a large amount of tribute. This perspective is appropriate to chiefdoms and early agrarian state societies. This structure is radically different from that of classical, proto-industrial and industrial states in which trade and competitive marketing linked with industry and world-wide commerce was responsible for the development of city-states. For example, the city-states of Italy during the Renaissance were associated with large-scale manufacture of textiles, metal-working and other crafts. Milan during the late twelfth century may have had as many as 80,000 persons. Of this large number, 20,000 were artisans. However, the majority of these city-states were small. Pisa, with spectacular naval achievements, consisted of no more than 10,000 people.

Transportation was a key factor. The size of an urban centre was dependent upon the amount of food that could be delivered to the town at a cost less than that of the food value. Accordingly, with low-cost shipping it was cheaper for Rome to obtain grain from Egypt and north Africa than from the Italian countryside. According to Hopkins (1978, pp. 43–4), a land journey by ox cart for 1 km cost the same as transporting the same weight 57 km by sea on a long voyage, and 5.7 km by river transport in AD 301. This explains, in part, the exceptional growth of Rome under the Roman Empire. Shipping in Egypt was also crucial for maintaining a national capital. Food could be shipped from various nomes to a capital city 700 km away. It also allowed the king to dispatch his troops quickly to quell rebellion or to send loads of grain to provinces blighted by famine. A famous historical example of the latter happened during a famine in Antioch dated to AD 362–3. Emperor Julian, in response, had 2600 tons of wheat, about 6700 cart loads, brought by road from two towns 80 and 160 km away. The cost of land transport for the distance of 160 km, according to Hopkins, would have raised the price by 50 per cent. This percentage creates what amounts to a 'transportation barrier' (Broshi 1979, p. 236). Given that riverine travel is five times cheaper, the transportation barrier would have been reached at a distance of about 800 km. Thus, without riverine transport, it would not have been economical to transport grain from the southern nomes of Egypt to Memphis.

Agricultural productivity in ancient Egypt and elsewhere, then, was limited. Productivity increased much later in time with the introduction of water-lifting devices, multiple cropping and perennial irrigation. Low productivity set a limit to the amount of grain that could be produced within the territorial reach of administrative centres.

It is from this perspective that I wish to examine the cities, towns and villages of ancient Egypt. This perspective differs from the locational models of urban geography. Such models have characteristically been generated within a context of industrial marketing economy. On occasions, they have been applied with a lack of regard to the structural differences between towns of early agrarian state societies and modern cities. Particularly important are differences in the scale of production and technology, and the pattern of economic transactions (see review by Crumley 1976; Crumley 1979). Archaeologists may indeed benefit from the approaches and techniques of urban geography. However, adjustments and modifications to take account of the differences in scale and structural relations are essential for a successful application. It is also inappropriate to evaluate the size of the towns and cities of early state-societies or chiefdoms by the standards of the cities of ancient empires or modern states. The origins of the modern town during the tenth century AD were related to the advent of commerce and workshops (e.g. cloth-making). According to Pirenne (1974, p. 154), 'Numbers of poor poured into the towns where cloth-making, the activity of which trade grew proportionately with the development of commerce, guaranteed them their daily bread.' Before that time, towns were merely fortified places and headquarters of administration (Pirenne 1974, p. 76). In western Europe, the great role played by commerce in post-medieval times must also be viewed in the light of the breakdown in a cultural order dominated by the divine power of the Church and later the erosion of royal authority, accompanied by the rise of a new power elite and a middle class. Consumerism and the concept of profit represented changes in values and world-view that created the basis for a new economic order dominated by manufacturing and commercial urban centres. It is instructive in this regard to refer to a system of production more akin to that of early agricultural societies, namely that of the Bemba of northern Zambia. According to Gudeman (1986, p. 101):

> The Bemba do not aim to accumulate a surplus over the years, and they do not believe that reinvestment is necessary to assure and increase future productivity. Technological change also has no place . . . for farming practices, as taught by the ancestors, need no revision.

What mattered was not profit but having ample food throughout the whole tribe or nation as an indication of social order and divine blessing. The motives for the development of early civilizations and cities might thus have been very different from that of modern societies. Even where trade was a basic ingredient in early states, the ideological and social context might have been radically different from that of post-medieval societies.

The emergence of towns and cities in early agricultural states was predicated upon the amount of resources that could be commanded by the chief or king, which in turn is bound up with the scope of his power to influence and command. To view towns and cities in any light other than that of dominance, mediation and control (cf. Wheatley 1972) misses the most crucial ingredient in the structure of early urban societies. Early urban settlements were primarily centres of power. Morphologically, the early urban settlements were distinguished from other settlements by relatively higher population density, a relatively high proportion of people engaged in non-agricultural activities, including an 'urban elite' holding managerial power, and a population aggregation greater than that of the largest village.

Early towns and cities were never exclusively 'urban' (see O'Connor, Ch. 34, this volume), including among inhabitants and within city limits a large proportion of farmers. At times, farmers were forcibly relocated to the vicinity of the city to provide vegetables and other perishable foods for city dwellers (O'Connor 1972b). Some farmers may have also been attracted to the city for protection and security.

The agricultural domain of a town was limited to the distance travelled by farmers to and from the city. In such societies a commuting distance by foot over about 5 km was impractical (Mills & Hamilton 1984, p. 19). Tribute from villages in the administrative zone of the town was transported on donkeys. The towns also had to be located close to the Nile to facilitate transport by water to and from the nation's capital or other towns.

The limitations of overland transport were crucial in restricting the size of towns and cities until the arrival of the railroad, the omnibus and the streetcar. For example, as late as 1790, New York City had a population of 50,000 people. The second largest city, Philadelphia, had just under 30,000 and no other city in the US had more than 20,000 people (Mills & Hamilton 1984, p. 20; see also Fletcher, Ch. 44, this volume).

Urbanization as we know it today is a very recent phenomenon. Cities have grown since the nineteenth century as a result of consumerism, mass-production and commerce. Modern cities have flourished as centres of profit-making in a context of individualism and competition. Technical advances in food production have also allowed a relatively small number of farmers to feed an urban population many times their size. Advances in transportation have also been crucial for modern urbanization. The phenomenal expansion of urbanization during the last two centuries is exemplified by the changes in the percentage of urban population in the coterminous United States between 1790 and 1980 (Mills & Hamilton 1984, p. 41). Of a population totalling 3.9 million people in 1790 no more than 5.1 per cent (200,000 people) lived in cities and towns (some with as few as 2500 people). Until 1830, the urban population still represented 8.8 per cent of the total population. In a span of a hundred years, the urban population climbed to 56.1 per cent and in 1980, 150 years later, the vast majority of people (73.7 per cent) lived in towns and cities. From 1790 to 1830, the percentage of urban population was within the range of pre-industrial societies. Sjoberg reports that the urban population in most pre-industrial countries is often about 5 per cent and rarely as high as 8–10 per cent of the population (Sjoberg 1960, p. 83). In fact, as late as 1920, the percentage of the population of the world outside Europe, North America, the USSR and Australia who resided in places with more than 20,000 people was 5.8 per cent, and by 1940 it was no more than 8.6 per cent, reaching 20.3 per cent in 1975 (Roberts 1979; see Fletcher, Ch. 44, this volume for ancient and modern African statistics).

The record of ancient Egyptian settlements

> Only a few comparatively well preserved but functionally rather special-
> ized settlements have so far been excavated, although there is still consider-
> able scope for settlement archaeology in Egypt in spite of the difficulties.
>
> (O'Connor 1972b, p. 79)

The record of ancient Egyptian settlements is derived from textual and archaeological data. There are inscriptions of town lists on temple walls. The lists have been critically examined with the help of other documents to provide more coherent information regarding the religious, economic or administrative functions of various towns (Gauthier 1925; Porter & Moss 1934–7; Gardiner 1947; Gardiner 1948; Montet 1957–61). Understandably, the data from a span of over 3000 years are patchy and in certain cases confusing. Small villages and hamlets are not likely to have been listed because they were not that important to the ideology of the state. Butzer (1976, pp. 74–5) lists 17 cities and 24 towns (large centres). In the following discussion the term 'capital city' is used to refer only to such national capitals as Thebes, Memphis and Tell el Amarna. The term 'town' will refer to capital centres of nomes or provinces, and the term 'village' to rural settlements.

The remains of ancient settlements are restricted to a number of mounds (*tell* or *kom*) where settlements from successive historical periods are superimposed. However, to date, examination of settlements (density, distribution, pattern of growth, layout) is sorely lacking. The situation is also complicated by differences in the location of cities, towns and villages. Villages and hamlets are likely to have been situated within the floodplain. Towns and cities were often located by the river since water transport was closely associated with urban centres. Accordingly, lateral shifts in the position of the channel of the Nile had an impact on the preservation of many towns (Butzer 1976). Villages, on the other hand, were often obliterated by violent floods. In addition, the siltation of the floodplain since the Old Kingdom is likely to have covered many older settlements with a thick layer of mud.

Methodology

> Whatever explanation we invent at any moment is a partial connection, and its richness derives from the richness of such connections as we are able to make.
>
> (Bronowski 1978, p. 96)

The empirical record of settlements of ancient Egypt is scanty. Fortunately, a few investigators have begun to undertake the thorny task of reconstructing the urban landscape of ancient Egypt (Kemp 1972b; O'Connor 1972b; Butzer 1976; Kemp 1977b; Kauffman 1981; O'Connor, Ch. 34, this volume). In this chapter, I build on their contributions, approaching urban settlements as a social phenomenon. Various estimates are generated using a model that links the various attributes of settlements to political organization, agricultural productivity, transport and taxation (tribute). Agricultural productivity in ancient civilizations was limited by pre-industrial technology and heavily dependent upon human labour (unlike modern agro-industrial production in which fossil energy and machinery play a critical role). Distance and volume of transport were constrained by the limitations set by foot, donkey and boat transport. Nevertheless, transport by donkey and boat were essential for the emergence of cities and towns and indeed the management of Egypt as a single political entity. The model is also based on an ideological model of ancient Egyptian society in which a divine king owned the land and served as a mediator between gods and people, coming to the rescue of provinces blighted by famines or disaster and serving as the embodiment of an ancestral god who gave Egypt agriculture. The divine king functioned as an active symbol of the dynamics of the agricultural cycle, giving life from dead seeds and reviving the earth during inundation after the season of drought. Limitations on manufacture and commerce were placed by a social order restricting access to elite goods to the king and the chiefs under his rule. There was no compelling incentive, then, for the type of phenomenal explosion of trade and manufacture that followed the collapse of the medieval [church] order in Europe. Egypt, characterized by national unity and central authority, was markedly different from Mesopotamia and Greece, where many city-states or rival nation-states created a political climate that permitted independent or semi-independent merchants to prosper.

Historical and ethnographic analogy plays a key role in fleshing the model with appropriate values for the variables that are necessary to operationalize the model. Whenever possible, data from medieval Egypt were consulted with due consideration for possible continuities and transformations. The nature of the data is such that no precise or certain conclusions can be reached. However, the results are informative and illuminating. No figures should be taken as final or exact. Nevertheless, they are highly suggestive of the most likely value of the parameters under discussion.

The urban population of ancient Egypt

> Only a minority lived in cities. By far the greater part of the population lived in peasant communities, and there were parts of Greece where urbanization never flourished. Most city states were small; about 10,000 was a normal population.
>
> (Jones 1968, p. 23)

It is difficult for us to imagine that the monumental civilizations of the past were not the work of very large populations. Surprisingly, the population of ancient Egypt is estimated at roughly 1.2, 2.1 and 3.2 million for the Old Kingdom, the New Kingdom and the Graeco-Roman period, respectively (Hassan In Press). Since urban dwellers were represented in most pre-industrial nations by 5–8 per cent of the population, the urban population during the New Kingdom is likely to have averaged between 105,000 and 168,000. The urban population of Egypt during the Old Kingdom would have been somewhere between 60,000 and 96,000 persons.

Number of villages in ancient Egypt

To estimate the number of villages in ancient Egypt, historical data from medieval and modern Egypt proved very useful (Table 33.1). Al-Maqrizi (AD 1364–1442) reports 956 villages in Upper Egypt and 1439 villages in the Delta at the time of the Ikhshids (AD 934–968. Russell (1966) reports 2261 villages in the 1400s in Upper Egypt and the Delta. After Mohamed Ali, who introduced perennial irrigation and cash crops in the early part of the nineteenth century, the number of villages climbed to 3860 in the 1920s (Toussoun 1924). It is very likely that villages may have increased during the early twentieth century as a result of agricultural intensification and extensification associated with an increase in the population of Egypt. From 1820 to 1859, the population of Egypt rose from 2.54 to 5.125 million. By 1907, the population increased to 11.3 million and later to 14.3 million in 1927. In 1947 the population was 19 million and in 1960, 25 million. Toussoun (1924) reports that at the time of Mohamed Ali there were 1758 villages in Upper Egypt. It is thus unlikely that the number of villages in Upper Egypt during Pharaonic times was greater than 956–1439.

Table 33.1 Textual estimates of the number of Egyptian villages in ancient and historical times

Period	No. of villages	Source
Persian	20,000	(Herodotus) Toussoun 1924
Pharaonic	18,000	(Diodorus) Toussoun 1924
Ptolemaic	30,000	(Diodorus) Toussoun 1924
Early Arab	10,000	(Ibn Al-Hakam) Toussoun 1924*
Ikhshid	2395	Al-Maqrizi[†]
AD 1420	2261[#]	Russell 1966
French	3962	Toussoun 1924
Mohamed Ali	3475[‡]	Toussoun 1924
Tawfik	3637	Toussoun 1924
Foad	3860	Toussoun 1924

[†] After Ibn Isa Boktor ibn Shifa who reported 956 villages in Upper Egypt and 1439 villages in the Delta

* Also Al-Maqrizi

[‡] Comprises 1717 villages in Lower Egypt and 1758 in Upper Egypt

[#] For Upper Egypt and the Delta

Town/village ratio

According to data provided by Al-Maqrizi, the ratio of town to village is 1:65. This ratio is less than that for Egypt during the 1920s, based on the frequency of various settlements in the Badari, Edfu and Minia, which can be estimated at 1:118.[1] The settlement frequency distribution is shown in Table 33.2.

That the ratio of villages to towns in Egypt during the 1920s–50s (118:1) is higher than the ratio of 65:1 reported by Al-Maqrizi for pre-modern Islamic Egypt is fully understandable because of a more than sevenfold increase in rural population. This increase would have led to an increase in the size of villages as well as the budding of new villages. The figure of 1:65 for the town:village ratio appears to be a reasonable estimate for ancient Egypt. At this ratio, the number of towns in Upper Egypt would have been close to 14–21. Thus, it can be assumed that the number of 39 large towns and cities listed by Butzer (1976) for Upper Egypt is probably too generous. If it is assumed that the ratio of towns to villages in ancient Egypt was close to that of pre-modern Egypt (1:65), the number of cities and towns listed by Butzer would imply about 3840 villages in Upper Egypt. This appears to be much more than warranted by analogy with a figure between 956 and 1439 villages in historical times (see above). At any time, the number of towns would have been less than that of the present archaeological traces of towns, since archaeological sites are the record of settlements from several time periods. Until this issue is clarified, I will ascribe towns only to the twenty-two nome capitals in Upper Egypt. Accordingly, the number of villages, using a ratio of villages to towns of 65:1, may be estimated at 1430 villages – an estimate between the figure of 956 villages for the Ikhshid period and that of 1758 villages at the time of Mohamed Ali (who ruled from 1805 to 1849).

Table 33.2 Frequency distribution of settlements in three regions in Upper Egypt

	Edfu	Badari	Minia	Average
Town	1	1	1	1
Large village	6	9	13	9
Small village	178	95	90	118

Size of ancient Egyptian villages

> The peasantry lived together in villages and hamlets, whence they could travel on foot or on donkey back to their fields.
>
> Lewis (1983, p. 65)

With a population of 14 million in 1927 and the number of villages totalling 3860 (Table 33.1), the average population size per village would have been about 3600 persons. By contrast, the number of villages and the population size of Egypt during the medieval Islamic period suggest that villages were occupied by 555–792 persons (Table 33.3). In general, the population averaged 2.67 million from 634–44 AD to 1820 AD, suggesting an average of about 725 persons per village.

Table 33.3 Population and number of villages in tenth- to nineteenth-century Egypt

	Total population	Rural population	No. of villages	Average village size
10th century	1,683,000	1,600,000	2395	668
15th century	3,200,000	3,040,000	3834	792
18th century	2,488,950	2,200,000	3962	555
1820s	2,536,400	2,300,000	3471	662

Table 33.4 Estimates of population and size of villages in ancient Egypt

	Total population	Rural population	Rural population in Upper Egypt	Average village size
Old Kingdom	1,200,000	1,140,000	633,000	452
New Kingdom	2,100,000	1,995,000	997,500	712
Graeco–Roman	3,200,000	3,040,000	1,216,000	868

Similarly, we may estimate the average size of villages in Upper Egypt from the number of villages and the size of rural population (Table 33.4). Assuming that there were 1400 villages in Upper Egypt and that the rural population represented 95 per cent of all Egyptians, we obtain an estimate of 452, 712 and 868 people per village during the Old Kingdom, the New Kingdom and Graeco-Roman Egypt, respectively. These figures are similar to those obtained for Egypt from the tenth century to the nineteenth century AD (Table 33.3). A report of a village of 475 persons in Ptolemaic times (Russell 1966) is well within the range estimated.

The size of ancient Egyptian cities and towns

[The Teaching for Merikare]
Multiply your partisans as neighbours; see, your towns are full of newly settled folk.

(Simpson 1973, p. 184)

Unfortunately, we do not have adequate archaeological estimates of the size of ancient Egyptian cities. Kemp's (1977a) overview underscores the pitiful state of our knowledge after more than 100 years of excavation. A detailed investigation of the number of houses and possible population size of Tell el Amarna led Kemp (1981) to conclude that Tell el Amarna was inhabited by 20,400 to 28,790 people, using an estimate of about 60 persons/ha. This is a much lower density than the density suggested for cities in ancient Mesopotamia ranging from 119 persons/ha to 300 persons/ha (Hassan 1981a, p. 66 with references).

Provincial towns were much smaller than the national capital. The areas of Kahun, Edfu, Hierakonpolis and Abydos are estimated at approximately 11, 9, 7 and 4.5 ha, respectively (Kemp 1977a, Fig. 6). The maximum population of such settlements using 60 persons/ha would have been 660, 540, 420 and 270 persons, respectively. Using a figure of 200 persons per hectare by analogy with Mesopotamia (see Hassan 1981a, pp. 66–7 for discussion), the population may be estimated at 2200, 1800, 1400 and 900 persons, respectively. These figures are more likely than those based on the population density of the capital city. Tell el Amarna thus may not have been typical of other Egyptian capitals, which is understandable considering that it had been built in the desert as a new city. Other Egyptian towns would have been more crowded. It is also possible that the area figure for provincial towns does not include areas buried under cultivation or destroyed by floods. In addition, the figures may not have included the areas once occupied by the houses of the farmers attached to the town.

Pending further archaeological investigations of Egyptian towns to determine their exact areal extent and patterning, an estimate of 1400–3000 persons is plausible. According to Sjoberg (1960, p. 83):

Numerous pre-industrial cities of consequence have undoubtedly sheltered little more than 10,000 and perhaps only 5,000 persons. For example, Lübeck dominated in the 13th century over all the cities of Germany with a population of 10,000 inhabitants.

Cairo in the tenth to eleventh centuries included only 25,000 people (Sjoberg 1960, p. 83).

An estimate of 20,000–40,000 persons for Memphis or Thebes would appear to be conservatively realistic, in part because the total urban population must be placed between 5 and 8 per cent of the total population (see also Sjoberg 1960). If the rural population was 1.5 million, the urban population would have been about 79,000–128,000. Assuming an average of 2200 persons for the population of each nome capital (42 in all), there would have been an estimated 92,000 urban population in the provinces. Thus, assuming 8 per cent as the maximum percentage of urban population, Memphis and/or Thebes would have had no more than 36,000 persons. It may be noted here that the largest cities of Early Dynastic Uruk in Mesopotamia were in the range of 30,000–40,000 (Hassan 1981a, p. 237). Other estimates for cities in Mesopotamia include a population of 24,000 for Ur in the late fourth millennium BC and 34,000 for the next millennium, 19,000 for Lagesh, 16,000 for Umma and 12,000 for Khafaje.

Settlement hierarchy

> The cities were Memphis, Thebes and (later) Pi-Ri'amese. Elsewhere, in any given region, the provincial capital was usually the most important administratively and probably the largest in population. It was surrounded by a zone of fairly large and densely concentrated villages.
>
> (O'Connor 1983, p. 21)

The villages of ancient Egypt probably ranged in size from large villages averaging 700–900 persons, medium villages numbering 500–600 persons and small villages at 250–400 persons, by analogy with villages in rural India based on an early census dating to 1901 (Lal 1984). It may also be noted that the ratio of the size of a village to the next bigger village is about 1:2 and 2:3 that of the bigger settlement. This pattern conforms to that for ancient rural settlements (Hassan 1981a, p. 248). The frequency of towns, large villages, medium villages and small villages can be roughly estimated as 1.5 per cent, 8 per cent, 24 per cent and 66.5 per cent (Table 33.5).

Table 33.5 Hypothetical settlement pattern in Upper Egypt during the New Kingdom

Settlement	Population size	%	Number	Total population
City/town	1400–3000	1.5	22	48,400
Large village	1400	8	117	163,800
Medium village	900	24	350	315,000
Small village	600	66.5	974	584,400
Total population	1,111,600			

Transport

> Hardly any country in ancient or modern times has been so dependent on its waterways as Egypt. Only local traffic between villages and to and from the river banks makes use of land routes on either side of the river.
>
> (Kees 1961, p. 96)

> The principal transport animal of ancient Egypt was the donkey.
>
> (Lewis 1983, p. 130)

The inhabitants of towns enjoyed a much higher standard of living than the peasants. If the income per capita per year in an ancient Egyptian town was approximately three times that of subsistence consumption (about 200 kg/person/year), as in many non-industrial nations, an urban population of 20,000 to 40,000 persons would have required 12–24 million kg of grain per year.

In Upper Egypt, the urban elite of 23 towns would have required no less than 30 million kg of grain (23 towns with 2200 persons each and an allotment of 600 kg of grain/capita). Since the total amount of revenue from Upper Egypt is estimated at 60 million kg, theoretically as much as 30 million kg could have been shipped to the nation's capital. An equal or greater amount could have also been procured from the Delta. The nation's capital might thus have enjoyed much greater riches than any nome's capital. If the revenue to the capital was 60 million kg, the average income per person would have been about 7–15 times that of a peasant and about 2.5–5 times that of a provincial administrator. The transport of as much as 12–60 million kg of grain each year to the nation's capital was a major undertaking. Nile boats in Islamic Egypt carried a load of 100–200 donkeys (Abu-Zayed 1987, pp. 92–3) or an average of approximately 20 tons. Hornell (1946, p. 215) also records that the large Nile cargo boats today have a maximum cargo capacity of 303 *ardebs* – about 40 tons. These figures are much lower than the carrying capacity of the largest Nile boats. In Roman times, such boats were some 20 m long by 3 m in beam, with a rated capacity of 18,000 *artabas*, or about 500 tons (Lewis 1983, p. 143). If the average cargo of a boat was 20–40 tons, transport of 30 million kg from Upper Egypt would have required a fleet of 1500–1750 boats. Thus each nome in Upper Egypt would have had to send 30–65 boats loaded with grain.

Transport from villages to nome capitals was by donkey. Each year, about 2.6 million kg were delivered on average to each nome capital (assuming revenue of about 60 million kg from Upper Egypt and 22 nomes plus the Fayum). Given an average of 65 villages supplying each capital town, the amount delivered from each village would have been 40 tons. Since a donkey could carry between 100 and 200 kg and may travel up to 20 km per day, a train of 7–14 donkeys could have transported the required amount over a period of one month from a village to the nome capital. Less time, or fewer donkeys, would have been required for villages situated at distances less than 20 km from the capital.

Urban locations in a rural landscape

> The hypothesis of maximization of administrative control over Nile Valley population by the designation of nome capital locations is a plausible interpretation of Ramesside goal orientation.
>
> (Kauffman 1981, p. 77)

The distance between nome capitals is in part a function of the radius required to support a principal (nome) town. In order to estimate this distance several assumptions can be made: (1) that a capital nome would on the average consist of 2200 persons, the number of inhabitants to carry on the administrative duties required to collect revenues and serve as an intermediary node between centralized power and the provinces (see above); (2) that the revenues collected to ship to the nation's capital is equal to that allocated to the nome capital (see above); and (3) that the income per person per year in the nome capital is equivalent to 600 kg/year (three times that of subsistence); (4) that agricultural productivity supports on average 80 farmers per km^2; and (5) that about 15 per cent of grain was reserved for taxes.

On average, each nome capital required about 2.60 million kg of grain (see above) in revenues. The total amount of grain production required to supply the revenues at a tax rate of 15 per cent amounts to about 17 million kg of grain. In Upper Egypt a total of 17 million kg of grain would have required an area of about 327–425 km^2. This corresponds favourably to 350 km^2 for the average area of a nome in Upper Egypt (Butzer 1976, pp. 74–5, Table 3).

The theoretical estimate of the area of a nome is derived as follows: (1) in Upper Egypt a total area of about 10,379 km^2 included approximately 900,000 *feddans* of arable land; (2) yield was approximately 450 kg/*feddan* during the Old Kingdom (Hassan In Press); and (3) the yield per km^2 of total land area (including non-agricultural land) may thus be estimated at about 40 tons of grain. The production of 17 million kg of grain requires an area of 327–425 km^2. At a higher yield of 600 kg/*feddan*, the yield per km^2 would have been 52 tons and the area required to produce 17 million kg of grain would have been 327 km^2.

The floodplain is narrow, averaging 10 km for both sides of the river, with a minimum of 2–3 km (at Aswan) and a maximum of 17 km at Beni Suef (Hamdan 1980, p. 685). Using the average width of 10 km, the length of the area supporting a capital nome would have been between 33 and 43 km. This figure also corresponds favourably to a mean river distance between nome capitals of 44 km estimated by Kauffman (1981, p. 68). It is also noteworthy that a donkey, the main means of overland transport (other than people), travels about 20 km/day. The distance between nomes might thus have been limited by how far a donkey can travel in a day.

Settlements and social interaction

> A dynasty is much more powerful at its centre than at its outlying regions.
> When it has extended its authority to its utmost limits, it grows weak.
>
> (Ibn Khaldun, 1375–9)

With an average of 65 villages in a hypothetical nome of 350 km^2 (see above), the average area of a village would have amounted to 5.4 km^2 (equivalent to a radius of 1.3 km). It has also been suggested above that the percentage of large villages would have been about 8 per cent of all settlements. This provides an estimate of five large villages that would have served as local markets and intermediary administrative nodes. The distance between such centres (assuming equal distance between them) would have been about 9.4 km. Any village would have been within a distance equal to, or less than, 4.7 km from any local market or minor official representatives of the state.

Nome capitals directly connected with the nation's capital were the most prominent seats of power in the rural landscape. They were the key links in the chain by which Egypt was integrated. The integration of nome capitals within a nation-state must have been one of the most problematic issues in the history of ancient Egypt because the linearity of the Nile valley stretched the domain of political control over 1296 km. Thebes, for example, was situated about 850 km from the northern Delta and about 440 km from Wadi Halfa in Nubia. Its situation was thus biased towards the southern part of Egypt. On the other hand, Memphis, at a distance of about 1100 km from the southern border of Egypt, was clearly biased towards northern Egypt. The two capitals may thus have been essential for the administration and consolidation of northern and southern Egypt, especially when the authority of the central government was at risk.

The range of territorial control exerted by a capital city was related to the distance over which food and warriors could be moved in a relatively short interval of time (perhaps a week and most probably less than a month). In summer, with etesian winds blowing from the north, a laden Nile cargo boat sailing south against the current could make 40 km a day (Lewis 1983, p. 143). Sail boats travelling between Egypt and Lebanon (a distance of about 500 km) took four days in one direction and ten days on the way back to Egypt against the current (between 50 and 125 km per day) (see also Kitchen, Ch. 35, this volume). Accordingly, Thebes, with a fleet capable of travelling a distance of 400 km in a matter of five to seven days, would have effectively controlled the valley to Malawi, slightly north of Assyut. More time would have been required to dispatch troops to nomes further north. The choice of Tell el Amarna near Malawi as the new capital of Akhenaten might have been in part due to its location approximately midway between Memphis and Thebes (see also Fletcher, Ch. 44, this volume regarding the relation between settlement location and logistics).

The logistic necessity of two polar administrative capitals expressed in the persistence of Memphis and Thebes harboured a potential for fission between southern Egypt and the Delta when central political, military or religious authority weakened. Middle Egypt, situated at the periphery of the effective range of the two capitals, would also have had the potential to emerge as an independent political centre. Nubia, at the extreme end of Egyptian influence to the south, also held the potential for political independence when the central authority of Egypt was reduced.

The history of Egypt provides repeated examples of the disintegration of centralized political power and the emergence of separate states in Upper and Lower Egypt. One of the notable examples was the emergence of the Herakleopolitan state ruled by kings from Ihnasya al-Medina (584 km from Thebes) in Middle Egypt during the First Intermediate (2134–2040 BC), which represented the first major breakdown in national unity. In the later years of the Old Kingdom, the provincial officials became hereditary holders of their posts and regarded their nomes as their own property. The aggrandizement of the power of the provincial ruler was at the expense of the centralized government that depended on the revenues sent from the nomes. A series of low Nile floods apparently worsened the situation. The nomarchs probably kept more for themselves and ultimately became sufficiently powerful to cede, fearing no major retaliation. Under Ramesses II, increasing contacts with the Near East required the establishment of a new capital in the eastern Delta – Pi-Ri'amese. Southern Egypt, at the periphery of the new centre of power, eventually became an independent territory under the hereditary rule of the priests of Karnak. A century later, during the reign of Ramesses XI (1100–1070 BC), the Nubians, emboldened by the weakening of Egypt, fought a battle for the Theban area. Egypt was eventually split between new kings in Lower Egypt, with a capital (Tanis) in the northeastern Delta controlling the country north of El-Hiba, and Theban high priests who controlled southern Egypt, south of El-Hiba (540 km north of Thebes).

The major capitals of Nubia/northern Sudan were effectively situated well beyond the range of Egyptian managerial power and direct control. For example, Kerma is located 385 km south of Halfa and Merwi 715 km south of Halfa (330 km from Kerma). To control the regions of such distant capitals required military expeditions that could only be attempted under stable political conditions at home and at great economic expense.

Final remarks

> [In Praise of the New City Called House-of-Ramesses]
> Its field is full of all good things, and it hath provisions
> and sustenance every day. Its ponds(?) are full of fishes,
> and its lakes of birds. Its plots verdant with herbage,
> and its banks bear dates. – Its granaries are full of barley
> and wheat, and they reach into the sky.
> . . . The small in it are like unto the great.
> (Poem from the New Kingdom (Pap. Anastasi), in Erman 1966, p. 206)

An awareness of the structural differences between towns and cities in early state society and commercial urban centres of later times is necessary for an understanding of early urbanization. The relations between incipient agriculture, a pre-industrial mode of transportation, divine kingship and centralized government form the basic structure shaping the size, location and hierarchy of towns in ancient Egypt and similar societies.

The social geography of Egypt was inseparable from the hegemony and power of the central state. The territorial principle of pre-industrial state societies has been well recognized since Ibn Khaldun by many sociologists and anthropologists (Balandier 1970, pp. 133ff). In Egypt, the territorial structure of the state was segmentary consisting of homologous, though hierarchical elements.

> In such societies the risk of cession and rupture is high. When the state is
> weakened, it does not bring the whole of society crashing down into ruin;
> it gradually contracts and the area it controls is finally limited to the region
> of which the declining capital is the centre. (Balandier 1970, pp. 138–9)

The dynamics of the political history of ancient Egypt may now be viewed from this perspective.

In modern times, advances in agricultural and transport technology, linkage to world markets and secularization mark an irrevocable change in the nature of Egyptian society. Today, urbanization is radically different from that predating the nineteenth century. Changes in the nature of urbanization, to be sure, had also occurred earlier in response to militarism during the New Kingdom and to the linkage to a global market since Roman times. In modern times, Cairo grew disproportionately as an administrative bureaucratic centre. Alexandria, as a port for exporting cotton, also assumed a certain prominence. Its location on the Mediterranean made it a favoured haven for Greek, Italian and other foreigners who played a key role in finance and trade from the reign of Khedive Ismail (1863–79) when Europe (mostly England and France) succeeded in putting a halt to the industrialization of Egypt. From that time on, urbanization in Egypt has been closely linked with governmental services and consumer economy.

Urbanization in contemporary Egypt is intimately associated with a rapid rate of population increase and migration from rural areas to towns. Since population increase has outpaced agricultural developments, Egypt no longer grows enough food for its people. Accordingly, the towns and cities of Egypt are no longer connected to the productivity of their territorial domain. The change to state-sponsored irrigation and agrarian policy since the nineteenth century has also marginalized provincial towns. Cairo, emerging as the capital city from the beginning of the Islamic period, became the centre of administration and, in medieval times, a major commercial node. Today, Cairo is one of the largest cities in the world. Unlike Pi-Ri'amese, Cairo cannot boast of verdant plots and lakes of birds. Its disproportionate size and crowded streets attest to the great attraction of this metropolis. At the same time the unchecked growth of Cairo requires a heavy investment in the infrastructure necessary to keep the city functioning (cf. Roberts 1979). As a result, the state is faced with the dilemma of providing the needed infrastructure while keeping taxes sufficiently low to encourage private enterprise and to minimize civil unrest. Urbanization comes at a price. More importantly, urbanization, since its inception, has been a political phenomenon. No study of cities, past or present, can ignore the links between cities and power.

Note

[1] The data were obtained from maps of the Survey Department of Egypt (Badari 1:25,000, No. 47/660,645; Minia 1:100,000, No. 150; Edfu 1:100,000, Nos. 24/72 and 24/78). The maps were prepared in 1934 (reissued 1952), 1956 and 1928 (revised in 1940) for Badari, Minia and Edfu, respectively.

Acknowledgements

The ideas expressed in this chapter were discussed in detail with Paul Sinclair during the seminar organized by him on 'Origins of Urbanization in East Africa' held in Uppsala, Sweden. His comments were useful in sharpening my views and in completing the manuscript. Editorial comments by Peter Ucko were extremely helpful in the production of the final version of this chapter. I am also indebted to Karl W. Butzer, whose work on the settlements of the Nile valley set the foundation for a cultural geography of ancient Egypt.

34   Urbanism in bronze age Egypt and northeast Africa

DAVID O'CONNOR

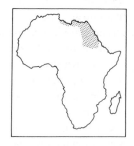

Introduction

The time span covered by this review of urbanism in Egypt and northeast Africa is coeval with the Egyptian Bronze Age (*c.* 3100–650 BC), a technically inexact but useful term (copper was dominant to *c.* 2000 BC, bronze relatively common thereafter) (Helck 1974, pp. 870–1; Grundlach 1979, pp. 881–2). Not all the non-Egyptian cultures discussed here were metal-producing[1] but all used metal to significant degrees. Prehistoric developments (before 3100 BC) are not covered, because the data are insufficient.

Geographically, coverage is extended beyond Egypt for two reasons. First, it is appropriate to do so in the context of this volume; and second, one's perspectives on Egyptian urbanism change productively when it is seen in the context of urban or proto-urban developments elsewhere in northeast Africa. The regions other than Egypt chosen for discussion share two attributes: (i) each had the environmental potential to support numerically large and socially complex societies that might develop urbanism; and (ii) substantial data on the culture of each region are available, if sometimes only indirectly through Egyptian pictures and texts. It is assumed that throughout most of the Bronze Age, environmental conditions were similar to those of today (Butzer 1976, pp. 13, 26–7; but cf. Grove, Ch. 1, this volume).

As to terminology, terms such as 'urbanism', 'city' and 'town' are notoriously difficult to define; and the most useful approach is perhaps to visualize urbanism as extending along a spectrum accommodating many variants, but maintaining some basic if minimal attributes (Trigger 1972, pp. 579–99; Wheatley 1972, pp. 601–37; Blanton 1981, pp. 392–400; Marcus 1983, pp. 195–242). It should be noted that the urban character of bronze age Egypt is not unanimously acknowledged. Many egyptologists use the term (for cited reasons) almost as a matter of course, but some well-informed outsiders remain sceptical (Kolb 1984, pp. 36–40). This chapter focuses on what has actually been found out about settlement types and their social and cultural roles in Egypt and the other regions, and what may be predicted about future discoveries. Individual readers may decide how far the use of 'urbanism' and 'proto-urbanism' meets the criteria they think essential. As well as individual settlements, settlement patterns will also be discussed, for the 'growth of cities is a manifestation of the growth of institutions capable of organizing large regions into integrated systems' (Blanton 1981, p. 393), and consequently regional settlement

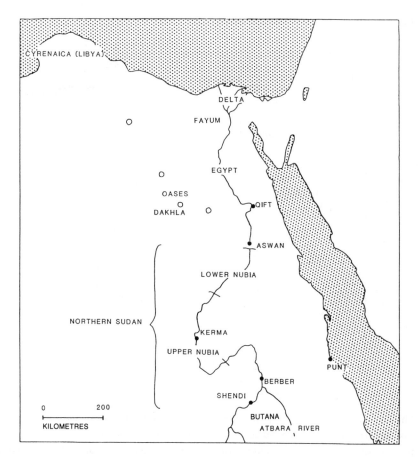

Figure 34.1 The relevant regions of northeast Africa.

patterns were intimately, if variously, related to the functions cities and towns were performing.

The regions: environments and cultural histories

Four regions are relevant: 'Libya', the environmentally favourable core of which was Cyrenaica; the western oases of Egypt; the Egyptian Nile valley; and the northern Sudan (as defined by Barbour 1961, Ch. 10, but including lower Nubia also), involving in this discussion riverine lands along the Nile (and Atbara), as well as some semi-arid and savanna lands in the northern Butana (Fig. 34.1). A fifth possibility – the central zone of the eastern Sudan (Barbour 1961, Ch. 14), which included in the Bronze Age the significant kingdom of Punt – is archaeologically too poorly documented to include (O'Connor 1983, pp. 270–1; O'Connor 1987, pp. 112–22; but see Kitchen, Ch. 35, this volume).

Table 34.1 Chronological and cultural chart

DATES B.C.	LIBYA Tjehenu, Tjemhu	Other Libyans	OASES Archaeological	Historical	EGYPT Period	Unitary Phase	Regional Phase	NUBIA Lower Archaeological	Historical	Upper Archaeological	Historical	BERBER-SHENDI Historical
3000					Early Dynastic	I	II	A-Group depopulation	T3 zty?			
2500		(Dakhla)	colonization	wḥ3t	Old Kingdom	III IV V VI		colonization C-Group Ia	Wawat Irtjet? Setjau?	Pre-Kerma Early Kerma	T3-nḥs Yam? Irtjet? Setjau?	Yam?
2000			colonization	wḥ3t	I.I.P. Middle Kingdom	XI XII XIII	VII–XI	Ib IIa colonization	Wawat	Middle Kerma	Kush (Yam?)	(Yam?)
1500	Libu, Mashwash	(Dakhla, Bahriya)	colonization	wḥ3t and its divisions	2.I.P. New Kingdom	XVIII XIX XX	XIII–XVII	IIb Colonization, Acculturation	Wawat	Classic Kerma Colonization, Acculturation?	Kush (Irem?)	Irem?
1000					3.I.P.	XXI XXII XXII– XXV		depopulation		Kurru Kingdom XXV	Kush Irem?	Irem?
500												

The environmental and, to some degree, the cultural differences between riverine Egypt and riverine northern Sudan have been unduly emphasized; there were also important similarities. The economy of each was based on an annually inundated floodplain (1105 km long, Egypt; 1750 km long, northern Sudan). Egypt had much more potentially cultivable land available – the estimated bronze age average has been calculated as 18,250 km^2 (Butzer 1976, Table 4, p. 83) – but the greater part of it may not have been densely settled and cultivated (Butzer 1976, pp. 80, 100–3). The Nubian population in the northern Sudan certainly had a markedly discontinuous pattern, but so perhaps did the Egyptian. Nubians were concentrated primarily in lower Nubia (350 km long), upper Nubia (390 km) and the Berber-Shendi reach (300 km), each subregion being separated from the others by long, thinly – or uninhabited – zones; yet Butzer, via a well-reasoned if as yet untested hypothesis, argues that for two-thirds of the Bronze Age only two Egyptian subregions were densely settled – Aswan to Qift (215 km long) and the Fayum mouth to Delta apex (200 km). The very long floodplain in between, and the wide Delta itself, were thinly settled. Actual population figures are difficult to gauge; the average for bronze age Egypt is estimated at 1.8 million (Butzer 1976, Table 4, p. 83); the northern Sudan's (by recent analogy, perhaps not a valid comparison?) would have been considerably less. Nevertheless, the historical perspective opened up is of considerable interest, since one might argue that the two widely separated Egyptian zones of dense settlement might have been as difficult to combine into and maintain as a political and cultural unity as was the case with the three Nubian subregions.

Sedentary life, highly differentiated society and the political and military centraliz-ation of territories that were large ('kingdoms', 'empires') or substantial (lesser kingdoms, 'city-states') are associated with the development of proto-urbanism and urbanism. Here again the differences between Egypt and the northern Sudan, while real, can be exaggerated.

Bronze age Egypt *was* a unitary state from 3100 BC onwards, dominated by a semi-divine pharaoh and an elite bureaucracy, yet this simple picture needs qualifying. The principal textual sources, all generated by the elite, and the grandiose archaeology associated with them, convey an impression of a totally pervasive government; but some, perhaps much, of social, economic and religious life – beyond the elite – may have been self-regulating. Moreover, the rise of subregional powers and even cultures in the three Intermediate Periods (Table 34.1), which are spaced throughout the Bronze Age, suggests a substantial instability in the apparently unitary system. These periods of regionalism were generated not by environmental change or foreign in-vasion, but by internal political and social factors which might have included a perennial difficulty in moving from the 'small-scale' to the 'large-scale' society (Bene-dict 1968, pp. 572–7) appropriate for the vast territory and administrative ambitions involved.

For the northern Sudan, regional and subregional capacity for the development of socially differentiated society, and large but politically and militarily centralized terri-tories, has been underestimated. The non-literate Nubians certainly had material – and implicitly social – cultures very different from Egypt's, and are more easily seen as divided up amongst themselves into culturally different groups (Table 34.1). The earliest bronze age one known – the A–Group of lower Nubia – probably did not represent a politico-military unity (Trigger 1976, pp. 42–469; contrary view, Williams 1986, pp. 13–18, 163–84), but thereafter two different historical scenarios can legitima-tely be suggested, and are summarized overleaf (O'Connor 1986, pp. 27–50; O'Connor 1987, pp. 99–136) (Table 34.2).

If hypothesis II is taken as more probable (O'Connor 1986, pp. 42–3; 1987, pp. 124–5, 135), one sees territorially large, politically centralized Nubian kingdoms, much closer to the Egyptian experience than is the case in hypothesis I. Possibly already dominated by a single ruler in Dynasty V (Emery, James & O'Connor Forthcoming), upper Nubia becomes, virtually, a unitary kingdom in Dynasty VI, capable of absorb-ing lower Nubia as well; indeed, the resulting entity was over 1000 km long. In the middle Bronze Age upper Nubia redeveloped into a unitary kingdom, of which the expansive kingdom of Kush (2.1.P.) (Table 34.1) was only one – the latest – phase. Within upper Nubia, socio-economic differentiation is visible by Early Kerma times, and becomes increasingly stronger; while the tombs of 'kings' are evident by Middle Kerma, and reach enormous size by Classic Kerma (Bonnet 1986, Ch. 4).

Environmentally and culturally, the other two regions are more special cases. The western oases depended entirely on tapping subsurface water, yet one at least was capable of supporting a large town – and numerous smaller settlements – in the early Bronze Age; all were Egyptian implantations, since the indigenes appear never to have

Table 34.2 Two possible scenarios

HYPOTHESIS I

Period		Lower Nubia	Upper Nubia	Berber-Shendi
Early Bronze	later Old Kingdom 1.1.P	C-Group Ia,b = Wawat, Irtjet, Setjau; three separate chiefdoms ephemerally uniting into a larger kingdom	Early Kerma/Middle Kerma = Yam, an important Kingdom/chiefdom; plus other chiefdoms (?)	?
Middle Bronze	Middle Kingdom	C-Group Ib, IIa = Wawat; dominated by Egyptian colonies	Middle Kerma = several (many?) chiefdoms, gradually coalescing into a unitary whole dominated by one (Kush)	?
Middle Bronze	2.1.P.	C-Group IIb, III = Wawat; chiefdoms emerging, then conquered by Kush	Classic Kerma = Kush; emergence of unitary (but unstable?) kingdom	
Late Bronze	New Kingdom	Acculturated Nubians = Wawat; dominated by Egyptian colonies	Acculturated Nubians? = Kush; dominated by Egyptian colonies; chiefdoms re-emerge (one, Irem = former Yam?) and periodically rebel	

Table 34.2 continued

Period		Lower Nubia	Upper Nubia		Berber-Shendi
			HYPOTHESIS II		
Early Bronze	later Old Kingdom 1.I.P.	C-Group IIa, b	Early Kerma/Middle Kerma	= Irtjet, Setjau; two substantial kingdoms coalescing into a unitary whole, capable of absorbing Lower Nubia	Yam, an important kingdom; plus several chiefdoms?
		= Wawat; a single substantial kingdom ephemerally integrated into a larger one based on Upper Nubia			
Middle Bronze	Middle Kingdom	C-Group Ib, IIa	Middle Kerma	= Kush, Shaat; two substantial kingdoms coalescing into a unitary whole, the former dominant	Yam? an important kingdom; plus several chiefdoms?
		= Wawat; dominated by Egyptian colonies			
Middle Bronze	2.I.P.	C-Group IIb, III	Classic Kerma	= Kush, a powerful, unitary kingdom	Yam?
		= Wawat; chiefdoms emerging, then conquered by Kush			
Late Bronze	New Kingdom	Acculturated Nubians	Acculturated Nubians?	= Kush, Kushite kingdom resists Egypt vigorously for generations (about 100 years), then dominated by Egyptian colonies	Irem (= former Yam?), a kingdom and chief opponent (and periodic trading partner?) of Egypt; plus other kingdoms/chiefdoms
		= Wawat; dominated by Egyptian colonies			

reached the level of complexity likely to generate (proto-)urbanism (Giddy 1987, pp. 76–7, 91–2, 97, 184–207). In ancient Libya, Cyrenaica depended on Mediterranean rains captured by its high *massif*; the Greek experience (after the Bronze Age) showed that cities could develop along the Cyrenaican coast and draw on substantial agricultural hinterlands (Boardman 1964, pp. 169–74), and upland towns could also have existed. The bronze age Libyans were basically pastoral nomads, but from early times had some degree of political centralization (Osing 1980, pp. 1015–33), while by the late Bronze Age there existed a hierarchical society, trading relationships with Egypt and the eastern Mediterranean and a high degree of political and military centralization – in fact, an aggressive 'nomadic state' was emerging with, conceivably, some tendency to urbanization (O'Connor 1990a, pp. 29–113).

Background

Urbanism in ancient Egypt had received comparatively little attention prior to 1972, when several essays on the topic (providing useful access to earlier literature) appeared in Ucko, Tringham & Dimbleby's *Man, Settlement and Urbanism* (Kemp 1972a, pp. 651–6; Kemp 1972b, pp. 657–80; O'Connor 1972a, pp. 681–98; Smith 1972, pp. 705–20). These reflected a developing interest in urbanism amongst egyptologists (Kemp 1977a; Bietak 1979b, pp. 97–144; Bietak 1981; Kemp 1981, pp. 68–78; Bietak 1984b, pp. 1233–49; Butzer 1984b, pp. 924–33; Kemp 1989). Substantial new excavations (most still current) opened up at some thirteen bronze age Egyptian sites and several surveys of settlement patterns were undertaken (Fig. 34.2).[2] The northern Sudan, so far as settlement archaeology is concerned, has been less well served. On the analytical side, Trigger's pioneering *History and Settlement in Lower Nubia* (Trigger 1965) still stands alone, and while many fortress-towns in the same subregion were (re-) investigated during the salvage campaign of the 1960s (Trigger 1976, pp. 68–77), these were Egyptian implantations and, in any case, have not been systematically analysed in detail as an expression of urbanism (however, cf. Kemp 1989, pp. 166–78). Settlement (as distinct from cemetery) types and distribution in upper Nubia are largely unknown – with the major exception of Kerma – while the Berber-Shendi reach remains archaeologically a *terra incognita* in the Bronze Age.

Elsewhere, recent surveys and excavation in Dakhla Oasis have proved very rewarding, but the other oases remain poorly documented; and bronze age Libya is completely unknown archaeologically, virtually all information having to be reconstructed from Egyptian textual and pictorial sources.

Even in Egypt problems should be noted. Excavational coverage of urban sites is still very thin, with most of the Delta and much of Middle Egypt unrepresented (Fig. 34.2). Organizationally, no nationally oriented strategy of urban archaeology has been brought into play, although the need for one has been eloquently stated (Bietak 1979a, pp. 156–60; Smith 1985); foreign institutes and individual projects in Egypt have not co-ordinated a programme of urban and settlement archaeology amongst themselves, while the Egyptian Antiquities Organization has to deal with a wide range of needs, of which promoting urban archaeology is only one. Two further issues require separate treatment.

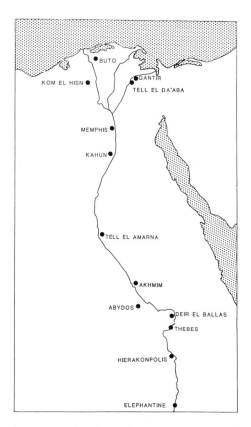

Figure 34.2 Egyptian bronze age urban sites under excavation or re–study.

Survival and recovery of urban and settlement sites

Evidently, archaeology will never deal with more than a fraction of the urban and settlement sites of Egypt and the northern Sudan, of the Bronze or any other age; but that fraction could be most informative if the present enthusiasm continues (and is extended to the northern Sudan), and is also so structured as to become a more co-ordinated and nationally oriented programme of survey, selective excavation and discussion. Two questions are fundamental in this regard: Can one estimate, in both regions, how many settlement sites have been lost beyond recovery? And can one hope to locate and analyse selectively representative samples of the remaining sites, many of which are inaccessible and often unknown as yet?

In Egypt, it has been argued that between Akhmim and Cairo (Fig. 34.2) the Nile has shifted from west to east, implying a major loss of floodplain settlement sites (Butzer 1976, pp. 33–85; Jeffreys 1985, pp. 48–51); on a smaller, more localized scale similar processes have occurred in the Delta, but appear not to have been significant in the northern Sudan. Throughout Egypt and (to a lesser degree?) the northern Sudan the rate of individual site destruction has increased greatly in recent times, e.g. as arable land is reclaimed, sites sought for new or expanding villages, factories and other developments, and gravel, sand and rock quarries expanded (Bietak 1979a, pp. 159, 197; van den Brink 1986, pp. 7 n. 2, 10 nn. 13, 12–13). These processes are inevitable; but all serious urban research must calculate their impact on the samples being dealt with.

As for surviving sites, currently inaccessible ones, as much as accessible ones, may eventually be subject to being located, mapped, sampled and perhaps selectively excavated. Inaccessible sites are buried under modern towns, intrusive sand dunes and, most typically, under floodplain sediment (Butzer 1961, pp. 65 (Abb. 1), 66–7; van den Brink 1986, pp. 12, 28–30). So far as the last is concerned, recent boring programmes at and around specific sites have shown that their buried strata and topography can be mapped and sampled (von der Way 1984, pp. 297–328; Hoffman 1986, p. 181; von der Way 1986, pp. 191–212; Jeffreys and Malek 1988, pp. 19–23), while technology for excavating below the omnipresent water-table has been successfully developed (von der Way 1986, pp. 209–12). Accessible sites above all require locating and mapping, and here aerial and satellite photography is being put to productive use (Bietak 1975, pp. 72–4; van den Brink 1986, pp. 10–11), although the study of crop-marks, familiar to European archaeology, has not been employed.

Sufficient work has been done for predictive theories about settlement location and distribution to emerge. In Egypt and the northern Sudan most settlements were on the floodplain (Bietak 1979b, pp. 100–2) and also in natural irrigation basins in the northern Sudan (Barbour 1961, pp. 141–2). Moreover, settlements would tend to concentrate on river levees (inactive or active), or on the sandy *geziras* of the Egyptian Delta, because all these features are the highest points and hence best protected from the annual inundation (Bietak 1979b, pp. 100–2). Within this general pattern of preference, settlements would also tend to be close to the Nile and its chief branches, to facilitate access to river-borne transportation.

Urbanism in Egyptian bronze age settlement patterns

Settlement patterns can both indicate the presence of urbanism and help define its changing character through time and space (Rouse 1972, pp. 95–108; Blanton 1981; Butzer 1984b, pp. 924–33), and a theoretical consensus has developed about the regional and subregional settlement patterns which are to be predicted for Egypt. According to this theory, all large towns are to be associated either with large temples and/or offices of national or provincial government. These two institutions – government, and temples as a special part of government – dominated the land-holdings on which the redistributive economy was based and were the chief employers of artisans and craftsmen, so other large towns could not, or at least would not, be allowed to develop outside the government centre–temple town matrix (Kemp 1972b, pp. 657–80; Bietak 1979b, pp. 128–33).

The theory allows for historical change. The deliberately founded government/ temple town was omnipresent in centralized periods, but in decentralized (intermediate) periods the market process might become freer and generate towns in its own right

(Bietak 1984, p. 1237). In these same periods insecurity also generated fortified towns, not necessarily all on the national government's initiative, and encouraged a contraction of settlement around them (Badawy 1975, pp. 194–203; O'Connor 1982, p. 17; O'Connor 1983, pp. 246–8). In the middle Bronze Age, it has recently been suggested, 'an extreme structured view of society' (Kemp 1989, p. 155) led to an urbanism based on a relatively rigid and uniform style of town plan that was the basis for 'an extensive programme of remodelling communities in . . . [a] strictly regimented fashion' (Kemp 1989, p. 157); while in the late Bronze Age, new and more open towns were founded on the floodplain adjacent to older ones, now inconveniently crowded, and perched on high tells (Kemp 1977a, pp. 189–94; Kemp 1977b; Kemp 1989, pp. 155–7, 202).

Evidently, this theory leaves little room for the possibility – which needs to be tested – that in all periods Egyptian society was largely self-regulating and capable of generating towns outside the governmental/temple town, e.g. as market centres, although the extent of 'free trade' alongside the generally redistributive, government-dominated Egyptian economy is still much debated (Janssen 1975, pp. 161 ff.; Janssen 1981; Janssen 1983, p. 283 n. 75; Kemp 1989, Ch. 6).

Both possibilities – towns created by government and temple, and others outside this matrix – could have resulted in either primate or rank size patterns (which one was typical of Egypt at different periods is still uncertain: compare Kemp 1977a, pp. 192, 198 with Wenke, Buck, Hamroush, Kobusiewicz, Kroeper & Redding 1988, p. 11; see also McIntosh & McIntosh, Ch. 37, this volume) and have involved similarly rational decisions as to location, thus generating similar settlement patterns. Thus in either case levees and *geziras* would be preferred, as would proximity to the river (see above), and major towns were likely to be located with reference to both significant riverine and land routes and to agricultural hinterlands which could be exploited (Bietak 1975, pp. 96–7; Bietak 1979b, p. 102). Nationally – at least for the late Bronze Age – a spatially logical locational pattern for the principal administrative centres has been identified (Kauffman 1981).

How does theory compare with actual case studies? The latter, so far, are rare. In one case, a subregional, late bronze age pattern (derived from textual data) of linear rank size settlements distributed over more than 2500 km² of arable floodplain was suggested; each major town (all were governmental/temple centres) was surrounded by a densely settled zone of agricultural villages (and other towns?), thinning away to extensive, sparsely occupied zones dedicated to animal-raising. Was this a typical pattern and, in any case, did the document employed really illustrate a representative, random sample of settlements throughout the subregion (O'Connor 1972a, pp. 690–6)? In a second case, the now invisible early bronze age settlement pattern over some 90 km² of floodplain was partially reconstructed from the exhaustively excavated desert edge *cemeteries* generated by those settlements. For some periods, a rank size pattern emerged, and the chief town was a governmental/temple centre; but the next rank of towns had no known governmental or temple function; and the smallest settlements lay furthest from the 'capital', corresponding perhaps to the 'agricultural/animal-raising' dichotomy noted above. But do cemeteries really reflect accurately the sizes and locations of settlements out on the floodplain? And might a closer analysis of the time element reduce the sharpness of the patterns (O'Connor 1972b, pp. 78–100; O'Connor 1974, pp. 28–9)?

Methodologically more secure are two surveys of the northeast Delta, focused on floodplain sites; only one – the smaller survey – involved actual checking in the field, and generated, over a 900 km² area, 1.5 times as many sites (81/53) as the larger survey had located in the same area (Bietak 1975; van den Brink 1986). The smaller survey covered a specific subregion with a rich agricultural hinterland and cut by a major Nile arm (the Pelusiac). Interestingly, early and late bronze age site distribution varied considerably (whether the pattern was primate or rank size could not be established); the former ran east–west across the north of the subregion, the latter northeast to southwest along the southern and eastern sides of the hinterland, generally following the Pelusiac arm (van den Brink 1986, Figs 2, 4). Why the two patterns differed is hard to explain (van den Brink 1986, p. 19), but this variability within a fairly coherent subregion is of great interest.

Evidently, many more case studies are required if a reliably based theory of settlement patterns for bronze age Egypt is to be developed.

Secular aspects of cities and towns

In the analysis of specific town sites there has been a more productive alliance of theory and application, especially in so far as their secular aspects are concerned. Topics of interest include the general function of each town (as centre of governmental or temple administration, for example), its area and population size, and its internal complexity, both occupational (cult areas vs. residential, administrative vs. crafts, for example) and socio-economic. An implicit issue throughout requires much more attention than it has so far received; in the absence of a detailed textual record about a town and its composition and life, how far can archaeology take us in these matters? Some major questions about Egyptian towns can only be answered (if at all) by textual data (Kemp 1984, pp. 20–7); but archaeology can illuminate important aspects of town life, and these will be discussed here.

Case histories are the best basis for discussion. Elephantine (Fig. 34.2), in the early and middle Bronze Ages, amply documents the complexity of a long-lived Egyptian town, but also shows how difficult it is to expose and interpret all or much of each major occupational phase. On an island, the town was never very large (2 ha in the early, 5 ha in the middle Bronze Ages?) (Kemp 1972b, pp. 661–2; Kemp 1989, pp. 149–57). The Old Kingdom town in Dakhla Oasis was first about 3.3 ha, and later at least 4.7 ha. Partly contemporary is a much smaller (1.24 ha?) Egyptian town at Buhen, lower Nubia; less complex, its pattern of growth and redevelopment (Dynasties IV and V) seems to correlate with periodic 'reforms' of the central governmental structure in far-off Memphis (Emery, James & O'Connor Forthcoming).

Kahun (14 ha?), the best excavated middle bronze age town, continues to attract discussion, but not agreement. Thus one scholar sees it as a self-sustaining temple town, the highest ranking inhabitant (and then only periodically) being the vizier or prime minister (Kemp 1972b, pp. 661–2; Kemp 1989, pp. 149–57); whereas another identifies it – and *all* such 'pyramid cities', built near royal funerary complexes throughout the early and middle Bronze Ages – as *the* royal residence and national capital of each reign, and hence presumably one of the largest towns (Stadelmann 1983, pp. 9–14). Yet the fascinating eastern Delta town of Tell el Da'aba, colonized by Canaanite settlers and reflecting both Egyptian and Canaanite city plans and building modes, had reached an estimated size of 200 ha by the end of middle bronze age times (Bietak 1984a, p. 5).

A number of relatively well-excavated towns (e.g. Deir el Ballas, Deir el Medineh) (Valbelle 1975, pp. 1028–34; Lacovara 1990) are of interest in late bronze age Egypt, but Tell el Amarna (440 ha) continues to receive the lion's share of attention, because it is extensively excavated, short-lived and highly differentiated internally. On the whole, the city is now considered to be typical of the 'organic' type of Egyptian town rather than the 'planned' type (Smith 1972, pp. 705–11; Kemp 1989, Ch. 17), and Kemp has convincingly reinterpreted major elements of its plan (Kemp 1976) and emphasized the representative character of its extensive residential zones (Kemp 1972b, pp. 668–76; Kemp 1977b, pp. 123–39; Kemp 1981, pp. 81–97; Janssen 1983). The latter in particular have been much discussed, particularly as regards their mixed character, akin to a 'series of self-contained and economically largely self-sustaining neighbourhoods', a 'pattern of separate neighbourhood units which must have been almost villages' (Kemp 1972b, p. 673). Detailed analysis of house plans and other features revealed a graded profile typical of a 'mature plan and housing range' (Kemp 1977b, pp. 128–33, 136), while eight basic house-types have been identified, forming three *Komfortklassen* (the highest, 7–9 per cent; the intermediate, 34–7 per cent; and the lowest, 54–9 per cent, of the whole) (Tietze 1984; Tietze 1985; Tietze 1986; cf. also Crocker 1985).

Yet the ambiguities created by the absence of a detailed textual record are clear. On archaeological grounds, one scholar estimates el Amarna's population as 20,400–28,790 (Kemp 1981, p. 97), another as 50,000–100,000 (Janssen 1983, p. 287). One argues that the greater households traded off agricultural surplus, especially to 'the occupiers of numerous smaller houses in their neighbourhoods', who in turn were craftsmen depending on the sale of their products for income (Kemp 1972b, pp. 670–4; Kemp 1989, pp. 305 ff.). But others suggest the smaller households were totally dependent on wages paid out (as a governmental function) by the larger households (Janssen 1983, pp. 280–2), each agglomeration or village-like unit corresponding to an *Arbeitsgruppe*, and with only about 1 per cent of el Amarna's population estimated to be economically independent workers (Tietze 1986, p. 78).

City as cosmos

Little attention has been paid to the cosmological roles of Egyptian cities in the Bronze Age, a surprising omission since in many cultures cities and towns, laid out and functioning so as to mimic the plan of the cosmos and its processes, have played a powerful role in maintaining the psychic or cognitive integrity of the society, and in helping to stabilize and perpetually renew its political structure and socio-economic system. Ancient societies believed that the 'city as cosmos' was a focus for the creative and revitalizing power of the cosmos, which surged through it and then diffused out into the worlds of humans and nature. The elite naturally manipulated this concept to reinforce its power; but society's broader religious needs were also involved (Wheatley 1971, especially Ch. 5; Lawrence and Low 1990).

Although it has been recently suggested that in late bronze age Egypt at least there was 'complete homology of the cosmic and the political sphere' and that the 'state [was] the exact imitation of . . . cosmic government on earth' (Assmann 1989, pp. 63, 65), it has not been realized that the royal cities (and perhaps others) gave to this concept a dramatic physical reality. The temple, integral to all towns, has long been recognized as representing the cosmos (Smith 1972, pp. 713–17; Assmann 1984, pp. 25–49); but I have advanced the thesis that the late bronze age royal city was laid out *as a whole* so as to replicate, and to function as, the cosmos.

The temple or temples received and passed on cosmic power. The palaces of the city, and especially the administrative palace – always adjacent to the main temple – mediated that power, organizing it so that it branched out along the appropriate channels into the social and natural worlds. To facilitate this every palace, like a temple, was modelled so as to represent a cosmos (O'Connor 1989, pp. 73–87; cf. also Uphill 1972, pp. 721–34; Kemp 1989, pp. 267–87). The city's inhabitants, as the first recipients of cosmic power, responded appropriately on behalf of Egypt and the world. Since the dead were considered part of society, even the elite tombs of the city were laid out and decorated so that they replicated the essential elements of the city, thus maintaining perpetually the correct relationships between subject and pharaoh, city and cosmos (O'Connor 1989, p. 11; O'Connor 1990b).

For example, at el Amarna the city is laid out so that the activities of the Sun-Disc, as cosmic ruler of the universe, and king, as ruler of Egypt and the world, are literally shown to be parallel. Periodically, the Disc emerges from his eastern 'horizon' (*akhet*) at the rim of the cosmos, and the king from his remote northern residential palace at the city's edge. Both process to the centre of the city (the king in a golden chariot gleaming like the Disc), adored by their creatures and subjects, represented by the city's inhabitants. At the centre, in a 'sacred city', Disc and king celebrate a mystic union, and the latter then emerges into the 'secular city' to carry out governance, while the former emerges into the cosmos to ensure its orderly continuation. When Disc and king depart, cosmos and city fall into quiet and darkness, awaiting the revitalizing return of the two lords (O'Connor 1989, p. 11).

Thebes was a much more traditional city, yet it also functioned as both secular city and cosmic symbol: Amon-Re, the imperial god, assumed the sun's form as cosmic ruler; the residential palace, like Amun-Re's horizon, was perhaps remote from the city proper; administrative palace and main temple were intimately linked; and great festivals were an annual event (Opet, and the festival of the Valley). These festivals involved temples, palaces, the city as a whole and – in the latter case – cemeteries in processional celebrations emphasizing the parallelism between Amun-Re's cosmic rulership and the earthly governance of pharaoh, and celebrating the unity, comprehensiveness and revitalizing power of the cosmos (O'Connor 1989).

Urbanism in northeast Africa in the Bronze Age

As suggested above, one at least of the western oases could support urban life (admittedly, implanted by Egypt), while in late bronze age Libya a nomadic state was taking shape. Egyptian sources refer explicitly to the 'cities/large towns' (*dmi*) of these Libyans in their Cyrenaican heartland, an indication that large-scale settlements existed (no such settlements are referred to with regard to a contemporary 'nomadic' people, the Shasu of Palestine; see O'Connor 1990a, pp. 63–6). However, archaeology has yet to locate these settlements and define the material culture of the Libyans as a whole.

It is necessary, therefore, to confine ourselves to two subregions where archaeology does provide information, albeit very fragmentary, on the emergence of proto-urbanism, and urbanism itself: Lower and Upper Nubia in the northern Sudan (Fig. 34.1; Table 34.2). Lower Nubia has periodically received intensive archaeological exploration, but it is clear that indigenous Nubian floodplain settlements were not systematically sought for, and are now lost beyond recovery (Lower Nubia is now a reservoir for the Aswan Dam). The prevalent impression that neither A–Group (early bronze age) nor C–Group (early and middle bronze age) peoples lived in substantial settlements is quite possibly mistaken. Nubian traditions in house architecture and settlement plan were certainly different from Egyptian (Bietak 1968, pp. 87–91; Nordstrom 1972, pp. 20–1; Gratien 1978, pp. 134–5, 185–7, 252; Bonnet 1986, Ch. 3), but some settlements may have been large and internally complex enough to be considered towns, especially as there is evidence for centralized indigenous political systems outside the periods of Egyptian colonization.

One possible index to the settlement pattern is the relatively well-surveyed and excavated cemeteries of lower Nubia (Trigger 1965). These indicate three primary zones of occupation for lower Nubians. Two at least each contained 'rulers' or elite cemeteries in A–Group times (Trigger 1965, p. 75; Williams 1986), hinting at substantial settlements nearby, and *one* relatively substantial settlement (unrelated to these two sites), built in rough stone on rectilinear lines (but only 0.15 ha in area) has been found (Lal 1967, pp. 104–9). In C–Group times it is noteworthy that in at least two of the three settlement zones, cemeteries spanning the same periods vary in size (Fig. 34.3). Aniba is particularly conspicuous (2.5 times as many graves as the average), but there are other conspicuous, if smaller, concentrations at Garf Husein, Dakka and Toshka; other cemeteries fall well below these sizes. The overall pattern could be interpreted as reflecting a rank size order of settlements on the adjoining floodplain, with a particularly substantial 'central place' at Aniba.

Of course, many dispersed, small settlements might have been making use of the same cemetery, but the indications of political and military centralization within the earlier C–Group (see above) hint at agglomerations into large settlements. Moreover, if the cemeteries directly reflect social custom, their relatively densely packed nature suggests that density and combination, not thinness and dispersion, would have been typical of C–Group settlements.

Two fairly substantial C–Group settlements have been excavated. Both were walled. One (El-Riqa) (Randall-MacIver & Woolley 1909, Ch. 2), of both stone and brick architecture, was primarily rectilinear in plan and had a complex history; overall, it

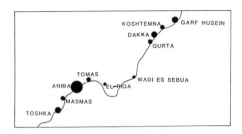

Figure 34.3   C-Group cemetery (= settlement?) patterns, lower Nubia.

occupied 0.25 ha. The other (Wadi es Sebua) was shorter-lived (C-Group IIa or IIb), and was built of rough stone masonry in both rectilinear and 'circular' house plans (Sauneron 1965); it occupied about 0.08 ha.[3] Both settlements obviously preferred concentrated to dispersed houses. They were in poorly settled regions, so settlements in more favoured areas may have been substantially larger, e.g. the assumed central place at Aniba might have been 0.5 ha or larger, a size to be compared with such early bronze age Egyptian towns as Elephantine (2 ha?), Buhen (1.24 ha?) and Ayn Asil in Dakhla (3.3/4.7 ha).

Upper Nubia was more environmentally favoured, probably had a larger population than lower Nubia and can reasonably be predicted to have contained large Nubian settlements on the basis of the most impressive bronze age Nubian settlement yet excavated, at Kerma (Fig. 34.1, Table 34.1). This town, as it may reasonably be called, the capital of a probably very large kingdom had a long and archaeologically complex history, but the *excavated* remains occupy about 3 ha, and the full extent may have been 6 ha or more. These areas compare favourably with the early bronze age Egyptian towns mentioned above, and even with middle bronze age Kahun, which at 14 ha was certainly a very substantial town for its period.

Throughout Kerma's history, a dense town plan (organized along central axes) was favoured, as were rectilinear houses, usually built in mud brick. Some Egyptian influence is detectable, but the resulting 'cityscape' was quite un-Egyptian. Monumental structures stood at the town centre, including an ultimately very massive cult-building occupying about 1000 m², with a palatial(?) complex adjoining it. Periodically, the town was supplied with very substantial fortifications (Bonnet 1986, Chs 2 and 3; Bonnet, Privati, Simon, Chaix & de Paepe 1988, pp. 9–13).

Kerma may be the largest middle (and early?) bronze age town in upper Nubia; but it cannot have been alone. Cemetery concentrations indicate other large settlements at Sai and elsewhere, and future surveys should expand our understanding of bronze age indigenous urbanism in a subregion where once it was not expected to have developed.

Conclusions

This review of the urban process in ancient northeastern Africa has necessarily high-lighted absent or negative evidence as much as actually recovered data. The importance of the negative evidence needs to be stressed: an understanding of villages and towns throughout this vast region must take into account what is *not* known, and how this shapes the understanding and interpretation of what is known, without being used as an excuse for groundless speculations. In every region discussed (except permanently drowned lower Nubia) much more data can and will be recovered, but the strategies and priorities intended to recover these data need to be highly focused on the critical issues, and need to avoid a random accumulation of duplicatory evidence.

Allowing for this negative evidence, however, one can say, on the positive side, that two points of major significance for the general study of early urban developments have emerged from the above review. First, definitions of urbanism must be relatively flexible, and indeed the process is as interesting for its varied manifestations as it is for its universally shared attributes. Northeast Africa is a particularly valuable region for the study of variation in settlement and urban patterns because the involved regions interacted with and influenced each other in spite of their environmental and cultural diversity.

Second, ancient Egypt potentially has a special value for research into both the utilitarian (in the Western sense) and the symbolic roles of towns and cities. First, it is clear that textual data (whether recovered, or to be recovered) can never provide a good basis for the reconstruction of the social and economic organization of ancient Egypt at any phase in its history. Only archaeological data will provide a sufficiently broad evidential basis for these purposes, and the evidence of the settlements and towns will be quite crucial in these regards. Second, Egyptian textual data *do* inform unusually well about the world-view of the Egyptians, and about their concepts concerning the relationships between society, state and cosmos; the symbolic richness of temples in these connections has been long realized, but that of palaces, towns and probably even villages has been almost completely disregarded, and potentially forms a most important field of study.

Notes

[1] At Kerma, in Upper Nubia, copper was being reduced from ores at the end of the Early Bronze Age (Bonnet 1986, p. 16).

[2] The sites in question are shown in Fig. 34.2. For introductions to each, see:

> Tell el Da'aba: Bietak 1984a; Bietak 1985.
> Qantir: Bietak 1983; Leclant & Clerk 1988.
> Buto: Altenmüller 1975.
> Kom el Hisn: Wenke, Buck, Hamroush, Kobusiewicz, Kroeper & Redding 1988.
> For the Delta in general see van den Brink 1988.
> Memphis: Zivie 1980; Jeffreys 1985; for more recent reports on work at Memphis see Jeffreys, Malek & Smith 1986, and subsequent volumes.
> Kahun: Arnold 1979. A Canadian project (under N. Millett) has recently begun a new survey and excavations at the site.
> Tell el Amarna: Kemp 1985; Kemp 1984–7; and preliminary reports by Kemp 1978, and subsequent volumes of the same journal.
> Abydos: Kemp 1972c; recent Pennsylvania-Yale excavations of urban remains (Fig. 34.4).

Figure 34.4 Pennsylvania–Yale expedition to Abydos, 1979; excavation of the Old Kingdom town.

Deir el Ballas: Eggebrecht 1974; for recent work Lacovara 1990.

Thebes: Stadelmann 1985. For recent work relevant to Thebes' urban remains see Leclant 1980 (under 'Région thébaine'), and see subsequent volumes.

Hierakonpolis: Adams 1977; Hoffman, Hamroush & Allen 1986.

Elephantine: Habachi 1975; new excavations, see preliminary reports by Kaiser, Grossman, Haeny & Jaritz 1970, and subsequent volumes.

Surveys: for recent surveys in the northeast Delta, see below; for survey (cemeteries only) in the Abydos-Thinis subregion, see Patch 1984.

[3] No scale is given on the map in Sauneron 1965 but the approximate scale can be worked out from the statement that the village wall was about 1 m wide (Gratien 1985, pp. 39–69).

35   The land of Punt

K. A. KITCHEN

Introduction

For over thirteen centuries (*c.* 2500–1170 BC) the historical and other records from ancient Egypt bear witness to the existence of a territory and people located in east Africa whose name is usually rendered as 'Punt' in most modern writings. Normal Egyptian hieroglyphic script gives only the consonantal framework of the words that it reproduces – P-w-n-t, whose real pronunciation remains unknown to us today (conceivably *Pewanet or *Epwonat).

Apart from Nubia, located on the Nile south of Egypt, from the First to Fourth Cataracts (Fig. 35.1) (and much better attested in Egyptian data), Punt is the sole African land with so ancient a history, traceable back into the third millennium BC, thanks to the often all-too-sparse Egyptian documentation, concerned as it is mainly with trade in exotic products from or via Punt.

History of Punt from Egyptian sources

Third millennium BC (Old Kingdom)

The earliest clear-cut reference to Punt comes at the height of the 'Pyramid Age', in the Vth Dynasty. On the so-called Palermo Stone (retrospective annals of Egypt's first five dynasties), the reference occurs late in the reign of Sahure (*c.* 2450 BC)[1] as follows:

> There was brought from: –
> The terraces(?) of the turquoise-land: 6000 [. . .].
> Punt: myrrh (*'ntyw*), 80,000 (measures);
> electrum, 6000 (measures);
> 2900 *sn-šsmt* (= ?); 23,020 staves.

Some sixty years later, there is a record (in a still later document, see Harkhuf, below) of 'a pygmy whom the God's Seal-bearer Bawerdjed brought from Punt in the time of (Djedkare) Isesi' (text, Sethe 1932, pp. 128:17–129:1; earlier translation, Breasted 1906–7, I, p. 160, no. 351). From tropical Africa, homeland of the pygmy peoples, the most direct route to Egypt would be down the Nile – possibly through Punt rather than originating from it, as shown below. A vase naming King Teti, founder of the VIth Dynasty, bears a figure symbolizing 'Punt' and a mention of myrrh (*'ntyw*), now in the museum at Berkeley, California (Leclant 1978, p. 70).

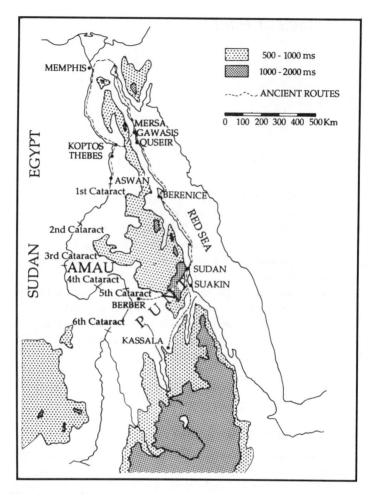

Figure 35.1 Egypt and Punt.

In the earlier years of Pepi II (*c.* 2270 BC), the expedition leader Harkhuf repeated Bawerdjed's exploit, bringing back from the deep south (Iam)[2] 'a pygmy (for) the dances of the god, from the land of the horizon-dwellers', whom the young king wanted to see 'more than the tribute of the mining-region (*bi3*) of Punt'.[3] As Harkhuf's expedition also returned down the Nile valley, his donkeys bringing incense and ebony among other things, this mention also implies an east African location for Punt.

Also under Pepi II, the expeditionary Pepi-nakht reports: 'the Majesty of my Lord sent me to the land (*or* desert) of the Asiatics, to retrieve for him (the body of) the . . . expedition-leader An-ankhti, who had been building a ship there, for (going to) Punt, when the Asiatic beduin ("sandfarers") slew him along with the army-detachment that was with him',[4] and how he in turn slew the bandits.

Nobody ever built boats far out in the desert for use on the Nile. These unruly Asiatic beduin will have belonged to the 'Arabian' desert, between the Nile and the Red

Sea. Thus, the luckless An-ankhti was almost certainly assembling a boat on the desert shore of the Red Sea (like his Middle Kingdom successors, see below), when he was set upon.

Hence, the total evidence under Pepi II indicates that products from (or via) Punt could reach Egypt either by the inland route (traded down the Nile), or by the sea route (expeditions south and back). So, wherever it was, Punt then occupied an area far south of Egypt that in the east could be reached by the Red Sea, and westward by ascending the valley of the Nile.

The contemporary remark by a man Khnumhotep that 'I went out with my masters, Tjety to Byblos [in Phoenicia] and Khui to Punt, and got back safely from these lands' reinforces the picture of early Egyptian travel to Punt, if it adds nothing else. Probably the same man Khui is the Khui known also from a graffito in Wadi Hammamat, the main route in Upper Egypt between the Nile and the Red Sea – this graffito may even have been a memento of his visit to Punt – by sea, in that case (Newberry 1938, p. 182).[5]

Early second millennium BC (Middle Kingdom)

In the reunited Egypt of the XIth Dynasty, Montuhotep III (Sankhkare) sent out an expedition to Punt in his eighth year (c. 1975 BC; date, see Kitchen 1989, p. 152). In charge was the high official Henu, who left an imposing rock-inscription (Couyat & Montet 1912–13, pp. 81ff., Pl. 31, no. 114; Porter & Moss 1952, p. 331) out in Wadi Hammamat, en route to the Red Sea. He gives the following account of his deeds:

> [My Lord] sent me out to despatch (or conduct – sbỉ) a ship to Punt, to fetch for him fresh myrrh from the rulers residing in the desert ('red land') because the dread of him was throughout the foreign land.
>
> Then I went out from Koptos, along the road which His Majesty had commanded for me; there was with me a force from Upper Egypt . . . [details are given] . . . four contingents of militia ('police') cleared the way before me, vanquishing any opposed to the King. Hunters, sons of the desert, were my bodyguards. . . .
>
> I went out with a force of 3000 men. . . . I provided a waterskin, pole, two jugs for water, and 20 loaves for each of them daily; asses were laden with sandals – as one wore out, another was ready(?).
>
> Now I made 12 wells along the valley floor, 2 wells in Idahet . . . (and) another in Iahetib. . . . Then I reached the sea. Then I made this ship, and I despatched (or conducted – sbỉ) it with all (kinds of) provisions when I had made for it a great oblation of cattle, bulls and gazelles.
>
> When I returned from the sea, I had achieved what His Majesty had commanded – I brought for him every product that I found on the shores of God's Land. I descended by Wadj and Ro-Hanu and I brought for him splendid stone blocks for temple statues.[6]

Given the location of this inscription, it is clear that Henu's considerable expedition took all necessary supplies to assemble a ship on the Red Sea coast, and to equip and provision it for a voyage to Punt. The verb *sbi* is ambiguous, but the total context might suggest that Henu did visit Punt personally.

Important data from the powerful XIIth Dynasty (some new, some long-known) fully confirm this inference. In the reign of Sesostris I (*c.* 1943–1898 BC), possibly in his 24th year (*c.* 1920 BC),[7] at least one expedition visited Punt, being based on the Red Sea port of Sa'waw,[8] from remains found close to and overlooking that inlet (XIIth Dynasty finds; Sayed 1977). These include several inscribed stelae, one formed from discarded limestone sea-anchors. On one fragment occur traces of the name of Sesostris I and the word 'ships' (Sayed 1977, Pl. 12b), on another the name 'Punt' (Sayed 1977, Pl. 13e), and on a third the phrase 'to the mining-region of Punt' (*bi3 n Pwnt*; Sayed 1977, Pl. 13b,c).

The triple stela-of-the-anchors set up by the Chamberlain Ankhu preserves further fragmentary allusions. The east side names Sesostris I and his reported opinion of Ankhu, higher than of 'any of his courtiers who are active at sea', with further broken allusions to '. . . settlement of Sa'waw(?), in the province of Koptos, to reach . . . this ship'. The traces on the centre block include:

> [Regnal Year?] 24, 1st Month of Winter, Day: . . . [the Superintendent of] ships' captains . . . to reach . . . with troops of recruits . . .; (*list of officials*) . . . 400 recruits; total, 400+*x* (people).

On the west side, mention is again made of

> the Superintendent of ships' captains, Superintendent of recruits, . . . sent to the mining-region (of) Punt. . . . I returned, . . . for the Majesty of King Sesostris I . . . ship(s) . . . their land (*h3st*), the products of God's Land with them . . . all that (the god) Tatonen had created, from everything of this land. (*Much, illegible*) . . . these products, which they had assembled, for revenue. . . .

A few hundred yards inland from this monument was found that of the vizier Intefoqer, also under Sesostris I. This also begins with the king's name, and states that:

> His Majesty commanded the Vizier (etc.) Intefoqer to construct this fleet at(?) the Koptos dockyards, (for) travelling (*sbi*) and reaching the mining-region of Punt, both to go safely and return safely, all their construction being (so well) provided to be good and sound beyond anything done in this land formerly. He did (this) most excellently, according as he had been commanded by the Majesty of the Palace. Now, the Herald, Montuhotep's son Ameny, was on the shore of the sea, constructing these vessels, along with the assembly from Thinis of southern Upper Egypt who were with him; and able-bodied men who were at the sea-shore as expeditionaries, along with the herald –

Retainers of the Lord [= King]	50 men
Stewards of the Assembly	1 man
Personnel of the crew of the Lord	500 men
Scribes of the great Assembly	5 men
Citizen-militia	3200 men

If these sources are combined, the following historical episode results. Possibly in Year 24 of Sesostris I, the vizier Intefoqer was commanded by the king to see to the building of several vessels in the Koptos dockyards, nearest point of importance on the Nile to Wadi Hammamat and its route to the Red Sea. An expedition of 3200 local people, 500 crewmen, 400 recruits (so, Ankhu), 5 scribes and one property-administrator, and 50 royal retainers (among others?) went through Wadi Hammamat to reach the shore of the Red Sea and to (re)assemble the Koptos-built ships at Sa'waw harbour (now Mersa Gawâsîs), for the actual voyage to Punt. The figure of 500 sailors might imply 10 ships, each crewed by 50 men; later, Queen Hatshepsut's vessels probably had about 40 men as crew (cf. Kitchen 1971, p. 203, n. 150). The intended destination was *bi3 (n) Pwnt*, 'the mining region (of) Punt'. Just what was mined there is not stated in the surviving fragments – New Kingdom sources might indicate gold. There can be little doubt that these are the fragments of records of a Red Sea visit to Punt.

Almost half a century later was set up a monument found long since in Wadi Gasus, only 3 or 4 miles from the Mersa Gawâsîs port. This and another document were found in a Graeco-Roman chapel, having been transferred thither from the seaport area in antiquity; it is republished by Sayed (1977, Pl. 8 opp. p. 140; cf. earlier sources, Porter & Moss 1952, p. 388 end). Dated to Year 28 of Amenemhat II (*c.* 1874 BC), this stela may be read:

> Adoring the god, giving praise to Haroeris-Re and to Min, (god) of Koptos, by the Noble and King's Sealbearer (etc.), Khentykhetywer, when he had returned safely from Punt, his expedition with him, safe and sound, and his ships resting at Sa'waw.

Here is fleeting but very clear evidence for a further substantial expedition ('ships', in plural) returning *from* Punt via the Red Sea, to the now known port of Sa'waw at Mersa Gawâsîs.

Other allusions at this period are still briefer and uninformative. A further stela from Wadi Gasus dated to Year 1 of Sesostris II (*c.* 1868 BC), set up by the sealbearer Khnumhotep, merely mentions 'setting his monument in God's Land' – but not why (a further Punt expedition?). In the fantasy-tale of the *Shipwrecked Sailor*, the Serpent on the magic isle calls himself 'Ruler of Punt', to whom myrrh belongs. The magic isle may have been inspired by the Isle of Zeberged, well down the Red Sea (Wainwright 1946; Wainwright 1948; Kitchen 1971, p. 192, n. 34). In the XIIIth Dynasty, a stela of Neferhotep I (*c.* 1730 BC) alludes conventionally to 'the odours of Punt' as mark of a god's presence (Breasted 1906–7, p. 335, no. 762).

Late second millennium BC (New Kingdom)

Here, our historical contacts are fourfold: (a) the famous Punt expedition sent by Queen Hatshepsut and immortalized in the beautifully wrought reliefs in her memorial temple; (b) expeditions undertaken by the Puntites themselves to Egypt (via the Red Sea coast), summarily depicted in the private tomb-chapels of high officials, dating from Tuthmosis III to Amenophis III; (c) fleeting allusions to Punt and Puntites under

(Akhenaten), Haremhab, Sethos I and Ramesses II; (d) the Punt expedition sent by
Ramesses III, briefly described in the Great Harris Papyrus.

Queen Hatshepsut

The queen announced the success of her expedition in a special sitting of her court in her
9th year (Sethe 1908–9, p. 349:10; earlier translations, Breasted 1906–7, II, p. 120, no.
292; Burkhardt 1984, p. 27). This probably implies that the entire undertaking occurred
within her Years 8 and 9, *c.* 1472/1 BC, on the currently likeliest dates for this period.
The motivation for her expedition appears to have been a desire to cut out the
middlemen in obtaining supplies of 'the marvels of Punt' – primarily aromatics such as
incense and myrrh, required for use in the temple cults. In his address to the queen, the
god Amun is made to remark:[9]

> I have assigned to you the whole of Punt, as far as the lands of the gods,
> God's Land. It had been heard (of), from mouth to mouth, in the reports of
> the ancestors. The marvels that were brought thence under your royal
> forefathers had been brought from one (hand) to another from time
> immemorial, to former kings in exchange for many payments – none
> reached it (= Punt) except for your explorers. But I will cause your
> expedition to reach it (i.e. directly).

As for the route to Punt, Amun then immediately adds: '(when) I have led them *by
water and by land*, opening up for them the difficult (*or* mysterious) roads.'[10]

Thus, besides travelling by ship (five vessels are shown), this expedition had some
overland travelling to do, at either end of its water-route, and probably at both ends.
The expedition was ordered by Theban Amun and welcomed back by Theban Amun,
hence it may have begun and ended at the Nile quays of Thebes. If so, Hatshepsut's
men – in traditional Old and Middle Kingdom fashion – may first have taken their boats
and goods through Wadi Hammamat to Sa'waw or Quseir, reassembled the five ships
on the Red Sea coast, and then sailed on to Punt. An old theory was that the fleet might
have sailed from Memphis down the Nile into the southeast Delta, then east via a
hypothetical canal (in Wadi Tumilat) to Suez and thence into the Red Sea (e.g. Breasted
1906–7, II, p. 103, no. 248). But this has been almost universally rejected under the
impact of the admirably careful study of the matter by Poesner (1938). On their return,
again, they would have transshipped everything overland from the seacoast to Koptos,
and have sailed thence ceremonially into Thebes.

However, the main journey was indeed by ship, as the superb reliefs make clear (Fig.
35.2).[11] On the outward voyage, three ships are to be seen in full sail while, before
them, two others are already at anchor in Punt, sails furled, while crewmen go ashore
by skiff, with jars of goods.[12] The texts above all this refer (in staccato fashion) to:

> Sailing on the sea, and making a good start for God's Land. Making
> landfall safely at the terrain of Punt, by the royal expedition in accord with
> the command of Amun, to fetch for him the marvels of every land . . .

That the ships sailed upon Red Sea waters is confirmed by the scenes themselves,
where the strips of water are populated with marine life mainly attested as denizens of

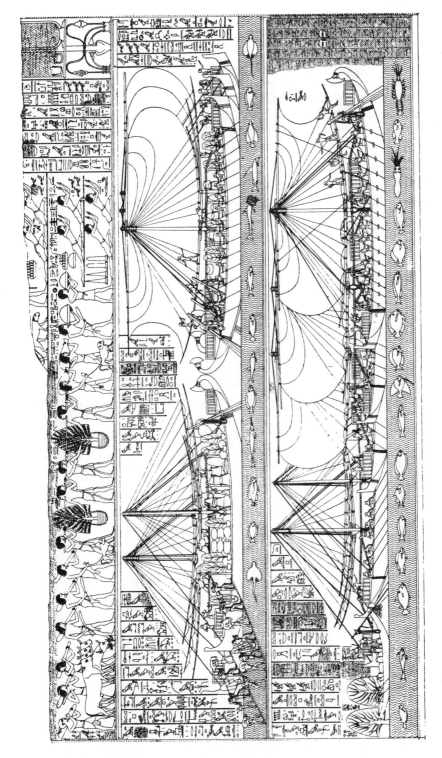

Figure 35.2 Queen Hatshepsut's Punt fleet: *below* arriving; *above* leaving.

the Red Sea and Indian Ocean (see Danelius & Steinitz 1967; and cf. Kitchen 1971, p. 193, n. 42).

A schematic representation of the land of Punt occupies the entire south end-wall, arranged in six superposed registers, to be 'read' from bottom to top (Fig. 35.3). Over a ribbon of sea-water, the first two registers show the Egyptian envoy meeting the local chiefs in Punt. In the first, the Egyptians present their gifts and trade-goods, here described as dedicated to the goddess Hathor (lady of anywhere 'abroad'):

> Arrival of the Royal Envoy in God's Land with the force in his charge, in the presence of the chiefs of Punt, (having been) sent with all kinds of good things from the Palace, for Hathor Lady of Punt and the well-being of Her Majesty.

With hands uplifted and followed by family and retainers, one such chief greets the visitors: 'The chief of Punt comes in obeisance, with bowed head, to receive this royal expedition.' Then they say:

> How come you have arrived here, in this land unknown to (other) people?
> Have you descended by the upper routes?
> (Or) have you voyaged by water and by land?

The only chief shown, along with his ample wife, are the only Puntites ever named in the Egyptian sources: 'Chief of Punt, Parahu; his wife, Atiya' (Sethe 1908–9, pp. 324:3–325:3; cf. Burkhardt 1984, p. 16, correcting Breasted 1906–7, II, nos. 254–8).

The chief's speech, of course, may be nothing more than Egyptian scribal invention. But it could reflect the response of Puntites if they had not seen Egyptian expeditions for some long time. The plural phrase 'chiefs of Punt' is repeatedly used (Sethe 1908–9, pp. 321:[9], 323:16, 324:3, 325:14, 330:2, 331:5, 332:7; contrast the singular with Parahu, 324:16, 326:2, 5). Thus, Parahu is either their chief spokesman, or the one first encountered by the Egyptians.

In the second register, the Egyptian envoy stands ceremoniously before his tent to receive in turn what the Puntite chief and delegation bring in exchange for the Egyptian goods – symbolized by a heap of myrrh, trays of rings of gold and pieces of ebony wood. The envoy's tent has space for the following text (Sethe 1908–9, p. 325:12–17; Breasted 1906–7, II, p. 108, no. 206; Burkhardt 1984, pp. 16–17):

> Preparing a tent for the Royal Envoy and his force at the myrrh-terraces of Punt, by the sea, to receive the chiefs of this land. Bread, beer, wine, meat and fruit – everything that is (found) in Egypt – is presented to them, as was commanded in the Palace.

Over the envoy may be read: 'Receiving the products ("tribute") of the Chief of Punt, by the Royal Envoy.' And over the chief, 'The Chief of Punt comes with his products ("tribute"), besides the sea, before the Royal [Envoy . . .] Palace – gold [of Amau], myrrh, [. . .]' (Sethe 1908–9, p. 326:2–12; Burkhardt 1984, p. 17; less complete, Breasted 1906–7, II, p. 108, nos. 261–2).

The upper four registers show the hewing of ebony, the collecting of myrrh and the removal of myrrh-shrubs, as well as illustrating the fauna (baboon, giraffe, rhino,

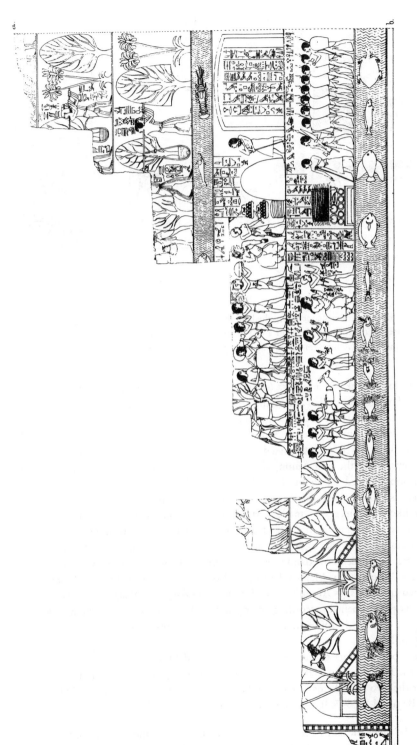

Figure 35.3 The land of Punt.

Figure 35.4 Fragments concerning the land of Punt: (a) carrying away ebony logs; (b) lower part of rhinoceros; (c) shrine of [Amun and Hatshepsut], offered to by Puntite chief (?); (d) Negro Puntite and pile-dwelling; (e) baboon up dom palm, cattle and herds of giraffe.

cattle, dogs, donkeys) and flora (including dom palms), besides domed pile-dwellings reached by ladders, and of course the Puntites themselves (Fig. 35.4a, b, d, e). At the far (left) end of the lowest of these registers can be seen traces of an Egyptian sacred shrine, before which a man (chief of Punt?) offers incense, along with rich offerings (Fig. 35.4c). This has been interpreted as a shrine containing (twin) statuary of Queen Hatshepsut and the god Amun, alleged to have been mentioned in a badly damaged inscription carved down the left edge of this scene.[13] That the queen's statue was present is certain; that it formed a group statue with Amun, patron of the expedition, is very likely: '[There was made a statue of ?the god], conjoined with a statue (of Hatshepsut, of) granite'; the rest of the text alludes to events already noted above. It is uncertain how far the Egyptians penetrated into Punt away from the seacoast. An apparent reference to overland travel occurs in Hatshepsut's account of her expedition's success: '[Now], My Majesty had [given] orders to travel to the myrrh-terraces, so opened-up are his (= Amun's) roads for his own sake(?), (so that) his haunts are known and his paths opened, according to my father Amun's command' (Sethe 1908–9, p. 352:2–7; cf. slightly different versions of Breasted 1906–7, II, no. 294 and Burkhardt 1984, p. 27).

The four registers of gathering the products of Punt run towards the right, back towards the adjoining wall and scenes of the five ships loading up and leaving Punt. Over the two ships being loaded can be read (Sethe 1908–9, pp. 328:17–329:12; transl. also Breasted 1906–7, II, no. 265 and Burkhardt 1984, p. 18):

Loading the ships very heavily with the marvels of the land of Punt: with (all kinds of) good herbs of God's Land and heaps of nodules of myrrh,

with trees of fresh myrrh, with ebony and pure ivory, with 'green' gold of
'Amau, with *tishepes* and *khesyt* wood, with *ihmt*-myrrh, incense and eye-
paint, with baboons, monkeys and hounds, with southern leopard-skins,
and with servants and their children.

Over two vessels in full sail back northwards may be found (Sethe 1908–9, pp.
329:15–330:6; transl. also Breasted 1906–7, II, no. 266 and Burkhardt 1984, pp. 18–19):

Voyaging and arriving safely, making landfall at Karnak Temple joyfully,
by the royal expedition, accompanied by chiefs of this land. They have
brought (things) the like of which has not been brought to other kings,
from the marvels of the land of Punt.

Arrival at Karnak in Thebes presupposes some kind of transshipment from the Red
Sea to the Nile – most likely back through Wadi Hammamat, exactly as in the Middle
Kingdom and again later under Ramesses III. The set of scenes ends with the queen
receiving the cargo, presenting it to Amun, an account of the undertaking delivered in
the royal court in Year 9, along with the official reception of tribute from Nubia,
making a veritable African *durbar* of the whole occasion.

Mid-XVIIIth Dynasty contacts

In his Karnak Annals, Tuthmosis III twice records receipt of goods from Punt. In Year
33 (*c.* 1447 BC):

Marvels brought to His Majesty from the land of Punt in this year:
Dried myrrh, 1685 *heqat*-measures; gold [of Amau?, . . . *deben*].

In Year 38 (*c.* 1442 BC):

Marvels brought to the might of His Majesty from the land of Punt:
Dried myrrh, 240 *heqat*-measures.[14]

The non-committal form of these brief chronicular entries does not reveal whether
these deliveries of aromatics and gold were brought by Egyptian expeditions (like
Hatshepsut's), or by Puntites coming to Egypt. The latter may here be the likelier case
for two reasons. First, the modest scope of the entries; and second, there is contemporary evidence for Puntites trading into Egypt, probably via Wadi Hammamat.

From the reigns of Tuthmosis III (*c.* 1470–1425 BC), Amenophis II (*c.* 1427–1401 BC)
and Amenophis III (*c.* 1391–1353 BC, or ten years later), there are four scenes of visiting
Puntites in the tomb-chapels of four Theban notables (two under Tuthmosis III).
Perhaps the oldest is from Tomb 39, of Puyemre, Second Prophet of Amun (references,
Porter & Moss 1960, p. 72(11), IV–VI). Here, Tuthmosis III sits in state, 'viewing the
weighing of great heaps of myrrh and receiving the marvels of Punt, namely ivory,
ebony, gold of Amau, and all (manner of) sweet herbs' (Fig. 35.5).[15]

Before the king, the upper two registers show Egyptian scribes recording the heaps
of myrrh, including a figure of 4716 *heqat*-measures[16] above these heaps, and part of a
further figure, 1305. . . . In the middle register are shown myrrh-trees, logs of ebony,
tusks of ivory, incense or myrrh made into a model obelisk, and gold in ring form.

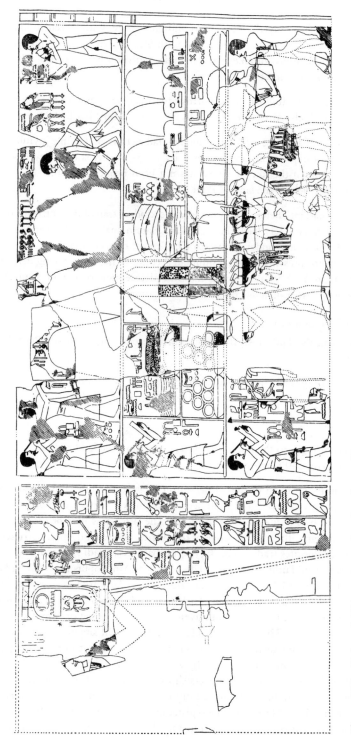

Figure 35.5 Tuthmosis III inspects myrrh and products of Punt, with Asiatic tribute (Tomb of Puyemre).

Figure 35.6 The products of Punt (Tomb of Rekhmire).

Figure 35.7 Puntite trade mission is welcomed on shores of the Red Sea (Theban Tomb 143).

The one long register in the tomb-chapel (No. 100) of the vizier Rekhmire (Fig. 35.6) shows the same items, plus leopard-skins, ostrich plumes and eggs, and live animals (baboon, ibex, monkey, cheetah), and bead-necklaces (material unknown) (Davies 1943, II, Pl. 17; Porter & Moss 1960, 207(4), I).

Tomb-chapel 143 (owner's identity unknown), under Tuthmosis III/Amenophis II, c. 1430/1420 BC, contains a scene of especial interest (Fig. 35.7). This shows Puntites arriving in two raft-like(?) boats, each having a black triangular sail. Goods unloaded include heaps of myrrh (or incense), a tree, ebony-logs, etc. Referring to the Egyptian welcoming delegation, a damaged text says: 'Travelling to [Thebes], going on the road (= Wadi Hammamat?), carrying thousands(?) of various [excellent] products of Punt – myrrh, incense, trees . . .' (Davies 1935; Porter & Moss 1960, pp. 255–7(6)). Here, clearly, is proof of two-way trade between Punt and Egypt; the Puntites could navigate the Red Sea coast route to Egypt, just as the Egyptians did the reverse.

Under Tuthmosis IV or Amenophis III, Amenmose (tomb-chapel 89) shows a similar scene (Fig. 35.8), but no ships (Davies 1940, p. 136, Pl. 25; Porter & Moss 1960, p. 182(14)). As Säve-Söderbergh (1946, p. 25) points out, a Sinai inscription of another

Figure 35.8   Receipt of myrrh and other Puntite products at the Red Sea (Theban Tomb 89).

official (Year 36 of Amenophis III, *c.* 1356 or 1346 BC) commemorates serving his king: 'I reached the seacoast, to announce the marvels of Punt, to receive aromatic gums, which the chiefs had brought . . . as revenue from lands unknown' (Gardiner, Peet & Cerny 1952, Pl. 66; Gardiner, Peet & Cerny 1955, pp. 165f., no. 211).

Other allusions, Dynasties XVIII–XIX

The tradition of Puntites bringing myrrh, etc., to Egypt appears to have continued for the next century or so.

In Year 36 of Amenophis III (*c.* 1345 BC), a Sinai inscription speaks of 'announcing the marvels of Punt' (parallel text, Edel 1983, pp. 183–5, Abb. 7–8), while a recently reconstituted text from Sinai of this period derives ebony from Wetjenat, *k3i* and *tisheps*-wood from [two lands. *lost*], and resin from Wekemet; Wetjenat is also attested as part of Punt in the great lists of Tuthmosis III noted below (Edel 1983, pp. 176–82, Abb. 6).

Under Akhenaten (*c.* 1340 BC), at his personal capital (El Amarna) in Middle Egypt, the official Meryre shows in his tomb (Fig. 35.9) people of Punt bringing myrrh and incense to be measured (Davies 1905, Pls 37, 40). A few decades later, King Haremhab caused to be carved at Karnak a scene of Puntite chiefs offering their products in bags, hence not identifiable (Wreszinski n.d., Pl. 60; cf. Breasted 1906–7, III, no. 38; other sources, Porter & Moss 1972, p. 183(551)).

In the XIXth Dynasty, references are again rather brief, but appear to presuppose continued interchange. Leaving aside generalities (inherited from the previous period), as in triumph-scenes, there is passing reference to Punt in the Nauri decree of Sethos I (*c.* 1290 BC) for his great temple at Abydos, thus:

Figure 35.9 Puntites bringing myrrh (Tomb of Meryre).

> The treasuries are full of valuables . . . myrrh is there from Punt, measured
> out by heaps. . . . Created for him (= Osiris) are fleets of ships to multiply
> herbs in his temple – their sheer number has covered the sea – each vessel
> 100 cubits long, laden with herbs from God's Land.[17]

Similar sentiments are expressed by Ramesses II (*c.* 1279–1213 BC). For his temple at
Abydos, likewise, he says that: 'he planted many gardens, planted with all (kinds of)
trees, all sweet and fragrant herbs, the plants of Punt' (Kitchen 1969–90, p. 514:16;
earlier transl., Breasted 1906–7, III, no. 527). A well-known hymn to Amun of this
general period (cf. also Säve-Söderbergh 1946, p. 28) reads:

> The dwellers of Punt come to you,
> God's Land is verdant for love of you.
> [To] you, [ships?] are brought by water, [laden] with gums,
> to make your temple festive with fragrances.

In the list of mining-regions inscribed in Luxor Temple, the personified Mountain of
Punt (No. 15) says to the king, 'I have come, I have brought you gum(s).'[18]

The Punt expedition of Ramesses III (c. 1184–1153 BC)

At some point in his reign, this king sent an expedition to Punt, described as follows in
the historical retrospect of his reign in the Great Papyrus Harris I:

> I constructed great transport vessels with towboats before them, equipped
> with strong crews . . . loaded with limitless goods from Egypt. They are
> innumerable, as myriads, despatched on the Red Sea.[19] They reached the
> land of Punt, unaffected by (any) misfortune, safe and respected. The
> towed transports and tugs were loaded with the products of God's Land
> . . . much myrrh of Punt, loaded by myriads, limitless. Their chiefs'
> children from God's Land returned in charge of their products ('tribute') to
> Egypt. They reached the desert land of Koptos, being kept safe. They
> moored safely, carrying the goods that they had brought. These were
> (re)loaded, overland, on donkeys and men, (then) loaded into ships on the
> River at the quay of Koptos, being despatched on downstream, arriving
> amidst festivity and presented as tribute in the Royal Presence as a
> marvel.[20]

This relatively matter-of-fact account indicates (as in earlier times) conveyance of Egyptian goods to trade for Punt's exotic products. It is clear and explicit about transshipment from the (Red) Sea overland (i.e., via Hammamat) back to the Nile at Koptos, precisely as is indicated for Middle Kingdom times, and most likely also for the XVIIIth and XIXth Dynasties. Of products, only myrrh is specified here; gums and resins are recorded from Punt in Ramesses III's memorial temple at Medinat Habu, and elsewhere in the lists of temple income and property in Papyrus Harris I.[21]

First millennium BC

After Ramesses III and the twelfth century BC, Punt simply drops out of view in our existing Egyptian historical sources. While mutual trading may well have continued unrecorded by the narrow range of often meagre sources for the later dynasties (c. 1070–332 BC), this near-total disappearance may well reflect the fall-off, then cessation, of trade relations. The very name of Punt does not recognizably recur in later sources from other cultural traditions (e.g. Old South Arabia, or Greek or Latin writers). The local political configurations in east Africa may well have changed so considerably that the entity 'Punt' was dissolved into other, local, social configurations.

Between Ramesses III and the Ptolemies (under whom occur only traditional mentions, of no historical value – see Herzog 1968, pp. 20–1 with references), there is so far only one significant reference, on a damaged stela of the XXVIth Dynasty, c. 600 BC.[22] This document may reflect greater Egyptian awareness of climatic conditions in the areas traversed by the Sudanese Nile, thanks to the brief political union of Egypt and Nubia from the Mediterranean south to Khartoum and even beyond, under the Kushite XXVth Dynasty (c. 715–664 BC). However that may be, the relevant legible parts of the stela run as follows:

> (3) . . . good. They said to [His] Majesty . . .(4) [all, illegible] (5) . . . in that mountain. Said the Majesty of?/His? Majesty, . . . (6) . . . difficult of roads(?), [. . . of] water, for an aeon of years it had not been trodden. (7) . . . the water. (8) . . . rained from the sky in . . . 4th Month of Winter, Day 12 (9) . . . very greatly (10) . . . entirely (11) . . . His Majesty. So, His Majesty's heart was greatly gladdened by it. . . . the army-force(s) thanked His Majesty (12) . . ., [saying]: (How) great is Your Majesty, O victorious King . . .! A great marvel has happened in Your Majesty's time; (13) this has not been seen or heard (before) – rainfall upon the mountain of Punt – (for) rain was a scarcity in the Southern provinces (14) . . . this month in which its rain was, (when) it was not the season (for it), even in the Delta towns; (15) your mother, (the goddess) Neith, has brought it for you – a Nile-flood to sustain your forces! (Then follow the king's thank-offering, and command to erect the stela.)

Here, a clear connection seems to be made between the rain on the mountains of Punt and the (subsequent) Nile inundation into Egypt, credited to the goddess Neith's benevolence. On this basis, Punt is regarded as including mountains on which rain fell to swell the Nile. Hence, in effect, Punt must include some part of the north/west Ethiopian highlands. On this monument, the location and activities of the Egyptian army remain obscure – on a raid into Napatan-dominated Nubia? If so, it is just conceivable that this monument is connected with the famous campaign of Psammetichus II into Nubia against the kingdom of Napata (c. 593 BC) (references Kitchen 1986, p. 406, no. 368 and n. 962).

Geographical location and extent of Punt

Even to the present day, despite over a century of discussion, the land of Punt is still 'of no fixed address' so far as scholarly consensus is concerned. In recent decades, three locations have been advanced, all in east Africa: (1) Within the Sudan, south of the Fifth Cataract of the Nile, between the White Nile and the mountains of east Sudan and Ethiopia that divide the Atbara drainage area from the Red Sea coast (Herzog 1968). (2) The same general area, but including the Red Sea coast north and south of the stretch from Port Sudan to Suakin, and the coastal mountains and passes westward through them (Kitchen 1971). (3) The formerly traditional location in Somalia (especially along its north coast), advocated by Sayed (1989). What, then, is the position?

First, as between positions (1) and (2), there can now be no serious doubt that the Egyptians reached Punt directly by way of the Red Sea route. The combined evidence from the XIth Dynasty (Hammamat texts), Sayed's discoveries of a Red Sea port and stelae (and older finds) from the XIIth Dynasty, the Red Sea marine fauna in Hatshepsut's reliefs of the XVIIIth Dynasty and the clear use of the Red Sea/ Hammamat/Koptos route under Ramesses III in the XXth Dynasty – all this proves access to Punt by sea, not just by the Nile. Therefore, the position (1) of Herzog is excluded, leaving positions (2) and (3). Any non-African location of Punt can be excluded on multiple grounds: the presence of giraffes, and likewise of rhinos (outside Africa, southeast Asia does not come into consideration as a possible location of Punt); the indirect trade from Punt down the Nile to Egypt in the Old Kingdom; rain falling in Punt going into the Nile. So, somewhere in east Africa running inland from the Red Sea coast is surely a certainty – but from which part of the coast?

Second, some features are not decisive. In east Africa, the occurrence of various kinds of *Boswellia* (frankincense) and *Commiphore/Balsamodendron* (myrrh) is widespread in east Sudan up to Ethiopia and Eritrea, and also in Somalia.[23] Again, dom palms and baboons can each be found in both Somalia and east Sudan/northeastern Ethiopia/ Eritrea; but the overlap of the dom palm with the hamadryas baboon (Hatshepsut) does favour Eritrea and east Sudan (Kitchen 1971, pp. 186f. & nn. 11, 15).

Third, features that do seem more conclusive. Here, it may be noted that the Egyptians obtained 'ebony' from Punt. Egyptian ebony is known (from analysis of actual specimens) to be *Dalbergia melanoxylon*, a wood attested in northwestern Ethiopia, bordering on northeastern Sudan, very close to positions (1) and (2) for Punt but not so good for (3) (see Kitchen 1971, p. 187, n. 13). Punt is also a supplier of gold and electrum, and had a 'mining-region' (Pepi II; Sesostris I). Also, Punt supplied 'gold of Amau'. The latter location is not finally fixed – but was accessible *both* from the Egyptian dominions in Nubia (south to the Fourth Cataract of the Nile) *and* from Punt. Given the effective boundary of Egypt's Nubian empire near the Fourth Cataract, a contiguous Amau could not possibly be anywhere remotely near a Punt in Somalia, over 1200 miles southeast as the crow flies. In fact, some have suggested[24] that Amau should be located in the area just east of the Third Cataract of the Nile. This location would entirely preclude any location of Punt south or east of eastern Sudan/Ethiopia. However, it seems (to this writer) quite incredible that the Egyptians should trade (i.e. pay for) Amau gold from the Puntites, if Amau were wholly and securely within the area of Egyptian rule, where the Egyptians could extract gold directly without paying anybody (using serf or convict labour). Neither a graffito found at Sabu (near the Third Cataract) nor the Luxor mining list proves that Amau is at the Third Cataract. 'Userhat of Amau', who left the graffito, may have come there from further southeast; the Nest-tawy of the Luxor list (before/? south of Amau) may be Napata, but this is neither proven, nor is Amau necessarily due north of it. An entirely preferable location for the gold of Amau would be around and east from Abu Hamed, and opposite the Nile (especially eastward) between the Fourth and Fifth Cataracts.[25] Thus, in the west, part of Amau may have fallen in, or close to, the southern Egyptian domain (hence presence of a man like Userhat); while eastward Amau extended along to the north of Punt, perhaps contiguous with its northernmost reaches. This well fits the positions (1), (2), of Punt, but rules out Somalia completely.

Finally, mention in the XXVIth Dynasty of rain falling on the mountain of Punt, and (ultimately) draining into the Nile, towards its inundation. This was only possible with rains that fell (or fall) upon the main, western bloc of the Ethiopian highlands, in a north–south line from north of Asmara down to the west of Addis Ababa on to Soddi (in the direction of Lake Rudolf). Rains here drain either to the coast or (largely) west and northwest into the Atbara, Blue Nile and more distantly the White Nile. Rain falling in Somalia (e.g., on high ground from Berbera westward) or on the adjoining section of the Ethiopian highlands (east of the railway-line from Djibouti to Dilo) could not (and cannot) possibly drain into any part of the Nile, as our evidence requires.

Thus, there is seemingly a virtually conclusive case for placing Punt between the Red Sea and the middle Nile, straddling the latter and the former's coast, occupying a large area on (and from) the north and northwest flanks of the Ethiopian highlands, in east Sudan; the supposed location in Somalia becomes increasingly next to impossible to sustain.[26]

Topography, archaeology, socio-political structure

Topography and archaeology

Occupying an area along the Red Sea coast from (perhaps) north of Port Sudan to northern Eritrea, and extending inland (along with the aromatic flora) perhaps as far as Kassala, and Er-Roseires southward, Punt may correspondingly (in its northern part) extend west from the coast via the gold-bearing mountains towards Berber just above the Fifth Nile Cataract, and so have adjoined the gold-bearing region of Amau (as argued above). A southward and westward reach of Punt to (or just west of) the White Nile then would straddle the route by which pygmies reached Egypt via Punt (down the Nile) in the Old Kingdom.

But within this entire area, what is known of Puntite settlements or place-names in either archaeology or texts? As for textual data, the great topographical lists of foreign places engraved (three versions) at Karnak under Tuthmosis III (*c.* 1450 BC) include a major African list, which (as others have long since noticed) consists of several distinct sections.[27] Here, in two of the three versions of the list, 'Punt' is the first of thirty place-names that appear to belong to this region,[28] being nos. 48–77. Unfortunately, no convincing identifications of these places can be offered at present.

The archaeology of this vast area is still in its beginnings. In recent decades, pioneering work in east Sudan and northern Ethiopia/Eritrea has revealed traces of local pottery-using cultures going back to the early first, the second and even third millennia BC and beyond – and at times having links both westward with the Nile valley and eastward along the Red Sea coast and linking up with the southern half of the Red Sea coast of Arabia (the Tihama region) (see Munro-Hay, Ch. 36, this volume). Adequate information on the form of settlements and distribution, funerary usages, etc. must await the impact of more extensive work in this vast area.[29] The Hatshepsut relief shows use of pile-dwellings (at least coastally?). Perhaps some day, traces will be found of postholes from structures, in village groupings.

Socio-political structure

On the basis of the Egyptian data, the comment can be brief. Parahu is termed 'chief of Punt' (the only one named). But apart from the two singular references to him thus, all other occurrences of the title are in the plural: 'chiefs of Punt . . . of this land' (see above). So, as with Nubian territories along the Nile, the Egyptians noted that Punt was an area ruled by (and divided up among) various local chiefs, and was not a unitary realm under one supreme ruler, to all appearances. There remains the pre-eminence of the chief Parahu (sole one named). As chief at the coast, the Egyptians perhaps dealt mainly with him; perhaps he acted as intermediary for chiefs inland. It is conceivable that he had some kind of superior status – *primus inter pares*? – but this can only be speculation. The main Puntite population was mixed. Besides the so-called 'Hamitic' type (like Parahu), not very different from the Egyptians in appearance, others represented were clearly of negro stock, in hues of brown and near-black. Parahu wore a continuous series of rings entirely encasing his right leg, as in some parts of the Sudan to modern times.

The pile-dwellings, clear presence of domesticated cattle and repeated references to chiefs (plural), may well indicate a country and culture of scattered villages (some, pile-dwellings), inhabited largely by cattle-herding pastoralists, trading in aromatics grown on the hill terraces, either down the Nile through intermediaries, or directly on the coast with visiting expeditions, or by their own emissaries on Red Sea boat-trips to Egyptian coasts. Gold was probably mined in the mountain ranges east of the Sudanese coast, and well to the southeast, as well as being traded from Amau in the north. Inland were stretches of terrain suited to giraffes, rhinos and leopards.

The products of Punt

The fullest list is that given in Hatshepsut's reliefs – herbs, myrrh resin and its trees, ebony, ivory, gold, other woods, incense, eye paint, fauna and people. Other references also mention gold and electrum, reflecting the mention of Punt and its mining-region under Sesostris I. Ramesses III mentions resin(?), *mnm* (not manna!) and gum. In literary references, the ubiquitous allusions to the odours of Punt emphasize the dominance of aromatics; gold is perhaps the second most important product, and ebony and other valuable woods third.

The eclipse of Punt

After the time of Ramesses III, early in the twelfth century BC, virtually all historical references to Punt (or expeditions) cease completely, and the name of Punt (except for one XXVIth-Dynasty mention) becomes an empty fossil in purely traditional lists and allusions. Punt seemingly disappeared from history. What happened?

In the first place, Egypt's later kings (other than the Kushite XXVth Dynasty) were all explicitly Delta-based. Only rarely between Ramesses III and the XXVIth Dynasty was Egypt politically united under rulers strong enough to mount expeditions to such distant lands as Punt. And even if such expeditions still just occasionally took place, they are not the kind of event to find any mention in the very narrow range of textual sources available to us during the period in question. Sources, in any case, are much sparser.

Second, the trade may, in fact, have died out for other reasons. During the first millennium BC, Egypt may have obtained supplies of aromatics from the neighbouring Levant, drawing on the trade that then came from Saba along the caravan route from Saba to Palestine. So, links between Egypt and Punt withered away. In terms of local culture, various successive cultural changes can be seen throughout the first millennium BC (on into the first millennium AD) in the local cultures bordering on the eastern Sudan, northern Ethiopia and Eritrea. By the ninth/eighth centuries BC, early pre-Axumite areas show two cultural provinces (east and west). Then middle pre-Axumite (about sixth–fourth centuries BC) shows us the culture of a unified realm, under a Sabean-acculturated ruling line. Then, late pre-Axumite disunity (again) runs through the Hellenistic into the early Roman period, probably ending in the rise of the realm of Axum itself.[30] It is most probable that a comparable (if different) series of changes operated through the centuries in the vast area of former 'Punt', just to the north and out west from the Axumite area. But such developments remain veiled from our gaze until the field archaeology of Punt is far more advanced and extensive than at present.

Notes

[1] Apparently the 'Year after the 7th numbering', which (if the 1st numbering was in the king's 2nd year) would correspond to Sahure's 15th (and perhaps last) year, if correctly read. Text,

Palermo Stone, verso 4:1, originally in Schäfer 1902; I use here the text in Sethe 1932, p. 246:3–5. cf. also, Gardiner 1945, p. 14.

[2] The earlier form of name of the land later known as Irem in the New Kingdom, at least as far south as the Dongola region, south of the Third Nile Cataract (northern Sudan), and just conceivably still further south; see Kitchen 1977, pp. 216–18 & Fig. 1; Vercoutter 1980. Again, the pygmy will have originated from well south of Dongola or beyond.

[3] Text, Sethe 1932, p. 128:15–16. On the term 'mine/mining-region of Punt', *bỉ3 (n) Pwnt*, cf. Sayed 1977, pp. 150, 162, 170:4, and especially 176–7.

[4] Text, Sethe 1932, p. 134:13–17; earlier translation, Breasted 1906–7, pp. 163f., no. 60f. Not needfully in Wadi Hammamat (cf. Posener 1938, p. 264).

[5] There is no support for the reading 'eleven visits'.

[6] We translate here from lines 10–15; previous translations, cf. Breasted 1906–7, I, pp. 208–11, nos. 427–33; Säve-Söderbergh 1946, pp. 11–12; Schenkel 1965, pp. 253–7, no. 426; Seyfried 1981, pp. 243–5; Lichtheim 1988, pp. 52–4, no. 21; cf. also, Kaplony 1969, pp. 25–7.

[7] Stela of Ankhu, central block, line 1: [?Regnal Year] 24, 1st Month of Winter, [Day . . .]; Sayed 1977, p. 161.

[8] Now to be located at Mersa Gawâsîs; see Sayed 1977, pp. 146–50 and maps 2, 3. Mersa Gawâsîs is only a few hundred yards south of the similarly named Mersa Gasus, where no ancient remains were found; both sites, cf. Kitchen 1971, p. 198, no. 16 & n. 78.

[9] Sethe 1908–9, p. 344:6–17; translations, etc., Breasted 1906–7, p. 117, nos. 286(end)–299(start); Burkhardt 1984, p. 25; cf. Säve-Söderbergh 1946, pp. 17–18; Yoyotte 1975, p. 46, who studies the term *smntyw* pp. 44–5, here translated 'explorers' – literally, 'gold-baggers' who explored the deserts for minerals, especially gold.

[10] Sethe 1908–9, p. 345:1–2, transl. Burkhardt 1984, p. 25. Note that Sethe read on the original *hr wb3 n.sn.* (not *mw*) *w3wt št3wt* as in Naville n.d., Pl. 84:13 top (s for second n). Thus the translation in Breasted 1906–7, II, no. 288 (start) is to be discarded. On *w3wt*, cf. Sethe 1908–9, p. 345, note b with reference to 338:5 (and note c). If *mw* were present, read: 'opening up difficult waters and roads'.

[11] Old reproduction, Mariette 1877, Pl. 6; standard one, Naville n.d., Pls 72–5; other references, Porter & Moss 1972, pp. 345f.

[12] These were not just water-pots or jars of rations, but rather would have contained various merchandise for trading with the Puntites; such vessels appear in other Egyptian pictures of shipping (Faulkner & Davies 1947). The function of such jars was discovered by G. F. Bass and colleagues, while excavating Canaanite shipwrecks (late second millennium BC) off the coast of southern Turkey, e.g. the Ulu Burun shipwreck (on which, cf. Bass 1986; Pulak 1988; Bass, Pulak, Collon & Weinstein 1989). My thanks go to Dr George F. Bass for his helpful personal remarks on the matter (Edinburgh, 1989). This is confirmed here by a minor text over the skiff, which says: 'Unloading the ships of tribute for (Hatshepsut's) "mother" (= Hathor), ship [by ship], for Hathor, Lady of Punt, for the well-being of Her Majesty' (Sethe 1908–9, p. 323:2–5); cf. also Burkhardt 1984, p. 15 & n.4, which corrects Breasted and others (who mistakenly read this as a present to Hathor *before* the fleet's departure).

[13] So Sethe 1908–9; cf. Simpson 1962, p. 60, with figure (land of Punt), p. 61, and Naville n.d., Pls 69, 70 left. Text, Sethe 1908–9, pp. 316–18, and his restoration (319–21); transl., Burkhardt 1984, pp. 14–15.

[14] Year 31 (*c.* 1449 BC), one may read of 'Arrival of emissaries from *Gnbtyw*, bearing their products ("tribute") of myrrh and *k3y*] . . .]' (Sethe 1908–9, p. 695:5–7; Breasted 1906–7, no. 474; Burkhardt 1984, p. 205). The location of *Gnbtyw* is uncertain. Some (e.g. Breasted) identify it with Punt; others, with Arabia (cf. Saleh 1972a; Saleh 1972b).

[15] Sethe 1908–9, p. 524, replaced by Davies 1922–3, I, Pls 30–4. The text adds: '(Also) reckoning

prisoners brought off by His Majesty through his victories' which applies not to Punt, but to the bottom row of Asiatic chiefs in the scene.

[16] The *heqat* 'was rather more than a gallon', about 4.54 litres (cf. Gardiner 1957, p. 198, no. 266:1).

[17] Text, Kitchen 1969–90, I, pp. 48:7, 9–10, 49:14–16; transl. also by Griffith 1927, p. 199. The boats would be about 180 feet long (a cubit = *c.* 20.6 inches, 523 mm, cf. Gardiner 1957, p. 199, no. 266:2).

[18] Text, Kitchen 1969–90, II, p. 619:13–14, no. 15; previous entry (no. 14) is 'God's Land', bringing precious stones.

[19] Lit. 'the great sea of the inverted water' – so named because the seasonal current bearing the ships south flowed in the opposite direction to the Nile.

[20] Papyrus Harris I, 77:8–17, in Erichsen 1933, pp. 94–5; transl., cf. (e.g.) Breasted 1906–7, IV, no. 407.

[21] Epigraphic Survey 1930–69, V, Pls 321A, 328–30; Kitchen 1969–90, V, pp. 321:11–12, 322:2 (and 'good gold of Amau', 321:14); Breasted 1906–7, IV, no. 29. Papyrus Harris I, 33b:12, 70b:14 (Erichsen 1933, pp. 39:5, 85:4), cf. Breasted 1906–7, IV, nos. 286, 389.

[22] First published by Petrie 1888, p. 107, Pl. 42:13; on this, see Posener 1938, p. 271 & n. 2, and Lloyd 1975, pp. 54f.

[23] Cf. already Kitchen 1971, pp. 185–6 and references. On South Arabian *boswellia* (in Dhofar), see also now Radcliffe-Smith 1980, p. 66; Mandaville 1980, pp. 87–8, Pls 1–3.

[24] Using the graffito of Userhat of Am(au), at Sabu near the Third Cataract: Vercoutter 1956, pp. 70–1; Posener 1958, p. 56; Vercoutter 1959, pp. 130–1, using the Ramesses II mining-regions list with the 'south–north' sequence, Nest-tawy (= Napata?), Amau, then Kush.

[25] Cf. gold-mines map, Vercoutter 1959, p. 129, map 2, east from Abu Hamed; cf. Säve-Söderbergh 1941, pp. 212–13.

[26] The suggested locations of toponyms in Punt (Tuthmosis III list) in Somalia (so, Sayed 1989, p. 164) are based on supposed equations between Greek, modern and Egyptian terms that are either imprecise or wholly unconvincing. Contrast (for location) the equally unconvincing treatment of the same list – looking in a totally different direction! – by Zylharz (1958). Neither author's equations can be credited either in detail or as a whole as their solutions are mutually exclusive.

[27] An observation made as long ago as 1886 by Brugsch, and subsequently by Zylharz (1958, p. 8) and Sayed (1989, p. 157).

[28] And *not* including nos. (1), 2–23, as wrongly stated by Zylharz (1958), who ignored the clear fact that the sequence in this list is Kush (upper Nubia), Wawat (lower Nubia, bordering on Egypt), Punt, Medjay (deserts north of Punt area, and east of the Nile), Kenset (perhaps originally west of Wawat) and Tjehenu (= 'Libya', the western deserts). On Kenset, cf. Zibelius (1972, p. 162), following Katznelson.

[29] For literature on what has been done, compare the following: Fattovich 1975; Fattovich 1978; Fattovich 1980; Fattovich, Marks & Ali Abbas 1984; Fattovich, Sadr & Vitagliano 1988.

[30] For the latest treatment of the overall dating of Axum, and a general account of that kingdom and its civilization, see Munro-Hay, 1989a, pp. 7–26; Munro-Hay 1991; Munro-Hay, Ch. 36, this volume.

36   State development and urbanism in northern Ethiopia

STUART MUNRO-HAY

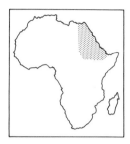

The earliest evidence for state formation

The rise of the Aksumite kingdom in northern Ethiopia in the first centuries BC/AD no longer seems so mushroom-like a phenomenon as has been represented in the past. Though considerable gaps remain in the record, Aksum's (Figs 36.1, 36.2) antecedents are now a little better known. The appearance of a complex society possibly of chiefdom status in the northern part of the region later controlled by Aksum, at Mahal Teglinos near Kassala in the Sudan–Ethiopian borderlands (Fig. 36.1), has now been confirmed archaeologically as far back as the late third to early second millennium BC (Fattovich 1988; Fattovich 1990). Possibly the stelae found at Mahal Teglinos are prototypes for the funerary monuments which later became a characteristic feature of Aksum.

It now seems very probable that the land of Punt, known to ancient Egyptian trading missions as a chiefdom accessible via the Red Sea during and even before this period, should be situated in this geographical area (Kitchen 1971; Fattovich 1988; Kitchen, Ch. 35, this volume), rather than further south in Arabia or Somalia, as has often been proposed (Fig. 36.1). Kitchen's suggestion was that Punt lay inland behind Port Sudan/Suakin, in the Berber/Kassala region (and see Kitchen, Ch. 35, this volume), and Fattovich, discussing work in the Gash delta, states that the evidence 'seems to confirm that this region was part of the land of Punt', and that 'Kassala was most likely the inland gateway to Punt' (Fattovich 1988). In this case, an identity has been provided for the earliest known archaeologically attested complex society in the Ethiopian border region.

Recent research has also confirmed that developments in Ethiopia in early pre-Aksumite times did not occur entirely in isolation. Pottery studies have suggested that the pre-Aksumite culture might owe something to Nile valley influences, specifically to the C-group/Kerma cultures (see O'Connor, Ch. 34, this volume), and in rather later times to Meroë/Alodia, as well as to contacts across the Red Sea on the Yemeni and Saudi coasts (Fattovich 1977; Fattovich 1978; Fattovich 1990). The Ethiopian plateau might have seemed a tempting habitat to people suffering from deteriorating ecological conditions in the Savanna/Sahel belt, and the movements of such groups might have imported certain cultural traditions onto the plateau, whilst others belong to a Red Sea cultural complex.

The plateau environment had certain advantages, and the region had evidently already been long occupied. An important site (Phillipson 1977b) for early Ethiopian archaeology is Gobedra, a rock shelter very close to Aksum (Fig. 36.2). Excavation

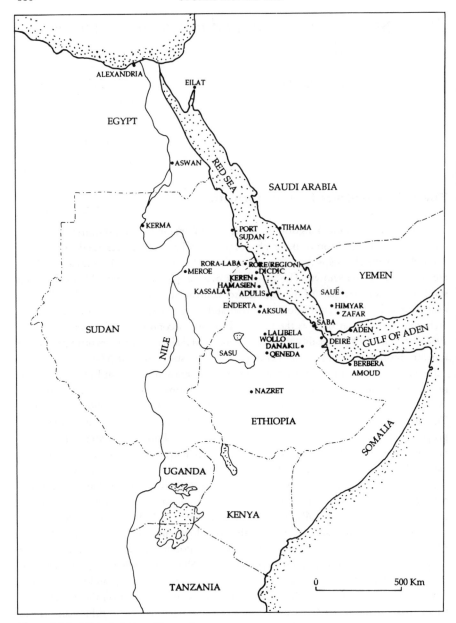

Figure 36.1 Ethiopia in its wider setting.

revealed that the upper levels were contemporary with the urban development of
Aksum, but the lower levels dated to 10,000–8,000 BC and contained a microlithic
industry. Pottery appeared apparently in the fourth millennium BC. Unfortunately, the
finger-millet seeds found in early levels at this site proved to be intrusive. But
nevertheless it is evident from the special position of the Ethiopian highlands with

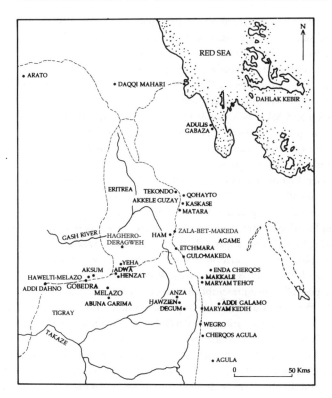

Figure 36.2 Ancient sites of Ethiopia.

regard to potential for cereal crops, and from the evidence already to hand concerning domestic animals (rock paintings, small sculptures and inscriptional evidence of Aksumite date), that agriculture and animal husbandry were vital factors behind the development on the Ethiopian plateau of early states, and, eventually, of the rise of Aksum itself to urban civilization (Phillipson 1990; Phillipson, Ch. 18, this volume).

The new discoveries in the Gash region and in the Tihama coastlands of Arabia are of major importance to an understanding of the eventual development of states in the Ethiopian highlands. The latest studies suggest that in the late second and early first millennium BC contacts existed between the Ethiopian plateau and both these regions. The eastern part of the Tigray plateau was included, with the Ona culture (Tringali 1965), in which pottery wares with Nile valley affinities appear for the first time in Eritrea, dating possibly to the second millennium BC, in a cultural complex extending from this part of Africa to the Arabian Tihama, in contact with peoples in the eastern Sudan and the Nile valley, while the western part was in contact with peoples along the Gash river, and later with the Sabaeans. These two regions were characterized by different pottery wares, which may reflect cultural if not ethnic divisions going back to the second millennium BC. There seem to have been no urban centres at this period, these appearing during the next phase, when the two regions became united culturally and politically under the D'MT monarchy (Fattovich 1989).

A monarchial society appeared on the Ethiopian plateau, in control of districts later ruled from Aksum, in the first half of the first millennium BC. Inscriptions which are usually dated to around the fifth–fourth century BC (Pirenne 1956; Drewes 1962, p. 91), but which may well date even earlier, perhaps to the eighth to fifth century BC in view of new discoveries in the Yemen (Fattovich 1990), refer to this polity as D'MT, and reveal that it was governed by rulers using the originally south Arabian religious/regal titles of MKRB and MLK (Caquot & Drewes 1955; Schneider 1961; Schneider 1973). The elite of this polity appear to have been considerably influenced, in their architecture, inscriptions, royal titulature and religion, for example, by elements emanating from the south Arabian kingdoms, particularly Saba, across the Red Sea (Schneider 1973; Schneider 1976b). However, notwithstanding the foreign influences apparent, however ephemerally, on the elite, the polity seems to have had a solid local base.

Comparisons of pottery and other material revealed by archaeology, as well as differences in locution in certain of the inscriptions as compared to those in the Sabaean language (Schneider 1976b), apparently indicate that this was an indigenous phenomenon, and not purely the foundation of south Arabian colonists, a theory previously in favour (but see Michels 1988, and below). Pottery types found at Matara and Yeha (Fig. 36.2) appear to have no resemblance to south Arabian material, but do have some Sudanese affinities. There are certainly impressive south Arabian imports; dressed stone building, writing and iron-working may well have been among the features introduced by Sabaeans. Fattovich (1990) considers that the plough was probably introduced from south Arabia during the D'MT period. But it is important to remember that there may have been a very long period of interaction among peoples on both sides of the Red Sea, both cultural and linguistic, from at least the second millennium BC (Fattovich 1990), and that the arrival of powerfully influential south Arabian traits in western Tigray must have had considerable antecedents as well. Certain features may have sprung from the mutual cultural experience on both sides of the Red Sea. Interestingly, it seems that words for 'plough' and other agricultural vocabulary are apparently of Agaw (Cushitic) origin in Ethiopian Semitic languages, and are not therefore likely to be words introduced by the south Arabians.

The relatively few excavations at sites belonging to the south Arabian-influenced pre-Aksumite period have revealed the trappings of this very complex society, with its well-developed artistic traditions, writing and the architectural remains of mainly religious or funerary installations. Some of these appear to have been of major importance, and exhibit an unmistakable connection with south Arabia. Most prominent is the famous temple at Yeha, and at the same site there are also a number of other buildings and tombs of the period (Anfray 1973a); the 'palace' of Grat Beal Guebra and the contents of a number of rock-cut tombs represent the upper strata of the contemporary society; as with most Ethiopian sites so far excavated, very little remains, or has yet been identified, from the humbler strata of society, whose dwellings would probably have been highly perishable, and whose tombs were doubtless little more than holes in the ground. The major town which developed here at this period is supposed to have covered some 75,000 m^2 (Fattovich 1977): Yeha may have been D'MT's capital, and some of the tombs found there may be royal. Michels (1988) notes that the soil in the Yeha valley, together with that in the plain facing the future capital, Aksum, is of excellent quality for cereal crop growth – strong reasons for the choice of these two places as major population centres. The basic, 'indigenous' settlement pattern of the area, characterized by regularly spaced small villages and hamlets, dominates in Michels' early and late pre-Aksumite phases, but in the middle pre-Aksumsite phase it was supplemented by a 'south Arabian' pattern in some places, where large nucleated communities emerged. Michels' interpretation of this 'south Arabian' pattern is in contrast to that of Schneider (1976b), and refers to the 'political, economic and cultural dominance' of 'the south Arabian colonists' (Michels 1988).

Further archaeological evidence from pre-Aksumite times comes from Hawelti-Melazo, near Aksum (Fig. 36.2) (de Contenson 1961), which seems to have been a minor ceremonial centre (Fattovich 1990), the early levels at Matara in Eritrea (Anfray 1967b), Kaskase in Eritrea, and from such sites as Addi Galamo (Caquot & Drewes 1955) and others (Ricci & Fattovich 1984–6). These few excavated pre-Aksumite sites – Addi Galamo was simply a cache – by no means reveal the whole picture; Fattovich (1990) has so far been able to identify some ninety sites altogether as belonging to the pre-Aksumite period.

The distribution of the pre-Aksumite sites suggests that the centre was in the Yeha/Aksum region, but the pre-Aksumite culture reached perhaps from the Rore region of Eritrea in the north to Enderta in the south (Schneider 1973, p. 389; Fattovich 1990). It seems most likely that the south Arabian features are owing to the establishment in Ethiopia of trading groups from across the Red Sea. Fattovich (1990) suggests that the route of south Arab penetration might have been via Aden, Dankalia and Makkale (Figs 36.1, 36.2). Such groups may have been installed to facilitate commerce with south Arabia, and will presumably have selected certain sites for their favourable position with regard to the routes by which goods moved from west to east towards the coast. There is no real evidence, however, for the political dominance formerly claimed for them.

The presence of these Sabaeans seems probable, from excavated material, at Matara, Yeha and Hawelti-Melazo (Schneider 1973, p. 388). The inscriptions of *mukarribs* of D'MT and Saba are known from Addi Galamo (Caquot & Drewes 1955, pp. 26–32), Enda Cherqos (Schneider 1961, pp. 61ff.), possibly Matara (a name LMN, attested there, may parallel MN from the other sites) (Schneider 1965, p. 90; Drewes & Schneider 1967, p. 91), Melazo (Schneider 1978, pp. 130–2) and Abuna Garima (Schneider 1973; Schneider 1976b, pp. 86ff.). Four rulers are known to date. The earliest may be W'RN HYWT, who bore the title *mlkn*, king, and who is attested at Yeha, Kaskase and elsewhere; he was succeeded by three *mukarribs*, RD'M, RBH and LMN (Schneider 1976b, pp. 89–93).

The end of D'MT is completely unknown. Possibly the region known as Tsiamo in later Aksumite inscriptions reflects the older polity, and it may have continued to survive, together with a number of other political groupings, until the rise of Aksum eventually unified the plateau and coastal plain. The Aksumite inscriptions of the early fourth century AD note a number of regions as being governed by rulers, all bearing the Ethiopic or Ge'ez title of *negus*, but by this time subject to the Aksumite *negusa nagast*, or king of kings. These are generally held to represent formerly independent kingdoms of the seacoast (Gabaza) and the plateau (Agwezat, etc.). It seems that the development of a number of these small states or chiefdoms on the plateau may have accompanied or succeeded the D'MT monarchy's existence in the region, and that these minor entities were all gradually incorporated into the expanding Aksumite kingdom. The major towns seem to have disappeared in the post-D'MT period, together with monumental inscriptions and buildings, art, and so forth. This reflects the collapse of the D'MT state, but nevertheless certain elements survived, such as the minor ceremonial centre at Hawelti-Melazo, and the regional settlement pattern of villages and hamlets remained much the same (Fattovich n.d.).

The apparent disappearance of the most distinctive south Arabian traits before the development of Aksum makes it impossible to say whether such features as the use of the disc and crescent as divine symbols, and of the south Arabian script as an inscriptional medium (curiously enough, for the Ge'ez language and not for Sabaean itself), is the result of a continued Ethiopian tradition, or of renewed contacts when Aksumite power expanded across the Red Sea to south Arabia itself. This latter is attested by about AD 200, by inscriptional material from south Arabia itself, while the *Periplus of the Erythraean Sea*, now generally dated to around AD 70, attests to a fairly developed commerce on both sides of the Red Sea at that date, with evident possibilities for cross-cultural exchange. The material evidence for Aksumite use of such south Arabian features as noted above appears only later; the obelisk at Matara and the pagan coins, which bear the disc and crescent, date to the late third century AD, and the use of south Arabian script for transcribing inscriptions is first attested even later, in the reign of Ezana or perhaps one of his immediate predecessors (Littmann, Krencker & von Lupke 1913b, inscription DAE 8).

The Aksumite kingdom

The geographical location of the town of Aksum, sited in the western part of the future Aksumite kingdom, doubtless reflects certain economic, political and commercial conditions which prevailed before the Aksumites were able to control overland routes and attain an outlet on the Red Sea coast at Adulis and possibly other ports. It seems likely that the original significance of the site sprang from the favourable quality of the local resource base, and from its ability to command certain interior trade routes. The suitability of the region is confirmed by the earlier interest shown in it; though Aksum itself has as yet yielded no evidence of pre-Aksumite occupation, there are many pre-Aksumite sites located in the immediate neighbourhood. The Aksumite plain, as already noted, is very fertile, and though requiring fertilization or fallow periods, the soils around Hawelti-Melazo are also quite adequate (Michels 1988). Abundant rainfall, the possibility of growing two crops per year and the development of large domestic animal resources, were certainly among the reasons behind Aksum's rise to prosperity. Another was the exploitation of trade from the interior. Together, these factors determined Aksum's future. Eventually the city lay at the heart of a network of routes (Fig. 36.1), running from the Nile to Adulis, to Aswan (Kosmas Indikopleustes, quoted by Wolska-Conus 1968, p. 356; Procopius, quoted by Dewing 1914 (1985)), to the land of incense called Barbaria (apparently the Somali coast, where incense can still be found) and through the Agaw lands towards Sasu (Wolska-Conus 1968, p. 362) beyond the Takaze.

What processes actually lay behind the formation of the Aksumite state? The only thing known is that by the mid-first century AD (Bowersock 1983, p. 70) Aksum appears as a *metropolis*, with a ruler entitled *basileus*, in the *Periplus of the Erythraean Sea*, a document which chooses very carefully those towns and rulers on which it bestows these rare titles. A large area of territory is sketched out, apparently belonging to Aksum and under the control of a certain Zoskales. This included a substantial region of the seacoast. How this situation arose is mere speculation.

A possible course of development is that in the Aksum region one of the successor states of the D'MT monarchy gradually developed. This polity, owing to its favourable position, grew increasingly prosperous, resulting in population expansion and a concomitant increase in military strength. The local rulers, who later bore the title *negus*, doubtless seized the occasion to secure new resources or control a wider network of trade routes. Other incentives may have played their part; an extra impetus could have been generated by the need for unity against neighbouring enemies, or by the rise of an exceptional leader. Eventually Aksum may have been able to gain an increasingly important role in the region, gradually assuming the position of *primus inter pares* among other neighbouring groups. Finally, the Aksumite state was able to absorb these neighbours, though often retaining traditional rulers as sub-kings of tributary status, until in the end the Aksumites controlled a very large area of modern Ethiopia.

There was yet a further stage of expansion. Inscriptions indicate that by *c.* AD 200 (Robin 1981; Robin 1984) the Aksumite kings were able to intervene militarily in internal struggles in south Arabia, and by the fourth century there is evidence for at least theoretical suzerainty over several groups in the Sudan, such as the Kasu, Noba and the Northern Cushitic-speaking Beja tribes. In the south, Agaw (Central Cushitic-speaking) peoples also became subject to the Semitic-speaking Aksumites. The expansion to the Adulite coastal region had permitted Aksum to convey goods originating in districts beyond the Nile or its tributaries to their own port on the Red Sea coast, and there were doubtless good economic reasons why Aksum felt the need to control parts at least of the Arabian kingdoms. The *Periplus* notes that the power of King Kharibael of Himyar and Saba, and the *tyrannos* Kholaibos of the southern coastal Mopharitic region (al-Ma'afir), reaching from their capitals of Zafar and Saué, was sufficient to allow them to control Azania, the east African coast to Tanzania, and its rich trade in ivory and tortoise-shell. Gradually, during the second century, Aksum must have begun to interest itself in weakening Himyarite maritime control, culminating in its allying with Saba and seizing certain areas formerly under Himyarite rule (Bafaqih & Robin 1980; Bafaqih 1983). By the early third century, Aksum had come to dominate the southern coast. With Rome as a powerful ally and trading partner, linked also by the Christian religion after about AD 330, Aksum's prosperity, based on firm geographical and historical realities, was maintained until events beyond the control of either power altered the whole political balance and trading structure of the ancient world in the later sixth/early seventh century.

The Aksumite cultural province, as far as reported sites can indicate (Fig. 36.2), was centred in Eritrea and Tigray, particularly the districts of the Akkele Guzay, Agame, and the region around Aksum and Adwa. Traces have also been found in Enderta, Hamasien, Keren and as far as the Rore plateau (Conti Rossini 1931), and even in Wollo

(Fig. 36.1) (Anfray 1970). Some of the largest extensions suggested for the kingdom seem unlikely; Doresse, for example (1971, p. 84), includes among 'the largest Aksumite ports' not only Adulis but Deirè, on the coast at the Bab al-Mandeb, and also notes (1971, p. 90) Mathew's statement that a structure excavated at Amoud south of Berbera suggested Aksumite building work. Such ideas, probably based on the *Monumentum Adulitanum* account of the campaign of an Aksumite king, cannot yet be confirmed.

Urbanism in Aksumite Ethiopia

The earliest surviving literary reference to Aksum, in the *Periplus of the Erythraean Sea* (Huntingford 1980; Casson 1989) and Ptolemy's Geography (Ptolemaeus 1932), together with some finds of early date from the site itself (Munro-Hay 1989a), indicate that the city was probably established at, or a little before, the beginning of the present era. The *Periplus* mentions a comprehensive selection of goods as being imported into Aksum. Ptolemy leads one to suspect a city with a king's palace at some time around the mid-second century AD. Archaeology has so far revealed little of this, but there is some early material; platform structures in the main cemetery at Aksum, and certain glass finds (Munro-Hay 1989a) indicate that further evidence for the existence of the city by the first century AD may now be expected. With more archaeological excavation, other early remains apart from the platforms may be discovered. Much of the other material excavated is at the moment difficult to date reliably and so remains inconclusive. In the immediate area of Aksum, Michels identified a number of villages whose produce was doubtless necessary to feed the capital's increasing population (Michels 1979).

This period, then, saw the rise of the city into the governmental centre for a considerable area of the Ethiopian plateau and the coastal plain. Two 'provinces' may be distinguishable, one in Akkele Guzay and Agame, the other in western Tigray, identifiable by differences in pottery and other elements. Tentative observations (Anfray 1974) suggest that sites on the north–south route from Qohayto to Agula, Degum and even to Nazret, constitute an eastern province (Figs 36.1, 36.2) which may have become the most prosperous in later Aksumite times. Aksum and the sites of the west, from Addi Dahno to Henzat and the Yeha region, may have enjoyed prosperity in the pre-Christian period (many stelae are associated with the sites), but compared unfavourably with the east later on. Throughout the expanded Aksumite kingdom, a number of flourishing urban communities appear to have grown up. Adulis, the chief Aksumite, and probably pre-Aksumite, port, and Aksum itself are special cases; but it seems, from archaeological and literary evidence, that a number of other towns became established on trade routes or crossroads, or wherever particularly favourable conditions were encountered. Water availability was an evident precondition (Anfray 1973b, p. 15, n. 5). The development of some degree of urbanism in Aksumite Ethiopia is an interesting phenomenon, but one which is not yet even partially documented. All that survives of many of the 'towns' are the traces of a few monumental structures such as temples, churches or elite residential/administrative buildings, and scatterings of pottery on the surface. These have been reported from the time of the earliest explorations in Ethiopia, but have only rarely been properly surveyed, much less excavated and planned. Excavation may yet provide some surprises, as it has already done at Matara, but in general these towns may not have been very large. Perhaps many were of little more than large village status, though Matara certainly seems to have been a sizeable community (Anfray 1963; Anfray & Annequin 1965; Anfray 1974). Nevertheless, the existence of some large towns bespeaks an agricultural output sufficient to provide the surplus necessary to support at least some town-dwellers engaged in specialist pursuits, and the availability of more or less efficient exchange and transport facilities on a regional scale.

It can be assumed from the apparently long existence of the towns, and from the fact that none were walled, that reasonably stable conditions prevailed in the country, both political and otherwise. This at least partly urbanized Aksumite society was in sharp contrast to the later situation in Ethiopia, when travellers remarked that the country contained no cities or substantial towns, only the mobile tented 'capital' which followed the emperor, and was moved to another region when it had exhausted the resources of a particular spot (Pankhurst 1961, pp. 137ff.).

The port-city of Adulis, where Paribeni (1907, p. 443) found ruins covering at least 20,000 m^2, had its harbour and customs point a short distance away at Gabaza (Fig. 36.2). This name may be identical with the kingdom of Gabaza, noted with its ruler SBL in an Aksumite inscription (DAE 8) as a tributary kingdom, but probably in earlier, pre-Aksumite, times, an independent entity. Adulis itself appears to have originated as a centre for the coastal people, called Adulitae by various ancient authors who continued to differentiate between them and the upland Aksumites. Gabaza-Adulis was the first point on the long trade route into the Sudan, and, favourably situated as it was in a bay on the Red Sea coast, had obvious opportunities to acquire wealth by trading from the earliest times. Fattovich (1989) includes the site among those of the ancient Eritrean coast/Arabian Tihama cultural complex.

Archaeological work at Adulis has revealed buildings ranging from large, formally planned mansion complexes and churches to smaller, organically developed housing areas of a few rooms (Paribeni 1907; Anfray 1974). The town lay a short distance inland from the actual harbour at Gabaza (Huntingford 1980, p. 20; Procopius, in Dewing 1985 (1914), p. 183). Kosmas Indikopleustes copied the famous *Monumentum Adulitanum* inscriptions for King Kaleb of Aksum from a stela and a stone throne placed at the entrance to the town, on the west side towards the road to Aksum. He also mentions that merchants from Alexandria and Eilat traded there (Wolska-Conus 1968, p. 364). On Kosmas' map, preserved in much later copies, the position of Adulis is shown with Gabaza a little to the south on the seashore, and another coastal town, Samidi, to the north (Wolska-Conus 1968, p. 367). Ptolemy mentions a town called Sabat, which he situates to the north of Adulis (Ptolemaeus 1932, p. 108, and map, where it is labelled Sabath). Perhaps it is identical with Kosmas' Samidi.

Though ancient origins have been proposed for Adulis (see above, and Munro-Hay 1982), a considerable amount more needs to be known about the earlier archaeological levels at the site. Nevertheless, Paribeni did find archaeological deposits of over 10 m depth in one of his exploratory trenches (Paribeni 1907, pp. 446ff., 566), and considered that substantial deposits represented a period before sustained contacts with other civilizations had developed.

On the plateau was the town of Koloë, noted above. Koloë town and Maste town were also noted by Ptolemy (Ptolemaeus 1932, p. 108) as among towns in the interior.

Koloë, which derived its importance from its position as the first inland market for ivory, may be identified with the present-day Matara in southern Eritrea. At this site the excavators (Anfray 1963; Anfray & Annequin 1965; Anfray 1967b; Anfray 1974) found numerous large mansion complexes, churches, tombs, and also excavated some domestic buildings in humbler residential areas. The site yielded the material remains of a very sophisticated way of life. The town's history, as revealed by the excavations, extends back into the pre-Aksumite period, but the early strata have only been cursorily investigated to date. Another site, Qohayto, further to the north – another possible candidate for Koloë – contains the ruins of impressive stone structures (Littmann, Krencker & von Lupke 1913a, pp. 148ff.). It remains unexcavated. Qohayto is most remarkable for a dam constructed with seven courses of dressed stone stepped back in typical Aksumite fashion, though it could even be of pre-Aksumite date, and which still retains water after the rains.

From Koloë the route from Adulis continued to Aksum and beyond; but relatively few sites have so far been identified to the west. The eastern highlands, in contrast, contain the ruins of numerous towns and villages, and it is evident that this region was a prosperous and populous region from pre-Aksumite days (Anfray 1973b, p. 20). The general homogeneity of the architecture and material goods of these ancient Ethiopian towns is apparent, and, despite regional differences in, for example, building stone and pottery types, the overall 'Aksumite' nature of the civilization is undeniable.

Although few details exist about the settlement pattern of the Aksumite kingdom outside the small area surveyed by Michels (1979), clusters of sites have been identified in particularly well-populated areas. The towns and villages along the main tracks (Fig. 36.2) south from Adulis towards Aksum, like Qohayto, Tekondo, Matara, Zala-Bet-Makeda, Ham, Etchmara, Gulo-Makeda, Haghero-Deragweh, Yeha/Dergouah and Henzat, and those further south along the route west of the escarpment from Maryam Tehot and Maryam Kedih, or the branch via Anza, Hawzien and Degum, at least as far as Cherqos Agula and Nazret (Anfray 1970), may have developed along with the main trade and supply routes and at cross-routes leading into the interior. Some such centres probably lay in areas of farming settlements, and acted as their market outlet and exchange points, and some perhaps supplemented this activity with specific local products or, if they were suitably situated, could provide services connected with the movement of goods along the main routes. Aksumite settlements also appear to the west and north of Adulis, and the inscription of Sembrouthes from Daqqi Mahari, and the buildings and coins from Arato (Piva 1907), confirm that this region belonged to the Aksumite hegemony.

However, it is impossible to suggest what the limits of the Aksumite kingdom may have been at its zenith in view of the lack of archaeological evidence. Conti Rossini (1931) notes ruins in northern Eritrea with possible Aksumite affinities, particularly the thrones at Dicdic and the carved stelae at Rora Laba with lion and ox sculptures, and Anfray (1970) describes apparently Aksumite columns from Qeneda, in Wollo, and tentatively parallels the lion sculpture at Tchika-Beret in southern Wollo with the well-known Aksumite lion-headed water-spouts. Anfray's survey is the most informative to date, but more work is required to define the limits of Aksumite penetration.

One feature often found in Aksumite town sites is the mansion-and-dependencies element. Archaeological work has been concentrated on these structures at Aksum, Adulis and Matara, since, like churches, their ruin-mounds are prominent and have accordingly attracted excavators. Such mansions were not only a feature of the towns, but also seem, at least in the case of Aksum itself, to have been distributed in their hinterland, perhaps representing local landlords' houses, rather like the contemporary Roman villas. These elite residences are found in quantity, according to the survey by Michels undertaken in 1974 (Michels 1979; Michels 1988) in and around the capital and in the region of a number of villages as far as Yeha. At present there is very little information about the possible function of the larger and smaller elite residences in the Aksum area, and one can only guess how to interpret them economically and socially. If more about their chronological development were known, it might be possible to trace whether the type was developed at Aksum and moved from the city and royal context first to other towns and then was adopted as the model for the country mansions of a landowner class, a sequence which might be plausible, or whether they originated elsewhere, perhaps in Adulis, with its greater exposure to foreign influences, spreading thence to Aksum and the countryside.

In the towns, the largest mansions probably housed the ruler of the region and acted as governmental and ceremonial centres. Their layout, with the separation of the imposing central pavilion on its podium and staircases, seems emphatically designed to impress, and the plans, with their projecting corners, are reminiscent of Kosmas' description of the 'four-towered palace of the kingdom Ethiopia' (Wolska-Conus 1968). The outer ranges of these complexes must have been partly used for occupation and partly for service activities. Ovens, a possible underfloor heating system, well-constructed drainage facilities, carved pillar bases and capitals, paved floors and other features indicate both domestic activities and a luxurious dwelling. Some rooms may even have been used for the manufacturing of items needed in everyday life. Anfray excavated one of these mansions just to the west of present-day Aksum, the so-called 'Château de Dungur', and when the results of this excavation are completely published, they will provide a much clearer idea of the nature of these structures (Anfray 1972).

The decline of Aksum

Over six hundred years of occupation evidently had a profound effect on the countryside around Aksum from which the town drew its subsistence. The use of wood and charcoal in manufacturing, cooking, heating and building, reduced the tree cover on the surrounding hills (Butzer 1981), and exposed the topsoil to degradation and erosion. The demand for food for an increased population may have subjected the surrounding lands to overcropping, leaving an exhausted soil in the proximity of the city and the immediate countryside. High flood levels recorded for the Nile (Butzer 1981) until c. AD 750 may also be significant, since they depended on the rains in Ethiopia. If the land had reached a state of advanced degradation during the late Aksumite period, even the heavier rains, though theoretically ideal for the growth of crops, would have contributed to the erosion on the slopes above the city and in the surrounding fields. Butzer found evidence for this in that material brought down by the run-off from the hillsides covered some of the Aksumite buildings in the town. In sum, it appears that difficulties in maintaining the food supplies may have been a significant factor in removing the capital elsewhere.

If it is true (see above) that in later Aksumite times the eastern province had become the most prosperous, Aksum may, even by the fifth and sixth centuries, have retained its position more by its ancient prestige as the royal, eponymous city of the kingdom than by any continuing special merit in its location. If, as the eastern towns grew richer, the remoter west, though the site of the capital, participated less in the new influx of wealth, commercial considerations alone may have suggested resiting the central place of the kingdom. But even more important events may have pre-empted this. It seems clear that the Aksumite state began to suffer external and internal political problems in the later sixth and the early seventh century. King Kaleb's Yemen seems to have cost Aksum both prestige and a considerable outlay in men and money, while, a little later and in more general terms, the political and commercial climate, after first the Yemen (c. AD 570) and then Jerusalem and Alexandria fell to the Persians (AD 614 and 619 respectively), must have severely affected Ethiopia's trade in the Red Sea, and accordingly its prosperity. The coinage, issued from the late third century, ceased apparently early in the seventh century (Munro-Hay 1984b). Coins of the later rulers have been found in quantity in apparently squatter occupation levels in the remains of some of the Aksumite mansions. Nothing reliably datable after the seventh century has been found in archaeological contexts in these structures, and the conclusion is that they were abandoned at that period.

There are suggestions that revolts may have further weakened the kingdom by cutting off certain internal resources and routes. The recorded traditions about the life of Muhammad and his followers report two revolts in Ethiopia under the *najashi* Ashama ibn Abjar (Guillaume 1955, pp. 153–5). The inscriptions of a certain military leader, the *hatsani* Daniel, found at Aksum (Littmann, Krencker & von Lupke 1913b, nos. 12–14), may corroborate such traditions about troubles in Ethiopia at this period, though they cannot yet be dated with any certainty. They indicate that Daniel was engaged in military campaigns, and not only another *hatsani*, Karuray(?), but a 'king of Aksum' is mentioned. Ashama ibn Abjar reportedly died in AD 630 and was, according to Ethiopian tradition, buried at Wegro, about 65 miles to the southeast of Aksum (Tamrat 1972, pp. 34–5). If this tradition can be accepted, the royal cemetery at Aksum may have been out of use by that date. Ethiopian and Arab traditions note the shift of the capital away from Aksum, assigning it to various reigns or periods (Hable-Sé 1972, p. 203; Tamrat 1972, pp. 35ff.).

There are further clues. Anfray (1974, p. 753), working at Adulis, found a thick layer of ashes over some structures, and deduced that the town's end had been brutal. In the northern part of the Aksumite dominion the Beja tribes, theoretically Aksumite subjects for a long period, eventually became independent of the *najashis* (al-Ya'qubi in Trimingham 1952, pp. 71–3) and may have caused trouble for some time before. Possibly the Ethiopians' inability to keep the sea-lanes free encouraged the Arabs to occupy the Dahlak islands, at least temporarily, around AD 702 (Hasan 1967, p. 30), though later Arab historians still include Dahlak in the dominions of the *najashis*.

None of this is definite, but in sum the evidence suggests that Aksum was finally abandoned as a capital in the first half of the seventh century. With the Arab take-over, around AD 640, of the routes and many of the destinations of Aksumite trade after the preliminary Persian incursions into Arabia and the eastern Roman world, the Ethiopian Christian kingdom had to change its direction. The Red Sea route itself soon became much less important when the Abbasid shift to Baghdad after AD 750 emphasized the role of the Persian gulf; it only revived when the Fatimids redeveloped it in the eleventh and twelfth centuries. The Aksumite cultural heritage, now bound firmly with Christianity, though no longer directed by a king of Aksum from Aksum itself, but by a *hadani* or *najashi* from elsewhere, continued its southern expansion, retiring from the north and the coast over the centuries. The process seems to have been gradual, since Arab writers long refer to the size and wealth of the *najashi*'s realm, and certain regions, though occupied by Muslims, still remained tributary.

By the mid-seventh century, then, Aksum had lost its political pre-eminence in the region of the Ethiopian plateau, the coastal plains and the Red Sea. The Ethiopian monarchy had left Aksum. The next recorded permanent capital was that of the *najashis* or *hadanis* who ruled from Ku'bar, a city mentioned in the ninth and tenth centuries by Arab writers as a great trading centre, but whose position is presently unknown. In the later tenth century the Ethiopian state may have almost succumbed to a usurping queen (Chennafi 1976), enabling the Agaw Zagwé dynasty eventually to seize control around AD 1137. But even then the churches of Lalibela, attributed to the Zagwé monarchs, and constructed near their capital city of Adafa or Roha, still indicate a strong continuity with the Aksumite cultural tradition.

37 Cities without citadels: understanding urban origins along the middle Niger

SUSAN KEECH McINTOSH &

RODERICK J. McINTOSH

The archaeology of the indigenous west African town is a sparsely populated field of enquiry, especially compared with the vast numbers of researchers involved in early urban phenomena elsewhere in the world. Part of the reason for this probably lies in the unimposing visual aspect of many early west African towns. They offer nothing approaching the impressive plazas and temples of Mesoamerica, the pyramids of Egypt or the ziggurats of Mesopotamia, all of which have proved irresistible to laymen and professionals alike for over a century. The perception that monumental public architecture is an essential defining characteristic of a city runs deep in Western culture. The use of architectural symbols to express, among other things, civic pride and identity can be traced in the Western tradition back beyond classical Greece and Rome to the city-states of Sumer. The title of this chapter is intended as a device to focus on the fundamental point that the way in which we define cities and the circumstances in which we are willing to recognize their presence are frequently controlled by various cultural and intellectual biases.

The presence of monumental public architecture is without doubt the most frequently cited criterion of urban status. It is not unusual to find statements in the literature on urban history that:

> one of the earliest structural elements of the ancient city was the walled citadel . . . [which] consisted of prominent structures containing the treasures of society and surplus food, and provided living space for a powerful and revered leadership class. . . . This complex of public buildings and temples formed a prominent, if not the dominant component of the ancient city. (Northam 1975, p. 36)

The sentiments behind Northam's recent identification of the citadel as the heart of the ancient city are echoes of deeply held beliefs about the comparative rise of cities by the majority of influential writers. Among these writers there is considerable consensus in the belief that monumentality was a necessary component of the social dynamics universal to the process of 'primary' urbanism. Wittfogel traced the rise of the early city to the imposition of despotic authority by 'earthly functionaries' of supreme gods over a population held in corvée bondage and to the need for 'adequate surroundings for worship and residence' (Wittfogel 1957, p. 41) for the despots. Weber sees cities arising after the 'Oriental patrimonial kingship' establishes control over a forced labour force capable of building on a vast scale (Weber 1956, pp. 1225–90; Weber 1958). Sjoberg (1960) defines his primeval 'constructed type' of pre-industrial city in terms both of a vast vassal population and of reinforcement of the elite's dominance of the masses by palaces and temples visually making reference to tradition and absolutes, such as the notion of king as intermediary with the city's gods. For Jacobsen, also, monumental architecture – especially the citadel – was a 'signpost to permanence' (Jacobsen 1976, pp. 180–6) reflecting and reinforcing the control ideology of the state.

Particularly influential was Childe, who used a trait-list approach to define 'city' archaeologically. Monumental public architecture figured prominently in Childe's list of urban criteria, although he also required the presence of nine other allegedly urban characteristics for a site to be accorded civic status (Childe 1950). Less circumspect was Kenyon, who declared Jericho to have been a city, based on a single criterion: the monumental 'defensive' walls surrounding the small (4 ha), eighth-millennium BC settlement (Kenyon 1957).

Writing is another essential feature that has regularly appeared on trait lists purporting to define urbanism, Childe's included. Sjoberg (1960, p. 33) went so far as to declare that 'the use of a writing system is the single firm criterion for distinguishing the city from other types of early settlement'. The ethnocentrism of this viewpoint has been remarked upon by Mabogunje (1968, p. 41). Although we must agree with Childe that the concomitant appearance in the archaeological record of writing and monumental architecture is clear evidence of a high level of social and economic complexity, it is certainly not correct to assume that increasing organizational complexity, leading to urbanism, will *necessarily* be manifested by these two features.

It is highly unlikely, in any case, that the great variety and variability which existed among early urban systems can ever be properly accommodated by attempting to define one, ten or even more individual features common to all of them. For one thing, the selection of criteria is too easily subject to various cultural and intellectual biases. For another, as Clarke commented:

> Complex systems cannot be specified by laundry-lists of attributes, whether physical or organizational, any more than a watch can be understood from a list of its parts.   (Clarke 1979, p. 438)

> The multiplicity of urban forms and functions represents a multidimensional structure which, while it may be collapsed into one dimension, arranged linearly and dichotomized endlessly, can only be done so with great arbitrariness and loss of information, to produce a classification useful only for limited purposes.   (Clarke 1979, p. 436)

As a result of an arbitrary, exclusionary characterization of urbanism, such as Sjoberg's, many researchers concluded that truly indigenous west African urbanism never existed. With particular reference to the western Sudan, it had been widely believed that towns did not appear until Arab-inspired trade from north Africa provided the requisite stimulus to economic reorganization (S. McIntosh & R. McIntosh

1988, pp. 110–14). The rise of cities in the western Sudan is commonly held to have begun in the late ninth century AD in connection with the trans-Saharan trade in gold, ivory and slaves, which moved north in exchange for salt, cloth and Mediterranean foodstuffs. The earliest cities in the western Sudan 'began as Arab trading posts and expanded into the capitals of African kingdoms whose prosperity depended on the trade routes' (Rayfield 1974, p. 179). In each case, a strong settlement of foreign traders, mostly Arab or Arabo–Berber, was present in the city's population. By this prevailing view, early towns did not originate in the western Sudan, and so cannot be called truly indigenous; they were a foreign element introduced as a result of the economic imperialism of north African Arabs. The seed of the earliest towns was an Arab trading settlement. The expansion of town life to the native populace was accompanied by conversion to Islam and the concomitant introduction of literacy and prominent religious architectural forms, all of which are considered among the hallmarks of the traditional western Sudanese town.

Contrary to this view, we have argued that there was an earlier, more completely African phase of urbanization (McIntosh & McIntosh 1983; McIntosh & McIntosh 1984; R. McIntosh & S. McIntosh 1988; S. McIntosh & R. McIntosh 1988). The remainder of this chapter focuses on this question by reviewing the archaeology of early urbanism at the key site of Jenne-jeno in Mali. We shall first be concerned to outline an approach to the archaeological recognition of urbanism that will be more useful and of broader applicability than earlier trait-complex definitions. Using this approach, we will go on to consider the evidence for indigenous town growth in the upper middle Niger of Mali, where we conducted fieldwork in 1977 and 1981 (Fig. 37.1). It is our

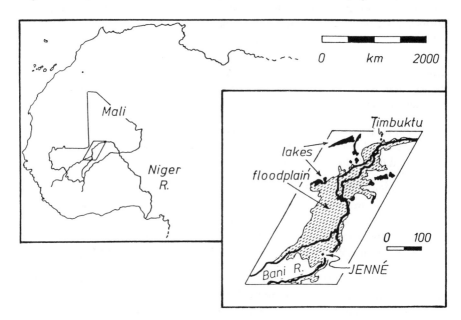

Figure 37.1 Map of the inland Niger delta, showing the location of Jenné and Timbuktu in relation to the area of annual inundation.

contention that the available archaeological evidence does not support historical recon-structions claiming a thirteenth- or fourteenth-century chronology for the development of towns in this area as a result of realignment of Arab-inspired trade routes. Rather, the evidence suggests a much earlier growth of towns, antedating the advent of the Arabs in north Africa. We close with a discussion of the factors which may have fostered early town growth in the middle Niger.

Identifying urbanism in the archaeological record

There has been an increasing awareness among archaeologists during the 1980s that large, complex sites should not be studied in isolation. A shift in research strategy from site-specific to regional investigative frameworks has taken place as researchers have appreciated the implications of an urban centre's functional interdependence with its complementary region, or hinterland. It is now widely acknowledged that a useful definition of urbanism must flow from what a city *does* – i.e. its performance of specialized functions in relation to a broader hinterland (Trigger 1971; Gugler & Flanagan 1978, p. 22). It is likely that the historical origin of towns lies in the need to concentrate in one place functions related to a wider area than a village, such as markets, administration or defence (Grove 1972). The evolutionary course of centralization of functions leading to urban sites can be quite varied, even within the regions of a single 'civilization' such as the Maya (Adams & Jones 1981).

In order to answer that question, we need to look at how human geographers, in particular, have explored the various types of relationship between functional centres and their surrounding areas. Among other things, they have demonstrated that, in general, the greater the level or variety of functions in a town, the larger its area of influence. With increasing complexity, a hierarchy of locations may develop with respect to any one type of activity, with higher-level or more specialized functions being performed at a small number of relatively large centres. One of the best-known models generated to describe the nature and functioning of urban hierarchies is Central Place Theory, which deals specifically with spatial relationships among the settlements in a hierarchical system. However, a rather more useful concept for archaeological applications is the rank–size rule.

Human geographers working in various parts of the world have observed a consist-ent relationship between the ranks and size of settlements in an urban system (Vining 1955; Berry & Garrison 1958; Berry 1961; Haggett, Cliff & Frey 1977). This relation-ship is described by the rule $P_r = P_1 \times 1/r$ where P_1 is the population of the city ranked 1, and P_r is the population of the settlement ranked r. Thus, a town of rank 5 would be expected to have one-fifth the population of the first-ranked city in the system. The rank–size relationship can also be described graphically by plotting settlement rank against population. If arithmetic scales are used for axes, the resulting graph is a curve (see Fig. 37.2). If the logarithms of size and rank are plotted, a straight line is produced. The formula in this case is written $\log P_r = \log P_1 - \log r$ (Bradford & Kent 1977, p. 60). The essence of the rank–size rule is that there are few cities with large populations and many with small populations. This relationship has been observed so frequently that it is accepted as an empirical regularity; the rank–size distribution is a recurring urban signature. Precisely why this should be so is not known. Some geographers suggest that the underlying mechanism is cost minimization and efficiency maximization; others believe that stochastic processes inherent in the growth of systems may be responsible. For our purposes, the proposed explanations for the rank–size rule are of less concern than its existence as a recurrent characteristic of urban systems.

Deviations from the rank–size rule are well known and of interest in their own right. The most noteworthy of these is the primate distribution, where the difference in size between the largest city and other settlements is much greater than that predicted by the rank–size rule. It is thought that primate distributions result from particular circumstances, such as dependence on a foreign power (e.g. a colonial situation), or very recent urbanization. Crumley (1976), following Berry (1961), has incorporated these

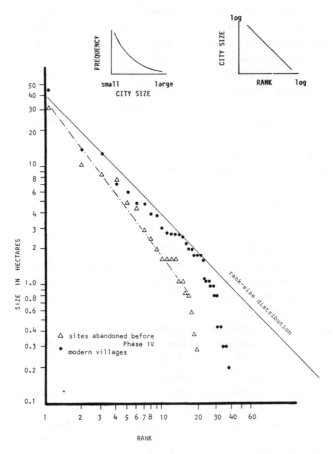

Figure 37.2 The distribution of contemporaneously occupied archaeological sites in the survey region closely approaches the ideal rank–size distribution (solid line). The graph of archaeological sites (Δ) is compared to the distribution of modern villages (●) in the same region. The small insets show the ideal rank–size curve plotted on arithmetic (left) and logarithmic (right) axes.

ideas into a developmental model for urbanism, moving from an early primate distribution through intermediate stages to a rank–size distribution in a well-established urban system. In her proposal that 'the size distribution curve itself is a reflection of that system's degree of urbanization' (Crumley 1976, p. 65) we find a potentially useful approach to the archaeological recognition of urbanism.

The application of this approach requires that the archaeologist first be able to identify a probable system of functionally interdependent settlements. Some archaeologists have used sophisticated mathematical tests of, for example, distance decay patterns in the frequency distribution of exchanged objects (Kimes, Haselgrove & Hodder 1982, pp. 113–14), to infer past territorial units and the presence of boundaries. Others, even in well-explored areas, must simply presume a city's region to be within a 35 km radius (one day's foot-travel distance) of the centre (Adams & Jones 1981, p. 308). In areas where there is a long history of excavation, interaction and interdependence among sites can often be inferred from functional differences observed at sites and from evidence of craft specialization and exchange. In regions where little or no relevant excavation data exist, such as the middle Niger, somewhat cruder tests must suffice. We inferred the existence of hierarchical interaction among sites by examining the diversity of artefacts and features present at individual sites (see below).

There is a difficulty, of course, in ascertaining whether all the sites under consideration functioned within the same system. Use of this method necessitates a credible degree of chronological control such that the contemporaneity of sites can be documented (Schacht 1981). The archaeologist must also present reasons for believing that apparently contemporaneous sites functioned as part of one system and not two or more overlapping systems. Finally, there is the thorny problem of the degree to which settlement population size (the statistic used by the originating geographers) is reflected in settlement area. The relationship is not straightforward. In ethnographic and ethnoarchaeological studies of relationship of settlement area and population, density patterns have been shown to vary with the functional level of a settlement in a hierarchical settlement system and average population-to-area ratio is of less interest than the range of distribution of density for understanding integration within the regional system (Hassan 1981; Schacht 1981; Sumner 1989). However, if these points can be reasonably met, the researcher can then go on to plot site rank against site size, in the hope that the resulting distribution will be either strongly primate or very nearly rank–size, signalling the past existence of an urban system. Problems encountered at this level of analysis will also be considered later in this chapter.

Urban origins in the middle Niger: a case study

The importance of the inland Niger delta, the southernmost basin of the middle Niger (Fig. 37.1), to economic and social development in the western Sudan cannot be overestimated. It is a remarkably fertile area in which large crops of wet rice, millet and sorghum can be produced. A staggering abundance and variety of fish is available from the Niger and its myriad tributaries. The growth and maintenance of northern middle Niger towns like Timbuktu were made possible by the import of staples grown in the inland delta (McIntosh & McIntosh 1980b; McIntosh & McIntosh 1986b). The inland Niger delta also served as a major thoroughfare for the transport of trade goods, such as kola, slaves, animal products and especially gold, from the southern forest regions of west Africa to the markets of northern Africa and Europe. European glass, north African pottery and Saharan salt moved south across the Sahara on camel caravan to the markets of Timbuktu and Jenné. This famous 'Golden Trade of the Moors', which flourished throughout much of the second millennium AD, relied upon water transport along the navigable inland Niger delta. It is not surprising that a trade centre of major proportions should have developed in this fertile area.

Historical mention of this trade centre does not occur before 1447, when an Italian merchant wrote that he had heard of the city-state (*civitate*) of Geni. Further references in the letter make it certain that the city in question is Jenné, located at the southwestern edge of the navigable inland delta (see McIntosh & McIntosh 1980b for a full discussion of historical references to Jenné). Later historical sources make it clear that by the sixteenth century Jenné was one of the principal intellectual and market centres of west Africa. A local seventeenth-century chronicler, al-Sa'di, wrote of Jenné, 'It is because of this blessed town that caravans come to Timbuktu from all points of the horizon' (al-Sa'di 1900, pp. 22–3). Scholars have pointed out that this is a most convincing tribute, since al-Sa'di was intensely jealous of the reputation of his own city, Timbuktu, of which Jenné was a rival in both fame and culture.

The origins of Jenné's economic and political development obviously lie much further back in time, but historical sources give us little clue as to what the chronology or causes of its growth might have been. The silence of Arab travellers and chroniclers on the subject of Jenné before the fifteenth century is baffling. Historians have interpreted it to mean that the city could not have been founded much before AD 1250 (Delafosse 1912, pp. 269–70; Levtzion 1973, pp. 157–9). However, this interpretation contradicts carefully preserved oral traditions which maintain that Jenné was founded centuries earlier. All transcribed accounts of the traditions agree that Jenné was founded in the eighth century AD, that the city was first situated on the site of Zoboro, and subsequently moved to its present location (al-Sa'di 1900; Monteil 1903; Delafosse 1912). The Ta'rikh al-Sudan provides the following account:

> In the beginning, the town had been built in a place called Zoboro; later it was moved to the spot where it still exists today. The former town was situated near the modern town in a southern direction. The town was founded by pagans in the mid-second century AH . . . the inhabitants did not convert to Islam until towards the end of the sixth century AH.
>
> (al-Sa'di 1900, p. 23)

The site of Zoboro is still well known to the inhabitants of Jenné; it is a mound situated 3 km southeast of Jenné and also known as Jenne-jeno ('ancient Jenne' in Songhay), Jenne-sire, Djoboro and Do-Djoboro. There is disagreement, however, over which city is indicated by the eighth-century foundation date: Jenné or Jenne-jeno (Zoboro). Also unknown is the duration of the occupation at Jenne-jeno. The traditions seem to imply that the move had taken place before the conversion to Islam of the twenty-sixth chief of Jenné, Koi Kombora, between AD 1200 and 1300. In fact, all we can state with confidence is that Jenne-jeno must have been abandoned by at least AD 1468, at which point Songhay conqueror Sonni Ali garrisoned his troops there (al-Sa'di 1900, p. 26). It was in the hope of clearing up the confusion over Jenne-jeno's chronology that we began excavating at the site in 1977.

The excavations

The results of the 1977 excavations at Jenne-jeno have already been published in detail (McIntosh & McIntosh 1979; McIntosh & McIntosh 1980a; McIntosh & McIntosh 1980b; R. McIntosh & S. McIntosh 1981). Here we supplement that information about the inhabitants' lifeways during the four occupation phases that we have defined for the site, using further data from research during 1981 at Jenne-jeno (McIntosh & McIntosh 1984; R. McIntosh & S. McIntosh 1988; S. McIntosh & R. McIntosh 1988, pp. 114–17; McIntosh & McIntosh In Preparation). The principal obstacle to gaining a representative view of all activities, professions and styles of life of the ancient community is the enormous size of the site. Measuring over $330,000 \text{ m}^2$ (33 ha) in surface area, Jenne-jeno is a tear-shaped mound rising up to 8 m above an abandoned channel of the Bani river, which now flows 4 km further to the southeast. Seasonal flooding of this abandoned channel surrounds Jenné and Jenne-jeno from September through December annually. A staggering variety of features and artefacts are strewn over the surface of the site: round and rectangular mud-brick foundations, funerary urns, concentrations of iron and slag, segments of a city wall, toy figurines of clay, copper ornaments, hundreds of sandstone grinding stones, and potsherds numbering in the hundreds of thousands. Careful examination of site topography and distribution of surface finds gives an approximate indication of functionally different areas at Jenne-jeno.

In the course of the 1977 and 1981 excavations, eleven units were excavated in dispersed sectors of Jenne-jeno. Diverse functional contexts – residential, craft, funerary and refuse – were sampled by these units. In addition, two outlying satellite tells were sampled. Excavation of these units permits a preliminary assessment of differences in the nature and chronology of deposits at various points on the mound. However, the very small area of the site excavated and the small number of units sunk makes the possibility of sample bias large.

Great care must be exercised when extrapolating from the excavated data to unexplored areas of the site. Hence, our tentative reconstruction of life at Jenne-jeno developed below is just that – very tentative indeed. We concentrated on those aspects of the site most likely to be revealed by rigorously controlled excavation of a relative handful of excavation units. These include site chronology (both radiocarbon and ceramic) and an investigation of the nature and depth of the deposits. Consideration of more complex issues such as specialist activities, housing and population densities and town layout were to a tentative degree addressed by the two large horizontal exposures of the 1981 season. The excavations did, however, yield some good preliminary information about the nature of economic and technological change, plant domestication, the introduction of iron and the possibility of early urban development in the inland Niger delta.

An excellent series of twenty-five radiocarbon determinations dates the occupation of Jenne-jeno from initial settlement at around 250 BC to abandonment by AD 1400 (Fig.

37.3). We have devised a three-phase preliminary chronology for the site on the basis of identification of discrete series of stratigraphic events as well as on significant changes in pottery. Material characteristics of the earliest phase (*c.* 250 BC – AD 99) were found in the six central units, indicating that the settlement was at least 25 ha in area by the end of that period. The Phase I/II economy seems to have been heavily reliant upon fish, reedbuck and domesticated cow (R. Klein & K. MacDonald, *pers. comm.*). During the 1981 season, several soundings into Phase I/II deposits produced many pieces of burnt clay with impressions of woven mat and wattle. Presumably, these are the remains of pole-and-mat structures smeared with a thick exterior coat of mud which was burnt in the course of an accidental fire. This new evidence supports our original suggestion that Jenne-jeno was permanently settled from the commencement of occupation, an

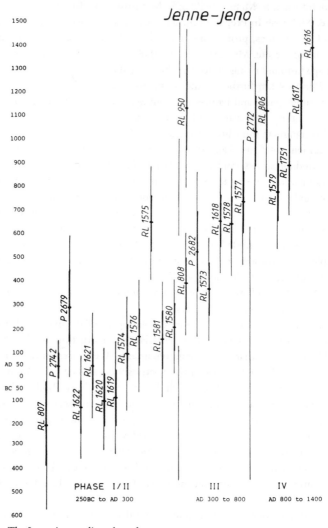

Figure 37.3 The Jenne-jeno radiocarbon dates.

interpretation based on the abundance of finely made pottery, large grindstones and slag mixed throughout the deposits. Our failure to find any sign of late stone age occupation in the course of excavation and extensive survey around Jenné suggests that the iron-using settlers at Jenne-jeno were among the earliest permanent inhabitants in the western inland Niger delta (McIntosh 1983, pp. 191–2).

Occupation deposits dated after *c.* AD 50 are marked by thick accumulation of collapsed mud-wall material. The economy throughout the sequence is little changed from that of the earliest occupation. The 1981 excavations revealed domesticated rice (*Oryza glaberrima*), millet and sorghum in the earliest deposits.

The appearance of crowded cemeteries and increasingly complex stratigraphy during Phase III (AD 300–800) indicate that the occupation of the site became increasingly intensive. Jenne-jeno probably reached its greatest areal extent in late Phase III. Thereafter, the site slowly began to decline. At its apogee, Jenne-jeno would have covered 33 ha. It is probable that the northern tell Hambarketolo was physically linked and functionally integrated with Jenne-jeno at the time of its florescence. The combined area of the two connected sites is 42 ha.

The cause of the decline and ultimate abandonment of Jenne-jeno and Hambarketolo is unknown. It appears that the beginnings of site abandonment antedate the thirteenth-century date for Jenné's Islamization reported by al-Sa'di, and may in some way be linked to an episode of dramatic decline at the time of the present millennium. However, the oral traditions for Jenne-jeno's abandonment should not be dismissed out of hand. It is possible that a new, Islamic Jenné was founded on a new site 'unpolluted' by pagan practices shortly after the king of Jenne(-jeno), or perhaps the community's elite, converted to Islam. If, as there is every reason to believe from the historical records, commercial control became vested in the hands of native Muslim merchants, the new Jenné would soon replace pagan Jenne-jeno as the hub of economic activity. Farmers, fishermen and craftsmen, who undoubtedly comprised the majority of Jenne-jeno's population, would have been attracted to Jenné as a growing market for their produce. Our hypothetical reconstruction of the decline of Jenne-jeno sees economic incentives at the new, Muslim, market centre of Jenné as the primary cause of Jenne-jeno's abandonment. This process was completed by at least the mid-fifteenth century.

Reconstructing lifeways at Jenne-jeno

Reconstructing the way of life of Jenne-jeno's ancient inhabitants is, of course, a highly speculative exercise. We are, however, on reasonably firm ground when dealing with subsistence and economy. As is the case today at Jenné, diet was heavily reliant upon cattle, fish and rice. This basic triad was present in the earliest levels at Jenne-jeno and throughout the deposits (R. McIntosh & S. McIntosh 1988, pp. 144–5).

Craft skills are evident in the earliest materials recovered at Jenne-jeno. The abundant iron and slag in the lowest levels indicates that some members of the community had the skill to smelt and smith the metal. Some members must also have had the time to obtain the necessary raw materials from sources as yet unidentified, but at least 50 km distant. The thin-walled, finely twine-impressed pottery in Phase I/II is superb, and it is quite possible that at least part-time specialists were engaged in its manufacture.

In Phase III, the evidence for craft specialization increases. Potters and smiths were joined by masons working initially in *tauf* (solid coursed mud) and later in unfired brick. Many stone beads and hundreds of sandstone grinders of uniform size and shape were found. Also present in Phase III were ornaments of copper and gold. We cannot at present say whether all these were imported ready-made from beyond the inland Niger delta or were crafted at Jenne-jeno from imported raw materials. Such large amounts of foreign materials at Jenne-jeno in Phase III certainly imply the existence of a well-organized trade system at this time (see below).

Neither the houses nor the thirty-four burials excavated to date at Jenne-jeno provided much indication of social or economic differences among the population. This impression of uniformity will probably be corrected by future work. Should evidence of social ranking at Jenne-jeno be forthcoming, it will not necessarily reflect the existence of authoritarian institutions such as a 'temple elite'. Authority in the community may have been dispersed, as it is in Jenné today, through various smaller institutions, such as craft associations, residential quarter associations and secular kin networks controlling trade (discussed in R. McIntosh In Press; R. McIntosh & S. McIntosh 1988, pp. 155–8). It may be that the position of chief (*koi*) in Jenné evolved out of the need for kin-based trading associations to centralize aspects of the administration of expanding commercial networks. Enquiries in Jenné today indicate that the chief's authority was economic in origin rather than political. This would explain why Jenné never appears, from historical sources, to have exerted any political hegemony over the western inland Niger delta.

We turn now to the question of how Jenne-jeno might have looked at its apogee in the late first millennium AD. The layout of house foundations found on the surface of the site and in the course of excavations suggests that residences were built close together with narrow alleys providing passage between houses. The effect was probably like a rabbit's warren of weaving alleys between tightly packed compounds of round and square houses linked by walls. There may have been an open market-place in a central location. The whole residential sector was enclosed by a wall built of solid rows of cylindrical mud brick and measuring 3.6 m in width at the base. The wall may have been the most prominent architectural feature at Jenne-jeno.

The wall was probably built during the latter half of the first millennium AD, according to information recovered during the sectioning of the wall in 1981. There is no evidence for external threats to the settlement at this time. It is entirely possible, however, that the wall was not built for defensive purposes. It may have been intended to protect Jenne-jeno from destructive floods. Or it may have served to control access to the market-place and trade. During the second millennium, for example, foreign traders were required to camp outside the walls of Jenné while their agents negotiated with the chief and merchants of the town. It is also quite possible that the wall was built to enhance civic identity and prestige.

In all likelihood, Jenne-jeno boasted a substantial population. Attempts at population estimation are tricky, however. Archaeologists working in other parts of the world have had great difficulty in establishing indices by which population could be determined from settlement data (Hassan 1981; Schacht 1981). Our approach to the question of Jenne-jeno's population will be to calculate population density for several existing towns in the vicinity of Jenné in order to explore the findings of Kramer (1982, pp.

170–81) and Sumner (1989, p. 638) that population density per hectare varies greatly according to functional level of a settlement within a hierarchical settlement system. One of the towns is Jenné itself, where a population of 9900 lives on a surface area of 44.8 ha (surface area is measured from air photos and includes both public and private space, residential and non-residential sectors). Jenné's population density is 221 persons per hectare. A more traditional hinterland town, Gomitogo, lacks the vast non-residential spaces characteristic of Jenné and has a much higher population density (2751 persons on 7.07 ha = 389/ha). Yet another density factor can be obtained by averaging the data available for fifteen settlements (excluding Jenné) located within 8 km of Jenné: 237/ha. These three density factors provide an indication of the range of population concentration on settlements in the Jenné region today.

Whether the population density at Jenne-jeno fell within this range is open to debate. But the fact is, we have too little excavation data to attempt to devise any other kind of population index: any formula using floor area or compound size is out of the question. Despite shortcomings, the calculated density factors do provide a ballpark estimate of Jenne-jeno's possible range of population (Table 37.1).

Table 37.1 Possible range of population at Jenne-jeno

	Density factor		
	A	B	C
Area	221/ha	237/ha	389/ha
Jenne-jeno (33 ha)	7293	7821	12837
Jenne-jeno and Hambarketolo (33 + 8.8 = 41.8 ha)	9238	9907	16260
Jenne-jeno cluster (includes 25 satellite sites within 1 km) (33 + 35.7 = 68.7 ha)	15183	16282	26724

The population of Jenne-jeno alone may have been between 7000 and 13,000. But our calculation really ought to take into account the site of Hambarketolo, which was occupied at the same time as Jenne-jeno and is connected to it by a causeway. It is very likely that the two sites functioned together as a unit. However, Hambarketolo is only one of twenty-five 'satellite' sites clustered around Jenne-jeno within a 1 km radius. Tradition in Jenné today maintains that all these sites together were called Jenné in the distant past, suggesting that all the settlements (plus Jenne-jeno) constituted a single entity. Thus, depending on how Jenne-jeno is defined, and which density factor is used, population estimates could range from around 7300 persons for Jenne-jeno in isolation up to almost 27,000 for the 'town complex'.

Thus far, we have not raised the question of Jenne-jeno's urban status. It was a very large settlement, without a doubt, and its inhabitants engaged in a variety of occupations, but did it function within an urban landscape? We have argued earlier that the most effective way to investigate the appearance and development of the precolonial situation in west Africa is not to excavate only the town site, but to document the hierarchy of settlements of which the town was the summit (see McIntosh & McIntosh 1984). As specific evidence of the emergence of such a hierarchy, we shall be looking for site size distributions which conform to the rank–size rule. A complementary concern is the investigation of inter-site diversity, reflected in the relative heterogeneity of arte-facts and features at individual sites. As a settlement becomes more urban, we assume that the inhabitants become more varied than their village counterparts in terms of wealth, social and ethnic background, and personal idiosyncrasies. This diversity should increase in some relationship to the position of the settlement within the urban hierarchy, and it should be archaeologically detectable.

The regional survey

Having reaffirmed our commitment to the regional perspective on urbanism, we now turn to the survey conducted over an 1100 km^2 area to the north and west of Jenne-jeno. This particular area was selected for investigation because it includes a representative cross-section of Jenne-jeno's rural hinterland with a wide diversity of landforms and vegetation. Boundaries of the survey region were arbitrarily delineated to coincide with the boundaries of aerial photographs of the area, with the exception of the eastern boundary provided by the Bani river. Our basic goal in the survey was to provide with minimum expenditure of time and money a base for quantitative and qualitative estimates of the character of archaeological sites in the survey region. To achieve this goal, survey was conducted on an explicit sampling basis using probability theory. For purposes of economy, the regional population of areas to be sampled was restricted to include only those elevated areas not subject to annual inundation. We made the assumption that the scanty traces of seasonal occupation that may exist on the floodplain have probably been obscured by alluviation. This assumption may be wrong, and it may discriminate against the seasonal or limited-activity sites of nomads, but this potential bias is at least explicit and was evaluated in 1977 and again in 1981. The net effect of this assumption was to reduce by $c.$ 90 per cent the regional population area to be surveyed. In neither survey year were any significant scatters of archaeologi-cal material found on the alluvium on the floodplain between one above-flood tell or landform and another.

In 1977, the survey region was first stratified geometrically into 12 squares measuring 9.5 × 9.5 km, which is the area covered by a single air photo (12 photos in all). Within each of these 12 blocks, the two different classes of non-inundated area were each sampled by a different, appropriate method: discrete mounds in the floodplain were numbered individually and a 20 per cent sample selected for investigation with the aid of a random number table (all floodplain mounds proved to be tells); other upland areas (e.g. dunes and levees) were gridded into consecutively numbered transects each measuring 2 × 0.5 km, and a systematic 20 per cent sample was chosen for careful, on-foot investigation. Analysis of the two different samples and inferences drawn from them were kept separate. The only exception to the above procedures concerned the area within a 4 km radius of Jenné, where all non-inundated areas were surveyed completely because a focus of interest was the growth and organization of urban Jenné/Jenne-jeno.

In 1981 we concentrated on the tell sites found within 4 km of Jenné. We selected a 50 per cent sample of the 65 sites thus represented. Half of the single, isolated sites were selected by a simple random sampling scheme. Half of the sites comprising each 'cluster' of cities were also selected by simple random sampling. For all sites discovered in the course of the survey, we recorded information on topographic situation (land-form, vegetation), soils, size and surface features and artefacts. Small surface collections of pottery were made so that the survey sites could be tentatively tied into the Jenne-jeno pottery sequence.

One of the startling conclusions of the survey was that, of 42 sites investigated in the course of the 1977 sample survey, and of 33 sites recorded in 1981, almost three-quarters had been abandoned by the end of Phase IV (AD 1400), and none was abandoned before Phase III. Almost all sites investigated are tells with deposits exceed-ing 2 m in height above the floodplain. Such an accumulation probably represents several centuries of occupation prior to abandonment. These conclusions receive some independent support from archaeological investigations by Bedaux at two small sites in the inland Niger delta. Both mounds appear to have been occupied from the eleventh through the fifteenth centuries AD and then abandoned (Bedaux, Constandse-Westermann, Hacquebord, Lange & van der Waals 1978). Preliminary as they are, these results imply that site density reached its greatest expression in late Phase III/early Phase IV, and thereafter began to decline. At its maximum, site density in the survey region may have approached ten times the density of occupied settlements in the same region today, judging from the 404 sites identified on air photographs.

Thus far, the survey data accord well with the excavation results: both indicate that Jenne-jeno and its hinterland were developing rapidly during Phase III (AD 300–800). Site density apparently reached a maximum sometime between *c.* AD 750 and 1150 at approximately the same time that Jenne-jeno achieved its maximum areal extent. We feel confident that these preliminary data reflect a degree of indigenous urbanism hitherto unsuspected for this region. This conclusion is supported by the distribution of site sizes and ranks, which closely approximates the rank–size rule. In Figure 37.2, we have plotted the logarithms of site size against the logarithms of site rank for those sites investigated in the course of the 1977 sample survey whose surface pottery indicated abandonment before the end of Phase IV (*c.* AD 1400). Since all the sites involved are tells with over 2 m of deposits, it is likely that most represent several centuries of occupation. It is therefore very probable, in our opinion, that these sites were contem-poraneous with Jenne-jeno in Phase IV.

Diversity among the Phase IV sites was measured by the number of different artefact features and classes noted in a careful examination of each site's surface. The presence of features such as iron-smelting furnaces, slag concentrations and settlement walls were recorded, as were non-mundane artefacts like fired, slipped bricks, ceramic bedrests, tuyères, iron artefacts, non-ferrous metals, net weights, spindle whorls, cowries, terracotta statuettes and jewellery items. In general, the number of different artefact and feature classes recorded varied directly with size (Fig. 37.4). If our procedure can be accepted as an admittedly crude, but nevertheless useful, approach to the investigation of site diversity, our expectation that diversity should increase in some relation to a site's position in the settlement hierarchy has been met. The additional fact that basic classes of material culture at Phase IV hinterland sites are virtually identical to those at

Jenne-jeno provides further evidence that the hinterland sites were integrated into a settlement hierarchy with Jenne-jeno as its apex.

We would be the first to acknowledge that there are serious problems with the analysis just described (discussed in full in McIntosh & McIntosh 1980b, part 2). Many of these problems plague any archaeological attempt to document past settlement hierarchies; a few are specific to the Jenné region. First, there is a major difficulty with using site area as a measurement of size in plotting rank–size distributions (Sumner 1989, pp. 638–9). Size is *correctly* plotted using population. Thus, we have had to make the quite unwarranted assumption that the predominant factor affecting site size is population, and that this relationship is consistent for all sites. In truth, however, this assumption can be more or less confidently made only for that portion of the site that actually houses the inhabitants, excluding any parts that may have been restricted to livestock or the dead, for example (the problem of 'functional size' is discussed in Johnson 1977, p. 495; alternatives to population/area ratios for ranking sites are given in Adams & Jones 1981, pp. 304–7). To a certain extent, this is controllable in the inland

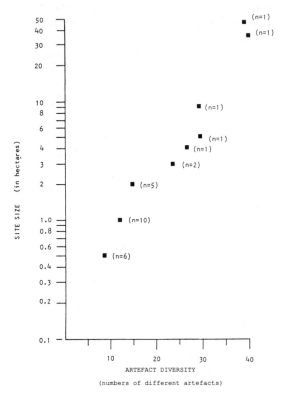

Figure 37.4 Artefact diversity, calculated by counting the number of different artefact classes present on the site surface, is plotted against site size for all pre-Phase V sites surveyed in 1981. The investigated sites constitute a 50 per cent random sample of all sites within a 4 km radius of Jenne-jeno. For values where n=1, the plotted artefact diversity value is an average calculated using all the density values for sites in a given size class (0.1–0.5 ha, 0.5–1.0 ha, 1–2 ha, etc.).

Niger delta because house foundations and funerary urns are often highly visible on the site surface.

An equally imponderable difficulty is the question of contemporaneity (Schacht 1981). A rank–size diagram like Figure 37.2 implies that the site sizes plotted were all achieved contemporaneously (and not just during the same *period*). While we can be fairly sure that most of the plotted sites existed at the same time, we cannot be sure that all of them reached their maximum areal extent at the same time. There is some evidence from Jenne-jeno, for example, that the site was only partly occupied by the middle of Phase IV: its functional size had decreased dramatically.

We also assume, in plotting rank–size distributions, that all plotted sites functioned within the same hierarchy. This is not a crippling problem with the Jenne-jeno survey data because the sites are all located within a 25 km radius, and historical sources indicate that, during the second millennium, sites within this region consistently functioned in a hierarchy with Jenné at its summit. Although delineating of *system boundaries* is perhaps not as confounding for Jenne-jeno as it is for other archaeological situations, the definition of *site boundaries* in the inland Niger delta poses a dilemma. Archaeological sites around Jenne-jeno cluster to an unusual degree. Only 23 per cent are single mounds situated more than 500 m from any other mound. The other 77 per cent of the sites occur in clusters of from two to fifteen mounds, all within shouting distance. This contrasts markedly with the settlement pattern of occupied settlements in the area today, where 87 per cent are single, isolated sites, and 13 per cent occur as paired villages, usually of two different ethnic groups. One of the purposes of the near-Jenné 1981 survey was to determine whether clusters of archaeological sites in the survey region represent sequential or simultaneous occupation, functional differences, ethnic differences, seasonal occupation or another factor entirely. It now appears to be a greater than ever possibility that most or all of the mounds in a cluster were contemporaneously occupied and functioned as parts of a single urban unit. 'Clustering', therefore, has serious implications for our original calculation of site size.

The lesson of these and other problems with the analysis is one of caution, we believe, not despair. We have not attempted to delineate detailed regional hierarchies or to employ locational theory to elucidate settlement patterns because we acknowledge that our data fall dismally short of the precision in chronology, size estimation and boundary recognition required for such analyses. We are, after all, dealing largely with the results of two field seasons conducted in an area about which virtually nothing was known archaeologically prior to 1977. In using the rank–size distribution and complementary studies of site diversity, we have attempted to demonstrate only that a settlement hierarchy existed in the upper inland Niger delta before AD 1400. We note with some gratification that the distribution is in no way primate (i.e. one major town and many small villages), yet a primate distribution is what we would expect if the development of the region was economically dependent on foreign empires, as the historical view of Jenné's origin contends. A primate distribution could also indicate an incipient, early, urban system (Crumley 1976, p. 65). What we see, however, is a distribution which closely approximates the rank–size rule, and so indicates a fairly developed, well-established degree of urbanism.

Regional trade and urban effects

The recognition of a mature settlement hierarchy in the Jenné region implies a long process of contact and interaction between different communities. We should add parenthetically that excavation and survey of the traditional town of Dia, some 100 km to the northwest, revealed not only a chronology of settlement and abandonment and a ceramic sequence virtually indistinguishable from that at Jenne-jeno, but also similar site 'clustering' (R. McIntosh & S. McIntosh 1988, pp. 150–1). The reasons for this interaction (intraregional in city hinterlands and between the regions of the middle Niger) and the factors responsible for the early emergence of towns like Jenne-jeno are undoubtedly complex. A comprehensive attempt to elucidate them would be impossible even after two long excavation seasons. Based on excavation data and later historical sources, however, we are able to suggest with some confidence that indigenous trade was a vital element in Jenne-jeno's development. We see the well-established settlement hierarchy in the Jenne-jeno region as a manifestation of the integration of communities into a formal, intra-regional economic network. Within this network, there probably existed a lively trade in local staples, including rice and fish, which could be exchanged for desired commodities from other regions, such as copper from the Sahara (Fig. 37.5).

Situated in an alluvial plain lacking in stone and iron ore, at the interface of two major vegetation zones (dry savanna and sahel), Jenne-jeno is a natural candidate for the early growth of inter-regional trade networks. Indeed, Phase I deposits strongly indicate early involvement in trade. Not only are the stone beads from the earliest deposits foreign to the inland delta, but there is also evidence that the iron must have been obtained from outside the delta, presumably by trade. To the best of our knowledge, there are no sources of iron ore in the inland Niger delta suitable for smelting. The presence of slag at Jenne-jeno and many other sites in the survey area suggests that either iron ore or bloomery iron, with some slag still adhering, was imported into the central delta. The latter possibility seems the more reasonable, since transport costs would be appreciably reduced by removing the weight of useless silicates at the source area. Smelting in the Jenné area would seriously reduce the tree cover of the inland delta, which was probably never great. There is historical documentation that in the nineteenth and twentieth centuries Jenné imported bloomery iron or iron preliminarily forged into bars from the Benedougou region near San. If, as we suspect, the Benedougou is the nearest source of abundant iron ore to Jenné, the iron trade between the two areas is likely to be of considerable antiquity, perhaps dating back to the foundation of Jenne-jeno.

Evidence that the exchange networks within which Jenne-jeno functioned had expanded by the fourth century AD is provided by copper ornaments in the earliest Phase III deposits. The three closest known sources of copper ore are in the Sahara: Akjoujt, Nioro and Aïr (Mauny 1961, p. 307). This evidence strongly implies that inter-regional trade for Saharan copper existed by the mid-first millennium AD. Other Saharan commodities carried in this early trade can only be guessed at: salt is a major possibility, given the historically documented demand in the western Sudan for Saharan salt and copper during the second millennium. Unfortunately, salt trade is difficult to document archaeologically (see also Alexander, Ch. 39, this volume). If Saharan copper and salt were reaching Jenne-jeno in any quantity by the fifth century AD, then it is reasonable to suggest that the navigable middle Niger was functioning as an important north–south transport axis by that date. The ease of riverine transport, at least seasonally, and the annual migration, by pirogue, of fisherfolk downstream to the Niger Bend (Sundstrom 1972) would have made this a natural early development.

Commodities sought by Saharan traders in exchange for copper and salt may have been largely agricultural, including rice from the Jenné region and fruit or other savanna products from the Benedougou. This riverine trade in staples is mentioned in the very first reference to Jenné. In AD 1447, Antonio Malfante wrote from north Africa regarding his informant's tales of the inland Niger delta:

> Every day he tells me wonderful things of these people. They have an abundance of flesh, milk, and rice, but no corn or barley. Through these lands flows a very large river, which at times of the year inundates all these lands. This river passes by the gates of Timbuktu. There are many boats on it, by which they carry on trade. (Crone 1937, p. 87)

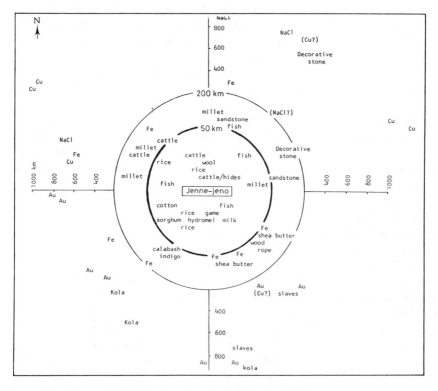

Figure 37.5 Diagram of principal resources available to the inhabitants of Jenne-jeno by trade, with an indication of distances from Jenne-jeno to the nearest known sources. The concentric circles delineate the trading spheres of immediate hinterland (0–50 km), intermediate markets (50–200 km) and distant markets (200 km).

Gold may also have been one of the savanna commodities moving along the exchange networks at this early time, confirmed by the find of a gold earring in Jenne-jeno deposits antedating AD 800.

This hypothetical reconstruction of the development of first-millennium inter-regional exchange along the Niger emphasizes Jenne-jeno's role as a producer of surplus staples, such as dried fish, fish oil and rice, which were potentially desirable to communities in the adjacent dry savanna and Saharan zones. Such a theory explains Jenné(-jeno)'s location more satisfactorily than do interpretations of the town's devel-opment that stress its excellent situation for riverine trade with the Niger bend or its defensible location. Indeed, Jenné is perhaps not in the best location for trade down the Niger. The most direct waterway from Jenné to the Niger, the Souman-Bani, is too shallow for riverine transport during four months of the year. Rather, Jenne-jeno's location is optimal with respect to three different requirements: proximity of a richly productive agricultural hinterland, access to the Benedougou savanna highlands to the southeast, and riverine transport, throughout most of the year, to the Saharan contact zone at the Niger bend. We suggest that Jenne-jeno's location at the southwestern extreme of the navigable *and* agriculturally productive inland delta promoted its growth as a trade centre where Saharan commodities like copper and salt could be traded for dried fish, fish oil and rice produced in the inland delta, and where savanna products, including iron from the Benedougou, could be obtained with a minimum of overland travel in exchange for salt, copper, rice, fish and other staples.

The historically documented existence of trade centres by the eleventh century in the agriculturally impoverished Niger bend area offers the first evidence, however circum-stantial, that the inland Niger delta was established as the agricultural support system for the Niger bend (McIntosh 1981). Al-Bakri mentions the towns of Safanku and Bughrat along the Niger route to Tirekka, located at the southward turning of the river (Cuoq 1975, p. 106). Tirekka's market attracted the merchants of Ghana and Tadmekka, the latter of which is described as 'a great town . . . better built than Ghana or Kawkaw. The inhabitants . . . import millet and all other cereals from the Land of the Blacks' (Cuoq 1975, p. 107). It is probable that sizeable settlements on the Niger bend – discovered during our 1983 survey in the Timbuktu region – could not produce enough food locally to maintain their population, as is the case in Timbuktu today.

More direct evidence for Jenne-jeno's participation in interregional trade during the first millennium AD will have to come from archaeological research. However, the aforementioned similarity of ceramics at late first-millennium BC Dia and Jenne-jeno and the presence of wares characteristic of Jenne-jeno Phase III throughout the second–eighth-century sequence at Soumpi in the lakes region south of the Niger bend surely cannot be coincidental. The above explanation for the town's growth is merely a hypothesis that attempts to account in a reasonable way for the archaeological fact that Jenne-jeno existed throughout the first millennium AD, that it was receiving copper, probably of Saharan origin, by the fifth century, and that it had grown into an urban centre of considerable proportions by the mid-first millennium AD.

Conclusion

It is customary to finish an exercise as frankly speculative as the above with disclaimers so broad as to make the reader believe the authors have no confidence whatsoever in their own results. This will not be the case here. We believe we have been moderate in our use of concepts developed by geographers. We have stated the special cautions attached to the use of archaeological data – and yet we believe that future work will bear out the usefulness of the principal points made in this chapter. To end our discussion we look to those issues most requiring future consideration and promising the most exciting results for the patient and persistent investigator.

All these issues centre on the integrative factors working in the intra-regional economy and settlement hierarchy. Many of the fundamental propositions of this chapter imply assumptions about the areal extent and fabric of contacts between communities within the Jenné region. We recognize a great similarity of artefacts at Jenne-jeno and at sites in the hinterland and assume that the similarity is not fortuitous. We presume to plot sites on a rank–size diagram knowing full well that this sample of sites represents only a fraction of all sites integrated within a formally bounded region. We assume this fraction reliably approximates the distribution of all sites. We have cleverly avoided the thorny problem of the tendency of ancient sites to cluster. On a chart of heterogeneity of surface remains, are these to be plotted as many small, simple sites, or as a few large, complex sites which also happen to be a composite of satellite sites? By our archaeologically useful definition of a town, what real difference is there between a large settlement contained on a single tell and a large settlement physically segmented into craft or ethnic quarters, or along lineage or other kinship divisions – while still *functioning* as an integral whole?

It is the search for underlying principles of urban integration at sites like Jenne-jeno that makes work on the indigenous African town every bit as vital as investigation of urbanism anywhere else in the world. Jenne-jeno happens not to have had a citadel and, indeed, we would be surprised to find coincidence in every detail at early cities in places and cultures as diverse as Sumer, bronze age China, Mesoamerica and west Africa. But beyond the level of details and of preconceived notions of what cities should look like, there will be distilled out processes in common to all these areas. We believe that the contribution of African research to this distillation will be considerable.

Acknowledgements

An initial version of this chapter was given at the University of California, Los Angeles, as part of a seminar organized by Merrick Posnansky in 1981 on 'The Indigenous African Town'. It was revised while the authors were Fellows at the Center for Advanced Study in the Behavioral Sciences in 1989–90. We are grateful for financial support provided by the National Science Foundation (BNS87–008649) to the Center and to us (BNS77–02157 and BNS80–04868) for the fieldwork on which the chapter is based. The research was conducted under the aegis of the Institut des Sciences Humaines, directed by Dr Klena Sanogo, to whom we are grateful for research permission and continuing support of the Jenne-jeno project.

38   *Urbanization and state formation in Ghana during the Iron Age*

JAMES ANQUANDAH

Introduction

An outstanding development in Ghana during the second millennium AD was the emergence of complex settlements in the form of states and towns.

A *state* may be defined as a relatively large territorial unit resulting from the amalgamation of smaller settlement units (such as theocratic and acephalous communities and principalities) under the rulership of a political head. The designation of such a ruler varies from one ethnic group to another. In Ghana, the titles used include *Omanhene, Mantese, Togbe, Atara,* and by the suffixes *-Na* and *-Wura*.

A *town* may be viewed as a complex settlement, compact in its outlay, and having a dense population of 2000–5000 or more people (and see Hassan, Ch. 33, this volume; O'Connor, Ch. 34, this volume). It often comprises a population diverse in its ethnic affiliation and political status or structure and in its agricultural, technological and industrial specializations and this population may perform functions in relation to both a localized and a broader hinterland (Mabogunje 1968; Rouse 1972; Smith 1972; Trigger 1972; Wheatley 1972; Evans 1976, p. 503; Posnansky n.d.; McIntosh & McIntosh 1984; McIntosh & McIntosh, Ch. 37, this volume).

In precolonial Ghana, there were few states that had towns. On the other hand, virtually all early towns constituted parts of states ruled by chiefs. In fact, the social function of the town as the seat of an *Omanhene* or a principal chieftain, and as a focus of socio-political life, was an important traditional factor distinguishing a town from a village (Barbour & Prothero 1961, pp. 250–5).

In tropical Africa, there are problems of data survival and retrieval, high research costs, problems of research funding and the fact that iron age societies were largely non-literate. It is indeed a herculean task to attempt to utilize the fragmentary archaeological data, the silent static residue from dynamic past human activities, for understanding and explaining urban and state-forming processes. As Binford states (1983a, p. 23):

> Archaeological data, unfortunately, do not carry self-evident meanings. . . . We need sites that preserve for us things from the past; but, equally, we need the theoretical tools to give meaning to these things when they are found: Identifying them accurately and recognizing their contexts in past behavior depends upon a kind of research that cannot be conducted in the archaeological record itself. That is, if we intend to investigate the relation-

ship between statics and dynamics, we must be able to observe both aspects simultaneously; and the only place we *can* observe dynamics is in the modern world, in the here and now.

In tropical Africa, where the rural population, in particular, has conservatively held on to the ancient traditions of building, metal-working, farming, ethnomedicine, politics and arts and crafts, etc., the *eclectic* strategy which dictates a multidisciplinary approach has much to recommend it.

For the purposes of discussing issues of iron age urbanism and state formation, this chapter focuses on the examples of Begho and Bono Manso in Akan Brong country (middle Ghana) and on the La and Shai of the Accra plains (Dangmeland) (Fig. 38.1).

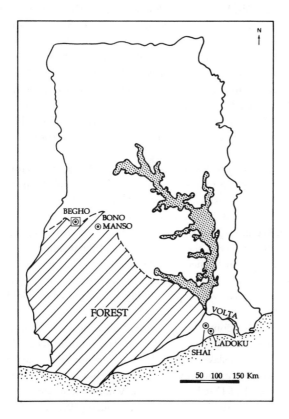

Figure 38.1   Map of middle Ghana and Dangmeland.

Written history

In the multidisciplinary scheme of things, one rich source of evidence that can be tapped is written history. For instance, the seventeenth-century Dutch writer, Abramsz, and the author of the eighteenth-century Arabic work *Khitab Chunja* (Wilks 1961), referred to the old Begho area as the location of a cosmopolitan trading town-state linking the Akan forest producers of gold, kola and ivory with the Sudanic trans-Saharan trading centres like Jenné (see McIntosh & McIntosh, Ch. 37, this volume). Hans Propheet, a Dutch cartographer who drew a map at Moure in 1629, indicated the Begho area as being famous for its textile industries (Kea 1982). Because of their proximity to the European coastal trade area, the La and Shai settlements received mention in several European written records. La/Laay was described in 1682 by Barbot as a 'town' (Barbot 1732). In 1838, Riis and Murdter visited and described Shai as comprising two large populous hill principalities (see Riis 1839). Zimmerman (1851) carried out an expedition to Shai (in 1850) and estimated its population around 1881 to be about 10,000. Two Danish medical and botanical scientists, Isert and Thonning, visited the Shai area in the 1780s and 1790s and documented the local people's traditional medical, nutritional and obstetrical skills and made a catalogue of names of Dangme plants and their uses (Schumacher 1828; Schumacher 1829; Adams 1957; Hepper 1976). The local names and uses of many of the plant specimens collected by Isert and Thonning are still extant today.

Besides, there are numerous references in records of European visitors to Shai during the period 1800–70 which show how the local Dangme people managed to cope with the difficult problem of a harsh environment characterized by a geological system that produces infertile soils and has poor water-preserving properties: they vigorously exploited the rich kaolin clays of the same geological systems to produce high-quality pottery that was sold widely in the Accra plains and the neighbouring area (Meredith 1812; Riis 1839; Windmann & Dieterle 1848; Kimble 1963). One missionary visitor to Shai in 1852 was carried away by his impressions and painted an exaggerated picture of 'big pottery villages in Shai, whose pots supply almost the whole Gold Coast' (Quarcoo & Johnson 1968, p. 55).

European writings also pointed to the ancient Shai and La as beneficiaries of organized trade with European nationals in gold and slaves. For instance, Barbot observed that in the Ningo-Lay area, slaves and gold were traded for velvets and printed calicoes, the gold being generally brought from Quahoe, which was rich in gold (Barbot 1732).

The Director-General of Dutch possessions, Van Sevenhuysen, wrote in May 1699 of Kpone, located close to the La/Lay area (Van Dantzig 1978, p. 70):

> After the urgent request of the under-king of Aquamboe, I have encouraged that trade at Ponnie for more than 1½ years and I propose that we should establish a fort or lodge there. It has provided us with very good slaves and abundant gold and it is of such importance. Much gold is being received there when the passages towards Accra are closed by the Upper King.

Ethnohistory and ethnography

The general approach of recent researchers on iron age Ghana has been to carry out studies on ethnohistory, ethnography, linguistics and ecological studies from an archaeological perspective and to use the data in formulating hypotheses that can be tested against independent archaeological evidence. The method has been to isolate and examine the evidence from systemic and subsystemic components related to such social aspects as population, settlement, subsistence, trade, metallurgy, arts and crafts and political control in order to ascertain the bearing of these on urbanism and state formation.

For instance, at Begho, linguistic tests conducted within the postulated parameters of the old township and its rural satellites revealed extreme linguistic diversity, attesting to the belief that the Akan, Guan, Senufo, Mande, Kulango and Grusi-Mo modern communities are descendants and residuary legatees of iron age peoples. Ethnohistoric narratives referred to Begho as a state ruled by an equestrian and palanquin-borne Akan chieftain and as a burgh having at least five multi-ethnic suburbs ordered along ethnic/functional lines, namely (Figs 38.1, 38.2):

Brong – the capital site and residence of the chief and his subchiefs and the main Akan populace;
Adwinfuo – the 'factory' or workshop sector and dormitory area of the artisans including coppersmiths and blacksmiths;
Gyetunidi or Dwabirim (Fig. 38.3) – embracing the actual trading area and the residential sector of specialist traders;
Kramo – the residence of Muslim Mande traders where presumably a mosque(s) built of mud must have stood;
Dapaa – the iron-smelting industrial area located on the outskirts of the township.

Ethnographic studies in the Begho area have shown that for a long time the Mo of Bonakyere have maintained the ancestral potting traditions; the Mande of Kokua have continued the traditions of spinning, dyeing and weaving cloth, an ancient practice in the Begho area that is attested to in the 1629 Dutch map; the Akan Brong pursue farming, hunting and trapping and also maintain old complex ethnomedical and nutritional systems that keep mortality rates down and so maintain demographic equilibrium; and throughout the area, blacksmithing as well as building by the indigenous puddling and wattle-and-daub methods are still extant (Posnansky 1973; Posnansky 1975b; Anquandah 1982a).

Similarly, at Bono Manso, ethnohistoric sources point to trade in gold, ivory and kola as stimulating urban and state evolution and that even though Manso lacked Begho's multifunctional suburbs, it also had a Kramo sector and an Akan royal capital site. The oral traditions also refer to the making and maintenance of paths for horses on which the Bono royals rode during state ceremonies and annual festivals. Manso duplicates, to some extent, Begho's picture of a continuing diversified complex of traditional specialist arts and crafts, subsistence economies and other activities (Effa-Gyamfi 1985).

The Dangme of La are an example of an ancient subethnic population that was displaced and transferred to the Labadi coast near Accra after a civil war with their Dangme kin group, the Dangme of Shai. Hence, the cultural continuity and the direct ethnographic link between old and present-day La has been broken. However, the Shai have continued to live within 2–5 km of their ancient hill settlements from which they were ejected by the British in 1892. In five modern Shai townships, Agomeda, Kodiabe, Doryumu, Ayikuma and Dodowa, which I have studied in detail from 1976 to 1986, there is a rich corpus of ethnohistory in the ancient Klama cult songs and oral traditions which are corroborated by ethnographic studies. Together, these sources show that the Dangme had:

1   a precolonial theocratic form of rule by a priest–chief called Lanimuo (Lord of La); this was replaced from the 1880s by a *mache* type of centralized monarchial system (Crowther 1915; Saxton 1925);
2   complex interrelated subsystems of traditional nutrition, herbal medicine and farming;

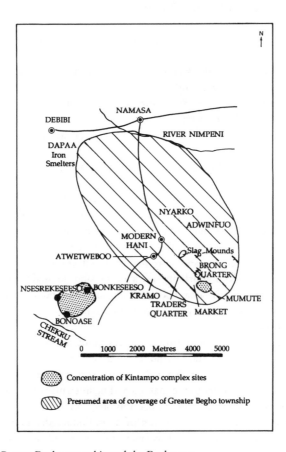

Figure 38.2   Greater Begho township and the Begho area.

3 a viable all-pervasive and dynamic ceramic industry;
4 an annual puberty rite called *dipo* which is tied to, and promotes, productive subsistence and technology because it requires the use of local crops, meat, raw materials and cult equipment;
5 a network of commerce with neighbouring areas, especially in pottery.

Archaeology

La and Shai in the Iron Age

The site of Old La is known in Dangme ethnohistory as Ladoku or 'Derelict La'. Radial transect surveys conducted there have shown that an area measuring 1.6 km by 1.1 km is densely covered by pottery and fragmentary remains of mud and wooden houses built on stone foundations. The pottery which is found on the surface and in the upper levels is seventeenth-century 'Classic Shai ware', slipped and smoke-glazed, with angular profile, imported from the Shai hill potting centres. Excavations have revealed an underlying earlier settlement level associated with 'Cherekecherete pottery', with flowing profiles and applied decoration belonging to the fourteenth and fifteenth centuries.

This earlier pottery is found on surface sites only in the Shai hills area, principally at Cherekecherete, Adwuku, Tetedwa, Mawubedzibe and Pianoyo. It would not be possible to trace 'Cherekecherete ware' on the low-lying plains of Old La near Dawhenya dam without deep area excavation, and it will therefore be some time before the parameters of the fifteenth-century settlement can be ascertained.

However, in 1977–9, excavation of a large incinerator located on the highest point of Ladoku revealed a large quantity of 'Classic Shai pottery' associated with abundant remains of *Bos* and ovicaprids, several thousand mollusca, numerous milling stones, copper and iron objects, local smoking pipes of the period 1640–80 and imported seventeenth- and eighteenth-century European pottery, glass beads, smoking pipes and *C. moneta* and *annulus* cowrie shells, probably used by the La as ornaments and currency. This site is dated by three C14 determinations as follows (Anquandah 1982a, pp. 143–4):

Upper levels with 'Classic Shai ware'
N – 2969 1660 ± 80 ad
N – 2970 1785 ± 70 ad
N – 3346 1680 ± 80 ad
Lower levels with 'Cherekecherete ware'
N – 2968 1400 ± 75 ad

Similar survey and excavation work has been carried out in the Shai hills where there are some fifteen iron age settlement units all having Dangme names, and spread over an area extending 6 km by 12 km. Three of these sites have produced only fifteenth-century Cherekecherete ware. The other sites have pottery spanning the period from the fifteenth to the eighteenth century.

The Shai evidence, like that of Ladoku, suggests urban development principally in the period AD 1600–1880 (Ozanne 1965a; Ozanne 1965b). How do we account for urbanism at this time? It appears that explanations may be found as much in internal as in external factors. The excavations revealed vigorous La/Shai–European trading activities. The La and Shai exported to local areas cattle, pottery and mollusca (used as lime for white-washing houses in Akanland) and obtained gold and slaves which were traded to European ships (Wilks 1961; Reindorf 1966). It is clear, however, that the expansion of the local potting industry and trade was paralleled by similar expansion in related crafts, industries, subsistence practices and socio-economic activities which tended to attract population into the Shai/La area. Shai pottery, sometimes exhibiting trademarks like the sun motif, is found distributed some 5–20 km in places such as central Accra, Akuapem and Ladoku. This suggests some standardization and evolution of a 'factory-type' industry. An analysis of the excavated pottery has shown that a number of present-day pottery functional types, including pots for pharmaceutical preparations, *dipo* puberty rite pots, palm wine-tapping pots and hearth pots were made in iron age times.

Moreover, the presence of ceramic floor tiles in early nineteenth-century house levels at Adwuku-Shai attests to increasing wealth and development of adjuncts of the ceramic industry including charcoal stoves, smoking pipes and building technology; Anquandah (1978; 1979; 1982a; 1982b; 1986; 1987; n.d.a) provides numerous references with regard to Shai and La. Actual archaeological data related to state formation are limited to studies on the ruins of the Shai-Hiowey mud-built royal palace and associated midden, which contain many European imported goods.

Begho

At Begho the ubiquitous 'elephant grass' (*Pennisetum purpureum*) conceals a 'hump and hollow' configuration of mounds representing house compounds, each compound having living-rooms, a store and a kitchen arranged around a rectangular courtyard, as suggested by the ethnographic model. There have been general surveys, study of surface material and counts of mounds from which it is estimated that there are some 1500 mounds representing ruins of houses in the various suburbs. The present-day village of Hani, located in the area, has a population of about 1200 and each household has some 10–12 residents. Assuming that some of the 1500 iron age mounds may be workshops and middens, and not house compounds, it is still possible, using the ethnographic parallel, to estimate Old Begho's population at its peak in the seventeenth century to have been around 10,000, which would make it one of the largest townships of iron age west Africa. Detailed radial transect surveys have been conducted in the three major suburbs of Kramo, Gyetunidi and Brong.

Nearly one per cent of the total number of mounds have been excavated by sampling the various suburbs. Fifteen radiocarbon dates have been obtained, spanning the eleventh century to the eighteenth century AD. It appears that the beginnings of the towns can be traced to the nuclear eleventh-century Nyarko quarter, an area covering about 1 km², and littered with slip and painted pottery of the period. At its peak in the seventeenth century, the densest area covered about 3 km², and the Kramo and Brong quarters, which were located 2 km apart in the fifteenth century, had expanded to meet at an emergent Gyetunidi market suburb, as outlined by Posnansky (1973; 1975b; 1979; n.d.), Anquandah (1975; 1981; 1982a), Shaw (1981b) and Sutton (1981).

The data from the excavations (summarized below) have shed some light on the great variety of specialist subsistence, technological, industrial, commercial and political activities of Begho's complex society:

over 2000 diverse iron implements from all the suburbs;

Numerous copper and copper alloyed objects and over 500 clay crucibles used for melting copper (Anquandah 1981);

Many spindle whorls and occurrences of dye holes used in the textile industry;

Ivory bracelets, carvings, etc., produced from the eleventh century AD onwards;

Many thousands of sherds of pottery comprising Begho ware manufactured in the vicinity, and three other wares traded from Buipe in Gonja, Bono Manso and Old Wenchi;

Large quantities of remains of wild fauna such as antelope, and domestic cattle, sheep, goats and pigs;

Stone-milling equipment;

Goods imported through long-distance commerce – sixteenth- to eighteenth-century German stoneware, Delftware, Chinese porcelain, some 450 Dutch and Venetian glass beads, bones and teeth of horses; stone and pottery discs thought to be used for weighing gold; and many local smoking pipes suggestive of tobacco importation on a large scale;

Pieces of royal heraldic ivory trumpets akin to the regalia of the modern Hani chief as well as royal ancestral shrine remains with fifty offering vessels, altogether pointing to the operation of a centralized monarchy at Old Begho;

Evidence of puddled mud and wattle-and-daub architecture; and evidence of Mande-type ceramic roof drain-pipes, indicating a variety of architectural technology, and reflecting the cosmopolitan nature of the township.

Research in the satellite areas surrounding Begho shows that it interacted with a hinterland extending to around a 25 km radius from the centre of Begho: Dapaa, the iron-smelting quarter, which produced iron goods for the town, is one of west Africa's largest smelting centres. Nsawkaw, Begho's successor state, has traditional shrines and monuments containing imported Mameluke Egyptian fifteenth-century brass bowls depicting Naski or Kufic arabic inscriptions.

It is evident that the Begho area, strategically located in the forest-grassland ecotone, enjoyed the best of both ecological zones.

Abundant local subsistence and mineral resources enabled 'neolithic' villages and early iron age settlements to flourish in the area, as indeed the four 'Kintampo complex' sites of the first to second millennium BC (Anquandah, Ch. 13, this volume; Stahl, Ch. 14, this volume) and the second-century AD iron-working site of Atwetweboo testify; and the ecotone was also a haven adaptable for both sudanic and forest trading peoples (Figs 38.2, 38.3).

The emergence of the Begho town-state was due as much to the trade-induced transfer of population from Mandeland, Ivory Coast, northern Ghana and Akanland as to local development of viable systems of food production, medicine, nutrition, crafts, technology and architecture based on local resources.

Bono Manso

Archaeological investigations at Manso have involved surveying large areas and studying types and distributions of pottery and occupation mounds, by both survey and excavations. Three urban phases are postulated on the basis of nine radiocarbon age determinations:

Early phase: thirteenth to fifteenth century AD, characterized by small low mounds representing wattle-and-daub houses each occupied by a family of 3–5 persons, containing slipped and painted pottery distributed over 2.3 km². A population of 4000 is postulated on the basis of some 230 located house units.

Middle phase: sixteenth to mid-seventeenth century AD, characterized by larger mounds with evidence of puddled mud houses continuously and compactly distributed, suggesting a density of some 8000–10,000 people, reckoning on ten persons to one house. This phase provides evidence of long-distance trade including imported domestic mica-coated pottery, seventeenth- to eighteenth-century European glass beads and pottery, and local smoking pipes.

Late phase: late seventeenth century to eighteenth century AD, characterized by larger and more concentrated mounds and pottery confined to half of the original area of iron age settlement, suggestive of greater population density coupled with greater political centralization (Effa-Gyamfi 1985).

The Bono Manso hypothesis of inception and development of urbanism after AD 1200 springing from improved agriculture, expanding local technology and commerce rests on a few items of excavated local and exotic goods, and rather heavily on the

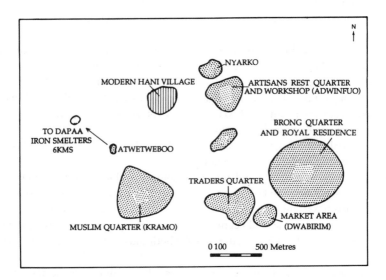

Figure 38.3 Begho town, AD 1000–1750.

typology and distribution of pottery and occupation mounds. Support for the hypothesis of state formation is unduly reliant on oral history. Local traditions state that Manso (meaning, literally, 'capital site') was the residence of Bono's paramount chief. It was also the seat of equestrian subchiefs who superintended Manso's seven satellite villages and hinterland tributary principalities – Amoman, Asekye, Dewoman, Nyafoman and Takyiman.

The traditions also refer to the existence of a number of commercial centres, namely, Kramokron, Ameyawkrom and Sempoakrom. The Bono Manso studies have involved a certain amount of 'urbocentric' as well as regional studies in which pottery from the urban phases of Manso have been traced to hinterland sites.

On the whole, the evidence adduced for complexity of production, specialization and settlement at Bono Manso is sparse as compared to the data from Begho.

Conclusion

A number of situations arise which are thought to lead to either transfers of population from one area to supplement population in another area, and/or concentration of population in a particular area and both are believed to stimulate the growth of complex settlements (Law 1977b, p. 264). Among these are:

1 synoecism or the amalgamation of small communities to form a township for purposes of defence;
2 voluntary immigration of people attracted by opportunities for wealth in an area of expanding commerce, agriculture and industry;
3 incorporation of refugees;
4 purchase of slaves; and
5 appropriation of slaves by violence.

It seems highly probable that in the turbulent state of politics and economics created by Akwamu political and economic imperialism in the Accra plains during the sixteenth and seventeenth centuries, the little Shai homesteads and villages would tend to come together in the relative security of the Shai hill fastnesses; this could have promoted urbanism and state formation.

It seems probable also that the development of large-scale local industries and trade, like potting in Shai, perhaps gold in La, and gold, ivory and kola in Begho and Bono Manso would tend to serve as a magnet, attracting immigrants from other areas, so paving the way to state and town development.

39   The salt industries of west Africa: a preliminary study

JOHN ALEXANDER

Enough is known about salt production and marketing in different parts of the world in historic times for the whole process from extraction to consumption to be considered as an industry, but it may seem foolhardy to attempt to study it in prehistoric times since salt, unlike the materials usually studied by archaeologists, only rarely survives even at the sites where it was obtained. Ethnographic evidence, however, suggests that it is possible to recognize both production and trading, and the results of work in Europe (Alexander 1987) make it useful to apply to west Africa the methods evolved in Europe to analyse prehistoric salt production. The questions and problems raised by such investigations are of some importance, for it seems likely that salt (sodium chloride) is one of the essential, but rare, commodities long needed by human communities and therefore a breaker of the barriers of self-sufficiency (Waldecker 1967, p. 9).

Consumption

1   To avoid sodium deficiency, human beings need at least 2 g a day and whilst this can be obtained from meat, blood, milk and urine, communities with largely cereal diets need a supplement. It can also be necessary for domestic animals. On the evidence of the last 1000 years, both in west Africa and Europe (Alexander 1975, p. 81), salt has been widely traded to arable farming communities for these purposes.
2   As is known from west Africa in recent times, fashion and social or religious observances can require particular kinds of salt to be obtained, either as a condiment or for offerings.
3   It is known from both Europe and west Africa that the development of trades in meat or fish, skins and hides may require quantities of salt as a preservative.
4   Salt, divorced from its culinary or industrial use, can be used as easily stored wealth and was often used in west Africa to pay tribute or as general currency (Abir 1970, p. 119; Hopkins 1973, pp. 47, 164).

Many communities do not control the sources of the salt they need because deposits are rare. There has therefore been widespread and large-scale trading in salt.

Production

If there is a demand for large quantities of salt then there will be large-scale production at sources of salt and these can be organized in a variety of ways (Gouletquer 1975, p.

197 for west Africa). The nature of west African salt industries, from extraction to marketing, can be demonstrated and compared to European ones. Mining and quarrying either involve deeply buried salt deposits or surface exposures, both of which leave considerable evidence for archaeologists. Extraction of salt can be carried out from seawater, salty springs, solutions made from salty earths or from salty vegetable ash (Barth 1857–8, p. 206). Evaporation methods either utilize natural (solar) heat or induce evaporation by boiling, involving much burning of fuel and making of containers (Riehm 1961). Both these methods leave archaeological evidence and are still practised in west Africa today.

Mining, if it is carried on at any depth or at any considerable scale, requires skilled specialist workers and an organization to maintain and feed them. Such organized production is also true of large-scale operations carried out under strong political/social control, as at Teghaza in Mauritania (Bovill 1968, p. 25; Skolle 1956, p. 313). Strong central control of a source may be visible in the wealth accumulated by the controllers, as seen in their settlements or cemeteries. But evaporation can, if deposits are easy to work and no special skills are needed, be carried out seasonally on a small scale by village communities or even families, as at Uvinza in Tanzania (Sutton & Roberts 1968, p. 47).

Trading

Whilst trading in salt will be broadly similar to, and often difficult to disentangle from, trade in other much-needed commodities (like iron), it seems likely that around any salt source two zones of salt dependency may be assumed, their shape depending upon neighbouring salt sources and local political entities. Inner zones with $c.$ 100 km radius from the source, can rely on the mechanism of local markets or the collection of salt direct from the source (Birmingham 1970, p. 164). Outer zones with up to a 1000 km radius from the source must rely on supplies by organized long-distance trading caravans with all their special requirements of guides, negotiated transit rights, overnight stopping-places with food and fodder markets (Vansina 1962; Cohen 1971). The 'Azalai' caravan from Bilma to Agades provides a west African example of long-distance trade (Pales 1950, p. 249). Where suitable water routes exist, especially those inland from the seacoasts, canoe transport could be used, as in Dahomey (Rivallain 1980, p. 149).

It is instructive to consider recent work done in western and central Europe before continuing to discuss west Africa. In Europe it is reasonable to assume that no major source of salt remains unknown and there is sufficient excavated evidence to provide a chronological framework for its prehistoric exploitation. A most interesting pattern has emerged (Gouletquer & Kleinmann 1978; Alexander 1982; Alexander 1987). The kinds of salt production reviewed above were all used in Europe in the first millennium BC. Some of the main inland sources in Austria, Germany and France were already being exploited in the third millennium BC (Nenquin 1964) and there was also some coastal exploitation in Britain (Pryor 1980). This continued through the second millennium and increased greatly after 1200 BC when both quarried rock-salt, and saltwater boiling salt, were being produced and three major inland centres can be recognized in central Austria (Salzkammergut), southeastern Germany (Saale basin) and eastern France (Moselle basin). In the Salzkammergut, at Hallstatt, between 1000 and 500 BC, deep mining shafts were dug (where the miner's equipment is preserved), and production was in terms of tons of salt won (Barth 1967, p. 254; Barth 1983), much more than was needed for local consumption. Since the cemeteries near the mines, and contemporary with them, have been extensively excavated and studied, the rich jewellery and fine metalwork from them suggest an 'outer trading zone' of some 500 km radius. Very large-scale production was taking place in the same period about Halle in the Saale basin (Kleinmann 1975; Gouletquer & Kleinmann 1978); here production was by boiling. There was also large-scale production in the Moselle basin with dumps of briquetage up to 17 m thick (Poncelet 1967; Bertaux 1972). In spite of much work on coastal saltworkings, especially in western France, very few have been shown to be earlier than 500 BC and it would seem that little exploitation of sea-water took place. The evidence therefore suggests much inland production over a 500-year period with long-distance trading from the three main centres mentioned above (Fig. 39.1).

After 500 BC the pattern changes dramatically (Fig. 39.2): the inland centres are either abandoned or have very much reduced output whilst the coastal exploitation by boiling develops from Spain to Denmark (e.g. Tessier 1975, pp. 52–6). It would appear that solar evaporation was employed on the Mediterranean coasts all through the millennium (Ponsich & Tarradell 1965). In southern England this has been shown to be seasonal (early summer) work carried out by local communities (Bradley 1975, p. 20). After the first century BC local salt-trading networks have also been identified (Morris 1981, p. 67). The Roman Conquest imposed a different and centralized control on most salt production and trading in western Europe.

For west Africa, it would seem possible (although it has not been attempted there before) to define the prehistoric salt industries, from a combination of evidence from

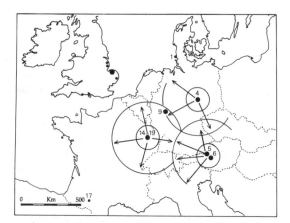

Figure 39.1 Centres of salt production in Europe before 500 BC (suggested trading areas). Numbers taken from Nenquin 1964: 4 Halle–Giebichenstein; 5 Hallein; 6 Hallstatt; 14 & 19 Sielle, Morsal.

the main sources of salt production, the settlements and burial sites of their controlling exploiters, and from long-distance trading routes identified as leading to them (see Connah 1991 for an archaeological study of the salt industry in east Africa).

In west Africa three chronologically distinct phases of salt production and trading can be tentatively suggested: before AD *c.* 400; AD *c.* 400–1800; 1800 – today.

Before AD *c.* 400

The salt industries of this period have not yet been studied but a number of suggestions can already be made. Salt would have been needed by agricultural communities. In the absence of the camel it is likely that the desert sources were not utilized and both savanna and forest zones would have to be supplied by boiling, or, in some parts of the coast and Lake Chad, by solar evaporation. Three sources of salt – salt earths, salty water (inland and sea) and plant ashes – are likely to have been in use. A pattern of supply to both seed and tuber/rhizome cultivators may well have existed southwards from the Manga and Dallol Fogha regions and northwards from the coasts, and over large areas extraction of salt from plant ashes (inefficient as it often is) may have been the main source of supply. Any organized extraction should be archaeologically visible. Trade inland from coastal exploitation would be more difficult to detect unless inland goods prove to be present in coastal cemeteries.

AD *c.* 400–1800

The introduction of the camel and the development of camel/pastoral communities in the Sahel and Sahara made available, probably for the first time, the rich rock-salt deposits of Mauritania and northern Mali (Teghaza, Taoudeni, Erebeb) and southern Algeria (Amadror) and, by evaporation, the salty earths and brines of Niger (Bilma,

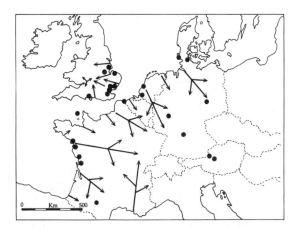

Figure 39.2 Centres of salt production in Europe after 500 BC (suggested trading routes).

Dirkou Djaba and Teggidda-n-Tesemt) (Gouletquer 1975, p. 47; Bernus & Bernus 1972, p. 31). Their exploitation, by the twelfth century (Mauny 1961), had captured much of the salt trade in the northern savannas and continued to dominate it until the eighteenth century. Further south in the savannas Gouletquer (1975) suggests that a different pattern of exploitation by boiling salty earths, especially in the Lake Chad, Manda region (Guigmi, Maine Soroa, Goudomaria and Dallol Fogha), took place. In Cameroon and Upper Volta, plant ashes were widely used instead (Lewicki 1974). Much of this trade was carried on over long distances of up to 1500 km and was controlled in the north by pastoral elites. Coastal salt-making and subsequent trading inland certainly flourished in the sixteenth century, but there is little evidence of long (more than 500 km) distance trading (Daaku 1971). Production seems likely to have been small-scale for local needs in the forest hinterland (Rivallain 1980). A suggested limit is shown in Figure 39.3.

AD 1800 onwards

A major change in salt trading came about with the arrival of cheaply produced salt from Europe (Fig. 39.4). With increasingly mechanized production its price on the west African coast dropped from *c.* £56 a ton in 1817 to £33 a ton in 1850 and to £1 a ton in 1940; as late as 1870, desert (rock) salt was still £100 to £120 a ton in Sokoto. As communications inland from the coast improved (and in 1950 salt was still sold in the interior at ten times its coastal price), the production of salt from the inland sources decreased and became a 'luxury' salt for those who could afford it for social, ritual or medicinal purposes (Newbury 1971). Though reasons for the changes are different from those of first-millennium BC Europe, some startling similarities in the decline of inland production and the rise of coastal trade into the interior can be seen by comparing Figures 39.1 and 39.2 with 39.3 and 39.4. Although no analogies must be drawn from these patterns, for the circumstances which caused them were different,

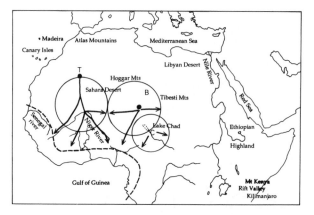

Figure 39.3 Salt production and trading in west Africa AD *c.* 400–1800. The dotted line shows the possible limit of coastal–inland salt trading.   Key: T Teghaza   B Bilma   C Chad.

they offer an instructive and cautionary comment on the interpretation of archaeological evidence.

Discussion

In west Africa the construction, in the nineteenth to twentieth century AD, of railways and roads from the coast inland and the establishment of large new ports, will presumably be noted by future archaeologists, as will the absence of similar means of communication along the east–west axis in the Savanna and Sahel. It is doubtful if this will be attributed to the political decisions of the colonial period unless literary evidence is available. Greatly increased contacts with Europe and the spread of a new religion, Christianity, would presumably be noted. It is more likely that decrease in inland salt production would be seen as part of the general decline in trans-saharan and trans-sahelian trading which took place after the collapse of the slave trade and the Islamic jehads. The collapse of production at the great desert salt sources would certainly be discovered through excavation, in the same way that changes in the first-millennium BC European salt-trading pattern – lacking any literary evidence – can only be inferred from the changes at the salt-making industrial centres. In Europe, as in west Africa, the actual trade in salt is at present archaeologically invisible. The changes in production in Europe seem most likely to have been caused by the large-scale movements of population in the period 600–300 BC in central Europe and the disruption of long-established trading routes and by changes in sea-levels, but this is very difficult to prove archaeologically and no attempt has yet been made to confirm it.

Whether there was a nostalgic longing for the taste of Hallstatt salt in central Europe as there still is for Saharan salt in the west African Sahel is, alas, unknown.

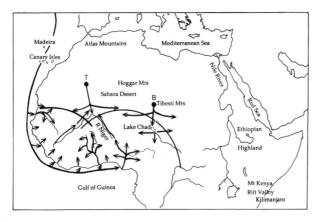

Figure 39.4   Suggested pattern of the salt trade in west Africa after AD 1800.
Key: T Teghaza;   B Bilma.

40　　Trade and politics on the eastern littoral of Africa, AD 800–1300

H. T. WRIGHT

Anthropologists seeking to understand the development of civilizations have focused on the earliest complex societies. These arose in arid river valleys and basins in both the Old World and the New with the emergence of progressively larger and more nucleated regional systems. The hierarchical societies which developed outside – and often in interaction with – these established centres have been attributed to entrepreneurs, missionaries, conquerors or undefined influences from the centres. Some researchers have proposed explanations of such developments using the same variables called upon to explain the primary examples: changes in population, subsistence, exchange, warfare or ideology. Such secondary or tertiary developments are deserving of more careful consideration, for any general explanation of the development of complex cultural systems should subsume cases arising under many different conditions. Perhaps the most striking contrasts with the nucleated primary civilizations are the dispersed archipelagic civilizations whose elements – scattered on islands in the world's seas or on oases in its deserts – are some of the smallest known hierarchical polities. The early polities of the southwestern Indian Ocean are an interesting nexus to consider, not simply because they are increasingly well understood, but because they are often explained solely in terms of the stimulus of outside entrepreneurs or missionaries. Let us consider, within the limits of presently available data, a wide range of both local and external factors which could have affected the development of these Indian Ocean polities.

My assumptions in this chapter are that both the local face-to-face communities, as well as the higher order regional and transregional networks, can be viewed as cultural phenomena in which both material and social relations are mediated by symbolic structures, and that these symbolic structures are altered by reassessments of material success and failure and by social experience. We can evaluate our propositions derived from systemic constructs about past phenomena based upon such assumptions with the material debris of past communities.

In recent history, the communities of the east coast of Africa, the nearby islands and the coasts of Madagascar have been closely related. Goods and people moved freely between the widespread towns, where Swahili and related languages were spoken. These languages are a group within the Bantu language family, perhaps originating from a common ancestor on the north coast of present-day Kenya (Nurse 1983), with many loan-words from Arabic, Persian and other languages. Both in the interior of eastern Africa, where related Bantu languages were spoken, and in Madagascar, where Malagasy (the closest relatives of which are found in Indonesia) was spoken, there were communities commercially related to the towns where Swahili-related languages predominated. In these towns, whereas women owned the homes and sometimes the gardens which they or their slaves worked, men owned craft and nautical technology and controlled much of the commercial and political life. Social relations, particularly those among men, were ordered by the tenets of Sunni Islam and its institutional contexts: mosque, class, descent group and Sufi brotherhood. Indeed, all political action was closely conditioned by the spatial prescriptions, accumulations of wealth and legal responsibilities mandated by Islam, such that politics and religion cannot be considered separately. One can reasonably ask whether the development of hierarchical polities in the southwestern Indian Ocean was a result of the establishment of settlements by Moslem traders seeking wealth or Islamic missionaries seeking converts. In short, were these principalities the simple result of colonization by Near Eastern seafarers?

Only in the past few years has it been possible to answer questions about the earlier phases of this maritime civilization, those dating between AD 800 and 1400. This is a result not of new documents supplementing our few written sources, but rather the growth of archaeology. Since the 1970s major works on key medieval towns in Kenya and Tanzania have been published (Chittick 1974; Chittick 1984; Horton 1984; Horton & Mudida, Ch. 41, this volume) and intensive archaeological research has begun in Mozambique (Morais 1984; Sinclair 1987) and the Comoro islands (Kus & Wright 1976; Chanudet & Vérin 1983).

Regrettably, archaeology has not yet contributed greatly to our knowledge of these centuries prior to AD 800. Though we know that peoples of the early Iron Age were near the coast around AD 200 (Soper 1967) and we have reason to expect that Roman and Sassanid traders would have visited the area – indeed there is documentation of the former visiting a port somewhere on the coast (Datoo 1970; Casson 1989) – material evidence is scanty. Similarly, although it is likely that the first Malagasy settled on Madagascar and perhaps the African coast during this time, archaeological evidence is lacking (Shepherd 1982; Vérin 1986). It is possible that earlier sites are located in completely different places from those later sites with visible architecture which have been the object of most archaeologists' investigations. Also, it may be that the sites are known, but that the earlier material is not yet recognizable. This ignorance, however, is not crippling, since it is likely that prosperity came to the coastal settlements only periodically before AD 800, as after. We must understand each period of prosperity – with its own distinctive social patterns, local production, long-range trade opportunities, means of navigation and consequent strategies of settlement location – in its own terms.

The ninth and tenth centuries

Evidence of communities during this period is now widely available. The recognition of such material at Kilwa, off the coast of Tanzania, by Chittick (1966b, pp. 5–10) was followed by reports of contemporary material from Unguja Ukuu on Zanzibar (Chittick 1966a), from Irodo on northeastern Madagascar (Battistini & Vérin 1966) and Manda on the north Kenya coast (Chittick 1967). More recently, related sites have been reported from southern Mozambique (Sinclair 1982) and the Comoros (Chanudet & Vérin 1983; Wright 1984; Wright 1986). All of these communities except those on Madagascar share a common ceramic tradition. Pottery from sites on the southern coast of Mozambique is very similar in form and surface decoration to that on the Lamu archipelago (Wilding 1977b), 2200 km of difficult sailing away. The common elements in this tradition are, first, a range of ring-built restricted jars or pots with scraped or lightly burnished surfaces and often with zigzag or triangular incised motifs, and second, ring-based bowls with in-turned rims often with red-slipped, burnished surfaces often with silvery graphite decorations. Contemporary Madagascan ceramics contrast in having a preponderance of spherical, neckless jars with impressions and wavy combing made with a shell. Thus far, the combed decoration is common only on Madagascar. The Madagascan sites, however, do have a variant of the red-slipped bowls found throughout the southwestern Indian Ocean. It is tempting to interpret the vast sphere of ceramic communality along the east African coast as an indication of ethnic communality, perhaps the first dispersion of Swahili-speaking peoples, but either the exchange of objects or the voyaging of craftsmen, both widely known in the region, could create this pattern of homogeneity. These alternative possibilities must be tested with technical studies of diverse samples of ceramics. It is further tempting to interpret the contrasting tradition on Madagascar as a stylistic manifestation of early Malagasy colonists, though in the absence of published contemporary material from Indonesia there is no way to evaluate such a proposal.

Most of the communities occupied during these centuries were small (Fig. 40.1). Chibuene in the far south was a seaside community covering at least 1 ha, with indications of fishing and sheep- and cattle-herding. Iron slag indicates local iron production (Sinclair 1982, pp. 152, 162; Sinclair, Morais, Adamowicz & Duarte, Ch. 24, this volume).

Far to the north, on a small island off the Tanzanian coast, was the village of Kilwa Ia (Chittick 1974, pp. 27–60). This community of rectangular post-houses with wattle-and-daub walls (Chittick 1974, p. 31) covered at least 1 ha. Shellfish-collecting and fishing were important (Chittick 1974, pp. 28, 36). Agriculture is not directly attested, but it is likely that the sorghum found in Kilwa Ib layers (Chittick 1974, p. 52) was already available. The production of iron (Chittick 1974, pp. 28, 37) and grinding of shell beads (Chittick 1974, pp. 28, 33, 38) were widespread in the village.

A day's sail to the east, on the Comoro archipelago, villages of the local 'Dembeni Phase' (Fig. 40.2) vary from small hamlets of less than ½ ha up to large villages of 5 ha (Wright 1984c). There is evidence of both reef and lagoon netting, spearing and angling of fish (Scott 1984), the exploitation of turtle and goats (Redding & Goodman 1984) and – thanks to the use of water flotation techniques – the cultivation of much rice, some millet, coconuts, a bean and a possible citrus fruit (Hoffman 1984). Mud-plastered pole-and-bamboo houses, probably rectangular, occurred in most villages. Local crafts, at least in the larger villages, include pottery and iron production. Further to the north of Kilwa, on the south end of Zanzibar, is the settlement at Unguja Ukuu (Chittick 1966a;

Clark & Horton 1985, pp. 11–12, 34, Fig. 19). This began, perhaps as early as the eighth century, as a village of perhaps 2 ha, but grew to cover about 10 ha during the ninth or tenth century; there is evidence of iron production and bead manufacture, but little evidence of substantial architecture. Smaller settlements are known on the north end of the island of Zanzibar at Mkokotoni (Clark & Horton 1985, p. 10) and opposite on the mainland at Mkadini (Chittick 1966a), but survey is yet insufficient to indicate whether there was simply a range of settlement sizes, as on the Comoros, or whether, in contrast, Unguja Ukuu was emerging as the major centre in the area, as Manda was to the north (see below).

Though the communities on the northern coasts of Madagascar have a different ceramic repertoire from these other communities, they were broadly similar in scale

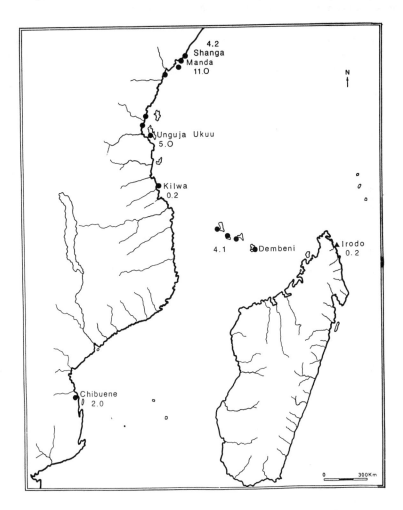

Figure 40.1 Distribution of ninth- to tenth-century coastal settlement showing the relative importance of imported wares.

and economy (Battistini & Vérin 1966; Wright 1986). For example, the village sites at Irodo – three on the beach and one on the estuary, each of which grew to cover about 1.5 ha by the time the settlement cluster reached its final form – were composed of 13 to 18 discrete shell concentrations, perhaps indicating organization into households or small neighbourhoods. The house form, however, remains unknown. Shellfish-collecting and fishing were evidently important at Irodo, but plant use is undocumented. One local craft widely in evidence was the working of chlorite-schist, primarily to create perforated discs probably used locally as net weights, but also to form vessels of the types exported to the African coast. Widespread survey efforts on the coasts of Madagascar revealed other sites including camp sites in rock shelters (Dewar 1987). However, on Madagascar, as on the Comoros and along the coast of Tanzania, the density of communities appears to have been very low.

This low density of villages contrasts with the pattern of settlement clusters found to the north. The south Kenya coast has little evidence of ninth–tenth-century use in spite of much survey effort (Wilson 1982). On the north Kenya coast, a number of smaller coastal sites, probably once villages such as those discussed above, surround the sites of

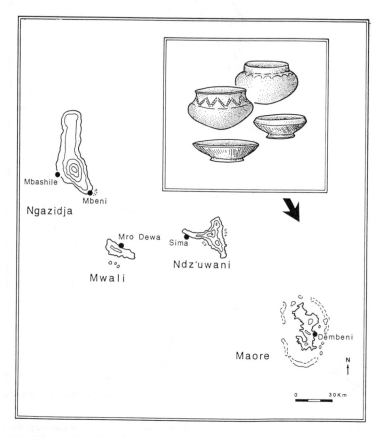

Figure 40.2   Distribution of some Dembeni-phase sites on the Comoro islands.

larger centres. The settlement of Manda has been the object of an extensive excavation programme (Chittick 1967; Chittick 1984), as has nearby Shanga (Horton 1984). The former covered at least 3.8 ha during the ninth century (Chittick 1984, pp. 7–9, Fig. 3), and exceeded 7 ha by the late tenth century. It had both wattle-and-daub construction and houses with walls of both coral rubble and baked brick (Chittick 1984, pp. 39–41). Water-screened samples indicate that fish and shellfish were major protein sources (Chittick 1984, p. 221), but sheep, goat and cows were important. Camel, cat and sea turtle occur as well (Chittick 1984, p. 215). The debris of iron-working and bead manufacture is also notable. During the same period, Shanga, some 15 km northeast of Manda across a sound, covered about 1.5 ha and had round wattle-and-daub-covered structures in one area and rectangular ones in another, the latter replaced with walls of coral set in mud during the tenth century (Horton 1984, pp. 215–26). The earliest layers have not yielded many faunal remains, but fish and domestic chicken become important during the ninth century and sheep or goat appear during the tenth (Horton 1984, pp. 231–9). Plant remains are not yet reported. Evidence of iron production, as well as beads and bead grinders, was recovered (Horton 1984, pp. 253–62). Other sites of the period were probably small villages, in contrast to more substantial settlements such as Manda and Shanga. Thus the available evidence shows that even early in the period under consideration, some communities had architectural differences indicating social differences, and that by the end of the period the central community – as we shall soon see, the one with much greater overseas trade involvement – had become much larger than any of its neighbours.

What can be said about the ideological and political organization of these communities? Had any of these communities yet accepted Islam? The evidence is limited. The one reported Chibuene burial appears to have been oriented correctly for Islamic funerary ritual (Sinclair 1987, p. 89). However, on the Comorian archipelago, there is evidence that the inhabitants of at least the island nearest Africa – Ngazidja or Grand Comore – had not yet accepted Islam. Salvage excavations by the author in 1986 at the small beachside village of Mbeni produced two burials with their heads to the southeast and lying on their backs, in contrast to the normal Islamic disposition of head to the east and body on the right side, facing Mecca. The one essentially intact individual exhibits physical details characteristic of east Africans today, and had his incisors removed in youth, a ritual practice widespread in east Africa today, and one not known among Moslems (Boulinier, pers. comm.). Note, however, that even if some Comorian communities were of African origin and were not Moslem, yet others might have come from elsewhere and might have already accepted Islam. From Kilwa the evidence is less clear. The one burial of Period Ia was disturbed, though its pit seems to have been oriented north–south, suggesting it was not Islamic (Chittick 1974, p. 36). Also, two pig tusks were recovered, although the occurrence of tusks alone does not indicate that pork was consumed (Chittick 1974, p. 51). On the other hand, a stone with an inscription in Arabic letters was recovered, suggesting that someone at Kilwa was literate in Arabic (Chittick 1974, pp. 131, 262). Unfortunately, no one has succeeded in reading the inscription. There is no evidence from Manda during these centuries that is relevant to the question of ideology. The particular loci and strata that should contain the remains of mosques have not yet been investigated. From Shanga, however, there is evidence that a small mosque was constructed before the tenth century (Horton 1987b). For areas to the south, also relevant to this issue, is the remarkable pattern, discussed below, in which many of the early mosques investigated to date seem to have been founded during the eleventh or twelfth centuries AD. No doubt there were Moslem families resident in the various earlier communities, as implied by al-Mas⁽ʿ⁾udi's description of his visit to the yet unlocated port of Kanbalu in the tenth century (Pellat 1962, pp. 84, 93–4). However, there is no evidence yet of congregations, of communities of the faithful, which were central to the villages and towns of recent centuries.

Given the small size of the communities discussed above, their relative isolation, their lack of substantial residences and the lack of Islamic institutions except perhaps in the far north, it is likely that they had an elementary political organization, perhaps involving no more than individuals of locally achieved status.

What is the evidence for a network of trade and exchange among the communities of the southwestern Indian Ocean during the ninth–tenth centuries AD? It is surprisingly rich. Export is probably indicated by the production in excess of local commodities. While iron tools, ceramics and shell beads could be locally consumed or exchanged, some of the chlorito–schist items from Irodo, the turtle products from Sima on Ndzuwani (Wright 1984, p. 51) and the ivory items like those found in Kilwa (Chittick 1974, pp. 434–5) could have been intended for long-range exchange. Indeed, al-Mas⁽ʿ⁾udi mentions the latter two commodities in his account (Pellat 1965, p. 321). In contrast to such exports, imports are easy to document archaeologically. Small bowls – typically white-glazed bowls sometimes with splashes of blue, green or lustre glaze (Chittick 1984, pp. 77–8) from the Near East, and, rarely, white porcelain bowls from China (Chittick 1984, pp. 66–7) – were probably sought as prestigious display pottery. Large jars, plain or green-glazed (the so-called 'Sassanian Islamic' ware) (Chittick 1984, pp. 71–6), perhaps contained valuable liquids such as oils or syrups. The tiny glass vials or beakers are thought to have contained ointments or perfumes (Chittick 1984, pp. 159–79). Fine metalwork was also imported (Chittick 1984, pp. 203–7). Other commodities such as cloth must have been important, but the sole archaeological evidence of such items is the rarity of spindle whorls on these sites in contrast to later periods (Chittick 1984, p. 218).

We can use quantities of imported ceramics as a proxy for imports in general, using an 'imported sherd ratio'. This ratio is defined as the number of imported sherds per 100 local sherds. It assumes that the discard of local jar and bowl fragments by domestic units was roughly constant in time and space in the region under discussion. This seems reasonable, since ceramic technology, ceramic form and food preparation habits changed very little throughout the region. On the first map (Fig. 40.1) one notes that there is not a simple decrease in the imported sherd ratio as one moves further to the south away from the Near Eastern sources of the imports. Manda on the far north does have a special position in the network. A ninth-century deposit on the beach, where ships' cargoes would have been unloaded and repacked, and broken pieces would have been discarded, has an imported sherd ratio of 38 (Chittick 1984, p. 221). In domestic refuse within the settlement, a context more comparable to those from more southerly sites (see below), this ratio is 11 (Chittick 1984, p. 233), still a remarkably high ratio of imported pieces to local pieces. By the end of the tenth century Manda's position as a 'break-in-bulk' point was further strengthened by the construction of the first of its 'sea-walls', massive footings for masonry buildings, perhaps factors' compounds. In contrast to Manda, other sites in the area have smaller ratios of imported ceramics (see Fig. 40.1). The nearby settlement of Shanga has a ratio of about 4.2 (Horton 1984, p. 310, Fig. 75). Further south, the large village of Unguja Ukuu has a ratio of about 5.0 (Clark & Horton 1985, p. 34), while nearby and smaller Kilwa Kisiwani has a ratio of only 0.2 (Chittick 1974, p. 302). The Comorian villages (Wright 1984, p. 26) have ratios averaging 4.1 and Chibuene in the far south (Sinclair 1982, pp. 152–9) has a ratio of about 2.0. It is possible that the differences result from sampling vagaries, but they seem more likely to have resulted from disparities in the local supplies of possible exports; for example, perhaps the turtles of the Comoros, the pearls of Zanzibar and the elephants of southern Mozambique gave local communities a trading advantage, while the beads made at Kilwa – similar to those from the other coastal communities – endowed no such advantage.

In sum, during the ninth and tenth centuries small local communities throughout the southwestern Indian Ocean were self-sufficient as a result of diverse local domestic and collected food sources and of their own capacity to make tools of iron and doubtless other materials. They had contacts with traders seeking exotic materials, offering craft products from the Near East and even China. Such craft products were probably used in social display, and would not have undermined the productive self-sufficiency of the villagers. There is no evidence that this trade was mediated by hierarchical political organizations or that it resulted in any pervasive acceptance of Islam.

The eleventh to thirteenth centuries

These three centuries saw fundamental changes in the ideological basis of society and the organization of human communities. While little is known of the coasts of Mozambique to the south during this time, much can be said about other parts of the African coast, the Comoros, and Madagascar. As far as we can tell, the basic subsistence economies did not change greatly. The same patterns of fishing and cultivation continued. Our few faunal samples indicate that cattle and the domestic chicken became more common, but no major changes are evident. Likewise, the local crafts of iron-working and pottery production changed little, though the pottery styles diverged slightly, with each component in the regional network decorating its jars and pots in locally distinctive ways. It might be supposed that the organization of production could have changed, even though the products were similar. However, the techniques of fishing, gardening, iron-working and potting indicated by the evidence are not amenable to intensification. Indeed, the techniques still in use today seem to be the same as those used during the tenth century. The herding of cows, the one form of production easily intensified, remained a minor element in the subsistence repertoires of the region until at least the fourteenth century.

Hierarchical settlement patterns become widespread (Fig. 40.3). To the north, Manda grew to cover at least 10 ha. Its 'sea-walls' were greatly expanded during the eleventh and twelfth centuries (Chittick 1984, pp. 19–35). Substantial masonry houses covered the western half of the site close to the port (Chittick 1984, pp. 35–51), while insubstantial rubble-footed housing seems to have occupied the eastern half (Chittick 1984, p. 53). Nearby Shanga also grew, though it probably did not reach its full extent of five occupied hectares until the thirteenth century when Manda had already diminished. Houses of coral and mud construction become widespread in the small town (Horton 1984, pp. 221–6). In contrast, there were a number of small villages without evident substantial architecture (Wilson 1982; Horton 1984, pp. 375–410). Down the coast to the south, many communities were founded or expanded greatly. Ungwana-on-the-Tana (Kirkman 1966, pp. 17–20, 55) became substantial; smaller communities were established at Gedi (Kirkman 1954, pp. 14–15, 23–58) and Mombasa (Sassoon 1980). On Zanzibar, Jongwe grew to cover 25 ha, with large houses of coral and mud

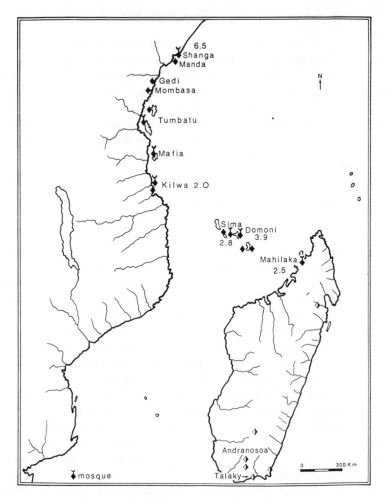

Figure 40.3 Distribution of eleventh- to thirteenth-century coastal settlements showing the relative importance of imported wares.

construction concentrated at its northeast end; small towns of 10 to 15 ha existed at Mkokotoni and at Ras Mkumbu and Mtamwe Mkuu on nearby Pemba (Clark & Horton 1985, pp. 8–10, 25–31). Kilwa expanded to cover about 30 ha during the eleventh century with mud-constructed buildings throughout the settlement, though in the centre of the settlement some buildings had coral block footings. By the thirteenth century some of these had substantial coral block masonry walls. Not surprisingly, large lime kilns are attested during this later period. Only 12 km to the south of Kilwa on another island was the smaller twelfth- to thirteenth-century town of Sanje ya Kati (Chittick 1966b, pp. 29–30). Not far to the north of Kilwa, Kisimani Mafia was founded (Chittick 1961). The kind of archaeological survey which might document contemporary smaller village sites on the islands of Pemba, Zanzibar, Mafia and Kilwa and on the nearby mainland is only just beginning.

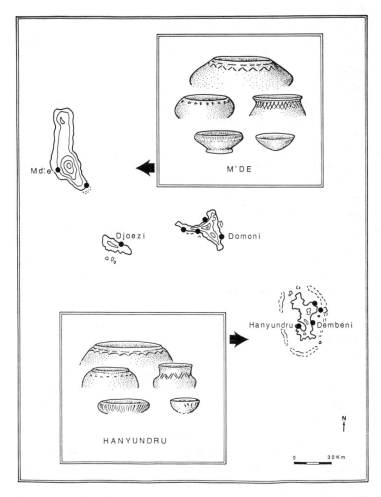

Figure 40.4 Occurrence of eleventh- to thirteenth-century ceramics of the M'de and Hanyundru phases.

On the Comorian archipelago (Fig. 40.4), the largest known centre of this period, Dembeni on Maore (Mayotte), reached its height during the eleventh or twelfth century, covering more than 14 ha and with indications of a surrounding wall on one side. Excavations have not yet been undertaken on the post-tenth-century remains on the site, but dressed stone blocks indicate that substantial buildings with stone footings were widespread. Contemporary with the expansion of Dembeni were three larger villages from 1.5 to 3 ha in an area on the coasts between 5 and 12 km to the north and west. Also, there were a large number of small hamlets of a hectare or less, some on the coast and some on the higher central ridges of the island, indicating that dry rice cultivators had cut deeply into the island's forests. That two coastal villages of the twelfth to thirteenth centuries are partly covered by layers of alluvium indicates that erosion was becoming a severe problem (Wright 1986). On the island of Ndzuwani (Anjouan), there were two towns on opposite sides of the island. Sima grew to cover about 8 ha and Domoni, though obscured by the still living town, must have been of similar or even greater size (Wright n.d.). On tiny Mwali (Moheli) was another town also of similar magnitude (Chanudet & Vérin 1983). Smaller village and hamlet sites are known on both islands. In contrast, on the large and still volcanically active island of Ngazidja (Grand Comore), only a few village and hamlet sites are known. It is possible that major towns, perhaps hidden by lava flows, remain to be discovered. It is also possible that, in the absence of a developed cistern technology, large populations could not be maintained on an island with few permanent water sources.

Very similar settlements existed on the northeast coast of Madagascar in the Bay of Ampasindava during the twelfth to fourteenth centuries. The town of Mahilaka (Vérin 1975, pp. 594–644) had a walled area of more than 60 ha, within which were a few stone wall structures scattered among many impermanent structures (C. Radimilahay, *pers. comm.*). The earlier ceramic traditions continued, and there is evidence of both iron-smelting and chlorite schist-working throughout the walled area. Late in this period a trapezoidal fortified residential compound enclosing 3.8 ha was built in the centre of the town (Vérin 1975, p. 626). Recent archaeological survey around Mahilaka by Radimilahy and the author recorded a number of contemporary settlement sites, all less than a hectare in size, both on the shore and islands of the bay and on high inland ridges. Elsewhere along the northern coasts are villages with ceramics similar to those of Mahilaka. Further south on Madagascar were communities participating in a different ceramic tradition emphasizing heavy basins with lugs and smaller red-slipped bowls. On the forested east coast, a few village sites have been found on estuary and river banks, but none have been investigated in detail. In the arid thorn forests of the south, however, several large villages and camp sites have been studied. Cattle and sheep/goat-herding and the hunting of tenrecs, a primitive insectivore, are documented (Rasamuel 1984), but no evidence of cultivation has been found. At one of these communities, the site of Andranosoa, multiple embankments partially defined an area of 30 ha, within which were concentrations of mud-covered impermanent housing (Radimilahy 1980). Most evidence of cattle use, iron-working and the discard of imported ceramics are in the south end of the site, suggesting socio-economic differences within this community. As will be discussed below, even these herders on the distant margins of the eleventh- to thirteenth-century world participated in the exchange network which spanned the Indian Ocean.

In sum, communities proliferated and population must have increased during the eleventh to thirteenth centuries. On the well-surveyed Comoros, there was a fourfold increase in the total area covered by settlements. On the relatively well-known Kenya coast a similar increase was achieved as a result of the spread of settlement to previously little-inhabited stretches of the coast. In all studied areas, towns – distinguished by contrasting substantial and impermanent architecture and sizes of 10 ha or greater – emerge as the dominant element in local settlement hierarchies.

The evidence of the widespread adoption of Islam during these centuries is consistent and compelling. By the twelfth century, if not before, Shanga (Horton 1984, pp. 113–21, 203–6; Horton 1987b), Kisimkazi (Chittick 1960), Kilwa (Chittick 1974, pp. 59–99) and Domoni and Sima on Ndzuwani in the Comoros (Knudstad n.d.) had small, well-built masonry mosques raised on high foundations. By the thirteenth century, the settlements of Ras Mkumbu on Pemba near Zanzibar (Kirkman 1959, p. 168, Figs 2, 3), Sanje ya Kati near Kilwa (Chittick 1966b, p. 30) and Hanyundru on Maore (Wright 1986) had small mosques, and a mosque was built at the larger town of Mahilaka on Madagascar (Vérin 1975, pp. 627–35). These mosques were small, ranging in interior size from 9.5 by 5.8 m at Sima to 14.0 by 7.5 m at Shanga. Most exhibit the distinctive long *qibla* axis and several have the central row of columns blocking a view of the mihrab later common in the region, but the deep mihrabs which have characterized the region's mosques to the present day, as well as panelled and corded decoration in cut coral, are not definitely attested earlier than the late twelfth- or thirteenth-century example at Shanga (Horton 1984, pp. 118–19, Fig. 28). By the twelfth and thirteenth centuries, cemeteries with Islamic modes of interment appeared at Shanga (Horton 1984, pp. 124–34), Kilwa (Chittick 1974, pp. 225–7), Domoni (Wright n.d.), Hanyundru (Wright 1986) and Bagamoyo, a village site on the island of Pamanze off the coast of Maore (Allibert, Argant & Argant 1983). Though the precise relation between town expansion and Islamic institutions is nowhere certain, several points are notable. First, Islamic institutions appeared at about the same time in larger communities throughout, a reach of about 1500 km. The date of Islamization is not correlated with increasing distance from the centres of Islam to the north. Second, there is no evidence of Islam in the interiors of either east Africa or Madagascar. Indeed, Islam was not widely accepted there before the nineteenth century and the impact of modern colonialism, even in areas of close commercial relations with Moslem traders. In the medieval period, Islamic institutions were accepted first in larger communities and only on the coasts.

This archaeologically derived construct both confirms and is amplified by the traditional histories of the towns, recorded variously between the sixteenth and the nineteenth centuries. For example, such sources report local dynasts bearing Moslem names at Pate near Shanga (Werner 1914/15), at Kilwa (Freeman-Grenville 1962, pp. 220–6) and at Domoni (Ottenheimer 1985, pp. 8–10, 21–4). The Kilwa dynasty is dated to before the thirteenth century by stratified occurrences of the coins of its rulers (Chittick 1974, pp. 269–301; Horton 1987b). In all three cases, these nobles' families were said to have come from prestigious centres to the north, but one must remember that aristocrats always emphasize such claims, even when their origins are hardly exotic. In all three traditions, these towns fought with nearby communities, defeats leading to destruction and abandonment, but rarely to clear domination of one town by another.

The settlement hierarchies evident in the archaeological record would thus seem to have manifested social and economic relations rather than effective political dominance. In spite of Islamic institutions and dynastic titles, these societies were ephemeral states at best.

What is the evidence of exchange among these widespread communities? All could have been locally self-sufficient in grain, coconuts, domestic animals and fish, though larger towns on small and no doubt over-cultivated islands such as Manda and Kilwa may have been forced to import some food. The receipt of imports – the same high-quality Chinese porcelains and stonewares and Near Eastern sgraffito bowls received by the wealthy towns – by southern Madagascar herders whose only surplus would have been animal products also suggests that such items were exchanged. The exports mentioned from the ninth to tenth centuries – ivory, turtle scutes, chlorite schist and other rare minerals – continued to be important, and by the fourteenth century Ibn Battuta mentions that gold was important in the trade of Kilwa (Freeman-Grenville 1962, pp. 27–32). Gold-working is archaeologically known from Zimbabwe (Summers 1969), but present evidence indicates a date no earlier than the thirteenth century (Phillipson 1977a, pp. 180–94). Slaves are not mentioned as a major commodity and it is possible that the supplying of 'Zanj' slaves to Iraq, known from the seventh century (Popovic 1976, pp. 56–60), either drew its supply from further north or had diminished. In return for such exports as these, ceramics, glass vessels and glass beads, fine metalwork, and perhaps cloth, oils and spices were imported, almost all from the Near East rather than the Far East. Ceramics are more evident in the archaeological record, but it is more difficult to assemble valid statistics on the proportions of imported to local ceramics for this period than it was for the preceding period. Those few imported sherd ratios that have been estimated range between 2.0 and 7.0, little different from comparable ratios for the prosperous communities of the ninth and tenth centuries. If future research sustains this pattern, the quantity of these goods consumed by families in each town, and thus any local opportunities and problems created by the trade, would not have increased greatly. Note, however, that there was nearly a four-fold increase in known settlement area, and thus population, in the surveyed areas on both the African coast and the Comoros. The seeming stability in imported pottery consumption must therefore indicate a comparable increase in the absolute amount of ceramics imported, and a similar increase in the number of voyages. This might well present more opportunities for piracy and, as a result, increase the number of political problems in the relations between the different towns.

Conclusion

Before the ninth century AD, African seafaring peoples had spread throughout the east coast of Africa and the Comoro islands; Indonesian seafarers had probably already reached Madagascar, if not Africa, by this time. A way of life sustained principally by rice, millet, coconuts, goats and fishing arose. During the ninth and tenth centuries AD, about the second and third centuries after the Hegira, the relatively small and isolated communities of the eastern littoral of Africa and the southwestern Indian Ocean were bound together by exchange networks involving people, local craft goods and materials, and imported goods from the Near and Far East. Though they must have been familiar with Moslem seafarers, only at the end of this period did a few of these communities, those on the north end of the Kenya coast, make Islam the central focus of town life. During the eleventh and twelfth centuries AD, about the fourth and fifth centuries AH, large towns grew up throughout the region, though there is no parallel increase in the participation of towns in trade. Small masonry mosques were built in the centres of many of these towns; by the thirteenth century, even small towns and villages are known to have had central mosques.

It remains to be considered whether the available evidence of the changing long-distance trade, the growth of towns and the development of Islam contradicts or sustains any of the possible explanations for the rise of hierarchically organized societies in the southwestern Indian Ocean.

Could participation in long-distance trade have encouraged the promotion of local elites seeking display goods and organizing local populations to produce surpluses for exchange? Most local communities participated in the exchange network for several centuries without any indications of increase in size or hierarchical complexity. The sole exceptions are Manda and Shanga on the Lamu archipelago, where this sort of process might have operated. The subsequent appearance of larger towns and central mosques in other areas does not correlate with indications of change in the exchange system. In short, however much long-range trade was a resource for coastal peoples, neither the inception of, nor changes in the magnitude of, this trade were a general impetus to the rise of hierarchy.

Could the arrival of Moslem dynasts or teachers, fleeing from the disturbed heartlands of the Near East with their followers, have introduced statecraft into the village societies of the Indian Ocean littoral? This is an idea manifest in the historical traditions of many of these towns. It cannot be conclusively evaluated without more precise knowledge of early mosques and palaces, but it is notable that mosques seem to appear in the larger communities at about the same time. One would expect colonizing princes and saints to establish themselves first in a few places, probably those closer to the centres of Islam. A simultaneous development would suggest that town growth and the adoption of Islamic institutions result from some process at work in the community network as a whole, rather than from exogenous factors.

Future research should concentrate on explanations for the phenomena under discussion in the processes which Renfrew has termed 'peer polity interaction' with specific reference to the bronze age Aegean (Renfrew & Cherry 1986), somewhat similar to processes proposed for southeast Asia by Wheatley (1975). The long-term growth of village societies along the littoral – initiated by a synthesis of African and southeast Asian maritime and agricultural technologies – would have been facilitated by growth in exchange relations with traders offering exotic manufactures in exchange for local materials of value to distant urban consumers. Display and redistribution of exotic goods would reinforce elite status, but as some communities prospered and others did not, instability and conflict would increase. Though individuals may have accepted Islam earlier in order to relate to Moslem traders, Islamic institutions would have been made central in community life only in order to stabilize relations among the emerging elites of the larger communities, and subsequently extended to bind villages and smaller centres more closely to the emerging towns. In the conflicts inherent in such extensions of control, refugees from elsewhere, providing active assistance as well as legitimacy, might well have been welcomed. Evaluation of such a broad proposal will require intensive archaeological survey in areas yet little known, and the application of precise techniques of excavation, absolute dating and economic and social analysis to a sample of settlements of the ninth to thirteenth centuries. However, it is not only more comprehensive coverage and more precise techniques that are needed. The proposals discussed above demand a rethinking of assumptions about explanation in history. Simply to specify key material or social changes thought to initiate cultural development is not enough. We need constructs about interaction between material and symbolic changes at local, regional and transregional levels of systemic organization in order to specify how such initial changes are manifested in actual development.

41 Exploitation of marine resources: evidence for the origin of the Swahili communities of east Africa

MARK HORTON & NINA MUDIDA

Introduction

The ethnic and economic origins of the Swahili towns are subjects of continuing controversy. The model of Asiatic colonization has been largely rejected by historians and archaeologists (Horton 1984; Nurse & Spear 1985; Horton 1987a; Pouwels 1987) but the identification of the particular African group that was involved has not been satisfactorily concluded (and see Wright, Ch. 40, this volume). For such identification two classes of archaeological evidence are particularly useful: pottery and faunal assemblages. The pottery of the early Swahili communities (called Tana tradition) can be compared to early and pre-iron age forms from the interior and general affinities suggested. Pottery can however be traded and indeed made by specialist groups that may not be entirely representative of the society as a whole.

More reliable inference may be drawn from faunal evidence. From stratified sequences, it is clearly possible to deduce the economic basis of the early Swahili communities, whether they were living off fish, marine mammals, hunted or domestic animals. The basic premise of such an analysis is one of dietary conservatism: that non-fish eaters will continue to shun fish, except in times of great food shortages. There is well-known ethnographic support for this in the Lamu archipelago (Fig. 41.1), where ex-pastoralists, such as the wa-Katwa clan, despite living adjacent to the rich fishing grounds in east Africa, still refuse to eat fish after at least 200 years of settlement on the islands.

There are at present two broad models for the 'African' origins of the Swahili. The first, promoted by Nurse and Spear (1985, p. 50), favours a Bantu-speaking agriculturalist origin from the Tana basin. These village communities – directly related to the early iron age settlers from the interlacustrine area and the Kwale hills – settled the coastline around AD 500. As riverine dwellers, they were able to expand their techniques to reef fishing with relative ease. The principal evidence for their existence is linguistic, with broad similarities between Proto-Swahili and other languages in the Sabaki cluster of the northeast coastal Bantu. Reconstructed Proto-Swahili contains a vocabulary that includes several words associated with sea-fishing, including traps, baskets, nets, lines, as well as whales and turtles (Nurse & Spear 1985, p. 107).

An alternative view suggests a pastoralist origin. This model has been developed by Allen (1983; 1984), who believed that the Swahili developed from a multi-ethnic society, dominated by a Segeju pastoralist elite, who operated an early state on the mainland opposite the Lamu archipelago. This state is remembered in the Shungwaya origin traditions (shared by many of the coastal societies). It operated long-distance trade networks into the interior and controlled island ports for the development of international trade. While pastoralists were not the only group in this Shungwaya complex, they were economically the dominant group. In Allen's model it would be surprising to find substantial evidence for the exploitation of marine resources on the early Swahili sites, at least in the Lamu archipelago.

The historical evidence covering the period is ambiguous. Mas'udi saw cattle used as beasts of burden by the Zanj as well as being ridden in war, but does not specify where. Camels were absent, however. But Mas'udi also refers to whaling and other forms of fishing (Freeman-Grenville 1962, p. 14). A ninth-century Chinese source described Bobali, probably on the Somali or north Kenyan coast, where the inhabitants 'stick a needle into the veins of cattle and draw blood, which they drink raw mixed with milk' (Duyvendak 1949, p. 13). A twelfth-century description of Zhongli also identifies a pastoral component where cattle and sheep were plentiful and consumed on special occasions. Small birds were caught with nets and their taste was delicious (Duyvendak 1949, p. 21). In Bibalo there were sheep and the inhabitants lived off the flesh and milk of camels while in Zengba camels were not noted and the meat was mutton (Hirth & Rockhill 1911, pp. 126, 128). Ibn Battuta saw sheep in Mogadishu, but dined upon fish, chicken and meat (Gibb 1962, p. 376). Portuguese sources noted fat-tailed sheep, cattle

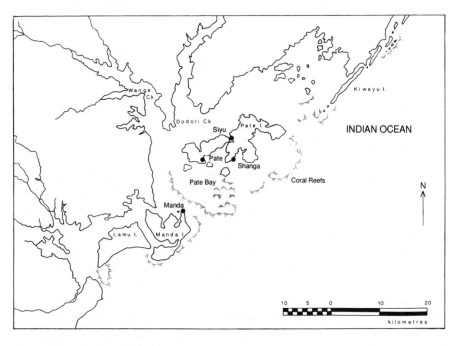

Figure 41.1   The Lamu archipelago.

and camels. In the sack of Mombasa in 1505 they captured camels and cattle and at Malindi in 1517 had 'plenty of round tailed sheep, cows and other cattle' (Freeman-Grenville 1962, pp. 110, 132). In the early fifteenth century horses, sheep and camels at Mogadishu were fed on dried fish according to eye-witness Chinese accounts (Duyvendak 1939).

The consumption of fish and other maritime products is also recorded in early sources. At Mulanda (Manda or Malindi), according to Idrisi, they salt and sell the catch (Lewis 1974, p. 118). At Badhuna, fish, shellfish, frogs, snakes, mice and a lizard with the Arabic name of *Umm Hubayun* – probably the monitor lizard – were eaten. At Bazawa (Barawa?), fish oil was of ritual importance as it was used to anoint standing stones (Lewis 1974, pp. 117–18). Ibn Battuta was given fish at Mogadishu (Gibb 1962, p. 376), but as part of a very large and varied menu. Early fifteenth-century Chinese descriptions of Barawa say that the country is infertile and inhabitants subsist entirely on fish (Duyvendak 1939). Gaspar de S. Bernadino records the hunting and eating of dugong at Siyu on Pate island in 1606 (Freeman-Grenville 1962, p. 163). Turtle-fishing is still practised by the Bajuni (Elliot 1925/6; Grottanelli 1947; Grottanelli 1955) using a technique whereby 'pilot fish' or remora are employed to locate the turtles, a technique which may have originated in southeast Asia.

Archaeological evidence provides a method of testing these two differing models of Swahili origins. Both Nurse & Spear and Allen point to the importance of the Lamu archipelago in cultural and linguistic terms. Archaeological survey has also identified several early sites, of which two, Manda (Chittick 1984) and Shanga (Horton Forthcoming), have been the subject of extensive excavation. At Shanga, where deposits were routinely screened (using a 5 mm mesh size) quantification of the faunal assemblage can be attempted. The stratification at Shanga spanned the eighth to early fifteenth century AD, with continuous occupation, enabling trends to be plotted over time. Shanga is one of the earliest sites so far identified on the east African coast.

Methodology

This chapter is concerned with the bones from trench 2 at Shanga, a 5 m by 5 m excavation. It has been chosen because the levels through the sequence were largely domestic (unlike the other trenches, which were often associated with religious and industrial activities). The levels were excavated with 100 per cent screening using the natural stratification and not arbitrary levels. From this excavation, 681 animal bones and 6009 fish bones were studied (Table 41.1). Over 250 individual contexts were identified and these were grouped into 12 phases, of around 50 years each, spanning *c.* AD 800 to *c.* AD 1400. The topmost levels ran through the courtyard of a stone house and those below, through mud and coral houses of successive rebuilds. The earliest levels comprised a short industrial phase (but also containing domestic rubbish pits) sealed by four phases of timber house, of which two were circular in plan.

Identification of the bones forms the essential first stage in any analysis and it is here that we encountered a complete absence of comparative collections of Indian Ocean fish species available in east Africa, noted in previous attempts to study fish bones from the

MARK HORTON & NINA MUDIDA

Ṣhanga + book

Table 41.1 Fish bones from trench 2 at Shanga

	Phase	1	2	3	4	5	6	7	8	9	10	11	12
Lethrinidae	*Lethrinus* spp.	13	53	37	99	154	154	317	402	270	316	188	14
Scaridae	*Leptoscarus vaigiensis*	12	31	11	40	66	30	112	220	141	129	87	15
	Scarus ghobban	1	6	1	25	11	11	40	64	62	29	106	7
	Scarus rubroviolaceus		3	1	6	2	1	3	6		6		
	Scarus niger	1	3	2	11	5	1	10	2		2	1	
	Calotumus carolinus		2	2	5	3						2	
	Hipposcarus harid			1									
Labridae	*Cheilio inermis*	1	4	3	10	6	5	36	44	30	24	9	
Haemulidae	*Plectorhinchus flavomaculatus*	9	72	51	130	68	64	80	61	45	12	5	
	Posadasys multimaculatum			1		10	33	20	25	6	6	25	13
	Plectorhinchus gaterinus		1	1	5	3	6	8	22	4	22	3	
	Plectorhinchus sordidus		1							6	8	5	5
	Plectorhinchus plagiodesmus				2				1	1			
	Plectorhinchus schotaf	2					2						1
Serranidae	*Epinephelus caeruleopunctatus*	1	2	10	7	2	4	12	11	17	7	6	1
	Promicrops lanceolatus	1	2	1	7	17	7	30	34	27	14	2	
	Plectropomus punctatus	1	2	11	4	8						1	
	Cephalopholis aurantia				10	8	1			3	5	3	
	Epinephelus fuscoguttatus		2									2	
	Dermatolepis striolatus									5			
	Vaviola louti										3	4	
Plotosidae	*Plotosus limbatus*	6	12	7	16	17	14	39	19	3	4	4	
Platycephalidae	*Papilloculiceps longiceps*		1	1	10	6	3	12	26	9	10		
Ariidae	*Arius* spp.		3	1	4	2		1	1	1	1	1	6
Lutjanidae	*Lutjanus vulviflamma*	1	2	1	5	10	7	9	17	4	17	10	
	Lutjanus argentimaculatus		2		3				2	1		1	2
	Lutjanus gibbus								1				
Siganidae	*Siganus sutor*	6	15	8	43	31	43	100	119	25	4		1
Sparidae	*Rhabdosargus sarba*				2	8	4	5	4	3	5	10	7
	Acanthopagrus berda						2	6	1	6		1	
Carangidae	*Alectis indicus*	6	2	2	3	11	1	18	25	26	7	8	
	Caranx sexfasciatus								1			2	3
	Carangoides sp.			3			1		11	11	2		
	Atule mate								1				
Acanthuridae	*Acanthurus lineolatus*	1	9	12	29	26	5	10	16	11	5	2	
	Naso hexacanthus				5			7	6		1		
Gerreidae	*Gerres acinaces*		2		2		1	4	2	1	14	3	3
Ephippidae	*Tripteredon orbis*					1			1	1	2		
Muraenidae	*Gymnothorax favagineus*	1	1		3				1	2	4	1	
	Gymnothorax undulatus					1		1	1				
	Lycodontis spp.					1		1	2	1	8		
Congridae	*Conger* sp.		4		2		2	1	3	1	6	2	
Sphyraenidae	*Sphyraena barracuda*			1	1				6	1	6	3	1
Carcharhinidae	*C. wheeleri + limbatus*				3		6	18	9	19	25	48	5
Stegostomatidae	*Stegostoma fasciatum*								3	2		3	
Dasyatidae	*Taeniura lymma*									1			
Albulidae	*Albula neoguinaica*					1							
Mugilidae	*Liza* spp.					2							
Ostraciidae	*Lactoria cornuta*							1					
Pomacanthidae	*Pomacanthus chyrsurus*	1	3										
Scorpaenidae	*Syanceia verrucosa*				1								
Lamnidae	*Isurus paucus*								1				
Platacidae	*Platax pinnatus*												1
	total: 6009	64	243	166	493	477	411	912	1170	736	702	550	85

region (Wright 1984, p. 51). A research collection was assembled with the gathering of two hundred specimens of fish from the vicinity of the site, during the course of the project. Two methods of collection were used: buying fish from the local fish market at Kizingitini at the east end of Pate island and fishing with our own boat on the reef using local nets, lines and spears. Collection of specimens was also accompanied by ethnographic observation of contemporary fish practice in the area and the collection of local species names. After acquisition, the fish specimens were measured, weighed, photographed, dissected and the flesh boiled off the bone. Marine mammals, as protected species, could obviously not be collected in this way and use had to be made of often incomplete specimens collected in the past. Work in the Osteology Laboratory of the National Museums of Kenya included species identification, using standard reference works (Smith 1950; Smith 1963; Carcasson 1977; Bock 1978; Fisher & Bianchi 1984; Wheeler & Jones 1989) from photographs and measurements taken at the time of collection.

The ecology of the Lamu archipelago

Shanga is located on the south side of Pate island, one of three islands in the Lamu archipelago (Fig. 41.1). The islands are exposed reefs, with a bedrock of coralline limestone and carbonate soils, frequently covered with a fine coral sand, which often build up to high dunes. Apart from these dunes, the islands are flat and have elevations of less that 10 m above sea-level. In general, the islands are very poor agriculturally, with little water and thinly developed soils that produce crops for only one or two seasons. The main cash crops produced today are coconuts and cashews, while a small number of stock animals are kept, including goats and cattle. The cattle are generally penned in the settlements at night and are taken out to graze as well as being hand-fed. In the nineteenth century, there was a very much larger population on the islands, which was supported by farming on the mainland, where large plantations were run, often using slaves (Brown 1985; Ylvisaker 1979). There were also large amounts of game on the mainland. Epidemics in the early part of the twentieth century reduced the population of the district; the plantations were abandoned and the populations retreated to the islands.

In contrast to these agricultural resources, the archipelago provided exceptionally rich fishing grounds. These range from offshore areas, especially exploiting pelagic fish, to the reef, which is particularly extensive off Pate island, to inshore sandy bays and estuaries, including two drowned river valleys that extend 30 km inland. Many of the villages in the archipelago, especially those that are Bajuni, rely on fishing for their basic protein supply (Grottanelli 1955).

Shanga is located on a narrow peninsula covered with sand-dunes fringed by a tidal estuary and mangrove forest. On the seaward side, the beach is flat and hard and the shelves shallow, so, at low tide, the water recedes about 1 km, leaving rocky pools, containing small fish and shellfish. The reef is a further 4 km off-shore and has a very complex structure, before the sea bottom falls away rapidly to the ocean floor. Pate Bay forms the area between reef and shore, a shallow sheltered lagoon with sea grasses and short outcrops of reef.

Fish bones

The general state of preservation of the fish remains was good, with tens of thousands of pieces recovered. Identification concentrated upon cranial fragments (which were particularly diagnostic) as well as vertebrae. For each identified bone, taxon, element, side of body, condition, age/size and evidence for burning/butchery were noted, along with archaeological information.

The systematic collection of fish bones from the stratification allowed for an analysis of trends in the use of different species and genera over time. Several methods were used to quantify fish biomass. Only around 10 per cent of fish bones from each context could be identified to the species level; postcranial bones in particular are extremely difficult to analyse. Minimum number analysis was attempted, but because of the selective nature of the identified sample this was found to be unreliable. As simple trends were being plotted, rather than overall biomass, it was decided to use identified bone counts in this analysis. The validity of this approach was supported by a simple plot of overall fish bone weight against identified bone numbers, for each phase. Here a very high correlation ($R = 0.98$) and a linear relationship was shown to exist between these two counts.

Identified fish species

Fifty-four different species were positively identified. All the identified species are found in the area of the northern Kenyan coast today (the Lamu archipelago is included in the FAO distribution lists for these species (Fisher & Bianchi 1984)); most were likely to have been caught in the Lamu archipelago.

By far the commonest fish exploited was Fam. Lethrinidae (see Appendix, 1 and Fig. 41.3), its proportion as compared to other fish increasing over time. Large fish were often decapitated, leaving butchery marks on the cleithrum, while the small fish seem to have been cooked whole, or sliced only once or twice. The presence of skull and vertebrae fragments indicates that these fish were processed on site.

The four commoner species of Fam. Scaridae (see Appendix, 2 and Fig. 41.3) have very different distributions over time: whereas *L. vaigiensis* declined in numbers, *S. ghobban* increased in popularity, while *S. rubroviolaceus* and *S. niger* were only found in very small proportions at the end of the sequence.

Of the six recorded species of Fam. Haemulidae (see Appendix, 4 and Fig. 41.4), *P. flavomaculatus* was very common in early phases, then declined steadily; in contrast, *P. multimaculatum* was common in the upper levels, while some of the other species of this family also showed distinctive and changing distributions over time.

E. caeruleopunctatus and *P. punctatus* (see Appendix, 5 and Fig. 41.5) declined in popularity after a certain time, whereas other species of the family Serranidae increased in frequency. Several individuals had massive heads, yet the presence of cranial fragments and vertebrae, some of which were burnt, indicates that the fish was generally processed on site.

Only one species of catfish was identified (see Appendix, 6 and Fig. 41.6), its frequency declining sharply over time.

Having been popular early on, the most common species of Fam. Carangidae (see

Appendix, 12 and Fig. 41.8), *A. indicus*, occurred only irregularly in later periods.

All the barracudas (see Appendix, 18 and Fig. 41.10) were very young individuals and, though relatively few in number and unevenly distributed through time, were possibly caught because, as today, they could be dried and smoked.

One serrated edge spine of a *Taeniura lymma* (see Appendix, 21) was found in the archaeological record despite the fact that the bone can inflict serious wounds on fishermen and is normally broken off as soon as the fish is caught, to avoid injury. The occurrence in this assemblage is therefore an unusual find.

The reef fish, Fam. Ostraciidae (see Appendix, 24) – nowadays considered a 'trash' fish – was found only in the earlier levels, as was also a single bone of *Syanceia verrucosa* (see Appendix, 26), whose venom from dorsal spines can be fatal.

Discussion

It is evident from this sample that the Shanga fish faunal assemblage consisted of a substantial range of taxa: 54 species in all, from 28 different fish families. Unidentified remains could add at least 10 more species to this list. The taxa revealed that all the identified fish were from the locally exploited marine population still inhabiting the shallow inshore waters and coral reefs around the site. The main families of fish which supplied the site all have good to excellent quality of flesh. These were mainly Lethrinids, Serranids, Scarids, Haemulids and Carangids; Siganids, Muraenids and Acanthurids were also important.

Some species have a distribution inshore and are associated with mangroves and estuaries, of which there is a considerable area adjacent to the site. The most significant family was the Lutjanidae which were exploited on a small scale throughout the sequence (see Appendix).

Fish from offshore areas are rare, especially in the early levels. *N. hexacanthus* which normally is found in deeper waters contributed less than 1 per cent. The exploitation of sharks and barracudas began after phase 9. Three species of identified shark are found both on coral reefs as well as in offshore waters, while the fourth, *I. paucus*, is found largely offshore. A possible deduction is that offshore fishing developed around phase 9, that is during the thirteenth century; there is no evidence for such practices in the early phases, nor for the exploitation of shoaling pelagic fish.

The occurrence of poor quality fish in the assemblage is significant. Included are both poisonous and semi-poisonous fish such as *S. verrucosa* and *T. lymma* as well as trash fish such as *L. cornuta* and *A. neoguinaica*. Whilst these may have been brought up accidentally in bottom trawls, the fact that they are brought back to the site for consumption suggests considerable food shortages. They occur generally in phase 8 onwards and it is significant that offshore species appear at the same point in the sequence, perhaps suggesting that the fish resources on the reef were becoming exhausted.

Most of the fish in the assemblage are shallow water-adapted, slow-moving and generally solitary individuals of moderate size. Most of the common species can be caught by spears and this reflects contemporary practice. Traps seem also to have been used, especially for the smaller sizes of fish that move in shoals. The relatively large numbers of *L. vaigiensis*, which are normally caught only by traps nowadays, suggests that traps were used from the very earliest phase. There is little evidence for the use of hand lines or nets on any scale and fish caught by these means today are rare in the assemblage.

There are variations in the proportions of fish species that were exploited in any one phase. In overall quantities, the larger the number of fish bones, the wider the range of species, and there is a clear relationship between the number of bones and number of species found in each phase. This suggests that the selection of fish was a largely random activity. Phase 9, for example, has the widest range of species as well as the largest number of bones.

But for individual families and taxa, there is clear patterning in the data. Long-term changes in the proportions of individual species and taxa can be observed from the archaeological record. These variations may be caused by cultural changes – changing preferences for one species above another, which are very difficult to reconstruct, or changing techniques in catching fish. But if the collection of reef species is considered to be a largely random activity, then these variations may in fact reflect changes in the structure of the fish population. The coral reef is a highly complex ecosystem and there may have been significant variations in populations, partly caused by human exploitation, but mainly through cyclical changes in habitat.

The fish assemblage from Shanga may give some indication of the presence and frequencies of different taxa over time. For example, two families show a similar pattern of decline: Plotosidae and Haemulidae. Both rely on crustaceans for their food and this habitat may have been reduced. The rapid decline in the consumption of Siganidae in phase 10 is all the more interesting as this fish is hardly ever caught nowadays. Perhaps it was overexploited in the thirteenth century and populations have never recovered. Present-day fish catches of *L. argentimaculatus* from Pate island are large, but the quantities of this taxon caught in the past seem to be less than 1 per cent.

The significance of fish in Swahili diet

These faunal data also allow an assessment of the overall significance of fish in the diet over time. From the same deposits, animal as well as fish bones were recovered and this allows for broad comparisons to be made (Fig. 41.2).

The quantity of fish bone deposited varied considerably over time and this may represent both archaeological and behavioural factors. From a relatively small excavation like trench 2, with fish bones largely concentrated in rubbish pits, variations in the domestic use of space may effect these patterns. The deposition rate for trench 2 was relatively smooth, with initially small quantities of fish bones deposited until phase 4, peaking in phase 9 and falling sharply thereafter. Broadly, fish-bone deposition was largely associated with mud-and-coral houses, but not with the early timber houses, or the later coral, rag and lime houses. Indeed, the quantities of fish found in the first and last phases suggest that, at these points, the inhabitants did not eat fish on a regular basis. A similar pattern was observed in the other much larger excavations, with relatively small numbers of fish in early levels and a peak in consumption in the thirteenth century, with numbers falling off thereafter.

Quantifying the first three phases in trench 2, there were only 473 identifiable elements (representing an occupation period between approximately AD 800 and 950) whereas in phase 4 (lasting to around AD 1000) there were 493 elements. Deposition rate for the first three phases is little more than 3 identifiable elements a year, while in phase 9 this rate rises to 23 elements a year. Extrapolating from identifiable elements to number of individuals is difficult but, on the basis of a 10 per cent survival rate, the difference in fish consumption rates would be roughly the equivalent of one fish a week to one a day in an area occupied by one or two individuals.

Comparison with animal bone rates shows a similar pattern. From trench 2 the only animal bones found in the first three phases were a single sea turtle bone and two chicken (*Gallus gallus*) bones. Only in phase 4 is the appearance of cattle (*Bos*) and sheep/goats (*Ovis/Caprini*) recorded and then in relatively small quantities. The changes in weight and numbers of identifiable bones for each phase show that only in the final phases does meat significantly replace fish as a protein supply.

It could be argued that this absence of meat-producing bones from trench 2 is not representative of the site as a whole. The bones from trenches 8, 9 and 10 have also been analysed in detail and a similar pattern emerges. The sequence from this area was divided into 21 phases, from the late eighth to the fifteenth centuries. Sheep/goat and cattle appear only in phase 3, the late ninth century, but in significant quantities only after phase 10, around AD 1050. Chicken is present from the beginning, at levels of around 10 per cent. In contrast to the absence of domesticates, there were small but significant quantities of hunted animals, both marine and terrestrial. Dugong (*Dugong dugon*) appears throughout the sequence in small but significant quantities, while sea turtle (probably green turtle, *Chelonia mydas*, but definitive identification is difficult) is common, especially at the beginning of the occupation, where it is found at levels in

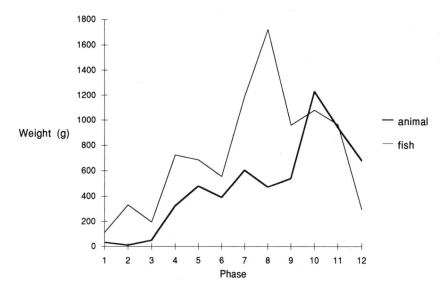

Figure 41.2 Weights of animal and fish bones from trench 2.

excess of 50 per cent of the total animal bone assemblage. There are also examples of Suni, Bush buck and Dik dik in these early levels.

In summary, the total quantity of bones deposited, both fish and animal, increases phase by phase, presumably indicating an increasingly protein-rich diet. In the earliest levels there is no evidence for sheep/goat or cattle and the only domesticated animal that appears to have been exploited is chicken. In contrast, fish, sea turtle and dugong bones are present from the earliest levels and must have provided a protein source for the inhabitants until the tenth century, supplemented by a number of wild animals hunted from the island rather than the mainland. Significant quantities of shells were also found in phase 1 and 2 levels, in particular *Potamides* spp., which are collected from mangrove swamps. These are rarely eaten today but are used for bait in fish traps and this was probably the pattern in the past.

Marine exploitation and the origin of the Swahili

The above evidence can be interpreted in two opposing ways. The first would be to suggest that a largely marine-oriented society lived in the Lamu archipelago during the eighth and ninth centuries AD. The food supplies were derived from the offshore reefs, using fish traps and spears, as well as from the estuaries around the site. In early levels proteins derived from fish and meat form a small part of the diet. The bulk of food derived from millets and legumes which, over time, as the community became richer, were replaced by protein-rich foods such as fish and domesticated and wild meat.

A second interpretation would postulate precisely the opposite view. This would assume that there were numbers of domestic animals at the beginning providing milk (and in the case of cattle, blood); this was the main protein supply rather than fish and meat. In many east African pastoralist societies meat is rarely consumed by slaughtering cattle and the number of bones from pastoralist sites is small. The inhabitants would be largely non-fish-eating, as can be suggested from the relatively rare occurrence of fish bones. The presence of both dugong and turtle (which traditionally do not form part of pastoralist fish taboos) might add weight to this hypothesis. Over time, the rising numbers of animal and fish bones are indicative of a general slackening of taboos and a greater reliance on meat rather than milk and blood.

We believe that the interpretation of Swahili origins should at present remain open, until many more sites are sampled and their faunal evidence studied in detail. The Shanga samples show that there are changes in diet over time which probably explain the diversity of the historical evidence. There may also be spatial variation, suggested from the faunal studies from the early levels on the Comorian sites (Wright 1984, p. 54). New evidence for this regional variation will undoubtedly result from the large number of sites currently being investigated on the east African coast by the SAREC Urban Origins Regional Cooperation Project (Sinclair 1989).

Marine resources, in particular fish, are of great economic importance to the Swahili nowadays, with numerous fisheries development programmes sponsored by donor countries. The archaeological evidence provides a long-term perspective on this resource and the cultural and ecological changes that have taken place during its exploitation by urban communities on the coast, over the last millennium.

Appendix

1 Fam. Lethrinidae (Emperors) (Fig. 41.3)

(a) *Lethrinus sanguineus*
(b) *Lethrinus lentjan*
(c) *Lethrinus* spp.

This family feeds on crustaceans and molluscs and occurs mainly around coral reefs and inshore waters up to 50 m in depth. They are slow swimmers and can be easily caught by spears and produce excellent meat.

Virtually every context with bones contained *Lethrinus* and this was by far the commonest fish exploited. The cranial bones of these three species are difficult to differentiate and it was decided to group them together. The proportion of Lethrinidae of the total increased over time. In phases 1, 2, 3 and 4, it remains around 20 per cent. Subsequently it peaks at phase 11 at 45 per cent of the total, before falling back to 17 per cent in the last phase.

Sizes of *Lethrinus* were estimated from every bone. The majority of bones are in the small size category (up to 25 cm), medium size follows (up to 40 cm), with very few large bones (up to 60 cm).

2 Fam. Scaridae (Parrot fishes) (Fig. 41.3)

(a) *Leptoscarus vaigiensis*
(b) *Scarus ghobban*
(c) *Scarus rubroviolaceus*
(d) *Scarus niger*
(e) *Calotumus carolinus*
(f) *Hipposcarus harid*

This family feeds on algae and sea grasses generally close to coral reefs and inshore lagoons. They are very territorial and often the most abundant species in inshore areas. They are caught most commonly in traps, occasionally by nets and spears. The flesh is soft and has to be eaten fresh.

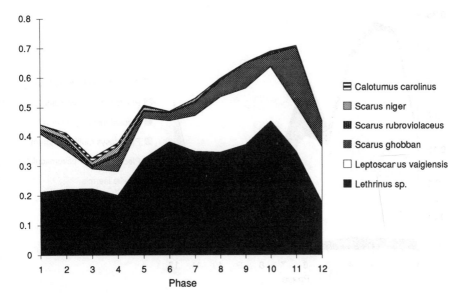

Figure 41.3 Lethrinidae and Scaridae.

Six species of parrot fish were identified and are listed above in their order of abundance. Two further species of this genus were suggested from fragments, but could not be identified through lack of comparative material. Vertebrae in the Scaridae family are very similar between species and cannot be used for identification.

Leptoscarus vaigiensis (Marbled parrot fish) outnumbers the other species, despite being the smallest in the parrot fish family, with a maximum standard length (st. l.) of 27 cm. *L. vaigiensis* was the only fish where sex could be determined as this species does not change sex, and mature and submature males have one to four canines projecting laterally from the premaxilla. *Scarus ghobban* (Blue-barred parrot fish) was also common and could be identified from its cranial fragments. From the size of bones, it was clear that individuals were in the initial stage of growth and the terminal stage (usually longer than 45 cm st. l.). *Scarus rubroviolaceus* (Ember parrot fish) and *Scarus niger* (Dusky parrot fish) were identified from cranial fragments. Bone size indicates that most individuals were in the terminal growth stage: over 26 cm st. l. for *S. rubroviolaceus* and over 20 cm st. l. for *S. niger*. *Calotumus carolinus* (Carolines parrot fish) was rare. There was one occurrence of a hyomandibular in a late level (phase 12) and a small group (left dentaries, articular, pharyngeal and premaxilla) in earlier levels (phases 2 to 5). The MNI counts for these phases were four individuals with a total of twelve bones, in terminal growth stage of over 20 cm st. l. *Hipposcarus harid* (Longnosed parrot fish) was represented by only one occurrence; the element was a complete maxilla of very distinctive morphology. Estimation of the size of this element places the individual in the initial growth phase, less than 30 cm st. l.

The four commoner species of Scaridae show a marked pattern of distribution over time. *L. vaigiensis* is commoner in the early phases, declines a little to 6.7 per cent in phase 3 and 8.1 per cent in phase 4, reviving to 18.9 per cent in phase 9 and then remaining at this level through the sequence. *S. ghobban* increases dramatically over time in popularity, from 1.6 per cent in phase 1 to 19.5 per cent in tr. 2:12. *S. rubroviolaceus* and *S. niger* decrease in popularity, from 1 per cent to 2 per cent initially, and dropping to tiny proportions after phase 8.

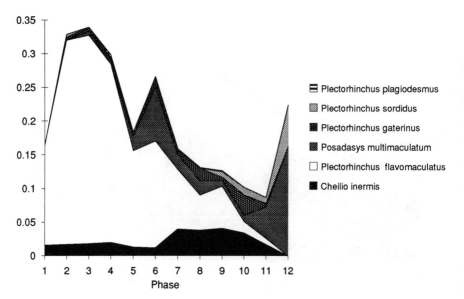

Figure 41.4 Labridae and Haemulidae.

3 Fam. Labridae (Wrasses) (Fig. 41.4)

(a) *Cheilio inermis*

Wrasses feed in shallow water, between 1 m and 10 m, on crustaceans and hard-shelled prey, on reefs and in weedy areas. They are caught nowadays by hook, line or spear and the flesh is considered of high quality.

This family is represented by only one species, *C. inermis* (Cigar wrasse). Fragments are well distributed through the stratigraphy; the commonest element was the lower pharyngeal while the vertebrae of *C. inermis* were very distinctive and were also recorded. The bones suggested medium-sized individuals, up to 40 cm. Total proportions of this fish remain stable, in the range 1.2 per cent to 2 per cent with a peak around 4 per cent in phases 8, 9, 10 and 11.

4 Fam. Haemulidae (Grunters, Sweetlips, Rubberlips) (Fig. 41.4)

(a) *Plectorhinchus flavomaculatus*

(b) *Pomadasys multimaculatum*

(c) *Plectorhinchus gaterinus*

(d) *Plectorhinchus sordidus*

(e) *Plectorhinchus plagiodesmus*

(f) *Plectorhinchus schotaf*

Haemulidae are coastal fish that are normally found around reefs. They feed on crustaceans and small fish, and can grow up to 80 cm, although they are more commonly 15 cm to 30 cm. Nowadays they are caught by handlines, spears or bottom trawls. The meat quality is excellent and is sometimes dried and salted.

Six species were recorded for the family Haemulidae, the first two, *P. flavomaculatus* (Lemon fish) and *P. multimaculatum* (Cock grunter) being the commonest. Although Haemulidae contributed significantly to the overall fish biomass from the site, their size was small to medium. Some species grow up to 90 cm (such as *P. plagiodesmus* and *P. schotaf*) but from this material no individual was greater than 60 cm (st. l.) in size.

P. flavomaculatus was very common in the earlier phases with over 30 per cent of the assemblage. From phase 3, the proportion declines steadily to only 0.9 per cent in phase 12. In contrast, *P. multimaculatum* (Cock grunter) is found generally in the upper levels. It first occurs significantly in phase 7, with 8 per cent, declining to levels of around 2 per cent rising to 4.6 per cent in phase 13. *P. gaterinus* increases marginally in popularity over time, with a maximum occurrence rate of 3.1 per cent in phase 11; *P. sordidus* was only found (apart from a single bone in phase 2) in the last four phases, at levels of around 1 per cent. *P. plagiodesmus* and *P. schotaf* are found so rarely that no changes can be deduced over time.

5 Fam. Serranidae (Groupers, Rockcods, Seabasses) (Fig. 41.5)

(a) *Epinephelus caeruleopunctatus*

(b) *Promicrops lanceolatus*

(c) *Plectropomus punctatus*

(d) *Cephalopholis aurantia*

(e) *Epinephelus fuscoguttatus*

(f) *Dermatolepis striolatus*

(g) *Variola louti*

Serranidae are large fish that can grow up to 270 cm, but more commonly around 50 cm. They are found in depths of between 5 m and 100 m around coral reefs and are predators on fish, crabs and lobsters. Nowadays, they are caught by spears, handlines, traps and nets and the meat is reasonable. *V. louti* can, however, be poisonous and is rarely eaten.

Seven species were identified, with one other in this family as yet unidentified. *E. caeruleopunctatus* (White-spotted rockcod) and *P. lanceolatus* (Brindle grouper) produced the largest number of fragments. *P. punctatus* (Marbled leopard grouper) and *C. aurantia* (Golden hind) are found intermittently, while *E. fuscoguttatus* (Blotchy rockcod), *D. striolatus* (Smooth grouper) and *V. louti* (Moontail seabass) were rarer. Serranids vary greatly in size from species to species; some like *P. lanceolatus*, can reach 270 cm with a weight of 400 kg while *E. caeruleopunctatus* only grows up to 55 cm. The Shanga assemblage represents only small and medium-sized individuals, up to around 60 cm st. l.

The distribution of this family is of some interest. There is a peak in phase 3 in both *E. caeruleopunctatus* and *P. punctatus*, which together add up to 13 per cent of the total. Figures of both fall off thereafter and do not contribute significantly to the diet. This contrasts to *P. lanceolatus*, which increases steadily over time, peaking at phase 10 with 3.7 per cent. *C. aurantia* has two peaks, one between phases 4 and 6, around 2 per cent and a second around 0.5 per cent at the end of the sequence. *V. louti* was only found in phases 11 and 12 in small quantities.

6 Fam. Plotosidae (Catfish) (Fig. 41.6)

(a) *Plotosus limbatus*

The catfish is found on estuaries and along open coasts, sometimes on coral reefs. Catfish feed off crustaceans and small fishes. The fish is not very commonly caught nowadays and the meat is poor. Fish are normally caught incidentally on bottom trawls and lines.

This family is represented by one species only, *P. limbatus* (Darkfin eel catfish). Fragments of pectoral spines are the commonest of the elements while the only portion of the opercular that escaped destruction is its articulation with the hyomandibular; this is, however, very distinctive in the different taxa and allows reliable identification. Little significant variation in the size of eel catfish was noted; most examples were the same moderate size, around 30 cm.

Over time, its distribution is very clear, declining from 9.8 per cent in tr. phase 1 to 0.7 per cent in phase 12. The fall is particularly strong after phase 8.

7 Fam. Platycephalidae (Flatheads) (Fig. 41.6)

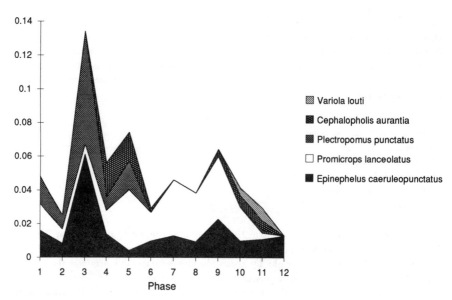

Figure 41.5 Serranidae.

(a) *Papilloculiceps longiceps*

Flatheads are found close to sand bottoms in the vicinity of coral reefs and are generally fished by lines or spears. Their meat is good.

One species, the Madagascar flathead, was found, persisting through most levels. The size range was moderate, around 50 cm. *P. longiceps* occurs between phase 2 and phase 11 at levels between 1 per cent and 2 per cent.

8 Fam. Ariidae (Sea catfish) (Fig. 41.6)

(a) *Arius* spp.

This genus has a wide distribution in coastal waters, especially around reefs, and feeds off invertebrates. Some species can grow to over 100 cm in length, and the meat is generally valued, especially as it can be dried and salted. It is caught by line or traps.

Because of the absence of comparative specimens, it was not possible to identify elements to species, of which there are twenty-three in the area nowadays. Fragments occur in the earlier phases at around 1 per cent, then reappearing in the final phase with a high 7.5 per cent.

9 Fam. Lutjanidae (Snappers) (Fig. 41.7)

(a) *Lutjanus vulviflamma*

(b) *Lutjanus argentimaculatus*

(c) *Lutjanus gibbus*

Lutjanidae are inshore fish, found in estuaries and shallow waters around mangroves and the rocky foreshore. Juveniles in particular are found in the mangrove swamps, while mature adults can range into the reef area. They live off invertebrates and small fish. *L. argentimaculatus* can grow up to 120 cm, with a normal length of around 80 cm; nowadays it is an important fish in the area. The other species are around 50 cm maximum length. The meat is excellent and can be dried and salted. They are mainly caught in traps, by lines and can sometimes be speared from the shore at night.

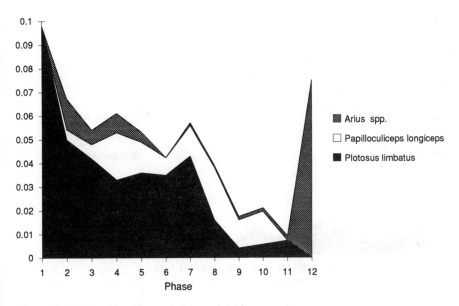

Figure 41.6 Plotosidae, Platycephalidae and Aridae.

Elements of *L. vulviflamma* (Dory snapper), one of the small Lutjanids, were found in moderate numbers and were from medium-sized individuals and occurred at a rate of around 2 per cent. The other two species were very rare. *L. argentimaculatus* (Mangrove red snapper) was found only at the beginning and the end of the sequence. *L. gibbus* (Humpback red snapper) was represented by a single bone in phase 9.

10 Fam. Siganidae (Fig. 41.7)

(a) *Siganus sutor*

Siganidae are herbivorous, living off algae close to rocks and corals. The fish reach sizes of 45 cm, but are generally around 30 cm. They are found in shoals and are thus generally caught using nets and traps.

S. sutor (Rabbit fish) was the only Saganid found in the assemblage; vertebrae constituted the predominant element. Skull fragments had little chance of survival as they were almost wafer-thin. Small individuals predominated. This was a reasonably popular fish, reaching levels of around 10 per cent. After phase 10, the proportion of this species falls off very rapidly, with only 1.3 per cent recorded in the final phase.

11 Fam. Sparidae (Seabreams) (Fig. 41.8)

(a) *Rhabdosargus sarba*

(b) *Acanthopagrus berda*

Sparidae live off small invertebrates and generally range close to sandy bottoms around reefs, in inshore waters and estuaries. They can grow up to 75 cm in length and produce excellent flesh. Nowadays they are fished using bottom trawls.

Two species of this family were found, although elements were rare. *Rhabdosargus* (Stumpnose seabream) was the most common, and could be identified from premaxilla and dentaries, while the *A. berda* (Picnic seabream) could be identified in addition from the articular to hyomandibular.

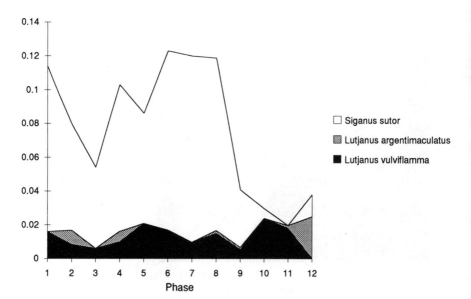

Figure 41.7 Lutjanidae and Siganidae.

Rhabdosargus had a bimodal distribution, peaking at 1.7 per cent in phase 5 and again at 8.7 per cent in phase 13.

12 Fam. Carangidae (Jacks, Trevallies) (Fig. 41.8)

(a) *Alectis indicus*
(b) *Caranx sexfasciatus*
(c) *Carangoides* spp.
(d) *Atule mate*

Carangidae are another coastal fish, living off fish and crustaceans in the reef area. They produce excellent flesh, which can be eaten fresh or dried and salted. They are caught by lines or nets and nowadays are highly valued. *A. indicus* grows up to 150 cm, or 22 kg in weight. Some species are pelagic and are found in large numbers offshore, close to the surface. The species represented in this assemblage are found more generally inshore.

Of the four species noted, *A. indicus* (Indian thread fish) is by far the most numerous. Element sizes and dentition changes suggest that most of the individuals were mature individuals of up to 60 cm st. l., while the largest were up to 150 cm st. l. It was very popular in the first phase, up to 9.8 per cent of the total. After this it occurs irregularly generally between 1 per cent and 3 per cent.

C. sexfasciatus (Bigeye trevally) occurred in the upper levels only. *A. mate* (Yellowtail scad) was probably recorded from one element, a dentary, from phase 9. *Carangoides* spp. was identified from dentary fragments, which could not be distinguished at species level. It was commonest between phases 8 and 10.

13 Fam. Acanthuridae (Fig. 41.9)

(a) *Acanthurus lineolatus*
(b) *Naso hexacanthus*

Acanthuridae are herbivorous, living off belgic algae in the vicinity of coral reefs and are fished

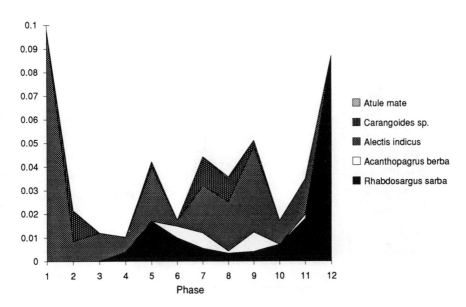

Figure 41.8 Sparidae and Carangidae.

using nets, spears and traps. *N. hexacanthus* is a deeper water fish, not generally found in less than 15 m of water, which lives off crab larvae and arrow worms. It is caught in traps.

This family is represented by two different genera: *Acanthurus lineolatus* (Surgeon fish) and *Naso hexacanthus* (Sleek unicorn fish). Medium-sized bones are characteristic of this family. *A. lineolatus* was initially common, with a peak in phase 3 of 7.3 per cent, but thereafter declining quickly in importance. *N. hexacanthus* occurs spasmodically.

14 Fam. Gerreidae (Fig. 41.9)

(a) *Gerres acinaces*

This species (Long-tailed silver biddi) lives in shallow water, especially around sandy bottoms and estuaries. It is generally caught by bottom trawls and the meat, eaten fresh, is moderately good. It occurred in moderate numbers and the size was generally 15–20 cm st. l. Its occurrence increases over time, peaking in the final phase at 3.8 per cent.

15 Fam. Ephippidae

(a) *Tripteredon orbis*

This is a coral reef fish, that can shoal in numbers of up to 500 individuals. It also ranges into estuaries and brackish rivers. A few elements of opercular and maxilla of this species (African spadefish) were found in the middle of the sequence (phase 7) and in the last few phases. Vertebrae and post-temporal elements can also be identified. All the bones were from fish of moderate size of around 30 cm.

16 Fam. Muraenidae (Morays) (Fig. 41.9)

(a) *Gymnothorax favagineus*

(b) *Gymnothorax undulatus*

(c) *Lycodontis* spp.

The species in this family are reef fish that live off crustaceans and small reef animals. They are mostly found in rocky areas, especially holes, and can be most easily caught by spears, although

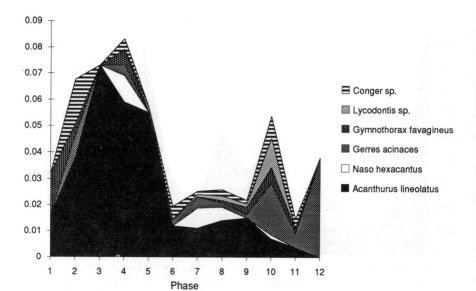

Figure 41.9 Acanthuridae, Gerreidae, Muraenidae and Congridae.

lines and traps are also used. The flesh is moderately good, but that of large individuals can cause poisoning.

Elements from both genera appear in the assemblage, although unevenly. *G. favagineus* (Honeycomb moray) was found at the beginning of the sequence and again around phase 11. *Lycodontis* spp. occurs around phase 11.

17 Fam. Congridae (Congers) (Fig. 41.9)
(a) *Conger* sp.
Congers are reef fish, that today are eaten locally but are not of commercial importance. *Conger* sp. (Conger eel) could be most easily determined by cranial and vertebrae fragments. It was rare, with a peak of 1.7 per cent in phase 2, then less than 1 per cent thereafter.

18 Fam. Sphyraenidae (Barracudas) (Fig. 41.10)
(a) *Sphyraena barracuda*
Barracudas are mainly found in the open sea and sometimes around reefs. They are voracious carnivores, feeding on small fish and can grow up to 180 cm. They are mainly caught by lines and are dangerous to fish.

This species (Great barracuda) could be identified from vertebrae, which were all small: definite evidence for very young individuals. One tooth and hyomandibular of a large barracuda were recorded in an upper level. This species was rare and mainly found from phase 9 onwards.

19 Fam. Carcharhinidae (Sharks) (Fig. 41.10)
(a) *Carcharhinus wheeleri* (Black-tailed reefshark)
(b) *Carcharhinus limbatus* (Black-tipshark)
and

20 Fam. Stegostomatidae
(a) *Stegostoma fasciatum* (Zebra shark)

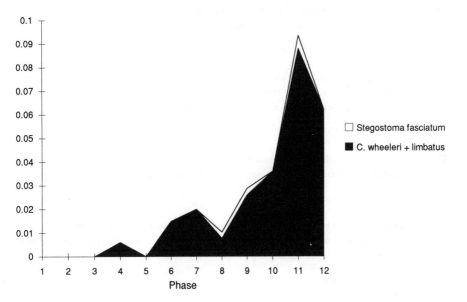

Figure 41.10 Sphyraenidae and Carcharhinidae.

Sharks live offshore and range into the reef and inshore areas to feed on fish, in particular squids and rays. They are caught using nets and lines. The meat is moderate, but can be dried and salted and nowadays this is an important source of portable food for long journeys.

Sharks can generally be identified from their vertebrae, although it is very difficult to relate them to particular species. The very small vertebrae of *Stegostoma fasciatum* seem to be characteristic. *Carcharhinus wheeleri* and *Carcharhinus limbatus* were identified from a single tooth. Numerous vertebrae of different sizes (0.5 mm to 30 mm in diameter) were noted but it is impossible to estimate size since small vertebrae can derive from the tail of large sharks.

The exploitation of sharks shows a very clear pattern, evident from vertebrae counts. They were found only significantly after phase 5, peaking with 48 vertebrae in phase 12, representing about 8 per cent of total occurrences. Identified bones of *S. fasciatum* occurred in only the upper levels.

21 Fam. Dasyatidae

(a) *Taeniura lymma*

T. lymma (Blue-spotted ribbontail ray) was recorded from a single serrated-edged spine which is normally rooted in the tail. Stingrays are cartilaginous fish and only the spine is likely to survive in the archaeological record; thus it is impossible to estimate accurately the importance of this family to the diet.

22 Fam. Albulidae (Bonefish)

(a) *Albula neoguinaica*

This species (Sharpjaw bonefish) occurred as rare fragments of parasphenoid and basibranchial tooth patches. It lives in shallow sandy bottom waters off molluscs, worms and small fish. The species is of little food value, because of its numerous small bones, and is caught today either as a sports fish, or for bait. Its rarity in the assemblage (phase 8) was therefore no surprise.

23 Fam. Mugilidae (Mullets)

(a) *Liza* spp.

The genus was recorded only once (phase 7), from a scapula and hyomandibular. This genus may have been more numerous, but owing to the skull fragility, elements do not survive. It is found in shallow waters, living off algae and is caught in nets.

24 Fam. Ostraciidae (Cowfish, Boxfish)

(a) *Lactoria cornuta*

The species (Longhorn cowfish) was identified from scale-plates which on living fish fuse together to form a carapace encasing the body. It was found rarely (phase 8). Today it is considered a 'trash' fish and only occasionally eaten when it is found in bottom trawls.

25 Fam. Pomacanthidae (Angelfish)

(a) *Pomacanthus chrysurus*

This species (Goldtail angelfish) was found in the lower levels only, as hyomandibular bones of small size. Fish of this species, a reef fish, are occasionally eaten today but the meat is not good.

26 Fam. Scorpaenidae

(a) *Syanceia verrucosa*

A single complete articular bone was found from this species (Stonefish) in phase 4. It is difficult to explain its presence; today this fish is not used for human consumption as the venom in the dorsal spines can cause death and serious injury.

27 Fam. Lamnidae (Sharks)

(a) *Isurus paucus*

A single tooth of *I. paucus* (Longfin mako) was found in phase 9. This is a little-known oceanic shark, distributed today mainly off Madagascar, but may range further north. It only approaches land to give birth. Its maximum size is 300 cm.

28 Fam. Platacidae

(a) *Platax pinnatus*

This species (Dusky batfish) was represented by a single hyomandibular from phase 12. It lives on coral reefs, but is nowhere particularly abundant. Its meat is edible, but not particularly palatable on account of foul feeding habits. It is rarely sold today, but may be occasionally caught in nets and lines.

42 Coast–interior settlements and social relations in the Kenya coastal hinterland

GEORGE H. O. ABUNGU

& HENRY W. MUTORO

Introduction

Settlement pattern studies are concerned with relics of human occupation in the past. In an archaeological record, these relics either appear in clusters or individually in the form of postholes, house floors, house foundations or as middens. On aerial photographs and topographic maps relics of past human occupation can be identified by the presence of circular or rectangular depressional features and stunted vegetation cover in the midst of a flourishing vegetation community. Past human settlements can also be identified in actual field observation as ruins: building structures, walled fortresses, moats, monuments and mounds.

Irrespective of their nature and conditions of preservation, past settlements are a reflection of human behaviour through time and space. The archaeological evidence that is found preserved in them can shed much light on our knowledge of past culture. The essential archaeological problem in the analysis and interpretation of settlement, however, is that architectural remains and other settlement data cannot be understood simply by their description, distribution, cultural attribution and chronology – as they have been from the early anthropological work of Morgan (1881) and Mindeleff (1890) through the first large-scale regional archaeological syntheses, such as Childe's (e.g. 1934) in Europe and Willey (1953) in South America up to the common archaeological survey work of today.

With the influence of modern cultural ecology, geography and sociobiology, settlement analysis has been transformed into a concern with environmental and ecological processes. Settlements are part of a complex integration of culture and ecology within a regional environment. As a result, settlement analysis in archaeology must attend not only to the physical layout of the environment, but also to the social and historical aspects of environmental interaction.

Settlement studies in east Africa

The history of the entire east African coastal region has for a long time generated racial controversy and debates among scholars because of the long contacts of that region with the outside world. Some regarded the key explanation for the origins and development of these coastal settlements as the result of the diffusion of ideas and material culture from the orient (e.g. Kirkman 1957; Kirkman 1964; Kirkman 1966; Chittick 1974; and see Wright, Ch. 40, this volume).

This assumption was due to the fact that many early researchers tended to assume that the northern coast of east Africa, and particularly that of Kenya, was never in close contact with its hinterland prior to the nineteenth century. This situation was attributed to various factors, ranging from: the coast being foreign, overseas-looking with nothing to do with the interior; the 'harsh' environment between the coast and the interior; the lack of enticing goods such as gold and copper in the interior to attract the coastal traders; to the restricted coastal zone as having been self-sufficient in goods required for the sustenance of this trade.

The coast of Kenya was thus seen as sea-facing, cut off from the rest of the African continent, and more or less a province of the Middle East (e.g. Garlake 1966; Chittick 1967; Chittick & Rotberg 1975; Posnansky 1975a; Chittick 1984).

Because of this assumption, little or no attention was paid in archaeological research to the evidence of social and economic relations within the region. For example, Kirkman (1957) found some seventeenth-century pottery in a test pit at the ruined settlement of Takwa on Manda island (Fig. 42.1); on the evidence of this single find, he dated the site and attributed its origins to Arab founders.

On the other hand, more recent work by regional archaeologists has concentrated on local and regional interaction. For example, Mutoro (1979) conducted an extensive archaeological survey of many deserted settlements on the north and south Kenya coasts, culminating in an extensive excavation of Takwa (Mutoro 1985).

Of the more than 10 million potsherds recovered from different parts of the Takwa settlement, the presence of five thousand foreign sherds attested to the significance of foreign contact. The foreign pottery was largely from Islamic countries – probably Arabia and Persia. Other pieces came from India, and still others from China. The history of contact was long – Chinese potsherds, consisting mostly of deep sea-green celadons of the tenth and twelfth centuries AD, were found several strata below the seventeenth-century Islamic potsherds.

Most importantly, however, this study provided significant evidence of regional economic relationships, indicated in the variety of wares from other settlements. Many potsherds found in contexts marking the earliest occupation period at Takwa are similar to those reported from the Manda site (Chittick 1984) and dated to the ninth century AD. This same type of local pottery, characterized by mixed triangular motifs has also been found in the Taita, Taveta, Pare and Usambara regions (personal observation and F. Chami, *pers. comm.*). This evidence therefore suggests that there were inter-ethnic contacts within and between the coastal societies themselves on the one hand and the interior societies on the other.

Because of the predominant interest in the wider context of inter-cultural relations, however, it is only recently that attention has been paid to this issue (see also Wright, Ch. 40, this volume). The earlier lack of concern was compounded by the fact that the local data were incomplete: local and regional analyses were limited to the description of local pottery from coastal settlements in isolation from other material culture objects in published and unpublished site reports.

Because the study of culture is a study of social and material environments, rather than simply of sites and artefacts, explanations about coastal settlements in east Africa need to pay attention to the inter- and intra-site relations on the coast, its settlements in the hinterland and beyond. Evidence for extra-societal, inter-ethnic contacts within this area may be exemplified by an analysis of the precolonial settlements, known as *makaya*, of the Mijikenda on the Kenya coastal hinterland and the settlements and ecology of the Tana river and delta (Fig. 42.1).

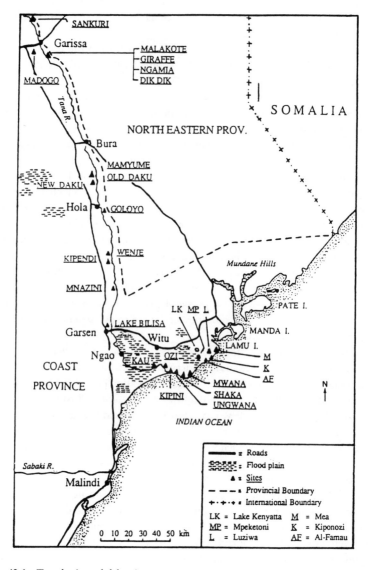

Figure 42.1   Tana basin and delta sites.

The Mijikenda *makaya*

The *makaya* (singular: *kaya*) were sacred, fortified settlements located right in the heart of a dense tropical rainforest on the Kenya coastal hinterland (Mutoro 1987). These settlements were distributed over a wide territory measuring approximately 65 km in width and stretching about 150 km from slightly north of latitude 3°S in Jilore in the north to latitude 4°30'S near the Kenya–Tanzania border (Fig. 42.2).

In an effort to understand processes of settlement formation and their social dynamics

Figure 42.2   Early settlements on the east African coast, including *makaya* settlements.

in the Kenya coastal hinterland, three kinds of evidence were used: site catchment and other forms of settlement analysis; the study of oral traditions; and the excavation of *makaya*.

Site catchment studies were carried out by walking transects and recording information as to the type of terrain, soils, vegetation cover and animals present. The resultant information was validated against Landsat satellite data. Three main ecological zones were discerned. The settlements were located on the coastal ridge in primary forest vegetation; the ridge provided security in the location of the *kaya* settlements. The lower slopes of the ridge, extending down to the plains, were farmlands and grazing grounds for the *kaya* inhabitants. The third zone covered a distance of up to 30 km and beyond and was interpreted as representing the area of regional trade and wider social interaction.

In order to analyse the relation of settlement distribution to environmental and social resources, a quantitative analysis using the nearest neighbour statistic was applied to the settlement data.

The first application was to data from the formative stage of the settlement prior to the tenth century AD, followed by analyses of later periods. It was assumed that there would be an even distribution of settlements if critical resources – security, water, food and shelter – were evenly distributed in the region and vice versa. However, the results showed that, in fact, there was clustering (e.g. nine *makaya* crowded together in a small area on a ridge). This pattern did not change very significantly during the second phase of settlement formation, although the spaces between *kaya* became filled with 'daughter' settlements.

These results were further examined by an analysis of hierarchical relations between the coastal hinterland settlements. For example, two sets of settlements were identified in the *kaya* region: the principal nine settlements that represent the nine Mijikenda ethnic groups and the smaller or 'daughter' settlements which developed from the nine.

Parent settlements were politically independent local units. Each was self-sustaining in many important respects. There were, however, occasions when representatives of their politico-religious councils, known as *kambi* and *mvaya*, converged from each of the nine *makaya* to discuss matters that affected the entire Mijikenda society, such as warfare and defence of the society, diplomacy, trade and funeral ceremonies (Mutoro 1988).

Oral traditions were used to determine the centres where such inter-*kaya* meetings took place. They indicated that the zone with the highest potential for interaction was within the Rabai-Ribe complex in which are *kaya* Rabai, *kaya* Ribe and *kaya* Giriama, while the zone with the least potential for interaction was around *kaya* Kauma (Fig. 42.2) (Mutoro 1988). When this result was considered within the context of the region as a whole, it was found that it would have been more cost-effective for all the representatives of the nine *makaya* to travel to any 'parent' *kaya* in the Rabai-Ribe complex than to any other *kaya*. It was also observed that in addition to having characteristics common to other *makaya* on the ridge, the *makaya* within the high-potential zone had additional characteristics that were unique to themselves (Mutoro 1987).

There were, however, also exceptions to this rule. A few 'daughter' settlements were located a considerable distance from the 'parent' settlements. A closer examination of these distant locations suggested that some, such as Pungu and Tiwi (Fig. 42.2), had been located for strategic reasons, namely to be in direct control of the trade of the Indian Ocean.

This geographical and ethnohistorical evidence was validated by data from archaeological excavation of the *makaya*. Evidence of interaction has been assessed by the presence of exotic goods not procurable within the region, and of artefacts and ecofacts from archaeological excavations of different *makaya* within the region. In cases where material culture objects were found to be local to the settlements, research has been carried out to determine the activity area locations at which they were produced. In the course of establishing such activity area locations, ethnoarchaeological studies have been used to 'predict' the location of such areas on the abandoned settlements. X-ray fluorescence methods have also been used to determine the different types of clays used in the production of pottery wares and their actual sources. Results have shown that many of the pottery wares were imported from the interior as well as from the neighbouring Swahili settlements, to supplement local wares (Mutoro 1990).

Coast–interior relations

In trying to understand the interaction of the coast of east Africa and its interior during the period AD 700–1890, Abungu (1988; 1989) has located and studied a group of sites on the Tana delta and along the northern Kenya coast. The most important of these is the town of Ungwana on the Tana delta; other significant sites include Mea, Luziwa, Kiponozi, Al-Famau, Mwana and Shaka (Fig. 42.1). Abungu used both historical and archaeological evidence and, in addition, attempted to equate these sites with the historical locations mentioned by sixteenth- and seventeenth-century Portuguese and Arab writers – a difficult task, especially in the absence of early maps and the fact that the names given to these sites, especially by twentieth-century writers such as Kirkman (1964; 1966), seem to have no historical validity.

Abungu also assessed the archaeological record for evidence that the Tana river basin had acted as a corridor into the interior. Sites were investigated along the course of the river (Fig. 42.1) from around its source (adjacent to Mt Kenya and the Rift Valley) via a narrow corridor of lush vegetation, to the delta on the coast. On the coast, as noted above, there existed a number of wealthy trading communities which participated in the Indian Ocean trade network; Ungwana, located at the present mouth of the Tana river, seems the most important.

Ungwana

Ungwana was one of the towns that had sprung up on the east African coast by the tenth century AD. Today, it is a 45-acre walled site situated on the northern shores of Formosa, or Ungwana Bay about 2 km east of the modern town of Kipini (Fig. 42.1). The ruins extend 500 m onto a coral ridge to the north. The site itself lies close to the former course of the Tana river, and about 2 km from the present Tana and Ozi rivers. The Tana flows into the Indian Ocean at Kipini, 128 km northeast of Malindi (Fig. 42.1). The river has changed its course many times, the last being in the late nineteenth century; during Ungwana's time, however, the river seems to have flowed into the ocean very close to the western edge of the town. Ungwana was excavated by Kirkman in the 1950s (Kirkman 1966).

The town was encircled by a town wall which enclosed ruins of eight mosques, numerous houses and several groups of large monumental tombs. Northeast of the town, and adjacent to the town wall, is located a large earthen mound reputed to be the burial place of Fumo Liongo, the Swahili poet-king who is also claimed by the Pokomo people of the Tana basin to be one of them.

The excavations by Kirkman took place at the main mosque (referred to as the Two Jamia), the mosque of the Domed Mihrab, the sea wall and at the gate adjacent to the Two Jamia (Fig. 42.3). Wilson (1978) also opened a sondage near the Domed Tomb, situated close to the mosque of the Domed Mihrab. From his excavations, Kirkman divided the town's life into six periods, with the beginnings of the settlement dated to the thirteenth century AD; it lasted until the seventeenth century, when it was deserted. While the date for its desertion was confirmed as early seventeenth century by field-work carried out by Abungu in 1986/7, its founding date is now seen to be much earlier than was first thought, sometime in the mid-tenth century AD.

Kirkman (1966) based his dates solely on imported pottery at a time when imported pottery as a dating material was still not well understood. It has now, however, emerged through further investigations that stratigraphic depths at Ungwana corre-

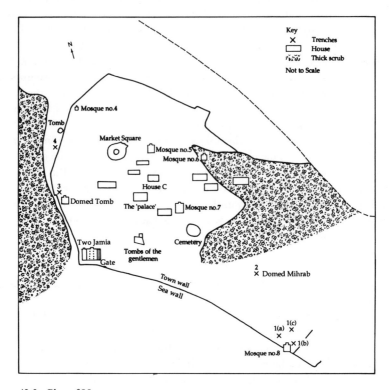

Figure 42.3 Plan of Ungwana.

spond closely to deposits excavated at other early coastal sites; among these are the island sites of Manda (Chittick 1984) and Shanga (Fig. 42.2) (Horton 1984; Horton & Mudida, Ch. 41, this volume), where early levels can now be dated both by imported Islamic and Far Eastern pottery, as well as by C14. On the basis of the imported pottery, Ungwana has now been divided into six periods, dating from AD 950 to AD 1600: Period I: 950–1150, Period II: 1150–1200, Period III: 1200–1350, Period IV: 1350–1450, Period V: 1450–1500 and Period VI: 1500–1600.

The area around the settlement, like most of the coastal strip, has fertile soils and enough rainfall for farming to be carried out all year round. The availability of good soils and adequate rainfall could have been one of the factors that influenced the location of the site, for it would have yielded a dependable surplus of food and, in case of scarcity, could have been a reserve for other Tana delta settlements.

Ungwana was well placed to tap the produce of the interior, especially along the lower and mid Tana, with the river serving as a waterway; it was probably a gateway community. Wherever trade is important to the growth of a region, the most influential communities will tend to develop and be situated at strategic locales for controlling the flow of merchandise. These communities flourish at the passage points into and out of distinct natural or cultural regions, and serve as 'gateways' which link their regions to external trade. Ungwana, located at the mouth of the Tana (a river that traverses the forested and sometimes arid region of the interior), would have been well suited as a gateway to interior commodities on the one hand and overseas trade on the other.

Although at present there is no good harbour, possibly owing to silting or land upheaval, there is a possibility that Ungwana possessed a deep-water harbour in the past. It is also clear that trade did not necessarily require a deep harbour, and that shallow ones are good for mooring and repair work on the types of boats likely to have been used (dhows). In any case, most of the settlements were actually situated in shallow areas. Thus the idea of a deep-water harbour is a present-day European navigational concept which did not apply in east Africa.

Water for domestic use was plentiful and was obtained from numerous wells found within the town; still today, Ungwana and the surrounding area produce fresh water a few metres below the ground. These wells, which can also be paralleled with others along the Swahili coast, are also similar to some of the inland types and as such are important in the study of the interaction between the coast and the interior, and of the part played by inland groups in the development of the towns. They suggest some architectural influence from the hinterland from areas such as Elwak and Wajir in northeastern Kenya.

At its peak Ungwana was very prosperous. It was a complex society, with a high occurrence of prestige goods. In the fourteenth to seventeenth centuries AD, the town centred on groups of stone houses with a mosque nearby. These groups – judging from the recent past and even the present Swahili settlement organization – were probably *mitaa* or wards, which are usually based on clan affiliation. However, it would be premature to refer to these groups of houses as *mitaa*, since it is still not clear how old this phenomenon is.

At the centre of the town was a large building which appears to have belonged to a wealthy person or ruler of some sort. The structure has been referred to as the 'palace'

(Fig. 42.3) (Abungu 1988), and its annex probably belonged to an important person and his relatives. Noteworthy is the delicate issue of rulers with 'palaces' in Swahili settlements, which has been questioned by, among others, Allen & Wilson (1979). It is only plausible, in the case of rulers, to view them not as all-powerful sultans wielding authoritarian rule over their subjects, but as successful traders who accumulated power through commercial ventures and through descent, with the first family settlers standing a good chance of being given the responsibility of leadership. The town wall was found to have been a later addition which enclosed a large settlement (45 acres), although the extent to which mud and thatch structures spread beyond the town wall is still not clearly defined.

Ungwana is not only older than has previously been thought, but it was also more important. Its strategic location on the mouth of the Tana favoured it in so far as coast–interior trade was concerned. Its power and wealth are represented in the prestigious buildings and imported goods found within the town. It seems possible that Ungwana was the centre of the powerful kingdom of Ozi.

The Tana basin and ceramic tradition

Parts of the Tana are areas of intricate ecological systems. They are rich in both flora and fauna and the Tana valley, in most cases, is heavily forested. On the high veld, the grassy environment is conducive to pastoralism. Symbiotic relationships have developed between inhabitants, and some groups have actually interacted so much that they have lost their original language and have taken that of their more powerful neighbours; in all these cases, the various groups maintain their individual economies. The present inhabitants are not the only ones who have lived in the area; the basin has many sites of earlier iron-using communities, some of whom cultivated, while others kept cattle or were hunter-gatherers.

The groups which can be recognized from seventh century AD had contacts with the coastal area (Abungu 1989). Pottery assemblages found on sites along the river are closely similar to those found in early levels at Ungwana and at other early sites along the coast such as Manda and Shanga; this pottery tradition also seems to extend to the Tanzanian and Mozambican coasts. It is a quite distinct assemblage which has been referred to by different names: Chittick (1974) referred to it as 'Early Kitchen ware', Wilding (1977a) as 'Swahili ware' and Horton & Mutoro (n.d.) as 'Tana ware'. The latter term will be used here.

The tradition of the pottery technology from this region has been divided into two facies, the river facies and the coastal facies, based on the study of fabric, decoration, surface treatment and form. This resulted in the coastal facies being divided into an early phase: Ungwana, Shanga and Manda; and a late phase: later Ungwana pottery. The early phase of the coastal material is nearly identical to the pottery found at the Tana basin sites; however, the late phase is also similar, yet there are a number of new motifs and forms. Some of the new forms are imitations of imported vessels. This late phase should be seen as a continuous development from the earlier one, with no discontinuity either in time or space. The Tana tradition has proved to be widespread (Abungu 1989).

Coast–interior relations: the Tana delta and basin

The first Swahili settlements developed along the northern Swahili coast, on the islands of Manda and Pate (Fig. 42.1), partly as a result of their strategic location in the Indian Ocean commercial world.

These early settlements were followed from the tenth century AD onwards by the rapid expansion of other settlements, both in the Lamu archipelago and on the Tana delta (Fig. 42.1). It appears that the juxtaposition of a number of distinct ecological zones, within the northern coast of Kenya and southern Somalia, stimulated regional symbiosis; this, in turn, provided a strong economic basis for the foundation of these island and mainland settlements. On the Tana delta, settlements like Ungwana appear to have become communities that maintained important positions in local affairs, and in relation to other delta and coastal sites, from the end of the first millennium AD to the beginning of the seventeenth century. However, to be able to take part in, and maintain, the level of trade, closer contact with the hinterland sources of raw materials for trade was necessary.

This relation between the coast and its hinterland is evidenced not only by the similarity in pottery tradition but also by trade goods, oral traditions of the various groups and the literature of early European writers.

The pottery traditions of the Tana river valley and the coastal sites were nearly identical. In addition, there is archaeological evidence for trade along the Tana; this includes imported glass beads, copper chains, aragonite beads, etc., but only one imported pottery sherd was found *in situ*, at Wenje in the mid Tana basin (Fig. 42.1). By coastal standards, there are few archaeological pointers of contacts in the form of trade goods.

There are three possible reasons for the scarcity of trade goods in the hinterland. First, that the goods which were traded were perishable; these could have included such things as salt, leather and cloth, and other organic materials which would not be visible in the archaeological record. Among the Pokomo, and along the Tana, a longstanding trade contact is recorded between the coast and the interior, which included items like ochre and salt; this trade involved Swahili traders and, at a later date, even Arabs joined the trade. This trade was not confined to the Pokomo and the Swahili coast; there was also trade between the Pokomo and Malakote, the Somali and other groups in the north. This trade involved the exchange of, among other things, goats, until the early part of the twentieth century.

Second, that there was an intricate system of trade organization which could have depended on preferences and value attachment to different goods. The hinterland groups probably never saw the need for porcelain, and so never acquired it. Still today, hunter–gatherers, pastoralists and, to some extent, even farmers of the region, do not attach much value to Chinese and European wares; but such wares are still seen as status symbols in the coastal towns.

Third, that the Swahili, as middlemen, probably needed to prevent prestige goods from reaching the interior, and instead replaced the imported goods with others, made at the coast, that were required in the interior. This could explain the portrayal of the interior as a wild place with fierce people, all probably propaganda to deter potential competitors.

Conclusion

In general, coast–interior relations seem to have been alliances between the groups
inhabiting the two regions, as attested by the evidence of oral traditions, environment
and archaeology. Indeed, it is reported in both Swahili chronicles and early Portuguese
writings that each and every Swahili town had a pact (alliance) with a particular group
from the interior. Such alliances served for protection, trade and other bilateral relations. Both the settlement data from the Mijikenda *makaya* and their outlying
villages in the coastal hinterland and the towns and ecological systems of the Tana river
and Tana delta demonstrate that the coast of east Africa was a region of autochthonous
dynamic social and economic integration, rather than simply a dependant of middle
eastern and oriental external influence.

43 Urban trajectories on the Zimbabwean plateau

Paul J. J. Sinclair,

Innocent Pikirayi, Gilbert Pwiti

& Robert Soper

Perceiving complexity: the case of the Zimbabwe state

In south-central Africa the problem of state formation has been interpreted from a number of clearly differentiated theoretical positions among historians, anthropologists and archaeologists which crosscut traditional disciplinary boundaries. Broadly speaking these may be divided into formalist approaches, which tend to concentrate on generalized patterns in the data, and substantivist approaches, which are concerned with the data in its specific material contexts (see Dalton 1981). Most recently, the development of historical and social relativist critiques (e.g. Hodder 1978a; Shanks & Tilley 1987), has caused the reappraisal of both cognitively oriented and materialist models in order to accommodate the situational variation in social processes that takes place at local and regional levels (Sinclair 1987).

In this rapidly changing theoretical context, disagreements are widespread and include the definition of the character of state as opposed to kingdom, confederation and chieftaincy and the nature of the processes which characterize state formation, whether, for example, a state is organized around a non-exploitative redistributary network or an oppressive class system, locally developed or externally stimulated. Much of this discourse is focused on the settlement of Great Zimbabwe (e.g. Huffman 1972; Garlake 1978; Beach 1980; Huffman 1981; Sinclair 1983; Huffman 1986b; Hall 1987; Sinclair 1987).

Because of an increasing emphasis on the particular historical conditions of the environment and the social landscape in social formation processes, there is now a greater need for more detailed archaeological information concerning the nature of social interactions in specific regions. Zimbabwe is fortunate in this regard, having a varied database built up by professional archaeologists for more than eighty years. The locational records of archaeological site surveys, combined with the detailed accounts from individual site reports, provide a rich matrix of evidence for such research.

This evidence naturally presents both unique possibilities and also problems for interpretation. It is possible for archaeologists to analyse aspects of a settlement system not accessible to historians and anthropologists, either because the data is prehistoric or because no records exist beyond material remains. But such research is conducted with great difficulty, as it is necessary to consider in any model of settlement dynamics, at whatever level, how specific features reflect both regional or wider influences and the local situation at individual sites.

This approach is especially problematic because the interpretation of variability in archaeological sites is severely limited by the lack of ethnographic or original accounts which could provide information that might reduce the daunting number of possible factors resulting in the nature and development of archaeological sites (e.g. Doran & Hodson 1975, pp. 94–7; Schiffer 1976). The problem is not confined to the interpretation of material remains, but extends to methodological problems, sampling in archaeological survey, excavation technique and in the selection of data for further analysis. In choosing a sample of sites for settlement analysis, for example, the archaeologist must consider a range of difficult questions regarding their comparability, based on such factors as whether they were living sites with a wide range of activities or single-purpose sites, and whether they were contemporary (Sinclair 1987, p. 50).

Because of the potential interplay of influences at different levels of observation, one promising approach is to take a holistic view of the larger analytical categories such as economy, ideology and social and political organization, gradually refining this view at successively smaller scales to consider how such general tendencies are deflected or modified by situational factors. The general model supported by this holistic approach conceives of a settlement pattern as a series of spatial contexts at successively smaller scales, each one 'nested' in the material and social context defined by its observational scale (Sinclair 1987, pp. 156–60).

Because this type of settlement analysis integrates social and environmental data in a historical context, the 'spatial finger prints' of present-day societies which are ethnographically well known can provide useful comparisons for interpreting certain aspects of past archaeological site distributions – as Butzer (1982, p. 238) has shown in suggesting six alternative regional models for hunter-gatherer settlement mobility in prehistory on the basis of ethnographic examples.

In regard to the behaviour of a population living in a hierarchically nested series of settlement groupings, it is clear that, given variation in group size and organization and the nature of the local environment, specific influences should not be considered as generalized conditions, but rather as situational factors that will vary in significance depending on the scale at which they are observed (Sinclair 1987, p. 33).

In contrast, simplistic interpretations favouring utilitarian explanations in accounting for intra-site distributions of artefacts appear increasingly ill founded. Their weakness is exposed by, for example, recent structuralist work on the organizing role of sets of cognitive rules which are best seen in a cultural frame of reference (see Arhem (1985) on the Maasai in relation to the empirical ethnoarchaeological work carried out by Ammerman, Gifford & Voorips (1977)). Such a fascinating range of interrelationships and the problems associated with them are lost if the primary considerations are the functional aspects of subsistence and the articulation of sites to surrounding territories. As Thornton (1980, p. 251) has observed, territory itself is as much an artefact as are tools or houses. Territory should therefore be seen at least at ground level as a cultural construct, and not merely in terms of utilitarian economic adaptation to a specific environment.

Inter-site analysis in a single area may not reveal extensive cultural variability, but from a different perspective it can provide a rich field for the consideration of inter-group relations in regard to environmental and political factors. Indeed, it is possible that phenomena expressed at different levels of organization may have demonstrable links: the distinction between shared space at site level and political space which is competed for at the regional level is one such possibility. As Thornton has suggested, 'Politicized territory is a specific social realization of the cultural images of space that serve to order many sorts of phenomena' (Thornton 1980, p. 251). In addition, environmental and climatological factors provide differential constraints and possibilities for each of the culturally, socially and politically constituted organizational levels; and the possibility of variation at different scales is even more apparent when localized production and extended networks of exchange are integrated into the analysis.

A multidimensional and holistic view also departs from the traditional distinction of time and space as organizing variables when considered at a large scale, for it is necessary to allow for differing degrees of spatial and temporal variation over a region. Ignoring such variability has been a problem in some ethnoarchaeological work, as pointed out by Gould (1980, pp. 32–4), which uses a crude form of the principle of uniformity to relate present and past activities in the form of direct analogies. The danger here is that such a deterministic approach which 'oppresses history' will obscure temporal variation in the society under study. A similar tendency of collapsing spatio-temporal variation by using a synchronic 'archaeological present' for behavioural interpretation of inadequately sampled archaeological materials is also widely prevalent.

Owing to the complexity of the factors operating in relation to both depositional and the post-depositional contexts, it is necessary to simplify the analytical frame of reference and artificially fix consideration of variation along a chronological dimension. Sinclair & Lundmark (1984) have attempted to overcome this problem by using a category of space–time units (square kilometres x radiocarbon years) in order to assess, albeit rather artificially, the spatio-temporal context of archaeological information. It may also be advantageous for the development of ethnoarchaeological studies to apply a similar set of spatio-temporal categories to ethnographic sources which have often tended to be framed in terms of an 'ethnographic present'.

Although spatial hierarchies may be regarded theoretically as the products of different combinations of social and environmental factors, the practical identification of such phenomena in the archaeological record is still in the first stages of development. In Zimbabwe, a disproportionate amount of research effort has been concentrated upon the capital itself. However, the work of Summers (1971) and the more recent work of Garlake (1978) and Sinclair & Lundmark (1984) have begun to assess the spatial extent of regional site distributions, as has a series of recent contributions which extend the analytical frame to surrounding areas such as Botswana (Denbow 1984; Denbow 1986), northern South Africa (Huffman 1986b; Huffman & Hanisch 1987; Maggs & Whitelaw 1991) and Mozambique (Sinclair 1987; Morais 1988) (Fig. 43.1). These are complemented by recent syntheses by Connah (1987) and Hall (1987) which introduce contrasting comparative elements into the discussion. The balanced treatment of economic and socio-political organization on the Zimbabwean plateau by Connah, comparing state systems from throughout the continent, contrasts with the intense fixation in South Africa on questions of ethnicity and boundedness of social groupings at the inter-site level and the extent to which the southern Bantu Cattle Pattern is reflected at the intra-site level (Huffman 1986a; Hall 1987; Maggs & Whitelaw 1991).

Interpretation of results is only just beginning but already it is becoming apparent that traditional archaeological foci on external influences – gold and other elite artefacts and their trade routes – and the interrelation of material culture, economy and environment should be examined in new ways.

Methodological and empirical considerations

Following intra-site analysis in Mozambique (Sinclair, Morais, Adamowicz & Duarte, Ch. 24, this volume), an attempt at developing a methodology for tackling inter-site problems was made during the early 1980s in the context of research on the Zimbabwe state, c. AD 1250–1450. The approach adopted (and see Sinclair & Lundmark 1984) included a computer-aided searching procedure to assess the potential clustering levels

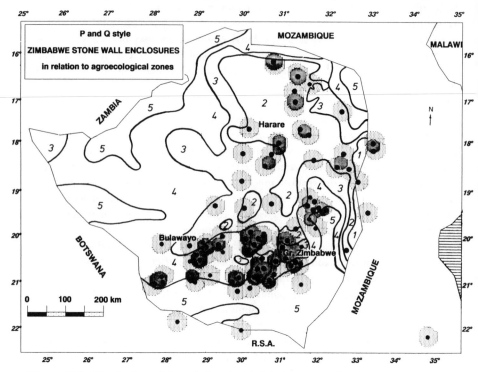

Figure 43.1 Distribution of P- and Q-style Zimbabwe stone wall enclosures in relation to agroecological zones (after Sinclair 1987). zone 1: highlands; zones 2–3: agriculturally suitable; zone 4: regular crop failures but good pasturage; zone 5: agriculturally unsuitable but good winter grazing

represented in a constellation of points, in this case farming community sites and stone buildings from the Zimbabwe state. It was possible to produce relative density maps of site distributions at selected clustering levels. Such clusters should be conceptualized within a given space–time framework as site contemporaneity cannot be included as an *a priori* assumption.

Most significant, however, is the very clear correlation which has been found between southern clusters of the Zimbabwe state and zone 4 in the agroecological survey of Zimbabwe (Fig. 43.1) (Sinclair 1987). This correlation is so clear that even the buffer zones between the clusters are also included within it. Two exceptions, the capital, Great Zimbabwe, which is in a relatively more productive agricultural region, and the drier, though iron-rich, area of Mt Buhwa, lend caution to facile generalizations.

There remains a strong impression that environmental factors of topography, soils and rainfall play an important role in the localization of southern clusters as a whole, but it seems clear that cluster spacing and the internal organization within clusters is much more the result of social and political factors. Indeed, when the clusters of the Zimbabwe state are viewed in a wider temporal frame of reference which incorporates the earlier Mapungubwe polity and the succeeding Mutapa state, it is apparent that significant continuities and also discontinuities exist in the record. This is especially clear if capital clusters are distinguished from provincial ones. The former show a relatively high site density and a chronologically limited existence of *c.* 200 years while the provincial clusters seem to have a more prolonged but less intensely settled character (Sinclair 1987).

It appears that what is being dealt with is a form of urbanism which, on the scale of the individual site, was constrained temporally. However, when a larger frame of reference is chosen, it can be seen that the settlement system as a whole maintained a series of urban settlements beginning from the late first millennium AD in the Limpopo valley with Bambandyanalo followed by Mapungubwe (Huffman 1988), and later, on the Zimbabwe plateau, by Great Zimbabwe. On the subregional level it is apparent from the large-scale clusters identified in the fuzzy-set analysis (Sinclair 1987), as well as historical documentation (see below), that the Zimbabwe state was succeeded in the west by the Torwa and Changamire states and in the north by the Mutapa state (see below).

This set of regional and local interrelations, from the period of Great Zimbabwe to that of the Mutapa state, suggests strongly that the elite settlements should be considered as essentially courts of paramounts and local chiefs which were occupied for single reigns, within the context of a larger social and political system that appears to have continuity from prehistoric to historic times (Sinclair 1987).

One element accounting for the dispersed pattern could be from the practice of collateral succession to chieftaincy with succeeding paramounts controlling (and accordingly building zimbabwe settlements) in different territorial subunits (wards or *maduhnu*) (Sinclair 1987, pp. 155–6). Collateral succession to chieftaincy is well attested in the ethnographic literature (Holleman 1952; Weinrich 1971) and acknowledged if not established in historical sources (Randles 1975; D. Beach, *pers. comm.*). Other forms of succession such as primogeniture, although apparently not as common, are known in

Shona society (D. Beach, *pers. comm.*) and can be expected to contribute to the complex of inter-site spatial relationships.

Current work is focusing on these differences, using a multidimensional approach that analyses archaeological survey data with environmental, ethnohistoric and ethno-graphic information in order to explore the dynamics of settlement relations in regional and local contexts. At the intra-site level a re-examination of the extensive urban settlement of Great Zimbabwe, following up on work by Huffman (1977), has recently been undertaken by a joint Swedish/Zimbabwean team. In order to obtain an adequate spatial coverage of the site, randomly chosen soil samples were collected from over 600 ha at a density of one per ha. Geophysical analysis, measurement of soil colour and geochemical analysis of phosphate concentrations were carried out over the whole town area. In addition, a micro-coring programme, consisting of drilling more than 200 cores of 50 mm diameter, was carried out in the western part of the site, and extended to the central valley area. This has permitted the interpolation of the stratigra-phy over an area of *c.* 20 ha. A compilation of preliminary results built up on the basis of the soil sampling, field walking and local information (W. Ndoro and D. Collett, *pers. comm.*), correlated with maps compiled by Whitty, Munro and Huffman (Files of the Great Zimbabwe Museum) permit an estimate of the developmental succession of the town (see Fig. 43.2).

It is only after these and other complex aspects of cultural and environmental context have been analysed that artefact and ecofact spatial variability can be considered in the context of status and power relations and influences, or indeed in terms of cognitive categories. The wide range of possible oppositions potentially applicable to the differ-ent archaeological distributions – for instance elite/peasantry, male/female, left/right, inside/outside the enclosure, as well as the differential location of status goods, food remains and work implements – provides a complex web of interpretive potentialities which need to be assessed empirically.

The building up of a database from the results of statistical sampling, which will allow the application of various methods to assess the goodness of fit between different interpretations and the archaeological data, is both advantageous and necessary. Only then will archaeologists in Zimbabwe be in a position to judge, from a position supported by archaeological data, the cognitive interpretations of spatial layouts at zimbabwe sites such as those of Huffman (1984) which have been roundly criticized by anthropologists (e.g. Blacking 1985) and historians (e.g. Beach 1991).

In a new development in northern Mashonaland further work is focusing on a multidimensional approach that analyses archaeological survey data with environmen-tal, ethnohistoric and ethnographic information in order to explore the dynamics of settlement relations in regional and local contexts. An examination of the rise of the Great Zimbabwe tradition on the northern plateau illustrates how the traditional preoccupation with external influence and relations, and functionalist settlement analy-sis, have obscured a fascinating and complex picture of organized and highly politicized social and economic relations within the Zimbabwe state.

Great Zimbabwe tradition settlement location: the environmental setting

The Great Zimbabwe tradition belongs to a period dating from around the eleventh century to the sixteenth century AD (Garlake 1973a; Huffman 1980b; Maggs 1984). It is associated with the beginnings and growth of complex systems contrasting markedly with earlier forms of social organization (Huffman 1979; Garlake 1982; Maggs 1984). The presence of stone walls in a variety of forms and styles, a broadly similar ceramic style which varies somewhat through space and time and a similar subsistence economy based on agriculture and livestock herding, with a particular emphasis on cattle, characterizes this tradition (Garlake 1973a; Garlake 1982).

Over 150 stone enclosures of this tradition are found on the Zimbabwe plateau but some have been reported in Mozambique, South Africa and Botswana. The main site is Great Zimbabwe, on the south-central part of the Zimbabwe plateau. In northern Zimbabwe the radiocarbon dates suggest an intrusion of this tradition on the basic populations of the Harare and Musengezi traditions. Cultural interaction has been suggested for some sites (Soper & Pwiti 1988; Thornycroft 1988).

The sites to be examined now – Nhunguza, Chisvingo and Yellow Jacket – are located on the northern part of the Zimbabwe plateau roughly 40 km north-northeast of Harare (Fig. 43.3).

Analysis of Great Zimbabwe tradition sites suggests that the state was organized as a three-tier structure, the different sites belonging to different levels within this hierarchical structure. The stone walls enclosed residential units of small groups of people, probably a ruling elite, and the walls themselves were probably a symbolic expression of power and prestige. Archaeological evidence has indicated that the enclosures known in Shona as *zimbabwe* were surrounded by commoner peasant settlements on whom the elite probably relied for subsistence and other needs.

Research on the distribution and location of sites of the tradition has been regional in scope. A pioneer study by Summers (1960) made a generalized national survey of the relationship between settlements and environment. A subsequent study (Summers 1971) focused on the importance of gold-mining and trade in the location of *zimbabwes*. Summers saw an almost complete accord between the distribution of the sites and gold fields, ancient mines and trade routes. This conclusion was challenged by Garlake (1978), who had made a more detailed examination of the evidence.

Garlake proposed that cattle herding was of paramount importance during the Zimbabwe phase and that the distribution of the sites reflected a pattern designed to take advantage of the differential seasonal availability of prime grazing on the highveld and lowveld of Zimbabwe. Livestock transhumance was therefore seen as one of the major variables in locational decisions. This proposal was supported by Sinclair (1984b) following excavations at Montevideo, near Great Zimbabwe.

Livestock transhumance as an important locational factor in the distribution of Great Zimbabwe tradition sites comes from Barker's (1978) study of Manyikeni in Mozambique. Barker indicated that the Manyikeni subsistence economy was heavily dependent on livestock, especially cattle, in an environment in which a successful agricultural economy was not possible. However, although livestock transhumance

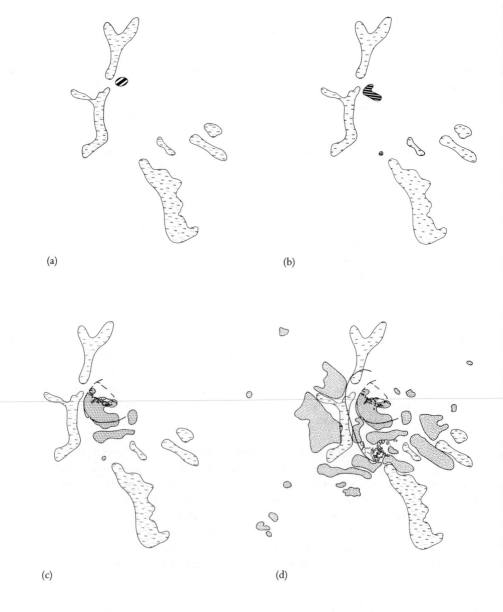

(a)

(b)

(c)

(d)

Figure 43.2 Preliminary diachronic model of the development of Great Zimbabwe:
43.2

(a) Period 1 AD 300–900. Early farming community: Gokomere tradition finds in valley (not shown) and Zhizo settlement on the hill slopes.

(b) Period 2. Later farming community Gumanye hilltop settlement and finds in valley. First stone walls *c.* AD 1000.

(c) Period 3. Expansion of stone built area. First perimeter wall and indications of settlement outside the wall *c.* AD 1150–1300.

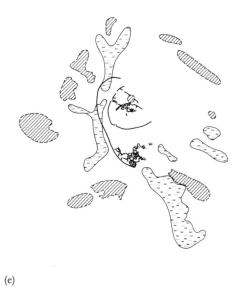

(e)

(f)

LEGEND

|||||| Zhizo site

Period 3/4

Post-Period 4

Marshy area

Drilled area

Walls

Daga pit

Quarry

0 100 200 300 m

(d) Period 4. Full development of Great Zimbabwe town both on hill and in valley. Outer perimeter wall differentiates lower and higher status areas *c.* AD 1300–1450. From 1450 hill abandoned but valley continues to be partially occupied.

(e) Period 5 post-AD 1700. Latest occupation with similar spatial pattern as before.

(f) Composite phase plan of urban development at Great Zimbabwe, showing drilled areas.

may have been of importance at this site, its significance to the whole range of Great Zimbabwe tradition sites should not simply be assumed, and has been questioned by Huffman (1979) and Thorp (1983).

Site catchment analysis

Site catchment analysis (SCA) was employed to investigate any correlations between settlement location and subsistence economy. SCA aims to understand the resources utilized by a site through detailed studies of the environment around it. The basic

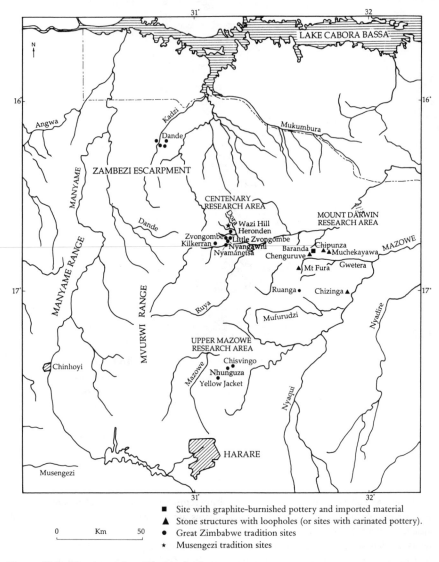

Figure 43.3   Sites in northern Mashonaland.

assumption is that agricultural communities would not exploit areas beyond a 5 km radius, while for hunter–gatherers, a 10 km radius has been proposed. The methodology applied in this research is based on Higgs & Vita Finzi (1970; 1972) as modified by Bailey & Davidson (1983). Criticisms made by Hodder & Orton (1976), Flannery (1976), Rossmann (1976) and Dennell (1980) on the use of SCA have been taken into account.

The method of SCA was thought to be particularly applicable to the Zimbabwean context because archaeology has established that the economy was mixed, based on the cultivation of sorghum, millet, cowpeas, ground beans and some rice, and the herding of sheep, goat and cattle. Further, it is clear that the settlements were permanent, as excavation at Nhunguza (Figs 43.3, 43.4) has indicated continual occupation for at least a generation (Garlake 1973b). Ethnographic observations (Bullock 1927; Kuper 1954; Bourdillon 1976) confirm that agricultural and herding pursuits were generally carried out around the settlements, falling within the arbitrary 5 km radius suggested for SCA.

Nhunguza, Chisvingo and Yellow Jacket (Figs 43.3, 43.4, 43.5, 43.6) lie in generally similar micro-environments characterized by rocky granite hills and large bare granite outcrops. The hills are interspersed with level plains and valleys, with seasonal and perennial streams cutting across the valleys. *Brachystegia* savanna woodland is the dominant vegetation, the grass dominating areas of major forest clearance. The domi-

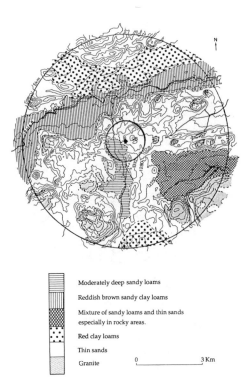

Moderately deep sandy loams

Reddish brown sandy clay loams

Mixture of sandy loams and thin sands especially in rocky areas.

Red clay loams

Thin sands

Granite   0   3 Km

Figure 43.4 Nhunguza site catchment distribution map.

nant soil types are coarse to fine sands and sandy loams of granitic origin. Some clays and clay loams originating from intrusive rocks like dolerite also occur. The area enjoys medium rainfall with an annual average of 700–800 mm. Altitude ranges from 900 to 1500 m above sea-level.

Soil types and agricultural potential

Within the individual site territories, six main soil types, ranging from granite-derived deep sandy loams, reddish brown clay loams, dolorite red clay loams through to coarse-grained sands, were identified. These soils differ in their agricultural potential according to moisture retention capacity, drainage and inherent fertility. Within the context of the technology of iron-using communities the ease with which the soil could be worked is also of importance. Ethnographic data suggest that because iron hoes were the major agricultural implement, lighter sandy soils would have been preferred to heavier clay soils. In any case these lighter soils were more suitable for the cultivation of crops as they produce higher yields.

Vegetation

The distribution of vegetation reflects soil variability with woodland clearing mostly in areas with moderately deep reddish brown sandy loams. Grass cover varies according

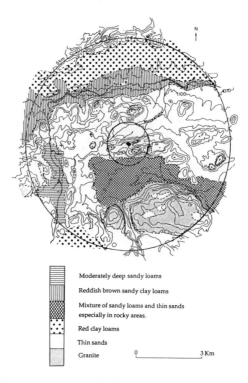

Moderately deep sandy loams

Reddish brown sandy clay loams

Mixture of sandy loams and thin sands especially in rocky areas.

Red clay loams

Thin sands

Granite

0   3 Km

Figure 43.5   Chisvingo site catchment distribution map.

to tree density, with heavier red clay loams supporting more grass, mainly due to poor drainage. These soils therefore support good grazing. The characteristic grass species include the dominant *Hyperrhenia* spp., *Themeda triandra*, *Heteropogon contrallus* and *Brachiaria* spp. The last three constitute the most suitable grazing especially during the wet summer months (October–April), but they tend to have a low protein content during the dry season (May–September). This leads to loss of condition in livestock, especially cattle. The *Hyperrhenia* species are only suitable for grazing during the early stages of growth in the wet seasons, especially after bush fires. In the dry season, however, grasses lose condition and the solution in modern times has been to provide supplementary feeds, and to graze cattle along rivers. Another solution has been to extend the grazing territory up to as much as 10 km. There seems no reason therefore to invoke transhumance as a strategy adopted by iron-using communities. Another relevant point is that the Sanga breed of cattle, evident in most Great Zimbabwe tradition faunal assemblages, is resistant to a seasonal low nutritional plane.

Discussion

The overall environmental picture is one offering a wide range of resources both for agriculture and pastoral pursuits (Table 43.1). Tsetse-fly is absent. In addition, there is a range of edible wild fruit and fauna, which could have been of some importance to the

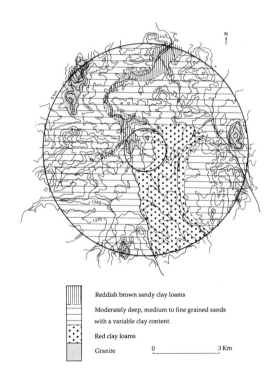

Figure 43.6 Yellow Jacket site catchment distribution map.

iron-using communities. An attempt was made to obtain estimates of the yield capacity of the site territories within a 1 and 2 km radius of the preferred soil types to gain some idea of the carrying capacity of each territory. Although these figures are based on historical and modern data, they do provide a reliable estimate (Tables 43.2, 43.3).

The picture that emerges from this research is significantly different from the classic theories of location being chosen in the context of gold-mining, external trade or transhumance. Instead, SCA suggests that proximity to suitable agricultural land, as well as grazing, was important. Two other variables, proximity to sources of permanent water and granite for building, presumably must also have been important factors. The overall scenario is of settled and self-sufficient communities.

Settlement patterns and the context of Great Zimbabwe tradition sites

The Centenary Research Area (Figs 43.1, 43.3, 43.7, 43.8, 43.9, 43.10) lies in north Zimbabwe some 25 km south of the Zambezi escarpment. The area is about 70 km to the north of the sites mentioned above. Here a group of five sites with stone walling and ceramics of the Great Zimbabwe tradition are situated within a 3 km radius of each

Table 43.1 Location of sites in relation to soil types, water and granite, in kms

Soil type	Nhunguza	Chisvingo	Yellow Jacket	Agricultural potential	Grazing
Moderately deep sandy loams	0	0	0	Good – prime cultivation	Good
Reddish brown sandy clay loams	0.2	2.2	0		
Sandy clay loams and thin sands especially in rocky areas	1.4	0.6	0	Good – but not easy to work with hoe – not suitable for traditional crops	Good
Red clay loams	2.4	3.5	0.4		
Thin sands	0	0	2.4	Poor – but possible cultivation	Rough grazing
Moderately deep, medium to fine-grained sands with a variable clay content	0	0	0	Good	Good potential
Granite	0	0.3	0		
Water	0.5	0.3	0.1		

Table 43.2 Comparison of catchment areas of Nhunguza, Chisvingo and Yellow Jacket

Site	1 km		2 km	
	Acreage	Yield estimate	Acreage	Yield estimate
Nhunguza Moderately deep sandy loams at 556 kg/ha	7.37 ha	4098 kg	19.25 ha	10,703 kg
Chisvingo Moderately deep sandy loams at 556 kg/ha	4.04 ha	2246 kg	32.17 ha	17,889.3 kg
Yellow Jacket Moderately deep medium to fine-grained sands with a variable clay content	15.04 ha	8801.5 kg	32.55 ha	18,097 kg

Table 43.3 Estimates of carrying capacity (nos. of individuals per year)

Territory radius	Nhunguza		Chisvingo		Yellow Jacket
	Uncorrected	Corrected	Uncorrected	Corrected	
1 km	22	22	13	9	49
2 km	82	62	99	66	101

other. Their study has provided information on the context and settlement pattern of the Great Zimbabwe tradition in this area.

Great Zimbabwe tradition sites have previously been studied largely in isolation, giving a very restricted picture of their significance and little or no idea of the populations which supported them. The survey area was delimited by an arbitrarily determined radius of 5 km from the sites of Zvongombe and Little Zvongombe (Fig. 43.3), with the aim of including a meaningful catchment area.

The greater part of the area consists of rolling terrain with scattered hills and outcrops rising to over 1200 m above sea-level, divided by the valleys of three small streams namely Tsatsi, Kamorirari and Makwrabeti, which converge to the east as tributaries of the river Dora. In the south-central part of the area is more broken country with larger hills. Geologically, the majority of the area is formed by granites and granitoid gneisses with limited intrusions of dolerite, notably Wazi Hill in the north. Soils are mainly greyish and sandy, derived from the granite, with areas of brown or red soils derived from dolerite or gneisses. Current land use is commercial farming, the main crop being tobacco. Much of the area is extensively cultivated on a fallow cycle of about four years in the case of tobacco, but the broken country mentioned above allows for only limited areas of cultivation.

Zvongombe North and South are on a substantial hill, Zv. South on the highest point and Zv. North in a saddle below the highest peak. Heronden is on the crest of a broad watershed with no upstanding rocks but some low outcrops almost flush with the ground surface. Little Zvongombe is on a slight eminence, the highest point for some distance around but with no steep approaches. Nyangawni is on a fairly gentle slope, not dominating in any way.

The survey

The survey was designed to cover 10 per cent of the survey area, using a random stratified sampling strategy based on 250 m quadrants (survey units), with the aim of providing a statistical estimate of site density and preferred location at successive stages. It was particularly concerned to investigate the settlement patterns of villages contemporary with the Great Zimbabwe tradition of stone structures. The area was first stratified into four land forms (Fig. 43.7): (1) rocky hills (6 per cent of stratified area); (2) arable land (56 per cent); (3) arable land interspersed with rock outcrops (27 per cent) and (4) river valleys (11 per cent). Individual quadrants were walked systematically by

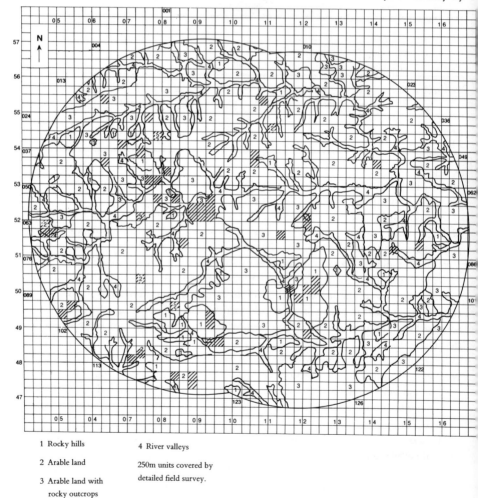

1 Rocky hills

2 Arable land

3 Arable land with rocky outcrops

4 River valleys

250m units covered by detailed field survey.

Figure 43.7 Centenary Research Area: topography and drainage.

teams of up to 6 or 7 people and all sites recorded on standard proforma. Surface scatters of potsherds with concentrations of three or more sherds per m^2 were classified as sites.

Within the survey area, but outside the statistical sample investigated, there are a number of sites which include seven rock painting sites, several Musengezi tradition burials and some hilltop sites with Musengezi pottery, the most important of which is Wazi Hill (Soper & Pwiti 1988).

The cultural succession

Apart from rock painting sites and a fairly general scatter of middle to late stone age artefacts mostly of quartz, the main cultural stages are as follows:

Early Gokomere tradition

Four sites have been located, of which the most important are Wazi Hill and Zvongombe East. The pottery can be assigned to phase 2 of the Early Iron Age and perhaps phase 3 in the case of Zvongombe East. On Huffman's classification (1971) the pottery can be assigned to phase 2 of the Early Iron Age and perhaps phase 3 in the case of Zvongombe East. These may belong to the Coronation/Maxton phases but the samples are too small for detailed analysis and comparison. Dates of AD 810 ± 80 and AD 860 ± 140 have been obtained from Wazi and Zvongombe East respectively.

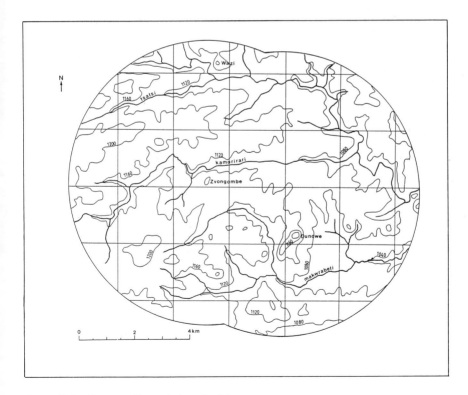

Figure 43.8 Centenary Research Area: land forms.

Musengezi tradition (Fig. 43.9)

Sites include burials in rock shelters and clefts, usually with complete pots, and occupation sites of which the most important is Wazi Hill. This is a village covering approximately 1 ha with up to 70 cm of deposits and early iron age material stratified beneath; on the hilltop itself is at least one house with Great Zimbabwe tradition sherds among predominantly Musengezi pottery. The distribution of the Musengezi tradition covers a wide area of northern Zimbabwe from north of Harare to the Zambezi escarpment. The only three previously available dates fell around the end of the thirteenth century AD. New dates from Wazi Hill extend this range to the sixteenth century, providing a convincing overlap with the Great Zimbabwe tradition.

Great Zimbabwe tradition (Fig. 43.10)

The Great Zimbabwe tradition sites, on the basis of architecture, ceramics and radiocarbon dates, belong to the Great Zimbabwe phase contemporary with the later stages of Great Zimbabwe itself.

Survey results

Apart from the stone structures, there are a number of surface sites with relatively high frequencies of graphite-burnished sherds but without stone walls. The sites are all on

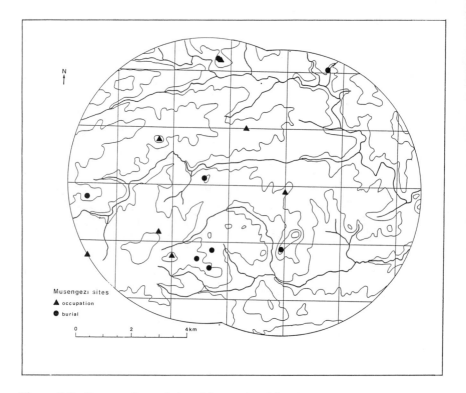

Figure 43.9   Centenary Research Area: Musengezi tradition sites.

cultivated land where the pottery is highly fragmented so that diagnosis of vessel shape is uncertain. However, one of the sites in the Nyamanetsa area in the south has one neck sherd with incised herringbone decoration consistent with Great Zimbabwe typology, while petrographic analysis shows a number of links between pairs of individual sherds from the *zimbabwes* themselves and several of the surface sites (Muringaniza 1989). More recent pottery from this part of the country, while still imperfectly known, does not appear to include a significant proportion of burnishing, so these sites may be provisionally attributed to the Great Zimbabwe tradition.

The sites comprise relatively small (30 x 40 m diameter) concentrations of sherds, occasionally accompanied by soil discoloration suggesting a ploughed–out midden. These can be reasonably attributed to homestead sites occupied for a limited period.

Discussion

Although the sample size is still rather small, it can be seen that Musengezi burials are all situated on rocky hills or outcrops providing the necessary shelters or clefts, while settlement sites are on hills or on, or immediately adjacent to, outcrops (Figs 43.8, 43.9). The size of these settlement sites is generally uncertain, since the hilltop and outcrop sites are usually represented by a sparse scatter of sherds among the rocks. One

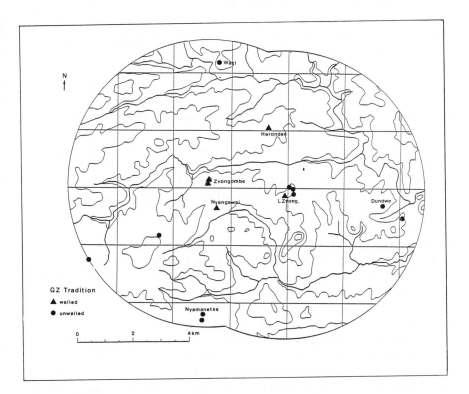

Figure 43.10   Centenary Research Area: Great Zimbabwe tradition sites.

site has a thin scatter of sherds extending over some 50 m, whereas Wazi, as mentioned above, covers perhaps 1 ha.

The stone structures must of their nature be adjacent to granite sources on hills or outcrops providing suitable exfoliated granite (Fig. 43.9). However, available stone appears very limited in the case of Heronden and Nyangawni. The size of Heronden is unknown, having been destroyed and the stone removed without record in the 1950s; Nyangawni has only one low section of wall 10 m long, perhaps reflecting the shortage of stone.

The unwalled sites with probable Great Zimbabwe tradition pottery are all in open situations, either on clear arable land or in the vicinity of outcrops but still in the open (Figs 43.8, 43.10). One site, however, is situated around outcrops along a relatively gentle ridge crest; another exception is Wazi Hill but this, as indicated above, is basically a Musengezi settlement, within which is at least one house with Great Zimbabwe tradition affinities and a limited amount of Great Zimbabwe tradition pottery. Great Zimbabwe tradition sites have not been found in the broken hilly part of the research area where Musengezi sites are relatively common.

There is a clear preference for the grey sandy granite soils, the main exception being again Wazi Hill where dark brown clayey soil underlies the Musengezi/early iron age occupation layers within the hill complex and early iron age material lies on the surface of the red-brown soils south of the hill. One site was located on reddish soils. Two early iron age sites are found on the brown soils. The heavier red arable areas appear to be lacking in sites. This observation is important in the light of the data obtained from site catchment analysis discussed above.

Musengezi sites appear to have a more general distribution than Great Zimbabwe tradition sites in the survey area. Chronologically, it is likely that the Musengezi tradition covers a wider time bracket than the Great Zimbabwe tradition in this region, but the effects of this on site density and distribution would depend on population density and duration of site occupation, both of which are unknown in the absence of more precise dating. The initial impression of the distribution of Great Zimbabwe tradition sites, based on the stone structures, was of a fairly close cluster of settlements. The nearest known related site is Kilkerran 15 km to the southwest and beyond that the Dande cluster over 50 km to the northwest and Ruanga a similar distance to the southeast (Fig. 43.3). The recognition of unwalled sites, ceramically related to the *zimbabwes* and distinct in ceramics and physical setting from the Musengezi sites, modifies this initial impression. Thirteen sites fall into this category, of which five are tightly grouped within 450 m or less of Little Zvongombe. The others are more widely scattered up to 4 km or more from the nearest stone structure. The true nature of the settlement pattern is still difficult to discern, since only a very small sample of the research area has been examined and it is not known whether or not such sites extend further into the surrounding area. In addition, there is no dating from any of the surface sites to prove their contemporaneity with all or any of the stone structures, nor has the contemporaneity of the stone structures with each other been demonstrated.

However, a scenario consistent with the evidence may be advanced, even if it is rather speculative: (1) The stone structures form a coherent contemporary complex rather than successive settlements. This is suggested by their varying nature, physical position and extent of adjoining occupation, which would support different but perhaps complementary social functions. (2) Around these were scattered small individual homesteads, probably agricultural in nature, perhaps also with livestock. These extend to the limits of the survey area and may (or may not) extend considerably further. (3) Most of these minor sites are ceramically mutually distinct from the Musengezi communities, some of which must have coexisted with them. Wazi Hill does show clear Great Zimbabwe tradition influence within a substantial Musengezi community, the hilltop residence suggesting that it is an important representative of the Great Zimbabwe tradition.

The picture thus far, then, suggests a group of more important Great Zimbabwe tradition communities, perhaps a 'political elite', though this may entail an unacceptable level of supposition, supported by a network of small subordinate settlements. These could have established themselves among a pre-existing native Musengezi population.

It is still not clear what happened to both the Great Zimbabwe and Musengezi tradition communities during the periods coinciding with the historical period but new evidence from 50 km east of the Centenary Research Area reveals possible relationships with the Mutapa state.

The historical period in northern Zimbabwe: archaeological evidence for the Mutapa state

Introduction

Archaeological evidence from northern Zimbabwe during the historical period provides clear evidence of the social and cultural complexity already noticed for the preceding ('prehistoric') Zimbabwe state (Sinclair 1987). The first Portuguese visited the Zimbabwe plateau at the beginning of the sixteenth century and reported the existence of a fully developed Mutapa state with trading links to the coast. The earliest written sources referred to events mostly in the northern parts of the country. This is the same period covered by Shona oral traditions, spanning the period from the late fifteenth century to the beginning of the present century.

Previous scholars have tended to use these historical sources in a way which gave them greater authority than available archaeological data. Abraham (1961) believed that whatever information was derived from oral traditions could be verified accurately from Portuguese written sources. As a result, the concept of the Mutapa state is a historical construct (Beach 1980; Mudenge 1988); no integrationist approach as suggested by Dymond (1974) exists. Broad themes and issues such as local and regional interactions, conflict, collapse and decline remain to be investigated. Only Beach (1987) provides useful guidelines as to how archaeologists can best handle written sources especially those relating to events of the last century.

Integrationist studies should adopt a processual dimension: documents should be used to delineate social variables such as ethnicity, religion, politics, occupation and economy; historical archaeology should be used to investigate the problems concerning the spatial scale of socio-cultural processes and to explain the generation or specificity of cultural material (Hodder 1978a).

In northern Zimbabwe a number of issues or processes can be investigated within the framework of historical archaeology – this archaeological information being in no way subservient to written or oral traditional sources.

The site of Baranda: a case study

The site of Baranda (Figs 43.3, 43.11, 43.12) is named after the owner of today's farm situated in the Chesa small-scale farming area about 8 km to the east of the Mt Darwin service centre. Geologically, the site lies very close to the northern extension of the gold belt. The soil cover is light grey and sandy, referred to by the local farmers as *mashapa* (and see below) to characterize its agriculturally less productive potential.

Most of Baranda's 15 to 20 ha is occupied by six small-scale farms (Fig. 43.11). Because of this, as well as the results of soil erosion, house structures have been destroyed (Fig. 43.12). However, from excavation of 57 1 x 1 m test pits across the site and surface collection from almost 100 5 x 5 m units (Pikirayi In Preparation), the evidence from pole-impressed *daga* lumps and hardened clay floor material was sufficient to indicate that the site was an aggregate of cone and cylinder houses, with several open spaces, some with almost no artefacts (possibly, therefore, marketplaces?), and some with dense accumulations of objects (stalls?), as well as some houses used for storage.

A variety of imports at Baranda include beads, glassware and ceramics. These imports have been dated mostly to the sixteenth and seventeenth century but some span a period up to the nineteenth century (R. Wilding, *pers. comm.*; H. Wright, *pers. comm.*). The ceramics include Near Eastern, Far Eastern and European (mostly Iberian) glazed wares, giving proof of Portuguese links with the site. Beads from the Cambay region of India have also been recovered in large quantities.

It is important to note that burnished graphite pottery made from local clays is far more abundant than imported wares. Initial typological analysis of this pottery shows that the majority of the motifs are similar to those of Period 4 of the Great Zimbabwe tradition sites (Robinson, Summers & Whitty 1961). This Period 4 marks the fullest expression of the development and spread of Great Zimbabwe tradition sites to most parts of the plateau.

It seems, therefore, that at Baranda either there must have been a continuation of Great Zimbabwe tradition in the area, or that the local potters adopted the motifs of their predecessors. Whichever is the case, there is no evidence from coastal sites that such local pottery was traded.

The only settlement of the size of Baranda mentioned in the historical record comes from Portuguese sources of the sixteenth and seventeenth centuries (Theal 1893–1903, II, pp. 393–5). The Portuguese mention a trading market called 'Massapa', close to Mt Fura, which, they said, was frequented by 'Moors' (presumably Swahili speakers, possibly in the early part of the sixteenth century). 'Massapa' is likely to derive from a misspelling by the Portuguese of *mashapa* – the name for the local soil of the area – which, by then, had become associated with a particular settlement rather than the area as a whole. These same Portuguese sources report that they eliminated these people, and Massapa became their possession. Massapa is also said to have been close to the Mukaradzi river, its valley often associated with gold-mining activities. The same

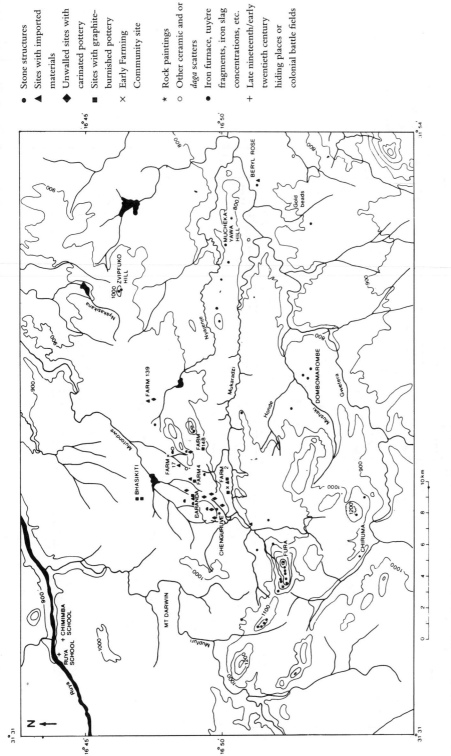

Figure 43.11 Some of the main sites in the Mount Darwin Research Area.

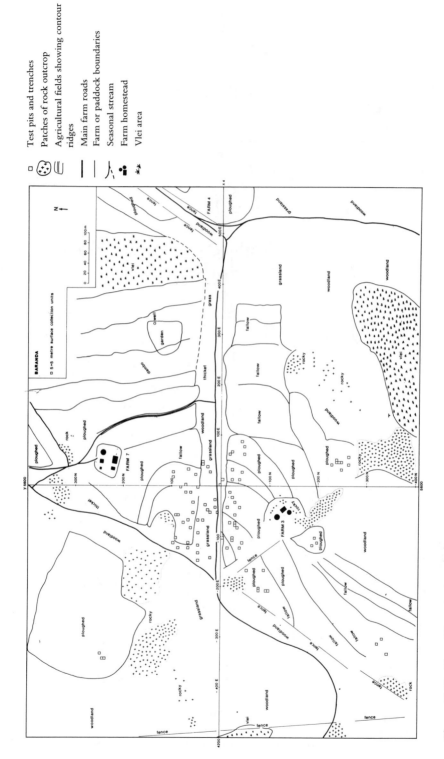

Figure 43.12 Plan of Baranda site.

sources report that Massapa (as well as other Portuguese trading settlements in the area) were abandoned in the late seventeenth century, following attacks by the Rozvi army led by Changamire.

Baranda in a local and regional context

The archaeological evidence therefore provides information concerning both cultural continuity and interaction. Baranda (the Portuguese 'Massapa') can only be understood in terms of its relationship with other sites found in the locality. These sites comprise a cluster of smaller sites containing similar graphite-burnished pottery to that found at Baranda and, in some cases, also sherds of imported pottery of broadly the same date as at Baranda.

Also found within the locality of Baranda are sites mostly located on hills which, in the area south of the Mukaradzi valley, become mountainous (Fig. 43.11). These sites are difficult of access, the closest to Baranda being at Chenguruve hill, less than 1 km to the southwest, and others, including Muchekayawa (Figs 43.3, 43.11, 43.13), only 10 km away. They appear either as ordinary pole-impressed *daga* concentrations associated with carinated pottery (but no graphite-burnished wares), or as stone structures with 'loopholes' (Pikirayi In Press) but with the same carinated pottery. Only a few

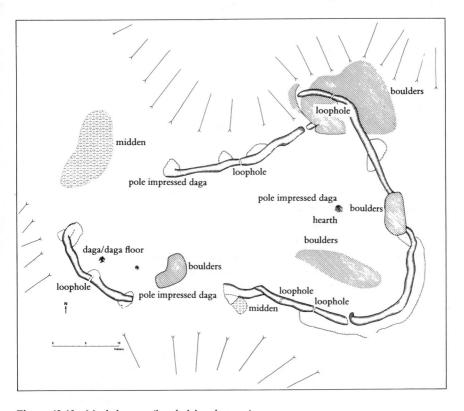

Figure 43.13 Muchekayawa 'loophole' enclosure site.

imported beads and ceramics dating to the sixteenth and seventeenth century have been recovered from some of these sites and the ashy middens associated with them. Clearly, the activities taking place at the sites must have had a bearing on what was happening at Baranda and the other sites with graphite-burnished wares.

The distribution of such hill and mountainous sites is not confined to the locality of Baranda but broadly coincides with the middle and lower basins of the Mazowe and Ruya rivers (Fig. 43.3).

Some of these hilltop sites are mentioned in Portuguese written sources (Theal 1893–1903, II, IV, VI, VII) in connection with the civil wars of the Mutapa state at the beginning of the seventeenth century (Beach 1980). Chizinga mountain, for example, was referred to as a rebel stronghold. Survey of part of the mountain revealed a loopholed stone structure – no doubt a fortification – and sites with small amounts of carinated pottery.

Archaeological evidence for the Mutapa state

Datable imports into northern Zimbabwe are a way of identifying the Mutapa state with particular archaeological sites, as well as the always predominant domestic pottery types found on them. It is not known exactly how these imports were used – whether some of them found their way to royal capitals or whether they were predominantly for Portuguese domestic consumption. However, there is one report (Theal 1893–1903, VI), from the beginning of the seventeenth century, that Mutapa Gatsi Rusere asked for some porcelain as part of his dues from Portuguese traders.

Such foreign imports not only yield information about the nature and extent of local and regional interactions – with all their social and economic implications – but they also demonstrate that major northern Zimbabwe rivers, such as the Mazowe and Ruya, must have formed trade routes.

Archaeological evidence can also shed light on the problem of the decline of the ('prehistoric') Zimbabwe state and the rise of the Mutapa state. As we have seen, the ceramic evidence recovered from the site of Baranda can, at least in part, be interpreted as demonstrating a continuity of tradition (through the continuing use of similar pottery motifs). Such continuity must be seen in the context of chronological development, since some of the imports found in association with the locally produced pottery give sure evidence of being relatively late in date. Thus, there existed at least by the sixteenth century both internal continuity and external contacts.

That there was considerable internal cohesion within the Mutapa state is shown by the fact that it only came to an end at the beginning of the twentieth century. It was able to survive both external threat from the Portuguese and internal conflict generated by the succession system (Mudenge 1988) – such internal and external factors sometimes even coming together, for example when the Portuguese interfered with court politics. Both Beach (1980) and Mudenge (1988) have argued that the state was able to adapt to changing socio-political circumstances while still retaining its name and identity.

Until the twentieth century, the Mutapa state never experienced a rapid, significant loss of its established level of socio-political complexity. Before then – as the archaeological evidence of the hilltop fortifications, and the paucity of imported goods found in them, reflects – the greatest challenge to its authority had been at the end of the sixteenth century and beginning of the seventeenth, but this was eventually overcome, and the state returned to independent existence by the end of the latter century.

Conclusions

In regard to Great Zimbabwe tradition sites, it is clear that data of considerable utility for the analysis of the social, political and economic relations of this dynamic form of settlement organization can be obtained through a multidimensional approach. The results of the site catchment analysis underline the importance of the immediate environment around the Great Zimbabwe tradition sites, as the data reveal the importance of agriculture as a more acceptable economic basis of the type-sites than previously assumed long-distance trade, gold-mining or livestock transhumance. And the detailed archaeological surveys around Great Zimbabwe tradition sites have presented a new set of possible cultural relationships and locational detail *vis-à-vis* the preceding and contemporary cultural traditions, with the strong suggestion of links between the Great Zimbabwe tradition and the historical Mutapa state.

The potential of an approach which assesses the various interactions between ideology, economy and political relations and environmental contexts at different scales of observation has barely been tapped. Useful generalizations must wait until the explication of specific sets of circumstances concerning settlement development in this region are more fully explored.

Acknowledgements

The geophysical and geochemical analyses were carried out with the assistance of H. Frej and K. Persson of the Stockholm Laboratory for Scientific Archaeology. We thank Alicija Grenberger for the illustrations of Great Zimbabwe and L. Adamowicz for the spatial distribution map.

44   Settlement area and communication in African towns and cities

ROLAND FLETCHER

Introduction

The purpose of this chapter is to provide a broad comparative view of the settlement size of indigenous African towns and cities. The size of the settlements and their overall residential pattern are discussed in relation to issues of information management and the role of external economic influence. Generalized plans of the settlements are presented at standard scales to facilitate comparability.[1] What will eventually be needed is a survey of the kind begun for towns and cities in the UK by Lobel (1969; 1974). In Africa, archaeology will be the crucial source for much of the information (Connah 1987, pp. 2–3, 14–15). The research on Mgungundlovu (Parkington & Cronin 1986), Begho (Posnansky n.d.), Benin (Connah 1975) and Jenne-jeno (McIntosh & McIntosh 1979; McIntosh & McIntosh 1980b; McIntosh & McIntosh, Ch. 37, this volume) illustrates the essential role of archaeology even for historically documented settlements.

Method

In this survey I have included settlements from north Africa, Egypt, the Sudan and Ethiopia as well as sub-Saharan Africa. With the expansion of Islam into west Africa and along the east African coast there seemed little reason to segregate the Islamic north from the rest of Africa. These comparisons help to put the great west African cities in perspective as giants of their kind. The Christian literate tradition of Ethiopia produced an unusual yet clearly African urban form, notable particularly for the enormous scale of the settlements which were successive locations for the mobile imperial capitals (Horvath 1969; Pankhurst 1979).

The settlements illustrated range in time from Meroe in the third century AD to Tananarive (Figs 44.3, 44.4), Addis Ababa (Figs 44.5, 44.6) and Ibadan (Figs 44.5, 44.6) in the nineteenth century AD. No recent colonial period settlements in Africa have been included. However, plans of London and Paris in AD 1800 and New York in AD 1840 (Fig. 44.6), prior to the enormous size increase of the Industrial Revolution, are provided for comparison with the indigenous African towns and cities. The terms 'town' and 'city' are used without rigorous definition. They occur frequently in the literature and the range of settlements to which they apply is a matter of common knowledge. For comparison I have included villages such as Ogol of the Dogon (Fig. 44.1) (Griaule 1965) and Ambohimasina/Ambohitriniarivo (Fig. 44.3) in Madagascar (Arnaud 1970), the enclosures of Bigo in Uganda (Figs 44.1, 44.4, 44.6) used from the thirteenth to the sixteenth century AD (Posnansky 1969, p. 135) and the military kraal of Mgungundlovu (Figs 44.1, 44.2) which was the Zulu 'capital' between AD 1829 and 1838 (Parkington & Cronin 1986). The plans were obtained primarily from published sources. I have made no attempt to seek out unpublished material. Nor have I sought original published plans, though Hull (1976) was useful as a guide to finding earlier reports. My purpose is only to offer a preliminary comparison not a definitive atlas. The figures use the scales provided in the referenced sources. I have not attempted the task of meticulously checking all the plans and their scales but have given examples of some problem cases. For instance, there are markedly different scales for plans of early Mombasa (Fig. 44.2) and differences of site shape of Koumbi Saleh (Fig. 44.3). As I note below, the same settlement can be reported with different scales and even a different form in different publications.

I accepted the edges of the settlements as represented in the published plans as an indicator of the size of the settlement. Without this assumption one cannot begin to make comparisons of the kind usual in the literature. We frequently make judgements of relative size, that 'such and such' a settlement was very large, or 'the site is extensive'. These declarations assume that settlements have recognizable edges. They also presume that in broad terms the definition of settlement boundaries is consistent. These premises suffice for general comparisons (Fletcher 1986). Overall settlement size can be considered without knowing the position of every building and without an exact definition or even a rigorously consistent rule for identifying the edge of a settlement.

Methodological issues: factors affecting the accuracy of area estimates

The presentation of observational statements

Copying tends to create error. While we should strive to control this problem it is almost inevitable that the repeated copying, standardization and reduction of plans for publication will lead to scale divergence for plans of the same settlement. I have used Mombasa as an example not because it is especially heinous or unusual but because it is, if anything, a rather modest case. The danger with relatively modest cases of error is that ordinary observation will not even hint that something is amiss. I refer to the Mombasa plans as a modest case because I have seen other instances where the scales have been 'out' by a very large margin. The usual cause has been mislabelling of the scale interval. A scale meant to represent 1 km divided into five intervals of 200 m each can be spectacularly transformed by a simple draughting error. If the total length of the scale is misinterpreted as the interval length, any area estimate from that scale will be in error by a multiple of 25!

The second major problem is caused by errors of estimation in the initial report of the size of a settlement. Observers are not always even reasonably accurate and sometimes wish to exaggerate. Explorers are known who have exaggerated their measured scale plan by a factor of 3. The usual tendency to talk in terms of rounded figures, as with the

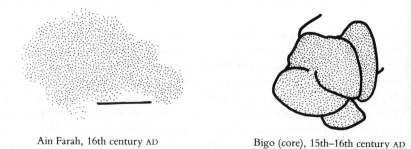

Ain Farah, 16th century AD

Bigo (core), 15th–16th century AD

Zinchera, 1st century AD

Meroe (core), 1st–3rd century BC

Ogol du Bas et Haut, 1940s–1950s AD

0 ——————— 500 m

Mgungundlovu, AD 1828–36

Figure 44.1 African settlements less than 0.5 km².

Conventions for all figures

Walls, ditches and banks are marked by a continuous line which simplifies the boundary.

Settlement area: stippled fill does not necessarily represent built space. It is merely a fill for the conventionally recognized area of the settlement. This convention has also been used when the density and arrangement of occupation is either unclear or unknown.

In settlements with large amounts of well-defined open space, such as Mgungundlovu (Figs 44.1, 44.2) and Ouagadougou (Figs 44.4, 44.6) the stippling does indicate the approximate location of groups of structures.

For dispersed, low-density residential occupation, a heavy dot stipple has been used – for example, Kampala (Figs 44.5, 44.6).

Topography: steep slopes integral to boundaries of the settlement are marked by hachures.

Coastlines are marked by a thin line.

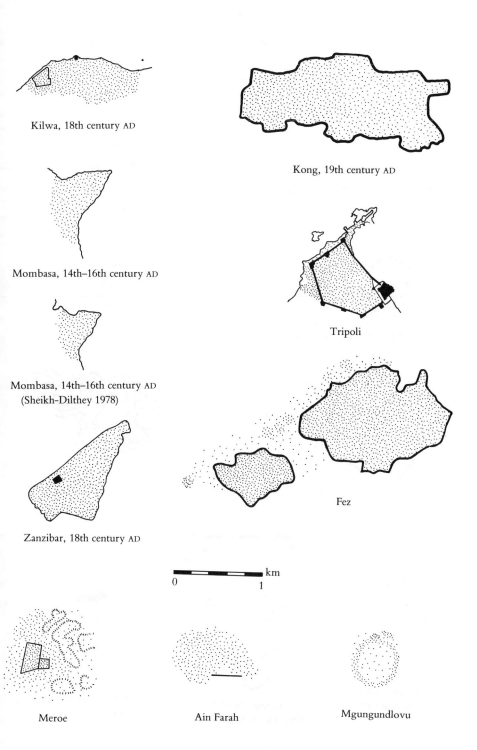

Kilwa, 18th century AD

Kong, 19th century AD

Mombasa, 14th–16th century AD

Mombasa, 14th–16th century AD
(Sheikh-Dilthey 1978)

Tripoli

Fez

Zanzibar, 18th century AD

0 — 1 km

Meroe

Ain Farah

Mgungundlovu

Figure 44.2 African towns and cities less than 5 km².

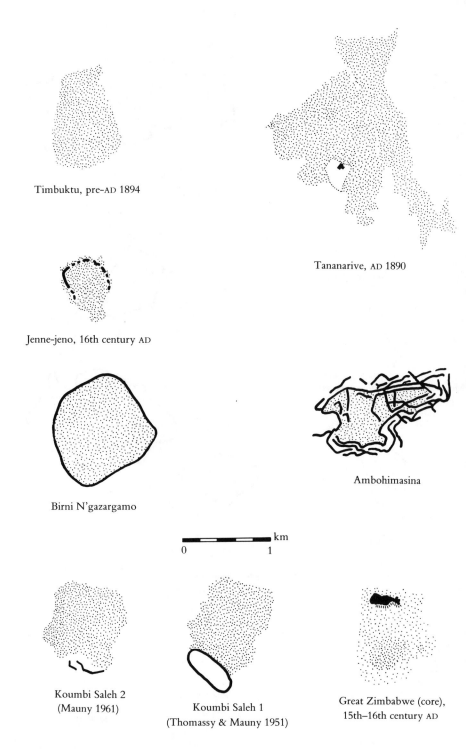

Figure 44.3 African towns and cities less than 5 km².

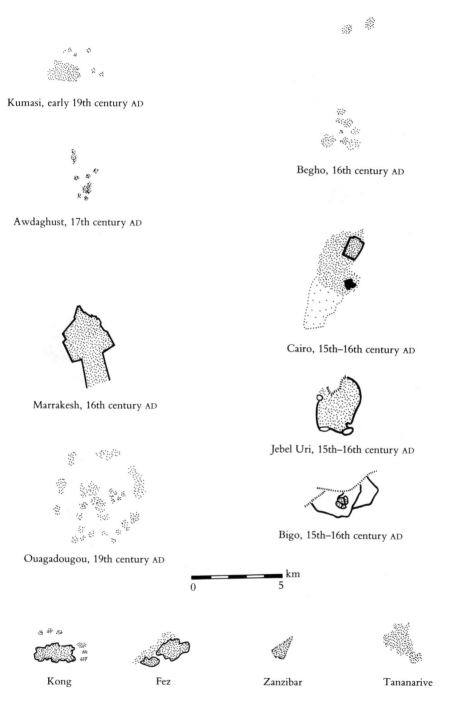

Kumasi, early 19th century AD

Begho, 16th century AD

Awdaghust, 17th century AD

Cairo, 15th–16th century AD

Marrakesh, 16th century AD

Jebel Uri, 15th–16th century AD

Ouagadougou, 19th century AD

Bigo, 15th–16th century AD

0   5   km

Kong   Fez   Zanzibar   Tananarive

Figure 44.4 African towns and cities less than 20 km².

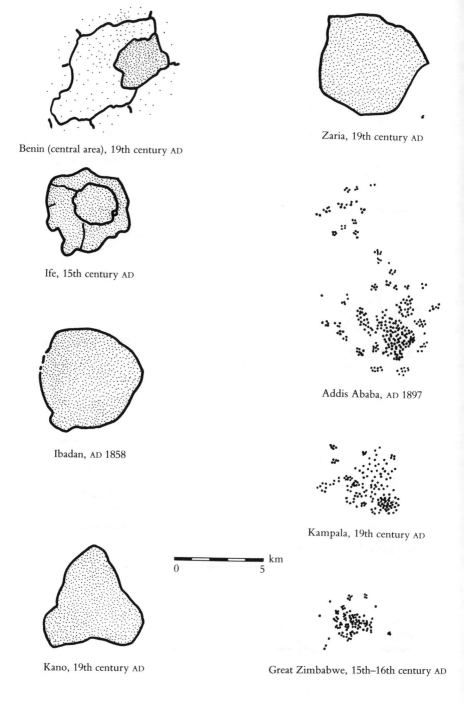

Benin (central area), 19th century AD

Zaria, 19th century AD

Ife, 15th century AD

Ibadan, AD 1858

Addis Ababa, AD 1897

Kampala, 19th century AD

Kano, 19th century AD

Great Zimbabwe, 15th–16th century AD

Figure 44.5 African towns and cities less than 50 km².

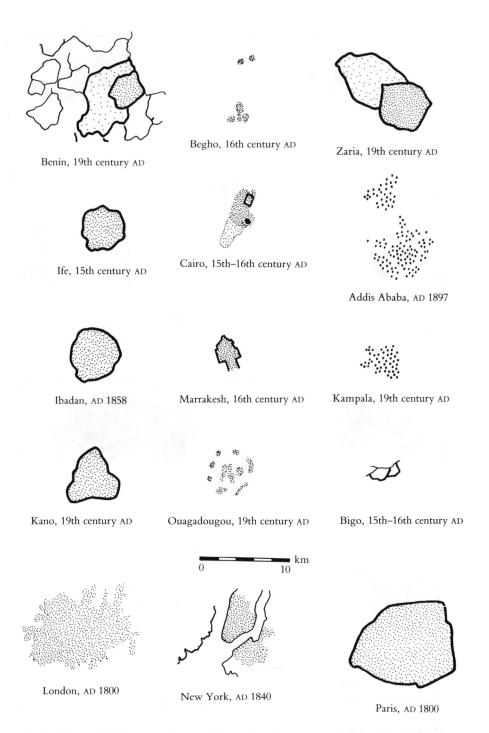

Benin, 19th century AD

Begho, 16th century AD

Zaria, 19th century AD

Ife, 15th century AD

Cairo, 15th–16th century AD

Addis Ababa, AD 1897

Ibadan, AD 1858

Marrakesh, 16th century AD

Kampala, 19th century AD

Kano, 19th century AD

Ouagadougou, 19th century AD

Bigo, 15th–16th century AD

km
0   10

London, AD 1800

New York, AD 1840

Paris, AD 1800

Figure 44.6 Large pre-industrial African towns and cities compared to London, Paris and New York in the early nineteenth century AD.

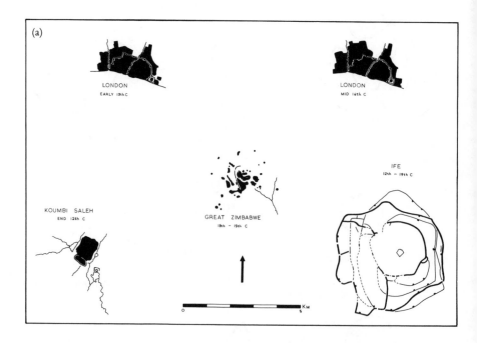

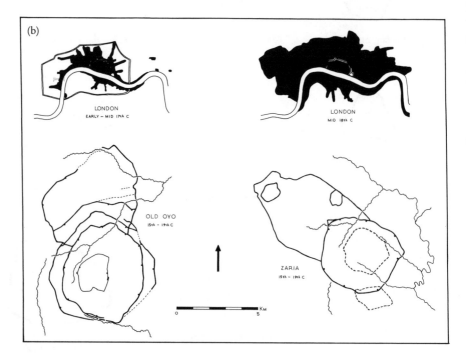

Figure 44.7a, b African towns and cities in comparison to the growth of pre-industrial London.

Zulu kraals, is also an invitation to exaggeration. The problem is that rounded figures cannot be generally supposed inaccurate. The risk is that some will be wildly inaccurate but may be the only available source until archaeological excavation and/or surface survey can clarify our knowledge of the settlement.

Another factor which may catch the unwary, but ought not to surprise archaeologists, is that settlement plans change with further research and the site areas reported frequently increase. The best recent example is the area for Great Zimbabwe, which has markedly changed as a result of the research of Huffman (1977). This has also led to a necessary reassessment of the nature of the site, which must now be considered as a dispersed palimpsest occupation (Sinclair, Pikirayi, Pwiti & Soper, Ch. 43, this volume). It is not always clear what is involved. The plans of Ife published in 1967 and 1970 by Willett are substantially different in detail, displaying the real difficulties of surveying a site which is both occupied and heavily vegetated. There are two plans of Koumbi Saleh (Fig. 44.3), both of which have been published by Mauny. But the particulars of the boundaries and the inclusiveness of the plans are different in the two reports, apparently as successive observations have been made of the site. Different judgements of site plan may also follow from different practices of generalizing the boundaries of a scatter of occupation debris.

Ambiguity of definition

There are not infrequent cases where a well-known site is actually part of a site group. Jenne-jeno is a good example. Careful surveys by McIntosh & McIntosh (1980b) have shown that the main mound lies at the centre of a cluster of occupation areas (see also McIntosh & McIntosh, Ch. 37, this volume). If these are of very different date, specifying the maximum size of a settlement is not a serious problem. But where there is no such time differentiation the designations of site area may be rather arbitrary. Fez (Figs 44.2, 44.4) consisted of two walled areas and surrounding suburbs in the fourteenth century AD but is properly reported as a single occupation area covering 3.0–3.5 km^2. Just because discrete occupation areas are recognizable it does not mean that each has to be referred to as a separated settlement. The moot question remains – at what point do we decide that the edge of a settlement has been reached and that other occupation spaces are discrete outlying settlements? Awdaghust (Fig. 44.4) can be perceived as quite extensive (1.5–2.0 km^2), if the locality containing the various mounds is considered as the areal extent of the settlement. According to McIntosh & McIntosh (1980b), however, the area of Awdaghust was approximately 12 ha (30 acres), the size of the main southern mound. Though there may be reason to exclude the open spaces around the mounds from the estimation of its area because the mounds are of very different dates, the open space in itself is not sufficient to restrict the estimates of area to separate residential loci. Ouagadougou (Figs 44.4, 44.6) has large open areas within its confines but we do not therefore split that town into its subcomponent suburbs to obtain area estimates. Similarly Begho (Figs 44.4, 44.6) can be described by a single area value (2.0–2.5 km^2) incorporating its various discrete residential localities. The issue merges into two others – where is the edge of settlement and how do we specify the limits of a settlement with dispersed occupation?

Ambiguity is inherent in defining the edge of a settlement. While there is a sense in which we know where such a limit should be recognized, it is not always easy to give a consistent specification for our choice. One problem is that the limits for different settlements are not of the same kind. Paris in AD 1800 (Fig. 44.6) can be delimited by the old Fermier General customs boundary wall. It was a bounded settlement, in the same sense as Zaria or Benin, with open ground including parks and farm land within the boundary. London (Fig. 44.6), by contrast, was not bounded, resembling the open pattern of African towns such as Kumasi (Fig. 44.4) or Tananarive (Fig. 44.3). There is a tendency to regard the limit of built space as the edge of the settlement (as in the London illustration in Fig. 44.6) but this is not consistent with the definition of the bounded cases. Open space is part of the interaction pattern of any settlement. In London, estates such as Richmond Park and Epping Forest became contiguous with the city in the nineteenth and early twentieth century as public recreation facilities. They became part of the traffic pattern of the city in the same way as the fields on the south side of the Thames were contiguous with and part of the medieval city as a recreation and market area (Brooke 1975).

Outside the main area of Kumasi (Fig. 44.4) there were various estates and shrines (Bowdich 1966, pp. 322–3). Quite how much regular daily movement of personnel occurred in the periphery of the settlement is hard to judge but should not be underestimated.

The remaining issue to be clarified is the problem of the relationship between natural features and estimates of settlement area. In the plans of London, Paris and Ouagadougou substantial river channels are regarded as part of the total settlement area. But when Roman London was restricted to the north bank of the Thames, an area estimate would not include the width of the river. The status of a natural phenomenon such as a river changes as a settlement grows. Prior to the nineteenth century AD New York and Brooklyn (Fig. 44.6) were patently two distinct settlements separated by the Hudson. But by AD 1840 the relative size of the two built areas and the role of the river as an aid to commercial communication give the appearance of a single urban area which includes a stretch of river. At present some arbitrary point in time must be chosen to switch from two separate settlement area estimates to one much larger aggregate estimate. Because it is arbitrary, such a size change can cause inconsistencies in the arguments based on comparative settlement size. Obviously there are criteria of relative scale, position and function which we use to designate whether or not open space is part of total settlement area. Proportionately huge open spaces are part of Begho and Mgungundlovu because of the route access and interaction functions of those central areas. Fez is recognized as one settlement because the space between the two walled areas was relatively small and filled by suburbs. Koumbi Saleh is supposed to be the Muslim partner of a Soninke royal town called El-Ghaba (Shinnie 1965, pp. 47–9). But the latter has not been found in close proximity; on our current knowledge the two towns would seem to have been too far apart (more than a kilometre) to be regarded as one settlement. The judgement involves an assumption about the degree of interaction between the communities in the two settlements. Such judgements are made constantly in the descriptions of settlement size and we should be watchful for potential inconsistencies. In Africa these effects will need to be watched carefully when some comparisons are being made between dual towns, such as the Soninke case mentioned above, towns astride major topographic features such as Ouagadougou and the characteristics of well-defined single settlement areas.

Settlements with dispersed occupation are a problem because they can be hard to recognize. Great Zimbabwe illustrates the problem of a dispersed settlement not being recognized despite many years of fieldwork. Assessing how the community dealt with scarce local resources such as salt and water becomes a very different issue when a 4–5 km² low density occupation is being considered rather than a compact 50–70 ha settlement. There may be other substantial settlements with dispersed occupations in Africa which we have not yet recognized on the ground. The changes in Bono Manso from a large dispersed settlement to a more compact settlement of less than 1 km² (100 ha) could not be readily perceived until the fieldwork by Effah-Gyamfi (1978; 1979). In an equivalent sized compact settlement the changes would tend to be more conspicuous. Likewise even the scale of a dispersed settlement as large and substantial as Old Oyo was not apparent until extensive ground surveys were carried out (Soper & Darling 1980; Agbaje-Williams & Onyango-Abuje 1981).

As a general rule the area of an open settlement should be presumed to include a periphery of open spaces, service function localities and dumps, unless there is strong evidence to the contrary (Fletcher 1986). An assessment of the overall behavioural factors affecting settlement size has to refer to this total of built area and occupation area within which the aggregate activity of the community occurred. Its archaeological identity should be the general scatter of debris which marks a site. The peripheral zone of a settlement can be recognized as a low density scatter of occupation debris of the kind recognized at the Hohokam site of Snaketown in Arizona (Wilcox, McGuire & Sternberg 1981).

For other research purposes different definitions of settlement space may be appropriate. There is no single, proper definition of settlement area that will be applicable to analyses of group behaviour. The definition used in this chapter is not universally requisite. More detailed, socially oriented studies of inter-residential activity use more specific definitions of settlement area (Whitelaw 1983).

Interaction/communication constraints and the size of settlements

Africa contained some of the more extensive agrarian cities with literate administrations. Though these cities were exceeded in size by the settlement areas of the imperial giants such as Changan during the Tang dynasty (Skinner 1977), Yuan Peking (Bouillard 1929) and Abbassid Baghdad (Le Strange 1924), which lay in the size range between 70 to 100 km² in area, the African examples are of equivalent extent to most of the relatively large urban settlements possessing literacy elsewhere in the world. Zaria (Figs 44.5, 44.6), including its northwestern extension, covered about 50 km² and Addis Ababa in 1897 spread over about 25–30 km² (Figs 44.5, 44.6). However, the overall tendency was for the large settlements to have relatively low average residential densities and comparatively small population sizes. Zaria consisted of a low density enclosure with a higher density core walled area; residence in Addis Ababa was almost entirely dispersed. As a comparison, New Kingdom Thebes in the sixteenth century BC was a dispersed settlement covering approximately 30–40 km^2. Occupation lay primarily along the Nile, around the main temples on the east bank, scattered in patches across the floodplain and concentrated along the western cliffs where the funerary temples were located (Trigger, Kemp, O'Connor & Lloyd 1983, p. 216).

In Africa prior to AD 1850, as in Europe (Fletcher 1986, p. 64), most settlements generally did not exceed 20–30 km^2. Even at this size there are relatively few examples. Most of the towns were less than 10 km^2 in extent, the majority less than 5 km^2 and the predominant size would, on a rough estimation, be around 1 to 2 km^2 or less. Jenne-jeno is referred to as a 'large mound' and covers about 33 ha (McIntosh & McIntosh 1980b, p. 63).

Comment

This distribution conforms to the overall pattern of settlement size behind a 100 km^2 communication limit (Fletcher 1981, Figs 6, 7, p. 112; Fletcher 1986). Most settlements are less than 10 km^2 in extent and some reach sizes of 15–30 km^2 (Fig. 44.7a). Few attain areas of about 50–60 km^2 (Fig. 44.7b) and scarcely any compact pre-industrial settlements ever approach areas of 70–100 km^2 (approximately 30–45 miles). The majority of settlements lie in the lower third of the range of possible sizes for towns and cities with non-industrialized means of communication and interaction.

The implication of the similar settlement size distribution in Africa and elsewhere in the world is that the large settlements over 30 km^2 in extent were inherently difficult to manage. Given that the various regions had very different economic systems, we cannot ascribe the relative frequencies of settlement size to the effect of specifics of resource supply. Resource supply cannot in general be proposed as a factor directly affecting settlement area. Community size is the intervening variable but has no direct correlation to settlement size (Fletcher 1981). A more succinct explanation would be that the relative scarcity of large settlements results from a marked increase in communication difficulties as settlements increase in extent (Fletcher 1981, pp. 112–13, 116–17; Fletcher 1986, p. 70).

Resource supply has an effect but it is regionally specific. The number of settlements in Africa over 15–30 km^2 in extent is very small and none appears to exceed 50–60 km^2 even on a generous definition of settlement limits. It is the absolute number of very large settlements in a region which is a function of resource supply. The resource constraint apparently delimits the number of large community aggregates which a region can support and therefore the probability of a very large case arising. China, with numerous settlements and a long history of urban growth, has produced more very large cities than any other region. The relative frequency with which settlements of different size persist has therefore to be ascribed to some internal variable which is equally applicable in all regions. The constraint produced by the internal communication capacity of the communities is the most straightforward candidate. No matter what resources the communities command the growth of their settlements is constrained by the limits on their capacity to manage the flow of information and services within the settlement.

Interaction/communication issues

In general, compact settlements larger than 150 ha (1.5 km²) use or possess traces of information storage systems. Writing and the 'quipu' (Ascher & Ascher 1981) are two examples of the diversity of such systems. Smaller settlements do not apparently require the same scale of information management (Fletcher 1986). Most African settlements conform to this pattern, for example Garamantian Zinchera (Fig. 44.1) in north Africa with an area of 25 ha and Mgungundlovu (Figs 44.1, 44.2) in southern Africa at 25 ha. But there are some conspicuous, extremely large settlements which do not fit these expectations. In some cases the reports may be suspect. The great Zulu war kraals which were the capitals of Shaka and Dingaan were said to be 3 miles in circumference or about 1 mile in diameter (Bryant 1949, pp. 472–3; Ritter 1957, p. 236; Oliver 1971, p. 99). Denyer states that Zulu war towns were often over 1 km in diameter (Denyer 1978, p. 72). At the most these reports indicate settlements covering 200 ha. A cautious estimate from Denyer would give 82 ha. Even this is three to four times larger than the actual area of Mgungundlovu which could not be regarded as one of the minor *mfecane* of the nineteenth-century Zulu. Some caution is needed about very large, rounded figures as reports of settlement size. There are, however, several cases for which the area reports are clearly reliable. They are of interest for an understanding of the internal mechanics of community life and might be explicable in two different ways.

(1) Dispersed occupation or low density occupation apparently allows large settlements like Great Zimbabwe (Fig. 44.5) (Huffman 1977) and Bigo (Figs 44.4, 44.6) (Posnansky 1969), covering about 4 km², to occur without the evident use of information storage. This is to be expected if the residential densities were only in the range of the highest possible average rural regional densities for human populations. Obviously rural regional populations have not needed literacy to manage interaction at relatively low densities over extensive areas, as in many regions of west Africa (Goody 1956; Netting 1965; Denyer 1978, p. 74). Settlements with dispersed or low density occupation at the lower end of the density scale for residential communities should not therefore be subject to a size constraint set by operational limits of their communication systems. Material aids for information storage and management may, therefore, only be crucial for the maintenance of large compact settlements over 150 ha. Dispersed and low density occupation does not apparently generate the same demands on communication coherence as compact relatively high density residence. On this basis Old Oyo would be one of the major African settlements which went along the trajectory to low average residential densities as various factors such as trade offered the impetus towards increased community size. We need to look carefully at the workings and layout of Benin, which can also be understood as a dispersed settlement occupying the enclosures around the central walled area of Benin city (Figs 44.5, 44.6). Prior to the mid-fifteenth century AD there were palace locations scattered outside the line of the current innermost city wall (Connah 1975, pp. 89, 243). Later palace sites follow the same pattern (Roese 1981, p. 170). Ryder has remarked that the pre-Ewuare settlement may have been dispersed (Connah 1975, p. 249). We might therefore view Benin as a dispersed settlement which developed a clearly defined central district with the area around the

Ewedo palace as its compact core. On the ground the form of Benin is not evident to outsiders because the thick forest vegetation masks the various enclosures and places a visual emphasis on the innermost walled enclosure.

There is an interesting corollary which needs further investigation. The compact core of a dispersed settlement may conform to the limit for compact communities. The recognized core of Great Zimbabwe covers about 50–70 ha (Hall & Neal 1902; Garlake 1973a, p. 18), though this does not appear to be clearly definable on Huffman's (1977) map. Specifying what constitutes the core area of a settlement is therefore a primary research issue. Other cases should be closely inspected. A possible example is the nineteenth-century AD royal enclosure, or *kibuga*, in Kampala (Gutkind 1963, pp. 13–15) which is usually said to have covered an oval approximately a mile by half a mile, about 100–130 ha. The only other example that I am familiar with is outside Africa. The Cahokia site in the Mississippi valley is a large dispersed settlement which covered about 12 km^2 between AD 1050 and 1500 (Fowler 1975). Its palisaded core area is just less than 1 km^2 (100 ha). If a communication constraint affects the core of dispersed settlements this may be of relevance for our understanding of other African settlements such as Bigo.

(2) We may need to broaden our taxonomy of indigenous information storage systems. The degree of their usage remains a problem to be assessed in more detail than I can manage here. In Abomey, a census record was said to have been kept using small stones stored in bags in the royal palace (Argyle 1966). Some care must be taken not to casually reject or accept this report. It has some odd inconsistencies, as Herskovits notes (Argyle 1966, p. 94). But we must also beware that literate chauvinism is not leading us to ignore a corrupted description of a potentially significant system resembling the basics of the Inca 'quipu'. When the palace of Benin was sacked in AD 1897 the famous Benin bronzes were found stored as an index of information on court precedent (Willett 1983, p. 65). Ogualo, one of the rulers of Benin, is said to have introduced metal-casting as a way of recording events (Crowder 1966, p. 63). Given such indications, were any other sectors of the administration served by equivalent procedures using perishable materials? A major topic for future research ought to be the nature, scale and function of indigenous African information systems and their relationship to settlement size, residential density and the resource base which maintained the communities.

The other major alternative is to seek an explanation in terms of external economic influence generating secondary urban growth. This should not be used as a generaliz-ation to explain all African urban development but has to be considered seriously in west Africa and parts of east Africa. Proximity to intense outside influence is apparent in the cases of Kumasi, Abomey and Old Oyo.

In settlements close to regions where literacy was present, local administrations could be managed by literate outsiders. After all, Nestorian Christians acted as scribes and administrators for the Mongol Khans in the fourteenth century AD (Rockhill 1900, pp. 101–7, 150, 168). The question remains whether such outsiders would have a significant impact on the hierarchical control of aggregate interaction levels within large settle-ments. For instance, Old Oyo lay on the border with the literate Islamicized states to the north. Muslim preachers had been in the region around Old Oyo before the re-establishment of the capital in the sixteenth to seventeenth century AD (Crowder 1966, pp. 61–2). We have to consider the possibility that literates from the north may have served the administration in Old Oyo.

It is more apparent, however, that intense economic and political influence may set up the growth and concentration of population under stresses generated both by new sources of wealth and by the introduction of massive differentiation of wealth and power. The residential concentration, population growth and settlement expansion of the Yoruba towns during the wars of the nineteenth century AD is a classic example. In the Kiriji war, the British were selectively supplying machine weapons to the combatants (Ajayi & Smith 1964, p. 12). Ibadan is a remarkable case of a settlement which grew to enormous size through its effective commercial and economic exploitation of proximate, outside influences. The Islamic and European influences on the towns of the forest belt in west Africa had begun in the sixteenth century AD with the expansion of the slave trade. These external connections were used to great effect by the rulers of Benin and the Fon of Dahomey, among others.

Combinations of exceptional military power and commercial advantage may perhaps serve to sustain large settlements which would not otherwise be able to manage coherent communication and interaction within their resident communities. It remains an open issue whether compact settlements of over 1.5 to 2 km^2 in extent can be sustained after an initial growth triggered by external economic influence. Given the form of Old Oyo, Great Zimbabwe and probably Benin, the development of a dispersed community pattern with marked spatial segregation may be very informative about the strains inherent in this type of settlement growth. Comparison with the growth of the Celtic oppida of Europe (Collis 1975; Collis 1984) and the transalpine influence of the classical world on the distribution of trade and power (Wells 1984) should provide a fascinating complementary insight into the processes of external stimulus to growth.

Conclusion

Africa has been the location of several major pre-industrial urban systems and possesses a number of settlements of considerable areal extent, such as Old Oyo in Nigeria. The central issue which needs clarifying is the relationship between information storage and settlement growth. The large indigenous African cities outside the regions where literacy was present reached sizes which were usually attained only by the settlements of literate communities elsewhere in the world. To what degree the size of the largest African settlements was made feasible by different interaction patterns based on low occupation densities and by the influence of powerful external economic input needs further examination. The African urban communities provide a critical test case of the role of interaction and communication factors in the growth and restriction of settlement size and community residence patterns.

Note

[1] Restrictions on use of diagrams:

(a) Since diagrams are presented with the scales provided in the original source, they should not be presumed to be absolutely correct. The plans do not come directly from a professional geodesic survey.

(b) All these plans have been redrawn at least once and we must assume that most have been enlarged and reduced on several occasions. While they provide relative size indicators, any new measurements for research should be taken from as primary a source as possible.

(c) When more detailed assessment is needed, simple intercomparability cannot be assumed. Neither the limits of built space nor structural boundaries such as walls necessarily provide a basis for consistent cross-comparable analysis of the details of settlement form. Some enclosed settlements, for instance the Yoruba towns, contain large amounts of open space (Mabogunje 1962). Market-places can lie outside town gates. Major residence units and religious establishments may be located a short distance away from the apparent, obvious edge of a settlement, as in early nineteenth-century AD Kumasi (Fig. 44.4).

(d) There is a potential class of settlement without definable edges. These have very low occupation densities. In Africa dispersed occupation occurs in the savanna, especially in west Africa. The countryside is covered with widely separated residence units. The occupants perceive themselves to be living in settlements with definable edges, but those limits are not necessarily apparent on the ground. Two residence units close to each other can belong to different named communities. The Lobi-Dagati of northwestern Ghana (Goody 1956) and the Kofyar of Nigeria (Netting 1965) offer good examples.

A few great settlements, identified by clearly recognizable centres, also display this pattern of occupation, among them nineteenth-century AD Kampala (Figs 44.5, 44.6) (Gutkind 1963) and Addis Ababa (Figs 44.5, 44.6) (Gleichen 1898). Average residential densities for selected areas of the settlements can be estimated but specifying the actual area of the settlement becomes rather difficult. The available plans suggest that some limits to the settlements can be recognized. We should beware, however, of this assumption as it may merely derive from illustrative conventions. All plans are observational statements and must be treated as such.

(e) This is neither an inclusive nor an exhaustive list of African towns and cities. Some major settlements have been excluded because I could not find a published plan. Mbamza Congo (Balandier 1968; Randles 1968), also referred to as São Salvador, is the notable example. Others, though well known, have been excluded because I have used another example to represent the class or region to which they belong; Gedi (Kirkman 1954), for example, has not been used for the east African coast example. A few settlements, though famous and consequential for our knowledge of African towns and cities, do not appear because the number of diagrams I could include is finite and other settlements had priority for the pan-African comparisons I wished to make. Settlement details, dates and illustrations are taken from:

Addis Ababa   AD 1897 (Gleichen 1898)
Ain Farah   16th century AD (de Neufville & Houghton 1965)
Ambohimasina/Ambohitriniarivo   18th century AD (Arnaud 1970)
Awdaghust   17th century AD (Robert 1970)
Begho   16th century AD (Posnansky n.d.)
Benin   19th century AD (Roese 1981)
Benin (central area)   19th century AD (Connah 1975)
Bigo   15th–16th century AD (Shinnie 1965)
Bigo (core)   15th–16th century AD (Posnansky 1969)

Birni N'Gazargamo   19th century AD (Bivar & Shinnie 1970)
Cairo   15th–16th century AD (Lapidus 1966)
Fez   14th century AD (Le Tourneau 1961)
Great Zimbabwe (core)   15th century AD (Garlake 1973a)
Great Zimbabwe   15th century AD (Huffman 1977; Connah 1987)
Ibadan   AD 1858 (Mabogunje 1968)
Ife   15th century AD (Willett 1970)
Jebel Uri   15th–16th century AD (Arkell 1946)
Jenne-jeno   16th century AD (McIntosh & McIntosh 1979)
Kampala   19th century AD (Gutkind 1963)
Kano   19th century AD (Moody 1970)
Kilwa   18th century AD (Chittick 1974)
Kong   19th century AD (Abasaka 1976)
Koumbi Saleh 1   before AD 1240 (Thomassy & Mauny 1951)
Koumbi Saleh 2   (Mauny 1961)
Kumasi   early 19th century AD (Bowdich 1966)
London   AD 1800 (Freeman 1966)
Marrakesh   16th century AD (Jemma 1971)
Meroe (core)   1st–3rd century AD (O'Connor 1967)
Mgungundlovu   AD 1828–36 (Parkington & Cronin 1986)
Mombasa (Mvita)   14th–16th century AD (Berg 1968; Sheikh-Dilthey 1978)
New York   AD 1840 (Hoyt 1939; Ford & Rowe 1951)
Ogol du Bas et Haut   AD 1940s–1950s (Griaule 1965)
Old Oyo   15th century AD (Soper & Darling 1980)
Ouagadougou   19th century AD (Hull 1976)
Paris   AD 1800 (Gallois 1923)
Tananarive   AD 1890 (Robequain 1958)
Timbukto   before AD 1894 (Tymowski 1979)
Tripoli   16th century AD (Lezine 1968)
Zanzibar   18th century AD (Hoyle 1967)
Zaria   15th–19th century AD (Sutton 1976b)
Zinchera   1st century AD (Daniels 1968)

Acknowledgements

My thanks to the staff of Mechanical Engineering, University of Sydney, especially Dr Andre Lozzi and Dr John Gal for their help with the use of the CADDS system. Mr Frank Szanto kindly prepared the programme. Bobby Oakley assisted with the data management. This chapter was revised while I was a Visiting Fellow at Clare Hall, Cambridge in 1988–9. My thanks to the Fellows of Clare Hall for the congenial milieu. Thurstan Shaw and David Phillipson kindly commented on the chapter while it was in preparation.

The data collection was funded in part by the Australian Research Grant Scheme (later the ARC). Much of the data were collected in Fisher Library, University of Sydney and the Library of the University of California at Los Angeles.

References

Abir, M. 1970. The Amoleh. In *Pre-colonial African Trade: essays on trade in central and eastern Africa before 1900*, Gray, J. R. & D. Birmingham (eds), 119–38. London: Oxford University Press.

Abraham, D. P. 1961. Maramuca: an exercise in the combined use of Portuguese records and oral tradition. *Journal of African History* 2, 211–25.

Abraham, R. C. 1933. *The Tiv People*. Lagos: Crown Agents for the Colonies.

—— 1940. *A Dictionary of the Tiv Language*. London: Crown Agents.

—— 1958. *Dictionary of Modern Yoruba*. London: University of London Press.

—— 1962. *Dictionary of the Hausa Language*. London: University of London Press.

Absaka, M. 1976. A review on Dyula town culture and society of a trader in west Africa. *African Studies* 10, 295–334.

Abungu, G. H. O. 1988. Ungwana and the Tana. In *Urban Origins in Eastern Africa*, Sinclair, P. J. J. & S. Wandibba (eds), 50–2. Stockholm: Swedish Central Board of National Antiquities.

—— 1989. Communities on the river Tana, Kenya: an archaeological study of relations between the delta and the rivers basin, AD 700–1890. Unpublished PhD thesis, University of Cambridge.

Abu-Zayed, M. M. Ali 1987. *The Nile and Egypt* (in Arabic). Cairo: Dar el-Hidaia.

Adamowicz, L. 1985. Report and comments on the progress of the CIPRIANA 81/85 Archaeological Project – Nampula Province. *Textos para Debate* 6.

—— 1987. Projecto 'CIPRIANA' 1981–1985. *Trabalhos de Arqueologia e Antropologia* 3, 47–144.

—— 1990. Newly discovered stone age and early iron age sites in Nampula Province, northern Mozambique. In *Proceedings of the 1990 Workshop, Harare and Great Zimbabwe*, Sinclair, P. J. J. & G. Pwiti (eds), 137–96. Stockholm: Swedish Central Board of National Antiquities.

Adams, B. 1977. Hierakonpolis. In *Lexikon der Ägyptologie, II*, Helck, W. & W. Westendorf (eds), 1182–6. Wiesbaden: Otto Harrasowitz.

Adams, C. D. 1957. Activities of Danish botanists in Guinea. *Transactions of the Historical Society of Ghana* 3, 30–46.

Adams, R. E. W. & R. C. Jones 1981. Spatial patterns and regional growth among Classic Maya cities. *American Antiquity* 46, 301–22.

Adamson, D. A., F. Gasse, F. A. Street & M. A. J. Williams 1981. Late quaternary history of the Nile. *Nature* 287: 50–5.

Adeniji, K. O. 1983. Review of endangered cattle breeds in Africa. Animal genetic resources in Africa, high potential and endangered livestock. In *2nd OAU Expert Committee Meeting on Animal Genetic Resources in Africa: November 1983, Bulawayo, Zimbabwe*, 24–30. Nairobi: Organization of African Unity.

Adu, I. F. & L. O. Ngere 1979. The indigenous sheep of Nigeria. *World Review of Animal Production* 15, 51–62.

Agbaje-Williams, B. & J. Onyango-Abuje 1981. Archaeological work at Old Oyo: 1979–81. *Nyame Akuma* 19, 9–11.

Agheyisi, R. N. 1986. *An Edo-English Dictionary*. Benin City: Ethiope Publishing Corporation.

Agnew, S. 1972. Environment and history: the Malawian setting. In *The Early History of Malawi*, Pachai, B. (ed.), 28–48. Bristol: Longman.

Agorsah, E. K. 1990. Ethnoarchaeology: the search for a self-corrective approach to the study of past human behaviour. *The African Archaeological Review* 8, 189–208.

Ahmed, K. A. 1984. *Meriotic Settlement in the Central Sudan*. Oxford: British Archaeological Reports.

Ajayi, J. F. A. & R. Smith 1964. *Yoruba Warfare in the 19th Century AD*. Cambridge: Cambridge University Press.

Akinkugbe, O. O. 1978. A comparative phonology of Yoruba dialects, Işękiri, and Igala. Unpublished PhD thesis, University of Ibadan.

Al-Gihaz al-Markazi lil-T'bia wal-Ihsa 1966. The population problem in UAR (in Arabic). *Risalet el-'ilm*, April–June 1966. Cairo, Egypt.

Al-Maqrizi, Taqai eldine Ahmed Ibn Ali (1441). *Al-Mawa'z wal-I'tibar bi-zikr al-Khitat wal-Athar* (in Arabic). Bulaq, Egypt.

al-Sa'di 1900. *Ta'rikh es-Sudan*. Paris: Adrien-Maisonneuve.

al-Tunisi, M. O. 1845. *Voyage au Darfour*. Paris: Benjamin Duprat.

—— 1851. *Voyage au Ouadday*. Paris: Benjamin Duprat.

Alberro, M. & S. Haile-Mariam 1982a. The indigenous cattle of Ethiopia. *World Animal Review* 41, 2–10.

—— 1982b. The indigenous cattle of Ethiopia. *World Animal Review* 42, 27–34.

Aldridge, S. n.d. Unpublished manuscript, Livingstone Museum, Livingstone, Zambia.

Alexander, J. A. 1970. The domestication of yams: a multi-disciplinary approach. In *Science in Archaeology: a survey of progress and research*, Brothwell, D. & E. Higgs (eds), 229–34. New York: Praeger.

—— 1975. The salt industries of Africa: their significance for European prehistory. In *Salt: the study of an ancient industry*, de Brisay, K. W. & K. A. Evans (eds), 81–3. Colchester: Colchester Archaeological Group.

—— 1980. The spread and development of iron using in Europe and Africa. In *Proceedings of the 8th Panafrican Congress of Prehistory and Quaternary Studies*, Leakey, R. E. & B. A. Ogot (eds), 327–30. Nairobi: International Louis Leakey Memorial Institute for African Prehistory.

—— 1982. The prehistoric salt trade in Europe. *Nature* 300, 577–8.

—— 1984. Early frontiers in southern Africa. In *Frontiers: southern African archaeology today*, Hall, M., G. Avery, D. M. Avery, M. L. Wilson & A. J. B. Humphreys (eds), 12–23. Oxford: British Archaeological Reports.

—— 1987. *The Production of Salt and Salt-trading in Central and Western Europe in the 1st Millennium B.C.* Rome: Studi di paletnologia in onore di S. M. Puglisi.

—— 1988. The Saharan divide in the Nile valley: the evidence from Qasr Ibrim. *African Archaeological Review* 6, 73–90.

Alexander, J. & D. G. Coursey 1969. The origins of yam cultivation. In *The Domestication and Exploitation of Plants and Animals*, Ucko, P. J. & G. W. Dimbleby (eds), 405–25. London: Duckworth.

Alexander, J. E. 1838. *An Expedition of Discovery into the Interior of Africa*. 2 vols. London: Henry Colburn.

Ali Hakem, A. M. & A. R. M. Khabir 1989. Sarourab 2: a new contribution to the Early Khartoum tradition from Bauda site. In *Late Prehistory of the Nile Basin and the Sahara*, Krzyzaniak, L. & M. Kobusiewicz (eds), 381–5. Poznan: Poznan Archaeological Museum.

Allan, W. 1972. Ecology, techniques and settlement patterns. In *Man, Settlement and Urbanism*, Ucko, P. J., R. Tringham & G. W. Dimbleby (eds), 211–26. London: Duckworth.

Allen, J. de V. 1983. Shungwaya, the Mijikenda and the traditions. *International Journal of African Historical Studies* 16, 455–85.

—— 1984. Shungwaya, the Segeju and Somali history. In *Archaeology and History: proceedings of the*

Second International Congress of Somali Studies, 1983, Labahn, T. (ed.), 35–72. Hamburg: Buske.

Allen, J. de V. & T. H. Wilson (eds) 1979. *Swahili Houses and Tombs of the Coast of Kenya*. London: Art and Archaeology Research Papers.

Allibert, C., A. Argant & J. Argant 1983. Le site de Bagamoyo (Mayotte). *Etudes Océan Indien 2*, 5–40.

Allison, P. A. 1962. Historical inferences to be drawn from the effect of human settlement on the vegetation of Africa. *Journal of African History* 3, 441–9.

Allsworth-Jones, P. A. 1982. Kariya Wuro 1981: faunal report. *Zaria Archaeological Papers* 4, 6–9.

Altenmüller, H. 1975. Buto. In *Lexikon der Ägyptologie, I*, Helck, W. & E. Otto (eds), 887–9. Wiesbaden: Otto Harrasowitz.

Althusser, L. & E. Balibar 1970. *Reading Capital*. London: New Left Books.

Ambrose, S. H. 1980. Elmenteitan and other late pastoral neolithic adaptations in the central highlands of east Africa. In *Proceedings of the 8th Panafrican Congress of Prehistory and Quaternary Studies*, Leakey, R. E. & B. A. Ogot (eds), 279–82. Nairobi: International Louis Leakey Memorial Institute for African Prehistory.

—— 1982. Archaeological and linguistic reconstructions of history in east Africa. In *The Archaeological and Linguistic Reconstruction of African History*, Ehret, C. & M. Posnansky (eds), 104–57. Berkeley: University of California Press.

—— 1984a. The introduction of pastoral adaptations to the highlands of east Africa. In *From Hunters to Farmers: the causes and consequences of food production in Africa*, Clark, J. D. & S. A. Brandt (eds), 212–39. Berkeley: University of California Press.

—— 1984b. Excavations at Deloraine, Rongai, 1978. *Azania* 19, 79–104.

—— 1986. Stable carbon and nitrogen isotope analysis of human and animal diet in Africa. *Journal of Human Evolution* 15, 707–31.

Ambrose, S. H. & M. J. DeNiro 1986. Reconstruction of African human diet using bone collagen carbon and nitrogen isotope ratios. *Nature* 319, 321–4.

Ammerman, A. J., D. P. Gifford & A. V. Voorips 1977. Towards an evaluation of sampling strategies: simulated excavations of a Kenyan pastoralist site. In *Simulation Studies in Archaeology*, Hodder, I. (ed.), 123–32. Cambridge: Cambridge University Press.

Anati, E. 1968. *Rock Art in Central Arabia, Vol. 2*. Louvain: Institut Orientaliste.

Andah, B. 1976. The development of the Ghanaian Volta basin. *West African Journal of Archaeology* 6, 1–11.

—— 1978. Excavations at Rim, upper Volta. *West African Journal of Archaeology* 8, 75–138.

—— 1979a. The later Stone Age and Neolithic of upper Volta viewed in a west African context. *West African Journal of Archaeology* 9, 85–117.

—— 1979b. Iron Age beginnings in west Africa: reflections and suggestions. *West African Journal of Archaeology* 9, 135–50.

—— 1979c. The Quaternary of the Guinea region of west Africa: an assessment of the geomorphic evidence. *West African Journal of Archaeology* 9, 9–46.

—— 1980a. L'Afrique de l'ouest avant le 7e siècle. In *Histoire générale de l'Afrique, I*, Ki-Zerbo, J. (ed.), 641–71. Paris: UNESCO.

—— 1980b. Coastal evolution of west Africa during the Quaternary. In *West African Culture Dynamics: archaeological and historical perspectives*, Swartz, B. K. & R. Dumett (eds), 17–36. The Hague: Mouton.

—— 1982. Urban 'origins' in the Guinea forest with special reference to Benin. *West African Journal of Archaeology* 12, 63–71.

—— 1983. The Bantu phenomenon: some unanswered questions of ethnolinguistics and ethnoarchaeology. *West African Journal of Archaeology* 13, 1–21.

—— (ed.) 1990. *Cultural Resource Management: an African dimension*. Ibadan: Wisdom Publishers.

Andah, B. & O. Ajayi 1981. The place of geomorphic features in the Quaternary of the Guinea region of west Africa: with special reference to Ibadan environs. *West African Journal of Archaeology* 11, 25–51.

Anfray, F. 1963. La première campagne de fouilles à Matara, près de Senafe (Nov. 1959 – Janv. 1960). *Annales d'Ethiopie* 5, 87–166.

—— 1967a. Les sculptures rupestres de Chabbe dans le Sidamo. *Annales d'Ethiopie* 7, 19–32.

—— 1967b. Matara. *Annales d'Ethiopie* 7, 33–53.

—— 1968. Aspects de l'archéologie éthiopienne. *Journal of African History* 9, 345–66.

—— 1970. Notes archéologiques. *Annales d'Ethiopie* 8, 31–42.

—— 1972. L'archéologie d'Axoum en 1972. *Paideuma* 18, 60–78.

—— 1973a. Les fouilles de Yeha, Mai–Juin 1973. *Documents pour Servir à l'Histoire de la Civilisation Ethiopienne* 4, 35–8.

—— 1973b. Nouveaux sites antiques. *Journal of Ethiopian Studies* 11, 13–27.

—— 1974. Deux villes axoumites: Adoulis et Matara. *Atti del IV Congresso Internazionale di Studi Etiopici (Roma 1972)*, 748–53.

Anfray, F. & G. Annequin 1965. Matara, deuxième, troisième et quatrième campagnes de fouilles. *Annales d'Ethiopie* 6, 49–85.

Angel, J. L. & J. O. Kelley 1986. Description and comparison of the skeleton. In *Prehistory of Wadi Kubbaniya, Vol. 1: The Wadi Kubbaniya Skeleton: a late palaeolithic burial from southern Egypt*, Wendorf, F. & R. Schild (eds), 53–70. Dallas: Southern Methodist University Press.

Ankermann, B. 1905. Kulturkreise und Kulturschichten in Africa. *Zeitschrift für Ethnologie* 37, 54–84.

Anozie, F. N. 1979. Early iron technology in Igboland (Lejja and Umundu). *West African Journal of Archaeology* 9, 119–34.

Anquandah, J. 1965. Ghana's terracotta cigars. *Ghana Notes and Queries* 7, 25.

—— 1975. State formation among the Akan of Ghana. *Sankofa* 1, 47–59.

—— 1976a. Boyasi hill – a Kintampo 'neolithic' village site in the forest of Ghana. *Sankofa* 2, 92.

—— 1976b. Excavation at Boyasi Hill, Kumase – a preliminary report. *Nyame Akuma* 8, 33–5.

—— 1978. The Accra Plains Archaeological and Historical Project. Report on 1976/77 field work. *Nyame Akuma* 12, 24–7.

—— 1979. The Accra Plains Archaeological and Historical Project. *Nyame Akuma* 15, 14–20.

—— 1981. Excavations at the smith's quarter of Begho, Ghana. *West African Journal of Archaeology* 11, 131–44.

—— 1982a. *Rediscovering Ghana's Past*. Harlow: Longman.

—— 1982b. Archaeological reconnaissance and excavations in the Shai hills, Ghana. *Nyame Akuma* 21, 15–17.

—— 1986. Ethnoarchaeological clues to Ghana's great past. *Universitas* 8, 113–30.

—— 1987. *Accra Plains Dangmeland: a study of iron age sites and related modern settlements*. University of Ghana Monographs and Papers in African Archaeology no. 3. Legon.

—— n.d.a. Urban and state origins in Dangmeland – an archaeological and historical study. Seminar Paper, Institute of African Studies, Legon, 1981.

—— n.d.b. Excavation at Boyasi Hill, a preliminary report. Unpublished paper, 1977. Department of Archaeology, Legon.

Anzani, A. 1926. Numismatica aksumita. *Rivista Italiana di Numismatica* 39, 5–110.

Appia, B. 1965. Les forgerons du Fouta-Djallon. *Journal de la Société des Africanistes* 35, 317–52.

Argyle, W. J. 1966. *The Fon of Dahomey: a history and ethnography of the Old Kingdom*. Oxford: Clarendon Press.

Arhem, K. 1985. *The Symbolic World of the Maasai Homestead*. Uppsala: Uppsala University Press.

Arkell, A. J. 1937a. An extinct Darfur hoe. *Sudan Notes and Records* 20, 146–50.

—— 1937b. The Tigda or reaping knife in Darfur. *Sudan Notes and Records* 20, 306–7.

—— 1946. Darfur antiquities III. *Sudan Notes and Records* 27, 185–202.

—— 1949. *Early Khartoum*. London: Oxford University Press.

—— 1951. The history of Darfur, A.D. 1200–1700. *Sudan Notes and Records* 32, 37–70, 207–38.

—— 1952. The history of Darfur, A.D. 1200–1700. *Sudan Notes and Records* 33, 129–55, 244–75.

—— 1954. Four occupation sites at Agordat. *Kush* 2, 33–62.

—— 1961. *A History of the Sudan: from the earliest times to 1821*. London: Athlone Press.

—— 1968. The valley of the Nile. In *The Dawn of African History*, Oliver, R. (ed.), 7–12. London: Oxford University Press.

Arkell, A. J., B. Fagan & R. Summers 1966. The Iron Age in sub-Saharan Africa. *Current Anthropology* 7, 451–84.

Arkell, A. J. & P. J. Ucko 1965. Review of predynastic development in the Nile valley. *Current Anthropology* 6, 145–66.

Armstrong, R. G. 1964. *The Study of West African Languages*. Ibadan: Ibadan University Press.

—— 1967. *A Comparative Wordlist of Five Igbo Dialects*. Ibadan: Institute of African Studies, University of Ibadan.

Arnaud, R. 1970. Villages de l'Ambohimarina. Archéologie des Hautes Terres et de l'Afrique orientale. Revue du Musée d'Art et d'Archéologie. *Taloha* 3, 113–26.

Arnold, D. 1979. el-Lahun. In *Lexikon der Ägyptologie, III*, Helck, W. & W. Westendorf (eds), 909–11. Wiesbaden: Otto Harrasowitz.

Arnold, E. 1985. *Ceramic Theory and Cultural Process*. Cambridge: Cambridge University Press.

Ascenso, J. C. 1966. Outlines of the oil palm breeding programme in Portuguese Guinea. *Euphytica* 15, 268–77.

Ascher, M. & R. Ascher 1981. *Code of the Quipu: a study in media, mathematics and culture*. Ann Arbor: University of Michigan Press.

Aschwanden, H. 1982. *Symbols of Life: an analysis of the consciousness of the Karanga*. Gweru: Mambo Press.

Assmann, J. 1984. *Theologie und Frommigkeit einer früheren Hochkultur*. Mainz: Kohlhammer.

—— 1989. State and religion in the New Kingdom. In *Religion and Philosophy in Ancient Egypt*, Allen, J., J. Assmann, A. Lloyd, R. Ritner & D. Silverman (eds), 55–88. New Haven: Yale Egyptological Studies.

Atherton, J. H. 1972. Excavations at Kamabai and Yagala rock shelters, Sierra Leone. *West African Journal of Archaeology* 2, 39–74.

—— 1979. Early economies of Sierra Leone and Liberia: archaeological and historical reflections. In *Essays on the Economic Anthropology of Sierra Leone and Liberia*, Dorjahn, V. & B. L. Isaac (eds), 27–43. Philadelphia: Institute for Liberian Studies.

—— 1980. Speculation on the functions of some prehistoric archaeological materials from Sierra Leone. In *West African Culture Dynamics: archaeological and historical perspectives*, Swartz, B. K. & R. Dumett (eds), 259–75. The Hague: Mouton.

Aumassip, G. 1975. La poterie de Batalimo. In *Recherches préhistoriques en République Centrafricaine*, de Bayle des Hermens, R. (ed.), 221–34. Nanterre: Labethno.

—— 1984. Ti-n-Hanakaten, Tassili-n-Ajjer, Algérie, Bilan de 6 campagnes de fouilles. *Libyca* 28/9, 115–27.

Austen, R. A. 1987. *African Economic History*. London: James Currey.

Avery, D. H. & P. Schmidt 1979. A metallurgical study of the iron bloomery, particularly as practised in BaHaya. *Journal of Metals* 31, 14–20.

Avery, G. 1984. Late holocene avian remains from Wortel, Walvis Bay, SWA/Namibia, and some observations on seasonality and Topnaar Hottentot prehistory. *Madoqua* 14, 63–70.

Badawy, A. 1975. Festungsanlage. In *Lexikon der Ägyptologie, II*, Helck, W. & W. Westendorf (eds), 194–203. Wiesbaden: Otto Harrasowitz.

Bafaqih, M. A. 1983. Le Yemen. Unpublished PhD thesis, Sorbonne, Paris.

Bafaqih, M. A. & C. Robin 1980. The importance of the inscriptions of Jabal al-Mis'äl (in Arabic). *Raydán* 3, 9–29.

Bahuchet, S. & H. Guillaume 1982. Aka–farmer relations in the northwest Congo basin. In *Politics and History in Band Societies*, Leacock, E. & R. Lee (eds), 189–211. Cambridge: Cambridge University Press.

Bailey, G. N. & I. Davidson 1983. Site exploration territories and topography: two case studies from palaeolithic Spain. *Journal of Archaeological Science* 2, 87–115.

Bailloud, G. 1959. La préhistoire de l'Ethiopie. *Cahiers de l'Afrique et de l'Asie* 5, 15–43.

Baines, J. & J. Malek 1984. *Atlas of Ancient Egypt*. Oxford: Phaidon.

Balandier, G. 1968. *Daily Life in the Kingdom of Kongo from the Sixteenth to the Eighteenth Century*. London: Allen & Unwin.

—— 1970. *Political Anthropology*. New York: Random House.

Ballmann, P. 1980. Report on the avian remains from sites in Egyptian Nubia, Upper Egypt and the Fayum. In *Loaves and Fishes: the prehistory of Wadi Kubbaniya*, A. E. Close (ed.), 307–10. Dallas: Southern Methodist University.

Balout, L. 1955. *Préhistoire de l'Afrique du nord*. Paris: Arts et Métiers Graphiques.

Banks, K. M. 1984. *Climates, Cultures and Cattle: the holocene archaeology of the eastern Sahara*. Dallas: Southern Methodist University Press.

Barbot, J. 1732. A description of the coast of north and south Guinea. *A Collection of Voyages and Travels, Vol. 5*, Churchill, A. & J. Churchill (compilers). London: A. & J. Churchill.

Barbour, K. 1961. *The Republic of the Sudan: a regional geography*. London: University of London Press.

Barbour, K. & R. M. Prothero (eds) 1961. *Essays on African Population*. New York: Praeger.

Barendsen, G. W., E. S. Deevey & L. J. Gralenski 1957. Yale national radiocarbon measurements III. *Science* 126, 917–18.

Bargery, G. P. 1934. *A Hausa–English Dictionary*. London: Oxford University Press.

Barich, B. E. 1980. Pour une définition du néolithique en Afrique du nord et du Sahara. *Proceedings of the 8th Panafrican Congress of Prehistory and Quaternary Studies, Nairobi, 1977*, Leakey, R. E. & B. A. Ogot (eds), 271–2. Nairobi: International Louis Leakey Memorial Institute for African Prehistory.

Barker, G. 1978. Economic models for the Manyikeni Zimbabwe, Mozambique. *Azania* 13, 71–100.

Barley, M. W. 1977. *European Towns*. London: Academic Press.

Barley, N. 1983. *Symbolic Structures: an exploration of the culture of the Dowayos*. Cambridge: Cambridge University Press.

Barnes, H. B. 1926. Iron smelting among the Ba-Ushi. *Journal of the Royal Anthropological Institute* 56, 189–94.

Barradas, L. 1961. Chronologia do Quaternario do sul de Moçambique. *Boletim do Instituto de Investigação Científica de Moçambique* 2, 374–88.

—— 1967. A primitiva Mabone e suas immediacoes. *Monumenta* 3, 23–41.

Barros, P. de 1986. Bassar: a quantified, chronologically controlled, regional approach to a traditional iron production centre in west Africa. *Africa* 56, 148–74.

Barth, F. (ed.) 1978. *Scale and Social Organization*. Oslo: Universitetsforlaget.

Barth, F. E. 1967. Prähistorische Knieholzschaftungen aus dem Salzberg zu Hallstatt. *Mitteilungen der Anthropologische Gesellschaft in Wien* 46, 254–72.

—— 1983. Mining at Hallstatt. Unpublished paper given at the London conference on 'Hallstatt and the Western Celts'.

Barth, H. 1857–8. *Travels and Discoveries in North and Central Africa.* 5 vols. London: Longman.

Barthelmé, J. W. 1985. *Fisher-hunters and Neolithic Pastoralists in East Turkana, Kenya.* Oxford: British Archaeological Reports.

Bar-Yosef, O. & A. Belfer-Cohen 1989. The Levantine 'PPNB' interaction sphere. In *People and Culture in Change: proceedings of the second symposium on upper palaeolithic, mesolithic and neolithic populations of Europe and the Mediterranean basin,* 59–72. Oxford: British Archaeological Reports.

Bass, G. F. 1986. A bronze age shipwreck at Ulu Burun (Kas): 1984 campaign. *American Journal of Archaeology* 90, 269–96.

Bass, G. F., C. Pulak, D. Collon & J. Weinstein 1989. The bronze age shipwreck at Ulu Burun: 1986 campaign. *American Journal of Archaeology* 93, 1–29.

Bate, D. M. A. 1947. An extinct reed-rat (*Thryonomys arkelli*) from the Sudan. *Annals and Magazine of Natural History* 11, 65–71.

—— 1953. The vertebrate fauna. In *Shaheinab,* Arkell, A. J. (ed.), 11–19. Oxford: Oxford University Press.

Battistini, R. & P. Vérin 1966. Irodo et la tradition vohemarienne. *Revue de Madagascar* 36, 11–32.

Battistini, R., P. Vérin & R. Rason 1963. Le site archéologique de Talaky, cadre géographique et géologique, les travaux de fouille, notes ethnographiques sur le village. *Annales de la Faculté de Lettres et Sciences Humaines de l'Université de Madagascar* 1, 113–28.

Baudet, J. & P. Laurenti 1976. Traceurs isotopiques et situation météorologique. *La Météorologie* 6, 213–21.

Baumann, H. 1975. *Die Volke Afrikas und ihre traditionellen Kulturen: Studien zur Kulturkunde, 1.* Wiesbaden: H. Baumann.

—— 1979. *Die Volke Afrikas und ihre traditionellen Kulturen: Studien zur Kulturkunde, 2.* Wiesbaden: H. Baumann.

Beach, D. N. 1980. *The Shona and Zimbabwe, 900–1850: an outline of Shona history.* Gweru: Mambo Press.

—— 1987. Documents and African society on the Zimbabwean plateau. *Paideuma* 33, 129–45.

—— 1991. Where you are the angels fear to tread: cognitive archaeology and imaginary history at Great Zimbabwe. Seminar paper, History Department, University of Zimbabwe.

Beattie, J. 1971. *The Nyoro State.* Oxford: Oxford University Press.

Beauvilain, A. 1983. Un élevage résiduel: les taurins du nord Cameroun. *Revue Géographique Camerounaise* 4, 39–44.

Beavon, K. S. O. & A. V. Hall 1972. A geotaxonomic approach to classification in urban and regional studies. *Geographic Analysis* 4, 407–15.

Bedaux, R. M. A., T. S. Constandse-Westermann, L. Hacquebord, A.-G. Lange & J. D. van der Waals 1978. Recherches archéologiques dans le delta du Niger. *Palaeohistoria* 20, 91–220.

Belai Giday 1987. *Currency and Banking in Ethiopia.* Addis Ababa: The author.

Bell, B. 1970. The oldest records of the Nile floods. *Geographical Journal* 136, 569–73.

—— 1971. The dark ages in ancient history. *American Journal of Archaeology* 75, 1–26.

—— 1975. Climate and the history of Egypt: the Middle Kingdom. *American Journal of Archaeology* 79, 223–69.

Bellamy, C. V. & F. W. Harbord 1904. West African smelting house. *Journal of the Iron and Steel Institute* 66, 99–126.

Bellwood, P. 1979. *Man's Conquest of the Pacific.* New York: Oxford University Press.

Bender, B. 1981. Gatherer-hunter intensification. In *Economic Archaeology: towards an integration of ecological and social approaches,* Sheridan, A. & G. Bailey (eds), 149–57. Oxford: British Archaeological Reports.

Bender, M. L. 1971. The languages of Ethiopia. *Anthropological Linguistics* 13, 165–288.

—— 1975a. *Omotic: a new Afroasiatic language family.* Carbondale: Southern Illinois University.

—— 1975b. Nilo-Saharan overview. In *The Non-Semitic Languages of Ethiopia*, Bender, M. L. & H. C. Fleming (eds), 439–83. East Lansing: Michigan State University Press.

—— 1982. Livestock and linguistics in north and east African ethnohistory. *Current Anthropology* 23, 316–17.

—— 1983a. Introduction. In *Nilo-Saharan Language Studies*, Bender, M. L. (ed.), 1–10. East Lansing: Michigan State University Press.

—— 1983b. Remnant languages of Ethiopia and Sudan. In *Nilo-Saharan Language Studies*, Bender, M. L. (ed.), 336–54. East Lansing: Michigan State University Press.

—— 1988. Core and periphery in Nilo-Saharan. Handout accompanying presentation at the 19th African Linguistics Conference, Boston.

Bendor-Samuel, J. & R. Hartell (eds) 1989. *The Niger-Congo Languages.* Lanham: Universities Press of America.

Benedict, B. 1968. Societies, small. In *International Encyclopaedia of the Social Sciences 14*, Sills, D. (ed.), 572–7. New York: Macmillan.

Bennett, P. R. 1983. Adamawa–Eastern: problems and prospects. In *Studies in African Linguistics, Vol. 1*, Dihoff, I. (ed.), 23–48. Dordrecht: Foris Publications.

Bennett, P. R. & J. P. Sterk 1977. South-central Niger-Congo: a reclassification. *Studies in African Linguistics* 8, 241–73.

Bent, J. T. 1892. *The Ruined Cities of Mashonaland.* London: Longman.

Berg, F. J. 1968. The Swahili community of Mombasa 1500–1900. *Journal of African History* 9, 35–6.

Berglund, A.-I. 1976. *Zulu Thought Patterns and Symbolism.* London: C. Hurst.

Bernhard, F. O. 1962. Two types of iron smelting furnace on Ziwa Farm (Inyanga). *South African Archaeological Bulletin* 17, 235–6.

Bernstein, H. & J. Depelchin 1978. The object of African history (a materialist perspective). *History in Africa* 5, 1–19.

—— 1979. The object of African history (a materialist perspective). *History in Africa* 6, 17–43.

Bernus, E. 1983. Place et rôle du forgeron dans la société touarègue. In *Métallurgies africaines: nouvelles contributions*, Echard, N. (ed.), 237–51. Paris: Société des Africanistes.

Bernus, E. & S. Bernus 1972. Du sel et des dates. *Etudes Nigériennes* 31, 31.

Berry, B. J. L. 1961. City size distributions and economic development. *Economic Development and Culture Change* 9, 573–87.

Berry, B. J. L. & W. L. Garrison 1958. Alternate explanations of urban rank–size relationships. *Annals of the Association of American Geographers* 48, 83–91.

Berry, S. 1989. Social institutions and access to resources. *Africa* 59, 41–55.

Bertaux, J. P. 1972. Etudes sur le briquetage de la Seille. *Bulletin de l'Académie et de la Société Lorraine des Sciences* 11, 168–81.

Berthoud, G. 1965. Essai historique sur les Ganawuri du plateau (nord du Nigeria). *Bulletin Annuel du Musée et Institut d'Ethnographie de la Ville de Genève* 8, 15–38.

Bhila, H. H. K. 1982. *Trade and Politics in a Shona Kingdom.* London: Longman.

Biberson, P. 1963. Human evolution in Morocco, in the framework of the paleoclimatic variations of the Atlantic Pleistocene. In *African Ecology and Human Evolution*, Howell, F. C. & F. Bourlière (eds), 417–47. New York: Wenner Gren Foundation.

Bietak, M. 1968. *Studien zur Chronologie der nubische C-Gruppe.* Vienna: Oesterreichische Akademie der Wissenschaften.

—— 1975. *Tell ed-Dab'a II.* Vienna: Oesterreichische Akademie der Wissenschaften.

—— 1979a. The present condition of Egyptian archaeology. *Journal of Egyptian Archaeology* 65,

156–60.

—— 1979b. Urban archaeology and the 'town problem' in ancient Egypt. In *Egyptology and the Social Sciences*, Weeks, K. (ed.), 97–140. Cairo: American University in Cairo Press.

—— 1981. Das Stadtproblem im alten Aegypten. In *150 Jahre Deutsches Archäologisches Institut 1829–1979*, 68–78. Mainz: Phillip von Zabern.

—— 1983. Ramesstadt. In *Lexikon der Ägyptologie V*, Helck, W. & W. Westendorf (eds), 128–46. Wiesbaden: Otto Harrasowitz.

—— 1984a. Tell ed-Dab'a 1983/84. *Jahreshefte des Österreichischen Archäologischen Institut in Wien* 55, 1–9.

—— 1984b. Stadt(anlage). In *Lexikon der Ägyptologie V*, Helck, W. & W. Westendorf (eds), 1233–49. Wiesbaden: Otto Harrasowitz.

—— 1985. Tell ed-Dab'a. In *Lexikon der Ägyptologie VI*, Helck, W. & W. Westendorf (eds), 321–33. Wiesbaden: Otto Harrasowitz.

Binford, L. R. 1981. Behavioral archaeology and the Pompeii Premise. *Journal of Anthropological Research* 37, 195–211.

—— 1983a. *In Pursuit of the Past*. London: Thames & Hudson.

—— 1983b. *Working at Archaeology*. New York: Academic Press.

—— 1984. *Faunal Remains from Klasies River Mouth*. London: Academic Press.

Binford, L. R. & S. Binford (eds) 1968. *New Perspectives in Archaeology*. Chicago: Aldine.

Birmingham, D. 1970. Early African trade in Angola and its hinterland. In *Pre-colonial African Trade*, Gray, R. & D. Birmingham (eds), 163–74. London: Oxford University Press.

Bishop, W. W. 1963. The later Tertiary and Pleistocene in eastern equatorial Africa. In *African Ecology and Human Evolution*, Howell, F. C. & F. Bourlière (eds), 246–75. New York: Wenner Gren Foundation.

Bishop, W. W. & J. D. Clark (eds) 1967. *Background to Evolution in Africa*. Chicago: Chicago University Press.

Bivar, A. D. H. & P. L. Shinnie 1970. Old Kanuri capitals. In *Papers in African Prehistory*, Fage, J. D. & R. A. Oliver (eds), 289–302. Cambridge: Cambridge University Press.

Blackburn, R. H. 1973. Okiek ceramics: evidence for central Kenya prehistory. *Azania* 8, 55–70.

Blacking, J. 1969. Songs, dances, mimes and symbolism of Venda girls' initiation schools: part 3, Domba. *African Studies* 28, 149–99.

—— 1985. The great enclosure and domba. *Man* 20, 542–3.

Blanton, R. 1981. The rise of cities. In *Supplement to the Handbook of Middle American Indians, I: Archaeology*, Sabloff, J. (ed.), 392–400. Austin: University of Texas Press.

Blench, R. M. 1989a. New Benue–Congo: a definition and proposed internal classification. *Afrikanistische Arbeitspapiere* 17, 115–47.

—— 1989b. The evolution of the cultigen repertoire of the Nupe of west-central Nigeria. *Azania* 24, 51–63.

—— n.d. Lesser-known African tuber crops and their role in prehistory. Unpublished ms.

Blench, R. M. & A. E. Edwards 1988. *A Dictionary of the Momi Language*. Cambridge: The authors.

Blench, R. M. & K. Williamson 1987. A new classification of Bantoid languages. Paper for the 17th Leiden Colloquium on African Languages.

Bloch, M. & P. Vérin 1966. Discovery of an allegedly neolithic artifact in Madagascar. *Man* 2, 240–1.

Boardman, J. 1964. *The Greeks Abroad*. Harmondsworth: Penguin Books.

Bock, K. R. 1978. *A Guide to Common Reef Fishes of the Western Ocean*. London: Macmillan.

Boessneck, J. 1988. *Die Tierwelt des alten Ägypten*. Munich: C. H. Beck.

Bohannan, L. & P. Bohannan 1953. *The Tiv of Central Nigeria*. London: International African

Institute.

Bohannan, P. 1954a. The migration and expansion of the Tiv. *Africa* 24, 2–16.

—— 1954b. *Tiv Farm and Settlement*. London: H. M. Stationery Office.

Bohannan, P. & L. Bohannan 1958. *Three Source Notebooks in Tiv Ethnography*. New Haven: Human Relations Area Files.

Bond, G. 1963. Pleistocene environments in southern Africa. In *African Ecology and Human Evolution*, Howell, F. C. & F. Bourlière (eds), 308–34. New York: Wenner Gren Foundation.

Bonnefille, R. & G. Riollet 1988. The Kashiru pollen sequence (Burundi): palaeoclimatic implications for the last 40,000 yr BP in tropical Africa. *Quaternary Research* 30, 19–35.

Bonnet, C. 1986. *Kerma: territoire et metropole*. Cairo: Institut français d'archéologie orientale du Caire.

Bonnet, C., B. Privati, C. Simon, L. Chaix & P. de Paepe 1988. *Kerma 1988–1986–1987–1987–1988*. Geneva 46.

Bonte, P. 1981. Marxist theory and anthropological analysis: the study of nomadic pastoralist societies. In *The Anthropology of Pre-capitalist Societies*, Kahn, J. S. & J. R. Llobera (eds), 22–56. London: Macmillan.

Bontinck, F. 1972. *Histoire du royaume du Congo (c. 1624): traduction annotée du Ms. 8080 de la Bibliothèque nationale de Lisbonne*. Louvain: Nauwelaerts.

Boston, J. S. 1968. *The Igala Kingdom*. Ibadan: Oxford University Press.

Bouillard, G. 1929. *Note succincte sur l'histoire du territoire de Peking et sur les diverses enceintes de cette ville*. The Museum of Far Eastern Antiquities.

Boulos, L. & M. N. el-Hadidi 1984. *The Weed Flora of Egypt*. Cairo: American University in Cairo Press.

Bouquiaux, L. (ed.) 1980. *L'Expansion bantoue*. Paris: Société d'Etudes Linguistiques et Anthropologiques de France.

Bourdillon, M. 1976. *The Shona Peoples*. Gweru: Mambo Press.

Bovier-Lapierre, P. 1926. *Une nouvelle station néolithique (El Omari) au nord d'Helouan (Egypte)*. Cairo: Congrès International de Géographie.

Bovill, E. 1968. *The Golden Trade of the Moors*. London: Oxford University Press.

Bowdich, T. E. 1966. *Mission from Cape Coast Castle to Ashantee*. London: Cass.

Bowen, T. J. 1857. *Central Africa: adventures and missionary labors in several countries in the interior of Africa, from 1849 to 1856*. Charleston: Southern Baptist Publication Society.

Bower, J. R. F. 1973a. Early pottery and other finds from Kisii district, western Kenya. *Azania* 8, 131–40.

—— 1973b. Seronera: excavations at a stone bowl site in the Serengeti National Park, Tanzania. *Azania* 8, 71–104.

—— 1976. New light on the East African Neolithic. In *Proceedings of the Panafrican Congress of Prehistory and Quaternary Studies, 7th Session, Addis Ababa, December 1971*, Abebe, B., J. Chevaillon & J. E. G. Sutton (eds), 47–9. Addis Ababa: Provisional Military Government of Socialist Ethiopia, Ministry of Culture.

—— 1978. Culture, environment and technology: preliminary results of an archaeological study in Kenya. *Proceedings of the Iowa Academy of Science* 85, 41–4.

—— 1984a. Settlement behavior of pastoral cultures in east Africa. In *From Hunters to Farmers: the causes and consequences of food production in Africa*, Clark, J. D. & S. A. Brandt (eds), 252–60. Berkeley: University of California Press.

—— 1984b. Subsistence-settlement systems of the Pastoral Neolithic in east Africa. In *Origin and Early Development of Food-producing Cultures in North-eastern Africa*, Krzyzaniak, L. & M. Kobusiewicz (eds), 473–80. Poznan: Polish Academy of Sciences & Poznan Archaeological Museum.

—— 1986. A survey of surveys: aspects of surface archaeology in sub-Saharan Africa. *African Archaeological Review* 4, 21–40.

Bower, J. R. F. & T. J. Chadderdon 1986. Further excavations of pastoral neolithic sites in Serengeti. *Azania* 21, 129–33.

Bower, J. R. F. & C. M. Nelson 1978. Early pottery and pastoral cultures of the central Rift Valley. *Man* 13, 554–66.

Bower, J. R. F., C. M. Nelson, A. F. Waibel & S. Wandibba 1977. The University of Massachusetts' later stone age/pastoral neolithic comparative study in central Kenya: an overview. *Azania* 12, 119–43.

Bowersock, G. W. 1983. *Roman Arabia*. Cambridge, Mass.: Harvard University Press.

Boyd, R. 1978. A propos des ressemblances lexicales entre langues Niger-Congo et Nilo-Saharien. *Société d'Etudes Linguistiques et Anthropologiques de France* 65, 43–94.

Bradbury, R. E. 1959. Chronological problems in the study of Benin history. *Journal of the Historic Society, Nigeria* 1, 263–87.

Bradford, M. G. & W. A. Kent 1977. *Human Geography*. Oxford: Oxford University Press.

Bradley, R. 1975. Salt and settlement in the Hampshire-Sussex borderland. In *Salt: the study of an ancient industry*, K. W. de Brisay & K. A. Evans (eds), 20–5. Colchester: Colchester Archaeological Group.

Braidwood, L. & R. J. Braidwood 1969. Current thoughts on the beginnings of food production in southwestern Asia. *Mélanges de l'Université Saint-Joseph* 15, 147–55.

Braidwood, R. J. 1962. The earliest village communities of southwestern Asia reconsidered. *Atti del VI Congresso Internazionale della Società Preistorica e Protostorica I*, 115–26. Florence: Sansoni.

Brain, C. K. 1981. *The Hunters or the Hunted? An introduction to African cave taphonomy*. Chicago: University of Chicago Press.

Brandt, S. A. 1980. Archaeological investigations at Lake Besaka, Ethiopia. In *Proceedings of the 8th Panafrican Congress of Prehistory and Quaternary Studies*, Leakey, R. E. & B. A. Ogot (eds), 239–43. Nairobi: International Louis Leakey Memorial Institute for African Prehistory.

—— 1984. New perspectives on the origins of food production in Ethiopia. In *From Hunters to Farmers: the causes and consequences of food production in Africa*, Clark, J. D. & S. A. Brandt (eds), 173–90. Berkeley: University of California Press.

—— 1986. The upper Pleistocene and early Holocene prehistory of the Horn of Africa. *African Archaeological Review* 4, 41–82.

Brandt, S. A. & N. Carder 1987. Pastoral rock art in the Horn of Africa: making sense of udder chaos. *World Archaeology* 9, 194–213.

Breasted, J. H. 1906–7. *Ancient Records of Egypt, I–V*. Chicago: University of Chicago Press.

Brelsford, V. W. 1949. Rituals and medicines of Chishinga ironworkers. *Man* 49, 27–9.

Brenac, P. 1988. Evolution de la végétation et du climat dans l'Ouest-Cameroun entre 25.000 et 11.000 ans BP. *Institut Français de Pondichery, Travaux du Section Scientifique et Technique* 25, 91–103.

Breuil, H. 1944. II Parte das primeiras impressoes duma viagem de estudos arqueologicos no sul de Moçambique. *Moçambique Documentario Trimestral* 40, 39–48.

—— 1948. The White Lady of the Brandberg, South West Africa, her companions and her guards. *South African Archaeological Bulletin* 3, 2–11.

Brewer, D. J. 1987. Seasonality in the prehistoric Faiyum basin based on the incremental growth structures of the Nile catfish (Pisces: *Clarias*). *Journal of Archaeological Science* 14, 459–72.

—— 1989a. *Fishermen, Hunters, and Herders: zooarchaeology in the Fayum, Egypt (c. 8200–5000 bp)*. Oxford: British Archaeological Reports.

—— 1989b. A model for resource exploitation in the prehistoric Fayum. In *Late Prehistory of the Nile Basin and the Sahara*, Krzyzaniak, L. & M. Kobusiewicz (eds), 127–38. Poznan: Poznan

Archaeology Museum.

Briggs, G. W. G. 1941. Crop yields and food requirements in Tiv Division, Benue Province, Nigeria. *Farm and Forest* 5, 15–20.

Brock, B. & W. Brock 1965. Iron working among the Nyiha of southwestern Tanzania. *South African Archaeological Bulletin* 20, 97–100.

Bronowski, J. 1973. *The Ascent of Man*. London: Britsh Broadcasting Corporation.

—— 1978. *The Origins of Knowledge and Imagination*. New York: Yale University Press.

Brooke, C. N. L. 1975. *London 800–1216: the shaping of a city*. London: Secker & Warburg.

Brookes, I. A. 1989. Early holocene basin sediments of Dakhleh Oasis region, south-central Egypt. *Quaternary Research* 52: 139–52.

Broshi, M. 1979. The population of western Palestine in the Roman–Byzantine period. *Bulletin of the American Schools of Oriental Research* 236, 1–10.

Brown, H. W. 1985. History of Siyu: the development and decline of a Swahili town on the northern Kenyan coast. Unpublished PhD thesis, Indiana University.

Brown, J. 1977. Anti-sorcery rituals of an Mberre blacksmith. *Kenya Past and Present* 8, 36–8.

Browne, W. G. 1799. *Travels in Egypt, Syria and Africa*. London: Longman & Rees.

Brunache, P. 1894. *Au centre de l'Afrique: autour du Tchad*. Paris: Alcan.

Brunton, G. 1928. The Badarian civilization, Pt I. In *The Badarian Civilization and Predynastic Remains near Badari*, Brunton, G. & G. Caton-Thompson, 1–68. London: Bernard Quaritch.

—— 1930. *Qau and Badari, III*. London: Bernard Quaritch.

—— 1937. *Mostagedda and the Tasian Culture*. London: Bernard Quaritch.

—— 1948. *Matmar*. London: Bernard Quaritch.

Brunton, G. & G. Caton-Thompson 1928. *The Badarian Civilization and Predynastic Remains Near Badari*. London: Bernard Quaritch.

Bryant, A. T. 1949. *The Zulu People, as they were before the White Men Came*. Pietermaritzberg: Shuter & Shooter.

Bucher, K. 1980. *Spirits and Power*. Oxford: Oxford University Press.

Budack, K. F. R. 1977. The /Aonin or Topnaar of the lower !Khuiseb valley and the sea. *Khoisan Linguistic Studies* 3, 1–42.

Bulliet, R. W. 1975. *The Camel and the Wheel*. Cambridge, Mass.: Harvard University Press.

Bullock, C. 1927. *The Mashona*. Cape Town: Juta and Co.

Bulman, J. C. 1985. A nutritional evaluation of the tuber of the plant *Cyperus esculentus*. Unpublished MSc dissertation, Department of Nutrition, King's College, University of London.

Burchell, W. J. 1822. *Travels in the Interior of Southern Africa*. 2 vols. Glasgow: The University Press.

Burgess, W. E. & H. R. Axelrod 1974. *Pacific Marine Fishes: fishes of Taiwan and adjacent waters*. 2 vols. Hong Kong: T. F. H. Publications.

Burkhardt, A. 1984. *Urkunden der 18: Dynastie, Übersetzung, Hefte 5–16*. Berlin: Akademie-Verlag.

Burkill, H. M. 1985. *The Useful Plants of West Tropical Africa, Vol. 1: Families A–D*. Kew: Royal Botanic Gardens.

Burney, D. A. 1987. Late holocene vegetation change in central Madagascar. *Quaternary Research* 28, 130–43.

Butterman, J. M. 1979. Luo social formations in change: Karachuonyo and Kanyamkago, *c.* 1800–1945. Unpublished PhD thesis, Syracuse University.

Butzer, K. W. 1959. Die Naturlandschaft Ägyptens wahrend der Vorgeschichte und der dynastischen Zeit. *Akademie der Wissenschaften und der Literatur in Mainz, Abhandlungen der Mathematisch-Naturwissenschaftlichen Klasse* 2, 1–80.

—— 1961. Archäologische Fundstellen Ober- und Mittelägyptens in ihrer geologischen

Landschaft. *Mitteilungen des Deutschen Archäologischen Instituts, Abteilung Kairo* 17, 54–68.

—— 1976. *Early Hydraulic Civilization in Egypt: a study in cultural ecology.* Chicago: University of Chicago Press.

—— 1980a. The holocene lake plain of north Rudolf, east Africa. *Physical Geography* 1: 42–58.

—— 1980b. Pleistocene history of the Nile valley in Egypt and lower Nubia. In *The Sahara and the Nile: quaternary environments and prehistoric occupation in northern Africa*, Martin A. J., W. Faure & H. Faure (eds), 253–80. Rotterdam: A. A. Balkema.

—— 1981. Rise and fall of Axum, Ethiopia: a geo-archaeological interpretation. *American Antiquity* 46, 471–95.

—— 1984a. Long-term Nile flood variation and political discontinuities in Pharaonic Egypt. In *From Hunters to Farmers: the causes and consequences of food production in Africa*, Clark, J. D. & Ş. A. Brandt (eds), 102–12. Berkeley: University of California Press.

—— 1984b. Siedlungsgeographie. In *Lexikon der Ägyptologie V*, Helck, W. & W. Westendorf (eds), 924–33. Wiesbaden: Otto Harrasowitz.

Cable, C. n.d. Forager–farmer interactions in Kenyan prehistory or 'What happened to the hungers?' Seminar paper, Department of History, University of Nairobi, 1987.

Cadet, D. L. & N. O. Nnoli 1987. Water vapour transport over Africa and the Atlantic Ocean during summer 1979. *Quarterly Journal of the Royal Meteorological Society* 113, 581–602.

Cagnolo, C. 1933. *The Akikuyu.* Nyeri: Mission Printing School.

Cahen, D. 1976. Nouvelles fouilles à la pointe de la Gombe (ex-pointe de Kalina), Kinshasa, Zaïre. *L'Anthropologie* 80, 573–602.

—— 1978. Vers une révision de la nomenclature des industries préhistoriques de l'Afrique centrale. *L'Anthropologie* 82, 5–36.

Cahen, D. & G. Mortelmans 1973. *Un site tshitolien sur le plateau des Bateke (République du Zaïre).* Tervuren: Musée Royal de l'Afrique Centrale.

Calvocoressi, D. & N. David 1979. A new survey of radiocarbon and thermoluminescence dates for west Africa. *Journal of African History* 20, 1–29.

Camps, G. 1968. *Amekni, néolithique ancien du Hoggar.* Algiers: Centre de Recherches Anthropologiques, Préhistoriques et Ethnographiques.

—— 1974. *Les Civilisations préhistoriques de l'Afrique du Nord et du Sahara.* Paris: Doin.

Cane, S. 1989. Australian aboriginal seed grinding and its archaeological record: a case study from the Western Desert. In *Foraging and Farming: the evolution of plant exploitation*, Harris, D. R. & G. C. Hillman (eds), 99–119. London: Unwin & Hyman.

Caquot, A. & A. J. Drewes 1955. Les monuments recueillis à Maqalle. *Annales d'Ethiopie* 1, 17–51.

Caratini, C. & P. Giresse 1979. Contribution palynologique à la connaissance des environnements continentaux et marins du Congo à la fin du Quaternaire. *Comptes Rendus de l'Académie des Sciences* 288, 379–82.

Carcasson, R. H. 1977. *A Field Guide to the Coral Reef Fishes of the Indian and West Pacific Oceans.* London: Collins.

Carr, C. 1985. *For Concordance in Archaeological Analysis.* Prospect Height: Waveland Press.

Carter, P. L. & C. Flight 1972. A report on the fauna from the sites of Ntereso and Kintampo Rock Shelter Six in Ghana: with evidence for the practice of animal husbandry during the second millennium B.C. *Man* 7, 277–82.

Casanova, J., C. Hilaire-Marcel, N. Page, M. Taieb & A. Vincens 1988. Stratigraphie et paléohydrologie des épisodes lacustres du Quaternaire récent du rift Suguta (Kenya). *Comptes Rendues de l'Académie des Sciences* 307, 1251–8.

Casanova, J., A. M. Lezine & C. Hilaire-Marcel 1988. L'épisode humide de l'Holocène ancien dans le Sahara occidental: données polliniques et isotopiques. Paper presented to the

International Geological Correlation Programme 252 meeting on the evolution of deserts, Cassis, France.

Cashdan, E. A. 1984. The effects of food production on mobility in the central Kalahari. In *From Hunters to Farmers: the causes and consequences of food production in Africa*, Clark, J. D. & S. A. Brandt (eds), 311–27. Berkeley: University of California Press.

Cassidy, F. G. & R. B. Le Page 1967. *Dictionary of Jamaican English*. Cambridge: Cambridge University Press.

Casson, L. 1989. *The Periplus Maris Erythraei*. Lawrenceville: Princeton University Press.

Castro, S. 1956. *Pinturas rupestres do Niassa*. Lourenço Marques: Boletim da Sociedade de Estudos de Moçambique.

Caton-Thompson, G. 1928. The Badarian civilization, Pt II, The predynastic settlement: North Spur Hemamieh. In *The Badarian Civilization and Predynastic Remains near Badari*, G. Brunton & G. Caton-Thompson, 69–116. London: Bernard Quaritch.

—— 1931. *The Zimbabwe Culture: ruins and reactions*. Oxford: Clarendon Press.

—— 1934. The camel in Dynastic Egypt. *Man* 34, 21.

Caton-Thompson, G. & E. W. Gardner 1934. *The Desert Fayum*. London: Royal Anthropological Institute of Great Britain and Ireland.

Celis, G. & E. Nzikobanyanka 1976. *La Metallurgie traditionnelle au Burundi: techniques et croyances*. Tervuren: Musée Royal de l'Afrique centrale.

Chaix, L. 1980. Note préliminaire sur la faune de Kerma (Soudan). *Genava* 28, 63–4.

Chaix, L. & A. Grant 1987. A study of a prehistoric population of sheep (*Ovis aries* L.) from Kerma (Sudan): archaeozoological and archaeological implications. *Archaeozoologia* 1, 77–92.

Chang, T. T. 1989. Domestication and spread of the cultivated rices. In *Foraging and Farming: the evolution of plant exploitation*, Harris, D. R. & G. C. Hillman (eds), 408–17. London: Unwin Hyman.

Chanudet, C. 1988. *Contribution à l'étude du peuplement de l'île de Moheli*. Moroni: Centre de la Recherche Scientifique.

Chanudet, C & P. Vérin 1983. Une reconnaissance archéologique de Moheli. *Etudes Océan Indien* 2, 41–58.

Chaplin, J. H. 1961. Notes on traditional smelting in Northern Rhodesia. *South African Archaeological Bulletin* 16, 53–60.

—— 1962a. A preliminary account of iron age burials with gold in the Gwembe valley, Northern Rhodesia. In *Proceedings of the 1st Federal Science Congress, Salisbury May 18th–22nd 1960*, Boughey, A. S. (succeeded by Robins, P. A.) (ed.), 397–406. Salisbury: Mardon Printers.

—— 1962b. Notes on some sites in Soli history. *Northern Rhodesia Journal* 5, 50–5.

Chapman, S. 1966. A Sirikwa hole on Mt Elgon. *Azania* 1, 139–48.

Charoenwongsa, P. & D. Bayard 1983. Non Chai: new dates in metal-working and trade from northeastern Thailand. *Current Anthropology* 24, 521–3.

Chase, A. K. 1989. Domestication and domiculture in northern Australia: a social perspective. In *Foraging and Farming: the evolution of plant exploitation*, Harris, D. R. & G. C. Hillman (eds), 42–54. London: Unwin Hyman.

Chennafi, M. el-. 1976. Mention nouvelle d'une 'reine Ethiopienne' au IVe s. de Hegire /Xe s. ap. J.-C. *Annales d'Ethiopie* 10, 119–21.

Chenorkian, R. 1983. Ivory Coast prehistory: recent developments. *African Archaeological Review* 1, 127–42.

Chikwendu, V. E., P. T. Craddock, R. M. Farquar, T. Shaw & A. C. Umeji 1989. Nigerian sources of copper, lead and tin for the Igbo-Ukwu bronzes. *Archaeometry* 31, 27–36.

Chikwendu, V. E. & C. E. A. Okezie 1989. Factors responsible for the ennoblement of African yams: inferences from experiments in yam domestication. In *Foraging and Farming: the evolution of plant exploitation*, Harris, D. R. & G. C. Hillman (eds), 344–57. London: Unwin Hyman.

Childe, V. G. 1934. *New Light on the Most Ancient East: the oriental prelude to European prehistory*. London: Kegan Paul.

—— 1936. *Man Makes Himself*. London: Watts.

—— 1950. The urban revolution. *Town Planning Review* 21, 2–17.

Childs, S. T. & P. R. Schmidt 1985. Experimental iron smelting: the genesis of a hypothesis with implications for African prehistory and history. In *African Iron Working: ancient and traditional*, Haaland, R. & P. Shinnie (eds), 121–41. Oslo: Norwegian University Press.

Chilver, E. M. 1961. Nineteenth-century trade in the Bamenda Grassfields, southern Cameroons. *Afrika und Ubersee* 45, 233–58.

—— 1981. Chronological synthesis: the western region, comprising the western Grassfields, Bamum, the Bamileke chiefdom and the central Mbam. In *Contribution de la recherche ethnologique à l'histoire des civilisations du Cameroun*. 2 vols, Tardits, C. (ed.), 453–73. Paris: CNRS (Centre National de la Recherche Scientifique).

—— n.d. Thaumaturgy in contemporary traditional religion: the Nso' case. Ms, 1985.

Chippindale, C. 1990. Editorial. *Antiquity* 64, 3–13.

Chittick, H. N. 1960. *Annual Report of the Department of Antiquities*. Dar es Salaam: Government Printer.

—— 1961. *Kisimani Mafia: excavations at an Islamic settlement on the east African coast*. Dar es Salaam: Ministry of Education, Antiquities Division.

—— 1966a. Unguja Ukuu: the earliest imported pottery and an Abbasid dinar. *Azania* 1, 161–3.

—— 1966b. Kilwa: a preliminary report. *Azania* 1, 1–36.

—— 1967. Discoveries in the Lamu archipelago. *Azania* 2, 37–67.

—— 1974. *Kilwa: an Islamic trading city on the east African coast*. 2 vols. Nairobi: British Institute in Eastern Africa.

—— 1979. Excavations at Delorain Farm. *Azania* 14, 162–3.

—— 1983. Barawa. *Nyame Akuma* 22, 22.

—— 1984. *Manda: excavations at an island port on the Kenya coast*. Nairobi: British Institute in Eastern Africa.

Chittick, H. N. & R. I. Rotberg (eds) 1975. *East Africa and the Orient: cultural syntheses in pre-colonial times*. New York: Africana Publishing Co.

Christaller, J. G. 1933. *Dictionary of the Asante and Fante language called Twi*. Basel: Basel Evangelical Missionary Society.

Claes, P. 1985. Contribution à l'étude de céramiques anciennes des environs de Yaoundé. Unpublished MA thesis, Brussels Free University.

Clapperton, H. 1829. *Journal of a Second Expedition into the Interior of Africa, from the Bight of Benin to Soccatoo*. London: John Murray.

Clark, C. & M. Horton 1985. *The Zanzibar Archaeological Survey: 1984–85*. Zanzibar: Ministry of Information, Culture and Sports.

Clark, J. D. (ed.) 1957. *Third Panafrican Congress on Prehistory, Livingstone, 1955*. London: Chatto & Windus.

—— 1962. Africa, south of the Sahara. In *Courses towards Urban Life*, Braidwood, R. & G. Willey (eds), 1–33. New York: Wenner Gren Foundation.

—— 1967a. The problem of neolithic culture in sub-Saharan Africa. In *Background to Evolution in Africa*, Bishop, W. W. & J. D. Clark (eds), 600–27. Chicago: University of Chicago Press.

—— 1967b. *Atlas of African Prehistory*. Chicago: University of Chicago Press.

—— 1969. *The Kalambo Falls Prehistoric Site, I*. Cambridge: Cambridge University Press.

—— 1970. *The Prehistory of Africa*. London: Thames & Hudson.

—— 1971. *A re-examination of the evidence for agricultural origins in the Nile valley. Proceedings of the Prehistoric Society* 37, 34–79.

—— 1974. *The Kalambo Falls Prehistoric Site, II.* London: Cambridge University Press.

—— 1976. Prehistoric populations and pressures favoring plant domestication in Africa. In *Origins of African Plant Domestication*, Harlan, J. R., J. M. J. De Wet & A. B. L. Stemler (eds), 67–105. The Hague: Mouton.

—— 1980. The origins of domestication in Ethiopia. In *Proceedings of the 8th Panafrican Congress of Prehistory and Quaternary Studies*, Leakey, R. E. & B. A. Ogot (eds), 268–70. Nairobi: International Louis Leakey Memorial Institute for African Prehistory.

—— 1983. The 9th Pan African congress on prehistory and related studies: Jos, Nigeria, 11th to 17th December, 1983. *Nyame Akuma* 23, 1–4.

Clark, J. D. & S. A. Brandt (eds) 1984. *From Hunters to Farmers: the causes and consequences of food production in Africa.* Berkeley: University of California Press.

Clark, J. D. & G. R. Prince 1978. Use-wear on later stone age microliths from Laga Oda, Haraghi, Ethiopia and possible functional interpretations. *Azania* 13, 101–10.

Clark, J. D. & M. A. J. Williams 1978. Recent archaeological research in southeastern Ethiopia (1974–5): some preliminary results. *Annales d'Ethiopie* 11, 19–44.

Clark, J. D., M. A. J. Williams & A. B. Smith 1973. The geomorphology and archaeology of Adrar Bous, central Sahara: a preliminary report. *Quaternaria* 18, 245–97.

Clark, J. G. D. 1977. *World Prehistory in New Perspective.* Cambridge: Cambridge University Press.

Clarke, D. L. 1968. *Analytical Archaeology.* London: Methuen.

—— 1977. *Spatial Archaeology.* London: Academic Press.

—— 1979. Towns in the development of early civilizations. In *Analytical Archaeologist*, Clarke, D. L. (ed.), 435–43. New York: Academic Press.

Clayton, R. (ed.) 1964. *The Geography of Greater London.* London: Institute of Education.

Clayton, W. D. 1976. The chorology of African mountain grasses. *Kew Bulletin* 31, 273–88.

Cline, W. 1937. *Mining and Metallurgy in Negro Africa.* Menasha: George Banta.

Clist, B. 1986. Le néolithique en Afrique centrale: état de la question et perspective d'avenir. *L'Anthropologie* 90, 217–32.

—— 1987a. La fin de l'âge de la pierre et les débuts de la métallurgie du fer au Gabon: résultats préliminaires des travaux de terrain de 1986–1987. *Nsi* 2, 24–8.

—— 1987b. 1985 fieldwork in Gabon. *Nyame Akuma* 28, 6–9.

—— 1987c. Early Bantu settlements in west-central Africa: a review of recent research. *Current Anthropology* 28, 380–2.

—— 1988. Un nouvel ensemble néolithique en Afrique centrale: le groupe d'Okala au Gabon. *Nsi* 3, 43–51.

—— 1989a. Archaeology in Gabon, 1886–1988. *African Archaeological Review* 7, 59–95.

—— 1989b. Vestiges archéologiques de fontes du fer dans la province du Woleu-Ntem au Gabon. *Nsi* 6, 79–96.

Clist, B., R. Oslisly & B. Peyrot 1986. Métallurgie ancienne du fer au Gabon: premiers éléments de synthèse. *Muntu* 4–5, 47–55.

Close, A. E. 1980. Current research and recent radiocarbon dates from northern Africa. *Journal of African History* 21, 145–67.

—— 1984. Current research and recent radiocarbon dates from northern Africa, II. *Journal of African History* 25, 1–24.

—— 1988. Current research and recent radiocarbon dates from northern Africa, III. *Journal of African History* 29, 115–76.

—— 1989. Lithic development in the Kubbaniyan. In *Late Prehistory of the Nile Basin and Sahara,*. Krzyzaniak, L. & M. Kobusiewicz (eds), 117–25. Poznan: Poznan Archaeology Museum.

Clutton-Brock, J. 1974. The Buhen horse. *Journal of Archaeological Science* 1, 89–100.

—— 1987. *A Natural History of Domesticated Mammals*. Cambridge: Cambridge University Press.

—— (ed.) 1989a. *The Walking Larder: patterns of domestication, pastoralism and predation*. London: Unwin Hyman.

—— 1989b. Cattle in ancient north Africa. In *The Walking Larder: patterns of domestication, pastoralism, and predation*, J. Clutton-Brock (ed.), 200–6. London: Unwin Hyman.

Coetzee, J. A. 1967. Pollen analytical studies in east and southern Africa. *Palaeoecology of Africa* 3, 1–146.

Coghlan, H. H. 1956. *Notes on Prehistoric and Early Iron in the Old World*. Oxford: Oxford University Press.

Cohen, A. 1971. Cultural strategies in the organization of trading diaspora. In *The Development of Indigenous Trade and Markets in West Africa*, C. Meillassoux (ed.), 266–81. Oxford: Oxford University Press.

Cole-King, P. A. 1973a. *Kukumba Mbiri Mu Malawi: a summary of archaeological research to March, 1973*. Zomba: Department of Antiquities.

—— 1973b. Zomba range: an early iron age site. In *Occasional Papers, 14*, 51–70. Zomba: Department of Antiquities.

Collett, D. P. 1984. The pottery. *Azania* 19, 83–7.

—— 1985. The spread of early iron-producing communities in eastern and southern Africa. Unpublished PhD thesis, University of Cambridge.

—— 1987. A contribution to the study of migrations in the archaeological record: the Ngoni and Kololo migrations as a case study. In *Archaeology as Long-term History*, Hodder, I. (ed.), 105–16. Cambridge: Cambridge University Press.

—— n.d. Cultures, transformations and politics: the archaeology and anthropology of Bantu settlements. Paper presented at Department of Archaeology, University of Cambridge, 1986.

Collett, D. P. & P. T. Robertshaw 1980. Early iron age and Kansyore pottery: finds from Gogo Falls, South Nyanza. *Azania* 15, 133–45.

—— 1983a. Problems in the interpretation of radiocarbon dates: the Pastoral Neolithic of east Africa. *African Archaeology Review* 1, 57–74.

—— 1983b. Pottery traditions of early pastoral communities in Kenya. *Azania* 18, 107–25.

Collis, J. 1975. *Defended Sites of the Late La Tène in Central and Western Europe*. Oxford: British Archaeological Reports.

—— 1984. *Oppida: earliest towns north of the Alps*. Sheffield: Department of Prehistory and Archaeology, University of Sheffield.

Colson, E. & M. Gluckman (eds) 1951. *Seven Tribes in Central Africa*. Oxford: Oxford University Press.

Colyn, M. M. 1987. Les primates des forêts ombrophiles de la cuvette du Zaïre; interprétations zoogéographiques des modèles de distribution. *Revue de Zoologie Africaine* 101, 183–96.

Comrie, B. 1981. *The Languages of the Soviet Union*. Cambridge: Cambridge University Press.

Connah, G. 1975. *The Archaeology of Benin*. Oxford: Clarendon Press.

—— 1976. The Daima sequence and the prehistoric chronology of the Lake Chad region of Nigeria. *Journal of African History* 17, 321–52.

—— 1981. *Three Thousand Years in Africa: man and his environment in the Lake Chad region of Nigeria*. Cambridge: Cambridge University Press.

—— 1985. Agricultural intensification and sedentism in the firki of N. E. Nigeria. In *Prehistoric Intensive Agriculture in the Tropics*, Farrington, I. S. (ed.), 765–85. Oxford: British Archaeological Reports.

—— 1987. *African Civilizations: precolonial cities and states in tropical Africa: an archaeological perspective*. Cambridge: Cambridge University Press.

—— 1991. The salt of Bunyoro: seeking the origins of an African kingdom. *Antiquity* 65, 479–94.

Connor, D. R. & A. E. Marks 1986. The terminal Pleistocene on the Nile: the final nilotic adjustment. In *The End of the Palaeolithic in the Old World*, Straus, L. G. (ed.), 171–99. Oxford: British Archaeological Reports.

Conti Rossini, C. 1931. *Chrestomathia Arabica Meridionalis epigraphica edita et glossario instructa*. Rome: Istituto per l'Oriente.

Cook, T. L. 1969. Some tentative notes on the KòHúmónò language. *Research Notes (Ibadan)* 2, 3.

Cooke, C. K. 1963. Report on excavations at Pomongwe and Tshangula caves, Matopo hills, Southern Rhodesia. *South African Archaeological Bulletin* 18, 73–151.

—— 1966. Account of iron smelting techniques once practised by the Manyubi of the Matobo District of Rhodesia. *South African Archaeological Bulletin* 21, 86–7.

Cooke, H. 1975. The paleoclimatic significance of caves and adjacent landforms in western Ngamiland, Botswana. *Geographical Journal* 141, 430–49.

Coppens, Y. 1965. L'époque haddadienne: une page de la protohistoire du Tchad. *Revista de la Facultade de Letras* 9, 3–8.

—— 1969. Les cultures protohistoriques et historiques du Djourab. In *Actes du Premier Colloque International d'Archéologie Africaine, Fort-Lamy, Decembre 1966*, 129–46. Fort Lamy: Institut National Tchadien pour les Sciences Humaines.

Coppens, Y. & F. C. Howell 1976. Mammalian faunas of the Omo Group: distributional and biostratigraphical aspects. In *Earliest Man and Environments in the Lake Rudolf Basin: stratigraphy, paleoecology, and evolution*, Coppens, Y., F. C. Howell, G. L. Isaac & R. E. F. Leakey (eds), 177–92. Chicago: University of Chicago Press.

Coquery-Vidrovitch, C. 1975. Research on an African mode of production. *Critique of Anthropology* 4/5, 38–71.

Cornevin, M. 1982. Les Néolithiques du Sahara central et l'histoire général de l'Afrique. *Bulletin de la Société Préhistorique Française* 79, 439–50.

Coursey, D. G. 1967. *Yams: an account of the nature, origins, cultivation and utilisation of the useful members of the Dioscoreaceae*. Tropical Agriculture Series. London: Longmans, Green.

—— 1976. The origins and domestication of yams in Africa. In *Origins of African Plant Domestication*, Harlan, J. R., J. M. J. De Wet & A. B. L. Stemler (eds), 383–408. The Hague: Mouton.

Coursey, D. G. & C. K. Coursey 1971. The new yam festivals of west Africa. *Anthropos* 66, 444–84.

Couyat, J. & P. Montet 1912–13. *Les Inscriptions hiéroglyphiques et hieratiques du ouadi Hammamamat*. Cairo: Imprimerie de l'Institut Français d'Archéologie Orientale.

Crabb, D. W. 1965. *Edoid Bantu Languages of Ogoja*. Cambridge: Cambridge University Press.

Crader, D. C. 1984. *Hunters in Iron Age Malawi: the zooarchaeology of Chenchere rockshelter*. Lilongwe: Malawi Department of Antiquities.

Cranstone, B. A. L. 1972. Environment and choice in dwelling and settlement: an ethnographic survey. In *Man, Settlement and Urbanism*, Ucko, P. J., R. Tringham & G. W. Dimbleby (eds), 487–503. London: Duckworth.

Crocker, P. 1985. Status symbols in the architecture of el-Amarna. *Journal of Egyptian Archaeology* 71, 52–65.

Crone, G. R. 1937. *The Voyages of Cadamosto*. London: Hakluyt Society.

Crowder, M. 1966. *The Story of Nigeria*. London: Faber & Faber.

Crowther, S. 1915. Memorandum. Ghana National Archives Colonial Records. Accra.

Crumley, C. 1976. Toward a locational definition of state systems of settlement. *American Anthropologist* 78, 59–73.

—— 1979. Three locational models: an epistemological assessment for anthropology and archaeology. In *Advances in Archaeological Method and Theory, Vol. 2*, Schiffer, M. (ed.), 143–73. New York: Academic Press.

Cruz e Silva, T. 1979. A preliminary report on an early iron age site: Matola IV/68. In *Proceedings of the 8th Panafrican Congress of Prehistory and Quaternary Studies*, Leakey, R. E. & B. A. Ogot (eds), 349. Nairobi: International Louis Leakey Memorial Institute for African Prehistory.

Cuoq, J. M. 1975. *Receuil des sources arabes concernant l'Afrique occidentale du VIIIe au XVIe siècle*. Paris: CNRS (Centre National de la Recherche Scientifique).

Daaku, K. 1971. Trade and trading patterns of the Akan in the 17th and 18th centuries. In *The Development of Indigenous Trade and Markets in West Africa*, Meillassoux, C. (ed.), 68–81. Oxford: Oxford University Press.

Dahl, O. C. 1951. *Malgache et Maanjan*. Oslo: Egede Instituttet.

Dalton, G. 1981. Anthropological models in archaeological perspectives. In *Pattern of the Past*, Hodder, I., G. Isaac & N. Hammond (eds), 17–41. Cambridge: Cambridge University Press.

Dalziel, J. M. 1937. *The Useful Plants of West Tropical Africa*. London: Crown Agents for the Colonies.

Danelius, E. & H. Steinitz 1967. The fishes and other aquatic animals on the Punt-reliefs at Deir el-Bahri. *Journal of Egyptian Archaeology* 53, 15–24.

Daniel, F. de F. 1936. The horse in native hands. *Nigerian Field* 5, 52–6.

Daniel, G. 1978. *One Hundred and Fifty Years of Archaeology*. London: Duckworth.

Daniels, C. M. 1968. Garamantian excavations, Zinchera 1965–67. *Libya Antiqua* 5, 113–94.

Danilova, L. V. 1971. Controversial problems in the theory of precapitalist societies. *Soviet Anthropology and Archaeology* 9, 269–328.

Darling, P. J. 1974. The earthworks of Benin. *Nigerian Field* 39, 128–37.

Datoo, B. A. 1970. Rhapta: the location and importance of east Africa's port. *Azania* 5, 66–75.

David, N. 1981. The archaeological background of Cameroonian history. In *Contribution de la recherche ethnologique à l'histoire des civilisations du Cameroun*, Tardits, C. (ed.), 79–99. Paris: CNRS (Centre National de la Recherche Scientifique).

—— 1982. Early Bantu expansion in the context of central African prehistory. In *Expansion bantou*, Bouquiaux, L. (ed.), 609–44. Paris: CNRS (Centre National de la Recherche Scientifique).

David, N., R. Heimann, D. Killick & M. Wayman 1989. Between bloomery and blast furnace: Mafa iron-smelting technology in north Cameroon. *African Archaeological Review* 7, 183–208.

David, N. & A. S. MacEachern 1988. The Mandara Archaeological Project: preliminary results of the 1984 season. In *Le Milieu et les hommes: recherches comparatives et historiques dans le bassin du Lac Tchad*, Barreteau, D. & H. Tourneux (eds), 51–80. Paris: ORSTOM (Institut Français de Recherche Scientifique pour le Développement en Coopération).

David, N. & J. Sterner 1989. The Mandara Archaeological Project 1988–89. *Nyame Akuma* 32, 5–9.

Davies, J. G. n.d. (1942–9) The Bi Rom. Ms., Bexhill-on-Sea.

Davies, N. de G. 1905. *The Rock Tombs of El Amarna II*. London: Egypt Exploration Society.

—— 1922–3. *The Tomb of Puyemre at Thebes, I–II*. New York: Metropolitan Museum of Art.

—— 1935. The work of the graphic branch of the expedition. *Bulletin of the Metropolitan Museum of Art, New York*, Nov. Part II, 46–9.

—— 1943. *The Tomb of Rekh-mi-re at Thebes, I–II*. New York: Metropolitan Museum of Art.

Davies, N. M. & N. de G. Davies 1940. The tomb of Amenmose (no. 89) at Thebes. *Journal of Egyptian Archaeology* 26, 131–6.

Davies, O. 1962. Neolithic cultures of Ghana. In *Actes du IVe Congrès Panafricain de Préhistoire et de l'Etude du Quaternaire, Section III, Pré- et protohistoire*, Mortelmans, G. & J. Nenquin (eds), 291–302. Tervuren: Musée Royal de l'Afrique Centrale.

—— 1964. *The Quaternary in the Coastlands of Guinea.* Glasgow: Jackson.

—— 1966a. Comment. *Current Anthropology* 7, 470–1.

—— 1966b (1963). The invasion of Ghana from the Sahara in the early Iron Age. In *Actas del V Congreso Panafricano de Prehistoria (Tenerife)*, 27–42. Santa Cruz de Tenerife: Museo Arquelogico.

—— 1967. *West Africa before the Europeans.* London: Methuen.

—— 1980. The Ntereso culture in Ghana. In *West African Culture Dynamics: archaeological and historical perspectives*, Swartz, B. K. & R. Dumett (eds), 205–25. The Hague: Mouton.

—— n.d. Excavations at Ntereso, Gonja, northern Ghana. Final Report, Pietermaritzburg, Natal Museum, 1973.

de Barros, P. 1986. Bassar: a quantified, chronologically controlled, regional approach to a traditional iron production centre in west Africa. *Africa* 56, 148–74.

—— 1988. Societal repercussions of the rise of traditional iron production: a west African example. *African Archaeological Review* 6, 91–113.

de Bayle des Hermens, R. 1975. *Recherches préhistoriques en République Centrafricaine.* Nanterre: Labethno.

de Contenson, H. 1961. Les fouilles de Haoulti-Melazo en 1958. *Annales d'Ethiopie* 4, 39–60.

—— 1981. Pre-Aksumite culture. In *General History of Africa, II*, Mokhtar, G. (ed.), 341–61. Paris: UNESCO.

de Foresta, H., D. Schwartz, R. Dechamps & R. Lanfranchi 1990. Un premier site de métallurgie de l'âge du fer ancien (2110 bp) dans le Mayombe congolais et ses implications sur la dynamique des écosystèmes. *Nsi* 7, 10–12.

De Heinzelin, J. 1955. Observations sur la genèse des nappes des gravats dans les sols tropicaux. *Publications de l'Institut National pour l'Etude Agronomique du Congo-Belge* 64, 1–37.

De Heusch, L. 1982. *The Drunken King, or the Origin of State.* Bloomington: Indiana University Press.

de Maret, P. 1978. Chronologie de l'âge du fer dans la depression de l'Upemba en République du Zaïre. Unpublished PhD thesis, University Libre du Bruxelles.

—— 1980. Ceux qui jouent avec le feu: la place du forgeron en Afrique centrale. *Africa* 50, 263–79.

—— 1982a. Belgian archaeological project in Cameroon (July-August 1981 fieldwork). *Nyame Akuma* 20, 11–12.

—— 1982b. New survey of archaeological research and dates for west-central and north-central Africa. *Journal of African History* 23, 1–15.

—— 1985. Recent archaeological research and dates from central Africa. *Journal of African History* 26, 129–48.

—— 1986. The Ngovo group: an industry with polished stone tools and pottery in lower Zaïre. *African Archaeological Review* 4, 103–33.

—— 1990. Phases and facies in the archaeology of central Africa. In *A History of African Archaeology*, Robertshaw, P. (ed.), 109–34. London: James Currey.

de Maret, P. & B. Clist 1985. Archaeological research in Zaïre. *Nyame Akuma* 26, 41–2.

de Maret, P., B. Clist & C. Mbida 1983. Belgian archaeological mission in Cameroon 1983 field season. *Nyame Akuma* 23, 5–6.

de Maret, P., B. Clist & W. Van Neer 1987. Résultats des premières fouilles dans les abris de Shum Laka et d'Abeke au nord-ouest du Cameroun. *L'Anthropologie* 91, 559–84.

de Maret, P. & F. Nsuka 1977. History of Bantu metallurgy: some linguistic aspects. *History in Africa* 4, 43–65.

de Maret, P., F. Van Noten & D. Cohen 1977. Radiocarbon dates for west central Africa. *Journal of African History* 18, 481–505.

De Morgan, J. 1897. *Recherches sur les origines de l'Egypte.* Paris: Ernest Leroux.

de Neufville, R. L. & A. A. Houghton III 1965. A description of Ain Farah and Wara. *Kush* 13, 195–204.

De Ploey, J. 1965. Position géomorphologique, genèse et chronologie de certains dépôts superficiels au Congo Occidentale. *Quaternaria* 7, 131–54.

—— 1969. Report on the Quaternary of the western Congo. *Palaeoecology of Africa* 4, 65–8.

De Wolf, P. 1971. *The Noun Class System of Proto-Benue-Congo*. The Hague: Mouton.

Deacon, J. 1984. *The Later Stone Age of Southernmost Africa*. Oxford: British Archaeological Reports.

Debono, F. 1945. Helouan-El Omari: fouilles du Service des Antiquités, 1943–1945. *Chronique d'Egypte* 21, 50–4.

—— 1948. El-Omari (pré d'Helouan), exposé sommaire sur les campagnes des fouilles 1943–1944 et 1948. *Annales du Service des Antiquités de l'Egypte* 48, 561–9.

—— 1956. La civilisation prédynastique d'El Omari (nord d'Helouan). *Bulletin de l'Institut d'Egypte* 37, 329–39.

Decary, R. 1951. *Moeurs et coutumes des Malgaches*. Paris: Payot.

Dechamps, R., R. Lanfranchi, A. Le Cocq & D. Schwartz 1988. Reconstitution d'environments quaternaires par l'étude de macrorestes végétaux (Pays Bateke, R. P. du Congo). *Palaeogeography, Palaeoclimatology, Palaeoecology* 66, 33–44.

Decret, F. & M. Fantar 1981. *L'Afrique du nord dans l'antiquité*. Paris: Payot.

Degerbol, M. 1967. Dogs from the Iron Age (*c.* AD 950–1000) in Zambia with remarks on dogs from primitive cultures. In *Iron Age Cultures in Zambia*, Fagan, B. M. (ed.), 198–207. London: Chatto & Windus.

Delafosse, M. 1900. Sur les traces probables de civilisation égyptienne et d'homme de race blanche à la Côte d'Ivoire. *L'Anthropologie* 9, 431–51, 543–68, 677–90.

—— 1912. *Haut-Sénégal-Niger* 3. Paris: Maisonneuve-Larose.

Delany, M. J. & D. C. D. Happold 1979. *Ecology of African Mammals*. London: Longman.

Delibrias, G., P. Giresse, R. Lanfranchi & A. Le Cocq 1983. Datations des dépôts holorganiques quaternaires sur la bordure occidentale de la Cuvette congolaise (R. P. du Congo): correlations avec les sédiments marins voisins. *Comptes Rendus de l'Académie des Sciences* 296, 463–6.

Denbow, J. 1973. Malowa rockshelter: archaeological report. In *Occasional Papers, 14*, 5–49. Zomba: Department of Antiquities.

Denbow, J. R. 1983. Iron age economics: herding, wealth, and politics along the fringes of the Kalahari desert during the early Iron Age. Unpublished PhD thesis, Indiana University.

—— 1984. Cows and kings: a spatial and economic analysis of a hierarchical early iron age settlement system in eastern Botswana. In *Frontiers: southern African archaeology today*, Hall, M., G. Avery, D. M. Avery, M. L. Wilson & A. J. B. Humphreys, 24–39. Oxford: British Archaeological Reports.

—— 1986. A new look at the later prehistory of the Kalahari. *Journal of African History* 27, 3–28.

Dennell, R. 1980. The use, abuse and potential of site catchment analysis. In *Catchment Analysis: essays on prehistoric resource space*, Findlow, F. J. & J. E. Ericsson (eds), 1–11. Los Angeles: University of California Press.

Denton, D. 1982. *The Hunger for Salt: an anthropological, physiological and medical analysis*. Berlin: Springer-Verlag.

Denyer, S. 1978. *African Traditional Architecture*. London: Heinemann.

Derefaka, A. A. 1980. Cordage, fabric, and basketry of the Tichitt tradition, a later prehistoric complex of the southwestern Sahara. *West African Journal of Archaeology* 10, 117–53.

Devisse, J., A. O. Babacar, T. M. Bah, J. Bouchud, G. S. Colin, N. Ghali, A. Launois, S. Lebecq, C. Meillassoux, B. Moussie, C. Richir, D. Robert-Chaleix, C. Vanacker & S. Van-Campo 1983. *Tegdaoust III: Recherches sur Aoudaghost (campagnes 1960–1965)*. Paris: Editions

Recherche sur les Civilisations.

Dewar, R. E. 1987. Malagasy roots. *Natural History* 87, 51.

—— 1988. Malagasy roots. *Natural History* 97, 51.

Dewing, M. B. 1985. *Procopius' History of the Wars*. London: Loeb.

Dez, J. 1965. Quelques hypothèses formulées par la linguistique comparée à l'usage de l'archéologie. *Taloha* 1, 197–214.

Diblasi, M. C. 1980. Kwamboo: an early iron age occurrence in the eastern highlands of central Kenya. Paper presented at the 79th annual meeting of the American Anthropological Association, Washington D. C.

Dickinson, R. W. 1975. The archaeology of the Sofala coast. *South African Archaeological Bulletin* 30, 84–105.

Digombe, L., P. R. Schmidt, V. Mouleingui-Boukosso, J.-B. Mombo & M. Locko 1987a. L'âge du fer ancien au Gabon. *L'Anthropologie* 91, 711–17.

—— 1987b. Gabon: the earliest Iron Age of west central Africa. *Nyame Akuma* 28, 9–11.

—— 1988. The development of an early iron age prehistory in Gabon. *Current Anthropology* 29, 179–84.

Dillon, R. G. 1973. Ideology, process, and change in pre-colonial Meta' political organisation (United Republic of Cameroon). Unpublished PhD thesis, University of Pennsylvania.

Dimmendaal, G. J. 1978. The consonants of Proto-Upper Cross and their implications for the classification of the Upper Cross languages. Unpublished PhD thesis, Department of African Linguistics, Leiden.

Dineur, B. & E. Thys 1986. Les Kapsiki: race taurine de l'extrême-nord camerounais, I. Introduction et barymétrie. *Revue d'Elevage et de Médécine Vétérinaire des Pays Tropicaux* 39, 435–42.

Diop, L.-M. 1968. Traditional iron working and Iron Age in Africa. *IFAN* (Bulletin de l'Institut Fondamental d'Afrique Noire) B, 10–38.

Dombrowski, J. C. 1970. Preliminary report on excavations in Lalibela and Natchabiet caves, Begemeder. *Annales d'Ethiopie* 8, 21–9.

—— 1971. Excavations in Ethiopia: Lalibela and Natchabiet caves, Begemeder Province. Unpublished PhD thesis, Boston University.

—— 1976. Mumute and Bonoase: two sites of the Kintampo industry. *Sankofa* 2, 64–71.

—— 1980. Earliest settlements in Ghana: the Kintampo industry. In *Proceedings of the 8th Panafrican Congress of Prehistory and Quaternary Studies*, Leakey, R. E. & B. A. Ogot (eds), 261–2. Nairobi: International Louis Leakey Memorial Institute for African Prehistory.

—— n.d. Early settlers in Ghana. Unpublished Inter-Faculty Lecture, 1980. University of Ghana, Legon.

Dombrowski, J. C. & B. Priddy 1978. Pottery decorating tools of the Kintampo industry. *West African Journal of Archaeology* 8, 165–7.

Domenichini-Ramiaramanana, B. & J. P. Domenichini 1983. Madagascar dans l'Océan Indien avant le XIIe siècle: présentation de données suggérant des orientations de recherche. *Nouvelles du Centre d'Art et d'Archéologie* 1, 5–19.

Doran, J. E. & F. R. Hodson 1975. *Mathematics and Computers in Archaeology*. Edinburgh: Edinburgh University Press.

Doresse, J. 1971. *Histoire sommaire de la Corne orientale de l'Afrique*. Paris: Geuthner.

Dorst, J. & P. Dandelot 1970. *A Field Guide to the Larger Mammals of Africa*. London: Collins.

Douglas, M. 1966. *Purity and Danger: an analysis of concepts of pollution and taboo*. London: Routledge & Kegan Paul.

—— 1970. *Natural Symbols: explorations in cosmology*. London: Penguin.

—— 1990. The pangolin revisited: a new approach to animal symbolism. In *Signifying Animals:*

human meaning in the natural world, Willis, R. G. (ed.), 25–36. London: Unwin Hyman.

Doutressolle, G. 1947. *L'Elevage en Afrique Occidentale Française*. Paris: Larose.

Downes, R. M. 1971. *Tiv Religion*. Ibadan: Ibadan University Press.

Drew, S. F. 1954. Notes from the Red Sea hills. *South African Archaeological Bulletin* 9, 101–2.

Drewes, A. J. 1962. *Inscriptions de l'Ethiopie antique*. Leiden: Brill.

Drewes, A. J. & R. Schneider 1967. Documents épigraphiques de l'Ethiopie. *Annales d'Ethiopie* 7, 89–106.

Duarte, M. L. T., T. Cruz e Silva, J. C. Senna Martinez, J. M. M. Morais & R. T. Duarte 1976. *Iron Age Research in Mozambique: collected preliminary reports*. Maputo: Instituto de Investigação Cientifica de Moçambique.

Duarte, R. T. 1976. Three iron age sites in Massingir area, Gaza Province, Moçambique and their importance in the southern Mozambique Bantu settlement. In *Iron Age Research in Mozambique: collected preliminary reports*, Duarte, M. L. T., T. Cruz e Silva, J. C. Senna Martinez, J. M. M. Morais & R. T. Duarte (eds), 1–29. Maputo: Instituto de Investigação Cientifica de Moçambique.

—— 1988. Arqueologia de idade do ferro em Moçambique. *Trabalhos de Arqueologia e Antropologia* 5, 57–73.

—— 1991. Northern Mozambique in the Swahili world. An archaeological approach. Unpublished Fil. lic. thesis, University of Uppsala.

Dudgeon, G. C. 1911. *The Agricultural and Forest Products of British West Africa*. London: John Murray.

Dumas, R. 1980. Contribution à l'étude des petits ruminants du Tchad. *Revue d'Elevage et de Médécine Vétérinaire des Pays Tropicaux* 33, 215–33.

Duyvendak, J. J. L. 1939. Voyages de Tcheng Houo à la côte Orientale de l'Afrique. In *Monumenta cartographica Africae et Aegypti, Vol. 4.4*, Kamal, Y. (ed.), 1411–16. Cairo: Youssouf Kamal.

—— 1949. *China's Discovery of Africa*. London: School of Oriental & African Studies.

Dymond, D. P. 1974. *Archaeology and History*. London: Thames & Hudson.

Earthy, E. 1933. *Valenge Women: the social and economic life of the Valenge women of Portuguese East Africa*. London: Oxford University Press.

Echard, N. 1965. Note sur les forgerons de l'Ader (Pays Hausa, République du Niger). *Journal de la Société des Africanistes* 35, 353–72.

—— 1983a. Avant-propos. In *Métallurgies africaines: nouvelles contributions*, Echard, N. (ed.), 11–14. Paris: Société des Africanistes.

—— 1983b. Scories et symboles: remarques sur la métallurgie hausa du fer au Niger. In *Métallurgies africaines: nouvelles contributions*, Echard, N. (ed.), 209–24. Paris: Société des Africanistes.

—— (ed.) 1983c. *Métallurgies africaines: nouvelles contributions*. Paris: Société des Africanistes.

Edel, E. 1983. *Beiträge zu den ägyptischen Sinaiinschriften*. Göttingen: Vandenhoeck & Rupprecht.

Edmunds, W. M. & E. P. Wright 1979. Groundwater recharge and palaeoclimate in the Sirte and Kufra basins, Libya. *Journal of Hydrology* 40, 215–41.

Effah-Gyamfi, K. 1978. Bono Manso: a study of early Akan urbanism. Unpublished MA thesis, University of Ghana, Legon.

—— 1979. Bono Manso Archaeological Research Project – 1973–76. *West African Journal of Archaeology* 9, 173–86.

—— 1981. Excavation of an early iron age occupation site at Samaru-West Zaria. *Zaria Archaeological Papers* 3, 6–54.

—— 1985. *Bono Manso: an archaeological investigation into early Akan urbanism*. Calgary: University of Calgary Press.

Eggebrecht, A. 1974. Deir el Ballas. In *Lexikon der Ägyptologie I*, Helck, W. & W. Westendorf (eds), 1025–7. Wiesbaden: Otto Harrasowitz.

Eggert, M. K. H. 1980. Der Keramikfund von Bondongo-Losombo (Région de l'Equateur, Zaïre) und die Archäologie des äquatorialen Regenwaldes. *Beiträge zur allgemeinen und Vergleichenden Archäologie* 2, 381–427.

—— 1981. Historical linguistics and prehistoric archaeology: trend and pattern in early iron age research of sub-Saharan Africa. *Beiträge zur Allgemeinen und Vergleichenden Archäologie* 3, 277–324.

—— 1983. Remarks on exploring archaeologically unknown rain forest territory: the case of central Africa. *Beiträge zur allgemeinen und Vergleichenden Archäologie* 5, 283–322.

—— 1984. Imbonga und Lingonda: zur frühesten Besiedlung des zentralafrikanischen Regenwaldes. *Beiträge zur Allgemeinen und Vergleichenden Archäologie* 6, 247–88.

—— 1985. Katuruka und Kemondo: zur Komplexität der frühen Eisentechnik in Afrika. *Beiträge zur Allgemeinen und Vergleichenden Archäologie* 7, 243–63.

—— 1987a. Imbonga and Batalimo: ceramic evidence for early settlement of the equatorial rain forest. *African Archaeological Review* 5, 129–45.

—— 1987b. On the alleged complexity of early and recent iron smelting in Africa: further comments on the preheating hypothesis. *Journal of Field Archaeology* 14, 377–82.

—— 1987c. Archäologische Forschungen im zentralafrikanischen Regenwald. In *Die großen Abenteuer der Archäologie, Vol. 9*, Niemeyer, H. G. & R. Pörtner (eds), 3217–40. Salzburg: Andreas.

—— 1988. Archäologie und Keramik-Ethnographie im äquatorialen Regenwald Zaïres. In *Töpfereiforschung zwischen Archäologie und Entwicklungspolitik*, Vossen, R. (ed.), 25–38. Töpferei- und Keramikforschung 1. Bonn: Habelt.

Eggert, M. K. H. & M. Kanimba 1987. Recherches archéologiques et ethnographiques dans la Région de l'Equateur (Zaïre), de la Cuvette, de la Sangha et de la Likouala (Congo): rapport préliminaire. *Annales Aequatoria* 8, 481–7.

Eggert, R. K. 1987. *Das Wirtschaftssystem der Mongo (Äquatorregion, Zaïre) am Vorabend der Kolonisation: eine Rekonstruktion*. Berlin: Reimer.

Ehret, C. 1967. Cattlekeeping and milking in eastern and southern African history: the linguistic evidence. *Journal of African History* 8, 1–17.

—— 1968. Sheep and Central Sudanic peoples in southern Africa. *Journal of African History* 9, 213–21.

—— 1974. *Ethiopians and East Africans: the problems of contact*. Nairobi: East African Publishing House.

—— 1979. On the antiquity of agriculture in Ethiopia. *Journal of African History* 20, 161–77.

—— 1982a. Linguistic inference about early Bantu history. In *The Archaeological and Linguistic Reconstruction of African History*, Ehret, C. & M. Posnansky (eds), 57–65. Berkeley: University of California Press.

—— 1982b. Population movement and culture contact in the southern Sudan, c. 3000 BC to AD 1000: a preliminary linguistic overview. In *Culture History in the Southern Sudan*, Mack, J. & P. Robertshaw (eds), 19–48. Nairobi: British Institute in Eastern Africa.

—— 1983. Nilotic and the limits of Eastern Sudanic. In *Nilotic Studies, Part Two*, Vossen, R. & M. Beckhaus-Gerst (eds), 377–421. Berlin: Dietrich Reimer.

—— 1984. Historical/linguistic evidence for early African food production. In *From Hunters to Farmers: the causes and consequences of food production in Africa*, Clark, J. D. & S. A. Brandt (eds), 26–35. Berkeley: University of California Press.

—— 1989. Subclassification of Nilo-Saharan: a proposal. In *Topics in Nilo-Saharan Linguistics*, Bender, M. L. (ed.), 35–50. Hamburg: Buske.

—— In Progress. Nilo-Saharan: a comparative-historical reconstruction.

Ehret, C., T. Coffman, L. Fliegelman, A. Gold, M. Hubbard, D. Johnson & D. Saxon 1974. Some thoughts on the early history of the Nile–Congo watershed. *Ufahamu* 5, 85–112.

Ehret, C. & M. Posnansky (eds) 1982. *The Archaeological and Linguistic Reconstruction of African History*. Berkeley: University of California Press.

Eiwanger, J. 1978. Erste Vorbericht über die Wiederaufnahme der Grabungen in der neolithischen Siedlung Merimde-Benisalame. *Mitteilungen des Deutschen Archäologischen Institut, Abteilung Kairo* 34, 33–42.

—— 1979. Zweiter Vorbericht über die Wiederaufnahme der Grabungen in der neolithischen Siedlung Merimde-Benisalame. *Mitteilungen des Deutschen Archäologischen Institut, Abteilung Kairo* 35, 23–57.

—— 1980. Dritter Vorbericht über die Wiederaufnahme der Grabungen in der neolithischen Siedlung Merimde-Benisalame. *Mitteilungen des Deutschen Archäologischen Institut, Abteilung Kairo* 36, 61–70.

—— 1982. Die neolithische Siedlung von Merimde-Benisalame: Vierter Bericht. *Mitteilungen des Deutschen Archäologischen Institut, Abteilung Kairo* 38, 67–82.

—— 1984. *Merimde-Benisalame I: Die Funde der Urschicht*. Mainz: Philipp von Zabern.

—— 1988. *Merimde-Benisalame II: Die Funde der mittleren Merimdekultur*. Mainz: Philipp von Zabern.

Ekechukwu, L. C. 1989. A new furnace type from the north of Igboland. *Nyame Akuma* 32, 20–1.

Ekholm, K. 1972. Power and prestige: the rise and fall of the Kongo kingdom. Unpublished PhD thesis, Uppsala University.

—— 1981. On the structure and dynamics of global systems. In *The Anthropology of Precapitalist Societies*, Kahn, J. & J. R. Llobera (eds), 241–62. London: Macmillan.

el Hadidi, M. N. 1980. Vegetation of the Nubian desert (Nabta region). In *Prehistory of the Eastern Sahara*, Wendorf, F. & R. Schild (eds), 345–51. New York: Academic Press.

el Hadidi, M. N. & I. Springuel 1978. Plant life in Nubia (Egypt). I. Introduction: plant communities in the Nile islands at Aswan. *Tackholmia* 9, 103–9.

—— 1989. The natural vegetation of the Nile valley at Wadi Kubbaniya. In *Prehistory of Wadi Kubbaniya, Vol. 2: Stratigraphy, Paleoeconomy, and Environment*, Wendorf, F., R. Schild & A. E. Close (eds), 243–51. Dallas: Southern Methodist University Press.

Elderkin, E. D. 1983. Tanzanian and Ugandan isolates. In *Nilotic Studies*, Vossen, R. & M. Bechaus-Gerst (eds), 499–522. Berlin: Reimer.

Elenga, H. 1987. Les Plateaux Bateke (Congo): paléoenvironnements quaternaires d'après l'étude (palynologique) du sondage du bois de Bilanko. Diplôme d'Etudes Approfondies, Université Aix-Marseilles.

Elenga, H., A. Vincens, P. Giresse & D. Schwartz 1987. Les Plateaux Bateke (Congo): palynologie, paléoflores et paléoclimats au Quaternaire récent. Paper presented to the Xe Symposium de l'Association de Palynologues de Langues Françaises, Bordeaux.

Eliade, M. 1971. *The Forge and the Crucible: the origins and structures of alchemy*. New York: Harper & Row.

Ellen, R. 1982. *Environment, Subsistence and System*. Cambridge: Cambridge University Press.

Elliot, J. A. G. 1925/6. A visit to the Bajun islands. *Journal of the Asiatic Society* 25, 10–22, 147–63, 245–63, 338–58.

Ellis, D. U. 1980. Comments on the advent of plant cultivation in west Africa. In *West African Culture Dynamics: archaeological and historical perspectives*, Swartz, B. K. & R. Dumett (eds), 123–37. The Hague: Mouton.

Elphick, R. 1977. *Kraal and Castle: Khoikhoi and the founding of White South Africa*. Newhaven: Yale University Press.

Elugbe, B. O. 1989. *Comparative Edoid: phonology and lexicon*. Port Harcourt: University of Port

Harcourt Press.

Emery, W. B., T. G. H. James & D. O'Connor Forthcoming. *The Old Kingdom Town at Buhen.*

Epstein, H. 1971. *The Origin of the Domestic Animals of Africa.* 2 vols. New York: Africana Publishing Corporation.

Epstein, H. & I. L. Mason 1984. Cattle. In *Evolution of Domesticated Animals*, Mason, I. L. (ed.), 6–27. London: Longman.

Erichsen, W. 1933. *Papyrus Harris, I: Hieroglyphische Transkription.* Brussels: Fondation Egyptologique Reine Elisabeth.

Erman, A. 1966. *The Ancient Egyptians: a source book of their writings.* New York: Harper Torchbooks.

Evans, J. D. 1976. Village, town, city: some thoughts on the prehistoric background to urban civilization in the Aegean and Italy. In *Problems in Economic and Social Archaeology*, Sieveking, G. de G., I. Longworth & K. E. Wilson (eds), 501–12. London: Duckworth.

Evans-Pritchard, E. E. 1937. *Witchcraft Oracles and Magic among the Azande.* Oxford: Clarendon Press.

Fabre, J. & N. Petit-Maire 1988. Holocene climatic evolution at 22–23°N from two lakes in the Taoudenni area (northern Mali). *Palaeogeography, Palaeoclimatology, Palaeoecology* 65, 133–48.

Facciola, S. 1990. *Cornucopia: a source book of edible plants.* Vista, Calif.: Kampong Publications.

Fagan, B. 1961. A collection of nineteenth-century Soli ironwork from the Lusaka area, Northern Rhodesia. *Journal of the Royal Anthropological Institute* 91, 228–50.

—— 1965. *Southern Africa in the Iron Age.* London: Thames & Hudson.

—— 1969a. Excavations at Ingombe Ilede, 1960–62. In *Iron Age Cultures in Zambia, Vol. 2*, Fagan, B. M., D. W. Phillipson & S. G. H. Daniels (eds), 57–161. London: Chatto & Windus.

—— 1969b. Early trade and raw materials in south central Africa. *Journal of African History* 10, 1–13.

Fagan, B. & F. L. Van Noten 1971. The hunter-gatherers of Gwisho. *Sciences Humaines 74.* Tervuren: Musée de l'Afrique Centrale.

Fagan, B. & J. E. Yellen 1968. Ivuna: ancient salt-working in southern Tanzania. *Azania* 3, 1–43.

Fagg, B. 1969. Recent work in west Africa: new light on the Nok culture. *World Archaeology* 1, 41–50.

—— 1972. Rop rock shelter excavations, 1944. *West African Journal of Archaeology* 2, 1–12.

FAO 1980. *Report on the Second FAO/UNFPA Expert Consultation on Land Resources for Populations of the Future.* Rome: Food and Agriculture Organization.

—— 1987. *Trypanotolerant Cattle and Livestock Development in West and Central Africa.* 2 vols. Rome: Food and Agricultural Organization.

FAO/UNESCO 1973. *Soil Map of the World, Sheet VI-3: Africa.* Paris: UNESCO.

Fardon, R. 1988. *Raiders and Refugees.* Washington: Smithsonian Institution Press.

Fattovich, R. 1975. The contribution of Nile valley's cultures to the rising of Ethiopian civilization: elements for a hypothesis of work. *Meroitic Newsletter* 16, 2–8.

—— 1977. Some data for the study of cultural history in ancient northern Ethiopia. *Nyame Akuma* 10, 6–18.

—— 1978. Traces of a possible African component in the pre-Aksumite culture of northern Ethiopia. *Abbay* 9, 25–30.

—— 1980. *Materiali per lo studio della ceramica pre-aksumita etiopica.* Naples: Istituto Orientale di Napoli.

—— 1982. The problem of Sudanese-Ethiopian contacts in antiquity: status quaestionis and current trends of research. In *Nubian Studies: proceedings of the Symposium for Nubian Studies, Selwyn College, Cambridge, 1978*, Plumley, J. M. (ed.), 76–86. Warminster: Aris & Phillips.

—— 1988. The contribution of recent field work at Kassala (eastern Sudan) to Ethiopian archaeology. Paper read at the Tenth International Conference of Ethiopian Studies, Paris.

—— 1989. Remarks on the later prehistory and early history of northern Ethiopia. In *Proceedings of the Eighth International Conference on Ethiopian Studies*, 85–104. Addis Ababa: Institute of Ethiopian Studies.

—— 1990. Remarks on the pre-Aksumite period in northern Ethiopia. *Journal of Ethiopian Studies* 23, 1–33..

Fattovich, R., A. E. Marks & Ali M. Abbas 1984. The archaeology of the eastern Sahel, Sudan: preliminary results. *African Archaeological Review* 2, 173–88.

Fattovich, R., K. Sadr & S. Vitagliano 1988. Società e territorio nel delta del Gash (Sudan), 3000 a. Cr. – 300/400 d. Cr. *Africa (Rome)* 43, 394–453.

Faulkner, R. O. & N. de G. Davies 1947. A Syrian trading venture to Egypt. *Journal of Egyptian Archaeology* 33, 40–6.

Faure, H. & J. Y. Gac 1981. Will the Sahelian drought end in 1985? *Nature* 291, 475–8.

Ferguson, W. 1967. Muturu cattle of western Nigeria. *Journal of the West African Science Association* 12, 37–44.

Fernald, M. L. & A. C. Kinsey (revised, R. C. Rollins) 1958. *Edible Wild Plants of Eastern North America*. New York: Harper & Row.

Fiedler, L. & J. Preuss 1985. Stone tools from the inner Zaïre basin (Région de l'Equateur, Zaïre). *African Archaeological Review* 3, 179–87.

Filipowiak, W. 1966. Expédition archéologique Polono-Guinéenne à Niani (Guinée). *Africana Bulletin* 4, 116–27.

Fisher, H. J. 1972a. The horse in the Central Sudan. I. Its introduction. *Journal of African History* 13, 369–88.

—— 1972b. The horse in the Central Sudan. II. Its use. *Journal of African History* 14, 355–79.

Fisher, W. & G. Bianchi 1984. *FAO Species Identification Sheets for Fishery Purposes (Western Indian Ocean): fishing area 51*. 4 vols. Rome: Food and Agricultural Organization.

Fitzpatrick, J. F. J. 1910. Some notes on the Kwolla district and its tribes. *Journal of the African Society* 10, 16–52.

Flannery, K. 1976. Empirical determination of site catchments in the Oaxaca and Tehuacen. In *The Early Mesoamerican Village*, Flannery K. (ed.), 103–17. New York: Academic Press.

Fleming, H. C. 1983a. Chadic external relations. In *Studies in Chadic and Afroasiatic Linguistics*, Wolff, E. & H. Meyer-Bahlburg (eds), 17–31. Hamburg: Buske.

—— 1983b. Surma etymologies. In *Nilotic Studies*, Vossen, R. & M. Bechaus Gerst (eds), 523–55. Berlin: Reimer.

Flenley, J. R. 1979. *The Equatorial Rain Forest: a geological history*. London: Butterworth.

Fletcher, R. J. 1981. People and space. In *Pattern of the Past*, Hodder, I., G. L. Isaac & N. Hammond (eds), 97–128. Cambridge: Cambridge University Press.

—— 1986. Settlement archaeology: worldwide comparisons. *World Archaeology* 18, 59–83.

Flight, C. 1970. Excavations at Kintampo. *West African Archaeological Newsletter* 12, 71–3.

—— 1973a. A survey of recent results in the radiocarbon chronology of northern and western Africa. *Journal of African History* 14, 531–54.

—— 1973b. The prehistoric sequence in the Kintampo area of Ghana. In *Sixième Congrès Panafricain de Préhistoire, Dakar 1967*, Hugot, H. J. (ed.), 68–9. Chambéry: Les Imprimeries Réunies.

—— 1976. The Kintampo culture and its place in the economic prehistory of west Africa. In *Origins of African Plant Domestication*, Harlan, J. R., J. M. J. De Wet & A. B. L. Stemler (eds), 211–21. The Hague: Mouton.

Flint, J. E. 1974. Economic change in west Africa in the nineteenth century. In *History of West*

Africa, Vol. 2, Ajayi, J. F. Ade & M. Crowder (eds), 387–91. London: Longman.

Foley, R. 1988. Hominids, humans and hunter-gatherers: an evolutionary perspective. In *Hunters and Gatherers 1: History, Evolution and Social Change*, Ingold, T., D. Riches & J. Woodburn (eds), 207–21. Oxford: Berg.

Folorunso, C. A. 1983a. An ethnoarchaeological study of the Ushongo hill-top 'prehistoric' settlement. Paper presented to the 9th Pan-African Congress for Prehistory and Related Studies, Jos, Nigeria.

—— 1983b. Human occupation of the Tse-Dura rockshelters. Paper presented to the 9th Pan-African Congress for Prehistory and Related Studies, Jos, Nigeria.

—— 1989a. Recherches sur la continuité du peuplement Tiv dans la vallée de Katsina-Ala (Bassin de la Bénué au Nigéria): sondages sur le site ancien d'Ushongo et d'ethnoarchéologie de l'habitat actuel. Unpublished PhD thesis, University of Paris I, Sorbonne.

—— 1989b. The Tiv compound: practising ethnoarchaeology at Ushongo, Benue State of Nigeria. Paper presented to the Conference in Honour of Professor Thurstan Shaw, Ibadan, Nigeria.

—— 1989c. La poterie Tiv: étude ethnographique à Ushongo (Etat Bénué du Nigéria). Paper presented to the Conference in Honour of Professor Thurstan Shaw, Ibadan, Nigeria.

Fontes, J. & F. Gasse 1989. On the ages of humid holocene and late pleistocene phases in north Africa – remarks on 'Late quaternary climatic reconstruction for the Maghreb (north Africa)' by P. Rognon. *Palaeogeography, Palaeoclimatology and Palaeoecology* 70, 393–8.

Fontes, J., F. Gasse, Y. Callot, J. C. Plazeat, P. Carbonnel, P. A. Dupeuble & I. Kaczmarska 1985. Freshwater to marine-like environments from holocene lakes in northern Sahara. *Nature* 317, 608–10.

Forbes, J. 1950. *Metallurgy in Antiquity*. Leiden: E. J. Brill.

Forbes, R. H. 1933. The blackman's industries. *Geographical Review* 23, 230–47.

Ford, E. & B. Rowe 1951. *Graphic Geography 1: Regions and Man*. Sydney: Angus & Robertson.

Forde, C. D. 1934. *Habitat, Economy and Society*. London: Methuen.

Fortes, M. & E. E. Evans-Pritchard (eds) 1940. *African Political Systems*. Oxford: Oxford University Press.

Fouche, L. 1937. *Mapungubwe: ancient Bantu civilization on the Limpopo*. Cambridge: Cambridge University Press.

Fowler, M. L. 1975. A pre-Columbian urban center on the Mississippi. *Scientific American* 233 (2), 93–101.

Francaviglia, V. & A. M. Palmieri 1983. Petrochemical analysis of the 'Early Khartoum' pottery: a preliminary report. *Origini* 12, 191–205.

Francis-Boeuf, C. 1937. L'industrie autochtone du fer en Afrique Occidentale Française. *Bulletin du Comité d'Etudes Historiques et Scientifiques de l'Afrique Occidentale Française* 20, 403–64.

Frank, A. G. 1967. *Capitalism and Underdevelopment in Latin America*. London: Penguin.

Frank, B. 1981. Zur Bedeutung des Pferdes bei den Ron oder Challa (Plateau-Staat, Nigeria). *Tribus* 30, 135–43.

Frankfort, H. 1948. *Kingship and the Gods*. Chicago: University of Chicago Press.

Franklin, H. 1945. The native ironworkers of Enkeldoorn District and their art. *Native Affairs Department Annual* 22, 5–10.

Fredoux, A. & J. P. Tastet 1988. Stratigraphie pollinique et paléoclimatique de la marge septentrionale du Golfe de Guinée depuis 200,000 ans. *Institut Français de Pondichery, Travaux de la Section Scientifique et Technique* 25, 175–83.

Fredoux, A., J. P. Tastet, J. Maley & C. Guilmette 1989. Caracterisation palynologique du stade isotopique 5 et présence de *Podocarpus latifolius* en Côte d'Ivoire au Pléistocène supérieur. Paper presented to 1er Symposium Palynologie Africaine, Rabat.

Freeman, T. W. 1966. *The Conurbations of Great Britain*. Manchester: Manchester University Press.

Freeman-Grenville, G. S. P. 1962. *The East African Coast: select documents from the first to the earlier nineteenth century.* Oxford: Clarendon Press.

FRELIMO 1972. *Historia da Africa.* Dar es Salaam.

Fricke, W. 1979. *Cattle Husbandry in Nigeria: a study of its ecological conditions and social-geographical differentiations.* Heidelberg: Geographisches Institut der Universität Heidelberg.

Fried, M. 1960. On the evolution of social stratification and the state. In *Culture in History*, S. Diamond (ed.), 713–31. New York: Columbia University Press.

Friede, H. M. 1977. Iron age metal working in the Magaliesberg area. *Journal of the South African Institute of Mining and Metallurgy* 77, 224–32.

Friede, H., A. Hejja & A. Koursaris 1982. Archaeo-metallurgical studies of iron smelting slags from prehistoric sites in southern Africa. *Journal of the South African Institute of Mining and Metallurgy* 82, 38–48.

Friede, H. M. & R. H. Steel 1977. An experimental study of iron-smelting techniques used in the South African Iron Age. *Journal of the South African Institute of Mining and Metallurgy* 77, 233–42.

—— 1988. Notes on an iron smelting pit furnace found at Bultfontein iron age site 41/85 (central Transvaal) and on general features of pit furnaces. *South African Archaeological Bulletin* 43, 38–41.

Friedman, J. 1974. Marxism, structuralism, and vulgar materialism. *Man* 8, 444–69.

Frobenius, L. 1913. *The Voice of Africa: being an account of the travels of the German Army African exploration expedition in the years 1910–1912.* 2 vols. London: Hutchinson.

Fyle, C. N. & E. N. Jones 1980. *A Krio–English Dictionary.* Oxford: Oxford & Sierra Leone University Presses.

Gabel, C. 1976. Microlithic occurrences in the Republic of Liberia. *West African Journal of Archaeology* 6, 21–35.

Gabriel, B. 1976. Neolithische Steinplätze und Paläokologie in den Ebenen der östlichen Zentralsahara. *Palaeoecology of Africa* 9, 25–40.

—— 1977. *Zum ökologischen Wandel im Neolithikum der östlichen Zentralsahara.* Berlin: Freie Universität, Berliner Geographische Abhandlung.

—— 1986. *Die östliche libysche Wüste im Jungquartär.* Berlin: Institut für Geographie der Technischen Universität.

Gailey, C. W. 1985. The state of the state in anthropology. *Dialectical Anthropology* 9, 65–85.

Gallois, L. 1923. The origin and growth of Paris. *The Geographical Review* 13, 345–67.

Gardin, J. 1979. *Une archéologie théorique.* Paris: Hachette.

—— 1980 *Archaeological Constructs: an aspect of theoretical archaeology.* Cambridge: Cambridge University Press.

Gardiner, A. H. 1945. Regnal years and civil calendar in Pharaonic Egypt. *Journal of Egyptian Archaeology* 31, 11–28.

—— 1947. *Ancient Egyptian Onomastica.* 2 vols. Oxford: Oxford University Press.

—— 1948. *The Wilbur Papyrus, Vol. 2: Commentary.* Oxford: Oxford University Press.

—— 1957. *Egyptian Grammar.* Oxford: Oxford University Press.

Gardiner, Sir A. H., T. E. Peet & J. Cerny 1952. *The Inscriptions of Sinai, I.* London: Egypt Exploration Society.

—— 1955. *The Inscriptions of Sinai, II.* London: Egypt Exploration Society.

Gardner, I. 1980. *Abuan–English, English–Abuan Dictionary.* Port Harcourt and Jos: University of Port Harcourt Press & Nigeria Bible Translation Trust.

Garlake, P. S. 1966. *The Early Islamic Architecture of the East African Coast.* Nairobi: British Institute in Eastern Africa.

—— 1973a. *Great Zimbabwe*. London: Thames & Hudson.

—— 1973b. Excavations at Mhunguza and Ruanga ruins in northern Mashonaland. *South African Archaeological Bulletin* 27, 107–43.

—— 1976a. An investigation of Manekweni, Mozambique. *Azania* 11, 25–47.

—— 1976b. Excavation of a Zimbabwe in Mozambique. *Antiquity* 50, 146–8.

—— 1978. Pastoralism and Zimbabwe. *Journal of African History* 19, 479–94.

—— 1982. *Great Zimbabwe Described and Explained*. Harare: Zimbabwe Publishing House.

Gasse, F. 1980. Late quaternary changes in lake-levels and diatom assemblages on the south-east margins of the Sahara. *Palaeoecology of Africa* 12, 333–50.

Gasse, F., P. Rognon & F. E. Strict 1980. Quaternary history of the Afar and Ethiopian Rift lakes. In *The Sahara and the Nile: quaternary environments and prehistoric occupation in northern Africa*, Williams, M. A. J. & H. Faure (eds), 361–400. Rotterdam: Balkema.

Gates, G. M. 1952. Breeds of cattle found in Nigeria. *Farm and Forest* 11, 19–43.

Gathercole, P. & D. Lowenthal 1990. *The Politics of the Past*. London: Unwin Hyman.

Gauthier, H. 1923–31. *Dictionnaire des noms géographiques, contenu dans les textes hiéroglyphiques, I–VIII*. Cairo: Institut Français d'Archéologie Orientale.

Gauthier-Pilters, H. & A. I. Dagg 1981. *The Camel: its evolution, ecology, behavior, and relationship to man*. Chicago: University of Chicago Press.

Gautier, A. 1968. Mammalian remains of the northern Sudan and southern Egypt. In *The Prehistory of Nubia, Vol. 1*, Wendorf, F. (ed.), 80–99. Dallas: Fort Burgwin Research Center & Southern Methodist University Press.

—— 1976a. Freshwater mollusks and mammals from upper palaeolithic sites near Idfu and Isna. In *Prehistory of the Nile Valley*, Wendorf, F. & R. Schild (eds), 349–64. New York: Academic Press.

—— 1976b. Animal remains from localities near Dishna. In *Prehistory of the Nile Valley*, Wendorf, F. & R. Schild (eds), 365–7. New York: Academic Press.

—— 1976c. Animal remains from archaeological sites of the terminal palaeolithic to Old Kingdom age in the Fayum. In *Prehistory of the Nile Valley*, Wendorf, F. & R. Schild (eds), 369–81. New York: Academic Press.

—— 1980. Contributions to the archaeozoology of Egypt. In *Prehistory of the Eastern Sahara*, Wendorf, F. & R. Schild (eds), 317–44. New York: Academic Press.

—— 1982. Prehistoric fauna from Ti-n-Torha (Tadrart Acacus, Libya). *Origini* 11, 87–127.

—— 1983. Animal life along the prehistoric Nile: the evidence from Saggai I and Geili (Sudan). *Origini* 12, 50–115.

—— 1984. Archaeozoology of the Bir Kiseiba region, eastern Sahara. In *Cattle-keepers of the Eastern Sahara: the Neolithic of Bir Kiseiba*, Wendorf, F., R. Schild & A. E. Close (eds), 49–72. Dallas: Southern Methodist University.

—— 1987. Prehistoric men and cattle in north Africa: a dearth of data and a surfeit of models. In *Prehistory of Arid North Africa: essays in honor of Fred Wendorf*, Close, A. E. (ed.), 163–87. Dallas: Southern Methodist University Press.

Gautier, A. & W. van Neer 1989. Animal remains from the late palaeolithic sequence at Wadi Kubbaniya. In *The Prehistory of North Africa, Vol. 2: Palaeoeconomy, Environment and Stratigraphy*, Close, A. E. (ed.), 119–58. Dallas: Southern Methodist University Press.

Gavua, K. 1985. Daboya and the Kintampo culture of Ghana. Unpublished MA thesis, University of Calgary.

Geary, C. 1976. *We: die Genese eines Häuptlingstums im Grasland von Kamerun*. Wiesbaden: Franz Steiner.

Gell, A. 1988. Technology and magic. *Anthropology Today* 4, 6–9.

Gerhardt, L. 1983. *Beiträge zur Kenntnis der Sprachen des Nigerianischen Plateaus*. Glückstadt: J. J. Augustin.

Germeraad, J. H., C. A. Hopping & J. Muller 1968. Palynology of tertiary sediments from tropical areas. *Review of Paleobotany and Palynology* 6, 189–348.

Gibb, H. A. R. 1962. *The Travels of Ibn Battuta AD 1325–54, Vol. 2*. London: Hakluyt Society.

Giddy, L. 1987. *Egyptian Oases*. Warminster: Aris & Phillips.

Gifford, D. P., G. L. Isaac & C. M. Nelson 1980. Evidence for predation and pastoralism at Prolonged Drift: a pastoral neolithic site in Kenya. *Azania* 15, 57–8.

Gifford-Gonzalez, D. P. 1984. Implications of a faunal assemblage from a pastoral neolithic site in Kenya: findings and a perspective on research. In *From Hunters to Farmers: the causes and consequences of food production in Africa*, Clark, J. D. & S. A. Brandt (eds), 240–51. Berkeley: University of California Press.

Gifford-Gonzalez, D. P. & J. Kimengich 1984. Faunal evidence for early stock-keeping in the central Rift of Kenya: preliminary findings. In *Origin and Early Development of Food-producing Cultures in North-eastern Africa*, Krzyzaniak, L. & M. Kobusiewicz (eds), 457–71. Poznan: Polish Academy of Sciences & Poznan Archaeological Museum.

Gillespie, R., F. A. Street-Perrott & R. Switsur 1983. Post-glacial arid episodes in Ethiopia have implications for climate prediction. *Nature* 306, 681–3.

Gilman, A. 1976. A later prehistory of Tangier, Morocco. *American School of Prehistoric Research, Bulletin 29*. Cambridge, Mass.: Harvard University Press.

Ginter, B. & J. K. Kozlowski 1983. Investigations on neolithic settlements. In *Qasr el-Sagha 1980*, Kozlowski, J. (ed.), 37–67. Warzawa-Krakow: Panstwowe Wydawnictwo Naukowe.

—— 1984. The Tarifian and the origins of the Naqadian. In *Origins and Early Development of Food-producing Cultures in North-eastern Africa*, Krzyzaniak, L. & M. Kobusiewicz (eds), 247–60. Poznan: Polish Academy of Sciences & Poznan Archaeological Museum.

—— 1986. Kulturelle und palaeoklimatische Sequenz in der Fayum-Depression: eine zusammenfassende Darstellung der Forschungs-arbeiten in den Jahren 1979–1981. *Mitteilungen des Deutschen Archäologischen Institut, Abteilung Kairo* 42, 9–23.

Ginter, B., J. K. Kozlowski, M. Litynska & M. Pawlikoswski 1988. Field report from the excavation of the sites MA 21/83 and MA 21a/83 near Armant in Upper Egypt in 1986. *Mitteilungen des Deutschen Archäologischen Institut, Abteilung Kairo* 44, 95–101.

Ginter, B., J. K. Kozlowski & M. Pawlikoswski 1985. Field report from the survey conducted in Upper Egypt in 1983. *Mitteilungen des Deutschen Archäologischen Institut, Abteilung Kairo* 41, 15–41.

—— 1987. Investigations into Site MA 6/83 and MA 21/83 in the region of Qurna-Armant in Upper Egypt. *Mitteilungen des Deutschen Archäologischen Institut, Abteilung Kairo* 43, 42–66.

Ginter, B., J. K. Kozlowski & J. Sliwa 1979. Excavation report on the prehistoric and predynastic settlement in El-Tarif during 1978. *Mitteilungen des Deutschen Archäologischen Institut, Abteilung Kairo* 35, 92–9.

Giresse, P. 1978. Le contrôle climatique de la sedimentation marine et continentale en Afrique Centrale Atlantique à la fin du Quaternaire: problèmes de correlation. *Palaeogeography, Palaeoclimatology, Palaeoecology* 23, 57–77.

Giresse, P., G. Bongo-Passi, G. Delibrias & J. C. Duplessy 1982. La lithostratigraphie des sédiments hémipelagiques du delta profond du fleuve Congo et ses indications sur les paléoclimats de la fin du Quaternaire. *Bulletin de la Société Géologique de France* 24, 803–15.

Giresse, P., Kinga-Mouzeo & D. Schwartz Forthcoming. Les ruptures d'équilibre de l'environnement quaternaire du Bassin du Congo, leurs incidences sur la sédimentation océanique. In *African Continental Sediments*, Lang, J. & C. A. Kogbe (eds). London: Pergamon Press.

Giresse, P. & R. Lanfranchi 1984. Les climats et les océans de la région congolaise pendant l'Holocène. Bilans selon les échelles et les méthodes de l'observation. *Palaeoecology of Africa* 16, 77–88.

Gledhill, J., B. Bender & M. T. Larsen 1988. *State and Society: the emergence and development of social hierarchy and political centralization*. London: Unwin Hyman.

Gleichen, Count 1898. *With the Mission to Menelik*. London: Edward Arnold.

Glover, I. 1990. *Early Trade between India and Southeast Asia*. Hull: Centre for Southeast Asian Studies.

Godelier, M. 1972. *Rationality and Irrationality in Economics*. London: New Left Books.

Goodall, E. 1946. Domestic animals in rock art. *Transactions of the Rhodesia Scientific Association* 41, 57–62.

Goodfriend, G. A. 1988. Mid-holocene rainfall in the Negev desert from 13C land snail shell organic matter. *Nature* 333, 757–60.

Goodman, M. 1970. Some questions on the classification of African languages. *International Journal of African Linguistics* 36, 117–22.

Goodman, S. M. & J. J. Hobbs 1988. The ethnobotany of the Egyptian Eastern Desert: a comparison of common plant usage between two culturally distinct Bedouin groups. *Journal of Ethnopharmacology* 23, 73–89.

Goodwin, A. J. H. & C. Van Riet Lowe 1929. The stone age cultures of South Africa. *Annals of the South African Museum* 27.

Goody, J. R. 1956. *The Social Organisation of the LoWiili*. London: H. M. Stationery Office.

—— 1971. *Technology, Tradition and the State in West Africa*. London: Oxford University Press.

Gott, B. 1982. The ecology of root use by the Aborigines of southern Australia. *Archaeology in Oceania* 17, 59–67.

Goucher, C. L. 1981. Iron is iron 'til it is rust: trade and ecology in the decline of west African iron-smelting. *Journal of African History* 22, 179–89.

—— 1983. Technological change in Bassar iron production. *Nyame Akuma* 23, 36.

—— 1984. The iron industry of Bassar, Togo: an interdisciplinary investigation of African technological history. Unpublished PhD thesis, University of California at Los Angeles.

Gould, R. A. 1980. *Living Archaeology: new studies in archaeology*. Cambridge: Cambridge University Press.

Gouldsbury, G. & H. Sheanne 1911. *The Great Plateau of Northern Rhodesia*. London: Edward Arnold.

Gouletquer, P. L. 1975. Niger: country of salt. In *Salt: the study of an ancient industry*, de Brisay, K. & K. A. Evans (eds), 47–51. Colchester: Colchester Archaeological Group.

Gouletquer, P. L. & D. Kleinmann 1978. Salle. *Mitteilungen der Anthropologische Gesellschaft in Wien* 108, 1–45.

Gowland, W. 1912. The metals in antiquity. *Journal of the Royal Anthropological Institute* 42, 276–87.

Gowlett, J. A. J., R. Hedges, I. Law & C. Perry 1987. Radiocarbon dates from the Oxford AMS system: archaeometry datelist 5. *Archaeometry* 29, 125–55.

Grace, G. W. 1967. The effect of heterogeneity on the lexicostatistical text list: the case of Rotuman. In *Polynesian Culture History*, Highland, G. (ed.), 289–302. Honolulu: Bernice P. Bishop Museum.

Gramly, R. M. 1975. Pastoralists and hunters: recent prehistory in southern Kenya and northern Tanzania. Unpublished PhD thesis, Harvard University.

—— 1978. Expansion of Bantu speakers versus development of Bantu languages *in situ*: an archaeologist's perspective. *South African Archaeological Bulletin* 33, 107–12.

Grandin, B. E. 1980. Small cows, big money; wealth and dwarf cattle production in southwestern Nigeria. Unpublished PhD thesis, Stanford University.

Gratien, B. 1978. *Les Cultures Kerma: essai de classification*. Villeneuve-d'Ascov: Université de Lille III.

—— 1985. Le village fortifié du groupe C à Ourdi es-Seboua Est, typologie de la céramique.

Cahier de Recherches de l'Institut de Papyrologie et d'Egyptologie, Sociétés Urbaines en Egypte et au Soudan 1, 39–70.

Grébénart, D. 1979a. La préhistoire de la République du Niger: état actuel de la question. In *Recherches sahariennes I*, 37–70. Paris: CNRS (Centre National de la Recherche Scientifique).

—— 1979b. Recherches sur la préhistoire au Niger. In *Recherches sahariennes I*, 207–24. Paris: CNRS (Centre National de la Recherche Scientifique).

—— 1983. Les métallurgies du cuivre et du fer autour d'Agadez (Niger) des origines au début de la période médiévale: vues générales. In *Métallurgies africaines: nouvelles contributions*, Echard, N. (ed.), 109–25. Paris: Société des Africanistes.

—— 1987. Characteristics of the final Neolithic and Metal Ages in the region of Agadez (Niger). In *Prehistory of Arid North Africa: essays in honor of Fred Wendorf*, Close, A. E. (ed.), 287–316. Dallas: Southern Methodist University Press.

—— 1988. *Les Premiers Métallurgistes en Afrique Occidentale (les origines de la métallurgie en Afrique Occidentale)*. Paris: Errance.

Green, S. 1975. Sudanese radiocarbon chronology: a provisional date list. *Nyame Akuma* 6, 10–24.

Greenberg, J. H. 1964. Historical inferences from linguistic research in sub-Saharan Africa. In *Boston University Papers in African History 1*, Butler, J. (ed.), 1–15. Boston: Boston University Press.

—— 1966. *The Languages of Africa*. The Hague: Mouton.

—— 1971. Nilo-Saharan and Meroitic. In *Current Trends in Linguistics, Vol. 7: Sub-Saharan Africa*, Berry, J. & J. H. Greenberg (eds), 421–42. The Hague: Mouton.

Greenwood, P. H. 1968. Fish remains. In *The Prehistory of Nubia, Vol. 1.*, Wendorf, F. (ed.), 100–9. Dallas: Fort Burgwin Research Center & Southern Methodist University Press.

Gregersen, E. A. 1967. Linguistic seriation as a dating device for loanwords, with special reference to west Africa. *African Language Review* 6, 102–8.

—— 1972. Kongo-Saharan. *Journal of African Languages* 11, 69–89.

Gregory, S. (ed.) 1988. *Recent Climatic Change, Part 3: Tropical and Southern Africa*. London: Bellhaven.

Grey, D. & H. Cooke 1977. Some problems in quaternary evolution of landforms of northern Botswana. *Catena* 4, 123–33.

Griaule, M. 1965. *Conversations with Ogotemmli: an introduction to Dogon religious ideas*. London: Oxford University Press.

Grieg, R. C. H. 1937. Iron smelting in Fipa. *Tanganyika Notes and Records* 4, 77–81.

Griffith, F. Ll. 1972. The Abydos decree of Seti I at Nauri. *Journal of Egyptian Archaeology* 13, 193–208.

Grigson, C., J. A. J. Gowlett & J. Zarins 1989. The camel in Arabia – a direct radiocarbon date, calibrated to about 7000 BC. *Journal of Archaeological Science* 16, 355–62.

Grottanelli, V. L. 1947. Asiatic influences on Somali culture. *Ethnos* 4, 153–81.

—— 1955. *Pescatori dell'Oceano Indiano*. Rome: Cremonese.

Grove, A. T. 1983. Evolution of the physical geography of the east African Rift Valley region. In *Evolution, Time and Space: the emergence of the biosphere*, Sims, R. W., J. H. Price & P. E. S. Whalley (eds), 117–55. London: Academic Press.

—— 1988. Lake levels in tropical Africa with special reference to Lake Chad and to future research needs. Unpublished. International Geological Correlation Programme no. 252.

—— 1989. *The Changing Geography of Africa*. Oxford: Oxford University Press.

Grove, A. T. & R. A. Pullan 1963. Some aspects of the pleistocene paleogeography of the Chad basin. In *African Ecology and Human Evolution*, Howell, F. C. & F. Bourlière (eds), 230–45. Chicago: Aldine.

Grove, A. T., F. A. Street & A. S. Goudie 1975. Former lake levels and climatic change in the Rift

Valley of southern Ethiopia. *Geographical Journal* 141: 177–202.

Grove, A. T. & A. Warren 1968. Quaternary landforms and climate on the south side of the Sahara. *Geographical Journal* 134, 194–208.

Grove, D. 1972. The function and future of urban centres. In *Man, Settlement and Urbanism*, Ucko, P. J., R. Tringham & G. W. Dimbleby (eds), 559–65. London: Duckworth.

Grundlach, R. 1979. Kupfer. In *Lexikon der Ägyptologie III*, Helck, W. & W. Westendorf (eds), 881–2. Wiesbaden: Otto Harrasowitz.

Gudeman, S. 1986. *Economics as Culture: models and metaphors of livelihood.* London: Routledge & Kegan Paul.

Guenther, M. G. 1975. The trance dancer as an agent of social change among the farm Bushmen of the Ghanzi District. *Botswana Notes and Records* 7, 161–6.

Gugler, J. & W. Flanagan 1978. *Urbanization and Social Change in West Africa.* Cambridge: Cambridge University Press.

Guillain, M. 1856. *Documents sur l'histoire, la géographie et le commerce de l'Afrique orientale, 1.* Paris: Arthus Bertrand.

Guillard, J. 1965. *Golonpoui.* Paris: Mouton.

Guillaume, A. 1955. *The Life of Muhammad: a translation of Ibn Ishaq's 'Sirat Rasul Allah'.* Oxford: Oxford University Press.

Guthrie, M. 1962. Some developments in the prehistory of the Bantu languages. *Journal of African History* 3, 273–82.

—— 1967–71. *Comparative Bantu.* 4 vols. Farnborough: Gregg Press.

Gutkind, P. C. W. 1963. *The Royal Capital of Buganda.* The Hague: Mouton.

Haaland, R. 1980. Man's role in the changing habitat of Mema during the old kingdom of Ghana. *Norwegian Archaeological Review* 13, 31–46.

—— 1985. Iron production, its socio-cultural context and ecological implications. In *African Iron Working: ancient and traditional*, Haaland, R. & P. L. Shinnie (eds), 50–72. Oslo: Norwegian University Press.

Haas, H. & C. V. Haynes 1980. Discussion of radiocarbon dates from the Western Desert. In *Prehistory of the Eastern Sahara*, Wendorf, F. & R. Schild (eds), 373–8. New York: Academic Press.

Habachi, L. 1975. Elephantine. In *Lexikon der Ägyptologie, I*, Helck, W. & E. Otto (eds), 1217–25. Wiesbaden: Otto Harrasowitz.

Hable-Selassie, S. 1972. *Ancient and Medieval Ethiopian History to 1270.* Addis Ababa: Department of History, Haile Selassie I University.

Haggett, P., A. Cliff & A. Frey 1977. *Locational Analysis in Human Geography.* New York: John Wiley & Sons.

Hall, M. 1981. *Settlement Patterns in the Iron Age of Zululand.* Oxford: British Archaeological Reports.

—— 1987. *The Changing Past: farmers, kings and traders in southern Africa, 200–1860.* Cape Town: David Phillip.

Hall, M. & A. B. Smith (eds) 1986. *Prehistoric Pastoralism in Southern Africa.* Vlaeberg: South African Archaeological Society.

Hall, M. & J. Vogel 1980. Some recent radiocarbon dates from southern Africa. *Journal of African History* 21, 431–55.

Hall, R. N. & W. Neal 1902. *The Ancient Ruins of Rhodesia.* London: Methuen.

Hamdan, G. 1980. *Shakhsiat Misr* (in Arabic). Cairo: Alam el-Kutub.

Hamilton, A. 1973. The history of the vegetation. In *The Vegetation of East Africa*, Lind, E. M. & M. E. S. Morrison (eds), 188–209. London: Longman.

—— 1976. The significance of patterns of distribution shown by forest plants and animals in tropical Africa for the reconstruction of upper pleistocene palaeoenvironments: a review. *Palaeoecology of Africa* 9, 63–97.

—— 1982. *Environmental History of East Africa: a study of the Quaternary*. London: Academic Press.

Hamilton, A., D. Taylor & J. C. Vogel 1986. Early forest clearance and environmental degradation in southwest Uganda. *Nature* 320, 164–7.

Hanish, E. O. M. 1980. An archaeological interpretation of certain iron age sites in the Limpopo/ Shashi valley. Unpublished MA thesis, University of Pretoria.

Harlan, J. R. 1969. Ethiopia – a center of diversity. *Economic Botany* 23, 309–14.

—— 1971. Agricultural origins: centers and noncenters. *Science* 174, 468–74.

—— 1989 Wild-grass seed harvesting in the Sahara and sub-Sahara of Africa. In *Foraging and Farming: the evolution of plant exploitation*. Harris, D. R. & G. C. Hillman (eds), 79–98. London: Unwin Hyman.

Harlan, J. R. & J. M. J. De Wet 1972. A simplified classification of cultivated sorghum. *Crop Science* 12, 172–6.

Harlan, J. R., J. M. J. De Wet & E. G. Price 1973. Comparative evolution of cereals. *Evolution* 27, 311–25.

Harlan, J. R., J. M. J. De Wet & A. B. L. Stemler (eds) 1976. *Origins of African Plant Domestication*. The Hague: Mouton.

Harlan, J. R. & J. Pasquereau 1969. Décrue agriculture in Mali. *Economic Botany* 23, 70–4.

Harlan, J. R. & A. B. L. Stemler 1976. The races of sorghum in Africa. In *Origins of African Plant Domestication*, Harlan, J. R., J. M. J. De Wet & A. B. L. Stemler (eds), 465–78. The Hague: Mouton.

Harris, D. R. 1969. Agricultural systems, ecosystems and the origins of agriculture. In *The Domestication and Exploitation of Plants and Animals*, Ucko, P. J. & G. W. Dimbleby (eds), 3–15. London: Duckworth.

—— 1976. Traditional systems of plant food production and the origins of agriculture in west Africa. In *Origins of African Plant Domestication*, Harlan, J. R., J. M. J. De Wet & A. B. L. Stemler (eds), 311–56. The Hague: Mouton.

—— 1989. An evolutionary continuum of people–plant interaction. In *Foraging and Farming: the evolution of plant exploitation*, Harris, D. R. & G. C. Hillman (eds), 11–26. London: Unwin Hyman.

Harris, D. R. & G. C. Hillman (eds) 1989. *Foraging and Farming: the evolution of plant exploitation*. London: Unwin Hyman.

Hartley, C. W. S. 1970. *The Oil Palm (Elaeis guineensis Jacq.)*. 2nd edn. London: Longmans, Green.

Harvey, P. & A. T. Grove 1982. A prehistoric source of the Nile. *Geographical Journal* 148, 327–36.

Hasan, Y. F. 1967. *The Arabs and the Sudan*. Edinburgh: Edinburgh University Press.

Haskell, H., S. K. McIntosh & R. J. McIntosh 1988. Archaeological reconnaissance in the region of Dia, Mali. Final report to the National Geographic Society.

Hassan, F. A. 1979. Demography and archaeology. *Annual Review of Anthropology* 8, 137–60.

—— 1980. Prehistoric settlements along the Main Nile. In *The Sahara and the Nile: quaternary environments and prehistoric occupation in northern Africa*, Williams, M. A. J. & H. Faure (eds), 421–50. Rotterdam: Balkema.

—— 1981a. *Demographic Archaeology*. New York: Academic Press.

—— 1981b. The Predynastic of Egypt: subsistence-settlement studies in the Nagada-Khattara region. Final Report to the National Science Foundation, Washington, D. C.

—— 1984a. Environment and súbsistence in predynastic Egypt. In *From Hunters to Farmers: the causes and consequences of food production in Africa*, Clark, J. D. & S. A. Brandt (eds), 57–64. Berkeley: University of California Press.

—— 1984b. A radiocarbon date from Hemanieh [sic], Upper Egypt. Nyame Akuma 24/5, 3.

—— 1985. A radiocarbon chronology of neolithic and predynastic sites in Upper Egypt and the Delta. African Archaeological Review 3, 95–116.

—— 1986a. Holocene lakes and prehistoric settlements of the western Faiyum, Egypt. Journal of Archaeological Science 13, 483–501.

—— 1986b. Desert environment and origins of agriculture in Egypt. Norwegian Archaeological Review 19, 63–76.

—— 1988. The Predynastic of Egypt. Journal of World Prehistory 2, 135–85.

—— In Press. Population ecology and civilization in ancient Egypt. In Historical Ecology, Crumley, C. (ed.). Santa Fe, New Mexico: School of American Research.

Hassan, F. A. & G. T. Gross 1987. Resources and subsistence during the early Holocene at Siwa Oasis, northern Egypt. In Prehistory of Arid North Africa: essays in honor of Fred Wendorf, Close, A. E. (ed.), 85–103. Dallas: Southern Methodist University Press.

Hassan, F. A. & R. G. Matson 1989. Seriation of predynastic potsherds from the Nagada region (Upper Egypt). In Late Prehistory of the Nile Basin and the Sahara, Krzyzaniak, L. & M. Kobusiewicz (eds), 303–15. Poznan: Poznan Archaeology Museum.

Hassan, F. A. & B. Stucki 1987. Nile floods and climatic change. In Climate, History, Periodicity and Predictability, Rampino, M. R., J. E. Sanders, W. S. Newman & L. K. Königsson (eds), 37–46. New York: Van Norstrand Reinholt.

Hastenrath, S. & J. E. Kutzbach 1983. Paleoclimatic estimates from water and energy budgets of east African lakes. Quaternary Research 19, 141–53.

Hastorf, C. A. & M. J. DeNiro 1985. Reconstruction of prehistoric plant production and cooking practices by a new isotopic method. Nature 315, 489–91.

Hather, J. G. 1988. The morphological and anatomical identification and interpretation of charred vegetative parenchymatous plant remains. Unpublished PhD thesis, Institute of Archaeology, University College, London.

Hatton, J. S. 1967. Notes on Makalanga iron smelting. Native Affairs Development Annual 9, 39–41.

Haumesser, J. B. 1975. Some aspects of reproduction in the Red Sokoto goat. Comparison with other tropical and subtropical breeds. Revue d'Elevage et de Médécine Vétérinaire des Pays Tropicaux 28, 225–33.

Haumesser, J. B. & P. Gerbaldi 1980. Observations sur la reproduction et l'élevage du mouton Oudah nigérien. Revue d'Elevage et de Médécine Vétérinaire des Pays Tropicaux 33, 205–13.

Hayes, W. C. 1965. Most Ancient Egypt. Chicago: University of Chicago Press.

Haynes, C. V. 1987. Holocene migration rates of the Sudano–Sahelian wetting front, Arba'in desert, eastern Sahara. In Prehistory of Arid North Africa: essays in honor of Fred Wendorf, Close, A. E. (ed.), 69–84. Dallas: Southern Methodist University Press.

Haynes, C. V., C. H. Eyles, L. A. Pavlish, J. C. Ritchie & M. Rybak 1989. Holocene palaeoecology of the eastern Sahara: Selima Oasis. Quaternary Science Reviews 8, 109–36.

Hays, T. R. 1974. 'Wavy line' pottery: an element of nilotic diffusion. South African Archaeological Bulletin 29, 27–32.

—— 1976a. An examination of the Sudanese Neolithic. In Proceedings of the Panafrican Congress of Prehistory and Quaternary Studies, 7th Session, Addis Ababa, December 1971, Abebe, B., J. Chevaillon & J. E. G. Sutton (eds), 85–92. Addis Ababa: Provisional Military Government of Socialist Ethiopia, Ministry of Culture.

—— 1976b. Predynastic Egypt: recent field research. Current Anthropology 17, 552–4.

Hays, T. R. & F. A. Hassan 1974. Mineralogical analysis of 'Sudanese Neolithic' ceramics. Archaeometry 16, 71–9.

Hayward, E. 1921. Round about Panyam. London: Church Missionary Society.

Hayward, R. J. (ed.) 1990. Omotic Language Studies. London: School of Oriental African Studies.

Haywood, A. H. W. 1912. *Through Timbuctoo and across the Great Sahara.* London: Seeley Service.

Head, B. V. 1887. *Historia Nummorum.* Oxford: Clarendon Press.

Hecky, R. E. & E. T. Degens 1973. *Late Pleistocene–Holocene Chemical Stratigraphy and Paleolimnology of the Rift Valley Lakes in Central Africa.* Woods Hole, Mass.: Woods Hole Oceanographic Institute.

Hedinger, R. 1987. *The Manenguba Languages (Bantu A.15, Mbo Cluster) of Cameroon.* London: School of Oriental and African Studies.

Heine, B. 1973. Zur genetischen Gliederung der Bantu-sprachen. *Afrika und Übersee* 56, 164–85.

—— 1984. The dispersal of the Bantu peoples in the light of linguistic evidence. *Muntu* 1, 21–35.

Heine, B., H. Hoff & R. Vossen 1977. Neuere Ergebnisse zur Territorialgeschichte der Bantu. In *Zur Sprachgeschichte und Ethnohistorie in Afrika: neue Beiträge afrikanistischer Forschungen,* Möhlig, W. J. G., F. Rottland & B. Heine (eds), 57–72. Berlin: Reimer.

Helbaek, H. 1955. Ancient Egyptian wheats. *Proceedings of the Prehistoric Society* 21, 93–5.

—— 1960. Comment on *Chenopodium* as a food plant in prehistory. *Berichte der geobotanischen Forschungenstitut Rubel Zürich* 31, 16–19.

Helck, W. 1974. *Die altägyptischen Gaue.* Wiesbaden: Reichert Verlag.

—— 1975. Bronze. In *Lexikon der Ägyptologie, I,* Helck, W. & E. Otto (eds), 870–1. Wiesbaden: Otto Harrasowitz.

Henneberg, M., M. Kobusiewicz, R. Schild & F. Wendorf 1989. The early neolithic, Qarunian burial from the north Fayum desert (Egypt). In *Late Prehistory of the Nile Basin and the Sahara,* Krzyzaniak, L. & M. Kobusiewicz (eds), 181–96. Poznan: Poznan Archaeology Museum.

Hepper, F. N. 1976. *The West African Herbaria of Isert and Thonning.* London: Royal Kew Gardens.

Herbert, E. W. 1984. *Red Gold of Africa: copper in precolonial history and culture.* Madison: University of Wisconsin Press.

—— Forthcoming. Paradigm of procreation: technology and gender in African iron making. Conference on African Material Culture, Bellagio, May 1988.

Herskovits, M. J. 1926. The cattle complex in east Africa. *American Anthropologist* 28, 1–137.

—— 1938. *Dahomey: an ancient west African kingdom.* 2 vols. New York: Augustin.

Herzog, R. 1968. *Punt.* Glückstadt: Augustin.

Hesse, R. 1937. *Ecological Animal Geography: an authorized, rewritten edition based on 'Tiergeographie auf ökologische Grundlage',* by Richard Hesse, Allee, W. C. & K. P. Schmidt (eds). London: Chapman & Hall.

Heusch, L. de 1982. *Rois nés d'un coeur de vache.* Paris: Gallimard.

Hiernaux, J. 1968. Bantu expansion: the evidence from physical anthropology confronted with linguistic and archaeological evidence. *Journal of African History* 9, 505–15.

Hiernaux, J., E. Maquet & J. De Buyst 1968. Excavations at Sanga 1958. *South African Journal of Science* 64, 113–17.

Higgs, E. S. 1967. Environment and chronology: evidence from mammalian fauna. In *The Haua Fteah (Cyrenaica) and the Stone Age of the South-east Mediterranean,* McBurney, C. (ed.), 16–44. Cambridge: Cambridge University Press.

—— (ed.) 1972. *Papers in Economic Prehistory.* Cambridge: Cambridge University Press.

Higgs, E. S. & C. Vita Finzi 1970. Prehistoric economy in the Mount Carmel area of Palestine: site catchment analysis. *Proceedings of the Prehistoric Society* 86, 1–37.

—— 1972. Prehistoric economies: a territorial approach. In *Papers in Economic Prehistory,* Higgs E. S. (ed.), 27–36. Cambridge: Cambridge University Press.

Hill, H. E. & J. Evans 1989. Crops of the Pacific: new evidence from the chemical analysis of organic residues in pottery. In *Foraging and Farming: the evolution of plant exploitation,* Harris, D. R. & G. C. Hillman (eds), 418–25. London: Unwin Hyman.

Hill, M. 1981. The Senegambian monument complex: current status and prospects for research. In

Megaliths to Medicine Wheels, Wilson, M., K. Road & K. J. Hardy (eds), 419–30. Calgary: University of Calgary Press.

Hillman, G. C. 1984. Traditional husbandry and processing of archaic cereals in recent times: the operations, products and equipment which might feature in Sumerian texts. Part I: The glume wheats. *Bulletin on Sumerian Agriculture* 1, 114–52.

—— 1989. Late palaeolithic plant foods from Wadi Kubbaniya in Upper Egypt: dietary diversity, infant weaning, and seasonality in a riverine environment. In *Foraging and Farming: the evolution of plant exploitation*, Harris, D. R. & G. C. Hillman (eds), 207–39. London: Unwin Hyman.

Hillman, G. C. & M. F. Davies 1991. Domestication rate in wild wheats and barley under primitive cultivation: preliminary results using field measurements of selection coefficient, and the archaeological implications. In *Préhistoire de l'agriculture: nouvelles approches experimentales et ethnographiques*, Anderson–Gerfaud, P. C. (ed.), 157–222. Valbonne: Centre de Recherches Archéologiques.

Hillman, G., E. Madeyska & J. Hather 1989. Wild plant foods and diet at late paleolithic Wadi Kubbaniya: the evidence from charred remains. In *The Prehistory of Wadi Kubbaniya, Vol. 2: Stratigraphy, Paleoeconomy and Environment*, Wendorf, F., R. Schild & A. E. Close (eds), 162–242. Dallas: Southern Methodist University Press.

Hindess, B. & P. Hirst 1975. *Precapitalist Modes of Production*. London: Routledge & Kegan Paul.

—— 1977. *Mode of Production and Social Function: an autocritique of precapitalist modes of production*. London: Macmillan.

Hirth, F. & W. W. Rockhill (eds) 1911. *Chau Ju-Kua: his work on the Chinese and Arab trade in the twelfth and thirteenth centuries, entitled 'Chu-fan-chi'*. St Petersburg: Publishing House of the Imperial Academy of Sciences.

Hitchcock, R. K. 1982. Patterns of sedentism among the Basarwa of eastern Botswana. In *Politics and History in Band Societies*, Leacock, E. & R. Lee, 223–67. Cambridge: Cambridge University Press.

Hitchcock, R. K. & J. I. Ebert 1984. Foraging and food production among Kalahari hunter/gatherers. In *From Hunters to Farmers: the causes and consequences of food production in Africa*, Clark, J. D. & S. A. Brandt (eds), 328–48. Berkeley: University of California Press.

Hobley, C. W. 1910. *Ethnology of the Akamba and Other East African Tribes*. London: Cass.

—— 1922. *Bantu Beliefs and Magic*. London: Witherby.

Hodder, I. 1978a. The contribution of the long term. In *Archaeology as Long-term History*, Hodder, I. (ed.), 1–8. Cambridge: Cambridge University Press.

—— 1978b. Simple correlations between material culture items with other aspects of society. In *Spatial Organization of Culture*, Hodder, I. (ed.), 3–24. London: Duckworth.

—— 1982. *Symbols in Action*. Cambridge: Cambridge University Press.

—— 1986. *Reading the Past*. Cambridge: Cambridge University Press.

—— (ed.) 1989. *The Meanings of Things: material culture and symbolic expression*. London: Unwin Hyman.

Hodder, I. & C. Orton 1976. *Spatial Analysis in Archaeology*. Cambridge: Cambridge University Press.

Hodgson, A. G. O. 1933. Notes on the Achewa and Ngoni of the Dowa District of Nyasaland Protectorate. *Journal of the Royal Anthropological Institute* 63, 123–64.

Hoffman, E. S. 1984. Dembeni phase botanical remains. *Azania* 19, 48–9.

Hoffman, M. 1986. A preliminary report on 1984 excavations at Hierakonpolis. *Newsletter of the American Research Center in Egypt* 132, 13–14.

Hoffman, M., H. Hamroush & R. Allen 1986. A model of urban development for the Hierakonpolis region from predynastic through Old Kingdom times. *Journal of the American*

Research Center in Egypt 23, 175–88.

Hoffmann, C. 1965. A word list of Central Kambari. *Journal of West African Languages* 2, 7–31.

Holl, A. 1983. La question de l'âge du fer ancien de l'Afrique occidentale: essai de méthode. Paper presented at the Colloque sur l'Histoire de la Métallurgie Africaine du Fer, Paris.

—— 1985. Subsistence patterns of the Dhar Tichitt Neolithic, Mauritania. *African Archaeological Review* 3, 151–62.

—— 1986. Neolithic communities of the Dhar Tichitt, Mauritania: socioeconomic organization and settlement dynamics. In 'The Longest Record: the human career in Africa', 47. Conference Abstracts, University of California, Berkeley.

—— 1987. Mound formation processes and societal transformation: a case study from the Perichadian plain. *Journal of Anthropological Archaeology* 6, 122–58.

—— 1988. *Houlouf I: archéologie des sociétés prohistoriques du bassin tchadien.* Oxford: British Archaeological Reports.

Holleman, J. F. 1952. *Shona Customary Law.* Cape Town: Oxford University Press.

—— 1953. *Accommodating the Spirit amongst some North-eastern Shona Tribes.* Cape Town: Oxford University Press.

Holmes, D. L. 1988. The predynastic lithic industries of Badari, Middle Egypt: new perspectives and inter-regional relations. *World Archaeology* 20, 71–86.

Hooghiemstra, H. & C. O. Agwu 1988. Changes in the vegetation and trade winds in equatorial northwest Africa 140,000–70,000 yr BP as deduced from two marine pollen records. *Palaeogeography, Palaeoclimatology, Palaeoecology* 66, 172–213.

Hopkins, A. G. 1973. *An Economic History of West Africa.* London: Longman.

Hopkins, K. 1978. Economic growth and towns in classical antiquity. In *Towns in Societies*, Abrams, P. & E. A. Wrigley (eds), 35–78. Cambridge: Cambridge University Press.

Hornell, J. 1946. *Water Transport: origins and early evolution.* Cambridge: Cambridge University Press.

Horton, M. 1984. The early settlement of the northern Swahili coast. Unpublished PhD thesis, University of Cambridge.

—— 1987a. Early Muslim trading settlements on the east African coast: new evidence from Shanga. *Antiquaries Journal* 67, 290–323.

—— 1987b. The Swahili corridor. *Scientific American* 257 (Sept.), 86–93.

—— Forthcoming. *Shanga: excavations at a trading settlement on the east African coast, 1980–88.* Nairobi: British Institute in Eastern Africa.

Horton, M. & H. Mutoro n.d. Tana ware: ceramic tradition on the east African coast. Ms, 1987.

Horton, R. n.d. Environment and people: some formative processes. Unpublished paper, University of Port Harcourt, 1985.

Horvath, R. J. 1969. The wandering capitals of Ethiopia. *Journal of African History* 10, 205–19.

Houlihan, P. F. 1986. *The Birds of Ancient Egypt.* Warminster: Aris & Phillips.

Howe, R. W. 1966. *Black Africa.* New York: Walker & Co.

Howell, F. C. & F. Bourlière (eds) 1963. *African Ecology and Human Evolution.* New York: Wenner Gren Foundation.

Hoyle, B. S. 1967. *The Seaports of East Africa.* Nairobi: East African Publishing House.

Hoyt, H. 1939. *The Structure and Growth of Residential Neighbourhoods in American Cities.* Washington: Federal Housing Administration.

Huard, P. 1960. Contribution à l'étude du cheval, du fer et du chameau au Sahara oriental. I: Le fer. *IFAN* (Bulletin de l'Institut Français d'Afrique Noire) 22, 136.

—— 1964. Nouvelle contribution à l'étude du fer au Sahara et au Tchad. *IFAN* (Bulletin de l'Institut Français d'Afrique Noire) 24, 297–397.

—— 1966. Introduction et diffusion du fer au Tchad. *Journal of African History* 7, 377–404.

Huffman, T. N. 1970. The early Iron Age and the spread of the Bantu. *South African Archaeological Bulletin* 25, 3–21.

—— 1971. A guide to the Iron Age of Mashonaland. *Occasional Papers of the National Museums of Rhodesia* 4, 20–44.

—— 1972. The rise and fall of Zimbabwe. *Journal of African History* 13, 353–66.

—— 1977. Zimbabwe: southern Africa's first town. *Rhodesian Prehistory* 7, 9–14.

—— 1979. Test excavations at Naba and Lanlory, northern Mashonaland. *South African Archaeological Bulletin* 27, 14–46.

—— 1980a. Ceramics, classification and iron age entities. *African Studies* 39, 123–74.

—— 1980b. Corrected radiocarbon date for the Iron Age of Rhodesia. In *The Shona and Zimbabwe 900–1850*, Beach, D. N. (ed.), 321–5. Gweru: Mambo Press.

—— 1981. Snakes and birds: expressive space at Great Zimbabwe. *African Studies* 40, 131–50.

—— 1982. Archaeology and ethnohistory of the African Iron Age. *Annual Review of Anthropology* 11, 133–50.

—— 1984. Expressive space in the Zimbabwe culture. *Man* 19, 593–612.

—— 1986a. Cognitive studies of the Iron Age in southern Africa. *World Archaeology* 18, 84–95.

—— 1986b. Iron age settlement patterns and the origin of class distinctions in southern Africa. In *Advances in World Archaeology 5*, Wendorf, F. & A. E. Close (eds), 291–338. New York: Academic Press.

—— 1988. Southern Africa to the south of the Zambezi. In *General History of Africa, III*, Frasi, M. L. & I. Hrbak (eds), 664–80. London: Heinemann/UNESCO.

—— 1989. *Iron Age Migrations: the ceramic sequence in southern Zambia*. Johannesburg: Witswatersrand University Press.

Huffman, T. N. & E. O. M. Hanisch 1987. Settlement hierarchies in the northern Transvaal: Zimbabwe ruins and Venda history. *African Studies* 46, 79–116.

Huffnagel, H. P. 1961. *Agriculture in Ethiopia*. Rome: Food and Agriculture Organization of UNESCO.

Hugot, H. J. (ed.) 1973. *Sixième Congrès Panafricain de Préhistoire, Dakar, 1967*. Chambéry: Les Imprimeries Réunies.

Hull, R. W. 1976. *African Cities and Towns before the European Conquest*. New York: Norton.

Hulstaert, G. 1962. L'extraction de l'huile chez les Mongo. *Aequatoria* 25, 41–2.

—— 1966. *Notes de botanique mongo*. Bruxelles: Académie Royale des Sciences d'Outre-Mer.

Hulthen, B. 1977. *On the Documentation of Pottery*. Lund: C. W. K. Gleeryp.

—— 1988. Report on a pilot investigation of ceramics from Mozambique and Zimbabwe. In *Analyses of Slag, Iron Ceramics and Animal Bones from Mozambique*, Sinclair, P. J. J., M. Tornblom, C. Bohm, B. Sigvalius & B. Hulthen (eds), 35–54. Stockholm: Eduardo Mondlane University & Central Board of National Antiquities, Sweden.

Huntingford, G. W. B. 1980. *The Periplus of the Erythraean Sea*. London: Hakluyt Society.

Hyman, L. M. 1970. *Essentials of Gwari Grammar*. Ibadan: Institute of African Studies.

Ibeanu, A. M. 1991. On the threshold of isolation: the dilemma of archaeological practice in Nigeria. *World Archaeological Bulletin* 5, 66–72.

Ibn Fartua, A. 1926. *History of the First Twelve Years of the Reign of Mai Idris Alooma of Bornu (1571–1583)*, trans. H. R. Palmer. Lagos: Government Printer.

Ibn Khaldun, T. 1947. *The Muqaddimah*. Princeton: Princeton University Press.

Ibrahim-Arirabiyi, F. 1989. A comparative reconstruction of Akpes lects: Akoko North, Ondo State. Unpublished MA thesis, University of Port Harcourt.

Ikoro, S. M. 1989. Segmental phonology and lexicon of Proto-Keggoid. Unpublished MA thesis, University of Port Harcourt.

ILCA 1979. *Trypanotolerant Livestock in West and Central Africa*. 2 vols. Addis Ababa: International Livestock Centre for Africa.

Ingold, T. 1980. *Hunters, Pastoralists and Ranchers: reindeer economies and their transformations*. Cambridge: Cambridge University Press.

Inskeep, R. R. 1965. *Preliminary Investigation of a Proto-historic Cemetery at Nkudzi Bay, Malawi*. Livingstone: The National Museums of Zambia.

—— 1969. The archaeological background. In *The Oxford History of South Africa*, Wilson, M. & L. Thompson (eds), 1–49. Oxford: Clarendon Press.

Irstam, T. 1944. *The King of Ganda*. Stockholm: Ethnographic Museum.

Irvine, F. R. 1961. *Woody Plants of Ghana: with special reference to their uses*. London: Oxford University Press.

Isichei, E. 1977. *Igbo Worlds*. London: Macmillan.

—— (ed.) 1982a. *Studies in the History of Plateau State, Nigeria*. London: Macmillan.

—— 1982b. Introduction. In *Studies in the History of Plateau State, Nigeria*, Isichei, E. (ed.), 1–57. London: Macmillan.

Issawi, B. 1976. An introduction to the physiography of the Nile valley. In *Prehistory of the Nile Valley*, Wendorf, F. & R. Schild (eds), 3–22. New York: Academic Press.

Izard, M. 1983. Le royaume Yatenga et ses forgerons: une recherche d'histoire du peuplement (Haute-Volta). In *Métallurgies africaines: nouvelles contributions*, Echard, N. (ed.), 253–79. Paris: Société des Africanistes.

Jacobs, A. H. 1965. The traditional political organization of the pastoral Masai. Unpublished DPhil thesis, Oxford University.

Jacobsen, T. 1976. *The Treasures of Darkness*. New Haven: Yale University Press.

Jacobson, L. 1980. The White Lady of the Brandberg: a reinterpretation. *Namibiana* 2, 21–30.

Jakel, D. 1977. Runoff and fluvial formation processes in the Tibesti mountains as indicators of climatic history in the central Sahara during the late Pleistocene and Holocene. *Palaeoecology of Africa* 10/11, 13–44.

Janssen, J. 1975. Prolegomena to the study of Egypt's economic history during the New Kingdom. *Studien zur Altägyptischen Kultur* 3, 127–85.

—— 1981. Die Struktur der pharaonischen Wirtschaft. *Göttinger Miszellen* 48, 59–77.

—— 1983. El-Amarna as a residential city. *Bibliotheca Orientalis* 40, 273–88.

Jasny, N. 1944. *The Wheats of Classical Antiquity*. Baltimore: Johns Hopkins University Press.

Jeffreys, D. 1985. *The Survey of Memphis I*. London: Egypt Exploration Society.

Jeffreys, D. & J. Malek. 1988. Memphis 1986, 1987. *Journal of Egyptian Archaeology* 74, 15–29.

Jeffreys, D., J. Malek, & H. S. Smith 1986. Memphis 1984. *Journal of Egyptian Archaeology* 72, 1–14.

Jeffreys, M. D. W. 1947. Notes on twins, Bamenda. *African Studies* 6, 189–95.

—— 1948. Stone age smiths, Fungom tribe, Bamenda. *Archive für Völkerkunde* 3, 1–9.

—— 1952. Some notes on the Bikom blacksmiths. *Man* 75, 49–51.

—— 1961. Oku blacksmiths. *Nigerian Field* 26, 137–44.

—— 1962. Some notes on the Kwaja smiths of Bamenda. *Man* 47, 152–3.

—— n.d.a. Unpublished 1942 report on the local iron industry, Bamenda Division. Bamenda Provincial Archives, Cameroon.

—— n.d.b. Unpublished 1942 addenda to B. 2142/64 of 12th Feb. 1942. Bamenda Provincial Archives, Cameroon.

Jelinek, J. 1985. Tilizahren, the key site of Fezzanese rock art. *L'Anthropologie* 23, 125–65, 223–75.

Jemkur, J. F. 1989. Traditional iron smelting methods by the Berom of Plateau State, Nigeria. *Nyame Akuma* 32, 21–4.

Jemma, D. 1971. *Les Tanneurs de Marrakesh*. Alger: Centre de Recherches Anthropologiques, Préhistoriques et Ethnographiques.

Jenewari, C. E. W. 1983. *Defaka: Ijo's closest linguistic relative*. Port Harcourt: University of Port Harcourt Press.

Jochmann, H. 1910. Die Buschmannzeichnungen in Deutsch-Sudwestafrika. *Die Woche* 3.

Johnson, G. A. 1977. Regional analysis in archaeology. *Annual Review of Anthropology* 6, 479–508.

Johnson, M. 1977. Census, map and guess-estimate: the past population of the Accra region. In *African Historical Demography, Vol. 1*, Fyfe, C. & D. McMaster (eds), 272–94. Edinburgh: University of Edinburgh Centre of African Studies.

Johnson, M. H. 1989. Conceptions of agency in archaeological interpretation. *Journal of Anthropological Archaeology* 8, 189–211.

Johnston, H. H. 1913. A survey of the ethnography of Africa and the former racial and tribal migrations in that continent. *Journal of the Royal Anthropological Institute* 43, 375–421.

Jones, C. E. R. 1989. Archaeochemistry: fact or fancy? In *The Prehistory of Wadi Kubbaniya, Vol. 2: Stratigraphy, Paleoeconomy, and Environment*, Wendorf, F., R. Schild & A. E. Close (eds), 260–6. Dallas: Southern Methodist University Press.

Jones, E. 1968. *Towns and Cities*. New York: Oxford University Press.

Jones, G. I. n.d. Tribal distribution in southern Nigeria. Ms.

Jones, R. & B. Meehan 1989. Plant foods of the Gidjingali: ethnographic and archaeological perspectives from northern Australia on tuber and seed exploitation. In *Foraging and Farming: the evolution of plant exploitation*, Harris, D. R. & G. C. Hillman (eds), 120–35. London: Unwin Hyman.

Joussaume, R. 1981. L'art rupestre de l'Ethiopie. In *Préhistoire africaine*, Roubet, C., H.-J. Hugot & G. Souville (eds), 159–75. Paris: Editions APDF.

Jungraithmayr, H. & K. Shimizu 1981. *Chadic Lexical Roots*. Berlin: Reimer.

Junker, H. 1928. Bericht uber die von der Akademie der Wissenschaften in Wien nach dem Westdelta Entsendete Expedition. *Denkschrift Akademie Wissenschaft Philosophische-Historische Klasse* 28, 14–24.

—— 1929. Vorbericht über die Grabungen auf der neolithischen Siedlung von Merimde-Benisalame. *Anzeiger der Akademie der Wissenschaften in Wien, Philosophisch-Historische Klasse* 66, 156–250.

—— 1930. Vorbericht über die Grabungen auf der neolithischen Siedlung von Merimde-Benisalame. *Anzeiger der Akademie der Wissenschaften in Wien, Philosophisch-Historische Klasse* 67, 21–83.

—— 1932. Vorbericht über die Grabungen auf der neolithischen Siedlung von Merimde-Benisalame 1931/32. *Anzeiger der Akademie der Wissenschaften in Wien, Philosophisch-Historische Klasse* 69, 36–82.

—— 1933. Vorlaufiger Bericht über die Grabungen auf der neolithischen Siedlung von Merimde-Benisalame 1933. *Anzeiger der Akademie der Wissenschaften in Wien, Philosophisch-Historische Klasse* 70, 54–82.

—— 1934. Vorbericht über die funfte von der Akademie der Wissenschaften in Wien und dem Egyptiska Museet in Stockholm unternommene Grabung auf der neolithischen Siedlung Merimde-Benisalame vom 13. Februar bis 26. Marz 1934. *Anzeiger der Akademie der Wissenschaften in Wien, Philosophisch-Historische Klasse* 71, 118–32.

—— 1940. Vorbericht über die siebente Grabung der Akademie der Wissenschaften in Wien auf der vorgeschichtlichen Siedlung Merimde-Benisalame vom 25. Januar bis 4. bis April 1939. *Anzeiger der Akademie der Wissenschaften in Wien, Philosophisch-Historische Klasse* 77, 1–17.

Junod, H. A. 1912–13. *The Life of a South African Tribe (The Thonga)*. London: David Nutt.

Juwayeyi, Y. M. 1981. The later prehistory of southern Malawi: a contribution to the study of technology and economy during the later stone age and iron age periods. Unpublished PhD thesis, University of California, Berkeley.

Kadomura, H. & N. Hori 1990. Environmental implications of slope deposits in humid tropical Africa: evidence from southern Cameroon and western Kenya. *Geographical Report (Tokyo Metropolitan University)* 25, 213–36.

Kaiser, T. & B. Voytek 1983. Sedentism and economic change in the Balkan Neolithic. *Journal of Anthropological Archaeology* 2, 323–53.

Kaiser, W. 1982. Stadt und Tempel von Elephantine. Neunter/Zehnter Grabungsbericht. *Mitteilungen der Deutschen Archäologischen Institut, Abteilung Kairo* 38, 271–345.

—— 1987. Stadt und Tempel von Elephantine. 13/14 Grabungsbericht. *Mitteilungen der Deutschen Archäologischen Institut, Abteilung Kairo* 43, 75–114.

Kaiser, W., P. Grossmann, G. Haeny & H. Jaritz 1970. Stadt und Tempel von Elephantine. Erster Grabungsbericht. *Mitteilungen des deutschen archäologischen Institut, Abteilung Kairo* 26, 87–139.

Kajale, M. D. 1988. Ancient plant economy at chalcolithic Juljapur Garhi, district Amraoti, Maharashtra. *Current Science* 57, 377–9.

Kammerer, A. 1926. *Essai sur l'histoire antique d'Abyssinie.* Paris: Librairie Orientaliste Paul Geuthner.

Kaplony, P. 1969. Bermerkungen zu funf Texten der ersten Zwischenzeit und der späteren 11. Dynastie. *Mitteilungen des Deutschen Archäologischen Institut, Abteilung Kairo* 25, 22–32.

Kauffman, B. 1981. The maximal covering location problem as a simulation of decision making in Ramessid Egypt. Unpublished MA thesis, University of Chicago.

Kaufman, E. M. 1985. *Ibibio Dictionary.* Leiden: Cross River State University, Ibibio Language Board, Nigeria & African Studies Centre, Leiden.

Kea, R. A. 1982. *Settlement, Trade and Polities in the 17th Century Gold Coast.* Baltimore: Johns Hopkins University Press.

Kees, H. 1961. *Ancient Egypt, a Cultural Topography,* London: Faber & Faber.

Kemp, B. 1972a. Fortified towns in Nubia. In *Man, Settlement and Urbanism,* Ucko, P. J., R. Tringham & G. W. Dimbleby (eds), 651–6. London: Duckworth.

—— 1972b. Temple and town in ancient Egypt. In *Man, Settlement and Urbanism,* Ucko, P. J., R. Tringham & G. W. Dimbleby (eds), 657–80. London: Duckworth.

—— 1972c. Abydos. In *Lexikon der Ägyptologie, I,* Helck, W. & E. Otto (eds), 28–41. Wiesbaden: Otto Harrasowitz.

—— 1976. The window of appearance at el-Amarna, and the basic structure of this city. *Journal of Egyptian Archaeology* 62, 81–99.

—— 1977a. The early development of towns in Egypt. *Antiquity* 51, 185–200.

—— 1977b. The city of el-Amarna as a source for the study of urban society in ancient Egypt. *World Archaeology* 9, 123–39.

—— 1981. The character of the south suburb at Tell el 'Amarna. *Mitteilungen der Deutschen Orient-gesellschaft zu Berlin* 113, 81–97.

—— 1984. In the shadow of texts: archaeology in Egypt. *Archaeological Review for Cambridge* 3, 20–7.

—— 1984–7. *Amarna Reports: I, II, III, IV.* London: Egypt Exploration Society.

—— 1985. Tell el-Amarna. In *Lexikon der Ägyptologie, VI,* Helck, W. & W. Westendorf (eds), 309–19. Wiesbaden: Otto Harrasowitz.

—— 1989. *Ancient Egypt: anatomy of a civilization.* London: Routledge.

Kendall, R. L. 1969. An ecological history of the Lake Victoria basin. *Ecological Monographs* 39, 121–76.

Kense, F. J. 1979. Daboya: report on the 1979 season. *Nyame Akuma* 15, 20–2.

—— 1980. The Kintampo and Daboya: a preliminary note. *Nyame Akuma* 17, 38–9.

—— 1983a. *Daboya project update: more dates and evidence for a 'Kintampoid' culture.* Nyame Akuma 22, 10–11.

—— 1983b. 1983 field report on Daboya, Ghana. *Nyame Akuma* 23, 8–10.

—— 1983c. *Traditional African Iron-working.* Calgary: University of Calgary.

—— 1985a. The initial diffusion of iron to Africa. In *African Iron Working: ancient and traditional,* Haaland, R. & P. L. Shinnie (eds), 11–27. Oslo: Norwegian University Press.

—— 1985b. Western Gonja Archaeology Project: preliminary report. *Nyame Akuma* 26, 18–20.

—— In Press. Settlement and livelihood in Mampurugu, northern Ghana: the archaeological evidence. In *Papers in Honour of P. L. Shinnie,* Sterner, J. & N. David (eds). Calgary: University of Calgary Press.

Kenyatta, J. 1938. *Facing Mount Kenya.* London: Secker & Warburg.

Kenyon, K. 1957. *Digging Up Jericho.* London: Ernest Benn.

Keteku, E. n.d. The Iron Age in Ghana. MA project, University of Calgary, 1987.

Khan, M. 1988. The prehistoric rock art of northern Saudi Arabia: a synthetic approach to the study of the rock art from Wadi Damm, northwest of Tabuk. Unpublished PhD thesis, University of Southampton.

Killick, D. J. 1987. On the dating of African metallurgical sites. *Nyame Akuma* 30, 39–41.

Killick, D. J., N. van der Merwe, R. B. Gordon & D. Grébénart 1988. Reassessment of the evidence for early metallurgy in Niger, west Africa. *Journal of Archaeological Sciences* 15, 367–94.

Kimble, D. 1963. *Political History of Ghana.* Oxford: Oxford University Press.

Kimes, T., C. Haselgrove & I. Hodder 1982. A method of the identification of the location of regional cultural boundaries. *Journal of Anthropological Archaeology* 1, 113–31.

Kinahan, J. 1984. The stratigraphy and lithic assemblages of Falls rock shelter, western Damaraland, Namibia. *Cimbebasia* 4, 13–27.

—— 1986. The archaeological structure of pastoral production in the central Namib desert. In *Prehistoric Pastoralism in Southern Africa,* Hall, M. & A. B. Smith (eds), 69–82. Vlaeburg: South African Archaeological Society.

—— 1990. Four thousand years at the Spitzkoppe: changes in human settlement and landuse on the edge of the Namib desert. *Cimbebasia* 12, 1–14.

—— 1990. The impenetrable shield: HMS *Nautilus* and the Namib coast in the late 18th century. *Cimbebasia* 12, 23–62.

Kinahan, J. & J. C. Vogel 1982. Recent copper-working sites in the !Khuiseb drainage, Namibia. *South African Archaeological Bulletin* 37, 44–5.

Kingdon, J. 1982. *East African Mammals: an atlas of evolution in Africa, Vol. 3, Part D (Bovids).* London: Academic Press.

Kiriama, H. O. 1986. Prehistoric iron smelting technology in east Africa. Unpublished MPhil thesis, University of Cambridge.

—— 1987. Archeo-metallurgy of iron smelting slags from a Mwitu tradition site in Kenya. *South African Archaeological Bulletin* 42, 125–30.

—— n.d. The social context of iron use in Bantu Africa. To be submitted to *Utafiti.*

—— In Press. The archaeology and early history of Kisii district, Kenya. *Utafiti* 2 (Occasional papers of National Museums of Kenya).

Kirkman, J. S. 1954. *The Arab City of Gedi: excavations at the Great Mosque. Architecture and finds.* London: Oxford University Press.

—— 1957. Historical archaeology in Kenya: 1948–1956. *African Journal* 37, 16–18.

—— 1959. Excavations at Ras Mkumbuu on the island of Pemba. *Tanzania Notes and Records* 53, 161–78.

—— 1964. *Men and Monuments on the East African Coast.* London: Butterworth Press.

—— 1966. *Ungwana on the Tana*. The Hague: Mouton.

Kislev, M. E. 1989. Pre-domesticated cereals in the Pre-Pottery Neolithic A period. In *People and Culture in Change: proceedings of the Second Symposium on Upper Palaeolithic, Mesolithic and Neolithic Populations of Europe and the Mediterranean Basin*, 147–51. Oxford: British Archaeological Reports.

Kitchen, K. A. 1969–90. *Ramesside Inscriptions, I–VIII*. Oxford: Blackwell.

—— 1971. Punt and how to get there. *Orientalia* 40, 184–207.

—— 1977. Historical observations on Ramesside Nubia. In *Ägypten und Kusch*, Endesfelder, E., K.-H. Priese, W. F. Reineke & S. Wenig (eds), 213–25. Berlin: Akademie-Verlag.

—— 1986. *The Third Intermediate Period in Egypt (1100–650 BC)*. Warminster: Aris & Phillips.

—— 1989. Supplementary notes on 'The basics of Egyptian chronology'. In *High, Middle or Low?*, Astrom, P. (ed.), 152–9. Gothenburg: Paul Astroms Forlag.

Kiyaga-Mulindwa, D. 1983. Moeng I: a Tswapong early iron age site in central Botswana. Paper presented to the 9th Pan-African Congress for Prehistory and Related Studies, Jos, Nigeria.

Kjekshus, H. 1977. *Ecology Control and Economic Development in East African History*. London: Heinemann.

Klapwijk, M. A. 1974. A preliminary report on pottery from the north eastern Transvaal. *South African Archaeological Bulletin* 29, 19–23.

Klein, R. G. 1984. The prehistory of stone age herders in South Africa. In *From Hunters to Farmers: the causes and consequences of food production in Africa*, Clark, J. D. & S. A. Brandt (eds), pp. 281–90. Berkeley: University of California Press.

—— 1986. The prehistory of stone age herders in the Cape Province of South Africa. In *Prehistoric Pastoralism in Southern Africa*, Hall, M. & A. B. Smith (eds), 5–12. Vlaeberg: South African Archaeological Society.

Klein, R. G. & K. Scott 1986. Re-analysis of faunal assemblages from the Haua Fteah and other late quaternary archaeological sites in Cyrenaican Libya. *Journal of Archaeological Science* 13, 515–42.

Kleinmann, D. 1975. Salt springs in the Salle valley. In *Salt: the study of an ancient industry*, de Brisay, K. W. & K. A. Evans (eds), 45–6. Colchester: Colchester Archaeological Group.

Klejn, L. S. 1973. Marxism: the systemic approach, and archaeology. In *The Explanation of Culture Change: models in prehistory*, Renfrew, C. (ed.), 691–710. London: Duckworth.

Klusemann, K. 1924. Die Entwicklung der Eisengewinnung in Afrika und Europa. *Mitteilungen der Anthropologische Gesellschaft in Wien* 54, 120–40.

Knudstad, J. n.d. The early mosques at Sima and Domoni. *Azania*.

Kobishchanov, Y. 1979. *Aksum*. University Park: Pennsylvania State University Press.

Koelle, S. W. 1854a. *Polyglotta Africana*. London: Church Missionary Society.

—— 1854b. *African Native Literature*. London: Church Missionary Society.

Köhler, O. 1953/4. Das 'Pferd' in den Gur-Sprachen. *Afrika und Übersee* 38, 93–110.

Köhler-Rollefson, I. 1988. The introduction of the camel into Africa with special reference to Somalia. *Working Paper No. 24*. Somali Academy of Sciences and Arts.

Kolb, F. 1984. *Die Stadt im Altertum*. Munich: Beck.

Kone, K. 1948. Le boeuf du lac Tchad de la région de N'Guigmi. *Bulletin de la Service d'Elevage Indigène des Animaux d'Afrique Occidental Française* 1, 47–65.

Kopotoff, I. (ed.) 1987. *The African Frontier*. Bloomington: Indiana University Press.

Kozlowski, J. K. & B. Ginter 1989. The Fayum Neolithic in the light of new discoveries. In *Late Prehistory of the Nile Basin and the Sahara*, Krzyzaniak, L. & M. Kobusiewicz (eds), 157–79. Poznan: Polish Academy of Sciences & Poznan Archaeological Museum.

Kramer, C. 1982. *Village Ethnoarchaeology: rural Iran in archaeological perspective*. New York: Academic Press.

Kromer, B., M. Rhein, H. Bruns, H. Schoch-Fischer, K. O. Münnich, M. Stuiver and B. Becker 1986. Radiocarbon calibration data for the 6th to the 8th millennia BC. *Radiocarbon* 28, 954–60.

Kropelin, S. 1987. Paleoclimatic evidence from early to mid-holocene playas in the Gilf Kebir (south west Egypt). *Palaeoecology of Africa* 18, 189–208.

Kropp-Dakubu, M. E. 1976. On the linguistic geography of the area of ancient Begho. In *Languages of the Akan Area*, Trutenau, H. (ed.), 63–91. Basel: Communications from the Basel Africa Bibliography.

Krzyzaniak, L. 1991. Early farming in the middle Nile basin: recent discoveries at Kadero (Central Sudan). *Antiquity* 65, 515–32.

Krzyzaniak, L. & M. Kobusiewicz (eds) 1984. *Origin and Early Development of Food-producing Cultures in North-eastern Africa*. Poznan: Polish Academy of Sciences and Poznan Archaeological Museum.

Kumm, K. 1910. *From Hausaland to Egypt, through the Sudan*. London: Constable.

Kuper, A. 1980. Symbolic dimensions of southern Bantu homesteads. *Africa* 50, 8–23.

—— 1982. *Wives for Cattle: bridewealth and marriage in southern Africa*. London: Routledge & Kegan Paul.

Kuper, A. & P. Van Leynselle 1978. Social anthropology and the Bantu expansion. *Africa* 48, 335–52.

Kuper, H. 1954. *The Shona Ndebele of Southern Rhodesia*. London: International African Institute.

Kuperus, J. 1985. *The Londo Word: its phonological and morphological structure*. Tervuren: Koninklijk Museum voor Midden-Afrika.

Kurashina, H. 1973. Investigations along the Nanyangu. In *Occasional Papers, 14*, 71–89. Zomba: Department of Antiquities.

Kus, S. M. & H. T. Wright 1976. Notes préliminaires sur une reconnaissance archéologique de l'île de Mayotte. *Asie du Sud-est et le Monde Indul-indien* 7, 123–35.

Küsel, U. S. n.d. *Primitive Iron Smelting in the Transvaal*. Study No. 3. Pretoria: National Cultural History and Open Air Museum.

Kutzbach, J. E. 1980. Estimates of past climate at Palaeolake Chad, north Africa, based on a hydrological and energy-balance model. *Quaternary Research* 14, 210–23.

Kutzbach, J. E. & F. A. Street-Perrott 1985. Milankovitch forcing of fluctuations in the level of tropical lakes from 18 to 0 kyr BP. *Nature* 317, 130–4.

Lacovara, P. 1990. *Deir El-Ballas: preliminary report on the Deir El-Ballas Expedition, 1980–1986*. Indiana: Eisenbrauns.

Laird, M. & R. A. K. Oldfield 1937. *Narrative of an Expedition into the Interior of Africa by the River Niger*. 2 vols. London: Bentley.

Lal, B. 1967. Indian Archaeological Expedition to Nubia, 1962: a preliminary report. In *Fouilles en Nubie, Vol. 2 (1961–1963)*, 104–9. Cairo: Organisme Général des Imprimeries Gouvernementales.

Lal, M. 1984. *Archaeology of Population*. Varanasi: Banaras Hindu University.

Lambert, N. 1983. Nouvelle contribution à l'étude du chalcolithique de Mauritanie. In *Métallurgies africaines: nouvelles contributions*, Echard, N. (ed.), 63–87. Paris: Société des Africanistes.

Lamprey, R. H. 1984. Maasai impact on Kenya savanna vegetation: a remote sensing approach. Unpublished PhD thesis, University of Aston in Birmingham.

Lamprey, R. H. & R. Waller 1990. The Loita-Mara region in historic times: patterns of subsistence, settlement and ecological change. In *Early Pastoralists of South-western Kenya*, Robertshaw, P. T. (ed.), 16–35. Nairobi: British Institute in Eastern Africa.

Lancaster, I. N. 1979. *Quaternary Environments in the Arid Zone of Southern Africa*. Johannesburg: University of the Witwatersrand.

—— 1987. Formation and reactivation of dunes in the south-western Kalahari: palaeoclimatic implications. *Palaeoclimatology of Africa* 18, 103–10.

Lancel, S. 1978. Fouilles de Carthage 1976–77: la colline de Byrsa et l'occupation punique. *Comptes Rendus de l'Académie des Inscriptions et Belles Lettres*, 300–31.

Lander, R. 1830. *Records of Captain Clapperton's Last Expedition to Africa*. London: Colburn, Bentley.

Lane, D. A. 1962. The forest vegetation. In *Agriculture and Land Use in Ghana*, Wills, J. B. (ed.), 160–9. London: Oxford University Press.

Lanfranchi, R. & D. Schwartz 1990. Evolution des paysages de la Sangha (R. P. du Congo) au Pleistocène supérieur. Bilan des observations archéologiques, géomorphologiques, pédologiques et paléobiologiques. In *Paysages quaternaires de l'Afrique Centrale Atlantique*, Lanfranchi, R. & D. Schwartz (eds), 248–59. Paris: ORSTOM (Institut Français de Recherche Scientifique pour le Développement en Coopération).

Langdon, J. & P. Robertshaw 1985. Petrographic and physico-chemical studies of early pottery from south-western Kenya. *Azania* 20, 1–28.

Lanning, E. C. 1954. Genital symbols on smiths' bellows in Uganda. *Man* 54, 167–9.

Lapidus, I. M. (ed.) 1966. *Middle Eastern Cities*. Berkeley: University of California Press.

Last, J. T. 1883. A visit to the Wa-Itumba iron-workers and the Mangaheri, near Mamboia, in east-central Africa. *Proceedings of the Royal Geographical Society* 5, 581–92.

Law, R. 1976. Horses, firearms and political power in pre-colonial west Africa. *Past and Present* 72, 112–32.

—— 1977a. *The Oyo Empire c. 1600 – c. 1836*. Oxford: Oxford University Press.

—— 1977b. Towards a history of urbanization in pre-colonial Yorubaland. In *African Historical Demography, Vol. 1*, Fyfe, C. & D. McMaster (eds), 260–71. Edinburgh: University of Edinburgh Centre of African Studies.

—— 1980. *The Horse in West African History*. Oxford: Oxford University Press.

Lawrence, D. & S. Low 1990. The built environment and spatial form. *Annual Review of Anthropology* 19, 466–76.

Le Quellec, J. L. 1985. Les gravures rupestres du Fezzan (Libya). *L'Anthropologie* 89, 365–83.

Le Strange, G. 1924. *Baghdad during the Abbasid Caliphate from Contemporary and Arabic and Persian Sources*. Oxford: Clarendon Press.

Le Tourneau, R. 1961. *Fez in the Age of the Marinides*. Norman: Oklahoma University Press.

Leach, E. 1976. *Culture and Communication*. Cambridge: Cambridge University Press.

Leakey, L. S. B. 1936. *Stone Age Africa*. London: Oxford University Press.

—— 1977. *The Southern Kikuyu before 1903*. 3 vols. London: Academic Press.

Leakey, M. D. 1943. Notes on the ground and polished stone axes of east Africa. *Journal of the East Africa and Uganda Natural History Society* 17, 182–95.

—— 1945. Report on the excavations at Hyrax Hill, Nakuru, Kenya Colony, 1937–38. *Transactions of the Royal Society of South Africa* 30, 271–408.

Lebeuf, A. M. D. & A. Holl 1985. Fouilles archéologiques de Houlouf (Nord-Cameroun). *Nyame Akuma* 26, 5–7.

Lebeuf, A. M. D., J.-P. Lebeuf, Fr. Treinen-Claustre & J. Courtin 1980. *Le Gisement sao de Mdaga (Tchad): fouilles 1960–1968*. Paris: Société d'Ethnographie.

Lebeuf, J.-P. 1969. *Carte archéologique des abords du lac Tchad*. Paris: CNRS (Centre National de la Recherche Scientifique).

—— 1980. *Travaux archéologiques dans les basses vallées du Chari et du Logone 1936–1980*. Paris: Académie des Inscriptions et Belles-Lettres.

—— 1981. *Carte archéologique des abords du lac Tchad, Supplément*. Paris: CNRS (Centre National de la Recherche Scientifique).

Lebeuf, J.-P. & M. Griaule 1947. Fouilles archéologiques dans la région du Tchad. *Journal de la*

Société des Africanistes 18, 1–116.

Lechaptois, M. 1913. *Aux rives du Tanganyika*. Algiers: Maison-Carée.

Leclant, J. 1956. Le fer à travers les âges. *Annales de l'Est* 16, 83–91.

—— 1978. L'exploration des côtes de la Mer Rouge. A la quête de Pount et des secrets de la Mer Erythrée. *Annales d'Ethiopie* 11, 69–73.

—— 1980. Fouilles et travaux en Egypte et au Soudan, 1978–1979. *Orientalia* 49, 346–420.

Leclant, J. & G. Clerk 1988. Fouilles et travaux en Egypte et au Soudan, 1986–1987. *Orientalia* 57, 307–404.

Lee, R. B. 1979. *The !Kung San: men, women and work in a foraging society*. Cambridge: Cambridge University Press.

Lefébure, C. 1979. Introduction: the specificity of nomadic pastoral societies. In *Pastoral Production and Society*, L'Equipe écologie et anthropologie des sociétés pastorales (ed.), 1–14. Cambridge: Cambridge University Press.

Leo Africanus, J. 1956. *Description de l'Afrique*. Trans. A. Epaulard. Paris: A. Maisonneuve.

—— 1969. *A Geographical Historie of Africa*. New York: Da Capo Press.

Letouzey, R. 1968. *Etude phytogéographique du Cameroun*. Paris: Lechevalier.

—— 1985. *Notice de la carte phytogéographique du Cameroun au 1:500,000*. Toulouse & Yaounde: Institut de Recherches Agronomiques.

Lévi-Strauss, C. 1958. *Anthropologie structurale*. Paris: Plon.

—— 1966. *The Savage Mind*. London: Weidenfeld & Nicolson.

—— 1970. *The Raw and the Cooked: introduction to a science of mythology I*. London: Jonathan Cape.

Levtzion, N. 1973. *Ancient Ghana and Mali*. London: Methuen.

Levtzion, N. & J. F. P. Hopkins 1981. *Corpus of Early Arabic Sources for West African History*. Cambridge: Cambridge University Press.

Lewicki, T. 1974. *West African Food in the Middle Ages*. Cambridge: Cambridge University Press.

Lewis, B. 1974. *Islam: from the Prophet Mohammed to the Capture of Constantinople, Vol. 2*. London: Macmillan.

Lewis, C. A. 1988. Periglacial features in southern Africa: a review, 1987. *Palaeoecology of Africa* 19, 357–70.

Lewis, N. 1983. *Life in Egypt under Roman Rule*. Oxford: Clarendon Press.

Lewis-Williams, J. D. 1981. *Believing and Seeing: symbolic meanings in southern San rock art*. London: Academic Press.

—— 1982. The economic and social context of southern San rock art. *Current Anthropology* 23, 429–49.

—— 1984. Ideological continuities in prehistoric southern Africa: the evidence of rock art. In *Past and Present in Hunter-gatherer Studies*, Schrire, C. (ed.), 225–52. Orlando: Academic Press.

Lezine, A. 1968. Tripoli: notes archéologiques. *Libya Antiqua* 5, 55–67.

Lezine, A.-M. 1989. Late quaternary vegetation and climate of the Sahel. *Quaternary Research* 40, 317–34.

Lezine, A.-M. & J. Casanova 1989. Pollen and hydrological evidence for the interpretation of past climates in tropical west Africa during the Holocene. *Quaternary Science Reviews* 8, 45–55.

Lhote, H. 1952. La connaissance du fer en Afrique occidentale. *Encyclopédie Mensuelle d'Outre-Mer*, 269–72.

—— 1959. *The Search for the Tassili Frescoes: the rock paintings of the Sahara*. London: Hutchinson.

—— 1984. Chronologie de l'art rupestre nord-africain et saharien. *L'Anthropologie* 88, 649–54.

Lichtheim, M. 1988. *Ancient Egyptian Autobiographies, Chiefly of the Middle Kingdom: a study and anthology*. Gottingen: Vandenhoeck & Ruprecht.

Liesegang, G. 1975. Archaeological sites on the Bay of Sofala. *Azania* 7, 147–59.

Lima, A. 1967. Le fer en Angola. *Cahiers d'Etudes Africaines* 17, 345–51.

Linares de Sapir, O. 1971. Shell middens of lower Casamance and problems of Diola protohistory. *West African Journal of Archaeology* 1, 23–54.

—— 1976. 'Garden hunting' in the American tropics. *Human Ecology* 4, 331–49.

—— 1981. Diola wet rice cultivation. *Africa* 51, 557–95.

Lindblom, G. 1920. *The Akamba in British East Africa*. Uppsala: Appelbergs.

Lindquist, P. I. 1984. *Archaeology in Mozambique*. Stockholm: Swedish Central Board of National Antiquities.

Lineham, S. 1972. Climate, wind and weather. In *Malawi in Maps*, Agnew, S. & M. Stubbs (eds), 26–7. London: University of London Press.

Littmann, E. 1913. *Deutsche Aksum-Expedition*. Berlin: Reimer.

Littmann, E., D. Krencker & T. von Lupke 1913a. *Vorbericht der deutschen Aksum Expedition, Vol. 2*. Berlin: Reimer.

—— 1913b. *Vorbericht der deutschen Aksum Expedition, Vol. 4*. Berlin: Reimer.

Livingstone, D. A. 1967. Postglacial vegetation of the Ruwenzori mountains in equatorial Africa. *Ecological Monographs* 37, 25–52.

—— 1971. A 22,000-year pollen record from the plateau of Zambia. *Limnology and Oceanography* 16, 349–56.

—— 1975. Late quaternary climatic change in Africa. *Annual Review of Ecology and Systematics* 6, 249–80.

—— 1984. Interaction of food production and changing vegetation in Africa. In *From Hunters to Farmers: the causes and consequences in food production in Africa*, Clark, J. D. & S. A. Brandt (eds), 22–5. Berkeley: University of California Press.

Livingstone, D. A. & W. D. Clayton 1980. An altitudinal cline in tropical African grass floras and its palaeoecological significance. *Quaternary Research* 13, 392–402.

Livingstone, D. L. & C. Livingstone 1865. *Narrative of an Expedition to the Zambezi and its Tributaries*. London: John Murray.

Lloyd, A. B. 1975. Once more Hammamat inscription 191. *Journal of Egyptian Archaeology* 61, 54–66.

Lobel, M. D. (ed.) 1969. *Historic Towns: maps and plans of towns and cities in the British Isles*. Oxford: Lovell Johns Ltd.

—— (ed.) 1974. *Historic Towns, Vol. 2: Cambridge*. London: Scholar Press.

Locko, M. 1987. Les sources archéologiques de la métallurgie du fer au Gabon. *Nyame Akuma* 29, 23–6.

Lombard, M. 1971. *L'Islam dans sa première grandeur (VIIIe–IXe siècle)*. Paris: Flamarion.

Lonsdale, J. 1981. States and social processes in Africa: a historiographic survey. *African Studies Review* 24, 139–225.

Lothaire, H.-J. 1907. Notes sur le régime économique. In *Les Bangala (Etat Ind. du Congo)*, Van Overbergh, C. (ed.), 364. Bruxelles: De Wit & Institut International de Bibliographie.

Lubell, D., P. Sheppard & M. Jackes 1984. Continuity in the Epipalaeolithic of north Africa with special emphasis on the Maghreb. In *Advances in World Archaeology 3*, Wendorf, F. & A. E. Close (eds), 143–91. New York: Academic Press.

Lwanga-Lunyiigo 1976. The Bantu problem reconsidered. *Current Anthropology* 17, 282–6.

Mabogunje, A. L. 1962. *Yoruba Towns*. Ibadan: Ibadan University Press.

—— 1968. *Urbanization in Nigeria*. London: University of London Press.

McCosh, F. W. J. 1979. Traditional iron-working in central Africa with some reference to the ritualistic and scientific aspects of the industry. *Zambezia* 7, 159–60.

McCurdy, G. G. 1924. *Human Origins: a manual of prehistory*. New York: Appleton.

MacDonald, K. C. 1989. The identification and analysis of animal bones from west African sites. Unpublished PhD thesis, Rice University.

MacDonald, K. C. 1992. The domestic chicken (*Gallus gallus*) in sub-Saharan Africa: a background to its introduction and its osteological differentiation from indigenous fowls (*Numidinae* and *Francolinus* sp.). *Journal of Archaeological Science* 19, 303–18.

McHugh, W. P., G. G. Schaber, C. S. Breed & J. F. McCauley 1989. Neolithic adaptation and the holocene functioning of tertiary palaeodrainages in southern Egypt and northern Sudan. *Antiquity* 63, 320–36.

McIntosh, R. J. 1983. Floodplain geomorphology and human occupation of the upper inland delta of the Niger. *Geographical Journal* 149, 182–201.

—— In Press. Early urban clusters: arbitrating social ambiguity. *Journal of Field Archaeology*.

McIntosh, R. J. & S. K. McIntosh 1981. The inland Niger delta before the empire of Mali: evidence from Jenno-jeno. *Journal of African History* 22, 1–22.

—— 1988. From *siècles obscurs* to revolutionary centuries in the middle Niger. *World Archaeology* 20, 141–65.

McIntosh, S. K. 1981. A reconsideration of Wangara/Palolus, Island of Gold. *Journal of African History* 22, 145–58.

McIntosh, S. K. & R. J. McIntosh 1979. Initial perspectives on prehistoric subsistence in the inland Niger delta (Mali). *World Archaeology* 11, 227–43.

—— 1980a. Jenne-jeno, an ancient African city. *Archaeology* 33, 8–14.

—— 1980b. *Prehistoric Investigations in the Region of Jenne, Mali*. Oxford: British Archaeological Reports.

—— 1981. West African prehistory. *American Scientist* 69, 602–13.

—— 1983. Current directions in west African prehistory. *Annual Review of Anthropology* 12, 215–58.

—— 1984. The early city in west Africa: towards an understanding. *African Archaeological Review* 2, 73–98.

—— 1986a. Recent archaeological research and dates from west Africa. *Journal of African History* 27, 413–42.

—— 1986b. Archaeological reconnaissance in the region of Timbuktu, Mali. *National Geographic Research* 2, 302–19.

—— 1988. From stone to metal: new perspectives on the later prehistory of West Africa. *Journal of World Prehistory* 2, 89–133.

—— In Preparation. *Jenne-jeno: the second season of excavation and survey*. University of California Monographs in Anthropology. Berkeley: University of California Press.

McLaren, F., J. Evans & G. Hillman 1990. Identification of charred seeds from epipalaeolithic sites in S. W. Asia. In *Proceedings of the 26th International Symposium on Archaeometry, Heidelberg 1990*, Wagner, G. & E. Perricka (eds), 797–806. Basel: Birkhaus.

MacMichael, H. A. 1912. *The Tribes of Northern and Central Kordufam*. Cambridge: Cambridge University Press.

—— 1922. *The History of the Arabs in the Sudan*. Cambridge: Cambridge University Press.

Madsen, T. 1982. Settlement systems of early agricultural societies in east Jutland; Denmark. *Journal of Anthropological Archaeology* 1, 197–236.

Maggs, T. 1980. The iron age sequence south of the Vaal and Pongola rivers: some historical implications. Iron Age research in Mozambique. Collected preliminary reports. *Journal of African History* 21, 1–15.

—— 1984. The Iron Age south of the Zambezi. In *Southern African Prehistory and Palaeoenvironments*, R. G. Klein (ed.), 329–60. Rotterdam: Balkema.

Maggs, T. & G. Whitelaw 1991. A review of recent archaeological research on food-producing communities in southern Africa. *Journal of African History* 32, 3–24.

Mahachi, G. 1991. Conference Report. *PAST* 12, 5–7.

Mainga, M. 1973. *Bulozi under the Luyana Kings: political evolution and state formation in pre-colonial Zambia.* London: Longman.

Maistre, C. 1895. *Travers l'Afrique du Congo au Niger, 1892–3.* Paris: Hachette.

Maître, J. P. 1971. *Contribution à la préhistoire de l'Ahaggar, I: Tefedest centrale.* Algiers: Centre de Recherches Anthropologiques, Préhistoriques et d'Ethnographiques.

Malbrant, R., P. Receveur & R. Sabin 1947. Le boeuf du lac Tchad. *Revue d'Elevage et de Médécine Vétérinaire des Pays Tropicaux* 1, 37–42, 109–29.

Maley, J. 1980. Les changements climatiques de la fin du Tertiaire en Afrique: leur conséquence sur l'apparition du Sahara et de sa végétation. In *The Sahara and the Nile: quaternary environments and prehistoric occupation in northern Africa,* Williams, M. A. J. & H. Faure (eds), 63–84. Rotterdam: Balkema.

—— 1981. *Etudes palynologiques dans le bassin du Tchad et paléoclimatologie de l'Afrique nord-tropicale de 30,000 ans à l'époque actuelle.* Paris: ORSTOM (Office de la Recherche Scientifique et Technique d'Outre-Mer).

—— 1982. Dust, clouds, rain types and climatic variations in tropical north Africa. *Quaternary Research* 18, 1–16.

—— 1983. Histoire de la végétation et du climat de l'Afrique nord-tropicale au quaternaire récent. *Bothalia* 14, 377–89.

—— 1987. Fragmentation de la forêt dense humide africaine et extension des biotopes montagnards au Quaternaire récent: nouvelles données polliniques et chronologiques: implications paléoclimatiques et biogéographiques. *Palaeoecology of Africa* 18, 307–34.

—— 1989. Late quaternary climatic changes in the African rain forest: forest refugia and the major role of sea surface temperature variations. In *Palaeoclimatology and Palaeometeorology: modern and past patterns of global atmospheric transport,* Leinen, M. & M. Sarnthein (eds), 585–616. Dordrecht: Kluwer Academic Publications.

—— 1990. Histoire récente de la forêt dense humide africaine et dynamisme actuel de quelques formations forestières. In *Paysages quaternaires de l'Afrique Centrale Atlantique,* Lanfranchi, R. & D. Schwartz (eds), 367–82. Paris: ORSTOM (Institut Français de Recherche Scientifique pour le Développement en Coopération).

Maley, J. & P. Brenac 1987. Analyses polliniques préliminaires du Quaternaire récent de l'Ouest Cameroun: mise en évidence de refuges forestières et discussion des problèmes paléoclimatiques. *Mémoire de Travaux de l'Ecole Pratique des Hautes Etudes* 17, 129–42.

Maley, J., G. Caballe & P. Sita 1990a. Etude d'un peuplement résiduel à basse altitude de *Podocarpus latifolius* sur le flanc congolais du massif du Chaillu: implications paléoclimatiques et biogéographiques: étude de la pluie pollinique actuelle. In *Paysages quaternaires de l'Afrique Centrale Atlantique,* Lanfranchi, R. & D. Schwartz (eds), 336–49. Paris: ORSTOM (Institut Français de Recherche Scientifique pour le Développement en Coopération).

Maley, J. & D. A. Livingstone 1983. Extension d'un élément montagnard dans le sud du Ghana (Afrique de l'Ouest) au Pléistocène supérieur et à l'Holocène inférieur: premières données polliniques. *Compte Rendue de l'Académie des Sciences, Paris, Séries 2* 296, 1287–92.

Maley, J., D. A. Livingstone, P. Giresse, N. Thouveny, P. Brenac, K. Kelts, G. Kling, C. Stager, M. Haag, M. Fournier, Y. Bandet, D. Williamson & A. Zogning 1990b. Lithostratigraphy, volcanism, palaeomagnetism, and palynology of quaternary lacustrine deposits from Barombi-Mbo (West Cameroon): preliminary results. *Journal of Volcanology & Geothermal Research* 42, 319–35.

Malinowski, B. 1934. *Coral Gardens and their Magic.* Bloomington: Indiana University Press.

—— 1948. *Magic, Science and Religion and Other Essays.* Boston: Beacon Press.

Mandaville, J. P. 1980. Frankincense in Dhofar. In *The Scientific Results of the Oman Flora and Fauna Survey 1977 (Dhofar),* 87–9. Journal of Oman Studies, Special Report 2.

Manessy, G. 1972. Les noms d'animaux domestiques dans les languages voltaïques. In *Langues et techniques, nature et société approche linguistique, Vol. 1*, 301–20. Paris: Klincksieck.

Manhire, A. H. & J. E. Parkington 1986. Cattle, sheep and horses: a review of domestic animals in the rock art of southern Africa. In *Prehistoric Pastoralism in Southern Africa*, Hall, M. & A. B. Smith (eds), 22–30. Vlaeberg: South African Archaeological Society.

Marchesseau, J. 1967. Etude minéralogique et morphologique de la 'stone line' au Gabon. *IFAN* (Bulletin de l'Institut Fondamental d'Afrique Noire) 29, 862–5.

Marcus, J. 1983. On the nature of the Mesoamerican city. In *Prehistoric Settlement Patterns*, Vogt, E. & R. Leventhal (eds), 195–242. New Mexico: University of New Mexico Press.

Mariette, A. 1877. *Deir-el-Bahari*. Leipzig: Hinrichs.

Marks, A. E., M. A. Abbas, T. R. Hays & Y. Elamin 1983. Preliminary report of the Butana Archaeological Project. The 1982/3 field season. *Nyame Akuma* 22, 26–7.

Marks, S. 1980. South Africa: the myth of the empty land. *History Today* 30, 7–12.

Marshall, F. B. 1986. Aspects of the advent of pastoral economies in east Africa. Unpublished PhD thesis, University of California, Berkeley.

—— 1990. Cattle herds and caprine flocks: early pastoral strategies in south-western Kenya. In *Early Pastoralists of South-western Kenya*, Robertshaw, P. T. (ed.), 205–60. Nairobi: British Institute in Eastern Africa.

Marshall, L. 1969. The medicine dance of the !Kung Bushmen. *Africa* 39, 347–81.

Marx, K. 1973. *Grundrisse*. Harmondsworth: Penguin.

Masao, F. & H. Mutoro 1988. The east African coast and the Comoro islands. In *General History of Africa, III*, Frasi, M. L. & I. Hrbak (eds), 586–615. London: Heinemann/UNESCO.

Mason, I. L. 1976. Report of the mission to the Kuri cattle of Lake Chad. *Ark* 3, 196–200.

—— (ed.) 1984a. *Evolution of Domesticated Animals*. London: Longman.

—— 1984b. Goat. In *Evolution of Domesticated Animals*, Mason, I. L. (ed.), 85–99. London: Longman.

—— 1988. *A World Dictionary of Livestock Breeds, Types and Varieties*. Wallingford: Commonwealth Agricultural Bureau International.

Mason, R. J. 1952. South African iron age pottery from the southern Transvaal. *South African Archaeological Bulletin* 7, 70–9.

—— 1955. Notes on the recent archaeology of the Scherz basin, Brandberg. *South African Archaeological Bulletin* 10, 30–1.

—— 1974. Background to the Transvaal iron age new discoveries at Olifantspoort and Broederstroom. *Journal of the South African Institute of Mining and Metallurgy* 74, 211–16.

Masquelier, B. M. 1978. Structure and process of political identity: Ide, a polity of the Metchum valley (Cameroon). Unpublished PhD thesis, University of Pennsylvania.

Mathewson, R. D. 1967. Chukuto and Kisoto. In *Archaeology in the Volta Basin, 1963–66*, York, R. Y., R. D. Mathewson & C. Flight (eds), 23–7. Legon: Department of Archaeology.

Mauny, R. 1952. Essai sur l'histoire des métaux en Afrique occidentale. *IFAN* (Bulletin de l'Institut Français d'Afrique Noire) 14, 545–95.

—— 1953. Autour de l'historique de l'introduction du fer en Afrique occidentale. *Encyclopédie Mensuelle d'Outre-Mer*, 109–10.

—— 1961. *Tableau géographique: navigations mediévales de l'ouest africain au moyen age d'après les sources écrites, la tradition orale et l'archéologie*. Dakar: IFAN (Bulletin de l'Institut Français d'Afrique Noire).

—— 1970. Le périple d'Hannon, un faux célèbre concernant les navigations antiques. *Archéologia* 37, 78–80.

—— 1973. Datation au C14 des sites ouest-africains de l'âge du fer. In *Sixième Congrès Panafricain de Préhistoire, Dakar 1967*, Hugot, H.-J. (ed.), 533–9. Chambéry: Les Imprimeries Réunies.

—— 1978. Trans-Saharan contacts and the Iron Age in west Africa. In *The Cambridge History of*

Africa, Vol. 2: From c. 500 BC to AD 1050, Fage, J. D. (ed.), 272–341. Cambridge: Cambridge University Press.

Meadow, R. H. 1980. Animal bones: problems for the archaeologist together with some possible solutions. *Paléorient* 6, 65–77.

Meadows, M. 1984. Later quaternary vegetation history of the Nyika plateau, Malawi. *Journal of Biogeography* 11, 223–33.

Meek, C. K. 1931a. *Tribal Studies in Northern Nigeria*. 2 vols. London: Kegan Paul.

—— 1931b. *A Sudanese Kingdom*. London: Kegan Paul.

Mehlman, M. J. 1986. The African 3-age system and stone age realities, with particular reference to the 'MSA' in northern Tanzania. In 'The Longest Record: the human career in Africa', 62–3. Conference Abstracts, University of California, Berkeley.

Meillassoux, C. 1975. *Femmes, greniers et capitaux*. Paris: Maspero.

—— 1981. *Maidens, Meal and Money: capitalism and the domestic community*. Cambridge: Cambridge University Press.

Meneses, P. 1988. Idade da Pedra em Mozambique. *Trabalhos de Arqueologia e Antropologia* 5, 3–56.

Menghin, O. 1932. Paläolithische Funde in der Umgebung von Merimde-Benisalame. *Anzeiger der Akademie der Wissenschaften in Wien, Philosophisch-Historische Klasse* 69, 89–99.

Meniaud, J. 1912. Géographie économique. In *Haut-Sénégal-Niger, Soudan Français, Vol. 1*, Clozel, M. F. J. (ed.). Paris: E. Larose.

Mercer, J. 1976. *Spanish Sahara*. London: George Allen & Unwin.

Meredith, H. 1812. *An Account of the Gold Coast of Africa*. London: Hurst, Rees, Orme & Brown.

Merrick, H. V. & F. H. Brown 1984. Obsidian sources and patterns of source utilization in Kenya and northern Tanzania: some initial findings. *African Archaeology Review* 2, 129–52.

Meyerowitz, E. L. R. 1951. *The Sacred State of the Akan*. London: Faber & Faber.

Mgomezulu, G. G. Y. 1978. Food production: the beginnings in the Linthipe/Changoni area of Dedza District, Malawi. Unpublished PhD thesis, University of California, Berkeley.

Michels, J. W. 1976. Settlement-pattern survey in the region of Axum. *Annales d'Ethiopie* 10, 325.

—— 1979. Axumite archaeology: an introductory essay. In *Axum*, Kobishchanov, Y. (ed.), 1–34. University Park: Pennsylvania State University Press.

—— 1988. Regional political organization in the Axum-Yeha area during the pre-Axumite and Axumite era. Paper read at the 10th International Conference of Ethiopian Studies, Paris.

—— 1990. Review article on *Excavations at Aksum* by S. Munro-Hay. *African Archaeological Review* 8, 177–88.

Migeod, F. W. H. 1924. *Through Nigeria to Lake Chad*. London: Heath Cranton.

Milburn, M. 1986. Incipient cultivation in the neolithic Sahara: some queries. *Africa* 41, 292–304.

Mille, A. 1970. Contribution à l'étude des villages fortifiés de l'Imerina ancien (Madagascar). Thèse de IIIème Cycle, Clermont-Ferrand.

Miller, D., M. Rowlands & C. Tilley 1989. *Domination and Resistance*. London: Unwin Hyman.

Miller, N. 1991. The Near East. In *Progress in Old World Palaeoethnobotany: a retrospective view on the occasion of 20 years of the International Work Group for Palaeoethnobotany*, van Zeist, W., K. Wasylikowa & K.-E. Behre (eds), 133–61. Rotterdam: A. A. Balkema.

Mills, E. S. & B. W. Hamilton 1984. *Urban Economics* (3rd edition). Glenview, Ill.: Scott, Foresman & Co.

Mindeleff, C. 1890. Localization of Tusayan clans. *US Bureau of American Ethnology, Annual Report, 1897–98*, 639–52.

Möhlig, W. J. G. 1979. The Bantu nucleus: its conditional nature and its pre-significance. *Sprache und Geschichte in Afrika* 1, 109–42.

—— 1981. Stratification in the history of the Bantu languages. *Sprache und Geschichte in Afrika* 3, 251–316.

—— 1989. Sprachgeschichte, Kulturgeschichte und Archäologie: die Kongruenz der Forschungsergebnisse als methodologisches Problem. *Paideuma* 35, 189–96.

Molet, L. 1948. Forge Malgache. *Bulletin de Madagascar* 248, 725.

Monino, Y. 1983. Accoucher du fer: la métallurgie gbaya (Centrafrique). In *Métallurgies africaines: nouvelles contributions*, Echard, N. (ed.), 281–310. Paris: Société des Africanistes.

Monod, T. 1975. Introduction. In *Pastoralism in Tropical Africa*, Monod, T. (ed.), 1–183. London: International Africa Institute.

Monteil, C. 1903. *Monographie de Djénné.* Tulle: Mazierie.

Monteny, B. A. 1986. Forêt équatoriale, relais de l'océan comme source de vapeur d'eau pour l'atmosphère. *Vielle Climatique Satellitaire* 12, 39–51.

—— 1987. *Contribution à l'étude des interactions végétation–atmosphère en milieu tropicale humide.* Paris: ORSTOM (Institut Français de Recherche Scientifique pour le Développement en Coopération).

Montet, P. 1957–61. *Géographie de l'Egypte ancienne.* 2 vols. Paris: Klincksieck.

Moody, H. L. B. 1970. *The Walls and Gates of Kano City.* Lagos: Nigerian Department of Antiquities.

Moore, A. 1983. The first farmers in the Levant. In *The Hilly Flanks and Beyond: essays on the prehistory of southwestern Asia presented to Robert Braidwood, November 15, 1982,* Young, T. C., P. E. L. Smith & P. Mortensen (eds), 91–111. Chicago: Oriental Institute.

—— 1985. The development of neolithic societies in the Near East. *Advances in World Archaeology* 4, 1–69.

Morais, J. M. M. 1976. Prehistoric research in Mozambique. In *Iron Age Research in Mozambique: collected preliminary reports*, Duarte, M. L. T., T. Cruz e Silva, J. C. Senna Martinez, J. M. M. Morais & R. T. Duarte (eds), 1–2. Maputo: Instituto de Investigação Científica de Moçambique.

—— 1978. *Tentative de definicao de algumas formacoes socio-economicas em Moçambique de 0 a 1500.* Maputo: Centro de Estudos Africanos, Universidade Eduardo Mondlane.

—— 1984. Mozambican archaeology: past and present. *African Archaeological Review* 2, 113–28.

—— 1988. *The Early Farming Communities of Southern Mozambique.* Stockholm: Eduardo Mondlane University & Swedish Central Board of National Antiquities.

Morais J. M. M. & P. J. J. Sinclair 1980. Manyikeni: a Zimbabwe in southern Mozambique. In *Proceedings of the 8th Panafrican Congress of Prehistory and Quaternary Studies,* Leakey, R. E. & B. A. Ogot (eds), 351–4. Nairobi: International Louis Leakey Memorial Institute for African Prehistory.

Moreau, R. E. 1966. *The Bird Faunas of Africa and its Islands.* London: Academic Press.

Morgan, L. H. 1881. Houses and house life of modern aborigines. In *Contribution to North American Ethnology* 4, 310–19. Washington: Department of the Interior.

Mori, F. 1974. The earliest Saharan rock-engravings. *Antiquity* 48, 87–92.

Morris, E. L. 1981. Ceramic exchange in western Britain. In *Production and Distribution: a ceramic viewpoint,* Howard, H. & E. L. Morris (eds), 67–75. Oxford: British Archaeological Reports.

Morrison, J. H. 1982. Plateau societies' resistance to Jihadist penetration. In *Studies in the History of Plateau State, Nigeria,* Isichei, E. (ed.), 136–50. London: Macmillan.

Mortelmans, G. 1962. Archéologie des grottes Dimba et Ngovo. In *Actes du IVe Congrès Panafricain de Préhistoire et de l'Etude du Quaternaire, Section III, Pré- et protohistoire,* Mortelmans, G. & J. Nenquin (eds), 407–25. Tervuren: Musée Royal de l'Afrique Centrale.

Morton, G. R. & J. Wingrove 1969. Constitution of bloomery slags, part 1: Roman. *Journal of the Iron and Steel Institute* 207, 1556–69.

—— 1972. Constitution of bloomery slags, part 2: Medieval. *Journal of the Iron and Steel Institute* 210, 478–88.

Mudenge, S. I. 1988. *A Political History of Munhumutapa*. Harare: Zimbabwe Publishing House.

Muhle, C. G. 1981. The historical development of the chiefdom of We (southern Fungom). In *Contribution de la recherche ethnologique à l'histoire des civilisations du Cameroun*, Tardits, C. (ed.), 383–92. Paris: CNRS (Centre National de la Recherche Scientifique).

Mukarovsky, H. 1976–7. *A Study of Western Nigritic*. 2 vols. Vienna: Institut für Ägyptologie und Afrikanistik, Universität Wien.

Multhauf, R. F. 1978. *Neptune's Gift*. Baltimore: Johns Hopkins University Press.

Munro-Hay, S. 1982. The foreign trade of the Aksumite port of Adulis. *Azania* 17, 107–25.

—— 1984a. *The Coinage of Aksum*. New Delhi: Manohar.

—— 1984b. Aksumite chronology: some reconsiderations. *Jahrbuch für Numismatik und Geldgeschichte* 34, 134–44.

—— 1989a. *Excavations at Aksum*. London: British Institute in Eastern Africa.

—— 1989b. The al-Madhariba hoard of gold Aksumite and late Roman coins. *Numismatic Chronicle* 149, 83–100.

—— 1991. *An African Civilisation, the Aksumite Kingdom of Northern Ethiopia*. Edinburgh: Edinburgh University Press.

Munson, P. J. 1968. Recent archaeological research in the Dhar Tichit region of south central Mauritania. *West African Archaeological Newsletter* 10, 6–13.

—— 1970. Corrections and additional comments concerning the Tichit traditions. *West African Archaeological Newsletter* 12, 47–8.

—— 1976. Archaeological data on the origins of cultivation in the southwestern Sahara and their implications for west Africa. In *Origins of African Plant Domestication*, Harlan, J. R., J. M. J. De Wet & A. B. L. Stemler (eds), 187–209. The Hague: Mouton.

—— 1977. Africa's prehistoric past. In *Africa*, O'Meara, P. (ed.), 62–82. Bloomington: Indiana University Press.

Murdock, G. P. 1959. *Africa: its peoples and their culture history*. New York: McGraw-Hill.

Muringaniza, J. 1989. Petrographic analysis of Great Zimbabwe tradition pottery and its relationship with other contemporary pottery traditions in northern Mashonaland. Unpublished BA thesis, University of Zimbabwe.

Muriuki, G. 1974. *A History of the Kikuyu*. Nairobi: East African Publishing House.

Musa Muhammed, I. 1986. *The Archaeology of Central Darfur in the 1st Millennium AD*. Oxford: British Archaeological Reports.

Musonda, F. B. 1976. The Late Stone Age in Ghana in the light of excavations along the Voltaian scarp. Unpublished MA thesis, University of Ghana.

Mussi, M., I. Caneva & A. Zarattini 1984. More on the terminal Palaeolithic of the Fayum depression. In *Origin and Early Development of Food-producing Cultures in North-eastern Africa*, Krzyzaniak, L. & M. Kobusiewicz (eds), 185–91. Poznan: Poznan Archaeology Museum.

Mutoro, H. W. 1979. A contribution to the study of cultural and economic dynamics of the historical settlements on the Kenya coast with particular reference to the ruins at Takwa, north Kenya coast. Unpublished MA thesis, University of Nairobi.

—— 1985. The spatial distribution of the Mijikenda kaya settlements on the hinterland of the Kenya coast. *Transafrican Journal of History* 14, 78–99.

—— 1987. An archaeological study of the Mijikenda kaya settlements. PhD thesis, University of California, Los Angeles.

—— 1988. A nearest neighbour analysis of the Mijikenda on the Kenya coast. *Kenya Journal of Sciences* C, 5–17.

—— 1990. The kaya as a sacred site. Unpublished paper presented to World Archaeological Congress 2, Barquisimeto, Venezuela.

Muzzolini, A. 1983. L'art rupestre du Sahara central: classification et chronologie. Le boeuf dans la préhistoire africaine. Thèse 3ème cycle, Université de Provence, Aix-en-Provence.

—— 1986. *L'Art rupestre préhistorique des massifs centraux sahariens.* Oxford: British Archaeological Reports.

—— 1990. The sheep in Saharan rock art. *Rock Art Research* 7, 93–109.

Nachtigal, G. 1971. *Sahara and Sudan.* London: H. Hurst.

Naville, E. H. n.d. *The Temple of Deir el-Bahari, III.* London: Kegan Paul, Trench, Trubner & Co.

Needham, S. & J. Evans 1987. Honey and dripping: neolithic plant food residues from Runneymead Bridge. *Oxford Journal of Archaeology* 6, 21–8.

Nelson, C. M. 1980. The Elmenteitan lithic industry. In *Proceedings of the 8th Panafrican Congress of Prehistory and Quaternary Studies*, Leakey, R. E. & B. A. Ogot (eds), 275–8, Nairobi: International Louis Leakey Memorial Institute for African Prehistory.

Nenquin, J. 1963. *Excavations at Sanga 1957: the protohistoric necropolis.* Tervuren: Musée Royal de l'Afrique Centrale.

—— 1964. *Salt in Prehistoric Europe.* Dissertation Archéologique 6, University of Ghent.

Netting, R. Mc. 1965. Household organization and intensive agriculture: the Kofyar case. *African* 35, 422–9.

—— 1968. *Hill Farmers of Nigeria.* Seattle: University of Washington Press.

Neumann, K. 1987. Middle holocene vegetation of the Gilf Kebir, S. W. Egypt: a reconstruction. *Palaeoecology of Africa* 18, 179–88.

Newberry, P. E. 1938. Three Old-Kingdom travellers to Byblos and Pwenet. *Journal of Egyptian Archaeology* 24, 182–4.

Newbury, C. 1971. Prices and profitability in early 19th century west African trade. In *The Development of Indigenous Trade and Markets in West Africa*, Meillassoux, C. (ed.), 91–106. London: Oxford University Press.

Newman, P. 1980. *The Classification of Chadic in Afroasiatic.* Leiden: University Press.

Newton, L. E. 1980. More Kintampo culture finds in the forest zone of Ghana. *Nyame Akuma* 16, 7–8.

Newton, L. E. & S. R. J. Woodell 1976. A newly discovered site for the Kintampo culture. *Sankofa* 2, 19–22.

Ngcongco, L. D. 1979. Origins of the Tswana. *Pula* 1, 33–7.

Ngere, L. O. 1983a. The White Fulani (Bunaji) of Nigeria. Animal genetic resources in Africa: high potential and endangered livestock. In *2nd OAU Expert Committee Meeting on Animal Genetic Resources in Africa, November 1983, Bulawayo, Zimbabwe*, 67–77. Nairobi: Organization of African Unity.

—— 1983b. The Gudali of Nigeria – review. Animal genetic resources in Africa: high potential and endangered livestock. In *2nd OAU Expert Committee Meeting on Animal Genetic Resources in Africa, November 1983, Bulawayo, Zimbabwe*, 77–81. Nairobi: Organization of African Unity.

Ngere, L. O., I. F. Adu & I. O. Okubanjo 1984. The indigenous goats of Nigeria. *Animal Genetic Resources Information* 3, 1–9.

Nicholson, S. E. 1978. Climatic variations in the Sahel and other African regions during the last five centuries. *Journal of Arid Environments* 1, 3–24.

Nicolaisen, J. 1963. *Ecology and Culture of the Pastoral Tuareg.* Copenhagen: Nationalmuseets Skrifter Ethnografisk Raekke.

Nkwanga, E. B. 1991. Efforts to mitigate the effects of isolation – World Bank initiatives in Nigera. *World Archaeological Bulletin* 5, 73–6.

Nkwi, P. N. 1976. *Traditional Government and Social Change: a study of the political institutions among the Kom of the Cameroon Grassfields.* Fribourg: University Press.

Nordstrom, H. A. 1972. *Neolithic and A-Group Sites: the Scandinavian Joint Expedition to Sudanese*

Nubia, III. Stockholm: Scandinavian University Books.

Northam, R. M. 1975. *Urban Geography.* New York: John Wiley & Sons.

Nurse, D. 1983. History from linguistics: the case of the Tana river. *History in Africa* 10, 207–38.

Nurse, D. & T. Spear 1985. *The Swahili: reconstructing the history and language of an African society, 800–1500.* Philadelphia: Pennsylvania University Press.

Nzewunwa, N. 1985. *The Niger delta: prehistoric economy and culture.* Oxford: British Archaeological Reports.

O'Connor, A. 1983. *The African City.* London: Hutchinson.

O'Connor, D. 1967. Sudan. Monumental centers. *Encyclopaedia of World Art XIII*, 662–74. New York: McGraw Hill.

—— 1972a. The geography of settlement in ancient Egypt. In *Man, Settlement and Urbanism*, Ucko, P. J., R. Tringham & G. W. Dimbleby (eds), 681–98. London: Duckworth.

—— 1972b. A regional population in Egypt to *circa* 600 B.C. In *Population Growth: anthropological implications*, Spooner, B. (ed.), 78–100. Cambridge, Mass. & London: Massachusetts Institute of Technology Press.

—— 1974. Political systems and archaeological data in Egypt: 2600–1780 BC. *World Archaeology* 6, 15–38.

—— 1982. Cities and towns. In *Egypt's Golden Age: the art of living in the New Kingdom 1558–1085 BC*, 17–24. Boston: Museum of Fine Arts.

—— 1983. New Kingdom and Third Intermediate Period, 1552–664 BC. In *Ancient Egypt: a social history*, Trigger, B. G., B. J. Kemp, D. O'Connor & A. B. Lloyd, 183–278. Cambridge: Cambridge University Press.

—— 1986. The locations of Yam and Kush and their historical implications. *Journal of the American Research Center in Egypt* 23, 27–50.

—— 1987. The location of Irem. *Journal of Egyptian Archaeology* 73, 99–136.

—— 1989. City and palace in New Kingdom Egypt. *Cahier de Recherches de l'Institut de Papyrologie et d'Egyptologie de Lille, Sociétés Urbaines en Egypte et au Soudan* 11, 73–87.

—— 1990a. The nature of Tjemhu (Libyan) society in the later New Kingdom. In *Libya and Egypt c. 1300–750 B.C.*, Leahy, A. (ed.), 29–113. London: School of Oriental and African Studies, Center of Near and Middle Eastern Studies and the Society of Libyan Studies.

—— 1990b. Demarcating the boundaries: an interpretation of a scene in the tomb of Mahu, el-Amarna. *Bulletin of the Egyptological Seminar (New York)* 9, 41–51.

O'Laughlin, B. 1975. Marxist approaches in anthropology. *Annual Review of American Anthropology* 4, 341–70.

O'Mahoney, K. 1970. Salt trail. *Journal of Ethiopian Studies* 8, 147–53.

Ochieng', W. R. 1971. *A Precolonial History of the Gusii of Western Kenya.* Nairobi: East African Publishing House.

Odner, K. 1971. Usangi Hospital and other archaeological sites in north Pare mountains, northeastern Tanzania. *Azania* 6, 89–130.

—— 1972. Excavations at Narosura, a Stone Bowl site in the southern Kenya highlands. *Azania* 7, 25–92.

Ogot, B. A. 1967. *History of the Southern Luo, Vol. 1: Migration and settlement 1500–1900.* Nairobi: East African Publishing House.

Oguagha, P. A. 1982. The 'conquest hypothesis' in Igbo–Igala relations: a re-examination. *West African Journal of Archaeology* 12, 55–61.

Oguagha, P. A. & A. I. Okpoko 1984. *History and Ethnoarchaeology in Eastern Nigeria: a study of Igbo–Igala relations with special reference to the Anambra valley.* Oxford: British Archaeological Reports.

Ogundele, S. O. 1989. Settlement archaeology in Tivland: a preliminary report. *West African Journal of Archaeology* 19, 83–91.

Ohiri-Aniche, C. In Preparation. A reconstruction of Proto-Igboid-Yoruboid-Edoid. University of Port Harcourt.

Oikawa, A. 1991. Japanese archaeological site databases and data visualization. *World Archaeological Bulletin* 5, 100–7.

—— 1992. Japanese archaeological site databases and data visualization. In *Archaeology and the Information Age*, Reilly, P. & S. Rahtz (eds), 58–64. London: Routledge.

Okafor, E. E. 1983. Metallurgy in ancient Igboland. *Nyame Akuma* 23, 14–15.

—— 1984. Ancient mines in the north of Igboland. *Nyame Akuma* 24/5, 14–15.

—— 1988. More iron working sites in Nsukka. *Nyame Akuma* 30, 29–30.

—— 1989. Eguru Anube malla Orba: blacksmith clan among the Orba. *Nyame Akuma* 32, 24–7.

—— n.d.a. Origin and development of iron working in west Africa. BA project, University of Ibadan, 1977.

—— n.d.b. A study of iron working in Orba, Nsukka. MSc project, University of Ibadan, 1984.

—— Forthcoming. Archaeological investigations in Opi, Orba, Umunda and Owerre-Elu.

Okigbo, B. N. 1980. Plants and food in Igbo culture. 1980 Ahiajoku Lecture. Owerri, State Ministry of Information, Culture Division.

Okoro, J. A. 1989. An investigation of iron smelting sites in Gambaga and the implications for iron age studies in Ghana. Unpublished MPhil thesis, University of Ghana.

Oliver, P. (ed.) 1971. *Shelter in Africa*. London: Barrie & Jenkins.

Oliver, R. 1962. *A Short History of Africa*. Harmondsworth: Penguin.

—— 1966. The problem of the Bantu expansion. *Journal of African History* 7, 361–76.

Oliver, R. & A. Atmore 1981. *The African Middle Ages 1400–1800*. Cambridge: Cambridge University Press.

Onyango-Abuje, J. C. 1980. Temporal and spatial distribution of mesolithic cultures in east Africa. *Proceedings of the 8th Panafrican Congress of Prehistory and Quaternary Studies, Nairobi, 1977*, Leakey, R. E. & B. A. Ogot (eds), 288–92. Nairobi: International Louis Leakey Memorial Institute for African Prehistory.

Opsomer, J. E. n.d. (*c.* 1955). Les cultures coloniales. In *Encyclopédie du Congo Belge I*, 424–632. Brussels: Bieleveld.

Osborn, D. J. & I. Helmy 1980. The contemporary land mammals of Egypt (including Sinai). *Fieldiana Zoology* 5.

Osing, J. 1980. Libyen, Libyer. In *Lexikon der Ägyptologie, III*, Helck, H. & W. Westendorf (eds), 1015–33. Wiesbaden: Otto Harrasowitz.

Oslisly, R. & B. Peyrot 1988. Synthèse des données archéologiques des sites de la moyenne vallée de l'Ogooué (province du Moyen Ogooué et Ogooué Ivindo), Gabon. *Nsi* 3, 63–8.

Ottenheimer, M. 1985. *Marriage in Domoni*. Prospect Park: Waveland Press.

Ottino, P. 1983. L'ancienne succession dynastique malgache (l'example merina). In *Les Souverains de Madagascar*, Raison-jourde, F. (ed.), 223–63. Paris: Kathala.

Ottino-Kellum, M. 1969. Découverte d'une herminette néolithique à Madagascar. *Bulletin de Madagascar* 272, 1–4.

Owen, R. B., J. W. Barthelme, R. W. Renaut & A. Vincens 1982. Paleolimnology and archaeology of holocene deposits north-east of Lake Turkana, Kenya. *Nature* 298, 523–9.

Ozanne, P. C. 1965a. Ladoku: an early town near Prampram. *Ghana Notes and Queries* 7, 6–7.

—— 1965b. Adwuku: a fortified hill-top village in Shai. *Ghana Notes and Queries* 7, 4–5.

—— 1969. The diffusion of smoking in west Africa. *Odu* 2, 29–42.

Pachur, H. J. 1982. Das Abflussystem des Djebel Dalmar – eine Singularität? *Würzburger*

Geographische Arbeiten 56, 93–110.

Pachur, H. J. & G. Braun 1982. Aspekte paläoklimatischer Befunde in der östlichen Zentralsahara. *Geomethodica Veröffentlichung* 7, 23–54.

Pachur, H. J. & S. Kropelin 1987. Wadi Howar: paleoclimatic evidence from an extinct river system in the southeastern Sahara. *Science* 237, 298–300.

Pachur, H. J. & H. P. Roper 1984. Die Bedeutung paläoklimatischer Befunde aus den Flachbereichen der östlichen Sahara und des nördlichen Sudan. *Zeitschrift für Geomorphologie* 50, 59–78.

Pales, L. 1950. *Les Sels alimentaires: sels minéraux.* Dakar: Gouvernement Générale de l'Afrique Occidental Française.

Palmer, H. R. 1928. *Sudanese Memoirs, Vol. 2.* Lagos: Governement Printer.

Pankhurst, R. 1961. *An Introduction to the Economic History of Ethiopia from Early Times to 1800.* London: Lalibela House.

—— 1979. Ethiopian medieval and post-medieval capitals: their development and principal features. *Azania* 14, 2–29.

Paribeni, R. 1907. Ricerche sul luogo dell'antica Adulis. *Monumenti Antichi, Reale Accademia dei Lincei* 18, 437–572.

Park, M. 1954. *Travels of Mungo Park*, Miller, R. (ed.). London: J. M. Dent.

Parkington, J. & M. Cronin 1986. The size and layout of Mgungundlovu 1829–1838. In *Prehistoric Pastoralism in Southern Africa*, Hall, M. & A. B. Smith (eds), 133–48. Vlaeberg: South African Archaeological Society.

Pastouret, L., H. Chamley, G. Delibrias, J. C. Duplessy & J. Thiede 1978. Late quaternary climatic changes in western tropical Africa deduced from deep-sea sedimentation off the Niger delta. *Oceanologica Acta* 1, 217–32.

Patch, D. 1984. Preliminary report on the 1983 field season of the Pennsylvania-Yale Expedition to Abydos. *Newsletter of the American Research Center in Egypt* 126, 14–20.

Paulissen, E. & P. M. Vermeersch 1987. Earth, man and climate in the Egyptian Nile valley during the Pleistocene. In *Prehistory of Arid North Africa: essays in honor of Fred Wendorf*, Close, A. E. (ed.), 29–67. Dallas: Southern Methodist University Press.

Pearce, S. 1960. The appearance of iron and its use in proto-historic Africa. Unpublished MA thesis, University of London.

Pearson, G. W. 1987. How to cope with calibration. *Antiquity* 61, 98–103.

Pearson, G. W. & M. Stuiver 1986. High-precision calibration of the radiocarbon time scale, 500–2500 BC. *Radiocarbon* 28, 839–62.

Pellat, C. 1962. *Masʿudi. Les Prairies d'Or: traduction française de Meynard et Pavet de Courteille, revue et corrigée par C. Pellat, Vol. 1.* Paris: Société Asiatique.

—— 1965. *Masʿudi. Les Prairies d'Or: traduction française de Meynard et Pavet de Courteille, revue et corrigée par C. Pellat, Vol. 2.* Paris: Société Asiatique.

Penn, A. E. D. 1931. The ruins of Zankor. *Sudan Notes and Records* 14, 179–84.

Percival, J. 1936. Cereals of ancient Egypt. *Nature* 138, 270–3.

Perrott, R. A. 1982. A high altitude pollen diagram from Mount Kenya: its implications for the history of glaciation. *Palaeoecology of Africa* 14, 77–83.

—— 1987. Early forest clearance and the environment in southwest Uganda. *Nature* 325, 89–90.

Perrott, R. A. & F. A. Street-Perrott 1982. New evidence for a late pleistocene wet phase in northern intertropical Africa. *Palaeoecology of Africa* 14, 57–75.

Peters, J. 1985–6. Bijdrage tot de archeozoölogie van Soedan en Egypte. Unpublished PhD thesis, Rijksuniversiteit Gent, Fakulteit des Watenschappen.

Petit-Maire, N. (ed.) 1979. *Le Sahara atlantique à l'Holocène: peuplement et écologie.* Algiers: Centre de Recherches Anthropologiques.

——— 1980. Holocene biogeographical variations along the northwestern African coast (28–19°N): paleoclimatic implications. *Palaeoecology of Africa* 12, 365–7.

Petit-Maire, N., J. C. Celles, D. Commelin, G. Delibrias & M. Raimbault 1983. The Sahara in northern Mali: man and his environment between 10,000 and 3500 years bp (preliminary results). *African Archaeological Review* 1, 105–25.

Petit-Maire, N., G. Delibrias & C. Gaven 1980. Pleistocene lakes in the Shati area, Fezzan (27–30°N). *Palaeoecology of Africa* 12, 289–95.

Petit-Maire, N. & J. Riser (eds) 1983. *Sahara ou Sahel? Quaternaire recent du bassin de Taoudenni (Mali)*. Paris: Librairie du Museum.

——— 1987. Holocene paleohydrology of the Niger. *Palaeoecology of Africa* 18, 135–41.

Petrie, W. M. F. 1888. *Nebesheh*. London: Egypt Exploration Fund.

——— 1914. *Tarkhan II*. London: British School of Archaeology in Egypt and Bernard Quaritch.

——— 1920. *Prehistoric Egypt*. London: British School of Archaeology and Egyptian Research Account.

Peyrot, B. & R. Oslisly 1986. Recherches récentes sur le paléoenvironnement et l'archéologie au Gabon: 1982–1985. *L'Anthropologie* 90, 201–16.

——— 1990. Sites archéologiques associant pierres taillées, céramiques, coquilles marines et outils en pierre polie à Tchengué, province de l'Ogooué-Maritime (Gabon). *Nsi* 7, 13–19.

Phillipson, D. W. 1968a. The early iron age site at Kapwirimbwe, Lusaka. *Azania* 3, 87–105.

——— 1968b. The early Iron Age in Zambia – regional variants and some tentative conclusions. *Journal of African History* 9, 191–211.

——— 1969. Early iron-using peoples of southern Africa. In *African Societies in Southern Africa*, Thompson, L. D. (ed.), 24–49. London: Heinemann.

——— 1975. The chronology of the Iron Age in Bantu Africa. *Journal of African History* 15, 1–25.

——— 1976. *The Prehistory of Eastern Zambia*. Nairobi: British Institute in Eastern Africa.

——— 1977a. *The Later Prehistory of Eastern and Southern Africa*. London: Heinemann.

——— 1977b. The excavation of Gobedra rock-shelter, Axum. *Azania* 12, 53–82.

——— 1984. Aspects of early food production in northern Kenya. In *Origin and Early Development of Food-producing Cultures in North-east Africa*, Krzyzaniak, L. & M. Kobusiewicz (eds), 489–95. Poznan: Polish Academy of Sciences.

——— 1985a. *African Archaeology*. Cambridge: Cambridge University Press.

——— 1985b. An archaeological reconsideration of Bantu expansion. *Muntu* 2, 69–84.

——— 1990. Aksum in Africa. *Journal of Ethiopian Studies* 23, 55–65.

Picard, G.-C. 1991. *La Civilisation de l'Afrique romaine*. Paris: Presses Universitaires de France.

Pierre, C. 1906. *L'Elevage dans l'Afrique Occidentale Française*. Paris: A. Challamel.

Pigafetta, F. 1881. *A Report of the Kingdom of Kongo and of the Surrounding Countries, Drawn out of the Writings and Discourses of the Portuguese, Duarte Lopez, in Rome, 1591*. London: John Murray.

Pikirayi, I. In Press. Loopholed stone structures in a local and regional context. In *Proceedings of the Zanzibar Workshop of the Urban Origins in Eastern Africa Project, 1991*.

——— In Preparation. Excavations at Baranda field site, Mt Darwin, northern Zimbabwe.

Pirenne, H. 1974. *Medieval Cities: their origins and the revival of trade*. Princeton: Princeton University Press.

Pirenne, J. 1956. *Paléographie des inscriptions sud-arabes I*. Brussels: Paleis der Academien.

Piva, A. 1907. Una civiltà scomparsa dell'Eritrea e gli scavi archeologici nella regione di Cheren. *Nuova Antologia*, 323–35.

Plug, I. & E. A. Voigt 1985. Archaeozoological studies of iron age communities in southern Africa. In *Advances in World Archaeology 4*, Wendorf, F. (ed.), 189–238. London: Academic Press.

Podelewski, A.-M. 1966. *Les Forgerons mafa: description et évolution d'un groupe endogame*. Paris: ORSTOM (Office de la Recherche Scientifique et Technique Outre-Mer).

Pole, L. M. 1974a. *Iron-smelting in Northern Ghana*. Accra: National Museum of Ghana.

—— 1974b. Account of an iron smelting operation at Lawra, Upper Region. *Ghana Journal of Science* 14, 127–36.

—— 1975a. Iron smelting procedure in the upper region of Ghana. *Bulletin of the Historical Metallurgy Group* 8, 21–31.

—— 1975b. Iron working apparatus and techniques: upper region of Ghana. *West African Journal of Archaeology* 5, 11–39.

—— 1982. Decline or survival? Iron production in west Africa from the seventeenth to the twentieth centuries. *Journal of African History* 23, 503–13.

—— 1983. A Ruhr or rural industry? The scale of iron production in west Africa. Paper read at a meeting in London of the Museum Ethnographers' Group, 1983.

—— 1985. Furnace design and smelting operation: a survey of written reports of iron smelting in west Africa. In *African Iron Working: ancient and traditional*, Haaland, R. & P. L. Shinnie (eds), 142–63. Bergen: Norwegian University Press.

Poncelet, L. 1967. La briquetage de Seille. *Bulletin de l'Association des Amis de l'Archéologie Mosellane* 35, 1–20 .

Ponsich, M. & M. Tarradell 1965. *Garum et industries antiques de salaisons dans la Mediterranée occidentale*. Paris: Hachette.

Popovic, A. 1976. *La Révolte des esclaves en Iraq au IIIme/IXme siècle*. Paris: Paul Guethner.

Porter, B. & R. Moss 1934–7. *Topographical Bibliography of Ancient Egyptian Hieroglyphic Texts, Reliefs, and Paintings*. Oxford: Oxford University Press.

—— 1952. *Topographical Bibliography of Ancient Egyptian Hieroglyphic Texts, Reliefs and Paintings, VII: Nubia, Deserts and outside Egypt*. Oxford: Oxford University Press.

Porter, B., R. Moss & E. M. Burney 1960. *Topographical Bibliography of Ancient Egyptian Hieroglyphic Texts, Reliefs and Paintings, I: Theban Necropolis, Part I. Private Tombs*. Oxford: Oxford University Press.

—— 1972. *Topographical Bibliography of Ancient Egyptian Hieroglyphic Texts, Reliefs and Paintings, II: Theban Temples*. Oxford: Oxford University Press.

Portères, R. 1950. Vieilles agricultures de l'Afrique intertropicale: centres d'origine et de diversification variétale primaire et berceau d'agriculture antérieurs au XVIe siècle. *L'Agronomie Tropicale* 5, 489–507.

—— 1955. Les céréales mineures du genre digitaria en Afrique et Europe. *Journal d'Agriculture Tropicale et de Botanique Appliquée* 2, 477–510.

—— 1976. African cereals: *Eleusine*, fonio, black fonio, teff, *Brachiaria*, paspalum, *Pennisetum*, and African rice. In *Origins of African Plant Domestication*, Harlan, J. R., J. M. J. De Wet & A. B. L. Stemler (eds), 409–52. The Hague: Mouton.

Posener, G. 1938. Le canal du Nil à la Mer Rouge avant les Ptolémées. *Chronique d'Egypte* 13, 258–73.

—— 1958. Pour une location du pays Koush au Moyen Empire. *Kush* 6, 39–68.

Posnansky, M. 1967. Excavations at Lanet, Kenya 1957. *Azania* 1, 89–114.

—— 1968. Bantu genesis: archaeological reflexions. *Journal of African History* 9, 1–11.

—— 1969. Bigo Bya Mugenyi. *The Uganda Journal* 33, 125–50.

—— 1973. Aspects of early west African trade. *World Archaeology* 5, 149–62.

—— 1975a. Connections between the lacustrine peoples and the coast. In *East Africa and the Orient: cultural syntheses in pre-colonial times*, Chittick, H. N. & R. I. Rotberg (eds), 216–25. New York: Africana Publishing Co.

—— 1975b. Archaeology, technology and Akan civilization. *Journal of African Studies* 2, 24–38.

—— 1979. Excavation at Begho, Ghana 1979. *Nyame Akuma* 15, 23–7.

—— 1984. Early agricultural societies in Ghana. In *From Hunters to Farmers: the causes and consequences of food production in Africa*, Clark, J. D. & S. A. Brandt (eds), 147–51. Berkeley:

University of California Press.

—— n.d. The indigenous African town. *African Studies*, Fall 1980 Colloquium, Los Angeles, University of California.

Posnansky, M. & R. J. McIntosh 1976. New radiocarbon dates from northern and western Africa. *Journal of African History* 17, 161–95.

Pouwels, R. 1987. *Horn and Crescent: cultural change and traditional Islam on the east African coast, 800–1900.* Cambridge: Cambridge University Press.

Pradelles, C. H. 1975. Bangwa. La parenté et la famille dans une chefferie bamiléké du Ndé au Cameroun. Unpublished Doctorat de IIIième Cycle thesis, Paris.

—— 1986. Le champ du langage dans une chefferie Bamiléké. Thèse de Doctorat d'Etat. Paris: Ecole des Hautes Etudes des Sciences Sociales.

Preuss, J. 1986a. Die Klimaentwicklung in den äquatorialen Breiten Afrikas im Jungpleistozän: Versuch eines Überblicks in Zusammenhang mit Geländearbeiten in Zaïre. In *Geographische Forschung in Marburg: eine Dokumentation aktueller Arbeitsrichtungen*, Andres, W., E. Buchofer & G. Mertins (eds), 132–48. Marburg/Lahn: Marburger Geographische Gesellschaft.

—— 1986b. Jungpleistozäne Klimaänderungen im Kongo-Zaïre-Becken. *Geowissenschaften in unserer Zeit* 4, 177–87.

—— 1990. L'évolution des paysages du bassin intérieur du Zaïre pendant les quarante derniers millénaires. In *Paysages quaternaires de l'Afrique Centrale Atlantique*, Lanfranchi, R. & D. Schwartz (eds), 260–70. Paris: ORSTOM (Institut Français de Recherche Scientifique pour le Développement en Coopération).

Preuss, J. & L. Fiedler 1984. Steingeräte aus dem inneren Kongobecken und ihre geomorphologische Einbindung. *Beiträge zur Allgemeinen und Vergleichenden Archäologie* 6, 227–46.

Proceedings of the Angra Pequena and West Coast Claims Joint Commission 1885. Cape Town: Saul Solomon & Co.

Pryor, F. 1980. Excavation at Fengate, Peterborough, England: the third report. *Northamptonshire Archaeological Society Monograph* 1, 18–21.

Ptolemaeus, C. 1932. *Geography of Claudius Ptolemy, Translated into English and Edited by Edward Luther Stevenson.* New York: New York Public Library.

Pulak, C. 1988. The bronze age shipwreck at Ulu Burun, Turkey: 1985 campaign. *American Journal of Archaeology* 92, 1–37.

Purseglove, J. W. 1972. *Tropical Crops: monocotyledons 1.* New York: John Wiley & Sons.

—— 1976. The origins and migrations of crops in tropical Africa. In *Origins of African Plant Domestication*, Harlan, J. R., J. M. J. De Wet & A. B. L. Stemler (eds), 291–309. The Hague: Mouton.

Quarcoo, A. K. & M. Johnson 1968. Shai pots. The pottery industry of the Shai people of southern Ghana. *Baessler-Archiv* 16, 47–88.

Queval, R., J. P. Petit, G. Tacher, A. Provost & J. Pagot 1971. Le Kouri: race bovine du lac Tchad I. Introduction générale à son étude zootechnique et biochimique: origines et écologie de la race. *Revue d'Elevage et de Médécine Vétérinaire des Pays Tropicaux* 24, 667–87.

Radcliffe-Brown, A. R. 1952. *Structure and Function in Primitive Society.* London: Oxford University Press.

Radcliffe-Smith, A. 1980. The vegetation of Dhofar. In *The Scientific Results of the Oman Flora and Fauna Survey 1977 (Dhofar)*, 59–86. Journal of Oman Studies, Special Report 2.

Radimilahy, C. 1980. *L'Archéologie de l'Androy: travail d'études et de recherche.* Antananarivo: Centre d'Art et d'Archéologie.

—— 1988. *L'Ancienne métallurgie du fer à Madagascar.* Oxford: British Archaeological Reports.

—— 1990. Mahilaka: rapport préliminaire. In *Urban Origins in Eastern Africa: proceedings of the 1989 Madagascar workshop*, Sinclair, P. J. J. & J. A. Rakotoarisoa (eds), 41–6. Stockholm: Swedish Central Board of National Antiquities.

Raharijoana, V. 1988. Etude du peuplement de l'espace d'une vallée des Hautes Terres Centrales de Madagascar: archéologie de la Manadona (XVe–XVIe siècles). Thèse de Doctorat d'Etat, Paris, Sorbonne.

Rahtz, P. A. & C. Flight 1974. A quern factory near Kintampo, Ghana. *West African Journal of Archaeology* 4, 1–31.

Rakotovololona, S. 1990. Premiers résultats de la fouille d'Ankadivory. In *Urban Origins in Eastern Africa: proceedings of the 1989 Madagascar workshop*, Sinclair, P. J. J. & J. A. Rakotoarisoa (eds), 85–90. Stockholm: Swedish Central Board of National Antiquities.

Randall-MacIver, D. 1906. The Rhodesian ruins: their probable origin and significance. *Geographical Journal* 27, 4.

Randall-MacIver, D. & C. L. Woolley 1909. *Areika*. Philadelphia: University Museum, University of Pennsylvania.

Randles, W. G. L. 1968. *L'Ancien Régime royaume du Congo des origines à la fin du XIXe siècle*. The Hague: Mouton.

—— 1975. *L'Empire du Monomotapa du XVme au XIXme siècle*. Paris: Mouton.

Raphael, J. R. n.d. (*c.* 1915). *Through Unknown Nigeria*. London: Werner Laurie.

Rapp, J. 1980. Fouilles 1980 dans le gisement sao de Sou Blame Radjil (Nord-Cameroun). *Bulletin de la Société Anthropologique du Sud-Ouest* 15, 219–28.

Rasamuel, D. 1984. Alimentation et techniques anciennes dans le sud de Madagascar, à travers une fosse à odures du XIme siècle. *Etudes Océan Indien* 4, 81–109.

Rayfield, J. R. 1974. Theories of urbanization and the colonial city in west Africa. *Africa* 44, 163–85.

Redding, R. & S. Goodman 1984. Dembeni phase reptile, bird and mammal remains. *Azania* 19, 51–4.

Redman, C. (ed) 1986. *Qsar es-Sagahir*. London: Academic Press.

Rehder, J. E. 1986. Use of preheated air in primitive furnaces: comments on views of Avery and Schmidt. *Journal of Field Archaeology* 13, 351–3.

Reindorf, C. C. (1895) 1966. *The History of the Gold Coast and Asante*. Oxford: Oxford University Press.

Renel, C. 1910. *Contes de Madagascar, I: Contes merveilleux*. Paris: E. Leroux.

Renfrew, C. 1989. *Archaeology and Language: the puzzle of Indo-European origins*. Harmondsworth: Penguin.

Renfrew, C. & J. Cherry 1986. *Peer Polity Interaction*. Cambridge: Cambridge University Press.

Reynolds, B. R. G. 1968. *The Material Culture of the People of the Gwembe Valley*. Manchester: Manchester University Press.

Ricci, L. & R. Fattovich 1984–6. Scavi archeologici nella zona di Aksum. A. Seglamien. *Rassegna di Studi Etiopici* 30, 117–69.

Richards, A. I. 1951. The Bemba of north-eastern Rhodesia. In *Seven Tribes in Central Africa*, Colson, E. & M. Gluckman (eds), 164–93. Oxford: Oxford University Press.

—— 1956. *Chisungu: a girl's initiation ceremony among the Bemba of Zambia*. London: Tavistock.

Richards, P. 1983a. Ecological change and the politics of African land use. *African Studies Review* 26, 1–72.

—— 1983b. Farming systems in west Africa. *Progress in Human Geography* 7, 4–39.

Richardson, J. L. & A. E. Richardson 1972. History of an African Rift lake and its climatic implications. *Ecological Monographs* 42, 499–534.

Riehm, K. 1961. Prehistoric salt boiling. *Antiquity* 35, 18–21.

Riis, A. 1839. *Der evangelische Heidenbote*. Basel: Basel Evangelical Missionary Society.

RIM 1989. *Livestock and Land Use in Niger and Anambra States, Nigeria*. 2 vols. Abuja: Resource

Inventory and Management Ltd.

—— 1991. *Nigerian National Livestock Resource Survey*. 5 vols. Abuja: Resource Inventory and Management Ltd.

Riser, J., C. Hilaire-Marcel & P. Rognon 1983. Les phases lacustres holocènes. In *Sahara ou Sahel?*, Petit-Maire, N. & J. Risir (eds), 65–86. Marseilles: Lamy.

Rita-Ferreira, A. 1975. *Povos de Moçambique: historia e cultura*. Oporto: Afrontamento.

—— 1982. *Fixacão Portuguesa e historia pre-colonial de Moçambique*. Lisbon: Instituto de Investigação Cientifica Tropical.

Ritchie, J. C., C. H. Eyles & C. V. Haynes 1989. Sediment and pollen evidence for an early to mid-holocene humid period in the eastern Sahara. *Nature* 314, 352–5.

Ritter, E. A. 1957. *Shaka Zulu*. New York: Putnam.

Rivallain, J., 1980. Le sel dans les villages côtiers et lagunaires du Bas-Dahomey: sa fabrication, sa place dans le circuit du sel Africain. *Annales de l'Université d'Abidjan* Ic 8, 143–67.

Robbins, L. H., S. McFarlin, J. T. Brower & A. E. Hoffman 1977. Rangi, a late stone age site in Karamoja district Uganda. *Azania* 12, 209–33.

Robequain, C. 1958. *Madagascar et les bases dispersées de l'union française*. Paris: Presses Universitaires de France.

Robert, D. S. 1970. Les fouilles de Tegdaoust. *Journal of African History* 11, 471–93.

Robert, S. & D. Robert 1972. Douze années de recherches archéologiques en République Islamique de Mauretanie. *Annales de la Faculté des Lettres et Sciences Humaines, Université de Dakar* 2, 195–233.

Robert-Chalex, D. & M. Sognane 1983. Une industrie métallurgique ancienne sur la rive mauritanienne du fleuve Sénégal. In *Métallurgies africaines*, Echard, N. (ed.), 45–57. Paris: Société des Africanistes.

Roberts, A. D. 1973. *A History of the Bemba*. Madison: University of Wisconsin Press.

Roberts, B. 1979. *Cities of Peasants*. Beverly Hills: Sage Publications.

Roberts, N. 1989. *The Holocene: an environmental history*. Oxford: Blackwell.

Robertshaw, P. 1982. Eastern Equatoria in the context of later eastern African prehistory. In *Culture History in the Southern Sudan*, Mack, J. & P. Robertshaw (eds), 89–100. Nairobi: British Institute in Eastern Africa.

—— 1989. The development of pastoralism in east Africa. In *The Walking Larder: patterns of domestication, pastoralism and predation*, Clutton-Brock, J. (ed.), 207–14. London: Unwin Hyman.

—— (ed.) 1990. *A History of African Archaeology*. London: James Currey.

—— n.d. The prehistory of pastoralism in Kenya. Unpublished seminar paper, 1984. School of Oriental and African Studies, University of London.

Robertshaw, P. & D. P. Collett 1983. The identification of pastoral peoples in the archaeological record: an example from east Africa. *World Archaeology* 15, 67–78.

Robertshaw, P., D. P. Collett, D. Gifford & N. B. Mbae 1983. Shell middens on the shores of Lake Victoria. *Azania* 18, 1–43.

Robertshaw, P., T. Pilgram, A. Siiriäinen & F. Marshall 1990. The archaeological survey and prehistoric settlement patterns. In *Early Pastoralists of South-western Kenya*, Robertshaw, P. T. (ed.), 36–51. Nairobi: British Institute in Eastern Africa.

Robertson, D. W. 1968. *Chaucer's London*. New York: Wiley.

Robin, C. 1981. Les inscriptions d'al-Mis'ál et la chronologie de l'arabie méridionale au IIIe siècle de l'ère chrétienne. *Comptes Rendus: Académie des Inscriptions et Belles-lettres* April–June, 315–39.

—— 1984. Les Abyssins en Arabie meridionale (IIe–IVe s). Paper read at the Eighth International Conference of Ethiopian Studies, Addis Ababa.

Robinet, A. H. 1967. La Chèvre Rousse de Maradi. *Revue d'Elevage et de Médécine Vétérinaire des*

Pays Tropicaux 20, 129–86.

Robinson, K. R. 1961. Two iron-smelting furnaces from the Chibi Native Reserve, Southern Rhodesia. *South African Archaeological Bulletin* 16, 20–2.

—— 1964. Dombozanga rockshelter, Mtengwe river, Beit Bridge, Southern Rhodesia: excavation results. *Arnoldia* 1, 1–13.

—— 1966. Bambata ware: its position in the Rhodesian Iron Age in the light of recent evidence. *South African Archaeological Bulletin* 21, 81–5.

—— 1970. *The Iron Age of Southern Lake Area of Malawi*. Zomba: Department of Antiquities.

—— 1973a. *The Iron Age of the Upper and Lower Shire, Malawi*. Zomba: Department of Antiquities.

—— 1973b. The pottery sequence of Malawi briefly compared with that already established south of the Zambezi. *Arnoldia* 6, 1–11.

—— 1977. *Iron Age Occupation North and East of the Mulanje Plateau, Malawi*. Limbe: Department of Antiquities.

—— 1979. *The Nkhota-kota Lake Shore and Marginal Areas, Malawi: an archaeological reconnaissance*. Limbe: Department of Antiquities.

—— 1982. *The Iron Age of Northern Malawi: an archaeological reconnaissance*. Limbe: Department of Antiquities.

Robinson, K. R., R. Summers & A. Whitty 1961. Zimbabwe Excavations, 1958: some general conclusions. *Occasional Papers of the National Museums of Southern Rhodesia* 3, 226–333.

Roche, E. 1979. Végétation ancienne et actuelle de l'Afrique centrale. *African Economic History* 7, 30–7.

Rockhill, W. W. (ed.) 1900. *The Journey of William of Rubruck*. London: Hakluyt Society.

Rodney, W. 1970. *A History of the Upper Guinea Coast 1545–1800*. Oxford: Oxford University Press.

Roese, P. M. 1981. Erdwle und Grben im ehemaligen Königreich von Benin. *Anthropos* 76, 166–209.

Rognon, P. 1987. Late quaternary climatic reconstruction for the Maghreb (north Africa). *Palaeogeography, Palaeoclimatology and Palaeoecology* 58, 11–34.

Roscoe, J. 1923. *The Bakitara or Bunyoro*. Cambridge: Cambridge University Press.

Rosemund, C. 1943. Iron smelting in Kahama District. *Tanganyika Notes and Records* 16, 79–84.

Rosevear, D. R. 1974. *The Carnivores of West Africa*. London: Trustees of the British Museum (Natural History).

Rosset, J. P. 1987. Palaeoclimatic and cultural conditions of neolithic development in the early Holocene of northern Niger (Air and Tenere). In *Prehistory of Arid North Africa*, Close, A. E. (ed.), 211–34. Dallas: Southern Methodist University Press.

Rossignol-Strick, M., W. Nesteroff, P. Olive & C. Vergnaud-Grazzini 1982. After the deluge: Mediterranean stagnation and sapropel formation. *Nature* 295, 105–10.

Rossman, D. C. 1976. A site catchment analysis of San-Lorenzo-Vercroz. In *The Early Mesoamerican Village*, Flannery, K. (ed.), 95–102. New York: Academic Press.

Roubet, C. 1968. *Le Gisement du Damous el Ahmer*. Travaux du Centre de Recherches Anthropologiques, Préhistoriques et Ethnographiques en Algérie. Paris: Arts et Métiers Graphiques.

—— 1970. Prospection et découvertes de documents préhistoriques en Dankalie (Ethiopie septentrionale). *Annales d'Ethiopie* 8, 13–20.

—— 1978. Une économie pastorale, pré-agricole en Algérie orientale: le Néolithique de tradition capsienne. *L'Anthropologie* 82, 583–6.

—— 1979. *Economie pastorale préagricole en Algérie orientale: le Néolithique de tradition capsienne*. Paris: CNRS (Centre National de la Recherche Scientifique).

Rouse, I. 1972. Settlement patterns in archeology. In *Man, Settlement and Urbanism*, Ucko, P. J., R. Tringham & G. W. Dimbleby (eds), 95–107. London: Duckworth.

Routledge, W. S. & K. Routledge 1910. *With a Prehistoric People: the Akikúyu of British East Africa*. London: Edward Arnold.

Rowlands, M. J. 1979. Local and long distance trade and incipient state formation on the Bamenda plateau in the late 19th century. *Paideuma* 25, 1–20.

—— 1985. Notes on the material symbolism of Grassfields palaces. *Paideuma* 31, 203–13.

Rowley-Conwy, P. 1988. The camel in the Nile valley: new radiocarbon accelerator (AMS) dates from Qasr Ibrim. *Journal of Egyptian Archaeology* 74, 245–8.

—— 1991. Sorghum from Qasr Ibrim, Egyptian Nubia, c. 1800 BC - AD 1811: a preliminary study. In *New Light on Early Farming: recent developments in palaeoethnology*, Renfrew, J. M. (ed.), 191–212. Edinburgh: Edinburgh University Press.

Rudner, J. 1957. The Brandberg and its archaeological remains. *Journal of the South West African Scientific Society* 12, 7–44.

Russell, J. C. 1966. The population of medieval Egypt. *Journal of the American Research Center in Egypt* 5, 69–82.

Rustad, J. 1980. The emergence of iron technology in west Africa, with special emphasis on the Nok culture of Nigeria. In *West African Culture Dynamics: archaeological and historical perspectives*, Swartz, B. K. & R. Dumett (eds), 227–45. The Hague: Mouton.

Ryder, M. L. 1983. *Sheep and Man*. London: Duckworth.

—— 1984. Sheep. In *Evolution of Domesticated Animals*, Mason, I. L. (ed.), 63–84. London: Longman.

Saad, E. N. 1983. *Social History of Timbuktu*. Cambridge: Cambridge University Press.

Saleh, A. A. 1972a. The *Gnbtyw* of Thutmosis III's annals and the south Arabian *Geb(b)anitae* of the classical writers. *Bulletin de l'Institut Français d'Archaeologie Oriental au Caire* 77, 245–62.

—— 1972b. Some problems relating to the Pwenet reliefs at Deir el-Bahari. *Journal of Egyptian Archaeology* 58, 140–58.

Samuel, R. (ed.) 1981. *People's History and Social Theory*. London: Routledge & Kegan Paul.

Sandelowsky, B. H. 1977. Mirabib – an archaeological study in the Namib. *Madoqua* 10, 221–83.

—— 1983. Archaeology in Namibia. *American Scientist* 71, 606–15.

Sandelowsky, B. H., J. H. Van Rooyen & J. C. Vogel 1979. Early evidence for herders in the Namib. *South African Archaeological Bulletin* 34, 50–1.

SARQ 1980. Arquelogia e conhecimento do passado em Mozambiwque. *Trabalhos em Arqueologia e Anthropologia* 1. Maputo: Universidade Eduardo Mondlane.

Sassoon, H. 1963. Early sources of iron in Africa. *South African Archaeological Bulletin* 18, 176–80.

—— 1964. Iron-smelting in the hill village of Sukur, north-eastern Nigeria. *Man* 64, 174–8.

—— 1980. Excavations at the site of early Mombasa. *Azania* 15, 1–42.

Sauneron, S. 1965. Un village nubien fortifié sur la rive orientale de Ouadi es-Sebou. *Bulletin de l'Institut Français d'Archéologie Orientale* 63, 161–7.

Säve-Söderbergh, T. 1941. *Ägypten und Nubien*. Lund: Hakan Ohlssons Boktryckeri.

—— 1946. *The Navy of the Eighteenth Egyptian Dynasty*. Uppsala: A.-B. Lundequistska Bokhandeln.

Saxon, D. 1980. The history of the Sahri river basin, ca. 500 BC–1000 AD. Unpublished PhD thesis, University of California at Los Angeles.

—— n.d. Linguistic evidence for the early history of the Chad basin. Unpublished seminar paper, 1975.

Saxton, Lt Commander 1925. Historical survey of the Shai people. *Gold Coast Review* June–Dec., 127–45.

Sayed, A. M. A. H. 1977. Discovery of the site of the 12th dynasty port at Wady Gawasis on the

Red Sea shore. *Revue d'Egyptologie* 29, 138–78.

—— 1989. Were there direct relationships between pharaonic Egypt and Arabia? *Proceedings of the Seminar for Arabian Studies* 19, 155–66.

Schacht, R. 1981. Estimating past population trends. *Annual Review of Anthropology* 10, 119–40.

Schadeberg, T. C. 1981. The classification of the Kadugli language group. In *Nilo-Saharan*, Schadeberg, T. C. & M. L. Bender (eds), 291–306. Dordrecht: Foris Publications.

Schadeberg, T. C. & M. L. Bender (eds) 1981. *Nilo-Saharan*. Dordrecht: Foris Publications.

Schaefer, R. P. 1987. *An Initial Orthography and Lexicon for Emai: an Edoid language of Nigeria.* Bloomington: Indiana University Linguistics Club.

Schafer, H. 1902. *Ein Bruchstuck altägyptischer Annalen*. Berlin: Akademie der Wissenschaften.

Schapera, I. 1971. *Married Life in an African Tribe*. Harmondsworth: Penguin.

Schenkel, W. 1965. *Memphis, Herakleopolis und Theben*. Wiesbaden: Otto Harrasowitz.

Schiffer, M. B. 1976. *Behavioral Archaeology*. New York: Academic Press.

Schild, R., M. Chmielewska & H. Wieckowska 1968. The Arkinian and Shamarkian industries. In *The Prehistory of Nubia, Vol. 2*, Wendorf, F. (ed.), 651–767. Dallas: Fort Burgwin Research Center & Southern Methodist University Press.

Schild, R. & F. Wendorf 1989. The late pleistocene Nile in Wadi Kubbaniya. In *The Prehistory of Wadi Kubbaniya, Vol. 2: Stratigraphy, Paleoeconomy, and Environment*, Wendorf, F., R. Schild, & A. E. Close (eds), 15–100. Dallas: Southern Methodist University Press.

Schmidt, P. R. 1974. An investigation of early and late iron age cultures through oral tradition and archaeology: an interdisciplinary case study in Buhaya, Tanzania. Unpublished PhD thesis, Northwestern University.

—— 1975. A new look at interpretations of the early Iron Age in East Africa. *History in Africa* 2, 127–36.

—— 1978. *Historical Archaeology: a structural approach in an African culture*. Westport: Greenwood Press.

—— 1980. Steel production in prehistoric Africa: insights from ethnoarchaeology in West Lake, Tanzania. In *Proceedings of the 8th Panafrican Congress of Prehistory and Quaternary Studies*, Leakey, R. E. & B. A. Ogot (eds), 335–40. Nairobi: International Louis Leakey Memorial Institute for African Prehistory.

—— 1981. *The Origins of Iron Smelting in Africa: a complex technology in Tanzania*. Brown University.

—— 1983. An alternative to a strictly materialist perspective: a review of historical archaeology, ethnoarchaeology and symbolic approaches in African archaeology. *American Antiquity* 48, 62–79.

Schmidt, P. R. & D. H. Avery 1978. Complex iron smelting and prehistoric culture in Tanzania. *Science* 201, 1085–9.

—— 1983. More evidence for an advanced prehistoric iron technology in Africa. *Journal of Field Archaeology* 10, 421–34.

Schmidt, P. & S. T. Childs 1985. Innovation and industry during the early Iron Age in east Africa: the KM2 and KM3 sites of northwest Tanzania. *African Archaeological Review* 3, 53–94.

Schmidt, P. R., L. Digombe, M. Locko & V. Mouleingui 1985. Newly dated iron age sites in Gabon. *Nyame Akuma* 26, 16–18.

Schneider, H. K. 1981. *The Africans: an ethnological account*. Englewood Cliffs: Prentice-Hall.

Schneider, R. 1961. Inscriptions d'Enda Cerqos. *Annales d'Ethiopie* 4, 61–5.

—— 1965. Notes épigraphiques sur les découvertes de Matara. *Annales d'Ethiopie* 6, 88–92.

—— 1973. Deux inscriptions Sudarabiques du Tigré. *Bibliotheca Orientalis* 30, 385–9.

—— 1976a. Les débuts de l'histoire Ethiopienne. *Documents pour Servir à l'Histoire de la Civilisation Ethiopienne* 7, 47–54.

—— 1976b. L'inscription chrétienne d'Ezana en écriture sudarabe. *Annales d'Ethiopie* 10, 109–17.

—— 1976c. Documents épigraphiques de l'Ethiopie – V. *Annales d'Ethiopie* 10, 81–93.

—— 1978. Documents épigraphiques de l'Ethiopie – VI. *Annales d'Ethiopie* 11, 129–32.

Schnell, R. 1977. *Introduction à la phytogéographie des pays tropicaux, 4: La Flore et la végétation de l'Afrique tropicale, R. P. du Congo*. Paris: Gauthier-Villars.

Schofield, J. F. 1948. *Primitive Pottery*. Cape Town: South African Archaeological Society.

Schulken, K. 1922. Das Togopony. Unpublished inaugural dissertation, University of Hanover.

Schumacher, F. C. 1828. Beskrivelse af guineiske Planter, som er fundne af danske Botanikere. *Det Kongelige Danske Videnskabernes Selskabs Naturvidenskabelige og Mathematiske Afhandlinger*, Tredie Deel 1ste stykke, 21–248.

—— 1829. Beskrivelse af guineiske Planter, som er fundne af danske Botanikere. *Det Kongelige Danske Videnskabernes Selskabs Naturvidenskabelige og Mathematiske Afhandlinger*, Fierde Deel Andet stykke, 1–236.

Schwartz, D. 1988a. *Histoire d'un paysage: le lousseke. Paléoenvironnements quaternaires et podzolisation sur sables Bateke: quarante derniers millénaires, région de Brazzaville, R. P. du Congo*. Paris: Etudes et Thèses de l'ORSTOM (Office de Recherche Scientifique et Technique d'Outre-Mer).

—— 1988b. Some podzols on Bateke Sands and their origins, People's Republic of Congo. *Geoderma* 43, 229–47.

—— 1990. Relations sols–relief–variations paléo-climatiques en Afrique centrale. In *Paysages quaternaires de l'Afrique Centrale Atlantique*, Lanfranchi, R. & D. Schwartz (eds), 186–92. Paris: ORSTOM (Institut Français de Recherche Scientifique pour le Développement en Coopération).

Schwartz, D., G. Delibrias, B. Guillet & R. Lanfranchi 1985. Datations par le 14-C d'alios humiques: Hge Njilien (40,000–30,000 B. P.) de la podzolisation sur sables Bateke (Rep. Pop. Congo). *Compte Rendue de l'Académie des Sciences* 300, 891–4.

Scott, L. 1982. A late quaternary pollen record from the Transvaal bushveld, South Africa. *Quaternary Research* 17, 339–70.

Scott, S. L. 1984. Dembeni phase fish remains. *Azania* 19, 49–51.

Scudder, T. 1962. *The Ecology of the Gwembe Tonga*. Manchester: Manchester University Press.

Seignobos, C. (ed.) 1987. *Le Poney du Logone*. Paris: Institut d'Elevage et de Médécine Vétérinaire des Pays Tropicaux.

Seligman, C. G. & B. Z. Seligman 1932. *Pagan Tribes of the Western Sudan*. London: Routledge & Kegan Paul.

Senna Martinez, J. C. 1976. A preliminary report on two early iron age traditions from the southern Mozambique coastal plain. In *Iron Age Research in Mozambique: collected preliminary reports*, Duarte, M. L. T., T. Cruz e Silva, J. C. Senna Martinez, J. M. M. Morais & R. T. Duarte (eds), 1–47. Maputo: Instituto de Investigação Científica de Moçambique.

Servant, M. 1973. Séquences continentales et variations climatiques: évolution du bassin du Tchad au Cénozoique supérieur. Unpublished PhD thesis, University of Paris.

Servant, M. & S. Servant-Vildary 1980. L'environnement quaternaire du bassin du Tchad. In *Sahara and the Nile: quaternary environments and prehistoric occupation in northern Africa*, Williams, M. A. J. & H. Faure (eds), 133–62. Rotterdam: A. A. Balkema.

Servant-Vildary, S. 1978. *Etude des diatomées et paléolimnologie du bassin tchadien au Cénozoïque supérieur*. Paris: ORSTOM (Office de la Recherche Scientifique et Technique d' Outre-Mer).

Sethe, K. 1908/9. *Urkunden der 18. Dynastie*. Leipzig: Hinrichs.

—— 1932. *Urkunden des Alten Reiches, Vol. 1*. Leipzig: Hinrichs.

Seyfried, K. J. 1981. *Beiträge zu den Expeditionen des Mittleren Reiches in die Ostwuste*. Hildesheim: Gerstenberg.

Shackley, M. L. 1985. Palaeolithic archaeology of the central Namib desert: a preliminary survey of chronology, typology and site location. *Cimbebasia*, Memoire 6.

Shaw, P. A., H. J. Cooke & D. S. G. Thomas 1988. Recent advances in the study of quaternary landforms in Botswana. *Palaeoecology of Africa* 19, 15–26.

Shaw, T. 1944. Report on excavations carried out in the cave known as 'Bosumpra' at Abetifi, Kwahu, Gold Coast Colony. *Proceedings of the Prehistoric Society* 10, 1–67.

—— 1963. *Archaeology in Nigeria*. Ibadan: Ibadan University Press.

—— 1966a. Recent archaeological work in Nigeria. *West African Archaeological Newsletter* 5, 9–11.

—— 1966b. Discussions on terminology. *West African Archaeological Newsletter* 5, 39–53.

—— 1967. Resolutions on terminology. *West African Archaeological Newsletter* 7, 33–7.

—— 1969. On radiocarbon chronology of the iron age in sub-Saharan Africa. *Current Anthropology* 10, 226–31.

—— 1970. *Igbo-Ukwu*. London: Faber.

—— 1973. Finds at the Iwo Eleru rock shelter, western Nigeria. In *Sixième Congrès Panafricain de Préhistoire, Dakar 1967*, Hugot, H. J. (ed.), 190–2. Chambéry: Les Imprimeries Réunies.

—— 1975. *Why 'Darkest' Africa? Archaeological light on an old problem*. Ibadan: Ibadan University Press.

—— 1976. Early crops in Africa: a review of the evidence. In *Origins of African Plant Domestication*, Harlan, J. R., J. M. J. De Wet & A. B. L. Stemler (eds), 107–53. The Hague: Mouton.

—— 1977. Hunters, gatherers and first farmers in west Africa. In *Hunters, Gatherers and First Farmers beyond Europe: an archaeological survey*, Megaw, J. V. S. (ed.), 69–125. Leicester: Leicester University Press.

—— 1978. *Nigeria: its archaeology and early history*. London: Thames & Hudson.

—— 1978–9. Holocene adaptations in west Africa: the Late Stone Age. *Early Man News* 3/4, 51–82.

—— 1981a. The Nok sculptures of Nigeria. *Scientific American* 244, 154–66.

—— 1981b. Towards a prehistoric demography of Africa. In *African Historical Demography, Vol. 2*, McMaster, C. & D. Fyfe (eds), 581–606. Edinburgh: University of Edinburgh Centre of African Studies.

—— 1985a. The prehistory of west Africa. In *History of West Africa*, Ade Ajayi, J. F. & M. Crowder (eds), 48–86. Harlow: Longman.

—— 1985b. Always something new from Africa. *Antiquity* 59, 209–13.

—— 1988. The Guinea Zone. In *General History of Africa: Africa from the seventh to eleventh century, Vol. III*, M. El Fari & I. Hrbek (eds), 461–87. London: Heinemann/UNESCO.

—— 1989. The academic profession and contemporary politics: the World Archaeological Congress – politics and learning. *Minerva* 27, 58–125.

—— 1990. The prehistory of west Africa. In *General History of Africa: Methodology and African prehistory, Vol. I* (abridged edn), J. Ki-Zerbo (ed.), 264–73., 611–30. London: Heinemann/ UNESCO.

—— n.d. Rainfall and exogamy in the Sahara: adaptations to the holocene environment. Unpublished manuscript, 1979.

Shaw, T. & S. G. Daniels 1984. *Excavations at Iwo Eleru, Ondo State, Nigeria*. Ibadan: West African Journal of Archaeology Monograph.

Sheik-Dilthey, H. 1978. Alt-Mombasa: Interethnische Beziehungen einer ostafrikanischen Hafenstadt. *Anthropos* 73, 673–716.

Shepherd, G. 1982. The making of the Swahili: a view from the southern end of the east African coast. *Paideuma* 28, 129–48.

Shimizu, Kiyoshi 1980. *Comparative Jukunoid*. 3 vols. Vienna: Afropub.

Shinnie, P. L. 1965. *Ancient African Kingdoms*. London: Edward Arnold.

—— 1966. Meroe and west Africa. *West African Archaeological Newsletter* 6, 12–16.

—— (ed.) 1971. *The African Iron Age*. Oxford: Clarendon Press.

Shinnie, P. L. & F. J. Kense 1989. *Archaeology of Gonja, Ghana: excavations at Daboya*. Calgary: University of Calgary Press.

Siiriäinen, A. 1971. The iron age site at Gatung'ang'a, central Kenya. *Azania* 6, 199–222.

Simmonds, N. W. 1966. *Bananas*. London: Longmans, Green.

Simoons, F. J. 1960. *Northwest Ethiopia: peoples and economy*. Madison: University of Wisconsin Press.

—— 1965. Some questions on the economic prehistory of Ethiopia. *Journal of African History* 6, 1–13.

Simpson, W. K. 1973. *The Literature of Ancient Egypt*. New Haven: Yale University Press.

Sinclair, P. J. J. 1981. An archaeological outline of two social formations of the later Iron Age of Zimbabwe and Mozambique. Paper presented to the 10th International Union of Pre- and Proto-historic Sciences Conference, Mexico City.

—— 1982. Chibuene, an early trading site in southern Mozambique. Festschrift for J. Kirkman. *Paideuma* 28, 149–64.

—— 1984a. Rescue excavation of a furnace at Gokomere Mission, Zimbabwe. *Cookeia* 1, 15–26.

—— 1984b. Some aspects of the economic level of the Zimbabwe state. *Zimbabwea* 1, 48–53.

—— 1985. *An Archaeological Survey of Northern Mozambique. Part I, Nampula Province*. Uppsala: Department of Cultural Anthropology, Uppsala University.

—— 1986. *An Archaeological Survey of Northern Mozambique. Part II, Cabo Delgado Province*. Uppsala: Department of Cultural Anthropology, Uppsala University.

—— 1987. *Space, Time and Social Formation: a territorial approach to the archaeology and anthropology of Zimbabwe and Mozambique, c. 0–1700 AD*. Uppsala: Societas Archaeologica Upsaliensis.

—— 1988. *The Mombasa Specialist Workshop 1st–6th August 1988*. Stockholm: Swedish Central Board of National Antiquities.

—— 1989. Urban origins in eastern Africa: a regional cooperation project. *World Archaeological Bulletin* 3, 33–51.

—— 1990 The earth is our history book: archaeology in Mozambique. In *The Excluded Past: archaeology in education*, Stone, P. & R. MacKenzie (eds), 152–9. London: Unwin Hyman.

—— 1991. Archaeology in eastern Africa: an overview of current chronological issues. *Journal of African History* 32, 179–219.

Sinclair, P. J. J., M. Kokonya, M. Meneses & J.-A. Rakatoarisoa 1992. The impact of information technology on the archaeology of southern and eastern Africa – the first decades. In *Archaeology and the Information Age*, Reilly, P. & S. Rahtz (eds), 30–41. London: Routledge.

Sinclair P. J. J. & H. Lundmark 1984. A spatial analysis of archaeological sites from Zimbabwe. In *Frontiers: southern African archaeology today*, Hall, M., G. Avery, M. Avery & M. L. Wilson (eds), 277–88. Oxford: British Archaeological Reports.

Sinclair, P. J. J., J. M. M. Morais & B. Bingham 1979. The archaeology of Mozambique and Zimbabwe. Paper presented to a symposium, International Louis Leakey Memorial Institute for African Prehistory, 1979.

Sinclair, P. J. J., N. G. Nydolf & G. W. Nydolf 1987. *Excavations at the University Campus Site, 2532 Dc 1, Southern Mozambique*. Stockholm: Eduardo Mondlane University & Swedish Central Board of National Antiquities.

Sjoberg, G. 1960. *The Preindustrial City, Past and Present*. Glencoe: Free Press.

Skinner, G. W. (ed.) 1977. *The City in Late Imperial China*. Stanford: Stanford University Press.

Skinner, N. 1979. Domestic animals in Chadic. In *Papers in Chadic Linguistics*, Newman, P. & R. M. Newman (eds), 175–98. Leiden: Afrika-Studiecentrum.

—— 1984. Afroasiatic vocabulary: evidence for some culturally important items. *Africana Marburgensia*, Special Issue.

Skolle, J. 1956. *The Road to Timbuktoo*. London: Victor Gollancz.

Smith, A. B. 1974. Preliminary reports of excavations at Karkarichinkat nord and Karkarichinkat sud, Tilemsi valley, Republic of Mali, Spring 1972. *West African Journal of Archaeology* 4, 33–55.

—— 1975a. A note on the flora and fauna from post-palaeolithic sites of Karkarichinkat nord and sud. *West African Journal of Archaeology* 5, 201–4.

—— 1975b. Radiocarbon dates from Bosumpra cave, Abetifi, Ghana. *Proceedings of the Prehistoric Society* 41, 179–82.

—— 1980a. Domesticated cattle in the Sahara and their introduction into west Africa. In *The Sahara and the Nile: quaternary environments and prehistoric occupation in northern Africa*, Williams, M. A. J. & H. Faure (eds), 489–503. Rotterdam: Balkema.

—— 1980b. The neolithic tradition in the Sahara. In *The Sahara and the Nile: quaternary environments and prehistoric occupation in northern Africa*, Williams, M. A. J. & H. Faure (eds), 451–65. Rotterdam: Balkema.

—— 1986. Review article: cattle domestication in north Africa. *African Archaeological Review* 4, 197–203.

Smith, E. & M. Dale 1920. *The Ila Speaking People of Northern Rhodesia*. London: Macmillan.

Smith, Sir G. E. 1915. *The Migrations of Early Culture*. Manchester: Victoria University.

Smith, H. 1972. Society and settlement in ancient Egypt. In *Man, Settlement and Urbanism*, Ucko, P. J., R. Tringham & G. W. Dimbleby (eds), 705–20. London: Duckworth.

—— 1985. Settlements in the Nile valley. In *Mélanges Gamal Eddin Mokhtar*, Posener-Krieger, P. (ed.), 287–94. Cairo: Institut Français d'Archéologie Orientale du Caire.

Smith, J. 1968. *Colonial Cadet in Nigeria*. Durham, N. C.: Duke University Press.

Smith, J. L. B. 1950. *The Sea Fishes of Southern Africa*. South Africa: Central News Agency.

—— 1963. *The Fishes of Seychelles*. Grahamstown: Rhodes University Press.

Smith, M. G. 1972. Complexity, size and urbanization. In *Man, Settlement and Urbanism*, Ucko, P. J., R. Tringham & G. W. Dimbleby (eds), 567–74. London: Duckworth.

Smith, S. E. 1980. The environmental adaptation of nomads in the west African Sahel: a key to understanding prehistoric pastoralists. In *The Sahara and the Nile: quaternary environments and prehistoric occupation in northern Africa*, Williams, M. A. J. & H. Faure (eds), 467–87. Rotterdam: Balkema.

Smolla, G. 1976. Archaeological research in the coastal area of southern Mozambique. In *Proceedings of the Panafrican Congress of Prehistory and Quaternary Studies, 7th Session, Addis Ababa, December 1971*, Abebe, B., J. Chevaillon & J. E. G. Sutton (eds), 265–70. Addis Ababa: Provisional Military Government of Socialist Ethiopia, Ministry of Culture.

Soper, R. C. 1967. Kwale: an early iron age site in south-eastern Kenya. *Azania* 2, 1–17.

—— 1971a. Early iron age pottery types from east Africa: comparative analysis. *Azania* 6, 39–52.

—— 1971b. A general review of the early Iron Age in the southern half of Africa. *Azania* 6, 5–37.

—— 1975. Some comments on the site of Old Oyo. Eyewitness accounts and archaeological observations. *The Archaeologist* 2, 47–52.

—— 1976. Archaeological sites in the Chyulu hills, Kenya. *Azania* 11, 83–116.

—— 1982. Bantu expansion into east Africa: archaeological evidence. In *The Archaeological and Linguistic Reconstruction of African History*, Ehret, C. & M. Posnansky (eds), 223–38. Berkeley: University of California Press.

Soper, R. C. & P. Darling 1980. The walls of Old Oyo. *West African Journal of Archaeology* 10, 61–81.

Soper, R. C. & G. Pwiti 1988. Preliminary report on excavations at Wazi Hill, Centenary, northern Zimbabwe. *Zimbabwean Prehistory* 20, 16–20.

Southall, A. 1965. A critique of the typology of states and political systems. In *Political Systems and the Distribution of Power*, Banton, M. (ed.), 113–38. London: Tavistock.

—— 1973. The density of role-relationships as a current index of urbanization. In *Urban Anthropology: cross-cultural studies of urbanization*, Southall, A. (ed.), 71–106. New York: Oxford University Press.

Sowunmi, M. A. 1985. The beginnings of agriculture in west Africa: botanical evidence. *Current Anthropology* 26, 127–9.

Springuel, I. V. 1981. Studies on the natural vegetation of the islands of the First Cataract at Aswan, Egypt. Unpublished PhD thesis, Aswan Faculty of Science, Asyut University.

Spruytte, J. 1971. Le cheval et le char de l'Egypte ancienne. *Plaisirs Equestres* 51, 171–6.

Stadelmann, R. 1983. Pyramidenstadt. In *Lexikon der Ägyptologie, V*, Helck, W. & W. Westendorf (eds), 9–14. Wiesbaden: Otto Harrasowitz.

—— 1985. Theben. In *Lexikon der Ägyptologie, VI*, Helck, W. & W. Westendorf (eds), 465–73. Wiesbaden: Otto Harrasowitz.

Stahl, A. B. 1984. A history and critique of investigations into early African agriculture. In *From Hunters to Farmers: the causes and consequences of food production in Africa*, Clark, J. D. & S. A. Brandt (eds), 9–21. Berkeley: University of California Press.

—— 1985a. Reinvestigation of Kintampo 6 rock shelter, Ghana: implications for the nature of culture change. *African Archaeological Review* 3, 117–50.

—— 1985b. The Kintampo culture: subsistence and settlement in Ghana during the mid-second millennium BC. Unpublished PhD thesis, University of California at Berkeley.

—— 1986. Early food production in west Africa: rethinking the role of the Kintampo culture. *Current Anthropology* 27, 532–6.

—— 1989. Plant food processing: implications for dietary quality. In *Foraging and Farming: the evolution of plant exploitation*, Harris, D. R. & G. C. Hillman (eds), 171–94. London: Unwin Hyman.

Stannus, S. N. 1914. Angoni smelting furnace. *Man* 14, 131–2.

Starkey, P. H. 1984. N'dama cattle – a productive trypanotolerant breed. *World Animal Review* 50, 2–15.

Stayt, H. A. 1931. *The Bavenda*. London: Oxford University Press.

Stemler, A. B. L. 1980. Origins of plant domestication in the Sahara and the Nile valley. In *The Sahara and the Nile: quaternary environments and prehistoric occupation in north Africa*, Williams, M. A. J. & H. Faure (eds), 503–26. Rotterdam: Balkema.

Stemler, A. B. L. & R. H. Falk 1980. A scanning electron microscope study of cereal grains from Nabta Playa. In *Prehistory of the Eastern Sahara*, Wendorf, F. & R. Schild (eds), 393–9. New York: Academic Press.

Steponaitis, V. P. 1978. Location theory and complex chiefdoms: a Mississippian example. In *Mississippian Settlement Patterns*, Smith, B. D. (ed.), 417–53. New York: Academic Press.

Sterk, J. P. 1977. Elements of Gade grammar. Unpublished PhD thesis, University of Wisconsin.

Stewart, J. 1973. The lenis stops of the Potou Lagoon languages and their significance for pre-Bantu reconstruction. *Research Review (Ghana)* Supplement 4, 1–49.

Stewart, J. L. 1937. *The Cattle of the Gold Coast*. Accra: Government Printer.

Stobbs, A. R. & A. Young 1972. Natural regions. In *Malawi in Maps*, Agnew, S. & M. Stubb (eds), 40–2. London: University of London Press.

Stoops, G. 1967. Le profil d'altération au Bas-Congo (Kinshasa). *Pédologie* 17, 60–105.

Street, F. A. 1979. Late quaternary lakes in the Ziway-Shala basin, southern Ethiopia. Unpublished PhD thesis, University of Cambridge.

Street, F. A. & F. Gasse 1981. Recent developments in the quaternary climatic history of the Sahara. In *The Sahara: ecological change and early economic history*, Allan, J. A. (ed.), 7–28. Outwell: Middle Eastern and North African Studies Press.

Street, F. A. & A. T. Grove 1976. Environmental and climatic implications of late quaternary lake-level fluctuations in Africa. *Nature* 261, 385–90.

Street-Perrott, F. A., D. S. Marchand, N. Roberts & S. P. Harrison 1989. *Global Lake-level Variations from 18000 to 0 Years Ago: a paleoclimatic analysis.* Washington: United States Department of Energy.

Street-Perrott, F. A. & N. Roberts 1983. Fluctuations in closed basin lakes as an indicator of past atmospheric circulation patterns. In *Variations in the Global Water Budget*, Street-Perrott, A., M. Beran & R. Ratcliffe (eds), 331–45. Dordrecht: Reidel.

Street-Perrott, F. A., N. Roberts & S. Metcalfe 1985. Geomorphic implications of late quaternary hydrological and climatic changes in the northern hemisphere tropics. In *Environmental Change and Tropical Geomorphology*, Douglas, I. & T. Spencer (eds), 165–83. London: Allen & Unwin.

Stuiver, M. & G. W. Pearson 1986. High-precision calibration of the radiocarbon time scale, AD 1950–500 BC. *Radiocarbon* 28, 805–38.

Summers, R. 1950. Iron age cultures in Southern Rhodesia. *South African Journal of Science* 47, 95–107.

—— 1960. Environment and culture in Southern Rhodesia. *Proceedings of the American Philosophical Society* 3, 266–92.

—— 1969. *Ancient Mining in Rhodesia and Adjacent Areas.* Salisbury: National Museums and Monuments of Rhodesia.

—— 1971. *Ancient Ruins and Vanished Civilizations of Southern Rhodesia.* Cape Town: Bulpin.

Sumner, W. M. 1989. Population and settlement area: an example from Iran. *American Anthropologist* 91, 631–41.

Sundstrom, L. 1972. *Ecology and Symbiosis: Niger waterfolk.* Uppsala: Studia Ethnographica Upsaliensia.

Sutton, J. E. G. 1973a. The eastern African 'Neolithic'. In *Sixième Congrès Panafricain de Préhistoire, Dakar, 1967*, Hugot, H. J. (ed.), 88–90. Chambéry: Les Imprimeries Réunies.

—— 1973b. *The Archaeology of the Western Highlands of Kenya.* Nairobi: British Institute in Eastern Africa.

—— 1974. The aquatic civilisation of middle Africa. *Journal of African History* 15, 527–46.

—— 1976a. Iron working around Zaria. *Zaria Archaeological Papers* 8, 18.

—— 1976b. The walls of Zaria and Kufena. *Zaria Archaeological Papers* 11, 1–19.

—— 1977. The African Aqualithic. *Antiquity* 51, 25–34.

—— 1981. Population estimates from selected African iron age sites. In *African Historical Demography, Vol. 2*, McMaster, C. & D. Fyfe (eds), 607–53. Edinburgh: University of Edinburgh Centre of African Studies.

—— 1982. Archaeology in west Africa: a review of recent work and a further list of radiocarbon dates. *Journal of African History* 23, 291–313.

—— 1985. Temporal and spatial variability in African iron furnaces. In *African Iron Working: ancient and traditional*, Haaland, R. & P. Shinnie (eds), 164–98. Oslo: Norwegian University Press.

—— 1987. Deloraine and the Rift Valley sequence. *Nyame Akuma* 29, 34–6.

—— 1990. *A Thousand Years of East Africa.* Nairobi: British Institute in Eastern Africa.

—— 1991. The international factor at Igbo Ukwu. *African Archaeological Review* 9, 145–60.

Sutton, J. E. G. & A. Roberts 1968. Uvinza and its salt industry. *Azania* 3, 45–86.

Tackholm, V. 1974. *Students' Flora of Egypt.* Cairo: University of Cairo.

Tackholm, V. & M. Drar 1941. *Flora of Egypt, Vol. 1.* Cairo: Faculty of Science, Fouad I University.

—— 1950. *Flora of Egypt, Vol. 2.* Cairo: Faculty of Science, Fouad I University.

Talbot, M. R. 1981. Holocene changes in tropical wind intensity and rainfall: evidence from south-east Ghana. *Quaternary Research* 16, 201–20.

Talbot, M. R., D. A. Livingstone, P. G. Palmer, J. Maley, J. M. Melack, G. Delibrias & S. Gulliksen 1984. Preliminary results from sediment cores from Lake Bosumtwi, Ghana. *Palaeoecology of Africa* 16, 173–92.

Tamrat, T. 1972. *Church and State in Ethiopia 1270–1527*. Oxford: Clarendon Press.

Tanaka, J. 1976. Subsistence ecology of central Kalahari San. In *Kalahari Hunter-Gathers: studies of the !Kung San and their neighbors*, Lee, R. B. & I. DeVore (eds), 98–119. Cambridge, Mass. & London: Harvard University Press.

Tardits, C. 1980. *Le Royaume bamoum*. Paris: Armand Colin.

—— (ed.) 1981a. *Contribution de la recherche ethnologique à l'histoire des civilisations du Cameroun*. 2 vols. Paris: CNRS (Centre National de la Recherche Scientifique).

—— 1981b. Le royaume bamoum. In *Contribution de la recherche ethnologique à l'histoire des civilisations du Cameroun*, Tardits, C. (ed.), 401–20. Paris: CNRS (Centre National de la Recherche Scientifique).

Taylor, G. 1926. Native iron-workers. *Native Affairs Development Annual* 4, 53.

Terray, E. 1974. Long distance trade, exchange and formation of the state: the case of the Abron kingdom of Gyamon. *Economy and Society* 3, 315–45.

Tessier, J. 1975. Proto-historic saltmaking sites in the Pays de Retz (France). In *Salt: the study of an ancient industry*, de Brisay, K. W. & K. A. Evans (eds), 52–6. Colchester: Colchester Archaeological Group.

Tessmann, G. 1929. Die Mbaka-Limba, Mbum und Lakka. *Zeitschrift für Ethnologie* 60, 305–52.

Tewe, O. O., S. S. Ajayi & E. O. Faturoti 1984. Giant rat and cane rat. In *Evolution of Domesticated Animals*, Mason, I. L. (ed.), 291–3. London: Longman.

Theal, G. M. 1893–1903. *Records of South Eastern Africa*. 9 vols. Cape Town: Government of Cape Colony.

Thomas, E. & K. Williamson 1967. *Wordlists of Delta Edo: Epie, Engenni, Degema*. Ibadan: Institute of African Studies.

Thomassy, P. & R. Mauny 1951. Campagne de fouilles à Koumbi Saleh. *IFAN* (Bulletin de l'Institut Français d'Afrique Noire) 13, 438–62.

—— 1956. Campagne de fouilles à Koumbi Saleh. *IFAN* (Bulletin de l'Institut Français d'Afrique Noire) 18, 117–40.

Thompson, E. P. 1978. *The Poverty of Theory and Other Essays*. London: Merlin Press.

Thornton, R. J. 1980. *Space, Time, and Culture among the Iraq of Tanzania*. New York: Academic Press.

Thornycroft, C. 1988. Report on an excavation at Castle Kopje, Wedza District. *Zimbabwean Prehistory* 20, 29–36.

Thorp, C. 1983. Late iron age faunal remains. *Nyame Akuma* 22, 37–8.

Tietze, C. 1984. Die Bewohner der Amarna. *Das Altertum* 30, 225–32.

—— 1985. Amarna. Analyse den Wohnhäuser und soziale Struktur der Stadtbewohner. *Zeitschrift für altägyptische Sprache und Altertumskunde* 112, 48–84.

—— 1986. Amarna (Teil II). Analyse der ökonomische Beziehungen der Stadtbewohner. *Zeitschrift für Altägyptische Sprache und Altertumskunde* 113, 55–78.

Tilley, C. 1982. Social formation, social structure and social change. In *Symbolic and Structural Archaeology*, Hodder, I. (ed.), 129–54. Cambridge: Cambridge University Press.

Todd, J. A. 1976. Studies of primitive iron technology. Unpublished PhD thesis, University of Cambridge.

—— 1979. Studies of the African Iron Age. *Journal of Metals* 31, 39–45.

—— 1985. Iron production by the Dimi of Ethiopia. In *African Iron Working: ancient and traditional*, Haaland, R. & P. Shinnie (eds), 88–101. Oslo: Norwegian University Press.

Todd, J. A. & J. A. Charles 1978. Ethiopian bloomery iron and the significance of inclusion analysis in iron studies. *Journal of the Historical Metallurgy Society* 12, 63–87.

Tomlinson, R. W. 1973. *The Inyanga Area, an Essay in Regional Biogeography*. Salisbury: University of Rhodesia.

Tourneux, H. 1987. Les noms des équides en Afrique Centrale. In *Le Poney du Logone*, Seignobos, C. (ed.), 169–205. Paris: Institut d'Elevage et de Médécine Vétérinaire des Pays Tropicaux.

Toussoun, O. 1924. *Memoire sur les finances de l'Egypte depuis les Pharaons jusqu'à nos jour*. Cairo: Société Royale de Géographie d'Egypte.

Traill, A. 1978. Research on the non-Bantu languages. In *Language and Communication Studies in South Africa: current issues and directions in research enquiry*, Lanham, L. W. & K. P. Prinsloo (eds), 117–37. Cape Town: Oxford University Press.

Treinen-Claustre, F. 1982. *Sahara et Sahel à l'âge du fer: Borkou, Tchad*. Paris: Société des Africanistes.

Tremearne, A. J. N. 1912. *The Tailed Head-hunters of Nigeria*. London: Seeley Service.

Trevor-Roper, H. 1963. The rise of Christian Europe. *The Listener*, 28 November, p. 871.

Trifonov, V. 1991. Why so little is known about modern Soviet archaeology: archaeological data in the USSR. *World Archaeological Bulletin* 5, 77–85.

Trifonov, V. & P. M. Dolukhanov 1992. Archaeological data in the USSR – collection, storage and exploitation: has IT a role? In *Archaeology and the Information Age*, Reilly, P. & S. Rahtz (eds), 65–9. London: Routledge.

Trigger, B. 1965. *History and Settlement in Lower Nubia*. New Haven: Yale University Press.

—— 1969. The myth of Meroe and the African Iron Age. *African Historical Studies* 2, 23–50.

—— 1972. Determinants of urban growth in pre-industrial societies. In *Man, Settlement and Urbanism*, Ucko, P. J., R. Tringham & G. W. Dimbleby (eds), 575–99. London: Duckworth.

—— 1976. *Nubia under the Pharaohs*. London: Thames & Hudson.

—— 1983. The rise of Egyptian civilization. In *Ancient Egypt: a social history*, Trigger, B. G., B. J. Kemp, D. O'Connor & A. B. Lloyd, 1–69. Cambridge: Cambridge University Press.

—— 1989. *A History of Archaeological Thought*. Cambridge: Cambridge University Press.

Trigger, B., B. Kemp, D. O'Connor & A. Lloyd 1983. *Ancient Egypt: a social history*. Cambridge: Cambridge University Press

Trimingham, J. S. 1952. *Islam in Africa*. London: Oxford University Press.

Tringali, G. 1965. Cenni sulle 'Ona' di Asmara e dintorni. *Annales d'Ethiopie* 6, 143–52.

Troquereau, P. J. A. 1961. Les ressources animales de la République du Dahomey. Report to the Government of the Republic of Dahomey.

Tucker, A. N. & M. A. Bryan 1956. *The Non-Bantu Languages of North-eastern Africa. Handbook of African Languages, Vol. 3*. London: International African Institute.

Tylecote, R. F. 1962. *Metallurgy in Archaeology*. London: Edward Arnold.

—— 1965. Iron smelting in pre-industrial communities. *Journal of Iron and Steel Institute* 203, 340–8.

—— 1970. Iron working at Meroe, Sudan. *Bulletin of the Historical Metallurgy Group* 4, 67–72.

—— 1975a. The origin of iron smelting in Africa. *West African Journal of Archaeology* 5, 1–9.

—— 1975b. Iron smelting at Taruga, Nigeria. *Journal of the Historical Metallurgy Society* 9, 49–56.

—— 1976. *A History of Metallurgy*. London: Edward Arnold.

—— 1980. Furnaces, crucibles and slags. In *The Coming of the Age of Iron*, Wertime, T. A. & J. D. Muhly (eds), 183–228. New Haven: Yale University Press.

—— 1982. Early copper slags and copper-base metal from the Agadeg region of Niger. *Journal of the Historical Metallurgical Society* 16, 58–64.

—— 1983. Archaeometallurgical finds and their significance. In *Métallurgies africaines: nouvelles contributions*, Echard, N. (ed.), 1–11. Paris: Société des Africanistes.

—— 1987. *The Early History of Metallurgy in Europe*. London: Longman.

Tylecote, R. F., J. N. Austin & A. E. Wraith 1971. The mechanism of the bloomery process in shaft furnaces. *Journal of the Iron and Steel Institute* 209, 342–63.

Tymowski, M. 1979. *Historia Mali*. Warsaw: Ossolineum.

Tyson, P. D. 1987. *Climatic Change and Variability in Southern Africa*. Cape Town: Oxford University Press.

Ucko, P. J. 1987. *Academic Freedom and Apartheid: the story of the World Archaeological Congress*. London: Duckworth.

—— 1992. Foreword. In *Archaeology and the Information Age: a global perspective*, Reilly, P. & S. Rahtz (eds), vii–xi. London: Routledge.

Ucko, P. J., R. Tringham & G. W. Dimbleby (eds) 1972. *Man, Settlement and Urbanism*. London: Duckworth.

Udo, R. K. 1966. Transformation of rural settlements in British tropical Africa. *The Nigerian Geographical Journal* 9, 129–42.

—— 1982. *The Human Geography of Tropical Africa*. Ibadan: Heinemann.

Uphill, E. 1972. The concept of the Egyptian palace as a 'ruling machine'. In *Man, Settlement and Urbanism*, Ucko, P. J., R. Tringham & G. W. Dimbleby (eds), 721–34. London: Duckworth.

Valbelle, D. 1975. Deir el-Medineh. In *Lexikon der Ägyptologie, I*, Helck, W. & E. Otto (eds), 1028–34. Wiesbaden: Otto Harrasowitz.

Valentia, G. (Viscount) 1809. *Voyages and Travels to India, Ceylon, the Red Sea, Abyssinia and Egypt, in the Years 1802–1806*. London: William Miller.

van Beek, G. W. 1969. *Hajar bin Humeid: investigations at a pre-Islamic site in south Arabia*. Baltimore: Johns Hopkins University Press.

Van Dantzig, A. 1978. *The Dutch and the Guinea Coast 1674–1742*. Accra: Ghana Academy of Arts and Sciences.

van den Brink, E. 1986. A geo-archaeological survey of the north-eastern Nile delta, Egypt. *Mitteilungen des Deutschen Archäologischen Institut, Abteilung Kairo* 43, 7–31.

—— 1988. *The Archaeology of the Nile Delta: problems and priorities*. Amsterdam: Netherlands Foundation for Archaeological Research in Egypt/Uitgeverij.

van der Merwe, N. J. 1977. Production of high-carbon steel in the Iron Age. In *Proceedings of the 8th Panafrican Congress of Prehistory and Quaternary Studies*, Leakey, R. E. & B. A. Ogot (eds), 331–4. Nairobi: International Louis Leakey Memorial Institute for African Prehistory.

—— 1980. The advent of iron in Africa. In *The Coming of the Age of Iron*, Wertime, T. A. & J. D. Muhly (eds), 463–506. New Haven: Yale University Press.

van der Merwe, N. J. & D. H. Avery 1982. Pathways to steel. *American Scientist* 70, 146–55.

—— 1987. Science and magic in African technology: traditional iron smelting in Malawi. *Africa* 57, 143–72.

van der Merwe, N. J. & D. J. Killick 1979. Square: an iron smelting site near Phalaborwa, Johannesburg. *South African Archaeological Society, Goodwin Series* 3, 86–93.

Van der Plicht, J. & W. G. Mook 1989. Calibration of radiocarbon age by computer. *Radiocarbon* 31, 805–16.

Van Grunderbeek, M.-C., E. Roche & H. Doutrelepont 1982. L'âge du fer ancien au Rwanda et au Burundi: archéologie et environnement. *Journal de la Société des Africanistes* 52, 5–58.

Van Heekeren, H. R. 1958. *The Bronze–Iron Age of Indonesia*. s'Gravenhage: M. Nijhoff.

Van Moesieke, D. 1929. Monographie agricole du district de la Lulonga (Equateur). *Bulletin Agricole du Congo Belge* 20, 395–439.

van Neer, W. 1984. Faunal remains from Matupi cave, an iron age and late stone age site in northeastern Zaïre. *Academiae Analecta* 46, 59–76.

—— 1989. Fishing along the prehistoric Nile. In *Late Prehistory of the Nile Basin and the Sahara*, Krzyzaniak, L. & M. Kobusiewicz (eds), 49–56. Poznan: Poznan Archaeology Museum.

Van Noten, F. 1977. Excavations at Matupi cave. *Antiquity* 51, 35–40.

—— 1979. The early Iron Age in the interlacustrine region: the diffusion of iron technology. *Azania* 14, 61–80.

—— 1982. *The Archaeology of Central Africa*. Graz: Akademische Druck- und Verlagsanstalt.

—— 1985. Ancient and modern iron smelting in central Africa: Zaïre, Rwanda and Burundi. In *African Iron Working*, Haaland, R. & P. L. Shinnie (eds), 102–20. Oslo: Norwegian University Press.

Van Riet Lowe, C. 1943. Subsidio para a pre-historia de Moçambique. *Moçambique, Documentario Trimestral* 36, 7–12.

van Zeist, W. & W. Waterbolk-van Rooijen 1985. The palaeobotany of Tell Bougras, eastern Syria. *Paléorient* 11, 131–47.

Van Zinderen Bakker, E. M. 1951. Archaeology and palynology. *South African Archaeological Bulletin* 23, 80–7.

—— 1976. Tentative vegetation maps of Africa south of the Sahara during a glacial and an interglacial maximum. *Palaeoecology of Africa* 9, colour map in frontispiece & Pl. IV.

Van Zinderen Bakker, E. M. & J. A. Coatzee 1972. A re-appraisal of late quaternary climatic evidence from tropical Africa. *Palaeoecology of Africa* 7, 151–81.

—— 1988. A review of late quaternary pollen studies in east, central and southern Africa. *Review of Palaeobotany & Palynology* 55, 155–74.

Vansina, J. T. 1962. Long distance routes in central Africa. *Journal of African History* 3, 375–90.

—— 1965. *Oral Tradition*. London: Routledge & Kegan Paul.

—— 1979a. Bantu in the Crystal Ball. *History in Africa* 6, 287–333.

—— 1979b. Finding food and the history of precolonial equatorial Africa: a plea. *African Economic History* 7, 9–20.

—— 1980. Bantu in the Crystal Ball II. *History in Africa* 7, 293–325.

—— 1984. Western Bantu expansion. *Journal of African History* 25, 129–45.

—— 1989. Western Bantu tradition and the notion of tradition. *Paideuma* 35, 289–300.

Vaufrey, R. 1933. Notes sur le Capsien. *L'Anthropologie* 43, 457–83.

—— 1938. L'âge de l'art rupestre nord-africain. *Jahrbuch für Prähistorische und Ethnographische Kunst* 12, 10–29.

—— 1946. Le Néolithique de tradition capsienne au Sénégal. *Rivista di Scienza Preistorica* 1, 18–32.

Vedder, H. 1938. *South West Africa in Early Times*. London: Frank Cass.

Vercoutter, J. 1956. New inscriptions from the Sudan. *Kush* 4, 66–82.

—— 1959. The gold of Kush. *Kush* 7, 120–53.

—— 1980. Le pays Irem et la pénétration égyptienne en Afrique (stele de Sai S. 579). In *Livre du centennaire 1880–1980*, Vercoutter, J. (ed.), 157–78. Cairo: Institut Français d'Archéologie Orientale.

Vercruisse, E. 1984. *The Penetration of Capitalism: a west African case study*. London: Zed.

Vérin, P. 1975. *Les Chelles anciennes du commerce sur les côtes nords de Madagascar*. Lille: Service de Reproduction des thèses, Université de Lille III.

—— 1977–8. Une nouvelle documentation sur l'histoire des côtes de l'ouest de l'Océan Indien. *Etudes d'Histoire d'Afrique* 9/10, 213–16.

—— 1986. *The History of Civilization in North Madagascar*. Rotterdam: A. A. Balkema.

—— 1989. Malgache et Swahili, culture de frange et interférences. In *Le Swahili et ses limites, ambiguité des notions reçus*, Rombi, M. F. (ed.), 175–8. Paris: Ministrie des Affaires Etrangers.

Vermeersch, P. M. 1978. *Elkab II*. Leuven: University Press.

—— 1984 Subsistence activities in the late palaeolithic site of el-Kab (Egypt). In *Origin and Early*

Development of Food-producing Cultures in North-eastern Africa, Krzyzaniak, L. & M. Kobusiewicz (eds), 137–42. Poznan: Polish Academy of Sciences & Poznan Archaeological Museum.

Vermeersch, P. M., E. Paulissen & W. van Neer 1989. The late palaeolithic Makhadma site (Egypt): environment and subsistence. In *Late Prehistory of the Nile Basin and the Sahara*, Krzyzaniak, L. & M. Kobusiewicz (eds), 87–116. Poznan: Poznan Archaeology Museum.

Vidal, P. 1987. Les activités archéologiques en Centrafrique, 1986–1987. *Nsi* 2, 20–3.

Vidal, P. & R. de Bayle des Hermens 1983. Le site archéologique de l'île de Toala sur la haute Ouham (République Centrafricaine): néolithique et l'âge du fer. *L'Anthropologie* 87, 113–26.

Viereck, A. 1967. The Damaraland culture. *Journal of the South West African Scientific Society* 21, 13–31.

Vierich, H. I. D. 1982. Adaptive flexibility in a multi-ethnic setting: the Basarwa of the southern Kalahari. In *Politics and History in Band Societies*, Leacock, E. & R. Lee (eds), 213–22. Cambridge: Cambridge University Press.

Vincent, P. L. 1966. Les formations meubles superficielles (colluvium) au sud du Congo et au Gabon. *Bulletin du Bureau de Recherches Géologiques et Minières* (Paris) 4, 53–111.

Vining, R. 1955. A description of certain spatial aspects of an economic system. *Economic Development and Culture Change* 3, 147–95.

Vinnicombe, P. 1976. *People of the Eland: rock paintings of the Drakensberg Bushmen as a reflection of their life and thought*. Pietermaritzburg: University of Natal Press.

Vivian, B. C. 1990. Origins of the Asante Research Project: 1989–1990 excavations at Asantemanso. *Nyame Akuma* 34, 19–22.

Vogel, J. O. 1971. *Kamangoza*. Nairobi: Oxford University Press.

—— 1972. On early iron age funerary practice in southern Zambia. *Current Anthropology* 13, 583–6.

—— 1973. Some early iron age sites in southern and western Zambia. *Azania* 8, 25–54.

—— 1974. Later iron age hoe blades from Simango, southern Zambia. *Current Anthropology* 15, 198–9.

—— 1975a. *Simbusenga*. Nairobi: Oxford University Press.

—— 1975b. Kabondo Kumbo and the early Iron Age in the Victoria Falls region. *Azania* 10, 49–75.

—— 1980. The iron age pottery of the Victoria Falls region. *Zambia Museums Journal* 5, 41–77.

—— 1982. An early iron age burial from Chundu, Zambia. *Zambia Museums Journal* 6, 118–25.

—— 1984. An early iron age settlement system in southern Zambia. *Azania* 19, 61–78.

—— 1986. Micro-environments, swidden and the early iron age settlements of south-western Zambia. *Azania* 21, 85–97.

—— 1990. The cultural basis, development and consequences of a socially mediated trading corporation in southern Zambezia. *Journal of Anthropological Archaeology* 9, 105–47.

Vogt, J. 1966. Le complexe de la stone-line: mise au point. *Bulletin du Bureau de Recherches Géologiques et Minières* (Paris) 4, 3–51.

Voigt, E. A. (ed.) 1981. *Guide to Archaeological Sites in the Northern and Eastern Transvaal*. Pretoria: Transvaal Museum.

—— 1986. Iron age herding: archaeological and ethnoarchaeological approaches to pastoral problems. In *Prehistoric Pastoralism in Southern Africa*, Hall, M. & A. B. Smith (eds), 13–21. Vlaeberg: South African Archaeological Society.

Voigt, E. A. & A. von den Driesch (1984). Preliminary report on the faunal assemblage from Ndondondwane, Natal. *Annals of the Natal Museum* 26, 95–104.

Voigt, E. A. & I. Plug (eds) 1981. *Early Iron Age Herders of the Limpopo Valley*. Pretoria: Transvaal Museum.

von den Driesch, A. 1986. Tierknochenfunde aus Qasr el-Sagha/Fayum (Neolithicum Mittleres

Reich). *Mitteilungen des Deutschen Archäologischen Institut, Abteilung Kairo* 42, 1–8.

von den Driesch, A. & J. Boessneck 1985. *Die Tierknochenfunde aus der neolithischen Siedlung von Merimde-Benisalame am westlichen Nildelta*. Munich: Institut für Palaeoanatomie, Domestikationsforschung und Geschichte der Tiermedizin.

von der Way, T. 1984. Untersuchungen des deutschen archäologischen Instituts Kairo im nördlichen Delta zwischen Disuq und Tida. *Mitteilungen des Deutschen Archäologischen Institut, Abteilung Kairo* 40, 297–328.

―― 1986. Tell el-Fara'in/Buto. *Mitteilungen des Deutschen Archäologischen Institut, Abteilung Kairo* 42, 191–212.

Vossen, R. & M. Bechaus-Gerst (eds) 1983. *Nilotic Studies*. Berlin: Reimer.

Wadley, L. 1979. Big Elephant shelter and its role in the holocene prehistory of central South West Africa. *Cimbebasia* 3, 1–76.

Wainwright, G. A. 1946. Zeberged: the shipwrecked sailor's island. *Journal of Egyptian Archaeology* 32, 31–8.

―― 1984. Zeberged: a correction. *Journal of Egyptian Archaeology* 34, 119.

Waldecker, B. 1967. Sel et salines en Afrique. *Bulletin du Centre d'Etude des Problèmes Sociaux Indigènes* 75/6, 9–54.

Wallerstein, I. 1974. *The Modern World-System*. New York: Academic Press.

Wandibba, S. 1980. The application of attribute analysis to the study of later stone age/neolithic pottery ceramics in Kenya. In *Proceedings of the 8th Panafrican Congress of Prehistory and Quaternary Studies, Nairobi, 1977*, Leakey, R. E. & B. A. Ogot (eds), 283–5. Nairobi: International Louis Leakey Memorial Institute for African Prehistory.

―― 1984. Petrological investigation of pottery in Kenya. Report prepared for the Ford Foundation.

Warnier, J.-P. 1975. Pre-colonial Mankon: the development of a Cameroon chiefdom in its regional setting. Unpublished PhD thesis, University of Pennsylvania.

―― 1981. L'histoire précoloniale de la chefferie de Mankom. In *Contribution de la recherche ethnologique à l'histoire des civilisations du Cameroun*, Tardits, C. (ed.), 421–36. Paris: CNRS (Centre National de la Recherche Scientifique).

―― 1983. Sociologie du Bamenda pré-colonial – Cameroun. Unpublished thèse de Doctorat d'Etat, Université de Paris X.

―― 1984. Histoire du peuplement et genèse des paysages dans l'ouest camerounais. *Journal of African History* 25, 395–410.

―― 1985. *Echanges, développement et hiérarchie dans le Bamenda pré-colonial: Cameroun*. Wiesbaden: Franz Steiner Verlag.

Warnier, J.-P. & I. Fowler 1979. A nineteenth-century Ruhr in central Africa. *Africa* 49, 329–51.

Washbourn, C. K. 1967. Late quaternary lakes in the Nakuru-Elmenteita basin, Kenya. Unpublished PhD thesis, University of Cambridge.

Watson, P. J., S. A. LeBlanc & R. L. Redman 1971. *Explanation in Archaeology: an explicitly scientific approach*. New York: Cambridge University Press.

Wayland, E. J. 1934. Rifts, rivers, rains and early man in Uganda. *Journal of the Royal Anthropological Institute* 64, 333–52.

Weber, M. 1956. *Economy and Society*. New York: Bedminster Press.

―― 1958. *The City*. Glencoe: Free Press.

Weinrich, A. K. H. 1971. *Chiefs and Councils in Rhodesia*. London: Heinemann.

Weischoff, H. A. 1941. *The Zimbabwe-Monomatapa Culture in South East Africa*. Menasha: George Banta.

Wells, P. S. 1984. *Farms, Villages and Cities: commerce and urban origin in late prehistoric Europe*.

Ithaca: Cornell University Press.

Wembah-Rashid, J. 1969. Iron workers of Ufipa. *Bulletin of International Committee of Urgent Anthropological Research* 11, 65–72.

Wendorf, F. 1968a. Late palaeolithic sites in Egyptian Nubia. In *The Prehistory of Nubia, Vol. 2*, Wendorf, F. (ed.), 791–953. Dallas: Fort Burgwin Research Center & Southern Methodist University Press.

—— 1968b. Summary of Nubian prehistory. In *The Prehistory of Nubia, Vol. 2*, Wendorf, F. (ed.), 1041–59. Dallas: Fort Burgwin Research Center & Southern Methodist University Press.

—— 1968c. Site 117: a Nubian final palaeolithic graveyard near Jebel Sahaba, Sudan. In *The Prehistory of Nubia, Vol. 2*, Wendorf, F. (ed.), 954–95. Dallas: Fort Burgwin Research Center & Southern Methodist University Press.

—— 1989. Introduction. In *The Prehistory of Wadi Kubbaniya, Vol. 2: Stratigraphy, Palaeoeconomy and Environment*, Wendorf, F., R. Schild and A. E. Close (eds), 1–11. Dallas: Southern Methodist University Press.

Wendorf, F., A. E. Close, A. Gautier & R. Schild 1990. Les débuts du pastoralisme en Egypte. *La Recherche* 21, 436–45.

Wendorf, F., A. E. Close & R. Schild 1985. Prehistoric settlements in the Nubian desert. *American Scientist* 173, 132–41.

Wendorf, F. & F. Hassan 1980. Holocene ecology and prehistory in the Egyptian Sahara. In *The Sahara and the Nile: quaternary environments and prehistoric occupation in northern Africa*, Williams, M. A. J. & H. Faure (eds), 407–19. Rotterdam: Balkema.

Wendorf, F., R. Said & R. Schild 1970. Egyptian prehistory: some new concepts. *Science* 169, 1161–71.

Wendorf, F. & R. Schild 1976a. *Prehistory of the Nile Valley*. New York: Academic Press.

—— 1976b. The use of ground grain during the late Paleolithic of the lower Nile valley, Egypt. In *Origins of African Plant Domestication*, Harlan, J. R., J. M. J. De Wet & A. B. L. Stemler (eds), 269–88. The Hague: Mouton.

—— 1980. *Prehistory of the Eastern Sahara*. New York: Academic Press.

—— 1984a. Conclusions. In *Cattle-keepers of the Eastern Sahara: the Neolithic of Bir Kiseiba*, Wendorf, F., R. Schild & A. E. Close (eds), 404–28. Dallas: Southern Methodist University Press.

—— 1984b. The emergence of food production in the Egyptian Sahara. In *From Hunters to Farmers: the causes and consequences of food production in Africa*, Clark, J. D. & S. A. Brandt (eds), 93–101. Berkeley: University of California Press.

—— 1986. Conclusions. In *The Prehistory of Wadi Kubbaniya, Vol. 1: The Wadi Kubbaniya Skeleton: a late palaeolithic burial from southern Egypt*, Wendorf, F., R. Schild & A. E. Close (eds), 71–4. Dallas: Southern Methodist University Press.

—— 1989. Summary and synthesis. In *The Prehistory of Wadi Kubbaniya, Vol. 3: Late Palaeolithic Archaeology*, Wendorf, F., R. Schild & A. E. Close (eds), 768–824. Dallas: Southern Methodist University Press.

Wendorf, F., R. Schild & A. E. Close (eds) 1984. *Cattle-keepers of the Eastern Sahara: the Neolithic of Bir Kiseiba*. Dallas: Southern Methodist University Press.

—— (eds) 1989. *The Prehistory of Wadi Kubbaniya, Vols 2 & 3: Stratigraphy, Paleoeconomy, and Environment* and *Late Palaeolithic Archaeology*. Dallas: Southern Methodist University Press.

Wendorf, F., R. Schild & H. Haas 1979. A new radiocarbon chronology for prehistoric sites in Nubia. *Journal of Field Archaeology* 6, 219–23.

Wendt, W. E. 1972. Preliminary report on an archaeological research programme in South West Africa. *Cimbebasia* 2, 1–61.

Wenke, R., P. Buck, H. Hamroush, M. Kobusiewicz, K. Kroeper & R. Redding 1988. Kom el-

Hisn: excavation of an Old Kingdom settlement in the Egyptian Delta. Journal of the American Research Center in Egypt 25, 5–34.

Wenke, R. J., P. Buck, J. R. Hanley, M. E. Lane, Janet Long & R. R. Redding 1983. The Fayyum Archaeological Project: preliminary report of the 1981 season. *American Research Center in Egypt Newsletter* 122, 25–40.

Wenke, R. & M. Cassini 1989. The epipaleolithic–neolithic transition in Egypt's Fayum depression. In *Late Prehistory of the Nile Basin and the Sahara*, Krzyzaniak, L. & M. Kobusiewicz (eds), 139–56. Poznan: Poznan Archaeology Museum.

Wenke, R. J., J. E. Long & P. E. Buck 1988. Epipaleolithic and neolithic subsistence and settlement in the Fayyum Oasis of Egypt. *Journal of Field Archaeology* 15, 29–51.

Werner, A. 1914/15. A Swahili history of Pate. *Journal of African History* 14, 148–66, 278–97, 392–413.

Werth, E. 1939. Emmer und Gerste aus dem 5. Jahrtausend v. Chr. und andere vorgeschichtliche Kulturpflanzenfunde. *Botanischen Gesellschaft* 57, 453–62.

Wertime, T. 1973. The beginnings of metallurgy: a new look. *Science* 182, 875–87.

Westermann, D. 1927. *Die westlichen Sudansprachen und ihre Beziehungen zum Bantu*. Berlin: de Gruyter.

Westphal, E. O. J. 1971. The click languages of southern and eastern Africa. In *Current Trends in Linguistics, Vol. 7: Sub-Saharan Africa*, Berry, J. & J. H. Greenberg (eds), 367–420. The Hague: Mouton.

Wetterstrom, W. 1986. Ecology and agricultural intensification in predynastic Egypt. Final Report to the National Science Foundation, Washington D. C.

Wheatley, P. 1971. *Pivot of the Four Quarters*. Chicago: Aldine Publishing Company.

—— 1972. The concept of urbanism. In *Man, Settlement and Urbanism*, Ucko, P. J., R. Tringham & G. W. Dimbleby (eds), 601–37. London: Duckworth.

—— 1975. Satyanrta in Suvarnadvipa: reciprocity and redistribution in ancient southeast Asia. In *Ancient Civilizations and Trade*, Sabloff, J. A. & C. C. Lamberg-Karlovsky (eds), 227–83. Albuquerque: University of New Mexico Press.

Wheeler, A. & A. Jones 1989. *Fishes*. Cambridge: Cambridge University Press.

Wheeler, T. S. & R. Maddin 1980. Metallurgy and ancient man. In *The Coming of the Age of Iron*, Wertime, T. A. & J. D. Muhly (eds), 99–126. Newhaven: Yale University Press.

White, F. 1981. The history of the Afromontane archipelago and the scientific need for its conservation. *African Journal of Ecology* 19, 33–54.

—— 1983. *The Vegetation of Africa*. Paris: UNESCO.

White, S. 1974. Iron production and iron trade in north and central Liberia: history of a major indigenous technology. Paper presented to the 6th Liberian Studies Conference, Madison, Wisconsin.

Whitelaw, T. 1983. People and space in hunter-gatherer camps: a generalizing approach to ethnoarchaeology. *Archaeological Review from Cambridge* 2, 48–66.

Whyte, R. O. 1977. The botanical Neolithic Revolution. *Human Ecology* 5, 209–22.

Wickens, G. E. 1975. Changes in the climate and vegetation of the Sudan since 20,000 BP. *Boissiera* 24, 43–65.

Wieschoff, H. A. 1941. *The Zimbabwe Monomotapa Culture in South East Africa*. Menasha: G. Banta.

Wilcox, D. R., T. R. McGuire & C. Sternberg 1981. *Snaketown Revisited*. Tucson: Arizona State Museum.

Wilding, R. F. 1977a. The ceramics of the north Kenya coast. Unpublished PhD thesis, University of Nairobi.

—— 1977b. *Ceramics of the Lamu Archipelago*. Nairobi: University of Nairobi.

—— 1989. The pottery. In *Excavations at Aksum*, Munro-Hay, S. (ed.), 235–316. London: British

Institute in Eastern Africa.

Wilks, I. 1961. The northern factor in Ashanti history: Begho and the Mande. *Journal of African History* 2, 25–34.

—— 1966. A note on the chronology and origins of the Gonja kings, Ghana. *Notes and Queries* 8, 26–8.

—— 1975. *Asante in the 19th Century*. Cambridge: Cambridge University Press.

Willcocks, W. 1889. *Egyptian Irrigation*. London: E. & F. N. Spon.

—— 1904. *The Nile in 1904*. London: E. & F. N. Spon.

Willett, F. 1967. *Ife in the History of West African Sculpture*. London: Thames & Hudson.

—— 1970. Ife and its archaeology. In *Papers in African Prehistory*, Fage, J. D. & R. A. Oliver (eds), 303–26. Cambridge: Cambridge University Press.

—— 1971. A survey of recent results in the radiocarbon chronology of western and northern Africa. *Journal of African History* 12, 339–70.

—— 1983. Who taught the smiths of Igbo Ukwu? *New Scientist* 98, 65–8.

Willey, G. R. 1953. *Prehistoric Settlement Patterns in the Viru Valley, Peru*. Washington: US Government Printing Office.

Williams, B. 1986. *The A-Group Royal Cemetery at Qustul: Cemetery L*. Chicago: Oriental Institute of the University of Chicago.

Williams, D. 1969. African iron in the classical world. In *Africa in Classical Antiquity*, Thompson, L. & J. Ferguson (eds), 62–80. Ibadan: Ibadan University Press.

—— 1974. *Icon and Image: a study of sacred and secular forms of African classical art*. London: Allen Lane.

Williamson, K. 1970. Some food plant names in the Niger delta. *International Journal of American Linguistics* 36, 156–67.

—— (ed.) 1972. *Igbo-English Dictionary: based on the Onitsha dialect*. Benin: Ethiope Publishing Corporation.

—— 1973. *Benue-Congo Comparative Wordlist, Vol. 2*. Ibadan: West African Linguistic Society.

—— 1989a. Linguistic evidence for the prehistory of the Niger delta. In *The Early History of the Niger Delta*, Alagoa, E. J., F. N. Anozie & N. Nzewunwa (eds), 65–119. Hamburg: Buske.

—— 1989b. Niger-Congo overview. In *The Niger-Congo Languages*, Bendor-Samuel, J. & R. Hartell (eds), 3–45. Lanham: Universities Press of America.

—— In Preparation. Comparative Ijo.

Williamson, K. & K. Shimizu. 1968. *Benue-Congo Comparative Wordlist, Vol. 1*. Ibadan: West African Linguistic Society.

Willis, R. 1981. *A State in the Making: myth, history and social transformation in pre-colonial Ufipa*. Bloomington: Indiana University Press.

Wills, W. H. 1988. *The Agricultural Transition in the American Southwest*. Santa Fe: School of American Research Press.

Wilson, G. & M. Wilson 1945. *The Analysis of Social Change*. Cambridge: Cambridge University Press.

Wilson, G. T. & R. W. Felkin 1882. *Uganda and the Egyptian Sudan*. 2 vols. London: Sampson Low, Marston Searle & Rivington.

Wilson, J. 1960. Egypt to the New Kingdom. In *City Invincible*, Kraeling, C. & R. M. Adams (eds), 124–64. Chicago: University of Chicago Press.

Wilson, J. C. 1970. Preliminary observations on the Oropom people of Karamoja, their ethnic status, culture and postulated relation to the peoples of the Late Stone Age. *Uganda Journal* 34, 125–45.

Wilson, M. 1957. *Rituals of Kinship among the Nyakusa*. London: Oxford University Press.

—— 1959. *Communal Rituals of the Nyakusa*. London: Oxford University Press.

—— 1977. *For Men and Elders*. London: International African Institute.

Wilson, T. H. 1978. *The Monumental Architecture and Archaeology North of the Tana River*. Nairobi: National Museums of Kenya.

—— 1982. Spatial analysis and settlement on the east African coast. *Paideuma* 28, 201–20.

Windmann & Dieterle, Basel Mission archives, 1848 (quoted in Quarcoo & Johnson 1968, p. 55, n. 11).

Winter, J. C. 1981. Bantu prehistory in eastern and southern Africa. An evaluation of D. W. Phillipson's archaeological synthesis in the light of ethnological and linguistic evidence. *Sprache und Geschichte in Afrika* 3, 251–316.

Wirth, R. 1938. Urbanism as a way of life. *American Journal of Sociology* 144, 1–24.

Wise, R. 1958a. Iron smelting in Ufipa. *Tanganyika Notes and Records* 51, 106–11.

—— 1958b. Some rituals of iron making in Ufipa. *Tanganyika Notes and Records* 51, 232–8.

Wittfogel, K. A. 1957. *Oriental Despotism*. New Haven: Yale University Press.

Wolff, E. & H. Meyer–Bahlburg 1983. *Studies in Chadic and Afroasiatic Linguistics*. Hamburg: Buske.

Wolff, H. 1969. *A Comparative Vocabulary of Abuan Dialects*. Evanston: Northwestern University Press.

Wolska–Conus, W. 1968. *La Topographie chrétienne*. Paris: Cerf.

Woodburn, J. 1968. An introduction to Hadza ecology. In *Man the Hunter*, Lee, R. B. & I. DeVore (eds), 49–55. Chicago: Aldine-Atherton.

Wotzka, H.-P. 1990. Studien zur Besiedlungsgeschichte des äquatorialen Regenwaldes Zaïres: die archäologische Keramik des inneren Zaïre-Beckens und ihre Stellung im Kontext der Bantu-Expansion. Unpublished PhD thesis, University of Hamburg.

Wreszinski, W. n.d. *Atlas zur altägyptischen Kulturgeschichte, I–III*. Leipzig: Hinrichs.

Wright, H. T. 1984. Early seafarers of the Comoro islands: the Dembeni phase of the IXth–Xth centuries AD. *Azania* 19, 13–59.

—— 1986. Early communities on the island of Mayotte and the coasts of Madagascar. In *Madagascar: society and history*, Kottak, C., J.-A. Rakotoarisoa, A. Southall & P. Vérin (eds), 53–88. Durham: Carolina Academic Press.

—— n.d. Early Islam, oceanic trade, and town development on Nzwani: the Comorian archipelago in the XIth to XVth centuries AD *Azania*.

Wright, H. T. & J. A. Rakotoarisoa 1990. The archaeology of complex societies in Madagascar: case studies in cultural diversification. In *Urban Origins in Eastern Africa: proceedings of the 1989 Madagascar workshop*, Sinclair, P. J. J. & J. A. Rakotoarisoa (eds), 21–31. Stockholm: Swedish Central Board of National Antiquities.

Wykaert, A. 1914. Forgerons païens et forgerons chrétiens au Tanganyika. *Anthropos* 9, 371–80.

Yellen, J. E. 1976. Settlement patterns of the !Kung: an archaeological perspective. In *Kalahari Hunter-Gatherers: studies of the !Kung San and their neighbors*, Lee, R. B. & I. DeVore (eds), 47–72. Cambridge, Mass. & London: Harvard University Press.

Yellen, J. E. & R. B. Lee 1976. The Dobe-/Du/da environment: background to a hunting and gathering way of life. In *Kalahari Hunter-Gatherers: studies of the !Kung San and their neighbors*, Lee, R. B. & I. DeVore (eds), 27–46. Cambridge, Mass. & London: Harvard University Press.

Ylvisaker, M. 1979. *Lamu in the Nineteenth Century: land, trade and politics*. Boston: Boston University African Studies Center.

York, R. N. 1974. Excavations at Dutsen Kongba near Jos, Nigeria. Preliminary note. *Nyame Akuma* 4, 17–20.

—— 1978. Excavations at Dutsen Kongba, Plateau State, Nigeria. *West African Journal of*

Archaeology 8, 139–63.

Youatt, W. 1837. *Sheep: their breeds, management, and diseases.* London: Baldwin & Cradock.

Yoyotte, J. 1975. Les *sementiou* et l'exploitation des régions minières à l'ancien Empire. *Bulletin de la Société Française d'Egyptologie* 73, 44–55.

Zacharia, S. and H.-G. Bachmann 1983. Iron smelting in west Africa: Ivory Coast. *Journal of the Historical Metallurgy Society* 17, 1–3.

Zeitlyn, D. n.d. Mambila dictionary. First draft 1986, computer printout.

Zeuner, F. E. 1963. *A History of Domesticated Animals.* London: Hutchinson.

Zibelius, K. 1972. *Afrikanische Orts- und Völkernamen in hieroglyphischen und hieratischen Texten.* Wiesbaden: Reichert.

Zimmerman, J. 1851. Vierteljahrbericht. Basel Mission Archives.

Zivie, C. 1980. Memphis. In *Lexikon der Ägyptologie, IV,* Helck, W. & W. Westendorf (eds), 24–41. Wiesbaden: Otto Harrasowitz.

Zohary, D. 1969. The progenitors of wheat and barley in relation to domestication and agricultural dispersal in the Old World. In *The Domestication and Exploitation of Plants and Animals,* Ucko, P. J. & G. W. Dimbleby (eds), 47–66. Chicago: Aldine-Atherton.

Zohary, D. & M. Hopf 1988. *Domestication of Plants in the Old World: the origin and spread of cultivated plants in west Asia, Europe, and the Nile valley.* Oxford: Clarendon Press.

Zohary, M. 1966. *Flora Palaestina Part I.* Jerusalem: The Israel Academy of Sciences and Humanities.

—— 1973. *Geobotanical Foundations of the Middle East.* Stuttgart: Gustav Fischer Verlag.

Zvelebil, M. & P. Rowley-Conwy 1986. Foragers and farmers in Atlantic Europe. In *Hunters in Transition,* Zvelebil, M. (ed.), 67–93. Cambridge: Cambridge University Press.

Zwernemann, J. 1983. *Culture, History and African Anthropology.* Uppsala: Uppsala University Press.

Zylharz, E. 1958. The countries of the Ethiopian empire of Kash (Kush) and Egyptian Old Ethiopia in the New Kingdom. *Kush* 6, 7–38.

Index[1]

Abagusii people 487–8, 494–7
Aborigines Australian: languages 134; burning of land 182
Abyssinia 21
Abyssinian oat (*Avena abyssinica*) 59
acacia 173, 178–9, 183, 187, 190, 195–6, 360; *Acacia albida* 460; *Acacia nilotica* 178, 460; *Acacia sayel*, 460; *Acacia tortiles* 460
Acacus region 228–9, 232, 236
Accra plains (Dangmeland) 241–3, 643, 646, 648, 651
Adamawa: language family 128–9, 130, 142; region 89, 95, 98–100
adaptation: environmental xxiv, 16, 53, 104, 238, 286, 358, 381, 706; hunter-gatherer, in southwest Kenya 362–3, 366, 370; of livestock 18, 75, 79, 84–7, 90–2; 'Nilotic adaptation' 227–9; of sorghum 53; hunter-gatherer, in Egypt 165–97; hunter-gatherer, in west Africa 262; social 286, 326, 456
addax 199, 208
Aden 338, 613
aerial photography 35, 694
aerial yam ('up-yam') 19; linguistic evidence 146, 152
Afar depression 41–2
African archaeology (as a discipline) xxx–xxxiv, 1–2, 9, 30–1, 289–90, 326–7, 410; bibliographical practices xxix–xxxi, geographical approaches 24; and the imposition of foreign terminology xxxii, xxxiv, 2–3, 8, 254, 452; political context of 7, 12; terminology 2–9, 452
African bread fruit (*Treculia africana*) 248
African spadefish (Ephippidae) 676, 690
Afroasiatic language phylum 18, 73, 79, 82, 92, 126, 128, 134–7, 353; classification 134; origins of 127, 135–7; pre-proto 135; proto 135
Agadez region 92, 334, 433, 464, 466
Agaw peoples 614
Agikuyu people: *see* Kikuyu
agricultural: mode of production 245–6; specialization 390; tools 175, 237, 253, 263, 277–9, 343, 346, 403, 407, 463–4, 528–30, 542; techniques: *see* cultivation techniques.
agriculture 2–4, 8, 16–20, 23, 61, 272, 336–7, 395, 459–60, 484, 487, 491, 514, 645–6, 650,

711; arboriculture 272; as a concept 240; in the definition of the neolithic 3, 6, 302; on the east African littoral 660, 662, 664, 667; in Egypt 165, 197–226; in Ethiopia 344–57; external introduction vs indigenous development 9–10; incipient 568; in Kenya 358–71; linguistic evidence 18, 244, 353; in Mozambican prehistory 417–28; amongst Nilo-Saharan speaking peoples 108–21; role in state formation 551, 556, 610, 613; role in urbanization 558–9, 566, 616, 649; in the Sahara 227, 234–39; as a social phenomenon 240; Tiv 274–88; in west African prehistory 240–54, 272–3; on the Zimbabwean plateau 710–14, 731; *see also* cultivation; domestication; horticulture
Agwezat, kingdom of 613
Aïr region 118, 122–5, 228–9, 236, 251, 638
Akan Brong country 643–4, 648–9
Akan people 246, 645
Akhenaten: *see* Tell el Amarna
Akjoujt region 334, 433, 466, 638
Aksumite kingdom 609, 614–21; pre-Aksumite period 348, 609–14; society 346, 348; suzerainty 615
Alexandria 569, 617, 620
Algeria 6, 655
Amala river 361
Amau region 588, 594–6, 603–4
Amration tradition: *see* Nagada I
Anaguta people 101
Anambra: State 150; valley 455
Angas people 95–6
Angelfish (Pomacanthidae) 676, 692
Angola 10, 49, 80, 372
antelope 61–2, 214, 362, 365, 374, 376; dama 208; dik dik 684; duiker 266, 270; eland (*Tragelaphus oryx*) 61; oribi 365; oryx 199, 208; reedbuck 365, 630; royal antelope 266; *see also* gazelle; hartebeest
anthropology: *see* ethnography
Anufo people 100
anvil 439, 476–7, 480–1, 510, 513, 515, 518, 529–30, 532, 539, 547
aqualithic, in north Africa 232–234
aquatic resources, exploitation of 15, 182, 262, 346, 392, 398, 426–7, 674, 682: *see also* riverine resources
Arabia 22, 26, 58, 65, 77, 348, 351–2, 604, 614–15, 695
Arabic 148, 150; language family 128, 659
archaeology (as a discipline) 1–2; 'western' 1; archaeology vs history 1; education xxxiv, 429; nature of the evidence 642–3, 705;

---

1. Note that with a few exceptions the names of authors and other persons referred to in the text are excluded from this index.

periodisation, problems with 2, 330; its role in the present 12, 386, 428; site-specific vs regional investigative frameworks 625; theory 15; *see also* experimental archaeology

archaeometallurgical techniques 331; experimental reconstruction 461, 468–77; radiographic analysis: of iron 332; residues, analysis, of 435–45, 449

Arkell: *see* 'Khartoum Mesolithic'; Darfur

Arkinian lithic industry 166, 184–5, 192

Armant-Gurna area 191, 220

art 27–8, 62–4, 68, 89, 267, 269, 614; representation of domesticated animals 63–5, 68–71, 75, 77, 80, 85, 87, 89, 92, 199, 234–6, 259, 350–4, 374; *see also* rock art

artefact diversity, analysis of 636

Asantemanso 453–4

Ashanti people 27, 546

Asia 56, 66, 233, 279; central Asia 78, 80; east Asia 432; southeast Asia 4, 62, 200, 479–80; western Asia 65–6, 68; *see also* Far East

Assyut 552, 553, 567

Astaboran language family 105–6, 109, 112, 114; pre-proto- 125; proto- 106, 117

Aswan 167, 170, 185, 193, 553, 566, 572, 583, 614

Atbara region 106, 604

Atlantic: Ocean 37, 129–30; culture 10; language family 128

auroch (*Bos primogenius*) 66, 172–3, 179, 181, 185, 188

authority: *see* power

autochthonous: *see* indigenous

Awash River 35

Azande people 540

Azania 615

Azawad region 39, 41

Bacama people 103

Badari region 202, 562

Badarian tradition 203–4, 214–17

Bade [Bedde] people 95–6, 103

Bahr-al-Ghazal 41, 107, 114–15

Ballanan lithic tradition 179

baLozi people 405

Bamileke people 525

Bamoum kingdom 100, 536

banana 140, 324

Banda 129, 258, 267

Bandama river 241

Bani people: *see* Samba

Bani river 624, 629, 634

Bantoid language family 130, 131, 141–2

Bantu xxxiii, 46, 53, 91; 'Homeland' Project 274; Centre International des Civilisations Bantou 9; cultural diversity 494–8; cultural history 275, 289; cultural unity of 492–4, 707; language family 79, 128, 140, 143, 145, 323, 493, 658; migration 2, 10–12, 48, 127,

290, 323, 326, 365, 386, 389, 434, 484, 489–93, 497–8, 658, 673; racial connotations of 8; the role of cattle in Bantu society 67; speaking peoples 67, 361, 479, 487–8, 497

Banyabwisha (Hutu) people 468–77

baobab tree (*Adansonia digitata*) 248

Barbaria, the land of incense 614

barley 58–9, 164, 175, 198, 200–1, 346, 349, 355; six-row hulled barley 200–2, 208, 213–14, 216, 218, 223; two-row barley 200, 208

Barracuda (Sphyraenidae) 676, 691

Bassar: region 434, 436, 453–4; people 525

Batalimo-Maluba Horizon (pottery) 308–11, 321–2, 325–6; radiocarbon dating 311

Batéke Plateau 48, 298, 306

Bauchi: Plateau 94, 96; State 95, 101

Bazaruto archipelago 418–19, 427

beads 209, 258, 726; aragonite 703; copper 383; glass 342, 382–3, 388, 390, 394, 419, 426–7, 488, 649–50, 670, 703; gold 403; Indian glass 397; iron 465; shell 390, 403, 660, 664; stone 255, 260, 267, 632, 638

Bedde people: *see* Bade

beer 58, 278, 349; production of 55

Begho ware 649

Beja: language family, 134; peoples 615

belief, systems of: *see* cosmology; ideology, religion

bellows 389, 452–3, 458, 461–3, 473–4, 475, 480–1, 494, 500, 509, 510, 513, 519, 529, 532, 547

Bemba people 400, 406, 500, 504, 557

Bena people 500

Benedougou region 638–40

Benin 46, 76, 95, 292; kingdom of xxxiv, 151; Republic of 241

beniseed (*Sesamum indicum*) 276

Benue: Niger/Benue region 11; river 37, 39, 46, 122–5, 241, 274; State 275; valley 99, 275, 280

Benue–Congo language family 19, 79, 127–9, 143–4, 152; classification of 131–2; (new) Benue–Congo 130–1, 139, 146; proto 139, 140, 145, 147

Benye-Mikebwe people 468–77

Berber: language family 128, 134–5; people 21, 90, 331, 432; region 604, 609

Berom people 94–7, 101, 453, 455

Berta [Bertha] language family 105, 133

Betsileo people 478, 481

Betsimisaraka 480

birds: coot (*Fulica atra*) 174; crane 62; exploitation of 181, 199, 362, 365; garganey 181; geese 62–3, 174; quail 62; Suni 681; teal 181; water fowl 62, 174, 188, 195, 207–8, 210–11 214; *see also* fowl

Bisa 397

bistort 211; swamp bistort (*Polygonum senegalense*) 178–9

Blue Nile river 18, 41, 106, 108, 344, 347, 604
Blue spotted ribbontail ray (*Dasyatidae*) 676, 692
boar (*Sus scrofa*) 65
Bodélé depression 36, 41
Bokélé plateau 306, 308
bone artefacts 209, 260, 262, 338–9, 342, 363, 381
bonefish (Albulidae) 676, 692
Borgu region 88, 95, 98
Borno region 95, 97
Bornu 338–40, 461
botanical remains 154–64, 171, 186–7, 189, 197, 203, 208–9, 213–14, 216, 219–20, 222–4, 260, 262–3, 323–5, 349, 355–6, 412, 660; as evidence of climate 39; identification and preservation 19
Botswana 12, 20, 38, 386–90, 436, 707, 711
bread 354–5; injera (flat sour bread) 349, 354, 356; Ethiopian dabbo 355
bridewealth 91, 97, 494
bronze metallurgy 463
buffalo 73, 258, 362–3
building: materials 248, 256, 282, 631–2, 649, 663, 667, 726; technology 259–60, 282, 286–7, 648–50, 663, 665–6, 688
buildings: *see* structural remains
bulrushes (*Schoenoplectus* spp.) 177, 179
burial 28, 212, 216–19, 226, 239, 287–8, 341–3, 348, 358, 399, 401, 421, 423, 463–5, 487, 663, 699, 721–4; funerary ritual, 401, 403–4, 407–8; in ancient Egypt, 552, 582; *see* frontispiece; *see also* grave goods; mortuary cults
burning, of land 182, 192, 199, 278
Busira river 294–6, 306
Butana region 228, 232
Bwanje river valley 391

Cairo 167, 212, 214, 563, 569, 577, 737, 739, 749
calabash 18, 112, 115, 120
camel 65–6, 355–6, 460, 663, 674–5; C14 dating 66; as transport 350–1, 355
Cameroon 43, 45–6, 48–50, 72, 76–7, 85, 95, 98–9, 101, 153, 261, 263, 322–3, 336, 338, 343, 435, 455, 482, 512–50, 656
Canids 223; *Canis lupus arabs* (wolf) 64; *see also* dog
Cape Mogador 26
caper (*Capparis* sp.) 175, 190
caprines: *see* goat
Capsian 237–8; tradition 6
Carthage 432–3
Caspian Sea 36
cassava 150, 276–9; linguistic evidence for 140
cat 61, 663; domestic cat (*Felis catus*) 63; *Felis silvestris libyca* 63
catfish: *Clarias* 169, 173–4, 178, 181, 184–5

188, 195, 197–8, 207–8, 211, 214; Plotosidae 676, 686; sea catfish (Ariidae) 676, 689; *Synodontis* 184, 188, 208, 211, 214
catstail, or reedmace (*Typha* spp.) 177, 179
cattle 7, 20, 61, 64, 70, 72–78, 85, 199–200, 207–8, 211, 214, 216–17, 223, 230–1, 234–6, 255, 260, 342, 350–1, 354–5, 356, 363, 365–7, 381–2, 388, 390, 392, 395–7, 398, 417, 419, 427, 460, 589, 594, 630–1, 647–8, 660, 663, 665, 668–9, 674–5, 702, 711–12, 715, 717; Afrikander 67; Ankole 67; Baoule 72; as bridewealth 494, 91; cattle complex 11; dwarf shorthorn (*muturu*) 73–5, 83; dwarfed taurines 89; as a form of wealth 389; Fulani humped 67, 91; humpless long-horned 72, 75–6, 85–7, 351; humpless short-horned 66, 74, 85, 92, 351; *n'dama* 75–6, 78, 85; *see* cattle; humpless longhorn cattle 75; indigenous domestication 18; introduction into Africa 18; *Keteku* 72; *kuri* 76–7, 85; linguistic evidence 73–4, 110–15; *pape* 77; representation in the faunal record 203; rinderpest 75, 362; in the Saharo-Sudanese Neolithic 116, 118, 120, 122; Sanga 67, 78, 717; tax on 552; trypanotolerance 74–5, 85; wild 172, 188; zebu (*Bos indicus*) 66–7, 75, 77–8, 86; West African Dwarf 87
Celtis sp.: *see* Hackberry
centralised polities 26, 101–2, 514, 527, 554, 609–12, 615, 658–72, 710; peer polity interaction 671
ceramic late stone age 261–73; *see also* epipalaeolithic; late stone age; neolithic
cereals 16–8, 53–61, 197, 200, 203, 205, 208–11, 216, 219–20, 222–3, 250, 346, 353, 378–9, 611, 640, 670; as an offering in burial 216; cultivation of 236–40, 353–4, 356; domestication 53–60, 248–9; linguistic evidence 110–11, 115; in the Saharo-Sudanese Neolithic 116, 120, 123; tax on 552; wild 229, 232
Chad 13, 36, 54, 75, 83, 88, 107, 118, 250, 335–6, 338, 462, 464; basin 336, 459; *see also* Lake Chad; Palaeolake Chad; Perichadean plain
Chadic language family 73, 93, 128, 134–5; proto 73
chaff 216, 223
Chaillu Massif 48
Chamba people 100; *see also* Samba Leeko 99
chamomile (Compositae) 175, 177
change: *see* under environment; society; culture; political
Changamire state 710
Chari-Nile language group 53
chat (*Catha edulis*) 346, 350
Chemchane depression 39
chemical analysis: allozyme-electrophoresis 160; biochemical analysis of human and

animal bone 70; geochemical analysis 43; infra-red spectroscopy 159–60, 161–2
Cherekecherete pottery 647
Chewa people 405, 500–1; migration of 396, 398
chicken (*Gallus gallus*): *see* fowl
chickpeas 59, 356
chieftaincies 15, 23, 100–1, 283, 399, 403, 513–14, 522, 527, 536–7, 540, 542, 554–9, 573, 594–6, 605, 606, 609, 614, 628, 632, 642, 645, 651, 705, 710
Chifumbaze complex 386
Childe G.V.: *see* 'Neolithic Revolution'; urbanism
China 641, 664, 695, 743
Chishinga people 500, 502
Chokwe people 500, 501, 503
Chondwe ware 484
chromatographic techniques 162
church 352, 557, 559, 616–19, 621
Chyulu hills 488
city: *see* town
Clark J.D.: *see* urbanism
class 659; differentiation 428; interests 429
Classic Shai ware 647
climate: in the central African rainforest 291, 293–4; change 13–14, 228 climatic correlations in Africa 13; Holocene 32–42, 182; late Pleistocene in north Africa 227; in Malawi 391; monsoon 14, 182; in the Nile valley 168; rainfall 32, 36–7, 182, 241, 361, 459; role in the adoption of agriculture 238; role in migration 16; role in urbanisation 21; temperature 32, 34; 48–50
club-rush (*Scirpus maritimus/S. tuberosus*) 175–9
coconut 153; linguistic evidence 144
cocoyam 151, 243, 276; cultural significance of 150; linguistic evidence 140, 151; new (*Xanthosoma mafaffa*) 149, 153; old (*Colocasia esculenta*) 149, 153; ritual significance 150; *Urginea altissima* 544
coffee 346, 350, 354
colonial attitudes 2, 7, 15, 22–3, 349, 437, 457
commerce 557; in the Aksumite period 614; *see also* trade
communication: networks 267–8, 269, 537; in an urban environment 732, 742–6
Comoro islands 29, 414, 660–1, 665, 667–8
complexity, social xxxiv, 8, 24–5, 30–1, 230, 411–12, 622, 671, 725, 730
complex society: *see* centralized polities; chieftaincies; in state
conger fish (Congridae) 676, 690–1
Congo 43, 45–6, 48, 304, 311, 322
Congo basin 21, 434–5
Congo river: *see* Zaïre river
Congo-Zaïre basin 291, 294, 296, 298, 319, 321–3, 325–6
cooking 264, 266, 495, 505; structures 282, 286; vessels, decoration of 506, 507, 510

copper 638–9, 694; ore 639; trade 638, 640
copper artefacts 390, 397, 403, 408, 632, 638, 647, 649, 704
copper metallurgy xxxiv, 347, 383, 433, 463, 466; radiocarbon dating 334
cosmology 506–12, 524–8; processes of material transformation 504–6, 513, 539–42; role of the town/city in ancient Egypt 581–2
cotton 245, 249, 276, 278, 356
cowfish (Ostraciidae), 676, 692
cowrie shell 394, 408, 488, 635
craft specialization 21, 554–5, 627, 631–2, 641
crocodile 208, 214, 217, 231, 362
Cross River 74
crossbreeding 72, 86
cucurbits (Curcurbitaceae) 112, 118–19, 164
cultivation 8, 56, 162, 251, 370, 395–8; incidental propagation 199; linguistic evidence for 152; *see also* agriculture
cultivation techniques 242, 245, 177–9; burning, of land 182, 192, 199, 278; crop rotation 244, 278; decrue (hydraulic) system 56, 252; 'fadama' (floodplain) 245; fallow 250, 719, 614; fertilization 242, 244, 614; flood retreat (residual moisture) 242, 244–5; interdigitation 242; mulching 242; ridging 242; shifting 242, 244; slash and burn 247; swidden systems 248, 251, 252; terracing 242; transplanting of rice 56; *see also* irrigation
cultural: classification, of iron production 502, 504; determinism 458; differentiation 118, 386, 611; diffusion 233; evolution vs environmental determinism 4; units 11, 233 *see also* ethnicity; socio-cultural
culture historical approaches 10, 13, 25, 275, 289, 359, 412, 493; problems with 11–12
Cunene river 372
Cushitic language family 108, 128, 134–5, 353, 359; Old East African Cushitic 135
Cushitic speaking peoples 135, 489
Cyperaceae 50; *Cyperus* 170, 189; *Cyperus conglomeratus* 208; *Cyperus-Panicum* 183
Cyrenaica (Libya) 227, 571, 576

D'MT monarchy 611, 613–15
Dahomey Gap 46, 241, 292, 653, 746
Dakhlah Oasis 38, 228–9, 571, 574, 580, 584
Dakoid language family 129, 131
Dambwa ware 484
Danakil depression 344–5, 347
Darfur 122–5, 434, 459–67
Darfur-Wadai 109
date palm 178
Dâures (Brandenburg) massif 372–4
deep sea coring 13
defence 25, 101–2, 555, 625, 651, 698
Defoid language family 129, 131

deforestation 437, 457, 466 *see also* reforestation

demography: *see* population

dendrochronology 203

'desert kernel' (Kernwuste) hypothesis 230

diet xxxiv, 70, 167, 219, 240, 248, 421, 631, 680; carbohydrate 178; ethnographic evidence for 246; evidence of diet in the neolithic and palaeolithic 164; starch 178

diffusion 2, 9–13, 138, 233–4, 239, 241, 304, 432, 137; of domestic ruminants 61, 72, 75, 114; of iron production 432–3, 453, 459, 465–6

diffusionist approaches 22, 234, 331, 334–5, 432–3, 694–5

digging stick 175, 253, 277–8

Dimi people 436

Diola people 245–6

Djado region 228, 235

Dobe region 64, 177

dog 64, 171, 185, 207–8, 217, 223, 225, 350, 460, 596; *Canis familiaris* 188; domestication 352; *see also* Canids

Dogon region 733

dom palm (doum palm) 175, 177, 179, 196, 218, 596, 603

domestication xxxiv, 3–4, 240, 243, 302, 350, 354; adoption of domesticates in the Nile valley 166–7, 197–226; adoption of domestic animals in Africa 61–103, 356; of cereals 53–60, 248, 249, 251; as a concept 237; gene pool divergence 160; of indigenous cucurbits 119; incipient, in the Nile valley 199; linguistic evidence for domestic animals 71–103; of plants 8, 19; 246–7, 251; of pulses 153; radiocarbon dating 235; redomestication of the horse 88, 91, 103; *see also* entries under individual genera/species

Domoni 666–9

donkey (*Equus asinus*) 61, 65, 179, 350, 460, 596; C14 dating 65; as transport 350, 355, 557, 559, 565–6, 588, 602

Dowayo [Namji] people 76

Drakensburg 49

dromedary: *see* camel

duck 62, 174, 181

Dugong (*Dugong dugon*) 675, 681–2

Dusky batfish (Platacidae) 676, 693

dwarfing: as an environmemtal adaptation 90–1; of the goat 91; of the horse 89–90, 103

dye, use of sorghum 56

East African Rift Valley: *see* Rift Valley

ebony (*Dalbergia melanoxylon*) 588, 594–7, 603, 606

ecological approaches: *see* ethnoecology and palaeoecology

economy, interrelation of economic and

environmental variables 410; *see also* production; trade; markets

Edo people 151

egalitarianism 377

Egypt 10, 13, 15, 25, 32, 38, 62–6, 68–9, 75, 77, 79–80, 86, 89–90, 118–19, 165–228, 234, 349–50, 432, 456, 551–605, 610, 622, 732; interaction with Punt 587–606; interrelationship with Nubia 572–3; the role of textual data 585

Ancient Egyptian language family 133–5

Elkabian lithic industry 185

electron microscopy 439

electrum 604, 606

elephant 61, 342, 375, 421

Elmenteitan tradition 369–70, 487; lithic artefacts, 365, 367, 370; obsidian hydration dating 368; pottery 358, 364–5, 370; radiocarbon dating for 368; settlement 370

emperor fish (Lethrinidae) 676, 678, 683

Ennedi region 38, 107, 122–5, 228, 230

Ennedian language 105

ensete (*Ensete edule*) 19, 241, 346, 350, 356

environment 32–52, 67, 167–70, 180, 192, 197, 211, 225, 227, 241–2, 290–4, 297, 338, 344–6, 357, 359–62, 381, 391–2, 418, 571–2, 716–17; human control and exploitation 15, 182, 192, 199, 278, 242, 245, 247, 253, 279, 421, 450, 457–8, 466; montane systems 48–50; and society xxxiii, 13–17; 27, 29, 31, 193, 225, 232, 237–8, 239, 242, 244, 250, 265, 290–1, 331–2, 379, 382, 410–11, 426–7, 456, 465, 491, 537, 570–4, 584–5, 644, 694, 698, 702, 705–11, 731; *see also* climate

environmental: adaptation of livestock 18, 75, 79, 84–7, 90–2; change 1–2, 16, 169, 180, 266, 294, 369, 572; degradation/deterioration 171–2, 182, 436, 466, 619; determinism 4, 239, 695, 706

epipalaeolithic: as a concept 6; in Egypt 165, 168–9, 181, 183–99, 210, 212, 221, 225, in the Sahara 227–34; *see also* ceramic late stone age; late stone age; palaeolithic

equatorial rainforest of central Africa 14, 19, 52, 241, 247; archaeology of 289–327; as a barrier 292; as a human habitat 290

Eritrea 344, 346, 604, 611, 615

Eritrean coast/Arabian Tihama cultural complex 617

Erythraean culture 10

Ethio-Semitic language family 128, 353

Ethiopia 18–19, 21, 34–9, 42, 49, 53, 56–9, 68, 74–5, 77, 85–6, 106, 108, 134, 135, 251, 344–57, 434, 436, 601, 605–6, 609–21, 732; geophysical regions of 344–5

Ethiopian: highlands 73, 107–8, 116, 348, 604, 610–11; plateau 232, 609, 611

ethnic: names for food plants 152; succession paradigm 372, 374, 377, 384, 416

ethnicity xxxiii, 12, 97, 118, 233–4, 238, 275,

379, 386, 412, 493, 637, 660, 695–6, 707, 726
ethnoarchaeology xxxiii, 478, 627, 699, 706; 'ethnographic present', problems with 707; *see also* ethnography
ethnoecology 177, 242, 246
ethnography 1–2, 17, 19, 20, 71–87, 93, 99, 189, 379, 383, 645–6; of agricultural societies 71–103, 254, 274–88, 324; of hunter-gatherers 174, 176, 378; of iron production 494–6, 512–51; *see also* ethnoarchaeology
Europe 2, 13, 59, 233, 436, 569, 628, 657, 726, 743; prehistoric salt production 654–5; European names for food plants 152
evaporation 32, 37
evapotranspiration 14, 186
exchange 31, 269, 330, 384–5, 408, 427, 537, 658; networks 28, 267, 272, 390, 426, 482; *see also* trade
experimental archaeology: iron production 434, 455, 461
Eze-Leja (the chief priest of Leja) 439, 440

Fakhurian lithic tradition 179
Far East 670–1, 726
farming: *see* agriculture
faunal remains 16, 19, 167, 169, 179, 187–8, 197, 203, 207–8, 214, 216–20, 223–4, 255, 258, 262–3, 297, 324, 341, 342, 356, 362, 365–7, 376, 381, 384, 390, 392, 412, 417, 419, 421, 660, 663, 665, 678–93; preservation of 5; study of 15
Fayum 167, 183–4, 186, 190, 193, 198, 227, 552–3, 571, 572; *see also* site index
Fayum A industry/culture 186, 204–11
Fayum B industry/culture 186
feral 103; horse 88, 91
fertility: as a concept in iron production 495–6, 502–4, 513, 515, 522–9, 533, 541, 544–5; agricultural 26, 242, 249, 529, 716
Fez 735, 737, 740–1, 749
Fezzan region 92, 228, 235–6
Fipa people 500–1, 503, 508, 510
fish 167, 171, 173, 179, 181–2, 188, 195–6, 207–8, 211, 214, 217, 220, 223, 232, 342, 362, 363, 392, 630–1, 638, 640, 660, 663, 670, 675–93; drying and salting 675, 688; drying and smoking 174, 181, 196; preservation of 203; *see also* under family/genera/species
fishing 20, 173–4, 178, 180, 184–5, 188, 192, 195, 198, 206–8, 210–11, 214, 229, 232, 238, 247, 259, 271, 343, 365, 370, 392, 660, 662, 665, 670, 674; shellfish gathering 426; technology 173, 181, 185, 223, 232, 260, 262, 673, 686–7
Flathead fish (Platycephalidae) 676, 681, 687
flax (*Linum*) 200, 208, 210, 213–14, 216, 218, 223, 349

flora: *see* botanical remains
flotation 171, 366
food processing: detoxification 176, 279; among the Tiv 275, 279; in the west African late stone age 266, 269, 272
food production: *see* agriculture; foraging
forest refugia 45
Fouta Djallon 59; hills 253; people 481
fowl 350, 352; domestic fowl (*Gallus gallus*) 62, 663, 665; fowling 365; red junglefowl 62; sacrifice of 529, 530
Frankincense (*Boswellia*) 603
fruit crops 240, 276, 279
Fulani people 27, 253
FulBe people 77, 78, 86, 96, 100, 102, 128; jehad 101
Fundong 514–18, 523
funerary practices 403–4; *see also* burial
Fur [For] language family 105, 107, 110–12, 117, 128, 132–3; pre- 125
furnaces 302–3, 325, 333–5, 389–90, 395, 397, 435–7, 449, 451–4, 455, 457, 462–3, 474, 475, 481, 494, 502, 509, 518–22, 524, 529, 547, 550, 635; bowl 326, 329, 435, 439, 443, 494, 500, 503; construction 461, 472–3, 508; decoration 506–7, 510; low-shaft 435, 500–2, 503; tall-shaft 435, 500–3; typology of 435, 452, 458

Gabaza, kingdom of 613
Gaberi people 99
Gabon 9, 45, 289, 292, 299–300, 302–4, 323, 325, 454
Gambia 453–4
Gambia river 241, 253
Garamantes people 92
Gash delta 609; region 611
Gatung'ang'a ware 485, 488; radiocarbon dating 488
gazelle 61, 185, 188, 199, 207, 211, 217, 219, 475, 589; 'pet' gazelle 217, 219; red-fronted 181; dorcas gazelle (*Gazella dorcas*) 172–3, 179, 181, 185, 208, 223; *see also* antelope
gender relations: among the Abagusii 494–6; among the Kikuyu (Agikuyu) 3, 493–6; among the Tiv 276–7; on the East African littoral 659
geographical models: Central Place Theory 625; distance decay patterns 627; nearest neighbour analysis 698; rank size rule 625–6, 634–5, 637, 641; site catchment analysis 697, 714–18, 724, 731; geography: biogeography 43; human 24, 280, 264, 556
geomorphology 13, 250; of the central African rainforest 291, 293; of Malawi 391; of the Nile valley and delta 168
Ghana 10, 17, 27, 39, 41, 43, 45–6, 48, 93, 148, 241, 255–6, 258, 292, 335–6, 434–5,

454, 457, 640, 642–51, 748; Gonja, 101; intensification in the late stone age 261, 273
giraffe 374, 461
glass artefacts 408, 726
glazed sherds iron industry ('Chap group industry') 514–43
goat 18, 20, 67, 70, 72, 79, 81–4, 86, 113, 200, 208, 214, 216–17, 223, 234, 255, 265–6, 272, 276, 350, 356, 367, 377, 427, 494, 660, 668, 670, 677, 681, 715; desert goat 83; domestic goat (*Capra hircus*), 68; dwarf goat 81–2, 86, 260; dwarfing 91; ibex 199; linguistic evidence for 82, 111, 114–15; Maltese 81–3, 87; milking 81, 83; Nubian/Zaraibi 81–3, 87; resistence to disease 92; in the Saharo-Sudanese Neolithic 120; Sahel 83; savanna goat 81, 83–4, 86; scimitar-horned (*Capra aegagrus*) 68; Sokoto Red 83, 87; trade 702; trypanotolerance 87; West African Dwarf 81–3; West African long-legged 83; wild 416; *see also* ovicaprids
Gokomere (Ziwa) tradition 418–19, 712, 721; pottery 427–8, 484
gold 27, 591, 594–9, 604, 606, 624, 628, 632, 640, 644, 648, 651, 670, 695; mining 711, 718, 726, 731; trade in 708, 711
Gold Coast 644
gourd 18, 112, 115, 120, 248
grain: *see* cereals
granary 111, 118, 120, 205–6, 208, 210, 214, 215–16, 220, 229, 258, 276, 279
Grand Erg Occidental 41
grave goods 342–3, 403–4, 407, 465
Great Lakes 9–11
Great Zimbabwe tradition 711–25, 731; radiocarbon dating 711, 721
Greece 62, 559
grinding stones 116, 118, 120, 175, 181, 185, 190, 206, 207, 232, 237, 266, 269, 300, 324, 342, 368, 394, 399, 518, 629–30, 647, 649
groundnuts 245, 276, 278; linguistic evidence 140
grouper fish (Serranidae) 676, 685, 686
grunter fish (Haemuliidae) 676, 679–80, 683–4, 685
Grusi-Mo people 645
Guan people 645
Guinea 39, 50, 86, 244, 246, 248, 250–1, 262
guinea fowl (*Numida meleagris/N. ptilorhynca*) 61–2, 258, 260
Guinea highlands 252
Guinea yam (*Diocorea cayenensis, D. rotundata*) 19, 146–8, 241, 248; linguistic evidence 147, 152
Guinea, Gulf of 39, 52
Guinea-Bissau 245
Gumban culture 8
Gur people 128–30
Gur language family 93, 128, 143
Gurage people 346, 350

Gwembe Tonga people 405, 406

Hackberry (*Celtis* sp.) 51, 258–9, 263, 264
Hadza people 136; language 128, 134
Halfan lithic tradition, 179
Hamitic migration 10, 235
Harappan civilization, script 55
Harar area 345–6, 351–2
hare 181, 188, 208, 376
hartebeest 179, 181–2, 185, 188, 199, 207, 365; *Acelaphus buselaphus* 172–3; *see also* antelope
harvesting 278; of root foods 178, 190
Hausa people 27, 88, 145, 245; slavers 94; traders 128; Emirates 102
Hausa country 88, 128, 245
Haut Ogooué 453–4
Haya people 500
hearths 206, 211, 213, 222
hierarchy, social 11, 21, 246, 283–4, 390, 554–5, 572, 573, 632, 658, 671
hippopotamus 171, 179, 181–2, 185, 188, 208, 214, 217, 231, 342, 362–3
history, nature of the evidence xxxiv, 22; *see also* oral history
hoes 253, 263, 277, 403, 407, 463–4, 528–30, 542
Hoggar region 122–5, 228–9, 232–5, 236
Holocene, climate and vegetation 13–14, 18, 32–52, 234, 238, 291, 293–4, 338, 346, 413, 415–17; in Egypt 168; in the Nile valley 170; forest expansion 46; the Great Wet Phase 228–9
Horn of Africa 77, 79–80, 86, 435
horse (*Equus caballus*), 65, 88–103, 350, 675; in art 92; Barb horse 89–91; dégénéresence 89; disease resistance 91; Dongola 89; dwarfing 89–91, 103; feral 88, 91, 103; fodder 91–2; Fulani 98; linguistic evidence 93; Oriental 89–90; as prestige animal 17, 88, 97; redomestication 88, 91, 103; ritual role 97; role in state formation 88–9, 100–3; as transport 350; trypanotolerance 88, 91, 103; in warfare 17, 88–9, 94, 100–3
horticulture 255, 272; *see also* agriculture; cultivation
human morphology, change in at the end of the pleistocene 168–9, 226
Hungorob Ravine 373, 374–81
Hungorob pottery 381
hunter-gatherers 7–8, 16, 20, 258, 299, 338, 343, 358–9, 362, 374, 392, 395–6, 426, 702; in Egypt 16, 165–97 epipalaeolithic hunter-gatherers in the Sahara 227–34; hunting technology 174, 263, 265; late stone age 261–6, 270, 386; in Mozambican prehistory 413–17; settlement 364, 706
hyaena 62, 199
hybridization 54, 57–8, 248; of oil palm 248
Hyksos people 65
hyrax 376

ideology 11, 411; analysis of 413; change in
    658, 665; of iron production 478–81; of the
    state 558; on the east African littoral 663
Igala people 95, 98
Igbo people 28
Igbo-Ukwu 28, 95, 97; see frontispiece
Igboland 98, 150, 455
Ijo people 130
Ijoid language family, 128–30, 139, 141–2
Ikelemba river 294–5, 305, 306
Ila people 500–2, 504–5
Imbonga Horizon (pottery) 304–5, 311, 319,
    321, 322, 325, 326; radiocarbon dating 308
Imerina people 481
inbreeding, of African domestic animals 91
incense 588, 592, 595, 597–9, 606, 614; see also
    frankincense 603
incense tree (Canarium schweinfurthii) 248, 258,
    263–5, 300, 324, 329
India 53–5, 57–9, 62, 66, 77, 79, 86, 435, 479,
    480, 482–3, 564, 695, 726
Indian Ocean 26, 29–30, 32, 77, 482, 592, 660,
    665, 670–1, 675, 697, 703
indigenous: African archeologists xxxiii, 6;
    agriculture in Mozambique 428; agriculture
    in west Africa 253; copper production 382;
    development of iron production 433, 491;
    development of iron technology 331;
    domestication of animals 61; exploitation of
    ovicaprids 234; innovation xxxiv, 10; iron
    production 449, 451, 456; plant
    domestication 346; urban development
    27–9; urbanism in Nubia 583–4; urbanism
    in west Africa 623, 635, 641
Indo-European language phylum 106, 108,
    128; Proto-, 106, 109
Indonesia 480–1, 660
Indonesian people 481; contact between
    Indonesia and Africa 479–80, 483; migration
    to Madagascar 479
information storage 744–6
Inhambane region 413
inscriptions: Aksumite 351, 353, 355, 613,
    615, 617; Harrappan (on pottery) 55;
    Himyaritic 348, 353; Naski or Kufic arabic
    649; Sabaean 612–13; of the D'MT
    monarchy 613
interdisciplinary/multidisciplinary approaches
    30–1, 230, 409–10, 703, 710
interglacials 293
invention 9, 22, 304
Irigwe people 95–6, 101–2
iron age (as a concept) xxvi, 8–9, 452;
    definition of 330; 'Pastoral Iron Age' 7; see
    iron using/producing societies
iron artefacts 335, 365, 369, 403, 463–4,
    527–8, 635, 645, 647, 649; trade in 664
iron ore 333, 395, 436–7, 451, 465, 504, 540,
    549, 638; ownership 469, 471; preparation
    451, 471, 529; prospecting and extraction

468–71, 494; protection of 471; ritual
    prohibition associated with extraction 469;
    specialist ore hunters 468
iron production xxxiv, 5, 9, 270, 302–4,
    325–6, 332, 333, 347, 389–90, 395, 417, 427,
    449–67, 498, 631, 638, 660, 663, 665, 668;
    cast iron 451; cultural classification of
    501–2, 504; decline of 436, 456–7;
    ethnographic evidence 451, 455, 512–50;
    experimental reconstruction 461, 468–77;
    external introduction vs indigenous
    development 331, 432–3, 456, 465–6, 491;
    extraction 389; fuel 397, 436, 455, 461, 465,
    471, 521, 530, 547, 549; historical evidence
    461; introduction into northern Ethiopia
    612; labour 436, 457; linguistic evidence for
    353; origins of 79–83, 432, 453, 456, 465–6,
    612; origins of, in west Africa 330–2; in
    prehistoric Kenya 84–94; in prehistoric
    Madagascar 478–83; procurement of
    materials 333, 461; radiocarbon dating 303,
    336–7, 390, 433–4, 517–18; residue analysis
    435–45, 449; ritual and taboo 457, 469, 473,
    481, 494–5, 502–10, 512–43; secularization
    of 539; slag 335, 343, 389, 395, 436, 440,
    463, 530, 549, 629, 635; smelting 9, 333,
    389, 397, 432–51, 457–8, 461, 462, 472–5,
    480–1, 494–5, 499–500, 501–10, 515,
    518–30; smithing (forging) 333, 389, 457–8,
    462, 472, 475–7, 515, 530–5; social
    organization of 457; specialization 472; steel
    435–6, 451, 483; technology vs ritual in the
    study of 499, 510, 512–13, 535–8; tools 333,
    521, 547–8, 716; typological approaches 9,
    332, 435, 452, 458; use of lime 437;
    wrought iron 450; see also bellows; furnaces;
    tuyères
iron using/producing societies 7, 9, 271, 279,
    290, 299, 325–6, 330, 368, 370, 463, 487–8,
    490–1, 499–512; in Botswana 386–90; in
    Cameroon 512–50; in Kenya 484–98; in
    Madagascar 478–83; in Malawi 391–8; in
    Nigeria 432–48; pottery 494; settlement
    15–98; in the Sudano-Sahelian zone 330,
    343; in west Africa 449–58; in Zaïre 468–77;
    on the Zimbabwean plateau 716, 722–3
irrigation 22, 54, 202, 241, 244, 395, 560, 569,
    see also cultivation techniques
Islam 84, 87, 94, 100, 659; Islamic Egypt
    561–2, 565, 569; Islamic expansion 732;
    Islamic funerary ritual 663, 669; Islamic
    influence on urbanization 24, 27, 624–5,
    628, 631, 669–71; Islamic trade 479, 483,
    657, 665, 671, 695, 700
Islamization 246, 628, 631, 663–5, 669, 671,
    745
Isnan cultural tradition 180
isotopic analysis 43; isotope ratios in snail
    shells 38; nitrogen isotope analysis 368
Isu 515–20, 521, 522, 524–5

Ithanga hills 485
ivory 597, 606, 624, 644, 651, 664, 670
Ivory Coast 50, 100, 242, 255–6, 258, 272, 436, 649
Izon 144

J. Marra 37–8, 57, 106–7, 460
J. Si 460, 462
J. Simiat 460, 462
J. Tagabo 460, 462
Jack fish (Caringidae) 676, 689
Jenn 624, 628, 632–3, 636, 638–9, 644
Jericho 623
Jerusalem 620
Jongwe (Tumbatu) 666
Jos 49, 102
Jos plateau, 57, 94–5, 97, 100–2, 455
Juba river 345, 347
Jukun people 95, 102; see also Koroafa

Kadugli language family 133
Kalahari 29, 35, 38, 40–1, 57, 64, 378
Kalambo ware 484–5
Kalanga-speaking groups 386
Kalenjin people 487–9; Sot Kalenjin 488
Kampala 738–9, 745, 748–9
Kamba people 500
Kanyamkago hills, 360, 363
Kano 27, 94–5, 102, 143, 738–9, 749
Kanuri country 245
Kaonde people 400, 500–1
Kapeni ware 394–8
Kapwirimbwe ware 484
Kapwirimbwe/Lydenburg/NC3/Roan Antelope tradition 485
Karanga people 503, 506, 510
Kasu people 615
Kay Ladio pottery 302
Kebbi region 88, 95
Kel Tamasheq 206
Kenya 13, 15, 20, 25, 35, 37, 49, 57, 85, 344, 351, 358–71, 392, 414, 421, 426–7, 484–98, 658–71, 669, 671, 672, 694–704
Kerma kingdom: see site index
Kgatla people 500, 504
Khoikhoi people 68
Khoisan language family 126, 128, 133–5
Khoisan-speaking peoples 80
Khushmaan Ma'aza Bedouin 189
Kibangian climatic phase 44–6, 293–4; see also Holocene
Kikuyu (Agikuyu) people 494–7, 500, 503–5, 508, 510
Kilungu hills 485–6, 488
Kilwa island 667; see also site index
Kinga people 500
Kinshasa 296, 298, 306
kinship 426, 495–6, 555; descent 404, 407, 494, 659; endogamy 482; exogamy 233, 494; in the Kenyan coastal hinterland 701–2;

kin-based production 245, 246; kin-based trading associations 632; polygamy 246; Tiv 277, 282–4
Kintampo complex 255–61, 265–71, 649; distribution of sites 257, 646; pottery 258, 267–8, 270; radiocarbon dating for 256; see also site index
Kir language family 114; proto 116–18
Kir-Abbaian language branch 105–6, 111–12, 114, 115; proto-, 106, 115–17, 125
Kivu region (Zaïre) 468–77
Kofyar people 95–6
kola (Cola acuminata/C. nitida) 19, 140, 143, 147, 628, 644, 651
Kolokuma people 146
Koman language family 108, 113–15, 132–3; proto- 117
Kongo kingdom 10, 28
Kontagora country 88
Koptos 588–92, 601–2
Kordofanian language family 73, 128, 130
Kordofanian-speaking peoples 82
Kordufan 462, 464–5
'Koroafa' [Jukun] 102
Kru language family 128–30
Kubbaniyan tradition 171, 199
Kuja river 363
Kulango people 645
Kuliak language branch 105–7, 111–12, 133; pre-proto 125; proto- 117
Kumasi area 271
Kunama language family 105, 107–10, 113, 117, 128
Kunama-Ilit 133
!Kung San 64, 177, 217, 220; see also San
Kush, kingdom of 573
Kwa language family 79, 128–30, 143–6, 152, 253; New Kwa 130
Kwale hills 673
Kwale ware 392, 417–18, 421, 423, 426–7, 484–5, 488, 490

lactose intolerance 67
lake levels 52; calculation of past rainfall 36–8; at the end of the Pleistocene 40; regression of 39; sediments 43, study of 13, 33, 35
Lake Abhé 35, 42
Lake Abiyata 35
Lake Besaka 346, 356
Lake Bosumtwi 39, 41, 45–6, 48
Lake Chad 9, 35, 41, 53, 76–7, 80, 83, 86–7, 122–5, 251, 271, 338, 459, 463, 465, 655–6
Lake Chilwa 38
Lake Langano 35
Lake Malawi 12, 391, 392–4
Lake Malombe 393
Lake Moeris 167
Lake Naivasha 35, 37, 41
Lake Nakuru-Elmenteita 35, 37
Lake Ngami 35

Lake Nyanza 427
Lake Rudolf: see Lake Turkana
Lake Shala 35, 42
Lake Tumba (Lac Tumba) 294–8, 306
Lake Turkana (Rudolf) 35, 37, 41, 232, 344, 347, 356; basin 69
Lake Victoria 35, 37, 51, 83, 359–60, 362–3, 370, 485–6
Lake Ziway 35, 42
Lake Ziway-Shala 41
Lamu archipelago 414, 427, 671, 673–5, 678–93, 696, 703; ecology of 677
land: economic importance of 23; ownership 403, 559; tenure 245; use 253, 381, 384–5
Lanet ware 487–8
language and prehistory xxxiii, 1, 71–137; correlation of language phyla with peoples 18, 234; correlation of linguistic and archaeological evidence 11, 227, 234, 323, 326–7, 358, 489, 491–2; see also linguistics
late stone age 9, 227, 296, 298, 330, 346, 366, 386, 396, 487, 721; as a concept 7; in the Sudano-Sahelian zone 330, 334–5, 338–9, 341, 343; in west Africa 261–73; see also palaeolithic; epipalaeolithic; ceramic late stone age; neolithic
legumes 200, 213, 250, 356, 682; see also individual genera/species
Leja 438, 441–5
Lelesu ware 392, 484
Lemek valley 359, 361, 366–8, 370
lentils 59, 200–1, 213, 218, 222, 350
Leopoldian climatic phase 44–5
Leptadenia shrubs 170, 183
Levant 16, 165, 200–1, 234
Liberia 74, 242, 544
Libya 40, 118, 571, 573–4, 583
Libyan desert 228, 230
Likwala-aux-Herbes river (Likouala-aux-Herbes) 294–5, 305, 306, 311, 314, 321, 327
Limpopo valley 29, 709
linguistics: comparative linguistics 71–2; glottochronology 117, 126, 234, 326; historical linguistics 290, 326; lexicostatistics 126, 326; loan-words and 'borrowing' 109, 114, 140, 146, 151, 658; 'mass-comparison' 126; methodology 126–8; neo-classical comparative linguistics 492; principle of least moves, 106, 108; problems with the data 135; the 'Swadesh list' 126; see also language and prehistory
Linia river 339
literacy 624; see also writing
lithic artefacts 4, 44, 167, 185, 187, 191, 202, 206, 211, 230, 253, 279, 296–7, 335, 341, 342, 358, 364, 366, 369, 375–6, 396, 426, 488; Acheulean 4; adzes 238; Aurignacian 4; backed bladelets 171, 185, 187; bifacially flaked 253; bifacially retouched tools 297, 298; burins 185; Chellean 4; Djokocien

lithic industry 296; Elmenteitan tradition 364–5, 367, 487; as evidence for the domestication of cereals 55; Fayum A tradition 207; flake industries 262; gloss-edged trapezoids 17, 55; ground stone 4–5, 19, 238, 250, 260, 262, 270, 300, 302, 328, 347, 356; microliths 180, 185, 227, 233, 237–8, 250, 253, 256, 258, 262–3, 297, 299, 346, 356, 362, 366, 415, 610; Moerian tradition 212; Mousterian 202; outils écaillés 365; polished stone 3, 255, 258–9, 267, 269, 270, 298–9, 301–2, 304, 335, 341, 342, 517; projectile points 223, 253, 296; scrapers 185, 335, 356, 362; Tarifian lithic industry 191; thumbnail scrapers 375; typology 25; see also Ballanan industry; Qarunian industry; Shamarkian industry
locust-bean trees (Parkia spp.) 276
Logone 98–9, 103
Logone river 37; Logone-Shari river 32, 34
long distance trade 10, 15, 28, 30, 80, 355, 388, 390, 396–8, 479, 638–9, 649–50, 656, 659, 664, 671, 674, 701; in salt 653–5, 695; see also trade
long-tailed silver biddi (Gerreidae) 676, 690
Longwe pottery 396, 398; radiocarbon dating 396
Lopori river 294–5, 306
Lua river 305, 306
Luangwa tradition 423
Lulonga river 294, 295, 305, 306
Lunga people 500
lungfish (Protopterus aethiopicus) 362
Lungu people 501, 503
Luo people 361; pottery 493
Lurio river 414, 426
Lydenburg tradition 417

Maasai people 361, 369, 487–9, 510–11, 706; settlement 367
Maasailand 369
Maban language family 105, 107, 109–10, 112, 129, 133; pre-proto- 125; proto- 117
Madagascar 29, 432, 479–83, 658–60, 662, 665, 669–70, 733
Mafa people 482
Mafia island 667
Maghreb 75, 227–8, 234, 237
magic 283, 540; in association with iron production 499, 510, 512–13, 522–30, 533–43
maize 57, 243, 276, 279; linguistic evidence for 140
Makua people 397
Malagasy: culture 478–80; language 658; people 480, 659–60
Malakote people 703
Malawi 25, 29, 38, 391–8, 403, 435, 484, 537–8, 553, 567

Mali 27, 32, 39, 56, 91, 94, 100, 206, 232, 335, 391–8, 624, 655
Maluekian climatic phase 44–5
Mamba-Kassenga people 468–77
Mambila plateau 98
Mampurugu area (Nigeria) 453–5
Manda Island 696, 703; *see also* site index
Manda region 656
Mandara mountains 98
Mande language family 128–33, 146, 246
Mande people 101, 645
Mandeland 649
mango (*Irvingia gabonensis*) 248
Maniema region (Zaïre) 468–77
manioc 243, 323
Mapungubwe polity 709
Mara region 20, 359, 361, 366–70
Maravi pottery 426
Maringa river 295, 305, 306
market 28, 97, 406, 457–8, 513, 537, 552, 566–7, 578–9, 618, 625, 628, 631–2, 640, 649, 653, 677, 727, 741, 748; 'pre-market' 245; world market 429, 556, 568–9
Mashonland 710, 714
material culture, cultural identity of 399–408; *see also* specific artefactual types
material transformation: *see* cosomology
Matola tradition 417, 427
Mauritania 39, 41, 233, 250–1, 334, 433, 653, 655
Mawudzu pottery 396, 398; radiocarbon dating for 396
Mayo Kebbi river 37
mayweed (*Anthemis*) 223–4
Mazowe river 730
Mberre people 500–1
medicine 64, 146, 218, 525–6, 529–31, 533, 535, 540–1, 544–50, 646, 650; plants 543–7; healer 543
Mediterranean 10, 30, 38, 63, 65, 168, 569
Mekeyir: *see* Shabo language
Mellala Sebkha 41
Mema, kingdom of 466
Merga 228, 231
Merina people 478
Meringa river 294
Meroitic kingdom 24, 26; *see also* site index
Mesoamerica 91, 622, 641
mesolithic 8; 'Khartoum Mesolithic' 227, 232–4; *see also* Fayum B
Mesopotamia 555, 559, 563–4, 622
Meta people 527
Middle East 80, 85–6
migration 2, 10, 12, 148, 202, 364, 416, 484, 651, 657; frontier theory 12; of game in the Nile valley 198; of hunter-gatherers in the Egyptian Holocene 183; in the Levant 200; of pastoral peoples into East Africa 358; rural/urban 569; seasonal 245; trade induced 649; *see also* Bantu; Chewa; Hamitic

millet: *Bracharia deflexa* 59, 61, 200, 241, 243–5, 250–1, 346, 388, 426, 460, 494, 627, 631, 640, 660, 670, 682, 715; Banbara groundnut 241; cultivation 251; *Digitaria* spp. 58, 241, 243; finger millet (*Eleusine coracana*) 17, 57–8, 241, 243, 251, 346, 349, 354, 358, 610; fonio millet 251; kertsing's groundnut 241; pearl millet (*Pennisetum* spp.) 17, 56, 58–9, 241, 249, 251, 274, 343, 562; wild 178–9
mobility, hunter-gatherer 264–6, 267, 269, 272, 706
Moerian tradition 205, 211–24; economy 220, 222; pottery 212, 215; radiocarbon dating 211, 221–2
mollusca 188, 232, 392, 647–8; giant land snail (*Achatina achatina*) 263–4, 270; *Unio* 179; C13 analysis 41; isotope ratios in snail shells 38; Red Sea 201
Mombasa 392, 414, 425, 485–6, 666, 675, 733, 735, 749
Momboyo river 294–5, 305
Monapo tradition 421; pottery 423–4, 425
monumental architecture 348, 616, 622, 624; as a focus of archaeological research 659
Moors 27, 727; 'Golden Trade of the Moors' 628
moray fish (Muraenidae) 676, 690
Moroa people 95
Morocco 13, 26, 56, 65, 82, 87, 229
mortars 171, 180; wooden 190
mortuary cults, in ancient Egypt 552, 582; *see also* burial
mosque 645, 659, 663, 669, 671, 700–1
Mossi people 333
Moyen Ogooué 453–4
Mozambique 11, 25, 29, 409–29, 659–60, 665, 702, 707–8, 711
Mukaradzi river 726
Mulanje plateau 391–2, 397
mullet (Mugalidae) 676, 692
Mumuye people 76
Musengezi tradition 711, 722; burial 722–3; pottery 721
Mutapa state 709, 725–31
Mwahavul people 95, 97, 101
Mwitu tradition ('Early Iron Age Industrial Complex of Eastern and Southern Africa'/'Chifumbaze complex') 484–5, 487–8
myrrh (*Commiphore/Balsamodendron*) 587, 589, 591–2, 594–5, 599–603, 606, 607

Nagada region 222, 552
Nagada I (Amration) tradition 203–4, 217
Nagada II/Naqadian (Gerzean) tradition: economy 222; pottery 221; radiocarbon dating 221
Nahron people 378
Naivasha region 366

Nambib desert 20, 372–83, 385
Namibia 20
Nampula region (Mozambique) 413, 415–16, 418, 421
Nampula tradition 416, 421; pottery 422, 424
Natal 55, 64, 70, 426–7
native Americans: Apache, domestication of the horse 91; transition to farming in the American southwest 197; use of Chenopodium and Rumex seeds 189
Nderit ware: see Olmalenge pottery
Ndjilian climatic phase 293
Ndop plain 513; chiefdoms 536; iron industry 514, 520, 537
Near East 453, 568, 664, 670, 671, 726
neolithic xxxi, xxxiv, 2, 9, 491; as a concept 3–8, 254, 261, 298, 302; el Adam type 120; el Ghorab type 120; el Kortein type 120; el Nabta type 120; the 'Guinea Neolithic' 4; in the central African rainforest 297–304, 325, 326; in the Fayum 204; houses at Nabta PLaya 154; Kintampo 'neolithic' 261; in the Levant 200; the 'Neolithic Revolution' 4, 21, 237–8, 254; Pre-Pottery Neolithic A 200; pre-pottery Neolithic B 200, 202, 234; in the Sahara 234–9; Saharo-Sudanese Neolithic 104–25, 232, 233; settlement, in the Nile valley 202; technology 326; in west Africa 260; Wet Phase 228, 231–2, 234, 237; see also: ceramic late stone age; epipalaeolithic; Fayum A tradition
Néolithicisation 6
Ngoko river 294–5, 305, 306, 312, 321–2
Ngong hills 486, 488
Ngoni people 500–1
Ngovo group (pottery) 299, 302, 322
Niger 11, 36, 56, 83, 95, 118, 232, 334–5, 433, 453–4, 481, 655
Niger delta 18, 27, 39, 80, 139, 146, 250, 253; inland, 627–8, 638
Niger river 30, 32, 34, 41, 56, 91, 95, 97, 122–5, 241, 244–5, 252–3, 624, 640
Niger-Congo language phylum 18–19, 53, 73, 79, 82, 93, 126, 128–30, 133, 135, 137–9; classification 126, 130; as a concept 128; origins of 136–7; proto- 82, 127; relationship with Nilo-Saharan 133
Niger-Congo speaking peoples 136
Nigeria 14, 27–8, 35, 45, 55–6, 73–4, 76–7, 83, 89, 92, 94, 98, 101, 139–53, 148, 245, 250, 270, 274–88, 272, 292, 335–6, 338, 432–48, 544, 748
Nile monitors (Varanus niloticus) 362
Nile perch (Lates niloticus) 184–5, 188, 208, 211, 217, 342
Nile river 10, 15, 26, 30, 32, 34–5, 38, 54, 75, 80, 106–7, 118, 122–5, 232, 552, 577, 587, 591–2, 597, 603–5, 619, 743; annual flood variation 193; delta 77, 194; Sudanese Nile 229

Nile valley 13, 14, 16, 165–227, 229, 238, 347, 350, 465–6, 555, 571, 588–9, 609, 611
Nilo-Saharan language phylum 18, 73, 79, 82, 92–3, 104, 106–10, 114, 120, 126, 129–34, 135, 234; classification of 72, 104, 117, 133–4; culture history 120; origins of 18, 136, 137; proto- 108
Nilo-Saharan speaking peoples 104–25; agriculture 109, 115
Nilotic language family 133, 359
Nilotic-speaking peoples 73, 487–9
Njilian climatic phase 44–5
Njulunga people 508
Nkhudzi pottery 397–8
Nkope ware 392, 394–7, 484
Noba people 615
Nok culture 336, 433, 453, 455, 466
nomadism 8, 227, 230–1, 236, 238, 334, 372–85, 460, 552, 576, 583
noog (Guizotia abyssinica) 346, 349
Northern Sudanic language family 18
Nsukka 92–3, 97, 433, 436–48, 444, 446–7
Nubia 93, 181, 184, 194, 228, 232, 347, 350–1, 567–8, 571–3, 587, 597, 603, 605; Egyptian colonization of 583; interrelationship with ancient Egypt 572–3; settlement patterns 574; urbanization 583–4
Nupe people 88, 95, 97–8, 145
nut-grass 177, 179, 199; wild (Cyperus rotundus) 174–5, 218
Nyakusa people 500, 504–5
Nyandarua hills 485–6, 488
Nyanza district 20, 360
Nyiha people 500
Nyoro people 500–1, 508–9, 511

obsidian artefacts 362, 364, 366, 369, 487
obsidian hydration dating 348, 363, 366, 368
oedema 545–6
Ogoni 146, 150, 153
Ogooué river 302, 304–5
oil palm (Elaeis guineensis) 18, 243, 246–8, 250, 258, 260, 263, 299, 302, 324, 329, 514; cultivation 265; domestication 324; hybridization 248; linguistic evidence 140, 143, 152
Okala ware 300, 302, 322, 328
Okiek people 488
Oldishi tradition 367, 370; pottery 358, 366
Olmalenge pottery (Nderit ware) 358, 370
Oltome tradition 364; pottery 363
Oman 419
Omotic language family 128, 134–5, 353
Ona culture 611
Ondo 95, 97
One World Archaeology Series xxvii–xxviii, 289
Ongamo people 488–9
Ongota [Birale] language 135
oral history 1, 23, 98, 397, 468, 478, 481, 518, 631, 645–6, 651, 698, 704

Orange river 372
Oropom language 135
ostrich 188, 214, 375
otter 181–2
Ouagadougou 737, 739, 740–2, 749
Ouham river 298
ovicaprids 7, 207, 211, 236, 258, 265, 342, 367, 647; *see also* sheep and goat
oxygen isotope Stage five 50
Oyo 38, 41
Ozi river 699
Ozi, kingdom of 702

palaeobiological studies 16–17, 38, 43–5, 52
palaeoecology 1, 338; of Africa in the late Quaternary 43–52; of the central African rainforest 293–4
Palaeolake Chad/Megachad 35–7, 39, 338
Palaeolake Nakuru 37
palaeolithic 409; as a concept 6; evidence of diet in the late palaeolithic 164; late palaeolithic hunter-gatherer subsistence in the Nile valley 170–80; *see also* epipalaeolithic; late stone age
palm oil 144, 153; *see also* oil palm
palynology 14, 43, 44, 48, 50, 250, 293–4, 297; of lake sediments 45
Panafrican Congress on Prehistory 5, 9, 437
Panicum 170
Pape people 76
papyrus (*Cyperus papyrus*) 177, 179
parrot fish (Scaridae) 676, 679, 683
pastoralism 19, 20, 61, 66, 70, 72, 77, 80, 235, 238, 255, 574, 673–4, 702; agro-pastoralism 419; emergence of, in east Africa 358–70; external introduction vs indigenous development 378, 384; herd management practices 367; in Kenya 19; in the Nambib desert 372, 385; nomadic pastoralism 20; occupationally specialized pastoralists 84; 'pastoral Neolithic' 6–7; 'post-pastoral' foragers, 359; relations of production 379; stock rotation 382
Pate Island 675, 677, 680, 696, 703
peas 200–1, 213; cowpea 253, 259–60, 715; pigeon pea 253
pear, native (*Dacryodes edulis*) 248
pedology 14, 43–5, 293; FAO/UNESCO studies 14; geochemical analysis 710; geophysical analysis 710; podsolization 46, 718–19
Pemba island 666–7, 669
pepper 276, 278
Perichadean plain 330–43
Persia 480, 695
Persian language 658
Persians, the 21, 620–1
personal adornment 258, 265, 267, 269, 335, 347, 365, 465, 649; *see also* beads
Phragmites 170, 190

Pibor river 35
pig 208, 214, 223, 352, 362, 365; domestic (*Sus domesticus*) 65; forest 270; semitic prohibition of 352
Pikunda-Munda Horizon (pottery) 311–19, 321, 322, 326, 328; radiocarbon dating for 314
Piti 95–6
plantain 243; linguistic evidence for 140
playa lakes 38, 154
Pleistocene, climate and environment 13–14, 18, 34, 169–82, 227, 291, 338, 346; climate in Egypt 168; climatic fluctuations 293; environment in the Nile valley 170
Pliocene 291
plough 237, 346, 352–3, 356, 612
pluvials 13, 293; 'interpluvials' 293
Pokomo people 699, 703
political organization 246, 280, 390, 411, 413, 454, 458, 514, 559, 572–6, 645, 663–4, 650, 726; *see also* power
polity: *see* centralized polities
pollen analysis: *see* palynology
pony 88–103 Bariba 89, 100; Chamba 99–100; dwarfing 89–90, 91; in Egyptian art 89; Kotokoli 100; Plateau pony 94, 96–8; as prestige animal 97; ritual role 97; role in state formation 100–3; 'Sara'/'Laka' 98–9; in warfare 96–9; *see also* horse
population: in ancient Egypt 572; change 658; estimation of settlement population 627, 632–3; growth 746; in Nubia 572; role in the adoption of agriculture 238; study of 25, 562–3
Portuguese 62, 140, 144, 153, 699, 725, 727; textual evidence 730; traders 730
pottery 4–5, 20, 55, 157, 238, 250, 253, 279–80, 291, 296–303, 339, 342, 346–8, 356, 368, 372, 374–5, 379, 381–2, 390, 401–2, 420, 464, 610, 630–1, 635, 640, 648, 650, 660, 664, 673; correlation of pottery traditions with peoples 660; correlation cluster link analysis 491; in the definition of food production 19; in the definition of the 'Neolithic' 3, 298; early pottery in the central African rainforest 297–327; as evidence for change in culinary style 266; figurines 255–6, 267, 341, 342, 354, 629, 635; graphite burnished wares 726, 729, 730; green glazed wares 419; Levantine (in Egypt 201; linguistic evidence for 110; petrographic analysis 723; in the Saharan epipalaeolithic 230–2; in the Saharo-Sudanese Neolithic 116, 118, 120, 122, 232–3; thin section analysis 412; tin glazed wares 419; typology 25, 412, 484; social context of 492–4; in the west African late stone age 262, 264, 266, 267–8, 270–1; X-ray fluorescence analysis 699; *see also* specific pottery traditions: Begho; Cherekecherete; Classic Shai; Gatung'ang'a;

Gokomere (Ziwa); Kapeni; Kintampo; Kwale; Lanet; Lelesu; Longwe; Maravi; Mawudzu; Moerian; Monapo; Musengezi; Nampula; Nkhudzi; Nkope; Tana; Tarifian; Urewe; Zhizo
power, political: 15, 21–4, 100–1, 389, 411, 466, 496, 526, 552, 557, 614–15, 711; centralization of 22, 26, 554–5, 566–8, 572–4, 578, 581–2, 746
production 2, 31; 'African mode of production' 30, 410; division of labour 230, 411; exploitation of surplus production 100; mode of production 245–6, 410–11; relations of production 379; surplus production 30; see also iron production; agriculture
property, transfer of 404, 407–8
proto-languages 72, 108–9, 112–13, 127, 133, 137, 139–40, 152
Punpun phase, radiocarbon dating 263
Punt, the land of 571, 587–609; Egyptian textual evidence 587–603; location of 603; socio-political structure 604–5
pygmy animal species 91

Qarunian lithic industry/tradition 186–91, 202, 205
Qena 168, 170, 180–2, 202, 222, 226, 552–3; province of 194, 197
Qift 553–4, 571, 572
Quaternary 13, 43, 52; arid phases 45
Queen Hatshepsut 592–6
Quseir 588, 592
quern 190, 206, 271

Rabbit fish (Siganidae) 676, 681, 683–4, 690
racial classification 9; ideas 11
radiocarbon dating xxix, 4, 7, 43–4, 118–19; errors 52; of food production 19; of the Egyptian Neolithic 202–3; of lake sediments 33, 35; of molluscs 35
Red Sea 26, 82, 87, 108, 344, 347, 391, 588–9, 591–2, 597–9, 600, 603–5, 609, 612, 614–15, 617, 620–1
Red Sea hills 116, 168, 173, 179, 183, 344
reed, common (Phragmites australis) 177, 179
reforestation 44, 46; see also deforestation
religion 25, 246, 352–3, 512, 522, 525, 539, 543, 559, 612, 615, 621, 628, 631, 657, 659, 726; see also Islam
Rhodesia 7; see also Zimbabwe
rice 56, 242–4, 246, 249, 627, 631, 638, 640, 660, 670, 715; African rice 241, 252; Asian rice 58, 252; cultivation techniques 245; décrue (hydraulic) cultivation 56, 252; estuarine rice production 244; swamp rice cultivation 245; transplanting 58; West African rice (Oryza glaberrima) 58, 245, 631
Rift Valley, the 30, 50, 344–6, 356, 359, 362, 366, 391, 487–8

rinderpest 362
Rio de Oro 228, 235
ritual 378, 400; associated with iron production 469, 473, 481, 494–5, 502–10, 512–43; funerary 401, 403–4; healing practices 377; role of the horse 97
rock art 17, 20, 64, 68, 70–1, 75, 77, 85, 87, 92, 199, 234–6, 238, 289, 372, 374–5, 377–8, 383–4, 413, 721; the 'Bubaline period' 235–6 rockcod (Serranidae): see grouper fish
rodents 171, 259, 266, 270; African giant rat (Cricetomys gambianus) 63; black rat (Rattus rattus) 63; grasscutter/cane rat (Thryonomys swinderianus) 63; house mouse (Mus domesticus) 63; Norway rat (Rattus norvegicus) 63
Roman empire 26, 556, 615
Ron people 94–6
Rongo people 500–1
root foods 16, 175–6, 196–7, 203, 209, 218, 240, 243, 324; see also tubers
rubberlip fish (Haemulidae): see grunter fish
Ruki river 294, 295–6, 305, 307
Rukwa basin 37
Rutshuru area 468–9
Ruya river 730

Sa'waw (at Mersa Gawâsîs) 590–2, 607
Saba 606, 610; kingdom of 612–13, 615
Sacred Lake 50–1
Sahara 6, 10, 14, 19, 27, 39–42, 54, 57, 63–5, 91–2, 104, 107, 116, 118, 182, 200, 232–4, 251, 272, 227–39, 459, 638, 640, 655
Saharan Atlas 228, 235
Saharan language family 105, 110–12, 128, 129, 132–3; proto- 107–8, 117, 124–5
Sahel 27, 35, 57, 104, 107, 182, 200, 232–3, 265, 269, 272, 459, 609, 638, 655, 657; sahelian vegetation 14, 36, 41
Sahelian language family 105, 107, 114; proto- 107, 109, 111–17, 234
salt (sodium chloride) 271, 355, 624, 628; consumption 652; economic importance 405; extraction 653; as a preservative 652; production 405, 407–8, 652–7; social significance 405; trade in 405, 638–40, 653–5, 703
Samba 101–3
Samba Leeko [Chamba] 95, 99–100
sampling 629, 634–5, 706, 710; random sampling 24, 413, 421–2
San 61, 64, 386, 389; see also !Kung San
Sancul (Swahili) tradition 426
Sandawe language 128, 134–5
Sangha river 294–5, 305, 311, 314, 319
Sanghai [Songay] language family 129
Sasanian Islamic ware 419, 664
Saudi Arabia 79, 86, 609–10; see also Arabia

savanna 14, 16, 48, 56, 58, 96, 183, 241, 250–1, 253, 255, 263, 272, 297, 302, 360, 372, 460, 487, 609, 638, 640, 655, 657; *Brachystegia* savannah woodland 715; forest-savanna mosaic 241; Guinea savanna grassland 275
Save river 414, 419, 428
Seabass (Serranidae): *see* grouper fish
seabream fish (Sparidae) 676, 688–9
secularization 539, 568
sedentism xxxiv, 8; in the Egyptian Neolithic 220; in the west African late stone age, 265, 269, in west Africa 255; origins of, in the Sahara 228–30; semi-sedentism 247
sedge 174, 178–9, 211, 213; *Scirpus tuberosus* or *maritimus* 189
sedimentology 293
Selima oasis 38
Semitic language family 134–5
Senegal 57, 250–1, 335
Senegal river 32, 34, 56, 241, 250, 252–3
Senegambia 252
Senufo people 645
Serengeti 361, 366
Serir Calanscio 228, 231
Setswana-speaking people 386, 389
settlement 15, 29, 253, 296, 645, 665, 705–6; Aksumite 348; analysis of 705–6; boundaries, definition of 637, 733, 740–2, 748; expansion 745–6; Fayum A tradition 204; Great Zimbabwe tradition stone enclosures (*zimbabwes*) 711–25, 729; growth, in the Nile valley 167; hierarchy 25, 30–1, 388, 390, 419, 552, 564, 568, 625, 633, 635–8, 665, 669–70, 698, 706; linguistic evidence 111; in Malawi 391–8; Mijikenda Makaya 696–9, 704; nucleation 15, 30; of the Oltome phase, 364; organization 280–2, 365, 367, 385, 388, 491, 495, 496, 566–9, 632, 706, 731; in the Saharan epipalaeolithic 229–30; in the Saharo-Sudanese Neolithic 118, 120; sites, recovery of 577–8; Tiv 274–88; in the west African late stone age 269
settlement location 15; Great Zimbabwe tradition 711–18; in ancient Egypt 565–8; role of environmental factors 709; role of socio-political factors 709
settlement patterns 275, 358, 378, 427, 694; Aksumite 618; in Egypt 564, 578–80; epipalaeolithic of the Nile valley 184–5; in the Kenyan coastal hinterland 698; late palaeolithic/epipalaeolithic, in the Nile valley 192; on the east African littoral 662; in pre-Aksumite Ethiopia 612–13; problems with the evidence 271; Qarunian 190; relationship to the nature and function of towns 570
sexual dimorphism, amongst hunter-gatherers in the Egyptian Pleistocene 168–9

sexual prohibition and iron production 494, 502–10, 526–7, 535, 542
Shabo [Mekeyir] language 135
shamanism 378, 539
Shamarkian lithic industry 166, 184–5, 192
Shari river 37
shark: Carcharhinidae 676, 691; Lamnidae 676, 692–3
Shati depression 40
shea butter tree (*Butyrospermum paradoxum*) 248
sheep 18, 20, 67, 72, 78–80, 86, 113, 200–1, 207, 216, 217, 223, 234–6, 255, 265, 272, 350, 352, 356, 377, 419, 427, 475, 494, 660, 663, 668, 674, 685, 715; Asiatic mouflon (*Ovis orientalis*) 69; Barbary (*Ammotragus lervia*) 185, 229; domestic (*Ovis aries*) 69; fat-rumped 78, 80–1, 86; fat-tailed 70, 78, 80–1, 86, 352–3, 675; linguistic evidence 111, 114–15; radiocarbon dating 235; representation in art 69–70; in the Saharo-Sudanese Neolithic 120; thin-tailed hair 70, 78–9, 86; thin-tailed wool 78, 79, 80, 86; trypanotolerance 83; wild 416; *see also* ovicaprids
shell middens 262, 264, 362–3, 381, 409, 417
shellfish 362–3, 418, 426, 662–3, 675
Shendi 572, 573, 574
Shire: highlands 391–2, 395–6; valley 391–2, 394
Shoa 344, 350
Sholio [Moroa] people 94
Shona people 386, 403, 405, 500–1, 710, 711; oral traditions 726
Siberia 135
Sierra Leone 242, 245–6, 261–2, 292, 453–4
Silsillian lithic tradition 179
Simyen mountains 344
Sinai 201
site catchment analysis 368, 696, 714–16, 724, 731
slaughtering patterns 367
slavery 12, 92, 101, 677; the slave trade 23, 624, 628, 643, 648, 651, 657, 670
sleek unicorn fish (Acanthuridae): *see* surgeon fish
smoking pipes 649–50
Smith, E.: *see* diffusionist approaches
Snagha river 305
snakes 171, 375
snapper fish (Lutjanidae) 676, 687–8
social: aspects of food production 20, 240; complexity 24, 230; context of agriculture 244; interaction xxxiv, 269, 566–9, 699, 705, 726; relations 475, 480, 482, 494–5, 658–9, 697–704, 706; reproduction, role of iron 528, 542; *see also* hierarchy
social-cultural change, analysis of 2–3, 237, 410, 498, 618
Socotra island 75

soil 14, 242, 244, 253; erosion 241; creep 45
soil studies: *see* pedology
Sokoto 95, 97; Sokoto–Rima basin 245
Soli people 403
Somali people 703
Somalia (Somaliland) 65, 344, 419, 426, 603, 605, 614, 674, 703
Somana 414, 426
Songay language family: *see* Songhai
Songhai empire 94, 100
Songhai [Songay] language family 105, 107, 110–12, 117, 125, 128, 129, 133, 136, 145
sorcery: *see* magic
Sorghum 17, 53–9, 61, 157–62, 164, 200, 237, 241, 243–5, 249–51, 388, 421, 426, 460, 627, 631, 660, 715; domestication 251; Guinea corn (*Sorghum bicolor*) 17, 53–7, 275, 278; hybridization 54; radiocarbon dating 155; wild 162
Sot Kalenjin: *see* Kalenjin
Sotho–Tswana-speaking groups 386
South Africa 7, 12–14, 67, 409, 412, 428, 434, 436, 707–8, 711
South Nyanza 362–6, 370
spectrometry, pyrolysis mass 175
spindle whorls 209, 334, 635, 649, 664
star apple (*Chrysophylum albidum*) 248
state, definition of 642, 705
state formation 23–4, 30, 428, 555–6; formalist vs substantivist approaches 705; the influence of long-distance trade 30; in iron age Ghana 642–51; in pre-Aksumite and Aksumite Ethiopia 609–16; role of the horse 88–9, 100–3
steel: *see* iron production
statistical/computer modelling: correlation cluster link analysis, 491; correspondence analysis 420; information technology 413; quantitative analysis 24
stone age 4–5, 296, 328, 415; in Mozambique, 413, 415–17; the South African 'Middle Stone Age' 4, 296; *see also* epipalaeolithic, late stone age, palaeolithic
stone tools: *see* lithic artefacts
stonefish (Scorpaenidae) 676, 692
storage 167, 174, 179, 181, 190, 196, 209, 211, 214, 224–5, 239, 247, 265, 726; of information 744–6; of sorghum 56; of starch by rhizomes 179; structures 154, 156, 205–6, 210, 212–3, 216–17, 220–1, 229–30, 276, 279, 286, 288, 300, 378, 388; vessels 238, 264, 266, 379
structural remains 155–6, 212–14, 217–22, 229–30, 232, 255–6, 258, 378–88, 392, 395, 420, 464, 467, 618–19, 629, 631, 637, 648, 650, 660, 663–4, 666–8, 675, 694, 726, 729
Suakin 603, 609
subsistence 8, 30, 202; change in 265, 658; Fayum A, Egypt 207–11; in the central African rainforest 323–5; *see also* agriculture; fishing; hunter-gathering; horticulture
succession: collateral succession 709; primogeniture 709
Sudan 17, 38, 41, 54, 57, 63, 65, 75, 80, 86, 106–7, 118, 145, 227–8, 252–3, 432, 464, 568, 571–2, 574, 588, 603, 604, 610, 615, 617, 623, 627, 638, 732
Sudanic language family 80, 102, 105, 107, 110–15, 128, 133; proto- 107–11, 113–18, 140, 149, 234
Suguta valley 35
Sukur 95, 98, 434
Sunni Islam 659
surgeon fish (Acanthuridae) 676, 679, 689, 690
Surtic culture 10
Swahili 15; language 658, origins of 673–4, 682; culture 29; migration 660
Swahili tradition: *see* Sancul tradition
Swaziland 436
sweet potatoes 276, 278
sweetlip fish (Haemulidae): *see* grunter fish
sword lily/corn-flat (*Gladiolus*) 248
sycamore fig (*Ficus sycomorus*) 214, 218
symbolic: anthropology 11; approaches 12; aspects of iron production 499, 502–10, 512–43; structures, role in mediating social relations 658
Syria 68

Taita hills 485–6, 695
Takezze river 344, 347
tamarisk (*Tamarix*) 170, 183, 187, 190
Tana river 485–6, 696, 699, 703; basin 673, 700, 702; delta 696, 699, 703
Tana ware (Early Kitchen ware/Swahili ware) 673, 702
Tanala people 481
Tananarive 732, 736–7, 741, 749
Tanzania 14, 20, 38, 75, 134, 325, 358–9, 369, 392, 414, 417, 421, 426–7, 433–5, 485–6, 488, 615, 659, 662, 702
Taoudenni depression 39, 41–2
taphonomy, site 177
Tassili region 235–6
Tatoga people 369
taurines: *see* cattle
taxation: in ancient Egypt 559, 566; *see also* tribute
technology 9; change 2, 272; late palaeolithic in the Nile valley 171, 175, 180–1; military 102; *see also* entries under agriculture; fishing; hunting; iron
teff (*Eragrostis tef*) 19, 241, 346, 349; wild (*Eragrostis pilosa*) 58
Temoro people 480
Ten [Ganawuri] people 95, 97
territoriality 8, 192–3, 230, 238–9, 555–7, 568–9, 572–3, 615, 627, 642, 706–7, 709
Thar desert 57
thermoluminescence 433

Thonga people 500, 504, 511
Tibesti, 35, 37, 39, 41, 92, 107, 116, 122–5, 228, 230–2, 237
Tigray plateau 611–12, 615
Tigre 344, 346
Tilemsi river 39
Timbuktu 39, 100, 624, 627–8, 639–40
Tirekka 640
Tiv 95, 99, 150, 274–88; the *Tor* Tiv 283
Tivoid language family 131, 132
tobacco 276, 719–20
Togo 46, 100, 241, 292, 434–6, 525
Torwa state 709
Toutswe (Zhizo) pottery 388–90
town/city 10; the 'African town' 30; as a centre of power 552, 557, 567, 578, 581–2; cosmological role of the town in ancient Egypt 580–2; definition 21–2, 570, 642, 732; nome capital (Egypt) 552, 559, 561–8; population studies 562; provincial 552; ratio of towns to villages in ancient Egypt 561–2; spatial organization within towns 31; temple towns 26; typology of 24; *see also* urbanism; village; walled settlements
trade 21, 102, 245, 267, 330, 369, 405, 419, 427–8, 458, 479, 514, 555, 559, 615–20, 630, 639–40, 644–5, 701, 703, 708, 718, 725, 727, 744; in the Aksumite period 614–15; between Punt and Egypt 599, 601, 605; European 374; goods 488; hinterland trade 15; of horses 97; Indian Ocean network 699; influence on urbanization 29, 30; kin-based 632; regional 698; role in the development of hierarchical polities; 658–72; role in urbanization 648, 650; of salt 651–6; trans-Saharan 27, 606, 623, 628, 644, 657; *see also* exchange; long distance trade
transhumance 116, 378–80, 384, 711, 718, 731; transhumant settlement 120
Transjordan 201
transport 17, 559; in ancient Egypt 557–8, 564–6, 568; role in state formation 556; use of domestic animals 350–1, 357; water transport 271, 350, 355, 557, 559, 565–6, 588, 601, 639
Transvaal 29, 386, 388, 426–7
Transvaal ware 484
tree crops 240, 250, 265; linguistic evidence 143–5
trevaly fish (Caringidae): *see* Jack fish
tribute 92, 355, 555, 557, 588, 597; *see also* taxation
tropical forest: *see* equatorial forest
trypanosomiasis 67, 360
trypanotolerance: in cattle 85; in sheep 83; of goats 87; of the horse 88, 91, 103
Tshitolien phase 296, 298
Tshuapa river 294–6, 305, 306
Tsimihety people 481
Tuareg people, 198, 333; use of Chenopodium

(*C. vulvaria*) 189
tubers, 16–17, 146–51, 164, 174, 177, 184, 189–90, 199, 209, 218, 224, 248, 263, 324; *Cyperus* spp. 181, 218–19; linguistic evidence for 146–51; *Scirpus* spp. tubers 176; southeast Asian vs indigenous tubers 153; use of burning to stimulate growth 182; *see also* root crops
Tumbatu: *see* Jongwe
Tupuri 99
turtle, 185, 188, 208, 214, 217, 223, 232, 660, 663–5, 670, 673, 675, 682
tuyères 303, 333, 389–90, 395, 433, 449, 451–2, 454, 457, 461, 463, 494, 505, 519, 521–2, 524, 529–30, 540, 550, 635
typological approaches 25, 409–10, 412; *see also* entries under furnaces; iron production; lithic artefacts; pottery; towns; urbanism

Ubangi river 292, 294–5, 305, 306, 321
Ugab river 372
Uganda 14, 28, 57, 67, 107, 135, 358, 485, 733
Ukpwa 515–16, 518, 542
ungulates 171, 181, 198, 362, 365; *see also* antelope; individual genera/species
Upper Guinea 292
Upper Volta 656
Urban Origins in Eastern Africa Project xxxiv, 413, 682
urbanism/urbanization xxxiv, 2, 21–31, 80, 348, 428; in Aksumite Ethiopia 616–19; in ancient Egypt 551–85; communication issues 732, 742–6; definition 21, 25, 570, 585, 622, 623, 625; on the east African littoral 671; in Europe 556–7; external influence vs indigenous development 27–9, 623–5; functional characteristics 25; in Ghana 642–51; in Libya 583; multidisciplinary approaches 709; non-nucleated urban centre 27; in Nubia 583–4; origins of 551–8, 694; origins of Swahili towns 672; regional approaches to 625–7, 634–41; role of agriculture 650; role of trade 650; typolgical approaches to 22; the 'urban revolution' 21; in west Africa 623–41; Yoruba 27–8; on the Zimbabwean plateau 705–31; *see also* town; walled settlements
Urewe pottery 365, 370, 484–5, 490–1
Usambara mountains 485–6, 695
Ushi people 500

vegetational history: of Africa in the late Quaternary 43–52; of the central African rainforest 293–4
Venda people 500–1, 505, 508
vetch (*Vicia sativa*) 214
Victoria Falls 35; region 399, 400–1, 406
village 4, 11, 154, 215–16, 218, 232, 269, 300, 311, 314, 323, 347, 390, 395, 406, 408, 461,

488, 551–2, 554–5, 557, 559–62, 564–6, 579, 581, 586, 604, 613, 617, 625, 634, 642, 660–1, 663, 665, 667–9, 671, 673–4; *see also* town
violence, as a concept in iron production 522–9, 537–40, 542
Volta river 241; basin 102

Wadi Akhdar 228–9
Wadi Hammamat 589, 591–2, 596, 606
Wadi Howar 38, 228, 231, 460
Wadi Kubbaniya 164–6, 169–80, 184–5, 189–90, 218, 226
Walia ibex (*Capra ibex walie*) 68
walled settlements 629, 632, 663, 668–9, 711–25, 729, 742, 744, 748
Walvis Bay 381–3
Wandibba 6–7
warfare 21, 239, 527, 658, 698; role of the horse 17, 88–9, 94, 100–3; role of the pony 96–9
water balance/hydrological budget 37
water buffalo: domestic (*Bubalus bubalis*) 68; wild Indian water buffalo (*Bubalus arnee*) 68
water cistern technology 258, 668
water lily (Nymphaceae) 175, 178–9, 190
wateryam (*Dioscorea alata*) 146, 148; linguistic evidence 140, 152
We 513, 516–17, 519, 522, 524–5, 527, 537
wealth: accumulation of 23; transfer of 404, 407–8
weapons 9, 334–5, 527
weaving 265, 284, 645
Webi Shebele river 345, 347
Western desert (Egypt) 154–64, 173, 182–4, 197, 200, 211, 229–31
wetland resources 169, 177, 203, 224; *see also* aquatic resources
whales 381, 673
wheat 198, 200, 213, 245–6, 349; einkorn 200; emmer 59, 200–1, 203, 208, 213–14, 216, 218, 222–3, 354–5
White Nile river 18, 35, 108, 602–4
wildebeest 362
wine 144, 248, 355, 530; palm wine 150, 648; raphia wine 529, 531, 535, 545–7; linguistic evidence 144
wine palm (*Raphia hookeri*) 18; linguistic evidence 140, 144, 152
witchcraft 150, 526–7, 541–2; *see also* magic
wolf: *Canis lupus arabs* 64; *Vulpes* 207

Wollo people 616, 618–19
women: adornment among the Karanga 507, 510; their role in subsistence among the Tiv 276–7
World Archaeological Congress xxvii, xxxii
world system (as a theoretical model) 30
Wrass fish (Labridae) 676, 684, 685
writing 744–5; introduction into northern Ethiopia 612; in the definition of urbanism 623; *see also* literacy
Wum 515–16, 537, 542, 545, 547

yam (*Dioscerea* spp.) 242–6, 250, 275–7, 323; cultivation 19, 265, 323; cultural significance 148; detoxification 247; domestication 246–7; linguistic evidence 140, 146, 147; seed yam tradition 244; yellow yam (*Dioscorea cayenensis*) 246; *see also* aerial yam; cocoyam; Guinea yam; wateryam
Yao people 397
Yaounde 269, 299, 306
Yemen 55, 356, 609–10, 620
Yoruba people 27–8, 88, 95, 98
Yorubaland 97, 145

Zagros mountains 237
Zaïre 25, 45, 263, 270, 272, 294, 302, 403, 468–77, 485, 489
Zaïre (Congo) river 292, 294–5, 305, 306, 321–2, 327; basin 28
Zambezi river 35, 292, 391, 501, 708
Zambia 14, 392, 409, 435, 484, 491, 557
Zangon Katab 102
Zanzibar 427, 659–61, 665–7, 669, 735, 737, 749
Zanzibar/Inhambane floral mosaic 427
zebra 365, 374
Zebra shark (Stegostomatidae) 676, 691–2
Zhizo (Toutswe) people 388–9; settlement 712; *see also* Toutswe (Zhizo) pottery
Zimbabwe 10, 12, 14, 20, 24–5, 29, 70, 386, 388–9, 392, 409, 411, 414, 427, 484, 501, 506, 670, 705–31, 742
Zimbabwe state 389, 411, 709–10
Zimbabwe tradition 388, 419
Ziwa ware: *see* Gokomere ware
Ziway-Shala basin 37, 39
Zizyphus sp. 156–7, 163, 190
Zulu people 500, 504, 744

Site Index[1]

Abu Ballas **228**–30
Abu Hussein **228**, 231
Abydos 226, 552, **553**–4, 563, 577, 585–6, 600
Addi Galamo 613
Adrar Bous **228**–9, 236–7
Adulis 347–8, **610–11** 614, 616–19
Adwuku 647, 648
Afikpo 250, 274
Afunfun 334
Ain Farah **460**, 465, 734, 735, 748
Akira **486**, 488
Akjoujt region 334, 433, 466, 638
Aksum (Axum) 26, 346, **347**, 348, 354–5, 606, 608–21
Akyekyemabuo 258
Al-Famau 699
Amekni **228**–9, 232, 236
Amkoundjo **335**, **338**; radiocarbon dating 337, 340
Andranosoa **666**, 668
Aniba 583–4
Apreku 258
Arlit **228**, 236
Armant 184, 191, 204, 220–2, 224, 552–3
Armazia, 426; radiocarbon dating 430
Atfih 552–**3**
Atwetweboo **646**, 649
Awdaghust 737, 740, 748
Azelik 334–**5**; radiocarbon dating 337

Ba'ati Facada **347**, 351–2
Badari **166**, 202, 204, 214, 217–24, **553**, 561–2, 569
Bagamoyo 669
Baha 433, **441**
Bambandyanalo 709
Baranda ('Massapa') **714**, 726–30
Barawa 426, 675
Batalimo 298–9, **306**, 308–11, 319, 321, 325–7; radiocarbon dating 300, 311
Begho 27, **643**, 643–4, 648–50, 732, 737, 739, 740–1, 748; radiocarbon dating 648; see also Begho ware
Benin 27, 46, 76, 148, 150, 292, 732, 738–9, 741, 744, 745–6, 748
Bigo 28, 733–4, 737, 739, 744–5, 748
Bilene **414**; radiocarbon dating 430
Binda **274**, 280, 285, 287
Bir Kiseiba 66, 182, 200, **228**, 230, 238
Birni N'gazargamo 736, 749

Bochianga 463
Bokuma **306**, 308; radiocarbon dating 308
Bono Manso **643**, 645, 649–51, 742; radiocarbon dating 650
Bonoase 256, **257**–8, **262**, 267–8, **646**
Bora **460**, 462, 464–5
Bornu **339**–40; radiocarbon dating 340
Boso-Njafo **306**–9; radiocarbon dating 308
Bosumpra 250, 258, **262**, 264, 267; radiocarbon dating 263
Bosumtwi 265
Bou-Alem **228**, 235
Boyasi hill 256, **257**–8, 262, 267
Buhaya 434, **441**, 485
Buhen 26, 65, 580, 584
Bweyorere 28

Carthage 26, 432–3
Chabbe **347**, 351
Chenguruve **714**, 727, 729
Cherekecherete 647
Chibuene 62, **414**, 419–20, 425, 427–8, 660, **661**, 663, 665; radiocarbon dating 430–1
Chipunza **714**
Chirombo Iron Age Village 395
Chisvingo 711, **714**–16, 719
Chizinga **714**, 730
Chongoene **414**; radiocarbon dating 430
Christian Village 256, **257**
Chundu **400**–1, 403, 407–8
Coptos 552–3
Cynopolis 552–**3**

Dabakala 256, **262**, 272
Daboya 256–7, **262**, 268, 270–1, **335**–7, 434, **453**–4, **440**
Daima **262**, 272, **339**, 343, 463, **464**–5, 467; radiocarbon dating 339–40
Dakka 583
Dambwa 392, 401, 484
Deir el Ballas 577, 581, 586
Deloraine farm **486**–7
Dembeni 660, **661**–2, **666**–7
Dendara 552, **553**–4
Dia 638, 640
Dibeira West 184
Do Dimi **441**; radiocarbon dating 338, 433
Dongo **306**, 309–11
Dutsen Kongba **262**–4, 270, 272

Edfu 552, **553**–4, 561–3, 569
Ekne Wan Ataran 334–**5**; radiocarbon dating 338

---

1. Note that figures in bold signify the pages with location maps for sites.

El Adam **228**–9
El Ghorab **228**–30
El Kortein **228**–9
El Omari **166**; radiocarbon dating 203, 214
El Riqa 583–4
El Tarif **166**, 191, 202, 221
El-Kab **166**, 185, **553**–4
Elephantine **553**–4, 577, 580, 584, 586
Esh Shaheinab 64, 68–9, **228**
Esna 349

Facada **347**, 351
Falls Rock Shelter 375–7
Fayum 167, 183–4, 186–8, 190–1, 193, 198,
    201–2, 203, 204–14, 216, 225, 227–8, 552,
    565, **571**–2; FS-1 **166**, 190, 204, 207–8, 209;
    FS-2 **166**, 187–90, 209; Kom K 205–6,
    209–10; Kom W 204–5, 207, 208–10; Upper
    K 206, 208–10, 216, 220; radiocarbon dating
    187, 207

Garf Husein 583–4
Gatare forest 485
Gatung'ang'a 485–**6**; radiocarbon dating 488
Gedi **666**, 748
Gilf Kebir 38, **228**–9, 231
Gilgil River burial site **486**–7
Gobedra 346, 347, 354–5, 609
Gogo Falls **359**–60, 362–3, 365–7, 369, 371;
    radiocarbon dating 364
Gokomere 392; *see also* Gokomere tradition
Gomene **414**, 426
Great Zimbabwe 10, 21, 29, 413–14, 419, 428,
    705, **708**–14, 717, 718–19, 722–5, 731, 740,
    747
Grotte Capeletti 66, **228**, 236
Gurgussom **347**
Gwisho 298

Hajar bin Humeid 356
Hani 436, **441**, 648–9
Hanyundru **666**, 667
Happy Rest, the 68
Hassi el Abiod **228**, 233
Haua Fteah 69, **228**, 236
Hawelti-Melazo 613–14
Hemamieh **166**, 203, 214, 217, 219–21;
    radiocarbon dating 215
Heronden **714**, **723**, 724
Hierakonpolis 26, 552, **553**–4, 563, 586
Hola Hola **414**, 418, 426
Hyrax Hill 488

Ibadan 151, 732, 738–9, 746, 749
Ibo Island **414**, 425
Ibonzi 297–8, **306**
Ife 27–8, 45, 738–40, 747, 749
Igbo-Ukwu 28, **95**, 97
Igbo Richard: radiocarbon dating 92

Ikawaten 334
Imbonga 305, **306**–7; radiocarbon dating 308;
    see also imbonga pottery
In Talaylen **335**; radiocarbon dating 337
Ingombe Ilede 403
Inhambane 413–**14**, 419, 427; radiocarbon
    dating 431
Irodo 658, 660–**1**, 664
Isamu Pati Mound 64
Isu 515, 518; see also main index
Iwo Eleru, 17, 45, 55, 250, **262**, 263–4, 269

J. el Beid **228**, 229
J. Mao **460**, 462, 464–5, 467
J. Sahaba **228**, 239
J. Shaqadud 62, 65, 232
Jenne-jeno 27, 62, 252, **335**, **453**–4, **464**, 466,
    624, 628–41, 732, 736, 740, 749;
    radiocarbon dating 338, 628–9
Jenne-sire 628

Kabondo **401**–2
Kadero 17, 204, 214
Kahun 26, **553**, 563, 577, 580, 584–5
Kalambo Falls 400
Kamabai 250, **262**–4
Kamiranzovu 50–1
Kango 304, **305**
Kanjera West 363
Kapeni **393**, 396; see also Kepeni ware
Kapwirimbwe 406, 484, 485
Karkarichinkat **262**, 272
Karnak 552, **553**–4, 568, 597, 600, 605
Kashiru 50–1
Kaskase **611**, 613
Kassala (Mahal Teglinos) 604, 609–**11**
Katoto 403
Kerma 26, 64, 69, 568, **571**, 573–4, 584–5,
    609–**10**
Kgaswe 388, 390
KH3 **166**, 222–4
Khartoum 34, 35, 55, 63, 181, 227–**8**, 232–4,
    602
Kilkerran **714**, 725
Kilwa **414**, 419, 425, 427, 659–61, 663–70,
    735, 749
Kintampo 17, 68, 250, 253, 255–72, 649;
    radiocarbon dating 263
Kiponozi 699
Kokasu cave 263–4
Kom el Hisn 577, 585
Kom Ombo **166**, 170, 173
Koro Toro 463–**4**
Koualessis **306**, 328; radiocarbon dating 304
Koumbi Saleh 27, 733, 736, 740–1, 747, 749
Kumasi 268, 271, 737, 741, 745, 748–9
Kursakata **339**; radiocarbon dating 339–40
Kwale 485–**6**, **697**; radiocarbon dating 485 *see*
    also Kwale ware
Kwamboo 485

Ladoku (Old La) 643; radiocarbon dating 647
Laga Oda 346–7, 356
Lagesh 564
Lake Besaka 346–7, 356
Lalibela **610**
Lamek **361**
Lanet **486**, 488; *see also* Lanet ware
Launay **228**–29
Leja 439, **440**–5
Les Saras 304, **306**; radiocarbon dating 304
Likwala **306**; radiocarbon dating 319
Lopé 299, 302–4, 328; radiocarbon dating 300, 304
Lumbo 425–6; radiocarbon dating 429
Luxor 222, 552, 601, 604
Luziwa 699

Mahalapye **387**–8
Mahilaka 483, **666**, 668–9
Makalia **486**–7
Makhadma **166**, 181, 184
Makodu **387**, 389–90
Makohere **414**, 421
Makokou **306**, 328; radiocarbon dating 304–5
Maluba **306**, 324; radiocarbon dating 311
Mampurugu 454–5
Manda (Malindi, Mulanda) 485, **656**, 659, **663**–5, 670–1, **674**–5, 695, **696**, 700, 702
Manyikeni 410, 413–15, 419, 428–9, **708**, 711
Mapungubwe 29, 419, 709
Massingir **414**, 417, 427
Matara **611**–14, 617–19
Mathendous **228**, 231
Matmar **166**, 204, 214, 218–20, 222
Matola **414**–15, 417–18, 427; radiocarbon dating 430
Matope Court 392
Matupi 297, **306**
Maunatlala **387**, 390
Mawudzu **393**, 396–7; see also Mawudzu pottery
Mbandaka 291, **306**, 305
Mbashile **662**
Mbeni **662**–3
Mdaga **336**, **339**, 342–3, 463–4; radiocarbon dating 337, 339–40
Mea 699
Medinat Habu 602
Mejiro cave (Old Oyo) 250
Melville Koppjes 436, **441**
Memphis 552–3, 556, 559, 563–4, 567, 577, 580, 585, **588**, 592
Meniet **228**, 236
Merimde **166**, 201–3, 212–15, 217, 551, **553**
Meroe 24, 432–3, 435, **441**, 465–6, 485, **610**, 732, 734–5, 749
Meru 488
Mgungundlovu 732–5, 741, 744, 749
Minia **553**, 561–2, 569
Mitula **306**, 319, 322; radiocarbon dating 319

Mkadini 661
Mkokotoni 661, 665
Moanda 303–**6**, 328; radiocarbon dating 303–4
Mobaka **306**, 319, 322; radiocarbon dating 319
Moeng I **387**, 389–90
Montevideo 711
Mostagedda **166**, 204, 214, 219
Mouila 303; radiocarbon dating 304
Mozambique island **414**, 425
Mro Dewa **662**
Muchekayawa **714**, **727**, 729
Muhekani **414**, 421–2, 423, 426; radiocarbon dating 429
Mumute 256, **257**–8, **262**
Munda **306**, 311–13, 319, 321, 324, 326; radiocarbon dating 318
Murrapania **414**, 421–3; radiocarbon dating 430
Mutawania **414**, 421–2; radiocarbon dating 430
Mwakoni **414**, 421, 423
Mwana 699

Nabta Playa 16, 154–64, 182, 184, 200, **228**–30, 232, 238; radiocarbon dating 154–7, 161
Naga ed Der 218
Nagada **166**, 204, 221–2, 224, 552, **553**–4
Nagada South Town 221, 224, 552
Nakwaho **414**, 416, 422; radiocarbon dating 429
Namialo 421, 423–4
Namikopo **414**, 421–2; radiocarbon dating 430
Namolepiwa **414**, 421, 423–5; radiocarbon dating 430
Nampula **414**, 421, 427; see also Nampula region; Nampula tradition
Narosura **359**, 366
Nasiyaya 394
Natchabiet **347**, 355–6
Nazret **610**, 616, 618
Ndondondwane 62–4, 68
Ngamuriak **361**, 367–8, 371
Ngovo **262**, 270, 272, 299, 302, **306**, 329; radiocarbon dating 300
Ngungu 299, **306**
Nhachengue **414**, 419; radiocarbon dating 430
Nhunguza 715, 719
Niani 27
Nkhudzi Bay 397; see also Nkhudzi pottery
Nkope **393**; See also Nkope ware
Nkukoa Buoho 258
Nok **335**–6, 433–4, **439**, **453**, 455, 466; radiocarbon dating 337
Nokara **335**; radiocarbon dating 337
Ntereso 68, 256, **257**–8, **262**, 267–8, 270, 434, **439**; radiocarbon dating 271
Nyamanetsa **714**, **723**
Nyangawni **714**, **723**, 724

Obobogo **262**, 269, 272, 299–302, **306**, 322, 324, 329; radiocarbon dating 301
Okala 299–300, 302, **306**, 328; radiocarbon dating 300
Opi 433, 437, 438, **441**, 446; radiocarbon dating 438–9
Orba 437; radiocarbon dating 439
Otoumbi 303–**6**; radiocarbon dating 304
Owerre-Elu 437; radiocarbon dating 438–9
Oyem (2) 303; radiocarbon dating 304

Pangane **414**, 426
Pate 669, **674**–5, 677, 680, 703
Phalaborwa **441**
Pi-Ri'amese **553**, 564, 568, 569
Pikunda **306**, 311, 315–18, 319, 322, 326; radiocarbon dating 319
Pilkington Bay 51
Pokomo **697**, 700, 703
Pont Drift 63
Port Sudan **588**, 603, 604
Prolonged Drift 69, **359**, 365
Pumpuano **527**

Qasr el-Sagha **166**, 204, 208
Qasr Ibrim 26, 66, 351
Qohayto **611**, 616, 618

Rafin Ndoko **335**; radiocarbon dating 337
Ras Hafun 419, 428
Ras Mkumbu **666**, 667, 669
Riane 416, 421–2; radiocarbon dating 429
River Denis site **306**, 322, 328
Rombo **486**, 488
Rop 92, **262**–4, **336**; radiocarbon dating 337
Ruanga **714**, 725

Saggai **228**, 232
St Antonio de Tanna (wreck) 425
Sakuzi 299; radiocarbon dating 299–300
Salasun **486**, 488
Samun Dukiya **336**
Sancul 419, 425–6
Sandwich Harbour 381, 384
Sanga 28, 67, 78, 403, 717
Sanje ya Kati 667, 669
Saqqara 552–**3**
Sarourab **228**–9
Schroda 64, 388
Sekkiret valley 334
Serkama **347**, 352–3
Seronera **486**, 488
Serowe **387**–8
Serra Mesa 424
Shaka 699, 744
Shanga 29, **661**–3, 665–**6**, 669, 671, **674**–93, **697**, 701, 702
Shaqadud **228**
Shongweni 55

Shum Laka 298–9, **306**; radiocarbon dating 297
Sihi 66
Silver Leaves 417
Sima **662**, 664, **666**, 668–9
Simbusenga 403
Site 8905 180
Site TO 17 395
Siyu 675
Snake Rock 376–8
Sopie cave **262**–4
Sou (SII) radiocarbon dating 339–40
Sou Blam Radjil (SI) **339**; radiocarbon dating 337–40
Soumpi 640

Taforalt **228**–9
Tagalagal **228**–9
Takwa 695
Talaky 483, **666**
Tanis 552–**3**, 568
Taruga **336**, 432, 435, 437, **441**, **464**, 466; radiocarbon dating 338, 433
Taukome **387**–8
Tchengu 299–300, **306**
Tegdaoust 27, 92
Teguef n'Agar **336**; radiocarbon dating 338
Tekondo **611**–18
Tell el Amarna 552–**3**, 559, 563, 567, 577, 581
Tell el Da'aba 577, 581, 585
Tetedwa 647
Tetewabuo 258
Thebes 191, 552–**3**, 559, 563–4, 567–8, 577, 582, 586, **588**, 592, 597, 599, 742
Ti-n Hanakaten **228**
Ti-n-Torha 119, **228**–9, 232, 236
Tichitt 251, **262**, 272
Tikene Bassoura **336**; radiocarbon dating 338
Tikinyia 424–5
Toala Island 298, **306**
Toshka 583–**4**
Tototo 422; radiocarbon dating 429
Toukh 64, 69
Toungour **336**, 463–**4**; radiocarbon dating 338
Toutswe **387**–8
Tse Dura **274**–5, 279–80, **441**
Tyeral 334

Uan Muhuggiag **228**, 236
Ukpo Eze mound 93
Ukpwa 516, 518, 542
Umundu 437–**40**, 441; radiocarbon dating 437–9
Unguje Ukwu **414**
Ungwana 29, 666, **696**, 698–702
University Campus 413, 417; radiocarbon dating 431
Urewe: see Urewe pottery
Uri **460**, 465, 467, 749
Uruk 564

Usangi hospital 485
Ushongo **274**, 279, 286; radiocarbon dating
    280

Vilanculos Bay **414**, 418–19

Wajir **697**, 700
Wazi Hill **714**, 719, **721**–5
We **515**, 525; *see also* main index
Wenje 703
Wima **460**, 462, 467

Xai Xai **414**; radiocarbon dating 430
Xakota **414**, 416, 421–3; radiocarbon dating
    429
Xokas 426; radiocarbon dating 429

Yagala **262**–4

Yala 485
Yeha **306**, **347**–8, 612–13, 616, 618–19
Yellow Jacket 711, **714**–15, 717–18
Yengema 250

Zala-Bet-Makeda **611**, 618
Zambezi Farm **400**–1, 408
Zaria 738–9, 741–2, 747, 749
Zengba 674
Zhongli 674
Zitundo **414**, 417, 427; radiocarbon dating
    430–1
Ziwa 392; see also Gokomere tradition
Ziwa Farm 503
Zoui **335**; radiocarbon dating 337
Zvongombe **714**, 721, **722**–5